LAROUSSE
Dictionary of
WINES
of the World

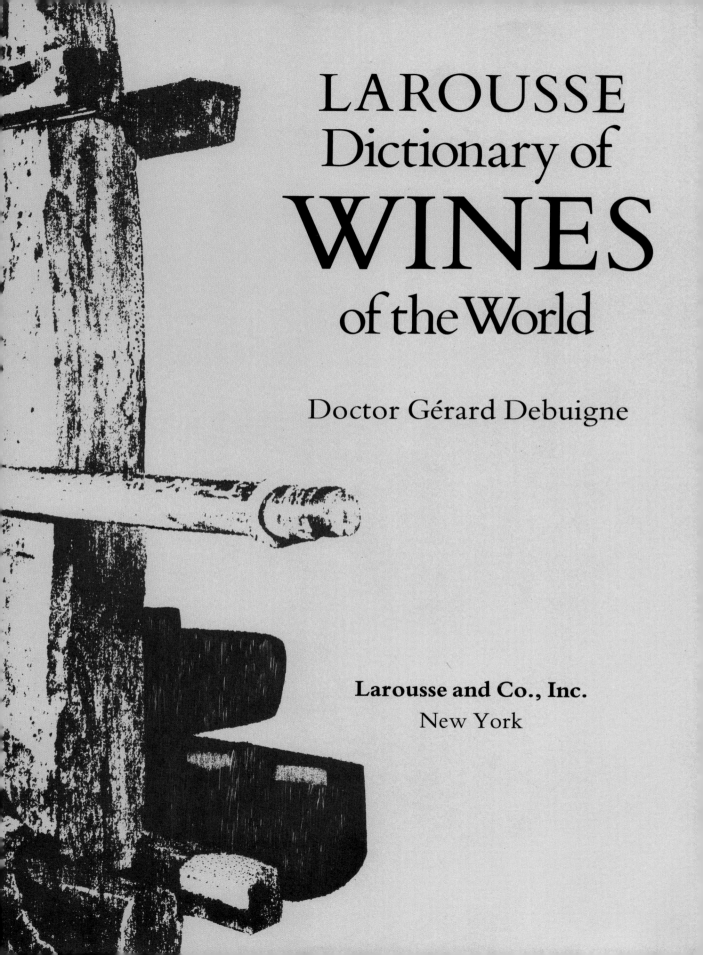

LAROUSSE
Dictionary of
WINES
of the World

Doctor Gérard Debuigne

Larousse and Co., Inc.
New York

Originally published under the title LAROUSSE DES VINS
© Copyright Librairie Larousse Paris 1970
© Copyright English text The Hamlyn Publishing Group Limited 1976
© English edition first published in Great Britain
by The Hamlyn Publishing Group Limited

First published in the United States by
Larousse and Co, Inc., 572 Fifth Avenue, New York, N.Y. 10036 1976

ISBN 0–88332–044–4
Library of Congress Catalog Card Number: 75–44852

Printed in Spain by Mateu Cromo, Madrid

Drinking horn (Germany, 15th Century). Musée de Cluny. Phot M.

FOREWORD

Since Genesis, wine has always existed side by side with man and played a role in the events of his life: communion wine, votive wine, wine of honour. . . .

Olivier de Serres, in his *Théâtre d'Agriculture,* wrote in 1600: 'After bread comes wine, the second element given by the Creator for the preservation of life and the first celebration of his excellence'. A gift from heaven certainly, but from a heaven which is far from always merciful! Wine is also a product of man's endeavour and – above all – a work of art.

Today, the art of the vigneron is not only based on tradition but has become a true science, tempered by an intelligent, empirical instinct. The *Larousse Dictionary of Wines of the World* permits the man of today, always pressed for time, to learn rapidly and without long research the successive phases of the creation and life of wine; the different vinicultural regions and the 'races' of wines; the indispensable technical details of vinification and legislation affecting wine as well as the vocabulary used by wine-lovers.

Many subjects are now so complex that it can be almost impossible to know everything about any one. This is the case with wine. There is no living person who could hope to embrace all the knowledge related to it. This book does not pretend to treat such a vast and profound subject in depth but, by putting within everyone's reach all the essential facts, it will engender a respect and love for this noble and mysterious juice of the grape.

September at the château of Saumur from Les Très Riches Heures du Duc de Berry. *Musée Condé, Chantilly.* Phot. Giraudon.

abondance Abondance is the wine liberally diluted with water that is sometimes given to children in French schools.

acescence Also known as *piqûre,* this disease is caused by acetic bacteria which attack all fermented liquids, notably wine, making them sour and acid.

acid (malic) An element found mostly in unripe grapes which gives them a characteristic sour★ taste. The quantity of malic acid decreases as the fruit ripens because of the part it plays in the respiratory processes of the plant. These processes accelerate when the temperature rises, which is why grapes contain little malic acid in hot years and too much in cold years.

Under the influence of certain bacteria, malic acid decomposes during malo-lactic fermentation★. This results in a reduction in the overall acidity of the wine.

acid (sorbic) The use of this acid, in the form of potassium sorbate, is officially limited to a maximum of 200 mg per litre. It is used as a partial substitute for sulphur dioxide★ as a sterilising agent and deoxidant. Sorbic acid is especially useful in the treatment of sweet wines when sulphur dioxide has to be used to prevent refermentation★. Sulphur dioxide sometimes produces a noticeable smell and taste in the wine, an undesirable effect that can be greatly reduced by the substitution of a quantity of sorbic acid. However, as sorbic acid is effective only as a fungicide and an inhibitor of yeasts and ineffective against bacteria, it must always be used in conjunction with sulphur dioxide.

Sorbic acid also has several drawbacks.

If the acid solution is not fresh it can impair the taste of the wine; bacteria may attack it and cause it to decompose which results in a very disagreeable taste comparable to that of geranium stalks; and lastly, resistant yeasts sometimes develop at the bottom of the bottle and form unpleasant lumps of deposit. Sorbic acid should, therefore, only be used immediately before bottling on wine that has been stabilised and is completely free of bacteria.

acidification The process of adding tartaric acid to must, or citric acid to wine, when a very hot and sunny year has produced a wine deficient in acidity. Without this corrective measure the wine would lack balance and freshness and would not keep well. Acidification is not a chemical process, it is simply the correction of a deficiency in substances which are normally constituent parts of the wine. Citric and tartaric acid are both natural products.

acidity (fixed) The combination of all the organic acids normally contained in the fruit and also present in the wine, e.g. malic acid★, tartaric acid and lactic acid.

acidity (real) This is expressed by chemists as pH, which, without going into technical details, can be said to represent the intensity of a wine's acidity. Some acids have a more active acidity than others, which is why wines with the same total acidity★ can have different pH ratings. For acid solutions pH is graded from 7 to 0, 7 being absolute neutrality and 0 absolute acidity. The lower a wine's pH, the higher its acidity. According to a French oenologist named Jaulmes, wines have a pH of between 2·7 and 3·9. The first figure would represent a very acid wine and the second, a very neutral and flat one.

acidity (total)   The total or overall acidity of a wine is composed of all the free and combined acid substances present in it, i.e. its volatile acidity★ and its fixed acidity★. The health and longevity of wine depend on its acid content as do the qualities known as freshness and nerve★, or crispness. Acidity itself depends on the condition of the grapes. In cold years they are still relatively unripe at harvest time and the resulting wine has too much acid, tasting tart and green★. In some cases deacidification★ is legally permitted as a corrective measure for excessive acidity. In hot years, on the other hand, overripe grapes make wine with a low acid content which has to be corrected by acidification★. A well-balanced, reasonably long-lived wine should have a total acidity of 4–5 g per litre.

Two wines with the same overall acid content can taste completely different owing to the different nature of their constituent acids. If tartaric acid predominates, for example, the wine will have a rough taste. This, however, disappears quite quickly as, with the advent of cold weather, the tartaric acid is changed into insoluble potassium bitartrate.

acidity (volatile)   Volatile acids are those which can be separated from the wine by distillation. Wine normally contains only a small quantity, from 0·3–0·4 g per litre. Any increase in this proportion is evidence of microbial adulteration, which is why French law statutorily prohibits the sale of wines showing 0·9 g of volatile acidity in the vineyard and 1 g in the shops. The principal constituent element of volatile acidity is acetic acid (or vinegar) which can make wine practically undrinkable. It begins by tasting piquant, or sharp, and later becomes distinctly sour★. Volatile acidity always increases with age and produces a piqué wine. There is no remedy, especially as dépiquage, chemical correction of the sourness, is strictly forbidden by law. When the volatile acidity of a wine is strong enough (about 0·7 g) to be noticeable in taste, the wine is said to be feverish, and later sour and piqué.

Africa   As vines can only be grown in a temperate climate, the only parts of this vast continent that produce wine are the temperate zones of the north (Morocco★, Algeria★ and Tunisia★) and the south (South Africa★).

age of the vine   This has a very great influence on the quality of wine. A plant takes three years to produce its first grapes and from ten to twelve years to make a respectable wine. The greatest wines have always been made from vines between twenty and forty years old. Vignerons say: 'You need old vines for great wines'.

aggressive   An aggressive wine 'attacks' the taste buds, either with an excessive acidity caused by unripe grapes or with an excess of tannin due to a prolonged fermentation period.

Ahr   A small river in western Germany which joins the Rhine from the west just north of Coblenz. The vineyards perched on the steep hillsides of the river valley are planted almost entirely with the Pinot Noir of Burgundy, locally known as Spätburgunder. They are the most northerly vineyards in Europe. Their pale red wines, which are delicious and have a fine bouquet, are the best red wines of Germany (which produces very few). The wines are rarely exported, and are best drunk slightly chilled in their native region around the towns of Ahrweiler, Neuenahr and Walporzheim.

aigre   A disorder giving wine a sour taste

Electric pH meter for measuring the acidity of wines. Ecole Nationale d'Agriculture de Montpellier. Phot. M.

caused by the *Mycoderma aceti*★ bacteria which turn wine into vinegar. It occurs most frequently in barrels which are not filled properly and in which the wine lost by evaporation is not replaced with sufficient care or regularity – leaving the bacteria the air they need for their development. Acetic bacteria are even more liable to develop when the temperature exceeds 30°C and this accounts for the frequency with which the malady occurs during the summer months.

A sour taste in a wine is immediately noticeable. When a proportion of the acetic acid combines with alcohol it produces a sharp taste, which is even more unpleasant. The correction of this fault is forbidden by French law, as is the sale of such wine.

Ain-Bessem-Bouira Algerian wines grown south-east of Algiers on limestone or schistose soil at an altitude of about 500 m. The red wines are very full-bodied (at least 13° alcohol), bright and supple, with a pleasant, well-rounded flavour. The rosés, which are also fairly alcoholic, are a pretty bright pink, almost cherry-red, colour and are fruity and easy on the palate. Ain-Bessem-Bouira wines were once classified VDQS★.

Ain-el-Hadjar A small Algerian vineyard in the department of Oran whose wines were once VDQS★. They are grown high up on the plateaus, at altitudes of between 600 and 1200 m. The wines, which can be red, rosé or white, are generally of good quality and keep well in bottle. The reds are very full-bodied (13·8°) and well balanced, with a delicate bouquet and mellowness. The equally full-bodied whites and rosés are fragrant and fruity.

Aix-en-Provence (Coteaux d') The wines produced around the ancient city of Aix qualify for the VDQS★ label. They are made from the classic grapes of Provence★, i.e. Grenache, Carignan, Cinsault and Mourvèdre for the red and the rosé, and Clairette, Ugni and Muscat for the white. They are pleasant, fruity, full-bodied wines.

Alameda A county in northern California★ east of San Francisco Bay. The main vineyards are situated in the Livermore Valley, around the town of Livermore. The fine gravelly soil seems ideally suited to fine white European grapes such as Sauvignon, Sémillon, Pinot Blanc and Chardonnay. The region's output is almost entirely white, and its wines are among the best in California. The best-known vineyards are Concannon, Cresta Blanca and Wente Brothers.

alcohol The alcohol content of a wine is formed during fermentation of the must. The natural grape sugar is converted by yeasts into roughly equal amounts of alcohol and carbon dioxide★. The alcoholic strength of the wine is usually between 8 and 14°, sometimes 15°. Normal fermentation cannot produce a strength of more than 15°, consequently a wine with more than 15° of alcohol (i.e. 15% by volume) has invariably been fortified in some way with extra alcohol. Wines which have been subject to mutage★ can have an alcoholic strength of 18–22°. One degree of alcohol is produced by roughly 17 g of sugar per litre for white wine and 18 g for red. Thus a 10° wine will have been made from juice containing 170 g of sugar per litre if white, 180 g if red.

Alcohol sustains other constituent elements of the wine and also contributes greatly to its longevity. A wine rich in alcohol is more agreeable to the palate, although ultimately more tiring to the drinker. Unfortunately, alcoholic strength was once, in the public mind, synonymous with quality, and until quite recently the degree of alcohol was a popular criterion of excellence. Nowadays, the wine-buying public is more discerning and generally prefers lighter, less full-bodied wines.

The alcohol content of a wine depends on various factors: the species of grape; the nature of the soil (wine grown on limestone, for example, is generally richer in alcohol than wine grown on pebbly, siliceous soil); the climate (a hot, dry climate tends to produce wines with more body); and lastly the vintage (wines grown in a hot year usually have a relatively high alcohol content). The alcohol should never dominate the taste of the wine, but should always blend perfectly with the other elements. Chaptalisation★ can therefore be a very risky operation. The addition of

sugar to the grape juice in order to increase the wine's alcohol content may disturb the natural balance between its various elements and result in a harsh, unbalanced and mediocre wine. Wines rich in alcohol are characterised by the English words vinous★, heady★, full-bodied★, generous★ and spirituous. (Their French equivalents are *vineux, capiteux, corsé, généreux* and *spiritueux*.)

ALCOHOL (TOTAL) The expressions total alcohol, acquired alcohol and potential alcohol are sometimes used in reference to vins blanc liquoreux (sweet white wines). The total alcohol is the sum of the acquired alcohol and the potential alcohol. Thus Sauternes★, for example, has an official minimum alcohol content of 13°, of which at least 12·5° is acquired alcohol. This means that Sauternes must have at least 12·5° of real alcohol, the remaining 0·5° being 'potential' alcohol, i.e. sugar. As

same name. It is a member of the Muscat★ family, a fact evident in both its bouquet and its taste. The best wine is produced on the island of Elba, particularly around the town of Portoferraio, whose name it sometimes bears. It is a smooth dessert wine that has a wide reputation. It is not unlike a port, although it is lighter in body and possesses a fine aroma of Muscat.

Algeria All the vineyards of this former French colony were planted by French colonisers who settled in the country from 1842 onwards. As phylloxera★ ravaged the vineyards in the south of France, planting was begun on a massive scale in Algeria, on both hills and plains. Today, the principal varieties of grape are Carignan, Cinsault, Grenache, Cabernet, Morastel, Mourvèdre and Pinot for red wines, and Faranah, Clairette, Ugni Blanc and Aligoté for white.

Until recently Algerian wines were used

Vineyards of the Mitidja, Algeria. Phot. OFALAC and Ministry of Information, Algiers.

it takes 17 g of sugar per litre to produce one degree of alcohol, the extra 0·5° would be obtained by adding 8·5 g of sugar to each litre of grape juice (a quantity which is, in fact, often exceeded).

Likewise, 11° of Monbazillac's★ official 13° total alcohol content must be acquired alcohol with the remaining 2° of potential alcohol being produced by 34 g of sugar per litre. Quarts-de-Chaume★ must have 13° of total alcohol, of which 12° is acquired alcohol, etc.

Aleatico An Italian grape which produces a red, usually sweet, wine of the

as the basis of French vins de coupage★, or blended wines. Made as they were from common, extremely prolific vines, they were for a long time merely mass-produced vins ordinaires (table wines). However, several wines grown in the mountain regions gradually improved in quality until they finally qualified for the important VDQS★ label. This was the result of more than a century's work by pioneers from the Languedoc, Jura and Burgundy regions of France, who gradually adapted their grapes and methods of vinification to the soil and climate of Africa.

*Vineyards of the Mitidja,
Algeria.* Phot. OFALAC
and Ministry of
Information, Algiers.

The red wines, always full and generous, were sometimes remarkably good, with a pronounced bouquet and a certain quality. They had the additional advantage of maturing quickly. Some of the white wines, although they were not well known, were light and fruity but lacked vigour.

Algerian wines have not been officially entitled to the VDQS label since the country's independence in 1962, as French wine laws can no longer be enforced. Algeria is now expected to define the quality of its own wines in accordance with the standards established by the international wine laws.

Besides table wines, Algeria, since 1880, has produced mistelles★ (wines used in the preparation of apéritifs), and has been France's chief supplier since 1910. The country also manufactures vins de liqueur★, or fortified wines, of its own. Some of them, such as those made from Muscat grapes on the hills of Harrach and the estate of the Trappist order at Staouéli, are excellent.

Since its independence, the young Algerian State has tried to maintain the wine production which was previously so important to the country. However, in the area of Algiers and Tizi-Ouzou where viticulture remains one of the most important agricultural activities, numerous vines, particularly the Mitidja, have been abandoned due to the inexperience of the new proprietors. This region produces well-balanced reds which are often fruity. The region of El Asnam (Orleansville) produces vigorous, highly-coloured wine. The best are still from the Côtes du Zaccar★. Wines from the regions of Médéa★ and Ain-Bessem-Bouira★ also have a very fine reputation. The old department of Oran which produces more than two-thirds of the Algerian harvest has some of the best Algerian wines. The region of Mostaganem★ makes fine, fruity wines on the chalky slopes of the Haut-Dahra★ and robust wines on the plain. South of the Béni-Chougran mountains, Mascara★ and Coteaux de Mascara are well-known names of wines from the vineyards of Ain-el-Hadjar★ and the Mountains of Tessalah. Finally, the region around Tlemcen★ produces some fine wine, especially Coteaux de Tlemcen.

Exportation is the only outlet for production as the Moslem population does not drink wine, according to the rule of the Koran. About 90–100% of Algerian wine has always been exported, the majority of it to France.

alliaceous Having the smell and taste of onion or garlic. This develops when sulphur dioxide★ which is used as an antiseptic combines, under certain conditions, with the alcohol of the wine.

Aloxe-Corton This commune at the foot of what is locally known as 'la Montagne' is the starting point of the really great crus of the Côte de Beaune★. The Aloxe-Corton appellation officially includes some vineyards in the Ladoix-Serrigny and Pernand-Vergelesses★ communes. The red and white wines are equally well known.

In great years the red wines are for many wine-lovers the most revered of all Côte de Beaunes, and are certainly the ones which age best. They are magnificent Burgundies, firm, well balanced and potent with a full, well-rounded bouquet that has a slight flavour of kirsch.

The white wines are very full-bodied and have great vitality. They are a marvellous golden colour and have a faint aroma of cinnamon. The whites rank with the best Meursaults★, and according to some admirers often even surpass them.

The crus are Corton (red and white) and Corton-Charlemagne (white only). Wines labelled simply with the communal appellation Aloxe-Corton are, although excellent, less distinguished and full-bodied; they mature more quickly, but also age sooner. (See Index.)

Alsace The vineyards of Alsace rise in terraces on the slopes between the Vosges mountains and the Rhine valley. Stretching from Wasselonne, near Strasbourg, in the north to Thann, near Mulhouse, in the south, they cover an area just over 100 km long and from one to five km wide. Facing east, south and south-east, they perch picturesquely on hillsides whose altitude varies from 200–450 m, sheltered from the cold, humid, north-westerly winds by the Vosges mountains. There are about 100 viticultural communes, two-thirds of which are in the Haut-Rhin department and the remaining third in the Bas-Rhin. The most famous are Ammerschwihr, Barr, Eguisheim, Riquewihr, Kaysersberg, Mittelwihr and Ribeauvillé.

The distinctive feature of these eminent vineyards is their originality. The varied composition of the soil (gneiss and granite, pink sandstone, clay and limestone, alluvium, sand and gravel), the diversity of the micro-climates, and the variety of the vines give them a character all of their own. One feature peculiar to the wines of Alsace, and almost unique among French

wines, is that they are generally named after the grape from which they are made, and not, as elsewhere, after their cru★ ('growth' or place of origin) – which would seem to support Olivier de Serres' remark that 'Le génie du vin est dans le cépage', i.e. the spirit, or essence, of wine lies in the grape. As exceptions to the general rule Alsace does, nevertheless,

The village of Ammerschwihr, Haut-Rhin, and its vineyards. Phot. Candelier.

have a few crus such as Pfersigberg d'Eguisheim, Kaeferkopf, Kanzlerberg and the Rangen of Thann. This last is the most full-bodied of Alsatian wines. Its ferocity is such that a local curse runs 'Que le Rangen te frappe!' (May Rangen strike you!).

The vine was apparently introduced to Alsace a little later than to most other areas, but vineyards are recorded in 119 different Alsatian villages between AD 650 and 890. The wines of Alsace, as many and varied then as now, enjoyed a great reputation in the Middle Ages, especially in the Nordic countries to which they were exported from the Rhine. Despite the incessant ravages of various wars, Alsatian vignerons have always shown great perseverance in replanting their vineyards. After the occupation of 1870 the planting of noble grape varieties was discouraged in favour of inferior but more prolific vines. However, since 1918 the vineyards have been re-establishing their traditional high standards, and today about three-quarters of the vines are noble varieties.

The Gewurz grape. Phot. M.

13

Nearly all the wines of Alsace are white, and most are dry. Wines produced from common varieties are Knipperlé★, Chasselas★ and Goldriesling. The noble vines produce a unique and marvellously varied range of white wines, from the very dry to the almost sweet and from the fresh and light to the heady. They are Sylvaner★, Riesling★, Traminer★, Gewurztraminer★, Pinot Blanc or Clevner, Pinot Gris★ or Tokay d'Alsace, and Muscat★. There are also some wines made by blending either common or noble wines, e.g. Zwicker★ and Edelzwicker★.

Red wines are rare in Alsace, but are nonetheless excellent. They are in fact made from the Pinot Noir (which the Alsatians, incidentally, call Burgunder) from which the great Burgundies are made – a sufficient guarantee of breeding and distinction.

Rosé or clairet★ wines (Schillerwein) are made from either the Pinot Noir or the Pinot Meunier grape, and are fresh, dry and pleasantly fruity.

Lastly, mention should be made of the magnificent vin de paille★ that used to be made in the Colmar region but which unfortunately no longer exists.

ALSACE, APPELLATION D'ORIGINE CONTRÔLÉE Alsace has only recently (1962) qualified for an appellation contrôlée of its own. The official appellation is Alsace or Vin d'Alsace, accompanied, as is customary, by the name of the grape from which the wine was made. The variety of grape is in some cases followed by the name of the commune which produced the wine: there are ninety-three such communes in the Haut-Rhin and Bas-Rhin departments.

The words Grand Vin or Grand Cru, or similar indications of superior quality, are also used, but are only authorised for wines made from noble grapes whose musts are rich enough in sugar to attain 11° of alcohol by natural fermentation. It is in fact legally permitted for Alsatian wines to be enriched or fortified with up to 2·5° of extra alcohol if the regional committee of experts judges it necessary.

amber A word generally used to describe the golden yellow colour of certain old white wines. This colour should never be accompanied by a taste of maderisation★. The amber tinge is caused by oxidisation of the wine's colouring-matter★ (which, although scarcely visible in young white wines, is nonetheless always present). In a young wine the colour is a fault.

Amboise The vineyards of Vouvray★ and Montlouis★ include several communes grouped around Amboise and its famous château. The white, red and rosé wines made there are all entitled to the appellation Touraine★ followed by Amboise. The white wines produced by the Nazelles and Pocé-sur-Cisse communes are excellent. These communes are on the edge of the official Vouvray area, and their wines were in fact once sold under the name of Vouvray. The other white wines, all grown on the micaceous chalk of Touraine, are also extremely good, possessing elegance and a fine fruity flavour.

The Limeray and Cangey communes produce mostly red and rosé wines. The rosés, made from Cot grapes combined with Gamay and Cabernet, are particularly good. The white wines should have 10·5° of alcohol, the rosés 10° and the reds 9·5°. Amboise wines are produced in fairly small quantities, and are almost all consumed locally.

amer (bitter) The name of a disease (also called amertume) which sometimes affects wines in bottle, particularly red Burgundies. Their taste, though at first negligible, later becomes decidedly bitter, and the colouring-matter★ solidifies and forms a deposit. The disease usually affects wines of low acidity, acting on their glycerine and tartaric acid content. In the early stages of the disease, wine can sometimes be treated by pasteurisation★.

Certain varieties of grape have a definite light bitterness which, far from being offensive, is rated highly. This is the case with the Mauzac grape (Gaillac★, Blanquette de Limoux★) and the Clairette grape (la Clairette★) of Languedoc whose bitter aftertaste makes it a desirable ingredient of quality vermouths.

amoroso A sweetened oloroso sherry made especially for the British market. The full-bodied amoroso called East India gets its name from the days when the

Aerial view of the château of Amboise and the Loire valley. Phot. Beaujard–Lauros.

sailing ships carried casks of sherry to the East Indies and back. The sea air and constant rolling motion were supposed to improve the sherry. Brown sherry is a very dark and sweet amoroso.

ample An 'ample' wine has a full, generous taste and its aroma, bouquet and flavour are rich, well rounded and perfectly balanced.

Ancenis (Coteaux d') This vineyard covers the hillsides around the town of Ancenis on the right bank of the Loire. In addition to the predominant Muscadet★ and Gros-Plant★ vines, the vineyard is planted with a proportion of the Gamay grape of Beaujolais and the Cabernet of Anjou, whose wines are supple, light and greatly admired. They should be drunk while young.

Vineyards of the Loire, Oudon near Ancenis. Phot. M.

15

CABERNET D'ANJOU

APPELLATION CONTRÔLÉE   NICOLAS

The vineyard also produces wines which are made from the Chenin Blanc (or Pineau de la Loire) and the Pinot Gris (or Beurot), locally known as Malvoisie. All these wines are VDQS★ and are supple and fresh, with a pleasant bouquet.

Anjou   An old French province whose limits correspond more or less to the present Maine-et-Loire department. Its vineyards continue the viticultural region of Touraine★ to the west along the Loire, covering the hillsides that border the river and its tributaries. They also enjoy a mild climate. The wines of Anjou have always had a great reputation and have been exported to England in great quantities since 1199. Although the white wines are the best known, there is a great variety to choose from, each with a character of its own. There are dry, medium-dry and sweet whites, and pétillant★, sparkling red and rosé wines. For viticultural purposes Anjou is usually divided into four sub-regions: Saumur★, Coteaux de la Loire★, Coteaux du Layon★ and Coteaux de l'Aubance★.

ANJOU, APPELLATION D'ORIGINE CONTRÔLÉE   The red, white and rosé wines which qualify for the Anjou appellation must be produced within the legally-defined limits of the region and made from the following grapes: Pineau de la Loire (or Chenin Blanc) for white wines, Cabernet Franc and Cabernet-Sauvignon for red wines and Cabernet Franc, Cabernet-Sauvignon, Pineau d'Aunis, Gamay, Cot and Groslot for rosés.

ANJOU (MOUSSEUX)   Sparkling wines that can be either white or rosé. The official grape variety for the white is Pineau de la Loire, but in practice certain red grapes (Cabernet, Gamay, Cot, Groslot and Pineau d'Aunis) are also allowed, vinified as for white wine, up to a maximum proportion of 60%. The rosé must be made from Cabernet, Cot, Gamay and Groslot grapes. These wines must all have 9.5° of alcohol before their liqueur de tirage★ is added.

ANJOU (ROSÉ D')   Anjou produces a great many rosé wines that qualify for the Anjou appellation, all of which have a suppleness, fruitiness and freshness that have deservedly won them great popularity. Only rosé made exclusively from the Cabernet grape is entitled to the Cabernet d'Anjou appellation. Rosés are produced in most parts of Anjou, but particularly around Brissac in the Coteaux de l'Aubance★, around Tigné in the central area of the Coteaux du Layon★, and in the Saumur★ region. The latter produces only Cabernet rosés, which are entitled to the appellation Cabernet de Saumur.

Anjou rosés make good carafe wines, being well balanced, fruity and light, sometimes slightly moelleux★, and best drunk within a year of the vintage. Cabernet d'Anjou has an attractive colour, is fresh and fruity and should have an alcoholic strength of at least 10°. Its liveliness and fruitiness are best appreciated when young. The production of rosés in Anjou has undergone a remarkable expansion, increasing some 80% in the last ten years.

announcement of vendange   A proclamation formerly used to notify growers to begin harvesting the grapes. They were forbidden to start the harvest before that moment. This constraint led to the production of quality wines by not allowing the picking of grapes before they were mature. The decision to announce the vendange was based on the appearance and taste of the grapes (modern analytical methods of checking maturation did not

The hillsides of Layon in Anjou. Phot. M.

then exist), and also conformed to local custom.

In Burgundy the vendange began 100 days after the flowering of the vines. Today, the ancient words are proclaimed by the president of the Jurade of Saint-Emilion standing symbolically at the top of the Tower of the King; 'People of Saint-Emilion and the seven communes, the Jurade proclaims the beginning of the vendange. Open the heavy doors of the cuves and begin the picking'.

appellation d'origine Wines labelled *à appellation d'origine* are always designated by a precise geographic term which leaves no doubt where they come from. It may be an entire region (Burgundy), a town (Nuit-Saint-Georges), a château in Bordeaux (Château d'Yquem) or a climat★ in Burgundy (Richebourg).

French legislation obliges producers to comply with stringent requirements for their wines being classed appellation d'origine. These wines are divided into strict official categories drawn up by an organisation called l'Institut National des Appellations d'Origine (INAO★). The categories are: vins à appellation d'origine contrôlée★, vins délimités de qualité supérieure★ (VDQS) and vins à appellation simple. The superior category is represented by the appellation d'origine contrôlée (AOC) under which are classified practically all the great wines of France. Then come the vins délimités de qualité supérieure (VDQS), excellent regional wines which must meet certain standards of quality although not as high as those for AOC wines. Finally, the third category, the wines à appellation simple, includes only a few representatives. The wines of Alsace were classed in this category for a long time, but they have now graduated to the AOC class. The white, red and rosé still wines of Champagne are included in this category.

On wine menus the wines of appellation d'origine must never be mixed with ordinary wines but should always have a special heading.

appellation d'origine contrôlée (AOC) The INAO★ has laid down strict rules for the admission of all the great wines which are included in this prestigious classification. The area of pro-duction must be clearly defined, and all the wine's contributing factors are carefully controlled and specified – variety of grape, minimum amount of sugar in the must and of alcohol in the wine, maximum yield per hectare, methods of pruning, viticulture and vinification. Although these rules are based on long-standing tradition and local practice, they are in no way opposed to scientific innovations provided they bring about an improvement in the quality of the wine. Conformity to the rules is strictly enforced by representatives both of the INAO and the Répression des Fraudes★.

All the famous French crus are AOC wines, and all of them must carry the words 'Appellation Contrôlée' clearly on their label (one exception being Champagne). When being transported, these wines must be accompanied by transit documents and by certificates indicating any particular modifications they have undergone, and the title must also figure on declarations of harvest and stocks, prospectuses, bills of sale and on all containers. France has more than 150 AOC wines.

Arbois Arbois and Château-Chalon are the most famous vineyards in the Jura★ department of France. Several communes share the highly-prized appellation contrôlée of Arbois, the best known being Pupillin, Montigny-les-Arsures, Mesnay and Les Arsures. Although they had been well known for many centuries, Pasteur really made the wines of Arbois famous when he settled there to engage upon his research into the fermentation and diseases of wine, which he afterwards described in his 'Etudes Sur le Vin'.

The red wines of Arbois are fine and generous, the whites are low in alcohol and dry with a highly individual bouquet. The vineyard also produces sparkling wine (made by the Champagne method), vin de paille★ and vin jaune★ which is almost on a par with Château-Chalon★. The most famous of its quality wines, however, is probably Arbois rosé, an excellent, fruity, dry wine with an attractive light ruby colour that verges on *pelure d'oignon*★. There is a record of it being served at the Royal tables as early as 1298. A local saying about these excellent wines is that '*Plus on en boit, plus on va droit*' (the more one

Following two pages: celebration of the proclamation of the wine-harvest at Saint-Emilion. Phot. Renè-Jacques.

17

drinks, the straighter one walks) – a saying which it is tempting to put to the test!

Argentina The Argentine vineyards have been expanding rapidly for the last forty years, and their output is now roughly equal to that of Algeria, i.e. 155,000 hl a year. Argentina is the chief producer as well as the chief consumer of wine in South America★. Very little of its wine is exported as practically the entire annual production is consumed locally. The wines, which are all cheap and full-bodied, are harvested in the Mendoza and San Juan districts not far from the Chilean border, at the foot of the Andes due west of Buenos Aires. The red wines are generally better than the whites and the rosés.

Armenia The principal wine-growing centres of this Soviet republic are Etchmiadzin, Ashtarak and Jerevan. The largest vineyard lies around Jerevan and extends as far as Anipemza in the north, and Artachat in the south. The local wine-growers have managed to cultivate various frost-resistant species of grapes on irrigated volcanic soil in the mountainous regions (Lori, Chirak and Zangezour). Although most Armenian wines are dry,

General view of Arbois. Phot. Beaujard-Lauros.

the country is well known for its port-type wine, which is sold in the USSR as 'Portvein'.

aroma Aroma is the distinctive smell which a wine exudes. In French it is also called *fruit, parfum, bouquet primaire* and *bouquet originel*. Aroma is essentially a product of the grape, since it originates from substances that form in the grape skin as it grows. Each species of grape, therefore, has its own particular aroma which is more or less pronounced according to species, soil and vintage. Red and white Burgundies, for example, have technically speaking no aroma, since with one or two exceptions the juice of their grapes has, when freshly picked, only a very slight smell.

The most characteristic aroma is that of Muscat★ grapes, but the Cabernet, Traminer, Syrah and Malvoisie varieties are also quite distinctive. A great deal of aroma is lost during fermentation, and dry★ wines rarely have as much aroma as wines which have retained a certain amount of their natural sugar. Aroma also tends to fade with time. It first combines with the developing bouquet★ and then is superseded by it.

aromatic An aromatic wine is one that gives off a powerful aroma★. Only fruity wines are really aromatic, as aroma depends largely on the grapes from which the wine is made.

artificial wines Various artificial beverages have at one time or another been invented and sold as wine to the public, mostly at the end of the last century during the wine shortage caused by the devastation of French vineyards by oidium★, phylloxera★ and mildew★. Some were made from dried Greek and Turkish raisins, others were simply vins de sucre★ which had nothing to do with grapes at all. Others still were 'improved' vins de sucre. Two, three or even four cuvées★ were made from the same crop by running off the first wine and then pouring sugar, water and other ingredients on to the residue left in the vat to make it ferment again. Also, a 'white wine' was made by adding large quantities of sulphuric acid to extremely coarse, poor quality red wine and thus neutralising its colour.

Vendange at Mendoza in Argentina. Phot. Aarons.

A famous case of falsifying wines occurred recently at Limoges, where the defendant, who had been concocting 'wine' out of purely chemical substances, received a harsh sentence.

assemblage The blending or combining of wines in a vat, e.g. the vin de goutte★ with the vin de presse★ from the same cuvée★, or vat. Wines from different vats are also blended in order to achieve an overall uniformity of the vineyard's production. Assemblage is also used as a technique for the correction★ of wines. Different vintages from the same vineyard are blended to maintain a consistent character and quality from one year to the next. This method is standard practice in Champagne★, but as it requires enormous and costly reserve stocks, as well as a great deal of storage room and much extra labour, it is not really a viable proposition for the average vigneron.

Asti Asti, situated south of Turin, is one of the most important centres of the Italian wine industry. It is best known abroad for its sparkling wine Asti Spumante, which is made from the Canelli Muscat grape

21

(named after a village near Asti) cultivated on the surrounding hills. This grape makes pale, sweet wine with a low alcohol content and a very pronounced aroma★, which is also used in the manufacture of Italian vermouths.

Asti also produces good quality red wines from Barbera and Freisa grapes, and from the excellent Grignolino and Nebbiolo varieties.

Asti Spumante   A very popular sparkling wine (*spumante* literally means 'foaming') made at Asti★. The method of production differs from those generally used in France for sparkling wines in that the basis of the final product is not wine but must, i.e. unfermented grape juice. Another difference is that the carbon dioxide which causes the effervescence is, in the Asti method, produced by the first fermentation, whereas in other methods the sparkle does not develop until secondary fermentation, either in bottle (Champagne method★ and German method★) or in vat (the cuve close★, Charmat process).

At Asti the must of Muscat★ grapes is stored in cellars under refrigeration, which effectively prevents it from fermenting. It is then decanted and transferred to hermetically sealed vats where it is left to ferment and produce the carbon dioxide that forms the wine's effervescence. The great advantage of this method is that it allows the Muscat grapes to retain their characteristic taste and aroma. Great care and delicacy is usually needed to make sparkling wines from Muscat grapes. If they are vinified as for dry wines, i.e. if all their natural sugar is used up in the first fermentation, they will lose their distinctive aroma when extra sugar is added to cause the secondary fermentation.

astringent   Another word used by wine-tasters to describe this trait is tannic, since astringency is generally caused by an excess of tannin★. Astringent wine makes the mouth and face pucker up and can sometimes cause an involuntary grimace. It is thus sometimes said to have 'bite'. Astringent wines are also called harsh★, hard★, angular and thick.

Aubance (Coteaux de l')   An Anjou★ vineyard that stretches from the Loire to the Layon along the Aubance, which is a tributary of the Loire. Although its wines were until the sixteenth century more highly prized than those of the neighbouring Coteaux de Layon★, the latter have since gradually come to be preferred by wine-lovers.

The Aubance shares with the Layon vineyards its schistose soil and its vines, the Pineau de la Loire variety. The white wines entitled to the appellation Coteaux de l'Aubance are usually medium dry, fruity and delicate, with a pleasant earthy taste (*goût de terroir*★). Although they have less strength, vitality and firmness than Layon wines, they nonetheless have a certain character of their own. The best-known domaines, or estates, are at Mûrs, Saint-Melaine, Soulaines and Vauchrétien.

The overall production of Coteaux de l'Aubance is not great, and is consumed locally. The commune of Brissac, which is also in the Coteaux de l'Aubance area, produces a great quantity of rosé and Cabernet rosé under the regional appellation Anjou.

Ausone (Château)   A premier grand cru classé★ of Saint-Emilion. Although it is doubtless only a legend, local tradition has it that Château Ausone occupies the site of the property where the Roman poet Ausonius lived in the fourth century. Château Ausone is a very fine wine that is generous and elegant.

austere   An austere wine does not lack good qualities, but has a high tannin content which tends to obscure its taste and bouquet. It is also a little too rough to please all palates. Immature Médocs, for example, often have this characteristic. It is also said that such a wine is 'severe' and its good qualities are often hidden beneath this severity.

Australia   Vines are not indigenous to Australia. The first ones were planted near Sydney in New South Wales in about 1788. Today the states of Victoria and South Australia both cultivate vines more extensively than New South Wales, and 50% of their production consists of fresh eating-grapes and raisins. As in Europe, the vines were successfully regrafted on to American rootstocks when the vineyards were devastated by phylloxera★.

In the last few years great technical

progress has been made in Australian vinification methods, particularly in the preparation of Australian 'sherry', a fortified wine made in the same way as genuine sherry.

Wines resembling European ones are designated under the appellations claret, Burgundy, Bordeaux, Moselle, etc. But these traditional names are quickly being replaced by labels indicating the grape and viticultural region. The principal vineyards are found in the following regions:

Hunter Valley Produces a Burgundy-type wine which improves with age and can be kept for a long time in bottle.

Central and North-East Victoria Produces dessert wines of the Muscat, Madeira and port types as well as some light, white wines and good full-bodied reds.

Western Victoria Produces light, white wines of the Riesling and Champagne types and also more robust whites and vigorous, flavourful reds.

South and South-East Australia Produces quality red wines.

Adelaide The region around this city is known for its Bordeaux-type flavourful reds as well as delicate whites and sherry-type dessert wines, both vintage and tawny.

Barossa Valley, Eden Valley, Clare One of the largest Australian vineyard areas. Full-bodied reds, light aromatic Rieslings and dessert wines are produced.

Swan Valley There are many small producers, but only four or five large vineyards. The Burgundy-type wines are vigorous and full-bodied and, like those of the Hunter Valley, have a very characteristic aroma.

Murray Valley Sweet wines and Muscats are produced all along the Murray River as are dry, supple, mild whites of the Moselle and Sauternes types, sherry-type wines and also a large quantity of light rosé and red table wines. During the last few years more noble grapes have been planted in many districts, particularly at Cadell, Mildura, Nildottie, Lexton and Langhorne Creek.

Riverina District Forty viticultural enterprises produce red wines, dry and sweet whites and sherry-type dessert wines.

Austria The vineyards of Austria have suffered a great deal from the successive wars fought on her soil, and the remains of the Austro-Hungarian empire were stripped of many good wine-growing regions (such as the Tyrol which is now partly Italian). Today, the total annual production more or less meets national demand and very little Austrian wine is exported.

The best Austrian wines are white. The red ones, made from Spätburgunder (Pinot Noir) grapes, are in no way remarkable, and are all consumed locally. The

Austria: Wolkersdorf vines, near the Czech border. Phot. Ségalat.

23

white wines are in quite another class. Made from Riesling, Sylvaner, Gewürztraminer and Müller-Thurgau grapes, together with several local varieties such as Rotgipfler and Veltliner (which is rather like Traminer★ though with less aroma and flavour), they have certain similarities with the wines made in the neighbouring districts of southern Germany and the Italian Tyrol. They are light, dry, fresh, fruity wines which should be drunk young.

Gumpoldskirchener, produced south of Vienna, is probably the best-known Austrian wine today. Loved by generations of Viennese, it is a clear, fragrant, fruity wine and, although it has never been a great one, is always very agreeable. Loibner, Kremser and Dürnsteiner wines are grown and harvested on the steep banks of the Danube

A tavern-keeper savours the new wine of Gumpoldskirche, near Vienna. Phot. Rapho.

to the east of Vienna, and are generally excellent. In addition, the region immediately around Vienna produces good carafe wines that are drunk in the cafés of Vienna and Grinzing. The best of these carafe wines (Nassberger, Wiener and Grinzinger) are sometimes bottled and exported.

Auvergne The wines of Auvergne are classified with those of the Loire★ and are VDQS★. Despite efforts to promote and improve viniculture in the region, the vineyards now cover only one-third of their former area, and wine production has decreased proportionately. Most of the vineyards lie south and south-east of Clermont-Ferrand, though there are also a few in the area between Châtel-Guyon and Issoire. They are divided into three main production areas: the Clermont-Ferrand district, which produces the once-famous crus Chanturgues★ and Corent; the Issoire district, in which the good and fruity wines of Boudes are grown; and the Riom district, with its well-known fruity cru Châteaugay.

Auvergne wines are usually red, sometimes rosé, and are made from Gamay grapes. They are good quality, fresh, pleasant wines with a fine bouquet, and should be drunk young. Local demand for them is great, particularly in the region's many spa towns.

Ayse A Savoie★ cru from the Bonneville region. The sparkling wine of Ayse has great character but also a reputation for 'breaking legs'. To qualify for the appellation Mousseux de Savoie, followed by the name Ayse, the wine must be made from Gringet, Altesse and Roussette d'Ayse (at least 30%) grapes. It is made either by the Champagne method★ of bottling before secondary fermentation, or by the local method of spontaneous fermentation.

Azay-le-Rideau Not far from Tours in the valley of Indre, the flinty soil of Azay-le-Rideau's limestone hills produces a white wine that has been famous for many centuries. Several communes share the appellation (which must always be

The château of Azay-le-Rideau. Phot. Lauros-Geay.

25

Azay-le-Rideau: the first wine festival (1968). Phot. Léah Lourié.

preceded by the word Touraine). Saché, where Balzac wrote *'Le Lys dans la Vallée,'* enjoys the greatest reputation. Production is very low, which is a pity as the wine is dry, fresh and fruity, and is considered one of the best dry white wines of Touraine. Its official minimum alcohol content is 10°.

Azerbaijan Vines have been grown in this Soviet Republic for many hundreds of years. They were even mentioned by the Greek geographer Strabon, who was born in 58 BC. The methods used by Azerbaijani vignerons in the Middle Ages indicate an advanced knowledge of viniculture. The vine-shoots were trained along growing props (young trees) or bunches of reeds tied together in threes, or spread out on the sandy soil. In the colder areas they were covered with earth in winter and carefully loosened again in spring. There is even some evidence of grafting. The entire crop

was made into wine and, given the sophistication of their vinicultural techniques, it was probably extremely good.

With the adoption of Islam as the country's religion, the wine industry declined, and it was only in the nineteenth century that it slowly began to revive.

Today, some forty varieties of grape are cultivated, the best of which are Ag Shany and Gara Shany, both grown on the sandy peninsular of Apsheron. The chief vine-growing areas are, in order of importance: Shamkhor, Shemakha, Kirovabad, Tauz and Agsu (near Shemakha). Wine is also produced all over the Nagorno-Karabakh district from Norashen-Shakhbuz to Paragachai. The most important product of the region is a Soviet port-type wine called 'Portvein'. Azerbaijan's white vins ordinaires are pleasant and light, especially Báyan Shirei. There is also a very velvety red wine called Matrassa.

B

Badacsony A well-known Hungarian vineyard situated on the western shore of Lake Balaton. In ancient times it was the property of the Grey Friars, and was divided into small lots in the seventeenth century. Badacsony is a sarcophagus-shaped hill 400 m high on which the vines grow in terraces giving the area a Mediterranean atmosphere. The peasants say that only the vines 'which are reflected in the mirror of Lake Balaton' give good wine as the undersides of the leaves receive reflected light from the lake.

The wine of Badacsony has been re-nowned for some years. It is often said that the fire of ancient volcanoes burns in it and that the Romans knew and appreciated its flavour. Altars erected to the Roman God of wine, the 'Liber Pater', have been discovered in the course of excavations. The old wine presses★ are constructed on Roman foundations, and the knife used in the vendange which is passed down from generation to generation resembles the implement used by the Romans. The largest wine cellar in Hungary is found in the community of Badacsonylabdi. It contains more than a million and a half litres.

The best-known wines of Badacsony are the Badacsonyi Kéknyelu, a white wine of the Kéknyelu grape (whose name means blue sleeve), and the Szürkebarat (grey friar). But the region also produces other good white wines from the Rizling (Riesling), Furmint and other grapes, and also remarkable dessert wines.

Baden A wine-growing area of south-west Germany★ bordered by Switzerland on the south and Alsace on the west. The many vineyards planted with different varieties are found at the foot of the Black Forest facing the Rhine Valley. Since the Second World War, considerable effort has been made to regroup and replant the vineyards. The dominant grape varieties are the Müller-Thurgau, the Gutedel (Chasselas) and Pinot Noir, each representing about one-fifth of the total. Pinot Gris, Pinot Blanc, Sylvaner and a little Riesling account for the rest. Almost all of the wine is produced in modern co-operative cellars.

The very varied wines of Baden, which used to be consumed only locally, are now gaining favour on the German market and

18th-century house at Badacsony. This type of building comprised a cellar, cave and press, and was used only in the harvest period.
Phot. J.-L. Charmet.

27

are starting to be exported to other countries. Some of the better-known wines of the area are: the Seeweine of Lake Constance; the good cru of Kaiserstuhl, produced on a sort of volcanic island to the west of Freiburg; the Markgräfler grown between Freiburg and Switzerland from the Gutedel; and the Mauerweine produced around Baden-Baden and sold in bocksbeutels like the wines of Franconia.

Bandol The wines of Bandol, which have one of the four appellations contrôlées of Provence★, grow on terraced hillsides (called *restanques*) between La Ciotat and Toulon.

The vineyard's four principal communes are Bandol, La Cadière-d'Azur, Sanary and Le Castellet. The area also includes Le Beausset, Saint-Cyr, Ollioules and Evenos. Wooded hills shelter the vineyard against cold winds from the north, and the proximity of the sea reduces any sudden change of temperature so that the vineyard rarely suffers from extremes of heat or cold. Apart from vines, the arid flint and limestone soil produces nothing but pine trees and scrub.

Bandol's red wine has always been held in high esteem, even in quite distant

countries – in fact travelling by sea seemed to suit it extremely well and gave it a smooth texture and bouquet that were much admired. It is made from a combination of Mourvèdre, Grenache and Cinsault grapes. As all its most distinctive qualities are contributed by Mourvèdre, the viticultural authorities have decreed a gradual increase in the proportion of this variety (now at least 20%) in an attempt to restore the red wine's former reputation.

To qualify for its appellation the red wine must mature for at least eighteen months before being bottled. At the end of this period it is a fine, generous, robust and well-balanced wine with an attractive dark colour, a distinctive velvety texture and an aroma of violets whose strength varies in proportion to the amount of Mourvèdre grape in the wine's composition. It ages well, acquiring a characteristic bouquet, and is arguably the best red wine of Provence.

The white wine, which is mostly produced around Sanary, is also excellent. It is made from Clairette (50%) and Ugni Blanc grapes and is dry (but not acid), fresh and full-bodied.

The rosé is fruity, supple and fresh and is steadily increasing in popularity. The official maturing period for both white and rosé is at least eight months.

banvin (right of) In feudal days, the time in which the lord could sell his own wine before his vassals had the right to market theirs. The exact number of days was generally determined by custom and varied greatly from one fiefdom to another. The lord owned the oven, the mill and the wine press which his subjects used as a right of their tenure. The lord also sold the wines to other areas and searched for new outlets when the local production was large. In exchange for this last service he was granted the right of banvin, dating from the end of the Carolingian period (AD 987).

The term 'banvin' also means the notice authorising the sale of wine by the subjects on the lord's territory.

Banyuls This Roussillon★ wine is the most famous and perhaps the best French AOC vin doux naturel★. The Banyuls area lies at the extreme south of France on the

Spanish frontier. It is bordered by mountains on every side, those to the east plunging straight into the Mediterranean. This stretch of rocky coast is the most picturesque part of the Côte Vermeille.

The vineyard is divided into four communes, Banyuls, Cerbère, Port-Vendres and Collioure, and is extremely difficult to cultivate as it consists of very steep hillsides that rise to an altitude of 300 m, and extend to the very edge of the cliffs that fall to the sea. The vines have to be grown in terraces in order to withstand the torrential rains and the *tramontane* (a north wind). The vignerons use an interesting system of channelling water called *pied de coq*. The soil itself is hard to work, consisting mainly of shale with a thin covering of arable earth which has to be brought up to the top of the vineyard every year.

Banyuls wine is traditionally made from the Grenache Noir grape. Like all vins doux naturels, alcohol is added to the wine, a process which enables it to retain the full flavour of the grapes. The alcohol is added to bring fermentation to a halt before all the wine's natural grape sugar has been converted into alcohol. If a dry wine is desired, the mutage★ is left until all the sugar has been fermented.

There are two appellations d'origine contrôlée: Banyuls and Banyuls Grand Cru★.

Besides being an apéritif and dessert wine that bears comparison with the most famous wines of its category made in other countries (notably Germany), Banyuls is also a good accompaniment to certain main dishes. It is a warm, racé★ wine with breeding and elegance.

BANYULS GRAND CRU   This red wine is subject to much stricter regulations than the Banyuls. Certain features of its preparation are officially specified and rigorously adhered to, such as the species of grape; obligatory égrappage★, or destalking; a minimum five days' maceration of grape juice and skins before mutage★; and, above all, at least thirty months maturing 'in wood'. The wine is first put in small casks to mature in contact with the air, and later transferred to large, hermetically-sealed wooden ones (*foudres*) to complete the process. In addition, the wine is tasted, before being bottled, by a panel of inspectors appointed by the INAO★.

Barbaresco   One of the best red wines of the Italian province of Piemonte. It is made from the Nebbiolo grape and produced in limited quantities around the two communes of Barbaresco and Neive. Although the production area is similar to that of the neighbouring Barolo★ and they both come from the same grape, Barbaresco is very different. A lighter wine, it matures more quickly and after two or three years in bottle takes on a *pelure d'oignon*★ tint. It is an excellent and distinctive wine which is classed among the best of Italy. Unlike Barolo, which is generally sold in Burgundy-shape bottles, Barbaresco is often found in the Bordeaux-type.

Barbera   A red wine made from the Barbera grape in the Piemonte region of Italy. It is a good table wine with colour, body and plenty of bouquet and flavour.

Vendange near Banyuls on hills overlooking the sea. Phot. Rapho.

29

Barbera is a wine of no great distinction, and is best drunk young and as an accompaniment to Italian food. It sometimes referments in bottle and becomes moustillant★, which, although it may be strange to subtler palates, suits the people of Piemonte very well.

Bardolino A very good light red wine from the province of Verona in Italy, produced at the eastern end of Lake Garda. Like its neighbour Valpolicella★, it is made from Corvina, Negrara and Molinara grapes. Hardly more coloured than a dark rosé, it is a delicious, fruity wine that rarely has an alcohol content of more than 11°. Bardolino is at its best between one and three years of age.

Barolo Barolo is possibly the best red wine of Italy and is made from the Nebbiolo grape. Both full-bodied and long-lasting, it is not unlike the wines of the Côtes-du-Rhône★, and sometimes reminiscent of Hermitage★ and Côte-Rôtie★. It is produced in the Piemonte region on eight communes around the village of Barolo, south of Turin. It is usually kept in cask for three years before being bottled (in Burgundy-shaped bottles), and improves even more if left longer. Barolo is strong (from 12–14°) and has an attractive deep red colour. It is always a good wine and often a great one.

barrique A large barrel, or cask, that varies in size from one region to another (it is often advisable to ascertain its capacity before purchase). A barrique usually holds 228 litres (in the Nantes and Côtre d'Or regions, for example). In Bordeaux it holds 225 litres, an ancient tradition officially established by a law of 1866; and a bordelais tonneau★ holds 900 litres, or four barriques. In Touraine and Anjou it is equal to 232 litres, and in Languedoc, to a third of a muid★. In some regions (e.g. Burgundy) it is also known as a pièce★.

Barsac This commune, which is part of the Sauternes vineyard, is traditionally and officially entitled to the two appellations Barsac and Sauternes★. Barsac is as outstanding a wine as Sauternes, and is made with the same meticulous care. The differences between the two are, in fact, few and subtle: Barsac is less gras★ and less sweet, but also fruitier and more aromatic when young. The premiers crus of the 1855 classification★ are Châteaux Climens and Coutet, but the seconds crus are also excellent – Châteaux Myrat, Doisy-Daëne, Doisy-Dubroca and Doisy-Védrines. (See Index.)

Baux-de-Provence (Coteaux des) The wines of this region have recently qualified for the VDQS★ label. The red and rosé wines are made from Grenache, Carignan, Cinsault and Mourvèdre grapes, the white wines from Clairette, Ugni and Muscat varieties, all of which are well suited to a sunny climate. The wines have breeding and elegance.

Baux-de-Provence (Coteaux des) The wines of this region have recently qualified for the VDQS★ label. The red and rosé wines are made from Grenarche, Carignan, Cinsault and Mourvèdre grapes, the white wines from Clairette, Ugni and Muscat varieties, all of which are well suited to a sunny climate. The wines have breeding and elegance.

Béarn This former French province covered almost the same area as the present-day department of Basses-Pyrénées. Its vine-growing area, which forms part of the Sud-Ouest★ region, covers picturesque hillsides between the *gaves*, or mountain streams, of Pau and Oloron, sometimes reaching a height of

300 m. It has a great many communes, including Jurançon, Gan, Lasseube, Monein, Salies-de-Béarn, Bellocq and Oraas. In the north-east the vineyard extends to the border of the Hautes-Pyrénées department and slopes down to the Adour valley around Lembeye, Crouseilles, Conchez and Portet.

Béarn is mainly known for its appellation contrôlée wines: the great Jurançon★ and its close rival Pacherenc-du-Vic-Bihl★, and the red wine of Madiran★. However, it also produces some VDQS★ sold as vins de Béarn. Most of these wines, which can be either red, white or rosé, are vinified in co-operative cellars. The reds and rosés are good wines that are consumed locally and much praised by visitors. They are made mainly from Tannat grapes, in combination with Bouchy and Pinenc and sometimes Manseng and Courbu Rouge. The dry white wines are made from various grapes such as Baroque, Courbu Blanc, Sémillon and Claverie but output is only about 15% of total red and rosé production. Rousselet du Béarn, which is made near Pau, is probably the most pleasant of these white wines.

Beaujolais The southernmost vineyard of the Burgundy region and also the largest, covering about 15,000 ha. It is situated entirely in the Rhône department, except for the canton of Chapelle-de-Guinchay which is in Saône-et-Loire. The picturesque hillsides of Beaujolais lie on slopes overlooking the Saône valley and rise to heights of 500 and even 600 m.

The predominant variety of grape is the Gamay. Although this grape is also grown in both the Auvergne and Loire regions, it is only in Beaujolais that it develops all its qualities (particularly its fruitiness) to the fullest. This is probably due to the granitic soil of the area since, on clay and limestone soil elsewhere in Burgundy, the same grape makes relatively ordinary wine. A small quantity of white Beaujolais is produced, made like all white Burgundies from Chardonnay grapes.

Beaujolais is the ideal carafe wine, pleasant, smooth and refreshing. It should always be served chilled, which is rare for red wine. For many years Beaujolais was drunk only by the inhabitants of Lyons, but since then the charm of its youth and freshness has won it widespread popularity. Beaujolais' nine crus are, from north to south: Saint-Amour★, Juliénas★, Chénas★, Moulin-à-Vent★, Fleurie★, Chiroubles★, Morgon★, Brouilly★ and Côte-de-Brouilly★. Other Beaujolais appellations are Beaujolais★, Beaujolais supérieur★ and Beaujolais-Villages★.

BEAUJOLAIS and BEAUJOLAIS SUPÉRIEUR These appellations apply to red, rosé and white wines grown all over the Beaujolais area. For Beaujolais, red wines must be at least 9° in alcohol content

31

and white wines, 9·5°; for Beaujolais supérieur, red wines must be 10° and white wines, 10·5°. Maximum yield per hectare may not exceed 50 hl for Beaujolais and 45 hl for Beaujolais supérieur.

BEAUJOLAIS-VILLAGES Certain wines from the best areas of the vineyard are entitled to the appellation Beaujolais-Villages, or Beaujolais followed by the name of their commune, e.g. Jullié, Emeringes, Leynes and Bellevue. (See Index.) The great charm of these unpretentious, fruity and smooth Beaujolais is their youth. They should therefore be drunk within about a year of the vintage, and always slightly chilled (never at room temperature) to bring out the fruity flavour.

The Hospice de Beaune (view from the courtyard).
Phot. Aarons-L.S.P.

Beaumes-de-Venise A commune that lies a little to the south of Rasteau★ in the Vaucluse department and produces an excellent appellation contrôlée Muscat wine made, like other vins doux naturels★, by mutage★ of the must with alcohol. But whereas Rasteau wine is made almost exclusively from Grenache grapes, Beaumes-de-Venise Muscat can only be made from Muscat-à-petit-grains, a small-graped vine also called Muscat de Frontignan. The vineyard is part of the southern Côtes-du-Rhône region and extends from Beaumes-de-Venise to Aubignan.

Although relatively and undeservedly little known, owing to low production,

Beaumes-de-Venise is one of the best French vins doux naturels. It is golden, sweet (although less so than Frontignan★) and, above all, has exquisite finesse and a marvellous aroma. It ages well, preserving all its finesse and aroma.

Beaune This small, picturesque city is historically, spiritually and commercially one of the great centres of the Burgundian wine industry. It is famous for its magnificent Hôtel-Dieu, an almshouse that was founded in 1443 and has its own vineyards. These produce very fine wines (the *vins des Hospices de Beaune*) which have been famous for centuries and are sold to the public at the wine auctions that take place in the Hôtel-Dieu each November. This annual sale is an important event for wine merchants everywhere, and its proceeds are devoted to the maintenance of the Hôtel-Dieu and its charitable activities.

Some 95% of Beaune's wines are red. However, all its wines, both red and white, are distinguished, graceful and well balanced. The whites have a pronounced bouquet while the reds vary a great deal according to the conditions of their growth (soil, climate, etc.). Some are vigorous and firm, some are velvety and fine, and some again combine finesse with a warm, strong flavour. Erasmus, the humanist philosopher, felt he owed his recovery from ill-health to Beaune, and wrote, 'Fortunate Burgundy! You should be called the Mother of Men since you give them such milk!'

The most famous crus are Grèves, Fèves, Marconnets, les Bressandes, Cras, Clos de la Mousse, Clos du Roi and Clos des Mouches (which produces a remarkably good white wine). (See Index.)

Belgium Vines were introduced to Belgium by the Romans, who planted them principally along the Meuse and Escaut rivers. The most extensive vineyards seem to have been established in the ninth century around Liège and Huy. (It was on the hills overlooking Huy, incidentally, that the last Belgian wine made from grapes grown in the open air was produced, in 1947.) There is mention of vines growing in Namur and Tournai in the tenth century, and in Brussels, Bruges and Malines in the eleventh.

Today, Belgian wine is quite different as

Cultivation of grapes in a glasshouse near Brussels. The wine is made from the 'Royal' grape. Phot. Actualit.

it is made entirely from hothouse-grown grapes vinified by co-operatives. Hothouse cultivation made its first appearance in 1865 near Brussels, in Hoeilaart and Overijssel, where the grapes were sold as fresh fruit. It was not until about 1954, following an unusually large production, that a hothouse owner had the idea of making wine from his crop.

The grapes used are the Frankenthal, Royal and Colman varieties with a small quantity of Chasselas★. Belgian wine is mostly white, sometimes rosé or sparkling. It is made of 95% red grapes and 5% white (the white wine can therefore be called blanc de noirs★). Vintage is totally unimportant as the grapes are always grown in hothouses and are sheltered from changes of climate. Belgian wine should be consumed early and does not keep well.

The hothouse cultivation of Belgian grapes used to be protected by internal taxes which virtually prohibited other European varieties. Since the formation of the EEC, however, these taxes have been abolished and Italian and French grapes are now being sold in increasing quantities on the Belgian market. Today, the government subsidises vine-growers who uproot their vines and plant something else, so viticulture is no longer an economic proposition.

Bellet A tiny vineyard in Provence★ with its own appellation contrôlée. Surrounded by the acres of carnations and other flowers that are grown on the perimeter of the commune of Nice, it lies on hills overlooking the Var valley at a height of 250–300 m. The slopes of these hills are very steep, which means that the vineyard has to be cultivated by hand.

Bellet produces very little wine. Not long ago the vineyard was reconstructed and divided among several owners, one of whom subsequently installed equipment that could vinify the whole crop at once. The wine, which can be red, rosé or white, is excellent, and has a distinctive character. Most of the grapes grown are exclusive to the vineyard: Folle-Noire, Braquet and Cinsault for the red and rosé (there is, however, a large number of supplementary varieties authorised for rosé); Rolle, Roussan, Spagnol or Mayorquin for the white.

The red wine is light, fine and delicate, and has an attractive ruby colour. The rosé is also light and elegant, and has an aroma of iris root. The white wine has a lot of character, having nerve★ and elegance with a fine aroma and freshness remarkable in a southern wine. This is probably due to the cold winds that come from the Alps and to the altitude of the vineyard.

bentonite A special kind of clay (silicate of aluminium) which is extracted from deposits in Wyoming and South Dakota in the USA. Used in fining, it causes proteins in solution to flocculate and to form deposits in the bottle. It has very good results when used in large quantities to clarify the wine. Unfortunately, it robs the wine of other substances which contribute to its fullness and sometimes imparts an earthy taste when used indiscriminately.

Bergerac A vineyard that covers most of the Bergerac area of Dordogne. Its wines are classed among those of the Sud-Ouest★ and are entitled to the appellation d'origine contrôlée Bergerac. The vineyard produces red wines which, despite a reputation dating from the Middle Ages, are relatively little known outside their place of origin. Those grown on the right bank of the Dordogne (of which Pécharmant★ is the best known) have more finesse and suppleness, while those grown on the left have more body, colour and tannin.

The wines are made from Cabernet, Merlot and Malbec grapes (all Bordeaux varieties) and contain from 9–12° of alcohol. The white wines are subtle, mellow, rarely dry (except for Panisseau★), and are made from Sémillon, Sauvignon and Muscadelle grapes. Rosette★ is one of the best-known crus. Monbazillac★ should also be mentioned here. It is the region's most famous wine, and has its own appellation contrôlée. Bergerac also produces some rosé wines.

Berry The old French province of Berry, which, with its capital, Bourges, lies at the very heart of France, is today divided into the two departments of Cher and Indre. Its wines have always been highly esteemed: Gregory of Tours mentioned them in 582, and in 1567, Nicolas of Nicolay wrote in his *Description Générale des Pais et Duché de Berry* that, 'The dry, stony region abounds in very good wine that keeps a long time'. Today, four Berry wines have appellations d'origine contrôlée: Sancerre★, Ménetou-Salon★, Quincy★ and Reuilly★. Châteaumeillant★ has a VDQS★ label. The red and rosé wines with these appellations are made from Pinot and Gamay grapes, the white from Sauvignon.

Bikavér One of the most famous red wines of Hungary★, produced on the hills of the village of Eger about 100 km northeast of Budapest. It is made from the excellent Hungarian grape Kadarka, together with a few French varieties such as Cabernet and Gamay. The vineyard was severely damaged by phylloxera★ in 1880, but fortunately not completely destroyed. Bikavér (which means 'bull's blood') is a magnificent, full-bodied, generous wine with an attractive deep red colour and a very distinctive bouquet. It is considered the best red wine of Hungary.

Blagny A hamlet in the Côte de Beaune★ region whose vineyard is divided between Meursault★ and Puligny-Montrachet★, giving rise to an unusual situation: the climats★ in the Puligny area have the appellation Puligny-Montrachet, and those on the Meursault side, Blagny or Meursault-Blagny. The white wine of Blagny is similar to Meursault, though it has an elegance and delicacy more like that of Puligny. The red wine is fine and delicate and not unlike Volnay★.

blanc (vin) White wine. The vinification of white wine differs greatly from that of reds, being more difficult and unpredictable. More precautions must be taken when gathering the grapes and they have to be transported to the vatting sheds without being crushed in the process. There they must be pressed immediately, stalks and all.

The first juice obtained, moût de goutte★, is separated from the skins and put in barrels. Then the rest of the grapes are crushed, a longer process than that for reds because the must has a tendancy to expand. However, it is necessary to press quickly in order to avoid contact with the air which can cause yellowing and maderisation. The moût de presse★ then joins the moût de goutte in the vat and the important sulphur dioxide★ is added. This is left standing for six to twelve hours during which time the must separates from the sediment. Next comes a light racking and transferrence of the juice into new oak barrels (which give the necessary tannin to the wine) for fermentation. This process is always more laborious and delicate than for the red wine as the yeasts need essential elements found in the parts of the grape

'The Vendange' by Goya.
Prado Museum, Madrid.
Phot. Scala.

which have been eliminated by cleansing.

The fermentation lasts at least two or three weeks and must be carried out at a temperature of 15–18°C. Occasionally the fermentation stops completely until the spring. Each day the wine must be inspected and analysed and the barrels rolled in order to stir up the dregs and stimulate the yeast. Sweet white wines are even more difficult to make because of their richness and sugar content. When the wine

has finished fermenting, it is placed, like most wines, in barrels.

blanc liquoreux (vin) The fermentation of white wines is always longer and more difficult than that of red wines. The problem is even more complicated when making vin blanc liquoreux or sweet white wines. The must comes from grapes which have been subject to pourriture noble★ and thus contain a large amount of

35

Vineyards of the Limoux region (Aude). Phot. M.

sugar. All this sugar cannot be transformed into alcohol; when the must attains an average alcoholic content of 14–15° the yeast stops working, the alcoholic fermentation ceases and a significant quantity of natural sugar still remains in the wine. Certain sweet wines contain 14° of acquired alcohol and thus retain nearly 90 g of sugar per litre. In this case a large dose of sulphur dioxide★ must be added to avoid a secondary fermentation.

Before the Second World War there was a great demand for sweet white wine. To make as much as possible despite musts which did not contain enough sugar, certain wine makers stopped the fermentation at 12°, for example, in order to safeguard the remaining sugar. In order to do this they had to use even stronger doses of sulphur dioxide. Besides sugar, sweet white wines also contain gums and a lot of natural glycerine which gives them a special oily, fat consistency. The principal sweet white wines are those of Bordeaux (Sauternes★, Barsac★, Cérons★, Sainte-Croix-du-Mont★ and Loupiac★), Monbazillac★, certain Anjou★ and Touraine★ wines and the famous rare Trockenbeerenauslese of the German vineyards of the Rhine and Moselle.

Blancs (Côte des) One of the most renowned vineyards of Champagne situated south-east of Epernay. It is called the White Coast because white Chardonnay grapes are almost the only crop grown. The wines show remarkable finesse and delicacy. This vineyard contains the following famous crus: Cramant, Avize, Oger, Mesnil-sur-Oger and Vertus. Cramant and Avize are the best known. They produce Blancs de Blancs★ which are extraordinarily subtle and delicate and have a lot of breeding. Cramant is a rare cru which is sold under its own name from vines harvested solely on its territory without being mixed with those coming from other crus.

Blancs de Blancs An expression that simply means 'white wine made from white grapes', and could, strictly speaking, be applied to any such wine. Its real importance as a qualitative description is in Champagne, where it is used to distinguish wine made exclusively with white Chardonnay grapes from other Champagnes (Blanc de Noirs★) made with Pinot Noir grapes, or with a mixture of the two. Blancs de Blancs are mainly produced in the Côte des Blancs★ region of Epernay, at Cramant, Mesnil and Avize. They are remarkably delicate, fine, light wines of a pale green-gold colour. Recently the expression has begun to be used, incorrectly, in regions other than Champagne.

Blancs de Noirs An expression used in the Champagne region meaning 'white wine made from black grapes'. This is not as contradictory as it sounds, for a grape's colouring-matter is contained in its skin, and the juice of black grapes is almost always quite colourless. (Vines that produce grapes with coloured juices are called *teinturiers*.)

The volume of Pinot (black grapes) grown in Champagne is estimated to be about four times that of Chardonnay (white grapes). Black grapes are grown for various reasons: they are more resistant to spring frosts and also to mold, which in humid years can affect grapes either before or during the harvest. They also have more body, more *sève*★ and a higher alcohol content than Blancs de Blancs★, and keep their whiteness longer.

There are in fact very few absolutely pure Blancs de Noirs. The equivalent of from an eighth to a quarter of their volume in Blancs de Blancs is usually added in order to make them lighter, finer and easier to convert into sparkling wine. There is also some Champagne made from 75–80% white grapes, as well as pure Blancs de Blancs.

Blanquette de Limoux A well-known sparkling white wine of Languedoc★ which has an appellation contrôlée and is made from the Mauzac grape (sometimes associated with the Clairette), grown in rocky limestone soil around Limoux. Previously, the Mauzac was called 'Blanquette' because of the fine, white down which covered the undersides of the leaves. Thus the origin of the name of the delicious Blanquette de Limoux. Three principal centres produce it, the most important being around Limoux, another near Saint-Hilaire, and a third, more to the south

The Blanquette is obtained by a very moderate pressing – one hl of wine from 150 kg of fresh grapes. The production is therefore very small. In the sixteenth century, the monks of the Abbey of Saint-Hilaire discovered that the wine of Blanquette, when put in small pitchers, became naturally pétillant★ (semi-sparkling) and, by the time of Louis XIII, it was already much in demand. Today, at the co-operative which makes a large amount of the wine, the fermentation of the must is done by the rural method★ of a second fermentation taking place in the bottle. The natural sugar remaining in the wine after the first fermentation provokes the spontaneous formation of the froth. This produces elegant sparkling wine, light and golden, marrowy and fruity, with a particularly pleasant aroma.

Blayais A vineyard on the right bank of the Gironde estuary opposite the Médoc★ region. Its wines are sold under the following appellations contrôlées: Blaye or Blayais (red and white), Côtes de Blaye (white) and Premières Côtes de Blaye (red and white). The white wines are pleasant and usually dry. Côtes de Blaye is full-bodied, sometimes marrowy, crisp and fine. Premières Côtes de Blaye is rather more marrowy. The red wines have an attractive colour and are moelleux, fruity, supple, and ready for bottling relatively soon after fermentation.

bloom A fine waxy dust containing yeasts which collects on grapes and other fruits like the plum. It comes off when the grape is rubbed. The yeasts which activate alcoholic fermentation reside permanently in the vineyards and are transported by wind or insects onto the grape and invade the must when the vendange★ is pressed. However, certain of the yeasts can be harmful which is why the must has to be sterilised with sulphur dioxide★.

Bolivia Vineyards cover only about 2000 ha of the country and are concentrated around La Paz. The vines, which originated in the Canary Islands, generally produce heavy red and white wines ranging from 13–15° in alcohol. Some fortified wines are also produced. All the Bolivian wines are consumed locally.

Bonnezeaux One of the grand crus of the Coteaux du Layon★ region, made in the commune of Thouarcé on the right bank of the Layon river. Like Quarts-de-Chaume★, another vineyard in the

Bonnezeaux: general view of the Layon vineyard. Phot. M.

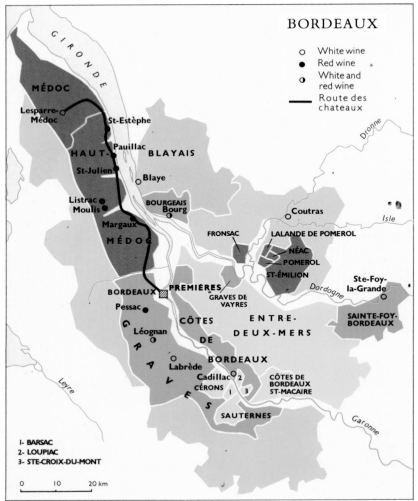

BORDEAUX

- ○ White wine
- ● Red wine
- ◑ White and red wine
- — Route des chateaux

GIRONDE

MÉDOC

Lesparre-Médoc

St-Estèphe

HAUT-

Pauillac

BLAYAIS

St-Julien

Blaye

Listrac

Moulis

BOURGEAIS
Bourg

Coutras

Margaux

Isle

MÉDOC

FRONSAC

LALANDE DE POMEROL

NÉAC

POMEROL

ST-ÉMILION

Dronne

Ste-Foy-la-Grande

BORDEAUX

PREMIÈRES

GRAVES DE VAYRES

Pessac

Dordogne

SAINTE-FOY-BORDEAUX

CÔTES

ENTRE-

DEUX-MERS

Léognan

DE

BORDEAUX

Labrède

Cadillac 2

CÉRONS 1 3

CÔTES DE
BORDEAUX
ST-MACAIRE

SAUTERNES

Garonne

Leyre

1- BARSAC
2- LOUPIAC
3- STE-CROIX-DU-MONT

0   10   20 km

following the Garonne and Dordogne rivers and their common estuary, the Gironde. The vines grow mainly on rocky, hilly land as the marshy, alluvial soil near the rivers is not suited to quality production.

Bordeaux is divided into several viticultural areas: Médoc★, Graves★ and Sauternes★ on the left side of the Garonne and Gironde, and Blayais★, Bourgeais★, Fronsac★, Pomerol★ and Saint-Emilion★ on the right bank of the Dordogne and the Gironde.

Entre-deux-Mers★ is found between them in the triangle formed by the Garonne and the Dordogne. The wines of Entre-deux-Mers include Premières Côtes de Bordeaux, Côtes de Bordeaux-Saint-Macaire★, Graves de Vayres★ and Sainte-Foy-Bordeaux.

The grapes of Bordeaux are the Cabernet, Malbec and Merlot for the reds, and the Sauvignon, Sémillon and Muscadelle for the whites.

BORDEAUX: APPELLATIONS D'ORIGINE CONTRÔLÉES There are numerous Bordeaux wines which are AOC: thirty-four reds, twenty-three whites and two rosés. This does not seem an excessive amount when one considers the diversity of fine Bordeaux wine. There are three categories of appellations:

General name: Bordeaux or Bordeaux

same region, it has its own appellation contrôlée. The vineyard, with its schistose soil and steep hills, is barely 3 km by 500 m. The wine of Bonnezeaux has in its way as much distinction as its rival Quarts-de-Chaume. It is as tender★, fragrant, smooth and vigorous as the latter, and is mainly distinguished by its characteristic fruity aroma and flavour. It ages extremely well. The principal domaines are la Montagne and Château de Fesles.

Bordeaux The wines of Bordeaux have been highly regarded through the ages – the Romans first spread their fame, they were prized by the English in the Middle Ages and, by the eighteenth century, the reputation of Bordeaux wines was known around the world.

The Bordeaux vineyards are located wholly within the Gironde department,

Poster by Hervé Morvan (1957). Bibl. de l'Arsenal. Phot. Lauros-Giraudon.

le monde entier boit du
BORDEAUX

vous aussi

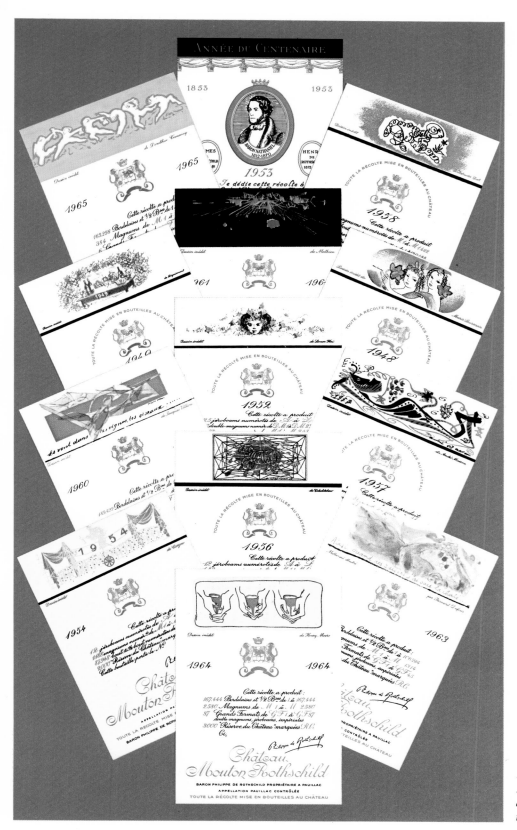

Each year Château Mouton–Rothschild employs a famous artist to provide a design on the theme of wine.

The wine port of Bordeaux.
Phot. Lauros-Geay.

supérieur (red, white, rosé or clairet) some-times followed by the name of the com-mune it comes from.

Regional name: corresponds to the geo-graphical area of the vineyard: Médoc (red), Graves (red and white), Entre-deux-Mers (white), etc.

Communal name: less common, and more reputable: Margaux (red), Pauillac (red), Sauternes (white), etc.

BORDEAUX and BORDEAUX SUPÉRIEUR The white, red and rosé wines falling under this category are of medium quality, sometimes unsteady but make good table wines. The red Bordeaux must have a minimum of 9.5° alcohol and the whites, 10°. The Bordeaux supérieurs, which keep well, must have a minimum of 10.5° for the reds and 11.5° for the whites.

These wines come from areas of Bor-deaux which do not have their own particular appellation, e.g. the districts of Coutras and Guitres. The vineyard owners also use these appellations in a bad year when they think their wine is not of sufficient quality to merit its particular appellation or for the part of their harvest which exceeds the hectarage limit set by law.

BORDEAUX CLAIRET Clairet, a clear, pale red wine, was for a long time the only kind of wine usually available. The relatively recent red and white are made by methods which are much more sophisticated than those which wine-makers used to employ. However, the red wine of Bordeaux is still called claret in Britain.

Today, the Bordelais are trying to re-vive the old clairet, which should not be confused with a rosé wine. It is made from a red wine which undergoes a very short fermentation period, which does not allow all the tannin to dissolve in the must. The result is a supple, round wine with a pleasant bouquet. The clairet, not having much tannin, has very little astringency – a feature which is appreciated by drinkers of young wines. It is also fresh and fruity, and can be drunk in its first year. Clairet does not age well.

BORDEAUX-CÔTES-DE-CASTILLON This appellation covers the wines of Castillon-la-Bataille, Saint-Magne-de-Castillon and Blèves-Castillon, communes that lie on the right bank of the Dordogne. The red wines, which sometimes have the appel-lation Bordeaux supérieur-Côtes de Cast-illon, have a rich colour and are generous and full-bodied. They can be drunk young.

BORDEAUX-HAUT-BÉNAUGE An appel-lation that applies to nine communes in the Entre-deux-Mers★ region. They were once part of the old county of Bénauge, which because of its dark and gloomy forests used to be known as the Black

Bénauge. Today, much of the forest has given way to vineyards which produce an agreeable white wine.

BORDEAUX MOUSSEUX   These are white and sometimes rosé wines made by the Champagne method★ of secondary fermentation in bottle. They are entitled to the AOC Bordeaux and are very pleasant and fruity if made from selected grapes and prepared with great care and attention.

bottle (bouteille)   The history of the manufacture and use of the bottle is chronicled by James Barrelet in his work '*La Verrerie en France de l'époque gallo-romaine à nos jours*', (Librairie Larousse). He reports that, at first, a leather bottle called a *boutiaux*, which could be attached to the saddle of a horse, was used to carry wine. At the time of the Renaissance, the French imported Italian bottles made of very thin, dull glass and protected by wicker casing. They were used to serve wines at the table.

At the beginning of the seventeenth century, the French began to produce thick glass bottles called 'green glass' or 'black glass' which could be used for serving, transporting and storing the wine. This was an extremely important invention for the future of French wines, and for their prestige.

The shape of the bottle was the same for all wines. At first, the base of the bottle was in the shape of an onion and then, little by little, became cylindrical (like a Benedictine bottle). During the first part of the nineteenth century, the traditional bottle was continually refined (Burgundy type), and at the same time a particular shape was created for certain crus. In 1800 the 'Bordeaux' and 'Champagne' shapes could be distinguished. The first machine-made bottles were used in Cognac in 1894, and standardisation of different types of bottles began. Today, the most widely-used bottles are those of Burgundy, Bordeaux, Champagne and the Rhine, and they appear in clear or tinted glass (green, yellow or yellow-brown).

BOTTLES (CAPACITY OF)   This varies a little depending on the region. Burgundy, Bordeaux, and Anjou bottles contain 7·5 dl, Alsatian 7·2 dl and Champagne 8 dl. The Angevine filette (Anjou half bottle) contains 3·5 dl and the Beaujolais 'pot' 4·5 dl.

There is more variation in the contents of Champagne bottles. The split contains 2 dl, the pint 4 dl, the bottle 8 dl, the magnum two normal bottles, the Jeroboam four bottles, the Rehoboam six bottles, Methuselah eight bottles,

Left: the Malbec or Cot grape, a variety much used in making Bordeaux wines.
Phot. M.

The Bordeaux vineyards.
Phot. Atlas-Photo.

From left to right: wine or liqueur bottle often found in the press rooms of Hungarian vignerons. It holds 2 litres. Phot. J.-L. Chamet. Glass oval bottle with hunting scene. Germany around 1600. Musée des Arts Décoratifs. Phot. Lauros-Giraudon. Flat, stoneware bottle decorated with the coat of arms of Liosel. Beauvaisis, second half of the 16th century. Height 25 cm. Musée de Sèvres. Phot. Lauros-Giraudon.

Salmanazar twelve bottles, Balthazar sixteen and Nebuchadnezzar twenty.

bottle sickness A wine should never be drunk immediately after being bottled. It should be left to settle for one to three months depending on the wine, a length of time the specialists call the 'bottle sickness' period. All the operations the wines have gone through (fermentation, etc.) have made the delicate wine somewhat unbalanced. Even the most well-bottled wine is subjected to an unsettling aeration which temporarily hides its bouquet and its other attributes. When the oxidising effect of the air has disappeared the wine regains its delicate equilibrium, then if it is a wine which profits from ageing, the wine begins to take on its new qualities.

bottle washing Despite the care taken in cleaning bottles, a little deposit sometimes remains on the inside. The old remedy of scouring is very good. The cleaning agent should be put in the bottle with a little water, then shaken vigorously to loosen the lees and tartar which stick to the inside. Afterwards, the bottle should be rinsed twice with water, and left to dry in an upside down position.

bouchonné A term used to describe a wine which tastes 'corky'. This taste is so disagreeable and noticeable that it needs no description. A corky tasting wine is not usually the result of a mistake when making the wine, but rather a faulty cork. The taste comes from the cork itself and is due to parasites living in the bark of the cork oaks. The best corks, which come from Spain, especially Catalonia, rarely produce this result. Sometimes, the taste is even worse and comes from mould which has developed in the cells of the cork.

For storage, the bottles must always be laid down to avoid drying out the cork. It is also very bad to keep changing the bottle from an upright to a horizontal position.

If the odour of the cork is faint, it is enough to throw away the first few inches of wine, as the rest of the bottle is usually undamaged. But a wine which is really bouchonné should not be drunk. Restauranteurs and hosts should try to safeguard their guests from this disappointment by always discreetly smelling the cork before serving the wine.

bouquet The fragrant smell of a wine which develops with maturity. The bouquet is one of the great charms of a fine wine and one of the subtlest pleasures for the drinker. Bouquet is the result of a combination of the aroma★ of the grape and a more complex fragrance which develops after the wine has undergone fermentation.

The secondary fragrance, which is affected by the action of the yeasts, is flowery or fruity, or both. Thus, for example, the bouquet which is so pleasant in Beaujolais can be characterised as follows: Saint-Amour, peach, reseda; Juliénas, peach, raspberry; Brouilly, peony, prune, etc.

The bouquet is further developed by oxidation while the wines are maturing in barrels, then to a lesser degree during ageing in bottles. As a result of these changes the wine gives off a smell which is extremely subtle, fragile and complex. To appreciate this bouquet to the fullest, the gourmet adroitly turns the glass in his hand and inhales the aroma time and again.

The fragrances found most often have been classed into a series forming the 'fragrance spectrum'. Plant fragrances, often used to describe young wines, are floral (rose, jasmine, hyacinth, lilac, orange blossom, violet, peony, reseda, pink, lime, etc.) or fruity (peach, apricot, apple, almond, raspberry, banana, blackcurrant and cherry).

Vegetable odours appear in the bouquet of older wines – mushroom, truffle, undergrowth, humus, etc. Old wines which have recently reached their fullness are often described in terms of animals: venison, pheasant and musk deer (like certain admirable old Burgundies). Spices like pepper, sandalwood, clove and vanilla are also mentioned, as are the odours like fine tobacco (certain Châteauneufs-du-Papes), resin, coffee and toasted almond (old white Burgundies).

The wines from northern vineyards which have a temperate climate usually have a higher acid content and also more bouquet than those from warmer southern regions, which have little acidity. In the same way, wines from rocky, chalky soil which receive little sun have more bouquet than those made from more fertile land.

Certain oenophiles can determine the area and grape from which a wine comes and its approximate year merely by smelling the bouquet. When the bouquet ex-

pands slowly, taking a long time to reveal itself, it is said that the bouquet has a 'long nose'. On the other hand, if the bouquet is not apparent or fades quickly, it is said to have a 'short nose'.

Bourgeais   A vineyard that lies on the right bank of both the Dordogne and the Gironde rivers, facing the Médoc★ district. Its wines are sold under the appellations contrôlées Bourg or Bourgeais and Côtes de Bourg. The white wines are dry, medium dry or sweet. The red wines are full-bodied, well balanced, robust and age well. They are excellent table wines.

bourgeois (crus)   The great diversity of Médoc★ wines has led to a natural classification, based on usage of the different crus. They are divided according to merit into crus paysans, crus artisans, crus bourgeois ordinaires, bons bourgeois, bourgeois supérieurs and, lastly, into grands crus. These latter, representing the aristocrats of wine, were classified in 1855 into five categories, called crus classés.

The crus bourgeois were classified in 1858, in a work by M. d'Armailhacq, into thirty-four bourgeois supérieurs, sixty-four bons bourgeois and about 150 bourgeois. Today they are referred to simply as the 'bourgeois supérieurs' and the 'bourgeois'. In 1932, 100 were officially recognised by the courtiers★ of the region. Châteaux Gloria, Phélan-Ségur, Sémeillan and Fourcas-Dupré are among the crus bourgeois supérieurs. Certain crus of some years are called crus exceptionnels. However, this easily misleads the public because, in fact, the crus exceptionnels are officially listed under the five crus classés. These are the Chateaux Angludet, Bel-Air-Marquis-d'Aligre, Chase-Spleen, la Couronne, Moulin-Riche, Poujeaux-Theil and Villegorge.

Bourgogne aligoté   This appellation is given to those white wines grown in Burgundy★ which come from the Aligoté grape (with or without Chardonnay). The minimum alcoholic content must be 9·5° and the maximum yield per ha, 45 hl.

Bourgogne ordinaire and **Bourgogne grand ordinaire**   These appellations concern the red, rosé and white wines produced in the Burgundy★ area. The red

wines come from the fine Pinot and Gamay grapes (in the Yonne, the César and the Tressot). The whites come from the Chardonnay and Pinot Blanc, the Aligoté and the Melon de Bourgogne (in the Yonne and the Sacy). The minimum alcohol content must be 9·5° and the maximum yield per ha, 45 hl.

Bourgogne passe-tous-grains This appellation is only applied to those red wines made in Burgundy★ from two-thirds Gamay Noir and one-third Pinot grapes. The minimum alcohol content must be 9·5° and the maximum yield per ha, 45 hl.

Bourgueil Formerly, almost all of the Bourgueil country was part of the province of Anjou, and later it was included in the modern viticultural classification with Touraine★.

The vineyards extend in a line for twenty km between Saint-Patrice and Saint-Nicolas-de-Bourgueil, as well as along the Loire (La Chapelle, Chouzé).

The soils have a different composition, going from south to north: alluvium deposited by the Loire, then gravel terraces and thick sands, and finally the coast, where limestone-clay covers micaceous chalk. The wines grown on gravelly soil

Saint-Nicolas de Bourgueil

APPELLATION CONTRÔLÉE ★NICOLAS★ CHARENTON. VAL-DE-MARNE

Vendange at Bourgueil.
Phot. Phedon-Salou.

are the lightest, with more finesse and bouquet, and can be drunk young. The wines of the coast are more full-bodied, harder when young and must mature before they can be drunk.

Most of the communes produce wines of both the coastal and rocky varieties (the volume of wines from rocky soil is greater). Yet, Ingrandes produces only wine from rocky soil, and Benais, the wines of the coast. The grape, like at Chinon★, is the Cabernet Breton (or Cabernet Franc).

It is difficult to separate Bourgueil from Chinon. Both are located in the 'Kingdom of Grandgousier' and their red wines bear such a resemblance to each other that it is sometimes difficult to tell them apart. Bourgueil takes longer to mature than Chinon, but it has more body while still being fresh and delicate. Its strongest characteristic is a magnificent bouquet of raspberries (Chinon has a violet bouquet), and it is often compared to the bon crus bourgeois of the Médoc★. Bourgueil has, in any case, a singular virtue, if one believes the Prior who said in 1089, 'This wine makes sad hearts happy'. There are two appellations contrôlées: Bourgueil and Saint-Nicolas-de-Bourgueil.

bourru (vin) A vin bourru is one which has not yet deposited its yeasts and impurities at the bottom of the barrel. The wine is therefore full of insoluble matter and still contains unfermented sugar. It has a cloudy appearance.

This sparkling or semi-sparkling grape juice used to be much in demand and was the speciality of certain regions. Unfermented wines are still bought and sold at the time of the vendange. Parisians favour the macadam★, the unfermented wine of Bergerac★, and not so long ago it was esteemed an honour for members of the trade to handle the unfermented wine of Gaillac★. In autumn the unfermented wine of Alsace, the Neuer Susser, comes each day to Paris from the vendange and is quickly consumed.

bouteilles, mise en (put in bottles) Some large houses refuse to deliver their wines in barrels but insist on bottling it on the premises. Bottling is an important job which, if done at the wrong time, can utterly destroy the best wines.

Analysis determines the maximum expansion of the wine in the barrel, its clearness and stability. The most favourable time is always chosen to bottle as the bottling period only lasts a maximum of six weeks. March and September are generally the favoured months. The temperature should be constant, the weather dry and barometric pressure stable. Traditional wine-makers wait for a north wind which they believe is a sign of good atmospheric conditions. The bottling must be carried out rapidly with all equipment meticulously clean.

A wooden spigot or a siphon can be used to transfer the wine from cask to bottle. A siphon with a plastic spout is preferable, as the wooden spigot tends to stir up the wine each time the tap is closed. The corking must always be done so as to leave the least possible amount of air between the wine and the bottom of the cork. Then the bottles are left standing for twenty-four hours so that the corks will adhere well to the neck of the bottles. Next the wine is laid down for at least a month (the 'bottle sickness'★ period) before it is delivered for consumption.

The wine-maker who likes to have the adventure of bottling his own wine must wait till he judges the wine is in the right state for bottling. Wine must not travel in hot weather as a refermentation may occur, nor in cold weather as the wine may freeze en route. After transport, white wines should rest from eight to ten days, and red wines from ten to fifteen days, before being drunk.

Bouzy A village in Champagne★ which has given its name to the Côte de Bouzy, the south-eastern slope of the Montagne de Reims★ that runs into the Marne★ valley. Bouzy is an excellent cru of Champagne and produces an exquisite (though not, of course, sparkling) red wine. This is made in very small quantities, and unfortunately is rather delicate and does not travel well.

In good years Bouzy is a magnificent wine that would seem to justify the famous quarrel between Champagne and Burgundy in the seventeenth century which was begun by Fagon★, the king's doctor. It is a fine, garnet-coloured wine with a distinctive bouquet of peaches (a characteristic of Champagne wines first noted by the Marquis de Saint-Evremond). After

several years in bottle, this powerful, warm and well-balanced wine is sometimes hard to distinguish from an excellent Burgundy.

Brazil Although vines have been planted since the Portuguese conquest, it was not until the Italian immigration after the First World War that viticulture really started to develop. The chief vineyard area is in the south of the country in the state of Rio Grande do Sul, but the regions of Sao Paulo, Santa Catarina, Rio de Janeiro and Minas Geraes also produce some wine. The American hybrid Isabella is the most widely-planted grape. It produces a vin ordinaire which is often a good, but never a great, wine.

brilliance A very attractive visual quality, especially in white and rosé wines

Bottling wine in a private cellar at Savigny-lès-Beaune (Burgundy). Phot. M.

when they are absolutely limpid. Wines that have clarity and brilliance, however, are not always perfect. The processes (collage★, filtering★ and racking★) necessary to clarify a wine during vinification may impair both the aroma★ and bouquet★ of the wine.

Brouilly One of the most famous Beaujolais★ crus. The appellation applies to wines made in the communes of Odenas, Saint-Lager, Cercié, Quincié and Charentay, which are grouped around the Montagne de Brouilly. Brouilly is a typical Beaujolais, fruity★ and tender★ with a pronounced bouquet. It should be drunk young, as these distinctive qualities fade with age.

Mount Brouilly (Beaujolais).
Phot. M.

Brouilly (Côte de) One of the better wines of Beaujolais★, Côte de Brouilly comes from the vineyard which occupies the slopes of the renowned Montagne de Brouilly. The position of the vineyard and its granitic soil produce a particularly fine wine.

It is produced in the communes of Odenas, Saint-Lager, Cercié and Quincié. The wine is a beautiful dark purple colour, high in alcohol and fleshy★, but also fruity★ and fragrant. Although a little firm when young, it can be drunk then or after several years when it becomes truly exquisite. As Côte de Brouilly ages, it loses some of its fruitiness but develops its bouquet.

Bué Although it covers only a small area, this commune of the Cher is well known for its wine, which has the right to the appellation contrôlée Sancerre★. This area produces the well-known crus of Chêne-Marchand, Chemarin and Poussie. The vines of Poussie, the ancient property of the Abbey of Bué, grow both on clay and dry limestone which gives the wines good bouquet, equilibrium and longevity.

Buena Vista A historical vineyard of Sonoma★, California, founded just after the gold rush by the colourful Hungarian Count Agoston Haraszthy, who preferred to renounce his title to become 'the Colonel'. He has been called 'the father of modern Californian viticulture' because of his strong influence on the vineyards of that state. The winery of Buena Vista has suffered a series of misfortunes including the destruction of the caves during the great San Francisco earthquake.

Today, Buena Vista again produces Premium Wines. Most of the time, the wines carrying the Buena Vista label are sold under the name of the grape they come from (Varietal Wines), but there is also some wine that carries two special appellations, Rose Brook and Vine Brook.

Bugey Bugey was the home of the renowned Brillat-Savarin. Its small vineyard, which carries the VDQS★ label, is located in the department of Ain between Beaujolais★ and Savoie★ and has recently been reducing its production. The red and rosé wines come from the Gamay, Pinot Noir and Gris, Poulsard and Mondeuse grapes. These very agreeable wines are generally light and fruity and somewhat similar to a Beaujolais. The white wines are made from the Chardonnay, Altesse, Aligoté, and Mondeuse Blanc. They are light and refreshing, like many of the Savoie wines. The best crus are the Virieu and Montagnieu. Only the white wines from Altesse and Chardonnay grapes can be called Roussette de Bugey.

Bulgaria Viticulture is an important part of the Bulgarian economy and a considerable effort is being made to modernise it. After Italy, Bulgaria is the second largest European exporter of fresh grapes. A large quantity of wine is also exported, especially to the USSR, Czechoslovakia and East Germany.

Vineyards are found as high as 500 m and sixty-three varieties of grape are grown, of which three-quarters are used to produce table wines. The other varieties are used to make dessert wines: Asenovgrad (a sort of Malaga made in the town of the same name), Madara, Slavianka, Tchirpan, Tyrnovo and Melnik.

There are six principal wine-growing areas in Bulgaria:

The Valley of the Roses (Kazanlyk region) with the great centres of Karlova and Troian. It produces the Rozentaler Riesling (Riesling of the Valley of the Roses), and the Karlovski Misket, an amber-coloured muscat.

The South-west (Kjustendil region) The vine, cultivated around Sandanski and Melnik, produces the Melnik, a very sweet and agreeable wine containing up to 35% sugar.

Thracia The most important vineyards are found along the Maritsa between Dimitrovgrad to the east and Thtiman to the west, with the Stara Zagora–Sliven line as the northern boundary. Within this principal zone there are two regions of production around Plovdiv and Tchirpan. The Plovdiv region produces Bolgar, Pamid (red wine), Pirinsko (red wine from the Pirine grape, near Plovdiv) and Trakia (red wine). Tchirpan produces a dessert wine of the same name.

The Banks of the Danube possess rich vineyards whose largest centres are Vidin and Silistra. Vidin produces the Gymza, a well-known red wine.

The Coast of the North Sea The two towns of Varna and Pomerie produce a white wine called Dimiat.

The Tirnovo region in northern Bulgaria gives its name to a well-known dessert wine.

Despite their careful preparation, all the white wines of Bulgaria lack freshness because of the latitude of the country. The red wines, however, have recently become very good table wines which often attain the level of red French VDQS★ and are classed, most of the time, with those of Romania and Hungary, and have a similar astringency.

Bué: the domaine of La Poussie with its natural amphitheatre. Phot. M.

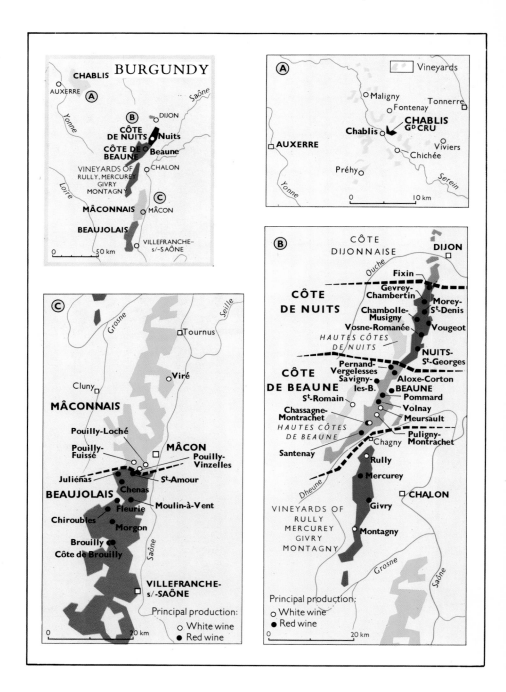

Burgundy Without doubt, the cultivation of the vine began in Burgundy in the Gallo-Roman period and perhaps even earlier. However, the Burgundy vineyards are certainly the work of the monasteries. From the twelfth century, thanks to the monks of Cîteaux, the fame of the wine of Burgundy was widespread. The vineyard of Lower Burgundy, with Auxerre as its capital, was known outside the region before that of Upper Burgundy. In the fourth century, St Germain had inherited some vineyards from her parents in Auxerre, and a piece of this ancient vineyard still exists (Clos de la Chainette★).

It was only towards the thirteenth century that the wines around Beaune began to be appreciated outside their area. Beaune established the universal reputation of the wines of Burgundy and, upon the death of Philip Augustus, the vineyards of Beaune were considered 'the great riches of the duchy of Burgundy'. At the beginning of the eighteenth century the first *maisons* (houses) of wine were founded at Beaune, then at Nuits and Dijon. The *négociants*★ greatly extended the scope of commerce for the wines and were largely responsible for spreading their reputation.

The vineyards of Burgundy today extend into four departments: Yonne, Côte-d'Or, Saône-et-Loire and Rhône. These are divided into five subregions: Chablis★ (Yonne department); Côte d'Or★ (department of the Côte-d'Or) comprising the Côte de Nuits★ and the Côte de Beaune★; Côte Chalonnaise★(department of Saône-et-Loire); Mâconnais★ (department of Saône-et-Loire) and Beaujolais★ (department of Saône–et–Loire and Rhône).

BURGUNDY: APPELLATIONS D'ORIGINE CONTRÔLÉES Of all the French regions

A village in Burgundy: Rochepot and its 12th-century château. Phot. Aarons–L.S.P.

Burgundy: Château Vougeot. Phot. M.

'The Drinker' by Watteau.
Musée Cognacq-Jay.
Phot. Giraudon.

which produce wine, Burgundy has the largest number of appellations contrôlées. Particularly in the Côte de Nuits and the Côte de Beaune, there are many villages which themselves have numerous crus or climats★, each with its own characteristic and distinctive personality. The legislation then only had to follow the 'usage and tradition' of the area. There are four categories of appellations:

Generic or regional appellations   These are designated wines which are grown in the Burgundy area and which all have the right to the appellation: Bourgogne★ rouge and blanc and Bourgogne rosé or clairet; Bourgogne aligoté★ (white); Bourgogne ordinaire★, or Bourgogne grand ordinaire★ (red and white); Bourgogne passe-tous-grains★ (red).

Sub-regional appellations   This appellation is applied only to wines produced in a particular subregion of Burgundy: Côtes de Beaune-Villages★ (red); Mâcon and Mâcon supérieur★ (red and white); Mâcon Villages★ (white); Beaujolais★ and Beaujolais supérieur★ (red and white); Beaujolais-Villages★ (red).

Communal appellations   Many of the Burgundy villages can legally give their name to the wine grown on their territory: Fleurie★, Beaune★, Volnay★, Nuits-Saint-Georges★, Meursault★, Chablis★, etc.

Appellations of crus   The vineyard of each commune is divided into small vineyards called climats★ in Burgundy. Certain of the best-known vineyards are called by their particular name: e.g. Chambertin, Musigny and Clos de Vougeot. Often the communal appellation is followed by the name of the climat or the expression premier cru, e.g. Chambolle-Musigny-les-Amoureuses.

BURGUNDY: APPELLATION BOURGOGNE   This is applied to red and white wines produced in the Burgundy area. For the rosés, the appellation becomes Bourgogne clairet or Bourgogne rosé. For the red wines, the authorised grapes are the Pinot; in the Yonne, the César and the Tressot; in the Mâconnais and Beaujolais, the Gamay noir à jus blanc. For the white wines, the grapes are the Chardonnay★ and the Pinot Blanc★. The minimum alcohol content for the Burgundies is 10° for the reds and the rosés, and 10·5° for the whites. The maximum yield is 45 hl per ha.

Under certain conditions, the names of Marsannay or Marsannay-la-Côte of the Upper Côtes de Nuits and Upper Côtes de Beaune can be added to the appellation Bourgogne (red, white and rosé).

Buzet (Côtes du)   A small VDQS★ area of the south-west of France, located to the east of Agen on the left bank of the Garonne, and includes the eight communes of the canton of Lavardac. The viticultural co-operative of Buzet-sur-Baise is well equipped to vinify the production of all the wine-growers in the district.

The region produces good quality red wines which are agreeable and full of bouquet. They come from the Merlot, Cabernet Franc, Cabernet Sauvignon and Malbec grapes. This last variety is being eclipsed more and more by the Merlot, a variety which up till now was used mostly in Bordeaux, and which makes fine wines with a good bouquet. A small amount of white wine is produced from grapes used in Bordeaux: Sémillon, Sauvignon and Muscadelle. The grape-growing area is presently being enlarged.

C

Cabernet Franc This grape has different names depending on the region. It is called Bouchet or Gros-Bouchet in Saint-Emilion and Pomerol, Bouchy in Madiran, and Breton in Touraine and Saumur. It is a hardy variety with small bunches of thin-skinned, bluish-black grapes. It grows well on most soils except chalky ones. The wine from this grape has a lively, sparkling colour like that from the Cabernet-Sauvignon★, but with less bouquet. On the other hand, it takes less time than the Cabernet-Sauvignon to clear after fermentation. The Cabernet Franc is often combined with other varieties in Gironde and the south-west but in the Loire★ it is the sole grape used for Chinon★, Bourgueil★, Saint-Nicolas-de-Bourgueil★, Saumur-Champigny★ and several other reds and rosés.

Cabernet-Sauvignon A typical grape of Bordeaux, principally of Médoc★ and Graves★ where it accounts for 50–70% of the grapes producing good crus. It is also called Petit-Cabernet (Médoc and Graves), and Petit Bouchet (Saint-Emilion★ and Pomerol★). The Cabernet-Sauvignon is often mixed with the Cabernet Franc★, Merlot and Petit-Verdot but very rarely with the Malbec.

The Cabernet-Sauvignon prefers poor, dry soil and it grows in small bunches of little, thick-skinned, bluish-black grapes. This grape produces a dark-coloured wine full of tannin, which is harsh in a young wine but which with time takes on body, suppleness and a very delicate bouquet of violets. Cabernet-Sauvignon has been planted in many other countries by those attempting to imitate the wines of the

Far left: the Cabernet Franc grape, a 'noble' variety found in different regions of France. Phot. M.

Left: the Cabernet-Sauvignon, a characteristic grape of Bordeaux and especially of the Médoc. Phot. M.

Médoc. In California good quality wines have been produced but, elsewhere, the results have not been so successful.

Cabrières One of the appellations of the Coteaux du Languedoc★, classified VDQS★. The red wine, vin vermeil, of Cabrières was known in Montpellier as early as 1357 and was a favourite of Louis XIV. It is an excellent rosé, fruity and full-bodied. It is made mainly from the Carignan and Cinsault grape.

café wines Simple, light, red wines which are easily drunk at the counter or, like table wines, from a carafe. They are very agreeable when served slightly chilled. These wines are made by a short vinification process which gives them a pleasant suppleness. Many of the red wines coming from the Côtes du Rhône and Languedoc are treated in this way. They are also called 'one night wines' because their fermentation time is no longer than a night (from twelve to fourteen hours).

The commune of Saint-Saturnin in the Hérault, and that of Saint-Cécile-les-Vignes in Vaucluse, are well known for their café wines.

Cahors The red wine of Cahors, classified VDQS★, is one of the best wines of south-west France. Well known even at the time of the Romans, it was completely overshadowed by the Bordeaux wines until Louis XVI ended the privilège de Bordeaux★ in 1776. Phylloxera★, then the frost of 1956, almost extinguished the doughty vines, but they soon revived.

Cahors is produced by forty communes on the two banks of the River Lot, both up and down stream from Cahors, in the centres of Cahors, Luzech, Puy-l'Evêque, Catus, Montcuq and Lalbenque. The principal grape (60–80%) is the Malbec, also called the Auxerrois. It is sometimes blended with the Jurançon Rouge, Abouriou, Merlot and others.

Cahors is perhaps the most colourful of French wines. It is a brilliant, dark crimson colour, almost black, which is similar to the deep velvety red of the better wines of Valteline in northern Italy. The Italian wines can be drunk when very young while the Cahors should mature three to five years before being bottled, and is not at its best for another five to ten years thereafter. An aged Cahors is a splendid wine, harmonious and firm without being

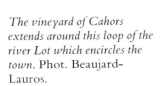

The vineyard of Cahors extends around this loop of the river Lot which encircles the town. Phot. Beaujard-Lauros.

hard, and full-bodied with an inimitable bouquet.

The USSR★ gives the name 'Cahors' to something very different – vins de liqueur★ which are dark red, almost black in colour, very sugary and containing about 16° alcohol. The vines which make this wine (also called Karop or Kagor) are descended no doubt from grapes imported a long time ago from Quercy. The addition of alcohol, used to make the Russian version, was probably the idea of a resident of Cahors who used the process with his wine so that it would make the trip to Russia without damage. This expensive wine, which is very much in demand in Russia, has for a long time been that used for the Mass in the Orthodox Church. Even though it is nothing like the French original, the Russians have adopted the name of Cahors for one of their most precious wines.

California   California accounts for 90% of the vineyard acreage of the United States. Less than half of its enormous production is actually used for wine; the rest is made into dried raisins or consumed as table grapes. Two-thirds of total wine production (about six million hl) consists of vins de liqueur★ (Muscatel, Angelica, sherry and port).

The vineyards of California are divided into three distinct regions. The first, which produces mainly table grapes, is found around San Francisco along the northern coast of the Pacific. It is divided into several grape-growing areas, the principal ones being, from north to south: Mendocino, Sonoma★, Napa★, Alameda★ (principally in the Livermore Valley), Santa Clara★ and San Benito★.

The second region, in the interior of the State, includes the San Joaquin and Grand valleys and, from north to south, the vineyards are those of Sacramento, San Joaquin, Madero, Fresno and Tulare. This region produces primarily dried raisins, table grapes and lots of cheap sweet wines.

The third region extends further south, eastwards of Los Angeles, to the foot of the San Bernardino mountains, and produces mostly vins ordinaires, comparable to the French wines of the Midi★ region.

The indigenous wild vines were growing to the west of the Rocky Mountains when the first European grape varieties

were brought to California by the Spanish Franciscan monks. They planted them to the north of San Francisco (this variety, which has since been named 'Mission', produces only a mediocre wine). But it was a Hungarian immigrant who brought to California the beginnings of modern viticulture. The dynamic Count Agoston Haraszthy (called more familiarly 'the Colonel') is rightly known as 'the father of California wine-making'.

The red wines of California come principally from the following grape varieties: Zinfandel, Carignan, Alicante-Bouschet, Grenache, Mission, Mataro (a common, very productive variety of Spanish origin) and Petite-Syrah (which probably comes from the same family as the French Hermitage). The majority of white wines come from the Sultana or Thompson Seedless (which gives a clear wine without much aroma and a neutral taste, but very inexpensive) and other varieties like the Sauvignon Vert, Burger and Palomino (this last, while excellent for sherry, makes a mediocre table wine).

During the last twenty years, great progress has been made in the production of Californian table wines. The areas planted with good European varieties (Cabernet, Pinot, Riesling, Sémillon) have been extended considerably. The better wineries rival those of Europe from the point of view of technique and equipment. The sometimes arbitrary methods of naming wines are becoming more uniform, so that they can now be classified in three categories: mediocre vins ordinaires, which are simply called reds, whites or rosés; wines which still carry the generic names coined at the beginning of Californian wine-making like 'California Chablis' and 'California Burgundy' (there is no law which regulates the percentage of Chardonnay for the 'Chablis' or of Pinot Noir for the 'Burgundy' contained in these wines, but they are of good quality); and finally, the 'Premium Wines' which represent the aristocracy of Californian wines and are of excellent quality. They are called 'Varietal Wines' because they carry the name of the grape variety from which they are made (for example, Pinot Noir and Cabernet-Sauvignon) and correspond in a way to the French AOC wines. The name of a winery added to that of the grape gives a further guarantee of quality.

Certain producers date their wines, although a vintage year does not have the same importance as in France because the character of Californian wines does not vary very much from one year to another. The stability of the climate gives a consistant quality with no surprises. The vintage year, then, is simply an indication of age, a guarantee of the maturity of the wine.

As well as table wines, California produces a great quantity of sparkling wines which are made for the most part by the Champagne method★. Many of them are mediocre because there is no legal supervision as in France. But some made from the Chardonnay and Pinot Blanc, in well-known wineries (like Almaden, Beaulieu, Korbel and Paul Masson), are of excellent quality. The sparkling wines of California are sold under the name 'California Champagne' and 'Sparkling Burgundy'. The American vins de liqueur★ which are produced in large quantities are generally made from different grapes and by different vinification methods than their European counterparts. However, there are five or six producers, including Almaden and Louis M. Martini, who make sherry and port according to the traditional Spanish or Portuguese methods.

Canada All the Canadian vineyards are found around Niagara between Lake Erie and Lake Ontario (except for a few widely-dispersed vineyards in British Columbia). There are only about 8000 ha planted to vines, which produce some 250,000 hl of wine. The climate of this peninsular formed between the two lakes is very temperate, and conditions are very favourable for the cultivation of the vine.

One of Champlain's companions, Jean de Poutrincount, planted several feet of vines, but the real origins of Canadian viticulture date from 1811 when a German named John Schiller began planting vines and making wine near Toronto. Today, the wines resemble those which are produced in the United States in the nearby state of New York. They are made from some of the same varieties: Concorde, Catawba, Niagara and Delaware. Since the end of the Second World War, some experiments have been tried with hybrids★ of French origin. Most of the production still consists of sweet dessert wines but the demand for table wines is becoming stronger.

Capri One of the most popular dry white wines in southern Italy. Capri is produced not only on the island of Capri but also on the neighbouring island of Ischia and on the nearby mainland. (These other areas, incidentally, often make better wine than Capri itself.) The quality of Capri varies according to individual vineyards. The best wine is probably not exported.

capsule A capsule is the metallic or paper wrapper around the cork and neck of a bottle of wine, and as such has a purely decorative function. When opening a bottle, the capsule should be cut cleanly under the ridge round the top of the bottle. Wine should never come into contact with it when being poured, as this might give it an unpleasant 'capsule taste'.

capucine A wooden receptacle in which the vignerons of Lorraine carry their drinking wine to work every day. A capucine holds two litres and is produced in the shape of a round-bellied bottle with a long neck. It is made of pieces of wood held together by metal rings, like a barrel. The capucine inspired the creation of the *Confrérie des Compagnons de la Capucine*, whose declared mission is to uphold and protect the wines of Lorraine★.

carafe wines Young, cheap, unpretentious wines that are served in carafes and not in bottles. Carafe wines are often excellent, light, fresh wines, providing they are genuine vins de pays★.

carbon dioxide (CO₂) This gas is a waste product which is encountered several times during the life of a wine.

It is present during alcoholic fermentation★ when the sugar decomposes into alcohol and carbon dioxide. One hl of must produces about 4·5 hl of carbon dioxide. The gas, being heavier than air, can collect in the cellars and it is necessary to provide good ventilation during the fermentation period.

Carbon dioxide is also formed during malo-lactic fermentation★. It is responsible for the slight effervescence found in certain wines like Crepy★ and Gaillac perle★ which undergo their malo-lactic fermentation in bottle.

It also causes the light sparkle of wines bottled on their lees, and the sparkle in Champagne★ and other sparkling wines made by other methods such as the rural★, German★, cuve close★ and the Asti★ process. It is also injected into carbonated sparkling wines.

carbonic maceration A method of vinifying red wines used mainly in Beaujolais★. The grapes are put in the cuve without being crushed. The result is an intracellular fermentation by which part of the sugar is converted into alcohol without the aid of yeasts. At the same time, a small amount of grapes at the bottom of the cuve has undergone alcoholic fermentation as the skins have been broken by the weight of grapes above. The ingredients in the skin of these grapes diffuse throughout the pulp creating aromatic substances which would not appear in wine vinified in the normal way.

After several days of maceration the grapes are crushed and normal fermentation takes place. As a result of this method, very fragrant wines having only a small volatile acid content are produced. They mature quickly and conserve well.

Carbonnieux (eau minérale de) Not a mineral water, but an excellent wine made in Graves★. According to an almost certainly apocryphal story, Benedictine monks used to sell the white wine from their domaine★ of Carbonnieux under this name at the court of the Turkish Sultan, where the Moslem laws of abstinence were supposedly in force.

Carthagène Carthagène is a vin de liqueur★, or fortified wine, traditionally made by vignerons in the south of France for their private consumption. It is made in very small casks and in small quantities, as the only alcohol available to the vignerons is the amount officially allowed to distillers. To every five litres of Grenache grape juice (which is very rich in sugar), one litre of 96° proof alcohol is added, and the mixture is then left on the lees for the winter (clarification occurs spontaneously). After one year in cask the wine has acquired a golden colour, is sweet (200–250 g of natural sugar per litre) and has an alcohol content of 16°.

Once, only *eau-de-vie de vin* or wine spirit was used. Nowadays *eau-de-vie de marc* (spirit made from grape pulp) is sometimes used as well, and makes a harsher, much less fine wine.

Similar wines are made in Champagne and Burgundy (Ratafia★ and Riquiqui) as well as in Charentes which produces Pineau des Charentes★, a much less sweet wine than Carthagène, and made with Cognac rather than *eau-de-vie*.

casse brune A disease that commonly affects white wines and is caused by oxidation. As a preventive measure, doses of sulphur dioxide★ are added to the grape juice before fermentation.

casse ferrique A disease that can occur when the iron content of a wine exceeds 10–12 mg per litre. Oxidation causes the ferric salts of the wine to crystallise, which in turn makes either the tannin or the protein content do the same. According to the appearance of the wine, two types of casse are distinguishable, casse bleue and casse blanche. Both of these appear soon after the wine has been exposed to the air (during racking or filtering, for example).

Casse bleue gives red wine a purplish colour, and white wine a leaden tinge and a black precipitate of ferric tannate.

Casse blanche makes the wine look milky and opalescent due to the formation of ferric phosphate, which causes flocculation of the protein compounds.

Ideally, to avoid casse ferrique, no part of any machine used for vinification should be made of iron. In practice, this is virtually impossible since iron is used all over the vineyard, in metal buckets used by the grape-pickers, the crushing apparatus, the chains in the presses, the pipes used for racking and transferring wine from one vat to another and even in the cement from which some vats are made. Iron buckets have now been replaced by plastic ones, and wherever iron is absolutely unavoidable, it is sealed and protected with a layer of varnish. The use of enamelled, plastic-coated, or stainless steel vats is becoming more and more widespread. When the damage has already been done, French law authorises treatment with citric acid, which dissolves the crystallised ferric salts that were the original cause of the casse. The most effective treatment, however, is potassium ferrocyanide, known as blue-fining★.

Cassis An AOC Provence★ vineyard with an exceptional geographical situation. It rises in tiers around the little port of Cassis, surrounded by massive limestone rocks and open to the sun and sea in the south. In winter it is sheltered by the hills from the cold north winds, and in summer the sea air tempers the fierce heat of the sun. The vineyards were considerably developed during the reign of Henri IV (although vines had been grown there many years before) and Cassis has been highly regarded ever since.

The white wine, made from Ugni Blanc, Clairette, Doucillon, Marsanne, Sauvignon and Pascal Blanc grapes, has always been better known than the red. It is very dry though not acid, and has finesse, freshness and character. It is also a perfect accompaniment to *bouillabaisse*, a fish soup which is a speciality of Provence. Particular care must be taken during harvesting and vinification to ensure its clarity★ and brilliance★ and to prevent it from turning yellow.

The red and rosé are made from Grenache, Mourvèdre, Carignan and Cinsault grapes. The red, when successful, is a good wine with a warm and velvety taste. The rosé, although an attractive, supple and fruity wine, has never achieved the reputation of white Cassis.

Castelli Romani A generic name for an immensely varied range of popular Italian table wines that go particularly well with the Roman cuisine. Although lacking great distinction, they are very pleasant, particularly the dry white wines that are served young in carafe. They are produced south-east of Rome around the villages of Frascati, Marino, Rocca di Papa, Velletri, Albano, Genzano, Ariccia and Grottaferrata. The best known is Frascati★.

categories of wine It is easy to get lost in the maze of official French appellations, which are both numerous and definitive, although they were partly devised to protect the customer.

Basically, French law divides wine into three categories: wines with appellations d'origine★, vins de consommation courante★ (which are administered by the Institut des Vins de Consommation Courante), and imported wines.

cave (cellar) The role played by the cave in the preservation and evolution of

APPELLATION CASSIS CONTRÔLÉE

La Ferme Blanche

Cave of Saint-Emilion. Phot. René-Jacques.

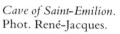

wines has always been important. Columelle outlined the principal components of the ideal cave: 'facing north, away from the baths, the oven, cooking pit, cistern . . .' In Caton he advised having good caves 'in order to reach the peak of perfection'. However it was Chaptal, the great chemist, who gave the definition of the perfect cave in his 1807 work *Art de Faire le Vin*. The cave must face north so as to protect it from great variations in temperature which would occur if it faced south. It must be very low and cool. The best temperature, which should remain constant all year round, is from 9–12°C (as is the case in the best caves of Champagne★,

Saumur★ and Vouvray★). If necessary, the ventilators should be closed during extreme hot or cold spells, and the floor should be covered with sand which can be moistened in the summer.

The cave should be sufficiently, but not excessively, ventilated. There must also be constant humidity, but not too much; an excess would provoke mould on the casks and corks, and the wine would acquire a bad taste, becoming weak and characterless. Lack of humidity results in dried-out barrels and consequent seepage of the wine through the pores.

The cave should be dim, as bright light dries out the wine. Nearby vibrations are very harmful as they stir up the lees★ and force them into suspension in the wine which can encourage acidity or sourness. Finally, the cave must be clean, free of refuse and any substances which produce an odour (like vegetables, fruits, oil, fuel, etc.) or other matter susceptible to fermentation. Neither vinegar nor green wood should be placed in the cave.

This is the kind of cave still found in some old houses, but it is rare to find these conditions in the cellars of today's oenophiles. It is adviseable, though, to have a 'cellar book' in which to keep track of each wine and to record from whom and for what price it was brought, when it was served and with what dishes. A special column reserved for tasting observations is also worthwhile and often amusing.

If real cellars are not available, special metallic or wooden racks or solid shelves should be used. The bottles must be lying face down so that the wine bathes the cork. Only bottles of Cognac, *eaux-de-vie*, port, apéritifs and liqueurs should be standing.

The beginner can make a good start with a cave of 300 or 400 bottles. Most wine producers sell their wines in cases of six and twelve bottles. All the purchases should have labels with the name, vintage, date and price.

Cérons Bordered by Barsac★ on the south and Graves★ on the north and west, the vineyards of Cérons are situated on the left bank of the Garonne in the area of the great white wines. The appellation Cérons also includes the communes of Podensac and Illats. The grapes and harvesting are as in Sauternes, with successive and careful picking.

Cérons is a very fine and elegant wine. Less sweet than Sauternes, it is lighter, more vigorous and also fruitier. A part of the harvest is vinified into an excellent fruity dry or semi-dry wine which is classed among the best Graves, while keeping the strong characteristics of the Sauternes-Barsac. The best crus include the Châteaux of Cérons and of Calvimont, Lamouroux, Haut-Mayne and Grand Enclos du Château de Cérons.

Chablis The northernmost vineyard of Burgundy is positioned around the little village of Chablis. The Cistercian monks living in the Abbey of Pontigny in the twelfth century did much to develop its reputation. However, its clear, dry, very fine and fruity white wines have been widely appreciated since the ninth century.

Before the phylloxera★ invasion and the destruction of the vineyards, the region produced one-third of the total production of Burgundy. Replanted in the famous area of the grand crus, the present vineyards suffer from exposure to springtime frost, which in certain years causes considerable damage. In 1957 the vineyards were almost completely destroyed by frost, but the vignerons have obstinately continued production in spite of these trials. First they burned fires among the vines, and more recently organised a network of heaters in the vineyards. Re-

Chablis, the northernmost Burgundy vineyard, has organised an effective system of fighting spring frosts with propane heaters. Phot. M.

search is underway to develop other, more sophisticated devices.

The only grape used for Chablis is the Chardonnay★, the grape of all the great white wines of Burgundy. The soil of the vineyards, which stretch along the hillsides bordering the Serein, is well suited to grape-growing. It is flinty, based on the chalky limestone of the Upper Jurassic period. Chablis, light, dry and vigorous, is an excellent accompaniment to seafood.

CHABLIS: APPELLATIONS D'ORIGINE CONTRÔLÉES   The Chablis area has four appellations: Chablis Grand Cru, Chablis Premier Cru, Chablis and Petit Chablis. The appellations Chablis Grand Cru and Chablis Premier Cru should be followed by the climat of origin. The maximum authorised yield per hectare is 40 hl except for Chablis Grand Cru, which is only 35 hl. The minimum alcohol content is 11° for Chablis Grand Cru, 10.5° for Chablis and 9.5° for Petit Chablis.

chabrot or **chabrol**   In certain provinces of France, such as the Midi, it was formerly the custom to put a little wine in the main dish or soup before serving it. This custom, termed *chabrot*, now survives mainly in folklore although it is still practised regularly in Béarn.

chai A building located above ground where the vinification operations take place. The names *cellier* or, in certain provinces, *cuverie* are also used. The chai must be protected from extremes of temperature. The ceiling should be arched and have lofts above it, and the walls should have small glass windows which are not exposed to the south. The chai must always be kept clean and free from products susceptible to mould or fermentation like green wood or vinegar.

chai (master of the) A person of considerable importance in all the notable vineyards. The success of a wine depends on his valuation and is subject to his authority alone. The master has absorbed twenty centuries of observation, research and tradition. While the master of the chai makes use of scientific knowledge in handling the wine, he also follows age-old traditions. He understands that the seasons, the cold, the moon, the sap and many other things still have an unpredictable and mysterious influence on the wine.

He alone decides the best moment for racking and bottling, and he alone determines if a new wine shows indications of a promising future. No instrument, no matter how sophisticated, can replace the trained eye, the sense of smell and the infallible taste of the master of the chai, who reigns in the cave wearing a black jacket and leather apron.

Chaînette (Clos de la) A well-known vineyard situated at the heart of the town of Auxerre in the grounds of the departmental psychiatric hospital. It contains the remains of the vine belonging to St Germain which was bequeathed to her in the fourth century by her parents. The wines of Auxerre were greatly renowned in ancient times and the manuscripts of the Middle Ages commended them. The wines of Clos de la Chaînette were served at the tables of the kings of France and they still are of exceptional quality today.

Chambolle-Musigny A commune of the Côte de Nuits★ which produces mostly red, and a little white, wine. The Musigny white is excellent, but unfortunately very rare.

Musigny and Bonnes-Mares are the most esteemed vineyards. The appellations such as les Amoureuses and les Charmes, which always precede the name of Chambolle-Musigny, also produce remarkable wines.

More feminine than Chambertin, the red wines of Chambolle-Musigny have an incomparable bouquet and suavity and many oenologists claim that they are the best and most delicate of the Côte de Nuits.

chambrer (to bring to room temperature) An expression dating from the eighteenth century which means that the wine is brought from the cellar temperature to room temperature. Rooms of that time would seem cold to those

Master of the chai with his traditional apron and the symbols of his trade, pipette and tastevin. Phot. M.

accustomed to central heating and the temperature of the cellar would not be more than 10–12°C.

To chambrer a wine thus originally meant to bring it to a temperature of 14°C (rarely higher), which was the ideal drinking temperature. In time, the expression has gradually changed in meaning and today it is often used in the sense of 'to heat a wine', a practice which will destroy it.

Champagne (the region) It is impossible to really appreciate Champagne without knowing the region from which it comes. Champagne would never have attained its perfection without several conditions unique to the region. Legislation has, among other things, severely limited the area of production of Champagne and certain areas which used to supply their harvest to the Champagne shippers have thus been excluded. The vine was cultivated in Champagne from the beginnings of the Christian era and, by the Middle Ages, the wine was already well known. At that time, the still red and white wines of the area were renowned and became involved in a famous quarrel between advocates of Champagne and Burgundy.

The vineyards of Champagne are situated in three departments, chiefly the Marne, the Aube and Aisne, and several hectares of the Seine-et-Marne. The centre is found in the Marne vineyard which is divided into three large areas: the Montagne de Reims★, Valley of the Marne★ and Côte des Blancs★.

Champagne is the perfect illustration of Olivier de Serres' dictum, 'the air, the soil and the growth are the fundamentals of the vineyard'. In Champagne these three elements unite to produce an incomparable wine. The Champagne area has a very favourable climate despite its location in a latitude which is the most northern for the cultivation of the vine. The rivers and forests assure a constant humidity, the winters are relatively mild, and the summer and autumn often sunny. Thus the vines receive a maximum of warmth and sunlight. The chalky subsoil is counterbalanced by the affect of acids in the soil and ensures perfect drainage. However, this subsoil has also permitted the construction of the caves which are indispensable to the making of Champagne, and there are 200 km of underground galleries.

The noble★ grape varieties which have existed in Champagne from the Middle Ages are vigorous and their wines have a very great finesse. These are chiefly the Pinot Noir and the white Chardonnay. The Pinot Noir produces the great red wines of Burgundy; here it is made into white wines (Blanc de Noirs★). The Chardonnay, also grown in Burgundy, produces in Champagne wines which have finesse, freshness and lots of sparkle (Blanc de Blancs★). The Pinot Meunier produces a less fine wine and is used in the second crus.

In Champagne, crus do not have the same importance as in other areas. Most of

Champagne: The Smiling Angle, 13th century. Rheims Cathedral. Phot. Lauros-Giraudon.

Following two pages: Champagne vineyards. Phot. René-Jacques.

Map labels:

Aisne
SOISSONS
Vesle
AISNE
Trigny
REIMS
Mⁿᵉ DE REIMS
Mailly-Champagne
Verzenay
Verzy
Villers-Marmery
Trépail
Ambonnay
Bouzy
Reuil
Chᵃᵘ-Thierry
V. OF THE MARNE
4 3
Ay
ÉPERNAY
2
Moussy
Cramant
Avize
Oger
Le Mesnil-s/-Oger
CÔTE DES BLANCS
Vertus
Tours-s/-Marne
CHÂLONS-s/-MARNE
Pᵗ Morin
SEINE-
Gᵈ Morin
ET-
MARNE
Marais de Sᵗ-Gond
M A R N E
Marne
Vitry-le-François
Aube
Nogent-s/-Seine
Marcilly-le-Hayer
Seine
A U B E
Montgueux
TROYES
Brienne-le-Chᵃᵘ
Bar-s/-Aube
Bar-s/-Seine
Landreville
Polisot
Les Riceys

1. **Chouilly**
2. **Mareuil-s/-Ay**
3. **Cumières**
4. **Damery**

▨ Vineyard

—— Department boundary

0   20 km

---

the idea of a cru exists despite everything, because the best houses blend their wines from the vines coming from the three most important areas (the Montagne de Reims, Valley of the Marne and Côte des Blancs).

Champagne (the wine) A wine for feasting, a wine for celebrating, Champagne occupies a cherished place among the wines of France. Present at the *petits soupers* of the Regency period, appreciated by the beautiful Pompadour 'who became more beautiful after drinking it', this pale golden wine is always praised. It is not surprising that the sale of Champagne has more than doubled in ten years and 124 million bottles were sold in 1973.

There is only one Champagne. Other sparkling wines (which can also attain a very high quality) are called vins mousseux★. The Champagne method★, where the second fermentation takes place in bottle, is used for many of the sparkling wines, and some are good enough to have the right to an appellation d'origine contrôlée, e.g. Vouvray mousseux, Saumur mousseux and Saint-Péray mousseux.

But apart from this fermentation method, the wine must undergo a series of special steps before it can be called Champagne. These include the vendange, pressing, first fermentation and blending, all of which must be done with delicate precision.

Only those wines which are produced in the limited area of Champagne and come from the grapes of that area have the right to the appellation Champagne. The grapes are harvested when mature, but not overripe, and are handled with extreme care to avoid colouring the must, especially when using black grapes. Careful hand-picking is the rule here.

Then comes the pressing. The large houses buy the grapes and prefer to use their own premises (called *vendangeoirs*) for pressing. The grapes are never crushed prior to being pressed. This is for obvious reasons, especially with the black grapes, because the end product should be a clear, unblemished juice.

The Champagne presses are unique, being wide and shallow and forcing the juice to leave the skin quickly without dissolving the colouring matter. About 4000 kg are generally pressed at a time,

---

the wines of Champagne are made traditionally from a mixture of wines coming from different crus. Each house has its favourite proportions and blends and strives to produce a consistent style of wine each year. Nevertheless, there are Champagnes (generally coming from the small producers and not the great houses) which are made from the grapes grown on a single commune, e.g. Cramant, Avize, Le Mesnil, Ay and Mailly. On the other hand,

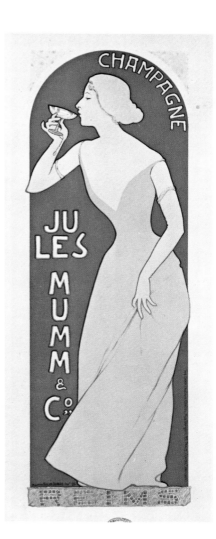

Two advertising posters (around 1900) by Alphonse Mucha (left) and M. Réalier-Dumas. Bibl. de l'Arsenal. Phot. Lauros-Giraudon.

The 'mountain' of Rheims and the Champagne vineyards. Phot. Lauros.

giving first 20·5 hl of cuvée, then 4 hl of the first taille and 2 hl of the second taille. Only the cuvée is generally used for the best wines, the tailles making quality still wines. The first fermentation usually occurs in the same way as all other white wines.

The wine ferments either in Champagne casks of 205 litres or in large, modern, glass vats. This produces a still wine which is soon clarified by the cold of winter. A racking then separates the deposits.

The period from January to the beginning of March is the crucial time in the constitution of the cuvée as it is then that technique begins to give way to art. There are no crus in Champagne and it is only the way the wine is blended that accounts for differentiation among the various types. Each house has a personal recipe for the cuvée, which brings together the wines that have complementary qualities and which is also designed to produce the type of Champagne appreciated by its clientele. In a normal year the cuvée is composed of about one-quarter of wine from the Ay region (which gives it finesse and racé★), one-quarter of wines from the Marne Valley (body and vigour), one-quarter from the Montagne de Reims (freshness and bouquet) and one-quarter of wines from the Côte de Blancs (grace, elegance and finesse). The proportions vary depending on whether the year is hot or cold.

This idea of marrying the various Champagne wines is attributed to Dom Perignon★. Only Champagne made from white grapes can be called 'Blanc de Blancs'★.

CHAMPAGNE BEATER A barbarous instrument similar to a swizzle stick which suppresses the bubbles in Champagne, removing all the spirit and ruining the distinctive taste.

CHAMPAGNE METHOD (MÉTHODE CHAMPENOISE) A method used to make French sparkling wines which are appellation contrôlée (except for a few made by the rural method★). The principle seems simple enough. It is to encourage a secondary fermentation in a hermetically-sealed bottle by adding sugar to the wine base which has been obtained by the usual process of vinification. In decomposing, the sugar gives off carbon dioxide which remains dissolved in the wine, and cannot escape. In practice, it is a very delicate operation to produce the sparkle and it took several centuries to perfect the method. At the beginning of the last century, the breakage of bottles was very high at 15–20% and in 1828, 80% of the bottles were broken.

The Champagne method, as it is practised in Champagne, is a collection of strict rules, which is not adhered to in the preparation of Mousseux. From the vendange to the maturing, excluding the composition of the cuvée, there runs a rigid, traditional chain of discipline which allows no flexibility.

The expression méthode champenoise on a label of Mousseux simply means that the wine is made by a secondary fermentation in bottle followed by a dégorgement★, or removal of the sediment. The wine must be in bottle for nine months to merit the vins à appellation d'origine title and four months for the wines without appellation (instead of the minimum of twelve months for Champagne).

The Champagne method proceeds as follows. After it has been left standing for a certain period, the still wine is bottled (usually when the sap starts to rise in the spring), and the liqueur de tirage★ is added. The second fermentation slowly takes place after the bottles are laid down. Then the delicate operation of remuage★ begins in order to collect the deposit and lees. Afterwards, the bottles are left for the necessary time, then subjected to the operation of dégorgement to remove the deposit. Next, the 'dosage' takes place in which the liqueur d'expédition★ is added (the dosage depending on the desired taste), filling up the space emptied by the dégorgement. The bottles then receive their final corks by machine and bound solidly by a steel muzzle.

CHAMPAGNE ROSÉ Instead of the classic pale golden wine, Champagne rosé reflects the colour of rubies. It is made according to a traditional and ancient recipe and was much in demand in the Russian and German courts of the nineteenth century. Champagne rosé is not made in the same way as other rosé wines of France. It is a process unique to Champagne.

When the cuvée is made up, a very small

Champagne labels and collars.

quantity of red Champagne wine is added until the desired colour is reached. This operation is very delicate as care must be taken not to alter the initial character of the cuvée. The red wine must be from the Champagne region and a beautiful vintage Bouzy★, colourful and full-bodied, is usually chosen. This small addition of red wine to the cuvée must be made before the racking and in the presence of authorised witnesses. A rosé Champagne is a good quality Champagne that can attain perfection with some brands.

CHAMPAGNE VINTAGES   Only the best years are declared vintages in Champagne (those for example, as the old saying goes, 'when the vines have had 100 days of sun'). On the other hand, each house only has the right to declare as vintage a maximum of 80% of its collection and the minimum obligatory maturing period must be at least three years after the vendange. For these three reasons, vintage Champagne is of superior quality to average wines sold under each trademark.

Vintage in Champagne is not as important as in some other wines. The producers of Champagne strive to make a superior wine each year. To accomplish this, they blend a mélange of wines coming not only from the different areas of Champagne, but also from different years. All the non-vintage wines are made from a blending of several harvests whose good and bad qualities balance each other. Thus, a very strong wine, for example, will be mixed with a light year, and this is why there is practically no difference among wines of different years produced under the same brand, excluding the vintage years.

Wine-lovers should be warned that they will find resemblances between two different brands of Champagne of the same vintage year, but not between two non-vintage years. The Champagnes of 1870 were the first to have a vintage printed on the label. Then around 1880 it became more common. The most recent vintages have been 1937, 1943, 1945, 1947, 1949, 1952, 1953, 1955, 1959, 1961, 1962, 1964, 1966 and 1969.

Champigny   A little hamlet located in the commune of Souzay which produces the AOC Saumur-Champigny, the best red wine of Saumur and all of Anjou. The area of appellation comprises the communes of Chacé, Dampierre, Parnay, Saint-Cyr-en-Bourg, Saumur, Souzay and Varrains. The Saumur-Champigny, renowned as early as the Middle Ages, resembles its cousins of Touraine★, Chinon★ and Bourgueil★, but is more full-bodied. Certain connoisseurs find it has the aroma of a Médoc and is fleshy like a Beaune with a fruitiness all of its own. Ranging from 10–12° alcohol, it has a beautiful dark ruby colour, and is firm and generous with a blooming bouquet of wild raspberries and strawberries. In good years, it is an excellent wine to lay down.

chantepleure   A term used in the Vouvray area to describe the wooden tap used for removing wine from the cask. The word is derived from the impression that the tap 'sings' as it is being opened, and that the wine 'cries' as it is being removed. A little before the Second World War, Vouvray created the *Confrérie des Chevaliers de la Chantepleure* whose members are reunited twice a year during the winter and summer solstices in the caves of the Bonne Dame.

Organised tour of a cave. The miniature train of Mercier Champagne. Phot. Veronese, ©SPADEM.

Chanturgues A well-known wine of the Auvergne★ which is produced in very small quantities today and seems to turn up only in the coq au vin of Chanturgues. Chanturgues is an agreeable wine of the Gamay grape, is cherry red, light, fruity and delicate and keeps well. In the record years it has a lot of body and richness with a velvety feel and a pleasant, strong, violet bouquet.

chapeau (hat) The name given to the solid elements of the vendange (skins, stones, etc.) which are raised by the release of carbon dioxide and float on the surface of the must during fermentation. They take the form of a floating hat, *chapeau flottant*, or a submerged hat, *chapeau submergé*. As the colouring matter is found in this hat it is necessary, in order to have coloured wine, to put the must in contact with it. The hat can be bathed in the juice by pumping the juice from the base of the vat, or it can be pushed down with a wooden instrument from time to time. It is also possible to keep it in the centre of the must by using a special system.

chaptalisation An operation which is also called sugaring. The process has for some years been the subject of a passionate controversy. The addition of sugared substances to an insufficiently rich must is not new. At first, honey was used and, around 1790, sugar was first introduced at Clos de Vougeot when the wine lacked *vinosité naturelle* or natural vinosity★. But it was Chaptal (1756–1832) who was the real promoter of sugaring the vendange and who gave his name to this operation.

To have the right to an appellation, a minimum degree of alcohol is demanded for the wines, which varies according to region. Certain bad years produce musts that are insufficiently sugared and which will not therefore produce enough alcohol, resulting in poor quality. The sugaring operations are strictly regulated by law. All the controls stipulate that the musts have to reach, before enrichment, a minimum level of natural sugar. Only cane and beetroot sugars are allowed, never glucose, and it is forbidden to use more than 3 kg of sugar per hl of vendange. (1700 kg of sugar in 1 hl of vendange adds 1° of alcohol.)

Chaptalisation is not allowed in the south of France. The addition of an excess of sugar is very harmful to the wine as the finesse and bouquet are altered and the wine becomes disproportioned. Nevertheless, a wine increased in alcohol by 0.5–1° by sugaring, when the must was originally very low in sugar, is certainly improved. Although the added sugar, under the influence of yeast, is transformed into alcohol, it also creates aromatic substances like glycerine★. The wine has more finish and bouquet while, without sugar, it was thin and deceptive.

Chardonnay One of the finest white grape varieties. It has been the most important in Champagne and Burgundy since ancient times and has given its name to a tiny village in the Mâcon area. In Champagne, where it has existed since the height of the Middle Ages, it is called *fromenteau* because of its wheaten colour.

The Chardonnay produces small, shining, golden grapes, full of a delicious, white, sugary juice from which Champagne and all the great white wines of Burgundy are made, e.g. Montrachet, Meursault, Chablis and Pouilly-Fuissé. It thrives on clay and limestone hills facing

The Chardonnay grape.

Chassagne-Montrachet The great white wines produced by this commune of the Côte de Beaune★ have an obvious relationship with those of the neighbouring village of Puligny★. The king of all these noble wines, the Montrachet★, is grown in about an equal area in these two communes, as is Bâtard-Montrachet.

The elegant and fruity Criots-Bâtard-Montrachet is only produced in the Chassagne area. As in Puligny, these superb wines only carry the name of their vineyard and not that of the commune.

The great white wines of Chassagne and Puligny have in common a light aroma of almonds or hazelnuts, delicacy and finesse and also the ability to mature gracefully. On the whole, Puligny wines are more delicate than the robust Chassagnes.

Chassagne-Montrachet also produces excellent whites and reds carrying the appellation Chassagne-Montrachet followed by the name of the climat★. Certain of the white wines are remarkably like the Chassagne-Montrachet les Ruchottes, Cailleret and Morgeot. The red wines are full-bodied with an excellent bouquet and resemble certain wines of the Côte de Nuits. The best crus include Chassagne-Montrachet, Clos Saint-Jean, Morgeot, la Boudriotte and la Maltroie.

Chasselas There are several varieties of this white grape (sometimes rosé), most of them making a very good table grape (Moissac, for example). The wine made from the Chasselas is not really remarkable, except when it is cultivated in a cold climate. It is commonly grown in Alsace★ where it produces a popular, agreeable wine with little acidity which is best when drunk chilled and young. It is bottled early, at the end of the winter following the harvest, and retains a very pleasant, light sparkle caused by carbon dioxide which dissolves in the new wine.

In France, the Chasselas is the grape of the Pouilly-sur-Loire★ and Crépy★ of Savoie wines. In Switzerland, the Chasselas is widely grown and is made into the Fendant of Valais and the Dorin of the canton of Vaud. It is also grown in the Bade★ area south of Freiburg, where it is called Gutedel.

château A name used traditionally in the Gironde area to designate a vineyard or

Chasselas Doré grape.
Phot. Lauros.

east and south-east, where it develops its best qualities and finesse. These conditions exist on the Côte-d'Or and in Champagne, especially on the Côte des Blancs★.

The grape is often called Pinot Chardonnay although it is not related to the Pinot family. It is referred to by this name in California where it produces a good white wine. The Chardonnay should not be confused with the Pinot Blanc, which comes from a mutation of the Pinot Noir; the Pinot Blanc produces wine totally inferior to the Chardonnay (the best is perhaps the Pinot d'Alba in the Piemonte). The Chardonnay itself produces absolutely remarkable wines which are clear, light and fine. Outside Champagne and Burgundy, the Chardonnay is found in several vineyard areas, e.g. Lyon★, Jura★ and Châtillon-en-Dois★.

charpenté A wine which has enough alcohol to give it a good body, and is also rich in other elements, is said to be 'well-built' or *charpenté*. It is always one of a good year made from grapes which have achieved a high degree of maturity.

cru★ having a certain importance, and which has the appropriate buildings for making wine and an impressive dwelling. A judgement of 1938 ruled that the word château in Gironde is synonymous with domaine, clos or cru.

The degree of 30th September, 1949 detailed that the wines sold under the name of château must come from such an estate. This decree abolished the misuse of the word by reserving it for vineyards distinguished as such by custom or charter.

The INAO★ is always watchful to see that this measure is enforced to protect the consumer, because the word château itself exercises a magical attraction, and wines are often preferred when presented under this name.

CHÂTEAU (MISE EN BOUTEILLES AU) 'Bottled at the château' appears on the label as a guarantee of authenticity for the consumer. It was first developed in the Gironde during the last half of the nineteenth century. The wines thus designated are always quality wines, grown solely on the land where they are bottled.

Château-Chalon This extraordinary wine of the Jura★, endowed with a communal appellation, is certainly the quintessence of the celebrated vins jaunes★. The Savagnin or Naturé is the only grape variety used in this vineyard which comprises four communes: Château-Chalon, Minétru, Nevy-sur-Seille and Domblans. It is only in this part of the Jura that the wine is produced in any great quantity. The Savagnin favours the blue, chalky soil covered with limestone scree which is found at Château-Chalon and in the upper hills of Arbois (at Pupillin in particular).

The Savagnin must be protected from cold winds and needs a lot of sun. At Château-Chalon, it nestles in the deep hollows which are natural hothouses. The area of production of Château-Chalon is thus very restricted and one must admire the incomparable quality of this wine which has survived through the centuries despite the problems of the vineyards and the wine-making. Château-Chalon is truly the prince of the vins jaunes because, even if others were to follow the same vinification process, it would still emerge as the most perfect and graceful.

Château-Chalon, in its flask-shaped

Above: the cliffs of Château-Chalon; in the foreground, ancient vines trained on poles. Phot. Cuisset.

Below: Château-Chalon: vineyards of the 'prince of vins jaunes'. Phot. Hétier.

special bottle, the clavelin★, is a rare and fascinating wine the colour of golden amber. Its astonishing bouquet is strong and penetrating. Its characteristic nutty flavour has a lingering aftertaste and conserves well. Certain cellars keep Château-Chalon more than a century and the wine never loses its excellent qualities.

Château-Grillet The production of this exceptional vineyard of the Côtes du Rhône★ is without a doubt the smallest of the appellations contrôlées in France, producing about a dozen barrels (225 litres) from two hectares. As at Condrieu★, the only grape is the Viognier which is planted on stony terrain that makes hard work for the vigneron. It is harvested when very ripe.

The suave and unique Château-Grillet which is the result of this toil is golden and flamboyant, generous and fragrant with an exquisite delicacy and a sensation of being sweet and dry at the same time. It is an unpredictable wine which sometimes keeps well several years, but which often has a tendency to dry out and maderise★.

Châteaumeillant The Berry area produces these good VDQS★ reds and rosés. The vineyard, already extensive in the twelfth century, was very prosperous after the introduction of the Gamay grape around 1830. Sadly, phylloxera★ destroyed all the vines and today's production is still quite small.

Located about sixty km south of Bourges, the vineyard, planted mainly with the Gamay, is found in the communes of Châteaumeillant, Reigny, Saint-Maur and Vesdun in the Cher, and those of Champillet, Feusines, Néret and Urciers in the Indre. In bad years a certain proportion of Pinot Noir and Pinot Gris are sometimes added to reduce the acidity of the Gamay, and also to raise the degree of alcohol.

The red is a quality wine, especially in good years. The rosé (called vin gris) is excellent. Dry, fruity and light, its popularity is now increasing to what it was in the past.

Châteauneuf-du-Pape A prestigious name that is well deserved by this superb wine, the pride of the vineyards of the left bank of the southern Côtes du Rhône★. The majestic château, now in ruins, which was erected by the papacy in the fourteenth century, has given its name to the vineyard. The soil, the old river bed of the Rhône, is covered with sun-scorched pebbles – an environment which would appear to be unsuitable for the cultivation of the vine; in fact, it is said that this hostile soil wears out an iron plough in two hours.

Although only the Syrah grape is used in Hermitage★, thirteen grape varieties are involved in making the marvellous Châteauneuf. These include the Grenache, Clairette, Cinsault, Mourvèdre and Bourboulenc.

The purple-robed Châteauneuf is a

Châteauneuf-du-Pape: the grapes of this famous cru grow on inhospitable soil full of round stones scorched by the sun. Phot. M.

forceful wine, ardent and warm, whose incomparable bouquet combines the smell of burning raspberry and iodine. A little harsh at first, this magnificent wine develops its unique qualities and subtle bouquet with time.

The best vineyards include Château Fortia, Domaine de Mont-Redon, Cabrières-les-Silex, Château des Fines-Roches, Château Rayas and la Solitude. There is also a very rare white Châteauneuf-du-Pape which accounts for only 1% of production.

Châtillon-en-Diois A small vineyard on the left bank of the Rhône valley in the department of the Drôme which produces red, rosé and white wines having the right to the label VDQS★. The reds and rosés come from the noble★ grape companions: the Syrah (the Hermitage grape), Gamay (the Beaujolais grape) and Pinot Noir (the Burgundy grape).

This is not sparkling wine like that of the nearby Die★, so proud of its Clairette title, and is delicious, fruity, fine and elegant. Sadly, these wines are produced in very small quantities (around 1000 hl).

Chavignol Well known for its *crottin*, a delicious goat cheese, Chavignol is no less famous for its wine, which has the right to the appellation contrôlée Sancerre★. The reputation of Chavignol was already quite widespread in the Middle Ages for the abundance and excellence of its wines, and has never diminished. Chavignol has several very good vineyards: la Comtesse, Cul de Beaujeu and la Garde.

Chénas People complain that the vine has replaced the old oak trees (*chênes*) which gave this commune of Beaujolais★ its name, and for some this has been a source of regret. The vineyards, located to the east and south of Chénas, also have the right to the appellation Moulin-à-Vent★.

The village of Chavignol among the vineyards of Sancerre. Phot. M.

Chénas is an excellent Beaujolais with a fruity and generous bouquet, but is lighter than Moulin-à-Vent.

Cheval-Blanc (Château) A grand cru of Saint-Emilion★ which, although very generous and full-bodied, is also fine and velvety with a delicious bouquet. It has, without a doubt, the strongest bouquet of the wines of Saint-Emilion. Although the wine matures quickly in bottle, it can also be kept for a long time without losing its qualities.

Chianti This famous Italian wine has a well-known, straw-covered bottle, the *fiasco*, which has done much to popularise it around the world. Nevertheless, it is the wines of lesser quality which are presented in these special bottles, so it is true that for

certain of them, 'the habit makes the monk'. The very good Chiantis are sold in classic Bordeaux bottles carrying an authentic vintage and need no special bottle dressing to be appreciated.

In Tuscany, Chianti is the ordinary table wine (nearly always red) that is drunk young, generally in carafe. It is served in all the restaurants of Florence and suits the Italian cuisine admirably.

Chianti is made by a special method of vinification called *governo* which gives it a very particular character. A part of the harvest (about 10%) is not pressed, but laid to dry on straw screens. At the end of November this reserved part, whose juice is concentrated, is crushed and left to ferment, then it is added to the rest of the Chianti which has already undergone normal fermentation. The whole solution is left in a closed vat until spring. The slightly sparkling wine which emerges lightly tickles the tongue and is fresh and agreeable.

The Classic Chianti, grown on barren, dry hills between Florence and Siena, is a very different wine. It is one of the best Italian wines, being firm, steady and full-bodied with a fine bouquet. It improves considerably with age. This Chianti is made from two grape varieties, San Gioveto and Cannaiolo, to which is added a little Trebbiano Blanc and Malvasia Blanc, which were formerly cultivated at a high altitude amidst the olives. The area of appellation covers four communes, Greve, Radda, Castelina and Gaiole, and a part of six others. The Classic Chianti is never bottled outside the zone of production. It carries the seal of the association of producers and often the name of the vineyard, such as Barone Ricasoli (Brolio, Meleto) and Conte Serristori (Machiavelli).

Many Chiantis, however, are produced outside the classic zone in six legally delimited regions: Rufina and Montalbano (the best), Colli Fiorentini and Colli Pisani (quality product, but limited). The two others, Colli Senesi and Colli Arentini, produce mediocre wines which are often mixed with others coming from the rest of Italy to furnish most of the cheap Chiantis. There is also a white Chianti which comes from the Trebbiano (called Ugni Blanc in France). It is a dry, golden, agreeable wine which is rather full-bodied and without great distinction.

Chiaretto or **Rosato del Garda**   A rosé wine produced south of Lake Garda between Milan and Verona which is certainly one of the best rosés of Italy. The best Chiarettos are made around the villages of Padenghe, Manerba and Moniga (in the region of Brescia) from the local red grapes: Gropello, Marzemino and Schiava. The Chiarettos from the east bank of Lake Garda (in the region of Verona) are equally good but of a totally different character. They are made from the Corvina, Negrara and Molinaro grapes which also give the red, light Bardolino★. These last rosés are mostly sold under the name of Chiaretto although the two appellations Chiaretto and Chiarello are almost used indiscriminately.

The Chiaretto is a delicious, pale rosé wine, fresh and light, which generally has 10–11° alcohol. It is now being exported and, if it is young and served chilled, may be very agreeable, but never as good as in its country of origin.

Chile   Although less productive than those of Argentina, the Chilean vineyards yield the best wines of South America★. Chile is the oldest viticultural region of Latin America, and the vine was cultivated there before 1600. Today's vineyards, however, are more recent, dating no earlier than 1850 when the French varieties imported from Europe were planted for the first time. Thus the majority of Chilean wines (at least the best of them) come from grapes of European origin: Cabernet, Sémillon, Riesling, Pinot, Sauvignon, Merlot, Malbec and Folle-Blanche (here called Loca Blanca).

Chilean viticultural and vinification methods are largely inspired by those used in Bordeaux and adapted to a climate similar to the Mediterranean type and to a volcanic soil, which is totally different.

The vineyards are found in the central part of Chile between 30° and 40° latitude, an area tempered by the polar waters of the Humboldt current crossing the Pacific. The best vineyards are located in the centre of this region not far from Santiago. The two best areas are the Aconcagua and Maipo Valleys, which are mainly planted in Cabernet. Chile has two other large viticultural regions, one in the north, the other in the south. The northern region, which extends from the Atacama Dessert

Chinon: the vineyard of 'Clos de l'Echo'. Phot. M.

to the Choapa River, is planted in Muscat and gives generous wines high in alcohol. They are often drunk in the same manner as Madeira, port or sherry. The southern region is found between the Maule and Bio-Bio Rivers. It produces red and light white wines which are low in alcohol. The main grape is the Pais, a Spanish grape by origin and one of the oldest planted in Chile.

Chile produces around 70% red wines and 30% white. The good Chilean wines, which really deserve to be exported, come from noble★ grapes and often bear the name of the grape on their label. The others are sold as 'Sauternes', 'Chablis', 'Borgona' (Burgundy) and 'Rhine'. Finally, Chile also produces sparkling wines, some of which are remarkable and others, a little too sweet.

Chilean wines are classified by age into four categories. The first includes those wines less than a year old. The second, the *especiales*, are two years old. The label *reservado* designates four-year-old wines which are generally of good quality. Finally, the best Chilean wines, the 'Gran Vino', are six years old or more, and are excellent.

Chinon The sprawling vineyard of Chinon occupies both the left bank of the Loire★ and the two banks of the Vienne. The soils are comparable to those of Bourgueil: gravelly terraces on the sides of the Vienne and the Loire, limestone and clay slopes and micaceous chalk below. As at Bourgueil, the wine from the gravelly area gives the informed connoisseur a different taste than those from the coast. This red wine, '*pour intellectuels*' as it is called, is produced by Chinon and several communes which have the right to the appellation contrôlée Chinon. These include Beaumont-en-Véron, Cravant, Avoine and Savigny, not forgetting Ligré, the birthplace of François Rabelais, a great lover of 'this good Breton wine'. Chinon, like Bourgueil, comes from the Cabernet Franc★ which is locally called Cabernet Breton.

Chinon is ruby red in colour, fresh, dainty and supple, with a violet bouquet. Lighter and more tender than the Bourgueil, it is drunk earlier but fades more quickly. On the other hand, certain years can be preserved up to forty years in bottle. The wines of Ligré are full-bodied and gain a very beautiful bouquet with

age. The region of Chinon also produces an excellent rosé from the Cabernet which is dry and light and has an agreeable bouquet, making it one of the best of Touraine★.

Chiroubles Situated in the heart of Beaujolais★, this charming hillside village produces an excellent fruity wine which is tender and full of charm with all the characteristics typical of its area. It should be drunk young and chilled.

Chusclan This commune does not benefit from a proper appellation contrôlée but it has the right to add its name to that of the Côtes du Rhône★ printed in identical characters on the label. The vineyard occupies five different areas in the department of Gard, on the right bank of the Rhône north of Tavel and west of Orange.

The wine produced is a remarkable rosé, strong and very fruity with an aroma of prunes and acacia. It resembles Tavel★ and Lirac★, but is more virile. Sadly, the atomic centre of Marcoule is gradually encroaching on the vineyards and soon there will probably be no more of this delicious, aromatic rosé.

The co-operative of Chusclan also produces an excellent red wine which has title only to the appellation Côtes du Rhône.

clairet A very light red wine which is quite different from a rosé.

Clairette A southern variety of grape, white or rosé, mostly cultivated in the south of France in the departments of Hérault, Gard, Var, Vaucluse, Drôme and the Lower Alps, and also to some extent in California. The origin of the name is not known. In the Drôme, the Clairette produces the celebrated Clairette de Die★, a sparkling wine which has long been respected. In Die, the pure Clairette wines are often made by the Champagne method★, while the Clairette wines blended with Muscat★, which are produced in much larger quantities, are made by the old rural method★ perfected by the modern technique of filtration under pressure. Trans, near Draguignan, used to make a sparkling Clairette of the same type.

In the Mediterranean climate, Clairette gives a wine of high alcoholic content (12–14°) as many of the grapes are picked when very ripe. The Clairette is also mixed

La Clape, the appellation of vineyards located between Narbonne and the sea. In the background, a dovecot. Phot. M.

with other varieties in the white wines of Palette★, Cassis★ and Bandol, as well as in the rosé of Tavel and the red wine of Châteauneuf-du-Pape★.

The Clairette wines maderise★ very quickly, which is considered a fault, although in former days when vermouth was in vogue, they were much in demand as an ingredient. The Clairette of Languedoc★, like that of Bellegarde, possesses nearly all the characteristics of a pure Clairette wine.

Clairette de Die The Roman emperors, according to Pliny, were very fond of the Clairette Dea Augusta (the Roman name of Die). On the rocky hills of Saillans at Châtillon-en-Diois, around the little village of Die in the valley of the Drôme, lie vineyards whose golden grapes are related to the southern Côtes du Rhône. The delicious and exhilarating AOC wine Clairette de Die is made from the Clairette grape, which gives it lightness and freshness, and the Muscat which gives it bouquet and its particular character. It is a golden, semi-sparkling wine, marrowy or sweet and very fruity with an extremely delicate aroma of Muscat and rose.

The Clairette de Die is made in two ways, by the Champagne method★ of second fermentation in bottles, or the rural method★ where the bubbles form spontaneously in the bottle as a result of the natural sugar remaining in the wine after fermentation and without the addition of a liqueur de tirage★. The second method, though delicate and troublesome, makes a much superior sparkling wine. The fine bouquet of Muscat is totally preserved and the wines have more sparkle, and are fruitier, than those made by the Champagne method. Today, the vignerons are perfecting the method by eliminating the light cloudiness which sometimes occurs as a result of filtration under pressure before bottling.

Clairette du Languedoc This white wine of the Hérault must be made only from the Clairette grape to qualify for the appellation contrôlée. The Clairette, a classic white grape of southern vineyards, produces a wine in good soil which is very full-bodied and high in alcohol. The Clairette of Languedoc is a pretty, almost golden coloured wine, dry and full-bodied

with a slightly bitter aftertaste peculiar to this grape. It is used as a base for quality Vermouths.

The wine maderises★ very quickly and takes on a 'rancio'★ taste which is very unique. The word rancio must be specified on the label as a notification that the wine has aged naturally for at least three years and contains 14° of alcohol.

The production area includes the following communes: Aspiran, Paulhan, Adissan, Fontès, Cabrières, Péret and Ceyras. The Gard also produces a Clairette of the same type near Nîmes called the Clairette de Bellegarde.

Clape An appellation given to some of the Coteaux du Languedoc★ wines classified VDQS★ having a long-standing reputation. The vineyard lies in the hollow of a massive limestone range between Narbonne and the sea. The wines, reds and rosés, are colourful and the reds age well. Quality white wines are also produced.

clarity Although this is a quality ·demanded by many drinkers, the processes the wine is subjected to in order to attain a

Clarity: racking is one of the operations performed to obtain a clear wine. Caves in Beaune. Production Calvet. Phot. Rapho-Feher.

perfect clarity may rob it of its charm and bouquet. Thus racking, fining and filtering are often not even used for the great wines.

Classification of 1855 A classification of vineyards of the Médoc had been operating since the beginning of the eighteenth century. Several classifications (like those of Jullien in 1816) distinguished four or five categories of crus as well as bourgeois★ and paysans★. But it was not until the Great Paris Exhibition of 1855 that the classification of Bordeaux wines became official. The courtiers★ of Bordeaux (who act in an official capacity) were told to furnish a 'complete and satisfactory display' of the wines of the department. Essentially based on prices which the wines had commanded over the years, the Classification of 1855 grouped wines of different style but of the same quality. Astonishingly enough, after more than a century the classification still has a certain value.

Actually, the methods of cultivation, vinification and breeding of the wines are similar in all the great vineyards. Only the different soil gives each wine its personality and quality. A well-grounded classification like this normally remains constant with only a few exceptions (some crus have subsequently been demoted or promoted; others not classified in 1855 are now sold at the same price as the classified crus).

One can only criticise the classification for concerning itself solely with the wines of the Médoc and Sauternes and only one Graves (Haut-Brion), and for having totally ignored Saint-Emilion, Pomerol and other Bordeaux appellations, and the rest of the Graves. The classification recognised four red grand premier crus, Château Lafite-Rothschild, Château Margaux, Château Latour and Château Haut-Brion, and for the whites, only one grand premier cru, the prestigious Château d'Yquem. All the Médoc crus classified in 1855 in five categories should be considered as old nobility, but the superieur and unclassified bourgeois crus often give the wine-lover as much pleasure.

clavelin The name of a special squat bottle which holds the vin jaune★ of Jura. Its capacity is 6 dl.

climat A term used in Burgundy to distinguish a particular vineyard area. In each village the vineyard is divided into climats. Thus the Côte d'Or, which is only forty km long and four km wide, has sixty appellation contrôlées and each of them comprises from twenty to fifty climats, each so unique in area that those seeking to define them could only follow the traditional usage and classification. Some of the climats have been very famous since ancient times: Chambertin, Montrachet, Clos de Vougeot and others. The climat of Burgundy is the equivalent of the Bordeaux château.

collage (fining) The traditional and ancient practice used since Roman times to clear the wine and give it a desirable clarity★. Before the wine is bottled, several different substances are introduced which combine with the tannin★ to cause precipitation of these undesirable particles in suspension. The principal agents used for this process are de-fibred beef blood, gelatin, casein, isinglass (used mainly for white wines) and fresh egg whites (used for quality red wines). There must, however, be sufficient tannin present to balance the protein content. When there is insufficient tannin, part of the protein content stays in suspension in the wine and forms a kind of white veil. It is over-fined – a disastrous accident which can only be rectified by addition of tannin or bentonite★.

Blue fine is used in certain countries to eliminate iron, which is responsible for casse ferrique★ (iron clouding). Potassium ferrocyanide must be added to the wine as it forms a heavy insoluble compound with the iron. This substance, called *bleu de Prusse* (Prussian blue), is then precipitated with the fining substance.

colouring matter The colouring matter of red grapes is due to pigments of the tannins in the skin. The pulp is colourless except for several varieties of grapes called *teinturiers* (Gamay teinturier for example). Analysis shows that the colouring matter is peculiar to each grape variety. When they are fresh, the cells of the skin retain the pigment and pressing red grapes produces a juice which has very little colouring (vin gris) or no colour at all (Champagne★).

The pigments are insoluble in cold

Left: collage using a manual pump at Courthézon, Vaucluse; right: traditional collage in Burgundy. Phot. M.

water but may well dissolve in alcohol. This is why the longer a wine ferments, the more pronounced the colour as the pigment slowly dissolves in the alcohol formed by the fermentation process.

Besides furnishing colour, the pigments also contribute to the formation of the fruitiness of young wines and the bouquet of old wines. Later, the pigment matter becomes insoluble when oxidised, which explains why brownish deposits are found at the bottom of old bottles. Although colouring matter does not seem to appear in white wines, it is nonetheless present and is quite visible in maderised★ wines, which take on a yellow tint.

comet (wines of the) Since ancient times, comets have been considered as auspicious occurrences. Among other things, they are supposed to produce wines of exceptional quality in the years they appear. The 'wines of the comet' were always very much in demand and had an enviable place in the hierarchy of grand crus.

The passing of the comet, 1811. Coloured engraving. Bibl. Nat. Phot. B.N.

The Rhône at Condrieu. The 'Côte-Chérie' tiers of terraces on the river banks are planted with Viognier Doré, which make the suave wines of Condrieu and the rare Château-Grillet. Phot. M.

Whatever the case, the wines of the comet of 1811 have left a reminder which is as celebrated as the beautiful comet which appeared that year. But an exceptional summer and autumn, splendid and warm, should perhaps also account for some of the excellence of the wines of that year.

complete wine　A wine which is perfectly constituted. It unites all the qualities – bouquet, elegance, finesse, breeding and harmony. It is the wine of great years.

composition of wine　This is very complex as at least sixty elements are known and still others have not been identified. The principal constituents are alcohol, acids, tannins, colouring matter and pectins. There are also salts (phosphates of potassium, calcium and iron, potassium sulphate, etc.), metalloids (chlorine, fluorine, iodine, silicon, zinc, copper) and vitamins (especially B and C). Finally, about 75–85% is water.

Condrieu　An appellation of the Côtes du Rhône★ which includes three communes of the right bank of the Rhône: Condrieu, Vérin and Saint-Michel. The area is sometimes called Côte-Chérie. Condrieu is a unique and very rare white wine which only few have enjoyed since it

travels poorly. It is only made in this area, and comes from one grape, the Viognier or Viognier doré, which is harvested late. This grape gives a very rich must whose fermentation is rarely finished before the arrival of frost.

After careful preparation, the wine is bottled in spring and some is left in casks for eighteen months following fermentation. The first process gives a marrowy taste because of the sugar remaining in the wine. The second gives a dry wine which has a remarkable delicacy and suppleness due to the glycerine which is formed during the long fermentation (certain wine-makers obtain this second type of wine in the harvest year). The Condrieu should be drunk when young as it ages poorly, drying out and maderising★.

It is a splendid, full-bodied wine with a penetrating, suave bouquet, unique like the neighbouring, even more exceptional, Château-Grillet★.

consommation courante (vins de)　These so-called 'table wines' are regarded as being suitable for everyday consumption. Well chosen, they do not strain the stomach or head and have the best taste next to the appellation contrôlée★ and VDQS★ wines. By law, they must mention their alcoholic content and satisfy requirements such as minimum degree of alcohol, absence of toxic substances, normal content of volatile acid, etc. They are sold in capped bottles or from the barrel and their quality is controlled by the Institut des Vins de Consommation Courante. They are also subject to the Répression des Fraudes Commission. The wines are divided into two categories: vins de pays★ and vins de coupage★.

Constance A wine produced in the Republic of South Africa by a small vineyard belonging to the State. It is located not far from the village of Cap and was planted around 1700 by the Dutch Governor, Simon Van der Stel. The vineyard was called Great Constantia in honour of the governor's wife whose name was Constance. The French Protestant émigrés contributed to the establishment of the vineyards.

The wine of Constance enjoyed an incredible vogue in the nineteenth century in France and England and the heroes of Balzac often honoured it! Today's production is only a few hundred hectolitres and it is almost impossible to obtain. Good, often very good, the wine is sweet, suave and fine with a light muscadet perfume (due to the Muscadelle of Bordeaux planted by the French Protestants). However, compared with today's wines, it does not seem to measure up totally to its former glory.

co-operative The wine-making co-operatives had modest beginnings around 1900, after the start of the first dairy co-operatives. Their prime objective was to sell the harvest, and stock in cellars the excess production which would lower the price. Little by little, the vignerons began to make wine together. The co-operative formula offered great practical advantages to the small producers, removing the need for expensive individually-owned wine casks, which demanded costly and delicate upkeep. It also resulted in economy of work, more care in the vinification and storing of wine, and liberated space previously devoted to wine-making.

The co-operative offered its members modern techniques, used modern equipment and assured them of a quality product. The small producers benefited because they often found it impossible to acquire modern equipment or even to maintain the old equipment. This formula was very successful, especially in the Midi, in the Languedoc area and in North Africa.

The method is particularly valuable for making table wines (vins de consommation courante★), wines of genuine appellation and vins de pays★ but, although certain co-operatives made laudable efforts to conserve the individuality of the wines, it is not compatible with the idea of personal art and particular vineyards which characterise the famous crus. Today, there are about 1100 caves including 250,000 members. They make between 25 and 30% of French wine (around 15 million hectolitres of which 12 million is vin de consommation courante). The rest, about 3 million hectolitres, is divided equally among the VDQS★ and the AOC★ wines.

Corbières This VDQS★ wine, coming from limestone hills south-east of Carcassonne in Languedoc-Roussilon, is very popular.

Red, rosé and white wines are produced but the reds are by far the best known. The grapes are the typical ones of the region: mainly . Carignon, but also Grenache, Cinsault and Terret Noir in varying

The vineyard of Corbières stretches to the foot of the walls of Carcassonne. Phot. Hétier.

*Corbières: 11th-century
Roman chapel on the outskirts
of Lézignan (Aude). Phot. M.*

*Stripping cork (Portugal).
Phot. Loirat.*

proportions for the reds and rosés, and Clairette for the white wines. The rosés are full-bodied, nervous★ and fruity. When they are well made, the reds are a beautiful, sombre colour, full-bodied and fleshy, acquiring very quickly a particular bouquet which is refined with age. A well-known saying about this wine is, 'The wine of Corbières has an accent'.

Corbières and Corbières Supérieurs are found in the department of Aude, and the Corbières du Roussillon in the Pyrénées-Orientales. Corbières must have 10° of alcohol and Corbières Supérieurs, 12°. Fitou★, an appellation contrôlée wine, is produced by the best communes of Corbières.

The Corbières du Roussillon are full-bodied, fine-flavoured wines which come from the same grapes as the Corbières, with the addition of the Malvoisie and Macabéo.

Corent   A wine of the Auvergne★ which now exists mainly in legend, like the Chanturgues★. Both are produced in the area of Clermont-Ferrand and made from the Gamay noir à just blanc. Corent has a very pale tint and great charm. It is usually found as vin gris (that is, when it can actually be found).

cork (bouchon)   The cork is the ideal seal for wine. No other natural or manufactured material can match it, and attempts to stopper wines with plastic corks

have failed miserably. A cork should allow the wine to breathe so that it keeps well, but should also continue to expand. The proper supple cork clings remarkably well to the neck of the bottle and, most important, does not rot.

Specialists use different types of cork for individual wines. A supple cork, for example, is used for wines to be drunk young, a stronger cork for wine to be conserved longer and white wines subject to maderisation★.

The idea of the cork stopper is attributed to Dom Perignon★. He is said to have been inspired by the Spanish pilgrims who used large pieces of cork to seal their gourds. Prior to that, either a layer of oil was floated on the wine or hemp impregnated with oil was put over the top.

It is dangerous to economise on the quality of the cork. It should be of top quality and at least 4–4½ cm long. The cork should never be soaked in hot water before use as it will lose its elasticity. It should, instead, be soaked in cool water for about twelve hours.

corkscrew The invention of this instrument apparently dates from the time when all wines, even non-sparkling ones, began to be sealed with cork★ stoppers as opposed to oil-soaked hemp. The first corks, used by Dom Perignon★ for his Champagne, could probably be eased out by hand, aided by the wine's effervescence.

Corkscrews are first recorded around the end of the seventeenth century, but the name of their inventor remains unknown. Nowadays, corkscrews are available in many different shapes and designs, and are usually worked by a screw, lever or gas. Whatever their form, the principal requirement is that they should be functional and, above all, allow the wine to be uncorked slowly, gently and carefully.

Cornas The vineyard of this Côtes du Rhône★ commune is found on the right bank of the Rhône nearly facing Valence. It only produces appellation contrôlée red wines made from the Syrah. Cornas is a little bitter when young, but acquires an agreeable suppleness when mature. Not as noble or aromatic as its neighbour Hermitage, it is nevertheless a wine of great quality, especially when mature. Full-bodied, heady and substantial, it has a characteristic earthy taste. It has been much in demand and appreciated for a long time. Its deep ruby colour prompted Louis XV to call it 'a very good black wine'.

correction of wines Each year the local oenological stations specify corrections which can discreetly improve the imperfections resulting from a harvest in bad weather while preserving the natural composition of the wine. All the changes are limited and controlled by law. Certain wines must establish a normal level of acidity, some by adding acid and others by reducing it. Insufficient sugar may be corrected by chaptalisation★.

Other problems might be an excess or insufficiency of tannin, calling for fining or the addition of tannin respectively. Sometimes the wine lacks colour which is remedied by heating a part of the vendange to release colouring matter★. Finally, the method of assemblage★, as used in Champagne, can also be employed. Two wines coming from the same soil, but of a different year, sometimes complement

each other admirably and give a steady, complete wine.

Corsica Nothing is mediocre on this beautiful island, and the wines that it produces are no exception to the rule. They are all excellent, or at least original. They used to be consumed only on the island, but are now exported.

The principal grape is the Vermentino (Malvoisie), as well as other indigenous varieties: Nielluccio, Rossola, Bianca, Sciaccarello, Barbarosso and Carcajolo. The continental varieties represent about 15% of the acreage and have only been planted since the last century: Alicante, Grenache, Carignan, Cinsault and Muscat.

Wine is produced all over the island and, although the Corsican wines are not subject to the French legislation of the Continent, they are regulated under an unique legal statute dating from 1801. The coastal area has most of the good vineyards. The vineyard of Cap Corse, which is as well known outside the island, produces full-bodied white, rosé and red wines. The celebrated sweet Cap Corse wine, made from Muscat and Malvoisie,

Corsica: the vineyard of Patrimonio, in the Bastia region. Phot. Rapho.

83

is marrowy and delicate and has made it famous. But there are other famous coastal producers: Coteaux de Saint-Florent, which produces without a doubt the best Corsican wines, especially the famous Patrimonio★, and has been AOC★ since 1968; the region of Bastia (with the excellent wines of Vescovato and Cervione); Balagne (Calvi and Calenzana), where the Sciaccarello reigns; Sartène and its strong VDQS★; Ajaccio and its belt of vineyards; Piana which, besides delicious rosés, gives perfumed Muscats; Bonifacia and others.

The interior of the island also produces some interesting, although less esteemed, wines. These are found around Bastelica, Corte and Omessa.

The Corsican wines are well made considering they come from such a poor, flinty soil. Delicious when young, they also age admirably and acquire a delicate

Costières du Gard, on the right bank of the Rhône. Phot. M.

bouquet. The often dry white wines are full of finesse and fragrance and certain of them resemble Hermitage★. The red wines have a remarkable bouquet. Nearly all are heady and strong and possess a particular finesse. Some of them resemble Côtes-du-Rhône★, especially Chateauneuf-du-Pape★. The exquisite rosés are a lovely colour with a fruity, warm taste, blending pepper and smoke.

Since 1968, Patrimonio has been appellation contrôlée and sometimes classified VDQS.

Cortaillod A Swiss wine which comes from the Lake Neuchâtel area around the village of Cortaillod. It is made from the Pinot Noir of Burgundy which is the only grape allowed in the canton. It is an agreeable pale red wine, fresh and fruity.

Cortese A dry white wine produced from a grape of the same name in the Piemonte region of Italy. It is an extremely pleasant wine, pale, light and fresh, which should be drunk young.

Costières-du-Gard An appellation which groups the red, rosé and white wines classed VDQS★ from this vineyard. The production area is located on the right side of the Rhône Valley south of Nîmes, between Beaucaire and Vauvert.

The vineyard, planted on rolling gravel which reflects the heat of the sun, includes the usual varieties grown in the Midi and the Côtes du Rhône including the Grenache, Syrah and Carignan. The full-bodied reds have a rich aroma resembling the Côtes-du-Rhône.

The white wines, coming from the Clairette, are fine and fruity if the vendange is not too late.

Cot A red grape which is known by a variety of different names – Malbec in Gironde, Auxerrois at Cahors, Cot in Touraine and Quercy, and so on. It is gradually being replaced by the Merlot variety in the best Gironde vineyards, but is still planted in Bergerac★, Côtes de Duras★ and many VDQS★ crus of the Sud-Ouest★ region. It is traditionally the principal variety of grape (70–80%) grown in the Cahors vineyard. In Touraine it is chiefly grown in the Cher valley, at Mesland★ and Amboise★. In Anjou★ it is combined with Groslot, Gamay and Cabernet grapes to make rosé d'Anjou★.

Unlike most other grapes, which grow from offshoots of the previous year's growth, Cot grapes grow from offshoots of old, tough wood which is an advantage in regions where spring frosts occur. It is most productive on clay and limestone soil. The wine it produces has good colour and body, but is slightly lacking in bouquet and flavour. It does, on the other hand, combine well with other, finer, varieties – it contributes colour and moelleux★ to wine and makes it mature more quickly.

Côte Chalonnaise An area in Burgundy that takes its name from the town of Chalon-sur-Saône. It is a natural extension of the Côte de Beaune vineyards, and shares with them the same soil, methods of viticulture and vinification and commercial traditions. The region has four appellation contrôlées (Côte Chalonnaise is not itself an appellation): Rully★, Mercurey★, Givry★ and Montangy★.

The authorised grape varieties for these wines are those grown in the Côte d'Or: Chardonnay★ for white wines and Pinot Noir★ for red. A certain quantity of Aligoté is also grown in the region and, as elsewhere in Burgundy, the wine made from it is entitled to the appellation Bourgogne Aligoté★. Another grape grown here is Gamay which is made into Bourgogne passe-tous-grains★ with Groslot grapes in a ratio of 2:1. It also produces the wines of appellation Bourgogne ordinaire and Bourgogne grand ordinaire★.

Côte de Beaune The Côte de Beaune represents the southern half of the famous Côte d'Or★ vineyards, and stretches from Ladoix in the north to Santenay in the south, covering an area of 2800 ha. Unlike the Côte de Nuits★, whose wines are almost all red, it is chiefly notable for its magnificent white wines, which are the best in Burgundy★. Some of the reds are also excellent, and the area as a whole produces more red wine than white.

Red Côte de Beaune wines have charm and finesse; they are more subtle, less powerful, and more feminine than those of the Côte de Nuits. They are also ready for drinking sooner, but do not keep as long. The white wines have exceptional breeding and distinction. Many find their smoothness and delicate aroma unequalled by any other wine.

Appellations are either names of communes (e.g. Beaune) or of crus (e.g. Montrachet). The most important communes of the Côte de Beaune are Aloxe-Corton★, Pernand-Vergelesses★, Savigny-les-Beaune★, Beaune★, Pommard★, Volnay★, Meursault★ and Blagny★, Chassagne-Montrachet★, Puligny-Montrachet★ and Santenay★.

Other, lesser known communes also produce excellent wines, some of which certainly deserve to be better known by the wine-buying public. They are, from north to south, Ladoix (red and white), Chorey-les-Beaune (red and white), Mon-thelie (red), Saint-Romain (red and white), Auxey-Duresses (red and white), Dezize-les-Maranges, Sampigny-les-Maranges and Cheilly-les-Maranges (red and white). The last three of these communes are in the Saône-et-Loire department.

Ladoix-Serrigny Although this commune has its own appellation, its wines are usually sold under the name Côte-de-Beaune Villages★ and the best under that of the neighbouring Aloxe-Corton, whose characteristics they share. The wines of Ladoix-Serrigny are light and have a charming bouquet.

Chorey-les-Beaune mainly produces red wines which can be sold under their own appellation or that of Côte-de-Beaune-Villages.

Monthelie has several premiers crus whose names can be added to that of the commune: Sur La Velle, Les Vignes Rondes, Le Meix Bataille, Les Riottes, La Taupine, Le Clos-Gauthey, Le Château-Gaillard, Les Champs-Fulliot, Le Cas Rougeot and Duresse.

Vineyard of Monthélie, near Beaune in Burgundy.
Phot. Rapho.

Saint-Romain produces robust reds and fruity whites sold under the AOC Saint-Romain. Some of the production is also sold as Côte-de-Beaune-Villages.

Auxey-Duresses Before the appellation laws the wine was sold as Volnay★ or Pommard★. Some of the climats have the right to the name Côte-de-Beaune accompanied by the name of the commune. At present these include: Les Duresses, Les Bas-des-Duresses, Reugne, Les Grands-Champs, Climat-du-Val (or Clos-du-Val), Les Ecusseaux and Les Bretterins (the climat of La Chapelle is divided between Les Bretterins and Reugne).

Saint-Aubin Positioned on the hills behind Puligny-Montrachet★ and Chassagne-Montrachet★, this commune produces red and white wines having the appellation Saint-Aubin or Saint-Aubin-Côte-de-Beaune or Côte-de-Beaune-Villages. The best climats are allowed to carry the name of their cru in addition to that of the commune: La Chatenière, Les Murgers-des-Dents-de-Chien, En Remilly, Les Frionnes, Sur-le Sentier-du-Clou, Sur Gamay, Les Combes and Champlot.

Dezize-les-Maranges These fruity, light red and white wines are sold under their proper name or under Côte-de-Beaune-Villages.

Cheilly-les-Maranges These red and white wines are often blended with those of other communes and sold under the name Côte-de-Beaune plus the name of the commune. The best crus, Les Maranges and Clos-du-Roi, can label their wines Sampigny-les-Maranges and Sampigny-les-Maranges-Clos-du-Roi.

CÔTE DE BEAUNE: APPELLATION CÔTE-DE-BEAUNE A wine bearing on its label the name Côte-de-Beaune without mention of the commune or village is a wine coming from the Beaune area, and less prized, evidently, than those which only carry the name Beaune on the label. The Côtes-de-Beaune are red or white and must have 10·5° alcohol for the reds and 11° for the whites.

Côte-de-Beaune-Villages This appellation is completely different from Côte-de-Beaune. It is applied exclusively to red wines made from a combination of at least two wines from certain communes in the

Côte de Beaune area (but not Beaune itself). They have an alcoholic strength of 10·5°.

Côte de Nuits Occupies about 1200 ha from Dijon to Prémeaux, but the grand crus begin at Fixin. Most of the production is red wine which has great breeding. Some excellent white wines are made at Musigny, Vougeot★, Morey-Saint-Denis★ and Nuits-Saint-Georges★, but they have not attained the excellence of the great red wines.

Like all the Burgundy★ wines, these possess the personality of their climat★, and have in common great breeding, firmness, sumptuous colour, rich bouquet and the ability to mature well. The appellation may be that of the commune (Gevrey-Chambertin★) or the cru (Romanée-Conti). The communes of the Côte de Nuits are: Fixin★, Gevrey-Chambertin, Morey-Saint-Denis, Chambolle-Musigny★, Vougeot, Vosne-Romanée★ and Nuits-Saint-Georges.

Côte d'Or The Côte d'Or forms the most important and the most beautiful area of Burgundy★. Its soil produces the prestigious red and white wines whose names are universally known: Romanée-Conti, Chambertin and Montrachet★. This great viticultural region is divided into two sub-regions: Côte de Nuits★, which produces almost exclusively the great red wines, and the Côte de Beaune★ which produces both great reds and whites.

There are also two parallel regions, the upper Côtes de Nuits and the upper Côtes de Beaune, which produce appellation wines and can, under certain conditions, add their name to the Côte d'Or appellation. From Dijon to Santenay, the Côte de Nuits and the Côte de Beaune forms a nearly continuous line of hills 200–500 m high. These hills, facing east and south-east, are protected from the wind and receive a maximum amount of sun. The best crus are harvested at 250–300 m.

The soil is extremely varied and complex which explains the many crus of Burgundy: white marl, favourable to great white wines like Montrachet; the iron- and limestone-rich soils of the Côte de Beaune; and argillo-siliceous-limestone and iron-bearing soils of the Côte de

Nuits. The only grape varieties approved for the great appellations of the communes and climats are the Pinot Noir for the red wines, and Chardonnay for the whites.

The Aligoté grape, mainly grown in the Upper Côtes, only has the right to the appellation Bourgogne Aligoté★.

Côte-Rôtie On the right bank of the Rhône, bordering the hills south of Lyons, is the celebrated vineyard of the Côte-Rôtie, whose width is no greater than 400 metres. The grapes are grown on the two communes of Tupin-Semons and Ampuis. Two noble★ grapes, the red Syrah and the white Viognier (about 20%) are grown on the acidic soil. The wine of the Côte-Rôtie is a great one, praised as early as the first century. It is a beautiful purple colour, full-bodied and generous, with a unique bouquet combining the fragrance of violet and raspberry.

The Côte-Rôtie is as sumptuous as its rival Châteauneuf-du-Pape★, but has greater distinction.

The best crus of the Côte-Rôtie are the Côte-Brune and the Côte-Blonde, which produce several wines. Those of the Côte-Brune are full-bodied and keep for a long time, whereas the wines of the Côte-Blonde do not age as well, but are lighter and more tender.

Côtes d'Agly A vineyard lying between those of Maury★ and Rivesaltes★ on the hills bordering the Agly, a small, turbulent river in the Roussillon★ area.

The soil is composed chiefly of clay and limestone and is planted with noble★ vines (Grenache, Muscat and Malvoisie) which, scorched by the sun and buffeted by the north wind, produce heady vins doux naturels★. These are either red (when the pulp is left with the grape juice during fermentation) or white (when the pulp is removed before fermentation).

Côtes d'Agly wines are often vinified in very modern co-operative cellars. They have an attractive colour, generosity★, distinction, and an aroma faintly reminiscent of stones warmed in the sun.

Côtes de Bordeaux-Saint-Macaire
The area entitled to this appellation is the continuation to the south of the Premières Côtes de Bordeaux★ vineyards. It covers several communes and adjoins the famous

crus of Sainte-Croix-du-Mont★. The appellation only applies to wines made from noble★ grapes grown on clay and gravel soil. These are picked when over-ripe, and there are strict regulations concerning their vinification. The sweet white wines obtained are full-bodied and delicate and have a distinctive fragrance. Their particular character makes them as suitable for serving with desserts as they are for fish dishes, and even some white meats.

Côtes de Canon-Fronsac This appellation is given to wines grown on the best slopes of the Fronsac★ vineyards, particularly on the hill of Canon. These wines have a fine dark colour, plenty of body and a distinctive, slightly spicy flavour. They

Village and vineyard of the Côte de Nuits. Phot. Atlas-Photo.

Côte-Rôtie, on the right bank of the Rhône, south of Vienna. Phot. M.

resemble both Pomerol★ and Burgundy★ wines, and are highly esteemed, especially in northern Europe. They are at their best a few years after bottling. The main crus are Châteaux Canon, Comte and Gaby.

Côtes de Duras   The name of this vineyard overlooking the Dropt Valley is one of the appellations contrôlées of the Sud-Ouest★. It lies to the north of the Lot-et-Garonne department between the Bordeaux region and the Bergerac vineyards and comprises about fifteen communes. Although Côtes de Duras is best known for its white wines, it also produces some reds made from the Cabernet, Merlot and Malbec grapes. These are good table wines of an unexceptional character with a minimum official alcohol content of 10°.

The white wines are distinctly superior in quality and have a correspondingly high reputation. They are made from the usual local grape varieties, Sémillon, Sauvignon and Muscadelle, with a proportion of Mauzac and sometimes Ugni Blanc, a grape grown all over the south of France. These wines are slightly sweet and have a distinctive and very pleasant aroma. Their official minimum alcohol content is 10·5°.

Côtes-de-Fronsac   This appellation applies to wines grown in the general Fronsac★ area which, although less fine than the wines of Côtes de Canon-Fronsac★, greatly resemble them in other respects, particularly in colouring and body. The principal crus are Châteaux Lavalode, Tasla and la Rivière.

Côtes de Haut-Roussillon   Planted on dry, stony soil known as *terre d'Aspres*, this appellation contrôlée vineyard in the Roussillon★ region produces vins doux naturels★ made from Grenache, Muscat and Malvoisie grapes, and comprises about forty communes between the valleys of the Tech and Têt. The region has been renowned for its fortified wines since Pliny the Elder praised them and compared them to Falerno. Overrun and destroyed by the Saracens, the vineyard was gradually reconstructed around the local monasteries and castles – so well that by the eleventh century its wines had regained their former reputation and were being served at the royal tables of France, Aragon, Majorca and Spain.

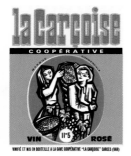

Côtes-du-Haut-Roussillon are generous wines with a very delicate and original bouquet that develops during a long period of maturation. They can be either red or white.

The Haut-Rousillon region also produces some full-bodied red wines made from Carignan grapes. They have an alcoholic strength of 12° and are used in the preparation of apéritifs.

Côtes-de-Provence   The domain of these VDQS★ wines extends from Marseilles to Nice on extremely varied terrain. In this fortunate country, the sun conditions the wine, the soil being only of relative importance. Thus the vine is found on both hills and plains, thrusting its roots into chalky soil mingled with flint.

Three principal regions produce the Côtes-de-Provence: la Côte (from la Ciotat to Saint-Tropez), the northern border of the Massif de Maures and the Argens valley.

The rosés are the most popular, and their vogue is due for the most part to the many tourists who identify the wine with the sun and holidays. They are excellent dry wines, fruity, full-bodied and fragrant, whose clear and pretty colour sometimes hints of gold. They are especially suited to the cuisine of the south.

The red wines, less known, are full-bodied, having a beautiful glowing colour and an enjoyable bouquet. Their character depends on the area of origin. For example, the wines of Taradeau, Pierrefeu and Puget-Ville are particularly heady, while those of Saint-Tropez and Gonfaron are agreeably supple. The reds are made from a variety of grapes: Grenache, Cinsault, Mourvèdre, Carignan, Pécoui-Touar and Oeillade. They age well, but can also be drunk young.

The white wines, which come mainly from the Clairette and the Ugni Blanc, are dry, full-bodied, fruity and pale gold in colour. They maderise★ quickly and should be drunk young.

There is an official classification of crus of Côtes de Provence. The principal ones are the domaines of Moulières, Aumerade, Minuty and la Croix; the châteaux of Selle and Sainte-Roseline; Clos Mireille, Cigonne and Bastide-Verte.

Côtes de Toul   This narrow vineyard, one of the two appellations of Lorraine★, is

Côtes-de-Provence; vineyards at Croix-Valmer. Phot. M.

perched on the limestone hills overlooking the Moselle around the village of Toul. There are nine communes, of which Lucey, Bruley and Ecrouves produce wines classified VDQS★. The grapes used are the Pinot Noir, Meunier, the Gamay of Toul and of Liverdun, as well as 20% maximum of secondary grapes such as the Aubin Blanc and Aligoté.

The Gamay of Liverdun, a variety adapted from the Gamay of Beaujolais, has become the principal variety today, increasingly replacing the Pinots which were, in the old days, the traditional grape of Lorraine. The region used to provide its harvest for Champagne before the legal limitation of production for that area. Today, most of the wine produced is a vin gris★ of a very pale colour which is quite light. The 8·5° minimum fixed by law is seldom exceeded. It is best drunk young, although it can be kept for several years. This is a very agreeable wine, fresh, aromatic and fruity with a touch of acidity much admired in the area. The red and white wines are much rarer and practically impossible to find.

Côtes du Forez   One of the appellations of Lyon which merits the VDQS★ label. The red and some rosé wines come from the Gamay. They are consumed locally.

Côtes-du-Jura   This regional appellation contrôlée, applied to the wines which originate in the chalk and gravel of the Jura★ hills, covers twelve cantons: Villers-Farlay, Salins, Arbois, Poligny, Sellières, Voiteur, Bletterans, Conliège, Lons-le-Saunier, Beaufort, Saint-Julien and Saint-Amour (not to be confused with the Saint-Amour cru of Beaujolais).

The appellation applies to white, dry, full-bodied wines having a particular perfume, and generous reds with bouquet and finish. When the Poulsard grape dominates, the red wines have little colouring, but are very fine. The Trousseau gives more colour and body. The rosés are dry and fruity, but have perhaps a little less character than the reds. Under this appellation are also found the vins jaune★, vins de paille★ and vins mousseux★.

Côtes du Luberon   This vineyard, located east of Avignon and north of Durance on the slopes of Luberon, is somewhat similar to the nearby Côtes du Ventoux★. The vignerons have made great efforts and met with the same success as their neighbours at Ventoux by gradually replacing the Carignan with the Grenache and the Cinsault.

The Côtes-du-Luberon wines merit the VDQS★ label. The reds and rosés resemble

Vines of Côtes du Luberon.
Phot. Brihat-Rapho.

those of Ventoux and come from the same grape varieties. The rosé is particularly delicious. The whites, made from the Clairette and Bourboulenc, are produced in just as large quantities. These are fruity wines which should be drunk young.

Côtes du Marmandais These VDQS★ wines of the Sud-Ouest★ are produced on the two banks of the Garonne in the cantons of Marmande and Seyches. The region is, in a sense, a prolongation of the Entre-deux-Mers area on the right bank of the Garonne, and of Sauternes on the left bank. The grape varieties planted on these sunny slopes are very varied. Interest has been mainly local in these red and white, good quality wines up till now.

Côtes du Rhône From Vienne to Avignon, the vineyards planted on the slopes of the two banks of the Rhône link those of Burgundy and Provence. No other vineyard offers such diversity as this to the wine drinker. More than 110 communes located in six departments are covered by the general appellation Côtes du Rhône. They produce wines which, for the most part, have only this appellation in common and include dry whites, sweet whites, light reds, robust reds, rosés, sparkling wines, vins doux naturels★ and vins de paille★.

The vineyard is divided into two parts, north and south, separated by a region without vines between Valence and the gorge of Donzère. The northern Côtes du Rhône is found on a narrow band of slopes overlooking the Rhône. The southern part is mostly laid out on both sides of the river as far as the department of Gard on the right and those of Vaucluse and Drôme on the left.

The terrain of the two is very different. The northern vineyards lie on steep slopes, while those of the south are planted on such arid, rocky soil as to defy nature.

A great variety of grapes are used, twenty being authorised including Syrah, Grenache, Mourvèdre, Cinsault, Clairette, Roussanne, Marsanne and Viognier. The following crus are recognised as the best of the northern region. On the right bank, Côte-Rôtie★, Condrieu★, Château-Grillet★, Saint-Joseph★, Cornas★ and Saint-Péray★; on the left bank, Hermitage★ and Crozes-Hermitage★. The southern Côtes-du-Rhône crus include, on the left bank, Châteauneuf-du-Pape★, Gigondas★, Vacqueyras, Cairanne, Vinsobres, Rasteau★, Beaumes-de-Venise★ and Die and its Clairette★ and on the right bank, Tavel★, Lirac★, Chusclan★ and Laudun★. Besides the appellation Côtes-du-Rhône, the same region of the Rhône valley offers a certain number of VDQS wines which are sold under their proper name. On the left bank these are Châtillon-en-Diois★, Haut-Comtat★, Coteaux-du-Tricastin★, Côtes-du-Ventoux★ and Côtes-du-Luberon★, and on the right bank, Côtes-du-Vivarais★ and Costières-du-Gard★.

CÔTES-DU-RHÔNE: APPELLATION The appellation Côtes-du-Rhône is given to a large quantity of wines which are usually generous and heady, and which when made well are good table wines. They particularly complement the food of the Midi region or other highly-seasoned dishes. These whites, reds and rosés come from a mélange of wines in the northern and southern part of the Côtes du Rhône.

Today, nearly all the wine sold under the single appellation Côtes-du-Rhône come from the southern part: Vaucluse, Drôme and Gard. The best wines have the right to their own appellation and certain communes can use their own name, like

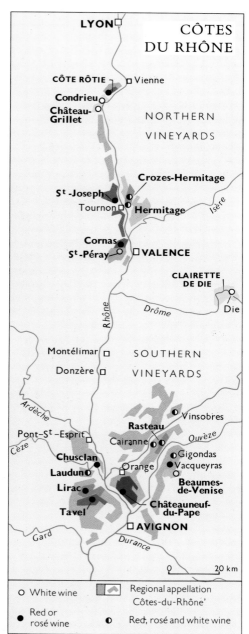

CÔTES DU RHÔNE

LYON

CÔTE RÔTIE — □ Vienne
Condrieu □
Château-
Grillet ○

NORTHERN
VINEYARDS

Crozes-Hermitage
St -Joseph □
Tournon □ ○ Hermitage
Isère

Cornas ●
St -Péray ○ □ VALENCE

CLAIRETTE
DE DIE
Rhône *Drôme* ○ Die

Montélimar □ SOUTHERN
Donzère □ VINEYARDS

Ardèche
◐ Vinsobres
Rasteau
Pont-St -Esprit □ Cairanne ◐◐ *Ouvèze*
Cèze
Chusclan ◐ Gigondas
Laudun ○ □ Orange ● Vacqueyras
Lirac ● ○
Beaumes-
Tavel ● de-Venise
Châteauneuf-
du-Pape
□ AVIGNON
Gard
Durance
0 20 km

○ White wine | Regional appellation Côtes-du-Rhône'
● Red or rosé wine | ◐ Red, rosé and white wine

Châteauneuf-du-Pape and Tavel. By contrast, certain communes can only use their name when it is preceded by Côtes-du-Rhône, for example Gigondas, Cairanne, Chusclan and Laudun.

Côtes du Ventoux This appellation derives from a vineyard in the Rhône valley of the same name. It is situated on the slopes of a mountain in the department of Vaucluse where the vines are protected from the cold winds and exposed to the sun. Thanks to the efforts of the vignerons, who have tried to improve the grape varieties and the methods of vinification, the wine of the Côtes du Ventoux has become one of the best VDQS★ of the Rhône valley.

The reds and rosés come from the Carignan (not more than 50%), the Grenache, Syrah, Mourvèdre and Cinsault grapes. The rosés have a rich bouquet, are fruity and nervous★ with finesse and freshness. The reds are an attractive, clear, ruby red. The whites, made principally from the Clairette and Bourboulenc, are produced in similar quantities.

Côtes du Vivarais A vineyard of the Ardèche department situated on the right bank of the Rhône around Orgnac, whose chasm is a favourite tourist attraction. It produces red, rosé and white wines from the classic grapes of the region – the Grenache, Syrah, Mourvèdre and Cinsault for the reds and rosés, and Clairette, Bourboulenc and Picpoul for the whites. The fresh and fragrant Côtes-du-Vivarais are classified VDQS★. When the grapes are more vigorous and the wines contain at least 11° of alcohol, the name of the commune can follow the appellation Côtes-du-Vivarais, for example Orgnac, Saint-Montant and Saint-Remèze.

Côtes du Zaccar Included under this appellation are the Algerian wines produced around Miliana south-west of Algiers which were labelled VDQS★ before Algerian independence. The red, rosé and white wines are grown on limestone-clay soil at an altitude of 400–900 m and share a common, unique bouquet.

The colourful, full-bodied reds were fleshy, sometimes having a raspberry fruitiness. They were counted among the best in Algeria. The whites, made mainly from the Faranah, were generally excellent, fruity and very flavourful.

coulant (vin) A wine which provides a very smooth sensation, also described as 'glissant' or 'slippery'. It is rich in glycerine★, harmonious and stable and no one element (alcohol, tannin or acid) predominates.

Coulée-de-Serrant This, along with Roche-aux-Moines★, is the most delicious

Following two pages: 4th-century Roman mosaic depicting boys gathering grapes, transport by cart and treading. Detail. Santa Costanza, Rome.
Phot. Hamlyn Group Michael Holford.

of the Savennières★. The appellation Coulée-de-Serrant must be preceded by Savennières. The domaine, enclosed by walls, only covers three hectares. On this schistose soil of a well-exposed hill, the Pineau de la Loire flourishes, and was always a favourite of Louis XIV and, later, the Empress Josephine. The wine used to be semi-dry or sweet and was harvested late so that the grapes could be conserved by the sun. Today, dry wine is made and no-one complains. It has kept its old delicacy and elegance and has also acquired a certain vigour.

CLOS
DE LA
Coulée de Serrant

APPELLATION SAVENNIÈRES · COULÉE DE SERRANT CONTROLÉE

B.C.A. Mme A. JOLY, Propriétaire · Château de la Roche-aux-Moines
SAVENNIÈRES (M.-&-L.) France
PRODUCT OF FRANCE   Mise en Bouteilles au Château   ESTATE BOTTLED

Coulée de Serrant: general view of the vineyards.
Phot. M.

coulure A vine disease. Sometimes, when the weather is bad during the period of the flowering of the vines, the flowers do not fully develop but dry up and fall off. Certain grapes like the Chardonnay are prone to this disease.

coupage (vins de) Offspring of several fathers, these blended wines have an undetermined origin. Their birthplace is in the cellars of wine *négociants*★, for they are made from the careful mixings of various wines. Algeria has always produced blended wines of high alcoholic strength. Vins de coupage always come from the same grapes, though hybrids are also permitted. Their alcoholic content must exceed 9.5°.

Many of the vins de coupage are the vins de marque★.

court en bouche (vin) A wine which may be excellent but which lacks vigour and imparts only a fleeting sensation to the tastebuds.

courtier An indispensable intermediary between the multitude of producers and the wine *négociants*★. The body of courtiers already existed at the beginning of the fifteenth century and the jurors of Bordeaux were officially given office in the sixteenth century. The profession today is controlled by the law of 31st December, 1949. The courtier thus inherits a great tradition and plays an important role, for he tours the vineyards and informs the *négociant* about interesting wines.

The work of the courtier calls for patient observation, great experience and correct judgement. One of the most enchanting tales of the courtier's infallibility is that of a Médoc cask whose certain indescribable taste could not be defined by anyone. The courtier tasted the wine and identified the flavours of iron, string, cardboard and ink. The cask was emptied and on the bottom was found the iron key to the chai which had fallen in. It was tied by string to a cardboard label on which was written in ink, 'Key to the chai'!

courtier gourmet-piqueur de vins The company of Courtiers Gourmet-piqueurs de Vins de Paris is a group of experts (from Paris) attached to the wine storehouses at Bercy. It is one of the oldest of such corporations that still exist. The gourmets, *magistrats de la vigne,* were officially elected jurors, similar to customs officers, whose job was to assure the proper movement of wine from place to place. The sanctions that they had the right to apply against abuses were severe and picturesque (if one can judge from the archives of the communes!).

The role of the gourmet consisted of serving as an intermediary between buyer and seller, then watching the packing and also accompanying the wine on its journey. He had to keep a precise register of the transportation of wine, subject to the control of the municipality and the corporation of vignerons. If the gourmet's function has disappeared, the title is still

carried proudly and legitimately by the modern courtiers.

crémant A Champagne which has less sparkle than usual. Its sparkle forms a 'cream' on the top of the glass (from which comes the name), and disappears very quickly. The crémant is located midway between a mousseux★ and a pétillant★. Its pressure is lower than the average mousseux wines (2.5–3 kg instead of around 5 for mousseux).

A well-made crémant is a good quality wine having the advantage over a normal Champagne of preserving its winey taste and a certain favourable sweetness. A crémant consequently comes principally from the best cuvées. It is a rare wine which is much sought after and very expensive. Unfortunately, very few houses still prepare the traditional crémant.

The word crémant should not be confused with the name of the commune of Cramant, a cru of the Côte de Blancs★, which is south-east of Epernay. This confusion easily arises as Cramant is one of the rare crus of Champagne. Funnily enough, there is actually a crémant of Cramant!

crème de tête An expression which formerly referred to the richest Sauternes carefully made from the earliest grapes. The first harvest, which was small, was composed almost exclusively of *pourris*, or rotten grapes, which were exceptionally rich in sugar (up to 500 g per litre) after attack by pourriture noble★. Subsequent harvests contained less and less of these grapes and the last, the queue, contained few or none at all.

Today, all the grand crus of Sauternes combine the portion of their harvest which they judge worthy to bear the name, and the rest is sold under the name of the château. The expression crème de tête has thus lost most of its importance as the grand crus no longer sell their individual first harvest under this name.

Crépy The wines of this appellation contrôlée of Savoie★ are grown on the banks of Lake Léman. They are the best known of the Savoie wines and the only ones drunk outside the region. The ancient vineyard occupies two limestone hills facing south and south-west on the communes of Loisin, Douvaine and Ballaison.

The Crépy comes from the Chasselas★ roux et vert which produces the celebrated Fendant in Switzerland. The Crépy is a delicious, very dry wine which has a light, natural sparkle found in perlant★ wines. By law it must have a minimum of 9.5° alcohol, but often exceeds this amount. It is clear, pale gold in colour with a hint of green, and the flavour is both elegant and charming, with body and an agreeable acidity. This acidity gives it, among other things, an astonishing vitality.

Crépy improves with age without maderising★, losing its acidity and fresh-

The Crépy of Savoie, like the Swiss Dézaley, is made from the Chasselas, a glorious grape in a cold climate, on the banks of Lake Léman.
Phot. Lauros-Atlas-Photo.

95

ness, but gaining a subtle perfume and taste of hazelnuts and violets.

Crozes-Hermitage An appellation of the Côtes du Rhône★ which designates the red and white wines produced by a dozen neighbouring communes of the celebrated hill of Hermitage★ on the left bank of the Rhône. The red wines come from Syrah and are close cousins of Hermitage, but with less colour and finesse. Their aroma of wild hawthorn and raspberry gives them undeniable charm. They do not keep as long as the Hermitage and become discoloured with age.

The white wines are made from the Roussanne and Marsanne and are less distinguished by their perfume and body than the whites of Hermitage. Very pale and light, they have an agreeable smell and taste of hazelnuts. Sweet in their youth, they become dry with age.

cru Applied to wine this word, which comes from the verb *croître*, to grow, designates a particular area and the wine produced in that area. In Bordeaux the word cru has a restricted meaning. It designates a château★ with particular standing and personality in the commune. The expression vin de cru therefore implies the notion of renown and superior quality. The château of Bordeaux is similar to the climat★ of Burgundy.

cru (grand) It has taken a long time to define the use of this term, except in Chablis★ where it can be applied to all the AOC wines. The decree of 27th June, 1964 clarified this by ruling that the use of the expression grand cru is forbidden except for Chablis, Saint-Emilion★, Banyuls★ and the wine of Alsace★, and its use must follow the precise conditions fixed by law. The Chablis Grand Cru are always the best of the appellation (Le Clos, Vaudésir, etc.). On the other hand, the Saint-Emilions Grand Cru are the wines which do not come from the classified crus, but which have been awarded this distinction following the recommendation of the tasting commission, and are classified above the wines which have the right to the appellation Saint-Emilion.

cru (premier) A term strictly reserved for those wines of appellation contrôlée which, according to regulation, are in a certain category of premier (first) crus. This is the case for the Burgundy appellations, particularly the communal appellations of the Côte de Nuits and Côte de Beaune, like Chablis, Mercurey, Givry, Rully and Montagny.

In Gironde it is termed premier cru classés, and the first four crus were classified in 1855 (Lafite, Margaux, Latour and Haut-Brion), the premier crus of Sauternes being classified in the same year.

Premier grand cru classé is authorised for certain domaines of Saint-Emilion classified by the decree of 1954, e.g. Ausone and Cheval-Blanc.

cru classé A term reserved for those crus which have been officially designated by the Institut National des Appellations d'Origine★. The crus of Bordeaux which were classified in 1855 have the right to be called cru classé. It is also applied to some AOC Bordeaux wines – Médoc, Sauternes, Graves and Saint-Emilion – and also to classified VDQS of the Côtes de Provence.

cuit (vin) Cooked wine is obtained from a concentration of must which has been heated in a cauldron. The vin cuit of Palette★, a Christmas treat in Provence, is excellent. A cooked taste is also a fault which is found in certain wines which have been warmed in the cuve either to start fermentation or to help those grapes which have been picked too late.

cuvage The area where the cuves are located, also called the *cuverie* or chai★. It can also mean fermentation.

cuvaison or **cuvage** The process of fermenting wine, that is, fermenting the vendange in a cuve★. This operation is most important as it determines the nature and quality of the wine.

The first phase is the delicate operation of pouring the vendange into the cuves. It is tempting to empty the grape-baskets and the carts into the cuves mechanically, and a number of machines have been devised for this purpose, though none are entirely satisfactory.

The choice of cuve and its capacity is also important, as is the vigneron's skill in controlling the alcoholic fermentation.

Several times a day, he tests the cuve with his mustmeter and tastevin. The cuvaison lasts from two days to three weeks according to region, the nature of the wine and its destination. Wines which are drunk young are fermented for less time than those which keep. Usually, however, the period is kept short. At Châteauneuf-du-Pape, for example, the cuvaison used to last until Christmas, just giving the wine sufficient tannin content and time to clear. It kept well but, in order to produce a fuller wine, it needed three years in cask before being bottled, and there was always the risk of the wine drying out. A successful wine therefore depends upon the balance between the time it spends fermenting and the period it remains in cask during the élevage★ process.

cuve The cuves used today are made of wood, cement or stainless steel. However, wood has always been the traditional material and many of the quality vineyards still use it. Wooden cuves have several drawbacks. They are expensive, their repair and detailed preparation before use demands a lot of hard work, and the white wines must be placed in casks or glass cuves after fermentation (thus doubling the necessary equipment). If the cuve is also used to store the wine after fermentation, it must be sealed to protect the wine from the air. Painting and varnishing the exterior to block evaporation also poses certain technical difficulties.

Wood cuves have their advantages, however. The white wine ferments, becoming finer and clearer, more quickly and thus can be sold more rapidly than those made in cement cuves. For the red wines, the wooden cuve is clearly superior as it allows the moderate amount of aeration they need before being bottled.

Cement cuves are less expensive and their upkeep and cleaning are easier. Wine can be kept in them after fermentation without risking oxidation. They do not take up as much space as the wooden cuves but may impart a taste of iron to the wine (casse ferrique★) and sometimes exhibit a certain porosity. The wooden cuve always had a very limited capacity (for fine wines it used to be no more than 100 hl) whereas the cement cuve took on gigantic quantities, from 600–800 hl. Many co-operative caves have thus bought these giant cuves

and the result is not worth waiting for. Such a mass is often attacked by bacteria (*Mycoderma aceti*★ and *Mycoderma vini*★) after fermentation because there is no cooling system.

There are now very expensive modern cuves made of stainless steel which are seen only at the great vineyards. They are extremely easy to maintain and the must in them can be cooled rapidly by interior or exterior cooling methods.

CUVE CLOSE A method of making mousseux wines which is also called the 'Charmat' process. The wines are considerably less expensive than those made by the Champagne method★. A solution of sugar and yeasts is added to the dry wine to obtain a second fermentation. But, unlike the Champagne method, it is not then bottled, and the sparkling level is instead reached in a vast hermetically-sealed vat (called a cuve close). The lining of this cuve is designed to resist the considerable pressure which develops during this second fermentation.

To clarify the wine, it is filtered under pressure and bottled immediately on leaving the filter. Sparkling wines are made in this way in two or three weeks and the delicate and expensive operations of the Champagne method are eliminated. This provides economy of time and manual labour. The mousseux obtained, however, is of inferior quality to those produced by the second fermentation in bottle, slowly and at a low temperature, following the method of Dom Pérignon★.

A cuve of Madeira.
Phot. Léah Lourié.

This method is often used in the Midi to make Muscats★ mousseux, whose base of vin ordinaire is enriched by the Muscat of Hamburg, a process which is not allowed in France for appellation wines.

CUVE FERMÉE A process used nearly everywhere in Gironde for fermenting red wines. The fermentation of grapes coming from Bordeaux varieties is more delicate than that for the Pinot Noir of Burgundy (Burgundy uses the cuve ouverte★ process). The quantity of the vendange is also greater than in Burgundy. The closed cuve allows a layer of carbon dioxide to form over the chapeau★ and protects the must from the risk of acescence★. The must is aerated by plunging the chapeau in and out of the wine at the beginning of fermentation before the yeast is added.

CUVE OUVERTE A process used generally in Burgundy during the fermentation period, which is facilitated by aeration. The floating chapeau★ is pushed down from time to time. Open, wooden cuves are usually used. They are equipped with a drapeau★ which allows heating or cooling of the must.

cuvé (overfermented) A wine cuvé has been left to ferment in the cuve★ too long and has an excess of tannin. It is thus astringent★ and dur★ and needs time to improve.

cuvée The quantity of wine which is made at the same time in a cuve★ or the total amount of wine which has fermented at different times in the same cuve. A cuvée also means the collection of wines from several cuves but which share the same origin. Première cuvée and seconde cuvée are expressions which describe the class and the relative quality of the wine.

cuver To ferment in a cuve★.

Cyprus The wine coming from this island, situated not far from the shores of Turkey and Syria, was celebrated as early as the Crusades. Commandaria, a golden wine produced from the vines planted by the Chevaliers of the Order of Templars around Limassol, was well known throughout the West. After the invasion of the Turks, viticulture languished, though without disappearing entirely, and did not really improve until the English arrived in 1878. By some miracle the vineyards escaped phylloxera★ and today viticulture is an important activity.

Cyprus now produces inexpensive, quality wines. The highly-coloured reds, full-bodied and rich in tannin, go well with spicy foods. The best are the Afames and Othello. The rosé called Kokkinelli is a dark-coloured, fresh, dry wine. The white wines have a unique taste – the best and driest are the Aphrodite and Arsinoé.

The best Cypriot wine is the Commandaria, produced by only twenty authorised villages, including Kalokhorio, Zoopiyi, Yerasa, Arjias and Mancas. This very sweet dessert wine is made from a mélange of red and white grapes and varies from village to village depending on the proportion of red and white grapes, vinification method and maturation time.

Cyprus also produces a great variety of sherry-type dessert wines of which Great Britain is the largest importer.

Grapes from Cyprus, planted in Madeira in the fifteenth century, produce the renowned Madeira wines, and legend has it that the Marsala of Sicily and Tokay of Hungary also originate from Cypriot vines.

Czechoslovakia Czechoslovakia has just over 20,000 ha of vineyards, and produces about 400,000 hl of wine a year. For a long time only dessert grapes were grown, but by the eighteenth century Czech wines had acquired a reputation and popularity that put them on a level with the best wines of Italy and Hungary. Today, wine is produced in the provinces of Bohemia, Moravia and Slovakia and practically all of it is consumed inside the country.

Bohemia's viticultural centre is Melnik, a town in the Elbe valley north of Prague whose red and white wines are considered the best in the region, and which also produces an extremely good sparkling wine. The wines of Moravia are mostly produced around Brno. In Slovakia, viticulture is still the principal livelihood of the peasants of Modra, Pézinok and Sviaty Jůz, and all the sunniest hillsides are traditionally reserved for their vines.

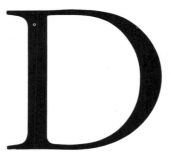

D

deacidification In a cold, rainy year, the grapes frequently do not ripen normally and the wine made from them is very acidic. Deacidification neutralises part of this excess acidity. It is only permitted under exceptional conditions and administered under the authorisation of the Ministry of Agriculture. Pure calcium carbonate is added to the must. Calcium is a natural product and, when the operation is performed correctly, it does not impair the quality of the wine.

débourbage The operation of separating the must from the sediment before fermentation when making white wine. The first racking after vinification is also called débourbage. This process usually takes place around December when the first lees are very thick and plentiful, and separate easily leaving the clear wine.

decanter A luxurious bottle into which vintage port, which ages in bottle, is transferred before serving. After years in bottle, the port needs to be decanted and aerated in an operation which is necessarily delicate because of the value of the wine. The decanters of olden days were made of glass, often inlaid with gold, and sometimes wore a gold medal around their necks. They were often carried in a container of precious wood. Modern decanters, usually made of glass, are also very elegant.

decanting A very delicate operation designed to transfer the wine, usually an old red one, from its original bottle to a carafe or decanter in order to separate it from its deposits which, if drunk, would impair digestion. The operation of decanting is actually a kind of racking. It is generally done by candlelight, the candle being placed behind the neck of the bottle so that the pourer can see when the wine first appears cloudy.

Despite the progress made in stabilising wines, it is impossible to prevent the deposits of tannin and colouring matter

Decanters of vintage port.
Phot. Casa de Portugal.

Dégorgement is one of the last steps in the preparation of Champagne. Caves Pommery. Phot. Lauros.

from collecting as the wine matures in bottle.

Decanting has both champions and opponents. Even if the operation is performed delicately and slowly, the oxidation which takes place may be so chemically violent as to destroy a very old wine whose equilibrium is always a little fragile. Actually, each wine poses a particular problem. The best general method is to stand the bottle up at least two hours before the meal in order to see if it needs decanting. Decanting should be done at the last moment, just before the time for drinking in the case of fragile wines, and a little before the meal for more hardy ones which may benefit from a moderate aeration (such as certain Médocs and Graves).

The adversaries of decanting do not want to risk killing a wine, as they say. They prefer to stand the bottle up two hours before it is drunk and uncork it. Then religiously, with infinite precaution, they pour it into the glasses, and often sacrifice the bottom of the bottle. They feel that if the wine needs aeration to develop all the subtle qualities of its bouquet, it will receive enough while being poured into the glass.

décuvaison The operation of transferring the wine from the cuve, where it has undergone alcoholic fermentation, into barrels. It takes place when most of the sugar has been transformed into alcohol.

definition of wine This was given in the first article of the decree of 3rd September, 1907: 'No drink can be held or transported with sale in mind, be put on sale or sold as wine, unless it is made exclusively from the fermentation of fresh grapes or the juice of fresh grapes'. It goes without saying that this legal French definition excludes drinks prepared with fruits other than grapes, and it also excludes drinks made with dried grapes, which is more important. Wines from other fruits have been made by defrauders, and wines from dried grapes are still produced in Greece and Italy.

dégorgement One of the last steps in the Champagne method★. The Champagne (or sparkling wine), having undergone second fermentation, accumulates deposits on the cork as a result of the turning of the bottle in the course of remuage★. These deposits must be removed. The operation used to be performed haphazardly, and, despite the ability of the workers, there was the risk of loss of gas as well as a certain amount of wine.

Today the process has been facilitated by using the freezing method. The neck of the bottle is frozen to a temperature of −16 to −18°C. Within a few minutes the sediment is encased in ice which a specialist removes by pulling out the cork. The wine lost using this process is insignificant. The space left by the removal of the deposit is immediately taken up by the liqueur d'expedition★ which is injected during the dosage★ operation.

dégustation (tasting) A simple, yet extremely complex, operation which is an art and perhaps even a science but, above all, an act of love.

Oenophiles are often as passionate about wine as are music lovers and painters about their respective interests. As art and music are discussed in terms of their own specific vocabulary, so too is wine even though the terms may seem bizarre, pretentious and ridiculous to the unacquainted.

Wine-tasting is not only a source of joy for the oenophile, and a subject of common interest among friends, it is also the most simple and sure test for the vignerons, *négociants*★ and *sommeliers*★. It is by successive tastings that they follow the state of the wine, observe its evolution and are thus certain of the quality of the product to be offered to the consumer.

Tasting affects three senses: sight, smell

and taste. The eye examines the colour (robe★) and the clarity★ of the wine, the nose appreciates the aroma★ and the bouquet★ while the palate distinguishes the diverse sensations from which one can judge the equilibrium of the elements in the wine (sugar, acidity, alcohol, tannin, glycerine, etc.) and the strength of these sensations.

The ability to judge objectively is a vital gift, and demands great concentration combined with the ability to recall and compare.

dentelle (lacy) This refers to a very fine, delicate wine of subtle aroma which is generally a white wine, such as Champagne.

Some old vignerons often say of an old wine '*qu'il tombe en dentelle*', meaning the wine has been killed by age and falls to pieces like an old cloak.

dépouillé The solid deposits contained in the wine after fermentation slowly drop to the bottom of the cask during the winter and form the lees. When the wine has become clear it is said to be dépouillé.

dessert wines Although neglected today, dessert wines were regarded as delicacies by our fathers, who could not conceive of an important repast without ending with such a wine. Sweet wines, fortified wines, Champagnes and the semi-dry sparkling wines can all be served with the dessert. The sweet white wines should be served very chilled, as they have a high sugar content, and the sparkling wines should also be served chilled but not icy.

Dézaley One of the best dry white wines produced in Switzerland. The Chasselas grapes from which it is made are grown on steep terraces facing Lake Geneva east of Lausanne in the Vaud canton. The wine of Dézaley possesses remarkable finesse, great distinction and generally deserves its high reputation.

discoloured A wine which looks badly tinted and whose colour has faded. This usually happens to very old wines when the colouring matter precipitates with ageing. But discoloured wine can also result from an excess of sulphur dioxide★, or animal charcoal which was used in fining.

diseases (wine) These are caused by bacteria. Aigre★, which sours wine, appears in the presence of air, but a number of bacterial fermentations develop in full, sealed casks and cause profound and often irreversible alterations in the wine. Diseases include tourne★, amertume★, graisse★ and mannite★. Improved hygiene as well as advances in oenological technology have considerably reduced their occurrence.

distinguished A distinguished wine is composed of pure and noble elements which unite in a perfect equilibrium.

Dôle A red Swiss wine produced in the Valais canton in the rocky valley of the Rhône. It is made from the Pinot Noir which is sometimes blended with Gamay and several local varieties. Many consider it the best red wine of Switzerland. It is richly coloured, full-bodied, keeps well and is not unlike the wines of Burgundy and those of the Côte-Rôtie.

dosage Adding a certain amount of sugar in the form of the liqueur d'expedition★ to Champagne★ after dégorgement★. The Champagne is then classified according to the amount of liqueur added: brut – contains from 0 to 0·25% or 0·5% of the liqueur; extra-dry, from 1% to 2%; sec, from 3% to 5%; demi-sec, from 6% to 10%; and doux, 8% to 14%.

Dégustation, Château d'Yquem.
Phot. Rapho-Weiss.

5

6

 1 *Haltica or flea-beetle*
 2 *Yellow spider*
 3 *Red spider*
 4 *Black rot (fungus)*
 5 *Mealy cochineal*
 6 *Vine leaves attacked by a*
   fungus
 7 *Grub of the Cochylis moth*
 8 *Ecaille martre*
 9 *Esca (fungus)*
10 *Excoriation*
11 *Meal moth*
12 *Leaf-roller moth*
13 *Iron wireworm, click beetle*
   larva
14 *greyworm, Noctuid larva*
   Phot. M.

10

11

2

3

4

7

8

9

12

13

14

In principle, brut does not contain any liqueur, but sometimes a small amount (0·25% to 0·5%) is added when it seems a little hard. Brut Champagne used not to be popular, but today it has many devotees. The French seem to prefer light brut Champagne, the English a full-bodied sec and the Nordic countries, a demi-sec or doux. The Americans used to favour sec but are now switching to brut.

A mediocre Champagne can easily mask its faults by the sweetness of the sugar. The liqueur used to be injected by hand, but the process is now performed quickly and automatically by special machines made of glass and copper.

doux In general the word doux describes an agreeable taste. Applied to wine, the word indicates the presence and taste of sugar in a rather large quantity.

It takes on a different meaning depending on the wine to which it is applied. The sweetness of a wine made from grapes attacked by pourriture noble★, such as a Sauternes or a Beerenauslese, is so marvellous that it is only found in exceptional climatic conditions. But it can also exist in a wine having natural unfermented sugar which is maintained by massive doses of sulphur dioxide.★ This process, which is used for certain white Bordeaux and cheap Liebfraumilch, began because of the demand from consumers for sweet wines. On the other hand, wine such as port, which has natural sugar remaining in the wine when fermentation has been arrested by the addition of alcohol, is legally defined as vin doux naturel★. As well as being sweet because of the sugar, they are also rich in alcohol. Still another sweetness in a wine, such as Marsala, may be caused by the addition of the juice of a very sweet grape.

Therefore, the word doux applied to wine is something very vague and imprecise. It is neither a good nor bad quality and depends on the wine it is applied to. The words demi-sec, moelleux★ and liquoreux describe the taste more precisely.

doux naturels (vins) This expression has an essentially fiscal value in France. It is applied to wines which are naturally rich in sugar, as a result of the addition of alcohol during fermentation, and thus are placed under a certain excise category.

These wines are all products of the Mediterranean sun. In France they are the Banyuls★, Maury★, Côtes-d'Agly★, Côtes-de-Haut-Roussillon★, Grand-Roussillon★, Rivesaltes★, Rasteau★ and the Muscats like Frontignan★ or Beaumes-de-Venise★.

The grapes from which these wines are made are the noble★ Grenache, Muscat, Macabéo and Malvoisie, which undoubtedly came from Spain or the Orient where they grew on arid coasts, burned by the sun on difficult soil. The local inhabitants have devoted themselves to the production of these wines from time immemorial.

The vins doux naturels, whether they be red, rosé or white, are rich in alcohol. The must possesses at least 250 g of sugar per litre. Fermentation is arrested by mutage★, or the addition of alcohol to the must. The wine preserves its fruitiness, a large proportion of its natural sugar and also a high degree of alcohol, often 22 or 23°. This method originated with the Saracens and is not unlike that for making Carthagène★, the liqueur of the Midi whose precise origin is unknown.

In a vin doux naturel the taste of alcohol blends with that of the wine. Sometimes the wine is left to mature in casks which are placed outside in the sun. This produces the exquisite Rancio★. The vins doux naturels are subject to very severe controls which must be observed by the vignerons.

Although they are muted with alcohol, they should not be confused with the vins blancs liquoreux★ produced in Bordeaux, the Loire (Sauternes, Quarts-de-Chaume, Vouvray, etc.) and in Germany (on the banks of the Rhine and the Moselle) which do not have alcohol added to them. They are simply the prized result of the natural fermentation of the juice of grapes which has been attacked by pourriture noble★.

The vins doux naturels belong to the category 'vins de liqueur' but are not included under the same fiscal bracket. They fall for the most part under the fiscal regulations applying to the specific wine.

drapeau Apparatus used to circulate water in the cuves★ during the fermentation period in order to reheat the must in a cold year or cool it in a hot year. Its use has been widespread in Burgundy since the very warm years of 1947 and 1949.

E

Egrappage by hand at Château Palmer in the Médoc. Egrappage results in a less astringent wine which is ready for drinking earlier. Phot. M.

éclaircissage A special vendage method used in Sauternes. When the grapes are mature the pickers skilfully remove half of them from the vines so that the remaining grapes receive more air and sunlight. They then ripen further and regularly attract pourriture noble★. The first grapes picked are made into an excellent dry white wine.

Edelzwicker A white Alsatian wine made from a blending of the noble★ grape varieties including Traminer, Riesling, Sylvaner and Pinot. The Edelzwicker is better than the Zwicker, the German word *edel* meaning 'noble' or superior. It is more full-bodied and fragrant, but is just as light and easy to drink. It makes a good carafe wine and goes especially well with sauerkraut.

égrappage Separating the grapes from the stalks before they are pressed or placed in the fermenting vats.

Egrappage has been practised in the Gironde since the eighteenth century, but has only come into general use in the Côte d'Or in the last thirty or forty years. It is also practised in the Loire (Bourgueil, Chinon, Champigny), the Côtes du Rhône (Hermitage, Cornas, Côte-Rôtie) as well as with grapes to be made into Chianti. On the other hand, it is not carried out in Beaujolais because of the short fermentation period. Egrappage is generally used for wines made from grapes which have a high tannin content (Cabernet, Pinot, Syrah and some Italian varieties) in order to make them less astringent and more drinkable.

In Bordeaux, where the grapes have a high tannin content, it is widely employed although some vignerons use it on only part of the harvest, depending on the maturity of the grapes, the varieties, soil and the year.

The practice of égrappage reduces the

total amount of the vendange, especially the marc. It gives the wine more marrow, finesse and colour and adds about one half degree of alcohol. On the other hand, flabby and flat wines should not have the stalks removed as they need the extra tannin to make them more firm and vinous.

Egrappage is performed mechanically by the *égrappoir* or *fouloir-grappe*, a machine that crushes the grape, then ejects the stalk after separating it from the juice and skin.

Egypt In ancient days the Egyptian wines were renowned, but at the beginning of this century they were practically nonexistent, and the few produced were poor. An Egyptian named Nestor Gianachis undertook the reconstruction of the vineyards. In 1903 he planted the first vines but it was not until 1931, after many attempts, that a decent wine was finally produced. Today, although production is still very limited, Egypt produces some interesting wines and efforts are being made to introduce them on the world market.

elegant All grand cru★ wines are elegant, which is not to say that less *racé*★ ones are not. The elegance of a wine is the result of the blending of different elements into a subtle harmony.

élevage The care lavished on newly-made wine to aid nature in improving its quality and to assure it a long life. It begins with the wine in cask, continues while it is bottled and during the maturing period until the time when the desired perfection is attained.

To begin, the warm new wine is not immediately sent to the cellar. Fermentation must have completely ceased and the temperature dropped below the minimum 20°C necessary for fermentation to occur. Also, before it is bottled, the wine must undergo several processes: ouillages★, débourbages★, soutirages★, collages★ and, finally, filtration★.

The period spent in cask varies according to the nature of the wine and the type of wine desired. Certain wines must mature for about two years before their bouquet is apparent (great Burgundies and Médoc). Others, like Beaujolais and Muscadet, are especially liked for their fruiti-

ness, and several months ageing is enough. On the other hand, the longer the fermentation, the longer the wine must mature in cask in order to remove the excess tannin. Today, however, wines tend to spend less time in cask than they used to. Wines which remain too long in cask dry out and lose part of their bouquet because of oxidation.

élevé (vin) A wine which is ready for bottling.

éleveur A word which has come into use only recently to describe the qualified specialist who cares for the wine from the time it is made until it is shipped from the cellar. The *éleveur* must know, among other things, the character, personality, vintage and origin of each wine.

emaciated A term which is applied to wine in the same sense as it is to humans. An emaciated wine has less substance or body due to repeated separations or racking of the clear wine from the deposits.

enemies of the vine The innumerable diseases which attack the vine pose one of the greatest problems of viticulture. Among the many enemies which impoverish the vine are insects, the innocent butterfly in the caterpillar and larval stages, as well as other larvae (cochylis, eudemis, pyrale, noctuelle), the may bug, red spiders and especially the dreaded phylloxera★ which ravaged the vineyards of Europe.

There are also the cryptogamic diseases caused by fungus, grey rot (pourriture grise★), apoplexy (esca), mildew and oidium★ (powdery mildew).

The vine can also suffer from attacks by physiological diseases: chlorisis (green sickness), leaf reddening (*rougeau*), coulure★, millerandage (shot berries★) and fan-leaf (*court-noué*).

Other enemies include lightning, hail and frosts.

Entre-deux-Mers The vast area occupying the triangle formed by the Garonne and Dordogne from their confluence at the mouth of Ambes to the eastern border of the Gironde department.

Several of the regions included in this territory produce special wines: Premières-Côtes-de-Bordeaux★,

Loupiac★, Sainte-Croix-du-Mont★, Côtes-de-Bordeaux-Sainte-Macaire★, Graves-de-Vayres★ and Sainte-Foy-Bordeaux★.

The name Entre-deux-Mers is applied uniquely to those dry white wines of at least 11·5° alcohol, produced on limestone, clay and gravel soil, from the noble★ grape varieties of Bordeaux. The wines are of excellent quality, particularly the dry whites which are quickly replacing the former sweeter ones due to consumer demand. Entre-deux-Mers is a fresh, fruity wine with its own particular *sève*★. It goes remarkably well with fish, especially oysters and hors-d'oeuvres.

The area also produces a red wine which is sold under the appellation Bordeaux or Bordeaux supérieur★.

entreillage (sometimes called *mise sur lattes*) After receiving the liqueur de tirage★ the bottles of Champagne are piled in horizontal lots in the cellars. Between each row, laths of wood have been skilfully placed by the cellarmen. In this position the second fermentation slowly takes place under a constant temperature of about 10°C. The slowness is indispensable for obtaining the persistent sparkle which is the trademark of Champagne. The sugar contained in the wine decomposes little by little into alcohol and carbon dioxide. This process takes between two and four months. Afterwards the wine is left to rest a while longer so that the deposits and lees from the dead yeasts will accumulate. The next step is the elimination of these deposits by the processes of remuage★ and dégorgement★.

enveloppé (vin) A wine whose alcohol and glycerine content overshadows the other elements, forming a kind of envelope around them so as to make it difficult to perceive their subtleties. This occurs in wines made from grapes of a high sugar content.

épanoui In full bloom, a term usually applied to the bouquet★ of a wine. The expanding bouquet reveals itself little by little until eventually it reaches its fullness.

épluchage Sorting the grapes by hand, just after picking and before they are crushed or pressed, in order to eliminate the damaged grapes. This is practised during the production of quality wines and is an extremely expensive operation because of the labour involved.

When the harvest is a healthy one and most of the grapes are at about the same stage of maturity, the operation can be performed very quickly. But this is not always the case, particularly in Champagne. In this northern climate the grapes often have difficulty ripening and the unripe grapes, which are acidic and low in sugar, must be discarded so that a sufficiently alcoholic wine can be made. Even more important, the rotten or

Entre-deux-Mers vineyards near Rozan. Phot. M.

Epluchage in a Champagne vineyard. Phot. M.

Sicilian vineyards at the foot of Mount Etna. Phot. Aarons-Z.F.A.

mouldy grapes which could impart a disagreeable smell or taste must be eliminated. Thus in Champagne the épluchage is an onerous, but necessary, task. It is performed at the vine itself. The grapes are deposited on wicker trays supported by two narrow wicker crates weighing 80 kg. The sorters cut the grapes with scissors and throw the healthy, ripe grapes in one basket and the green, mouldy, or damaged grapes into the other.

equilibrium   A wine in equilibrium has all its elements in perfect proportion to one another. The alcohol, acid and sugar are in perfect accord, with none dominating the others. Such a wine is also called balanced and harmonious. When a wine has an excess or lacks an element it is obviously termed unbalanced.

Estaing   A small vineyard of the Sud-Ouest★ situated in the Lot Valley on the three communes of Estaing, Coubisou and Sebrazac. The vineyards grow on terraces 300–450 m high which have been carefully constructed by vignerons over the centuries on the slopes of the deep valley. The vines benefit from warm, dry summers, but sometimes experience the rough winters of a continental climate.

The red wines are made mainly from the Fer★, locally called Mansois, and from the Gamay, Merlot, Cabernet, Négrette and Jurançon Noir. They are generally very delicate, excellent wines with a rich bouquet.

The best white wines are made from the Chenin Blanc, Rousselou and Mauzac. They are fine, dry, very pleasant wines which are enjoyed by both locals and

tourists, as are those of the neighbouring Entraygues. Both are classified VDQS★.

Est Est Est   A light, semi-dry, white Italian wine produced around the villages of Montefiascone and Bolsena, north of Rome. It is made from the Moscatello grape (or Moscato di Canelli) which is also used for Asti Spumante★ and the Italian vermouths.

The wine's curious name comes from an often recounted story about a wine-loving German bishop en route to Rome who sent his servant ahead to taste the various wines along the way. He was instructed to write the Latin word Est (is) on the wall of each inn whose wine was particularly good. After trying the wine at Montefiascone, the servant was not content to write Est but scribbled Est! Est!! Est!!! The poor bishop arrived and soon died of intoxication. The story is related on his tomb, which has been piously preserved.

Etna   The wines of Etna are the best table wines of Sicily. The vines grow on the slopes of the volcano and produce good quality red and white wines. The wines from the villages located at high altitudes like Nicolosi, Trecastagni and Zafferana are full-bodied and have a certain *racé*★.

Etoile (L')   This commune of the Jura★ which has a communal appellation contrôlée is the domain of white wine, with no red or rosé produced. The dry white wines have the characteristics of those of the region, but also possess a special delicacy which ranks with the best. The sparkling wines are fine and elegant, and the town also produces a small amount of vin jaune★ and vin de paille★.

évent   The French word meaning flat. A wine exposed to air takes on a different taste, and saying that a wine is flat is far from being a compliment. Such a wine is also described as mealy. A flat taste is acquired at the moment of bottling when the wine is unfortunately exposed to the air. The wine is then said to suffer from bottle-sickness as it appears rough, unbalanced and has a mealy taste which only disappears after a long, quiet rest during which the wine is sealed from the air.

F

Fagon Although he was Louis XIV's doctor it is not for this function that Fagon is renowned, but for his peremptory condemnation of Champagne. He did, however, recommend Burgundy, the wine of kings, to his patients.

Falerne The most famous wine of ancient Rome. Celebrated by Pliny and Horace, it was reputed to be immortal, preserving its splendour for more than a century and not revealing its inimitable, marvellous bouquet until after ten years. Its reputation continued for centuries and the best compliment that could be made to a wine was to compare it to Falerne.

Falerne is produced today on mountainous slopes north of Naples. Its red wine is a solid one and the agreeable white is dry, pale and fruity.

fat A wine containing a lot of glycerine★, an element which contributes to the wine's mellowness and smoothness. Certain wines, especially those made from grapes attacked by pourriture noble★, contain a large amount of glycerine. A fat wine appears oily and smooth and leaves traces (and is said to cry) on the glass.

fatigué (tired) Most wines are not very resilient and need time to recover after each step in the vinification process, e.g. after filtering and bottling, but a robust wine springs back quickly after each of these changes.

Faugères The red wines of this appellation are grouped under the Coteaux-du-Languedoc★ classified VDQS★. They are made north of Béziers not far from Saint-Chinian★. The excellent, full-bodied red wines are made principally from the Carignan, Grenache and Cinsault, while the white wines are made from the Clairette.

feeble A wine which lacks colour and alcohol. These anaemic wines are produced in bad years and, although they are often acceptable, they lack any real distinction.

feminine Feminine wines are full of grace, charm and elegance, such as Musigny. They are the opposite of virile★ wines.

Fendant The Swiss name of the Chasselas★ grape which, except for Pouilly-sur-Loire★, does not produce any remarkable wines. In the canton of Valais, very agreeable, clear, fresh, often fine and delicate wines are made from this grape. The wine is bottled early, before the end of the winter following the harvest, and preserves a light, pleasant sparkle because of the carbon dioxide which has dissolved in the young wine. It resembles Crépy★, which is also made from the Chasselas.

Fer A grape variety grown in the Aquitaine Basin from Landes to the Haut-Garonne. Its name is derived from the hardness of the wood. It is also called Fer Servadou, and Pinenc in the Basses-Pyrénées (where it produces Madiran★ and Tursan★), and blends well with the Tannat and Cabernet Franc. It is the characteristic red of Aveyron, where it is called Mansois, and makes Estaing★, Entraygues and Marcillac★.

If they are well vinified, the wines of this grape are excellent with an agreeable bouquet which hints of the countryside.

109

ferme A ferme wine is one which is full-bodied and vigorous, has a high tannin content and improves with age.

fermentation (alcoholic) The process by which grape juice becomes wine by the transformation of the sugar content of the must into alcohol and carbon dioxide by yeast. This was explained chemically by Gay-Lussac as $C_6H_{12}O_6 = 2C_2H_5OH + 2CO_2$ (glucose = ethyl alcohol + carbon dioxide).

Other elements are produced during the course of fermentation including glycerine★, volatile acids, succinic acid, esters and bouquet.

Must fermenting. Phot. M.

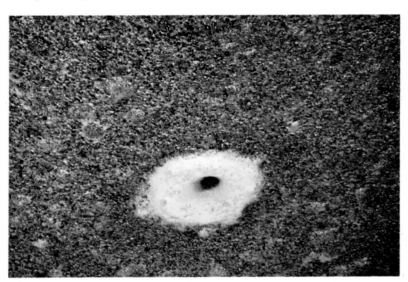

In 1857, Pasteur discovered that fermentation was caused by living organisms, the yeasts. Until that time people thought fermentation was a spontaneous action and classified it as a work of God. Since Pasteur's time, modern techniques have evolved and fermentation is not left to chance, but is carefully controlled. Constant surveillance is kept on the temperature of the must and the cellar.

Certain yeasts are selected and sulphur dioxide★ is used for sterilisation purposes. The fermentation of most wines lasts until almost all the sugar in the must has been used up. Fermentation stops when the wine reaches 14 or 15° alcohol. It can be halted by the addition of a foreign alcohol (mutage★) or by sterilisation with sulphur dioxide (used in the production of vins blancs liquoreux★).

fermentation (malo-lactic) This phenomenon sometimes takes place immediately after alcoholic fermentation★ but normally occurs in the spring 'when the sap is rising'. Under the action of certain bacteria the malic acid, which is normally present in the wine, is transformed into lactic acid and carbon dioxide. The wine then becomes slightly effervescent and disturbed. Lactic acid is much less acidic than malic, and the result is a deacidification of the wine as the percentage of malic acid is reduced.

When closely regulated, this process is very useful in the case of green★ and certain Swiss and Alsatian wines which contain too much malic acid.

The wines are best when bottled just after this secondary fermentation has take place, as they conserve a light sparkle due to the carbon dioxide. This is the case with Gaillac perlant★, Crépy★, the wines of Valais and the vinho verde★ of Portugal. Unfortunately this secondary fermentation cannot be regulated as closely as alcoholic fermentation.

When the wine has a normal amount of acidity, the occurrence of secondary fermentation can be a disadvantage. On the other hand, malo-lactic fermentation creates a taste of lactic acid which is slightly perceptible to the palate.

feuillette A measure used at Chablis in the Yonne of 132–136 litres. In Sâone-et-Loire and the Côte-d'Or, it holds 114 litres.

filtration A necessary operation to assure the clarity★ of wine. Unwanted deposits including dead yeast cells are caught in the filters. Filtering purifies the wine and kills certain microbial germs which could cause infection. It is best to carry out filtration at the same time as collage★ as certain protein substances which slip through filtration can show up again in the bottle.

Several kinds of filters are used, including the Chamberland-type candle filter, the hose filter lined with cotton which clears heavily-sedimented wines, and the Seitz filter which works through layers of asbestos.

fine In France the expression fine wine has become a synonym for a wine of appellation d'origine. A fine wine always has an inherent superiority because of its geographical origin, its grape and other factors which have given it remarkable individual characteristics.

Fine is also used in the sense of finesse. Finesse is usually attributed to a wine of class and distinction which has a delicate taste and a subtle aroma. Thus a full-bodied wine which has finesse is a great wine. Without finesse it can only be heavy and common.

Fitou A red AOC★ wine of Languedoc★ produced south of Narbonne by the better communes of Corbières★: Fitou, Caves-de-Treille, Leucate, Paziols, Tuchan, Cascatel and Villeneuve-des-Corbières. Fitou is made from Grenache and Carignan grapes (at least 75%) blended with some of the other classic grapes of the Midi. It is a generous, full-bodied, powerful wine of a beautiful, dark ruby colour which must be left in cask at least eighteen months to two years before bottling. It matures rapidly, casting off its tannic roughness and acquiring its own particular beautiful bouquet. It is really remarkable after five or six years.

Fixin This northernmost village of the Côte de Nuits produces vins fins de la Côte de Nuits★ as well as several great red wines, which are similar to those of Gevrey-Chambertin. The appellation Fixin can be followed by the term Premier Cru or the name of the following climats: les Hervelets, la Perrière, Clos du Chapitre and les Arvelets.

fleshy A fleshy wine has a lot of substance and firmness and imparts a full sensation to the palate. Such a wine always has a marvellous equilibrium between the alcohol, dry extract and glycerine content.

Fleurie The light and fragrant Fleurie evokes thoughts of flowers in spring. It is a very fruity Beaujolais★ which should be drunk chilled and young in order to appreciate its aroma and the taste of fresh grapes. In certain years Fleurie ages beautifully like Morgon★.

flor (vins de) A name applied to a certain group of very good wines whose fineness is due to special yeasts which form a thin veil (or flor) on the surface of the

Filtration: top, alluvial filter; below, plaque filter. Phot. M.

Fixin, a Burgundy vineyard near Gevrey-Chambertin. Phot. Giraudon.

Foulage in the Upper Douro (Portugal). The cuves are made of granite.
Phot. J.-Y. Loirat.

cask. The wine remains for six years or more under the veil without the cask being topped up. During this time it acquires an extremely original suave and powerful bouquet. The process is used in Spain to make sherry, and in France for the vins jaunes★ of the Jura area.

fondu Term for a balanced wine whose elements are all blended into a harmonious whole.

foulage (pressing) One of the first operations performed on the newly-harvested grapes when they arrive in the chai★ or cuvage★. Pressing or treading the grapes was practised even in ancient days by the Greeks, Egyptians, Hebrews, Romans and Gauls. During the pressing, care must be taken not to damage the stones or stalks as they are rich in tannin and oils necessary for the finesse of the wine. For this reason treading by feet is still practised for certain wines like port because it is gentler and more controlled than the mechanical pressers. The mechanical *fouloir-égrappoir* presses the grapes and removes the stalks at the same time.

White wines are always pressed in order to speed up the flow of the juice. It is not performed in Beaujolais where a tender and slightly tannic wine is desired.

foxy A word used to describe the smell and taste of wines made from hybrid vines, especially American ones. American root-stocks were imported into Europe as replacements after the phylloxera★ disaster, and some of these plants have a naturally 'gamey' smell or flavour in the grape, juice or wine. To the great relief of all vine-growers, however, these characteristics disappeared when European vines were grafted on to them.

The taste can also be imparted to wine by certain diseases. Champagne which is past its prime can also be foxy.

Franconia A German viticultural area located in the Main Valley around Würzburg. The best vineyards, located around the communes of Würzburg, Escherndorf, Iphofen, Randersacker and Rödelsee, belong to the German Government, five or six noble families and charitable organisations. As in the Baden area, several viticultural co-operatives have made great progress.

The wines of Franconia are dry, powerful, full-bodied and sometimes have a *goût de terroir*★ aftertaste. They are made from the Riesling, Sylvaner (which often makes the best wines of the area) and the Müller-Thurgau, a kind of hybrid of the Sylvaner and Riesling which makes common wines.

Würzburg produces, under the name of Steinwein, one of the best wines of the region from the Riesling or Sylvaner grown on steep slopes on the banks of the Main. Good Stein wines are dry, full-bodied, balanced and very agreeable. Franconian wines are traditionally sold in special bottles called Bocksbeutel, on which the name of the grape, the commune and vineyard are indicated.

Frangy The delicious Roussette de Frangy is a white wine of Savoie★ which must by law be made, like all Roussettes, from the Roussette grape (also called Altesse), the Petite-Sainte-Marie and the Mondeuse Blanche, with a maximum of 10% Marsanne. The Roussette grape is mainly grown at Seyssel★, and some at Marestel, Monterminod and Monthoux. Very little real Roussette, certified VDQS★ on the label, is produced in Savoie except at Seyssel. The Roussette de Frangy is a fresh, fragrant, smooth, agreeable wine whose only rival is the neighbouring Seyssel.

frank A frank wine is a pure, plain, well-balanced one which has a perfect aroma and taste. Such a wine is also said to be clean tasting.

Frascati One of the best-known white wines of Castelli Romani★, produced around the little town of Frascati, southeast of Rome. This golden-coloured, dry, full-bodied wine has an alcohol level of about 12° and makes an agreeable table wine which is particularly favoured by the Romans.

Freisa A red Italian wine produced in the mountainous area of Piemonte, east of Turin, from the grape of the same name. Freisa can appear in two guises – it can be a fruity red, often a little acidic and fresh when young, which rapidly takes on a remarkable bouquet and is best at around three years, or a fragrant, fruity, sparkling semi-dry, which is mostly favoured by Italians. As a result it is rarely exported in this form. The Freisa of Chieri is especially renowned.

fresh A fresh wine imparts a lively sensation to the palate. It is generally a young wine or has the attributes of one – fruitiness, vivacity, simplicity and an agreeable acidity. Fresh wines should be served chilled to reveal their best qualities.

Fronsac On the right bank of the Dordogne near Libourne, the vineyard of Fronsac, which includes several neighbouring communes, dominates the hills with its magnificent panorama.

Fronsac is famous throughout northern Europe for Charlemagne's château, as well as for its colourful, robust wines. The Duke of Richelieu, grand nephew of the celebrated minister of Louis XIII, later to be the Duke of Fronsac, was influential in making the wine popular at the French court.

The appellation Fronsac does not legally exist. Two appellation contrôlées belong to two distinct areas: Côtes de Canon-Fronsac★ and Côtes de Fronsac★.

Frontignan A Languedoc★ village well known for its incomparable Muscat★. The rocky hills are planted with the golden, small grape Muscat, also called Muscat doré de Frontignan. The famous Frontignan has been celebrated by Rabelais, Olivier de Serres and Voltaire. Like all vins

Frontignan. Phot. M.

doux naturels, Frontignan is muted with alcohol, a process which is especially good for the Muscat as it preserves its delicate and unique fruitiness.

Frontignan is a very generous wine having at least 15° alcohol. Its beautiful golden topaz colour, its suave aroma, its flavour which blends the taste of grapes and honey, make it a wine of great class and real distinction.

Fronton A VDQS★ wine of the Sud-Ouest★ and named after a small vineyard located north of Toulouse around the town of Fronton. Like its neighbour Villaudric★, Fronton was badly affected by the frost of 1956. The communes producing the wine are found in the departments of Haute-Garonne, (Castelnau-d'Estrefonds, Fronton, Vacquiers and

113

Saint-Rustice) and Tarn-et-Garonne (Nohic, Argueil and Campsas).

The strongly-coloured red wines are made from Négrette grapes blended with the Gamay, Cabernet, Fer, Syrah and Malbec varieties. The small quantity of white wines are made from Mauzac, Chalosse and Sémillon grapes.

frost (black) The frost that occurs in the middle of winter. Despite the precaution taken to cover the vines with earth, the frost is sometimes so intense that the buds frost over causing the vines to split. This occurred in Bordeaux in February 1956 and was a terrible disaster in Saint-Emilion and Pomerol. The extreme cold $(-25°C)$, arriving unexpectedly after a period of mild days, destroyed thousands of feet of vines.

frost (white) One of the nightmares of the vigneron as many of the world's good wines are made at the northernmost limit of the vine. Theoretically the danger of frost lasts for around six weeks in France and Germany, from 1st April to 15th May. However, there have been memorable exceptions. The vineyards of Pouilly-sur-Loire★ were ravaged on 28th May, 1961 and the vines of Chablis★ have been frosted in June. Only 3 or 4 degrees during these critical weeks is sufficient to partially or totally destroy a year's work and endanger future harvests.

The most threatened vineyards have taken precautions. Chablis, the vineyards of the Loire and the Moselle are equipped with oil heaters. The vineyards at the foot of the slopes are more exposed than those on the hills, but also produce less fine wines. The vignerons are slowly abandoning these spots, realising that in the end quality counts most.

fruity A fruity wine smells and tastes like fresh fruit. The word is also used to describe young wines, whose fruitiness in time will be replaced by bouquet★. Each grape variety has its own particular kind of fruitiness. The best-known fruity wines are Beaujolais, the wines of Alsace, Muscadet, Bourgueil and Chinon and the wines of California made from the Zinfandel grape, and, less pronounced, from the Riesling, Sylvaner and Pinot of California. The word musky★ is used to describe fruity Muscats.

full-bodied A full-bodied wine is one of good character, rich in alcohol, well coloured and with a pronounced taste. It is also said to have *corps* or body. The term *étoffé* is sometimes used to mean that there is sufficient glycerine★ content.

fumet The distinctive bouquet peculiar to a wine which has a great deal of personality, such as Châteauneuf-du-Pape★.

furry A furry wine imparts a unique sensation of velvety smoothness. It is mostly used to describe a fleshy wine with an exceptionally high glycerine content.

Warding off the frost: oil heaters. Phot. M.

114

G

Gaillac The region of Gaillac, in the Sud-Ouest★ area of France, has been engaged in viticulture since pre-Christian times. In fact it is said that the vine of Gaillac was the likely father of Bordeaux. Gaillac, which is particularly known for its sparkling wine, also produces mildly sparkling wines (perlant★) and still AOC★ wines, some dry and some sweet. They are made from the Mauzac grape (the same variety which gives the Blanquette de Limoux★) and from the grape with the curious name l'En de l'El (far from sight), to which the classic white varieties of the area are added.

The Tarn divides this area, which has a semi-mediterranean climate. The wines from the limestone slopes of the right bank are marrowy and full of bouquet, while those from the granite soil of the left bank are lively, dry and have nerve. This explains the diversity of the white wines of Gaillac, which are all well made.

Gaillac Mousseux is made by the rural method called *gaillacoise*. The sparkle is produced naturally without adding any sugar. Fermentation is slowly halted by successive filtrations. It is then left to mature for two or three years, at which time the wine is marrowy and fruity with a particular, delicate aroma. Wines made by the Champagne method★ have less charm and fruitiness.

The mildly sparkling or perlant wine of Gaillac is made by a completely different method. First, the must is left to ferment at a low temperature until it reaches the state of a dry white wine containing only a small amount of natural sugar. It is then left several months without racking until secondary fermentation begins, at which time it is bottled. The resulting wine is light, fruity and fresh with a special aroma.

The wines classified as Gaillac and Gaillac Mousseux must have at least 10·5° alcohol, while those called Gaillac-Premières-Côtes must contain a minimum of 11·5°. Attempts have been made for some time to produce quality red and rosé wines at Gaillac, such as those which used to be made at Cunac and Labastide by the process of carbonic maceration★.

Gaillac: the Tarn and the Saint-Michel Abbey, where the monks made the first wine of the cru. Phot. M.

Gamay A white-juiced red grape named after a hamlet near Puligny-Montrachet which is practically the only variety grown in Beaujolais★.

On the granitic slopes of Beaujolais it gives fine, aromatic, young wines which are much in demand today, while on the limestone-clay terrain of the rest of Burgundy it produces only ordinary wines. In 1395 Philip the Bold ordered 'the disloyal plant named Gamay' to be expelled from the kingdom. Happily for us, his subjects did not obey him.

Gamay rouge à jus blanc.
Phot. Larousse.

The Gamay is only planted in very good vineyards in Burgundy, where the Pinot Noir is king. When mixed with one-third Pinot Noir, Gamay produces Bourgogne-passe-tous-grains★. Gamay is also present in the wines of Lyonnais★, Saint-Pourçain★, Auvergne★, Châteaumeillant★ and Giennois★, but none of these wines have the finesse and bouquet of Beaujolais. In California, especially in the Napa★ and San Benito★ counties, it produces very agreeable wines which are sometimes superior to those made from the Pinot

Noir. They are sold under the name Gamay of Beaujolais.

gelée (vin de) Another name for the vin jaune★ of the Jura which, literally translated, means 'wine of the frost'. The Savagnin grapes are left on the vines until the first frost; the grape slowly withers up, concentrating its natural juices (passerillage★).

Gattinara A beautiful, red Italian wine made from the Nebbiolo grape, as are Barolo★ and Barbaresco★. Like these wines it comes from the Piemonte region, but from a different area north of Turin. Gattinara is an excellent wine which can be compared with the best Côtes-du-Rhône. Full-bodied and with a fine bouquet, it has an enveloping taste, and should not be drunk too young as its best qualities develop after some maturing. Unfortunately, production is very limited.

generous A wine such as Chambertin which is rich in alcohol. Such a wine is also said to be warm★ and vigorous and gives a sensation of well-being to the drinker. A generous wine is not, however, a heady one.

In Spain and Portugal, generous wines are usually muted with alcohol.

Georgia The viticultural region of the USSR furnishing the largest number of excellent quality wines and 20% of total production. Georgia has the third largest amount of land devoted to viticulture of the Soviet Republics. At Tchoudari, a vine 0·55 m in diameter with roots running under 2 m of soil covers an area of 80 sq m and each year produces 500 kg of grapes.

Grapes are grown at an altitude of 1000–1340 m which makes up for the unfavourable latitude of the area and accounts for the quality of Georgian wines. Some 400 varieties of grapes are cultivated of which sixteen are eventually made into wine. The vines are trained on horizontal poles, a method called *talavéri*.

Each Georgian province has its traditional viticultural methods. Kakhétie in the oriental part of Georgia is arid and must be irrigated. The vineyards cover about 100 km from Signakhi to Akhméta surrounding the Alazani Valley. Tsinandali and Moukouzani are the most important centres. This region produces notable wines (Kardanakhi, Mtsvane and Teliani), including good white wines (Naparéouli, Gourdjaani no 3, Tsolikaouri no 7 and Rkatsitéli), and excellent reds (Sapéravi, Teliani no 2 and Moukouzani no 4, one of the best of Kakhétie, resembling a Burgundy).

The red and whites of Tsinandali are the most famous Georgian wines. Tsinandali white no 1, for example, is a delicious dry wine.

The Kartélie region of Tbilissi grows the Tchinouri grape from which the white wine Gorouli-Mtsvane is made.

Imérétie (a region of Koutaisi) produces mainly white wines which are named after the grape from which they are made, e.g. Krakhouna, Tsitska and Tsolikaouri. The region also produces the red Khvantchkara, which was Stalin's favourite.

The western region of Gourie, located near Makharadzé, produces the white Djani and Tchkhavéri wines.

The seaside area of Abkhazie, close to Soukhoumi, mainly grows the Isabelle grape, while in the Valley of Bzyb, the Tsolikaouri of Imérétie is grown as well as the Isabelle.

Georgia also produces a sparkling wine called Soviétskoié.

German method A process of making sparkling wines which is more economical than the traditional Champagne method★ as it eliminates the delicate operations of remuage★ and dégorgement★. However, it differs from the cuve close★ process because the second fermentation takes place in bottle, as in the Champagne method, and not in a hermetically-sealed vat. After the second fermentation has occurred and the sparkle appears, the wine is transferred from bottle and pumped into a cold stainless steel vat where it is stabilised by nitrogen pressure. Then a certain amount of sugar is added (like the dosage of the classic Champagne method) and the wine is then filtered and bottled.

This process is only permitted in France for sparkling wines without controlled place names. The transfer into the vat and the filtering replace the process of dégorgement, but the delicate wine suffers from this treatment. It is far from the skilled and demanding task that the highly-trained *remuers* (men who turn the

bottles in the cellars of Champagne) perform.

Germany Germany's long viticultural tradition dates back to Roman times, when legions visited the Rhine and the Moselle. However, the country as a whole is not really suitable for vine-growing except in the valleys of the Rhine and its tributaries. German vineyards are situated further north than most vine-growing areas, and the vines are planted on hillsides overlooking the rivers so as to have maximum exposure to the sun. Only a few acclimatised varieties of vine are hardy enough to grow at this latitude, mainly Riesling, Sylvaner, Müller-Thurgau and, more rarely, Gewürztraminer, Rülander (Pinot Gris) and a few others. The variety of grape is usually specified on the wine's label. In general, Moselle and Rheingau wines are made from Riesling grapes, while Rheinhessen, Palatinate and Franconian wines are made from the prolific Sylvaner species.

Germany excels in the preparation of white wines, both sweet and dry, and these make up about 80% of her total output, which averages 4 or 5 million hl a year. Although the ordinary wines are unremarkable, the quality wines are outstanding, and have a distinctly original character. Relatively low in alcohol

*Vendange in Georgia.
Phot. Lauros-Hétier.*

*Following two pages: the transport of wine in cask, Chartres Cathedral, north aisle. 16th century.
Phot. Lauros-Giraudon.*

117

(usually between 8° and 11°), they are light, refreshing, fruity and pleasantly tart (though they sometimes show a touch of sweetness). They have great distinction, a delicate aroma, and often a remarkable clarity.

The white wines lend themselves extremely well to the preparation of sparkling wines, and the famous 'Sekt' industry has developed enormously since World War II. It is worth noting that German Sekt is agreeable only if it has been properly made from quality wine and has retained some of its character.

The greatest wines of the Rheingau★

further south on the west bank, near the border of Alsace. Other notable viticultural regions are the area north of the Rheingau between Rüdesheim and Coblenz, the Mittelrhein and the Baden★ vineyards on the outskirts of the Black Forest across the border from Alsace.

Moselle★ wines are produced in the valley of the Moselle River. Although completely different from the wines of the Rhine in character, they equal them in quality.

Distinctive wines are also produced on the banks of other tributaries of the Rhine: the wines of the Nahe★, which joins the

Vineyards growing on terraces along the left bank of the Rhine viewed from Bacharach.
Phot. Rapho.

and Rheinhessen★ are made in exceptional years from Riesling grapes grown in favourably positioned vineyards and affected by pourriture noble★. These sweet wines are extremely sought after, and are often sold by auction.

Rhine wines are produced in five regions of the Rhine valley, each having its own individual character. The wines of the Rheingau, on the east bank between Wiesbaden and Rüdesheim, are considered to be the best (one of them is the renowned Johannisberger★). They are helped a good deal by the vineyards' excellent position facing due south towards the Rhine. The Rheinhessen, which lies further south on the west bank, is the original home of Liebfraumilch★. The Palatinate★ lies still

Rhine from the west at Bingen; those of Franconia★, produced in the Main valley; and the wines of the Ahr★, which are red, and thus an exception.

German wines are usually sold in special, long, slim bottles (green for Moselle, yellowish-brown for Rhine wines). Others, such as Würzburger, Franconian Steinwein and Baden Mauerwein, come in squat, flask-shaped bottles with flat sides, called bocksbeutels.

The German system of appellations can be quite confusing. For quality wines the system is similar to the French one: they are called by the name of the town or village or origin (e.g. Rüdesheim, Johannisberg). The better wines also add the name of their particular vineyard (e.g.

120

Wine festival at Unkel, on the Rhine. Phot. Rapho.

Johannisberger Klaus, Rüdesheimer Berg Bronnen). There are a few exceptions to this rule, usually very famous wines which are known simply by the name of their vineyard (e.g. Steinberger from the Hattenheim commune, and Schloss Vollrads from the Winkel commune).

German wine labels also contain a certain amount of information which may seem esoteric, but in fact is quite important to the consumer. For example,

chaptalisation★ is allowed in Germany, mainly in bad years. (Fine wines, however, are not usually chaptalised.) The words *Natur*, *Rein* and *Naturwein* can only be applied to unchaptalised wines. *Wachstum*, *Creszenz* and *Gewächs* are the equivalents of the French cru★, and are followed by the owner's name. *Cabinet*, or *Kabinett*, can be translated as Special Reserve or Superior Quality, and *Schlossabzug*, *Originalabfüllung* and *Kellerabfüllung* correspond to the

From left to right: multicoloured engraved glass, 16–17th century; engraved glass, Bohemia, 18th century; ceramic flagon, 16th century. Musée des Arts Décoratifs. Phot. Giraudon.

French mise en château, i.e. château-bottled or estate-bottled. *Spätlese* means a wine made from 'late-picked' (i.e. over-ripe) grapes, and *Auslese*, one made from grapes affected by pourriture noble. *Spätlese* and *Auslese* wines are excellent sweet wines, and those marked *Beerenauslese* and *Trockenbeerenauslese* are even sweeter and richer. Lastly, the vintage of German wines is very important, as all northern

wonderfully. The climats are: Chambertin, Chambertin-Clos de Bèze, Charmes-Chambertin (or Mazoyères-Chambertin), Chapelle-Chambertin, Griotte-Chambertin, Latricières-Chambertin, Mazis-Chambertin and Ruchotes-Chambertin.

Gewürztraminer Traminer wines which are especially fragrant and heady.

Vineyards on terraces along the Rhine. View taken from the Lorelei rock looking towards Boppard. Phot. Lauros-Candelier.

vineyards are particularly dependent on good weather for the quality of their grape harvest and ultimately, of course, their wine.

Gevrey-Chambertin This Burgundian commune carries the prestigious name of Chambertin which is renowned throughout the world. The wines are an admirable blend of grace and vigour, strength and finesse, with a characteristic liquorice bouquet. The grand crus age

The word *Gewürz* means spicy. These are excellent, original wines, made from the grape of the same name, which also have the same seductive qualities as the Traminer. Their 'nose' and extremely aromatic taste are extraordinarily rich, sometimes even too exuberant. These qualities are even more marked after a late vendange, yet, in Alsace, the Gewürztraminers never attain the elegance of the Rieslings.

Germany and the Tyrol often produce excellent Gewürztraminers as does Cali-

fornia, but the aroma is never as pronounced as in the Alsatian wines.

Giennois (Coteaux du)

Today, the little village of Gien on the Loire★ is more famous for its pottery than its wines, but in former times, right up to the end of the last century, it was an important viticultural commune with more than 800 vignerons. Vines still grow on several hillsides and terraces around Gien, particularly at Bonny-sur-Loire, Beaulieu, Ousson, and Châtillon-sur-Loire.

The reds, rosés and whites, which are all consumed in the area, are VDQS★ but production is limited to 200–300 hl. The light, agreeable white wines made from the Sauvignon are generally the best, while the reds and rosés made from the Gamay are more ordinary.

Gigondas

Although the wine from this charming Provençal village, perched on the north side of Montmirail, does not have its own special appellation contrôlée, the name Gigondas can be added to Côtes du Rhône★ in the same print on the label.

The vineyards are located between Orange and the mountainous region of Ventoux, an area which enjoys a warm, dry climate.

Like all the southern Côtes du Rhône wines, the wines of Gigondas are made from numerous grape varieties. Grenache is the favourite, then Bourboulenc, Clairette, Cinsault, Mourvèdre and Picpoul. The vignerons no longer cultivate the

Carignan, as they wish to achieve a more supple wine.

Gigondas produces red, rosé and white wines. The dry, fruity, original rosé is very agreeable when young, but has a tendency

Gevrey-Chambertin: the vineyard and village.
Phot. Aarons-L.S.P.

The fortified village of Gigondas. Phot. M.

From left to right: German coloured glass; French glass; filigreed Dutch glass; Venetian-style glass, Belgium. All 17th century. Musée des Arts Décoratifs, Paris. Phot. Lauros and Lauros-Giraudon.

to maderise★ when it ages. The red is excellent. It is a powerful, full-bodied wine, having finesse, a certain elegance and is a beautiful, purple colour. Although a bit harsh when young, it acquires its true beauty after maturing at least two years.

Givry On the hills of the Côte Chalonnaise★, Givry produces excellent red wines related to Mercureys★. They have the same bouquet and finesse, but are lighter.

Glacier A white Swiss wine produced in the alpine valley of Anniviers in the canton of Valais. The wine receives a rather different treatment, as it is left to age high in the mountains for ten or fifteen years in small larch casks holding 37 litres. Glacier is a very special and, to some, surprising wine which has a certain bitterness when first tasted.

glass The choice of glass is quite important when tasting wine. Every major

viticultural region in France has created its own specially-shaped glass designed to show off its wine to the best advantage, e.g. there are glasses for red and white Burgundy, red and white Bordeaux, Vouvray and Alsatian wine. A glass should be simple and light. Its function is to hold wine rather than to decorate the table, and a lot of carving and ornamentation is merely an obstruction. Its texture should be thin for the same reason. Coloured glass deprives the enthusiast of his first pleasure, which is admiring the wine's colour. However rare and precious such glasses may be, they are never as suitable for a great wine as clear, shining crystal.

A glass should be of such a size that it need not be filled to the top, thus enabling one to release the wine's full bouquet, without fear of spilling, by a gentle circular movement of the hand. The shape is equally important. It should narrow slightly towards the rim in order to concentrate the bouquet, which a wide-topped glass would allow to escape. The traditional Champagne glasses are far from ideal as their width allows all the bubbles to escape, together with the Champagne's fine and subtle aroma, and would make even the greatest wine dull and flat. The most suitable glasses for Champagne are either fluted or tulip-shaped.

The stem of the glass, too, is important. It should be neither too thick nor too thin. Round ones are best to hold and they also make it easier to turn the glass and appreciate the wine's bouquet.

glycerine An element of wine responsible for smoothness and mellowness. Glycerine materialises during alcoholic fermentation★ and normally is present in wine at the level of 6–8 g per litre. Wines which undergo a slow fermentation have a higher level of glycerine.

The vins blancs liquoreux★ contain up to 20 g per litre but, in this case, the glycerine is not caused solely by alcoholic fermentation. *Botrytis cinerea*, the cause of pourriture noble★, has already produced some in the grapes. Must from grapes strongly affected by pourriture noble contains as much glycerine as 12 g per litre before alcoholic fermentation.

gouleyant A term which can be abused in oenophilic circles, probably because it sounds pleasing to the ear and esoteric to the uneducated. It simply means a fresh, light wine which glides easily and agreeably down the throat.

gourmet In wine parlance this refers to one who knows wines and how to taste them. The derivation of the word is found in the expression courtier gourmet – piqueur de vins★.

goutte When making white wines, moût de goutte is the juice which flows naturally from the grape after crushing and before pressing. In red wines the vin de goutte is the wine which runs from the cuves when fermentation has halted. This first juice accounts for about 85% of the volume. The rest is comprised of marc, which is returned to the press for the extraction of the vin de presse★.

grafting A method of vine propagation which has been used mainly since phylloxera★. It consists of attaching a graft (the shoot depending on the desired variety) on to a stock of American origin (Riparia, Rupestris, Vialla or Berlandieri) which is resistant to phylloxera. The most widely used is the English stock, as the American vines often make a disagreeable foxy★ tasting wine.

When grafting was first tried in France, there were many who feared that the marriage of the vines would weaken the traditional wines. The French oenologists

Grafting. Phot. M.

and vignerons have succeeded in classifying and selecting the stocks according to their aptitudes and preferences (precocity, affinity with the scion, exposition, soil, climate, etc.). But before grafting became a science there were many failures and some vineyards did not become revitalised until after forty years.

Certain famous vineyards resisted the practice of grafting for a long time. The prestigious vineyard of Romanée-Conti, for example, injected carbon sulphide into the soil until the Second World War but had to begin grafting during the Occupation when sulphur was not available.

Grafting does not affect the quality of a wine. Its influence is on the vigour of the vine, giving it more or less strength, and retarding or hastening the maturing of the grapes. Grafting has resulted in higher costs and modification of the method of vine cultivation.

grafting (English) A widely practised method in which the graft and stock are sectioned at complimentary angles by a special grafting machine so that they fit perfectly together in a V shape.

graisse A disease which attacks badly constituted or cared for white wines, which are poor in alcohol and tannin. The wine becomes oily and turgid, takes on a strange tint and tastes flat and faded. The treatment consists of trying to kill the bacteria by cleansing the wine with sulphur dioxide★ and to restore its clarity by energetic collage★ with tannisage★.

Grand-Roussillon This appellation contrôlée of Roussillon★ embraces all the vins doux naturels★ contained in the Grand-Roussillon region: Côtes d'Agly, Côtes-de-Haut-Roussillon, Maury and Rivesaltes.

Graves The vineyards of Graves are reputedly the cradle of Bordeaux★ wine. The wines of Graves, which have enjoyed an excellent reputation for hundreds of years, have always been called 'the wines of Bordeaux'.

The Graves region stretches the length of the left bank of the Garonne, between the river to the east and the forest of Landes to the west. It begins in the north at the Jalle de Blanquefort, the Médoc border,

and descends south to Langon, having twined around Sauternes. The average width of the vineyard is only twelve km and the length, sixty km. The name of the region comes from the terrain, called *grave*, which is a mixture of siliceous gravel, sand and a little clay.

Graves differs from other Bordeaux vineyards in that it produces both red and white wines (dry and sweet). The vineyards are customarily divided into two parts: red Graves in the north, and white in the south, but the separation is not really that clear-cut. The northern section also produces excellent quality white wines and the southern part, some reds. It is the nature of the soil that determines the grape grown. The pure *grave* is more favourable for red grapes, and *grave* mixed with other components is preferred for white vines.

Red Graves somewhat resembles the neighbouring Médoc. Both are made from the same grapes: Cabernet Franc, Cabernet-Sauvignon, Merlot and a small amount of Petit Verdot and Malbec. The extremely fragrant red Graves are elegant wines which keep well. They have more body and nerve than the Médocs, but do not possess their sweet fragrance and delicate mellowness. Pessac and Léogran (which also produce excellent white Graves) are the two main centres of production. But, unlike those of the Médoc, the communes of Graves do not have any particular appellation. Château-Haut-Brion, classified Premier Grand Cru in 1855, is the most glorious. Other crus also have a very good reputation, including Châteaux Pape-Clément, La Mission Haute-Brion and Haut-Bailly.

White Graves is grown mostly in the southern area, and is made from the same varieties as the neighbouring Sauternes: Sémillon, Sauvignon and Muscadelle. It is represented by a unique range of wines from dry to sweet (they become sweeter towards the south near Sauternes). The wines have *race*★ and are fine and fragrant, without being acidic like certain dry wines. In good years they age gracefully and, very rarely, maderize. Like the reds, the white Graves do not have a communal appellation. There are many good crus among them, including Château Carbonnieux, Domaine de Chevalier and Château Olivier. (See Index.)

GRAVES, APPELLATION GRAVES This regional appellation is applied to good quality red wines of the Graves area having an alcohol minimum of 10°.

GRAVES SUPÉRIEURS Applies to white wines (never red) which have a minimum alcohol content of 12°. The wines are generally sold with the name of the vineyard and the guarantee of authenticity *mise en bouteilles au château* indicated on the label. The appellation is often absent on the labels of certain well-known crus.

gress has been made since this revival and there are now more than 120 vineyards covering between 500 and 600 acres; the majority are in the south of England, though other areas include Lincolnshire, Norfolk and South Wales. Production is now approaching more than 170,000 bottles a year.

Most British wine is white, an exception being Beaulieu Abbey rosé, grown from Müller-Thurgau and Seyval B, grape varieties which resist disease, ripen early and suit Britain's damp climate. Quality is

Composed of a unique mixture of flinty pebbles, sand and a little clay, the 'graves' soil produces wines of longstanding repute. Phot. M.

GRAVES DE VAYRES An area of Bordeaux which is geographically part of Entre-deux-Mers★ occupying the left bank of the Dordogne, south-west of Libourne. It comprises the gravel-soiled areas of Vayres and Arveyres.

The white wines are fine and mellow with their own personal *sève*★. The supple, agreeable reds resemble the second crus of Pomerol.

Great Britain Viticulture in Britain is not an entirely new industry. There were extensive vineyards, in fact, attached to monasteries in the early Middle Ages and were it not for England's later trade ties with France, this level of wine production may have continued. However, it was not until 1952 that vines were commercially grown again on British soil. Much pro-

improving year by year though the British wine industry is presently handicapped by high excise duty and EEC restrictions covering the planting of new vines, introduced in response to overproduction in other European countries. It may therefore be a number of years before British wines make any impact on the European market.

Greece The ancient Greeks were great wine-lovers, praising it in their literature, religion and art. Ancient Greece is considered the mother of viticulture. The Greeks were the first to prune the vine and to observe that rough soil, which was unsuitable for growing other crops, paradoxically gave the best wines. When establishing a colony the first thing the Greeks planted was the vine.

127

Greece: high vines in Crete.
Phot. Loirat–Rapho.

Greece: vineyards at Corinth.
Phot. J. Bottin.

Little remains of this expertise today. Although vineyards are found in every part of Greece, a good part of the harvest is exported as fresh grapes or dried raisins (the celebrated Corinth grape). Around 5 million hl of wine is produced annually, mainly from the regions of Attica, the Peloponnese, Crete, Thrace, Corfu and the Aegean islands. Vineyards occupy 50% of the surface of the thin strip of land stretching along the Peloponnese coast.

The resin which is added to the famous white or red vin ordinaire Retsina gives the wine an aftertaste of burnt wood and turpentine. To the unaccustomed, it is sometimes considered undrinkable. Most of Greek wine is resinated as it helps to conserve it in the hot climate.

There are non-resinated wines made in the Peloponnese (around Achaia and Messini), Arcadia (around Tegee) and on the islands of Cephalonia, Santorin, Samos, Corfu and Zante. The unfavourable latitude and hot climate produce heavy wines, high in alcohol and full-bodied, which lack finesse, particularly the white wines.

The dessert wines, however, are often remarkable. The best known is the Muscat of Samos, a dry white wine which is very alcoholic (18°). Mavrodaphne, produced in several regions from the grape of the same name, is generally very good, especially that made near Patras.

green Wine made from unripe grapes tends to be over-acid, and is called 'green'. When the acidity is not obtrusive it can be pleasant, especially as it mellows to an agreeable freshness as the wine matures. Very young, immature wines often have a touch of greenness, even when made from sound grapes.

Grignolino An excellent Italian red wine, made from the grape variety of the same name in the Piemonte north of the village of Asti★ in the mountainous region of Monferrato. Produced in only small quantity, the Grignolino has its own very special taste and inimitable bouquet. Although it gives an impression of lightness it usually contains 13 or 14° alcohol.

gris (vin) Although not legally classified, this is a very light rosé made by treating a red harvest like a white one. The

process is used in Burgundy and the Loire (rosés of Saumur★ and Cabernet★) and in the east of France (Côtes de Toul★).

Until the eighteenth century, vignerons only made this kind of wine, as they lacked other means. On their arrival in the cuvage★, the grapes are immediately crushed and pressed, but less quickly than the whites.

Gros-Plant du Pays Nantais A very dry white VDQS★ wine which used to be kept for family and local consumption, but which during the past twenty years has been more widely known and drunk. The Gros-Plant (or Folle-Blanche) is made from a grape of the same name which has been in the region perhaps even longer than the Muscadet★.

The grape undoubtedly comes from the Charente where it used to be made into Cognac. However, because it is so susceptible to rot it is seldom grown any more in its area of origin.

In the Atlantic area of the Loire, the grape is grown in certain selected areas principally on siliceous soil around Lake Grandlieu (Saint-Philbert, Bouaye, Legé and Machecoul). It is also found around Loroux-Bottereau, Liré, Champtoceaux and in the Retz area where Muscadet is also cultivated.

The Gros-Plant is a light, fresh, almost colourless wine, usually containing about 9–11° alcohol. It can be kept but is best drunk young. It is always a bit green★ and never has quite the finesse of a Muscadet.

Vines of the Nantes area.
Phot. M.

129

H

hail One of the natural catastrophes which can harm the vineyard. If a hailstorm does not entirely destroy the vineyard, it still affects the quality of wine which is made from the damaged grapes. In a humid year mildew can more easily enter grapes whose skin has been broken by hail. In a dry year, on the other hand, the grapes become shrivelled and parched and the wine (especially the red) takes on what is called a 'taste of hail', a dry taste which is easily recognised.

Hailstones not only cut grapes and leaves, but often ruin the vines themselves. The vigneron must then prune the vine, a step which may have repercussions on the quality of the following year's wine. At-

tempts are made to fight off this calamity by shooting silver iodide into the air to prevent the formation of hailstones.

hard A term describing a wine which has an excess amount of acid or tannin. When the acid is not balanced by a high enough level of alcohol, which is often the case with young wines, it can be very disagreeable.

harsh A harsh wine is both astringent★ and rough on the tongue, and can even set one's teeth slightly on edge. These characteristics are caused by an excess of tannin, which is due either to a coarse variety of grape being used to make the wine or to bad vinification (cuvé★ wine). This tannin eventually precipitates, and the wine improves a little with age.

Other words used by connoisseurs to describe wines that contain excessive tannin are 'angular' and, when it impairs the delicacy of the wine's texture, 'thick'.

Haut-Brion (Château-) One of the four greatest red wines of Bordeaux and the only Graves officially classified in 1855 with the three greats of Médoc★ (Lafite★, Latour★ and Margaux★). Haut-Brion is a generous, powerful wine, but is also fine and elegant and has a very particular smoky taste. In good years it makes a wine which ages admirably. There is also a small quantity of white Château-Haut-Brion made, which is extremely full-bodied and powerful.

Haut-Comtat A vineyard of the left bank of the Rhône Valley which grows on six communes of the Drôme, around the little town of Nyons known for its olive

Grapes damaged by hail.
Phot. M.

trees and lavender. The vines, protected from cold winds by the mountains, grow on arid soil amongst the fragrant plants. The Grenache is the dominant vine (at least 50%) flanked by its habitual companions in the Midi: Carignan, Mourvèdre, Cinsault and Syrah. The VDQS★ reds and rosés are very fruity and agreeable, possessing a special aromatic bouquet.

Haut-Dahra The name given to the formerly VDQS★ wines of Algeria produced in the department of Algiers, west of Algiers between the coast and the Chelif river.

The vines are cultivated on a variety of terrains, the average at an altitude of 600 m. These highly-coloured red wines are powerful, fleshy and marrowy and have an alcohol content of at least 12°.

headache The true oenophile never has a headache from overdrinking, for as Brillat-Savarin aptly said, 'Those who stuff themselves or become inebriated do not know how to eat or drink'.

However, some suffer headaches after drinking certain white wines because of their sulphur dioxide★ content. The excess sulphur combines with the blood to cause this discomfort. About 10% of consumers are especially susceptible to sulphur, experiencing a headache and upset stomach even when the sulphur level is not extraordinary. Others who may experience headaches from rich red or white wines should stick to lighter ones.

heady A heady wine is one with a relatively high alcohol content, which makes it 'go to one's head'. The alcohol is sometimes masked by a high sugar content which may make the wine seem like a vin doux naturel★.

heavy The opposite of a harmonious, balanced wine. It is a wine which lacks finesse and has too much alcohol and tannin. The aroma and bouquet are thus completely hidden. Such a wine (and many of the vins ordinaires fall into this category) weighs heavily on the palate and stomach.

Hermitage or **Ermitage** The name given to the well-known red and white wines of the Côtes du Rhône★ which are

Tain-l'Hermitage and its terraced vineyards.
Phot. Pavlovsky-Rapho.

produced from vineyards growing on terraces in Tain-l'Hermitage. The name comes from a hermitage built in the reign of Blanche of Castille by the chevalier Gaspard de Stérimberg. Red Hermitage, made from the Syrah, is a generous, powerful wine which in its youth has the characteristic bitterness of wines made from this variety.

Rich purple in colour, it has a penetrating bouquet and its warm flavour lingers for a long time in the mouth. Red Hermitage takes several years to attain the height of its power and perfection. White Hermitage, made from Roussane and Marsanne grapes, is a full-bodied, fine wine of a beautiful gold colour which has a very characteristic aroma.

The region also produces a small quantity of the delicious, golden vin de paille★ which contains 15° alcohol and is made from grapes which are dried for at least two months on a bed of straw.

Hippocrates Was the most famous doctor of all time and the acknowledged father of medicine. Oenophiles remember him as the wise doctor who said, 'Wine is the best thing for man, whether he be healthy or sick, if taken in moderation'.

Vendange in Hungary in the Eger region. Phot. Charmet.

honour (wine of) A custom which is without doubt as old as wine itself. Wine offerings were presented by the ancients each time they wanted to honour someone, and the practice is still carried on today though on a less grandiose scale. Dating from the Middle Ages, bishops who owned vineyards would offer their best wines each time they received a distinguished visitor or the king himself. In those days of limited communication, the practice helped to disseminate the wine and spread the reputation of a particular vineyard. It was often after being appreciated as a 'wine of honour' that a cru was regularly served on the royal table.

In humbler homes the best wine was always reserved to honour any important visitor. Today in the country the best wine, colloquially called *derrière les fagots*, is kept for the visitor one wants to cordially welcome.

Grape-harvest celebrations at Kelebia, Hungary. Phot. Charmet.

Hungary This country traditionally had the largest viticultural area in Eastern Europe and produced excellent wines.

Viticulture has flourished in Hungary for a long time, becoming more advanced in the seventeenth century when colonies from Belgium and France were established. Although production has been surpassed by that of the USSR and Romania, the Hungarian vineyards have been in the process of expansion since 1959.

There are a number of viticultural areas. The mountainous region is found in the north, starting at Gyöngyös, north of Budapest, around the villages of Abasár, Visorita, Varkaz, Domoszló and Verpelét. Gyöngyös makes a white wine from the Chasselas grape, which is sweet like honey. At Gyöngyöstarjan there is a cave which was constructed in 1740 by French prisoners of war. Even in wartime, Hungary kept up its vineyards.

North-east of Gyöngyös is the important viticultural zone of Eger, known for its Bikavér★ and Egri Kádárka (two full-bodied reds which keep well) and also for the white wine Egri Leányka, and a Muscat★. This mountainous region ends near the Soviet frontier in the most famous vineyard, Tokaji-Hegyalia (see Tokay).

The vineyards of the great central plain, stretching between the Danube and Tisza, are centred around Kecskemèt which produces a good white wine, the Kecskemèti Léányka. The vines grow on sand-dunes and sandy soil and the region produces some 200,000–300,000 hl of wine, but it is best known for its *eaux-de-vie*.

The hilly area or Badacsony★, west of Lake Balaton, produces remarkable wines which have been famous for centuries.

A fourth area called the region of Szekszárd, located sixty km north-east of Pécs, is known for its Fleuré de Decs (produced in a little village of the same name), its Riesling of Szekszárd and its red wine of Kádárka.

Hungarian wines generally bear the name of the town or region of origin usually ending in 'i', e.g. Badacsonyi, Egri, Szekszárdi and Gyöngyösi. The grape name is sometimes added. For the red wines, these are the Vörös and Kádárka, and for the white (in order of quality) Furmint, Hárslevelü, Rizling (Riesling), Veltelini, Kéknyelü, Muskotály, Ezerjó and Léányka.

hybrid Viticulturally speaking, a hybrid is the result of crossing two varieties of grapes. Botanically speaking, hybridisation is a relatively new phenomenon, having been practised for only about 200 years. By selective breeding, it enables one to combine some qualities and to lose others; it also results in more vigorous and robust offspring. As far as the vine is concerned, hybridisation was first used in France after the phylloxera* attack as a means of warding off the insect. Laliman of Beaune replanted his vineyards with American vines which are resistant to phylloxera (Noah, Clinton, Elvira, Othello, etc.). However, as the wines were not appreciated, the next step was to cross the American vines with French ones by grafting. Thus a robust hybrid which could withstand phylloxera was created.

In France, hybrids bear the name of their 'inventor' plus a serial number (Seibel 5279, Couderc 4401, etc.). In other countries the hybrids are often called by the name of their parents whose characteristics they claim to possess, or by a name resembling that of a noble* parent. This creates a regrettable confusion, such as with Emerald Riesling and Ruby Cabernet in the United States, and, in Germany, Goldriesling, Mainriesling and Müller-Thurgau (sometimes presented under the name of 'Riesling und Sylvaner' or 'Reisling-Sylvaner' although it has not been proven that Müller-Thurgau is the result of the crossing of Riesling and Sylvaner).

In France, hybrid production is dying out, as the wines made from them are common and not much liked by wine-drinkers in other EEC countries. Moreover, the use of chromatography soon reveals wines made from hybrids. As a result, the vignerons are replacing more and more of their hybrids with the indigenous vine species.

Hypocras A drink, generally wine-based, which was in great vogue from the Middle Ages up to the time of Louis XIV. Hypocras was a mixture of white or red wine (or beer or cider in the homes of poorer folk), spices (cinnamon, cloves, nutmeg, etc.) and sugar. The famous Taillevent, Charles VII's master chef, left the recipe for posterity.

The nobles always preferred Hypocras

Popular Hungarian vessels: top, Transylvanian wine jugs (mid 19th century); centre, ceramic liqueur gourds (late 19th century); bottom, carved wooden gourd (late 19th century). Various colls. Phot. Charmet.

to wine and liked it enriched with raspberries and costly ingredients like amber. The mixture was clarified in a special filter and kept in air-tight containers.

I

Institut National des Appellations d'Origine (INAO) A unique institution which was created by the law of 30th July, 1935. Although it receives its power from the State, the INAO is a private organisation which brings together government officials (Agriculture, Justice and Repression of Frauds) with specialists in the wine field *(viticulteurs,* *négociants).* Its objective is to improve the quality of French wines and *eaux-de-vie,* and its primary task is to define the requirements which wines must meet to obtain an appellation d'origine contrôlée★ classification. Each step is defined, from the grape variety to the methods of vinification.

The INAO oversees and controls pro-

Irancy, Burgundy.
Phot. Beaujard-Lauros.

duction at every step; it educates, encourages and protects the consumer as well as the producer and subjects vignerons to a very strict discipline. Abroad, the INAO works to protect the French appellations, such as the case of the 'Spanish Champagne' in London where the INAO fought to safeguard the appellation 'Champagne'. After battling for three years it was victorious.

Iran Persia was one of the first countries to cultivate the vine in order to make wine. Even after the Moslem conquest, wine-making still flourished as is attested by Omar Khayyám's praise for the wines of his country.

The Syrah grape, from which Côte-du-Rhône wines are made, was, according to legend, brought to Europe from Persia during the Crusades.

Today the vine is mainly cultivated at the foot of the mountains, in the centre, the south-east and in the north around Alborz. Production is mainly in the form of table grapes which are locally consumed or exported as dried raisins. Only a very small amount of wine is made (around 3600 hl a year).

Irancy A small town south-west of Chablis★ whose vineyard, lying on well-exposed hills, used to be very famous. The wine was exported as early as the twelfth century and today the reds and rosés of Irancy are still excellent, especially the cru Palotte. However, only small sections of the old vineyard remain and production is greatly limited. Even the best restaurants of the region can not get enough to satisfy their clientele.

The wine of Irancy, like the other reds and rosés of Burgundy, is made primarily from the Pinot Noir. In fact the other regional varieties, the César and Tressot, are slowly disappearing.

In good years the red wine is excellent. It is a full-bodied, very fine wine of a beautiful purple colour and its own particular taste. It ages well and gradually unfolds its beautiful bouquet.

Unfortunately, the Pinot does not always mature perfectly in this northern part of Burgundy. Thus it is better in poor years to drink Irancy vinified into rosé, which is fresh and fruity and has an agreeable *goût de terroir*. Irancy has the right

to the regional appellation Burgundy to which it can add the name of the commune.

Irouléguy A VDQS★ wine and typical of the produce of the Basque country. It is produced by a very small vineyard in the Nive Valley located west of Saint-Jean-Pied-de-Port and stretches over seven communes, the principal ones being Saint-Etienne-de-Baigorry and Irouléguy. The vines perch on hills from 100–400 m high not far from the Spanish frontier. The small vineyard, which totals only about 40 ha, does not produce more than 1500 litres

a year of red and rosé wines, which are vinified at the co-operative cave of Irouléguy. The beautifully coloured red is warm and fruity and, like the other reds of Béarn, is made principally from the Tannat, with the addition of some Bouchy and Fer★.

Israel Israeli viticulture has only existed since the State was formed in 1949. From 1955 to 1961, wine production tripled (to 2,700,000 hl). However, the roots of viticulture in the area can be traced back to biblical times. It was revived around 1890

Vendange at Irouléguy.
Phot. Yan-Rapho.

after the Moslem occupation thanks to the efforts of Baron Edmond de Rothschild who began a viticultural experiment at Rishon-le-Zion, south-east of Tel Aviv.

Today, the two principal vineyards are Rishon-le-Zion and Zichron Jacob, south-east of Haifa. Vineyards have recently been planted further south in the regions of Lachish, Ascalon and Beersheba.

The grape varieties are those which adapt to the warm, dry climate of Israel. For the reds these are principally the Alicante, the Grenache, Carignan and Alicante Bouschet, and for the whites, the Clairette, the Muscat of Alexandria and the Frontignan. There is also some Cabernet-Sauvignon, Sémillon, Malbec and Ugni Blanc.

Israel has qualified technicians as well as twenty modern vinicultural installations, mainly co-operatives. The wines are well made and reasonably priced, good but never extraordinary. Most of the production is consumed locally, only about 6% being exported. Great Britain and the United States are the principal importers of Israeli wines.

The co-operative of Carmel Zion has an English branch called the Carmel Wine Company, which was founded in 1897. It also has an American branch, the Carmel Wine Co. Inc., New York.

Italy This has been a wine-producing country from time immemorial, and today accounts for about 20% of world production, rivalling France in actual volume produced. Every region of Italy produces wine, and from the Alps to Sicily there is a remarkable variety of climates, soil and grape varieties and vinicultural traditions. Many of these are ordinary wines without appellation, but are better than certain vins de consommation courante made in the French Midi. If, in recent years, the Italian vines have descended the hills to invade the plains, great progress has been made in vinicultural methods, particularly by the co-operatives. The result is a better balance in quality, and hybrids are now almost non-existent. The taste of the consumer is also changing, as in France, towards lighter, less alcoholic wines favouring rosés or semi-sparkling varieties.

Since the decree of 12th July, 1962 an appellation system inspired by the French classification has been organised for fine wines; the divisions are: *denominazione semplice, denominazione di origine controllata* (DOC), and *denominazione controllata e garantita* (the best wines). These appellations are placed under strict government control and the wines must adhere to stringent regulations regarding area of production, grape variety, production per hectare and alcoholic minimum.

Although the vine is cultivated all over Italy, certain regions are notable. In order of volume of production, they are the

Italy: one of the most famous crus of the 'country of wine', Aleatico is a dessert wine produced on Elba. A view of the island's main town, Portoferraio. Coloured engraving. Bibl. Nat. Phot. B.N.

Italy: Piemonte vineyards.
Phot. Lartigue-Rapho.

region of Pouilles, at the heel of the Italian boot, which produces very colourful and alcoholic common wines and some dessert wines, the Piemonte, second in production, but first in quality and famous for its Asti Spumanti★ and Barolo★, Sicily which, besides ordinary wines, produces dessert wines like the Marsala★, Tuscany, the source of Chianti★, Venetia, whose best wines are produced around Verona, and Campanie, producer of the famous Falerne★ and Lacrima Christi★.

Italian wines generally take the name of the town or province of origin or the name of the grape (with some exceptions like Est Est Est★ and Chiaretto★). The principal reds are: Barolo, Gattinara★, Barbaresco★ (made from the excellent Nebbiolo grape), Barbera★, Freisa★ and Grignolino★, all from the Piemonte; the Valtellina★ of Lombardy; Bardolino★ and Valpolicella★ of Verona; Santa Maddalena★, Lago di Caldaro★, Santa Giustina★ of the Italian Tyrol; the Lambrusco of Bologna; Chianti of Tuscany; and Gragnano of Naples.

The white wines are dry or semi-dry. Because of the latitude they are generally heavy except those of the Italian Tyrol in the north. Among the whites are the Cortese★ of Piemonte, the Lugana★ of Lake Garda, the Soave★ of Verona, the Terlano★ and Traminer of the Tyrol, the Orvieto★ and Est Est Est produced north of Rome, the Castelli Romani★, Capri★ and Lacrima Christi around Naples, and the Etna of Sicily.

The rosés are presented by the Chiaretto of Lake Garda and the Lagrein rosato★ of the Tyrol.

Marsala is the most famous dessert wine, but the Aleatico★ of the Isle of Elba is also excellent as is the Vino Santo★, produced mainly in Tuscany, as well as some in Trentin. There are in addition about six good Muscats. Asti Spumante, the king of the sparkling wines, is made by the Champagne method★ from Pinot Blanc or Gris.

The Italians attach little importance to vintage. The differences in quality from one year to the next are less marked than in French wines. Moreover, with the exception of about twelve, Italian wines do not improve after three years. Only wines made from the Nebbiolo (Barolo, Barbaresco, Gattinara, Ghemme, Valtellina) benefit from ageing. It is the same case with good Chiantis.

JK

Vin jaune is a speciality of the Jura. A view of an Arbois vineyard. Phot. Cuisset.

Japan The vine has been cultivated in Japan since the twelfth century, but viticulture did not assume any importance until the nineteenth century. Grape juice was used solely as an ingredient in medicines until the arrival of the Europeans and Americans. Despite research trips to France and California, the Japanese vineyards are far from achieving any real economic importance.

All the vineyards are located on the island of Hondo, mainly around Yamanashi, Osaka, Yamagata and Nagano. The humid climate is not favourable to the vine and the grapes must mature quickly because of the torrential rains in September. European, American and Asiatic vines (like the Japanese Koshu) are used. Unfortunately, the European varieties are vulnerable to cryptogamic diseases (mildew and oidium) because of the humid climate. The vines are never of great quality, except perhaps for those from the Sadoya vineyard in the Yamanashi region whose very agreeable wines are made from European varieties.

Jasnières A white wine of the Coteaux du Loir★ produced on the communes of Lhomme and Ruillé-sur-Loir. Made from the Pineau de la Loire, it is generally a dry wine which fills out in warm years and when aged. Jasnières is golden yellow in colour and is marrowy and delicate with a very fruity fragrance.

jaune (vin) This wine of the Jura★ and the glory of Château-Chalon★ is made from the Savagnin, a variety peculiar to the region. The vendange occurs late so that the grapes will be completely mature and the juice concentrated. As this is often after the first snows it is also called *vin de gelée*.

The special method of vinifying vin jaune may seem to defy all oenological rules. After the alcoholic fermentation, a year after the harvest, the wine is drawn off into thick oaken casks where it remains for six years without being topped up. During this ageing period, fixed by law, it acquires the inimitable *goût de jaune*. The wine is covered with a thick veil, formed by special yeasts peculiar to the Jura. In other places, a wine left under such conditions would turn to vinegar, but in this region it is transformed into a marvellous wine of a golden yellow colour, which has a curious nut-like bouquet. A similar process is used in southern Spain for sherry, Manzanilla and Montilla.

The vins jaunes are quite rare and

consequently expensive. As they must be aged six years before bottling a lot of capital is tied up. Moreover, the wine is sometimes inexplicably invaded by harmful bacteria. Finally, since the contents of the cask are subject to evaporation, the volume is diminished.

Vin jaune should never be served at the beginning of a meal. It is so powerful, full-bodied and penetrating that it would detract from the aroma and taste of any other wine following it.

Johannisberg   A famous German vineyard of the Rheingau★, which is located on one of the hilliest areas overlooking the Rhine. Production is insignificant in proportion to the world fame of Johannisberg, which has been considered for some time as a synonym for *racé*★ and refined elegance. The wine is all that, and as an assurance the name of the vineyard and the producer are specified on the label beside the word Johannisberg (the word *Dorf* next to Johannisberg signifies nothing more than 'village' in German).

The famous vineyards are Klaus, Vogelsang, Kläuserpfad, Kläuserberg and Hölle. The most famous is Schloss Johannisberg which was, according to legend, planted on orders from Charlemagne. The Austrian Emperor gave the vineyard to Metternich after the Congress of Vienna. The wines of Schloss Johannisberg are sold under two labels: the best known carries the coat of arms of the Metternich family; the other, a coloured picture of the château and vineyard. Different coloured capsules on the bottles distinguish the different wines: a red capsule for dry, less expensive wines; a green capsule for wines made from overripe grapes; a rose capsule for rare and costly wines only produced in certain years from grapes attacked by pourriture noble★. Some experts feel that the wines of Schloss Johannisberg are not living up to their reputation and that certain other Rheingau wines are better.

Juliénas   Documents reveal that Juliénas was making wine before the rest of Beaujolais was even planted. Juliénas is fresh and fruity and has a darker robe and more body than its neighbour Saint-Amour. It should be drunk young like most of the Beaujolais, although certain years profit from ageing.

Jullien   The author of *la Topographie de tous les vignobles connus*, written in 1816 and updated in 1822 and 1832. In this work Jullien gives a complete classification of all the existing crus so that the evolution of the French vineyards can be traced to the present day.

Jullien relied heavily on the topographical position of the vineyards as a basis for classification, e.g. 'dry wines are generally made from vineyards located above 47° of latitude', 'vins de liqueur are ordinarily made from vineyards situated below 39° of latitude and they contain a higher concentration of sugar the closer they are to the equator'.

The vineyard of Johannisberg and its château. Phot. Lauros-Atlas-Photo.

A Beaujolais village. Phot. L.S.P.-Aarons.

Jurançon vineyard. Phot. M.

Jura Within the limits of this department, from Port-Lesney to Saint-Amour, is found the viticultural region of the ancient province of Franche-Comté. The vineyard covers two well-positioned hills bordering the plain of Bresse on a line parallel with the Côte d'Or with the centre at Arbois. Although only eighty km long and six km wide, there is much originality and wine to satisfy every taste: red, white, rosé, sparkling wines, vin jaune★ and vin de paille★. Charles Quint, Francis I, Henry IV and Pasteur were among its admirers.

The vineyard is situated at an average altitude of 300 m on limestone and clay soil, and planted in three noble★ grape varieties peculiar to the Jura region: Trousseau and Poulsard for the red, and Savagnin or Naturé (called Traminer in Alsace) for the white and vin jaune. The Pinot Noir for red wine and Chardonnay for white are also cultivated.

The Jura has four appellations contrôlées: Côtes du Jura★ (whites, reds, rosés, vins de paille, vins mousseux), Arbois★ (whites, reds, rosés, vins jaunes, vins de paille, vins mousseux), L'Etoile (whites, vins jaunes, vins de paille, vins mousseux), and Château-Chalon★ (vins jaunes).

Jurançon Certainly the most illustrious of the appellations contrôlées of the Sud-Ouest★. The king of Navarre is said to have moistened the lips of his son, the future Henry IV, with the wine of Jurançon, and it was in demand throughout all of northern Europe until the French Revolution, thanks to the Dutch traders.

The Jurançon, pearl of Béarn, is produced south and west of Pau. The vineyards are dotted over the hills facing the south and south-east and are difficult to reach. The soil, whether it be sand, gravel, limestone or clay, is planted in grapes peculiar to the area: Petit-Manseng, Gros-Manseng and Courbu.

The vendange is performed late so that the grapes will be passerillaged★, and production is not more than 25 hl per hectare.

Jurançon is an extraordinary wine, without rival. It is a golden coloured, marrowy nectar that has a generous *sève*★, strong aroma and a light, spicy taste of cinnamon and clove. It gives the strange impression of hiding a certain acidity under the softness of its sugar. Jurançon is a wine which conserves and travels well. Sometimes very ripe, but not passerillaged, grapes are harvested and made into dry, nervy, fresh, fruity wines which are generally drunk in the year following the vendange. There is also a small amount of red Jurançon which is locally consumed. It is as old as the white, as is attested by documents reporting a gift made by Jeanne d'Albret in 1564 of 'a vine of Jurançon red and white'.

Knipperlé A small-grape variety grown in Alsace★ which every year is losing ground to the noble★ varieties. It attracts the pourriture easily and produces good quality wines which are fruity and supple.

Knipperlé is also cultivated in Germany and Switzerland under the name of *Räuschling*, but it is consumed locally in all areas of production.

FESTE BACCHIQUE

'The Feast of Bacchus' after Watteau. Print. Phot. Lauros–Giraudon.

L

Lacrima Christi A famous white Italian wine produced from vineyards growing on the volcanic slopes of Mount Vesuvius (a little red is also made). Its bouquet and taste as well as its pale golden colour somewhat resemble Graves. This wine, whose name means 'tears of Christ', is extremely rare and today there are hardly any vines on the slopes of Vesuvius. In 1816, Julien stated that very little was produced, and that the wine was reserved for the table of the king of Naples.

Lafite-Rothschild (Château) A premier grand cru classé of the Médoc★ which since the seventeenth century has been extraordinarily famous. Its old proprietor, M. de Ségur, was nicknamed the Prince of Vines. It was bought in 1858 for 5 million francs by Baron James de Rothschild and the nobility of the vines has never slackened. Many wine-lovers think that Château-Lafite is the best of all red wines,

or at least the masterpiece of the Haut-Médoc.

It is a perfect wine. Bright, velvety and generous, it has a delicate, suave taste and an exquisite finesse. It can be kept for a long time and still has all its qualities after forty years in bottle, and sometimes even after a century. Only the best cuvées are called Château-Lafite, the rest, although still of quality, are sold under the name Carruades-de-Château-Lafite-Rothschild.

Lago di Caldara An excellent red wine produced from vines growing on hills west and north of the small lake of the same name, which is located not far from Bolzano in the Italian Tyrol. Made from the Schiava Gentile, it is a light, lively, charming wine and is one of the best of the region.

Lagrein rosato A delicious, fresh and vivacious rosé, made around Bolzano in the Italian Tyrol from the local Lagrein, and which should be drunk young. It was called Lagreiner Kaetzer before the First World War when the region was part of Austria.

Lalande-de-Pomerol A vineyard growing north of Pomerol★ on gravelly and sandy soil which produces wines with the appellation contrôlée Lalande-de-Pomerol. The wines are generous and nervy like Pomerol, but have less finesse. The better crus, which can be compared with the second crus of Pomerol, include Château de Bel-Air (not to be confused with Château Belair, the premier grand cru of St. Emilion), Châteaux Grand-Ormeau, Commanderie, les Cluzelles and Perron.

Languedoc An ancient French province which extends from the Rhône delta to Narbonne and includes the coastal border of the departments of Gard, Hérault and the Aude. The last two departments are, by volume, the most important producers in France – most of the production consisting of vins de consommation courante★, which are often called 'wines of the Midi★'. But, besides these vins ordinaires, the region also produces AOC wines: Fitou★, Blanquette de Limoux★, Clairette du Languedoc★ and the suave Muscats★ of Frontignan★, Lunel★, Mireval★ and Saint-Jean-de-Minervois★. There are also VDQS wines: Corbières★, Corbières supérieurs★, Minervois★, Picpoul-de-Pinet★ and Coteaux-du-Languedoc★. This last appellation includes thirteen others.

Languedoc (Coteaux-du-) Under this VDQS appellation are grouped thirteen red and rosé wines coming from the hills of the Aude and Hérault departments (the whites do not merit the appellation) which are sold under the name Coteaux-du-Languedoc followed by their proper name, or solely by their proper name.

The majority of wines are made from Carignan, Cinsault and Grenache grapes and they must have a minimum alcohol content of 11°. They include the following appellations: Cabrières★. Coteaux-de-Vérargues, Faugères★, Coteaux-de-la-Méjanelle, Montpeyroux★, Pic-Saint-Loup, Saint-Chinian★, Saint-Christol,

Château Lafite-Rothschild. Phot. M.

Languedoc: the vineyards of Aigues-Mortes. Phot. M.

Languedoc: vineyards south of Sète. Phot. Lauros-Beaujard.

Château Latour. Phot. M.

Saint-Drézéry, Saint-Saint-Georges-d'Orques and Saint-Saturnin in the Hérault, and la Clape★ and Quatourze★ in the Aude.

These are excellent quality wines which have been famous since ancient times. Saint-Saturnin is well known for its light and agreeable *'vin d'une nuit'*. Saint-Christol, Saint-Drézéry, the Coteaux de Vérargues and Méjanelle mainly produce rosés. The first three appellations, along with Saint-Georges, were reputedly the best of the region in the last century.

Latour (Château) This premier grand cru classé of Pauillac★ is, with its rivals Château-Lafite-Rothschild★ and Châteaux-Margaux★, one of the three greats of the Médoc★. The dry, pebbly soil of the vineyard, planted in the noble★ varieties of Bordeaux, gives a small production but marvellous quality.

Château-Latour is always a robust, complete wine even in mediocre years, and reveals an exceptional richness in good years. It is a highly-coloured, full-bodied, astringent wine in its youth which, like all great wines, has a subtle taste of resin. On ageing it acquires a splendid bouquet and can be kept for a long time, easily for half a century.

Anyone who has drunk Château-Latour once in his life will not mistake it for another. Although there are a number of crus in France, and especially in Bordeaux, whose name includes 'Tour' or 'La Tour', the label of Château-Latour is unique, being inscribed with the picture of a lion standing atop a tower.

Laudun The vineyard of this village of the Côtes du Rhône★, found on the right bank of the Rhône, north of Tavel★ and Lirac★, produces very good, elegant, fruity reds and rosés, resembling Tavels and Liracs, and whites of excellent quality.

Laudun does not have a proper appellation contrôlée but its name can be added, in the same characters, to Côtes du Rhône on the label.

Lavilledieu A VDQS of the Sud-Ouest★ which scarcely exists any more as the winter of 1956 badly damaged the vineyards. The production area is located between Moissac and Montauban in the triangle formed by the Tarn and Garonne, and comprises the communes of Lavilledieu, Montech and Castelsarrasin.

Layon (Coteaux du) The vineyards of this Anjou★ appellation cover the hills bordering the little river of Layon, which flows into the Loire at Chalonnes. Only the area along the lower course of the Layon from Chavagnes and Thouarcé on the right bank, and from Rablay on the left, produce white wines which can claim the appellation.

Coteaux du Layon is the top producer in both quality and quantity in the Anjou

area and is well known outside the region. The Pineau de la Loire matures until October and is often attacked by the pourriture noble★. The wines range from dry to sweet, depending on the year and the grape, but are generally sweet. Tender and smooth, very fine and fragrant, they are usually a beautiful golden colour and are harmonious and full-bodied. They can approach the level of Sauternes, Barsac and the sweet German Rhine wines, while still preserving the fruitiness of the Loire wines.

The best communes are Beaulieu, Faye, Rablay, Rochefort, Saint-Aubin-de-Luigné, Quarts-de-Chaume★ and Bonnezeaux★. The famous crus of the Coteaux du Layon have a distinct appellation of origin.

Most of the production of Layon comprises white wines sold under the appellation Anjou, and also excellent rosés having the appellation Rosé d'Anjou★, as well as Cabernet d'Anjou.

lees Yellowish sediment deposited in the bottom of casks which is separated from the wine during racking. The lees consists of yeast cells and impurities from the wine, and smells like baker's yeast.

Young wines in barrels often have a pronounced taste of lees which disappears after racking. Such a taste is not necessarily a fault, in fact admirers of Muscadet and Swiss wines consider it a virtue.

lees (bottling on) Bottling on lees is a technique used for white wines such as Muscadet which are meant to be drunk young. It is practised to help the wines conserve their freshness and fruitiness. Such wines release a small amount of carbon dioxide which makes the tongue tingle agreeably. Normally, wine is bottled when it is clear, after a series of rackings to separate the wine from its lees or sediments. When the wine is bottled on its lees the yeasts use oxygen from the wine, thus protecting the wine from oxidation and consequent yellowing and ageing.

On the other hand, wine bottled on healthy yeasts is prone to a secondary malo-lactic fermentation★ accompanied by a release of carbon dioxide, part of which dissolves in the wine.

Wine which is bottled early and in cold

weather shows the same qualities; carbon dioxide is very soluble in cold wine and part of it remains in solution. Such wines are like those bottled after malo-lactic fermentation has finished. The Crépy★ of Savoie, Gaillac perlé★ and certain Alsatian wines, as well as the Swiss wines of Valais and Vaud (where the process is called the 'Neuchâtel method'), are made this way.

Bottling on lees is only carried out in good years because the secondary fermentation is always a dubious process, and the wine may be changed, attacked by diseases or developing a bad taste.

lees (wine) A sediment resembling fine sand which is especially visible in white wines and, although displeasing, should not be considered a fault. It is caused by crystals of potassium bitartrate (a compound of tartaric acid, one of the organic acids found in grapes) which precipitates when the wine is cold. The deposit usually appears in casks in winter, but sometimes a part of the potassium bitartrate content does not dissolve. The wine is then saturated with the compound which eventually deposits itself in the bottle; this precipitation improves the wine because it loses some of its acidity due to its tartaric acid content.

Liebfraumilch A German word meaning 'Our Lady's milk' and one of the best-known German wine appellations. It was originally applied to mediocre wine produced by the vineyard of Liebfrauenstift, near the Gothic cathedral in the town of Worms, in the Rhinehessen★. However, the word has now become a synonym for Rhine wine. It is no longer an appellation of origin and is not applied to wines of just one quality. Normally it is the mediocre, cheap wines of the Rhinehessen, sometimes

Wine with lees (below) and clear wine (above). Phot. M.

CHATEAU DU BREUIL

BEAULIEU
1966

APPELLATION CONTRÔLÉE
COTEAUX DU LAYON   NICOLAS CHARENTON .VAL-DE-MARNE

145

with those of the Palatinate★, which are sold under this name.

However, there are some quality wines sold as Liebfraumilch, but the name of the seller is the only way of distinguishing these.

Leichtenstein Two-thirds of the small amount of wine produced by this tiny, independent principality, situated between Switzerland and Austria, is called Vaduzer (after the capital, Vaduz). Vaduzer is a .light red wine which is so clear that it almost appears to be a rosé. It is made exclusively from the Blauburgunder grape. The best cru is Abtwingert, a vineyard of the Rote Haus. The principality also produces other wines, including Schaaner, Triesner and Balzner.

light When applied to wine, this term is the opposite of full-bodied and heavy and is therefore a compliment. A light wine usually contains little alcohol, which makes it easy to drink.

liqueur (vin de) Wine which has kept a large amount of its natural sugar thanks to mutage★ by alcohol. Port is one of the best-known wines in this category, but certain Madeiras★ made from the Malvoisie grape are also vins de liqueur.

In France, the title has a very precise meaning. It is only applied to those wines muted with alcohol and whose alcoholic content is not greater than 23°. All the vins doux naturels★ fall into this category: Banyuls, Côtes-d'Agly and Frontignan, for example. However, for tax purposes, vins de liqueur are classified as spirits, while vins doux naturels are not.

The mutage is performed before or during fermentation, the proportion of added alcohol depending on the appellation. The degree of alcohol must be mentioned on the label, although this is not the case with vins doux naturels.

liqueur d'expédition A mixture of old wine and cane sugar which is added to Champagne★ immediately after dégorgement★. The liqueur fills the empty space left by the expulsion of sediment which had amassed next to the cork. The amount of liqueur d'expédition injected depends upon the desired taste: brut, extra dry, sec, demi-sec or doux. Some-

times, certain brands of Champagne use Cognac.

This dosage is called liqueur d'expédition because it is one of the last steps performed before Champagne leaves the premises (actually, the bottles remain for a few weeks before being shipped).

liqueur de tirage Provokes the sparkle in Champagne★, and vins mousseux★ made by the Champagne method★. First, the amount of natural sugar in the still wine is measured; then a certain amount of cane sugar dissolved in old wine, the liqueur de tirage, is added. A good sparkle is expected when the wine contains around 25 g of sugar per litre. If the wine does not contain enough sugar there will not be enough bubbles; if it contains too much, the pressure will burst the bottle.

Formerly, the exact quantity of the liqueur to be added was not known and in some years there was a great loss due to broken bottles. An ordinary bottle will not support an internal pressure five to six times atmospheric pressure, which is that of sparkling wines. Thus, special bottles of a certain thickness are necessary. These are carefully filled with the wine mixed with the liqueur de tirage. They are then corked with a provisional cork and wire, and laid down to rest for some time.

Lirac The vineyard of this village of the Côtes du Rhône★ occupies dry, flinty hills north of its neighbour Tavel★. The appellation Lirac is applied to excellent, vigorous, fragrant rosés, which are not quite as good as the Tavel wines. Lirac is made from the same varieties as Tavel, as well as the Syrah, Mourvèdre and Ugni Blanc, and is vinified with the same care, whether it be at Château de Segries, Château de Clary or a co-operative.

Lirac also produces powerful and generous red wines having a pronounced bouquet from the same varieties as the rosés, and fine, fragrant white wines from the Clairette.

Listrac A commune of the Haut-Médoc★ producing red wines which, without being highly classified, are nevertheless very good wines of a pretty ruby colour, full of body and nerve and possessing a certain finesse and agreeable bouquet.

Listrac has several good crus bourgeois supérieurs (Châteaux Fonréaud, Fourcas-Dupré, Lestage, Sémeillan, Clarke) and several good crus bourgeois. The co-operative cave at Listrac vinifies a wine comparble to the crus bourgeois supérieurs.

lively A lively wine proclaims its vivacity and bursts with health. Young and clear, it stimulates the palate because of its agreeable, but never overbearing, acidity.

Loir (Coteaux du) This vineyard occupies well-exposed hills bordering the Loir north of Tours in the departments of Sarthe and Indre-et-Loire. Although located on the boundary between Touraine, Anjou and Maine, it is actually a Touraine★ vineyard with which it shares the same soil, climate and grapes.

The vineyard used to be more famous than it is today. Ronsard and Rabelais sang of the vineyard of La Chartre and Henri IV praised the wines of the area.

The white wines made from the Pineau de la Loire are the best known. They are a beautiful golden colour, fine and fruity, often lightly sparkling and keep well – somewhat resembling the Vouvrays. They have an alcohol content around 10°, and are mainly produced by the communes of Château-du-Loir, Saint-Paterne, Chahaignes, Bueil and Vouvray-sur-Loir. The red wines are colourful, generous and fragrant. Saint-Aubin, Chenu, Nogent and Saint-Pierre-de-Chevillé all produce good reds.

The region also produces rosé wines and some twenty communes produce wines of the famous cru Jasnières★.

Loire The longest river in France can boast many well-known châteaux as well as magnificent wines. The wines of the Loire are produced from more than 200,000 ha of vineyards. Vineyards flourish on both banks from its source to the Atlantic, growing on various soils, experiencing different weather and planted in many grape varieties.

The appellations d'origine contrôlées★ include those of Nivernais and Berry★, Sauvignon★, Pouilly-sur-Loire★, Sancerre★, Menetou-Salon★, Quincy★ and Reuilly★; those of Touraine★: Vouvray★, Montlouis★, Chinon★ and Bourgueil★; those of Anjou: Saumur★, Coteaux-de-la-Loire★, Coteaux-du-Layon★ and Coteaux-de-l'Aubance★; and, finally, in

Luynes, Indre-et-Loire. The château in autumn. Phot. Phédon-Salou.

147

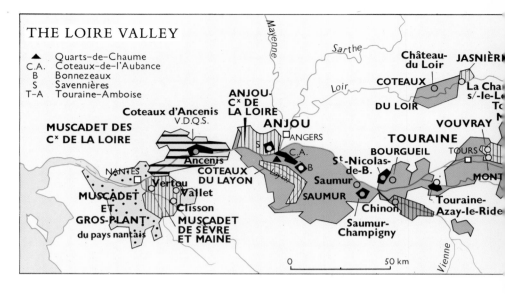

THE LOIRE VALLEY

▲ Quarts-de-Chaume
C.A. Coteaux-de-l'Aubance
B Bonnezeaux
S Savennières
T-A Touraine-Amboise

Mayenne

Sarthe

Loir

Château-du-Loir JASNIÈR

COTEAUX DU LOIR La Cha s/-le-Lo To

ANJOU-Cˣ DE LA LOIRE

Coteaux d'Ancenis V.D.Q.S.

ANJOU

ANGERS

VOUVRAY

MUSCADET DES Cˣ DE LA LOIRE

TOURAINE

BOURGUEIL

TOURS

S C.A.

Ancenis

St-Nicolas-de-B.

NANTES

COTEAUX DU LAYON

B

Saumur

MONT

Vertou

Saumur

MUSCADET ET GROS-PLANT du pays nantais

Vallet

Clisson

SAUMUR

Chinon

Touraine-Azay-le-Ride

MUSCADET DE SÈVRE ET MAINE

Saumur-Champigny

Vienne

0   50 km

the area of Nantes, the mischievous Muscadet★.

There are numerous VDQS★ wines from the Auvergne to Nantes: vins d'Auvergne★, Saint-Pourçain★, Château-meillant★, Coteaux-du-Giennois★, vins de l'Orléanais★, Montprés-Chambord-Cour-Cheverny, Coteaux-d'Ancenis★ and Gros Plant du pays nantais★.

Loire (Coteaux de la) The appellation contrôlée Anjou-Coteaux de la Loire is reserved for those communes located on the banks of the Loire★ around Angers:

Saint-Barthélemy, Brain-sur-l'Authion, Bourchemaine, Savennières★, La Possonnière, Saint-Georges, Champtocé and Ingrandes on the right bank; Montjean, La Pommeraye and a part of Chalonnes on the left bank. The vines grow on rocky hills next to the river and get plenty of exposure.

The white wines, made from the Pineau de la Loire, are not as sweet as those of Layon★. Fine and nervy, they are dry or semi-sweet and are always elegant wines with a fruity bouquet. The minimum alcohol content is 12°.

Ars-sur-Moselle. 'Vins de Moselle' is one of the two appellations reserved for the wines of Lorraine. Phot. M.

150

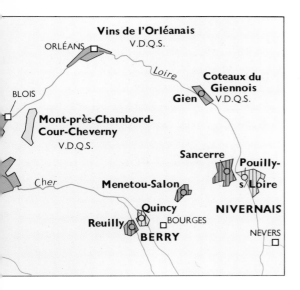

The village of Savennières has its own particular appellation contrôlée. The region also produces reds and rosés from the Cabernet which carry the appellation Anjou★.

The expression Coteaux de la Loire is also part of one of the three appellations contrôlées of the Nantes area, Muscadet des Coteaux de la Loire★.

Lorraine The wines of Lorraine, like those of Alsace, were at one time in great vogue. From the sixth to eighth centuries, the wines were in great demand and several of the large religious orders of Belgium and Luxembourg owned vineyards in the area. Later, the grapes were sold for making Champagne.

Today the vineyards possess only a shadow of their former glory. Wars, phylloxera★, disinterest by the youth in viticulture, and the replacement between 1904 and 1911 of most of the vineyards by orchards, have all taken their toll.

Although the vineyards only occupy about one-tenth of their area a century ago, some very good VDQS★ wines are produced. Two appellations designate the wines of Lorraine: Vins de la Moselle★ (Moselle) and Côtes-de-Toul★ (Meurthe-et-Moselle).

louche A louche wine is dull and feeble. This disorder may be caused by an incomplete alcoholic or malo-lactic fermentation or the onset of a microbial disease such as casse.

Loupiac This commune is situated on the right bank of the Garonne facing Barsac★. Although it is geographically part of the Premières Côtes de Bordeaux★, it forms a distinct region which has its own appellation.

Loupiac is a Sauternes-type wine made in the same way. Its qualities are similar to the neighbouring Sainte-Croix-du-Mont★. Full-bodied, fragrant and fine, Loupiac is an excellent, sweet white wine. The principal crus are those of the Châteaux of Ricaud, Gros, Loupiac-Gaudiet and Rondillon.

loyal A loyal wine is honest, sincere, and is also said to be frank. From a commercial point of view the expression designates a wine which can be delivered for sale without worrying about it undergoing any change. The complete expression is '*vin loyal et marchand*' (a loyal and saleable wine).

A tastevin is used to verify whether or not a wine is louche. Phot. M.

151

Lugana   A very pleasant dry white wine produced on the south bank of Lake Garda in northern Italy around the little village of Lugana. It is normally the best white in the region of the lake and is made from the Trebbiano, known in France as the Ugni Blanc (which is made into the white wine of Cassis). In Italy, the Trebbiano is also one of the two principal varieties from which Soave★ is made, and it also produces the white Chiantis★.

Lugana is a beautiful, pale golden coloured wine which is full-bodied and harmonious.

Lunel   A village between Nîmes and Montpellier in the Languedoc★ which produces an excellent AOC Muscat★. The production area includes the flinty terrains of Lunel, Lunel-Viel and Vérargues.

Like Frontignan★, the wine is made from the Muscat Doré and is a vin doux naturel of high quality, which is delicate and elegant. Although not as sweet as Frontignan, it has the same musky smell and taste of the grape.

Lussac-Saint-Emilion   This vineyard of the Lussac commune, which can add Saint-Emilion to its proper name, is found almost entirely on well-exposed hills. The wine is highly coloured and full-bodied and the good crus also have finesse. The principal Châteaux are those of Lyonnat, Bellevue,   Vieux-Chênes   and   Lion-Perruchon.

Lussac also produces white wine sold under the name Bordeaux or Bordeaux supérieur★.

Luxembourg   After leaving France and giving its name to certain wines of Lorraine★, the Moselle penetrates the Grand Duchy of Luxembourg before going on to Germany.

The wines of Luxembourg should not be ignored. Formerly part of the German Confederation, Luxembourg became independent in 1866 when Grand Duke Adolph of Nassau ascended the throne. Since then, Luxembourg has made great efforts to improve the quality of her wines. Viticulture is flourishing and production is

growing. Some 70% of the wine is consumed locally and the rest is bought by the Belgians.

Since 1935, the State has upheld a national standard, with every step in the vinicultural process subject to rigid standards and surveillance. The small neck label, the emblem of quality, is only awarded after severe controls.

As in Alsace, the wines of Luxembourg, which are nearly all white, are designated by the name of the grape from which they are made. They are light, clear wines which are low in alcohol and should be drunk chilled. Among them are Elbling, a popular, dry, refreshing vin de consommation courante; the light Riesling-Sylvaner which is mellower than Elbling and has a special fragrance; the supple, tender Auxerrois whose taste varies greatly from one year to the next, but unfortunately does not have any aroma; the slightly acidic, very fresh and fruity Pinot Blanc; the fragrant Ruländer (Pinot Gris) which is especially full-bodied in sunny years; the full-bodied, fragrant Traminer which has a touch of sweetness; and finally the fresh, distinguished Riesling which keeps well and has a discreet bouquet similar to that of German Moselle.

The most famous communes are Wormeldingen, Remich, Wintringen, Ehnen, Grevenmacher and Wasserbillig.

Lyons The third largest French city and a gastronomic capital which opens onto Beaujolais★ and the Côtes du Rhône★. From its founding as the Roman city Lugdunum in 43 BC until the advent of the railway, the town was known for its wine. It is often said that Lyons is watered not by two rivers, but by three: the Rhône, the Saône and the Beaujolais.

Lyonnais The Lyonnais region produces wines not unlike those of the neighbouring Beaujolais★. They share a similar geographical area, climate and grape variety – the white-juiced Gamay Noir.

There are three appellations among these VDQS★ wines: Vins du Lyonnais in

the Rhône department, Vins de Renaison-Côte Roannaise★ and Côtes-du-Forez★ in the department of the Loire.

The red wines under the appellation Vins du Lyonnais are fresh, fruity and light, but do not quite equal those of Beaujolais. The rosés are agreeable. The appellation also includes those whites made from the Chardonnay and Aligoté.

'The Vendage'. Apocalypse of Lorvão (1189), Torre do Tombo, Lisbon. Phot. Y. Loirat.

153

M

The château of Conches in the Mâconnais. Phot. René-Jacques.

Macadam The name under which the sweet white wines of Bergerac★ used to be sold. A good deal of the wine was sold in Paris and other large cities as vin bourru★.

Mâcon and Mâcon supérieur An appellation designating red, rosé and white wines. The white wines, made from the Chardonnay and Pinot Blanc, are dry, fruity and agreeable. They somewhat resemble the Pouillys, although with less finesse and body.

The reds and rosés are made from the white-juiced Gamay Noir, Pinot Gris or Pinot Noir. Nevertheless a 15% maximum of Gamay with coloured juice, or 15% of white vines (Gamay Blane, Aligoté, Pinot-Chardonnay) is tolerated. These make very good carafe wines which are fruity, like Beaujolais, but have more body.

Mâcon-Villages An appellation which is only applied to white wines, never reds. The wines having this appellation can sometimes add the name of the commune (e.g. Mâcon-Viré).

Mâconnais A vineyard around the city of Mâcon which had a very good reputation until the seventeenth century. The area stretches from a point near

Tournus through the Saône-et-Loire department to the limit of Beaujolais. Although production is mainly white wine, there are some excellent red and rosé table wines which are full-bodied and fruity. They are best when drunk young although they can be kept for a long time.

The famous Pouilly-Fuissé★, made from the Chardonnay grape, is the pride of Mâconnais. The two neighbouring appellations, Pouilly-Vinzelles★ and Pouilly-Loché★, although very similar in character and quality, do not attain the standard of Pouilly-Fuissé. The other appellations of Mâconnais are Mâcon and Mâcon supérieur★ for the reds, whites and rosés, Mâcon-Villages★ solely for whites and, since 1971, Saint-Véran.

Madeira A wine made on the Portuguese island of the same name. Some 25% of the cultivated area of Madeira is devoted to viticulture, the grapes being grown between 350 and 600 metres altitude.

Madeira, which has been famous for over 400 years, was a great favourite of Americans in the Colonial period. Ships called at the island on their way from Europe to America and took on board casks of Madeira for Charleston, Philadelphia, New York and Boston. The sea voyage seemed to improve the wine. British officers returning home after the American War of Independence brought with them a liking for the wine they had drunk in the Colonies.

Today, America and the Scandinavian countries are the principal importers of Madeira, with France also a good client.

Madeira is muted with alcohol like the vins doux naturels. The characteristic bouquet is obtained by a maturation period in heated cellars called *estufas*. There are various kinds of Madeira, ranging from very dry to very sweet and from a pale straw colour (Rainwater) to a sombre gold (Malmsey). Sercial, the dryest, often has a very special bouquet. It is excellent served chilled as an apéritif.

Vendange in the Mâconnais. Phot. René-Jacques.

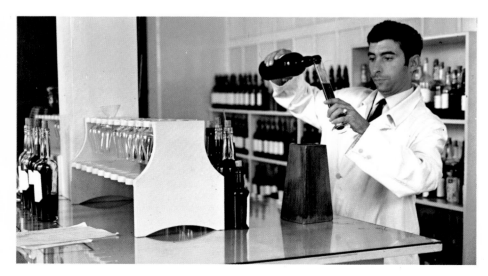

Oenological laboratory in Madeira. Phot. F. Roiter, Casa de Portugal.

Madeira: 19th-century mosaic 'azulejos', which depicts wine being transported by sled.
Phot. F. Roiter, Casa de Portugal.

Others include Verdelho which is less brilliant than Sercial, the sweeter and more golden Boal and the suave, fragrant dessert wine Malvasia (Malvoisie).

Madeira of Périgord The Dutch term for Monbazillac, which was an important trade item from the fourteenth century. The repeal of the Edict of Nantes sent 40,000 protestants from the region as immigrants to Holland. Relatives and, later, traders supplied them with their favourite wine which may have received its name from its physical resemblance to Madeira.

maderise To oxidise a wine. As one oenologist put it, 'a maderised wine is like rancid butter'. The term is usually applied to white and rosé wines. Maderised wine is quite apparent to the eye: white wine takes on a characteristic amber tint and rosé, a brickish colour. The taste is also altered. The wine acquires a Madeira-like flavour from which the term is derived.

Madiran A powerful red wine of the Sud-Ouest★ produced north-east of Pau and north-west of Tarbes in the Pyrenees, on the same communes as the Pacherenc-du-Vic-Bihl★. The red wine, which used to be so popular, lost favour for quite some time and is only just coming back into vogue, the vineyards having been re-planted some twenty years ago.

The Tannat grape gives the wine its dark colour and generosity, while the Bouchy or Cabernet Franc adds finesse. Although, from the beginning of the nineteenth century, the Tannat was nearly the only grape cultivated, the growers are now returning to the traditional varieties. The appellation contrôlée is given to wines made from the Tannat (30% to 50%), the Bouchy (50%) and the Pinenc (or Fer★) which contain 11° alcohol.

Wine from the Tannat is better in its youth, but conserves well. The wine used to be matured in cask for thirty-two months, but the period has been shortened to twenty months. The vigorous Madiran is sometimes compared to the Burgundies.

magnum A bottle whose capacity is double that of a normal bottle. It is often used for red wines and Champagne. Red wine is supposed to mature more slowly in larger bottles and can be kept longer. Thus reds of great years are often bottled in magnum. However, this bottling does not add any qualities to Champagne; on the contrary, the wine may wear out more quickly than in a normal-size bottle.

Malaga A famous Spanish fortified wine produced around the town of Malaga in Andalusia, southern Spain. It is a sweet, fragrant, generous, dark brown wine made from Pedro Ximénez and Muscat grapes. The best, called P.X., is sweetened by the addition of wine from Pedro Ximénez grapes which have been sun-dried.

The cheaper Malagas are sweetened with *arrope*, the juice of a grape which has been concentrated by boiling, and which yields only one-fifth of its original volume, imparting a brown tint and caramel taste to the wine. Malaga, like sherry, is matured by the Solera system.

Malta Most of the vineyards are found on the south coast of this island, with the majority of production consumed as table grapes. The Maltese wines, whether they be red or white, are very ordinary and often astringent and rough, totally lacking softness. The torrid summer and torrential rains are not conducive to the production of good quality wines.

However, the island does produce a sweet, full-bodied dessert wine from the Muscat grape which is exported to the United Kingdom.

Malvoisie   The wine originally bearing this name was made in Monemvasia, Greece, from the Malvoisie grape. As the grape was transported around the Mediterranean, its name was often changed, e.g., it was called Malvoisie in France, Malvagia in Spain and Malvasia in Italy. Malvoisie is not an appellation of origin but designates a wine made from the Malvoisie grape, whether it comes from Crete, Madeira or elsewhere. In Britain, such a wine is called Malmsey, and is a variety of Madeira.

mannite   Although rarely encountered in northern viticultural areas, this wine disease used to be quite common in the hot regions of the Midi and Algeria, where it caused a great deal of damage. The bacteria occurs in cuves which are warmer than normal and supplants the yeasts, imparting a strange, sickly sweet, sour taste to the wine.

Manzanilla   Although it legally has the right to the name sherry, Manzanilla is totally different, even though it is made from the same grapes and by the same methods. Some say the Atlantic sea breeze which blows through the vineyards and *bodegas* is the reason for this diversity.

Manzanilla is produced west of Jerez around the little town of Sanlucar de Barramedo. The word Manzanilla is the diminutive of Manzana, and is a combination of the Spanish for camomille and apple. However, Manzanilla has no connection with cider and even less with the herb camomille. When prepared for local consumption and not export, Manzanilla is a very clear wine of about 15–17° alcohol. It is an extremely dry wine with a very pronounced bouquet and a slightly bitter taste which some consider salty. Like sherry, Manzanilla becomes darker and its alcohol content rises when aged in casks. Some brown, full-bodied sherrys reach an alcohol level of 21°.

Manzanillas are classified into five types: Manzanilla Pasada, Manzanilla Olorosa, Manzanilla Fina, Manzanilla and Amanzanillado.

Marcillac   The wines from this Sud-Ouest★ vineyard north of Rodez have recently been classified VDQS★. The vineyards flank the hillsides in eleven communes including Marcillac-Vallon, Balsac, Clairvaux and Saint-Christophe-Vallon.

The excellent red wine, which ages well, is smooth and colourful with a raspberry bouquet. It is made from the Fer★, locally called 'Mansois', blended

with Gamay, Jurançon Noir, Merlot and Cabernet. The rosés and whites have less *race*★, the latter being made from Sémillon, Mauzac, Clairette and Muscat grapes.

Marcobrunn   A famous German vineyard which is one of the best of the Rheingau★. It takes its name from the *Marcobrunnen*, a charming little fountain which marks the boundary between the villages of Erbach and Hattenheim. Marcobrunner is a fruity, full-bodied wine with *race*★ and an astonishing bouquet.

Malaga: maturation caves.
Phot. Pedro Domecq.

157

The wines from Erbach are generally sold as Erbacher Marcobrunn, and those of Hattenheim as simply Marcobrunner.

Margaux This famous communal appellation of the Médoc★ is applied to the commune of that name as well as the neighbouring ones of Cantenac, Soussans, Arsac and Labarde. Margaux wines have a suave bouquet and are exceptionally delicate. Velvety and elegant, they are generous without being too full-bodied. The premier cru is Château Margaux★, followed by Châteaux Rauzan-Ségla, Rauzan-Gassies and Durfort-Vivens. (See Index.)

Damery and Hautvilliers, in whose abbey Dom Pérignon★ perfected the Champagne method★.

marque (vin de) Brand name wines without appellation of origin which are produced by blending, and are sometimes of good quality. Wines from different regions are selected by the négociant★ who blends them according to the amounts particular to each trademark. In order to avoid confusion with appellations of origin, certain words are prohibited on the label of these wines: *clos, château, tour, domaine, cru, mont, moulin, côte* and *camp* (but the word *monopole* is tolerated). The

Margaux, famous communal appellation of the Médoc. Phot. M.

Margaux (Château-) The premier cru of the commune of Margaux★ and one of the greatest red wines of Bordeaux. Château-Margaux is a delicate, velvety, suave, well-balanced wine with an incomparable bouquet. The vineyard also produces a small amount of white wine sold under the name 'Pavillon-Blanc-de-Château-Margaux'.

Marne (Valley of the) An important Champagne★ vineyard found between Epernay and Dormans★ on both banks of the river and continuing into the Aisne department.

The 'wines of the river' are light and tender and have been important commercially since the ninth century. Ay is the most famous cru, and others include Mareuil-sur-Ay, Avenay, Cumières,

alcohol degree must be stated on the label, although the name and address of the *négociant* does not.

Marsala The most famous of the Italian vins de liqueur★, obtained by mutage of the must with alcohol. The wine is produced around the village of Marsala in western Sicily. In the second half of the eighteenth century, several English families living on the island desired a wine similar to sherry and created Marsala.

The wine is a beautiful amber colour, sometimes dry, but often sweet. It is produced by a strictly delimited region from Grillo, Catarratto and Inzolia grapes.

The original Marsala, called Marsala Vergini or Solera, is a dry wine containing 17 or 18° alcohol which has been blended and aged in casks. A sweeter wine is obtained by adding *sifone*, a concentrated, sugary grape juice of a syrupy consistency.

The official names of the different types of Marsala are, besides Marsala Vergini, Italia, the lightest and cheapest of the Marsalas, containing about 5% *sifone* and 17° alcohol, and Marsala Fini or Italia Particolare (or I.P.). Many Marsalas are exported as Marsalas superiori. They have an alcohol content of 18° and can be dry or sweet depending on the amount of *sifone* added.

Many of the Italian apéritifs have a Marsala base, e.g. Marsala Chinato (with added quinine) and Marsala all'uovo (with eggs).

Marsannay-la-Côte A Côte-d'Or village famous for its rosé, made from the Pinot Noir, and which is one of the lightest, freshest and most delicious French rosés.

The formal appellation contrôlée is Bourgogne-Marsannay-la-Côte.

Mascara An appellation applied to Algerian★ wines produced south-east of Oran, which were classified VDQS★ before independence. The reds and rosés are generous and full-bodied but lack finesse, and the whites are rather ordinary. Mascara wines were made from grapes

growing on limestone hills about 200 metres high, while those having the appellation Coteaux-de-Mascara were cultivated at between 600–800 metres. These colourful reds are full-bodied, heady and velvety, having a violet fragrance, while the rosés and whites are both fragrant and fruity.

maturation (control of) Thanks to the work of the INAO★ and the Institut Technique du Vin, French viticulturists know the best moment at which to begin the vendange. A team of professionals regularly test the grapes on different parts of the vine, beginning some three weeks before the supposed date of the vendange. The specimens are analysed in the laboratory and the results sent to the mayor and published in the local papers.

Two curves represent the evolution of maturity: the decreasing curve is that representing acidity, and the increasing one, the sugar level. The level of maturity is the balance between sugar and acidity, which differs depending on the year and grape variety. During the final days of maturation, the grape juice often shows a daily increase of 10–20 g of sugar per litre.

Maury Perched on a hill in an arid valley bordered by the ridges of Corbières

The Marne valley from Epernay. In the foreground, the vineyards of Moët et Chandon. Phot. Lauros.

and Albèze is the little town of Maury, which lends its name to the famous vin doux naturel★ of Roussillon★. The vines grow on schistose, rocky hills scorched by the sun.

Maury is a great wine which is usually red. A vin doux naturel, it is velvety, sweet and powerful and is made from the Grenache Noir.

measures Officially, the litre, along with its multiples, is the only measure of volume recognised by law. But old mea-sures better adapted to the wines of different regions are still used.

The basis of each unit of measure is the container used by the labourers in the vineyards, and the measures therefore vary from region to region. As a result, we have the terms barrique★, muid★, pièce★, tonneau★, feuillette★ and tierçon.

méchage (fumigation) An operation which consists of releasing sulphur dioxide★ by burning a wick of sulphur. Fumigation of amphoras was practised by

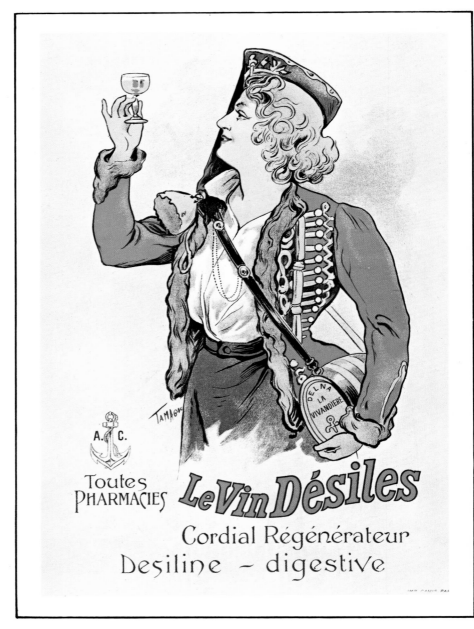

Poster advertisement for a medicinal wine. Coloured engraving by Tamagno (1900). Phot. Lauros.

160

the Romans, and for a long time it was the only source of sulphur dioxide at the disposal of the vigneron. The method is still used to sterilise casks. Before wine is transferred into a cask it is cleansed with about 3 g of sulphur per hl of capacity.

Médéa (Coteaux-de-) Algerian wines produced south of Algiers which were classified VDQS★ before 1958. The vineyard, located on sandy or chalky hills 600–1200 metres high, gives full-bodied reds having finesse and an agreeable bouquet. Although pleasant, the whites do not come up to the standard of the reds.

médecin (vin) A wine added to blends to improve feeble wines. Such a wine is usually very colourful, rich in alcohol, and has a high proportion of dry extracts.

Before it was appreciated as a wine in its own right, Corbières du Roussillon was greatly sought after for this purpose. Other wines in this category include Algerian wines, wines made from the Raboso grape and the red wines of Cahors★, called 'black wines' because of their sombre colour.

medicinal wines Along with vins de liqueur★ and highly spiced wines, these have been a speciality of Languedoc since as early as 1251, as an order from the King of England for clove and nutmeg wines from Montpellier attests. Montpellier's fame for producing medicinal wines is due, no doubt, to its school of medicine which was famous in the Middle Ages and inspired Arabian medicine. Medicinal wines are still used today, the proportion of wine being fixed by law at 80% of total volume. The best known are wines utilising coca, quinine, cola, gentian and the wines of Trousseau and Charité.

Médoc The Médoc occupies a triangular peninsula bordered by the Atlantic on the west, the Gironde estuary on the east and a line connecting Arcachon and Bordeaux on the south. Vineyards only occupy the eastern part of the Médoc, covering an area about eighty km long and ten km wide.

The Médoc is divided into two regions: the Haut-Médoc, from Blanquefort to Saint-Seurin-de-Cadourne, and the Bas-Médoc which stretches from the northern

limit of the Haut-Médoc to the estuary, and has its centre at Lesparre.

The subsoil of the Médoc, consisting of clay, flint and hard limestone, is covered by a pebbly layer called *grave* which, although not very fertile, is especially suited to the vine. The best wine is made from vines growing on this gravelly crust facing the river. (The wines from the recently deposited alluvial soil are not entitled to the appellation Médoc, and are sold as Bordeaux★ or Bordeaux supérieur★.) The principal grapes are the Cabernet Franc, Cabernet-Sauvignon, Merlot and Malbec.

The Médoc only produces red wines and these have a great reputation. A bit astringent in youth because of their high tannin content, they have vigour, bouquet and finesse and keep very well. All the elements are balanced, and they possess certain dietetic qualities which have earned them the respect of many doctors.

There is no Bas-Médoc appellation, the wines of this region being called Médoc. The wines of the Haut-Médoc, which are usually superior to the Médocs, have the appellation Haut-Médoc.

Montpellier: the school of medicine for which medieval Languedoc was famous because of its medicinal wines.
Phot. Bottin.

161

Médoc: view of Château Palmer. In the foreground, a worker prunes the vines.
Phot. M.

The best regions of the Haut-Médoc, where the illustrious crus are found, also have a communal appellation. The most famous are Margaux★, Saint-Julien★, Pauillac★, Saint-Estèphe★, Listrac★ and Moulis★. (See Index.)

Menetou-Salon An AOC applied to wines from this commune south of Sancerre★, as well as several neighbouring communes including Morogues, Parassy, Aubinges and Soulangis. The Sauvignon grows very well on the limestone hills of this Loire vineyard and produces wines similar to Sancerre, although with less finesse. The appellation is also used for reds and rosés made from the Pinot, but production is insignificant.

mer (vins pour la) A title which was formerly applied to the better Loire wines, produced between Blois and the coast, which were to be exported. In 1789 the Customs Department at Ingrandes imposed a heavy tax on wines shipped to Nantes and from there abroad. The vignerons of Touraine, Anjou and Orléans could not afford to pay this high duty on their excellent wines. As a result, Dutch and Belgian traders came up the Loire in barges as far as Rochefort and Ponts-de-Cé, and set off for the sea with their precious cargo of wines. As the better wines of the area, the *vins pour la mer* were

exported and the inferior wines, *vins de terre*, were sent to Paris, often to be blended. France for a long time neglected the wines of Saumur and Anjou for this reason. However, she has now made up for lost time.

Mercurey This appellation is applied almost exclusively to red wines produced on the communes of Mercurey, Saint-Martin-sous-Montaigu and Bourgneuf-Val-d'Or, on the Côte Chalonnaise★. The wines have a beautiful red robe, are warm and vivacious while remaining light, and have a bouquet similar to Cassis. Their finesse and distinction are similar to that of certain wines of the Côte de Beaune★. The appellation Mercurey can be followed, in some circumstances, by the expression premier cru or the name of the climat of origin. (See Index.)

The white wine is practically never sold commercially and is often very delicate.

Mesland The Mesland vineyard of Loir-et-Cher is geographically the final point of the Touraine vineyards. It extends over Mesland, Monteaux, Onzain and Chouzy and produces a large volume of white, red and rosé wines having the appellation Touraine, followed by the name of Mesland. The fine, light white wines made from the Pineau are delicious when young, but production is limited.

162

The region is particularly devoted to rosés made from the Gamay, which owe their delicacy to the granitic soil. The rosés of Touraine-Mesland are clear, light and fruity, especially in their youth. The best are dry, as the sweeter ones tend to lose their character. The whites and rosés must contain 10·5° alcohol, and the reds, 10°.

Meursault The great white vineyards of Burgundy begin at Meursault. Although the Côte de Nuits★ and the communes of the Côte de Beaune★, north of Meursault, produce good quality white wines, the Pinot-Chardonnay★ begins its reign at Meursault.

The white wines of Meursault, classed among the best whites of France, are both dry and marrowy. A rich, golden colour, limpid and brilliant, full-bodied and developing a rich bouquet, they are famous for their suavity. The best climats are les Perrières, les Genévrières, les Charmes and Goutte-d'Or. (See Index.)

Meursault also produces great reds which are fine, rich in bouquet and very powerful. They are little known, being eclipsed by the whites. The reds have the appellation Volnay-Sante-Nots and are made from the Meursault.

Mexico Although vineyards occupy about 10,000 ha, the country produces only about 40,000 hl of wine per year, three-quarters of production being sold as table grapes. The national drink of Mexico has an alcohol base fermented from cane sugar. As the tropical climate is not really conducive to the vine, the vineyards are mainly found on the peninsula of Lower California and in the Sierra Madre around Durango and Chihuahua, where the altitude helps to balance some of the defects imposed by climate.

The majority of Mexican wines are of mediocre quality, with the exception of those produced at Ensenada, on the US border around the old Spanish mission of Santo Tomás, but even these are no better than heavy vins ordinaires.

The principal producers of Mexican wines include the following firms: Compania Vinicola de Saltilla, Bodegas del Marques de Aguayo, Bodegas de Delicias and the best known, Bodegas de Santo Tomás in Lower California.

Midi (vin du) A Midi wine is usually a red ordinaire from the large production area of Languedoc★-Roussillon★ which includes the departments of the Aude,

Meursault and its vineyards.
Phot. Aarons-L.S.P.

163

The effect of mildew.
Phot. M.

until the railway penetrated the area that they became known in other parts of the country. The expression vin du Midi is not necessarily slighting. When well vinified and honestly prepared, the wines are a healthy, family drink. The most common grapes, the Aramon, Carignan, Oeillade and Petit-Bouschet, seem to have somewhat replaced the old noble★ varieties: the Muscat, Grenache, Macabéo and Malvoisie.

mildew A destructive mould seen for the first time in France in 1878 and believed to have been imported from America. It attacks the leaves (causing them to dry up and fall) and the grapes (making them turn brown and also drop). The survivors produce an acidic wine containing little alcohol. The treatment, which consists of spraying with copper sulphate, was discovered accidentally by a vigneron who habitually sprayed his vines blue with copper sulphate before the harvest to ward off plunderers. Only these grapes seemed to resist the mildew.

Copper was unobtainable during the Occupation, and other synthetic products such as Captane and Dithane were developed.

Hérault, Pyrénées-Orientales and Gard. The area accounts for more than half of France's total wine production.

Vineyards have flourished in this region from the eighteenth century, but it was not

General view of Minerve.
Phot. M.

Bottling in the caves of Thuir (P.-O.). Phot. M.

millerandage (shot berries) An ailment caused by incomplete fertilisation of the flowers of the vine, which results in very small grapes lacking pips.

mince (thin) An adjective describing a wine which is light in alcohol and has insufficient bouquet and flavour. A wine which is exceptionally thin is termed *maigre* or *grêle* (skinny).

Minervois This VDQS★ wine of Languedoc★ takes its name from the historic capital Minerve. Minervois occupies an immense circular area north of Corbières★ and west and north-west of Narbonne. The climate is warm and dry and the vineyards enjoy well-exposed positions on the hillsides and in the valleys. Roman soldiers, who colonised the Narbonne area, introduced viticulture and the wines rapidly became famous, being praised by Pliny the Younger and Cicero.

Although some whites and dry, fruity rosés are produced, the red wines are superior and, along with Corbières, are the best in the region. The reds are made from the traditional Languedoc grapes, Grenache, Cinsault and Carignan, and age well. They have a lively, red robe and are fine, fruity, delicate and well balanced with a characteristic bouquet and flavour.

mise en bouteilles à la propriété This phrase on a wine label attests that the wine was bottled by the producer in the same place it was vinified. Thus it is a guarantee of quality and authenticity; for example, it would not appear if a proprietor's wine was sent to a bottler.

Other terms have a similar meaning: *mise en bouteille au domaine* (or *mise du domaine*), *mise d'origine*, estate bottled and *mise en bouteilles au château*★ (used in the Gironde). In Burgundy, where there are few châteaux, the name of the wine *négociant*★ is referred to and this name becomes the guarantee of quality and authenticity.

On the other hand, the term *mise en bouteille par le propriétaire* or *mise en bouteille dans nos chais* is no guarantee that the wine has been bottled at the original château or domaine, nor is the mere mention of the name of a château or domaine.

mistelle The name given to the must of grapes to which alcohol has been added in a proportion of 5–10% to arrest fermentation. The operation is rigidly controlled, as is the use of mistelles. Before 1958, Algeria was a large producer of mistelles as the climate produced grapes having a high sugar content whose musts were powerful and rich in alcohol. The first mistelles were produced at Mostaganem in 1880 and, by 1910, Algeria was the largest producer of mistelles used in producing French apéritifs, and false Madeiras and Malagas as well. From 1940 Algeria continued to send mistelles to the French producers, but no longer made the vin de liqueur herself.

moelleux A white wine termed moelleux or marrowy is one whose sweetness is

vineyards, they are gradually being replaced by European varieties. The best white wine produced in Moldavia is the Aligoté, while Kaberné, which has a violet fragrance, and Bordeaux wines are the best reds.

The château of Monbazillac. Phot. M.

between that of a vin blanc liquoreux★ and a vin sec★. There is no precise rule for applying this term, but some consider that a wine containing 6–15 g of natural unfermented sugar should be considered moelleux.

Moldavia The second largest viticultural area of Russia and producer of one-third of all USSR wines.

The vine is cultivated in the valleys, particularly in the Dniestr valley around the towns of Kichinev, Oungheni, Rezina, Tiraspol and Bendery.

Although hybrids★ still dominate the

Monbazillac This famous, sweet white wine (vin blanc liquoreux★) of Dordogne is an appellation contrôlée of the Sud-Ouest★, which is sometimes wrongly classified as a Bordeaux. The vineyards flank the hills on the left bank of the Dordogne south of Bergerac★ in the communes of Monbazillac, Pomport, Colombier, Rouffignac and a section of Saint-Laurent-des-Vignes. The grapes are the same as those of Sauternes★: Sémillon, which gives flavour and moelleux★, Sauvignon, which assures finesse and body and Muscadelle, which gives a Muscat aroma.

As at Sauternes, the harvest is performed in successive stages when the pourriture noble★ has withered the grapes. Fermentation is slow, sometimes taking several months, during which time an important quantity of glycerine is produced which gives the wine its marvellous smoothness. Monbazillac contains a minimum of 12·5° alcohol and its sugar level varies from 30–100 g per litre. In good years Monbazillac is the richest of the French vin blancs liquoreux, containing 15–16° alcohol and 80–100 g of sugar per litre.

Monbazillac has been exported to northern Europe since the fourteenth century. The French émigrés of the region who fled to Holland after the revocation of the Edict of Nantes spread its fame and, in the eighteenth century, all the wine of Monbazillac was sent to Holland. In its youth Montbazillac has a lovely straw-coloured robe which becomes more or less amber with time, and the wine itself improves with age. This fine wine smells of honey and is particularly suave.

Although it bears some relationship to Sauternes, the two should not really be compared as each has very individual characteristics.

Mondeuse An excellent red and white grape which grows mainly in Savoie★ and the neighbouring region of Bugey★. The red Mondeuse produces a very good, fruity, light table wine whose bouquet, smelling of violet, raspberry and sometimes of truffle, develops with age. The delicious rosé of Montagnieu, a wine of Bugey, is made principally from the Mondeuse.

Montagne-Saint-Emilion The commune of Montagne has the privilege of adding Saint-Emilion★ to its name. Two distinct areas of the vineyard produce very different wines. The wine made from grapes grown on limestone soil found at higher altitudes are full-bodied, colourful and robust; the lower, flinty-clay soil gives a lighter, more supple wine resembling those of Pomerol★ and St Emilion. Some crus mix the two kinds of wine.

The best châteaux are Montaiguillon, Tours, Négrit, Roudier and Corbin.

Montagny An appellation of the Côte Chalonnaise★ applied to fresh, light, fragrant white wines made from the Chardonnay grape.

Montesquieu Venerated by the Bordelais, not only for his writings which include 'Esprit des Lois' and 'Lettres Persanes', but also for his love of the grape – as the vigneron of La Brède. He wrote, 'I do not want to make my fortune in the Court, I dream of making it from the value of my land.'

Montesquieu, the gentleman vigneron of La Brède. 18th-century French School, Musée du Château de Versailles. Phot. Giraudon.

Montilla An excellent Spanish wine made from vines growing on arid limestone hills around the villages of Montilla and Los Moriles, south of Cordoue. Until recently most of the production was sold to Jerez as sherry (the word Amontillado originally was applied to the type of sherry made from the wine of Montilla) but Montilla has recently been given its own particular appellation.

Montilla is made from the Pedro Ximénez grape which, according to legend, is really the Riesling of the Rhine Valley, having been introduced in Spain by a German soldier named Peter Siemens. The wine produced from this grape is more alcoholic than that from the Palomino from which sherry is made.

Unlike sherry, Montilla is unfortified, as its own alcohol content is sufficiently high. Like sherry it is a flor★ wine, vinified in *bodegas* and aged by the Solera system. However, it is not aged in wooden casks in

its youth as sherry, but in enormous man-sized jars called *tinajas,* which are similar to Roman amphoras.

Montilla can be a Fino- or Oloroso-type sherry, the latter being rare. It is generally a clear, dry wine, which is perhaps easier to drink and more agreeable than Manzanilla and Fino sherry, because it has less body and bouquet. It is delicious as an apéritif and with sea food, and is served chilled as are all the dry, sherry-type wines.

Montlouis Opposite Vouvray★ between Tours and Ambiose, the charming village of Montlouis snuggles in a bend of the left bank of the Loire★. The white wines, made from the Pineau de la Loire, are similar to Vouvray, and were sold under that name until 1938. However, after a long lawsuit, Montlouis was forbidden to use the appellation Vouvray on her wines. The soil, grape and methods of viticulture and vinification are identical at Vouvray and Montlouis, but the Loire separates the two.

The wines of Montlouis offer the same range as those of Vouvray: secs, demi-secs, liquoreux, tranquilles, pétillants and mousseux. They have less body and more *sève*★ with an expanding aroma. They can be drunk as young and keep just as well because of their lightness and great finesse.

Montpeyroux VDQS★ reds and rosés of Languedoc★ produced on the hills north of Béziers. These are very good wines, especially the reds, being full-bodied and beautifully coloured.

Mont-près-Chambord-Cour-Cheverny This vineyard, whose name recalls two famous châteaux of the Loire, stretches twelve km south-west of Blois to the boundary of Sologne. Its wines have been classified VDQS★ since 1951. Four communes share the appellation: Mont-près-Chambord, Cour-Cheverny, Cheverny and Huisseau-sur-Cosson. The characteristic grape, the Romorantin, grows well in the flinty soil, but a mixture of the Sauvignon and Pineau de la Loire is also authorised. These white wines, nearly all of which are vinified at the co-operative of Mont, are light, rarely surpassing 11° alcohol. Sec, sometimes demi-sec, agreeable, fresh and fruity, they are mainly

Château de Cheverny: the grounds and facade.
Phot. Giraudon.

consumed locally, although a few make their way to Paris.

Montrachet The greatest white wine of Burgundy, a title no-one disputes. This dry, sumptuous, powerful, velvety wine is absolutely perfect. Everything is admirable, from its pale golden robe tinged with green to its suave bouquet and rich flavour. Montrachet is certainly the best vin blanc sec, as Château-d'Yquem is the best vin blanc liquoreux.

Montravel An appellation contrôlée of the Sud-Ouest★ applied to white wines produced on the right bank of the Dordogne in the canton of Vélines. Although it occupies an area of Bordeaux, Montravel is not a Bordeaux appellation.

The region of Montravel has been called the cellar of Montaigne. Montaigne was born at Saint-Michel and seems to have been an admirer of the wines, of which he said, 'drinking little and moderately is too much of a restraint on the gifts of this God'.

Made from the Sémillon, Sauvignon and Muscadelle, the white wines of Montravel are divided into three appellations contrôlées: Montravel, the wine of the plain containing 10·5° alcohol, Côtes-de-Montravel and Haut-Montravel, both containing at least 11° and often more. These are moelleux or liquoreux wines of undeniable charm, which are fine and well balanced with a particular sève★ or vigour and fragrance.

An excellent red wine is also produced around Vélines under the appellation contrôlée Bergerac★.

Monts-du-Tessala An appellation applied to a group of Algerian★ wines produced south of Oran, which were classified VDQS★ before independence (Oued Imbert Lauriers Roses, M'Silah, Crêtes des Berkêches and Parmentier). These wines, made from grapes harvested on various soils at about 600 m altitude, were among the finest of Oran. A beautiful red colour, with a subtle raspberry fragrance, the wines of Tessala are full-bodied like all the Algerian wines, but they are also fine, delicate, fruity, velvety and smooth.

Morey-Saint-Denis The great red wines produced by this commune have distinction and a rich strawberry, violet or sometimes truffle bouquet.

The famous climats are Bonnes-Mares, Clos Saint-Denis, Clos de la Roche and Clos de Tart. The cru Bonnes-Mares is applied to the communes of Morey-Saint-Denis and Chambolle-Musigny.

Morgon The wine of Morgon is completely different from the other crus of Beaujolais. Some say it has too much Burgundy and not enough Beaujolais. With its deep garnet colour, currant and kirsch bouquet, generous and robust constitution, full, firm body and its ability to age well, it is evidently in a class apart from the other Beaujolais. Morgon is not as fruity as other Beaujolais but lasts a lot longer. In describing a wine similar to Morgon, the term *morgonne* is used. Le Py, a hill overflowing with vines, is the pride of Morgon.

Morocco This country was producing wine even in the days of ancient Rome.

Montaigne, son of Montravel.
Musée Condé, Chantilly.
Phot. Giraudon.

The principal viticultural areas are found in the eastern part of the country around Berkane and Oujda, Taza, Fèz, Meknès, Rabat and Casablanca. Others are located in the south between Safi and Mogador, along the Tensift wadi and in the mountainous region of Bon Assida.

Morocco has no grand crus, and reds and rosés make up the majority of production as the whites have a tendency to maderise in the hot climate. The country also produces sparkling wines, dessert wines and vins gris (vin gris de Demnate). The fragrant, heady reds are made from the Cinsault, Carignan, Grenache and Alicanti-Bouschet.

The north-east region produces the Muscat of Beikani and excellent rosés similar to those of Algeria. In the centre, Taza makes a wine which is used for blending. The reds produced in Meknès have the best reputation of Moroccan wines – they are full-bodied, colourful and have a characteristic fragrance. East of Rabat, the colourful Dar Bel Hamri is made around Sidi Slimane.

Although the red wines made around Casablanca are drunk very young, they can improve with age. Dry and fruity vins gris, considered a speciality of the country, are produced at Boulaouane and El Jadida.

Although some appellations of origin are printed on Moroccan wine labels, the system has nothing to do with the French classifications. The Moroccan Ministry of Agriculture has inaugurated quality control for wines and vines. Only healthy wines which meet the specified standards, which include an alcohol level of at least 11°, are eligible for export.

Moselle Before joining the Rhine at Koblenz, the Moselle flows past miles of different vineyards. In France, it passes the VDQS★ wines of Lorraine which have the appellation Vins de la Moselle★; further on, it passes the wines of Luxembourg★; and finally it reaches Germany, where it gives its name to world-famous vineyards.

The German vineyards, planted almost exclusively in Riesling, occupy steep slopes alongside the river starting at Trèves. The most favoured wines come from that part of the valley (Middle Moselle) which extends from Trittenheim to Traben-Trarbach. The best communes are Piesport, Bernkastel, Graach, Wehlen, Zeltingen and Brauneberg.

Moselle vineyards are also found in the valleys of its two small tributaries, the Sarre and Ruhr, in the communes of Wiltingen, Kanzem, Oberemmel, Ockfen, and Ayl (Sarre), and Maximin Grunhaus and Eitelsbach (Ruhr). The official name of the region is Mosel-Saar-Ruhr.

170

In poor years the wines are thin, deceptive and often very acidic, but in good years they are, without doubt, the most fragrant, delicate and *racé*★ of all the German wines. Clear and limpid, with their characteristic bouquet which is both flowery and spicy, they have an incomparable distinction.

The label of Moselle wines bears the usual terms of German wines: the name of the commune, the name of the vineyard of origin and an indication of selected picking (Spätlese, Auslese, etc.).

Moselle (vins de la)   This appellation is applied to VDQS★ wines of Lorraine★ produced in three different areas of the Moselle department: Sierck in the north near the Luxembourg border, Metz and Vic-sur-Seille, near Château Salins.

The red, rosé and white wines are made from the Gamay of Liverdun, Auxerrois Blanc and Gris, Pinot Noir and Pinot Blanc, Sylvaner and Riesling. The wines differ depending on the area of production: Sierck, for example, produces mainly white wines, Metz, light rosés (clairet of the Moselle), and Vic-sur-Seille, vins gris. The whites and rosés are very light and fruity and sometimes have a disconcerting acidity; the reds are light, but have less charm (Vic, Ancy, Jussy).

Mostaganem and **Mostaganem-Keneda**   An appellation applied before independence to VDQS Algerian★ wines made east of Oran near the coast around Mostaganem, Mazagran, Rivoli, Cassaigne and the Dahra (a zone between the sea and the Chélif River). The best wines came from limestone or limestone-clay soil at about 500 m altitude. These extremely full-bodied wines which had an alcohol level of 13° were supple, fruity and delicate.

The wines from the flinty plateau situated between 100–200 m altitude were also supple, but had less finesse. In his book on the wines of Algeria, Paul Reboux wrote of the wine of Saoura (in the Dahra) that it was distinguished by 'its finesse, delicacy and vigour', and added, 'From this Bordeaux-shaped bottle flows a velvety liquid which Burgundy would not disown'.

mou (feeble, weak)   When applied to wine this adjective has the same meaning as

The confluence of the Moselle and the Meurthe. Phot. A. Perceval.

when applied to man. A mou wine is one which has no character. Lacking a normal level of acidity★ and tannin★, it is flat and insipid.·

mouldy Some wines smell and taste of mould. This serious fault, which cannot be rectified, is caused by a badly cleaned cask or one in which water has been left and which has been attacked by mould. Wine placed in the cask contracts the offensive smell and taste.

Wine not so badly affected is said to have a stagnant taste or to smell of the cask. A mouldy taste can also come from grapes attacked by pourriture grise★.

Moulin-à-Vent This Beaujolais wine takes its name from an old windmill overlooking the vineyard. The appellation Moulin-à-Vent is applied to wine produced by the communes of Romanèche-Thorins and Chenas★. Moulin-à-Vent is always a full-bodied wine with a dark ruby robe and is generally considered one of the best Beaujolais. In certain years the wines are splendid, with a bouquet, body and

distinction resembling the wines of the Côte d'Or★.

Moulis An appellation applied to red wines produced by this commune of the Haut Médoc★ and parts of six other communes, particularly Listrac★. The wines of Moulis have a very particular character due to the presence of a larger amount of limestone in the soil than is found in the rest of the Médoc. The Moulis are colourful, full-bodied and robust. They have a strong bouquet and accentuated flavour which does not exclude finesse.

In the classification of 1855, Moulis was not among the crus classés, but rather the crus bourgeois supérieurs, the excellent Château Chasse-Spleen being classified 'Cru exceptionnel'.

mousse (foam) This is the heart of Champagne★. It must be light, firm and abundant and quickly disappear in the glass, yet remain in the bottle so as to renew the pleasure each time the glass is filled. A quality Champagne, chilled just the right amount, will not explode noisily

Moulin-à-Vent, Beaujolais.
Phot. M.

when the bottle is opened and its cork will not leap from the bottle and hit the ceiling. A large, explosive foam is evidence of a poorly conducted champagnisation.

When the froth has died away in the glass, the effervescence of the wine is revealed as an incessant gushing of little, light bubbles. A large, heavy bubble is slurringly called 'toad's eye'.

Mousseux Grouped under this general term are different kinds of sparkling wine, some being of inferior quality which can give a bad name to the others. Champagne★, although a sparkling wine, should never be described as mousseux – it is Champagne.

Different processes are employed to make vins mousseux. The oldest is the rural method★, which was formerly used in several regions including Champagne, and is still practised at Gaillac★, Die★ and Limoux. The Champagne method★ is, by definition, that used today in Champagne and is employed for all the AOC French vins mousseux: Anjou★, Arbois★, Blanquette de Limoux★, Bordeaux★, Burgundy★, L'Etoile★, Montlouis★, Saint-Péray★, Saumur★, Seyssel★, Touraine★ and Vouvray★.

There is also a German method★ in which the operations of remuage★ and dégorgement★ are eliminated, and which may only be used for sparkling wines not having an appellation.

The cuvé close★ method (Charmat process) allows the fabrication of a cheap Mousseux, but its use is prohibited for French AOC sparkling wines. The method used at Asti★ is different, because the sparkle is obtained during the first fermentation, since the must – not still wine – is treated.

Finally, there are several sparkling vins mousseux made by the injection of carbon dioxide. These wines have large bubbles and none of the creaminess of Champagne which they pretend to imitate.

MOUSSEUX ROSÉ Some regions produce sparkling rosés which can be of very good quality. The sparkling rosés of Touraine are made exclusively from the black grapes of the Cabernet, as are those of Bordeaux. Burgundy also produces sparkling rosés which for some time enjoyed great popularity in England and the United States, but never had quite the same success in France.

moustillant, moustiller Terms used to describe a wine which releases a small amount of gas. This shortcoming is often found in young wines which prick the tongue slightly when tasted. This pricking or tingling is quite acceptable to many people when it is not exaggerated, as in a *vin nouveau* like Beaujolais.

A moustillant wine is the result of a refermentation caused by yeasts or malolactic ferments. As a result there is some carbon dioxide in solution. This light release of gas is often deliberately induced, especially in the case of vins perlants★.

muid A measure used for the sale of large volumes of wine. The quantity varies from one region to another: it is 685 litres in the Hérault, 608 litres at Montpellier and 260 litres in the Aisne.

Murfatlar The best wine of Romania★, cultivated and produced at Basarabi in the Dobroudja from Pinot Gris, Riesling and Chardonnay grapes. Between 1957 and 1962, Murfatlar was awarded forty-five different medals for excellence. Before 1914, the wine rarely had an alcohol level higher than 15°. However, since 1945, the methods have changed, and the wines are now sweeter and have a higher alcohol level, from 16–18°. Murfatlar has a complex, modern vinicultural plant which is remarkably well organised and mechanised.

Muscadet Since 1930 this light, supple, fruity white wine, which originates in the Nantes area, has been a favourite of wine drinkers in Paris, the rest of France and other countries. Muscadet is made from the Melon de Bourgogne grape, which derives its name from its round leaves, and which is hardly grown any more in Burgundy. The grape was brought into Brittany in the seventeenth century and planted in large quantities after the terrible winter of 1709, which destroyed the vineyard. And then the miracle occurred. This grape, which had produced only mediocre wines in other areas, found on the banks of the Loire its perfect soil and climate.

The grape is probably called 'Muscadet' in Brittany because of its slightly musky

Muscadet: the vineyard of Saint-Fiacre. Phot. M.

taste, but it has absolutely no relationship with the Muscadelle of Bordeaux.

The Muscadet is harvested early, before the grapes are overripe. Fermentation is conducted slowly and the wine is kept for a long time on its lees★. This method of vinification accounts for the bouquet, suppleness, fruitiness and the very pale, almost colourless, tint of the wine. Muscadet is never acid because, in a cold year (like 1963), the vignerons reduce the excess acidity by malo-lactic★ fermentation. Dry without being tart, Muscadet has a great deal of finesse, an indefinable yet personal fragrance, and charms with its youthful brightness and clarity.

MUSCADET: APPELLATIONS D'ORIGINE CONTRÔLÉES Legislation distinguishes three appellations contrôlées: Muscadet, Muscadet de Sèvre et Maine★ and Muscadet des Coteaux de la Loire★. The appellation Muscadet is applied to wines with an alcohol level of $9.5°$, yielding 40 hl per hectare and produced in the delimited area.

Between them, the two other appellations produce 90% of Muscadet. Bottling on lees★ is the special process by which the wine is made. It is not racked after fermentation, but is left on its sediment from which it gains its fruitiness and youthful character which are so appreciated. The wine preserves a small amount of dissolved carbon dioxide which makes the tongue tingle.

Muscadet des Coteaux de la Loire The limited area of production is situated around Ancenis on the rocky hills bordering each bank of the Loire. The communes producing the wine on the right bank are found in Loire-Atlantique (Ancenis, Thouarcé, Mauves and Le Cellier). Those on the left bank are in Loire-Atlantique (Saint-Sébastien-sur-Loire and Barbechat) and Maine-et-Loire (La Varenne, Liré and Champtoceaux). The Muscadet des Coteaux de la Loire is generally more full-bodied, drier and fruitier than the Muscadet de Sèvre et Maine★. Sometimes it seems a bit acid, but it retains its youthful character for a long time.

Muscadet de Sèvre et Maine This region located south-west of Nantes produces 75% of the total amount of Muscadet. Here the vine is king, stretching fifty miles over pebbly, flinty, clay soil. The region is divided into four principal cantons, Vertou, Vallet, Clisson and Loroux-Bottereau. The best and most famous Muscadet is produced in this area. It is very fine and light, delicate and supple.

Muscat There are numerous varieties of this grape, whose colours range from a pale yellow to bluish-black. But all possess, to a varying degree, the fragrance and inimitable musky taste so liked by its admirers.

The Muscat is found in the warm soils of Italy, southern France, Spain, Portugal,

Greece, Tunisia and the islands of the Aegean and Mediterranean (Elba, Sardinia, Sicily and Cyprus), as well as the more inclement areas of Alsace, the Tyrol and Hungary. Although the Muscat of Alexandria is the most productive, the best is the Muscat doré of Frontignan. There is also a Muscat of Hambourg which makes a good table grape, but only a mediocre wine; the red Aleatico of the island of Elba; the Muscadelle of Sauternes; the Muscat Ottonel of Alsace; and the Moscatello of Italy from which Asti Spumante★ and Est Est Est★ are made.

The Muscats must be vinified delicately as the essence of their charm and suave, fruity fragrance is capricious and ephemeral. For example, vins mousseux having a Muscat base (Clairette de Die★) should not be vinified à sec, but should finish their first fermentation before being bottled. For this reason, the rural method★ is superior to the Champagne method★, because it preserves the aroma and taste of the grape. At Asti★ the sparkling wines are obtained from the first fermentation. The fragrance of the exquisite French Muscats liquoreux is preserved by mutage★ with alcohol which interrupts fermentation.

Muscat (France) Fragrant vins doux naturels★ from the Muscat grape are produced in the south of France in the Languedoc★ and Roussillon★ areas. The most famous is the Muscat de Frontignan★, with its robe of golden silk. But there are also rivals, including the Muscats de Lunel★, Mireval, Saint-Jean-de-Minervois★ and Rivesaltes★. There is also the suave and fragrant Muscat of Beaumes-de-Venise★, produced on the left bank of the Rhône in the Vaucluse department from the Muscat doré, as is the Frontignan.

The fine and fresh Muscat d'Alsace is the only dry French Muscat. It has the characteristic aroma and musky taste of the Muscat, as well as great delicacy and distinction.

Muscat (Italy) Italy produces much appreciated Muscats from several varieties. The Aleatico grape makes a red, generally sweet wine. The best, Portoferraio, is produced on the island of Elba.

The Muscat of Canelli is the base for Asti Spumante★, the Italian vermouths

Muscat Blanc.
Phot. Larousse.

Around Taormin in Sicily the Muscat predominates in the vineyards. Phot. Hétier.

175

Muscat vines in Tarragona, Spain. Phot. Aarons.

and the Est Est Est★ of Montefiascone. The Giallo Muscat of Trenton and the region north of Adige produces a vin blanc liquoreux of the Sauternes type which contains 12–15° alcohol. There are also true vins de liqueur, very sweet and full-bodied (from 15–17°), which are made from local Muscats in Sardinia (Muscat de Cagliari), the island of Pantelleria, and Sicily (Muscat of Syracuse).

musky A wine having the special aroma of Muscat grapes is said to be musky. This pleasant aroma vanishes almost completely when the must is entirely fermented, e.g. when all its sugar has been converted into alcohol. For this reason, fermentation of wines with a Muscat base are either arrested before completion by the addition of alcohol (Muscat de Frontignan★, Rivesaltes★) or by using the rural method★ to produce a sparkling wine.

must The juice of unfermented grapes.

must meter An instrument which determines the sugar level of must or grapes by measuring the density. A table gives the corresponding sugar concentration. The must meter is used at harvest time as it can record the increase in the sugar level and thus the appropriate time the grapes should be picked. This simple method is not strictly precise. The control of maturation★ tests carried out at oenological stations in the different wine areas are much more reliable, as they examine the development of the principal constituents of the must, including the sugar and acid content.

mutage A special operation used in making vins doux naturels★ which consists of arresting fermentation by adding alcohol. In its original state the must has a natural sugar level of at least 250 g per litre (the equivalent of 14° alcohol), a characteristic of very sweet grapes which have often undergone passerillage★.

In order to arrest fermentation, pure alcohol of 90° is added to the must in a proportion of about 6–10% of the must's volume. There remains in the wine a quantity of natural grape sugar (40–150 g per litre) which is not converted into alcohol. The wines are then more or less sweet and always generous and rich in alcohol, some of them containing as much as 23°. Wines preserve the fruitiness of the fresh grape when fermentation is stopped early. This is particularly the case with the Muscats★, which lose more of their fragrance and fruity taste the longer fermentation is allowed to continue.

Thus mutage is performed on vins doux naturels by the addition of alcohol. For other purposes, fermentation can be arrested by treatment with sulphur dioxide★.

Mycoderma aceti The 'mother of vinegar' bacteria described by Pasteur★. It forms a greyish veil on the surface of wine in the presence of air (because the bacteria is aerobic). When the veil thickens, it wrinkles, becoming reddish. The bacteria develops rapidly and little by little transforms the alcohol of the wine into acetic acid and water. *Mycoderma aceti* is the bacteria responsible for creating wine vinegar★, but it turns wine sour.

Mycoderma vini A whitish veil of *Mycoderma vini* often develops on the surface of wines with a low alcohol content. It is easy to get rid of as it can only exist if air is present in the casks; regular ouillage★ is therefore an essential precaution. If this is not done, the alcohol is changed into carbon dioxide and water, and the fixed acidity slowly diminishes as a result of oxidation of the malic, lactic and succinic acids. The wine becomes faded, flat and feeble. *Mycoderma vini* is often accompanied by *Mycoderma aceti*★ which is more formidable, making the wine sour.

N

Nahe An important German viticultural area located around Bad Kreuznach on red sandstone slopes overlooking the Nahe, a tributary of the Rhine.

The white wines of Nahe, made from the Riesling and Sylvaner, are rich, full-bodied and often excellent. They can be compared to the better wines of the Rhinehessen★, like Niersteiner and Nackenheimer, with the added vivacity which characterises the wines of the Nahe. The most famous vineyard of the region is that of Schloss Böckelheim, south-west of Kreuznach, owned by the German government. Other excellent wines are produced around Bad Kreuznach, Niederhäuser, Norheim, Roxheim, Münster, Bretzenheim and Winzerheim.

Nantais The fatherland of Muscadet★ and the two famous VDQS★ wines Gros-Plant★ and Côteaux d'Ancenis★. These are the last vineyards the Loire passes before it flows into the Atlantic.

Napa A valley north-east of San Francisco, California★ which is famous for its vineyards. St Helena mountain, often still covered with snow in March, towers over the northern end of the valley, while the southern end is bordered by San Francisco Bay. The vineyards are cultivated on the gravelly soil of the valley and at the feet of the neighbouring hills.

Napa produces almost exclusively table wines, including a number of the best Californian wines. Excellent Cabernet-Sauvignons, good Pinot Noirs and Pinot Chardonnays, agreeable Chenin Blancs and other good wines are made in the valley. The wines of generic appellation 'Burgundy', 'Claret' and 'Chablis' are usually superior to those produced by the other Californian regions. Many famous 'wineries' are located in the Napa Valley, including Beaulieu, Inglenook, Charles Krug, Louis M. Martini and Beringer Bros, all old establishment, some dating from as early as 1860.

Some sparkling wine and 'sherry' is also vinified by certain producers.

nature (vins nature de la Champagne) Still (non-sparkling) wines from the delimited Champagne★ area and made from the authorised grapes. The expression Champagne nature, often used to designate these wines, is incorrect, as the appellation Champagne is legally reserved for the sparkling wines. Today the largest part of the vendange is vinified into Champagne. However, prior to the heyday of sparkling wine, the still wines of Champagne, the Clairets, whites and, especially, reds, had a very strong reputation.

The majority of vins blanc nature of

Nantais vineyards. Phot. M.

*Vendange, Château Matras
near Saint-Emilion.*
Phot. Peter Titmuss.

Vendange in Bordeaux near Néac. Phot. Atlas-Photo – J. Windenberger.

Champagne now come from the Côte dès Blancs★ and are made from white grapes, although occasionally a still Blanc de Noirs★ is found. These are dry, refreshing, charming wines, especially in good years, which should be drunk young.

Those made from the Mesnil grape are delicious, fruity and fine, while those of the Cramant have more body. Some houses prepare a vin blanc nature by blending several crus. However, the quality is often irregular as the true still white wines are made only with the must of the first and second pressings. Moreover, vins nature are often capricious and unstable and do not travel well.

The red wines of Champagne were very famous in the Middle Ages. In 1816, Julien classed them among the best fine wines of the kingdom and found them to have great finesse. Their bouquet and flavour could be compared with the best wines of Burgundy, which is not surprising as they are made from the same grape, the Pinot Noir. Certain vignerons still produce good reds at Cumières, Ambonnay and especially Bouzy★. They should generally be drunk young, although the good years age admirably. They are tender, smooth and fragrant.

Another still wine of Champagne is the extraordinary rosé of Riceys★ produced in the Aube department. It should not be confused with Champagne rosé★.

Néac   The wine of this appellation contrôlée comes from a vineyard found north of Pomerol★, between Lalande-de-Pomerol★ and Montagne-Saint-Emilion★.

These good quality wines are colourful, generous and fragrant, having both the *sève*★ of the Pomerols and the richness of Saint-Emilion. The premier crus (Châteaux Tournefeuille, Moncets, Siaurac, Belles-Graves and Teysson) are equal to the second crus of Pomerol.

négociant   The *négociant* is not a simple wine merchant. He plays a multiple role. He must first know how to choose wines, and judiciously select his purchases in the cellars with the aid of the courtiers. There is considerable risk attached to this profession, as it is almost impossible to predict how every wine will evolve.

The *négociant* must raise the wine. In this role he is called the *éleveur*★. This calls for the expenditure of a large amount of capital in order to purchase the young wine, as well as a great deal of talent and knowledge in order to raise it properly. He must also despatch the wine and make sure that it arrives at the point of sale in a drinkable state, and must also prospect for clients and arrange for sales.

Although many vignerons have all the facilities needed to raise, bottle and despatch the wine, there are many thousands who do not have the space or equipment. The *négociant*, in fulfilling these roles for them, assures that many marvellous wines, which otherwise would have been unknown, are brought to the attention of consumers.

nervosité (nerve)   This quality of a wine is based on its acidity. When the acidity is not excessive and is within the normal limits, the different sensations which can come from a wine are revealed more strongly. A nervous wine always has character.

New York   The vineyards of this state are neither numerous nor widespread. In terms of production it ranks second to California★, but there is a considerable difference in volume between them. Vineyards are found around Buffalo, Lake Erie and the Hudson Valley, but their main production effort is table grapes, as opposed to wine. A viticultural region of some importance is situated south-east of Rochester around two of the four Finger Lakes, Keuka and Canandaigua.

Most of the wines come from indigenous varieties planted around 1829 (Delaware, Catawba, Elvira, Concorde, Niagara and Isabelle) but, since the end of prohibition, hybrids★ of French origin (Baco, Coudero and Seibel) have been grown and attempts are now being made to cultivate European grape varieties in this area.

This region produces most of the sparkling wines made in the USA, as well as sweet and table wines. European appellations such as Burgundy, Sauternes, Port and Sherry, followed by their appellation, New York State, are used on the labels.

New Zealand Two Australian pioneers, James Busby and the Reverend Samuel Marsden, planted the first vines in New Zealand in 1830 at the Bay of Islands. Then, around 1835, the Marist Fathers introduced the vine at Hawke's Bay. Production remained small until the Second World War when imports of wines were reduced. Viticulture did not progress significantly until the 1950s, when the Australian companies MacWilliams and Seppelts invested heavily. Today, the most important viticultural areas are found on the North Island at Auckland and Henderson in the north and Hawkes Bay in the south.

Both white and red wines are produced, the whites being the better of the two. The whites are made from the Müller-Thurgau, Chardonnay and Chasselas and have an agreeable acidity which assures a certain vigour, a characteristic of New Zealand wines. The reds made from the Cabernet, and two hybrids, the Pinotage and Seibel 5437, have a tendency to be overacid. Chaptalisation★ is allowed because of the low level of sugar in the grapes.

Production was formerly geared to fortified wines and 'Sherry', but today's trend is towards light, white table wines.

Nuits-Saint-Georges This commune has given its name to the 'Côte de Nuits'. Certain plots of vineyards in the neighbouring village of Prémeaux are legally included in the commune of Nuits. A small quantity of excellent white wine is produced but Nuits is most famous for its reds, which are generous and well balanced, falling between the Gevrey-Chambertins and Chambolle-Musignys. They are less firm and vigorous than the Gevreys, but have more body and colour than the Chambolle-Musignys. Although they are vinified earlier than the Gevreys they keep just as well.

There are a number of climats on the two communes of Nuits and Prémeaux, including Saint-Georges, Vaucrains, les Cailles, les Pruliers, les Porrets, Clos de la Maréchale and Clos des Argillières.

The vineyard of Nuits-Saint-Georges. Phot. Aarons-L.S.P.

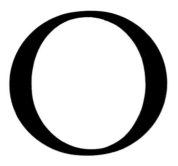

oeil-de-perdrix (partridge eye) A very light, indecisive colour attributed to lightly coloured vins gris★.

oenologist (from the Greek *oinos*, wine, and *logos*, science) A technician whose knowledge of wine is certified by a national diploma. The title of oenologist was officially recognised by the law of 19th March, 1955.

The oenologist can take total responsibility for vinifying and raising wines and is able to perform the most delicate analyses on the grape.

oenophile A person who loves wine and devotes much time and attention to it. The oenophile treats the study and selection of wine as a hobby, sometimes becoming involved to the point of making his own wine, or at any rate building up quite a respectable cellar.

As early as 210 BC, the Greek historian Polybe described the love of the Celts for wine and, in the first century AD, Diodore of Sicily wrote that the Greek wines had a good market in what is now France. The Phoenician colony of Massalia (Marseilles) supplied wine to the Gauls in the sixth century AD, and the beautiful wine vessel in the famous 'treasures of Vix' of Châtillon-sur-Seine dates from the same time, proving the interest its owner had in wine.

Office International de la Vigne et du Vin (OIV) An organisation which was created in 1924 and now has a membership of twenty-four countries, which accounts for about 90% of the world's vineyards. It has a considerable influence on governments and oenological organisations, which is not surprising in view of the calibre of its absolutely impartial experts.

The OIV first of all provides an information service to supply governments with official documentation. It is also a technical forum whose members exchange information on their researches and international experiments. Finally, it is an economic organisation which tries to align the legislation and rules of the different viticultural countries in order to arrive at a rational world viticultural policy.

Ohio The first vineyards of this viticultural state of the USA were planted by German immigrants east and west of Cincinnati along the Ohio River, whose steep banks resemble those of the Rhine. One of these planters, Nicholas Longworth, was particularly successful with his

Oenological laboratory at Saint-André-de-Cubzac, Gironde. Phot. M.

vines and did so much to further viniculture that, by the Civil War, Ohio was by far the largest wine producer in the United States, making highly respected wines, including sparkling wines, from the Catawba grape.

Today there is little evidence of these once-successful vineyards along the Ohio. The vines are now found on some islands and on the south shore of Lake Erie, particularly around Sandusky, an area which provides a mellowing influence on the climate, protecting the grapes from early frosts. Although it produces a large quantity of wine, Ohio has lost its former importance.

oidium A disease of American origin, provoked by a microscopic mould which attacks the leaves, flowers and grapes, covering them with a whitish, flour-like dust. The grapes are then prey to pourriture grise★. In 1846 oidium attacked the French vineyards and did enormous damage over the next few years. Production fell from 45 million hl in 1850 to 10 million in 1854.

A remedy, consisting of regular sprayings with sulphur dioxide★, was soon discovered, but not before several vignerons were ruined.

oily An oily wine has the appearance and consistency of oil and is caused by graisse★. It should not be confused with a fleshy wine, which owes its oily quality to a high level of glycerine★.

old When used in connection with wine, the term 'old' does not carry any derogatory implication – in fact, an old wine takes precedence over all others in the cellar, and however casually gourmets may treat young★ wines, they always respect an old one.

It is pointless to compare the merits of old and young wines, since they are essentially quite different. Generally speaking, wines are called old when they are between five and fifteen years of age. The great red and white Burgundies, the sweet wines of Bordeaux and the Loire, Monbazillacs, the great red wines of the Gironde, white and red Côtes-du-Rhône and vins jaunes★ should all be drunk within this period. Among these, some veterans can happily age fifteen or twenty years, or

Grapes attacked by oidium. Phot. M.

Casks in a maturing cave in the Côtes-du-Rhône. Phot. M.

even longer. This is always true of vins jaunes but, of others, only in good years.

If the qualities of youth are fruitiness and freshness, age gives a wine inimitable bouquet and flavour as well as subtlety. When a wine has lost some of its qualities with age, the French no longer call it simply *vieux*, but say *il vieillarde* (i.e. 'it is ageing'). This is half-way to the final stage of *sénilité*, by which time its beauty and quality have definitely gone, and various changes have taken place; it has oxidised, has deposited its colouring matter and tartrates, and lost its bouquet.

Orléans The reputation of this vineyard dates back to the seventh century, when the wine of Orléans conquered Paris. A large vineyard in the area, created by Saint Mesmin, received a gift from Clovis in tribute to its well-known wine. Orléans quickly became the great wine market of the region, and the Orléanais wines at the time of Louis XIII were compared to those of Bordeaux for their richness and reputation.

The red was the most famous at this time, although Villon praised the white wine of Mauves (Meung-sur-Loire). Although its importance lasted up to the end of the last century, vineyards are now only found in about fifteen communes, mainly on the right bank of the river below Orléans (Baul, Messas, Meung-sur-Loire and Beaugency).

The VDQS★ wines are white, red and rosé. The Pinot Meunier, here called 'Gris-Meunier', is by far the most cultivated variety. The Pinot Noir is also encountered, its name here being 'Auvernat', but it has been supplanted by the Gris-Meunier. A small amount of Chardonnay, Pinot Gris and Cabernet Franc are also cultivated. The clear reds are fresh and light and may be drunk in the year following the vendange. However, for some thirty years, the Pinot-Meunier has been vinified into rosé; this is the famous, fragrant Gris-Meunier made by pressing★ after a short maceration of the vendange.

Finally, Orléans uses its wine in making its celebrated vinegar.

Orvieto A very popular Italian white wine produced around the town of Orvieto in Umbria. The vineyards of Orvieto are quite unique, as most of the grapes are cultivated in a fashion the Italians call *coltura promiscua* – the vines are mixed among the apple trees and cabbage plots. The wine is often good, despite this fantastic method of culture. Always light, it is generally *abboccato* (demi-sec), more rarely *secco* (sec). It is sold in a squat, straw-covered bottle called a *pulcianelle*.

ouillage or **remplissage (topping up)** An operation which consists of keeping the casks constantly full of wine while they are in the cave. The first topping up is done when the wine has stopped fermenting. At first, wine of the same quality is added to the cask twice a week, then every fifteen days. An air pocket forms at the top of the cask for several reasons – cold makes the wine shrink in volume and some wine is lost in evaporation through the pores in the cask. Altogether, about 1% of the wine's volume is lost each month. If the casks were not topped up to replace the lost wine, harmful ferments would begin to alter the wine. At first this would be revealed as flor★, then by an increase in acidity *(piqûre)*.

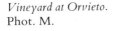

Vineyard at Orvieto.
Phot. M.

PQ

Pacherenc-du-Vic-Bihl This is the white relative of Madiran★, with which it shares the same terrain in the Pyrenees. It is made from Ruffiac, Manseng, Courbu, Sémillon and Sauvignon grapes, which grow at a high altitude like those of Jurançon.

The Pacherenc-du-Vic-Bihl is an AOC★ wine which must have a minimum of 12° alcohol. Lively and marrowy, it slightly resembles its rival, the Jurançon, which is generally sweeter. The wines that come from the area around Portet are the finest.

paille (vin de) Today this rare dessert★ wine is made almost exclusively in the Jura★ region. The Hermitage★ vineyards have almost stopped production, and it is no longer made in Alsace. The grapes from which it is made (the Jura's noble★ varieties: Savagnin, Trousseau, Chardonnay and Poulsard) are carefully picked and then laid on beds of straw (*paille*) for at least two months – sometimes until Christmas – during which time a slow concentration of their natural sugar takes place. The must from these grapes has an exceptionally high sugar content and, after a long and often difficult fermentation, results in a liquoreux★ wine with an alcoholic strength of 14 or 15°. Vin de paille is extremely rare, and few people have the good fortune to taste it on the spot. It is smooth and aromatic, and has a pronounced bouquet.

VIN DE PAILLE
19___

VICHOT-GIROD
PROPRIÉTAIRE A NEVY-SUR-SEILLE (JURA)

CÔTES DU JURA Appellation Contrôlée

Grapes hung to mature in the production of vin de paille.
Phot. Cuisset.

In the days when transporting wine was a hazardous undertaking, the parish priests in the north of France used to make their communion wine by the same process which, particularly in wet or cold years, enabled them to produce wines that were less acid than if the grapes had been pressed straight after the harvest.

generally considered the best, closely followed by those of Bad Dürkheim, Kallstadt, Leistadt and Königsbach. Most of the region's production consists of red and white vin ordinaire, with a predominance of white. A great deal of the wine it exports comes from the area between Neustadt and Bad Dürkheim, known as

Palatinate: a view of the vineyards from the Rhine. Phot. Candelier-Lauros.

Palatinate One of the four great vine-growing regions in Germany★, and in good years often the chief producer. Its viticultural tradition dates back many hundreds of years; the province was for a long time known as 'the cellar of the Holy Roman Empire'. Its name is derived from the Palatine Hill in Rome, where the Roman Emperors had their official residence.

Today, the Palatinate is bordered by the states of North Rhine-Westphalia to the north, the Rhine to the east and by Alsace-Lorraine to the south and west. The vineyards lie around the foot of a small chain of hills called the Haardt (a northern continuation of the Vosges mountains in eastern France) and also cover a large part of the fertile plain which borders the Rhine. The vineyards of Wachenheim, Forst, Deidesheim and Ruppertsberg are

Mittelhaardt, which produces a few red vins ordinaires and a great many white ones. The most noteworthy are made chiefly from Riesling grapes, and some others from Sylvaner.

The Rieslings from the best vineyards are extremely good, and are almost on a par with the excellent Rheingau★ wines. They are full-bodied, heady and aromatic, and have finesse, breeding and a marvellous bouquet. As in all German vineyards, the 'Beerenauslesen' are outstanding, and command high prices.

Palette A Provence appellation contrôlée which belongs to a small vineyard located on a part of the communes of Meyreuil, Tholonet and Aix-en-Provence. The vines are grown on soil derived from the Langesse limestone geological formation.

186

The red and rosé wines come for the most part (about 50%) from Grenache, Cinsault and Mourvèdre (not less than 10%) grapes. About 55% of the white wines are made from different varieties of Clairettes.

Palette wines are, for the most part, fine and elegant with a very pleasant freshness and lightness. The reds are warm, the rosés full of bouquet and the whites have great distinction. The best cru is Château-Simone. The vineyard also produces a sweet vin cuit★ which is greatly liked in the region and is traditionally drunk at Christmas. It is produced by heating the must in cauldrons before it is left to ferment.

palus This word, which is derived from the French for swamp, is used in Bordeaux to describe the recently deposited alluvial soil which lies along the river banks.

There are not many vines planted on this soil and the *palus* is rarely found in appellation contrôlée zones. The vines which grow on the *palus* are usually very productive but never give quality wines.

panier verseur The use of this wine basket for pouring wine is highly recommended for an old wine containing a little deposit. The deposit, which is mainly composed of tannins, colouring matter, potassium bitartrate and gums, sometimes adheres to the sides of the bottle, though more usually falls to the bottom. It is then mobile, and with each change of position is put in suspension in the wine.

A useful precaution when one is preparing an old bottle is to place it cautiously in the cellar in a wine basket, keeping it in the same horizontal position that it had in the cave. Thanks to the basket, each glass can be subsequently served with the necessary delicacy needed to avoid mixing the deposits with the wine. Some very refined baskets have a small handle which regulates the level of the bottle, thereby enabling the wine to be drunk to the last drop, leaving only the deposit. If the bottle is stored in an upright position and then placed into the wine basket immediately before serving, the deposits may be disturbed. In this case it is better to leave the bottle standing on the table and decant it.

It is not necessary to serve a young wine, which does not have a deposit, in a wine basket, however elegant this may look.

Panisseau A dry white wine produced around Sigoulès which merits the appellation contrôlée Bergerac★. It is one of the rare dry wines of the area. Unlike the marrowy wines of the Sud-Ouest★, it is picked early. It is an aromatic, nervy★, very agreeable wine.

Parsac-Saint-Emilion The commune of Parsac has the right to add Saint-Emilion to its proper name. Its rocky hills produce very colourful, full-bodied wines which have considerable bouquet. The principle châteaux are Langlade, Binet and Piron.

passerillage A very late vendange which can only take place in exceptional weather conditions and with certain thick-skinned grape varieties. It is necessary to leave the grapes on the vine past the normal maturation state. The grape shrinks up and looks withered, the contents, especially sugar, becoming concentrated. The quality of the must which is produced from this is remarkable. This overmaturing is done to obtain the strongly concentrated Muscats★ which are used for vins doux naturels★.

The vins de paille★ are also made from passerillage of the grapes, not on the ground but in closed, warm areas. The grapes are hung in barns or laid on clay or on beds of straw. In certain years, over-ripening is also used in Sauternes★, Anjou★ and Touraine★, but the wines have neither the character nor the quality of those obtained from grapes which have been affected by pourriture noble★.

Pasteur, Louis (1822–1895) He is justly considered to be the father of modern oenology. This illustrious scientist began his studies on wine at the request of Napoleon III, who wanted an investigation into the numerous changes which could alter a wine. The first step was to determine the exact nature of alcoholic fermentation by which wine is made. He also investigated diseases of wine and their treatment. The sum of this considerable work was reported to the Emperor at Compiègne in 1865 in his famous 'Studies on wine, its diseases and the causes which

Louis Pasteur in his laboratory.
Painting by Edelfeld (1887).
Phot. Musée Pasteur, Paris.

is a delicate operation, since the wine's qualities may be altered by heating it.

Patrimonio One of the best-known Corsican★ wines, produced around Saint-Florent between Ile-Rousse and Bastia. There is some good red wine, and the white is interesting, dry, fragrant and full-bodied. The most famous, however, is the rosé, which is of exceptional quality and generally considered the best in Corsica. It is full-bodied, quite powerful and has a delicious fragrance. Since 1968 Patrimonio has been entitled to an AOC★, subject to certain conditions. Principal varieties of grape are Nielluccio for red and rosé, and Vermentino, Ugni Blanc and Rossola for white.

Pauillac The small town of Pauillac, unchallenged viticultural capital of the Médoc★, lies between Saint-Estèphe★ and Saint-Julien★. The appellation Pauillac comprises parts of Saint-Estèphe, Saint-Julien and Clissac. Pauillac's magnificent red wines fully justify their prestigious reputation. In good years they have all the essential characteristics of true Bordeaux. They are full-bodied, moelleux★ and *séveux*★, have a fine, fragrant bouquet and age extremely well.

Of all the Bordeaux communes, Pauillac is outstanding for having had eighteen châteaux listed in the 1855 classification★. Two of them were premier crus, the prestigious Château Lafite-Rothschild★ and Château-Latour★, and the others included equally distinguished names, such as Mouton-Rothschild (now a premier cru), Pichon-Longueville, Pichon-Longueville-Lalande, Pontet-Canet and Batailley. (See Index.)

paulée Originally a *paulée* was a communal meal held every year in the Côte d'Or at the end of the grape harvest. Proprietors and vignerons were united around one table, and in each village people brought out their best bottles to drink with the substantial regional dishes. The tradition gradually fell into disuse, and then, after a long lapse, was revived by the city of Meursault in 1923. A *paulée* was instituted in Paris in 1932. It takes place every year in a big restaurant, and is attended by both wine-lovers and vineyard-proprietors.

prevoke it; new and old ways of keeping it'.

pasteurisation A method of stabilising wine which was named after Pasteur who, along with Appert and Gayon, pioneered the process. The wine is heated for a minute to a temperature of around 60°C (55°C for wines high in alcohol and acidity, 65°C for light wines). This process destroys the bacteria in the wine and acts as a cure for diseases caused by acetic and lactic bacteria. It has often been used not only to stabilise wine but also to age it artificially or treat casse★.

The only real pasteurisation is that done by putting bottles in a bain-marie. It destroys the development of bacteria but also, at the same time, any chance of improving the wine. This process is occasionally used for ordinary table wines. It

pays (vin de) A regional wine, usually made by blending, which is not subject to the appellation of origin controls. These wines, having an alcohol content of at least 8·5°, are hardly known outside their particular region as they are only consumed locally.

Vins de pays should not be confused with vins à appellation d'origine★. They are titled 'vins de pays du canton de . . .' unless the name of the canton is an appellation d'origine, in which case the name of the commune is substituted. If the commune is also an appellation d'origine the name of the locality is used, followed by the name of the department.

acquire with age. Certain light red and rosé wines possess this colour naturally.

Pérignon (Dom) A monk who was given the job of cellarer in the Abbey of Hautvillers in 1668, and occupied this post until his death in 1715. Popular tradition attributes him with the 'invention' of Champagne. The white wines of Champagne did, in fact, have a natural tendency to effervesce, a tendency which caused the local vignerons considerable annoyance and which remained largely unaffected by their various attempts to restrain it. Moreover, since the fashion at the time was for red wine, no-one bothered much about

The vines of Patrimonio.
Phot. Botin.

Pécharmant The appellation of some red wines of Bergerac★ produced on the hills near the town of Pécharmant, between the Dordogne and the main Bergerac-Périgueux road. The name (sometimes also written Pech-Charmant, meaning 'charming peak') applies to certain *parcelles*, or divisions, of the Saint-Sauveur, Creysse, Lembras and Bergerac communes, whose flinty, clay soil produces well-coloured, full-bodied warm wines with a characteristic *sève*★ and an alcoholic strength of at least 11°.

pelure d'oignon 'Onion-skin' is the name given to the slightly orange, reddish-brown or tawny tinge that some red wines

white, which was kept mainly for local consumption.

The fashion subsequently changed and people started to ask for white wine. (In those days it was called *clairet* or *fauvelet*, and was actually a pinkish or greyish colour, rather than white.) Dom Pérignon managed to create a really white wine a few years after taking up his cellarership. He studied the behaviour of its once-maligned effervescence, determined to transform the defect into a positive quality and to discover a method by which he could induce effervescence regularly and be certain of success every time.

His 'secret' was basically the addition of a certain, precise quantity of sugar to the

Above: the Abbey of Hautvillers; right: relief of Dom Pérignon in the gallery inaugurated in 1932 in honour of the inventor of Champagne. Phot. Lauros-Giraudon.

without proof, to have been the first to substitute cork for the stoppers made of oil-soaked hemp which had, until then, always been used for wine bottles.

perlant   A word which describes a wine with a very slight effervescence, somewhere between a still wine and a vin pétillant★. The best-known perlant wines are Fendant du Valais, Crépy★ and Gaillac perlé★. The wine is bottled immediately after malo-lactic fermentation★, which transforms the malic acid contained in young wines into lactic acid and carbon dioxide. The carbon dioxide is trapped in the wine and produces the attractive light effervescence. The process is helped by leaving the lees in suspension and bottling the wine early in cold weather after filtration.

still wine. The many hopeful imitators who tried to reproduce the wine after his death had a high percentage of burst bottles for their pains, and it was not until a century later that his methods and expertise were rediscovered by a French chemist and wine-lover named François de Châlons, who has undeservedly been forgotten.

Dom Pérignon's real and indisputable merit was to have invented, or at any rate perfected, the blending and 'dosing' of different crus in order to balance and combine their various qualities to the best advantage. He was gifted with an extraordinarily sensitive palate which could distinguish not only one wine from another, but also the species of grape from which each one was made, and he used this skill to produce blended and unblended wines of incomparable quality.

Among other ideas ascribed to him is that of using the famous *crayères* (underground cellars cut out of the chalk during the Roman occupation of Gaul), where the low temperature allowed wine to mature more slowly, and a fining method by which wine could be cleared of sediment without being decanted. (The formula, whose basic ingredients were crystallised sugar, wine and *eau-de-vie*, served in any case as liqueur de tirage★ and to ensure secondary fermentation.) Some people even attribute to him the invention of the long, thin glasses that some purists consider to be the only proper ones for Champagne, and he is also alleged, albeit

Pernand-Vergelesses   A small village in the Côte de Beaune on the borders of

PERNAND-VERGELESSES
LES VERGELESSES
APPELLATION PERNAND VERGELESSES CONTROLEE
Chanson Père & Fils
CHANSON PÈRE & FILS, NÉGOCIANTS A BEAUNE (COTE-D'OR)

the Aloxe-Corton★ commune. Certain divisions of the Pernand-Vergelesses vineyards produce excellent red or white wines, and these are entitled to the appellation Corton and Corton-Charlemagne.

The reds have warmth, firmness, longevity and a bouquet that has a distinct flavour of raspberries. When produced from a good rootstock, the red wines from the Ile des Vergelesses climat★ can, in good years, be compared with the best Cortons. The white wines have finesse and are excellent.

persistence The quality of a wine whose taste lingers pleasantly on the palate for some time after swallowing. Basically, a wine's bouquet is produced by its volatile elements, and its taste derives from the non-volatile ones (sugar, tannin, acids and their salts).

A *vin long* is one whose flavour persists on the palate, and is always a good wine; a *vin court* is merely average. Gauging the duration of their taste is a useful way of distinguishing different crus. The method is quite simple: after swallowing a mouthful of wine, count the seconds until the taste has completely disappeared from the palate. (A taste of tannin, which occasionally persists by itself, should be ignored.) The taste of red wine never lasts as long as that of white; even a very great red rarely lasts longer than eleven seconds. The following scale is a rough guide to the quality of wine: vin ordinaire: 1–3 seconds; good wine, 4–5 seconds; great wine, 6–8 seconds; very great wine, 8–11 seconds and more (the same as for dry white wines); vin blanc liquoreux★: 18 seconds; and the best Sauternes. Vouvray and Château-Chalon, 20–25 seconds.

pétillant (vin demi-mousseux) Semi-sparkling wine with more effervescence than vin perlant★ but less than vin mousseux★. Pétillant wine has a carbon dioxide pressure of not more than 2 or 2·5 kg at 20°C whereas the pressure of vin mousseux, like that of Champagne★, must be at least 4 and often 5 kg.

There are strict regulations governing the use of the word when applied to the AOC★ Loire wines (Vouvray, Montlouis, Touraine, Saumur, Anjou) made by the Champagne method★ of secondary fermentation in bottle. Wines from other vineyards, however, are unaffected by these rules, which is why some wines customarily called pétillant have no pressure at all, merely containing a small amount of dissolved carbon dioxide (for example, wines bottled on lees★, and immediately after malo-lactic fermentation★).

Pétrus (Château) Although there is no official classification of the wines of Pomerol★, the best of them is indisputably Château-Pétrus, an excellent wine that ranks with the premiers grands crus★ of Médoc★ and Saint-Emilion★.

Château-Pétrus is a 'complete' wine, velvety and admirably well balanced, with plenty of body and bouquet. Its quality is remarkably consistent and even a mediocre year produces good wine, although this should not be kept too long.

phylloxera This tiny aphid, *Phylloxera vastatrix*, is the most destructive of all vine pests. The species originated in the USA and was accidentally introduced into Europe in the course of some viticultural experiments in about 1864. From the Gard

Vine leaves attacked by phylloxera. Phot. M.

191

*'The Vendange' by F. Van
Valchenborch. Detail of a
spinet cover, late 16th century.*
Phot. Scola.

department of France, where it was first
noticed, it proceeded to ravage virtually
every vineyard in Europe, and some never
fully recovered. Vignerons tried various
countermeasures such as submerging★ the
vines, planting them in sand and injecting
the soil with carbon bisulphide, but despite
all their efforts these methods proved
useless. Finally, they tried grafting European vines on to American root-stocks,
which are immune to the insect, which
was finally successful. It was feared at first
that the imported strains would have a
detrimental effect on the taste of the wines
(see foxy★), but these fears were un-
founded and grafting has been standard
practice ever since.

The restoration of the vineyards of
France alone cost 1800 million francs, an
expense that was borne entirely by the
industry. The traditional structure of the
European vineyards was completely altered as a result of this reconstruction. For
some, like the Ile-de-France, the catas-
trophe was fatal and they disappeared
forever. The reconstituted vineyards did,
on the other hand, benefit from the re-
generative effects of technology.

Picpoul-de-Pinet   A white VDQS★
wine from Languedoc★ made mainly
(about 70%) from the Picpoul grape,
which gives it its name, with a proportion
of the white Terret and Clairette varieties.
This wine, produced by the Pinet commune and four or five others nearby, is
generous, dry but not acid, and the
ideal   accompaniment   to   Bouzigues
oysters.

pièce   A hogshead. A measure used in
the Burgundy region, roughly the equivalent of a barrique★ (i.e. 228 litres). Its
capacity does, however, vary from region
to region. In Mâcon it is 216 litres and in
Beaujolais, 214. The unit of measure used
in Chablis is the feuillette★.

pied de cuve   Thanks to the contrôle
de maturation★, the vigneron knows beforehand when the vendage will take
place and has time to prepare carefully
the base of his cuve. With this in mind,
he chooses from the best parts of the
vines several hundred beautiful, healthy,
ripe grapes. After destalking and pres-
sing★, the grapes are placed in a very clean
container. If necessary, the vigneron heats
the must to between 22 and 25°C. Alcoholic fermentation begins within twelve
hours, during which time the vigneron
takes care to aerate the must. The resultant
leaven, the pied de cuve, contains such a
high level of active yeast that 1 hl can
activate 40 hl of the vendange.

Pierrevert (Coteaux de)   The VDQS★
red and rosé wines from this Provence★
vineyard are made from the traditional
grapes of the region, combined with the
Syrah variety. The white wines, made
from Clairette, Marsanne and Roussane
grapes, are reminiscent of Côtes-du-
Rhône★. The appellation Clairet de Pierrevert applies to white and rosé wines
grown at Pierrevert, Manosque and

Sainte-Tulle. These are sometimes sparkling, and have a musky flavour.

pinard A French slang word (sanctioned by the Académie Française since 1943) for vins ordinaires rich in colour and tannin. The word received official recognition during the First World War, when Marshall Joffre called the wine drunk by the common soldiers 'le Général Pinard', and he was well qualified to assess its virtues since his father was a cooper in Rivesaltes, a famous vineyard near the Pyrenees.

As to the origin of the word, various theories have been suggested: some think it comes from *pino*, classical Greek for 'to drink'; others recall that, in the sixteenth century, a Burgundian named Jean Pinard was renowned as the best vigneron of his time, a fact noted in a book printed at Auxerre in 1607 and reprinted in Paris in 1851.

pinçant A pinçant wine has an excessive fixed acidity★ which makes it seem to 'pinch' the tongue. *Pointu*, or 'sharp', is used in the same sense.

Pineau d'Aunis A red grape grown mostly in the Vendôme and Loir-et-Cher departments of France, and sometimes known as Chenin Noir. Like Chenin Blanc, otherwise called Pineau de la Loire★, it is in no way related to the Pinot★ varieties. Its name comes from a small village in the commune of Dampierre not far from Saumur.

Pineau d'Aunis is probably descended from indigenous wild vines, and is generally acknowledged to be the ancestor of the famous Pineau de la Loire, which is itself the result of years of carefully selective cultivation by the vignerons of the Loire valley. It is one of the varieties grown for the red and rosé wines of Anjou★ and Saumur★.

Pineau de la Loire The only grape used for the great white wines of Touraine★ and Anjou★. It is also known as Chenin Blanc, which is what Rabelais called it. It is sometimes, mistakenly, written as Pinot de la Loire, although it has no connection with the Pinot family. The Pineau de la Loire is ideally suited to the Loire valley, being perfectly adapted to its climate and

able to grow on any kind of soil. Elsewhere, however, the wines it produces are not outstanding.

Pineau de la Loire is responsible for the great wines of Vouvray★, Montlouis★, Saumur★, Savennières★ and Coteaux-du-Layon★. The grape, during good years, is frequently attacked by pourriture noble★. It is harvested very late, sometimes during November, producing well-coloured wines with a wonderfully delicate bouquet. It also lends itself very well to the preparation of sparkling wines, e.g. the vins mousseux of Vouvray, Montlouis and Saumur.

Pineau des Charentes An AOC★ liqueur★ wine, Pineau des Charentes is made by muting with alcohol, in this case Cognac, and the must or grape juice is harvested in the Charentes vineyards. The method of preparation seems to have originated in the sixteenth century. Like Ratafia de Champagne★, Pineau des Charentes was for a long time made only for private consumption, and it was not until just before the Second World War that it was sold commercially. It can be drunk as both an apéritif and a dessert wine, and is extremely pleasant chilled. It can be either red or white, and has an alcoholic strength

Pineau de la Loire. In good years this famous grape may be attacked by pourriture noble, as is shown here. Phot. M.

193

of at least 16·5° (sometimes as much as 22°), masked by a deceptive smoothness.

Pinot Gris An Alsatian grape, a member of the great Pinot family. It is also incorrectly known as 'Tokay', which can cause confusion with the famous Hungarian wine. It is difficult to cultivate, and generally has a poor yield. The white wine it makes is full-bodied, heady, solid and powerful, but somewhat lacking in delicacy, and is most appreciated in its native region. In good years, however, it has more grace and an agreeable smoothness. The grape is also grown in Baden, Germany, where it is called Ruländer, and in northern Italy where it is one of the varieties used to make Terlano, one of the best white wines of the Tyrol.

Pinot Noir One of the most important red grapes, Pinot Noir has been the mainstay of the great red Burgundies since the Burgundian vineyards were first planted, producing the excellent wines of Romanée-Conti, la Tâche, Musigny, Chambertin, Clos-de-Vougeot and Pommard.

With Chardonnay★ it is one of the two principal varieties of grape grown in both Burgundy and Champagne. In the latter region, where it has been cultivated since the Middle Ages, it was given the name *morillon* (probably in reference to its colour, which is black 'as a Moor'), and used to make excellent red wines that rivalled

Pinot Noir, the great variety of Burgundy and Champagne. Phot. M.

194

those of Beaune★. Of these, only Bouzy★ and Cumières have survived to the present day. Nowadays, the production of Pinot Noir, which is grown mainly on the Montagne de Reims★, is roughly four times as great as that of Chardonnay, whereas in the Middle Ages the proportions were the other way round.

Pinot grapes are small, tight and blue-black, with a sweet and colourless juice. In Burgundy the skins are left with the juice while it ferments, the pigments contained in them dissolve as the temperature rises and give the wines their magnificent colour. In Champagne, Pinot grapes are never crushed; they are picked and then immediately placed in special presses whose large surface area enables them to be pressed very quickly. This is to prevent the juice from being discoloured by contact with the skins.

A proportion of Pinot is used in the preparation of the wines of Saint-Pourçain★, the Orléannais★, Châtillon-en-Diois★ and the Jura★, as well as the excellent red wines of Alsace★ and the exceptional rosés of Marsannay-la-Côte★, les Riceys★ and Sancerre★.

piquette When the vin de presse★ has been removed from the press, marc still

remains in the cuve. Water is added and, after about fifteen days, a thin, rather strong wine called piquette is produced which is usually consumed by the vigneron and his family. If the operation is repeated a second time, more acidic piquette is produced.

Piquette is also used in a derogatory way to describe wines which are low in alcohol but high in acidity

plein Full, a word used to describe a wine rich in alcohol, agreeably full-bodied and well balanced.

Pomerol The little vineyard of Pomerol, bordered to the east by the gravelly region of Saint-Emilion★, lies just outside Libourne on the right bank of the Dordogne. Vines have been cultivated in the Pomerol region since the Gallo-Roman era, but it was the Hospitalers of St John who really developed the vineyards when they established a Commandery there in the twelfth century. The vines were for a long time confused with those of Saint-Emilion, and it was not until the nineteenth century that their great reputation was finally established.

The soil of Pomerol is particularly suitable for the cultivation of vines, being composed of flint and gravel, clay and gravel, or sand, with an iron-bearing subsoil that gives the wine its particular *sève*★ or strength. The wines, all red, are made from the noble★ grapes, Cabernet Franc, Cabernet-Sauvignon (or Bouchet), Merlot and Malbec (or Pressac).

Pomerol is a generous, full-bodied, very attractive wine with a brilliant, dark ruby colour, a distinctive flavour and a marvellous velvety taste which fulfills the promise of its bouquet. It has been called 'a mesh of savours and aromas'. It has a curious similarity to Burgundy, but is more notable for combining the best qualities of the Médoc★ and Saint-Emilion. It has the finesse of the former and the *sève* and vigour of the latter.

The appellation Pomerol comprises the Pomerol commune and a small part of Libourne. Although there is no official classification of Pomerol crus, Château-Pétrus★ is generally acknowledged to be the best, followed by the Châteaux Certan, Vieux-Certan, la Conseillante, Petit-Village, Trotanoy, l'Evangile, Lafleur,

Pinot Meunier or 'Gris-Meunier' grape. The most popular variety around Orléans. Phot. M.

Above and right: Pomerol vineyards near Libourne. Phot. M. and René-Jacques.

Gaxin and La Fleur-Pétrus. (See Index.)

The Pomerol vineyards also extend into two neighbouring communes which produce wines that have more or less the same characteristics: Lalande-de-Pomerol★ and Néac★.

Pommard   Pommard, which is always red, is perhaps the best known of all red Burgundies, at any rate outside its native country. The commune from which it comes in the Côte de Beaune★ has, in fact, cultivated the vine for many hundreds of years, and in the days when vinification and conservation techniques were far from perfect, Pommard had two important qualities: it kept well and travelled without spoiling. It was therefore known far beyond the borders of Burgundy at a very early stage.

Besides possessing these qualities, all Pommards are full-bodied, vinous, well coloured and powerful, and acquire in ageing a flavour of truffles. Their taste has bite and fullness. These characteristics are more or less pronounced according to the climat: Argillières is lighter, Rugiens is very full-bodied and firm, and Epenots has finesse and breeding. Also worth mentioning are Clos-Blanc, les Arvelets, les Croix-Noires and la Platière. (See Index.)

Port The most famous, as well as the most widely known, of all liqueur* wines, port comes from a strictly delimited region in Portugal, the Upper Douro and its tributaries, including the Cima Corgo and the Baixo Corgo above and below the Rio Corgo. The vine-growing region of the Upper Douro covers barely 2500 square km and is particularly harsh and inhospitable. The ravines, enclosed by schistose mountains and mercilessly scorched by the sun, produce about 250–280,000 hl of port a year, which is strictly controlled by Portuguese wine laws. Due to the special character of the region, the variety of

grapes planted is of only secondary importance. There are about sixteen red varieties, including Avarelhão and Touriga, and six white ones, amongst which are Malvasia Fina, Moscatel, Rabigato and Codega. However, it is the soil and the climate which with skilful human assistance make port wine really what it is.

At the beginning of the eighteenth century, a commercial agreement was made between Portugal and Britain concerning the exchange of English wool and Portuguese wines, which had always been popular in England. Thus it was in response to the preferences of the British palate that the preparation of port was gradually established. Some Englishmen were such enthusiasts that, not content with having installed themselves as wine merchants in Oporto, they became vine-growers in the Upper Douro. One of the

Pommard, near Beaune.
Phot. Lauros-Beaujard.

Barge designed for the transport of casks from the Upper Douro to the town of Oporto. Phot. Casa de Portugal.

best known of these was the celebrated Joseph James Forrester who was born in Hull in 1809, came to Oporto in 1831 and was drowned in the Douro in 1861. His thirty years in Portugal were so full of achievement that the Portuguese made him a baron. One of his original ideas was to transport the wine casks from the vineyards to Oporto in flat-bottomed boats called *barcos rabelos*, which were able to negotiate the fierce torrents and rapids of the Douro. More important, he was the first to explore thoroughly the valley of the Douro, making a map of the vineyard area and conducting a geological survey.

Although grapes were traditionally trodden by foot in the Upper Douro, mechanical pressing is now gradually becoming the rule. Port is made by mutage★, like the vins doux naturels of France. Fermentation, which converts the must's natural sugar into alcohol, is stopped at a certain point by adding more alcohol, the timing depending on whether a sweet or dry wine is desired. Since 1907, the percentage of alcohol added to the wine has been legally fixed at a minimum of 16·5%, and must be in the form of a natural *eau-de-vie* made in the Douro vineyards.

After its arrival in Oporto, or rather in Vila Nova de Gaia, the capital's twin-city on the other side of the river, the wine is left in cask for three years, during which time it is constantly checked and examined by experts who decide which kind of port it is most suitable for – Tawny★, Vintage★, etc.

England has 95% of the vintage port market and used to be the chief importer of other types of port, but has recently been overtaken by France. The French usually drink port as an apéritif, an increasingly popular habit which accounts for the trebling of French imports over the last ten years. As an apéritif it should be white, dry and chilled. In England and Portugal it is more often served at the end of the meal, where its warm, smooth and generous nature has made it the traditional and perfect accompaniment and stimulant to after-dinner conversation.

The ideal age for port is generally considered to be between twenty and thirty years. Its qualities usually start to decline after forty years, although there are some marvellous exceptions. Once opened, a bottle should be consumed within a few days as if left longer, it tends to go flat and sour and loses its aroma.

There are a great many ornate and extremely expensive 'port glasses' on the market, but they should be avoided. Whatever kind of port is being served, the glasses should be clear, to show off its colour, and preferably tulip-shaped, i.e. closing a little towards the rim. They should never be filled more than two-thirds full, so that enough room is left to trap the bouquet.

Portugal Together with cork, wine is the country's chief export. Port★ and Madeira★ have long been known and admired the world over, and vinho verde★, long unknown outside its native country except by tourists, has recently started to appear in the rest of Europe. But as well as these famous wines, Portugal produces a considerable quantity of red, rosé and white vins ordinaires which are generally quite full-bodied and often pleasant.

The country's total annual production is about 15 million hl, of which three-quarters is red. Vinho verde accounts for 3 million hl, port for barely 280,000 hl, and Madeira, only 80,000 hl.

Portugal has fifteen viticultural regions including Madeira, which is an island off the west coast of Morocco. All Portuguese wines are subject to strict wine laws, and

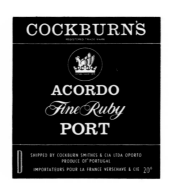

COCKBURN'S
REGISTERED TRADE MARK

ACORDO
Fine Ruby
PORT

SHIPPED BY COCKBURN SMITHES & CIA LTDA OPORTO
PRODUCE OF PORTUGAL
IMPORTATEURS POUR LA FRANCE VERSCHAVE & CIE 20°

198

Portugal: vineyards of the Upper Douro near Pinhão. Phot. Y. Loirat.

port, Madeira and vinho verde are very rigidly controlled. The regions of Dão, Colares, Carcavelos, Setubal and Bucelas produce characteristic wines whose production area is legally delimited and which have an official appellation of origin.

The Dão wines, considered the best of Portugal, are made from grapes growing along the banks of the Mondego. Most of the wines are red and are made from the Tourigo grape, which gives a sweet, slightly astringent wine. The less numerous white wines are made from the Dona Branca and Arinto grape and are light, fresh and fragrant with a beautiful blond colour. The Colares vineyards are situated

which is a perfect apéritif, dessert wine or accompaniment to cheese. The dry, astringent, pale yellow wines of Bucelas, north of Lisbon, are made from the Arinto grape.

Eight other regions of Portugal are in the process of being officially limited and classified AOC★. Pinhel produces light, agreeable clarets, and Lafões, red wines somewhat similar to the vinho verdes★. Bairrada, not far from Dão, makes the pétillant★ white or red Anadia and the Ruby of Bairrada. Other viticultural regions include Bucaco, Sangalhos, Alcobaca, Ribatejo and Torres Vedras.

Portugal also produces sparkling wines like Lamego, and rosés such as Mateus and Faisca (sold under the name Lancers).

Pouilly-Fuissé This excellent dry white wine from the Mâconnais★ vineyards is, like all the great white Burgundies, made from Chardonnay★ grapes. It is produced by four communes: Fuissé, Solutré-Pouilly, Vergisson and Chaintré.

It is a very attractive wine with a fine, greeny-gold colour and an exquisite, delicately shaded bouquet. It is vigorous and dry, though moelleux, and has a pronounced character of its own. Some people find it a little heavy and difficult to digest. It ages extremely well and may well improve after even twenty years in bottle.

on the seacoast close to Lisbon, growing in sandy soil which is difficult to cultivate. The Ramisco grape makes the wines of Colares full-bodied and velvety. They are kept in cask for two years and do not fully mature for at least five years. Unfortunately, the vineyards are slowly disappearing as a result of expanding tourist facilities. The Setubal region south of Lisbon produces the well-known Muscatel of Setubal whose pronounced aroma, colour and fruity taste are attributed to the special method of vinification, in which the stalks are left in the must and the wine is matured in cask for five or six years. The Muscatel of Setubal is a vin de liqueur

Pouilly Fumé An appellation contrôlée that applies only to Pouilly-sur-Loire★ wines made from Sauvignon★ (also known as Blanc Fumé) grapes. The appellation is sometimes Blanc Fumé de Pouilly. Nobody knows why Sauvignon should be called Blanc Fumé at Pouilly, though it may be because of its colour and smoky flavour. Whatever the reason, it makes excellent wines and has been responsible for Pouilly-sur-Loire's longstanding and well-merited reputation. Unfortunately, its success is not as widespread as it deserves to be, since annual production is not only low but is also sometimes drastically reduced by spring frosts.

It is an attractive, clear, green-tinted wine that has a minimum alcoholic content of 11° and a distinct character of its own. It has a pronounced, slightly spicy and musky fragrance and, although dry, is always pleasingly supple. It is ready to drink quite soon after bottling and loses none of its qualities with age. The best crus are les Loges, les Bas-Coins, Château du Nozet and les Bernadats.

Pouilly-Loché An appellation which applies to wines produced by the Loché commune, next to Pouilly★ in the Mâconnais★. It is a dry, fruity wine with the same characteristics as Pouilly-Fuissé★.

Pouilly-sur-Loire Celebrated for its wines since the Middle Ages, the vineyard of Pouilly-sur-Loire surrounds the village of the same name on the right bank of the Loire in the Nièvre department of France. The communes of Pouilly-sur-Loire, Saint-Andelain, Tracy, Garchy, Saint-Laurent, Saint-Martin and Mesves all produce wine entitled to this AOC★, but the first three are the most important. There is a great variety of soils, with marl and Kimmeridge clay predominating, as at Chablis★.

The appellation Pouilly-sur-Loire applies to wines made from Chasselas★ grapes, whereas the appellation Pouilly Fumé★ is restricted to wines made entirely from Sauvignon★ (or Blanc Fumé). Chasselas usually grows best in siliceous clay (on the hill of Saint-Andelain, for instance), a type of soil not altogether suitable for Sauvignon, which has largely taken over the best, or at any rate the most calcareous, slopes. Chasselas here produces

wines which are totally different from the ones it makes in Switzerland and Savoie (Crépy★). The region suits it perfectly and an expert has declared that, 'the soil of Pouilly is to Chasselas what Beaujolais is to Gamay'.

Pouilly-sur-Loire is a clear, light, fruity wine, very pleasant in its youth but lacking the character and distinction of Pouilly Fumé. It is fine and delicate and has a low acid content, a minimum alcoholic strength of 9° and occasionally a nutty flavour.

Pouilly-sur-Loire bailiffs at Saint-Emilion. Phot. René-Jacques.

Pouilly-Vinzelles Like those of Loché, the limestone-clay hills of the Vinzelles commune in the Mâconnais★ produce a dry white wine which has a well-deserved reputation and various similarities to Pouilly-Fuissé★. Like the latter, Pouilly-Vinzelles keeps for a long time without losing any of its bouquet or flavour.

pourriture grise (grey rot) *Botrytis cinerea*, responsible for the famous pourriture noble★ which attacks ripe grapes, also produces the disastrous pourriture grise (grey rot) which affects green grapes. It invades the immature grapes after a long

Above: pourriture grise;
below: pourriture noble. Phot.
M. and Weiss-Rapho.

period of humidity when many have split
– some may have burst as a result of the
flow of strong saps, others by insects. As
the fungus moves in and rapidly propagates, the grapes darken, become covered with a grey dust and fall.

The damage can be considerable. The
wine made from such an infected vendange will be of poor quality, having a
mouldy, 'oxide' taste and will reach old
age precociously.

Several methods can be used to treat
that part of the vendange which has been
infected by grey rot. If the must is heated
to 80°C the oxidising fungus will be
destroyed and the resulting wine is a bit
better than if the operation had not been
performed. However, bouquet is still
changed and the wine still ages rapidly.

Alternatively, the wine can be made a
rosé, in which case the musty taste acquired from the stalk and pulp during a
one- or two-day fermentation would not
be noticeable.

pourriture noble 'Noble rot' is the
literal translation of this French name for
the mould, *Botrytis cinerea,* which attacks
ripe grapes when the temperature and
humidity are favourable. Unlike pourriture grise★ or 'grey rot', it is heartily
welcomed by the vignerons, as it produces
exquisite and much sought after wine. At
first, small, brown marks appear on the
grape skin and these gradually grow to
cover the whole fruit until it is the colour
the Loire vine-growers call *'patte-de-lièvre'*
(hare's foot). The grape then turns a dark
purplish-brown, a stage known as *'pourri
plein'*, and finally withers, wrinkles and
looks shrivelled, or *'rôti'*. The grapes do
not all reach this final stage at the same
time, so the pickers have to go through the
vineyard very carefully at intervals and
only take those that are ready. The grapes
are picked individually with special
scissors, and the whole meticulous process
can last from September until the beginning of November.

Pourriture noble causes the composition
of the grape to change considerably; the
grape juice is condensed, causing a greater
concentration of the natural sugar, an
overall diminution of acids and the formation of gums and of citric and glut-
inic acids. Mere overripening, or
passerillage★, of the grapes does not

produce the same results. Ideally, *Botrytis* should attack really ripe grapes; if it comes too soon, it is less effective.

The fermentation of the grapes is extremely slow, as the activity of the yeasts is inhibited by the high sugar content of the must, and may take from several weeks to several months. This long period in vat produces a considerable quantity of glycerine★, which gives the wine exceptional smoothness. The wine has to be racked★ and topped up (ouillage★) frequently, and is usually bottled about three years after the vintage. All this complicated and painstaking preparation results in the great vins blancs liquoreux de pourriture noble – rare, delicious, and absolutely natural sweet white wines that are prized and admired the world over.

Although the wines made by pourriture noble in Sauternes★ are generally considered the best, the neighbouring vineyards of Loupiac★, Cérons★ and Sainte-Croix-du-Mont★ also produce their own, as do Monbazillac★ in Touraine★, the regions of Anjou★ and Alsace★, and the Rhine and Moselle valleys in Germany.

Premières Côtes de Bordeaux A region which stretches roughly sixty kl along the right bank of the Garonne from Saint-Maixant to Bordeaux, and consists of about thirty communes entitled to use the appellation. Loupiac★ and Sainte-Croix-du-Mont★, although geographically part of the region, qualify for their own appellation contrôlée.

Both red and white wines are produced, the red mainly in the south, and the white in the north of the district, with the Cambes commune on the dividing line. The white wines are made from Sémillon, Sauvignon and Muscadelle grapes, harvested as at Sauternes★. They are full-bodied, fine and fragrant, often moelleux★, sometimes liquoreux. Some people prefer them dry, and a small quantity is made to cater for this taste. The Langoiran and Cadillac communes produce what are probably the best white wines of the region. The red wines are warm and generous with a good colour. They are a little hard in their youth, but acquire suppleness and softness with age.

press There are various types of winepress in use. Ideally they should combine speed and economy of labour with efficiency. A bad press, for instance, could crush the grape stalks, which would make the wine taste very unpleasant. In ancient times, grapes were pressed by hand in linen

Winepress owned by Hattstatt (1687). Musée d'Unterlinden, Colmar. Phot. Lauros.

Automatic presses in a co-operative cave on the island of Oléron. Phot. M.

Automatic pressing. Phot. René-Jacques.

bags; later, in presses worked by levers and capstans; and by AD 23, screw-presses were in use. Grapes were always pressed before fermentation, and wine was generally rather pale. Today there are hydraulic presses, mechanical presses, horizontal and vertical presses and screw-presses. There is even a pneumatic press, in which the grapes are crushed against the sides of a cylinder by an expanding bag filled with compressed air.

presse (moût de, vin de) In the vinification of white wines, the moût de presse is the juice obtained from the grapes put in the press after the moût de goutte★ has been run off. In Champagne★, the juice from the last pressing of the must (about 7·5 litres per hl of must) is called rebêche★ and is not allowed to be sold commercially.

In the vinification of red wines, the vin de presse is that obtained by pressing the marc which is left after running the vin de goutte★ off from the vats of fermented

wine. The vin de presse has a higher tannin★ content and a higher volatile acidity★ than the vin de goutte, but a lower fixed acidity★. The percentage of vin de presse added to the vin de goutte varies according to the type of wine desired, and whatever is left over is sold without an appellation. To prevent white grapes being overpressed, a precise ruling obliges vine-growers to distil the remainder and sell it as alcohol to the State.

pressing An operation which consists of extracting the juice from grapes or the wine from marc by means of a press★. For white wines and vins gris★, the grapes are crushed and pressed as soon as they are picked. For red wines, the skins and stalks are left in the juice during fermentation to add colour and tannin★. They also form the marc, which is afterwards pressed to extract the vin de presse★, which varies in amount from about 10–20% of the vin de goutte★. In certain vineyards the marc is never pressed more than once, in order to avoid crushing the stalks which would give the wine an excessive tannin content and result in an unpleasant astringency known as *goût de rafle*.

privilège de Bordeaux A statute introduced by Henry III in 1224 gave the people of Bordeaux the right to protect their wine trade, i.e. the sale of the wine produced in Bordeaux and its immediate environs. The citizens interpreted this as

authorising them to forbid any wine from the inland areas of Aquitaine access to the port of Bordeaux before a certain date. This became known as the privilège de Bordeaux and, although it had no real legal basis, it nonetheless had the force of law for six centuries. The date they fixed was originally 11th November, then 30th November, and finally Christmas, by which time the foreign ships moored in the Gironde had long since made provision for their journeys – including, of course, stocks of Bordeaux wine.

This measure meant that there was, in seilles in about 600 BC. The Provençal viticultural tradition, therefore, goes back 2500 years, longer than any other French vineyard.

As in all southern vineyards, a great many varieties of grape are used: Grenache, Cinsault, Mourvèdre, Tibouren and Carignan for red wines, Clairette, Ugni Blanc and Bourboulenc for white. The INAO★ has divided them into two categories, authorised varieties and supplementary varieties. The proportion of the latter in any wine is strictly limited by law.

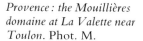

Provence: the Mouillières domaine at La Valette near Toulon. Phot. M.

effect, no foreign outlet at all for the wines of Cahors★, Gaillac★, Moissac and even the Médoc★. The only vineyard to get round this harsh law was Bergerac★, which could ship its wines to the sea on the Dordogne without having to go through Bordeaux. The privilege was abolished, after an enquiry which disclosed its origins, by an edict of Louis XVI in 1776.

This boycott by Bordeaux had a significant effect on rival vineyards. Moissac and Agen turned to producing fruit (prunes and table grapes), and Cahors dug up all its vines.

Provence The present vine-growing region of Provence is much smaller than was the former province of the same name, consisting nowadays of only the Bouches-du-Rhône, Var and Alpes-Maritimes departments. Vines were first planted there by Greeks from Phocea, who founded a colony on the site of present-day Mar-

The Ugni Blanc grape is widely used in Provence, particularly around Cassis. Phot. M.

Provence: vendange at Lorgues in the Var. Phot. M.

Provence has four appellations con-trôlées, Palette★, Cassis★, Bandol★ and Bellet★, and also four pleasant VDQS★, Côtes-de-Provence★, Coteaux-d'Aix-en-Provence★, Coteaux-des-Baux★ and Coteaux-de-Pierrevert★.

provignage Layering, a method once employed to propagate vines. A shoot of the growing vine is led down into the ground, where it eventually takes root. It is then cut from the main stem and replanted as a new rooted plant.

Puisseguin-Saint-Emilion The pebbly slopes of the Puisseguin commune, which is entitled to add the name Saint-Emilion★ to its own, produce firm, full-bodied wines that have a strong colour and keep well. The good crus also have a certain finesse. The best known are Chât-eaux des Laurets, du Roc-de-Boissac and Teyssier.

Puligny-Montrachet This village of the Côte de Beaune, together with the neighbouring one of Chassagne-Montrachet★, produces superlative dry white wines which are considered among the best in the world. The most famous of them, the great Montrachet★, is grown in both communes as is Bâtard-Montrachet, whereas Chevalier-Montrachet and Bienvenues-Bâtard-Montrachet are grown only in Puligny. Chevalier-Montrachet scarcely falls short of Montrachet's exceptional quality, equal-ling it in delicacy if not in body. Bienvenues-Bâtard-Montrachet is lighter than both of these, but has a certain elegance and a more fruity taste which have won it an enthusiastic following. These outstanding wines are sold under the name of their cru and not of their com-mune. Other wines, with equal breeding though less prestige, bear the name Puligny-Montrachet followed by the name of their particular climat★ (e.g. Puligny-Montrachet les Combettes, le Cailleret, les Folatières, les Pucelles and les Chalumeaux). (See Index.)

The red wines are produced in limited quantities (le Cailleret, for example) and have body, finesse and a smooth bouquet that develops with age.

Q

Quarts-de-Chaume One of the great white crus of Anjou★, made on the hillsides bordering the Layon★ and possessing its own appellation contrôlée. Its superior quality can be largely attributed to its quite exceptional location. It forms a part of the Rochefort-sur-Loire commune, and slopes down from the village of Chaumes to the banks of the river Layon, sheltered by hills from the north, east and west winds. Thus protected, the grapes ripen quicker and pourriture noble★ develops better than in the neighbouring vineyards. Even very ordinary years produce remarkably good wines, and good years are outstanding – the 1921 vintage, for example, will long be remembered.

Quarts-de-Chaume is a rich, powerful, velvety, sweet wine with exceptional qualities of both bouquet and taste. Some people claim to detect in it the flavours of amber, lime and apricots, and it has a slight, distinctive touch of bitterness which brings out its fragrance further. It is at its best several years after bottling, indeed it ages magnificently and is well worth waiting for. The principal domaines are l'Echarderie, Bellerive and Suronde. Annual production is extremely low, which is unfortunate as it is generally considered to be the greatest of all Anjou wines.

Quatourze The wines of this appellation are made in the Coteaux du Languedoc★ area and are classified VDQS★. They are either red or rosé, as the small quantity of white wine does not qualify for the appellation. The vineyard is situated on a pebbly plateau not far from the town of Narbonne in the Aude department. The red wines, which are undoubtedly the best, are full, warm and powerful, have a certain finesse and age well.

queue (vin de) The vin de queue is made from the last batch of grapes gathered in the Sauternes★ vineyards. The grapes are picked in successive stages, only the ones with pourriture noble★ being taken each time. In the end the only grapes left are those which have not been, and now never will be, affected by the mould and it is these which make the vin de queue.

A queue is also a measure of capacity equal to two pièces★, i.e. 2 × 228 litres. Lastly, *taille à queue*, or 'tail pruning', is a method of pruning vines.

Quincy A small vineyard of about 200 ha which lies in the commune of Quincy and part of Brinay on the banks of the Cher, to the west of Bourges in the Loire valley. The wine's distinctive character is largely due to the type of soil in the vineyard. Quincy is situated on a limestone plateau which, in prehistoric times, formed the riverbed of the Cher, and the soil is composed of the gravel and siliceous sand deposited by the river over a layer of clay of varying depth. This soil, which is

Quarts-de-Chaume: view of the vineyards. Phot. M.

otherwise barely suitable for cultivation, suits the Sauvignon★ grape extremely well. Sauvignon is the only variety planted in the Quincy vineyard and the wines made from it are AOC★. It is grafted on to an excellent vine-stock called Riparia which ripens quickly, giving Quincy an advantage over the nearby vineyards of Sancerre★ and Pouilly-sur-Loire★ in years of high humidity and late harvests.

Although Quincy keeps well, it is as good as it is rare when young, so that it is perhaps best to drink it as soon as it is found. It is a very dry wine with a good bouquet, a finesse imparted to it by the gravel of the soil and, besides the usual characteristics of wines made from Sauvignon, a particular and very agreeable flavour of its own. It has a minimum alcoholic strength of 10·5° and sometimes exceeds 11 or 12°, although in these cases the finesse of its fragrance is impaired.

R

racé A French word used to describe a wine that has all the characteristics of its 'race' or origins (variety of grape, soil, etc.). It implies more elegance and 'personality' than *type*, which is used for more ordinary wines. The equivalent phrase in English would be 'a wine of breeding'.

racking (soutirage) An operation which separates the clear wine from its deposits (or lees). It is a long and delicate process. First the wine is drawn off from the fermenting-vats into casks fumigated with sulphur dioxide★ and then, when the winter is well over, in about March or April, it is racked a second time, the lees now being mainly composed of tartric crystals. For wines which are going to remain in cask to mature, the third racking generally takes place around September. When wine is left in cask for more than a year, it is ouillaged★ as well as racked, i.e. more wine is added to replace that lost through evaporation and absorption by the wood.

rancio A name given to certain wines which acquire a particular bouquet and flavour in the course of a long and slow maturation in casks exposed to the sun. The process is a kind of beneficial maderisation★ which heightens and refines the qualities of the wine. Madeira, some Marsalas and the older French vins doux naturels★ are all included in this category. There is no precise legal definition of the term rancio. It is simply applied to all wines that have this particular colour and taste.

Rasteau This commune, which is situated in the south of the Côtes du Rhône★

Racking by pump. Phot. M.

region in the Vaucluse department, produces appellation contrôlée vins doux naturels★. Its vineyard covers the sunny hillsides between the Aygues and Ouvèze rivers, and consists of Rasteau and some parts of Sablet and Cairanne. It is mainly (90%) planted with Grenache vines.

Like all vins doux naturels, Rasteau is made by muting★ must with alcohol during fermentation. The must is then left to ferment with or without the grape skins and stalks, depending on whether a red or golden-coloured wine is desired. Rasteau is an excellent dessert wine, generous and sweet with a pronounced bouquet.

The commune also produces red, rosé and white wines sold under the regional appellation Côtes-du-Rhône.

Ratafia de Champagne A liqueur made by adding alcohol to the must of grapes from the Champagne★ region. The

Vines around Rasteau.
Phot. Lauros.

alcohol is either *eau-de-vie* from Champagne or from another source. Although the fruity tasting Ratafia is very agreeable, it is not often sold commercially, being highly taxed. Some prefer the appellation contrôlée Pineau des Charentes★, whose must is dosed with Cognac. Carthagène★ and Riquiqui are liqueurs of the same type made in certain areas for the personal consumption of the vine-growers. (In several European countries, particularly Spain, the designation Ratafia is used for those liqueurs made by the addition of alcohol to must.)

rebêche   The juice from the last pressing of Champagne grapes. Only the first few pressings are allowed to be made into Champagne★ and officially qualify for the name. According to present laws, every 4000 kg of grapes yields 26.66 hl of juice allowed to be used for Champagne, of which 20 hl are cuvée and 666 litres, the first and second tailles. The rebêche is the juice left in the marc gras, or pulp, after these pressings. It is extracted and made into a vin de consommation courante★ for the vine-growers and their employees. The remaining dry marc is made into *eau-de-vie de marc*, or grape brandy.

refermentation   The relatively high proportion of natural sugar remaining in vins blancs liquoreux★ after fermentation makes them liable to referment in bottle. This can result in clouded wine, a taste of lees, and corks which either leak or explode under the pressure of the carbon dioxide produced by fermentation. The tendency can be corrected by treatment with sulphur dioxide★, which is the only stabilising agent authorised by French law. Sulphur dioxide is only antiseptic, and thus effective, when pure, and it has to be added in fairly large quantities since a certain proportion always combines with the wine's sugar. The amount necessary varies from one wine to another, depending on the sugar content.

Nowadays, laboratories have equipment that can calculate the right dosage with complete precision, and thus avoid the unpleasant effects of excessive sulphur dioxide which gives wine a disagreeable and obtrusive taste and sometimes causes headaches. Overdosing was largely responsible for the decline in popularity of vins blancs liquoreux and other sweet white wines before this scientific accuracy was possible.

refrigeration, or cooling   Vignerons have long known that the coolness of cellars is beneficial to wine after fermentation: it helps the wine to clear, the lees to settle and excess tartric acid to precipitate. In really cold weather at Beanne, they used to take the barrels outside and roll them

Following two pages: detail of a fresco depicting a wine-harvest (c. 1400) from the Tower of the Eagle, Château Bon-Conseil, Trente, Italy.
Phot. Giraudon.

209

around on the ground; the wine would freeze around the sides of the barrel, trapping the deposits and leaving the clear, unfrozen wine to be racked off. Modern science has now largely superseded these methods, and refrigerated *cuveries* are both more reliable and more efficient.

Subjecting a wine to a temperature of around o°C causes its deposits to settle, so that after being filtered it becomes clear and stable. Refrigerated *cuveries* are indispensable for vinification in hot countries like Algeria and in the south of France, since to obtain a healthy and good quality wine the temperature should never really exceed 32°C. If the must from a crop which has been overexposed to the sun is not cooled down, the weakened alcohol yeasts★ will be supplanted by bacteria present in the fruit, which will seriously impair the wine and give it a high volatile acidity★ and an unpleasant bitter-sweet taste.

reginglard A local wine which is often a bit sour.

reheating of the must The best temperature for alcoholic fermentation is between 22 and 30°C. If the must is warmer than 30–32°C, the yeasts' action is impaired and the wine may suffer; below 22°C, yeasts act too slowly and sometimes not at all. In the first case the must has to be refrigerated★, and in the second, reheated to keep the yeasts active until fermentation is complete. Reheating is often necessary in cold countries where winter sets in relatively early. It can be carried out in two ways, either by taking a small quantity of must from the vat, heating it separately and then putting it back with the rest, or else by circulating warm water through pipes called drapeaux★ immersed in the must.

Remuage in a Champagne cave. Phot. J. Bottin.

remuage Remuage (from the verb *remuer*, to move, shift or stir) is an essential stage in the preparation of Champagne★. During secondary fermentation★, a deposit composed of dead yeasts and mineral salts settles on the side of each horizontally-placed bottle. In order to remove this deposit it must be worked down to the cork end of the bottle. This is an extremely delicate operation that requires specially-skilled workers called remueurs.

The bottles are stacked in wooden racks called *pupitres* which allow the angle of inclination to be adjusted. Every day the remueur takes hold of the base of each bottle and gives it a twist of a quarter-turn accompanied by a slight shake and a fractional change of angle (neck downwards) towards the perpendicular. A good remueur sometimes handles 30,000 bottles in one day.

This gradual progression from horizontal to vertical lasts about two or three months, at the end of which time the bottles are standing on their heads and the deposit has all collected on the corks, leaving the wine quite clear. The bottles are left like this for as long as the wine needs to develop and mature, which is sometimes several years.

The next stage is the removal of the deposit by dégorgement★.

Renaison–Côte Roannaise A VDQS★ wine produced in the Lyonnais★ vineyards. It is made from Gamay grapes and produced around the town of Roanne in about thirty communes on either side of the Loire in the Loire and Saône-et-Loire departments. It is a very pleasant red vin de pays★, and is fresh, light and best drunk young.

repression of frauds The *Service de la Repression des Fraudes et du Contrôle de la Qualité*, a sort of 'wine fraud squad', is a department of the French Ministry of Agriculture authorised by law in 1905. It is concerned with controlling the quality of all French wines, not only AOC★ and VDQS★, but also the vins de consommation courante★ which account for a large proportion of the country's total wine production. It is responsible for the application of various recent decrees which have laid down a higher minimum alcohol content for vins de pays★, it has prescribed the varieties of grape allowed in the composition of each wine, and set a lower limit for proportions of volatile acidity★ and sulphur dioxide★. A *casier vinicole* – a kind of 'vinicultural register' – has been set up for each department to help the administration deal with all the viti- and vinicultural information it collects, to give the necessary instructions at harvest-time and to forecast future developments for the benefit of both producer and consumer.

The Service was set up by decree in 1919, and consists of laboratory and administrative staff divided between a central office, travelling inspectors and teams of specialists. Its job is to clamp down on fraudulent marketing of goods and misleading advertising, and also to decide what 'additional substances' are permitted.

Reuilly An AOC★ wine of central France made in a vineyard on the banks of the Arnon, a tributary of the river Cher. The soil varies from marl and limestone, like that of Sancerre★, to gravelly sand like that of Quincy★, which is a commune ten km away on the banks of the Cher. The wine is produced by four communes: Reuilly and Diou in the Indre department, and Chéry and Lazenay in the Cher department. A long succession of medi-ocre vintages has unfortunately rather disheartened the vignerons, who now produce only a very small quantity of wine each year – which is a pity, as Reuilly possesses the same characteristics as other wines made from the Sauvignon★ grape, although it is perhaps less distinguished. It is fruity, full-bodied and dry, and reminiscent of both Sancerre and Quincy. A medium-dry Reuilly is sometimes made to suit local taste. The appellation also applies to rosé wines made from the Pinot grape.

Rheims The historic cathedral city of Rheims is, with Epernay, one of the two great commercial centres of Champagne★. The Montagne de Reims, which lies south-west of the city, is one of the principal vine-growing areas in the Marne department. It forms the southern side of the Vesle valley and faces north and east. According to tradition, it is the place where St Remi harvested the wine he presented to Clovis in order to establish good relations between them, and thus pave the way to the latter's eventual conversion.

The Montagne de Reims comprises the mountain proper (with the communes of Beaumont-sur-Vesle, Verzenay, Mailly and Sillery), the Petite Montagne de Reims (with Hermonville and Saint-Thierry), and the Côte de Bouzy★, which runs into the Marne★ valley (with Bouzy, Ambon-nay, Louvois and Tours-sur-Marne). The 'wines of Montagne' are full-bodied and have a pronounced bouquet and flavour.

Rheingau An important viticultural region in Germany which produces very high-quality white wines. The vineyards are perfectly situated at the foot of the Taunus range overlooking the Rhine – which at this point makes a curve of almost 180° – facing full south and catching the sunlight reflected from the river. The appellation officially includes the vineyards of Hochheim overlooking the Main (although these are, properly speaking, east of the Rheingau district) and the wines of Assmannshausen and Lorch, which are grown further north on the steep slopes of the Rhine gorges. Between Hochheim in the east and Rüdesheim in the west, there are fourteen villages which make Rheingau wine, and ten or eleven of these have great reputations: Erbach, Hattenheim, Winkel, Johannisberg★,

Rüdesheim, to name but a few. The success and renown of Rheingau, which some connoisseurs class among the best wine in the world, can largely be attributed to the Riesling grape, with which 70% of the region is planted.

The cheaper wines are usually chaptalised★ in order to attain the official alcoholic strength, and are entitled only to the name of the village which produces them (e.g. Rüdesheimer and Johannisberger). Certain world famous crus are sufficiently well known to have just one appellation, e.g. Steinberg★ (from Hattenheim), Schloss Vollrads (from Winkel), Marcobrunn★ and Schloss Johannisberg.

The best Rheingau wines, the rare and renowned Auslesen, Beerenauslesen and Trockenbeerenauslesen, are admirable dessert wines (especially those from the Steinberg, Johannisberg and Rüdesheim vineyards) on a par with the best Sauternes★, although less rich in alcohol. The other Rheingau wines are dry (but not excessively so), extremely fruity, and have a characteristic and inimitable bouquet.

A small quantity of good quality red wine is made at Assmannshausen, but it is very much an exception in this region of white wines.

Rheinhessen An important viticultural area of Germany whose capital is Mayence. The region is bordered on the east and north by the Rhine, on the south by the Palatinate★ and on the west by the Nahe★ valley. About 155 villages make their living by the vine, but only ten of them produce wine of really remarkable quality: Nierstein, Nackenheim, Oppenheim, Bingen, Dienheim, Bodenheim, Laubenheim, Guntersblum, Alsheim and Worms. The lesser quality wines are sold as carafe wines or a Liebfraumilch★ or Domtal (famous vineyards which have become generic names). Although Sylvaner is the dominant grape, the better wines are made from Riesling.

The communal wines produced in the Rheinhessen are often mediocre, being almost sickly sweet and smelling of sulphur dioxide★. But the fine wines made by the better communes are generally excellent, having a great deal of class and distinction. They are fruity and fragrant, distinguished and expansive and can be compared with the best wines of the Rheingau★. The best carry the name of the vineyard from which they come. The wines called Beerenauslesen are, like those of the Rheingau, splendid dessert wines comparable to Sauternes.

Riceys, Rosé des An excellent AOC★ wine made in the commune of les Riceys in the Aube department of France. Although the commune lies within the boundaries of the Champagne★ district,

Vineyards in Riceys, Champagne. Phot. M.

Rosé des Riceys is not a Champagne Rosé★ or pink champagne (although les Riceys produces this too), but a real rosé – and one that is particularly delicious. Vines have been grown in the commune since the beginning of the eighth century, and Rosé des Riceys has always been the most famous of all its wines.

The vineyard is situated on the steep sides of the Laignes valley, facing south and east. Some of these slopes are locally famous in their own right for the rosés they produce: la Velue, la Forêt and Violette, for instance. As at Chablis, the soil is pebbly clay and limestone, and many of the vineyards are equipped with heaters to combat the winter frosts.

The basic grape variety is the Pinot Noir of Champagne and Burgundy, together with a small proportion of Svégníe rose (a pink variety of the Jura Savagnin and the Traminer of Alsace) which gives the wine firmness, crispness and bouquet. The vinification of the wine is extremely delicate. The cuvaison, or vatting, is stopped the moment the wine has acquired a 'taste of rosé'; this may take anything from under two to four days. Only the vigneron's judgement can decide the right moment, and this requires great precision, as a few hours too long in vat can mean failure, producing a wine that is neither a rosé nor yet a red wine. The wine is bottled after eighteen months to two years in cask – and here again great precision is necessary, since if it stays too long in cask it turns the colour of *pelure d'oignon*★ and loses its characteristic and lovely deep rose colour.

Rosé des Riceys' only fault is its rarity. Justly rated among the best French rosés, it is a wine of breeding, originality, delicacy and great finesse, with a full bouquet and an exquisite, slightly nutty taste which persists for a pleasingly long time on the palate.

Riesling Riesling is without a doubt the most distinguished of all the noble★ grape varieties of Alsace★. It is a small-graped, unprolific vine that is not at all easy to cultivate, needing plenty of sunshine and exactly the right kind of soil. Given these, it produces excellent wine; without them, its wine can be acid and hard. The areas where it grows best are Eguisheim, Riquewihr, Ribeauvillé and Guebwiller.

Riesling wine is the best and most popular Alsatian wine. In great years it attains perfection, and shows outstanding breeding and distinction. It has few faults. It is a crisp, dry white wine with a delicate and subtle fragrance, and a smooth taste in which the flavours of lime, acacia and orange blossom are perceptible, with occasionally a touch of cinnamon. It is easy to drink, but without ill effects. It leaves both head and mouth fresh and clear.

Riesling is grown all over the world and, given the right conditions, always produces high quality wine. Besides being

Riesling, the most 'noble' of Alsatian grape varieties. Phot. M.

grown in Germany (in the Moselle★, Hesse★ and Palatinate★ vineyards) and in the Italian Tyrol, where it also makes good wines, it is cultivated extensively in most parts of central Europe. Riesling grapes also produce a fairly good wine in Chile, and in California produce a wine of distinction and bouquet called 'Johannisberg-Riesling'.

Rioja A viticultural region of Spain, near Pamplona, not far from the French border in the western Pyrenees. It takes its name from a tributary of the Ebro, the Rio Oja. The region produces more – and better – table wines than any other area in Spain. It is mountainous and has a harsh climate. The mountains at the northern

and southern ends of the valley are often still covered with snow at the end of April. The officially defined area of production includes Elciego, Fuenmayor, Cenicero and Ollauri, as well as Haro and Logroño, the two principal centres of the Rioja wine industry.

Rioja wines, particularly the red ones, have a curious similarity to those of Bordeaux. This is due to the emigration of several Bordeaux vine-growing families to the Ebro valley after the ruin of their own vineyards by phylloxera★ in the nineteenth century. They settled around Haro and Logroño, bringing with them their traditional methods of viti- and viniculture. Even now, the wines are made just as they were in Bordeaux more than eighty years ago.

The principal white grape varieties are Viura, Maturana, Calgrano and Turrantés, which make dry white wines of no great character or distinction. The red varieties – Garnacha (Grenache), Graciano, Mazuela and Tempranillo – are not quite what are usually called 'noble' grapes, but the wines they make are excellent, particularly in view of their price, which is always very reasonable. They are fine and light but quite full-bodied. None of them has a legally defined appellation of its own, which unfortunately means that one has to rely on the producer's name or the brand-name on the label. The best known are Marqués de Riscal, Marqués de Murrieta, Federico Paternina, Bodegas Bilbainas, Bodegas Franco-Españolas and La Rioja Alta, all of which usually appear under the initials CVNE (*Compañia Vinicola del Norte de España*).

Very little importance is attached to vintage, which is practically never specified. Quite a lot of producers do, however, call their young, light and inexpensive wines 'Clarete', while the descriptions 'Gran Reserva' and 'Imperial' are reserved for older wines, which are usually of excellent quality.

Ripaille A white cru of Savoie★ made from the Chasselas grape near the town of Thonon-les-Bains. Like most white wines of Savoie, it is a fresh, tart, dry wine and is rarely found outside its native area.

Rivesaltes A famous Roussillon★ vineyard, north of Perpignan, whose deep red earth produces excellent vins doux naturels★. It comprises about a dozen communes of which Salses, situated more or less in the centre of the area, has always been particularly renowned for its wine. Writing to the governor of the fort there, Voltaire said that it always gave him great pleasure to drink Salses, even though his feeble frame was not worthy of it. Rivesaltes makes two kinds of vin doux naturel, Rivesaltes and Muscat de Rivesaltes.

Rivesaltes is made from Grenache, Muscat, Malvoisie and Macabéo grapes, and can be either red or white (the latter vinified by fermenting the must without the pulp). It is a fine wine, and gets even better with age.

Muscat de Rivesaltes is made entirely from Muscat Doré (or Muscat de Frontignan) and Muscat d'Alexandrie grapes. It was in the Rivesaltes area that Muscat, probably of Spanish origin, made its first appearance when it was served at Pope Benedict XIII's table in 1394. It is an outstanding wine with finesse, a fruity taste and a marvellously fragrant bouquet – qualities which are earning it a steadily growing reputation among connoisseurs.

robe Robe is the word professional wine-tasters and connoisseurs use when referring to the colour of a wine. The colouring matter★ contained in the grape skins dissolves in the juice during fermentation and gives the wine its colour. This process can produce an enormous variety of colours, from dark to light. Red wines range from a deep cherry-red through bright red, ruby, garnet and purple to *rouge tuilé*★, or brick-red, and *pelure d'oignon*★. White wines vary from white to ochre, with intermediary shades of greenish-white, light yellow, lime, golden-yellow, straw and amber★. Rosé wines are gris★, bright pink, saffron-pink or brick-pink.

In red wines, a bluish tinge denotes a young wine (or one made from *teinturier* grapes), and a yellow tinge (tawny, rancio★ and *feuille-morte*, or autumn-leaf) an old one. In white wines, green denotes youth and a rusty colour is evidence of maderisation★.

robust A description applied to powerful, full-bodied wines which seem to assert

themselves on the palate with energy and authority. The words 'vigorous' and 'solid' describe more or less the same qualities.

Roche-aux-Moines A cru of the Savennières★ vineyard entitled, like Coulée-de-Serrant★, to add its own name to the appellation Savennières. It was given its name by monks from the abbey of Saint-Nicolas of Angers, who came and planted their vines on the hillsides there in the twelfth century, and now covers about 25 ha. Although it has much in common with the nearby Coulée-de-Serrant, it differs primarily in always being a dry wine. It is also less full-bodied and not as powerful, and should in general be drunk sooner. It does, however, share Coulée-de-Serrant's elegance and delicacy.

Romania The wines of the old Roman province of Dacia (present-day Romania) were famous even in very ancient times, as documents written in the third century attest. In the Middle Ages, the Romanian provinces sold wine to Russia, Poland and the Republic of Venice. Nowadays Romania has about 200,000 ha of vineyards, and her six wine-growing districts produce 4·5 million hl of wine a year.

Dobrudja or Dobrogea is the largest region, and the one which produces the most famous Romanian wine, Murfatlar★, which is grown near Basarabi and Nazarcea. Other well-known wines of the region are those produced at Ostrov in the south, and at Sarica and Niculitel in the Danube delta.

The Moldavian vineyards in the northeast are a continuation of the vineyards of Soviet Moldavia, and chiefly produce white wines. The best of these are Cotnari, Odobesti, Nicoresti, Panciu, Husi and Dealul-Mare ('Great Hill'), the last of which is rather like a French wine.

217

Munthenia, the region around the cities of Bucharest and Ploesti, produces the wines of Valea Călugărească, Urlati and Ceptura, while Oltenia, in the Olt valley, is known for its white wine, Drăgăsani, and Segarcea. Banat, in north-west Romania, produces only one wine worth mentioning, a red one called Minis, which is again not unlike a French wine.

Transylvania, in the west, has several wine-growing centres, amongst which are Alba Iulia, Aiud, Bistrita Năsăud and Tîrnaveni, the last of which produces a very pleasant white wine.

A southerly latitude is normally unfavourable to the production of white wines, but this is counterbalanced in Romania by the height at which the vines are grown, and the country produces more white wine than red. In recent years all Romanian wines have shown a definite improvement in quality. The most popular drink, incidentally, is a mixture of white wine and soda water, which is served very cold and called *sprit* (pronounced 'schpritz'). The reds are good table wines, despite a certain astringency.

Methods of vinification are the same as those used in Hungary★ and Bulgaria★. The wines tend to have a relatively high tannin content and are at their best with Romanian food, which is fairly strong and spicy.

rosé A rosé is never just a mixture of red and white wines, which is statutorily prohibited by French law. However, what is permitted is to mix red and white grapes, or their juice. Although rosé is mostly made only from red grapes, certain rosés are traditionally made by adding a small proportion of white grapes to the red. Until the eighteenth century, rosé was the only type of wine that could be made with complete success, but it suffered an eclipse when the vinification techniques for red wines became widespread in the nineteenth century. Recently, however, it has become more popular than ever.

Various methods are used to make rosé. The first consists of treating the red grapes as if they were white, i.e. pressing★ them as soon as they are picked, and separating the must from the skins and stalks before leaving it to ferment. The vins gris★ of Burgundy are made in this way, and so are the very pale rosés of Saumur and the

Loire valley. To obtain 'real' rosé, with a firmer, more pronounced colour, the crushed grapes are put in a vat and left to start fermenting. As the temperature of the juice rises and its alcohol content increases, the colouring matter★ in the skins dissolves and is absorbed by the liquid. The vigneron takes a sample of the juice every hour, and when he judges it to have reached the right depth of colour, he runs it off into another vat to complete its fermentation. The marc left behind is then pressed and its juice, which is now too dark for rosé, is used for red wine.

Another method is to 'bleed' the vats. After at least two hours of fermentation the vigneron turns the tap at the base of the vat and runs the juice out at intervals until it starts to get too dark. In both these cases it is often extremely difficult to judge the colour with accuracy. The period in vat (cuvaison) can vary from five or six hours to as many as forty-eight (as is the case in the Jura★, for example). The rosés of Tavel★, Provence★, Jura★ and les Riceys★ are all made by these methods. They have a good colour, are full-bodied and seem to retain the characteristics of the grapes they were made from. Rosés made from Pinot, for example, are always excellent, whether they come from the Côte-d'Or, Alsace or les Riceys.

Although some rosés have a long tradition behind them (les Riceys and Marsannay-la-Côte, for instance), a great number have appeared comparatively recently, in response to public demand. Vignerons also make rosé out of crops badly affected by pourriture grise★ to avoid the taste of mould the wine would acquire if vinified by the usual methods, i.e. left to ferment in contact with the grape skins.

Successful rosé vinification requires extremely accurate judgement and balancing of the various processes involved. In achieving a good, firm colour the wine may also acquire excessive tannin and become too heavy, but on the other hand the procedures employed when a pale, delicate colour is desired may well leave it lacking in bouquet. Despite their current popularity, rosés are not always up to standard. They sometimes have an unpleasant salmon-pink colour which is due to the grapes being picked too late or to the oxidisation of the colouring matter. In the

'Young Bacchus' by Caravaggio. Uffizi Gallery, Florence. Phot. Giraudon.

Midi, the proportion of white grapes sometimes rises above 20%, or the grapes are left to macerate too long before fermentation, and in both cases the wine is disappointing. Rosés have the further disadvantage of ageing badly. They must be bottled very early (in the February or March following the vintage) and drunk quite soon, generally within two years.

Rosette A white wine grown on hills just north of Bergerac★. The three classic vines of the Sud-Ouest★ region, Sémillon, Sauvignon and Muscadelle, grow on clay and siliceous-clay – types of soil which suit them particularly well. The appellation applies to wines produced by certain *parcelles*, or divisions, of the communes of Bergerac, Lembras, Creysse, Maurens, Prigourieux and Ginestet. It is a medium-dry, fruity wine with finesse, body (a minimum 12°) and character.

rouge (vin) Red wine is made in several steps. After the vendange the grapes are pressed★ and eventually separated from their stalks. The pressed grapes are put into a cuve★ where they undergo alcoholic fermentation★ caused by the action of certain yeasts, some naturally existing in the bloom on the grapes, and others added. This fermentation can take place in open or closed cuves. The vigneron must be sure that the must is aerated and that the temperature is between 25 and 28°C; if not, the yeast stops acting and it is sometimes necessary to reheat or refrigerate★ the must. The must has to be aerated in order to stimulate fermentation, and to help diffuse the colouring matter★ by putting the juice in contact with the chapeau★.

Finally, the vigneron must sterilise the grapes by adding sulphur dioxide★ and sometimes, acting on the advice of the oenological stations, he must make other additions to correct the must.

The length of the fermentation period varies from two or three days to three week's depending on the region and type of wine desired. After fermentation has ended the wine must be drawn off from the marc; this is the vin de goutte★. The marc is then pressed and yields the vin de presse. After blending in a cask, the young wine is sent to the cellars to mature in cask for a certain period before bottling.

roundness An agreeable quality of wines with a good alcohol★ and glycerine★ content and not too much acidity★, resulting in a generally 'well-rounded' sensation on the palate.

Roussillon This old French province, with Perpignan as its centre, consists of the department of Pyrénées-Orientales and a part of the Aude. As a wine-growing area, it presents several similarities to the neighbouring Languedoc★. It produces large quantities of vin ordinaire and several good VDQS★ table wines, amongst which are Corbières du Roussillon★ and Roussillon-Dels-Aspres★. Its main claim to fame, however, is that it produces three-quarters of all French vins doux naturels★, all with appellations contrôlées: Banyuls★, Rivesaltes★ and Muscat de Rivesaltes★, Côtes-d'Agly★, Maury★, Côtes-du-Haut-Roussillon★ and Grand-Roussillon★.

Roussillon-Dels-Aspres These wines greatly resemble the neighbouring Corbières★ and Corbières du Roussillon, and like them are VDQS★. The red wines have body, colour and warmth, and although they are made from the same grapes as Corbières du Roussillon, they have a particular flavour of their own, derived from the soil on which the vines are grown. The reds, rosés and whites must contain a minimum alcohol content of 11°.

Rully A very distinctive, dry, fruity, golden-yellow AOC★ wine made from Chardonnay grapes by the commune of Rully in the Côte Chalonnaise★. This wine, which lends itself remarkably well to effervescence, was the first sparkling wine to be made in Burgundy. Nowadays,

Typical vineyard area of Roussillon. Phot. Phédon-Salou.

sparkling Burgundies are widely known, though less appreciated in France than in other countries. The appellation Rully may in certain cases be followed by the words Premier Cru or by the name of a particular climat★. Rully also produces a little red wine of average quality.

rural method A very ancient method of preparing sparkling wines, employed before the Champagne method★ had been perfected, and nowadays scarcely in use at all except in Gaillac★, Die★ and Limoux★. With this method, the carbon dioxide★ is formed entirely by the natural grape sugar left in the wine, without the addition of any liqueur de tirage★. The procedure consists of slowing down, without actually stopping, primary fermentation (which converts grape juice into still wine) by repeated filtration and racking, and then bottling the wine when its remaining sugar content is judged sufficient to ensure a good *prise de mousse*, or secondary fermentation. Once the wine is bottled and firmly corked, fermentation slowly starts again, producing carbon dioxide which is trapped in the wine and remains in suspension as its 'sparkle'.

This method is in some respects similar to the one used at Asti★, where sparkling wines are also made by primary fermentation (although at Asti this takes place in vat), as opposed to the Champagne method, in which still wine is made to ferment twice. The wines it produces are excellent and marrowy with a very fine bouquet. The rural method is also the best way of preserving the characteristic aroma of Muscat★-based wines, such as Clairette-de-Die. It is, however, an extremely delicate operation which can go wrong in many ways. Fermentation may be either too fierce and make the bottles explode, or too weak, even non-existent. Refermentation★ sometimes occurs and quality may vary from one bottle to another. In addition, the wine is always slightly hazy. This is not due to solid deposits of lees and yeasts that can be collected on the cork and removed by dégorgement★ as in the Champagne method, but is a side-effect of the rural method itself, and can be eliminated by isobarometric filtration. At Die this filtration is carried out individually on each bottle.

Russian Soviet Federal Socialist Republic (RSFSR) Vineyards have flourished for a long time in the European part of this republic. They are planted on the banks of the Don and Kouban at Astrakan, Stavropol, and in the south at Saratov. European grape varieties were imported by Peter the Great. Today, the important viticultural centres are Tsimliansk, Derbent (Daghestan), the Kouban Valley (up to Maikop), Rostov-on-Don (which makes Tsimliansky, a sparkling wine) and the coastal areas of Novorossiisk, Touapsé and Sotchi, from which comes the good red wine Abraou-Diourso.

S

sables (vin de) One of the by-products of the desperate struggle against phylloxera★. When a vigneron of Vaucluse discovered that this destructive aphid was not able to survive in sand, people hurried to plant vines wherever they could find enough fine sand, e.g. around Saint-Laurent-de-la-Salanque in the Roussillon district, on the edges of the Thau d'Agde basin at Sète and on the dunes around Aigues-Mortes in the Gard department. The product, a vin de sables, was also made until quite recently near Soustons in the Landes region of south-western France.

The sandy islands of Oléron and Ré off the west coast of France, however, were producing this type of wine long before phylloxera had even been heard of – in fact, their wine was famous as early as the thirteenth century. Nowadays, the two islands make as much wine as ever, producing dry white wines which are greatly appreciated by visitors and tourists. The Ile de Ré also makes a curious-tasting red wine.

Sables-Saint-Emilion These wines are made in a vineyard just east of Libourne between Pomerol and Saint-Emilion. The soil is sandy and produces a wine which has the generosity of a Saint-Emilion and the suppleness and bouquet of a Pomerol. It is a pleasant wine that does not require a long vinification. The principal crus are Châteaux Cruzeau, Martinet, Doumaine and Gaillard.

sack One of the first names used in England for sherry★. It is also used for sweet wines resembling sherry, like Malaga sack and Canary sack.

Saint-Amour A popular red wine and one of the most pleasant Beaujolais★, produced in the region's northernmost commune. It has an attractive ruby colour and a delicate, fairly light bouquet.

Saint-Chinian The excellent red wine made in this village is one of the VDQS★ of the Coteaux-du-Languedoc★. The vineyard covers several pebbly hillsides in the north-west of the Hérault department, and produces an attractive ruby-coloured wine that is fairly full-bodied, but has a delicate bouquet which acquires depth with age.

Vin de sable. Vendange at Oléron. Phot. Léah Lourié.

222

Saint-Emilion The vineyard of Saint-Emilion is situated on the right bank of the Dordogne several kilometres from Libourne. It is one of the oldest in France and the chief producer of fine wines in the Bordeaux★ region. Louis XIV called Saint-Emilion 'the nectar of the gods'.

The appellation Saint-Emilion extends to all the communes formerly administered from Saint-Emilion: Saint-Laurent-des-Combes, Saint-Christophe-des-Bardes, Saint-Hippolyte, Saint-Etienne-de-Lisse, Saint-Sulpice-de-Faleyrens, Vignonet and Saint-Pey-d'Armens.

All Saint-Emilion wines have generosity, body and warmth, as well as an attractive, dark garnet colour and a fragrance reminiscent of truffles. More powerful than Mèdocs, they are sometimes called 'the Burgundies of Bordeaux'. An average tannin★ content ensures them a long life (sometimes thirty to forty years) without giving them the unpleasant astringency of wines that contain too much tannin.

Enthusiasts recognise two distinct kinds of Saint-Emilion: the wine grown on the hillsides, and the wine from the flat, gravelly parts of the vineyards. The *vin de côtes*, or hillside wine, is generous, full-bodied and firm (e.g. Château-Ausone★); the *vin de graves*, or gravel wine, has finesse, suppleness and a distinctive bouquet, and resembles Pomerol★ wines (e.g. Château-Cheval-Blanc★).

As in all the best Bordeaux vineyards, wines grown on the alluvial flats are excluded from the appellation. Only noble★ vines are grown: Cabernet Franc, Cabernet-Sauvignon (or Bouchet), Merlot and Malbec (or Pressac). It is interesting that the species of white grape called Saint-Emilion (or Ugni Blanc) is, despite its name, rarely found in the region.

The premiers grands crus classés are Château-Ausone and Château-Cheval-Blanc, followed by the Châteaux Beauséjour, Bélair, Canon, Figeac, la Gaffelière, Magdelaine, Clos Fourtet, Pavie and Trottevieille. (See Index.) In addition, six communes on the periphery of the Saint-Emilion area are officially permitted to add the name of Saint-Emilion to their own on their labels (although their name must always precede Saint-Emilion, and be printed in characters of the same size). These are Saint-Georges★, Montagne★, Lussac★, Puissegin★ and Parsac★, all of

Saint-Emilion: above, the Great Walls; below, the Jurates at the proclamation of the wine-harvest. Phot. René-Jacques.

Maturation cave, Saint-Emilion. Phot. M.

MIS EN BOUTEILLE AU CHATEAU

COS D'ESTOURNEL 1966
SAINT-ESTÈPHE
APPELLATION SAINT-ESTÈPHE CONTROLÉE
SOCIÉTÉ DES VIGNOBLES GINESTET PROPRIÉTAIRE A SAINT-ESTÈPHE

which are north of Saint-Emilion, and Sables-Saint-Emilion★, which lies west of Libourne.

Saint-Estèphe Very distinguished red wines made in the Médoc★. The grands crus (Châteaux Cos-d'Estournel, Montrose and Calon-Ségut) have great finesse. They are lighter in body than the neighbouring Pauillacs, but more fruity and supple. The appellation Saint-Estèphe also applies to a large number of secondary crus (classified in France as *crus bourgeois, crus artisans* or *crus paysans*) which make very good wines, especially those at the upper end of the scale (although they lack both the finesse and distinction of the classed growths).

Saint-Georges d'Orques One of the Coteaux-du-Languedoc★ VDQS★ wines. The area of production comprises the village of Saint-Georges and some parts of the neighbouring communes just outside Montpellier. The red wines, made mostly from Cinsault and Carignan grapes, have good texture and finesse and are very popular locally. They improve greatly with age.

Saint-Georges-Saint-Emilion The commune of Saint-Georges is officially entitled to add the name of Saint-Emilion to its own name on its labels. Its wines do in fact have all the characteristics of the

'*vins des côtes*' of Saint-Emilion: they are an attractive purplish-red colour, and are full-bodied and powerful without being coarse. Robust and well rounded, they age extremely well and retain a remarkable bouquet reminiscent of truffles. The best crus are Châteaux Saint-Georges-Macquin, Saint-Georges, Saint-André-Corbin, Samion and Tourteau.

Saint-Jean-de-Minervois Although still relatively unknown, this AOC★ Muscat wine from the Languedoc region is a vin doux naturel★ of excellent quality. It is both delicate and elegant, and dryer than other Muscats.

Saint-Joseph Wines made in the north of the Côtes du Rhône★ region, on the right bank of the Rhône facing the Hermitage★ vineyards. The vineyard's output is mainly red, made from Syrah grapes. These reds are very full-bodied, strongly coloured wines with a slightly bitter taste when young. Age refines their bouquet and often makes them excellent wines. The appellation also provides a small quantity of rosé and white wines made from Marsanne and Roussanne grapes. The crisp, fragrant white wines can show remarkable qualities in good years.

Saint-Julien A small commune in the heart of the upper Médoc★ region. (The appellation Saint-Julien also includes a few divisions of the Pauillac, Cussac and Saint-Laurent communes.) Saint-Julien is an excellent red wine, being supple and fine with a pronounced bouquet. In character it tends to be midway between Margaux★ and Pauillac★ wines. It is more full-bodied but has the same finesse as Margaux, and less full-bodied than Pauillac though its bouquet develops more quickly. It also keeps for a long time in bottle. The best-known châteaux are those of Ducru-Beaucaillou, Gruaud-Larose, Léoville-Las Cases, Léoville-Poyferré, Beychevelle and Talbot. (See Index.)

ling wine (by the Champagne method★) at the beginning of the nineteenth century. Saint-Péray-Mousseux has been extremely popular ever since, and is more widely known than the original, still Saint-Péray. It is one of the best French sparkling wines and some class it next to Champagne★. It has a deeper colour and more body than the latter, yet always preserves its characteristic aroma of violets.

Saint-Pourçain-sur-Sioule The Saint-Pourçain vineyards stretch for about thirty km, at a height of around 300 m, along hillsides bordering the Sioule, Allier

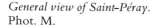

General view of Saint-Péray. Phot. M.

Saint-Nicolas-de-Bourgueil A commune in Touraine★ situated very near Bourgueil★. Although its wines are similar to the latter's, it has its own appellation contrôlée. The soil here is particularly favourable to the Cabernet Breton grape and brings out its best qualities. Saint-Nicolas-de-Bourgueil is usually rated higher than Bourgueil, which has less tannin and does not age as well.

Saint-Péray Situated on the right bank of the Rhône, opposite Valence, this Côtes du Rhône★ commune produces excellent dry white wine made from Roussanne and Marsanne grapes. Saint-Péray is a fine, crisp wine with an aroma of violets.

Saint-Péray was first made into spark-

and Boule rivers in central France. About twenty communes produce Saint-Pourçain, which is considered a Loire wine and has a VDQS★ label. The chief of these are Saint-Pourçain, Besson, Bramsat, Contigny, Chemilly and Bresnay. Although once served at the tables of the kings of France, its present reputation has for a long time been purely local.

The white wine is made from the Tresallier grape often found in the region (and known as Sacy in the Yonne department), of which the proportion is officially fixed at a minimum of 50%. To this are added the supplementary varieties Aligoté, Sauvignon, Chardonnay and Saint-Pierre-Doré (an unimportant species limited to a proportion of 10%). This

225

delicious, clear white wine has an attractive greenish-white colour. It is dry, light, fragrant and fine, with a fruity flavour that is curiously reminiscent of apples. Germany buys considerable quantities of it for use in the preparation of sparkling wines.

The red and rosé wines are made from Gamay and Pinot Noir. The red is very smooth and pleasant, a little reminiscent of Beaujolais, but with an agreeable *goût de terroir*★. The rosé is excellent, fresh and fruity, with an attractive, sometimes very pale colour (vins gris★). It is very popular with those who come to take cures at the nearby spas in the summer. The white, red and rosé should all be drunk young.

Saint-Véran This new Mâconnais cru received its title as an appellation contrôlée area on 6th January, 1971. The little village, formerly known as Saint Véran des Vignes, borders on Pouilly-Fuissé★, and the area of appellation includes seven communes: Chanes, Chasselas, Davaye, Prisse, Leynes, Saint-Amour and Saint Véran. The wine has the same subtle bouquet and taste of hazelnuts as its neighbour Pouilly-Fuissé.

Sainte-Croix-du-Mont The steep slopes of this commune overlook the right bank of the Garonne facing the Sauternes★ region. The regulations governing its

vinification procedure are the same – and as exacting – as those applied in Sauternes, and this has given its wine particular prestige among the other famous white wines of the right bank. Sainte-Croix-du-Mont is a lovely, clear, golden colour, is liquoreux and smooth, fine and fruity, and fully deserves its reputation.

Sainte-Foy-Bordeaux A region which occupies the north-east corner of the Gironde department on the left bank of the Dordogne. Although geographically a part of the Entre-deux-Mers area, its wines are quite different and have their own appellation. The white wines are moelleux★ or semi-liquoreux★, with a pleasant fragrance which has led to their being called 'the poor man's Sauternes'. Sometimes they are made dry or medium dry, and in these cases are similar to Anjou★ and Saumur★ wines. The red wines have good body and colour, and mature rapidly.

saints de glace These 'ice saints' are called *Eis Heilgen* in Germany, where they are the patron saints of the four days in May when the vignerons think their vines most susceptible to the spring frosts, particularly in the Moselle and Saar regions. From the 12th to the 15th May, Saint Pancras, Saint Servais, Saint Boniface and the cold Saint Sophie (*die kalte Sophie*) hold

the fate of the vineyards in their hands. It seems that the vines are in fact very rarely attacked by frosts after these dates.

San Benito A vine-growing county in California★ located east of Monterey Bay and south of San Francisco. The vineyards, which cover steep hillsides and the slopes of high valleys, have spread considerably in recent years as a result of the replanting around Paicine of the Almaden vineyard, which was forced out of Santa Clara★ by a housing development. Almaden is currently California's most important producer of 'premium wines' (i.e. quality wines), sparkling wines and sherry, which is made by the traditional Spanish methods. More than half of San Benito's vines are ungrafted French or German varieties (Chardonnay, Pinot Noir, Cabernet and Gewürztraminer), and the vineyard's future seems to be a promising one.

Sancerre Perched on a hilltop on the left bank of the Loire★, the tiny, picturesque town of Sancerre huddles round the remains of its feudal castle, overlooking the river and practically opposite Pouilly-sur-Loire★. The vineyards cover the neighbouring hills, which are composed of two kinds of soil: marly Kimmeridge clay, locally known as *terres blanches*, and dry limestone called *caillotes*. The appellation includes several villages around Sancerre, of which Amigny, Bué★, Champtin, Chavignol★, Reigny and Verdigny make the best-known wines. The superiority of these wines compared with others in the Sancerre region, although always discernible, is most evident in poor years.

Sancerre and its vineyards.
Phot. Lauros-Beaujard.

Sancerre owes its reputation to its dry white wine, which is made from Sauvignon grapes. Wines from the *terres blanches* take time to acquire their character and bouquet, but preserve them for a long time. They are fruity, supple and full-bodied. Those from the *caillotes* have great finesse and bouquet from the start, but lose their qualities more quickly. All the wines, however, justify the traditional oath taken by honorary vignerons of Bué: 'I swear I will drink the first glass of wine neat, the second without water, and the third just as it comes out of the barrel'.

Sancerre also produces red and rosé wines, which must be made from Pinot Noir grapes to qualify for the appellation. These wines were famous in the late Middle Ages, but nowadays Pinot is grown only on the slopes unsuitable for Sauvignon. The rosé is excellent, being pale, fruity and full-bodied, and it is considered one of the best Pinot rosés in France. The small output of red wine, made only in good years, is mostly consumed locally.

Santenay, at the border of the Côte-d'Or. Phot. Aarons-L.S.P.

sangria This is a refreshing drink made throughout Spain from oranges, lemons and wine; it is drunk with ice at the table or between meals. Additional sugar is often added to this fresh and pleasant drink, which is often deceptively strong at first.

Santa Clara A valley and county south of San Francisco Bay and Alameda★ in California★, named after an old Spanish mission established near San José. Santa Clara wines have long been known for their quality, but unfortunately there will soon be none of them left, as the vineyards are being encroached upon by the area's rapidly increasing population. Urban growth is gradually forcing the walnut trees from the valleys and the vines from the surrounding hillsides and replacing them with buildings. Many vineyards have succumbed completely or, like Almaden, have had to be replanted further south in a less populated area.

Nowadays, all that is left of the fine Santa Clara vineyards is a scrap of the old Almaden, a few insignificant patches of vines and the Novitiate of Los Gatos, a vineyard owned by Jesuits. Their production is primarily Communion wine, with a small quantity of good table wine and some dessert wines (e.g. Muscat Frontignan and Black Muscat).

Santa Maddalena An excellent red wine made in the Italian Tyrol as popular in Switzerland and Austria as it is in Italy. It is grown north-east of the town of Bolzano, and the vines are principally three varieties of Schiava (Schiava Gentile, Meranese and Grigia). The wine, which is a very pale cherry-red, is fresh, tender, light and fruity, and yet quite full-bodied.

Santenay The old and picturesque city of Santenay is on the boundary of the Côte d'Or★ and produces white and excellent red wines. The reds, which account for the bulk of wine production, resemble Chassagne-Montrachet and are ferme★, full-bodied, and moelleux★ with an original bouquet which improves with age. The best cru is Gravières. (See Index.)

The white wines are produced in small quantities and are fine and dry. They do not, however, enjoy the same reputation as the reds and are best drunk young.

Saumur Although the Saumur vineyards are officially in the Anjou★ district, they are more like an extension of Touraine★, having similar topography, identical methods of cultivation and vinification and, above all, the same type of soil (subsoil of Tufa chalk, out of which great underground cellars are cut, as at Vouvray★, and covered with pebbly, siliceous sand). The vines cover two lines of hills which meet at Saumur, where the best-known crus are to be found. One of the lines starts at Montsoreau and follows the course of the Loire, and the other stretches from Saix to Saumur along the banks of the Thouet and Dive rivers. Other areas of production are from Ranton to Pouançay on the right bank of the Dive, between Montreuil-Bellay and Saint-Hilaire-Saint-Florent on the left bank of the Thouet, and on a chalky hill further to the west (Puy-Notre-Dame and Vaudelnay). Altogether, thirty-seven communes produce AOC★ Saumur wine, the most famous being Montsoreau, Turquant, Parnay, Souzay, Dampierre, Saumur, Varrains, Chacé, Saint-Cyr-en-Bourg, Brézé, Epieds (part of the Bizay commune) and Saix. The wine of Saumur has been renowned since the twelfth century when it was exported in large quantities to the Netherlands.

The white wines, made from Pineau de la Loire grapes, are always dry or medium dry (to qualify for the appellation they must contain no more than 10 g of sugar per litre), and have a minimum alcoholic strength of 10°. They are remarkably light, fine, vigorous wines which keep extremely well – the best vintages always used to be buried in sand where they kept their youthful qualities for a particularly long time. Fruity and fresh, they have a smooth fragrance that deepens with age and a very original taste known as the *goût de tuf*, which derives from the subsoil and distinguishes them markedly from other Anjou wines. In rich years, the most sumptuous and fragrant sweet white wines are made from grapes which the sun has dried on the vine, or, even better, which have been attacked by pourriture noble★.

Apart from its still white wines, Saumur has since 1830 made fine and distinguished sparkling wines, which are produced in greater quantities than any other sparkling wine in France. The natural lightness of

The château of Saumur.
Phot. Hétier.

Saumur's wine makes it particularly suitable for this treatment, and the deep cellars cut out of the chalk under the vineyards are a further advantage in their vinification. The wines are made by the Champagne method★ of secondary fermentation in bottle. The same method is used to make pétillant★ wines, which have much less effervescence than the mousseux. Pétillant Saumurs are sold in the same bottles as the still wines, with a clamp over the cork.

A very small quantity of red Saumur is made (at Turquant, Montsoreau and Montreuil-Bellay), from Cabernet Franc and Cabernet-Sauvignon grapes. These are only harvested if the conditions are right for production from these varieties. The best known is made at Champigny★ and has the AOC Saumur-Champigny.

Finally, Cabernet de Saumur has become more and more popular during the last fifty years, benefiting from the current vogue for rosés. It is a fine, fruity, bright and refreshing wine made

Sauternes: the château of Maille. Phot. René-Jacqués.

from Cabernet Franc and Cabernet-Sauvignon. It is also extremely pale, as the grapes are not crushed but pressed as soon as they are brought in from the vineyards. With the eyes closed, it is sometimes very difficult to tell from the taste whether it is a white or a rosé wine.

Sauternes The small region of Sauternes, which produces world-famous vins blancs liquoreux★, lies a few kilometres from Langon on the left bank of the Garonne. The appellation contrôlée Sauternes includes, besides Sauternes itself, the communes of Bommes, Preignac, Fargues and Barsac★. The area is extremely fortunate in its soil which seems to produce only wines of exceptional quality. It is a mixture of pebbles and sand which give the wines finesse, limestone which gives strength and vigour, and clay which makes them smooth. The noble★ vines have a naturally low yield which is further reduced by severe pruning. The main variety, Sémillon, produces smoothness, Sauvignon adds body and a distinctive aroma, and the small proportion of Muscadelle contributes a subtle bouquet to the whole. The unique feature of the vineyard, however, is the way the grapes are harvested. They are cut from the vine individually, and only when absolutely ripe,

in a series of 'pickings' over a period of one or two months in late autumn. The warmth and humidity of the season favour the growth of *Botrytis cinerea*, the fungus that causes pourriture noble★.

The grapes affected by this mould over-ripen in a particular way, and provide a must which is rich in sugar, glycerine, pectins and other substances, resulting in an inimitable bouquet and flavour. The wine is liquoreux★ and rich in alcohol (officially at least 13°, but usually quite a bit more). It is also entirely natural. No extra sugar or alcohol is added to it, as the slightest 'enriching' of the must, even by legally permitted methods, would automatically mean the loss of the appellation. Sauternes is a smooth, sweet, golden wine that combines a rare strength with great elegance and finesse, and has a rich and delicate aroma of honey, lime and acacia. Sauternes crus were classified in 1855 with the eminent and universally-renowned Château d'Yquem★ in first place, followed by the Châteaux la Tour-Blanche, Lafaurie-Peyraguey, Clos-Haut-Peyraguey, Rayne-Vigneau and Suduiraut. (See Index.)

Sauvignon This white grape gives wines a special spicy taste. It is best grown in the Nivernais and Berry where it produces the celebrated 'wines of Sauvignon': Pouilly-Fumé and the white wines of Sancerre★, Menetou-Salon★, Quincy★ and Reuilly★.

In Bordeaux it is united with the Sémillon and Muscadelle to make Graves and the sweet wines of Sauternes. It is also found at Bergerac, Vic-Bihl and Cassis, where it adds distinction and aroma. In California it produces a full-bodied wine which has the same aroma and delicate taste as the French wines made from this grape.

Savennières A small village in the Coteaux de la Loire★ district on the right bank of the Loire which qualifies for its own appellation contrôlée. The vineyard is ideally situated on slopes of the river bank between the towns of la Pointe and la Possonnière. Its fine, golden wines are elegant, crisp, full-bodied and delicate, and have won a well-deserved and long-standing reputation. Their aroma suggests lime and quince. Usually dry, with occasional touches of softness, they are ready for drinking quite early but also keep well. Savennières has two outstanding crus, Coulée-de-Serrant★ and Roche-aux-Moines★. After these two, the best known are Bécherelle, Goutte-d'Or, Clos du Papillon and the Châteaux d'Epiré, de Camboureau, de Savennières and de la Bizolière.

Savigny-lès-Beaune This commune, located north-west of Beaune★, produces mainly light, fragrant red wines which should be drunk young. The best crus are Aux Vergelesses, les Marconnets, la Dominade and les Jarrons.

Savoie It is only recently, with the increase in the popularity of winter sports, that the vineyards of Savoie in south-eastern France have really begun to make a name for themselves. They are, however, of very ancient origin. The excellent Altesse vine species is said to have been brought back from Cyprus by a crusader, who introduced it very successfully all over the province.

Savigny-lès-Beaune.
Phot. Lauros Beaujard.

The Sauvignon, the white grape which is popular in the vineyards of central France.
Phot. M.

231

CONTRÔLÉES Savoie has only two AOC wines – Crépy★ and Seyssel★. Most of its other delicious wines are VDQS★ and have the appellations Vin de Savoie, Roussette de Savoie, Vin de Savoie Roussette, Vin de Savoie Mousseux or Mousseux de Savoie. The appellation Roussette de Savoie can only apply to wines made from Altesse, Petite-Sainte-Marie and Mondeuse Blanche grapes, with a maximum proportion of 10% Marsanne. Roussette de Frangy enjoys a well-deserved reputation.

The name of the grape can also be added to the appellation when the wine is made entirely from that variety (e.g. Mondeuse★). Some individual crus can also add their names – Ayse★, for example. There are many of these fresh and delicious Savoie crus: Marestel, Monthoux and Chautagne on the left bank of the Rhône, Monterminod, Chignin and Charpignat on the picturesque banks of the Bourget and in the Chambéry valley, and Abymes, Apremont, Montmélian, Arbin, Cruet and Saint-Jean-de-la-Porte on the right bank of the Isère and south-east of Chambéry.

scorching When grapes which have not attained their full maturity are exposed to intense periods of sunlight, they dry up, blacken and fall off the vine, and are said to be scorched.

sec (dry) A term applied to wines, usually white, which contain, or at least give the impression of containing, no sugar. Most people only notice the presence of sugar in a wine when the level is higher than 5 g per litre, and even the driest wines contain 1–2 g per litre. Entre-deux-Mers★, for instance, which has to be dry to qualify for its appellation, has an official maximum sugar content of 3 g per litre.

Acidity is another important factor as the higher a wine's acid content, the dryer it will taste. Similarly, a wine rich in glycerine★ will seem almost sweet even if it contains no sugar, as is the case with wines which have been harvested late and fermented very slowly.

As very dry white wines contain practically no residual sugar, there is no danger of their refermenting in the bottle. This means that they do not need the large doses

Savoie: the vineyard of Saint-Jean-de-la-Porte. Phot. Serraillier-Rapho.

It seems incredible that grapes should manage to ripen so rapidly at the very foot of snow-covered mountains, but the vines grown here are tough and have adapted themselves over the years to the harsh climate. The varieties grown are, for white wines, Altesse and Jacquère (a species only found in Savoie), Chasselas★ (also grown in Switzerland and at Pouilly-sur-Loire★), Petite-Sainte-Marie (Chardonnay), Mondeuse Blanche, Aligoté and Gringet; and for red wines, Mondeuse, Persan, Gamay-noir-à-jus-blanc and Pinot. The vine-growing region covers the Savoie and Haute-Savoie departments, and in general produces light-bodied, dry, fruity white wines with a pleasing touch of acidity. (In bad years this acidity is sometimes too pronounced.) There are also some good red and rosé wines made mainly around Chambéry and in the Chautagne area.

of sulphur dioxide★ given to other wines to prevent refermentation★, and are consequently always pleasant and easy to drink.

When applied to Champagne, dry (sec) is a precise qualitative description: Champagne sec (which the French call *goût americain*) contains a proportion of 3–5% liqueur d'expédition★ (authorised sweetener), and is thus not as dry as extra-dry or brut. The next in the scale, demi-sec, contains 6–10% liqueur d'expédition. (See Champagne★.)

séché Dried out, a term applied to a wine which has stayed too long in the barrel and lost its freshness and fruitiness, becoming dull and unattractive. Sometimes it even has a slightly bitter after-taste. The word can also apply to very old wines spoiled by too many years in bottle. Their colouring matter★ solidifies and they lose both bouquet and flavour. A *séché* wine produces an uncomfortable dry sensation on the palate, and can be positively unpleasant.

sève, séveux *Sève* literally means sap. A *séveux* wine has pronounced fragrance, as well as vitality and a certain alcoholic strength. *Sève* tends to fade after a certain number of years in bottle, so a *séveux* wine is always in its prime.

Seyssel White AOC★ Savoie★ wines grown in the Rhône Valley communes of Seyssel (in the Haute-Savoie department) and Seyssel-Corbonod (in the Ain). The long-established vineyards face south and south-west at a height of 200–400 m. The pronounced aroma of violets so characteristic of Seyssel wines is attributed to the soil, which is siliceous limestone and siliceous clay. This theory is borne out by the fact that the perfume-makers of Grasse for a long time extracted their essence of violets from irises growing on the right bank of the Rhône in the same area of the valley.

The only authorised vine is the Roussette and at Crépy★ the grapes are harvested late, at the peak of their ripeness. No more than 25 hl of wine is produced per hectare, and its minimum alcoholic strength is 10°. Seyssel is a delicious, pale golden wine, delicate and supple, with a distinctive aroma of violets.

SEYSSEL MOUSSEUX For this appellation the Molette and Bon Blanc (or Chasselas) grape varieties are authorised, although the wine must still contain a minimum proportion of 10% Roussette. Minimum alcoholic strength is 8·5° and maximum yield per hectare is 40 hl.

Seyssel mousseux, made by the Champagne method★, is an excellent, fine wine that has an enthusiastic following.

sharp Sharp is an adjective used when a wine's acidity★ is not balanced by its alcohol content. The acid completely dominates the taste, making it very strong and sour. Sharpness is generally a characteristic of wine made in years when cold weather has hindered the ripening of the grapes.

Sherry A pale gold or amber apéritif or dessert wine produced in southern Spain between Cadiz and Seville around the little town of Jerez de la Frontera. The controlled vineyard zone includes the communes of Jerez de la Frontera, Puerto de Santa Maria, Sanlucar de Barrameda, Chiclana, Puerto Real, Chipiona, Rota and

Sherry casks.
Phot. Pedro Domecq.

233

Trebujena. The Superior Sherry area is formed by a triangle linking Jerez de la Frontera, Sanlucar de Barrameda and Puerto de Santa Maria and includes the neighbouring communes of Rota and Chipiona. Manzanilla★ is produced on the Atlantic coast near Sanlucar de Barrameda.

The soil, more than anything else, determines the nature of the wine, the best being the *albarza*, an arid, white, chalky soil like that of Champagne which produces wines possessing great finesse and a splendid bouquet. The dominant grape is the famous Palomina which gives the best Finos and Amontillados. There are some six secondary varieties, including the Pedro Ximenez whose grapes are dried for two weeks in the sun after the vendange, giving a very strong, sweet wine used in varying proportions in blends called P.X. The vendange takes place in early September and the grapes are pressed after twelve or fourteen hours of exposure to the sun. The must is then brought into the *bodegas* where it is made into wine. The wine ferments until December when the experts decide on its destiny. Light, clear wine having a fine bouquet becomes Fino and Amontillado after adding *eau-de-vie de vin* until an alcohol content of 15·5° is obtained. The more full-bodied wine with less bouquet is fortified up to 17 or 18° and is called Oloroso or Cream Sherry.

The different wines are stocked in separate *criaderas* or nurseries for one or two years, or more. There, in three-quarters filled oak casks, the wines undergo an evolution caused by the indigenous yeast particles called the *flor*. Afterwards they are blended and aged in the *Solera* system. In time the sherry tends to darken slightly and the wine takes on its inimitable bouquet. It also becomes drier and, unlike other wines, richer in alcohol. Thus the Finos and Manzanillas, which began at 15·5°, can easily reach 21° after five years or more in cask.

Soave   One of the best dry white wines of Italy, produced east of Verona from the Garganega (90%), Trebbiano and Riesling vines, which are trained high above the ground on pergolas. Soave is made by two communes, the picturesque little town of Soave and the neighbouring village of Monforte. Virtually the entire harvest is vinified by the local co-operative (*cantina sociale*), which is one of the best equipped in Italy.

Soave is sold in tall green bottles similar to those used in Alsace, and is a pretty, green-tinted, straw colour. Light and fresh, dry but not acid, it is a delicious wine that has a faint almond-flavour, and should be drunk within three years.

sommelier   A wine-waiter. In certain restaurants the *sommelier* is the man in charge of all matters relating to the cellar and drinks generally. His jobs include ordering and receiving supplies, organising and constantly checking the cellars, advising customers and serving at table. Since the Belle Epoque it has become the custom in France for *sommeliers* to wear long aprons and short black jackets with a symbolic bunch of grapes embossed in gold on the lapel. The *sommelier*'s responsibilities are as great as the chef's; the *maître d'hôtel* can advise the customer on his choice of food, but only the *sommelier* has the knowledge and skill to suggest the most suitable wines.

The profession goes back an exceedingly long time – some might say even as

The head sommelier of a large Paris restaurant examining a Bordeaux in the cellar. Phot. Réalitiés.

far as Ganymede, who served ambrosia and nectar to the gods on Mount Olympus. Whatever its precise origin, the Merovingian and Carolingian kings (fifth to tenth centuries) were quick to adopt the idea from the courts of Rome and Byzantium and establish similar appointments at their own.

The derivation of the word is still disputed. Some people think a *sommelier*'s job was originally to receive the wine which was brought by *sommiers*, or *bêtes de somme* (pack-animals or beasts of burden; the origin of the obsolete English word 'sumpter'). Others assert that the word *somme* in Old French meant 'duty' or 'office', and that in great households the *sommelier* was the servant in charge of provisions: there was a *sommelier de panneterie* (bread-store) and a *sommelier d'échansonnerie* (wine-room). Although there does not seem to be a very clearly-defined distinction between the duties of the wine-room and those of the cellar, it seems that none of the great old households of ancient France ever dispensed with the services of this important functionary. Nowadays, when restaurants have no resident *sommelier*, the *patron* or manager should perform the services himself.

Sonoma One of the most important vine-growing counties in northern California★, Sonoma is situated north of San Francisco and borders San Francisco Bay in the south. Although the mission of Spanish Franciscan monks, from whom it takes its name, introduced vines there in the eighteenth century, viticulture did not really start to develop in the area until the arrival of Colonel Haraszthy, the 'father of Californian viticulture', who established the famous Buena Vista★ vineyard in the vicinity.

Both the climate and the soil of Sonoma vary a good deal, and vines are only grown in certain areas. The Pacific coast is too cold and rainy for them, but the northern part of the country, from Healdsburg to Asti in the Russian River Valley, has a climate similar to that of central Italy and its pebbly hills produce a great number of good quality red vins ordinaires (made from Zinfandel, Carignan, Petite-Syrah, Grenache and Mataro grapes) and several mediocre white ones. The best region

stretches across the middle of the county from San Francisco Bay to Guerneville, and includes Sonoma and Santa Rosa. Its climate is comparable to that of Burgundy in France, and is perfect for viticulture.

The biggest, 'wineries' are those of Buena Vista and Korbel, founded in 1881 by émigré Czechs of that name. The latter is concerned almost exclusively with the production of excellent sparkling wines which are made by the Champagne method★ and conform to the rigorous standards of quality that the Korbel brothers learned at the School of Viticulture at Melnik, near Prague.

sour A sour wine gives a very disagreeable sensation to the palate. It is acid, astringent and biting like an unripe apple.

South Africa Vines were first planted in this country when the Dutch colonised it in the seventeenth century. Its climate is favourable to viticulture, being similar to that of the Mediterranean area. The best-known vineyard, Groot-Constantia, which produces the once-famous Constantia★ wine, was planted in 1684.

Vendange near Cap (South Africa). Phot. Rapho.

The vineyards are clustered in the province of Cap and are divided into two distinct sections. The first, the coastal section, comprises the regions of Stellenbosch, Paarl and Wellington, the area from Malmesbury to Tulbagh, and finally the peninsula of Cap. The second is a high altitude area called Little Karoo. It extends from Ladysmith to Oudtshoorn between Drakenstein and Swartberg and includes Worcester, Robertson, Bonnievale and Swellendam. This second region produces mainly port- and sherry-type dessert wines, while the coastal region also produces dry red and white wines.

The vineyard of Paarl Valley, located just east of Cap, produces what are considered the best wines. But the wines of Cap have never recovered the popularity they enjoyed in the nineteenth century, particularly in France. They are mainly consumed locally.

South America Since the vine needs a temperate climate, it is mainly grown in the one-third of this vast continent which lies south of the tropic of Capricorn. Argentina★ is by far the largest producer and Chile★, which produces the best wines in South America, is the second largest. Vineyards are also found in Uruguay, where they are rapidly expanding, and in Brazil★, mainly in the southern region of Rio Grande do Sol. Although Peru lies north of the tropic of Capricorn, it also has some vineyards. The high altitude of the country compensates for its unfavourable latitude.

Spain Although vines are cultivated in almost every region of Spain, and the vineyards occupy an extensive area, the volume produced is much less than that of France or Italy. The arid soil and inhospitable climate limits production to around 25 million hl, about one-third of French production and half of the Italian.

Sherry is the only Spanish wine known to many, but it only represents 2% of the country's wine production. There is also a

Spain: a vineyard in Aragon.
Phot. J. Bottin.

wide range of reds, rosés, whites, sparkling wines, vins de liqueur and mistelles.

Vinification methods are still rather primitive in many areas and most of the wines fall into the table wine category and are drunk locally, as they are not bottled. These very inexpensive wines often surprise the visitor with their originality. The regions of Valencia and Aragon produce full-bodied, highly-coloured wines which are for the most part exported. They are used in Switzerland to give colour and alcohol to more anaemic wine. The best Spanish wines (particularly the reds) come from the Rioja★ region not far from the French border in the valley of the Ebro. The best of these wines resemble good Bordeaux.

The Atlantic region stretching from Galice to the Basque area produces well-known Spanish wines. Next is the important production area of Valdepenas★ south of Madrid in Nouvelle-Castille, followed by the Alicante region near Valence which produces a large quantity of red wine made from the Grenache grape, and also good rosés at Yecla. Several good quality reds and whites are produced around Barcelona (Panades, Perelada and Alella) and good reds, rosés and whites in Galice, which is located near the Portuguese border.

Catalonia produces a sparkling wine often labelled Xampan (pronounced Champagne). But Spain is most renowned for its fortified wines, especially sherry★, Manzanilla★ and Montilla★. Tarragona, south of Barcelona on the Mediterranean coast, produces a full-bodied, fortified red wine called Priorato in Spain and Tarragona when exported. Tarragona, like Malaga, has lost its once commercial importance, but is still a very agreeable wine.

stabilisation Being organic, wine is never really stable. The vigneron therefore has to use his skill to eliminate the ferments (or leavens) after fermentation, and to prevent their growth without impairing any of the wine's qualities or inhibiting its development. Cold weather has always helped vignerons to stabilise wines, though nowadays they also have modern refrigeration★ methods at their disposal. Heat, as used in pasteurisation★ and infra-red treatment, is also helpful, but must be used with great caution as it can easily

harm the wine. Another important process is racking, which separates the wine from the ferment-laden lees. But the vigneron's most important stabilising agent is sulphur dioxide★, which has been used since Roman times and is still indispensable.

Stabilisation also presents the vigneron with the extremely complex problem of achieving a lasting and perfect balance of the wine's elements (its present and future acidity, its sugar content and its colour) and also of eliminating all suspended matter (voltigeurs★) and preventing cloudiness. Each barrel, each year and each cru presents its particular problems, and has to be treated with great care, as each may react in a totally unforseen way.

Steinberg A well-known German vineyard located in the heart of the Rheingau★, which was created in the twelfth century by the Cistercian Saint

Saint Bernard, founder of the Abbey of Clairvaux and creator of two great vineyards, Steinberg and Clos de Vougeot. Miniature by Fouquet (c. 1445). Musée Condé, Chantilly. Phot. Giraudon.

Left: Schloss Ehrenfels.
Right: Schloss Vollrads and
vineyard in the Rheingau.
Below: Workers on their way
to the vineyards at Hochheim.
Phots. Colin Mahler.

Bernard of Clairvaux, who also established Clos de Vougeot. The wines of Steinberg are sold under different names as the wines, as well as the years, may vary considerably (e.g. Steinberger, Steinberger Kabinett, Auslese and Trockenbeerenauslese). But they all share the family traits of being full-bodied and powerful and having a delicate, expanding bouquet.

still A still wine is neither sparkling nor pétillant★. The term is generally used to describe the basic wine which is to be converted into sparkling wine to distinguish it from the finished product.

suave A word employed by connoisseurs to describe wines of refinement that have a delicate fragrance, perfect balance and great smoothness. It is often used in connection with the great vins blancs liquoreux★ of France.

submersion of vines In the course of the desperate fight against phylloxera★, it was noticed that the insect hibernated on the root of the vines. One of the remedies suggested was therefore to submerge the vines in water (in places where this was possible) and thus drown it. Many vignerons hastened to adopt this measure, which was not, however, as successful as they had hoped. The areas most favourable were, naturally, the low-lying plains of the Hérault, Aude, Gard and Bouches-du-Rhône departments. There are still a few hectares of these submerged vines near the Mediterranean coast.

Submersion in water, a technique used against phylloxera. Phot. M.

Sud-Ouest The Sud-Ouest (south-western) region of France produces an enormously varied range of wines that includes those of the former provinces of Aquitaine (except Bordeaux), Béarn, the Basque country and Languedoc. Its wines are officially divided into two categories, AOC★ and VDQS★.

The AOC wines are those of the Dordogne (Monbazillac★, Bergerac★ and Montravel★), Côtes-de-Duras★, Gaillac★ and the Basses-Pyrénées (Jurançon★, Madiran★ and Pacherenc-du-Vic-Bihl★).

There are a great many VDQS: Côtes-du-Buzet★, Côtes-du-Marmandais★, the wines of Tursan★, Cahors★, Béarn★, Irouléguy★, Fronton★, Villaudric★ and Lavilledieu★ and those of the Aveyron region (Entraygues, Fel, Estaing★ and Marcillac★).

sugar Grape juice contains two basic sugars, glucose and fructose, which are converted into alcohol by the action of yeasts★. A certain quantity of unfermented sugar is always left in the wine – even dry wines contain from 1–3 g of sugar per litre. In vins blancs liquoreux★, whose musts have a high sugar content, the amount of unfermented sugar left is very great as yeasts cannot work when the alcohol content of the must exceeds about 15°. Fermentation, therefore, comes to a halt of its own accord. In vins doux naturels★ the vigneron stops the yeasts' activity by adding alcohol to the wine himself in order to keep some of the natural sugar unfermented.

Another element always present in a wine which can make it taste sweet is glycerine★. Strictly speaking, it makes the wine moelleux★, but also gives an impression of sweetness.

sulphur dioxide (SO₂) Sulphur dioxide is an indispensible aid to vignerons at all stages of vinification, from vatting to bottling. Its use as an antiseptic dates back to Roman times, and it is still the only sterilising agent permitted by law. The work of Pasteur and other modern scientific developments have led to its widespread use by vignerons all over the world, and so far nothing better has been found for the purpose.

It has several functions. It kills bacteria and the germs of wine diseases without affecting the yeast cells that cause fermentation, and can therefore even be employed to sterilise must in the fermenting-vat. It is equally useful in the treatment of grapes that are not too badly damaged by pourriture grise★, as it eliminates the mould that causes casse brune★. It has also been found to improve the quality of must, making it richer in alcohol, fixed acidity★, extract content, flavour and colour.

Sulphur dioxide is particularly valuable in the preparation of vins blancs liquoreux★, sweet white wines whose high residual sugar content always makes them liable to a second fermentation in bottle, and its use for this purpose has become standard practice. Sulphur, as it is commonly called, is used in various forms, sometimes as a pressurised gas or as a powdered tablet, or, more commonly, as a solution of sulphur and water. A certain proportion of sulphur always combines with the wine's sugar (and in fact contributes to the bouquet), but it is only effective as an antiseptic when pure – which is unfortunately also when its flavour and smell becomes noticeable in the wine. It is usually at the bottling stage that vigernons tend to be heavy-handed out of a commendable desire to prevent oxidation or refermentation. Excess 'free' (uncombined) sulphur gives the wine an unpleasant smell and taste, can cause headaches and, in bad cases, sometimes causes the disagreeable smells of rotten eggs or garlic. In France the maximum dosage authorised by law is 450 mg per litre, and the proportion of free sulphur must not exceed 100 mg per litre – although some experts can often detect as little as 40 mg.

supple   A supple wine produces a pleasant sensation of smoothness and softness on the palate. Its alcohol★ and acidity★ are perfectly balanced, it has no excess tannin★, and contains a certain proportion of natural glycerine★. Suppleness is now an increasingly sought-after quality.

Switzerland   Switzerland is justifiably proud of its wines. The climate restricts vine-growing to sheltered areas in the hollows of its steep slopes and along the shores of its lakes, and the wines are chiefly the result of the great tenacity and unremitting labour of the vignerons.

About two-thirds of the country's total wine output is white and consumed locally. The rest, which is not a great deal, is exported to Germany and the United States, and very rarely to France or Britain where Swiss wine is virtually unknown. Total production never exceeds one million hl a year, and one-quarter is supplied by the Valais canton. On the other hand, Switzerland – despite its size – imports twice as much wine as Britain.

There are about 230 Swiss crus, but the legislation which governs their classification is different from that of France. Vines are grown in a dozen cantons, though only five of them are at all important: Valais, Neuchâtel, Vaud, Ticino and Geneva.

Valais, sometimes called 'the California of Switzerland', produces the best red wines and many of the best white ones. The vineyards are situated in the upper Rhône valley, stretching from Martigny at the foot of Mont Blanc to the northern end of the Simplon tunnel. Altogether it has seventeen crus, of which the best known are Dôle★, Hermitage, Johannisberg, Malvoisie, Arvine, Martigny, Glacier★ and a number of white wines called Fendant made from Chasselas★ grapes.

There are about 1000 ha of vineyards in the canton of Geneva located along the two banks of the Rhône, with the bulk on the right bank. The wines are grouped into large categories depending on the grapes and characterised by their origin, soil and aspect. Most of the vignerons belong to co-operatives (Cave de Lully, Cave de la Souche and Cave de Mandiment de Satigny). Among the wines produced are: Bouquet Royal, Coteaux de Lully and Perle de Mandiment, which are perlant★ wines from the Chasselas grape; Gout du Prieur, Clavendier and dry whites; Rosé Reine, Rosé de Pinot and rosés; and Clefs d'Or, Camerier and generous reds.

The canton of Neuchâtel, in the northwest of Switzerland, primarily produces white wines made from Chasselas grapes grown along the northern shore of Lake Neuchâtel. Often pétillant★, they are bright, fresh, pleasant wines, but are sometimes criticised for being 'sharp and green' in years of insufficient sunshine. Neuchâtel's red wine, which is made from Pinot Noir★ (its only authorised grape variety), is excellent. Many people find it

not unlike the French wine of Chiroubles★. The canton has about eighteen appellations, amongst which are Auvernier, Cormondrèche, Hauterive and Cortaillod★.

The wines of the Vaud canton are nearly all white and are made almost exclusively from Chasselas grapes. The most important vineyards are on the northern shores of Lake Geneva between Nyon and Lausanne (in a region known as La Côte), and then from Lausanne to beyond Vexey (the Lavaux region, which has the good cru Dézaley★). The region known as Chablais, with the well-known white crus Yvorne and Aigle, is also in this canton, as is the Côtes de l'Orbe near Neuchâtel.

Ticino is the Italian-speaking region around Locarno and Lugano. Its wines are mostly red vins ordinaires, and the best are made from Merlot grapes (one of the Bordeaux varieties).

Sylvaner Sylvaner is one of the principal vine varieties of Alsace, and produces good, average wine that has a certain charm. This pale, green-tinged wine is lively, light and refreshing – especially when it retains the light sparkle of its early youth – although it somewhat lacks bouquet and flavour. The best wine is made in Barr and around Rouffach, where it sometimes achieves a distinction that puts it on a par with Riesling★. The Sylvaner vine goes under different names in different parts of the world. It is very common in Germany, the Italian Tyrol and Austria, where its wines have more or less the same characteristics as those it makes in Alsace, and it is also grown in California and Chile.

Syria, Libya, Jordan As the Bible attests, the vine has been cultivated in these areas since ancient times, the wines of Helbon and Chalybon having been carried long distances by the caravans. Since the three countries embrace the Moslem religion, most of the production is consumed as table grapes or dried raisins, although some table wine and a little sparkling wine is made by Christian vigernons.

T

tannin An organic material found in the stones, skin and stalks of grapes. Normally the tannin contained in wine comes mainly from the skin and stones.

The quantity of tannin varies depending on the grape variety (the Cabernet, for example, is rich in tannin) and also on the vinification method. Egrappage★ (destalking), a short fermentation period, a moderate pressing, all lessen the strength of tannin in the wine. White wine has little tannin while red wine contains much more, especially when it has undergone a long fermentation.

Tannin forms deposits which are normally found in old red wines. A mature wine always contains less dissolved tannin than a young one. A normal amount of tannin is an indispensible element in wine as it contributes to the wine's steadiness and clarity. Too much tannin can be eliminated by the fining process. When the wine lacks tannin the process of tannisage★ is used to raise it to a normal level. The strength of tannin in a wine determines the use of certain expressions and terms such as astringent★, thick, thin★ and sour★.

tannisage A treatment sometimes necessary when a wine has a tannin deficiency, which may, for example, be due to unripe grapes. Tannin, a natural product derived from gallic acid, is added in order to prevent the wine from being thin★, and to facilitate the essential process of fining. Sometimes the wood of new oak casks itself imparts enough tannin to the wine to remedy the deficiency and can contribute considerably to its bouquet.

Tavel Tavel, in the Côtes du Rhône★ region, produces the most famous rosé in France. It was the favourite wine of François I and was praised by the poet Ronsard. The vineyard is situated in the Gard department on the right bank of the Rhône, not far from Avignon. A number of different vines are planted, the predominant variety being Grenache followed by Cinsault, Clairette Blanche and Clairette Rouge, Picpoul, Bourboulenc and a little Carignan. Only rosé wine qualifies for the appellation. Its colour – pale ruby with shades of topaz – deepens with age. Heady, dry and fruity, it is an elegant, fresh wine with a slightly pungent flavour and is quite different from other Côtes-du-Rhône wines. It is at its best when drunk slightly chilled. Although some people say it is the only rosé that keeps well, the vignerons themselves drink their Tavel within two years, and regard a bottle more than five years old as a curiosity.

Tavel. Phot. M.

A small quantity of red wine is also made in Tavel from the traditional grape varieties of the area, but is entitled only to the appellation Côtes-du-Rhône.

Tawny This kind of port★ is a blend of carefully selected wines from a legally defined area, and is always matured in cask. The name refers to the colour which all port acquires with age (whether originally red or white), and has come to mean a wine that has matured in cask, as opposed to vintage★ which matures in bottle. The object of the blending is to achieve a sustained and consistent quality from one year to the next. Vintage port, on the other hand, is always the product of one outstandingly good year, and is never blended.

The casks in which this eminent wine matures are usually made of Baltic oak or, failing that, of Portuguese or Italian chestnut. Their shape and volume (usually 550 litres) has been established by practical experience. The wine slowly oxidises as a consequence of the air which penetrates the wood, the colouring matter★ collects around the sides of the casks and the wine throws its deposit and gets lighter and lighter in colour. As it evaporates, the casks are continually filled up with younger wines which enrich the rest. The wine is bottled after a minimum of eight years in cask.

Chai of tawny port, Vila Nova de Gaia, Portugal. Phot. Y. Loriat.

These vinicultural techniques are continually being improved at the instigation of the Portuguese Wine Institute which exercises a strict control over this most important of Portugal's products. The method not only ensures a remarkably consistent quality, but also offers enthusiasts an ever-increasing range of bouquets, flavours and shades, from ruby to light tawny. Tawny port does not have to be served in a decanter★ as it has matured and thrown its deposit in cask. Its original bottle, with the seal of a reputable firm on it, does it ample justice. Port is traditionally passed clockwise around the table.

temperature of wine Temperature is a very important factor when serving wine. There is one golden rule: whether the wine is being chilled or brought to room temperature, it should be done slowly and gently. A young wine can more or less survive a sudden change of temperature, but an old and venerable bottle may be irreparably harmed. The barbaric practices of standing red wine on a corner of the stove or over a radiator, or immersing the bottle in hot water, are as reprehensible as they are harmful. Likewise, that of extra quick chilling by putting the bottle in the refrigerator or, worse still, in the freezer. Conditions were more satisfactory in the old days when the temperature of cellars was never higher than 12°C (which is by no means always the case today), and when living rooms were not overheated, as they nearly always are now. Two mistakes to be avoided at all costs are lukewarm red wine and frozen white wine. To be on the safe side, it is best simply to serve the wine at cellar temperature.

The temperature a wine should be served at depends primarily on the wine itself, on its age, the personal preferences of the guests and the temperature of the dining-room. However, some general rules always apply: young wines should be served at a lower temperature than old ones, and it is always better to serve a wine at slightly less than the ideal temperature, as it will get warmer during the meal. It should also be remembered that the warmer the room, the cooler the wine will appear to be, and vice versa.

Red wine, with one or two exceptions, should always be brought to room temperature. If the wine comes from an ideal cellar★ with a temperature not exceeding 12°C, two hours in the dining-room away from all sources of heat should be enough. This also leaves the guest the pleasure of releasing the bouquet and flavour of the wine himself by the warmth of his hand as he holds the glass.

Generally speaking, and according to the *code du sommelier*, red Bordeaux and Touraine wines are best at about 15–16°C, Burgundies and Côtes-du-Rhone at about 13–14°C, and Beaujolais and light regional wines a little cooler, at cellar temperature. Red vins doux naturels should also be served cool, owing to their alcohol and sugar content.

White wines should be drunk chilled, never frozen: from 6–11°C for dry wines and about 5°C for sweet wines. Château-Chalon and vins jaunes are exceptions and should be drunk at the same temperature as reds. Full-bodied white Burgundies (Corton Charlemagne, Montrachet and Meursault) also require a relatively high temperature, about 10–13°C, to bring out all their excellent qualities. Champagne is drunk chilled, at about 4°C, other sparkling wines even cooler at about 2°. Rosés, too, should be chilled even though the low temperature can often disguise their potency and lead the unwary to underestimate their alcohol content. To chill wine, the old system of an ice-bucket is always preferable to putting the bottle in the refrigerator.

tender A term applied to a wine that has little acidity but is delicate, fresh and light. Its character is not particularly pronounced and it is usually in the prime of its life. A tender wine pleases by reason of its softness and gentleness, and never imposes itself on the palate.

tenue 'Steadiness' is a rough translation of this word, which for the professional denotes a wine's resistance to cloudiness and casse★. For the wine-lover it means a good balance between the wine's various elements.

Terlano One of the best and most famous white wines of the Italian Tyrol. It is grown around the village of Terlano in the deep and picturesque gorges of the Adige, between Bolzano and Merano. Sold in tall, green bottles like the wines of

Alsace, Terlano is usually a dry white wine with a pale, greenish-gold colour. It is delicate and extremely pleasant, but has no great bouquet nor a particularly distinctive taste.

It is made from various grapes: Riesling, Pinot Blanc, Pinot Gris and Terlano (a local variety). Its quality and character depend on the relative proportions of these in its composition, something which can only be determined empirically.

terroir This word either means 'soil' or 'patch of ground', i.e. a particular plot of land that makes one cru different from another. There is also the expression *goût de terroir*, which means the characteristic though often indefinable flavour that a wine acquires from a particular type of soil.

thin A thin wine is like a thin person – it has less body★ and less substance than

September, the month of the grape and nut harvest. 15th-century miniature. Musée Condé, Chantilly. Phot. Giraudon.

245

normal. This is usually due to excess racking★ rather than any disease in the wine.

tierçon A measure of capacity that varies from region to region. In Languedoc it is a third of a muid★, i.e. 228 litres. It is mainly used for Muscat★ wines.

tisane à Richelieu This is a nickname given many years ago to Bordeaux. Louis XV sent Duke Armand de Richelieu, Marshall of France, to govern the province of Aquitaine as a rest from his exhausting life of pleasure at the court. Predictably, the Duke greatly appreciated the wines of Bordeaux, with whose help he soon resumed the life to which he was accustomed.

Tlemcen (Coteaux-de-) An Algerian★ wine made south-east of Oran near the Moroccan border, which was VDQS★ when Algeria was under French administration. Coteaux-de-Tlemcen is a mountain wine, grown on limestone at a height of 800 m. It is generous, full-bodied and firm, and has an attractive ruby colour (it is usually red, sometimes rosé). It also improves with age, acquiring moelleux★, finesse and a very pleasant velvety taste.

Tokay A world-famous Hungarian wine. Real Tokay, which is very rare, is one of the best white wines. It is produced by the small viticultural region of Tokaj – Hegyalja, located in north-east Hungary on the banks of the Bodrog, thirty km north-west of Nyiregyhaza. The wine is made mainly from the Furmint grape whose name came from the old French *forment* (the wine from the Furmint takes on a yellow tint like that of wheat).

The soil is composed of volcanic debris mixed with feldspar and the area is favoured by dry, sunny autumns which are conducive to the supermaturation of the grapes.

The special method of harvesting was discovered in the seventeenth century at Tokay as a result of the beneficial effect of the harvest being delayed one year because of war. The most common and least expensive Tokay is called Szamorodni. Its name, originally Polish, means 'as it grows'. To make it, the overripe grapes are added to the other grapes in the presses.

The quality depends on the year and it is always high in alcohol.

Another variety is the Tokay called Aszú, marvellously sweet and very rare and expensive. It contains a certain fixed proportion of carefully chosen grapes which have been attacked by pourriture noble★. The harvested grapes are laid on large tables and the dried, wrinkled grapes are separated from the others. From the pressing is obtained what is called the 'heart' of the wine which is kneaded into a sort of dough. This dough is added in variable quantities to the must of ordinary grapes which have already been pressed.

The quantity is specified on the label in terms of *puttonyos*. The *puttonyos* are 25-litre baskets used in the region. Depending on the number of *puttonyos* of chosen grapes added to a *fut* (136 litres), you get different labels – 'Aszu 2 puttonyos', 'Aszu 3 puttonyos' – up to six *puttonyos*. It follows that the more *puttonyos*, the better and more expensive the wine.

Tokay ferments in small casks which can be stored in very low cellars. (This has given the vignerons the opportunity to hide their wine in the course of many invasions.) Low cellars apparently make the best wine. Tokay is exported by the government in long-necked bottles of 5·0 dl. Its bouquet and unforgettable taste justify its reputation of being one of the best wines in the world. The best Tokay is grown on the commune of Tallya. Voltaire praised Tokay, saying 'Tokay, the golden liquid which fires the brain and inspires the most brilliant talk. Tokay leaps and sparkles on the brim of the glass'.

tonneau Before the invention of the *tonneau* or barrel (attributed to the Gauls), wine was kept in earthenware amphoras and carried in leather bottles. Amphoras had to be lined with pitch to make them watertight, which must have given the wine a very strong flavour. The resinous wines of Greece are probably the nearest we can get to the taste today.

Barrels have always been their present functional shape. The wood allows the wine to breathe, and also allows the evaporation necessary for its development. The rounded shape makes the barrels easy to move and, more important, facilitates the racking★ process as the lees remain in the bulge while the clear wine is drawn off.

Barrels are usually made of oak, which contributes considerably to the bouquet★, and white wines are often left to ferment in new oak casks to supplement their low tannin content. The small-scale vignerons of Bordeaux buy barrels second-hand from the great châteaux in the hope that some of the wine will have impregnated the staves and eventually improve the quality of their own. The barrels used for shipping wines are called *fûts perdus*, or lost casks, and are made of chestnut, not of oak.

The tonneau is also a trading unit in Bordeaux, although there is no actual barrel this size. It takes four barriques★ of 225 litres to make a tonneau of 900 litres.

Touraine This peaceful and attractive province, with its marvellous châteaux, is often called 'the garden of France'. Its vineyards date back to the sixth century, and its wines have been praised by a long line of French poets and writers, including Rabelais, Ronsard, Vigny, Balzac and Alexandre Dumas. The vineyards are mostly in the Indre-et-Loire department and produce a great variety of wines. The climate is particularly favourable to viticulture, as are the various types of soil found in the area. These range from granitic and pebbly sand over 'Touraine tufa' (the yellow chalk out of which the cellars at Vouvray are dug), to *aubuis*, the mixture of siliceous sand, clay and limestone at the foot of the hills which brings out all the best qualities of the Pineau de la Loire grape. This delightful region is justly renowned for the great white wines of Vouvray★ and Montlouis★ and the smooth red wines of Chinon★, Bourgueil★ and Saint-Nicolas-de-Bourgueil★.

The Coteaux du Loir★ vineyard, situ-

ated at the meeting point of the Touraine, Anjoy and Maine provinces, is also included in the Touraine viticultural region.

TOURAINE: APPELLATION D'ORIGINE CONTRÔLÉE To qualify for this appellation the delicate, fruity red wines of Touraine must be made from Cabernet Franc★ (locally known as Cabernet Breton) and certain other authorised, supplementary varieties: Cot, Malbec, Noble, Gris-Meunier, Pinot Gris and Gamay. The region's light, fruity rosés are made from Cabernet Breton, Cot, Gamay and Groslot. Both dry and sweet (sometimes sparkling) white wines are made from Chenin (or Pineau da la Loire) or, more rarely, Sauvignon. The minimum alcohol content is 9° for reds and rosés, and 9·5° for whites.

The alcohol content of Touraine pétillant★ (red, white or rosé) must be 9·5° before their secondary fermentation in bottle. The white is made from Pineau de la Loire, a white grape, whereas the red and rosé are made only from the red Cabernet variety.

Some Touraine wines are permitted to carry the name of their commune as well as the appellation Touraine (Azay-le-Rideau★, Amboise★ and Mesland★).

tourne A malady liable to affect badly made wines which are deficient in alcohol★ and acidity★ (having a pH greater than 3·5) and still contain a certain amount of

Cooper at work.
Phot. René-Jacques.

A Touraine vineyard between Azay-le-Rideau and Chinon after the vendange.
Phot. Lauros.

247

unfermented sugar, or wines made from damaged grapes. Wine affected in this way tastes extremely unpleasant, and is both sour and flat; it looks murky and has little, shiny threads which float about in it when the bottle is moved. Tourne bacteria attack the fixed acids, sugar, glycerine★ and, particularly, the tartric acid of a wine, so that its fixed acidity★ is reduced and its volatile acidity★ increased. The bacterial activity also releases carbon dioxide, which pushes out the staves at the bottom of the barrel and makes the wine froth as it is drawn out.

The disease can be prevented, and even in the initial stages halted, by dosing the wine with sulphur dioxide★ and tannin★, by racking★ it frequently with accompanying doses of sulphur dioxide, and by pasteurisation★.

traminer An Alsatian vine known elsewhere as Savagnin Blanc (or Rosé), one of the principal noble★ varieties of the Jura★. It derives its name from a village in the Italian Tyrol called Termeno, which was known as Traminer when it belonged to Austria. Its wine is never acid – sometimes even quite sweet – and has a pleasant aroma. It is a full-bodied, smooth, generous wine, with a very flowery taste and bouquet in which the flavours of rose and jasmine are the most distinct. Traminer is grown chiefly in the Rhine valley, the Italian Tyrol and in California. The best Traminers are called Gewürztraminers.

tuilé *Rouge tuilé*, or brick-red, is a colour often acquired by old wines whose constituent elements have become oxidised, and as such is a useful gauge of quality. The colour is normal, however, in Rancio★ wines.

Tunisia Wine production fell considerably following a phylloxera★ attack around 1936 which destroyed a large portion of the vineyards. Consumption in the country is minimal as the Moslem population do not drink alcoholic beverages. Although the table wines are fairly ordinary, except for some agreeable rosés, the vins de liqueur are remarkable, especially the Muscats. Made from the Muscats of Alexandria, Frontignan and Terracina, they contain a minimum of 17°

alcohol and at least 70 g of sugar per litre. These fragrant, powerful, fine Muscats are produced east of Bizerte between Ras-el-Djebel and Porto-Farina, and on the east coast in two other areas, between Kelibia and Menzel-Temin and between Beni-Aichoum and Beni-Khair.

Turkey Turkey produces very little wine – only 5% of the total grape harvest is vinified. Most of the crop is sold as fresh eating grapes, and a quarter is kept back to be dried and sold as raisins. Turkish vineyards are few and far between, and none of them is really big. They are grouped chiefly in the regions of Pergamum, Aydin-Tire-Izmir (which produces the best wine), Ankara, Gaziantep, Malatya, Kayseri, Konya and Niğde. In fact, Turkish wines are generally quite good: whether red or white, they are dry and pleasant – Buzbağ, Doluca, Kavaklidere, Marmara and Trakya are all good examples. Izmir is an excellent white wine, quite light and fruity, and should be drunk chilled. Sweet, Muscat-based wines like Miskit, on the other hand, are markedly less good than other Turkish wines.

Tursan A vineyard in the Sud-Ouest★ region whose origins go back to well before the fifteenth century, when it was considered the heart of the basco-béarnais *pays des vignes*. Its VDQS★ wines, which are mostly white, are produced on the hillsides of about forty communes in the Landes department, notably around Geaune and Aire-sur-Adour. A local variety called Baroque makes up 90% of Tursan's vines. Vinified in the cooperative at Geaune, the wines are improving all the time and are steadily increasing in popularity. They are crisp, smooth and very dry, and have a pronounced character of their own.

Tursan also makes red and rosé wines, although not in large quantities (less than 1000 hl out of a total of 8000 hl of VDQS wines annually). Like Madiran★ wines, these are made from Tannat grapes, which produce strongly-coloured, full-bodied wine with a high tannin content. As in Madiran, Tannat is combined with a certain quantity of Fer★ and Cabernet Franc★ grapes; the proportion of Cabernet Franc in the vineyards is being increased every year, as it suits Tannat particularly well.

U

Ukraine According to figures published in 1959, the republic has 379,000 ha of land under vine, which makes it the largest viticultural region in the Soviet Union. It produces 1,600,000 hl of wine a year. At first viticulture was practised mainly in the Dnieper, Boug and Dniester valleys, but around 1800 it started to spread out into the Steppes. At present, there are three main viticultural regions in the Ukraine: the subcarpathian region on the Hungarian border, which has Mukhachevo as its centre; the coastal region around Kherson, Odessa and Nikolaievsk; and most important of all, the Crimea, which specialises in large-scale production of sparkling wine – its annual output is twelve million bottles! There is a particularly well-equipped plant for the mass-production of this wine at the village of Massandra, near Yalta. The Crimea also produces dessert wines: Portvein, an imitation port, and various Muscats (Massandra and Zolota Balka).

USA When one considers wine production in the United States, California★ immediately comes to mind. Indeed, Californian vineyards are the most important and alone produce 80% of wine consumed. Nevertheless, there are a number of other wine-growing areas which, though less well known, account for about 14% of production (the rest is imported). These areas include, to the east, the states of New York★ and Ohio★ and to the west, on the Pacific coast, those of Washington★ and Oregon.

USSR According to figures published in 1964, there are 1,046,000 ha of vineyards in the Soviet Union, producing 9,800,000 hl of wine a year. They are mostly in the southern regions, and are planted mainly with Chasselas, Cabernet-Sauvignon, Pinot Gris, Riesling, Isabelle and Concorde grapes. In the extreme east of the Soviet Union there is also a variety of grape created by the naturalist Michurin which can withstand a temperature of −40°C (unfortunately, however, it is not immune to phylloxera★). The main Soviet viticultural regions are now, as in the past, Georgia★, whose wines have always been much admired, Moldavia★, which supplies a third of all Soviet wines, the Ukraine★,

Vinicultural co-operative in the Crimea. Phot. Novosti.

Vineyards on the banks of the Black Sea. Phot. Novosti.

Usakhe-Lauri No. 21, Kindzmareuli No. 22 and Ojaleshi No. 24. The Ukraine produces two wines of this type called 'Château Eyquem' and 'Barsac'.

There are several types of 'sweet' wine. Muscats are a speciality of the Crimea and of the viticultural complex at Massandra. Their alcohol content is from 12–16° and their sugar content varies from 20–30%. They are left to mature from two to four years before being delivered to retailers. The best are Krasnyi Kamen ('red stone') and Tavrida (made from Muscat Noir). There are also wines called 'Tokay', again produced mostly in the Crimea, made in the villages of Ai-Danil and Magarach. Some sweet wines are also made in Central Asia. 'Cahors' wines, which in the USSR are liqueur wines, are matured for at least three years before they are sold. The best known are the Shemakha of Azerbaijan, the Artashat of Armenia and the Yuzhno-berezhnyi of the Crimea, all of which have an alcoholic strength of 16° and a proportion of 18–20% sugar. The 'Cahors' of Uzbekistan is both stronger (17°) and sweeter (25% sugar) than these. Kiurdamir, made in Azerbaijan, has a velvety texture and a curious taste of chocolate. This category could also include sweet wines like the Crimean Pinot Gris, an amber-coloured wine (23% sugar and 13°), and the Georgian Salkhino No. 17, a dark, coffee-coloured wine with 30% sugar. Central Asian wines always have a high sugar content; the best are Iasman Salyk and Ter Bash from Turkmenistan, and Shirini from Tadzhikistan.

The 'fortified' wines have a strength of up to 20°, and are imitations of the famous liqueur wines of Spain, Portugal and Italy. Among the port-type wines, the best red ones are the Crimean Livadia and Massandra, and the best whites, the Crimean Yuzhnoberezhnyi and Surozh, the Armenian Aigeshat, the Georgian Kardanakhi No. 14, and Akstafa from Azerbaijan. The best 'sherry' is made in Armenia in the Ashtarak region. It is not unlike real sherry, having a deep golden colour, a fine and fruity bouquet and a slightly nutty flavour. The best 'Marsala' is produced in Turkmenistan. It slightly resembles Madeira and has an alcoholic strength of 18–19°. Soviet Madeira is mostly produced in the Crimea and Georgia – the Georgian Anaga No. 16 is tolerably good.

where almost all the sparkling wine is produced (in the Crimea) and Azerbaijan★, which has a long viticultural tradition. The RSFSR★ and Armenia★ also have vineyards of considerable importance.

In general, Russian wines are not helped by the continent's latitude and climate, particularly the white wines which tend to lack freshness. Those of Hungary★, Romania★ and Bulgaria★ are of distinctly superior quality. The USSR puts a lot of effort into the production of sparkling wines, which it calls, quite simply, 'Champagne'. This wine is in fact a passable imitation of Champagne, and can be very pleasant. In Moscow, Leningrad and other big cities there are special basement wine-shops where one can buy and drink it at leisure.

The Soviet Union also has a very wide and varied range of extremely pleasant dessert wines, which could provide serious competition if they were ever exported on the world market. These wines, of which there are a great number, can be divided into three categories: 'semi-sweet', 'sweet' and 'fortified'. The 'semi-sweet' wines have an alcohol content of less than 15°. The best are made in Georgia and have a distinctive aroma. Some are white, like Chkhaveri No. 1 and Tvishi No. 19, others are red, such as Khvachkara No. 20,

V

Valdepeñas An important viticultural centre in central Spain, situated south of Madrid near the city of Ciudad Real in the old province of New Castille, which was the home of Don Quixote de la Mancha. Although its name means 'valley of stones', the area is more like a large plain than a valley, and the soil, although arid, is not in fact particularly stony.

The extensive vineyards produce a very pleasant, pale, light-bodied red wine that is drunk young, particularly in Madrid, as a *vino corriente*, or vin ordinaire. It is cheap and usually served in carafes. The white wine is golden-yellow, full-bodied, fairly rough and much less agreeable. Until recently, Valdepeñas wines were rarely bottled or exported, and could only be sampled in Madrid.

Valpolicella An excellent red wine of northern Italy made from the same grape varieties as Bardolino★. Valpolicella is produced north-west of Verona on five communes: Negrar, Funane, Marano, San Pietro Incariano and Sant' Ambrogio. Ordinary Valpolicella is drunk in carafe in the first year.

The better wine, Valpolicella Superior, is bottled after eighteen months in cask, but should generally be drunk before the fifth year. It is a lively, fruity, velvety, light wine and, although rather full-bodied, possesses much finesse.

Valtellina A viticultural region in northern Italy★ near the Swiss border whose red wines are among the best of the country. The best are produced on five small mountainous slopes east of the town of Sondrio: Sassella, Grumello, Inferno, Grigioni and Fracia. The wines of this region are usually sold under their proper name, not under the appellation Valtellina. They are made from the famous Nebbiolo grape, called locally Chiavennasca, and is the grape from which the good reds of Piemonte are made.

The wines of Valtellina have a lot of personality. They are dark purple in colour – in fact, almost black – and are powerful and vigorous. They should not be drunk young as their beautiful qualities only develop after several years in bottle. A special wine of the area, called Spurzat, is transformed into a dessert wine reaching about 15 to 16° alcohol after it has aged a long time in bottle. It is marrowy and round with a colour bordering on orange.

velvety A velvety wine imparts a sensation of smoothness and softness to the palate because of its low acid content and fairly high level of glycerine★.

vendange The vendange, or grape-harvest, is a crucial time in the vineyard. After a year spent tending the vines, the vigneron finally gathers his grapes, which is the first stage of wine production. Thanks to the INAO★ and the Institut Technique du Vin (see control of maturation), the vigneron no longer has the burden of deciding when to start his harvest. The best compromise between the ripening times of different vine varieties, in regions where several varieties are combined to make a particular wine (in the Midi and Bordeaux areas, for example), is also calculated. The date of the harvest depends on the type of wine required. For dry wines the grapes are picked before they are fully ripe in order to preserve a pleasant touch of acidity. Sweet wines, on

the other hand, are made from overripe grapes that may have been attacked by pourriture noble★.

The main problem nowadays is labour, of which there is sometimes a disastrous shortage, and it is becoming more serious every year. There are special grape-picking machines in use in California, but they necessitate a rigorous pruning of the vines and, in any case, are not suitable for European vines or vineyards.

After the grapes have been picked they have to be brought back from the vineyards as quickly as possible to avoid oxidisation, and with the utmost gentleness to avoid damaging the grapes. This can pose problems for the vignerons, especially when the vineyards are on steep slopes – in the Valais region of Switzerland, for instance, they sometimes have to use cable-cars to bring the grapes down. Various kinds of receptacles are used to carry the grapes: tubs, baskets, hods, buckets, bags and wheelbarrows. Iron is always avoided, owing to the danger of casse ferrique★, and the materials used are the traditional wickerwork, wood and modern plastic.

véraison   A word used in the south of France for the last phase of a grape's development. At the *véraison* stage the grape has reached its maximum weight and volume but is not yet completely ripe; its sugar content begins to increase and its acidity decreases. In the period between *véraison* and full maturity the outside of the grape hardly changes at all, which used to make it extremely difficult to judge the right time to start the harvest. Nowadays, the local representative from the INAO★ or Institut Technique du Vin (see control of maturation) makes this much easier for the vignerons by deciding, and officially announcing, the best date for the harvest for each area.

Villaudric   This VDQS★ wine made in the Sud-Ouest★ region has a distinct resemblance to Fronton★. It is produced in fairly small quantities by the communes of Villaudric, Bouloc, Villemur, Fronton, Villematier and Villeneuve-les-Bouloc.

vin chaud   'Hot wine', a preparation which the French make in winter as a tonic for sufferers from colds and flu. It is made by gently heating sugar, cinnamon, one or two cloves and slivers of orange or lemon peel with a little water for seven to ten minutes. A bottle of table wine (Bordeaux, if possible) is added, and the mixture is brought to a fast boil. If the wine's alcohol content is sufficiently high, one can set the rising fumes alight. The concoction is ready when cool enough to drink.

vin de primeur The wine of the year, the new wine which generally appears after 15th December of the same year as the vendange.

Only certain wines can be offered so early in their youth, and have a corresponding freshness: Muscadet, Gros-Plant, Zwicker and Edelzwicker, Sylvaner, Gaillac, Beaujolais (but not the Beaujolais crus), Beaujolais-Villages, Mâcon Blanc and Rosé and the café wines.

vin de sucre A concoction that hardly deserves the name of wine. This artificial beverage was manufactured without using a single grape, mainly around 1903. The perpetrators of the fraud made a mixture of water, sugar and tartric acid to which, after fermentation, they added tannin and colouring matter. The Aimargues commune (which was by no means an exception) in the canton of Nîmes used nearly 450,000 kg of sugar for this purpose during September and October 1903. These deplorable operations were continued until 1907, when the honest vignerons started to stage violent demonstrations. The battle, fought mainly in the Languedoc, finally resulted in a law being passed in July 1907 prohibiting the 'watering' of wines. A decree in the same year also laid down the first legal definition for wine.

Another effect of this battle was to make the vignerons realise that they would have to band together to protect their produce. As a result, they formed the profession's first organised body, the *Confédération Générale des Vignerons*.

vinegar, wine Wine vinegar, which has been known since ancient times, owes a great deal to the work of Louis Pasteur, who established its production methods. For culinary purposes it is infinitely preferable to ordinary malt vinegar. Its preparation is based on the light, acid wines that used to be produced in great quantities in the region around Orléans in France, and it is now in fact one of that city's best-known products. The wine is poured into 230-litre oak casks, which are only half-full so that enough air can circulate. Every week ten litres of vinegar are siphoned off and replaced with the same quantity of wine. Care must be taken not to drown the *mère du vinaigre*, or vinegar 'culture', formed by *Mycoderma aceti*★ bacteria, which need

oxygen to survive. The vinegar has a distinctive flavour and contains the free organic acids of wine (malic, tartric and succinic).

Vinho verde The famous 'green wine' of Portugal. The name does not refer to its colour – there are both red and white vinhos verdes – but to its distinctive 'young' taste. About seven times as much red is produced as white, out of a total annual production of three million hl. The wines are made in the north of the country between Minho and the Douro in the districts of Moncao, Lima, Braga, Basto, Amarante and Penafiel. Each of these areas has its own traditional combination of grapes, but the most common varieties are the red ones: Vinhao, Borracal, Espadeiro and Azal Tinto. There are a great many different white varieties, the main ones being Azal blanco and Dourado.

Vinho verdes have been known for

many hundreds of years, and their production was subject to rigorous control as long ago as the eighteenth century. Today, their preparation is governed by strict regulations which affect the unusual methods of cultivation. The vines are grown on trellises supported by *enforcados*, which are usually living stems of chestnut or oak. They reach a height of anything from 1·5–5 m, and are never grown in vineyards as such but around the edges of fields, along the sides of paths and roads, and on

Following two pages: 'The Vendanges', 15th-century Dutch tapestry. Musée de Cluny, Paris. Phot. Lauros-Giraudon.

Véraison: the state of a grape at the moment it begins to ripen. Phot. M.

odd corners of unused farmland. The *enforcados* are pruned at the same time as the vines so that they do not deprive them of any sunlight. The wine can only be called vinho verde if it is made from vines grown by these methods.

The vinification procedures are unusual, too. Properties of the natural yeasts peculiar to the region cause a large amount of malic acid to be left in the wine after fermentation. This later provokes an intense malo-lactic fermentation★ which gives the wine its agreeable and characteristic sparkle. It is bottled early, around February or March. The wine is extremely refreshing, slightly effervescent, not very alcoholic and quite sharp. The white wines are bright and light-bodied, and are a perfect accompaniment to hors d'oeuvres and fish, besides being marvellously thirst-quenching. The red wines are more full-bodied and have a lovely bright colour, not unlike Beaujolais, and go extremely well with red meats.

vino santo A golden, very sweet, Italian dessert wine produced mainly in Tuscany, sometimes in Trentino and on the Greek island of Santorini. Various vines are used, but the most usual is Trebbiano. The grapes undergo supermaturation, either on the vine or in the chais★, in order to produce very concentrated musts with a high sugar content.

vinous, vinosity Rich in alcohol. It may seem superfluous to call a wine vinous, but it does have a real meaning in the sense that such a wine has a definite character, with a pronounced 'winy' flavour and bouquet.

vins délimités de qualité supérieure (VDQS) These letters or words are a guarantee of quality and describe regional wines made according to strict regulations which apply to the area of production, vines grown, alcoholic strength and maximum yield per hectare. Such wines are of excellent quality, and have been stringently checked and controlled by the INAO★ and the *Service de la Répression des Fraudes* (see repression of frauds). The vine-growers' unions themselves decide which wines should qualify for the label, and this is conferred only when their recommendations have been judged by an impartial commmission. The wines are always clearly labelled either with the words in full or simply with the initials VDQS.

vins fins de la Côte de Nuits Certain communes lying north and south of the line of grands crus are permitted under certain conditions to sell some of their wines as 'Vins fins de la Côte de Nuits'. They are Fixin, Brochon, Prissey, Comblanchien and Corgoloin. The official appellation 'Vins fins . . .' has recently been shortened to 'Cote-de-Nuits-Villages'.

vintage The year of vinification helps the gourmet★ to choose his wine. Certain years of distinction linger in the memory of oenophiles – years such as 1921, 1929, 1947 and 1949 (see table in appendix). Some specialists have observed that these are normally odd-numbered years. This seems true when considering 1943, 1945, 1953, 1955, 1957, 1959 and 1961, but the even years of 1942, 1950, 1952 and 1962 are also considered great. Within a ten-year period, three to five excellent years usually occur and one exceptional.

Sometimes wine-lovers tend to put too much weight on the year, forgetting that some years are relatively unheralded until the wines have matured, and years following famous ones are sometimes automatically overlooked. Wines coming after a mediocre year may be overestimated and not live up to their promise. In buying for a cellar it is best to follow this advice: 'Buy the petit cru in the great years and the grand cru in the lesser years'.

Vintage cave at Ferreirinha, Portugal. Phot. Cuisset.

Vintage port A Portuguese wine made in special years and bottled without being blended after two or three years in wood. Some vintage years have been 1921, 1924, 1927, 1934, 1947, 1950, 1955, 1960, 1964 and 1970. Usually not more than 10% of that year's harvest is reserved for vintage port.

After bottling, port must age slowly for at least ten years, during which time it acquires a special aroma and the bottle becomes encrusted with a white sediment. A special official label on the bottle guarantees the authenticity of the vintage. Port was a great British favourite in the nineteenth century.

The corkscrew is not used in opening port. Instead, special pincers are heated over a flame and used to slice the neck off. In this way no mustiness from the cork has a chance to mix with the wine, which can sometimes happen with the corkscrew method. After the ceremony of opening the bottle the wine is decanted so that it may aerate and be separated from its sediment.

virile A 'virile' wine is the opposite of a feminine★ one. It is powerful, vigorous and has great strength and character. Madiran★, Châteauneuf-de-Pape★ and the wines of the Côte de Nuits★ are all typical, virile red wines, while Pouilly-Fuissé is a typical white one.

Volnay Documentary evidence dates Volnay's great reputation back to 1250, and it has been called 'the most pleasing wine in all France'. Produced in the Côte de Beaune★, Volnay wines have great finesse, delicacy and rare distinction. They are well balanced, supple and light, and their aroma is fleetingly reminiscent of violets. They are the finest wines of the Côte de Beaune, just as Musignys are for their part the finest of the Côte de Nuits. Volnay only makes red wines. The best climats are les Caillerets, En Champans, Chevret, les Angles and Fremiets. (See Index.)

voltigeurs These are small particles of solid matter suspended in the wine which 'fly about' when the wine is moved or poured. They are composed of potassium bitartrate crystals, dead yeasts and solidified colouring matter★. Their existence usually has to be tolerated, unless too obtrusive. Absolute clarity in a wine is often obtained only at the expense of flavour.

Vosne-Romanée Despite its relatively low output, this is possibly the most outstanding viticultural commune in France. It produces incomparable red Burgundies whose names are synonymous with quality and distinction: Romanée-Conti, Richebourg, Romanée, la Tâche,

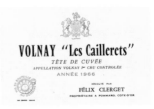

General view of Volnay.
Phot. Aarons-L.S.P.

Romanée-Saint-Vivant, Echezeaux and Grands-Echezeaux, seven of the most celebrated wines of Burgundy. They have brilliant colouring, a pronounced and subtle bouquet and exceptional smoothness and finesse.

Also worthy of mention are the following appellations: la Grande-Rue, les Suchots, Aus Malconsorts and les Beaux-Monts (which are always preceded by the name Vosne-Romanée). These all possess, though with less dazzling perfection than the seven mentioned above, the great characteristics of Vosne-Romanée wines, i.e. elegance, equilibrium and finesse of bouquet. (See Index.)

Vougeot Renowned for its world-famous cru Clos-de-Vougeot, this commune in Burgundy is also known on account of its picturesque castle, which is owned by the *Confrérie des Chevaliers du Tastevin*★ and used for their meetings.

Clos-de-Vougeot is a powerful, well-balanced wine which ages extremely well. Connoisseurs consider it one of the very best Côte d'Or wines. Vougeot also produces an excellent white wine, Clos-Blanc-de-Vougeot.

Vouvray Mounted like a precious jewel on the right bank of the Loire, Vouvray lies with its deep cellars cut into the chalk (sometimes hidden behind cave-like dwellings) and its valleys draped with vines. The vineyard comprises eight communes: Vouvray, Rochecorbon, Vernou, Sainte-Radegonde, Noizay, Chançay, Reugny and part of Parçay-Meslay.

The wines of Vouvray have been exported to Holland and Belgium for a long time, where they are enriched with must from Spain whose fermentation has been arrested with sulphur dioxide★. Then, following a secret recipe, fermentation begins again and sweet, highly alcoholic wines are produced.

Vouvray became a favourite on good

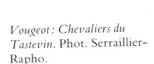

Vougeot: Chevaliers du Tastevin. Phot. Serraillier-Rapho.

258

French tables after phylloxera★ as the vine made a quick recovery.

Vouvray is made from the grape called Pineau de la Loire and takes on a different taste depending on the year, the aspect of the vineyard and the vinification method. Sometimes it is dry, light and lively, or full-bodied and powerful; at other times it is marrowy, fragrant and sweet and sometimes it tickles the nose and sparkles in the glass. It always has an amiable elegance and an exquisite freshness.

Still Vouvray must have 11° minimum alcohol. When young it is dry or semi-dry and gives great satisfaction, but reveals its splendour when kept for a few years. The 'heady' Vouvrays are made in great years although a cask of it can always be found, even in mediocre years.

Vouvray always keeps its freshness and fruitiness and is one of those astonishing wines which seems to have discovered the secret of eternal youth. Vigorous and solid, this golden, topaz-tinted wine has an extraordinary blend of aroma and taste reminiscent of acacia, fresh grapes, quince and almond.

Vouvray has a natural tendency to sparkle – a quality which is utilised in making semi-sparkling or sparkling wines, which must reach 9·5° before the second fermentation in bottle. Delicately fruity, supple and fragrant, they have a light sparkle which is produced by the natural sugar remaining in the wine after the first fermentation. This is enriched by cane sugar added as in the Champagne method★. Although prepared with a larger dose of sugar than that for the crackling or semi-sparkling wines, it is not an imitation Champagne. They are an attractive golden colour, finely perfumed, which preserve all the personality and grace of a still wine.

The sparkling wines of Vouvray, unlike other sparkling wines, improve with age and keep for a long time.

Aerial view of Vouvray. Phot. Lauros-Beaujard.

W-Z

Washington A wine-producing state in the extreme north-west of the USA★, bordered by Canada and the Pacific. The coastal region is relatively cold and damp and does not produce any outstanding wine. Further inland, however, the eastern part of the state has a continental climate and long, very hot summers. This region produces large quantities of strongly fortified liqueur★ wine and also, in the irrigated vineyards around Yakimo, some good table wines which are made from Sylvaner, Riesling, Pinot Noir, Pinot Blanc, Carignan, Concorde and Delaware vines (the last two being American varieties).

Y

Y A dry wine produced by Château d'Yquem★ which is a good deal less expensive than the sumptuous sweet white wine made by the same château.

yeasts One-celled micro-organisms responsible for turning grape juice into wine through the process of alcoholic fermentation★. The yeasts exist naturally on the skin of the grape or are trapped there by the bloom★. Thus alcoholic fermentation is often spontaneous and the role of the vigneron consists of observing the yeasts at work and making sure they have a favourable atmosphere.

There are several families of yeasts which work in different ways during the course of fermentation. Some can work at a low temperature, but a good fermentation point is between 25 and 28°C, which explains why it is necessary to reheat or cool the must depending on the climate.

The yeasts are slowly killed by the alcohol produced during the course of fermentation and their activity comes to a halt when the alcohol level reaches 15°. This characteristic is utilised in the mutage★ by alcohol of vins doux naturels.

The role of the yeast is not wholly confined to converting sugar into alcohol. The yeasts also attack other substances and create amino acids, glycerine, ethers and aldehydes. These elements give each wine its special character and aroma. For example, a special species of yeast gives vins de flor their particular taste.

YEASTS (SELECTED) Yeast cultures are sold under the name of famous viticultural areas, e.g. Burgundy, Beaujolais, Champagne, which are thought to give the particular characteristics of the wines of these regions. However, in reality, each grape variety and patch of soil has a complex mixture of yeasts in unknown proportions which there is no known way of calculating or reproducing.

If wines treated with the aforementioned yeasts seem to have the characteristics of the said wines during the first few weeks, these qualities tend to diminish rapidly. It is better to assure a good

fermentation with a good cuve base. The selected yeasts are best used in the case of defective white grapes which, after the necessary addition of sulphur dioxide★, need the added yeasts to ensure that fermentation begins and is maintained.

young This adjective takes on a different sense depending on the wine to which it is applied. If the wine is capable of maturing, it is called young or very young when it has not unfolded its qualities. If the wine has reached a certain age and is still lively and fruity it is also said to be young.

Certain wines should be drunk young as and some rare Chiantis. A young wine is not a vin de primeur★.

Yquem (Château-d') Words can hardly do justice to this magnificent wine of Sauternes★, the most famous sweet white wine in the world. The estate belongs to the Lur-Saluces family, who have supervised production of the wine for over two centuries. Château d'Yquem has a rich golden colour, a delicately fragrant aroma and an incomparable smoothness. Its quality is never less than perfect. In poor years the wine is simply sold under a regional appellation, i.e. Sauternes.

Château d'Yquem and its vineyards. Phot. M.

they acquire their personality and qualities very quickly and will not develop any further. It is therefore futile, even harmful, to conserve these wines for a long period.

The following wines should be drunk (generally) at around three and certainly before five years: all rosés, the dry whites of the Loire and Alsace, the white Burgundies, except the great appellations, the white Bordeaux, except the liquoreux and the Graves of good years, and the majority of white wines, with some exceptions. Red wines of good appellation should be conserved, except for some poor years. Nearly all the other reds can be drunk young, except in exceptional years, as well as Italian wines except the great reds from the Nebbiolo (Barolo, Gattinara, Barbaresco)

Yugoslavia The vine is found in all parts of this country, which is at the same latitude as Italy. Although total production is around six million litres, the wines never exceed the vin de pays★ level as far as quality is concerned. The following six republics contain important viticultural areas.

Serbia has vineyards in the Danube and Morava valleys, on the slopes of the Vojvodine and in the south. The Danube valley produces the Fruška Gora, an agreeable white wine, a table wine around Smederevo called the Smederevska and a dessert wine, the Smederevska Malaga. The Morava valley produces a white wine called Sicévačko around Negotin and Bagren, and Zupsko, a white or very fine rosé which is a speciality of Alexandrovac.

261

The Slovenian vineyard of Jerusalem in Yugoslavia. Phot. M.

Ružica is made in the Danube valley as an agreeable rosé and in Morava as a red. Finally, Vojvodine near Subotica on the Hungarian frontier produces the Rizling (Riesling) of Kraljev Berg.

Dalmatia produces two fruity wines around Mostar: the red Blatina and the full-bodied, dry, white Zilavka. It is also known for Prošek, a sweet, alcoholic red or white dessert wine, and Ružica, a rosé.

Slovenian viticulture used to be famous but is quickly dying out. The remaining vineyards are found in Istrie in the Drave valley where Bizelj and Cirček are produced for local consumption. Four wines are produced around Lutomer: Lutomer Riesling, Sylvanac, Traminac and Moslavac.

Macedonian vineyards are found throughout this republic, including the forest areas, and it is becoming an important viticultural area. The wines fit some-where between those of the Mediterranean and Central European areas. The red wines are made from several grapes of which the Serbian Prokupac is considered the national variety. It gives a rich, fleshy wine. The white wines are made from Zilavartea and Smerderevka grapes, the latter producing a quality wine in the Smederevo zone of Serbia. Macedonia also produces rosés and dessert wines.

Montenegro vines are cultivated on the hills and valleys of the Adriatic Coast in this mountainous country.

Croatia devotes only 5% of its area to viticulture. The best wines are found in Dalmatia and in the Save valley around Brod, Daruvar, Moslavina and Zagreb. The charming, slightly tart wines of the Save valley include Daruvar, Ivan Zelina and Okić-Plješivica. The Bermet and Karlovački Rizling are made around Karlovac.

Z

Zwicker A white Alsatian wine made from a blend of the must of different grapes, including noble★ varieties. The base is generally the Chasselas to which the Sylvaner is often added. The fact that it is a blended wine does not make the Zwicker a mediocre one, as the local viticultural syndicates demand certain standards of quality.

The Zwicker is a beautiful carafe wine, supple, light and easily drunk, but it lacks great character.

THE VINEYARDS OF FRANCE

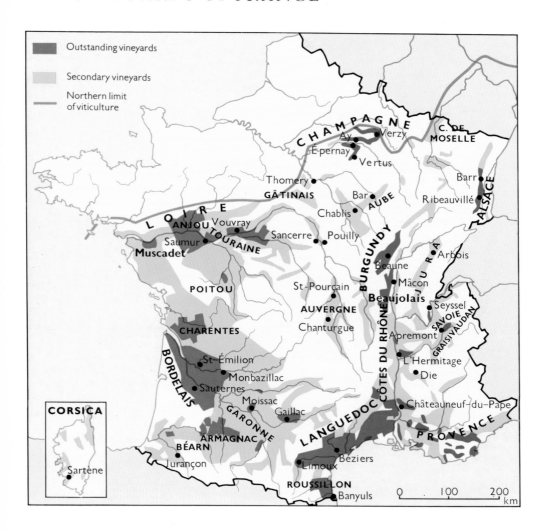

- Outstanding vineyards
- Secondary vineyards
- Northern limit of viticulture

CHAMPAGNE C. DE MOSELLE Ay Verzy Epernay Vertus Barr Thomery GÂTINAIS Bar AUBE Ribeauvillé ALSACE Chablis ANJOU Vouvray LOIRE Sancerre Pouilly TOURAINE Saumur Muscadet Beaune BURGUNDY Arbois JURA POITOU St-Pourçain Mâcon AUVERGNE Beaujolais Seyssel Chanturgue SAVOIE CHARENTES Apremont GRAISIVAUDAN BORDELAIS St-Émilion CÔTES DU RHÔNE L'Hermitage Monbazillac Die Sauternes GARONNE Moissac Gaillac Châteauneuf-du-Pape ARMAGNAC LANGUEDOC PROVENCE BÉARN Jurançon Limoux Béziers ROUSSILLON Banyuls CORSICA Sartène

0   100   200 km

BORDEAUX WINES

Classification of the crus of the Médoc

This is the official classification which dates from 1855. The wines are listed in each category, not in alphabetical or geographical order but according to merit. This classification has been the object of much criticism. Some wish to preserve it as it is, while others would change it completely. A third group favour a two-tier system in which the old classification would be treated as a historical souvenir and a new, flexible hierarchy would be created to exist parallel with the old one. This new classification could be examined each year and wines would move up or down depending on their quality that year. Wines would have a chance of promotion, a move which would have benefited Mouton-Rothschild which was only recently reclassified as a premier cru under the present system, a position it shares with Lafite-Rothschild, Margaux and Latour.

CHATEAUX	COMMUNES	*Deuxièmes crus*	
Premiers crus		Rausan-Ségla	Margaux
Lafite-Rothschild	Pauillac	Rauzan-Gassies	Margaux
Margaux	Margaux	Léoville-Las-Cases	Saint-Julien
Latour	Pauillac	Léoville-Poyferré	Saint-Julien
Mouton-Rothschild	Paulliac	Léoville-Barton	Saint-Julien
Haut-Brion	Pessac, Graves	Durfort-Vivens	Margaux

263

CHATEAUX	COMMUNES
Gruaud-Larose	Saint-Julien
Lascombes	Margaux
Brane-Cantenac	Cantenac
Pichon-Longueville (Baron)	Pauillac
Pichon-Longueville (Comtesse-de-Lalande-)	Pauillac
Ducru-Beaucaillou	Saint-Julien
Cos-d'Estournel	Saint-Estèphe
Montrose	Saint-Estèphe

Troisièmes crus

Kirwan	Cantenac
Issan	Cantenac
Lagrange	Saint-Julien
Langoa	Saint-Julien
Giscours	Labarde
Malescot-Saint-Exupéry	Margaux
Cantenac-Brown	Cantenac
Boyd-Cantenac	Margaux
Palmer	Cantenac
La Lagune	Ludon
Desmirail	Margaux
Calon-Ségur	Saint-Estèphe
Ferrière	Margaux
Marquis-d'Alesme-Becker	Margaux

Quatrièmes crus

Saint-Pierre-Sevaistre	Saint-Julien
Saint-Pierre-Bontemps	Saint-Julien
Talbot	Saint-Julien

Branaire-Ducru	Saint-Julien
Duhart-Milon	Pauillac
Pouget	Cantenac
La Tour-Carnet	Saint-Laurent
Rochet	Saint-Estèphe
Beychevelle	Saint-Julien
Le Prieuré	Cantenac
Marquis-de-Terme	Margaux

Cinquièmes crus

Pontet-Canet	Pauillac
Batailley	Pauillac
Haut-Batailley	Pauillac
Grand-Puy-Lacoste	Pauillac
Grand-Puy-Ducasse	Pauillac
Lynch-Bages	Pauillac
Lynch-Moussas	Pauillac
Dauzac	Labarde
Mouton-Baron-Philippe (called Mouton-d'Armailhacq since 1956)	Pauillac
Le Tertre	Arsac
Haut-Bages-Libéral	Pauillac
Pédesclaux	Pauillac
Belgrave	Saint-Laurent
Camensac	Saint-Laurent
Cos-Labory	Saint-Estèphe
Clerc-Milon	Pauillac
Croizet-Bages	Pauillac
Cantemerle	Macau

Classification of the crus of Sauternes and Barsac

This official classification dates from 1855 (see classification of 1855).

Grand Premier cru

Yquem	Sauternes

Premiers crus

La Tour-Blanche	Bommes
Lafaurie-Peyraguey	Bommes
Clos Haut-Peyraguey	Bommes
Rayne-Vigneau	Bommes
Suduiraut	Preignac
Coutet	Barsac
Climens	Barsac
Guiraud	Sauternes
Rieussec	Fargues
Rabaud-Sigalas	Bommes
Rabaud-Promis	Bommes

Deuxièmes crus

Myrat	Barsac
Doisy-Dubroca	Barsac
Doisy-Daëne	Barsac
Doisy-Védrines	Barsac
Arche	Sauternes
Arche-Lafaurie	Sauternes
Filhot	Sauternes
Broustet	Barsac
Nairac	Barsac
Caillou	Barsac
Suau	Barsac
De-Malle	Preignac
Romer-Lafon	Fargues
Lamothe-Bergey	Sauternes
Lamothe-Espagnet	Sauternes

Classification of the crus of Saint-Emilion

A century passed after the classification of 1855 before the wines of Saint-Emilion were ranked. After consultation with producers and the consent of the Institut National des Appellations d'Origine, the decree of 7th October, 1954 established the following classification for the crus based on their quality and reputation:

Saint-Emilion; Saint-Emilion Grand Cru; Saint-Emilion Grand Cru classé; Saint-Emilion Premier Grand Cru classé.
Although Château Ausone and Château Cheval-Blanc were classified 'Premier Grand Cru classé' they are considered as a special category.

CHATEAUX	CHATEAUX
Premiers Grands Crus classés	
A	
Ausone	Cheval-Blanc

B	
Beauséjour	Figeac
Beauséjour-Fagouet	La Gaffelière-Naudes
Bélair	Magdelaine
Canon	Pavie
Clos Fourtet	Trottevieille

Grands Crus classés

L'Angélus	Canon-la-Gaffelière
L'Arrosée	Cap-de-Mourlin
Balestard-la-Tonnelle	La Carte
Bellevue	Chapelle-Madeleine
Bergat	Le Châtelet
Cadet-Bon	Chauvin
Cadet-Piola	Clos des Jacobins
Clos la Madeleine	Lamarzelle
Clos Saint-Martin	Larmande
La Clotte	Laroze
La Cluzière	Lasserre
Corbin	Mauvezin
Corbin-Michotte	Moulin-du-Cadet
La Couspaude	Pavie-Decesse
Coutet	Pavie-Macquin

Le Couvent	Pavillon-Cadet
Croque-Michotte	Petit-Faurie-de-Souchard
Curé-Bon	Petit-Faurie-de-Soutard
La Dominique	Le Prieuré
Fonplégade	Ripeau
Fonroque	Sansonnet
Franc-Mayne	Saint-Georges-Côte-Pavie
Grand-Barrail-la-Marzelle-Figeac	Soutard
Grand-Corbin-d'Espagne	Tertre-Daugay
Grand-Corbin-Pécresse	La Tour-du-Pin-Figeac
Grand-Mayne	La Tour-Figeac
Grand-Pontet	Trimoulet
Grandes-Murailles	Trois-Moulins
Guadet-Saint-Julien	Troplong-Mondot
Jean-Faure	Villemaurine
Larcis-Ducasse	Yon-Figeac

Classification of Graves

The châteaux of Graves were ignored in the classification of 1855, except for Château Haut-Brion, which was ranked as a premier cru in company with the Médocs. In 1953 the Institut National des Appellations d'Origine officially classified the crus of Graves. This was confirmed by the Order of 16th February, 1959.

Premier Cru classified in 1855

Château Haut-Brion (Pessac)

Crus classified in 1959

CHATEAUX	COMMUNES
White Graves	
Carbonnieux	Léognan
Domaine de Chevalier	Léognan
Couhins	Villenave-d'Ornon
Olivier	Léognan
Laville-Haut-Brion	Talence
Bouscaut	Cadaujac
Latour-Martillac	Martillac
Malartic-Lagravière	Léognan

Red Graves	
La Mission-Haut-Brion	Talence
Haut-Bailly	Léognan
Domaine de Chevalier	Léognan
Carbonnieux	Léognan
Malartic-Lagravière	Léognan
Latour-Martillac	Martillac
Latour-Haut-Brion	Talence
Smith-Haut-Lafitte	Martillac
Olivier	Léognan
Bouscaut	Cadaujac
Fieuzal	Léognan
Pape-Clément	Pessac

Classification of the crus of Pomerol

No official classification of the wines of Pomerol exists. However, Château Pétrus is traditionally ranked first and the principal châteaux are more or less classified in the following order:

Premiers Grands crus

Château Pétrus	Ch.Gazin
Ch. Certan	Ch. Petit-Village
Vieux-Château-Certan	Ch. Trotanoy
Ch. la Conseillante	Ch. l'Evangile
Ch. Lafleur	Ch. la Fleur-Pétrus

Premiers crus

Dom. de l'Église	Ch. la Pointe
Ch. la Croix-de-Gay	Ch. Gombaude-Guillot
Ch. la Grave-Trigant-de-Boisset	Ch. Guillot
Clos l'Église	Ch. l'Église-Clinet
Ch. Latour-Pomerol	Ch. le Gay
Ch. Beauregard	Ch. la Grange
Ch. Certan-Marzelle	Ch. la Vraye-Croix-de-Gay
Ch. Clinet	Ch. Rouget
Ch. Nénin	

Deuxièmes Premiers crus

Ch. la Commanderie	Clos du Clocher

Ch. la Croix-Saint-Georges	Ch. Lacabane
Ch. la Croix	Ch. Moulinet
Ch. Plince	Clos René
Ch. de Salles	Dom. Haut-Tropchaud
Ch. Bourgneuf	Ch. Pignon-de-Gay
Ch. le Caillou	Clos Beauregard
Ch. l'Enclos	Dom. de Haut-Pignon
Enclos du Presbytère	Ch. Cantereau
Ch. Gratte-Cap	Ch. Mazeyres
Dom. de Tropchaud	Ch. Taillefer
Ch. la Violette	Ch. du Chêne-Liège
Ch. Lafleur-du-Gazin	

Deuxièmes crus

Ch. Bel-Air	Ch. Haut-Maillet
Ch. la Croix-Taillefer	Ch. Couprie
Ch. Ferrand	Ch. Franc-Maillet
Dom. de Mazeyres	Ch. Thibaud-Maillet
Enclos du Haut-Mazeyres	Ch. Hautes-Rouzes
Clos des Templiers	

CLIMATS OF BURGUNDY

It is not possible to rank the vineyards of Burgundy with such precision as those of Bordeaux. On the Côte-d'Or and at Chablis most of the vineyards are divided among a number of owners (more than sixty proprietors, for example, have a share of the famous Clos de Vougeot!). Well before the modern system of Appellations d'Origine Contrôlées an authoritative and exhaustive listing and classification of the crus was published in 1861 by the 'Comité d'Agriculture de l'Arrondissement de Beaune'.

The following list is inevitably incomplete. There are 419 climats recognised in the Côte de Nuits and twice as many in the Côte de Beaune! Although not official, the list mentions most of the 'climats' which the wine-lover is likely to encounter in more or less the order accepted by the majority of experts.

COMMUNES	CLIMATS
Côte de Nuits	
Fixin	Clos de la Perrière
	Les Hervelets
	Clos du Chapitre
	Les Arvelets
	Clos Napoléon
Gevrey-Chambertin	CHAMBERTIN
	CHAMBERTIN-CLOS DE BÈZE
	Charmes – Chambertin
	and Mazoyères – Chambertin
	Chapelle
	Griotte
	Latricières
	Mazis
	Ruchottes
	Clos Saint-Jacques
	Les Véroilles
	Aux Combottes
	Cazetiers
	Combe-aux-Moines
	Estournelles
	Lavaut
Morey-Saint-Denis	
	BONNES-MARES (a part)
	Clos de Tart
	Clos de la Roche
	Clos Saint-Denis
	Clos des Lambrays
Chambolle-Musigny	MUSIGNY
	BONNES-MARES (a part)
	Les Amoureuses
	Les Charmes
	Les Baudes
	Les Cras
	Derrière-la-Grange
	Les Fuées
Vougeot	CLOS DE VOUGEOT
	Le Clos Blanc-de-Vougeot
	Les Petits-Vougeots
Vosne-Romanée	ROMANÉE-CONTI
(and Flagey-Échezeaux)	RICHEBOURG
	LA TÂCHE
	ROMANÉE-SAINT-VIVANT
	ROMANÉE
	GRANDS-ÉCHEZEAUX

ÉCHEZEAUX	
	Les Malconsorts
	Les Beaux-Monts
	Les Perdrix
	Clos de la Maréchale
	Clos des Argillières
	Clos des Corvées
	Clos des Forêts
	Les Argilats
Côte de Beaune	
Aloxe-Corton	
(Ladoix and parts of	
Pernand-Vergelesses)	CORTON
	CORTON-CHARLEMAGNE
	CORTON-BRESSANDES
	CORTON-CLOS DU ROI
	Les Maréchaudes
	En Pauland
	Les Valozières
	Les Chaillots
	Les Perrières
	Les Meix
	Les Chaumes
	La Vigne-au-Saint
	Les Languettes
	Les Grèves
	Les Fiètres
	Les Fournières
	Les Renardes
Pernand-Vergelesses	
	Ile des Vergelesses
Savigny-lès-Beaune	Aux Vergelesses
	Les Marconnets
	La Dominode
	Les Jarrons
	Les Lavières
	Les Gaudichots
	Les Suchots
	La Grande-Rue
	Aux Brûlées
	Les Reignots
	Clos des Réas
Nuits-Saint-Georges	
(and Prémeaux)	Les Saint-Georges
	Les Vaucrains
	Les Pruliers

	Les Cailles
	Les Porets
	La Perrière
	Les Thorey
	Les Murgers
	Les Boudots
	Les Cras
	La Richemone
	Les Didiers
Beaune	Grèves
	Fèves
	Clos des Mouches
	Les Bressandes
	Marconnets
	Clos du Roi
	Champimonts
	Les Avaux
	Les Cras
	Clos de la Mousse
	Aigrots
	Les Cent-Vignes
	Les Theurons
	Les Sizies
	Toussaints
Pommard	Rugiens
	Épenots
	Rugiens-Hauts
	Petits-Épenots
	Clos Blanc
	Les Pézerolles
	Clos de la Commaraine
	Les Arvelets
	Les Boucherottes
	Les Argillières
	Les Charmots
	La Chanière
	Les Saussiles
	Les Chaponières
	Clos Micot
	Les Chanlins-Bas
	La Platière
	Les Fremiers
	Les Bertins
	Les Croix-Noires
	Les Poutures
	Les Combes-Dessus
	Clos du Verger
Volnay	CAILLERETS

Meursault

CHAMPANS
Les Angles
Clos des Ducs
Fremiets
Chevret
Les Mitans
Clos des Chênes
Les Santenots
Les Brouillards
En l'Ormeau
Carelle-sous-la-Chapelle
Pointe-d'Angles
Ronceret
Bousse-d'Or
En Verseuil

Meursault
PERRIÈRES
GENEVRIÈRES
CHARMES
La Pièce-sous-le-Bois
Les Santenots
Le Poruzot
Goutte-d'Or
Les Bouchères
Les Petures
Les Cras
La Jennelotte
Sous-le-Dos-d'Ane

Puligny-Montrachet
MONTRACHET (a part)
CHEVALIER-MONTRACHET
BÂTARD MONTRACHET
(a part)
BIENVENUES-BÂTARD-
MONTRACHET
Les Combettes
Les Pucelles
Les Folatières
Les Chalumeaux
Le Cailleret
Clavoillon
Champ-Canet
La Garenne
Sous-le-Puits
Hameau-de-Blagny
Les Referts
Les Levrons

Chassagne-Montrachet
MONTRACHET (a part)
BÂTARD-MONTRACHET

(a part)
CRIOTS-BÂTARD-MONTRACHET
Les Ruchottes
Cailleret
Morgeot
Les Chenevottes
La Boudriotte
Les Macherelles
Les Vergers
Clos Saint-Jean
La Maltroie
La Romanée

Santenay
Les Gravières
La Comme
Clos de Tavanne
Beauregard
Beaurepaire
La Maladière
Le Passe-Temps

Côte Chalonnaise

Mercurey
Clos du Roi
Les Voyens
Les Fourneaux
Les Montaigus
Les Combins
Clos Marcilly

Givry
Clos Saint-Pierre
Clos Saint-Paul
Clos Salomon
Clos du Cellier-aux-Moines

Rully
Margotey
Grésigny
Mont-Palais
Les Pierres
Vauvry
La Renarde

Chablis

Chablis Grand Cru
Vaudésir
Les Clos
Grenouilles
Valmur
Blanchots
Preuses
Bougros

Chablis Premier Cru
Monts-de-Milieu

Montée-de-Tonnerre
Chapelot
Vaulorent
Vaucoupin
Côte de Fontenay
Fourchaume
Les Forêts
Butteaux
Montmain
Vaillon
Sechet
Chatain
Beugnon
Melinots
Côte de Léchet
Les Lys
Beauroy
Troeme
Vosgros
Vogiros

Chablis and Petit Chablis
To merit the appellation, the wines must come from the twenty following communes: Chablis, Beine, Béru, La Chapelle-Vaupelteigne, Chemilly-sur-Serein, Chichée, Courgis, Fleys, Fontenay, Fyé, Ligny-le-Châtel, Lignorelles, Maligny, Milly, Poilly, Poinchy, Préhy, Rameau, Villy and Viviers.

Beaujolais
The wines from the thirty-five following communes are entitled to the appellation Beaujolais-Villages: Arbuissonnas, Beaujeu, Blacé, Cercié, Chanes, La Chapelle-de-Guinchay, Charentay, Chénas, Chiroubles, Durette, Émeringes, Fleurie, Juillé, Juliénas, Lancié, Lantigné, Leynes, Montmélas-Saint-Sorlin, Odénas, Le Perréon, Pruzilly, Quincié, Regnié, Rivolet, Romanèche-Thorins, Saint-Amour-Bellevue, Saint-Étienne-des-Oullières, Saint-Étienne-la-Varenne, Saint-Julien-en-Montmélas, Saint-Lager, Saint-Symphorien-d'Ancelles, Saint-Vérand, Salles, Vaux-en-Beaujolais, Villié-Morgon.

VINS DÉLIMITÉS DE QUALITÉ SUPÉRIEURE (VDQS)

R : red wine   **r** : rosé wine   **W** : white wine

	types	department of production
LANGUEDOC AND ROUSSILLON		
Corbières	R r W	Aude
Corbières supérieures	R r W	Aude
Corbières du Roussillon	R r W	Pyrénées-Orient.
Minervois	R r W	Hérault
Roussillon-dels-Aspres	R r W	Pyrénées-Orient.
Picpoul-de-Pinet	W	Hérault
Coteaux du Languedoc	R r	Hérault, Aude
Coteaux de la Méjanelle	R W	Hérault
Saint-Saturnin	R r	Hérault
Montpeyroux	R r	Hérault
Coteaux de Saint-Christol	R r	Hérault
Quatourze	R r W	Aude
La Clape	R r W	Aude
Saint-Drézery	R	Hérault
Saint-Chinian	R	Hérault
Faugères	R W	Hérault
Cabrières	r	Hérault
Coteaux de Vérargues	R r	Hérault
Pic-Saint-Loup	R r W	Hérault
Saint-Georges-d'Orques	R	Hérault
LOIRE		
Gros-Plant du pays nantais	W	Loire-Atlantique
Coteaux d'Ancenis	R r W	Loire-Atlantique
Mont-près-Chambord-Cour-Cheverny	W	Loir-et-Cher
Vins de l'Orléanais	R r W	Loiret
Coteaux du Giennois or Côtes de Gien	R r W	Loiret
Châteaumeillant	R r	Cher, Indre
Saint-Pourçain-sur-Sioule	R r W	Allier
Vins d'Auvergne Côtes d'Auvergne	R r W	Puy-de-Dôme
LORRAINE		
Vins de la Moselle	R r W	Moselle
Côtes de Toul	R r W	Meurthe-et-Moselle
LYONNAIS		
Vins du Lyonnais	R r W	Rhône
Vins de Renaison-Côte roannaise	R r	Loire
Côtes du Forez	R r	Loire
PROVENCE AND CORSICA		
Côtes de Provence	R r W	Var, Bouches-du-Rhône
Coteaux d'Aix-en-Provence	R r W	Bouches-du-Rhône
Coteaux des Baux	R r W	Bouches-du-Rhône
Coteaux de Pierrevert	R r W	Basses-Alpes
Sartène	R r W	Corsica
RHÔNE		
Châtillon-en-Diois	R r W	Drôme
Haut-Comtat	R r	Drôme
Coteaux du Tricastin	R r W	Drôme
Côtes du Ventoux	R r W	Vaucluse
Côtes du Luberon	R r W	Vaucluse
Côtes du Vivarais	R r W	Ardèche
Costières-du-Gard	R W	Gard
SAVOIE-BUGEY		
Vin de Savoie	R r W	Savoie, Haute-Savoie, Isère
Vin de Savoie + name of cru	R r W	Savoie, Haute-Savoie, Isère
Roussette	W	Savoie, Haute-Savoie, Isère
Mousseux de Savoie or Vin de Savoie mousseux	W	Savoie, Haute-Savoie, Isère
Vins du Bugey	R r W	Ain
Roussette du Bugey	W	Ain
SUD-OUEST		
Côtes du Buzet	R W	Lot-et-Garonne
Côtes du Marmandais	R W	Lot-et-Garonne
Vins de Tursan	R r W	Landes
Cahors	R	Lot
Vins de Béarn	R r W	Pyrénées-Atlant.
Rosé de Béarn	r	Hautes-Pyrénées
Rousselet de Béarn	W	Pyrénées-Atlant.
Irouléguy	R r W	Pyrénées-Atlant.
Fronton or Côtes de Fronton	R r W	Haute-Garonne, Tarn-et-Garonne
Villaudric	R W	Haute-Garonne
Lavilledieu	R W	Haute-Garonne, Tarn-et-Garonne
Vins d'Entraygues and du Fel	R r W	Aveyron
Estaing	R r W	Aveyron
Marcillac	R r	Aveyron

LIST OF FRENCH APPELLATIONS D'ORIGINE CONTRÔLÉES (AOC)

R: red wine **W**: white wine **r**: rosé wine

ALSACE

	W	R	r
Vin d'Alsace	W	R	r
Vin d'Alsace followed by the name of the grape	W	R	r
Vin d'Alsace Zwicker	W		
Vin d'Alsace Edelzwicker	W		
Vin d'Alsace followed by the name of several grapes	W	R	r
Vin d'Alsace Grand Vin or Grand Vin d'Alsace	W	R	r
Vin d'Alsace Grand Cru	W	R	r
Vin d'Alsace followed by the name of the commune of origin	W	R	r

BORDEAUX

	W	R	r
Barsac	W		
Blaye or Blayais	W		r
Bordeaux	W	R	
Bordeaux clairet or Bordeaux rosé			r
Bordeaux Côtes de Castillon		R	
Bordeaux Haut-Benauge	W		
Bordeaux supérieur	W	R	
Bordeaux supérieur clairet or Bordeaux supérieur rosé			r
Bordeaux supérieur Côtes de Castillon		R	
Bordeaux mousseux	W		r
Bourg, or Bourgeais, or Côtes de Bourg	W	R	
Cérons	W		
Côtes de Blaye	W		
Côtes de Bordeaux-Saint-Macaire	W		
Côtes de Fronsac		R	
Côtes de Canon-Fronsac, or Canon-Fronsac		R	
Entre-deux-Mers	W		
Graves	W	R	
Graves supérieurs	W		
Graves de Vayres	W	R	
Haut Médoc		R	
Lalande-de-Pomerol		R	
Listrac		R	
Loupiac	W		
Lussac-Saint-Émilion		R	
Margaux		R	
Médoc		R	
Montagne-Saint-Émilion		R	
Moulis or Moulis-en-Médoc		R	
Néac		R	
Parsac-Saint-Émilion		R	
Pauillac		R	
Pomerol		R	
Premières Côtes de Blaye	W	R	
Premières Côtes de Bordeaux	W	R	
Puisseguin-Saint-Émilion		R	
Sables-Saint-Émilion		R	
Sainte-Croix-du-Mont	W		
Saint-Émilion		R	
Saint-Émilion Grand Cru		R	
Saint-Émilion Grand Cru classé		R	
Saint-Émilion Premier Grand Cru classé		R	
Saint-Estèphe		R	
Sainte-Foy-Bordeaux	W	R	
Saint-Georges-Saint-Émilion		R	
Saint-Julien		R	
Sauternes	W		

BURGUNDY

	W	R	r
Aloxe-Corton	W	R	
Auxey-Duresses	W	R	
Bâtard-Montrachet	W		
Beaujolais	W	R	r
Beaujolais supérieur	W	R	r
Beaujolais-Villages	W	R	r
Beaune	W	R	
Bienvenues-Bâtard-Montrachet	W		
Blagny, or Meursault-Blagny	W	R	
Bonnes-Mares		R	
Bourgogne	W	R	
Bourgogne clairet or Bourgogne rosé			r
Bourgogne Marsannay		R	r
Bourgogne Hautes Côtes de Beaune	W	R	
Bourgogne rosé (or clairet) Hautes Côtes de Beaune			r
Bourgogne Hautes Côtes de Nuits	W	R	r
Bourgogne Passe-tous-grains		R	r
Bourgogne aligoté	W		
Bourgogne ordinaire or Bourgogne grand ordinaire	W	R	
Bourgogne ordinaire or Bourgogne grand ordinaire rosé (or clairet)			r
Bourgogne mousseux	W	R	r
Brouilly		R	
Chablis	W		
Petit-Chablis	W		
Chablis Grand Cru	W		
Chablis Premier Cru	W		
Chambertin		R	
Chambertin-Clos de Bèze		R	
Chambolle-Musigny		R	
Chapelle-Chambertin		R	
Charmes-Chambertin, or Mazoyères-Chambertin		R	
Chassagne-Montrachet	W	R	
Cheilly-lès-Maranges	W	R	
Chénas		R	
Chevalier-Montrachet	W		
Chiroubles		R	
Chorey-lès-Beaune	W	R	
Clos de la Roche		R	
Clos Saint-Denis		R	
Clos de Vougeot		R	

	W	R	r
Clos de Tart		R	
Corton	W	R	
Corton-Charlemagne	W		
Côte de Beaune	W	R	
Côte de Beaune-Villages		R	
Côte de Brouilly		R	
Criots-Bâtard-Montrachet	W		
Dezize-lès-Maranges	W	R	
Échezeaux		R	
Fixin	W	R	
Fleurie		R	
Gevrey-Chambertin		R	
Givry	W	R	
Grands-Échezeaux		R	
Griotte-Chambertin		R	
Juliénas		R	
Ladoix	W	R	
Latricières-Chambertin		R	
Mâcon	W	R	r
Mâcon supérieur	W	R	r
Mâcon-Villages	W		
Mazis-Chambertin		R	
Mercurey	W	R	
Meursault	W	R	
Montagny	W		
Monthélie	W	R	
Montrachet	W		
Morey-Saint-Denis	W	R	
Morgon		R	
Moulin-à-Vent		R	
Musigny	W	R	
Nuits, or Nuits-Saint-Georges	W	R	
Vin fin de la Côte de Nuits, or Côte de Nuits-Villages	W	R	
Pernand-Vergelesses	W	R	
Pommard		R	
Pouilly-Fuissé	W		
Pouilly-Loché	W		
Pouilly-Vinzelles	W		
Puligny-Montrachet	W	R	
Richebourg		R	
Romanée		R	
Romanée-Conti		R	
Romanée-Saint-Vivant		R	
Ruchottes-Chambertin		R	
Rully	W	R	
Saint-Amour		R	
Saint-Aubin	W	R	
Saint-Romain	W	R	
Sampigny-lès-Maranges	W	R	
Santenay	W	R	
Savigny, or Savigny-lès-Beaune	W	R	
La Tâche		R	
Volnay		R	
Vosne-Romanée		R	
Vougeot	W	R	

CHAMPAGNE

	W	R	r
Champagne			
Champagne rosé			
Rosé des Riceys			r
Vin nature de la Champagne (appellation not 'contrôlée')	W	R	r

CÔTES DU RHÔNE

	W	R	r
Château-Grillet	W		
Châteauneuf-du-Pape	W	R	
Clairette de Die	W, tranquille and mousseux		
Condrieu	W		
Cornas		R	
Côtes du Rhône	W	R	r
Côtes du Rhône (appellation followed by the names of the following communes: Rochegude, Saint-Maurice-sur-Eygues, Vinsobres, Cairanne, Gigondas, Rasteau, Roaix, Séguret, Vacqueyras, Valréas, Visan, Laudun)	W	R	r
Côtes du Rhône-Chusclan			r
Côte-Rôtie		R	
Crozes-Hermitage	W	R	
Ermitage, or Hermitage	W	R, vin de paille	
Lirac	W	R	r
Muscat de Beaumes-de-Venise	W		
Rasteau	W	R	r
Saint-Joseph	W	R	
Saint-Peray	W		
Saint-Peray mousseux	W		
Tavel			r

JURA

	W	R	r
Arbois	W	R	r, vin de paille, vin jaune, vin mousseux
Château-Chalon			vin jaune
Côtes du Jura	W	R	r, vin jaune, vin de paille, vin mousseux
L'Étoile	W, vin jaune, vin de paille, vin mousseux		

LANGUEDOC

	W	R	r
Blanquette de Limoux	W, mousseux		
Clairette de Bellegarde	W		
Clairette du Languedoc	W		
Fitou		R	
Muscat de Frontignan or Frontignan, or Vin de Frontignan	W		
Muscat de Lunel	W		
Muscat de Mireval	W		
Muscat de Saint-Jean-de-Minervois	W		

LOIRE

a) *Nivernais and Berry*

	W	R	r
Blanc fumé de Pouilly, or Pouilly fumé	W		
Menetou-Salon	W	R	r
Pouilly-sur-Loire	W		
Quincy	W		
Reuilly	W	R	r
Sancerre	W	R	r

b) *Touraine*

	W	R	r
Bourgueil		R	r
Chinon	W	R	r
Coteaux du Loir	W	R	r
Jasnières	W		
Montlouis	W		
Montlouis mousseux	W		
Montlouis pétillant	W		
Saint-Nicolas-de-Bourgueil		R	r
Touraine	W	R	r
Touraine-Amboise	W	R	r
Touraine-Azay-le-Rideau	W		

	W	R	r
Touraine-Mesland	W	R	r
Touraine mousseux	W	R	r
Touraine pétillant	W	R	r
Vouvray	W		
Vouvray mousseux	W		
Vouvray pétillant	W		

c) *Anjou*

	W	R	r
Anjou	W	R	
Anjou mousseux	W		r
Anjou pétillant	W		
Anjou-Coteaux de la Loire	W		
Bonnezeaux	W		
Cabernet d'Anjou			r
Cabernet de Saumur			r
Coteaux de l'Aubance	W		
Coteaux du Layon	W		
Coteaux du Layon + name of the commune of origin	W		
Coteaux de Saumur	W		
Quarts-de-Chaume	W		
Rosé d'Anjou			r
Rosé d'Anjou pétillant			r
Savennières	W		
Savennières-Coulée-de-Serrant	W		
Savennières-Roches-aux-Moines	W		
Saumur	W	R	

d) *Pays nantais*

	W	R	r
Muscadet	W		
Muscadet des Coteaux de la Loire	W		
Muscadet de Sèvre et Maine	W		

PROVENCE AND CORSICA

	W	R	r
Bandol or vin de Bandol	W	R	r
Bellet or vin de Bellet	W	R	r
Cassis	W	R	r

	W	R	r
Palette	W	R	r
Propriano	W	R	r

ROUSSILLON

	W	R	r
Banyuls	W	R	r, Rancio
Banyuls Grand Cru		R	
Maury		R	
Côte d'Agly	W	R	r, Rancio
Rivesaltes	W	R	r, Rancio
Muscat de Rivesaltes		R	
Côtes de Haut-Roussillon	W	R	r, Rancio
Grand-Roussillon	W	R	r, Rancio

SAVOIE

	W	R	r
Crépy	W		
Seyssel	W		
Seyssel mousseux	W		

SUD-OUEST

	W	R	r
Bergerac		R	r
Bergerac sec	W		
Côtes de Bergerac		R	
Côtes de Bergerac moelleux	W		
Côtes de Duras	W	R	
Côtes de Montravel	W		
Gaillac	W		
Gaillac mousseux	W		
Gaillac Premières Côtes	W		
Gaillac doux	W		
Haut-Montravel	W		
Jurançon	W		
Madiran		R	
Monbazillac	W		
Montravel	W		
Pacherenc-du-Vic-Bihl	W		
Pécharmant		R	
Rosette	W		

THE GOOD VINTAGES AND THE GREAT VINTAGES OF THE PRINCIPAL WINES

The good years are in roman, the great years in bold italic

ALSACE

1900	1911	1915	1918	1919	1920	1921	1923	1926
1928	*1929*	*1934*	1935	1937	1942	1943	*1945*	1947
1949	1953	*1959*	*1961*	1964	*1966*	*1967*	1969	*1970*
1971	*1973*	1974						

ANJOU AND TOURAINE

1900	1921	1928	1933	1934	1937	1943	1944	1945
1946	1947	1948	*1949*	1950	1952	1953	1954	*1955*
1957	1958	*1959*	1960	1961	1962	1964	1966	*1969*
1970	1971	1974						

WHITE BORDEAUX

1900	1904	1906	1914	1916	1919	*1921*	1924	1926
1928	*1929*	1934	*1937*	1942	*1943*	*1945*	*1947*	1948
1949	1950	1952	1953	*1955*	1957	1959	*1961*	*1962*
1966	*1967*	1969	1970	1971				

RED BORDEAUX

1900	1904	1906	1914	1916	*1920*	1921	*1924*	1926
1928	*1929*	*1934*	1940	1942	*1943*	*1945*	*1947*	1948
1949	1950	*1953*	*1955*	1959	1960	*1961*	*1962*	*1964*
1966	1967	1969	*1970*	1971	1973	1974		

WHITE BURGUNDIES

1904	1911	1915	1921	1923	1928	*1929*	1933	1934
1937	1942	1943	1945	1948	1950	1952	1953	*1955*
1957	1959	1961	1962	1964	1966	1967	*1969*	*1970*
1971	1973							

RED BURGUNDIES

1904	1906	1911	*1915*	1921	*1923*	1926	*1928*	*1929*
1933	1934	*1937*	1938	*1942*	1943	1945	*1947*	1948
1949	1952	1953	*1955*	1957	*1959*	*1961*	1962	*1964*
1966	1967	*1969*	1970	1971	1972			

CHAMPAGNE

1904	1906	*1911*	1914	1917	1919	1920	*1921*	1923
1926	*1928*	1929	1933	1934	1937	1942	1943	1945
1947	*1953*	1955	1959	1961	*1964*	*1966*	1969	1971

CÔTES DU RHÔNE

1904	1923	1926	*1929*	*1933*	1934	1942	1943	*1945*
1947	*1949*	1950	*1952*	*1954*	*1955*	*1957*	1959	1960
1961	1962	1964	1966	*1967*	*1969*	1970	1971	

NEW PARADIGMS FOR SOFTWARE DEVELOPMENT

William W. Agresti

IEEE Computer Society Order Number 707
Library of Congress Number 86-80959
IEEE Catalog Number EH0245-1
ISBN 0-8186-0707-6

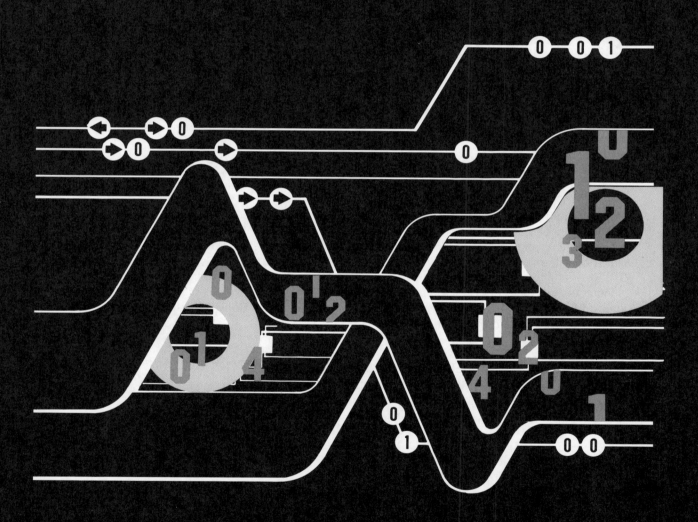

- PROTOTYPING
- OPERATIONAL SPECIFICATION
- TRANSFORMATIONAL IMPLEMENTATION
- CRITIQUES OF THE "WATERFALL" LIFE-CYCLE MODEL

 **IEEE COMPUTER SOCIETY**

 THE INSTITUTE OF ELECTRICAL
AND ELECTRONICS ENGINEERS, INC.
IEEE

COMPUTER
SOCIETY
PRESS

Published by IEEE Computer Society Press
1730 Massachusetts Avenue, N.W.
Washington, D.C. 20036-1903

COVER DESIGNED BY JACK I. BALLESTERO

IEEE Computer Society Order Number 707
Library of Congress Number 86-80959
IEEE Catalog Number EH0245-1
ISBN 0-8186-0707-6 (Paper)
ISBN 0-8186-4707-8 (Microfiche)

Order from: IEEE Computer Society   IEEE Service Center
            Post Office Box 80452   44 Hoes Lane
            Worldway Postal Center   Piscataway, NJ 08854
            Los Angeles, CA 90080

THE INSTITUTE OF ELECTRICAL AND ELECTRONICS ENGINEERS, INC.

To the Reader

This tutorial is designed for computer professionals who are interested in the *process* of software development. The conventional life-cycle (waterfall) model has been criticized recently on several fronts, including its inability to accommodate newer paradigms of software development, such as prototyping and end-user development.

The objective of this tutorial is to

- Expose the assumptions and limitations of the life-cycle model so that organizations will understand when it is appropriate and when it is not
- Explain, with examples, the new paradigms
  —Prototyping
  —Operational specification
  —Transformational implementation
- Show how the new paradigms interrelate to support process improvement by
  —Delivering executable objects early to the users
  —Applying automation
- Discuss the transition from the life-cycle model to a more flexible development process that accommodates these newer paradigms

The tutorial features 21 reprinted articles by outstanding authors, as well as extensive original material. An annotated bibliography of over 100 books and articles is included. These references are classified and organized to form a valuable guide to the literature for further study.

Your comments on this tutorial and your experiences with the software development process are of interest to the author in trying to cultivate the field of software process engineering. The author's address is

Dr. William W. Agresti
Computer Sciences Corporation
8728 Colesville Road
Silver Spring, MD 20910
(301) 589-1545

Acknowledgments

The authors of the reprinted articles must be acknowledged first for their contributions toward improving the process of software development.

Computer Sciences Corporation (CSC) supported the preparation of new material for this tutorial text. CSC colleagues—Victor Church, David Card, Gerald Page, Michael Plett, and Peter Belford—helped greatly through their support and encouragement. It is a pleasure to acknowledge the editorial assistance of Barbara Siegrist and the fine work of the Technical Publications Department.

The efforts of Chip Stockton and Margaret Brown of the IEEE Computer Society, Bill Carroll and Ez Nahouraii of the Computer Society Press Editorial Board, and the reviewers were instrumental in the development and production of this text.

And a very special contribution was made by Risa, Aimee, and Karen through their understanding.

Table of Contents

Part I. Introduction

The software development process is changing. As a process model, the conventional life-cycle (waterfall) paradigm has been influential and useful and has succeeded in focusing attention on the importance of software design. With an effective design, an organization would be spared the high cost of unraveling coding commitments later in the process.

But the conventional life-cycle model was formulated in an era that differed markedly from today's software development world. Convenient access to computers, development by users, and the availability of sophisticated support tools are prompting organizations to question their adherence to the conventional life-cycle.

Part II of this tutorial organizes and discusses various criticisms of the conventional life-cycle model, including its inadequate accommodation of

- Prototyping
- End-user development
- Reusability
- Uncertain requirements
- Constantly shifting requirements on large projects
- Natural intertwining of specification and design

Alternative software development paradigms—based on prototyping, operational specification, and transformational implementation—are introduced and shown to respond to the needs listed above. Parts III, IV, and V of this tutorial are dedicated to explaining these three paradigms.

To prepare for these later sections, the remaining three articles in Part I present the basics:

- What is the current paradigm?—Establishes the point of departure for the tutorial; defines the conventional life-cycle (waterfall) model; describes its assumptions and evolution into its current form

- What are the new paradigms?—Defines prototyping, operational specification, and transformational implementation; compares the process diagrams; shows how the three are related

- What is the framework of a more flexible process?—Describes a process that accommodates the new paradigms and allows the selection of project-specific activities and milestones

From the ideas and viewpoints expressed throughout this volume, the unifying themes of this tutorial emerge:

- Software should be produced by a *flexible* development process, allowing for the selection of different intermediate products, milestones, and activities for different projects

- Improvement in the software development process requires
  —Delivering *executable* objects *early* to the user and
  —Increasing the role of *automation*

The pursuit of these themes will contribute to the efficient production of the robust, reliable software that the world demands.

The Conventional Software Life-cycle Model: Its Evolution and Assumptions

William W. Agresti
Computer Sciences Corporation

Abstract

The conventional software development life-cycle model is briefly described. The model's evolution is traced through intermediate versions over the previous 30 years to its current form. Some fundamental assumptions of the model are identified because they are the bases for some of the disagreement over the model's suitability. The composition of the model is shown to reflect the state of software development at the time the model was formulated.

Introduction

This article establishes the point of departure for the remainder of the tutorial:

- What is the conventional software development life-cycle model?
- How did it evolve to its present form?
- What assumptions are built into it?

These topics are being discussed because they are the keys to understanding the criticisms of the model expressed in Part II. Those later critiques can be traced to

- Disagreement over the constituent elements of the model and their sequencing
- Belief that the model reflects the time period during which it evolved but is no longer appropriate
- Perception that the implicit assumptions of the model exclude newer paradigms of software development

The Conventional Life-Cycle Model

The conventional life-cycle (waterfall) model is shown in Figure 1 as a series of phases with validation and feedback at each phase. The most influential presentation of the waterfall model was in the landmark article by Barry Boehm in 1976 [Boehm 76]. Boehm and others have noted that the original version appeared in an article by W. W. Royce in 1970 [Royce 70].

The waterfall model has been stretched, shrunk, and otherwise modified since its inception. When we speak of the conventional life-cycle, we include all such variations that have preserved the essence of the waterfall model, i.e., that software is developed by the following sequence of general activities:

- Specification—A statement of "what" the software will do, following a detailed analysis of the requirements
- Design—"How" the software will meet the requirements; the structure of software units that perform specified functions
- Code—Implementation of the design in a programming language
- Test—Verification that the code executes without failure, and validation that the completed software is acceptable to the users

To this list may be added the phase of operations and maintenance (or evolution), to represent the working life of the software.

Every software development organization has its own variation of the waterfall model. The version in Figure 2, for example, stresses verification and validation at each phase. Detailed explanations of the conventional life-cycle model and its phases may be found in most software engineering textbooks (e.g., [Boehm 81] or [Jensen, Tonies 79]).

Evolution of the Conventional Life-Cycle Model

The life-cycle model has been related to cybernetics and general systems theory developed in the 1930s [Enger 81]. More specifically, it can be traced to the reductionist mode of inquiry that achieved prominence with scientific work on planning and logistics during and after World War II. By the early 1950s, these methods—systems analysis and operations research—were emerging as organized and systematic approaches to problem solving.

Today's life-cycle model was foreshadowed by early writers who had been associated with the systems approach. In 1956, Richard Canning's book *Electronic Data Processing for Business and Industry* [Canning 56] was motivated by practicality: now that high-speed computers were becoming available to companies, how should they be used? He specified the "systems engineering approach" for an organization to follow in installing a data processing system

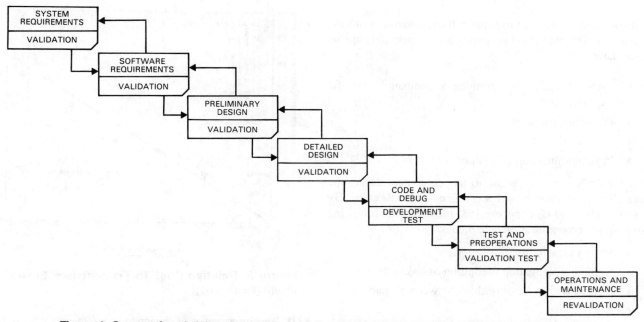

Figure 1. Conventional "Waterfall" Software Development Life-Cycle Model (From [Boehm 76])

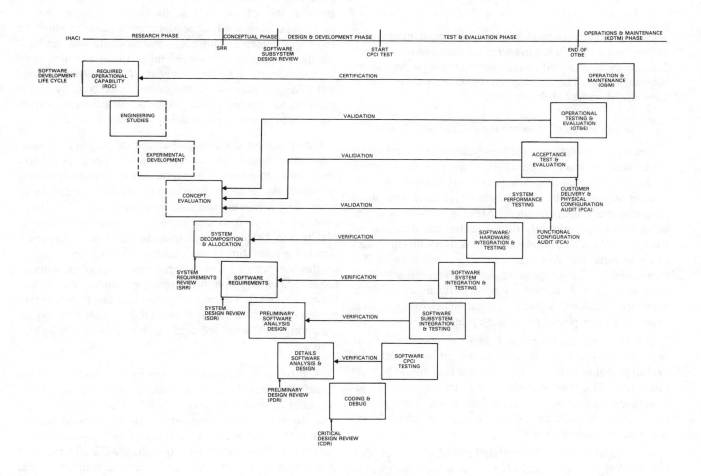

Figure 2. A Variant of the Conventional Software Life-Cycle Model (From [Jensen, Tonies 79])

(hardware and software) to support its information processing needs. The phases in his approach are remarkably apt 30 years later:

- Systems study (to determine a company's specific requirements)
- Preliminary design
- Detailed design
- Programming/acquisition/installation

As more companies began to use computers during the late 1950s, this early model was refined and elaborated. By 1963, Laden and Gildersleeve [63] identified the following steps in the emerging life-cycle model:

- Survey (feasibility)
- System investigation (definition of objectives)
- System design (relationships between all parts of the system)
- Programming
- Filemaking
- Preparation of clerical procedures (documentation)
- Program testing

Greater experience with software development practices during the late 1960s led to increased attention on intermediate products and verification steps to mark the transitions between phases. These additional refinements are evident in the waterfall model of Royce [70].

Assumptions of the Conventional Life-Cycle Model

Tracing the evolution of the life-cycle model revealed that it has been in place since 1970, with its basic structure established even earlier. The year 1970 is significant because it was one of the last years in which there were more programmers than computers [Musa 83]. Software was being developed primarily on expensive mainframe computers. As Musa [83] observed, "interaction with computers and computer software was primarily limited to skilled professionals." Language processors, debuggers, and operating systems were the only support software available to most organizations. Virtually no automated support tools existed for other phases of the life-cycle.

Because computers were an expensive resource, it made sense in 1970 that access to them should be preceded by careful planning so that time on the machine would be used effectively. The same planning and forethought should accompany the use of any expensive instrument. The waterfall model reflected this aspect of proceeding systematically and deferring implementation.

A principal virtue of the waterfall model was its recognition of design as a critical activity. Many examples have shown the expensive consequences of premature coding without adequate analysis and design (e.g., p. 39 of [Boehm

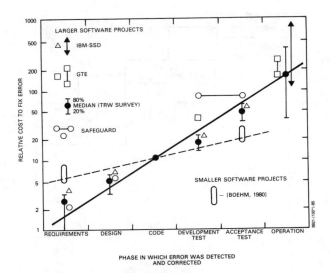

Figure 3. Relative Cost To Fix Software Errors (From [Boehm 81])

81]). The importance of design was effectively communicated because Boehm provided its economic rationale in the same article [Boehm 76] that explained the waterfall model. Figure 3 reproduces an updated version of the graph showing that the relative cost to fix errors on large projects increases exponentially depending on the phase in which the error was detected. This economic rationale was the basis for the assumption that successful software was developed by successively achieving subgoals at each phase [Boehm 81]. The subgoals were milestones corresponding to the completion of intermediate products, for example, a completed requirements specification or a completed design.

It may appear difficult to question the validity of these basic assumptions. The conventional life-cycle model has been shown to represent a careful and systematic approach in which the goal of developing successful software is attained by achieving subgoals in a particular order. However, some criticisms challenge even these assumptions. McCracken [81] cites examples to show that preparing detailed specifications is not effective. Peters is unequivocal on this subject: ". . . one cannot state a problem without some rudimentary notion of what the solution should be" [Peters 81, p.34]. The article by Swartout and Balzer in this section expresses a similar view on the inherent difficulty of separating the "what" of specification from the "how" of design.

Additional criticisms of these basic assumptions are founded on the differences in current software development practices compared to those of 1970. Currently, there are four times as many computers as there are programmers [Musa 83], and access to computers and software is no longer limited to people with specialized skills. The relative cost effectiveness of computer hardware technology has increased by a factor of 10,000 since 1970 [Musa 83]. A wide array of software development support tools are being used for every phase in the conventional life-cycle model. Of greater significance, some current tools and environments logically span several conventional phases, thereby challenging the usefulness of the life-cycle's partitioning into phases.

The theme of these observations is that the life-cycle model reflects the time period in which it evolved. Dramatic changes since then are prompting a reassessment of the model to determine if it is the appropriate paradigm.

References

Boehm, B.W., "Software Engineering," *IEEE Transactions on Computers*, vol. C-25, no. 12, December 1976, pp. 1226-1241

Boehm, B.W., *Software Engineering Economics*. Englewood Cliffs, N.J.: Prentice-Hall, 1981

Canning, R.G., *Electronic Data Processing for Business and Industry*. New York: John Wiley & Sons, 1956

Enger, N.L., "Classical and Structured Systems Life Cycle Phases and Documentation," in *Systems Analysis and Design-A Foundation for the 1980's*, W. W. Cotterman et al., eds., New York: Elsevier North-Holland, 1981, pp. 1-24

Jensen, R.W., and C. C. Tonies, *Software Engineering*. Englewood Cliffs, N.J.: Prentice-Hall, 1979

Laden, H.N., and T. R. Gildersleeve, *System Design for Computer Applications*. New York: John Wiley & Sons, 1963

McCracken, D.D., "A Maverick Approach to Systems Analysis and Design," in *Systems Analysis and Design—A Foundation for the 1980's*. W. W. Cotterman et al., eds., New York: Elsevier North-Holland, 1981, pp. 551-553

Musa, J.D., ed., "Stimulating Software Engineering Progress A Report of the Software Engineering Planning Group," *ACM Software Engineering Notes*, vol. 8, no. 2, April 1983, pp. 29-54

Peters, L.J., *Software Design: Methods and Techniques*. New York: Yourdon Press, 1981

Royce, W.W., "Managing the Development of Large Software Systems: Concepts and Techniques," *Proceedings, WESCON*, August 1970

What Are the New Paradigms?

William W. Agresti
Computer Sciences Corporation

Introduction

This article introduces and defines the three paradigms of this tutorial: prototyping, operational specification, and transformational implementation. The next three sections cover each paradigm in turn, showing the process diagram in each case. The final section discusses the relationships among the paradigms as they enforce the themes of delivering early executable objects to the users and automating the software development process.

Prototyping

Prototyping is the process of building a working model of a system or part of a system. It is a familiar practice in engineering, to obtain an early version of a product or system. Engineering prototypes can vary in size (scaled down or full size) and functionality (limited capability or a complete set of functions). In any case, the objective of prototyping is to clarify the characteristics and operation of a product or system by constructing a version that can be exercised.

Because software systems can be as complex as more traditionally engineered systems, it makes sense that prototyping has a useful role in software development. Prototyping can help considerably when the user's requirements for the system are not well understood. (I'll know what I want when I see it!) This situation is quite common, and the conventional life-cycle model does not adequately accommodate this uncertainty about system needs. Prototyping eases the communication between developers and users by allowing their discussions to focus on real behavior and actual user experiences in exercising the prototype.

The software development paradigm that incorporates prototyping is shown as the top half of Figure 1. The starting point, at the left side of the figure, is some notion of the user's needs. This may vary widely in formality and concreteness, ranging from a detailed requirements document to some vague ideas about a proposed system, obtained by interviewing prospective users. From this expression of needs, the prototype developer determines the objective and scope of the prototype. Often the prototype addresses aspects of the system—such as the user interface—that are difficult to specify through conventional means.

The prototype developers must consider what they intend to learn from building a prototype—for example, a better understanding of user requirements in certain areas, feasibility of a design approach, or understanding of system performance issues. It is important to write down the specific objectives of the prototype and the planned range of its capabilities. This informal "prototype statement of work" is the basis for planning the development of the prototype. This step is essential because, depending on the scope of the prototype, its development can be an expensive and time-consuming process. Effective planning will help ensure that the prototype is delivered in a timely manner. (There is nothing worse than a rapid prototype that isn't.) The development plan should maximize the use of very high level languages or screen management utilities to accelerate prototype development. (The article by Carey and Mason in this tutorial surveys such tools and techniques.)

The loop in the prototyping process in Figure 1 is the iterative revision of the prototype in response to user experiences. The number of traversals of this loop may vary. The initial delivery of the prototype may satisfy all the objectives of the prototyping effort. The developers may succeed in learning all that they intended through this first version. Alternatively, feedback from users may indicate that revising the prototype is necessary to obtain additional information.

When the objectives of the prototyping effort have been attained, a basic decision must be made: either refine the prototype into the complete system or begin a conventional development process, having benefited from building the prototype. The decision should be based on the costs and benefits of each alternative. Two key factors are

- How much functionality is already present in the prototype
- Will the design support a maintainable system (Is the prototype worth the investment of more effort?)

Figure 1 shows both alternatives. In the case of a throw-away prototype, the developers must still extract useful information from it to contribute to the requirements specification and design of the complete system.

The prototyping paradigm illustrates that prototyping can

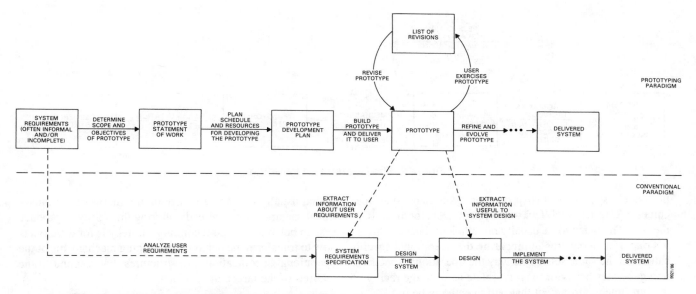

Figure 1. The Prototyping Paradigm and Its Relationship to the Conventional Software Development Paradigm

serve as a separate route to software development through the refinement process at the top of Figure 1. The article by Scharer in this tutorial discusses this paradigm in greater detail. Alternatively, prototyping can be joined to the conventional life-cycle model in a hybrid prototyping/waterfall paradigm. The article by Gomaa and Scott in this tutorial describes the use of prototyping in this role to clarify user requirements.

Operational Specification

An operational specification is a system model that can be evaluated or executed to generate the behavior of the system. An operational specification of a system is developed early in the development process, during what is typically the requirements analysis phase. However, because it is executable, the operational specification differs fundamentally from a traditional requirements specification and is the basis for a new paradigm of software development.

One way to understand the concept of an operational specification is to contrast it with a traditional requirements specification. The familiar advice to anyone preparing the latter is to describe "what" the system should do and not "how" it should do it. The focus is on the functions that the system should perform. The design process takes this specification and describes the "how"—that is, the internal structure of a system that the developers believe will deliver the required functionality.

A key feature of the conventional life-cycle model is its separation of external system behavior (the "what" of requirements specification) from internal system structure (the "how" of design). Separation of activities on this basis introduces many problems, to which the approach of operational specification directly responds. A later article in this tutorial by Swartout and Balzer explains the inherent diffi-

culty of extricating the "what" from the "how." They show by example that discussing the "what" of a system in any useful sense demands that design and implementation considerations be addressed. A second major problem with the rationale for separation in the conventional model is that is leaves too many issues to impinge on design decisions. The designer needs to consider

- Problem-oriented issues of decomposing high-level functions into successively lower levels
- Purely design issues such as information-hiding and abstraction
- Implementation issues such as system performance constraints and the feasibility of the design to be implemented in the target hardware-software environment

Preparing an operational specification requires using a different basis for separating early development activities. This approach acknowledges the intertwining of "what" and "how" considerations. The guiding principle is not to overwhelm system designers by requiring them to assess simultaneously the varied issues above. Instead, the separation is based on problem-oriented versus implementation-oriented concerns. The goal is to produce an operational specification that deals only with problem-oriented issues and to express it in some language or form that enables it to be executed, evaluated, or interpreted to reveal the behavior of the system. The resulting operational specification is a kind of prototype: one that generally produces all of the functional behavior of the system but does so by using different media than will be used in the delivered system.

Articles in this tutorial give examples of media for expressing operational specifications: languages such as GIST (Balzar, Goldman, and Wile) and PAISLey (Zave); seman-

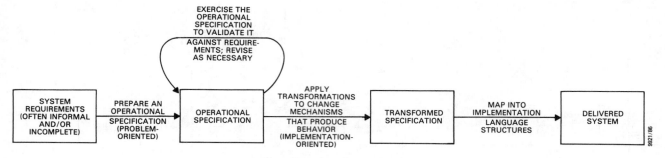

Figure 2. The Operational Paradigm

tic models such as virtual processors (Smoliar), state machines (Agresti), and Jackson System Development (Cameron). The behavior is usually not efficient, because that is not one of the concerns in preparing the operational specification. In the same sense, the way the operational specification generates behavior may not relate at all to the reality of the run-time environment that will eventually be used.

The operational specification resolves issues related to the behavior of the system using terms that are meaningful in the user's problem domain. After the operational specification is prepared, the implementation-oriented issues can be addressed, without the confounding effects (experienced in the conventional model) of still wrestling with the functional processing of the system. Thus, preparing an operational specification has implications for downstream activities and motivates a new paradigm for software development.

Figure 2 shows the new paradigm built around the preparation of an operational specification. From the system requirements, however informal or incomplete, the developers construct the operational specification. Because it is capable of exhibiting behavior, the operational specification can be exercised by both the developers and the users to begin validating that requirements are being met. The extent to which this validation step can substitute for later system testing depends on the capabilities of the language or system used to express the operational specification. (This issue is discussed in Zave's first article in this tutorial.) The key benefit, however, is that at least *some* validation of system behavior can occur early in the development process. This validation capability is more difficult with traditional, natural-language, static specifications that have no executable semantics.

The operational specification provides an opportunity to understand and clarify user needs early. With the conventional life-cycle model, the opportunity to experience system behavior is not available until much later in the process —after the implementation phase.

When the validation/revision loop in Figure 2 has resulted in a satisfactory operational specification, developers can begin to consider the implementation-oriented issues. One possibility, consistent with perceiving the operational specification as a prototype, is to revert to the conventional life-cycle model and begin the design phase. However, this option usually fails to capitalize on the merits of the operational specification as already offering the ability to produce system behavior. A more common strategy is for developers now to transform the behavior-producing mechanisms of the operational specification into structures that respond to the realities of the target environment.

The resulting transformed specification in Figure 2 is ultimately mapped into the implementation language to provide the solution system. Articles in this tutorial by Zave and Balzer et al. provide examples of how the remainder of this paradigm may evolve.

The steps involved in transforming the operational specification into a delivered system will, ideally, be assisted by automation in the future. A knowledge-based software "assistant" will guide the transformation process, guaranteeing correctness at each step so that the operational specification can be the single object on which validation and maintenance are performed. However, even without automated support, the operational paradigm has value by

- Separating the development process into problem-oriented and implementation-oriented phases
- Providing users with an executable system model early in the process that is useful for clarifying requirements and performing some early validation

Transformational Implementation

Transformational implementation is an approach to software development that uses automated support to apply a series of transformations that change a specification into a concrete software system. The transformational approach addresses the labor intensiveness of software development by using specialized computer software to transform successive versions of the developing system mechanically.

Figure 3 shows the software development paradigm based on transformational implementation. This paradigm represents a goal that is being pursued by many research and development projects (which are surveyed and classified by Partsch and Steinbrüggen in this tutorial). In practice, this automated paradigm has been realized in restricted application domains and at the level of individual programs. However, it is not now a generally available alternative for the production of large software systems.

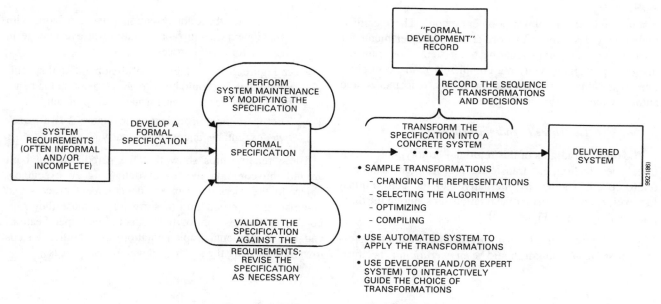

Figure 3. The Transformational Paradigm

The first step in Figure 3—developing a formal specification—is a major impediment to bringing this paradigm into widespread use. The specification needs to be expressed in some precisely defined way if there is to be any success at defining transformations that operate on it. At the same time, the specification must be understandable for users to validate that it meets their requirements. Meeting the contrasting demands for formality and understandability is difficult when coping with the size and complexity of the requirements for medium and large systems. Articles by Bauer and Cheatham et al. show how abstraction can make specifications more compact.

The characteristics of the formal specification affect the transformation phase that follows. For example, a specification may be expressed at a relatively high level—that is, in terms of objects, relationships, and operations in the user's domain. Such a specification enhances readability and validation but is far removed from its eventual realization as a concrete system executing in a particular run-time environment. Accordingly, the transformation phase in this case must include transformations that are level reducing; for example, to form data structures and to insert algorithms. A lower level formal specification may not require such transformations to be included in the transformation phase. In summary, a tradeoff exists between the work performed as part of developing the formal specification and the effort spent to transform the specification into a concrete system.

Figure 3 shows that the formal specification is the system baseline. It is

- The object that is validated against user requirements; under an ideal realization of this paradigm—that is, all transformations automated and correctness-preserving—the specification is the *only* object that needs to be validated

- The starting point for the transformation phase

- The object on which maintenance is performed; any change to the functioning of the system is expressed as a change to the specification, not to the code

The altered code is produced by a two-step process:

- First, appropriate changes are made to the "formal development," which is the record of the sequence of transformations and decisions that were used to convert the specification into the original code

- Second, the modified formal development is replayed to produce the new version of the system

There is no single path from formal specification to delivered system. The transformation phase in Figure 3 has many realizations, depending on such factors as

- The degree and nature of human interaction to guide the selection of the transformations to be applied

- The role of a knowledge-based software assistant to, for example, identify candidate transformations, choose data structures, or interrogate the user for any necessary constraints

The tutorial articles by Balzer, Kant and Barstow, and Cheatham et al. provide examples of different paths that have been taken in the development of real transformation systems. The common feature of the various alternatives in the transformation phase is the use of automation to apply the transformation rules. Because the rules are expressed formally, they can be studied separately to help ensure correctness and eliminate the introduction of contaminating side effects.

Three products emerge from the transformational paradigm of Figure 3: the formal specification, the delivered system, and the formal development record. The specification and the development record are necessary elements for maintaining and reimplementing the system. The transformational paradigm, while not completely realized in practice, is a valuable framework for efforts to formalize and automate the software development process.

The Three Paradigms Are Related

The three paradigms of this tutorial—prototyping, operational specification, and transformational implementation—reinforce one another as alternatives to the conventional life-cycle model. Consider the relationships among the three process diagrams in Figures 1 through 3:

- In Figure 3, the formal specification of the transformational paradigm should be an *operational* specification so that the transformation rules can work with behavior-producing representations at every stage in the transformation process.

- In Figure 2, the refinement of the operational specification ideally should be *automated* to obtain the benefits outlined for the transformational approach.

- The operational specification in Figure 2 *is* a *prototype*: executable and available early.

These relationships show that the paradigms are built around the common themes of delivering an executable object to the users early in the development process and automating the production of software. Because they support these themes, prototyping, operational specification, and transformational implementation are significant steps toward improving the software development process.

Framework for a Flexible Development Process

William W. Agresti
Computer Sciences Corporation

Abstract

The fundamental weakness of the conventional life-cycle model is identified as an imbalance of analysis versus synthesis due to the influence of the systems approach and the reality of software practices when the model was formulated. New software development paradigms—prototyping, operational specification, and transformational implementation—provide greater opportunity for synthesis. The extent to which these methodologies can be pursued within the life-cycle model is discussed. To obtain maximum benefit from new paradigms requires a more flexible development process. The framework for such a base process model is introduced.

Introduction

If the life-cycle model is flawed, what is the alternative? This article discusses the key characteristics of a more flexible development process—one that would begin to address the criticisms levied against the conventional model. The following topics are covered:

- The fundamental weakness in the conventional life-cycle model

- The responsiveness of prototyping, operational specification, and transformational implementation to this weakness

- The prospects for organizations to incorporate new development paradigms into their life-cycle-based methodologies

- The framework for a flexible development process

Fundamental Weakness of the Conventional Life-Cycle Model

Most debates between advocates and critics of the life-cycle model reveal a basic disagreement over the restrictiveness of the model. The critic charges that the life-cycle model cannot accommodate X, where X is prototyping, end-user development, etc. The advocate replies that the critic is interpreting the life-cycle much too rigidly—of course X can be accommodated!

Such different perspectives on essential and implied characteristics of the life-cycle model suggest that we look deeper to discover its true worth. Because software development requires major commitments of resources, it seems reasonable that organizations want to establish a set of systematic procedures to accomplish it and control it. The conventional life-cycle model is a basis for fulfilling these needs:

- The goal of developing software is accomplished by achieving subgoals (specification, design, etc.) in a prescribed order.

- The phase transitions serve as control points to review progress and intermediate products.

The fundamental weakness of the conventional life-cycle model is its imbalance between analysis and synthesis. The formulation of the model was strongly influenced by the systems approach, an analytical, reductionist pattern of problem solving [Sutherland 75; Agresti 86]. This approach was understandable in an era in which the opportunities for software synthesis were limited by hardware technology, access to computers, and availability of software support tools. As a consequence, the life-cycle process was very analytical, deferring hard commitment to code until later stages and thereby promoting efficient use of the relatively expensive mainframes of the period. This imbalance may be contrasted with the development process in more mature fields, like engineering, in which there is a rich interplay between analysis and synthesis (see, for example, the discussion of the engineering design process in [Beakley, Leach 72]).

The capability for synthesis has grown dramatically in recent years. The combination of sophisticated software support tools and convenient access by users to powerful microcomputers has enabled the rapid development of software. Martin [84] cites examples and applications of such tools. These advances support software development scenarios that are clearly outside even the broadest interpretation of the life-cycle model [McCracken, Jackson 81].

The capabilities for analysis and synthesis are more nearly in balance now. The conventional life-cycle model neither acknowledges nor exploits that balance.

Responsiveness of Prototyping, Operational Specification, and Transformational Implementation

The new paradigms presented in this tutorial—prototyping, operational specification, and transformational implementation—address the fundamental weakness in the conventional life-cycle model by providing synthesis in various forms. Prototyping and operational specification yield behavior-producing objects early in the development process. They contrast sharply with conventional, static representations of specification and design. Transformational implementation also provides for synthesis by automating the generation of concrete programs from specifications.

With these new paradigms, greater progress in software development can be expected. They add the elements of synthesis, thereby enabling an interaction with traditional analytical methods. Such interaction is a very natural route to progress in other domains. Consider the prospect of learning a new, complicated board game. It is common for players to study the rules only to a certain point, then strike out on their own. The early experience playing the game, even while not following all of the rules, is a more effective route to mastery than continuing to analyze the rules. The preference is for an alternative that involves active behavior to provide operational understanding. Prototyping and operational specification are alternatives for software development that offer similar advantages in the early stages.

Prospects for Organizations to Adopt New Paradigms

Many organizations that follow the life-cycle model also use prototyping [Boehm 81, p. 41]. The inclination is to question whether these "new paradigms" are not simply different practices that can be plugged into existing phases of the life-cycle. Prototyping, for example, has been most widely used to assist with understanding software requirements, especially when the user interface is a critical issue. Thus, prototyping can be integrated with the requirements specification phase of the conventional model. The information obtained by experimenting with the prototype is aded to the information obtained from traditional means (like user interviews) to help specify the software requirements.

It may appear that we have the best of both worlds: we can incorporate a new paradigm without perturbing the life-cycle model with which the developers are familiar. However, by remaining within the life-cycle model, we inherit its shortcomings, which limit the benefits that can be realized from new paradigms. The limitations are due to retaining the identical control points and intermediate products that are associated with the life-cycle model. To obtain the full benefit of prototyping, for example, the organization must be willing, at the end of requirements, to consider the alternative of evolving the prototype into the delivered system [Boar 84]. If the organization always discards the prototype and proceeds with traditional design and imple-

mentation, it may be missing an opportunity for more effective software development.

The life-cycle highlights only one dimension of the software development process, namely, the sequential activity phases. Orthogonal views of the process focus on configuration control and quality assurance. The key to reaping the maximum benefits from new software development paradigms is an organization's willingness to accept changes to intermediate products, reviews, and control points that it has come to expect with the conventional life-cycle model.

Framework for a Flexible Development Process

The endurance of the life-cycle model, in light of dramatic changes in other aspects of computer technology, has given it a sense of permanence that is unjustified. Its longevity is due, in part, to the considerable inertia in large organizations that have instituted software development practices according to phases in the model. Another reason is the inadequate attention and resources being allocated to process improvement and, generally, to software process engineering [Agresti 83]. Software engineering can benefit from defining the output of every software development project as both the software product *and* information on how to improve the process [Agresti 81]. With some notable exceptions (e.g., [McGarry 82] and [Thayer et al. 78]), there has been relatively little instrumentation of the software development process to obtain the data necessary for process improvement. With skilled personnel in high demand, organizations have generally not been willing or able to justify the commitment of resources to a basic program of process improvement.

Despite this entrenched position of the life-cycle model, it should be interpreted as only one class of responses to a more fundamental concern: the specification of an effective process model for software development. The central importance of such a "base" model to software engineering has been widely acknowledged [Musa 83; Riddle 84].

The flexible development process is offered as a base process model for software development. Its elements are as follows:

- Activities—e.g., interviewing users, prototyping the user interface, analyzing related designs, building an operational model, designing a performance experiment

- Intermediate products—e.g., operational model as a finite state machine, floppy disk with menu displays and sequences

- Control points—e.g., demonstrations of capabilities, reviews of intermediate products

- Baselines—i.e., sets of intermediate products constituting a controlled version of the system

Table 1. Identifiable Instances of the Flexible Development Process

Process Type	Process Drivers	Key Elements of the Flexible Development Process
A	User interface well understood. High degree of shared understanding of requirements between users and developers. No uncertainty about feasibility of developing the system.	Choose elements similar to those of conventional life-cycle.
B	Functional requirements well understand. User interface not well understood but not a significant component of the system.	Choose conventional life-cycle plus prototyping to clarify user interface in specification phase [Boehm 81].
C	Same as B above, only the user interface *is* a significant component of system.	Develop prototype as a major activity. Consider evolving prototype into complete system [Scharer 83].
D	Functional requirements not well understood. High interdependence between software and problems to be solved [Giddings 84].	User prototyping, operational specification, offline performance studies, experimentation, and project-specific control and integration points [Giddings 84].
E	High reuse of designs and code from completed systems.	Provide integration and review activities to manage reused materials [Silverman 85].
F	End-user development. Availability of implementation tool (fourth-generation language processor with data base inquiry and reporting facility) [McCracken 81].	Define activities for consultation between user and tool expert and for delivery of first skeletal version to user [McCracken, Jackson 81].

As a "base" model, the flexible development process supports customizing to individual software development projects. For each project, the manager and technical leader select elements (activities, control points, etc.) that will apply to the project. The choice of elements is influenced by the following process drivers:

- Legacy—Experience of the developers with the application area and the availability of related software products for potential reuse
- Tool support—Availability and effectiveness of software tools (for prototyping, automatic program generation, etc.) that are necessary to support various activities
- Interfaces—Nature of the software's relationships with other software, hardware, and data
- End-user involvement—Level and nature of user participation in development
- Requirements understanding—Degree to which the end users know what they want
- Operational characteristics of the software—Expected lifetime, patterns of use, need for documentation, ease of change, importance of reliability, performance requirements

Several patterns of development are identified in Table 1 as instances of the flexible development process. Also shown are the process drivers that characterize each pattern. For example, a Type A process (the conventional life-cycle) has the properties of well-understood requirements, no end-user involvement beyond the early stages, and little or no reused code [Silverman 85].

Table 1 offers an alternate way of expressing the theme of this tutorial: the conventional life-cycle model is being used when its assumptions for use (the process drivers for Type A) are not being satisfied. The other scenarios in Table 1, especially Types C and D, are much more realistic. Consequently, the corresponding development practices listed in the table should be considered in addition to those of the conventional life-cycle.

In selecting elements for a particular project, it should not be assumed that support tools such as fourth-generation languages are always the preferred route to development. The power of such languages can entice the user to begin development without understanding the existence of reusable code or the interfaces to other systems. The result can be a development activity that is out of control [Futures 85]. The selection of process elements must include adequate control points to provide feedback and visibility for the activities.

The relationships among the selected elements are expressed using a PERT chart [Turner et al. 78] or a process chart [Agresti 81]. The PERT chart has been used for systems engineering, that is, when both hardware and software are being developed and integrated concurrently. It has not been as necessary, however, when only software is being developed, because the life-cycle has taken its place. The PERT chart is intended for use when *different* projects are being planned [Turner, et al. 78]. The effect of new software development paradigms is that the life-cycle is no longer the only process model to follow. Use of the flexible development process will result in different development patterns that can benefit from a PERT chart or its equivalent to manage the activities, exploit concurrency, and identify milestones.

The flexible development process will certainly require more management effort, because the control points and intermediate products will vary among projects. Multimedia baselines will exist in which the controlled version of the system may be represented for example, by a design document plus a floppy disk of screen displays and sequencing options.

The approach of the flexible development process is to allow project managers to decide what constitutes *progress* in every software development project. No longer will every project be treated identically by equating progress with the lock-step procession of specification, design, code, and test. The message of this tutorial reinforces this approach: the new software development methods require a more flexible development process if they are to deliver maximum benefits.

References

Agresti, W.W., "Applying Industrial Engineering to the Software Development Process," *Proceedings, IEEE Fall COMPCON*, Washington, D.C.: IEEE Computer Society Press, 1981, pp. 264-270

Agresti, W.W., "Elements of Software Process Engineering," *Proceedings, ACM Computer Science Conference*, 1983, p. 73 (abstract only)

*Agresti, W.W., "The Conventional Software Life-Cycle Model: It's Evolution and Assumptions," (in Part I of this volume), 1986

Beakley, G.C. and H.W. Leach, *Engineering—An Introduction to a Creative Profession*. Second Edition. New York: Macmillan, 1972

Boar, B.H., *Application Prototyping*. New York: John Wiley & Sons, 1984

Boehm, B.W., *Software Engineering Economics*. Englewood Cliffs, N.J.: Prentice-Hall, 1981

Futures, "Controlling a 4GL Project," vol. 10, no. 1, Ken Orr & Associates, Inc., 1985

*Giddings, R.V., "Accommodating Uncertainty in Software Design," *Communications of the ACM*, vol. 27, no. 5, May 1984, pp. 428-434

Martin, J., *An Information Systems Manifesto*. Englewood Cliffs, N.J.: Prentice-Hall, 1984

McCracken, D.D., "A Maverick Approach to Systems Analysis and Design," *System Analysis and Design—A Foundation for the 1980's*. W.W. Cotterman, et al., eds. New York: Elsevier North-Holland, 1981

*McCracken, D.D. and M.A. Jackson, "A Minority Dissenting Position," *Systems Analysis and Design—A Foundation for the 1980's*. W.W. Cotterman et al., eds. New York: Elsevier North-Holland, 1981

McGarry, F.E., "Measuring Software Development Technology," *Proceedings, Seventh Annual Software Engineering Workshop*. NASA Goddard Space Flight Center, Greenbelt, Maryland, 1982, 34 pp.

Musa, J.D., ed. "Stimulating Software Engineering Progress—A Report of the Software Engineering Planning Group," ACM SIGSOFT *Software Engineering Notes*, vol. 8, no. 2, April 1983, pp. 29-54

Riddle, W.E., "Report on the Software Process Workshop," ACM SIGSOFT *Software Engineering Notes*, vol. 9, no. 2, April 1984, pp. 13-20

*Scharer, L., "The Prototyping Alternative," ITT *Programming*, vol. 1, no. 1, 1983, pp. 34-43

Silverman, B.G., "Software Cost and Productivity Improvements: An Analogical View," IEEE *Computer*, vol. 18, no. 5, May 1985, pp. 86-96

Sutherland, J.W., *Systems: Analysis, Administration and Architecture*. New York: Van Nostrand, 1975

Thayer, T.A., M. Lipow, and E.C. Nelson, *Software Reliability: A Study of Large Project Reality*. New York: North-Holland, 1978

Turner, W., J. Mize, and K. Case, *Introduction to Industrial and Systems Engineering*. Englewood Cliffs, N.J.: Prentice-Hall, 1978

---

*Paper included in this tutorial.

Part II. Critiques of the Conventional Software Life-cycle Model

The conventional life-cycle model has been the target of criticism in recent years. This section presents a representative sample of the most widely discussed weaknesses of the model.

Balzer, Cheatham, and Green discuss the lack of computer support for the critical, knowledge-intensive early phases in the conventional life-cycle model and the difficulty of performing maintenance on procedural source code. They propose an automation-based paradigm that provides for maintaining the specification (not the procedural code) and mechanically transforming the specification into code.

McCracken and Jackson offer two scenarios of software development that are clearly outside the conventional life-cycle model. This contribution is significant as a counterexample to the assertion that all software development can be viewed as a variation of the life-cycle model. The authors criticize the model for failing to accommodate end-user development and for failing to recognize that users generally do not know the system requirements in advance.

Swartout and Balzer observe that any development model (like the life-cycle) that separates specification from implementation is unrealistic. They give a simple example to show the difficulty of "pure" specification without including implementation decisions. The implication is that software development process models and tools should be designed to reflect this inevitable intertwining of specification and implementation.

Giddings calls attention to the relationship between software and the nature of problems to be computed (the universe of discourse). For domain-dependent software, about which there is uncertainty concerning the universe of discourse, the life-cycle model is not adequate. The author discusses this broad class of domain-dependent software and proposes a new development process that is appropriate.

Many other critical discussions of the conventional life-cycle model are listed in the annotated bibliography included in this tutorial.

This radical approach to software switches the noncreative aspects
of maintenance and modification from man to machine.
It could profoundly change computing.

Software Technology in the 1990's: Using a New Paradigm

Robert Balzer, Information Sciences Institute

Thomas E. Cheatham, Jr., Harvard University

Cordell Green, Kestrel Institute

One possible direction for Department of Defense software initiatives is toward incremental improvement in each portion of the existing software cycle. This is a conservative, evolutionary approach with a high probability of short-term payoff. It definitely deserves a major role in the DoD's initiatives.

But because it is based on the existing software paradigm, the evolutionary approach is ultimately limited by any weakness of that paradigm. Since this paradigm arose in an era of little or no computer support of the software life cycle, it is important to examine how appropriate this paradigm will be in the future.

In the past, computers were more expensive than people; now, people are more expensive. The gap will continue to widen as hardware costs plummet. Not only are people the expensive commodity, there is a shortage of those who are adequately trained. Furthermore, society's major sectors—commercial, governmental, and military—are becoming increasingly reliant on software. The speed with which this software can be produced, the functional complexity it can embody, and the reliability it can attain could become major factors in these sectors.

Two flaws and the maintenance problem

Thus, there is a clear need to investigate a software paradigm based on automation, which augments the effectiveness of the costly and limited supply of people producing and maintaining software. Unfortunately, the existing software paradigm is not a good candidate, because of fundamental flaws that exacerbate the maintenance problem.

First, there is no technology for managing the knowledge-intensive activities that constitute software development processes. These processes, which convert requirements into a specification and then into an implementation, are informal, labor intensive, and largely undocumented. Information about these processes and the rationale behind each of their steps is crucial for maintenance, but unavailable.

This flaw causes problems for other life-cycle phases, but is particularly acute for maintenance. The time lag and personnel changeover normally involved in maintenance preclude reliance on informal mechanisms, such as "walking down the hall," that are typically used in the other phases.

Second, maintenance is performed on source code, that is, the implementation. All of the programmer's skill and knowledge have already been applied in optimizing this form (the source code). These optimizations spread information. That is, they take advantage of what is known elsewhere and substitute complex, but efficient, realizations for (simple) abstractions. Both of these effects exacerbate the maintenance problem by making the software harder to understand, by increasing the dependencies among the parts (especially since these dependencies are implicit), and by scattering related information.

With these fundamental flaws—and the fact that our most junior people are assigned this onerous task—it is no wonder that maintenance is such a major problem in the existing software paradigm.

We must look elsewhere for an appropriate, automation-based software paradigm if we are to achieve orders-of-magnitude improvement. This search and the technology needed to support it represent a viable and important additional direction for the DoD's software initiative. As will be explained below, the technology needed to support an automation-based software paradigm does not yet exist. This is the reason the current paradigm persists and incremental improvements to it are an essential short-term component of the DoD's software initiative.

The rest of this article is devoted to the longer term, higher payoff, and higher risk task of shifting from the current informal, person-based software paradigm to a formalized, computer-assisted software paradigm.

Reprinted from *Computer*, November 1983, pages 39-45. Copyright © 1983 by The Institute of Electrical and Electronics Engineers, Inc.

Characteristics of the automation-based software paradigm

The nature and structure of this new software paradigm become evident as we examine the objectives it must meet.

Maintainability. Foremost among these objectives is maintainability, meaning not only activity to correct bugs, but also the much more important activity of enhancing the released system. As important as maintenance is today—and it is 80 to 90 percent of total effort—its importance will increase in direct proportion to our ability to handle it. The tremendous backlog of pent-

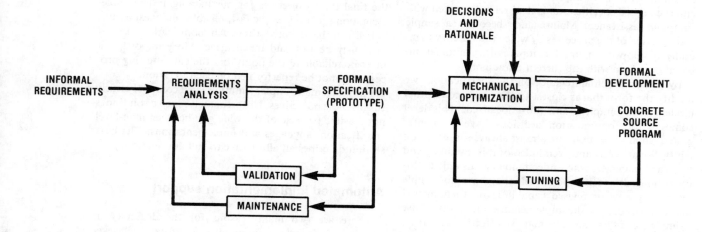

AUTOMATION-BASED PARADIGM

FORMAL SPECIFICATION
PROTOTYPING STANDARD
SPECIFICATION IS THE PROTOTYPE
PROTOTYPE VALIDATED AGAINST INTENT
PROTOTYPE BECOMES IMPLEMENTATION
IMPLEMENTATION MACHINE AIDED
TESTING ELIMINATED
FORMAL SPECIFICATION MAINTAINED
DEVELOPMENT AUTOMATICALLY DOCUMENTED
MAINTENANCE BY REPLAY

CURRENT PARADIGM

INFORMAL SPECIFICATION
PROTOTYPING UNCOMMON
PROTOTYPE CREATED MANUALLY
CODE VALIDATED AGAINST INTENT
PROTOTYPE DISCARDED
IMPLEMENTATION MANUAL
CODE TESTED
CONCRETE SOURCE CODE MAINTAINED
DESIGN DECISIONS LOST
MAINTENANCE BY PATCHING

(a)

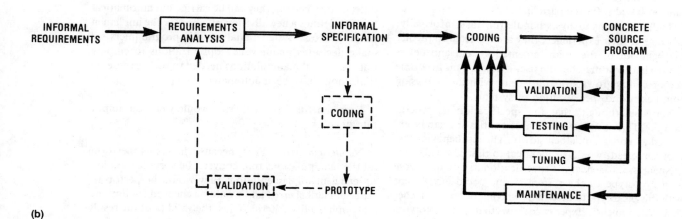

(b)

Figure 1. Paradigm comparison: (a) automation-based paradigm and (b) current paradigm.

up user demand for changes in existing systems is unanswered because of the delay and expense resulting from limited human resources.

Maintaining the specification. The two fundamental flaws in the existing paradigm—the spread of optimization information and the undocumented development processes, decisions, and rationales—that impede maintenance could be avoided with a new paradigm. In this new paradigm, maintenance is performed on the specification rather than the implementation (source program), and the revised specification is then reimplemented with computer assistance. Maintenance becomes a simple continuation of the processes by which the system was initially developed. Figure 1 compares this automation-based paradigm with the current paradigm.

By performing maintenance on the specification, we modify the form that is closest to the user's conceptual model, least complex, and most localized. This level comes before optimization decisions have been integrated, so modifications are almost always simple, if not trival. We are constantly reminded of this insight by end users and managers who understand systems only at this (unoptimized) specification level; they have no trouble integrating new or revised capabilities in their mental models. It is only at the implementation level that those "simple" changes can have massive effects, both structural and textual.

Thus, by maintaining the specification directly, we drastically simplify the maintenance problem. In fact, because end users understand this specification level and generate the new or revised capability requirements, they should be able, with suitable specification languages, to perform this specification maintenance themselves. This would fundamentally improve the software paradigm by employing a user-created and user-maintained specification as the interface between users and implementers.

The user as systems analyst. For this to become a reality, the end users must be given a means of ensuring that the specified system matches their intent, a means that avoids the delay and expense of producing an implementation. This feedback is the second objective of the automation-based software paradigm.

Today, systems analysts handle this task informally. Because of their experience, they are expected to predict the behavior of the unimplemented system and determine whether it matches the user's needs. This awesome responsibility grows more unrealistic with the increasing complexity and specialization of systems.

Suppose, though, that the specification is "operational." That is, it has a formal semantics and can be executed as a program, albeit slowly. Then its behavior, except for speed, would be identical to that of a valid implementation. Hence, the specification itself could serve as a prototype of the system. Users could experiment with this prototype to determine whether or not it matches their requirements. Experience shows that such prototypes normally lead users to improved perceptions of their needs. Thus, the resulting systems are more responsive to those needs.

Three objectives. Thus far, we've characterized the new, automation-based software paradigm as having formal specifications created and maintained by end users. These revised specifications become prototypes of the desired system and ensure that the system will be responsive to user needs.

But where is the automation in the automation-based software paradigm?

Its most obvious manifestation occurs in the implementation process. In this paradigm, the specification is reimplemented after each revision, which brings us to the final three objectives for our paradigm: The implementation process must be fast, reliable, and inexpensive.

If it is to be repeated after each modification, it must obviously be fast and inexpensive. More important it must be reliable to the point that the entire testing process need not be reperformed on each iteration.

Fully automatic implementation via a compiler clearly fulfills these objectives. Unfortunately, such a solution is not feasible because of the wide gap between high-level specification languages and implementations. The next section describes an alternative to full automation.

Automated implementation support

There are two main reasons for the difficulty in creating a fully automatic compiler to translate high-level specifications into efficient implementations. First, very little is known about how local optimizations influence global optimizations; second, the space of possible implementations is too large to search.

Existing compilers avoid these problems because their input is at a low enough level that purely local optimizations are sufficient. The systems analyst has already answered strategic questions about algorithm choice, control structure, representation selection, caching intermediate results, buffering, etc. In our new software paradigm, such implementation issues are specifically excluded from the specification; they must be addressed as part of the implementation process. Although some of these decisions can be automated through heuristic methods, a person must address those remaining.

After these decisions have been made, either by computer or by a person, they can be carried out automatically. This defines a new division of labor for the implementation process. Systems analysts and programmers still make decisions about which optimizations to employ, but the formal manipulations needed to realize these optimizations have been automated.

Four benefits. Such a division would yield four important benefits.

No clerical errors. First, because the system performs all the manipulations that convert the specification into an efficient implementation, they would be performed without clerical error and would be checked for any special applicability criteria. Thus, the validity of the resulting implementation is guaranteed by the *process* from which it is derived rather than by testing or correctness proofs.

Increased optimization. Second, by automating the manipulation of the program, developers are freed of this duty and the corresponding need to maintain consistency, which occupies the vast majority of current effort. They could spend more time considering optimization issues and, hence, do a better job. In fact, implementation could become cheap enough that developers would experiment with alternative implementations, thereby gaining experience and insight leading to better designs.

Better documentation. Third, since the developer's optimization decisions are explicitly communicated, both they and any automated optimization decisions can be recorded and used as documentation of the implementation process in any later maintenance. When maintenance is performed (by modifying the specification), the revised specification must be reimplemented.

Some modifications do not affect the set of optimizations to be employed. For these, the previously recorded optimization decisions (called the *development*) can be "replayed" to produce a new implementation.

Usually, however, modifications to the specification make some previous optimization decisions inappropriate and/or cause the set of decisions to be augmented. After the development has been suitably modified, it can be replayed to produce a new implementation and then used as documentation of the implementation during the next round of modification.

Reusable software. Finally, since maintenance has been simplified (by maintaining the specification and then reimplementing it) and the implementation process has been recorded (as the development) and is modifiable, the elusive goal of reusable software can be attained.

Software libraries—with the exception of mathematical subroutine libraries—have failed because the wrong things are in those libraries. They are filled with implementations, which necessarily contain many arbitrary decisions. The chance that such an implementation is precisely right for some later application is exceedingly small.

Instead, we should be placing specifications and their recorded development in libraries. Then, when a module is to be reused, the specification can be modified appropriately—that is, maintained—and its development changed accordingly. Thus, maintenance of both the specification and its development becomes the basis of reuse, rather than a fortuitous exact match with a previously stored implementation.

An automated assistant

Automated implementation support is a particular instance of the general role of automation in the automation-based software paradigm. This general role is to assist people in developing and maintaining software. This assistance involves recording the development activities, carrying out decisions made by people, and producing, accessing, and formatting the information needed to make those decisions.

These capabilities must be integrated into a single entity, an assistant that mediates and supports all software life-cycle development activities, as directed by the developers.

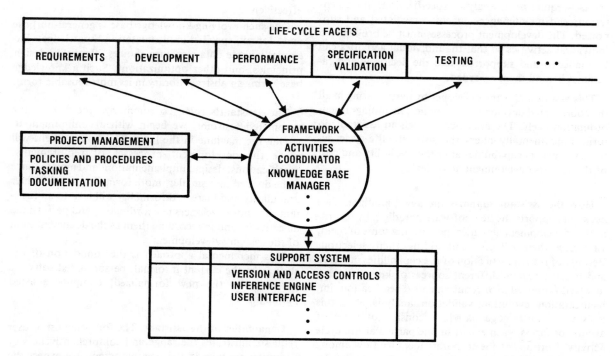

Figure 2. Generalized knowledge-based software assistant structure. (Adapted from Green et al., "Report on a Knowledge-Based Software Assistant," Technical Report KES. U.83.2, Kestrel Institute, Palo Alto, Calif., July 1983.)

COMPUTER

A development history. These activities are recorded to provide the corporate memory of the system evolution. The assistant uses this record to determine how the parts interact, the assumptions they make about one another, the rationale behind each evolutionary step (including implementation steps), how the system satisfies its requirements, and how to explain each of these to the developers of the system.

This knowledge base is dynamically acquired as a by-product of the development of each system. Again, it includes not only the individual manipulation steps, which ultimately lead to an implementation, but also the rationale behind those steps; the developers might have to explicitly state both. Explicit statement of the rationale by the developer might enable the automated assistant to select and perform a set of manipulations that achieves that objective for the developer.

A participating assistant. For the assistant to participate in the activities described above and not merely record them, the acitivities must be at least partially formalized; the most fundamental basis for automated support is formalization. Formalization allows the assistant to undertake responsibility for performing the activity, analyzing its effects, and, eventually, deciding which activities are appropriate. Individual development activities will become increasingly formalized, and so will coordinated sets of activities—thus accomplishing even larger development steps. In fact, the development process itself will be increasingly formalized into coordinated activities of multiple developers.

The automation-based software paradigm both facilitates and requires the existence of such an assistant. This is a consequence of having all the development processes—requirements analysis, specification, implementation, and maintenance—machine mediated and supported. The development processes must be broken into individual activities so that the individual activities can be mediated and supported, and the decisions and rationales behind them recorded.

This assistant aids the developer by participating in all the coordinated development activities, including the coordination itself. The existence of such an assistant, in turn, fundamentally alters the software life-cycle activities, since its capabilities alter the feasibility and cost of the various development activities.

How the assistant supports the new paradigm. This assistant supports the new software paradigm by recording the development activities, performing some of them, analyzing their effects, and aiding their selection. Because of the sophistication of the capabilities involved and because several different sources of knowledge are involved (knowledge of requirements, specification, implementation, evolution, validation, analysis, etc.), this assistant is knowledge based. It consists of a set of agents, or facets, each expert in one particular life-cycle activity. Portions of the corporate memory flow among these agents to initiate and coordinate their activity. Its general structure is shown in Figure 2.

Because the assistant mediates all development activities, it can support overall development as well as individual activities. It can coordinate one activity with another to maintain consistency; it can alert management if resources are, or are about to be, exceeded; it can help prevent maintainers from reexploring unfruitful implementations.

In short, by mediating all development activity and by being knowledgeable about that development, the assistant can help people apply whatever knowledge is relevant for their particular task. This is especially important on large projects in which it is currently difficult, if not impossible, for people to comprehend and assimilate all relevant information because it is fragmented, incomplete, or inconsistent.

Thus, the assistant is more than just the sum of its parts. It is an intelligent assistant that interfaces people to the computerized corporate memory, helps them perform their tasks, and coordinates their activities with each other.

The evolving assistant. The evolution of the software assistant and the incremental formalization of the development activities upon which it is based are the means of realization for the automation-based software.

As we learn how to formalize the various life-cycle activities, the assistant can incorporate them. Over time, this will allow developers to concentrate more and more on the higher level aspects of the development process, as the assistant takes over more of the low-level details. That is, as the development process is incrementally formalized, it can be increasingly automated. But since both the developer and the machine will be in the loop for the foreseeable future, suitable interfaces are necessary to allow the developers and the assistant to work together effectively.

One such evolving knowledge base is general-purpose and domain-specific implementation knowledge. Examples include data structure choices, algorithm design principles, and other optimizations. Such a knowledge base forms an abstract library in its most reusable form.

The assistant's role. To summarize the role of the automated assistant, we begin with a commitment to having the machine in the loop. This commitment will cause the development processes of requirements, specifications, design, implementation, and maintenance to be divided into smaller, more formal steps. This finer granularity and increased formality will lead to an assistant that aids developers in coordinating and performing all activities and in recording them as the documentation of the system's development.

This incremental approach is the foundation of the shift from the current informal, person-based software paradigm to the new formalized, computer-assisted paradigm.

Capabilities of the assistant. The following list of user requests illustrates the range and comprehensiveness of computer support in the new paradigm; we expect the assistant to fulfill such requests.

- Give the history of changes made to some module, along with the rationales for those changes.
- Find all methods for solving some domain-specific task (e.g., clustering methods).
- Find certain programs or rules, such as all rules that select data structures to implement ordered sets.
- Produce explanations of requirements, specifications, code, program derivations, etc.
- Provide help in debugging. For example, locate an inconsistency in a large rule base or in a large program specification that has been modified.
- Find some part of a program specification or requirement that a proposed change could affect.
- Find all relevant test programs that might be affected by a change in a specification so that a re-implementation can be retested.
- Monitor a program execution. For example, monitor a derivation to find all uses of an optimization rule that combines loops.
- Analyze alternative implementation paths to predict their likely cost.
- Analyze the execution of some program to see which operations are using large amounts of space or time.
- Analyze two nonintegrated programs to help to interface them.

The next list contains examples of some of the kinds of tools or capabilities that could carry out the above tasks, as well as many others.

- A monitor that measures performance, frequency of execution of program statements, data set sizes, etc. This information could be useful in deciding when pieces of a program should be recompiled. It could also help guide a smart, knowledge-based compiler in selecting appropriate implementations.
- An efficiency estimator that predicts which proposed implementation will be best, where the bottlenecks will be, or which pieces of the program should be made into modules.
- A help system that includes summarization and natural-language explanation capabilities for specifications and behavior tracers, etc.
- A tutor system to help maintenance personnel become familiar with existing specifications. Newcomers to the system could use the help, explanation, and program analysis tools to learn to modify specifications and requirements as needed.
- A deductive inference and simplification system to help optimize and analyze programs.
- A project management and communications system that sends out notices or reminders of bugs, changes, tasks, schedules, etc. It would have sets of procedures for handling common management situations.
- A requirements definition assistant that helps with requirements consistency, simplification, explanations, walk-throughs, trade-offs, etc., during requirements acquisition and modification.
- A verification tool to help verify the correctness or consistency of a new program optimization rule (since only transformations need to be verified).

Sociological effects of the automation-based software paradigm

Beyond the clear and dramatic benefits on the reliability and cost of producing software, the new paradigm might cause other less obvious, but equally profound, benefits.

Greater enhancements. First, systems will be enhanced after release to a much greater degree than they are at present. Today, maintenance tends to destroy structure, thus increasing the difficulty of further maintenance. Maintaining the specification should eliminate this problem. The pace of maintenance will be limited by the user's ability to generate and assimilate change rather than by technological constraints. Software will finally reach its potential; it will stay "soft" and modifiable rather than become ossified and brittle with age.

Because these systems will be able to evolve more, they will have longer lives. They will become larger and will integrate more capabilities. Evolution, rather than creation, will be the dominant programming mode.

No more standard packages. Because systems will be easier to modify, the standard packages that dominate today's market (due to cost and personnel limitations) will disappear. Users might start from a "standard" application, but they will personalize and augment it for their own purposes.

No more portability problem. Portability will disappear as a problem because the machine on which software runs will be just one of the decisions made during the implementation process. Like any other decision, it will be subject to change.

Personnel savings. Because the programmer's responsibility will be limited to decision-making, even very large systems will be implemented and maintained by a single programmer.

Increased user involvement. The most profound sociological effect will be the vastly increased involvement of end users in the specification process. Prototyping will be the means for debugging specifications before implementation; that is, evolution will also be the means for deriving an "initial specification." This will open up programming to a much wider population—many systems will be created and successfully used without proceeding beyond the prototype stage because the performance of the prototype itself will be adequate. ■

For further reading

Balzer, Robert, "Transformational Implementation: An Example," *IEEE Trans. Software Engineering,* Vol. SE-7, No. 1, Jan. 1981, pp. 3-14. Demonstrates feasibility of automation-based approach to building software.

Balzer, Robert, Neil Goldman, and David Wile, "Operational Specification as the Basis for Rapid Prototyping," *ACM Sigsoft Software Engineering Notes,* Vol. 7, No. 5, Dec. 1982, pp. 3-16. Describes role of prototyping in automation-based approach and presents an operational specification language for such prototyping.

Barr, Avron, and Edward Feigenbaum, *The Handbook of Artificial Intelligence,* Vol. 2, William Kaufman, Inc., Los Altos, Calif., 1982. This book covers the theory of the knowledge-based approach to software tools. In particular, Chapter 10, on automatic programming, surveys current and past research.

Cheatham, Thomas E., "Reusability Through Program Transformation," *Proc. IT&T Workshop Program Reusability,* Sept. 1983, pp. 122-129. Study on automated assistance in implementation via program refinement.

Cheatham, Thomas E., "An Overview of the Harvard Program Development System," in *Software Engineering Environments,* H. Hunke, ed., North Holland, New York, 1981. Demonstrates feasibility of automation-based approach to building software tools.

Hunke, Horst, ed., *Software Engineering Environments,* North Holland, New York, 1981. The traditional software engineering view of programming environments.

Green, Cordell, Jorge Phillips, Stephen Westfold, Tom Pressburger, Susan Angebrannt, Beverly Kedzierski, Bernard Mont-Reynaud, and Daniel Chapiro, "Towards a Knowledge-Based Programming System," tech. report KES.U.81.1, Kestrel Institute, Palo Alto, Calif., 1981. Demonstrates feasibility of automation-based approach to building software tools.

Green, Cordell, David Luckham, Robert Balzer, Thomas Cheatham, and Charles Rich, "Report on a Knowledge-Based Software Assistant," tech. report KES.U.83.2, Kestrel Institute, Palo Alto, Calif. July, 1983. An approach to defining an integrated, knowledge-based software assistant. The report formulates a technical plan for developing knowledge-based assistance for selected facets of the life cycle, including project management, requirements, specifications, implementation, testing, and documentation. Goals for the near, mid- and far terms are suggested for each facet.

Green, Cordell, and Steve Westfold, "Knowledge-Based Programming Self Applied," in *Machine Intelligence,* Vol. 10, Jean E. Hayes, Donald Michie, and YH. Pao, eds., John Wiley & Sons, New York, 1982, pp. 339-359. Prototype with an emphasis on self-description.

Kant, Elaine, and David R. Barstow, "The Refinement Paradigm: The Interaction of Coding and Efficiency Knowledge in Program Synthesis," *IEEE Trans. Software Engineering,* Vol. SE-7, No. 5, Sept. 1981, pp. 458-471. Study of automated assistance in implementation via program refinement.

Kedzierski, Beverly I., *Knowledge-Based Communication and Management Support in a System Development Environment,* PhD dissertation, tech. report KES.U.83.3, Kestrel Institute, Palo Alto, Calif., Aug. 1983. A knowledge-based system for project communication and management support.

Rich, Charles, and Richard C. Waters, "Abstraction, Inspection and Debugging in Programming," MIT AI Lab memo 634, MIT, Cambridge, Mass., June 1981. A prototype with an emphasis on program analysis.

Swartout, William, "The Gist Behavior Explainer," *Proc. American Association Artificial Intelligence Conf.,* Aug. 1983, pp. 402-407. A knowledge-based system for natural-language explanation of specifications.

Waters, Richard C, "The Programmer's Apprentice: Knowledge Based Program Editing," *IEEE Trans. Software Engineering,* Vol. SE-8, No. 1, Jan. 1982. Demonstration of feasibility of the automation-based approach to building software tools.

Robert Balzer, who helped form the University of Southern California Information Sciences Institute, is currently an associate professor of computer science and director of ISI's Software Sciences and Systems Division. The division combines artificial intelligence, database, and software engineering techniques to automate the software development process.

Before joining USC, Balzer spent several years with the Rand Corporation. He is a past president of ACM's Special Interest Group on Artificial Intelligence and was program chairman for the First National Conference of the American Association for Artificial Intelligence.

Balzer recieved his BS, MS, and PhD degrees in electrical engineering from the Carnegie Institute of Technology, Pittsburgh, Pennsylvania, in 1964, 1965, and 1966, respectively.

Thomas E. Cheatham, Jr., has been the Gordon McKay professor of computer science and director of the Center for Research in Computing Technology at Harvard University since 1969. For the past two years, he has also been chairman of Software Options, Inc., a Cambridge, Massachusetts, firm specializing in research in software technology. His current research interests include symbolic evaluation of programs, mechanical theorem proving for program verification, and the construction of systems for program development and maintenance.

Cheatham is a fellow of the American Academy of Arts and Sciences and a member of Sigma Xi and ACM. He received BS and MS degrees in mathematics from Purdue University, Lafayette, Indiana, in 1951 and 1953, respectively.

Cordell Green is director and chief scientist of the Kestrel Institute, where he leads the Chi knowledge-based software project. He previously directed the Psi program synthesis project at Stanford University. His early work at SRI in 1967 demonstrated how theorem proving formed a basis for logic programming, program synthesis, and problem solving. He has served as R&D program manager at DARPA, as area editor for *JACM*, and on the editorial board of *Cognitive Science.* He is a consulting professor of computer science at Stanford University, a consultant to Systems Control Technology, and member of the IEEE, ACM, and Tau Beta Pi.

Green received a BA and BS from Rice University, and an MS and PhD in electrical engineering from Stanford University.

Questions about this article can be directed to Robert Balzer, USC Information Sciences Institute, 4676 Admiralty Way, Suite 1001, Marina del Rey, CA 90291.

A Minority Dissenting Position

Daniel D. McCracken and Michael A. Jackson

We found the conference and workshop stimulating and useful, and we support many of its processes and conclusions.

However, we came to the meeting unprepared for the stultifying effect of the organizers' decision to structure the group's work around the concept of a system development life cycle.

The life cycle concept as promulgated in preconference mailings was that systems development consists of the following ten steps:

1. Organizational analysis

2. Systems evaluation

3. Feasibility analysis

4. Project plan

5. Logical design (produces general design specifications)

6. Physical design (produces detailed design specifications)

7. Program design

8. Implementation

9. Operation

10. Review and evaluation

Most attendees apparently found the life cycle concept comfortable. Several pointed out that there are many variations on the basic theme, but asserted that all life cycle concepts can be mapped onto each other. We would be interested in a demonstration of the latter assertion, which we doubt is true in any strict sense; if it is true, then we believe that the life cycle concept is probably, on balance, harmful. We adduce three groups of criticism.

A. Any form of life cycle is a project management structure imposed on system development. To contend that any life cycle scheme, even with variations, can be applied to all system development is either to fly in the face of reality or to assume a life cycle so rudimentary as to be vacuous.

The elaborate life cycle assumed as the basis for this conference may have seemed to be the only possible approach in the past when managing huge projects with inadequate development tools. (That it seemed to be the only choice, obviously did not prevent many such projects from failing.) It is foolish to use it as the basis for a certification effort that may be hoped to have a significant impact on the education of systems analysts for the next decade or more. During that time it seems highly probable to us that new development methodologies and implementation techniques will force--or rather permit--a complete re-evaluation of the assumptions built into the life cycle way of thinking.

B. The life cycle concept perpetuates our failure so far, as an industry, to build an effective bridge across the communication gap between end-user and systems analyst. In many ways it constrains future thinking to fit the mold created in response to failures of the past. It ignores such factors as the following, all of which are receiving rapidly increasing attention from both researchers and practitioners:

1. The widest possible development of systems by end-users themselves, limited only by the (rapidly improving) availability of development tools suited to the purpose. This is, of course, the optimum response to the communication gap: eliminate the need for communication.

2. Heavy end-user involvement in all phases of the application development process--not just requirements specification, but design and implementation also.

3. An increasing awareness that systems requirements cannot ever be stated fully in advance, not even in principle, because the user doesn't know them in advance-- not even in principle. To assert otherwise is to ignore the fact that the development process itself changes the user's perceptions of what is possible, increases his insights into his own environment, and indeed often changes that environment itself. We suggest an analogy with the Heisenbert Uncertainty Principle: any system development activity inevitably changes the environment out of which the need for the system arose. System development methodology must take into account that the user, and his needs and environment, change during the process.

What we understand to be the conventional life cycle approach might be compared with a supermarket at which the customer is forced to provide a complete order to a stock clerk at the door to the store, with no opportunity to roam the aisles--comparing prices, remembering items not on his list, or getting a headache and changing his mind about what to have for dinner. Such restricted shopping is certainly possible and sometimes desirable-- it's called mail order--but why should anyone wish to impose that restricted structure on all shopping?

C. The life cycle concept rigidifies thinking, and thus serves as poorly as possible the demand that systems be responsive to change. We all know that systems and their requirements inevitably change over time. In the past, severely limited by inadequate design and implementation tools as we were, there was little choice but to freeze designs much earlier than desirable and deal with changes only reluctantly and in large packets. The progress of system development thus moved along a kind of sawtooth, with a widely separated set of points being designated "completion of implemention," "completion of first set of modifications," etc. The term "life cycle," if it has any linguistic integrity at all, seems an odd way to describe this process. To impose the concept on emerging methods in which much greater responsiveness to change is possible, seems to us to be sadly shortsighted.

Here, as sketches only, are two scenarios of system development processes that seem to us to be impossible to force into the life cycle concept without torturing either logic or language or both.

1. (Prototyping.) Some response to the user's earliest and most tentative statement of needs is provided to him for experimentation and possibly even productive use, extremely early in the development process-perhaps 1% of the

way into the eventual total effort. Development proceeds step-by-step <u>with</u> <u>the</u> <u>user,</u> as he gains insight into his own environment and needs. A series of prototypes, or, what is perhaps the same thing, a series of modifications to the first prototype, evolves gradually into the final product. Formal specifications may <u>never</u> be written. Or, if specifications are needed, perhaps to permit a re-implementation to improve performance, the prototype itself furnishes the specifications.

This mode of operation is emphasized by some writers as being fundamental to the concept of Decision Support Systems; we believe it has even wider applicability.

2. A process of system development done by the end-user and an analyst in this sequence: implement, design, specify redesign, reimplement. The user is provided with an implementation tool <u>and</u> <u>one</u> <u>version</u> <u>of</u> <u>a</u> <u>system</u> <u>thought</u> to be <u>potentially</u> <u>useful</u> <u>to</u> <u>him.</u> By a process of experimentation, in occasional consulation with the analyst, the user carries out--essentially in parallel--the following activities:

   a. Learning the capabilities of the implementation.

   b. Learning the capabilities of the implementation tool.

   c. Designing his own desired system.

   d. Specifying his own desired system.

The <u>analyst</u> then works from the "specification," which in fact consists of a running functional model of the system, to produce a design that is then implemented by a programmer in some conventional language.

We claim that neither of these scenarios, nor many others that are readily imagineable, can be "mapped onto" the life cycle reproduced at the beginning of this note, or onto any other life cycle that is not vacuous. The life cycle concept is simply unsuited to the needs of the 1980's in developing systems.

Article

On the Inevitable Intertwining of Specification and Implementation

William Swartout and Robert Balzer
USC/Information Sciences Institute

"On the Inevitable Intertwining of Specification and Implementation" by W. Swartout and R. Balzer from *Communications of the ACM*, Volume 25, Number 7, July 1982, pages 438-440. Copyright 1982, Association for Computing Machinery, Inc., reprinted by permission.

Contrary to recent claims that specification should be completed before implementation begins, this paper presents two arguments that the two processes must be intertwined. First, limitations of available implementation technology may force a specification change. For example, deciding to implement a stack as an array (rather than as a linked list) may impose a fixed limit on the depth of the stack. Second, implementation choices may suggest augmentations to the original specification. For example, deciding to use an existing pattern-match routine to implement the search command in an editor may lead to incorporating some of the routine's features into the specification, such as the ability to include wild cards in the search key. This paper elaborates these points and illustrates how they arise in the specification of a controller for a package router.

CR Categories and Subject Descriptors: D.2.1. [**Software Engineering**]: Requirements/Specifications—*methodologies*
General Terms: Design, Documentation, Languages
Additional Key Words and Phrases: implementation

For several years we [1, 2, 3, 4] and others [5, 6, 7, 9, 10, 11] have been carefully pointing out how important it is to separate specification from implementation. In this view, one first completely specifies a system in a formal language at a high level of abstraction in an implementation-free manner. Then, as a separate phase, the implementation issues are considered and a program realizing the specification is produced. Depending on the development methodology being employed, this realization is produced either manually (Software Engineering), semiautomatically (Program Transformation), or automatically (High-level Languages and Automatic Programming). The key issue here is not how one arrives at the realization, but rather, that all current software methodologies have adopted a common model that separates specification from implementation.

Unfortunately, this model is overly naive, and does not match reality. Specification and implementation are, in fact, intimately intertwined because they are, respectively, the already-fixed and the yet-to-be-done portions of a multi-step system development. It is only because we have allowed this development process to occur, unobserved and unrecorded, in people's heads that the multi-step nature of this process was not more apparent earlier. Only with the appearance of development methodologies such as stepwise refinement and program transformation did this essential multi-step aspect become clear.

It was then natural, though naive, to partition this multi-step development process into two disjoint partitions: specification and implementation. But this partitioning is entirely arbitrary. Every specification is an implementation of some other higher level specification. Thus simply by shifting our focus to an earlier portion of the development, part of the specification becomes part of the implementation. This explains why it is so hard to create a good specification—one which is high level enough to be understandable, yet precise enough to define completely a particular class of behavior.

The standard software development model holds that each step of the development process should be a "valid" realization of the specification. By "valid" we mean that the behaviors specified by the implementation are a subset of those defined by the specification. However, in actual practice, we find that many development steps violate this validity relationship between specification and implementation. Rather than providing an implementation of the specification, they knowingly redefine the specification itself. Our central argument is that these steps are a crucial mechanism for elaborating the specification and are necessarily intertwined with the implementation. By their very nature, they cannot precede the implementation.

To distinguish such steps from valid implementation steps, we will call them *specification modifications*. They arise from two sources: physical limitations and imperfect foresight. We will consider these in turn.

This research is supported by the Air Force Systems Command, Rome Air Development Center under Contract No. F30602 81 K 0056. Views and conclusions contained in this report are the authors' and should not be interpreted as respresenting the official opinion or policy of RADC, the U.S. Government, or any person or agency connected with them.
Author's Present Address: William Swartout and Robert Balzer, University of Southern California, Information Sciences Institute, Marina del Rey, CA 90291.

The systems we implement employ physical devices (including computers). These devices have limitations (such as speed, size, and reliability) which are specific to the device. Often, one finds cost-effective partial solutions rather than total solutions. This introduces either a restriction that limits the domain of input (e.g., names can only be eight characters) or introduces the possibility of error. In the latter case, one must then define what to do when such errors arise. In either case, the semantics of the specification has been changed, and the alteration is only meaningful in terms of an already fixed implementation decision.

Clearly, such specification modifications cannot precede the implementation decisions they are predicated upon. These "imperfect implementations" are in fact quite common and include modifications due to finite resources or economic considerations and modifications that limit the domain of a specification to a subset of "expected" situations. One reason the specification modifications are not well recognized is that they are usually folded into the "initial" specification, which necessarily therefore also includes (implicitly) the associated implementation decisions, rather than existing explicitly as separate development steps.

The second source of specification modifications is our lack of foresight. The systems we specify and build are complex. We are unable to foresee all the implications and interactions in such systems. During implementation we examine these implications and interactions in more detail in terms of the more concrete implementation being created. Often we find undesirable effects or an incomplete description. This insight provides the basis for refining the specification appropriately. Which version of the specification is modified (i.e., where in the development the modification is inserted) depends upon which implementation decisions need to be reconsidered because of the new insight, and which implementation decisions it is dependent upon.

Such improved insight may (and usually does) also arise from actual usage of the implemented system. These changes reflect not only unanticipated implications and interactions in the implemented system, but also changing needs generated by the existence of the implemented system. Incorporation of these specification modifications is precisely the same as above, i.e., they must be integrated at some appropriate spot in the development.

Thus a much more intertwined relationship exists between specification and implementation than the standard rhetoric would have us believe. Implementation is a multi-step process. Each stage of this process is a specification for what follows. However, many of the steps in this development are not mathematically "valid." They do not implement the specification, they alter it. Many of these specification modifications arise from physical limitations of one form or another. Such "partial" or "imperfect" implementations provide the structure for elaborating the specification to handle the imperfections. The rest of the specification modifications arise from our lack of insight concerning the systems we are implementing. Inadequacies or incompletenesses are discovered during implementation and/or use, and result in the need to revise some appropriate version of the specification and reconsider some of the implementation decisions.

If we were to try to retain the old model of separation of specification from implementation, then we would have to define specification as that portion of the development process beyond which only valid implementation steps occurred (i.e., no specification modifications), and implementation was the rest. Unfortunately, such a distinction can only be made after the fact, and hence is not useful for system builders.

These observations should not be misinterpreted. We still believe that it is important to keep unnecessary implementation decisions out of specifications and we believe that maintenance should be performed by modifying the specification and reoptimizing the altered definition. These observations should indicate that the specification process is more complex and evolutionary than previously believed and they raise the question of the viability of the pervasive view of a specification as a fixed contract between a client and an implementer.

An Example

Consider the following specification of the controller for a package router:[1]

The package router is a system for distributing *packages* into destination *bins*. The packages arrive at a *source* station, which is connected to the bins via a series of *pipes*. A single pipe leaves the source station. The pipes are linked together by two-position *switches*. A switch enables a package sliding down its input pipe to be directed to either of its two output pipes. There is a unique path through the pipes from the source station to any particular bin.[2]

Packages arriving at the source station are scanned by a reading device which determines a destination bin for the package. The package is then allowed to slide down the pipe leaving the source station. The package router must set its switches ahead of each package sliding through the pipes so that each package is routed to the bin determined for it by the source station.

After a package's destination has been determined, it is delayed for a fixed time before being released into the first pipe. This is done to prevent packages from following one another so closely that a switch cannot be reset between successive packages when necessary. However, if a package's destination is the same as that of the package which preceded it through the source station, it is not delayed, since there will be no need to reset switches between the two packages.

There will generally be many packages sliding down the pipes at once. The packages slide at different and unpredictable speeds, so it is impossible to calculate when a given package will reach a particular switch. However, the switches contain sensors strategically placed at their entries and exits to detect the packages.

---

[1] This specification was obtained from [8].
[2] This is equivalent to viewing the router as a binary tree having switches as nodes, pipes as branches, and bins as leaves.

The sensors are placed in such a way that it is safe to change a switch setting if and only if no packages are present between the entry sensor of a switch and either of its exit sensors. The pipes are bent at the sensor locations in such a way that the sensors are guaranteed to detect a separation between two packages, no matter how closely they follow one another.

Due to the unpredictable sliding characteristics of the packages, it is possible, in spite of the source station delay, that packages will get so close together that it is not possible to reset a switch in time to properly route a package. *Misrouted* packages may be routed to any bin, but must not cause the misrouting of other packages. The bins too have sensors located at their entry, and upon each arrival of a misrouted package at a wrong bin, the routing machine is to signal that package's intended destination and the bin it actually reached.

When we received this specification, we considered it to be an excellent example of an abstract specification which had successfully separated the description of intended behavior from the implementation of that behavior. It was only during our attempt to formalize this example into our specification language that we came to the disturbing realization that the "excellent specification" was contaminated with many implementation decisions. For example, someone has made the decision to use gravity to move the boxes from one switch to the next. Alternately, this "package mover" could have been implemented by, say, a set of conveyor belts. If conveyor belts had been chosen, it might have been possible to make them more dependable than the gravity/chute implementation, and if so, the specification for the controller might not have to deal with "misrouted boxes" at all. Moving up a level, the choices of organizing the switches into a tree and making it binary are both implementation decisions. In fact, the package router could have been implemented using a gantry crane that would pick up boxes at the source and drop them in their appropriate bins. If that were the case, it would not have made much sense to talk about trees, switches, and package movers. Thus we can see that in this example (and we take it to be fairly typical) implementation decisions are made before specification is complete and these decisions can have a major effect on the further specification of the system. Turning things around, if we wanted a specification that contained no implementation commitments it would have to represent information about all the possible implementation technologies, a potentially enormous task.

The package router specification given above also illustrates how an implementation choice can force a modification to the specification. The goal of any package router is to distribute packages into their correct bins. However, particular implementation decisions already present in the specification presented (chiefly, the decision to slide boxes down chutes) introduce the possibility of boxes bunching up, preventing the system from routing all boxes to their correct destinations (because the switches do not and cannot have infinitely fast switching time). The notion of "misrouted boxes" must be introduced to specify what should happen when the goal cannot be achieved. If a different implementation decision had been made which assured that boxes would arrive correctly, the notion of misrouted boxes would be irrelevant.

Conclusion

From the standpoint of constructing aids for capturing the specification and evolution of programs, interleaving specification and implementation into a single development structure will result in a more coherent and realistic structure for making modifications. By contrast, if we attempted to construct such an aid keeping complete specifications and implementation separate, we necessarily would have trouble capturing specification changes like those described above which are forced by implementation decisions.

While the interleaving of specification and implementation seems to occur quite frequently in practice, work directed toward formal specification and aids for creating such specifications seems to have paid little attention to this phenomenon. We have attempted here to illustrate several situations where this interleaving plays an important part in the software development process. Therefore, our software development aids must begin to address these issues.

Received 11/81; revised 1/82; accepted 2/82

References
1. Balzer, R. M. Dataless programming. Full Joint Computer Conference, 1967, pp. 535–545.
2. Balzer, R. M., N. M. Goldman, and D. S. Wile. On the transformational implementation approach to programming. Proceedings of the Second International Conference on Software Engineering, October 1976, pp. 337–344.
3. Balzer, R. M., and N. M. Goldman. Principles of good software specification and their implications for specification languages. Proceedings of the Specifications of Reliable Software Conference, Boston, Massachusetts, April, 1979, pp. 58–67. (Also presented at the National Computer Conference, 1981.)
4. Balzer, R. M. Transformational implementation: An example. *IEEE Trans. Software Engineering 7*, 1 (Jan. 1981), 3–14. Also published as USC/Information Sciences Institute RR-79-79, May 1981.
5. Bauer, F. L. Programming as an evolutionary process. Proceedings of the Second International Conference on Software Engineering, Oct. 1976, pp. 223–234.
6. Burstall, R. M., and J. Darlington. Some transformations for developing recursive programs. Proceedings of the International Conference on Reliable Software, Los Angeles, Calif., April 1975, pp. 465–472.
7. Dijkstra, E. W. Notes on structured programming. In *Structured Programming*, Academic Press, New York, 1972.
8. Hommel, G. (Ed.) Vergleich verschiedener Spezifikationsverfahren am Beispiel einer Paketverteilanlage. Kernforschungszentrum Karlsruhe GmbH, August, 1980. PDV-Report, KfK-PDV 186, Part 1.
9. Knuth, D. E. Structured programming with goto statements. *Computing Surveys 6*, 4 (Dec. 1974).
10. Parnas, D. L. On the criteria to be used in decomposing systems into modules. *Comm. ACM 15*, 12 (Dec. 1972), 1053–1058.
11. Wirth, N. Program development by step-wise refinement. *Comm. ACM 14*, 4 (Aril 1971).

"Accommodating Uncertainty in Software Design" by R.V. Giddings from *Communications of the ACM*, Volume 27, Number 5, May 1984, pages 428-434. Copyright 1984, Association for Computing Machinery, Inc., reprinted by permission.

ACCOMMODATING UNCERTAINTY IN SOFTWARE DESIGN

Recognition that most software is domain dependent (DD) is extremely important because the most commonly used software life-cycle models are not adequate for DD software. The nature of DD software, and the need to manage its life cycle effectively, calls for a new approach to software design and the implementation of software development environments.

RICHARD V. GIDDINGS

A review of current literature would lead one to believe that the "software crisis" is a recent development. Such is not the case. There has always been a software crisis.

Software development techniques, which have matured little, require large amounts of highly skilled labor. Because the necessary labor has rarely been available, personnel with marginal skill levels have been, and are increasingly, in high demand.

The impact of the ongoing shortage of skilled labor is staggering. For example, it is estimated that up to 90 percent of the data processing intellectual effort in a large corporation is devoted to maintenance (namely, redesign, reprogramming, and error correction [6]).

Successful resolution of the software crisis requires a significant change in the manpower-intensive nature of the development process. It must be based on a redefinition of the process rather than on further value engineering. Such a redefinition must start by examining the basic assumptions about the nature of the software development process.

It has been recognized that software is not homogeneous, but only recently have software classifications begun to appear that are based on the relationship of the software to the environment within which it oper-

© 1984 ACM 0001-0782/84/0500-0428 75¢

A portion of this paper was originally published in the *Scientific Honeyweller 4,* 2 (June 1983), 11–13.

ates [5]. These classifications, one of which is proposed in this paper, provide an improved model for explaining program dynamics and developing life-cycle management strategies.

SOFTWARE MODELS AND LIFE CYCLES

Perhaps the most commonly used model of the software life cycle was developed by Boehm [2] and is shown in Figure 1. At a high level, the development process is viewed as a progression from problem definition to implementation to maintenance.

For many interesting classes of software, Boehm's life cycle does not adequately model the development process. Consider the following scheme that classifies software according to the way in which the universe of discourse (the class of problems to be computed) and the software interact.

Domain Independent (DI)

This class of software is distinguished by the independence of the problem statement and the universe of discourse (that is, solutions need to be verified but not validated). Figure 2 provides a model for this type of software.

For this class of software, the development process can be described as a search for one of many "good" solutions. The essential problem is proving that one has in fact obtained a solution (verification).

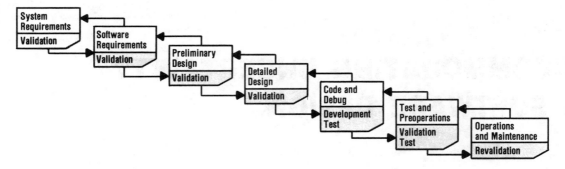

FIGURE 1. Boehm's Software Life Cycle

Examples of this type of software include numerical algorithms or, from a practical point of view, software developed under a contract with predetermined specifications and no ongoing responsibility for the developer other than bug fixing.

Domain Dependent Software (DD)

Two distinct types of software make up the class of DD software: experimental (DDEX) and embedded (DDEM). DDEX software is characterized by an intrinsic uncertainty about the universe of discourse (see Figure 3). The development process is embedded within a search for knowledge about the universe of discourse. The essential problem is producing software useful for testing a hypothesis or exploring unknown characteristics of the universe.

Examples of this class of software are models being used as vehicles for conducting research to discover information about a universe of discourse. In such efforts, one is trying to identify necessary data, data collection constraints (for example, accuracy or frequency), relationships, and systems dynamics.

The use of DDEX software may eventually lead to the development of a specification for software with other uses (for example, an economic model that can be used to improve decision making). However, that software would not be DDEX.

A model for DDEM software is shown in Figure 4. This software is characterized by interdependence between the universe of discourse and the software. The use of the software may change both the form and the substance of the universe of discourse and, as a result, the nature of the problem being solved.

Examples of DDEM software include business systems, office automation systems, software engineering systems, design automation systems, and successive generations of a large-scale operating system. In each of these, the development process is a search for a "good" problem statement. The essential difficulty lies in anticipating the impact of likely changes in the universe of discourse resulting from the introduction of the software.

An interesting phenomenon often associated with this type of development is that the introduction of the software serves as a catalyst for changes in its environment that far exceed those anticipated by the software designers. For example, some experts believe that 80 percent of the gain from office automation will result from concomitant factors such as work reorganization or job redesign, whereas only 20 percent will be derived directly from the application of advanced automation technology [4].

Domain Dependent Software Life Cycle

Historically, software methodologies have focused on programming techniques. Today, many focus on design. The few that address the entirety of Boehm's software life cycle rest on the a priori assumption that the designer has, or can obtain, a detailed understanding of the problem and can implement a solution and move on to another project leaving a rather mundane aspect—maintenance—to others.

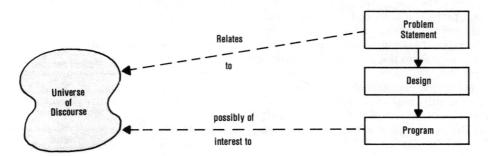

FIGURE 2. Domain Independent

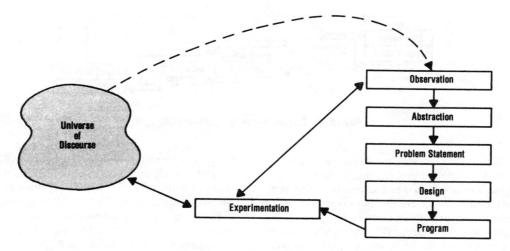

FIGURE 3. Domain Dependent Software—Experimental

For DD software, the above is only trivially true (that is, the designer knows the current problem statement but does not know the relationship between that problem statement and a problem statement that leads to a useful solution). Rather than implementing a solution, one is really refining a sequence of imperfect prototypes over an extended time (see Figure 5). For this reason, conducting experiments to validate the problem statement and to provide feedback for successive prototypes is an essential part of the development process.

Before proceeding, it is worth noting that one very common event is not explicitly represented in Figure 5. At some point, a prototype typically becomes useful to others besides the developers or experimenters. When this occurs, the prototype can be made available as a product or the specifications for the prototype can be used as the problem statement for a DI software development effort to produce a reengineered product. If the prototype is made available as a product, a "frozen"

copy of the software enters a maintenance phase limited to bug fixing.

Treating a product as a "spin-off" from the software development cycle with maintenance limited to bug fixing is useful for three reasons. First, it allows one to distinguish between bug fixing and program evolution. These two distinct activities have been traditionally clumped under the term, *maintenance*. Second, having made such a distinction, one can contrast management procedures designed to insure the short-term stability of a product with those designed to cope with a long-term process where continuing change is intrinsic. Third, one can conduct field evaluations as a check on the reliability of experimental validation efforts.

DOMAIN DEPENDENT SOFTWARE DEVELOPMENT LIFE-CYCLE IMPLICATIONS

Much of the current software crisis is a result of not recognizing and not managing the empirical, ongoing

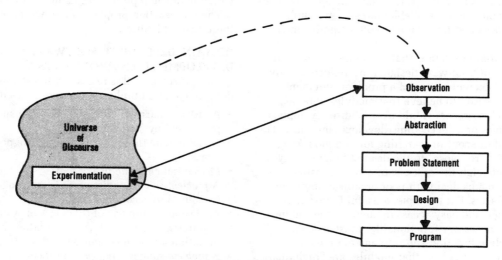

FIGURE 4. Domain Dependent Software—Embedded

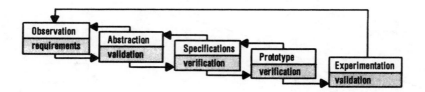

FIGURE 5. Domain Dependent Software Life Cycle

nature of DD software development (that is, using inappropriate DI development procedures). In fact, when one considers the perceptual and communication problems inherent in the software development process, DI software development may be quite rare.

Because the development of DD software is a process of refining prototypes, the basic management tradeoffs are both the total life-cycle cost and the time necessary to produce successive prototypes. Clearly, to be optimal, any methodology based on designing each of a sequence of prototypes from scratch will require a minimum amount of effort to build each prototype. Also, hierarchical system designs do not lend themselves to program evolution [5].

Using the tools and techniques available today, prototype development can be accomplished with very little effort for some types of problems. The trend toward using very high-level programming languages will increase the number and type of problems that can be effectively managed by building successive prototypes from scratch. However, for the foreseeable future, we will be faced with the recurring requirement of reducing the total life-cycle cost by increasing the probability that work invested in one prototype can be easily carried forward to succeeding prototypes.

One approach to protecting the investment made in any given prototype is to collect modules into libraries for reuse—either modules resulting from the structured design for each prototype or modules developed for other projects that happen to be accessible. However, module libraries of this type (that is, collections of modules that happen to be available) have been around since the 1950s and have failed to offer significant advantage.

The essential problem is that the individuality and creativeness of a software designer are reflected in the hierarchical decomposition of a problem statement. There is no reason to believe that modules obtained through such a process would ever be directly applicable to another, or a succeeding, development effort. The time and effort spent in searching for and modifying modules that are "close" to the desired functionality typically outweigh the cost advantages of reusing code.

Other problems deal with poor organization of the module libraries. For example, a useful library must provide quick and easy access to modules that might provide the necessary functionality, must specify clearly module function and implementation constraints, and must ensure that modules are "high quality."

As an alternative to the module library, Wasserman and Belady [8] proposed the establishment of a "software inventory." Later, Belady [7] proposed the concept of "evolved software." Parnas [7] described "designing software for ease of extension and contraction." I have proposed the idea of "component software" and, based on experience gained with the REAP system [3], the idea of a "component software development environment."

In each of the above proposals, the essential idea is to design software components for reuse. The internals of the components (parts or building blocks) are to be "unknowable" to the user, thus allowing the component designer the freedom to experiment with implementation strategies.

Each of these approaches offers the potential for overcoming the difficulties associated with the typical module library. However, significant problems remain.

The first difficulty with designing software components for reuse is identifying the components that should be provided. There is intuitive appeal to the idea that, for a given universe of discourse, there should be "optimal" sets of components. These sets are optimal in the sense that the cost of the component library (that is, component development cost; library development and operational costs; and cost of searching for a component, verifying its suitability, and incorporating it into a design) plus the total cost for a sequence of prototypes is minimized. The second difficulty is determining an effective environment within which to develop prototypes using components.

The next section proposes a method for addressing these two difficulties.

DOMAIN DEPENDENT SOFTWARE DEVELOPMENT ENVIRONMENTS

Before proceeding, it is necessary to establish definitions for a number of commonly used terms.

- A *task* is a narrowly focused activity usually performed by a single worker.
- A *tool* is something that facilitates the performance of a task.
- *Mechanization* is the use of tools.
- A *problem-solving environment* is an integrated set of tools used to accomplish a function.
- *Automation* is the use of that class of systems that requires no human intervention other than at initiation and at termination.
- A *problem-solving strategy* is a procedure followed by a human in obtaining some "end."

With these definitions, one can observe that

- Mechanization requires embedding a knowledge of tasks into the tools. Most existing software development environments focus on mechanization of software development tasks.
- Problem-solving environments require embedding a knowledge of ends, tasks, and problem-solving strategies into integrated systems (that is, they are "knowledge-based systems" or "expert systems").
- Automated systems require embedded knowledge of an end and an algorithm for achieving the end.

For all types of software, we are already seeing an increasing focus on the development of problem-solving environments because mechanization does not produce the productivity advantages of an integrated set of "intelligent" tools and, except for trivial cases, automation is not feasible.

Problem-Solving Environments and DD Software

The economics associated with managing the DD software life cycle are significantly different than those associated with the DI software life cycle. When one considers life cycles that typically extend over many years and may result in expenditures of millions of dollars, long-term cost tradeoffs are available that are often in conflict with the short-term nature of the DI development process.

The most important of these cost tradeoffs is the front-end development of problem-solving environments and management procedures designed to minimize the DD life-cycle cost. Cost reductions can be achieved in three complementary ways. First, a problem-solving environment can be designed to minimize the work invested in a sequence of prototypes (that is, an environment can be designed to increase the probability that effort invested in one prototype will be effectively utilized in successive prototypes; hence the cost can be prorated over a larger base). Second, a problem-solving environment can reduce the cycle time—the time from requirements analysis to experimental validation of a prototype. This reduced cycle time results in more effective products and reduced personnel costs. Third, a problem-solving environment can be designed for use by personnel with marginal data processing skills, thus conserving highly skilled manpower [3].

At present there are three forms an effective problem-solving environment may take:

(1) generic environments applicable to all software development,
(2) special-purpose environments for use with a specific universe of discourse (that is, a specific class of software development problems), or
(3) extensible environments that not only provide support for the development life cycle but are simply "extended" to produce prototypes and products.

It is my opinion that the development of generic environments, the bulk of current efforts, will not yield significant results. A problem-solving environment must have an embedded knowledge of ends, tasks, and problem-solving strategies; at a generic level, knowledge about software development can be embedded, but the amount of knowledge about any other universe of discourse will, by necessity, be small.

Special-purpose problem-solving environments have been shown to offer cost advantages and to hold significant potential for DD software. For example, the REAP system was built using a special-purpose environment designed specifically for use in building environmental systems. Overall development cost was reduced from an estimated $8 million to an actual $1.6 million [3]. Productivity of software development personnel was the equivalent of 1300 lines of production FORTRAN code per person-month at a cost of $2.84 per line of operational code. The end product, consisting of over 360,000 lines of FORTRAN code, is maintained by one person working part time at this task.

Extensible environments are interesting to think about; however, there are more questions than answers about cost and effectiveness. They are mentioned here primarily because the approach to problem-solving environment design described in the next section may also provide an approach to the design of extensible environments.

The Design of Problem-Solving Environments for DD Software

At this point, we need to return to the two issues left hanging earlier: how do we identify the set of components to be provided, and what is an effective problem-solving environment for using components? We can restate these issues a little more precisely as follows:

- Given a universe of discourse, how does one identify an "appropriate" set of components?
- Given that one has an "appropriate" set of components, what is the effect of changing the universe of discourse? (Or, given a set of components, what is the effect of adding or deleting components?)
- If there is a procedure for determining both of the above, does it make a difference how one selects a universe of discourse? (For example, if the universe of discourse I am interested in is the "class of all business problems," but I anticipate dealing also with the "class of all integrated circuit design problems," what is the effect of selecting a universe of discourse that is the union of those two sets?)
- How does answering the above affect the design of problem-solving environments?

Using concepts from formal mathematical model theory, one can formalize the first two of the above quite easily. In particular, the first two questions deal with "closure" and "consistency" of mathematical models.

Although it may not be obvious, the third question can be viewed primarily as a human factors tradeoff. Formal models can be easily developed for universes of discourse ranging from the class of all computable problems to a single, simple problem statement. As we shall see later, selection of the universe of discourse affects our ability to produce a model that is "easy to use" (in a sense defined later).

The fourth question boils down to, "If one goes to the effort of developing a formal model for a universe of discourse, can a problem-solving environment be developed that implements the formal model in a straightforward way and would such an implementation be usable?" The answer to this question is *yes*.

A methodology based on a formal modeling approach consists of four phases:

(1) describing the universe of discourse—an in-depth analysis of tasks, work flow, end-user behaviors (namely, problem-solving strategies), and organizational goals and objectives;
(2) developing a formal model;
(3) implementing the model;
(4) developing applications.

This approach is simplified by the following hypotheses:

(1) Human problem-solving strategies and behaviors can be represented as algorithms, which in turn can be represented as recursive functions (Church's thesis).
(2) The set of an individual's problem-solving strategies and cognitive processes, although dynamic, has a small cardinality.
(3) For any given class of problems, the cardinality of the set of human behaviors used to solve problems is small.

The first, a thesis that has held for 40 years, allows one to develop a formal model of the desired problem-solving environment and assures that it can be implemented in a straightforward manner. The second two, basic premises of cognitive psychology that have been studied since the turn of the century, allow one to build "easy to use" systems—easy to use in the sense that they

(1) minimize the number of end-user steps required to achieve a solution, and
(2) minimize impedance (that is, the steps a user is required to follow reflect both what tasks the user believes to be important and the order in which they should be performed).

It follows immediately that ease of use is not an abso-

lute measure. Rather, it is a measure with respect to a single problem domain and a specific class of end users. It also follows that the complexities associated with designing an "easy to use" system are related to human factors and cognitive psychology more than to data processing.

Several advantages are provided by formally modeling the problem domain and the behaviors of users that interact with that domain. First, a formal model provides the information necessary to build easy-to-use systems. Second, a formal model provides a natural way to identify and design "code" for reuse. Third, verification is simplified (that is, because the approach is constructive, one needs only to verify the correctness of the composition and, independently on a one-time basis, the model itself). Fourth, a formal model offers the potential of developing hardware and software architectures optimized for the universe of discourse.

For example, the nature of a "program" lends itself to the development of very high-level programming languages. Also, in my opinion, Wilner's [9] novel hardware architecture (particularly well suited to VLSI technology and avoiding the "Von Neumann bottleneck") would provide a good vehicle for the implementation of formal models.

Nested Development
The development of a problem-solving environment for DD software development adds confusion to the issue of life-cycle management. Because one is normally conducting two development efforts concurrently (that is, both the problem-solving environment and the application are DD software), there is a nesting of life cycles (see Figure 6). This nesting suggests the idea of extensible problem-solving environments and an approach to the design of that type of an environment (again, see Figure 6).

CONCLUSION
DD software development is an empirical, ongoing process. As such, it is not surprising that the front-end implementation of a problem-solving environment offers a high return-on-investment opportunity as well as a means for conserving skilled data-processing personnel and increasing product effectiveness.

Reusing tested, verified code is essential if software productivity is to be significantly improved by increasing our ability to effectively carry the investment in

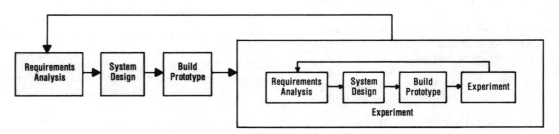

FIGURE 6. A Nested Development Cycle

one prototype forward to succeeding prototypes. However, reusable code will not be an accidental spin-off of current practices. Code with a high probability for reuse must be identified and designed for reuse, and an environment that encourages reuse must be created.

Special-purpose and extensible problem-solving environments (with their productivity improvements, better ability to conserve skilled manpower, and higher potential for reusing code) will be increasingly emphasized over generic problem-solving environments. The question of whether an optimal set of extensible problem-solving environments could be defined and extended to create special-purpose problem-solving environments will require a significant amount of research to resolve. However, if such a set were identified, software development costs could be significantly reduced.

Issues about the design of problem-solving environments can be formalized by means of model theory. Models derived through such a process could be directly implemented and hold the potential of offering alternatives to current practice.

REFERENCES

1. Belady, L.A.   Evolved software for the 80s. *Computer* (Feb. 1979), 79–82.
2. Boehm, B.W.   Software engineering. *IEEE Trans. Comput. C-25* (Dec. 1976), 1226–1241.
3. Giddings, R.V.   A graphics-oriented computer system to support environmental decision-making. In *Computer Graphics and Environmental Planning*, E. Teicholz and B. Berry, Eds. Prentice-Hall, Englewood Cliffs, N.J., 1983.
4. Hammer, M.   What is office automation? *Off. Autom.* Memo 12, Laboratory for Computer Science, Massachusetts Institute of Technology, Cambridge, Jan. 1980.
5. Lehman, M.M.   Programs, life cycles, and laws of software evolution. *Proc. IEEE 68*, 9 (Sept. 1980), 1060–1076.
6. Martin, J.   What to plan for to manage the future of your data center. *Can. Datasyst. 9*, 3 (Mar. 1977), 28–32.
7. Parnas, D.L.   Designing software for ease of extension and contraction. *IEEE Trans. Comput. SE-5*, 2 (Mar. 1979), 128–137.
8. Wasserman, A.I., and Belady, L.A.   Software engineering: The turning point. *Computer* (Sept. 1978), 30–39.
9. Wilner, W.T.   Recursive Machines. Rep. P.800054, Xerox Palo Alto Research Center, Palo Alto, Calif., June 1980.

CR Categories and Subject Descriptors: C.0 [**General**]: *system architectures*; D.1.1 [**Programming Techniques**]: Applicative (Functional) Programming; D.2.2 [**Software Engineering**]: Tools and Techniques—*software libraries, user interfaces*; D.2.6 [**Software Engineering**]: Programming Environments; D.2.9 [**Software Engineering**]: Management—*life cycle, productivity*; D.2 [**Software Engineering**]: Miscellaneous—*rapid phototyping, reusable software*

General Terms: Design, Economics, Human Factors, Languages, Management
Additional Key Words and Phrases: problem-solving environments

Author's Present Address: Richard V. Giddings, Manager, Local/Office Systems, Corporate Information Management, Honeywell Inc., Honeywell Plaza, Minneapolis, MN 55408.

Part III. Prototyping

Although it is a relatively recent addition to the software development lexicon, prototyping has received a great deal of attention in the literature (as the annotated bibliography attests). Much of the discussion revolves around the following issues:

- What is a (rapid) prototype?
- How does it compare with a final product?
- Is it release 1 of the system?
- Must it be discarded?
- How expensive is it to build?
- What should the prototype do?
- Can it be used within a conventional life-cycle?
- When should it be used?
- Does it replace a phase in the conventional life-cycle?
- Is it more properly a "breadboard," "brassboard," or "mockup"?
- How "rapid" is rapid prototyping?
- How is it assessed or evaluated for effectiveness?

The articles in this section have been selected to answer these questions. The reader should understand that the answers are not always the same—even for the definition of a prototype!

One view holds that every new software system is a prototype because it is one of a kind. Of course, in reality, every new software system is not tagged as a prototype. We are thus led to the view that a software prototype has more to do with *expectations* than with other definable characteristics:

> A software prototype is an executable object for which the users and developers have different expectations than they have for the corresponding delivered software product.

The expectations for prototypes often include less functionality or poorer performance than the delivered product will provide.*

Prototyping has been especially valuable as a way of giving users an early response to help them understand what they really want from the proposed system. The availability of microcomputers enables the rapid construction of display screens and operational scenarios for users. With user involvement throughout the development process, there is a much greater likelihood that the system will be accepted and used. Trying to specify user interface characteristics with prototypes is much more effective than with any narrative description.

The first article, by Taylor and Standish, addresses many of the basic questions raised above: What is prototyping? Why use it? What are the basic technical approaches, and what are its limitations?

Carey and Mason introduce some prototyping tools and techniques in the second article. They include a table that classifies the case studies of prototyping according to technique, tool, methodology, environment, and advantages cited.

Scharer presents some important, but often neglected, aspects of prototyping. She addresses the question "How do you prototype?" by providing a step-by-step procedure. The management and organizational impacts of prototyping are discussed.

Gomaa and Scott report on an example of prototyping a process management and information system for a semiconductor fabrication facility. Prototyping is being used in its most familiar role; to help specify user requirements. Experiences in implementing and exercising the prototype are discussed.

The final two articles report on case studies aimed at assessing the role and effectiveness of prototyping and prototypes. The experiment conducted by Boehm, Gray, and Seewaldt compared prototyping to specifying. The results identify the advantages of each method. Alavi combines field interviews with a laboratory experiment to discover the appropriate role for prototyping in a software development organization.

The annotated bibliography contains a host of references to prototyping, organized by application area, language, tool, and objective.

---

*Revisionist use of "prototype" to rationalize past failures is not recommended, as in "My, what lousy software this is!" "Oh, you mean you didn't know that this was only a prototype!"

INITIAL THOUGHTS ON
RAPID PROTOTYPING TECHNIQUES

Tamara Taylor and Thomas A. Standish

Irvine Programming Environment Project
Computer Science Department
University of California
Irvine, California 92717

A b s t r a c t

This paper sets some context, raises issues, and provides our initial thinking on the characteristics of effective rapid prototyping techniques.

After discussing the role rapid prototyping techniques can play in the software lifecycle, the paper looks at possible technical approaches including: heavily parameterized models, reusable software, rapid prototyping languages, prefabrication techniques for system generation, and reconfigurable test harnesses.

The paper concludes that a multi-faceted approach to rapid prototyping techniques is needed if we are to address a broad range of applications successfully --- no single technical approach suffices for all potentially desirable applications.

I n t r o d u c t i o n

When we are given a new computer system to build, we may find ourselves facing one of several possible sets of circumstances:

(1) In the best of all worlds, the system requirements are precisely stated, they reflect the true needs of the users, and it is known how to implement the system using techniques in the current state-of-the-art.

However, it is not always the case that things are as optimal as they are in case (1). For instance:

(2) The requirements may be perfectly stated but it may not be known how to build a system with the required properties. For example, we may specify that we want to build a "world champion chess program." We can state the requirements with complete precision, and there can be no doubt about whether the true needs of the users have been correctly and completely captured in the requirements statement. The rules of chess and of chess tournaments are clear, complete, and unambiguous. However, there does not exist the knowledge of how to build such a system in the current state-of-the-art in computer science. Here, we have a case where the "ends" sought are perfectly well specified, but the "means" are unknown.

Yet another case occurs when the "means" are adequate but the "ends" are unclear. For instance:

(3) The user may not really know what he needs and has no idea of how his needs may change later. E.g.,"My office procedures are too ad hoc. I need an office information system that will organize my transactions and will allow me to make decisions more effectively." In this case, there may be enough computer science techniques available in the current state-of-the-art to build office automation systems, but the "ends" to be served are too vague.

So we see, in general, that the user may either not know what he wants, or may describe what he wants in such vague unhelpful terms that the system is not really specified, or he may specify what he wants exactly, but computer science does not know how to build what he wants.

In some of these cases, having a precise specification language is of no help, since the user really doesn't know what statements to make in such a language --- that is, he can't articulate his needs if he doesn't know what they are regardless of whether or not there is a precise language for stating them.

Under some of the above circumstances, what may be needed is a learning process. System implementers may attempt to build a system they think meets the true user needs on an experimental basis. Then, they may attempt to expose the user to its behavior to allow the user to experience what it can do and to learn whether he thinks it satisfies his needs. Often, the user is able to articulate what he likes and dislikes about an actual working system that gives him concrete examples of behavior to judge, and often the chance to react to actual system behavior helps him to articulate statements of his needs, especially if he was previously unable to do so.

Thus, exposure to working systems is often a helpful learning method. Looking at a system design on paper may not be as effective as direct exposure to the system behavior, since the user can often understand the latter without technical training, whereas it takes technical training to examine a design and to imagine what its behavioral implications are.

If it is the case, then, that exposure to working system behavior is a useful idea, we may wish to find ways of producing such results rapidly and cheaply. This gives birth to the concept of rapid prototyping. Rapid prototyping techniques are just techniques for constructing working models of systems rapidly and cheaply. The aim is to accelerate our learning process about whether a system design meets user needs, and to do so as cheaply and rapidly as possible.

Here we can adopt the philosophy that, "Programs are like waffles --- the first one should always be thrown away." We can attempt to find ways of exchanging the increased power and capacity of the new generation of computers to get compression and ease of expression, since the latter is at a premium and the former may soon be cheap to acquire.

Rapid prototyping may also have a role to play in helping to improve software quality progressively during the software lifecycle.

During the software lifecycle it is usual to find activities such as: (1) requirements analysis, (2) specification, (3) design, (4) coding, (5) testing and integration, and (6) maintenance and upgrade.

Because we live in an imperfect world, each of these activities usually takes place in the context of imperfect predecessors. That is, we live in a world where requirements are never likely to be complete or accurate, designs are never likely to be correct, and implementations are never likely to satisfy the requirements and reflect the design intentions perfectly.

In such a world, we must resort to special measures in order to improve quality progressively. This yields various quality assurance disciplines such as design walkthroughs, independent validation, thorough testing at pre-release time and so forth. Even maintenance can be seen as an incremental activity that progressively improves software quality by, for example, removing bugs and upgrading the system to meet user needs better.

At a deeper level, we see that there are feedback loops between the activities in the lifecycle that help us incrementally to improve understanding and quality achieved at each stage. Thus, we may only really begin to understand the true system requirements when we are exposed to the behavior of an implementation. Cyclical exposure to the behavior of the artifacts we build may be necessary to achieve understanding of the true requirements, especially for a system we are trying to construct for the first time.

In this context, when we attempt to build systems with novel capabilities, we often imperfectly understand the true user needs. There is a learning process involved in articulating the true user needs, which involves exposing the user to a working initial version of the system and seeing if he is satisfied. Often, the user discovers that the requirements he originally stated need to be revised in light of the experience gained with a working model of the system. Here again, exposure to a working version of the system accelerates the learning process in which the user discovers and articulates his true needs.

We often see circumstances in which the requirements statements for a system get incrementally improved in just this fashion. However, if the true requirements are not discovered and articulated early enough in the software lifecycle there is often considerable wasted activity downstream. Designs and implementations are sometimes built to satisfy unstable requirements statements. As the requirements shift, the designs and implementations must be redesigned and reimplemented to track the changing requirements. This can be highly wasteful of resources as modules and portions of the system must be discarded and redone, and, perhaps worst of all, it is often sociologically disastrous to the morale of the designers and implementers who are forced to discard their previous work and are made to feel that their accomplishments may have little permanent value.

It would be highly useful, therefore, to find some methodology for learning about stable, accurate requirements as early as possible in the lifecycle in order to prevent as much downstream waste as possible and to prevent poor morale among project personnel due to shifting requirements. (This is not mere speculation. We know of companies who have lost whole project teams to their competitors the third time they were told to rewrite a system to meet changed requirements.)

If a methodology for requirements validation were available that involved static analysis of requirements statements and verification that requirements were complete, accurate, not over-constraining or under-constraining, and were truly reflective of user needs, we could apply such a methodology at great savings. However, no such satisfactory static analysis seems to have emerged and to have been successful.

Another approach is to consider the possibility that incremental learning via exposure to the behavior of working prototypes is a methodology for which we already have existence proofs, and to attempt to devise rapid prototyping techniques that enable rapid, cheap construction of working system prototypes (without much attention to efficiency or polish).

There are two more circumstances in which rapid prototyping techniques are of potential value.

First, rapid prototyping has to do with quick response to changing requirements after a system has been released as well as with initial articulation of correct, complete requirements. There are instances where the requirements for a system that we are perfectly happy with may change in a matter of hours and may need to be upgraded in a matter of hours in response. For example, if we suddenly discover that an electronic countermeasures device fails to protect adequately against certain surface-to-air missiles, the viability of a nation's air defenses may depend on reprogramming these devices rapidly.

Second, in some branches of industry and government, it is not uncommon that three to five years are spent building a system that may be subsequently determined to be non-responsive to user needs, and the system requirements analysis is iterated in succeeding procurement cycles. In this case, exposure of the user to working versions of the system still happens --- only it happens with very long cycle times in the learning feedback loop. This is the second circumstance in which a speed-up of the response time is important.

Thus, rapid prototyping has to do with more rapid effective development of initial versions of the system as well as with quick response to changing requirements in released systems during the maintenance and upgrade portion of the lifecycle.

Often, if we relax the optimization constraints on a system, we can build models at less expense than the expense of building the real system. Thus, partial models of the system can yield samples of system behavior adequate to determine responsiveness to user needs at a fraction of the cost of real systems. In addition, in building a prototype, often one need not model everything. Instead, one need only model things relevant to the functionality of the system as viewed by the user.

For example, the authors once built a model of an Automated Flight Service Station Information System incorporating aircraft weather and routing data to be used for pilots for preflight briefings. The prototype did not have on-line weather data, nor did it work for 4,000 terminals spread all over the continent, nor did it have all the airways and navigational aids in it. Rather, it had weather for one twelve hour period and airway and navigational aids only for the northeast corridor. Further, it modeled only what the user would do interacting at one terminal while getting weather, winds aloft, and navaid data, and while calculating and filing a flight plan. But it did model very accurately what the user could do at such a terminal, and was built at a very small fraction of the cost of building a real system (two man-weeks as opposed to who knows what?).

The database was resident in core rather than stored in large file structures on secondary memory, and so forth. The prototype was constructed in an extensible language and was used in a live demo at the Federal Aviation Administration in Washington, D.C.

During the demo, it was evident that potential users of the system could learn about whether the prototype satisfied their true user needs --- i.e. the prototype was a fully effective means of accelerating the learning process about the true system requirements at a fraction of the cost of experimentation with real systems. We cite this to illustrate our confidence that a basis already exists for a workable technology of rapid prototyping.

In the next section, we proceed to examine some possible technical approaches to the development of a set of useful rapid prototyping techniques.

Technical Approaches

What are some good techical approaches to rapid prototyping? Are there good general purpose techniques? In addition to such general techniques, are there situations where we must have well-adapted special purpose techniques in order to build prototypes rapidly and cheaply?

Are there ways to trade processing power for ease of construction? Can we devise good rapid prototyping languages that give us a promising means for accomplishing this?

What specific method shall we use to expose the user to the behavior of the prototype, and by what methodology can such exposure result in improvement of the requirement statements? Can we get traceability of the requirements and some specific methodology for completeness of enumeration or coverage? For each prototype can we automatically produce a test plan for running the prototype to check out the requirements systematically?

Here are some possible technical approaches:

Heavily Parameterized Models

Sometimes we can have a family of systems that differ from each other by variations in parameters or tables. For example, once we had a computer graphics system that modeled a radar air-traffic control system. The CRT displayed moving aircraft radar targets together with attached data blocks on a background map of the airspace. The system incorporated laws for moving the airplane targets to simulate a real-time radar air-traffic control system.

Then one day, some people from the St. Lawrence Seaway came by and mentioned that they needed a system for controlling ship traffic on the St. Lawrence Seaway. Could we give a demonstration of a system concept for controlling ships?

Another project group was able to substitute new display tables giving maps of the seaway, new symbols for ships, and new equations for ship motion starting with our air-traffic control system. In a matter of days, a live demonstration of the Seaway control system was working. This illustrates a technique for rapid-prototyping. It was only necessary to view the air-traffic control system as an instance of a more general system for moving "widgets". Once this view was adopted, it was trivial to respecialize the system to move ships instead of airplanes.

This yields the technique of rapid prototyping by generalization and respecialization. In general, we may wish to have heavily parameterized systems that can be specialized into particular prototypes by supplying appropriate parameters, tables, and subroutine packages.

Reusable Software

One way to gain leverage in constructing working systems rapidly is to make use of other people's work. The goal is to "stand on other people's shoulders, instead of stepping on their toes." By this means, we may advance more rapidly.

We already use other people's work when we call subroutines from a general subroutine library, or when we import packages of utilities in some language that runs on our own machine. FORTRAN is a frequently used medium for the exchange of programs since FORTRAN runs on nearly every machine. We also make use of other people's work when we implement algorithms drawn from the general computer science literature. Why write your own double hashing routine when, e.g. Knuth, has done all the good thinking to get it right and to make it efficient and when all you have to do is pay the cost of translation into your own programming language?

In a more powerful sense, if we can agree on interface and linkage conventions, it may be possible to have large libraries of modules that can be conveniently assembled. This requires assembly techniques and good languages, such as Ada, in which we can do information hiding, clean interface specification, and independent compilation. Perhaps Ada will give us the incentive to have large libraries of reusable software giving us reliable pieces we can assemble rapidly.

The recent Irvine Ph.D. thesis of Jim Neighbors, Software Construction Using Components, gives an approach to building systems out of reusable software components [Neighbors 1980, UCI-ICS, TR160]. In this approach, reuse of software results only from reuse of analysis, design, and code --- not just reuse of code. Sophisticated program transformation techniques are part of the approach as are careful specification of interfacing techniques for software components.

Prefabrication and System Generation

If we have to build prototypes with special device types included, such as special types of displays, we may need to have prefabrication methods for programming the device types easily. For example, if we have a two-dimensional incrementally updatable display, we may want ways of programming the usual sort of graphical user interface package that has capabilities such as windowing, clipping, menuing, inking, latching, cut-and-paste editing, hand written character recognition, and the like. It should be possible to define tables giving the menuing choices, and to have lots of these capabilities come in prefabricated form. There should be system generators that take parameters and tables as inputs and which generate a display interface according to the paradigm for the particular device. This would hasten the job of generating a display interface and would reduce the cost.

Restricting Functionality

To expose a user to a sample of working behavior of a system, often we do not have to model everything. Instead, we need model only the functionality that the user will see.

In a previously mentioned example (that of the pilot's flight service terminal), we needed only to model a single terminal (not 4000), a small portion of the airspace (the northeast corridor, not all of North America), and a single twelve hour period of weather (not real-time, on-line weather). This enabled potential users to get the feeling for how to use the system to request weather and winds aloft data, how to file flight plans, and how to get "airline captain quality" flight logs printed, without having to model everything.

Reconfigurable Test Harnesses

In some situations, such as testing satellites out on the ground, or testing any sort of "embedded" computer system that has to respond to sensor data in real-time, and that has to control devices --- we may have to simulate the environment of operation to see how a prototype behaves. This requires consideration of the properties of the "test harness" and the simulation of events that the prototype must respond to. It is not enough to have just a rapid prototyping language. Here we need mature consideration of reconfigurable test harnesses complete with event simulators and data collection capabilities.

Different embedded systems may need to be hooked up to different real or simulated devices in such a test harness. For example, we may want to attach real or simulated clocks, gyroscopes, and accelerometers to the test harness in which the embedded system prototype is being checked out. This requires us to have a technical approach to being able to reconfigure the test harness rapidly --- dropping and adding new peripherals using some cleanly specified interfacing techniques. Simulation, data collection, and data analysis capabilities clearly need to be included in order for such a system to be adequate to its task. (We are indebted to Dr. Stewart I. Schlesinger of the Aerospace Corporation and to Dr. Larry Druffel of the Defense Advanced Research Projects Agency for the origins of these ideas).

Rapid Prototyping Languages

Rapid prototyping languages may give us a general technique we can employ if our goal is to have a well-rounded set of rapid prototyping techniques.

The following list of possible characteristics and features of rapid prototyping languages represents an initial cut at our thinking on desirable features: (We are indebted to Dr. David A. Fisher of the Western Digital Corporation for some of these ideas.)

(1) Strongly extensible: (almost all of the following suggestions and characteristics address and expand upon the meaning of the phrase "strongly extensible").

(2) Program text is data: can have program writing programs and can execute programs that have been constructed as data values.

(3) Has interpreter, and is highly interactive. Evaluator is extensible and incrementally reprogrammable. Can overload evaluator functions and can incrementally extend standard system functions for printing, selection, assignment, equality, and the like. Explicit control over the read-eval-print loop.

(4) Run-time environment accessible as data structure in the language.

(5) Extended calling forms: self-replacing calls as well as value-returning calls. Command completion (or prompting with automatic fill-in) of calling forms (e.g., hit "escape" button and calling form fills in up to next point of ambiguity or next parameter position). Postponed definition of meaning. Use of syntax macros and program transformations to supply meaning and to show how to exchange the new for the known.

(6) Remove explicit representational dependencies: When we went from assembly language to high level languages we submerged things critical to the implementation such as register allocation and mappings between names and locations and we introduced application oriented things such as arithmetic expressions. Can we do more of this?

(7) Concept minimization: remove different ways of saying the same thing. E.g., T'FIRST, Array(Index), Function(Arg), and Record.Component are all different ways of saying "the X of Y" in Ada.

(8) Boundary removal: example --- use conceptually unbounded objects such as Iota(infinity), infinite sets, or unbounded arrays. Automatically allocate and use only that finite portion needed to compute results.

(9) More abstract primitives: non-determinism, backtracking, use of predicates in program forms (e.g., Gcd(x,y)= Max{d: d|x & d|y}).

(10) More powerful ways of defining things: In definitions, we always show how to exchange the new for the known. Already in extensible and ordinary programming languages, we have numerous ways of doing this. Function definition and calling, introducing new data definitions, introducing new operator definitions, and defining new notations each illustrate this principle. If we can use new calling forms and if we can introduce new ways of exchanging them for text with assigned meaning, we can have a very powerful handle on introducing compressed forms of expression of use in rapid prototyping. E.g., we may replace Gcd(x,y)=Max{d: d|x & d|y} with appropriate text in a programming language for computing the Gcd. The capability of manipulating programs as data and of having program writing programs opens up for us the possibility of powerful paradigms of exchanging new forms of expression (using predicates, sets, and other microworlds, for instance) with known executable program text.

(11) Data Extension Features: (a) can add new type and new operations on the type, (b) can give it all privileges of any initially supplied type including, (c) extend printing routines to print new type, (d) lexical recognition of literals of the new type, (e) assignment of values of new type, (f) equality defined on new type, (g) selection notation can perform selection on components of new type, (h) information hiding of its internal representation details, (i) extended appropriate new notation for operations on the new type.

(12) Use of expressions that compute locations which can be assigned values: E.g., (if x>0 then y else z end if) := 9.

(13) Extended control structures: tasking/rendevous, real-time, exceptions, continuously evaluating expressions, monitors and traps, interrupts and priorities, back-tracking, side-tracking.

(14) More user services: diagnostics, type checking, information hiding and encapsulation, increased number of safe transformations because there is more information in the language.

(15) More Powerful Concept of Types: Can we strengthen the type system with a more powerful form of definition invocation and recognition by attaching more advanced properties to objects, such as "type T is the set of all even integers between 2 and 256 except 56." Attribute attachment and textual substitution switched on attached types. E.g., (x) is (y) ==> if (y) is a (Boolean procedure) then Y(x); elsif (y) is a (constant) then x=y; elsif (y) is a (set) then (x) in (y); end if;, and so on.

(16) Artificially Intelligent Transformations: Script based programming, transforming plans of purposeful agents into programs. Calculus of program derivation and synthesis. Use of special micro-worlds such as sets, sequences, bags, heaps, trees, geometry, relations, total orders, etc.

(17) Strong Program Transformations: program transformation catalogue and semi-automatic system for chaining transformations (as in Dennis Kibler's Ph.D. Thesis, UC Irvine).

Coupling Rapid Prototyping into the Software Lifecycle

We have already mentioned that we need to have an explicit feedback methodology for taking the results of a user's exposure to the behavior of a working prototype and creating from them an incremental update to the requirements statements. Thus, rapid prototyping must feed <u>back</u> on the requirements. But can it also feed <u>forward</u> into downstream lifecycle activities?

One possibility is to have a strategy for reworking the prototype into a polished, production-engineered version of the system.

Incremental Redevelopment

If we have identified a working prototype that provides a core of functionality certified by the user to meet his perceived requirements, we may wish to extend the core into a complete system that displays the same core functionality.

Generally, there may be two sorts of incremental activities we need to perform to transform an initial core system into a complete, production-engineered final system:

(1) extending it functionally to a complete system by adding functionality that the user didn't see, which wasn't in the prototype, and which is needed to have a full operational capability, and

(2) altering or replacing inefficient pieces of the prototype to yield required performance efficiency.

Activity (2) may involve rewriting the system in an efficient systems programming language, using the program written in a rapid prototyping language as a "design".

Activity (1) is inherently a system design activity that requires knowledge of state-of-the-art system implementation techniques drawn from parts of software engineering independent of rapid prototyping and of known effectiveness in current practice.

We need to get some experience with some techniques for incremental redevelopment of a prototype to see what sorts of additional effort are required to rework prototypes into final systems. What are the ratios of effort involved to develop the prototype versus the effort involved to transform the prototype into a final system? What sorts of incremental activities are required during reworking, and how can they be scheduled and managed?

Feeding Design

Prototypes may perhaps best be used in some settings by not attempting to rework them into final systems, but rather by having them serve as an additional source of precise behavioral specification used as an input to a system design. In effect, they may serve as programs written in a <u>program design language</u> that are core designs for the larger system design. In this case, we do not care so much about running efficiency as we do about clarity of conceptual structure and extensibility to complete system designs.

Are there any incremental techniques for expanding a core design written in a program design language into a complete system design? Can the features of a good rapid prototyping language serve double duty by providing an attractive basis for program design languages as well? Could programs written in a rapid prototyping language be used directly as core designs for downstream design completion? Could we devise a new "inside-out" software design methodology based on such an approach?

Coupling with Requirements Review and Testing

It would be useful to have some systematic method for conducting a review of the system requirements that is closely coordinated with systematic examination of the behavior of a prototype. The reason this is important is that we are trying to use prototypes to check out whether the requirements are adequate, and we need some systematic way of performing this task, especially in cases where the requirements are lengthy or complex.

To get samples of the behavior of the prototype, we need to conduct a series of tests. Then we need to examine the behavior of the prototype revealed by the tests to see if that behavior meets the items of the requirements that it is supposed to satisfy.

Thus, we have a case where testing (which is used to extract behaviors) needs to be coupled with requirements review (which checks whether the elicited behaviors satisfy the relevant pieces of the requirements). Systematic traceability of the requirements to the tests that elicit the behaviors that are supposed to satisfy them seems to be called for.

While we have no particular ideas or approach to offer on this subject, we want to flag the issue and to suggest that it is important that it be addressed in the future in connection with rapid prototyping methodologies.

Limits of Prototyping

Up until this point in the discussion we have extolled prototyping, but what are the limits on what we should expect?

What do we not easily learn from prototypes? Here are some possibilties (kindly contributed by R. Kling):

(1) What it is like to live with the system for a while.

(2) How easy a real system will be to alter.

(3) How a system will behave when it is pushed to the extremes of performance (e.g., heavily loaded, various buffers nearly exhausted, displays saturated with data, etc.).

(4) How a system will interact with other elements in the software environment or related systems with which it should easily share data.

In general, there can be many different prototypes of a given target system. Each is like a selective shadow highlighting some features and losing details of others. To the extent that rapidly developed prototypes systematically distort since (a) they're designed to be plastic, (b) they're designed to be small, and (c) their interactions with other software will differ (by being more flexible and less easily interfaced, in some cases) rapid prototyping can lead users to misperceive what the target system may actually be like.

Thus, rapid prototyping may well be like democracy --- flawed, but far better than the available alternatives.

Conclusions

It is reasonable to conclude from our discussion that no single technical approach to rapid prototyping techniques can serve as a panacea --- universally applicable in all settings and fully sufficient to make prototyping cheap and rapid.

Rather, in some settings, such as the "test harness" setting for real-time, embedded systems, and the advanced two-dimensional, incrementally updatable display setting, we may need to take advantage of specially adapted rapid prototyping techniques, such as strongly parameterized system generation, reusable software, or easily reconfigurable test harnesses coupled with event simulators and data collectors.

Thus, the existence of rapid prototyping languages alone as a general purpose technique won't provide rapid, cheap construction of prototypes in all settings, even though they may considerably enhance prototyping in many general settings and even though they may feed downstream software lifecycle activities effectively.

This points to the conclusion that we must have a multi-faceted technical approach to rapid prototyping if we are to address a broad range of prototyping applications successfully.

This work was supported by the Defense Advanced Research Projects Agency of the United States Department of Defense under contract MDA-903-82-C-0039 to the Irvine Programming Environment Project. The views and conclusions contained herein are those of the authors and should not be interpreted as necessarily representing the official policies, either expressed or implied, of the Defense Advanced Research Projects Agency or the United States Government.

*Ada is a trademark of the United States Department of Defense (OUSDRE-AJPO).

INFORMATION SYSTEM PROTOTYPING: TECHNIQUES, TOOLS, AND METHODOLOGIES*

T.T. CAREY AND R.E.A. MASON

University of Guelph

ABSTRACT

"Prototyping" is frequently cited as an effective alternative technique to traditional approaches for the development of systems. This paper reviews recent literature on the subject and categorizes prototyping techniques that appear to be widely used. A large number of tools have been used for prototyping and they are discussed in relation to the technique employed and other factors in the programming environment. Issues of programming methodology raised by prototypes are also discussed.

RÉSUMÉ

Pour la création de systèmes d'information, on choisit souvent, plutôt que les approches traditionnelles, la méthode efficace des prototypes. Dans le présent rapport, nous examinons des documents récents traitant du sujet et rangeons en catégories les différents procédés de mise au point de prototypes les plus souvent utilisés. Un grand nombre d'instruments ont servi à l'élaboration de prototypes; ceux-ci seront étudiés par rapport aux techniques employées et aux autres facteurs relatifs à la programmation. Les points soulevés par les prototypes concernant la méthodologie de la programmation seront aussi analysés.

1. INTRODUCTION

Although the concept of the prototype is widely referenced in the recent computing literature, there appears to be little if any agreement on what a "prototype" is. In broad terms, the prototype attempts to present the user of a system with a relatively realistic view of the system as it will eventually appear. Users are thus able to relate what they see in the form of prototype directly to their requirements.

The use of prototypes appears to have advantages in user communication but raises other issues in system development. Different, non-traditional development tools may be required; the initial cost for the requirements phase of the development cycle may be greater; and there is the possibility of loss of distinction between phases and the development process. Despite such issues, there appears to be a growing consensus that prototypes form an effective component of an application development methodology.

In this paper we present a survey of the literature of application prototyping, and an analysis of the advantages of prototyping. Following distinctions made by Freeman[1], we discuss different categories of prototype techniques, the tools used to support these formal techniques, and some of the management or methodological issues they raise. An appendix summarizes these three parameters in prototype case studies from the literature. We restrict attention throughout to information systems as traditionally understood and as described by Wasserman[2]. Prototyping of systems software[3] is not considered in this paper.

1.1 Prototypes and system requirements
It is well understood that undetected errors that occur in the require-

*Received 9 July 1981; revised 21 December 1982

ments phase of system development are the most costly to repair in later stages. User approval of a requirement specification is mandated by most data processing managements as a means of correcting the requirement specification. Depending upon the application environment and the development methodology, the user may have access to a variety of developer-produced materials before certifying that his requirements have been correctly defined. Software blueprints[5] and SREM[6] are examples of specialized languages as a part of the users/developer interface for real time applications. These requirements languages presuppose sophisticated user representatives operating within the development methodology.

In conventional data processing environments, user participants in the development phase are normally middlé managers, and reliance upon such specialized skills is not appropriate. (Zahniser[4] and Mason[7] describe other differences between environments that affect the user / developer interface.) Requirements documentation presented to users can be broadly classified as one of the following three forms:

1. Textual lists of requirements that the proposed system must fulfil. Text description has been the traditional tool. Unfortunately, such descriptions, often lengthy and boring, are psychologically very distant from what the users will eventually receive. Even after significant effort on the part of the user to understand such documents, critical features of the system may not receive appropriate notice. For interactive systems textual description is clearly not an appropriate requirements specification technique.

2. An interpretive model of the proposed system. SADT[8] and USE[9] are examples of interpretive models. These techniques employ top down decomposition to manage relatively complex systems. They maintain distinction between functional specification and design and permit data analysis to be treated separately. Other features of interpretive models are discussed by Scharer[10] and finer classification appears in Peters and Tripp[11]. Again, however, on-line interaction is difficult to communicate with these models.

3. A working model, or prototype, of the proposed system. Prototypes, on the other hand attempt to present the user with a realistic view of the system as it will eventually appear. With prototypes a distinct attempt is made to produce a "specification" which users can directly experience. Communication with users, particularly the non-specialist middle management user, is a major motivator behind the recent interest in prototypes.

1.2 Prototyping as a folk fact: skimming the literature

David Harel's light-hearted article on folk theorems in computing[12] proposes as criteria for a folk theorem that it demonstrate popularity, anonymous authorship, and age. If we examine the assertion "Prototyping reduces specifications error," we can claim that it has the appropriate "folkishness," that is, it has been cited extensively in the literature[13-31]; in each case its origins are attributed either to folklore or the author's discovery,* and DP professionals will frequently state that they were doing it that way in 1401 Autocoder (relatively aged).

Furthermore, the multitude of prototype forms and labels attest to a genuine article of folklore. The assertion never having been proved in a rigorous sense, we are left with a folk fact rather than a folk theorem. Attempts to produce experimental evidence supporting the assertion,

*The lack of any cross-references to other prototype papers may be instructive as to the reading habits of both industry professionals and academics.

49

rather than simply testimonials, are plagued with the well-known difficulties of creating a long-term and controlled experiment in an industrial management setting of sufficient size to be statistically significant.

The general objectives within which prototypes are referenced in the professional literature are varied. Brittan[13] justifies prototypes in large part by bad example: "look what happens if we don't use them." There is consequently less interest for tools and techniques and more for a change in the attitudes behind the traditional development cycle and its limitations on user participation. Similarly, Berrisford and Wetherbe[14] and McLean[26] are concerned primarily with reducing the "adversarial" nature of a conventional requirements sign-off.

Another direction from which prototypes have been approached involves a specific tool that has made prototypes seem more cost-effective to the developers. Thus Davis and Tweedy[16], Kebel and Marling[20], Bishop and Gore[15], and Goodman[19] all mention prototypes as side effects of program development systems. Each of these systems encompasses a variety of automated techniques, which, as a byproduct, facilitate creation of working views of the system for user comment. Another class of tools frequently referenced is the new set of higher-level languages (sometimes labelled fourth-[29] or even fifth[32]-generation languages). These permit shorter development times for various functional applications. Their promoters have cited quick prototyping as one of the advantages of their use. This is particularly true of APL; see, for example, Jones and Kirk[24], and Martin[27].

Some considerations of prototypes are not directed at the requirements phase of the life cycle. Thus Jones[23] examines prototypes within a careful consideration of techniques for design defect removal. Rosenburger[30] is concerned with an early return on investment, so that a prototype representing 80% of functional capability, but only 20% of the development cost is recommended for its quick payoff to the users. (Some misgivings about this approach from a methodology viewpoint are mentioned in section 5). A measurement of requirements uncertainty is proved by Naumann, Davis, and McKeen[33], suggesting the circumstances under which the cost of a prototype can be most easily justified. The relationships among their situational variables and the point at which a prototype is recommended are recognized as dependent on local management policies and the availability of tools.

Our focus in this paper is on improving the final information system product through use of prototypes to illuminate more clearly the user's real needs. Thus we have not pursued the benefits of improved relationships between developers and users (it can be argued that prototypes merely enforce a communication pattern that should also exist in the traditional development cycle).

In addition, no attempt is made here to detail the relationship between improved product quality and eventual system cost. We are satisfied with the usual consensus that the earlier defects are removed from a product, the lower will be its eventual cost. The somewhat higher costs of development using prototypes are generally agreed by all the literature sources to be more than covered by either lower maintenance costs or better utility for the user.

2. PROTOTYPES AND SYSTEM REQUIREMENTS

From the point of view of enhancing system quality through better requirements specification, the advantages cited for prototypes fall into three categories: improved functional requirements, improved interaction requirements, and easier evolution of requirements. This list is adapted from the thorough description of decision support prototypes by Keen and Gambino[21].

2.1 Improved functional requirements

The prototype system reflects the developer's interpretation of the user's needs, captured previously in either formal or informal communication. When this communication has been distorted by various preconceptions or general unfamiliarity with the environment on either side, the prototype will frequently reveal how the misunderstanding will affect the product. This is particularly necessary for users with limited exposure to information system technology. The degree to which the prototype uncovers errors in functional logic, in addition to the range and type of function to be performed, is dependent on the particular technique employed, as considered in section 4.

2.2 Improved interaction requirements

The interaction requirements for a system are not always directly addressed in requirements specification. This is especially true if the clients are not the (direct) users. While the system may contain the correct functions, the design of the user interface may either discourage its use or introduce errors in usage.

A useful evaluative model for the user interface is Foley's[34] top-down interface design model. This model partitions the interface structure into successively more specific components: conceptual level, semantic level, syntactic level, and lexical level.

On the conceptual level one is concerned with the basic set of concepts underlying the user's view of the application. An example of a flaw in requirements at this level occurred in our development of a small application in which the requirements document specified certain files and certain tables of code interpretation. When the users began to interact with a preliminary version of the system, it became clear that the developer had conceptually separated the files and the tables, but the users did not distinguish them. They were surprised when the tables failed to function as files.

The semantic level deals with the information content that must pass between the user and the (machine) system, without specific regard for its format. When working through a demonstration, the user frequently notes that information is being requested that is not applicable to a given transaction type. Another common flaw at this level is a lack of information from the system for help or error recovery. While a prototype need not be expected to embody all the assistance features of the final program product, the developer can note where more information is likely to be needed.

The syntactic level deals with the structure and format of the interactions, including command syntax and screen layouts. Typical corrections to be incorporated include decreased space for titles, movement of total lines, syntax allowing for multiple report requests, etc.[35] Such alterations may often be made immediately by the analyst and rerun for the user.

At the lexical level one must define the actual command words, menu items, and display symbols. This defining can be related to the incorporation of the user's natural language, for example, renaming a command "insert" from "add," and the removal of the developer's natural language. In a detailed documentation of a prototype case Gomaa and Scott[18] cite examples of the latter problem: removal of expressions like "queue" and

"I6," which were foreign to the users. They give further examples reflecting the other levels.

Foley's model is designed to structure the development of the interface. We have found it a useful framework for the developer to analyse user reactions to a prototype. This is important at the conceptual and semantic levels, where the developer must be willing to interpret user difficulties as requiring re-examination of the application, rather than "educating" the user. (i.e., convert to the developer's conceptual model).

All the changes referenced above from our own studies[35] came after a requirements sign-off, which included printed copies of screen displays. There appears to be no adequate substitute in interactive applications for some kind of prototype to convey the nature of the proposed system. The level of detail in the prototype is partly a function of methodology, discussed in section 6.

2.3 Easier evolution of requirements

The evolution of requirements is of most concern in environments like decision support systems, where the user needs to employ the system in open-ended ways and no pattern of use can be accurately predicted until some experience is available. The case for this development pattern is well documented in standard texts like Keen and Scott Morton[36]. This evolutionary need can be met by successive product releases, but Keen and Gambino[21] note that a prototype methodology implies that the initial version is a program but not a program product in Brook's[37] sense. Accordingly, the initial development time is reduced, and the developer is specifically committed to a large degree of interaction while "version 0" is undergoing test. This testing can be confined to the hardier users. Users known to be reluctant to use the final version need not be exposed to version 0, which would likely confirm some of their fears about the developers not undestanding their application area.

In the summary chart of appendix A we have indicated which of these categories of advantage the authors have explicitly cited. As noted previously, the additional advantage of better relationships between users and developers was also frequently listed. The relationship of these categories to the choice of prototyping technique will be examined in the next section.

3. A CLASSIFICATION OF PROTOTYPING TECHNIQUES

Our literature survey and discussion with system developers* have led us to identify three categories of prototype techniques: scenarios or simulations, demonstration systems, and "version 0"[21] limited working systems.

A *scenario* or simulation presents to the user an example of actual system usage but only simulates the processing of user data or queries. That is, the eventual application logic is not developed, but a script is created that drives the screen for certain fixed entries, as if the system existed. Depending upon the tool used to build the scenario, some of the development work on the scenario may be applied to the production system, as seen in the next section.

A *demonstration* system processes a limited range of user queries or data, using limited files. Frequently, some portion of the system, especially screen displays, is carried over to the production system; these portions are commonly linked by a skeletal processing code, which will be replaced in the final product. Alternatively, the entire demonstration can be coded as a throw-away, as described by Gomaa and Scott[18]. In any case, the user chooses queries and data from a specified type or range.

*In particular, some of our terminology here is due to Art Benjamin of On-Line People.

A *version 0* prototype is a working release of the system intended to receive use under conditions approaching the production environment. While it is specifically designed as a test release, it is usually expected that the final product will build on version 0 by completing the implementation of functions, adding requested alterations, and generating the required documentation, etc. to convert the program into a product.

The three technique categories are clearly points of reference on a spectrum, but the distinction seems to be worth making. It clarifies the intent of a prototype and its expected benefits. A scenario will be expected to address interaction requirements and some functional requirements, although it cannot shed much light on application logic. A demonstration is likely to provide more insight into processing logic but may not be as useful for evolutionary requirements, because the user's exposure is of necessity limited. A related technique, incremental deliveries, has been described by Gilb[43], who distinguishes it from use of demonstrations and version 0.

The differing kinds of return expected from the investment in a prototype also suggest differing tool use. Tools for prototyping are described in the next section.

4. Tools Used for Prototyping

The use of prototypes has been advocated as cost-effective even in the absence of any special tools to support the various techniques[13,22]. But a number of tools do exist to support version 0, demonstrations, and scenario prototypes – some indirectly as by-products of higher-level languages or programming support environments and at least one directly as a requirements tool.

The time and cost of an initial version 0 of an application can be substantially reduced using higher level languages (also known as non-procedural, fourth-generation, even fifth-generation languages). These support applications data aggregates as primitive data types with appropriate built-in operations. When there is a good fit between these predefined structures and the application structure, these tools reduce the amount of programming required to develop an application over a traditional procedural language such as COBOL or PL/1. The most frequently referenced tool in the authors' literature search was APL[21,26,27]. Although this choice may be due more to the nature of the APL community than any other factors, ADF[19] and various other languages[27,29] are also proposed for a first working version.

The distinction between a version 0 prototype and a demonstration is as much the result of the environment in which it receives use as it is the functions provided. Thus, one would expect that demonstration prototypes could be conveniently constructed with tools such as ADF[19] and APL[19]. On the other hand, Berrisford and Wetherbe[14] found it productive to use a relational data base system to implement demonstrations, and several sources construct demonstrations essentially as by-products of programming support environments. This can provide facilities for macro commands (which are replaced once a design is verified) and program stubs to be later enhanced[17] or application generators based on traditional procedural languages[15,20].

The construction of a scenario prototype, since it provides less functionality than a demonstration prototype, must cost less than a demonstration if it is to be worthwhile. Using tools similar to those above, one can implement simple case logic to provide the desired actions when the values in the script are entered (and to ignore or reject all others).

Alternatively, one can use a special-purpose tool, which accepts example actions and automatically constructs the appropriate case logic.

In the chart of appendix A, we have attempted to summarize the literature cited, identifying in each case the prototyping technique employed and the major tool used. Appendix A provides additional comments to amplify the nature of the application development environment or application situation described in the citation.

One is struck in this summary by the wide variety of tools that have been used for prototyping. In their review of prototyping Naumann and Jenkins[44] also note the great variety of definitions of prototyping and the variety of tools employed in different situations. We believe this reflects the use of available tools in the absence of widely available integrated tool sets appropriate to a prototype-oriented development methodology. A tool that would support the evolution of a system prototype from specification through version 0 in an integrated manner is required. The Chevron Program Development System apparently provides such a facility through an "example editor"[16]. ACT/1 (25) allows a developer to script a screen flow by entering examples as a user would and then indicating the next screen to be displayed. In both cases it is envisioned that the screen designs can be transferred into the final product without recoding.

ACT/1 is one of small number of development tools specifically intended to apply an integrated prototype-oriented methodology to the development of information systems. Examples of the use of this and other tools were described in a workshop on rapid prototyping[45]. According to discussion at this workshop, there appears to be a trend towards development of integrated sets of tools which make use of prototypes. Such integrated tools raise many issues in the area of development methodology, some of which are discussed below.

5. METHODOLOGY ISSUES RAISED BY PROTOTYPING

The traditional system life cycle – requirements, design, implementation, test, integration, maintenance – reflects recognition of the need for an organized approach to system development with attendant milestones and approvals. Prototypes can be

1. incorporated into this cycle at the requirements phase (all techniques), or
2. used to bridge or merge the first two or three phases using demonstrations or version 0 in an iterative development, or
3. used to avoid the cycle altogether, when employed by end-users to create their own systems with little or no involvement from professional systems developers (version 0).

The issues raised by these choices are not trivial and include using a prototype as "throwaway" code or building upon it; preserving Brook's distinction between a program and a system product; the use of a prototype in documentation and maintenance; and the roles of development staff and users. In this section we discuss some of these issues.

5.1 Use of prototype materials in the product

Many proposals for prototypes assume that the traditional life cycle will be followed, so that at some point the users will agree to the requirements as specified by the prototype and supporting documentation. A design phase follows, which assumes the design of the prototype to be a black box that need not be examined. Some tools permit the screen display components to be transferred to later phases without recoding while the remainder of the program is replaced.

It is possible to think of the prototype in this instance as a part of the system documentation rather than an accessory to a specification document. In that case, one must consider maintenance of the system to nclude versions of the prototype, and the tools involved must support explicit version control. The cost involved in a version 0 prototype will sometimes make it unsuitable for this approach.

5.2 Iterative development

Other proposals for prototypes assert that the separation in time of requirements specification, design and implementation is either unnecessary or counter-productive, at least for certain application types. Peters[28,38] would encourage "hybrid" life cycles that merge specification and design. It is unlikely that a scenario prototype would be used alone here, since the extra cost of a demo or version 0 is treated as design expense.

Others feel just as strongly that their application environments require that the prototype be treated as part of the requirements process only (for example Gomaa and Scott[18]). We lack a sufficiently full understanding of those application characteristics that help determine when the phases need to be kept separate.

An important corollary issue is the necessity of allowing life-cycle time for converting a program into a system product. Keen and Gambino[21] suggest that the proportion of time required for these activities may be more or less independent of the implementation tool used. The checklist provided by Waters[39] is helpful in this regard; he distinguishes the specification of an application subsystem from the other subsystems required in a system product (recovery, control, monitor, etc.).

5.3 Prototypes and end users

Some authors suggest that an iterative development cycle as outlined above is well suited to end-users developing their own application systems. The existence of tools of sufficient simplicity and ease of change provides the user the opportunity to implement a version 0 prototype and evolve it to suit the requirements.

Like iterative development, we need a better grasp on the situations in which this is an appropriate choice, as well as a readiness to welcome such user involvement. The issue of fulfilling the requirements for a system product occurs here also. Suitable roles for professional system staff are evolving to address this need, in particular the concept of an Information Centre that helps users choose either a traditional development methodology or one of those outlined above. Martin[40] provides a helpful summary in this area.

It should be noted that the word prototype is also occasionally used for a test version demonstrated to users long after requirements sign-off, as part of system test. This seems to represent either an implicit iterative development cycle or a failure to include interaction requirements in the original specification.

Conclusion

We have examined some of the published accounts of prototypes as employed in information system development, and tried to categorize the techniques, tools and methodologies employed. The particular combination to be used in a given situation is determined by the application structure, the skills of the developers and users, and the tools and management practices available. Any prototype should be developed with a clear idea of the kinds of advantages it is hoped to achieve.

The current emphasis on prototyping represents, we believe, a return to basics in systems development, particularly in the domain of business information systems. Interest in prototyping reflects a recognition that traditional approaches to the management and conduct of systems development are not adequate. Prototyping, however loosely defined, reflects a renewed effort to meet user requirements for ever more complex system function in a more timely and productive manner.

It is our feeling that the prototyping approaches to system development should be expected to differ in different application domains. In the domain of business information systems there is reason to be optimistic that integrated tools that will have this desired effect are available and evolving.

REFERENCES

(1) P. Freeman, "A perspective on requirements analysis and specification," in *Tutorial on Software Design Techniques*, P. Freeman, and A.I. Wasserman, eds. IEEE Press, 1979, 86–96

(2) A.I. Wasserman, Information system design methodology, J. of ASIS 3/(1), 1980

(3) M.V. Zelkowitz, A case study in rapid prototyping," Soft. Pr. and Exp. 10, 1980

(4) R.A. Zahniser, "How to navigate the user fog," Computerworld, March 16, 1981

(5) P.H. Baucom, "Software blueprints," Proc. ACM Conference, 1978, 385–92

(6) M. Alford, "A requirements engineering methodology for real-time processing requirements," IEEE Trans. Software Eng., January 1977

(7) R.E.A. Mason, "A model of programming," Technical Report 80-001, Department of Computing and Information Science, University of Guelph, 1980

(8) M.E. Dickover, L.L. McGowan, and D.T. Ross, "Software design using SADT," Proc. 1977 ACM National Conference

(9) A.I. Wasserman, and S.K. Stinson, "A specification method for interactive information systems," in *Tutorial on Software Design in Techniques*, P. Freeman and A.I. Wasserman, eds. 1980, 187–96

(10) L. Scharer, "Pinpointing requirements," Datamation, April 1981

(11) L.J. Peters and L.L. Tripp, "A model of software engineering," Proc. ICSE 3, 1978

(12) D. Harel, "On folk theorems," CACM 23(7), 1980

(13) L. Bally, J.N.G. Brittan, and K. Wagner, "A prototype approach to information system design and development," Information Management 1, 1977

(14) T. Berrisford and J. Wetherbe, "Heuristic development: a redesign of systems design," MIS, March 1979, 11–19

(15) T.C. Bishop, and E.J. Grace, "CS magic improved program generation with interactive COBOL," Data Base 11(3), 1980, 56–63

(16) D.P. Davis and K.F. Tweedy, Chevron's integrated and automated approach to applications development," Data Base 11(3), 1980, 10–27

(17) Anon., Programming work-stations," EDP Analyzer 17(10), 1979

(18) H. Gomaa and D.B. Scott, "Prototyping as a tool in the specifications of user requirements," ICSE 5, 1981

(19) A.M. Goodman, IMSADF – a tool for programmer productivity," Data Base 11(3), 1980, 106–13

(20) K.N. Kebel and S.C.R. Morling, "Interactive program generator for IMS application," Data Base 11(3), 1980, 35–9

(21) P. Keen and T.J. Gambino, "The mythical man-month revisited," Proc. APL 1980, 630–48

(22) E. Keppel and D. Kropp, "Interactive programming by end-users," Proc. APL 77

(23) T.C. Jones, "A survey of programming design and specification techniques," Proc. of Conf. on Reliable Software, 1979, 91–103

(24) W.T. Jones and S.A. Kirk, "APL as a software design specification language," Computer Journal 23(3), 1980, 230–

(25) R.E.A. Mason and T. Carey, "Productivity experiences with a scenario tool," Proc. Compcon Fall 81, 1981

(26) E.R. McLean, "The use of APL for production applications," Proc. APL 1976, 303–7

(27) B.R. Martin, "Improving productivity with APL," Proc. Share 53, 1979

(28) L. Peters, "Relating software requirements and design," Proc. NCC 1980

(29) N.S. Read and D.L. Harmon, "Assuring MIS success," Datamation 27(2), 1981

(30) R. Rosenberger, "The information center – a productivity tool for end-user support," Proc. Share 53, 1979

(31) A.I. Wasserman, "User software engineering and the design of interactive systems," Proc. ICSE 5, 1981

(32) J.M. Grochoci, "Application generators anticipate requirements," Computerworld 15: SR/30-2, March 30, 1981

(33) J.D. Naumann, C.B. Davis, and J.D. McKeen, "Determining information requirements," J. of Systems and Software 1(4), 1980

(34) W. Myers, "Computer graphics: the human interface," Computer 13(6), 1980

(35) R.E.A. Mason, "Preliminary experiments with a requirements definition aid," Technical Report 80-0002, Department of Computing and Information Science, University of Guelph, 1980

(36) P. Keen and M. Scott Morton, *Decision Support Systems*. Addison-Wesley Publ. Co., 1978

(37) F.P. Brooks, *The Mythical Man Month*. Addison-Wesley Publ. Co., 1975

(38) L.J. Peters, "Relating software requirements and design," Proc. Software Quality and Assurance Workshop, 1978

(39) J. Waters, "Towards comprehensive specifications," Computer Journal 22(3)

(40) J. Martin, "Application development without programmers," Savant Institute, 1981

(41) J.N.G. Brittan, "Design for a changing environment," Computer Journal 23(1), 13–19

(42) E.R. McLean, "End users as application developers," MIS, December 1979, 37–46

(43) T. Gilb, "Evolutionary development," Software Engineering Notes, April 1981

(44) J.D. Naumann and A.A. Jenkins, "Prototyping: the new paradigm for systems development," MIS Quarterly, September 1982, 29

(45) W.V. Zilkowitz, ed., "Workshop notes, ACM SIGSOFT," Workshop on Rapid Prototyping, Columbia, Maryland, 19–21 April 1982

APPENDIX: SUMMARY OF CASE STUDIES

To illustrate the mix of techniques, tools, and methodologies, we summarize in the following table the characteristics of prototype case studies from the professional literature. The comments, especially under environment and advantages cited, represent our interpretations of the original experience.

Technique	Tool	Methodology	Environment	Advantages Cited	Reference
Scenario	Chevron PDS PL/1 base)	Simulation of screen operation post requirements	Information systems	Interaction	(16)
Scenario	ACT/1 Architect tool	Prototype in requirements phase	Information systems	Functional interaction	(25, 35)
Scenario and demonstration	APL	Advocates writing specifications in APL to be interpreted for verification	(Proposal only)	Functional	(24)
Scenario, demonstration, version 0	Dialogue design interpreter linked to DBMS	Prototype in requirements phase	Information systems research	Functional interaction	(31)
Demonstration	Interactive program (PL/1 base)	High level application generator, life cycle stage not stated	Information systems	Interaction functional	(20)
Demonstration ("mockup")	CSMAGIC (Cobol base)	Cobol generator, life-cycle stage not stated	Information systems	Functional interaction	(15)
Demonstration	Various	Iterative development ("hybrid" life-cycles merge specification and design)	Information systems		(28)
Demonstration	ADF	Prototype in requirements phase	Data base transactions	Evolutionary	(19)
Probably demonstration	Command language on programmer's workstation	Iterative development cycle: "throw away code"	Information systems	Functional	(17)
Demonstration	APL	Prototype in requirements phase	Production management	Functional interaction	(18)
Demonstration (occasional inadvertent version 0)	Relational DBMS	Iterative development ("heuristic development")	MIS	Functional	(11)
Version 0	Various	Iterative development (80% version)	Information systems	Early ROI. Use version 0 until version 1 produced	(30)
Version 0	APL	APL in design phase; encourage	Information systems	Functional interaction	(27)
Version 0	Local extension of APL	User programming	Data processing interactive forms	Functional	(22)
Version 0	APL	Iterative development cycle	Decision support	Functional interactive evolutionary	(21)
Version	APL or other high level language	Iterative development ("cooperative development") user programming	Decision support	Evolutionary	(26, 42)
Version 0	FOCUS	Iterative development cycle	MIS	Functional	(29)
Version 0	Various	Iterative development cycle, scaled-down production versions	Data processing (incl. batch)	Functional	(13, 41)
Version 0	Various	Prototypes for design defect removal (after specification)	Various	Functional interaction	(23)

The Prototyping Alternative

Laura Scharer

*The availability of powerful programming tools makes prototyping
a practical alternative to conventional methodologies
for the development of user-oriented business systems.*

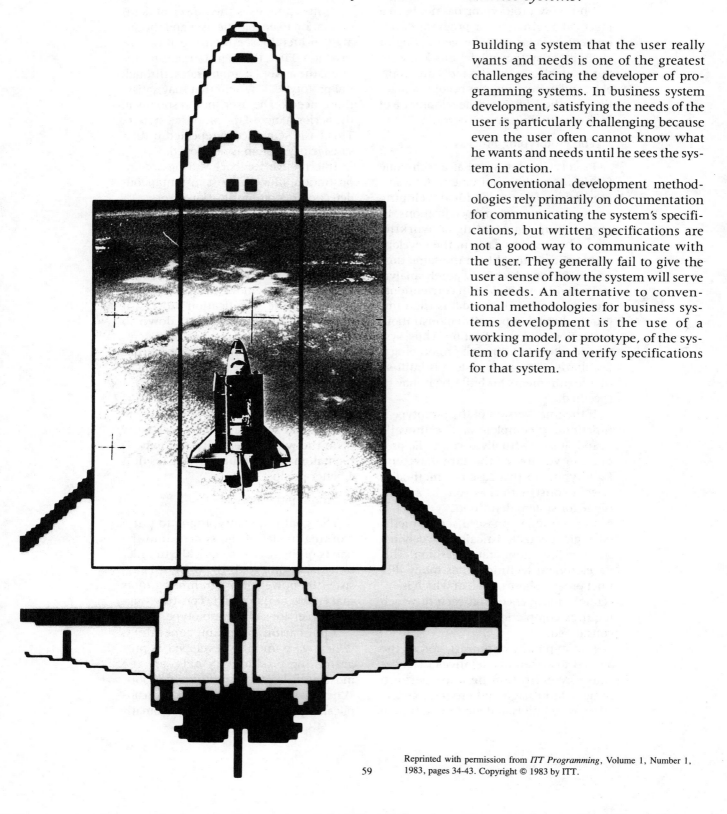

Building a system that the user really wants and needs is one of the greatest challenges facing the developer of programming systems. In business system development, satisfying the needs of the user is particularly challenging because even the user often cannot know what he wants and needs until he sees the system in action.

Conventional development methodologies rely primarily on documentation for communicating the system's specifications, but written specifications are not a good way to communicate with the user. They generally fail to give the user a sense of how the system will serve his needs. An alternative to conventional methodologies for business systems development is the use of a working model, or prototype, of the system to clarify and verify specifications for that system.

Reprinted with permission from *ITT Programming*, Volume 1, Number 1, 1983, pages 34-43. Copyright © 1983 by ITT.

The concept of prototyping is not new. In engineering, prototyping has long been a standard practice for developing and testing new products and systems. An engineering prototype can be either a scaled-down model or a full-sized version. A spectacular example of full-sized prototyping is the NASA space shuttle.

Until now, prototyping has not been a practical alternative for program development because tools for generating or changing a system model quickly were not available. Today, the tools are available, and prototyping has become a practical method for rapid development of high-quality business systems.

The Prototyping Process

Prototyping can serve as a technique for clarifying the requirements for a single system feature or for developing comprehensive system specifications. In prototyping, generating a working model begins very early in the development process, roughly in the same time period during which only purely analytical activities take place in conventional methodologies. The model is then improved through repeated demonstration, evaluation, and modification. Thus, system development through prototyping is peculiarly circular: a system is built so that requirements for building it may be specified.

If the final version of the prototype is functionally complete and technically sound, it may actually become the production version of the target system. Prototyping in this case is a method of system construction as well as a technique for system definition.

Conventional phase-discrete methodologies characteristically proceed in a straight-line, noniterative fashion. This development technique has many distinct project phases, each of which is executed in sequence, and each of which requires completion before the next is considered.

Prototyping, in contrast, forces the analyst to widen his iterative circle, because by definition he must perform some detail design and program generation as he builds and modifies a system model. In fact, prototyping opens up the whole world of design and construction to the analyst, allowing him the freedom to backtrack at any time. Knowledge that is not normally available until "later" phases can be applied to "earlier" phases.

Power of Demonstration

Prototyping uses the power of demonstration to enable the user and the analyst to literally see their specifications in action. First, the user states his needs. Then, the analyst demonstrates, through the prototype, a system that may satisfy those needs. The user then responds to the performance of the proposed system. This basic sequence is repeated until a satisfactory system is developed.

Interpretive feedback during a demonstration allows almost instantaneous detection of communication errors.

The demonstration is an active, hands-on process that involves the user in designing the system much more effectively than does reading abstract descriptions of the system. Because demonstration removes abstract descriptions from the specification process, it brings the user and analyst down to earth. The user is not responsible for creating a system; he only has to recognize what he wants or does not want when he sees it.

In prototyping, change and uncertainty are to be expected. Receptivity to change and acceptance of uncertainty open the way to creativity and experimentation, and presumably the result is a better product.

Prototyping Tools

The goal of prototyping is to put a working model of the system into the hands of the user very quickly. In order to achieve this goal, the analyst is assisted by powerful programming tools that enable him to rapidly construct successive versions of the prototype.

Application program generators, which were initially developed as programming productivity aids, are the most useful class of prototyping tools. When given the characteristics of an application, program generators automatically complete the detail work of system construction. They vary in their power and functional components, but their essential foundations are a strong data dictionary and a database management capability (Figure 1).

Prototyping tools must be easy to use and the programs that they generate must be real, working modules. Other functional criteria are quick program generation, nonprocedural specification, alterability, integrated functions, and error-free code.

The power of the tools determines how broadly prototyping can be applied. At the low end of the scale, individual components such as reports or screens can be refined using stand-alone report generators or screen-painting tools. At the upper end of the scale, fully integrated working systems can be generated.

If program generators are not available, proprietary application packages for common business functions such as order processing, receivables, and inventory can provide an excellent starting point for prototyping, often at suprisingly low cost. Application packages meet many prototyping criteria: they can be readied for installation quickly, they are normally parameter-driven and thereby changeable, and they form an integrated whole. The final version of a prototyped application package is a natural candidate for production.

Preliminary Fact-Finding

In prototyping, a small amount of analysis, known as preliminary fact-finding, must occur before the prototype can be built and refinement iterations can begin. This preliminary fact-finding replaces the first four steps in conventional methodologies (Figure 2).

The goal of preliminary fact-finding, which is the only purely investigative phase in prototyping, is to learn enough about the problem and its environment to determine whether the project should be carried out at all, and if so, to devise a practical approach to a solution. The specific tasks and deliverables associated with preliminary fact-finding are shown in Figure 3a.

A great deal of attention should be paid to the problem statement and the scope statement. They establish important project boundaries and require the understanding and approval of the users. A cost/benefit assessment is usually necessary to obtain management backing for the project.

By blending the first four tasks of conventional development, the formal reporting requirements are minimized. Also, preliminary fact-finding provides the first instance of the look-ahead feature of prototyping. The review of existing systems and the functional specifications occur before management is expected to judge project feasibility. Finally, the user is not asked to freeze the functional specifications during this phase. They can be revised or changed even after prototype refinement is under way.

Preliminary fact-finding should move quite quickly. Only those studies that are actually needed should be undertaken. Swift execution of this phase can substantially reduce the time required to develop a system.

Pregeneration Design

There is no analog to this phase in the conventional methodology. At this point in prototyping, attention is directed to a

Figure 1. Prototyping tools such as program generators vary in power and functional components. The essential components are a strong data dictionary and a database management capability.

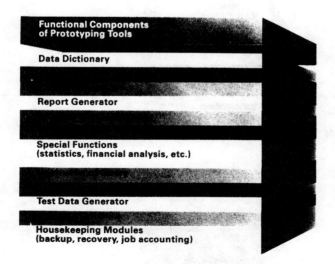

Functional Components of Prototyping Tools

Data Dictionary

Report Generator

Special Functions (statistics, financial analysis, etc.)

Test Data Generator

Housekeeping Modules (backup, recovery, job accounting)

physical, hands-on system rather than to the charts, diagrams, and other abstractions of general design. The tasks and deliverables of this phase are shown in Figure 3b.

The solution system proposal expands the approach statement from preliminary fact-finding into a list of functions, transactions, data elements, and user procedural responsibilities. The proposal should address all the needs discovered to this point.

A key difference between the prototype system proposal and a conventional specification document is that the system proposal is developed by the analyst specifically for the user. The analyst draws together a design, based on preliminary fact-finding and on his knowledge of systems, that he feels will satisfy the user's needs. The objective is to get the model into the hands of the user as soon as possible. The formality of asking the user to generate descriptions of the outputs and inputs is omitted in the interest of saving time.

The user's approval of the system proposal need only consist of a general agreement that the proposed data and functions are likely to be sufficient to meet his needs, and that the proposed procedural flow is practical and close to what he expected.

Technical approval should come from those who will be responsible for writing the production version of the system, if that is likely to occur, and from those who will be responsible for maintaining the system. At this point, the programming language, file structures, protocols, and hardware assignments that are likely to provide the foundation for the permanent system should be taken into consideration. The technical experts should warn the analyst if any parts of the proposed system could lead to unanticipated problems during system construction. They should also make known any subjective design preferences, especially if these could affect the form or style of the prototype.

Prototype Generation

This phase consists of generating and testing a baseline prototype, and developing a plan for its incremental growth (Figure 3c).

Figure 2. A conventional phase-discrete methodology for systems development proceeds in a fixed sequence of steps, each of which must be completed before the next step is undertaken. Prototyping has fewer steps and focuses on repeated refinement of a system model. The first four steps of the conventional methodology are replaced by a simpler fact-finding step in prototyping. When the prototype model is completed, it can be used as a specification guide for detail design in the conventional methodology, or the model itself can be put into production.

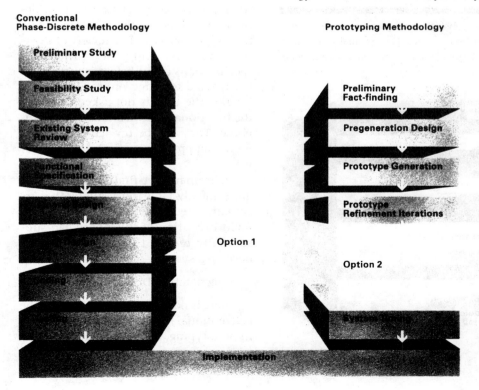

**Conventional
Phase-Discrete Methodology**

Preliminary Study

Feasibility Study

Existing System Review

Functional Specification

Option 1

Prototyping Methodology

Preliminary Fact-finding

Pregeneration Design

Prototype Generation

Prototype Refinement Iterations

Option 2

Implementation

Perhaps more challenging than actual prototype construction is deciding what subset of the total system to include in the baseline model. The functions selected to begin the prototyping should be meaningful to the user and help him to understand the prototyping process. They should be demonstrable in one sitting and comprehendible as one unit. In addition, it should be possible to build the selected functions relatively quickly (in a period of two days to two weeks), and they should establish a system style for report formatting, screen formatting, and interactive dialogues. Finally, the functions should provide a good foundation for future growth of the model.

An acceptable baseline prototype that meets these criteria consists of a key master database, an update of indicative information on this database, a report derived from the database, and a selective inquiry into the database.

Before embarking on prototype evaluation, a general plan for the continued growth of the prototype should be developed. The plan should ensure that all of the identified modules—at least those that require prototyping—are eventually added to the model. After the baseline model is constructed, functions that could affect the overall approach, integrity, or style of the system should be added. The areas of greatest uncertainty should be addressed first. The analyst will be able to find out early whether his perception of "normal case" processing matches that of the user.

Prototype Refinement Iterations

Iterations to refine the prototype are the fundamental processes of prototyping. In each iteration, new features are demonstrated and comments are solicited from the user (Figure 3d). Changes made during the previous iteration are reviewed. Unsatisfactory features are revised, and new ones are added.

This process of demonstration, review, refinement, and expansion is particularly rewarding because each iteration ends on a note of accomplishment and anticipation. Some specifications have been completed, and there is the anticipation of seeing new features in the next demonstration.

The ultimate goal of the iterations is, of course, to remove all uncertainty from the target system specifications. The physical model itself actually becomes the final system specification. It is supplemented by written documentation as needed.

A helpful tool during prototype refinement is a form called the prototype evaluation script (Figure 4). The form can be used to plan successive demonstrations and to record the questions or comments that arise during a demonstration. Afterwards, the form provides a checkoff list for the analyst as he changes the prototype to satisfy the stated needs of the user. Collectively, these prototype evaluation forms constitute a history of the maturing prototype. The reasons behind design decisions can be reconstructed should the need arise.

When a prototype is being evaluated by a large or dispersed group, it is useful to provide on-line comments with the prototype. Such electronic messaging is a convenience for the users. It also encourages them to make critical comments about the model [1].

A word of caution is in order. During prototype refinement, the analyst must remember that the project is still in the requirements definition stage. If necessary, new alternatives can be considered, project scope can be fine-tuned, and even the basic system approach can still be altered. The prototype can look so much like a final production system that even the analyst can be fooled.

Full-sized or Scaled Prototype?

What factors influence the decision of whether to build a full-sized production prototype or a scaled-down model? The decision must be made early in the prototype-generation phase, when the baseline model is being constructed and a growth plan is being considered. Generally, if only minor uncertainties remain about the system—for instance, style of formatting and dialogue—or if only isolated logic points require definition, then a full-sized prototype can be built.

If feasibility has not been established or a system approach is not certain, it is probably wiser to build a scaled-down model. Similarly, if available prototyping tools do not produce production-quality code and a rewrite of the system will be required, then scaling should be employed. The same is true if the prototype is to be written in a language or in a coding style that will be difficult to maintain.

Where scaling is employed, definition of individual requirements can pro-ceed quite rapidly. There is a drawback, however. A scaled-down model cannot become the full production system. When specification is complete, the system must be rewritten to production size and form. Of course, this could occur as another, full-scale program-generating exercise.

Figure 3. Tasks and deliverables for the four major steps of prototyping a business system are shown.

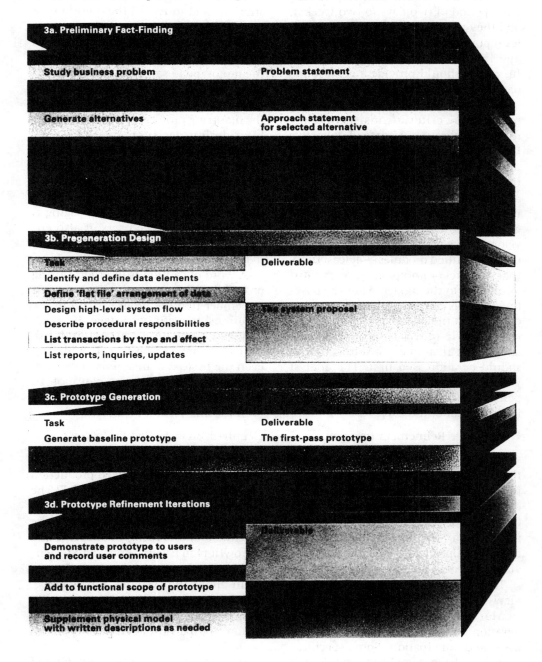

3a. Preliminary Fact-Finding

| Study business problem | Problem statement |
| Generate alternatives | Approach statement for selected alternative |

3b. Pregeneration Design

Task	Deliverable
Identify and define data elements	
Define 'flat file' arrangement of data	
Design high-level system flow	The system proposal
Describe procedural responsibilities	
List transactions by type and effect	
List reports, inquiries, updates	

3c. Prototype Generation

| Task | Deliverable |
| Generate baseline prototype | The first-pass prototype |

3d. Prototype Refinement Iterations

Demonstrate prototype to users and record user comments	Deliverable
Add to functional scope of prototype	
Supplement physical model with written descriptions as needed	

There are a number of ways in which a computer system may be scaled down:
- Reduce the database content.
- Simplify the database structures.
- Generate only necessary files.
- Generate smaller databases.
- Reduce logical flexibility.
- Generate only those functions that have significant specification uncertainties.
- Simplify data entry.
- Simplify outputs.
- Generate small transaction streams.
- Simulate interfaces.

Documentation

The major aim of prototyping is to specify a system. The system definition must be conveyed to all eventual users, including those not involved with the prototyping. If the prototype is a scaled-down model, it is necessary to be able to convey full system specifications to the technical team that is generating the production version.

Figure 4. A helpful tool during prototype refinement is a form called the prototype evaluation script. An excerpt from an evaluation script shows how the form is used to record user comments and to plan future demonstrations.

Prototype Evaluation		Page 1
System ORDER PROCESSING	Date 05 / 07 /83	
Demonstrator L. SCHARER	Evaluated by J. MAXWELL	
Demonstration Points	**Comments**	
Order status inquiry (pages 1 and 2)		
1. Is the most frequently accessed information on page 1?	CAN WE ALSO PUT ON PAGE 1: - SHIP DATE - BILL OF LADING NUMBER - CARRIER NAME	
2. Can the customer information be taken off?	NO! KEEP CUSTOMER DATA ON PAGE 1 AS SHOWN.	
3. Are the order status codes understandable?	INSTEAD OF USING NUMERIC CODES, TRY TO DEVELOP MNEMONICS. DEMONSTRATE NEXT TIME.	
4. Explain how to interpret shipping status information.	OK. NO FURTHER QUESTIONS.	
5. Ask about line-item sequence.	OK.	
6. General reaction to format.	MOVE SHIPPING SUMMARY TO THE TOP OF PAGE 1 RATHER THAN THE BOTTOM.	

Can a prototype serve as a self-documenting, external design package?

An answer is suggested by the "black box" problem that Weinberg uses in teaching students of systems analysis [2]. The students are given a computer program that models several systems. They are asked to conduct input-output studies of the model, trying different inputs and observing the outputs, without knowledge of internal structure. "One of the most important lessons I've learned from these experiments," Weinberg reports, "is how difficult it is to learn about the simplest models by this method."

Because evaluation of a prototype usually proceeds as if the prototype were a black box, Weinberg's observation should be heeded by proponents of prototyping. A prototype must be fully exercised in order to reveal all of its functions, and it is very difficult to develop a plan to do this. The transformations from input to output must be identifiable, and the meaning of the data must be understood. The impact of the system upon other systems must be perceived. And finally, if the model is scaled down, not all functions can be observed.

It is highly desirable, therefore, to supplement a prototype with supporting documentation. Information may be provided in a written document, in a data dictionary, or in explanation screens incorporated in the prototype itself. The prototype combined with its supporting documentation then becomes analogous to the general design documents of conventional development methodologies.

Supplementary information should include the purpose and goals of the system, processing logic that connects stimuli to responses, data element definitions, and, very importantly, complete specifications for any system feature that was scaled down during prototyping.

Definability and Prototyping

Prototyping has been presented as a technique for requirements definition and as a technique for system construction. When used for requirements definition, prototyping yields its highest dividends when there is low definability and little confidence in a proposed system solution [3,4]. Some factors that determine definability are database complexity, logical complexity, number of functions, and class of system. Environmental factors as well as internal system characteristics affect definability. As definability decreases, the usefulness of prototyping as a specification tool increases.

When a target system ranks high in definability, prototyping can be used to construct the production system directly. To employ prototyping for such "design-as-you-go" construction, system requirements should be almost self-evident, to the point that the system approach is somewhat predefined and analysis of alternatives is unnecessary.

Other characteristics that particularly qualify a system for full-scale production by prototyping are:

■ small number of functions, so the whole picture can be held mentally

■ stand-alone execution, with few (if any) requirements to interface with external systems

■ single-user specification, with no approval being necessary beyond that of the requesting user.

A surprising number of the new systems being developed for business applications today have characteristics that make them suitable for full-scale production by the prototyping technique.

This is in part because the proliferation of computing power—in the form of personal computers and office automation products—has created a new demand for single-user or limited-function systems.

Prototyping can also be used to clarify the definition of isolated system features or logic points before the prototypical construction of a full system. This approach can expedite development of systems that fall between the extremes of low and high definability. Many medium-sized business systems are in this category. An application itself (such as inventory, accounts payable, or order processing) may be standard, but the distinguishing characteristics of each organization's operating methods need to be accommodated.

Management of Prototyping

The methodology of prototyping emphasizes creativity, and accepts both uncertainty and change. The challenge of managing a prototyping project can be greater than that of managing a project undertaken with a conventional methodology. In fact, most of the gains in pro-

Figure 5. Organizational impact of prototyping may affect the entire systems and programming department. A typical organizational chart supporting conventional systems development separates systems analysis, programming, and technical support into distinct groups. With prototyping (right), application specialists can take a project from inception to completion, calling on a master analyst, programmer, or technician when help is needed.

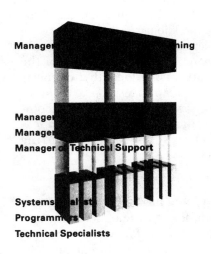

Manager ing

Manager
Manager
Manager of Technical Support

Systems Analyst
Programmers
Technical Specialists

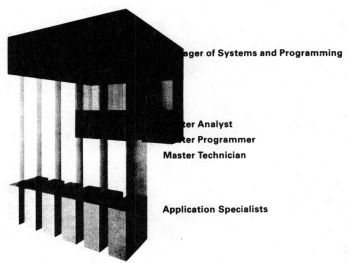

ager of Systems and Programming

ter Analyst
ter Programmer
Master Technician

Application Specialists

ductivity and quality that prototyping offers can be realized only if the activity is skillfully managed.

Probably the most crucial aspect of project control that the manager faces is deciding when the modeling process should end. During prototyping iterations, it can be predicted that the "99 percent complete" syndrome will often arise. Imposing a deadline, even an arbitrary one, will force some hard questions to be asked. Why is the model not acceptable to the user? Is an acceptable solution impossible to find? Is the user avoiding making a decision? Or is more time honestly justified?

Another problem that the leader of a prototyping project may face is securing the proper time and staffing commitments of the user. In his study, Canning notes the reaction of a former data processing manager who warns that prototyping requires more of the user's time than is expected [5,6]. Also, when the eventual user audience of a new system is large, an "experimentation group" may have to be assigned to evaluate how well the model works after the primary design group is satisfied with it. These considerations make user availability crucial to the success of a project.

Organizational Impact

The presence of program-generating tools, coupled with the prototyping approach, will undoubtedly lead to a new way of life, not just for analysts, but for the entire data processing department. In the traditional data processing department, systems analysis, programming, and technical programming support are separate specialties. Skills development is limited to specific disciplines. The manager of systems and programming is the only person who takes an overall view of development.

The traditional separation of analyst and programmer creates a rather artificial boundary during development. Players are not encouraged to cross that

Prototyping Experiences

After corporate management had endorsed a records retention policy, they asked for a computerized system to manage the records program. The basic need was for a database that could identify all records stored within the company, along with their location. An on-line add, update, and inquire function and a monthly report of the records on-hand were also desired. It was also necessary to have a notice that warned users that records under their jurisdiction were scheduled for destruction in the coming month. The requirements for the records system were developed in a 1.5 hour discussion and a system was delivered for inspection shortly after. Only a few minor changes were required following the user's review. Tne user asked for a simple messaging capability between terminals, and this was added to the system. It took about 26 hours to develop the prototype in a Wang OIS, BASIC, list-processing environment. To develop the same system by conventional means would have probably required from 120 to 150 hours.

The user requested a function that would assist in forecasting the number of acres that should be planted each year to produce the desired amount of custom-grown seed marketed by the company. The forecasting function had to consider several variables inputted by the user. It was estimated that designing and constructing the system by conventional techniques would require 120 hours. The user's forecasting method was unclear to the analyst, so a simple demonstration function was written in BASIC. After one review, the calculation algorithm was completed and a simple print function was added. The user declared that the prototype was exactly what he wanted. Total development time was 16 hours.

The printing and mailing department requested an automated support system for its supplies inventory and work-order billings. The user's needs were identified in a discussion of less than three hours. The basic needs were: perpetual inventory for materials and supplies; input of daily job tickets; monthly billing to customers; work-order performance analysis; inquiry functions for job status and charges to date; and monthly journal entry reports for the corporate general ledger. The analyst created a model system on the Wang OIS system, using BASIC, list processing, and Wang utilities. The model was quickly placed into production. Total development time was about 36 hours. The time required to construct the system with conventional development methodologies was estimated to be more than 200 hours.

These prototyping examples come from O.M. Scott & Sons, Inc. The records retention and the printing and mailing department projects were carried out by Richard Hopkins of O.M. Scott. Some interesting observations were drawn at the conclusion of the projects. First, the systems that were developed (curiously, no one called the technique "prototyping" during the development) were simpler and more straightforward than the analyst originally had expected. This raises the suspicion that the traditional methods of the analyst—and not the user—might be the source of the high degree of complexity in many business systems. Second, productivity gains were made even though powerful program generators were not available. Greater gains can be expected when more powerful tools are used in conjunction with prototyping.

boundary. Territorialism results, and special-interest groups develop. The need for formal communication increases, forcing an increase in unproductive paperwork. Such a situation is ripe for the compounding of errors.

With prototyping, the division of labor during development shifts away from programming and toward user contact, analysis, and design. This is achieved by replacing the analyst and programmer with application specialists—systems professionals who take a project from its inception all the way through prototype development, and, in many cases, on to production. Coordination is provided by the manager of systems and programming. A very small number of master analysts, master programmers, and master technicians can act as expert consultants to the application specialists (Figure 5).

The flow of system development in a conventional programming organization is in one direction, from user to analyst, and from analyst to programmer. As a middleman, the analyst sometimes actually becomes a barrier to communication. With prototyping, there is no middleman, and there is bidirectional communication between the user and the application specialist (Figure 6).

Costs and Potential Dangers

Although many production shops already have database management systems along with some elements of a total application generator, such as report writers and screen generators, additional software must usually be acquired to support prototyping. This cost can be amortized over several years.

Successful prototyping requires a strong project leader, one who possesses a great deal of systems savvy, good judgement about what to prototype and when, and extraordinary fluency with standard system applications. Achieving the benefits of prototyping is dependent to a great extent on the strengths of such an individual. Prototyping also requires a major investment of time from the most knowledgeable users, often management-level users.

There are certain potential pitfalls in prototyping. One is that in the haste to develop a prototype, the original business problem may not be thoroughly studied, and too little time may be devoted to generating and evaluating alternative solutions. There may be a tendency toward a quick fix by using existing systems, while opportunities to discover underlying problems and solve them innovatively may go unexplored. Finally, failure to develop a more conventional overall system plan before prototyping individual modules can cause system integration to suffer, especially where larger systems are built by prototyping one piece at a time.

Summary

Prototyping is promoted as a technique for more productive and more accurate system specification. Prototyping simplifies the system development methodology, exploits automation to assist the development process, and improves communications so the real needs of the user can be discovered during requirements definition. Through these strategies, prototyping becomes both a technique for generating high-quality systems and a philosophy for more productive use of resources over the lifetime of a system.

References

1. H. Gomaa, "Prototyping as a Tool in the Specification of User Requirements," Proceedings of the Fifth International Conference on Software Engineering, IEEE Computer Society, pp. 333–342, 1981.

2. G. Weinberg, *Rethinking Systems Analysis and Design*, Little, Brown & Co., Boston, 1982.

3. L. Gremillion and P. Pyburn, "Breaking the Systems Development Bottleneck," *Harvard Business Review*, Vol. 83, No. 2, pp. 130-137, 1983.

4. L.L. Scharer, "Pinpointing Requirements," *Datamation*, Vol. 27, No. 4, pp. 139-151, 1981.

5. R. Canning (Ed.), "'Programming' by End Users," *EDP Analyzer*, Vol. 19, No. 5, pp. 1-12, 1981.

6. Canning (Ed.), "Developing Systems by Prototyping," *EDP Analyzer*, Vol. 19, No. 9, pp. 1-14, 1981.

Prototyping as a Tool in the Specification of User Requirements

Hassan Gomaa
General Electric Co.
Syracuse, New York

Douglas B.H. Scott
I.P. Sharp Associates Ltd.
Toronto, Ontario, Canada

Abstract

One of the major problems in developing new computer applications is specifying the user's requirements such that the Requirements Specification is correct, complete and unambiguous. Although prototyping is often considered too expensive, correcting ambiguities and misunderstandings at the specification stage is significantly cheaper than correcting a system after it has gone into production. This paper describes how a prototype was used to help specify the requirements of a computer system to manage and control a semiconductor processing facility. The cost of developing and running the prototype was less than 10% of the total software development cost.

1.0 Introduction

In the past few years, the importance of Requirements Specification in the software life cycle has become widely acknowledged. The objective of this phase is to define what the system will provide for the user. The design phase defines how it is to be achieved.

Prototyping can be a powerful tool in assisting the requirements specification process. However prototypes are rarely developed because they are considered too expensive. For example, a panel session at the Fourth International Conference on Software Engineering dismissed prototypes on the grounds of cost [1]. However, correcting ambiguities and misunderstandings at the specification stage is significantly cheaper than correcting a system after it has gone into production.

This paper describes how a prototype was used to help specify the requirements of a computer system to manage a semiconductor processing facility which produces integrated circuits. The cost of developing and running the prototype was less than 10% of the total software development cost.

2.0 Problems in Specifying User Requirements

The Requirements Analysis and Specification phase of the software life cycle involves analyzing the user's requirements and then specifying a system to satisfy them.

The procedure usually followed in specifying a new computer system is to write a Requirements Specification and submit it for the approval of the users. The main problem with this approach is that users find it extremely difficult to visualize how the system will actually perform in their own environment just by reading a paper specification. This is particularly the case if the system is to be used by a wide spectrum of users, all of whom have different (sometimes conflicting) requirements, and some of whom have no previous experience of computer systems. These users often find a written specification dull to read and difficult to understand. Hence they are uncertain whether or not the proposed system meets their requirements. It is also very difficult to determine whether a Requirements Specification is complete, correct, consistent and unambiguous.

Furthermore, these problems are compounded by the fact that experience has shown that errors in requirements specification are usually the last to be detected and the most costly to correct [2]. Many data processing departments spend as much time maintaining existing computer systems as developing new ones, and many so-called 'maintenance' projects are in fact projects established to correct errors in the original Requirements Specification.

In recognition of these problems, various methods and tools have been developed to assist the requirements specification process. These tools fall into two main categories, system specification languages and graphical tools, or some combination of the two.

Reprinted from *The Proceedings of the 5th International Conference on Software Engineering*, 1981, pages 333-342. Copyright © 1981 by The Institute of Electrical and Electronics Engineers, Inc.

Use of a formal system specification language such as PSL (Problem Statement Language [3]) and RSL (Requirements Specification Language [4]) can help ensure that the specification is unambiguous and consistent. However, it cannot ensure that the specification is correct, i.e. the problem may have been correctly specified but it may not be the problem the user wants solved. Nor can it ensure that the specification is complete - a function or a set of functions may have been entirely omitted. One study identified that 20% of the errors in the requirements specification of several large software projects were due to missing information, and a further 30% were due to incorrect requirements [5].

Furthermore, a typical user who has to approve the requirements specification may well find it difficult to determine whether a specification written in a formal language does indeed satisfy his requirements.

For this reason other specification tools which have been developed are based on a graphical approach to specifying user requirements. A frequently used approach is based on information (or data) flow diagrams. This approach has been formalized in SADT [6], Structured Analysis [7] and SAMM [8], by adopting a hierarchical decomposition technique to decomposing the problem to be solved into several sub-problems with well defined interfaces between them.

One advantage of the graphical approach is that these diagrams are understandable to users who may then be able to provide valuable feedback to the developers. However, from the user's point of view, the best way to determine whether a system will satisfy his requirements is "hands-on" use of the system.

3.0 The Prototype Approach to Specifying User Requirements

The communication gap between the system developer and the user can be bridged by developing a prototype of the proposed system. With a prototype, the user can exercise the system just as though it were already operating in his own environment, and thereby provide vital feedback to the developer on the suitability of the specification.

Other branches of engineering frequently make use of prototypes, pilot plants and modelling techniques before putting complex systems into production. Prototyping can also help the software engineering process by producing application systems that are more user oriented.

A good time to develop a prototype is after a preliminary version of the Requirements Specification has been developed. At this stage, the developer believes he has a reasonable understanding of the user's problem and has completed his first serious attempt at proposing a system to satisfy the user's requirements.

The cost of making changes to a system increases significantly as the software development proceeds [2]. Consequently it is desirable to obtain the user feedback as early as possible in the software life cycle and definitely before the Requirements Specification is finalized. As the objective of the prototype is to maximize user feedback, the prototype should emphasize the user interface at the expense of lower level software which is not visible to the user.

After the prototype has been developed, users should be given ample opportunity to exercise it and to provide their feedback to the developers. Based on user feedback, further changes can be made to the prototype. Usually these changes are of a relatively minor nature, such as modifying output report formats or user prompts.

At some stage, which has to be carefully monitored and evaluated by user and developer, the benefits of further enhancements to the prototype are outweighed by the time and cost required for these modifications. At this stage, further development of the prototype is stopped. The temptation to continue development of the prototype after it has outlived its usefulness should be resisted. In particular, allowing the prototype to evolve into the delivered system is not recommended. The software engineering approach required to develop a production system is very different from that required to develop a prototype (see section 6). Hence maintainability is a much more important consideration in developing a production system than in a prototype.

Based on user feedback, the Requirements Specification is revised. This revised specification forms the basis from which the design and implementation of the system proceeds.

A prototype may also be used as a vehicle for training users on how to use the system. However, this requires that the prototype be kept up to date. The advantages of this approach have to be weighed against the additional cost of maintaining the prototype.

Prototyping is viewed as being complementary to other tools for analyzing and specifying user requirements. Thus a prototype can be used to help determine that the proposed system does in fact satisfy the user's requirements, i.e. to ensure that the specification is complete and correct. A requirements specification language may then be used to specify the user's requirements, ensuring that the specification is unambiguous and consistent.

4.0 Description of the Prototype

4.1 Introduction

The system under discussion, called PROMIS, is a Process Management and Information System for a semiconductor processing facility. PROMIS is a joint development of I.P. Sharp Associates and the General Electric Company, and the system is being installed in G.E.'s Solid State Applications Operation in Syracuse, N.Y..

PROMIS is a highly interactive system. Most user interactions with the system were explicitly prototyped. Some aspects of the system (such as interfacing with other computers) were not prototyped as it was felt that these requirements were generally clearly understood and would not benefit so much from prototyping.

The emphasis of the prototype was on prototyping user interactions with the system and not on performance. The prototype runs on an Amdahl 470 and the production system will run on a VAX 11/780. No attempt was made in the prototype to estimate what the performance of the production system would be. As the VAX has considerable spare capacity, performance was not considered a crucial factor.

4.2 Overview of the System

A semiconductor process (not to be confused with the software concept of a process) is the sequence of steps (typically 60-100) required to fabricate integrated circuit devices from bare silicon wafers (see Figure 1). In PROMIS, these processes are defined by a process engineer and stored on file.

A lot (i.e. batch) of silicon wafers (typically 25-50) is processed in the semiconductor processing facility as defined by the process. The processing for each process step is controlled by a process recipe which defines how a particular lot should be processed by the appropriate semiconductor equipment at a

given work center. Each recipe consists of 10-15 operations and is displayed to the equipment operator on the work center CRT. A typical process structure is shown in Figure 2.

A lot is moved through the work centers of the facility as directed by the process it is executing.

4.3 Overview of the Prototype

PROMIS has four major functions:

- Process Management

- Lot Tracking

- Lot History Analysis

- Facility Monitoring

All of these functions, apart from Facility Monitoring, were explicitly prototyped. It was felt that the requirements of Facility Monitoring (monitoring ambient temperatures, gas flows, gas pressures etc.) were generally clearly understood and would not benefit so much from prototyping.

PROMIS is a highly interactive system. In the prototype, a menu was provided as the means by which users selected functions to be executed. The menu was implemented as a three level command tree (see Figure 3). The objective was to provide a menu that is friendly to both novice and experienced users.

To select a function from the menu, the user may type the entire command name (e.g. LOT PROCESSING) or, starting with the first character, any unique substring of the command name (e.g. LOT or L). If the substring is not unique the system points out the ambiguity and reissues the prompt.

An experienced user may enter multiple commands on the same line. For example, L T V means that LOT PROCESSING (L) will be selected from level 1, TRACK OPERATIONS (T) will be selected from level 2, and VIEW LOT RECIPE (V) will be selected from level 3 of the command tree. Once a function at the lowest level of the command tree has been selected, the user is presented with simple English language prompts for any data that is required to execute that function.

The major groups of functions available to users are:

a) Process Management

These functions allow process engineers to create and modify semiconductor processes and their constituent recipes and operations. The process engineer is provided with a series of English language prompts to which he responds. For example to create a process, he is prompted for the overall characteristics of the process. He is then prompted for the recipe used at each process step.

b) Lot Tracking

These functions allow lots to be tracked in and out of work centers. Recipes are displayed at work center CRT's, enabling operators to process a lot on the work center equipment by following the operations described in the recipe.

The procedure for executing a process step at a work center is as follows:

1. TRACK IN. A lot is selected from the input queue for that work center and is tracked into the work center, i.e. transferred to the active list.

2. VIEW LOT RECIPE. The prototype automatically determines the recipe for that lot at that process step and displays it to the operator.

3. ENTER TEST RESULTS. If the recipe includes a test operation, the operator is prompted for each data item in turn, and the system performs range checks and pre-defined calculations on the test results.

4. TRACK OUT. The lot is tracked out of the work center, after which it appears in the input queue for the next work center.

c) Lot History Analysis

Each time a lot is tracked out of a work center a complete record of what happened to the lot is written out to file. This data may be later analyzed by a process engineer using an interactive query language to determine, for example, what factors affected lot yield. From this information, the engineer may modify this process with the objective of improving yield.

A more detailed description of the prototype is given in [9].

5.0 Experience with the Prototype

Users were given a two hour course and a practical demonstration of how to use the prototype. They were then given 2 weeks in which to experiment with the prototype.

Two methods were used to obtain the users' feedback: an evaluation form which they were asked to complete, and an on-line mechanism for entering (and reading) user comments. This allowed a user to enter his comments on-line, while using the prototype, and to review the comments of other users.

The main points revealed by developing and using the prototype were as follows:

1. In software development projects misunderstandings between developer and user tend to occur all too frequently, because of their different backgrounds. In this project, this type of misunderstanding was revealed through use of the prototype. For example, the developer thought that a semiconductor process could produce only one device, whereas it can produce many. This capability is required in the production system.

2. Ambiguities and inconsistencies in the Requirements Specification were identified, as the prototype was being developed, and corrected. Thus inconsistencies in the procedures for controlling process and recipe modification were discovered and corrected.

3. Omissions in the Requirements Specification were discovered when users asked for features which they considered essential, but were not available in the prototype. Examples of these omissions were the need for daily and weekly summary reports, and a user function to determine the lot to which an individual silicon wafer belongs.

4. Errors were discovered in the prototype which were due to incorrect or missing requirements. Thus in the prototype it was possible to start a lot before the process to fabricate it was fully defined. Furthermore it was

possible to track a lot out of a work center before test results had been entered. Both of these features should have been prohibited.

5. Some functions did not provide the user with the information he wanted. These were modified to provide additional or different information. An example of this is that although functions were provided to list the contents of individual processes and recipes, users requested the option of listing groups and summaries of processes and recipes.

6. Users were able to give valuable feedback as to which features of the system they found difficult or confusing to use. Users found certain command names confusing. Certain terminology such as 'queue' was also found confusing. Prompts requesting input included data type definitions (such as I6 for a six digit integer number) which were intended to help users. In fact these had the opposite effect and consequently were removed. Users also requested the capability to exit from a function prematurely and to return to the state they were at before entering the function.

7. In some cases the user was not sure how he wanted certain functions implemented. Developing the prototype helped him come to a decision on these. One of the major areas prototyped was the historical analysis of lot data. It was necessary to have a flexible and usable procedure. Although the proposed approach was flexible, it was not clear how usable it would be for process engineers. Some difficulty was experienced in using these features on the prototype and so the procedure is being modified.

8. Developing the prototype provided valuable insight to the developers on how the system should be designed, in particular how the system should be structured, how files and data should be structured and which algorithms should be used.

As user feedback was received, some relatively minor modifications were made to the prototype, primarily in the areas of report formats and user prompts. This enabled users to experience the results of their comments quickly. After five iterations, further development was cut off as it was felt that the primary benefits had been obtained from using the prototype.

A detailed analysis was then made of the user comments. Based on this, the Requirements Specification was significantly revised.

6.0 Implementation Aspects of the Prototype

The prototype was developed in APL by three people over a three month period. The total manpower spent on the prototype was 7 man months, which represents about 6% of the total estimated development effort of 10 man years. In addition, approximately $12,500 was spent in timesharing costs.

The main reasons why the development costs of the prototype were kept to this level are as follows:

a) Emphasis of the Prototype

The prototype emphasized the user interface to the system. The objective was to get the most benefit (i.e. user feedback) from the prototype. Consequently, not all aspects of the system were prototyped. In particular, frequently executed user functions were emphasized, not the exception conditions. Data validation, error handling and logging were not as comprehensive in the prototype as they are planned to be in the production system. Certain subsystems such as system recovery and facility monitoring were not prototyped at all, because they have little or no interaction with the user. Performance considerations were also ignored in the prototype.

b) Size of the Prototype

The prototype was developed by 3 people whereas the production system is being developed by a team of 12 people. A much more flexible and less formal development approach was therefore used for the prototype than that required for the production system.

c) APL Language

APL is an interpretive language with many powerful features for manipulating multi-dimensional arrays. Consequently APL programs are often much shorter than programs written in other languages. Because APL is interpretive, APL programmers tend to find it relatively fast to test their programs.

APL has often been criticized for resulting in unmaintainable code [10]. Whereas there is some justification for this criticism, it is possible to write readable programs in APL by observing a disciplined approach and a good programming style [11]. However, maintainability is by no means as important a consideration in a prototype as it is in a production system.

d) APL System

The APL system used, SHARP APL[12], has a number of features which assist program development. It has a file system which is easy to use. It also has a powerful report formatting utility, which facilitates writing and changing of sample reports, a valuable capability in any prototyping exercise. Furthermore, backup and recovery procedures are built into the system.

7.0 Conclusions

The use of a prototype was found to be an excellent method of evaluating the Requirements Specification.

The circulation of a written Requirements Specification to process engineers, management personnel, facility operators and supervisors yielded virtually no useful feedback. Unfortunately, the specification for such a system has to be quite lengthy to be complete, and prospective users often don't find the time to evaluate a written specification thoroughly. Even if they have the time, the task of carefully scrutinizing a 120 page document is difficult and boring, and is therefore not performed with the enthusiasm that is most conducive to good results.

Exercising a prototype system is interesting. Prospective users find it much easier to evaluate a working system than a paper document, and as a result are much more likely to obtain a system that will meet their requirements.

The cost of developing and running this prototype was less than 10% of the total software development cost. This demonstrates clearly that prototyping can be done economically. It is believed that this is also true for many other systems.

The feedback obtained from using the prototype was found to be extremely valuable, and more than justified its development. The changes made to the Requirement Specification, as a result of user feedback obtained through using the prototype, were of relatively low cost and would have been considerably more expensive to make had they been left to later in the software life cycle.

8.0 Acknowledgements

The authors gratefully acknowledge the major contributions of J.R. DeBolt, R.F. Johnston and I. Griggs in the Requirements Specification of PROMIS and the development of the prototype. Thanks are also due to L.J. Lambert and C.A. Shaw for their assistance in the Requirements Specification and the evaluation of the prototype.

9.0 References

1. W.P. Dodd,"Prototype Programs", IEEE Computer, February 1980.

2. B. Boehm,"Software Engineering - R and D Trends and Defense Needs" in Research Directions in Software Technology, MIT Press, 1978.

3. D. Teichrow and E. Hershey,"PSL/PSA: A Computer Aided Technique for Structured Documentation and Analysis of Information Processing Systems", IEEE Transactions on Software Engineering, January 1977.

4. T. Bell, D. Bixler and M. Dyer,"An Extendable Approach to Computer Aided Software Requirements Engineering", IEEE Transactions on Software Engineering, January 1977.

5. T. Bell and T. Thayer,"Software Requirements: Are They Really a Problem?", Proceedings of the 2nd International Software Engineering Conference, October 1976.

6. D. Ross and W. Schoman,"Structured Analysis for Requirements Definition", IEEE Transactions on Software Engineering, January 1977.

7. T. DeMarco,"Structured Analysis and System Specification", Yourdon Press, 1978.

8. S. Stephens and L. Tripp,"Requirements Expression and Verification Aid, Proceedings of the 3rd International Conference on Software Engineering, May 1978.

9. H. Gomaa and D. Scott,"An APL Prototype of a Management and Control System for a Semiconductor Fabrication Facility", Proceedings of the 1980 APL Users Meeting, October 1980.

10. E. Dijkstra,"The Humble Programmer", Communications ACM,

Vol. 15, No. 10, 1972.

11. B. Kernigham and W. Plauger,"The Elements of Programming Style", McGraw Hill, Second Edition, 1978.

12. P. Berry,"Sharp APL Reference Manual", I.P. Sharp Associates, 1979.

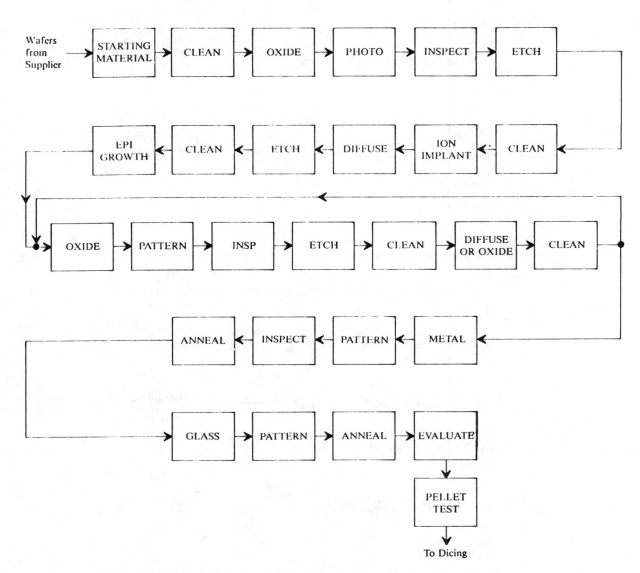

FIGURE 1 Example of Semiconductor Process

FIGURE 2

PROCESS ·STRUCTURE

PROCESS   PROCESS STEPS   OPERATIONS
                (RECIPES)

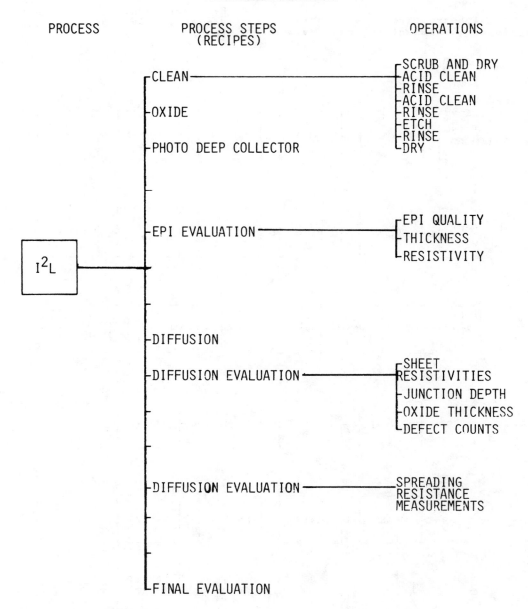

FIGURE 3

PROTOTYPE MENU STRUCTURE

LEVEL 1	LEVEL 2	LEVEL 3
PROCESS MANAGEMENT	PROCESS FUNCTIONS	ADD PROCESS
		CHANGE PROCESS
		DELETE PROCESS
		LIST PROCESS
		FULL-LIST PROC
		REC-LIST
		F-REC-LIST
		B-REC-LIST
		RECIPE XREF
	RECIPE FUNCTIONS	ADD RECIPE
		CHANGE RECIPE
		DELETE RECIPE
		LIST RECIPE
		F-REC-LIST
		B-REC-LIST
		RECIPE XREF
		OPERATION XREF
	OPERATION FUNCTIONS	ADD OPERATION
		DELETE OPN
		LIST OPN
		FULL-LIST OPN
		BRIEF-LIST OPN
		OPERATION XREF
LOT PROCESSING	MANAGING LOTS	START NEW LOT
		SPLIT A LOT
		REWORK LOT
		BACK UP LOT
		DISPLAY A LOT
		EDIT A LOT
	TRACK OPERATIONS	INTO WORK CENTER
		VIEW LOT RECIPE
		OUT OF WORK CENTER
		ATTACH TO WC
		WORK CENTER DISPLAY
		EQUIPMENT DISPLAY
		FIND LOT
		ENTER TEST RESULTS
	REPORTS	LOT
		FULL LOT
OUTPUT DATA	STATUS	LOT
		EQUIPMENT
		WORK CENTER
		WAFER INVENTORY
		TANKS GAS
		BACK LOG
	LOT HISTORY	DESCRIBE
		REPORT
	OTHER HISTORY	ALARM HISTORY
		FACILITY HISTORY
MESSAGE	DIRECTORY	
	SEND	
	COMMENTS	DESCRIBE
		WRITE
		READ

Reprinted from *IEEE Transactions on Software Engineering*, Volume SE-10, Number 3, May 1984, pages 290-302. Copyright © 1984 by The Institute of Electrical and Electronics Engineers, Inc.

Prototyping Versus Specifying: A Multiproject Experiment

BARRY W. BOEHM, TERENCE E. GRAY, AND THOMAS SEEWALDT

Abstract—In this experiment, seven software teams developed versions of the same small-size (2000–4000 source instruction) application software product. Four teams used the Specifying approach. Three teams used the Prototyping approach.

The main results of the experiment were the following.

1) Prototyping yielded products with roughly equivalent performance, but with about 40 percent less code and 45 percent less effort.

2) The prototyped products rated somewhat lower on functionality and robustness, but higher on ease of use and ease of learning.

3) Specifying produced more coherent designs and software that was easier to integrate.

The paper presents the experimental data supporting these and a number of additional conclusions.

Index Terms—Prototypes, requirements analysis, software engineering, software engineering education, software management, software metrics, specifications.

I. Introduction

A. Motivation

SHOULD the current specification-driven approach to software development be dropped in favor of an approach based on prototyping? There have been several recent proposals of this nature, and a great deal of discussion of the relative merits of the two alternative approaches.

Prototyping offers a number of attractive advantages, such as the early resolution of high-risk issues, and the flexibility to adapt to changing environmental characteristics or perceptions of users' needs. To date, however, there is not much information on whether the prototyping approach retains all of the advantages of the specification-driven approach, such as visibility and control of the software development process, and the ability to manage integration of many small programs into a large product. Nor is there much information on how the nature of a software product developed via prototyping compares with the nature of a product developed via the specification-driven approach.

In order to illuminate these and related issues, we undertook the experiment described in this paper. We had seven teams develop the same software product (a user-interactive software cost estimation model, comprising roughly 3000 Pascal source

Manuscript received April 15, 1983; revised January 5, 1984.

B. W. Boehm is with the Software and Information Systems, Division, TRW Defense Systems Group, Redondo Beach, CA 90278 and the University of California, Los Angeles, CA 90024.

T. E. Gray is with the Department of Computer Science, School of Engineering and Applied Science, University of California, Los Angeles, CA 90024.

T. Seewaldt was with the Department of Computer Science, University of California, Los Angeles, CA 90024. He is now with Universitaet Kaiserslautern, Kaiserslautern, West Germany.

instructions); four teams used a specification-driven approach, and three used a prototyping approach. The resulting data on the teams' experiences and products provide at least a start toward understanding the relative strengths and weaknesses of the prototyping and specifying approaches, and toward understanding how they may best fit into a next-generation software development methodology.

B. Background

At the beginning of every software project, the project manager is faced with a critical choice of approach. The primary choices are the following.

1) *Building and Fixing:* Proceed to build the full system with minimal or no specifications. Rework the resulting product as necessary until it satisfies its users.

2) *Specifying:* Develop a requirements specification for the product. Develop a design specification to implement the requirements. Develop the code to implement the design. Again, rework the resulting product as necessary.

3) *Prototyping:* Build prototype versions of parts of the product. Exercise the prototype parts to determine how best to implement the operational product. Proceed to build the operational product, and again rework it as necessary.

There are a number of variations on these three basic approaches, of course, but their essential distinctions are identified reasonably well in the above three options.

Approach 1, Building and Fixing, has been shown to work poorly on most projects of any reasonable size. This is largely because of the highly increased cost of fixing a software product once it is completed and operational [1]. The Specifying approach evolved to avoid the problems encountered in Building and Fixing [2]–[4] and led to the familiar "waterfall" model of software development most frequently seen today.

The Specifying approach has been highly successful in many application areas [5], [6]. However, it encounters difficulties in application areas in which it is hard to specify requirements in advance. This happens most frequently in human–machine interface systems, in which the requirements analyst often has to deal with user responses of the form, "I'm really not sure what I want, but I'll know it when I see it."

In such situations, the Prototyping approach appears attractive. A number of papers have proposed refinements of the waterfall model of the software life-cycle to incorporate prototyping options [7]–[9]. Some authors have gone so far as to suggest that prototyping options make all current life-cycle models completely obsolete and even harmful [10].

C. Open Questions

At this stage, however, not enough is known about the relative merits of specifying and prototyping to summarily reject either approach in favor of the other. The results of recent workshops such as the ACM–IEEE–NBS Workshop on Rapid Prototyping [11] indicate that a number of significant open questions still exist, such as the following.

What characterizes application areas in which prototyping is likely to be more successful than specifying?

What effect does prototyping have on a software project's effort distribution, schedule distribution, and productivity; and on the product's size, quality, maintainability, etc.?

How does prototyping change the mix of skills needed on a software project?

Is there need to adopt a mixed strategy using both specifying and prototyping? If so, when and how?

Clearly, such questions need to be further illuminated via analysis or experimentation before we can formulate definitive recommendations on the critical issue of specifying versus prototyping.

D. The Experiment

The experiment described here was designed to investigate such questions. It involved having seven teams develop their own versions of the same product, four teams using the specifying approach and three teams using the prototyping approach.

The product to be developed was an interactive version of the COCOMO model for software cost estimation [12]. The tables and equations in the model were the same for all projects, and provided an overall definition of the product's requirements. However, each team was to determine and create its own user interface to the model. A previous experiment [13] indicated that the interactive COCOMO model would be a suitable product for such an experiment. It is a reasonably sized job for an experiment, and the user interface constitutes the dominant portion of the product.

The experiment took place in early 1982 as part of a one-quarter first year graduate course in software engineering at UCLA. The four Specifying teams produced a requirements specification, a design specification, and an end product consisting of operational code, a user's manual, and a maintenance manual. The three Prototyping teams produced the same end products, but were required to produce and exercise a prototype by the midpoint of the course, rather than to develop specifications. All of the projects were instrumented to collect data relevant to the open questions above.

E. Outline of Paper

Section II of this paper describes the experimental project in more detail. Section III presents the experimental results. Section IV presents the resulting conclusions. Finally, Appendix A contains the project description given to the students, and Appendix B summarizes the primary lessons learned from an instructional standpoint.

II. The Experimental Project

This section discusses the key aspects of the experiment: the product developed; the project schedule and work environment; the organization into teams; the experimental data collection procedures; and some of the experimental limitations caused by the course schedule and teaching objectives.

A. The Product

Each team was to develop an interactive version of the COCOMO model for estimating the costs of a software product. The model accepts descriptions of the components of the future product in terms of their size, and their ratings with respect to 16 cost-driver attributes (e.g., hardware constraints, database size, personnel experience, use of tools and modern programming practices). It uses these to calculate the amount of time and effort (and resulting dollar cost) required to develop each component and the overall system, and provides a breakdown of the effort into the major development phases and activities.

The model algorithms and tables were provided in [12]; each team was to develop its own file system and user interface (see Appendix A). The user interface for such a product is considerably more extensive than the cost model algorithms. The user interface software must support the selective creation, addition, modification, query, and deletion of the cost-driver parameters describing each component of the software product whose costs are to be estimated. It must support the specification, generation, formatting, and dispatching of desired outputs: overall cost, effort, and schedule estimates, and their breakdown by component, by phase, and by activity. It must detect and provide messages for erroneous inputs, and provide some level of on-line help. There are also a wide variety of further options which may be included, and many alternative ways to accommodate inputs (menus, commands, tables, forms), display outputs, and support user control. Thus, there are a good many issues to be addressed via prototyping or specifying which have a significant influence on the nature of the project and its resulting product.

B. Project Schedule

The major milestones for each type of team were:

Week	Specifying Teams	Prototyping Teams
3	Requirements	
5		Prototype Demo
6	Design Spec Draft User Manual	
10	Acceptance Test User Manual Maintenance Manual	Acceptance Test User Manual Maintenance Manual
11	Project Critique Maintenance Vote	Project Critique Maintenance Vote

The requirements and design specifications were subjected to a thorough review by the instructors. This resulted in a set of Problem Reports returned to the project teams and discussed in a set of Requirements Reviews and Design Reviews. The prototypes were exercised by the instructors, who provided similar feedback on errors, suggested modifications, missing capabilities, etc.

The acceptance test consisted of the instructors' exercising each program to determine whether it performed all of the required capabilities, whether it handled error conditions with useful responses, and whether it exhibited a high degree of user-friendliness. Subsequently, the authors of this paper exercised each product in more detail, and each author rated it on a scale of 0 to 10 with respect to four particular citeria.

1) *Functionality:* The relative utility of the various computational, user interface, output, and file management functions provided by the product.

2) *Robustness:* The degree to which the user was protected from aborts, crashes, loss of working files, etc.

3) *Ease of Use (Or Lack of Frustration):* The degree of user convenience in performing desired functions, and the avoidance of overconstrained or unexpected program behavior.

4) *Ease of Learning:* The ease with which new users could master the product's workings and get it to do what they wished. This rating covered not only program prompts, help messages, and error messages, but also the user manual and associated job aids or "crib sheets" provided by the teams.

The project critiques were ten-page essays written by each student, addressing the question, "If we were to do the project over again, how could we do it better?" These critiques were analyzed for the degree of consensus among the participants on the most important factors influencing the project results.

The maintenance ballots asked each student to rate each of the other teams' products in the order in which they would prefer to have the product as their product to maintain. The average rating for each product was then calculated as an index of its maintainability. Twenty percent of each person's course grade was based on his product's maintainability rating.

C. Development Environment

The products were developed in UCB Pascal, using a UCLA VAX 11/780 running the Unix (TM: Bell Laboratories) operating system. The Unix environment provided excellent support for both documentation and code development functions. Some difficulties were the overload on the VAX at the end of the quarter combined with poor documentation of the separate compilation facilities in UCB Pascal, which made product integration and test much more complex and time-consuming than expected.

D. Team Organization and Staffing

At the beginning of the course, the students were given a description of the project, and a form to indicate their level of experience with Pascal, with Unix, and with programming; their grade point average; and their preference for which approach to use on the project. The instructors then selected teams based on the students' preferences and on experimental balance.

The 11 students expressing a preference for specifying were divided into four teams (S1–S4). The 7 students expressing a preference for prototyping were divided into three teams (P1–P3). The resulting team characteristics are given in Table I.

TABLE I
EXPERIMENTAL TEAM CHARACTERISTICS

Team	Specifying					Prototyping			
	S1	S2	S3	S4	Avg.	P1	P2	P3	Avg.
No. of people	3	3	2	3	2.75	2	3	2	2.33
Avg. programming experience (mo)	25	47	42	30	36	54	46	60	53
Avg. Pascal exp. (mo)	1	17	7	3	7	30	16	9	18
Avg. Unix exp. (mo)	0	1	12	5	4.5	3	4	0	2.3
Avg. grade point average	3.1	3.6	3.6	3.3	3.37	3.4	3.0	3.3	3.27

Each team was given the freedom to organize in whatever way the members found most appropriate. Most teams used a highly democratic consensus-based organization, with all members performing some design, some programming, some documentation, and some integration and test. Some teams had a single individual develop documents, such as the user's manual.

E. Experimental Limitations

The teaching objectives of the course introduced several experimental limitations which somewhat reduced the sharpness and representativeness of the results.

Technical Leveling: A pure experiment would have isolated the teams to minimize any cross-fertilization of ideas or technical leveling between projects. Here, our teaching objectives caused us to hold every requirements review, design review, and prototype exercise in front of the entire class. Thus, prototypers got some added insights from the specifiers' reviews, and vice versa. However, our impression is that the students did not significantly change their approaches as a result of this information.

Nonrepresentative Reviewing: In order to provide thorough feedback on specifications, and to show the value of early verification and validation, the instructors performed more thorough reviews of specifications than are performed on the typical project. The prototype exercises were also somewhat nonrepresentative in being one-shot exercises by expert users rather than sustained usage by nonexpert users.

Choice of Approach: The Specifying teams were staffed entirely with students who had expressed a preference for the Specifying approach, and similarly for the Prototyping teams. This is largely nonrepresentative of actual projects—although some students' critiques indicated that they would prefer taking the opposite approach if they were to do a similar project again.

Data Collection Procedures: The instructors explained to the students that their grade had nothing to do with the timesheet data they turned in, so there was no reason to falsify data. However, students occasionally exhibit procrastination and lapses in discipline. Thus, it was not too surprising that some of the timesheets were turned in late, with the attendant possibility that some of the data provided were created "from memory."

As stated above, these factors tend to reduce the sharpness and representativeness of the results. However, the net impression from the project critiques is that none of these factors played a critical role in the outcome of the experiment. Thus, the experimental results described below appear to transcend these acknowledged limitations. As a further point of perspective, it is worth noting that many conclusions reached in the software engineering field are still based on sample sizes of one project. Thus, a sample of seven reasonably comparable, moderately representative projects is not too bad.

III. EXPERIMENTAL RESULTS

A. Prototyping Versus Specifying

Product Size and Development Effort: The comparisons of the relative sizes of the products and the relative effort required to develop them produced a striking result: the prototyping teams' products were 40 percent smaller, on the average, and required 45 percent less effort to develop.

The products of the prototyping groups had an average size of 2064 delivered source instructions (DSI), while the products of the specifying groups had an average of 3391 DSI. The average development effort of the prototyping groups was 325 man-hours (MH), and for the specifying groups, 584 MH. Fig. 1 shows the relative results for each project and the averages by type of group.

Both differences might be partly due to the smaller average team size of the prototyping groups (2.33 persons versus 2.75), but comments in the project critiques indicate that the group type most significantly influenced these results. Specifically, the specifying people indicated that it was very easy to overpromise in their specifications. For example, when confronted with a review comment such as, "Some users would like to enter data by rows as well as columns," the specifiers would tend to say, "Sure, that's just another sentence in the spec." When confronted with this sort of comment in their prototype review, prototypers had a better feel for the programming implications, and tended to say, "We'll put that in if we have time."

The range of product sizes was from 1514 DSI to 4606 DSI (Table V below provides data on each project). The second largest product was 3391 DSI, so we consider the 4606 DSI product somewhat anomalous. Even so, the 3:1 range in product sizes in remarkable, considering that each team was developing essentially the same product. This range, and the comparable 3.4:1 range in project effort, tend to corroborate the ranges in [12, ch. 21] on the relative accuracy of early software sizing and costing efforts.

Overall Productivity: One of our hypotheses was that the prototyping projects would have higher "productivity" in terms of delivered source instructions per man-hour (DSI/MH), primarily because the prototyping teams did not have to expend the extra effort to develop requirements and design specifications. This hypothesis was not borne out by the experimental results: both the prototyping and specifying groups averaged roughly 6 DSI/MH, where the number of man-hours includes effort expended for all phases of the project, not just coding. The prototyping groups had an average productivity of 6.3 DSI/MH; the specifying groups, 5.8 DSI/MH.

The range in overall productivity for prototyping groups was from 6 to 6.5 DSI/MH; for specifying groups it was from 3.6 to 10, but with only one group (the same one that produced the largest product) exceeding 6.4 DSI/MH. As shown in Fig.

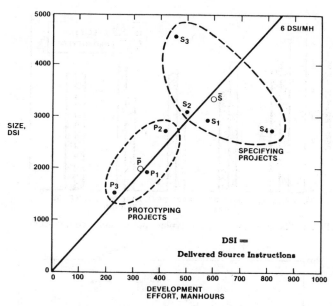

Fig. 1. Prototyping versus specifying: size and effort comparisons.

1, the development effort is generally proportional to the size of the developed product.

Note that the large variation in product size does not invalidate the DSI/MH productivity measure as an indicator of efficiency in producing code. Rather, it illustrates the need for further research into why ostensibly similar products can differ so dramatically in size, and therefore, development cost.

Coding Productivity: An unexpectedly large variation in coding productivity (DSI/programming MH) was observed. The low was 9.7 and the high was 33.8 DSI/MH. While the average for specifying teams (15.7) was 25 percent lower than that of prototyping teams (21), much of this difference is attributable to the pronounced team-size effect discussed in Section III-B.

Product Performance: Since the products of the prototyping groups were smaller and developed with less effort, one might think that they would rate correspondingly lower on performance. However, their overall performance was the same as the performance of the specifying groups (Fig. 2). The prototyped products were rated lower in overall functionality and in their tolerance of erroneous input, but correspondingly higher in their ease of learning and ease of use (i.e., the frustration caused by overconstrained or unexpected program behavior was less for the products of the prototyping groups). There was not a uniform dominance of prototyping or specifying projects on any of the performance ratings. Practically all the ratings were in the range of 3 through 7 (a "5" rating corresponded to an "acceptable" product), but there was considerable variation in ratings within the range in each group.

Maintainability Ratings: At the end of the quarter, students indicated which products they would prefer to maintain and ranked the products accordingly. The maintainability of the prototype group products was rated remarkably higher than the maintainability of the specifying group products. Therefore, the student's subjective evaluations did not confirm the hypothesis that the specifying approach leads to lower main-

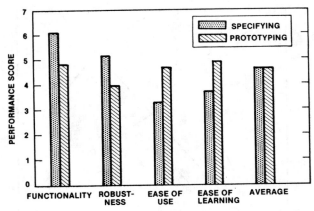

Fig. 2. Specifying versus prototyping: performance comparisons.

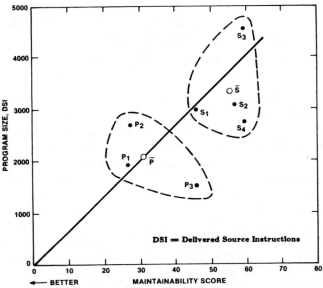

DSI = Delivered Source Instructions

Fig. 3. Maintainability rating versus size.

TABLE II
RANKING OF MAINTENANCE RATING CRITERIA

Factor	# Students Citing Factor
design	8
programming style	5
size of the product	4
documentation	3
product performance at acceptance test	2

effect" observed in [13], with major peaks of the total effort before the deadlines, is fairly distinct in the effort distribution of the specifying groups, the effort distribution by phase for the prototyping groups is much smoother. Especially at the end of the quarter, the programming, testing, and fixing effort of the prototyping groups did not peak, as it did for the specifying groups. Instead, the effort-peak for the prototyping groups at the end was mostly due to documentation effort.

Fig. 6 shows the effort distribution by activity in percent of the total effort for both group types. Proportionately, the prototype groups spent less time for designing and programming, more for testing, reviewing, and fixing. The higher effort needed to integrate the prototype products was confirmed by comments in the project critiques.

Going through the whole design process before coding seemed to simplify the integration by forcing developers "to think before coding." On the other hand, building a prototype had the advantage of "always having something that works."

Documentation Productivity: As mentioned already, no difference between the two groups in the overall productivity (DSI/MH) could be observed. However, there appeared to be a significant difference in the documentation productivity. The specifying groups produced, on the average, 2.8 pages per documentation MH, the prototype groups only 1.2 (Table III). An explanation for this effect might be that the members of the specifying groups were more motivated to write documents, for they chose their group type knowing that a lot of documents would have to be produced. In addition, the specifying groups had three deadlines where documents were to be presented, the prototype groups only one. Therefore, the "deadline effect" might have influenced the documentation productivity of the specifying groups more than the documentation productivity of the prototyping groups. Another explanation may be that a good deal of documentation was produced in the process of design; if the design man-hours are added to the documentation man-hours, the difference in pages/MH is reduced to 1.2 versus 0.9.

Retrospective Comments: In the follow-up questionnaire, the students were asked how their project outcome would have differed, if they would have belonged to a different group type. The answers of the students of the specifying groups were not uniform. Some would have expected a better product, some a worse product, if they had been in a prototyping group. On the other hand, the students of the prototyping groups mostly indicated that specifying would have increased the performance of their product and would have resulted in a faster development process. It is interesting that the data of the experiment generally did not confirm this expectation.

tenance costs. Somewhat paradoxically, however, the products of the prototype groups were judged worse as a basis for planning add-ons.

In exploring which factors influenced the maintainability rating, we compared the rating to the size of the products (Fig. 3). At first glance, it appears as if the students preferred to maintain smaller products. However, when asked in the follow-up questionnaire what the main criteria for their maintenance rating were, the students ranked the size of the products only third, and size was mentioned only as one factor besides design, programming style and documentation, and performance (see Table II).

Effort Distribution: During the development process, the groups had to meet different deadlines. The specifying groups had to hand in a requirements specification in the third week and a requirements and design specification in the sixth week. The prototype groups had to present their prototype for a prototype exercise in the fifth week. For both groups, the acceptance test took place in the tenth week after project start. Figs. 4 and 5 show the average effort distribution by phase and activity for both group types. While the "deadline

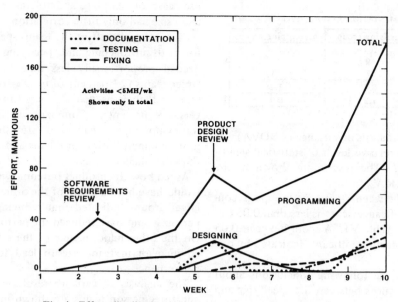

Fig. 4. Effort distribution by phase and activity: specifying groups.

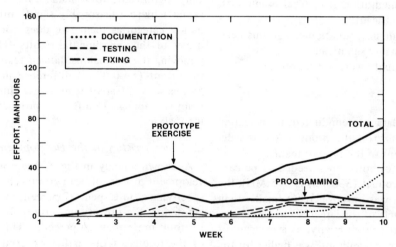

Fig. 5. Effort distribution by phase and activity: prototyping groups.

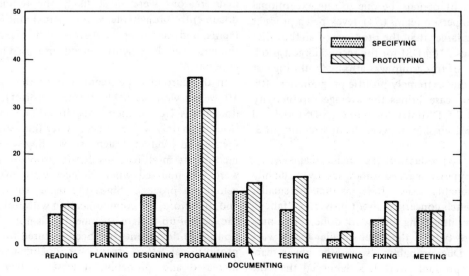

Fig. 6. Distribution of project effort by activity.

83

TABLE III
COMPARATIVE DOCUMENTATION PRODUCTIVITY

	specifying groups	prototyping groups
pages of documentation	161	54
MH for documentation	69	46
MH for design	67	13
productivity (page/MH)	2.8	1.2
pages/(design + doc. MH)	1.2	0.9

Analysis of Variance: An analysis of variance (ANOVA) was performed to determine the relative levels of statistical significance of the results above. The results are shown in the "Spec/Proto" column of Table V.

In general, a difference between treatment groups is considered significant if its significance score is less than 0.05 (indicated by two asterisks in Table V). A score between 0.05 and 0.10 is considered reasonably significant (indicated by one asterisk in Table V).

Table V thus summarizes the following conclusions about the significance of the differences between the specifying and prototyping groups:

- the differences in documentation size, total man-hours, and maintenance score are significant;
- the differences in program size, functionality, robustness, and ease of learning are reasonably significant;
- the differences in productivity were not significant.

B. Smaller Versus Larger Teams

A second analysis of the data was conducted, investigating the influence of the group size on the product and the development process, independent of the type of team.

Although the smaller teams of both types needed 41 percent less effort to develop their product (338 versus 575 MH), the average size of their products was only 8 percent smaller than the average size of the products of the larger teams (2690 versus 2921 DSI). Therefore, the productivity, as a measure of delivered source instructions per man-hour, was higher for the smaller teams than for the larger teams (7.5 versus 5.4 DSI/MH).

However, the almost equal average product size and the higher productivity might perhaps be due to one exceptional project: one of the two-person teams (S3) developed a product which was significantly larger than the products of all the other groups (4606 DSI versus 3164 DSI for the second largest product). The productivity of this group was also by far the highest (10 DSI/MH), due to one extremely prolific programmer. Removing this anomalous case brings the average productivity of smaller teams from 7.5 DSI/MH down to 6.25 DSI/MH and reveals a significant relationship between team size and product size.

The performance of the products of the smaller teams (again, independent of team type) was rated somewhat lower, mainly due to a lower functionality score. It seems that the smaller teams were not that much concerned about providing "fancy" functions, but more about getting their work done. (This may also have been because two of the three smaller teams were prototyping teams.) Due probably also to the lower manpower available, their products were less debugged than the products of the larger teams. On all the other factors—ease of

use, ease of learning, and tolerance of erroneous input, the team size had only little correlation.

Comparing the effort the teams spent for different activities, for both prototyping and specifying teams, the smaller teams needed proportionally less time for programming than the larger teams (27 percent of total effort versus 38 percent). As expected, they needed also less time for meetings (5 percent versus 9 percent). Comments in the project critiques and follow-up questionnaires confirm that the larger teams had more communication problems and communication overhead than the smaller teams.

Asked how the product outcome would have changed if they would have been a group of the other group size, people of the larger groups indicated that reducing their team size by one person would have reduced the performance of their products. On the other hand, people of the small teams did not expect an increase in team size to lead to an increase in product performance.

The analysis of variance results comparing the two-person and three-person teams are shown in the "Team Size" column of Table V. Most of the team size differences are not statistically significant; total man-hours and product functionality rating achieve a reasonably significant level. In the other evaluation categories team size does not appear to be a primary driver of the experimental results. However, as noted above, removing the anomalous data of team S3 yields a statistically significant ($s = 0.0039$) difference in product size across the groups with different team size. Thus, if we drop project S3, team size appears to influence product size more than development style.

C. Characteristics of the Development Process

As shown already in Fig. 6, the dominant activity in the development process of both group types was programming. The specifying groups spent 37 percent of their total effort for programming, the prototyping groups 30 percent. No other activity took more than 20 percent. This result conflicts with one of the results of the earlier experiment reported in [13], in which the percentages of effort for programming (12–17 percent) and documentation (27–32 percent) were reversed. The main reasons were most likely the requirements for more documents (project plans, test plans) and for updating documents, and the larger team sizes in the earlier experiment; and the improved documentation aids provided by Unix in the later experiment.

In the current experiment, due to the tight schedule (only 10 weeks were available for the project), the development documents (requirements specification and design specification) were only written once. After the software requirements review and product design review, they were not corrected to incorporate modifications due to problem reports. Also, they were not updated when changes were made during the development process. Since the team size was relatively small and, therefore, the communication within the groups was good, the lack of up-to-date documents was not critical. However, if up-to-date documents had been required for other reasons, the proportional effort spent for documentation would have increased and, probably, at least reached the programming effort.

TABLE IV
COCOMO ESTIMATES VERSUS PROJECT ACTUALS

Team	Man-Months actual	Man-Months predicted	Actual / Predicted
specifying	3.8	12	0.32
prototyping	2.1	6.6	0.32

In order to investigate whether the COCOMO model can be applied to this kind of class project, the data of the different products were entered in one of the products and a prediction was calculated. The results are shown in Table IV. Even allowing for the 30–40 percent difference due to nonproject activities explained in [12], a significant discrepancy remains. Several factors might have influenced this discrepancy. First, as mentioned above, no final version of the requirements and design specification was written and the documents were not updated. In addition, the fact that seven groups were working on the same kind of project simultaneously and the grade in the course was mostly based on the project outcome might have produced a much more competitive situation than is found in a normal program development environment. Also, the fixed schedule with no possibility for prolongation, imposed by the duration of the quarter, might have contributed to this effect.

Note that the COCOMO prediction offset was independent of the development style. For both specifying and prototyping groups, the model predicted the same percentage of the real effort. The mismatch between model estimates and project actuals is not overly surprising; in general, algorithmic cost models have a difficult time with small projects.

D. Characteristics of Products

Although all groups were given the same task, the product architectures differed significantly. They frequently seemed to be a reflection of the developer personalities (elaborate versus simple displays, terse versus verbose messages, free-form versus directed sequential inputs, etc.).

Most of the groups (6 or 7) developed a menu-driven system. Screen-oriented interaction was preferred to line-oriented interaction. The man–machine interface and the flexibility of the dialogue was very product- and architecture-dependent. In addition, competition stimulated man–machine interface frills.

The distribution of source code by function for products of both group types was almost the same (Fig. 7). Although the main purpose of the product was to calculate a cost, effort, and schedule estimation, the portion of code devoted to this purpose was very small (5–8 percent). The user interface turned out to be the most important part of the system. It took over 50 percent of the code. These results are consistent with the earlier results in [13].

The portion of code devoted to the file management system differs heavily between the products. It comprises anywhere between 5 and 40 percent of the code. Its size depends mostly on the provided capabilities and on how much file management functions of the operating system were used versus implementing a new file management system for the product. (The original directions to the teams said simply "develop a single-user file system for input data.")

In the number of delivered source instructions per person there was only little variation. With one exception (2303 for

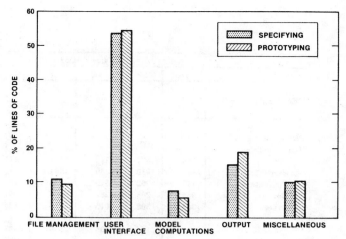

Fig. 7. Distribution of source code by function.

team S3), they were all in the range of 757–1055 DSI/person. The same is true for the overall performance of the products. With one exception (13.3 points), all products were rated between 17 and 21.3 points.

E. Some Other Observations

The organization of the team was left to the individual team members. Since no group leader was explicitly determined, every group followed more or less a democratic approach. Yet, the preferred organization was highly people-dependent. Four students mentioned in their critiques that the democratic approach worked well, while three students would have preferred to have a team leader.

The prototyping strategies were quite consistent over the prototyping groups. After building the prototype, no group started new to build the final product. Rather, 67–95 percent of the prototype code was used in the final product. The size of the prototypes was between 40–60 percent the size of the final product. An overall summary of project results is given in Table V.

IV. CONCLUSIONS

The results of this experiment provide some useful quantitative and qualitative information on the relative effects of the specifying and prototyping approaches on the development of a small applications software product. However, as indicated at several points earlier, initial experiments of this nature are not likely to provide definitive conclusions applicable to all project situations. The experimental results can be sensitive to exceptional individuals' performance or to experimental boundary conditions, or the results may depend on the size and nature of the software application. Therefore, the conclusions below should be considered suggestive rather than definitive. The conclusions are thus presented in project-specific rather than general terms.

A. Conclusions on Specifying Versus Prototyping

Prototyping tended to produce a smaller product, with roughly equivalent performance, using less effort. The prototyped products averaged about 40 percent smaller than the specified products, and required about 45 percent less effort. In performance, they rated somewhat lower on functionality

85

TABLE V
SUMMARY OF PROJECT RESULTS

	Specifying Teams					Prototyping Teams				ANOVA Significance	
	S1	S2	S3	S4	AVG.	P1	P2	P3	AVG.	Spec/Proto	Team Size
TEAM SIZE	3	3	2	3	2.75	2	3	2	2.33		
PROGRAM SIZE (Deliv. Source Inst.)											
File	64	622	246	714	411	45	356	204	201		
User Interface	1462	1910	2830	1064	1817	1123	1505	815	1148		
Compute	143	62	648	195	262	84	178	70	111		
Output	931	264	267	405	467	349	513	293	385		
Other	385	306	615	331	434	351	174	132	219		
TOTAL	2985	3164	4606	2809	3391	1952	2726	1514	2064	0.0674*	0.7891
Omitting S3 data					2986				2064	0.0668*	0.0039**
DOCUMENTATION (Pages)											
Rqts. Spec.	19	13	11	11	14	-	-	-	-		
Design Spec.	38	123	59	83	76	-	-	-	-		
User Manual	32	45	73	35	46	38	37	30	35		
TOTAL	165	231	181	179	189	58	49	56	54	0.0001**	0.3743
MANHOURS											
thru Rqts.	83	44	44	70	60	-	-	-	-		
thru Design	225	160	144	242	193	-	-	-	-		
thru Prototype	-	-	-	-	102	129	84	105	-		
Reading	29	33	40	72	43	21	24	43	29		
Planning	44	7	30	41	30	22	15	15	17		
Designing	81	46	59	82	67	16	13	12	13		
Programming	276	162	135	289	216	109	147	39	98		
Documenting	48	82	53	92	69	54	50	33	46		
Testing	45	49	55	29	44	27	75	46	49		
Reviewing	2	3	6	20	8	19	3	5	9		
Fixing	27	42	19	48	34	33	39	27	33		
Meeting	30	49	24	80	46	19	44	11	25		
Misc.	7	26	40	37	28	3	13	2	6		
TOTAL	589	498	459	789	584	323	422	232	325	0.0471**	0.0817*
PERFORMANCE											
Functionality	6.33	7	5	6	6.08	5.33	5	4	4.78	0.0799*	0.0799*
Robustness	4.67	5.5	6	4.33	5.13	4.33	4.33	3	3.89	0.0875*	0.7535
Ease of Use	2.33	4	2.67	4	3.25	6	5.33	2.67	4.67	0.2144	0.9133
Ease of Learning	3.67	3.5	4	3.67	3.71	5.67	5.33	3.67	4.89	0.0771*	0.6022
MAINT. SCORE (low is good)	45.5	57	59.5	59	55	21	27.5	45.5	31	0.0217**	0.6968
PRODUCTIVITY (DSI/MH)											
Overall	5.1	6.4	10	3.6	5.8	6	6.5	6.5	6.3	0.9727	0.1737
Coding	10.8	19.5	34.1	9.7	15.7	25	18.5	38.8	21		

and robustness, but somewhat higher on ease of learning and ease of use. Statistically, these differences were at least reasonably significant.

The main reason for this effect appeared to be that prototyping fostered a higher threshold for incorporating marginally useful features into a software product. The process of prototyping gave software developers a more realistic feel for the amount of effort required to add features to a project, and the lack of a definitive specification meant that prototypers were less locked into a set of promises to deliver capabilities than were the specifiers. In the somewhat rueful words of one of the specifiers, remarking on his team's efforts to fulfill the promises in their ambitious specification, "Words are cheap."

Prototyping did not tend to produce higher "productivity" if "productivity" is measured in delivered source instructions per man-hour. However, if "productivity" is measured in equivalent user satisfaction per man-hour, prototyping did tend to be superior. This conclusion reinforces the desire for a better productivity metric than the number of source instructions developed.

Again, this conclusion does not necessarily apply to every project situation. The value-of-information decision guidelines for software projects in [12, ch. 20] identify a number of situations in which the information value of a prototype will not be worth the investment in it. Even for projects similar to the one in this experiment, the specifying approach may be able to produce similarly concise products if the specification reviews are strongly focused on elimination of marginally useful product features.

Prototyping did tend to provide a number of benefits frequently ascribed to it. These included:

- products with better human-machine interfaces;
- always having something that works (at least for "build-upon" if not for throwaway prototypes);
- a reduced deadline effect at the end of the project.

Prototyping led to better maintainability ratings, but the effect was unclear. At the same time, participants' critiques indicated that specifications led to more coherent designs and that prototyping made it harder to plan additions.

Prototyping tended to create several negative effects. These included:

- proportionally less effort planning and designing, and proportionally more testing and fixing;
- more difficult integration due to lack of interface specifications;
- a less coherent design.

These effects become particularly critical on larger products. This suggests that, especially for larger products, prototyping should be followed by a reasonable level of specification of the product and its internal interfaces.

B. Conclusions on Team-Size Effects

Smaller teams produced smaller products with less effort and a higher "productivity" in DSI/man-hour. This conclusion is only statistically significant if the anomalous data for team $S3$ are removed from the analysis. The two-person teams spent smaller percentages of their effort in programming and meeting. Their products were rated somewhat lower on functionality, but about the same on ease of use, ease of learning, and robustness.

Some of this team-size effect may have accounted for some of the differences between the specifying and prototyping results, since the average size of prototyping teams was somewhat smaller (2.33 persons versus 2.75). However, the corroborative evidence from the project critiques indicates that the projects' results were strongly influenced by whether they used a specifying or a prototyping approach.

C. Conclusions on Other Software Engineering Effects

The "deadline effect" observed on a previous project [13] was corroborated. Also, this experiment corroborated the previous observation that most of a product's code is devoted to largely application-independent "housekeeping" functions.

The previous conclusion in [13] that "documentation is the dominant activity during software development" was not corroborated by this experiment. In fact, programming was the dominant activity during this experiment, due most likely to differences in project groundrules and team sizes. This result emphasizes the need for follow-up experiments to confirm conclusions reached during software engineering experiments.

The most effective software project organization in strongly dependent on the nature of the people on the project. Some people's critiques emphasized the need for a strong leader, as in the Chief Programmer Team approach. A larger number of people felt that a more democratic team approach was more effective.

The COCOMO model strongly overestimated the amount of effort required to develop the experimental products. The overestimates were typically by a factor of about 2.5, much larger than could be explained by not counting the typical 30–40 percent of the workday devoted to nonproject activities. Most likely, the extra productivity was a result of exceptional motivation of the people involved, both from the competitive-team aspects and from a Hawthorne effect.

Nothing succeeds like motivation. This was the major cause of both the high team productivity and the very high level of maintainability of their products. The software field in general needs a maintainability motivator similar in power to that of telling students, "20 percent of your course grade will depend on how much others want to maintain your product."

D. Future Research

It is clear that the large number of variables in the present experiment made it impossible to draw unambiguous conclusions. We believe it is equally clear that experiments such as this can make a significant contribution, particularly as others repeat them and thereby increase the sample size.

Subsequent experiments of this type should attempt to reduce the number of variables by:

- making all of the teams the same size (prohibit prime numbers of students per class!);
- more precisely defining the user-interface requirements, so that everyone implements close to the same functionality.

Several different directions for investigation were also suggested by this work.

- Further examinations of the effect of team size on programmer productivity and product size. Use the same development approach and environment, and a precisely defined product definition.
- Further examination of prototyping versus specifying approaches applied to different phases of a development project: definition of functional requirements, design decisions, and implementation decisions. In other words, how does the development approach affect the *nature* of the product, as distinct from the cost of development?

• Examination of the effect of implementation language choice on programmer productivity and product size. A series of class projects should be an excellent way to investigate this question. Of particular interest: comparison of interpreted and compiled languages.

• Examination of factors that influence the style of user-interface chosen by a particular designer, e.g., available development tools, assumptions about user environment, and personality traits of the designer.

• Investigation of the effect of turn-around time on programmer productivity. Is the effect linear or nonlinear? To what extent does it depend upon the programmer's expectations and previous experience?

• Examination of the "user-manual first" approach on product size, quality, and effort expended.

• Investigation of how accurately developers can predict final product size from requirements definitions. Also, how much does the existence of design specs improve accuracy of product size predictions?

• Further investigation of the effect of prototyping versus specifying on maintenance and enhancement costs.

• Further examination of the wide variations observed in coding productivity, with respect to both team size and development approach.

E. Summary

The results of this experiment indicate that both prototyping and specifying have valuable advantages that complement each other. For most large projects, and many small ones, a mix of prototyping and specifying will be preferable to the exclusive use of either by itself. In particular, the results indicate the following.

1) *The current specification-oriented model should not be completely scrapped, particularly on large projects.* The prototypers' experience indicated that interface and design specifications were still particularly valuable in supporting integration and change implementation.

2) *The current model needs to be reoriented to accommodate prototyping,* and such related techniques as incremental development. This involves establishing such new life-cycle milestones as a User Design Review (UDR) to achieve user validation of a prototyped user interface.

3) *Contracting for software acquisition needs to reflect the reoriented model.* This involves the use of competitive front-end prototyping and "fly-offs," and the organization of the development into a series of stabilized increments of functional capability.

4) *The bottom-line driver on selection of the specific mix of prototyping and specifying should be risk management.* Prototyping is not necessary on familiar projects where there is little risk of getting the wrong user interface, requirements, or design. Elaborate specifications are not necessary on smaller projects with good user-developer rapport, where there is little risk of botching the integration process or having an altercation over contract deliverables. Risk management considerations also drive most of the other key management decisions over the software life-cycle (how much to invest in analysis, simulation, new technology, testing, quality assurance, configuration management, etc.), leading to a final implication:

Software projects should develop, maintain, and follow a Risk Management Plan, which identifies potential high-risk issues, establishes plans for resolving them, and highlights risk-item resolution in project status reviews.

As a final note, it is worth reemphasizing the conclusion that the prototyping approach resulted in products that were easier to learn and use. For a field which is searching for ways to make its products more humane, this experiment indicated that the prototyping approach clearly has a great deal to offer.

APPENDIX A
PROJECT DESCRIPTION GIVEN TO STUDENTS

Project Objectives

The objectives of this two-quarter project are to develop and maintain a small software product (a version of the COCOMO software cost estimation model) as a team project. The product specifics for each quarter are the following.

Quarter 1 (Winter 1982): Develop an interactive version of the Intermediate COCOMO model, with the following capabilities:

• component-level project effort, schedule and cost estimation (basically, implementing the CLEF procedures in [12, Table 9-1, p. 148]);
• organic-mode projects only, with no adaptation estimation capability (simplification of [12, Table 9-1]);
• effort and schedule distributions by phase;
• single-user file system for storing and retrieving model inputs;
• easy to use by reasonably experienced, somewhat impatient user.

Quarter 2 (Spring 1982): Adapt the product of another team to provide the following additional capabilities:

• all three software development modes (organic, semidetached, embedded);
• adaptation effects;
• maintenance cost and effort estimation;
• effort distribution by activity;
• multiuser file system.
• user-interface enhancements.

Project Approach

Students will develop and maintain the product in three-person teams. Team selection and the types of teams available are covered in the Course Description. Specific schedules for each team's deliverable items are given in the Course Schedule.

Each program will be written in Pascal to run on the UCLA VAX-Unix system.

Product Acceptance

Acceptance tests for all teams' products will be performed on Wednesday, March 17. For preparation, each team shall provide three copies of a users' manual for their product on Monday, March 15.

The acceptance test shall consist of the instructors exercising the team's program to determine whether it:

- handles all cases specified in the objectives above;
- handles off-nominal conditions with useful error responses;
- exhibits a high degree of user-friendliness.

Product Deliverables

Each deliverable item shall be handed in at the classroom in three (3) copies at 4:00 PM of the designated day. Documents shall be page-numbered.

Day	Teams	Deliverable Items
Wed., Jan. 27	S	Requirements specification (see Course Notes for format)
Mon., Feb. 15	S	Requirements/Design spec and Draft Users' Manual (see Course Notes for format)
Mon., Mar. 15	S, P	Users' Manual (see Course Notes for format)
Wed., Mar. 17	S, P	Code and Maintenance Manual (Format TBD)

In addition, "P" Teams will prepare a prototype of their program to be exercised by the instructors on Wednesday, Feb. 10. Finally, each student will hand in two copies of their project critique (see Course Description for details) to either of the instructors by 4:00 PM, Wednesday, March 24.

Choice of Product to Maintain

A copy of each team's deliverable products (code, users' manual, maintenance manual) will be made available for review in (location TBD) during the period March 17-24. Each student is to review each of the other teams' products, and express his preference for which of the other teams' products he would prefer to maintain during the second quarter. A Product Choice form for expressing these preferences is attached; it is to be turned in with your project critique on Wednesday, March 24.

These evaluations will be used to determine:

- which product your team will receive to maintain during the second quarter;
- how well your team's first quarter product is rated for maintainability, as a component of your first quarter grade.

Time Sheets

Every Monday at classtime (4:00 PM), each student is to turn in a filled-out timesheet indicating how many hours during the previous week he spent performing the various project activities (reading, planning. . .). The results will be used for statistical purposes only; your grade will be based on your outputs and not on the number of hours you put in. A blank timesheet is part of this package.

Reviews

The Requirements Specifications produced by the "S" teams on Wednesday, January 27, will undergo a validation process by the instructors, resulting in a set of Design Problem Reports (DPR's) identifying problems found in the spec. (A sample DPR form is part of this package.) Copies of these DPR's will be provided to the "S" teams Monday morning, February 1. During the course period on February 1, a Software Requirements Review (SRR) will be held for each team, to determine the disposition of each DPR (required action, no action, redundant).

A similar process will be carried out for the "S" teams' Product Design specs and Draft Users' Manuals (Spec due Monday, February 15; DPR's returned Wednesday morning, February 17; Product Design Reviews during class February 17).

APPENDIX B
INSTRUCTIONAL LESSONS LEARNED

In this section we identify issues of specific interest to others who might wish to organize a course similar to this one. These comments are based on observations by the instructors as well as student critiques. They highlight a number of areas where we would make changes in any subsequent experiment.

Class Scheduling and Content

The project schedule was too tight for a one-quarter class, with test planning and study of software engineering papers referenced in lectures being the first casualties.

A second class was scheduled for the following quarter in order to examine maintenance and enhancement issues experimentally, but few students continued for the second class due to schedule conflicts.

Optimum scheduling of classroom lectures proved to be impossible: students wanted all lecture material prior to commencing the project.

There was insufficient lecture time for several important topics, e.g., coding and documentation standards, "user-manual first" strategy, and user-interface design issues.

While students considered the course very valuable, they complained that is was too much work, and that there was too much emphasis on the project and not enough on current software engineering literature.

The ideal situation would probably be a required three-course sequence: 1) lecture and reading; 2) product development; and 3) product maintenance.

Project Elements

Implementation of COCOMO cost-estimation equations was straightforward.

The file system was challenging due to lack of familiarity with Unix and the Pascal constructs needed to use operating system services.

The user-interface was challenging because the user-interface requirements were not given to students, and they were unfamiliar with user-interface design principles.

Terminal-independent, full-screen user-interfaces proved difficult due to poor documentation of relevant Unix library routines.

Project Requirements

Requirements definition for the user-interface and file system were too loose for close comparability of projects.

Ambiguity of system requirements led to competition among groups, and consequently overambitious goals. However, tighter requirements definitions for the user-interface might have subverted one of advantages of prototyping—the freedom to try more than one user-interface style.

While constraining the project to a more manageable scope and reducing the number of experimental variables, tighter requirements would also deprive students of useful lessons in system analysis and user-interface design.

Data Collection

The most important point regarding data collection is to insist that the student's timesheets be turned in on time, lest the student be forced to "recreate" the data at the end of the quarter.

It is also important to explain precisely which activities fall into which timesheet categories.

Project critiques were deemed very valuable by instructors, but varied widely in content; therefore, more specific guidelines should have been provided.

Documentation and Coding Standards

While the students were given relevant papers, relatively little emphasis was given to this subject in class. As a result, project results showed little attention to standards. Also, the amount of code documentation (i.e., comments) was highly variable.

We do not believe the lack of standards had any significant impact on experimental results; still, it is clear that more emphasis should be given to this topic in future classes.

Team Size and Experience

Our experience is inconclusive about the optimum team size from an instructional perspective. Small teams had fewer communication problems, but large teams benefited by more debate in design meetings.

The majority of students had less than a year of Pascal or Unix experience, but more important than amount of experience is its distribution. Instructors should survey the students to assist them in creating balanced teams.

Group Projects

Most students valued the group project experience; however, personality conflicts devastated one group.

Students were unsuccessful at inspiring less motivated team members, and they lacked effective methods for resolving conflicts. These problems can lead to unfair evaluation of individual students.

Since students ususally have relatively little experience with group projects, instructors should take pains to warn students that early meetings will be relatively unproductive, as team members try to get to know one another, and that they should make heavy use of electronic mail and design walkthroughs.

Examples of coordination problems that students should be made aware of include simultaneous update of one file by two team members, and two team members picking the same name for a file. Some of these problems can be minimized by using many small source files, combined via INCLUDE statements.

Design Reviews and Product Demonstrations

Letting everyone participate in reviews and demonstrations served our teaching goals very well, although our research goals were slightly compromised by doing this.

Members of both types of teams reported increased appreciation of specification and review techniques after seeing them in action.

Having two instructors review all documents and products provided much better feedback to students.

These sessions provided good opportunities to discuss alternate design decisions.

Development Environment

Use of a severely overloaded VAX 11/780 had an extremely negative impact on project development.

As contention for system resources increased (toward the end of the quarter) insufficient disk space often caused compiles to fail.

The Unix operating system and Berkeley Pascal were reasonable choices, although a more extended Pascal (e.g., one with strings) would have been preferred.

REFERENCES

[1] B. W. Boehm, "Software engineering," *IEEE Trans. Comput.*, pp. 1226–1241, Dec. 1976.
[2] H. D. Benington, "Production of large computer programs," in *Proc. Symp. Advanced Programming Methods for Digital Computers*, ONR, Washington, DC, June 1956, pp. 15–27.
[3] W. A. Hosier, "Pitfalls and safeguards in real-time systems with emphasis on programming," *IRE Trans. Eng. Management*, pp. 99–115, June 1961.
[4] W. W. Royce, "Managing the development of large software systems: Concepts and techniques," in *Proc. WESCON*, Aug. 1970.
[5] R. D. Williams, "Managing the development of large-scale reliable software," in *Proc. 1975 Int. Conf. Reliable Software*, IEEE/ACM, Apr. 1975, pp. 3–8.
[6] R. L. Glass, *Modern Programming Practices: A Report From Industry.* Englewood Cliffs, NJ: Prentice-Hall, 1982.
[7] M. M. Lehman, "Programs, life cycles, and laws of program evolution," *IEEE Spectrum*, Sept. 1980.
[8] P. Kerola and P. Freeman, "A comparison of lifecycle models," in *Proc. 5th Int. Conf. Software Eng.*, IEEE/ACM, Mar. 1981, pp. 90–99.
[9] B. W. Boehm, "Software design and structuring," in *Practical Strategies for Developing Large Software Systems*, E. Horowitz, Ed. Reading, MA: Addison-Wesley, 1975.
[10] D. D. McCracken and M. A. Jackson, "Life cycle concept considered harmful," *ACM SIGSOFT Software Eng. Notes*, pp. 29–32, Apr. 1982.
[11] M. Zelkowitz and M. Branstad, *Proc. ACM SIGSOFT Rapid Prototyping Symp.*, Columbia, MD, Apr. 1982.
[12] B. W. Boehm, *Software Engineering Economics.* Englewood Cliffs, NJ: Prentice-Hall, 1981.
[13] —, "An experiment in small-scale application software engineering," *IEEE Trans. Software Eng.*, pp. 482–493, Sept. 1981.

Edgar H. Sibley
Panel Editor

"An Assessment of the Prototyping Approach to Information Systems Development" by M. Alavi from *Communications of the ACM*, Volume 27, Number 6, June 1984, pages 556-563. Copyright 1984, Association for Computing Machinery, Inc., reprinted by permission.

A two-phased research project comparing the prototyping approach with the more traditional life cycle approach finds that prototyping facilitates communication between users and designers during the design process. However, the findings also indicate that designers who used prototyping experienced difficulties in managing and controlling the design process.

AN ASSESSMENT OF THE PROTOTYPING APPROACH TO INFORMATION SYSTEMS DEVELOPMENT

MARYAM ALAVI

Recently the traditional "life cycle" approach to information systems development has been under question [1, 2, 7]. A new approach to information systems development—prototyping—is gaining popularity among practitioners and academicians in the information systems field, and the term is appearing more frequently in the literature [1, 2, 11, 13].

Although common in hardware development, prototyping for information systems development is relatively new, and practical experience and published empirical studies in this area are limited. Except for isolated case studies [4, 6, 13], the effectiveness of the prototyping approach in organizational settings has not been studied. In fact, there is no unique definition for the term *information systems prototype*. Here, the following definition is adopted: An information systems prototype is an early version of a system that exhibits the essential features of the later operational system [13]. Some information systems prototypes may evolve into the actual production systems whereas others are used

only for experimentation and may eventually be replaced by the production system.

In this investigation of the effectiveness of the prototyping approach, user and designer attitudes are explored through field interviews and a laboratory experiment. Some practical suggestions for effectively using prototyping are presented in the conclusion.

PROTOTYPING APPLICATIONS: FIELD INTERVIEWS

Twelve information systems development projects using the prototyping approach in six organizations were analyzed. Industries and application projects are listed in Table I. The projects are further characterized in Table II.

In each organization and for each project, in-depth interviews with project managers and systems analysts were conducted—in all, 12 project managers and 10 systems analysts. In each interview, probing techniques were used to obtain a qualitative and complete understanding of the opportunities, problems, benefits, and shortcomings of prototyping.

Projects of varying size and scope were selected. The smallest in the sample was the accounts receivable system with an approximate project cost of $5000 and a project effort of 3 person-months. The chemical products costing and reporting system in the oil industry was the largest project at a cost of $630,000 and 88.9 person-months to develop. The nature of the systems studied ranged from transaction processing systems (e.g., accounts receivable, on-line calendar of events, registration, on-line telephone directory) to control systems (e.g., real estate development and management system, rail fleet management, and chemical products costing and reporting). All the projects were completed within the two years preceding the interviews and were considered to be successes by project managers and users.

Two sets of questionnaires were used. One set was used only in interviews with the project managers and contained structured questions for obtaining background information on the selected projects (e.g., scope, cost, effort). Another set of questionnaires was used with both project managers and systems analysts and contained open-ended questions with regard to the nature, perceived benefits, and shortcomings of prototyping.

GENERAL INTERVIEW FINDINGS

Perceived Benefits of Prototyping

The interviews revealed the following positive considerations with respect to prototyping.

Prototyping is real. An information systems prototype provides the user with a tangible means of comprehending and evaluating the proposed system and elicits more meaningful feedback from users in terms of their needs and requirements. As one project manager observed, "The users are extremely capable of criticizing an existing system but not too good at articulating or anticipating their needs."

Prototyping provides a common base line. Prototyping represents a common reference point for both users and designers by which to identify potential problems and opportunities early in the development process. It is also an effective way to draw out and clarify user requirements.

Users are enthusiastic. Prototyping is a practical way to cultivate and achieve user participation and commitment to a project. According to one systems analyst, "The ability to get a working system (the prototype) up and running in such a short time made the project very visible to the users. They felt that data processing was being responsive to their needs, and they in turn were very cooperative. The prototype helped us (the data processing group) gain credibility." Another project manager stated, "At the end of the prototyping process, the users were very satisfied with the development effort and the prototype. They felt they had some real influence in the design process."

TABLE I. Industries and Applications Using Prototyping

Industry	Applications
Education	Accounts receivable On-line calendar of events Registration system
Oil and gas	On-line journal processing and validation Chemical products costing and reporting On-line recruitment tracking Manpower utilization tracking On-line telephone directory Rail fleet management Crude transportation
Real estate development and management	Cash flow analysis and projection
State government	Personnel system

TABLE II. Some Characteristics of the Projects Studied

Application Projects	Approximate Project Cost[a] (dollars)	Approximate Project Effort[b] (person-months)	Project Development Duration (months)
Accounts receivable	5,000[c]	3	6
On-line calendar of events	not available	2	2
Registration system	10,000[c]	3	3
On-line journal processing and validation	216,000	30.6	13
Chemical products costing and reporting	630,000	88.9	21
On-line recruitment tracking	85,000	12	3
Manpower utilization tracking	560,000[d]	64	24
On-line telephone directory	70,000	11.3	6
Rail fleet management	295,000	41	14
Crude transportation	88,000	12.5	10
Cash flow analysis and projection	not available	0.9	3
Personnel system	50,000	7	9

[a] Cost figures present the total project costs (DP manpower, computer, and indirect costs) unless otherwise indicated.
[b] Only represents DP personnel time.
[c] Cost figure only represents DP manpower cost.
[d] The project involved five different sites. It was estimated that the total project cost would be $2.5 million upon completion of the system for all five sites.

Prototyping establishes better relationships. Users and data processing personnel seem to develop better communication and rapport, and a better appreciation for each other's jobs. This in turn leads to a better working relationship between the two groups.

Prototyping gets it right. Prototyping helps ensure that the nucleus of a system is right (i.e., performs as expected or required) before the expenditure of resources for development of the entire system.

Perceived Shortcomings of Prototyping

The following drawbacks were also found.

Prototypes can be oversold. Some project managers stated that by definition a prototype has limited capabilities and captures only the essential features of the operational system. Sometimes unrealistic user expectations are created by overselling the prototype, which may result in unmet user expectations and disappointment.

Prototypes are difficult to manage and control. Several project managers stated that due to the "newness" and nature of prototyping, there is a lack of know-how for planning, budgeting, managing, and control. Traditional life cycle approaches have specific phases and milestones and specific deliverables that are established before project initiation and are used as guidelines for project planning and control. Planning and control of prototyping projects are more difficult because the form of the evolving system, the number of revisions to the prototype, and some of the user requirements are unknown at the outset. Lack of explicit planning and control guidelines may bring about a reduction in the discipline needed for proper management (i.e., documentation and testing activities may be bypassed or superficially performed).

It is difficult to prototype large information systems. It is not clear how a large system should be divided for the purpose of prototyping or how aspects of the system to be prototyped are identified and boundaries set. In most cases, time and project resource constraints determine the boundaries and scope of the prototyping effort. However, more explicit guidelines and procedures are needed for prototyping large systems. Moreover, the internal technical arrangements of large information systems prototypes may be haphazard and inefficient and may not perform well in an operational environment with large amounts of data or large numbers of users.

It is difficult to maintain user enthusiasm. In some cases, user involvement and interest waned after the working prototype was developed. After high priority user requirements were satisfied by the prototype, users were not willing to spend time and resources to complete and "clean up" what was, in the minds of the designers, only an early version of the system. Instead, users wanted the design team to move on to a new project.

EXPERIMENTAL EVALUATION OF THE PROTOTYPING APPROACH

There were two basic limitations to the prototyping field interviews: (1) lack of a comparative analysis and evaluation of the perceived benefits and shortcomings due to unavailability of field data, and (2) unavailability of the users of the prototyped information systems for interviews with the researcher. To compensate, the second phase of the project consisted of a comparative evaluation of the prototyping versus the life cycle approach in a controlled laboratory environment for the purpose of obtaining data on user reactions and attitudes.

Experimental Setting

The experiment centered around a case analysis that involved developing an information system for support of a new plant investment decision in the chemical industry. Background, production, financial, and industry information were provided as well as price structure data and a detailed description of the company facing the investment decision. Detailed data on company history, cost, financial and market structures, and production history and projections were presented. In summary, a wide array of potentially relevant data was made available to the subjects.

Nine groups of 6 to 8 subjects each were formed. Half of the group members were asked to play the role of "user-managers" and decide whether or not to invest in the new plant, while the other half were instructed to assume the role of information system designer and develop a Management Information System for Investment Analysis and Planning (MISIAP) for the users. Half of the subjects playing the designer role were asked to use the prototyping approach; the other half were instructed to follow the life cycle approach.

Research Variables

The independent variable was, of course, the approach used—prototyping versus life cycle (Figure 1).

Three categories of dependent variables were investigated: (1) user evaluation of and satisfaction with the information system (MISIAP), (2) user and designer perceptions and attitudes toward the design process, and (3) the extent of use of the MISIAP in analyzing the case and arriving at decisions.

The first category of dependent variables was measured in terms of overall favorable evaluation, overall satisfaction, accuracy of output reports, ease of use, and helpfulness of the output reports.

User and designer perceptions and attitudes toward the design process (the second category of dependent variables) were measured in terms of ease of communication between user and designer, satisfaction with the level of user participation, degree of change in the user specifications, level of perceived conflict between the user and designer, user understanding of the information system throughout the design process, user influence on the design process, ease of control and management of the design process, and level of user commitment to the project.

The third category of dependent variables was measured in terms of extent of use as depicted in Figure 2. Figure 2 also provides an example of the five-point

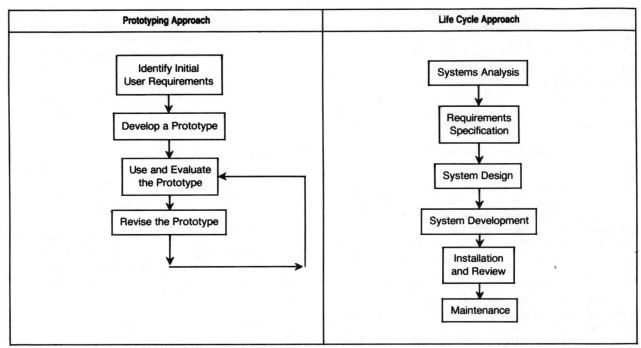

FIGURE 1. The Information Systems Development Approaches Investigated in the Study

Likert-type scales that were used as well in measuring the other two categories of dependent variables.

Subjects

The subjects of this experiment were drawn from the evening graduate student population of the College of Business Administration at the University of Houston. Ninety percent of the participating students had full-time professional positions with various organizations in the area. Two evening MBA classes were integrated for the purposes of the experiment: The subjects who played the role of users came from a course in general business and policy; those who played the role of the designers came from a graduate-level course in management information systems (MIS). The experiment was an assigned course project in both classes and

counted for 40 percent of the final course grade in each class.

The selection of this subject population was considered opportune for a number of reasons. First, it was felt that graduate business students would find role playing in a business case agreeable and were knowledgeable enough to feel comfortable analyzing the experimental case and making the new plant investment decision. Furthermore, it was felt that the training and academic backgrounds of the graduate MIS students provided them the skills necessary to develop the information system and profit from the experience. Also, since the experiment was assigned as a formal course project and constituted a major portion of the final course grade, the subjects were highly motivated and no resistance to the project was observed. Sixty-three

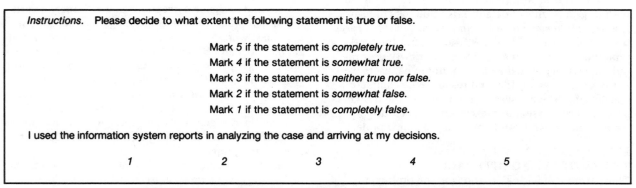

FIGURE 2. The Likert-Type Scale Used for Measuring the Extent of Use of MISIAP

subjects participated in the experiment: 29 in the role of systems analysts and 34 in the role of users.

Experimental Procedures

Nine user groups were formed from the graduate policy class and 9 systems analyst groups from the graduate MIS class. The user and systems analyst groups each consisted of 3 to 4 individuals. Each systems analyst group was randomly assigned to a user group, and each user/systems analyst team was randomly assigned to follow either the prototyping or life cycle approach.

Initially, neither the user groups nor the systems analyst groups were aware of the research question and the experimental nature of the project.[1] The policy students representing the users were told that the purpose of the exercise was to provide them an opportunity to make policy and strategic decisions in a specific case and learn about the computer and information processing technologies available to support managerial decision making. The systems analyst groups were advised that the project objective was to expose them to information systems development in a simulated real-world situation.

Case descriptions were distributed to each group. User groups were advised that their principal responsibility was to analyze the case and make the new plant decision and that they would be evaluated on the quality of their analysis and the investment decision. The principal responsibility of the systems analyst teams was to supply the information systems capabilities needed to support the users' decision and analysis.

Preexperimental Activities

The first preexperimental activity was the administration of a questionnaire to collect background and demographic information from the subjects. Next, the phases of the life cycle approach and the specific steps in each phase were reviewed in detail for the students who were asked to follow this approach. In addition, reading materials on the life cycle approach were assigned and discussed in class, and student questions regarding the approach answered. The prototyping approach was presented to the relevant students in a similar way.

Another preexperimental task was to teach the Inter-

active Financial Planning System (IFPS)[2] to the students playing the role of systems analyst. Through specific examples, students used IFPS in a "hands-on" mode. Homework assignments assured that all systems analyst students had a working knowledge and good understanding of IFPS capabilities and either the life cycle or prototyping approaches.[3] The elapsed time for the preexperimental activities was three weeks.

Experimental Session

To ensure that the prototyping and life cycle procedures were closely followed by the systems analyst teams, documentation forms corresponding to specific phases and activities of the two approaches were prepared and distributed. At the completion of each phase (four phases for the prototyping approach and six phases for the life cycle approach), each systems analyst team was required to use the forms to prepare and hand in documentation corresponding to that phase. The user and systems analyst teams were encouraged to meet as often as necessary. The elapsed time for the experimental session was seven weeks.

Postexperimental and Debriefing Sessions

After both the MISIAP and case analyses were complete, postexperimental questionnaires were administered to garner information in the following areas:

(1) user evaluation of and satisfaction with the information system developed,
(2) user and systems analyst subjects' attitudes and perceptions of the prototyping and life cycle approaches, and
(3) extent to which the information system was utilized by users in analyzing the case and arriving at the new plant investment decision.

Subjects were debriefed about the experiment and their questions about the project answered in general. Systems analyst subjects who had used the prototyping approach were debriefed on the life cycle approach and vice versa.

The poststudy session was concluded when the ques-

---

[1] The experiment and the research question were described to the subjects in the postexperimental session.

[2] IFPS is a modeling system developed and marketed by Execucom Systems Corporation in Austin, Texas.

[3] Postexperimental questionnaires indicated that the students felt they had adequate knowledge of IFPS and sufficient understanding of either the life cycle or prototyping approaches for design of their information systems.

TABLE III. Mean Scores[a] and Mann–Whitney U Test Results for the Dependent Variables Related to User Evaluation and Satisfaction with the Information System

Experimental Groups	Dependent Variables					
	Overall Favorable Evaluation of MISIAP	Overall Satisfaction with MISIAP	Timeliness of Output Reports	Accuracy of Output Reports	Ease of Use of MISIAP	Helpfulness of Output Reports
Users Exposed to Prototyping Approach	4.53	4.40	4.53	4.06	3.46	4.21
Users Exposed to Life Cycle Approach	3.42	3.21	4.53	2.64	3.07	3.14
Two-Tailed Probability	0.007[b]	0.011[b]	0.523	0.002[b]	0.345	0.007[b]

[a] Scores measured on 5-point Likert scales (1 = low, 5 = high).
[b] The difference between the means is statistically significant at $p < 0.05$.

TABLE IV. Mean Scores[a] and Mann–Whitney U Test Results for User Perceptions and Attitudes Toward the Design Process

	Dependent Variables			
Experimental Groups	Ease of Communication	Satisfaction with Level of User Participation	Perceived Conflict Between Users and Designers	User Understanding of Information Systems Project
Users Exposed to Prototyping Approach	3.86	4.20	1.36	3.66
Users Exposed to Life Cycle Approach	3.00	3.21	2.86	2.78
Two-Tailed Probability	0.13	0.0014[b]	0.0019[b]	0.11

[a] Scores measured on 5-point Likert scales (1 = low, 5 = high).
[b] The difference between the means is statistically significant at $p < 0.05$.

tionnaires were completed and all the subjects' questions were answered.

STATISTICAL ANALYSIS AND FINDINGS
The relationship between the independent variable (the information systems development approach) and the dependent variables (user evaluation and satisfaction with the information system, user and designer attitudes toward the design process, and utilization of the information system) was investigated by the Mann–Whitney U Test.[4] The Mann–Whitney U Test was used because the dependent variables were measured on Likert-type scales and because the sample sizes were relatively small.[5]

The mean scores and the results of the Mann–Whitney U Test for the dependent variables related to user evaluation and satisfaction with the information system are given in Table III. The statistically significant results indicate that, in general, user groups who used the prototyping approach had a more favorable evaluation of the information system and were more satisfied with it. In comparison to other user groups, they rated the system output higher in terms of accuracy and helpfulness to their analysis and decision making. No statistically significant differences between the two user groups were observed in terms of timeliness of output and ease of use.

The mean scores and results of the Mann–Whitney U Test for variables related to user perceptions and attitudes toward the design process are given in Table IV. In general, these results indicate that prototyping user groups had more favorable perceptions and attitudes toward the design approach, relative to life cycle users. The statistically significant results (at $p < 0.05$) show that prototyping user groups were more satisfied with

[4] This is one of the most powerful of the nonparametric tests, and it is a most useful alternative to the parametric test when the researcher wishes to avoid the *t* test's assumptions or when the measurement in the research is weaker than interval scaling.
[5] For user groups the sample sizes were 15 and 19, and for designer groups the sample sizes were 14 and 15.

their level of participation in the design process and perceived less conflict between the users and designers throughout the project. Although the results were not statistically significant, examination of the means indicates users of the prototyped system had a higher rating for ease of communication with the designers and reported a higher understanding of the design project.

The Mann–Whitney U Test result for the extent of actual use of information system output in making the new plant investment decision (Table V) was not statistically significant. However, the mean scores indicate a higher utilization of the system designed by the prototyping approach.

Analysis of data on designer attitudes and perceptions of the design process (Table VI) shows statistically significant differences between the prototyping and life cycle designer groups on only one item. The designers employing the prototyping approach perceived a higher degree of change in user specifications during the design process. Another interesting observation (although not statistically significant) is that prototyping designers had more difficulty managing and controlling the design process than did life cycle designers.

DISCUSSION OF FINDINGS
Interpretations of the research findings have to be qualified on two counts. First, the sample sizes, both in the

TABLE V. Mean Scores[a] and Mann-Whitney U Test Results for Extent of Use of MISIAP

	Dependent Variable
Experimental Groups	Extent of Use of MISIAP
Users Exposed to Prototyping Approach	3.66
Users Exposed to Life Cycle Approach	2.92
Two-Tailed Probability	0.11

[a] Scores measured on 5-point Likert scales (1 = low, 5 = high).

TABLE VI. Mean Scores[a] and Mann-Whitney U Test Results for Designers' Perceptions and Attitudes Toward the Design Process

Experimental Groups	Ease of Management and Control of Design Process	Frequency of Change in User Requirements
Designers Using Prototyping Approach	3.00	3.43
Designers Using Life Cycle Approach	4.00	1.34
Two-Tailed Probabilities	0.103	0.012[b]

[a] Scores measured on 5-point Likert scales (1 = low, 5 = high).
[b] The difference between the means is statistically significant at $p < 0.05$.

field interviews and in the experiment, were relatively small. Second, by the nature of laboratory experiments, the alternative design approaches—prototyping and life cycle—were compared in a less than realistic setting.

Business information systems to date have not met with unqualified success. Managers and users frequently complain about a low return on their large investment in computer-based information systems. Many of these systems are not fully used nor their full potential realized. Analysis of the reasons for failure indicates that basic problems are behavioral as well as technological. Users too often have a preconceived notion of what they want an information system to do and assume the designers have the same idea. In some situations, users may not be able to clearly identify their information processing problems and may not know what potential solutions exist. These conditions often set off a chain of misunderstandings both of the constraints imposed by the problems and the opportunities offered by their potential solution.

As users often have a difficult time visualizing what results an information system will produce, information systems designers need to develop ways of communicating and demonstrating such results before actually implementing the information system. Furthermore, once user requirements have been developed, the designer must convey to the user the logical design decisions that will have an eventual impact on the information system functions and the user. Such interactions have typically been missing, in part due to communication obstacles such as lack of a common language and a common frame of reference.

The prototyping approach seems to be effective in alleviating these behavioral problems in information systems development. Field interviews with practitioners of the prototyping approach, substantiated by the findings of the laboratory experiment, indicate positive user attitudes toward the information system and the design and development process. The experimental results suggest that prototyping increases the actual utilization of an information system by the users. Furthermore, information systems performance (as measured in terms of user satisfaction with the output and its perceived accuracy and helpfulness) was rated higher by users of prototyped systems than by users of systems developed by the life cycle approach. Field and laboratory observations suggest that prototyping makes communication between users and designers relatively easy and conflict free.

In the laboratory experiment, the experiences of designers using the prototyping versus the life cycle approach differed significantly on only one count—the perceived change in user requirements. The experiment also suggests that the designers of the prototyped information system experienced more difficulty managing and controlling the design process. These perceptions may be attributed to a higher level of user participation in the design process and more frequent changes in user requirements in the prototyping approach. Except for these two variables, no other noticeable differences between the two designer groups in the experimental setting were found. To some extent this conflicts with the field interview findings in which designers seemed to perceive improvements in communication and relationships with users when using the prototyping approach. The lack of difference between the two experimental designer groups may be attributable to the nature of laboratory experimentation. Another explanation may be that both user groups were highly motivated to work with the designer groups to complete the project, and hence, a high degree of communication and interaction between users and designers was observed by both experimental designer groups. However, more empirical research on the impact of prototyping on systems designers is clearly needed.

IMPLICATIONS FOR PRACTITIONERS
The research findings concerning the impact of the prototyping approach on designers and users of information systems provide some insight into the effectiveness of the prototyping approach. The field interviews in particular suggest the following guidelines for applying the prototyping approach.

Who should use prototyping. A prototyping effort should be undertaken by designers and users who are well informed about the prototyping approach. Prototyping philosophy and plans should be understood by both designers and users. In the laboratory experiment, designers who used prototyping reported a high level of change in user requirements compared to designers who used the life cycle approach. Frequent changes in user requirements may frustrate designers unless they are prepared to expect the change and view it positively.

Where to use prototyping. Prototyping is a new approach to information systems development, and like any organizational innovation, it needs a supportive organizational climate. Prerequisites to successful prototyping include technological tools that facilitate fast response to user requests and motivated and knowledgeable users and designers.

When to use the prototyping approach. Use the prototyping approach in the face of unclear or ambiguous user requirements. Prototyping seems to be effective in coping with undecided users and clarifying "fuzzy" requirements. Also, prototyping should be considered in situations where there is a need for experimentation and learning before commitment of resources to development of a full-scale system. A typical situation would be one in which innovative technical tools or approaches are used. In an example given by Canning [2], a company wanted to integrate three purchased packages into one system. Prototyping allowed them to experiment with different configurations and select the most effective way of linking the packages.

How to prototype. Manage and control the development of the prototype by planning the effort in advance (i.e., set cost, effort, and time limits). Set and enforce explicit procedures for control and coordination (e.g., deadlines for modifying and experimenting with the prototype, rules and criteria for documentation and testing). Failure to establish explicit procedures for managing and controlling the prototyping effort may result in designer frustration and dissatisfaction. In prototyping large projects, extra care should be taken; aspects of the system to be prototyped should be identified, and the possibility of using prototyping in conjunction with the traditional life cycle approach should be considered, as the milestones and control procedures offered by the life cycle approach seem to facilitate project management as a whole.

In summary, the prototyping approach offers an opportunity to achieve favorable user attitudes toward the design process and the information system. Furthermore, it facilitates fast response to user needs, allows clarification of user requirements, and offers an opportunity for experimentation. Although there are pitfalls and shortcomings, none seem troublesome enough to outweigh the potential benefits.

REFERENCES
1. Berrisford, T.R., and Wetherbe, J.C. Heuristic development: A redesign of systems design. *Manage. Inf. Syst. Q. 3*, 1 (Mar. 1979), 11–19. Proposes a major change to the life cycle approach to information systems development. An alternative approach, the heuristic development, is presented. Several case studies of heuristic development are discussed.
2. Canning, R.G. Developing systems by prototyping. *EDP Anal. 19*, 9, (Sept. 1981), 1–14. Defines software prototypes and describes their uses. Discusses technical and organizational requirements of prototyping. The application of prototyping approach in three large corporations is described.
3. Dodd, W.P. Prototyping programs. *Computer 13*, 2 (Feb. 1980), 81. Discusses the need for software program prototypes and describes the potential benefits of the approach.
4. Earl, M.J. Prototype systems for accounting, information, and control. *Account. Organ. Soc. 3*, 2 (1978), 161–170. Argues that many "principles" of MIS design fail to accommodate the complexities of organizational environment and learning. Three case studies are described, and a prototype procedure is presented.
5. Groner, C., Hopwood, M.D., Palley, N.A., and Sibley, W. Requirements analysis in clinical research information processing—A case study. *Computer 12*, 9 (Sept. 1979), 100–108. Contains a case study describing the use of computer system prototypes during the requirements analysis phase of clinical research information systems development.
6. Henderson, J.C., and Ingraham, R.S. Prototyping for DSS: A critical appraisal. In *Decision Support Systems*, M.J. Ginzberg, W.R. Reitman, and E.A. Stohr, Eds. Elsevier North-Holland, New York, 1982, pp. 79–96. Reviews the prototyping strategy and examines its use in the design and implementation of a model-based decision support system (DSS). Information requirements generated by prototyping approach are compared with the information requirements generated by a structured group process.
7. Keen, P.G.W. Adaptive design for decision support systems. *Database 12*, 1 (Fall 1980), 15–25. Argues that decision support systems should be designed through an adaptive process of learning, experimentation, and evolution. A framework for adaptive design is presented. A number of case studies are summarized in an appendix.
8. Keen, P.G.W. Value analysis: Justifying decision support systems. *Manage. Inf. Syst. Q. 5*, 1 (Mar. 1981), 1–16. Deals with justification of decision support systems, which by their very nature make traditional cost benefit analysis of little use. An alternative approach, value analysis based on prototyping and staged cost value assessment, is proposed.
9. Mason, R.E.A., and Carey, T.T. Prototyping interactive information systems. *Commun. ACM 26*, 5 (May 1983), 347–354. Presents a prototype methodology and development tool, which have been widely applied to the development of interactive information systems in the commercial data processing setting. The effectiveness of the methodology and relationship to other applications is discussed.
10. McCracken, D.D. Software in the 80's: Perils and promises. *Comput. World Extra* (Sept. 17, 1980), 5–10. Describes the problems in applications software development. It is argued that the root cause is that wrong application development tools are being used. A solution consisting of use of very high-level nonprocedural languages and prototyping is suggested.
11. Naumann, J.D., Davis, G.B., and McKeen, J.D. Determining information system requirements: A contingency method for selection of a requirements assurance strategy. *J. Syst. Softw. 1*, 4 (Dec. 1980), 29–44. Describes information requirements determination in terms of two stages: eliciting requirements and requirements assurance. The paper describes the selection of a strategy for information assurance that depends on environmental and project contingencies.
12. Naumann, J.D., and Jenkins, A.M. Prototyping: The new paradigm for systems development. *Manage. Inf. Syst. Q. 6*, 3 (Sept. 1982), 29–44. Reviews some of the published references to prototyping and presents a discussion of the underlying design concepts. A process model for information systems prototypes is developed. A discussion of the economics of prototyping and several examples are presented.
13. Sprague, R.H., and Carlson, E.D. *Building Effective Decision Support Systems.* Prentice-Hall, Englewood Cliffs, N.J., 1982. Covers conceptual and organizational issues related to design, development, and implementation of decision support systems.
14. Zelkowitz, M.W. A case study in rapid prototyping. *Softw. Pract. Exper. 10*, 12 (Dec. 1980), 1037–1042. Presents a case study in rapid prototyping using SNOBOL4. The goals of the experiment as well as some of the results are described.
15. Zelkowitz, M.V., Ed. Workshop notes. ACM SIGSOFT Workshop on Rapid Prototyping, Columbia, Md., Apr. 19–21, 1982. A collection of 31 papers on rapid prototyping.

CR Categories and Subject Descriptors: D.2.1 [**Software Engineering**]: Requirements/Specifications—*methodologies*; D.2.9 [**Software Engineering**]: Management—*life cycle*; D.2.m [**Software Engineering**]: Miscellaneous—*rapid prototyping*
General Terms: Design, Management
Additional Key Words and Phrases: assessment of prototyping approach

Received 8/82; revised 11/83; accepted 11/83

Author's Present Address: Maryam Alavi, Dept. of Systems and Strategy, College of Business Administration, University of Houston, 4800 Calhoun, Houston, TX 77004.

Part IV. Operational Specification

Unlike a conventional software specification, an operational specification can exhibit the behavior of the proposed software system. An operational specification is expressed in a language or form that allows it to be evaluated or interpreted to show system behavior. For example, it may describe the required system functioning as operations defined for an interacting set of computational processes (abstract machines). In this way, an operational specification may be thought of as a particular simulation model of the system—one that generates functional behavior but does not claim to do so efficiently. The articles in this section provide examples of languages and models for expressing operational specifications.

An operational specification addresses a key shortcoming of the conventional life-cycle, in which users and developers must wait well into the design phase before they have objects (e.g., modules or procedures) that are producing system behavior. By that time, design commitments have been made; if the system behavior is not acceptable, unraveling these commitments is costly. By contrast, an operational specification is available *early* in the process as a medium for users and developers to discuss the intended behavior of the system.

The relationship between an operational specification and fourth-generation languages (4GLs) should be clarified because the two approaches are sometimes perceived to be identical, or nearly so. A 4GL is nonprocedural, allowing users to state their intentions at a high level—for example, simply to print or display information without having to write procedures for data retrieval or formatting.*

Two aspects of the relationship between 4GLs and operational specification are as follows:

- The approach of operational specification is not limited to a particular application domain or run-time environment—both of which are factors in the selection of a 4GL. Zave, in the following article, makes this distinction.

- The operational specification is (generally) *not* the final, delivered system, whereas the "program" expressed in the 4GL (generally) *is* intended to be the

software solution. In this sense, a 4GL can obviate the need for an operational specification *if* the application domain and run-time environment are appropriate for its use.** With an operational specification, additional implemenation-oriented transformations are applied before the delivered system is produced.

The first article, by Zave, introduces the software development paradigm built around the method of operational specification. Comparisons are made to the conventional life-cycle paradigm. The article fairly treats the advantages and the disadvantages of both paradigms.

An operational specification is a prototype. In the second paper, Balzer, Goldman, and Wile illustrate this equivalence with an example using the GIST specification language. The article includes an insightful view of specification as providing various freedoms from design and implementation issues.

Smoliar's article addresses the representation of complex operational requirements for a system's reliability, growth, and availability. He develops an operational specification using P-nets to show the interaction of virtual machines that encapsulate system behavior. The essential element of an operational specification is present: a behavior-generating model formulated early in the software development process.

As Zave's paper makes clear, Jackson System Development (JSD) embodies the operational paradigm of software development. JSD rejects the top-down, function-oriented analysis in favor of explicitly modeling the behavior of the real objects that interact in the user's problem domain. Cameron, in this section, presents JSD examples that illustrate this operational approach.

The final two articles in this section offer case studies using operational specification in an embedded system (Zave) and a nonembedded system (Agresti). Zave's paper considers the special needs of requirements representation for embedded systems. The PAISLey specification language is defined and used on an example of a patient-monitoring system.

Agresti's nonembedded case study arises from the spacecraft flight dynamics environment. The operational specifi-

---

*4GLs have been used successfully by a variety of organizations, most often for applications that involve accessing and reporting from large data bases. In Part II of this tutorial, McCracken and Jackson describe a scenario of end-user development that is in use now with 4GLs as the implementation tool.

**Also, the efficiency may be less with a 4GL. One experiment reported that the 4GL implementation ran 30 times slower than the procedural language implementation (*Government Computer News*, June 21, 1985, page 33).

cation includes a model diagram and descriptions of behavior-producing processes. The article discusses two practical issues that will be important to organizations considering the use of operational specification:

- Under what circumstances is it likely to be effective?
- What were the observed benefits of using it?

The annotated bibliography lists some other articles that may be of interest. The open literature on operational specification is not as extensive as that on prototyping or transformational implementation. However, the articles in this section demonstrate that operational specification is a realistic alternative approach with distinct advantages over conventional methods.

"The Operational Versus the Conventional Approach to Software Development" by P. Zave from *Communications of the ACM*, Volume 27, Number 2, February 1984, pages 104-118. Copyright 1984, Association for Computing Machinery, Inc., reprinted by permission.

THE OPERATIONAL VERSUS THE CONVENTIONAL APPROACH TO SOFTWARE DEVELOPMENT

The conventional approach to software development is being challenged by new ideas, many of which can be organized into an alternative decision structure called the "operational" approach. The operational approach is explained and compared to the conventional one.

PAMELA ZAVE

For some years there has been a rough consensus on the proper phases of a software development project and on the decisions to be made during those phases. The conventional "software life cycle" has pervaded the field of software engineering, defining the terms we have used and shaping our perceptions of problems and their potential solutions.

More recently there have been complaints about the chronic problems of the conventional life cycle (e.g., [23]). Various new ideas for developing software have been emerging, but these ideas, such as executable specifications and program transformations, have no place in the conventional approach. They can, however, be organized into an alternative strategy called here the "operational approach." A number of current research projects based on the operational approach testify to its growing importance.

DESCRIPTION OF THE TWO APPROACHES

Any software development effort begins with a problem thought to be solvable by a computer system. When computer specialists become involved their first job is to investigate the problem; divergence between the two development approaches arises when those specialists begin to formulate a solution.

Either approach can be described as a sequence of decisions leading to a target system that can be installed and used. In both cases it may be necessary to back up, remake an earlier bad decision, and repeat the subsequent phases. In either case changes in customer needs may cause iteration of the entire sequence. Back-

A NEW APPROACH TO SOFTWARE DEVELOPMENT

Some of the most serious problems of software development were identified years ago but continue to resist practical solutions. Modern programming environments are designed to apply the latest technology to all aspects of software development, but because they do not offer comprehensive solutions to these chronic problems, only modest improvements in productivity can be expected from them.

Meanwhile several research projects, pursued independently, have incorporated an approach to software development so different in its organization of decision-making that unnecessary burdens on developers are eased and some of the usual trouble spots disappear entirely. The fundamental similarities among these projects have been obscured by many differences in style, emphasis, and application area. This article describes the essence of that approach, apart from the details of its instantiations.

The ideas presented here are relatively new and untried, and may not deliver in practice what they promise in theory. But they are interesting in their own right for the new perspective they provide, and if successful will yield substantial gains in software productivity—and cause major changes in the management of the development process.

tracking and iteration will not be considered until we compare the two approaches, however.

The Conventional Approach

The *conventional approach* to software development is pictured in Figure 1.

During the requirements phase, computer specialists formulate a system to solve the problem and define this system in the requirements specification. This specification treats the system as a "black box" describing all required characteristics of its external behavior ("what"), but no characteristics of the internal structure that will generate that behavior ("how"). The specification is almost always written in English, although natural language may be constrained by structure and supplemented by pictures, tables, formulas, etc. [15]. Figure 2 is a requirements specification for a trivial process-control system.

The design phase determines the internal structure of the software system, usually as a decomposition into modules of code. This is a top–down, hierarchical decomposition such that its modules will produce the required functions, be compatible with the hardware and software resources of the runtime environment, encapsulate information likely to change, meet the required performance constraints, and be implementable within the development environment. (For instance, it is often assumed that a module will be assigned to a single programmer.)

Figure 3 (p. 100) is a design for building the trivial process-control system in a runtime environment consisting of a single minicomputer running Pascal. Now the modules are treated as black boxes (only an English description of their externally visible behavior is given), but their interfaces (in this case, through procedure and function calls) are made explicit. A more substantial design might include preliminary allocations of resources and performance to modules, test plans [17], or axiomatic specifications of module behavior.

·The implementation phase turns the design into code executable in the runtime environment. This entails defining the internal mechanisms by which each module will meet its behavioral specification (and its performance/resource allocation), and mapping module mechanisms and interface properties into the implementation language. Figure 4 (p. 101) shows parts of a Pascal implementation of the trivial process-control system.

The preceding may seem to be a restrictive and even distorted picture of current software development practice. There are in fact many exceptions (see *Comparison of the Two Approaches*), some of them deliberate improvements to the conventional approach and some of them accidents caused by the deficiencies of the conventional approach. The point is that Figure 1 is the model upon which almost all theorizing and tool-building in software engineering are based. Its central principle is top–down decomposition of black boxes (starting from black-box requirements), from which all structure in Figure 1 devolves.

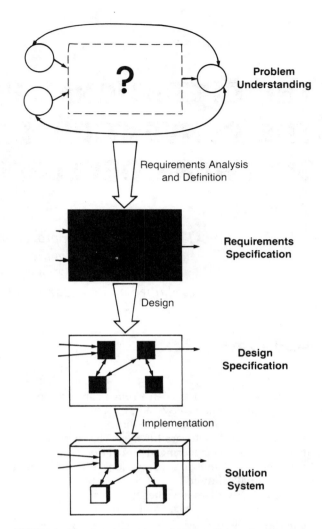

FIGURE 1. The conventional approach to software development is based on the principle of top–down decomposition of black boxes, and all its features can be derived from that philosophy.

The system must read a temperature sensor on each of 10 machines once every second. If a machine is hotter than 125°C, or if its temperature has risen more than 2°C in the last 5 intervals between readings, an alarm must be sounded until the condition ceases. Both the sensor values and the alarm activation flag are accessible as special-purpose hardware registers.

FIGURE 2. A requirements specification is supposed to describe all required characteristics of the external behavior of a system, but say nothing about the internal structure that will generate the behavior. It is almost always written in English (possibly constrained for the purpose or supplemented by graphics and formulas) because there is no suitable formal notation for the whole.

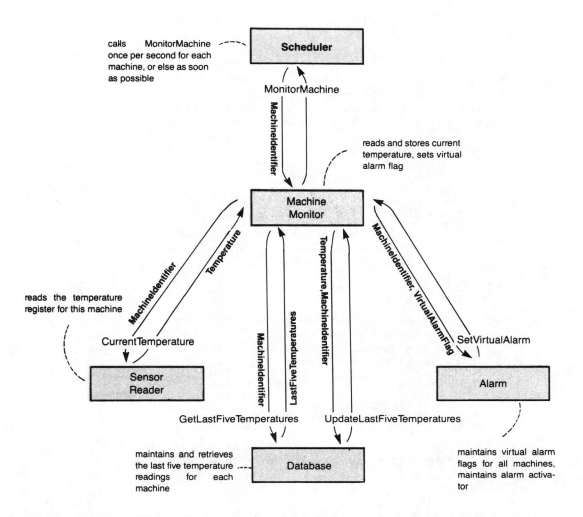

FIGURE 3. A design shows a decomposition of the system into modules of code. Although the interfaces between them are explicitly defined, each module is still a black box. The decomposition must meet functional, performance, resource, modifiability, and developmental requirements simultaneously; this design, for instance, is tailored to a single processor with adequate speed and a centralized memory.

The Operational Approach

The *operational approach* to software development is pictured in Figure 5 (p. 102).

During the specification phase, computer specialists formulate a system to solve the problem and specify this system in terms of implementation-independent structures that generate the behavior of the specified system. The operational specification is executable by a suitable interpreter. Thus external behavior is implicit in the specification (but can be brought out by the interpreter), while internal structure is explicit.

This description may make an operational specification sound like a design, but it is not. First of all the structures provided by an operational specification language are independent of specific resource configurations or resource allocation strategies (and can be implemented by a wide range of them), while designs actually refer to specific runtime environments. For in-

stance, the operational specification[1] of the trivial process-control system sketched in Figure 6 (p. 103) is organized in terms of asynchronously interacting parallel processes, virtual structures that can be implemented in a variety of ways. One way is to multiplex a single physical processor, effecting communication and synchronization through shared memory. Another is to use one physical processor per process, effecting communication and synchronization via messages sent across a data-communication link.

Each *machine-j-monitor* process is responsible for monitoring one machine. It goes through a sequence of discrete states, each of which is a member of the set "LAST-FIVE-TEMPERATURES," i.e., a five-tuple containing the recent history of the machine as known to

---

[1] The operational treatment of the process-control example will be carried out in PAISLey. For references and a summary of other operational specification languages, see *Some Instances of the Operational Approach.*

```
procedure MonitorMachine(Machine: MachineIdentifier);
    var ReadTemp: Temperature;
    RetrievedLastFiveTemperatures: LastFiveTemperatures;
    ComputedFlag: VirtualAlarmFlag;

    function FiveWayMin
        (TemperatureVector: LastFiveTemperatures): Temperature;
        var Min: Temperature;
        begin
            Min := TemperatureVector[1];
            for i := 2 to 5 do
                if TemperatureVector[i] < Min
                    then Min := TemperatureVector[i];
            FiveWayMin := Min;
        end;

    begin
        ReadTemp := CurrentTemperature(Machine);
        GetLastFiveTemperatures
            (Machine,RetrievedLastFiveTemperatures);
        ComputedFlag :=
            (ReadTemp >= 125.0)
            or
            ((ReadTemp -
                FiveWayMin(RetrievedLastFiveTemperatures))
                    >= 2.0);
        SetVirtualAlarm(Machine,ComputedFlag);
        UpdateLastFiveTemperatures(Machine,ReadTemp);
    end;

begin
    while true do
        for i := 1 to 10 do
            begin
                repeat ; until CurrentTime > Schedule[i];
                Schedule[i] := Schedule[i] + 1.0;
                MonitorMachine(i);
            end;
end.
```

FIGURE 4. A solution system consists of code executable in the runtime environment. Here is a fragment of a solution in Pascal. If the solution comes from implementing a design in the conventional approach, the internal mechanisms by which each module meets its behavioral specification are new, and the solution is the first version of the system to be executable. If the solution comes from a transformed specification in the operational approach, no new functions have been added since the specification phase.

the process-control system. The successor to each state is computed by evaluating the mapping:

(1) machine-j-monitor-cycle:
     LAST-FIVE-TEMPERATURES
     → LAST-FIVE-TEMPERATURES,

which is defined as:

(2) machine-j-monitor-cycle[hist] =
(3)   process-current-j-temperature
            [(hist,current-j-temperature)];

(4) current-j-temperature: → TEMPERATURE;

(5) process-current-j-temperature:
(6)   LAST-FIVE-TEMPERATURES
         × TEMPERATURE
         → LAST-FIVE-TEMPERATURES;
(7) process-current-j-temperature [(hist,temp)] =
(8)   proj[(1,(maintain-last-five-temperatures
                    [(hist,temp)],
(9)   maintain-virtual-alarm-j-flag
                    [(hist,temp)]
(10)   )
(11)   )];

(12) maintain-last-five-temperatures:
(13)   LAST-FIVE-TEMPERATURES
         × TEMPERATURE
         → LAST-FIVE-TEMPERATURES;

(14) maintain-virtual-alarm-j-flag:
(15)   LAST-FIVE-TEMPERATURES
         × TEMPERATURE
         → FILLER.

Lines 1, 4, 5–6, 12–13, and 14–15 are declarations that identify the domains and ranges of their respective mappings. Definitions use a simple functional syntax in which "[]" denotes application of a mapping to its argument and "()" denotes construction of a tuple. (Note that members of the set "$A \times B$" take the form "(a, b).") "proj" is an intrinsic mapping on two arguments, an integer and a tuple; the value of "proj[(i, t)]" is the ith component of the tuple t.

Functional syntax is an operational-specification-language structure that is independent of decisions concerning control and data, and can be implemented by a wide range of them. The two subexpressions whose values contribute the two components of the tuple on lines 8–10 can be evaluated sequentially or in parallel; nothing is said about how or where the values are stored before "proj" is applied to them.

At the end of the process step (after evaluation of "machine-j-monitor-cycle") the old state is *replaced* by the new value just computed. Replacement can later be implemented by modifying the data in place, by constructing a new value in scratch storage and then copying it, or by constructing a new value elsewhere and moving a pointer to refer to it.

Not only are the structures of an operational specification language independent of implementation-oriented decisions, but also the mechanisms (*usages* of the specification-language structures) in an operational specification are derived solely from the problem to be solved. They are chosen for modifiability and human comprehension without regard to any implementation characteristics whatsoever.

For instance, the process structure shown in Figure 6 is essentially a reflection of the real world in which the system will operate: one process per independent, asynchronous object. Each process interacts with and controls or senses only the object to which it corresponds.

For another instance, "maintain-last-five-temperatures" produces an updated value of the temperature history, while "maintain-virtual-alarm-j-flag" decides whether machine-j is cause for an alarm at this time

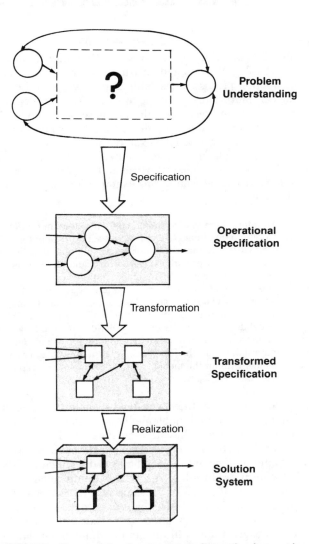

FIGURE 5. The operational approach to software development is based on separation of problem-oriented from implementation-oriented concerns, and all its features can be derived from that philosophy.

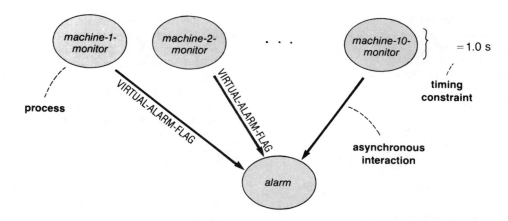

FIGURE 6. An operational specification is a complete and executable representation of the proposed system. It is described in terms of computational structures that are known to have a wide range of possible implementations, and its organization is based as closely as possible on the problem to be solved.

and so informs the *alarm* process ("maintain-virtual-alarm-j-flag" is evaluated only to cause this side effect on another process, so its value is always a place-holding constant). Thus each step of a *machine-j-monitor* process makes and responds fully to one sensor reading. Since the problem is to do this once per second, each step is constrained to take exactly this amount of time.

The principle of problem-oriented specification structure is a universal characteristic of the operational approach, as can be seen in this example from a very different domain:

- An information system should contain a computer-based representation (model) of real-world activities about which it provides information. It must also contain entities (functions) that answer various queries by examining the current state of the model. The model should be separated from the functions in the specification for a variety of reasons: (1) The model should be explicit so that it can serve as a basis for communication with the user. (2) The model defines the terms for the functions and implicitly circumscribes a set of possible functions. (3) The model is more stable than the functions, because the functions can change without the model's changing, but not *vice versa* [10, 22].

The structure of the operational specification is problem-oriented but not implementation-oriented. During the transformation phase the specification is subjected to transformations that preserve its external behavior, but alter or augment the mechanisms by which that behavior is produced, so as to yield an implementation-oriented specification of the same system. The goal of all research efforts in this area is to automate the transformations themselves, although selection of appropriate transformations will remain in human hands for the foreseeable future.

One type of transformation changes the modifiable and comprehensible mechanisms of the operational specification to equivalent ones lying at different points

in the trade-off space balancing performance (timing, reliability) and the various implementation resources (processors, memory, communication channels, *etc.*) involved. Some examples of these trade-offs:

- Most people understand (and would specify) Fibonacci numbers in terms of the equation "Fibonacci[n] = Fibonacci[$n - 1$] + Fibonacci[$n - 2$]," but they are far more efficiently computed by storing previous Fibonacci numbers rather than recomputing them.[2]

- If two processes have a producer–consumer relationship, their overall performance can often be improved by introducing buffering between them or even breaking each process into several stages and organizing a pipeline.

- An operational specification based on relational database theory may refer to the state of the database at some particular time in the past (when a given predicate was true). Although such a specification is directly executable, it requires a vast amount of storage, because no state of the database can ever be discarded. A transformation that eliminates this unreasonable use of storage entails noting which items are the subjects of "historical references," and adding extra structures to the database so that all relevant historical information is maintained in its current state [21].

Other transformations are needed so that specification structures can be mapped straightforwardly and efficiently onto a particular configuration of implementation resources. These transformations may introduce explicit representations of implementation resources, or resource allocation mechanisms, that were not present in the original specification.

Figure 7 shows a sequence of transformations on the operational specification of the process-control system. The result is an operational specification with the same structure as the design in Figure 3, because that seems to be the best organization for modules of code running

[2] For a transformation that does this *without* losing the structure of the original definition, see [32].

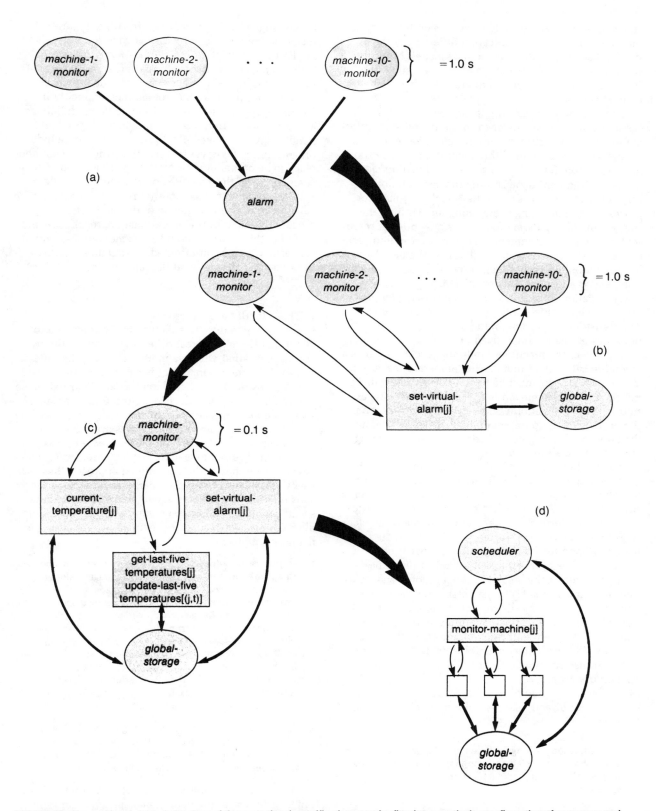

FIGURE 7. The problem-oriented structure of the operational specification must be fitted to a particular configuration of resources and resource-allocation strategies. This is accomplished by applying a series of automated transformations that preserve external behavior, but change the mechanisms producing the behavior.

on a single processor so as to solve this problem. (Note that the transformed specification differs from the design in that its modules are *not* black boxes, but fully specified executable structures.) In this example the same Pascal program will be the result of both development sequences.

Specification (a) has multiple asynchronous processes, each with the power to compute and store information, while the runtime environment has only a single processor and a monolithic memory unit. The transformation from (a) to (b) brings the specification closer to the environment by absorbing the computational role of the *alarm* process into the "machine-j-monitor" processes (as a mapping evaluation), and shifting the storage role of the *alarm* process to a new process representing the physical memory. This transformation preserves behavioral equivalence (because the old *alarm* process was idle except when responding to an interaction), and is a form of "inversion" [18, 19].

Specification (b) still has ten *machine-j-monitor* processes, each of which must take a step every second. The transformation from (b) to (c) reduces these ten processes to one parameterized process capable of monitoring any of the machines (and must cycle ten times a second to catch all of them). The temperature registers and history storage must be parameterized as well. This information is also moved to the *global-storage* process so that the specification will have two processes, one performing all computation but storing no information, the other performing no real computation but storing and retrieving all information.

Specification (c) now fits the physical resources of the runtime environment, but it has a process constrained to cycle once a second and no mechanism for enforcing that constraint. The transformation from (c) to (d) supplies a scheduler which interacts with a real-time clock so as to invoke the monitoring function (evaluate the mapping "monitor-machine") at the proper times.

The language of transformed specifications is basically the same as the language of operational specifications—it may be a subset or superset, but the framework remains. During the realization phase the transformed specification is mapped into the implementation language. The goal of all research efforts in this area is to deal with the challenging problems during specification or transformation, so that the realization step is a straightforward one.

Realization may entail making resource-allocation decisions not directly expressable in the specification language:

- If a specification language is based on relational database theory, and if the implementation language is a procedural one, then all the standard database operations must be implemented.

In other words, the realization creates a virtual machine on which the transformed specification can run.

More routinely, structures of the specification language must be mapped into structures of the implementation language. To go from Figure 7(d) to Figure 4, for instance, the *scheduler* process becomes a nonterminating Pascal program, and the *global-storage* process becomes the global variables in that program. (Note that interactions between the two become memory accesses via a bus but need not be programmed explicitly in Pascal.) Mapping evaluations become Pascal functions and procedures, in the course of which all residual parallelism is removed. Realization may also include programming low-level features that were too commonplace to be bothered with earlier, or translation of some components of the specification to hardware devices.

Just as top-down decomposition of black boxes can be considered the central theme of the conventional approach, the heart of the operational approach is separation of problem-oriented and implementation-oriented concerns via problem-oriented, executable specifications and transformational implementation.

Is There Really a Difference?

It is tempting to draw the picture in Figure 8, and to claim that there is no real difference between the two approaches—that we have merely changed the milestones. This view is incorrect because the four unlabeled boxes in Figure 8 could not exist. Their existence would imply a class of decisions preceding each milestone and another class of decisions following it—while in fact decisions from the two classes are interleaved.

The conventional approach places great emphasis on separating requirements (external behavior) from internal structure, but in the operational approach these are freely interleaved to get the operational specification. This interleaving is necessary to arrive at an executable specification, but it is also an expression of the inevitable coupling between *what* is being done and *how* it is being accomplished.

- Call-processing software in a telephone system must obtain a trunk line between two local exchanges before a long-distance voice connection can be made. If the trunk line is requested as soon as the long-distance number is dialed, the user of an overloaded network (in which there are no free trunk lines) will never hear the audible-ringing sound, nor will the called party's phone ring. If the trunk line is not requested until the called party has answered (on the grounds that trunk lines are scarce and valuable), users may find their calls aborted at this later point. Thus an internal mechanism affects the external behavior of the system.

- Almost any mechanism for processing transactions will impose limits on the sizes of certain input fields. The external behavior of the system includes what action it takes when these limits are exceeded [30].

The operational approach separates the problem-oriented structure of the operational specification from implementation considerations. In the conventional approach the design phase provides the high-level mechanisms that will produce the required behavior, but those structures must also fit the implementation envi-

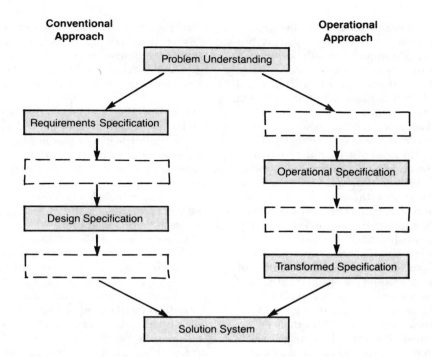

Conventional Approach

Operational Approach

FIGURE 8. An incorrect view. It is tempting to conclude that, as this picture suggests, the two approaches differ only in how the same sequence of decisions is divided and labeled. In fact there are fundamental differences between the two approaches in how decisions are ordered.

roment and meet the performance constraints. Thus designers must consider both problem-oriented and implementation-oriented issues together.

> The designer of a distributed system may wish to decompose into modules on the principle of information hiding [25, 27], but be unable to specify modules that extend across computers. This is because the effects of distribution on performance, reliability, and communication are too pronounced for this property to be left implicit in the design.

The conventional approach separates high-level (intermodule) mechanisms, which are determined during design, from low-level (intramodule) mechanisms, which are determined during implementation. Each mechanism is tailored for performance and resource consumption at the same time it is chosen to carry out a necessary function. In the operational approach all functional mechanisms have been chosen by the time the operational specification is complete, and optimizations of all types of mechanisms may be interleaved during the transformation phase.

Finally, the operational approach separates mechanisms from their realization in terms of the implementation language, while in the conventional approach intramodule mechanisms are interleaved with implementation-language decisions. This is inevitable, since the only way to record these mechanisms is to program them.

Yet another misconception is that an operational specification is no different from a program in a very high-level language (VHLL). A VHLL is a declarative language in which problems within a well-defined domain can be posed. Such a program is an input to an "application generator," which then generates a system to solve the particular problem for a fixed runtime environment. The operational approach is more widely applicable than the VHLL strategy because it requires neither a narrow domain (operational specification languages express solutions, not problems) nor a fixed runtime environment (transformations can be chosen so as to reshape the specification in many different directions).

COMPARISON OF THE TWO APPROACHES
Both approaches are idealizations of what is often a messy aggregation of compromises and retreats. Thus we will evaluate the potential of the two approaches on two separate grounds: (1) how the idealized decision sequence could be exploited if we could achieve it; and (2) how likely it is that the idealized decision sequence can be achieved without extensive backtracking.

How Can The Properties of the Two Approaches Be Exploited?
Validation (Building the Right System) A system development project cannot succeed unless the system

really solves the customer's problem. Since the proposed solution (described in the requirements specification or operational specification) is actually formulated by computer specialists, the proposal must be validated by the customer. "The customer" may be a large organization including end users familiar with the application but not with computer systems.

The conventional approach has the advantage that English requirements can be read and approved directly by customers. They can also form the basis of a legal contract. On the other hand, informal requirements are notorious for their incompleteness, inconsistency, and ambiguity. Indeed, these are the problems that first led computer scientists to look for specifications that were formal, and therefore subject to automated checks on their coherence.

Operational specifications are formal, and therefore seem to have the opposite characteristics: machine-processable but inaccessible to end users and other nontechnical people. Once a formal specification has been obtained, however, it is easy to summarize its properties informally in words or pictures. This can be done manually by a computer specialist whose heightened understanding (from dealing with the rigor of formal specification) should facilitate communication on all levels. It can also be done automatically; [29], for instance, describes a project to generate English narrative automatically from an operational specification.

Another important factor in user/analyst communication is the ability of the user to grasp and evaluate the concepts behind any proposal [36]. Experienced systems analysts report that an explicit operational model is much more helpful than black-box requirements, although doing a meticulous job on conventional requirements (e.g., [16]) may help just as much.

Recently the concept of prototyping has added a whole new dimension to the possibilities for user participation in system development. Prototyping is possible under both paradigms, but in substantially different forms.

In the operational approach the specification itself can be used as a prototype, since it is executable. This type of prototype can be produced rapidly [41] and will be produced as an integral part of the ordinary development cycle. It can only be used for demonstrations under tightly controlled "laboratory" conditions, however, because it will probably be missing low-level details, and will certainly lack the packaging, performance, etc., needed for a field trial.

In the conventional approach a prototype is produced by iterating the entire development cycle. This can result in a field-worthy prototype, but the conventional approach gives no particular guidance as to how to produce a prototype more rapidly than a product.

Verification (Building the System Right) Another major problem is to ensure that the delivered system is faithful to its specification. In the conventional approach, this can only be done through testing and/or formal proofs of correctness, each of which has well-known disadvantages. Program proving can only establish consistency between the design specification and the implementation, since the requirements are not formal. Furthermore, it has not been shown that proofs can be constructed by the average programmer in the context of a real development project.

Testing is a more common technique, and can be used to establish consistency between the implementation and the requirements specification (this is the sig-

TABLE I. Advantages of the Conventional and Operational Approaches*

	Conventional	Operational
Validation	Informal requirements can be understood directly by everyone	Formal specifications are rigorous, can be analyzed formally
		User has a model of the system to internalize and evaluate
		Operational approach makes rapid prototyping available automatically
Verification		Both testing and program-proving have well-known inadequacies
		Transformational implementation guarantees correctness
Automation		Transformation and realization are highly automatable
Maintenance		Operational approach addresses directly the structural conflict between efficiency and ease of maintenance
Management	Conventional approach provides organizationally useful milestones	Executable specification provides early results and accountability
	Managerial aspects of operational approach unexplored	

* Assuming that both approaches could be applied successfully to any project, the differing properties of the two approaches would still cause differences in the handling of certain chronic problems. Here advantages of the two approaches are summarized.

nificance of the test plan in [17][3]). Testing is an arduous process, however, and can never prove the absence of errors.

The philosophy of transformational implementation seeks to avoid either testing or verification by deriving the implementation from the specification using only transformations and mappings that have themselves been proven correct, i.e., proven to preserve behavioral equivalence. Compilation is such a transformation. We have little experience in using higher-level transformations (see *Weaknesses of the Operational Approach*), but the idea is so appealing, and the alternatives so inadequate, that it is certainly deserving of some enthusiasm.

Automation The conventional approach has successfully resisted automation for a long time. This is because early (preimplementation) system representations tend to be informal, and because each phase includes decisions about the mechanisms that will generate the required behavior—the automation of which can only be attempted through the techniques of artificial intelligence. Current interest in automated support for the conventional approach centers on integrated programming environments; these environments are useful for the implementation phase only, however, and do not claim to replace the creativity (synthesis) involved in writing a program.

In the operational approach the specification phase is labor-intensive, but its output is a formal object. This means that templates [37] and even components can be reused. This is also a once-promising idea whose luster has dimmed during years of failed attempts, but there is reason to hope that rigorous distinction between problem-oriented mechanisms and optimizations will enable it to work at last [1].

The transformation and realization phases of the operational approach are ripe for automation because all of the behavioral requirements have been translated into computational mechanisms by the time the operational specification is written. From this point on, the system is formally represented, and the decisions yet to be made concern efficiency, computational resource management, and language translation exclusively. The latter subjects can be understood analytically, and this knowledge can be turned into tools which supply everything but judgment.

Maintenance In the structure of software there is an inherent conflict between efficiency and ease of maintenance [3]. Efficiency suggests that information be distributed, while ease of maintenance suggests that it be localized.

- A "demon" is a procedure that is invoked whenever the state of the program satisfies a certain condition. The easily maintained, but inefficient, implementation is one that checks all demon triggering conditions whenever the state changes. The efficient, but hard-to-maintain, implementation is one that distributes knowledge of the demon to all

demon to all parts of the program where the state could change so as to make that demon's trigger true [21].

In other words, the decomposition suggested by the criteria of comprehensibility and modifiability (fortunately, these two seem to lead to the same decompositions) is not necessarily the same as the decomposition suggested by performance and efficient use of resources.

The conventional approach *per se* does nothing to alleviate this problem, since it supports only one decomposition. The conventional approach can be refined and altered to solve some aspects of it, however—even compilers solve low-level versions of the problem. One approach taken by the A-7 project led by David Parnas at the Naval Research Laboratory [9, 11, 12, 16, 24, 28] is to decompose on the basis of modifiability and then to regroup small logical units into other units, such as processes, chosen for resource-allocation purposes.

The operational approach addresses the structural conflict more directly by dividing development into two major phases exactly on these lines. The operational specification is optimized for maintainability, while the transformations break this structure down in favor of something more efficient.

Since an evolutionary cycle is a redevelopment of the system, the operational approach may promote automation of evolution as well as initial development. If the source of change is the system's required behavior, then the specification is modified, and the previous transformations can simply be reapplied to produce the modified implementation. Speed-ups here will improve responsiveness to changing user requirements [8]. If previous implementation decisions are at fault, then different transformations can be applied to the original specification. In either case the uniform language framework will improve traceability and change control. Note that neither proofs nor tests are robust in the face of change.

Management The conventional approach is well-suited to managerial and organizational needs. The requirements specification defines the interface between users and developers; the design specification defines the interface among the work of many programmers. No one has suggested which organizational structures or work assignments would be appropriate for the operational approach.

All potential advantages of the operational approach for management concern technical and psychological problems. For instance, the conventional approach does not yield executable code until late in development. Since we seldom feel sure of something until we see that it works (and rightly so), this means there is little accountability until it is too late. Nervous people are understandably overeager to produce code, neglecting the analysis and design phases. By prescribing an executable version of the system early in development, the operational approach offers a milestone which is both psychologically satisfying and subject to meaningful evaluation.

---

[3] It is interesting that one of the problems of conventional testing, namely determining whether the test output is correct, can be solved by the use of an operational specification as an oracle [34].

Can The Recommended Decision Sequences Be Achieved?

Weaknesses of the Conventional Approach The conventional approach stresses that all behavioral decisions should be made before any structural ones. This is an unrealistic and even undesirable expectation, since internal structure inevitably affects such external properties as feasibility, capacity, behavior under stress, and interleaving of independent events. Previous examples have illustrated this, as do the following:

- Ballistic missile-defense systems are at the outer limits of current computer technology. A necessary phase of the development of such systems is "preliminary design" to establish the feasibility of the proposed requirements. These preliminary designs are usually concealed from contractors bidding from the revised requirements.

- Software can be made fault-tolerant only if it has meaningful components whose failure can be detected and whose bad effects can be contained. To the extent that fault tolerance involves user participation, external behavior cannot be analyzed or defined without a virtual structure of components to which fault-tolerant properties can be attached.

Even if we could develop adequate behavioral requirements free of structural bias, there would be considerable difficulty in specifying them formally, since most formalisms introduce internal structure—if only to decompose complexity. Sets of axioms and finite-state machines are among the few representations that do not bias internal structure, but axioms have proven useful only for specifying *components* of complex systems, while finite-state machines (or regular expressions) have proven useful only for specifying very limited properties of complex systems. This problem is undoubtedly part of the reason why most conventional requirements are still written in English.

Another serious problem with the conventional approach is its reliance on a strategy of top–down decomposition for design. Basic methodological principles tell us that implicit decisions should be avoided, that if error-prone decisions must be made early then they should be subjected to early checks, and that individual decisions should be as orthogonal to others as possible. Top–down design leads to decomposition decisions most of whose consequences are implicit, makes the most global decisions earliest yet cannot validate them until the very end, and causes the top-level decisions to

affect all properties of the system [10, 22]. It seems that top–down hierarchical decomposition is an excellent way to explain something that is already understood [35], but a poor way to acquire understanding.

- Top-down design allocates both function and performance to modules. During implementation it may be discovered that no implementation of a module's functional requirements can meet its performance requirements, but there was no way to know this earlier.
- Consider the problem of printing, in order, the prime numbers up to 1000. Without prior knowledge of a solution there is no way to decide among these top-level decompositions [10]:

(1) "generate table of primes";
    "print table of primes"
(2) for $n := 2$ step 1 until 1000 do
        if "n is prime" then "print n" fi
(3) $n := 2$;
        while $n <= 1000$
        do "print n";
            $n :=$ "next prime after n"
        od

Note that these criticisms do not apply to verification of the *correctness* of a design decomposition (which can be accomplished top–down (see [26]), nor to TRW's Distributed Computer Design System [31], in which an exploratory "look-ahead" decomposition guides the final decomposition on the level above.

In the operational approach the primary decomposition of complexity is based on problem-oriented vs. implementation-oriented structure rather than hierarchical decomposition. Even within an operational specification, the most prominent structures tend to be discovered by methods other than top–down decomposition. Although it is true that hierarchical abstraction is often used within an operational specification to defer details, these details must be resolved before the specification phase comes to an end.

Weaknesses of the Operational Approach One apparent weakness of the operational approach is the need to reduce external behaviors to internal mechanisms before specifying them. This suggests to many that operational specifications are overconstraining and premature.

There can be no question that this is a danger, but results so far are promising. Particularly noteworthy is

TABLE II. Weaknesses of the Conventional and Operational Approaches*

Conventional	Operational
Conventional approach does not allow for the effect of system structure on system behavior	Operational approach presents a danger of premature design decisions
"Black-box" requirements are very difficult to specify	It may prove difficult to execute specifications with adequate performance
Top–down decomposition is difficult and risky	Transformational implementation is a new and undeveloped technology
	People may find it hard to guide transformations

* It may not be possible to apply both approaches successfully to any project. Here are the known feasibility problems on each side.

TABLE III. Some Instances of the Operational Approach*

	Jackson System Development Method	PAISLey Project	Gist Project	Applicative Programming
Domain of Origin	Data processing	Real-time systems	AI and database systems	Programming
Special Features	Specific method for obtaining operational specification	Explicit representation and transformation of concurrency and distribution	Very high-level specification language motivated by expressive power of English	Strong mathematical foundations
	Maintainability stressed Operational specification uses implementation language, transformations operate within implementation language	Formal and executable performance constraints Execution of incomplete specifications	Associative retrieval and historical reference Use of constraints to refine nondeterminism (as in common-sense reasoning)	Historical emphasis on efficient execution of the operational specification itself, including special-purpose hardware architectures
Automated Support	Specifications informal, not executable Transformations language-dependent	Complete integrated environment possible and being planned	Complete integrated environment possible and being planned	Specification environments exist Transformations being automated
Current Status	In real-world use	First tools being implemented Methods in research stage	Many tools implemented (including natural-language paraphraser, behavior explainer)	Transformations and special-purpose hardware in research stage, use without them stable
References	[19, 10, 22, 18]	[37–42]	[5, 14, 21, 4]	[2, 32, 13, 33, 6, 7]

* "Domain of Origin" refers to the source of a project's computational model and notational flavor. It does *not* delimit the domain of applicability of a project's techniques. In fact, in all four cases, broad applicability has been shown.

the Jackson System Development (JSD) method (Table III), which is the only instance of the operational approach to have well-developed procedures and guidelines for deriving the operational specification. JSD does not deal adequately with all aspects of system development, but JSD specification techniques are clearly comprehensive and JSD specifications are clearly implementation-independent.

Furthermore, structuring principles discovered by different research efforts do not seem to conflict with one another. We believe that, with further study of operational specifications, we shall arrive at a point where any case in which a behavior appears to have two different specifications will be seen to fall into one of two categories: (1) The two specifications actually produce subtly different behaviors. (2) Of the two specifications, one is clearly superior on solid methodological grounds having to do with the criteria of comprehensibility and modifiability. Thus the other form may be a suitable target for an optimizing transformation.

• An elevator controller receives inputs from request buttons at the various floors and from sensors in the elevator shaft; it controls the elevator motor and signal lights at the various floors. Each of the two functions (motor and lights) needs to know the "state" of the elevator (position, direction, outstanding requests), which can be computed by keeping track of the inputs. It may seem to be an arbitrary choice whether each function performs this computation for itself or whether the results of a single computation are shared by them, but it is not. If the computations are separate they may become somewhat unsynchronized, in which case the elevator's actual behavior may differ from the elevator's "intention" (as indicated by the lights) when race conditions occur. This will be discernable to the user [22].

• Two independent processes in the same system may happen to use some of the same external inputs. The input interface may send the inputs to one of the processes, which will then forward them to the other process. Alternatively, the input interface may replicate the inputs and send them to both processes. The latter is clearly better because it does not violate the original independence of the two processes [37].

The difficult aspect of the implementation-independence problem is that each existing operational specification language seems to be more abstract in some dimensions than in others. If future research fails to change this, however, it may be sufficient to choose a specification language for a particular problem that is implementation-independent and transformable in the properties most critical to the success of the system.

Another potential problem with operational specifications is that they may run too slowly for the kind of testing and demonstration we would like. The technical problems and opportunities here are well-known from the analogy with LISP. Techniques for speeding up LISP execution have ranged from special-purpose hardware to compilation of functions whose definitions have stabilized.

The other major weakness of the operational approach is that transformational implementation is a relatively untried approach, and the necessary theoretical supports are only beginning to be developed. The idea of program transformations has been with us for a long time (they are warmly endorsed in [20]), without noticeable impact.

The actual similarities between transformations of specification and of implementation languages are less than meets the eye, however. Although the line between operational specification languages and high-level implementation languages has grown fuzzy, there is still one clear difference: implementation languages are meant to be compiled automatically into the target code, without human intervention. This means that they *must* allow the programmer some control over use of physical resources, a necessity which complicates the languages and renders them less implementation-independent than specification languages.

> Dynamic structures of all kinds (data structures, processes, *etc.*) are much more difficult to analyze and transform than static ones. The primary reason for using dynamic structures is to conserve storage, a motivation that concerns implementation resources only. Problem-oriented specifications can always declare static structures up to the maximum capacity of the system, and use them as needed.

We conjecture that this inherent complication and implementation-dependence is what makes conventional programming languages difficult to transform. The transformational approach delays resource bindings for as long as possible—until after all necessary adjustments to the behavior-producing mechanisms have been made.

A final problem concerns current plans to have human users choose the transformations to be applied. It is not clear that, after several transformations, the specification will still be comprehensible enough to allow human intervention! Only further research and experience will determine whether or not this is a serious problem.

It may be worth mentioning that even without tools to support transformation, a form of the operational approach is already popular in some circles and has been applied successfully to projects under heavy time pressure. This is the use of shell programming on the UNIX[4] operating system to produce a prototype, followed by expansion and optimization in C.

SOME INSTANCES OF THE OPERATIONAL APPROACH

Despite their common philosophy, the projects summarized in Table III vary widely in style, emphasis, and accomplishments. An operational specification language, for instance, can use as its fundamental model of computation either parallel processes (PAISLey), updates and accesses to an associative database (Gist), or function evaluation (applicative programming). Any of these models can be tailored to a particular application domain by extension, i.e., by predefining structures native to that application.

My viewpoint is inevitably partisan, but the goal of this paper has been to clarify some legitimate and important distinctions. To do this it has been necessary to polarize two sets of ideas that can—and have been—combined in many ways. It has also been necessary to compare what is inherently incommensurate, for the conventional approach is a mature technology whose problems have either been solved or resisted many attempts at solution, while the operational approach is based on technology whose faults have not been filtered in this way. Nevertheless, I hope these means are justified by the ends of promoting general understanding and scientific debate.

Acknowledgments John Cameron will recognize many of our discussions in these pages; Mack Alford, Phil Cannata, Doug Comer, Dennis DeBruler, Peter Denning, Dick Kieburtz, John Manferdelli, Dave Parnas, Jim Weythman, Elaine Weyuker, and Jack Wileden all gave me valuable comments.

---

[4] Trademark of AT&T Bell Laboratories, Inc.

REFERENCES
1. Alford, M. Software requirements in the 80s: From alchemy to science. *Proc. ACM '80*, Nashville, TN (October 1980).
2. Backus, J. Can programming be liberated from the von Neumann style? A functional style and its algebra of programs. *Commun. ACM* 21 (August 1978), 613–641.
3. Balzer, R. Personal communication, April 1982.
4. Balzer, R.M. Goldman, N.M. and Wile, D.S. Operational specification as the basis for rapid prototyping. *ACM SIGSOFT Softw. Eng. Notes* 7, (December 1982), 3–16.
5. Balzer, R. and Goldman, N. Principles of good software specification and their implications for specification language. *Specifications of Reliable Software Conference*, Cambridge, MA (April 1979), 58–67.
6. Bauer, F.L. *et al.* Towards a wide spectrum language to support program specification and program development. *SIGPLAN Notices* 13, (December 1978), 15–24.
7. Bauer, F.L. *et al.* Programming in a wide spectrum language: A collection of examples. *Sci. Comput. Program 1.* (October 1981), 73–114.
8. Blum, B.I. The life cycle—A debate over alternative models. *Softw. Eng. Notes* 7 (October 1982), 18–20.
9. Britton, K.H. and Parnas, D.L. A-7E software module guide. *Naval Research Laboratory Memorandum Report* 4702, Washington, D.C. (December 1981).
10. Cameron, J.R. *JSP and JSD: The Jackson Approach to Software Development*, to be published.
11. Clements, P.C. Function specifications for the A-7E function driver module. *Naval Research Laboratory Memorandum Report* 4658, Washington, D.C. (November 1981).
12. Clements, P.C. Interface specifications for the A-7E shared services module. *Naval Research Laboratory Memorandum Report* 4863, Washington, D.C. (September 1982).
13. Darlington, J. An experimental program transformation and synthesis system. *Artif. Intell. 16* (March 1981), 1–46.

14. Goldman, N.M. and Wile, D.S. A relational data base foundation for process specifications. In: *Entity-Relationship Approach to Systems Analysis and Design*, P.P. Chen, ed. Elsevier North-Holland, New York, 1980, 413–432.
15. Heninger, K.L. Specifying software requirements for complex systems: New techniques and their application. *IEEE Trans. Softw. Eng. SE-6* (January 1980), 2–13.
16. Heninger, K.L. *et al.* Software requirements for the A-7E aircraft. *Naval Research Laboratory Memorandum Report. 3876*, Washington, D.C. (November 1978).
17. Hester, S.D., Parnas, D.L. and Utter, D.F. Using documentation as a software design medium. *Bell Sys. Tech. J. 60*, (October 1981), 1941–1977.
18. Jackson, M.A. *Principles of Program Design*, Academic Press, New York, 1975.
19. Jackson, M.A. *System Development*, Prentice-Hall, Englewood Cliffs, NJ, 1982.
20. Knuth, D.E. Structured programming with *go to* statements. *Comput Surv. 6* (December 1974), 261–301.
21. London, P. and Feather, M. Implementing specification freedoms. *Sci. Comput. Program. 2* (November 1982), 91–131.
22. Michael Jackson Systems Ltd. *Jackson System Development* (course manual), 1982.
23. McCracken, D.D. and Jackson, M.A. A minority dissenting position. *Systems Analysis and Design—A Foundation for the 1980's*, William W. Cotterman *et al.*, eds., Elsevier North-Holland, New York, 1981, 551–553.
24. Parker, R.A. *et al.* Abstract interface specifications for the A-7E device interface module. *Naval Research Laboratory Memorandum Report.* 4385, Washington, D.C. (November 1980).
25. Parnas, D.L. On the criteria to be used in decomposing systems into modules. *Commun. ACM 15* (December 1972), 1053–1058.
26. Parnas, D.L. The use of precise specifications in the development of software. *IFIP Congress*, Toronto, Ontario, August 1977, 861–867.
27. Parnas, D.L. Designing software for ease of extension and contraction. *IEEE Trans. Softw. Eng. SE-5* (March 1979), 128–138.
28. Parnas, D.L. *et al.* Interface specifications for the SCR (A-7E) extended computer module. *Naval Research Laboratory Memorandum Report* 4843, Washington, D.C. (January 1983).
29. Swartout, W. GIST English Generator. *Proc. National Conf. Artif. Intell.*, Pittsburgh, PA (August 1982), 404–409.
30. Swartout, W. and Balzer, R. On the inevitable intertwining of specification and implementation. *Commun. ACM 25* (July 1982), 438–440.
31. TRW Defense and Space Systems Group. Distributed computing design system/DCDS description. *Tech. Rep.* CDRL A004, Huntsville, AB, (August 1981).
32. Turner, D.A. The semantic elegance of applicative languages. *Proc.*
33. Wadler, P. Applicative style programming, program transformation, and list operators. *Proc. Conf. Funct. Program. Lang. Archit.* Portsmouth, N.H. (October 1981), 25–32.
34. Weyuker, E.J. On testing nontestable programs. *The Comput. J. 25, 4,* (1982), 465–470.
35. Wirth, N. On the composition of well-structured programs. *Comput. Surv. 6,* (December 1974), 247–259.
36. Yeh, R.T. *et al.* Software requirements: New directions and perspectives. *Software Engineering Handbook*, C.V. Ramamoorthy and C.R. Vick, eds., Van Nostrand Reinhold, New York, to appear.
37. Zave, P. The anatomy of a proc136s-control system. Submitted for publication, May 1982.
38. Zave, P. A distributed alternative to finite-state-machine specifications. Submitted for publication, December 1982.
39. Zave, P. An operational approach to requirements specification for embedded systems. *IEEE Trans. Softw. Eng. SE-8* (May 1982), 250–269.
40. Zave, P. Testing incomplete specifications of distributed systems. *ACM/SIGACT-SIGOPS Symp Princ. Distributed Comput.* Ottawa, Canada (August 1982), 42–48.
41. Zave, P. Case study: The PAISLey approach applied to its own software tools. Submitted for publication, June 1983.
42. Zave, P. and Yeh, R.T. Executable requirements for embedded systems. *Fifth Int. Conf. Softw. Eng.* San Diego, California. (March 1981), 295–304.

CR Categories and Subject Descriptors: D.2.1 [**Software Engineering**]: Requirements/Specifications—*methodologies*; D.2.2 [**Software Engineering**]: Tools and Techniques—*top-down programming*; D.2.4 [**Software Engineering**]: Program Verification—*validation*; D.2.9 [**Software Engineering**]: Management—*life cycle, productivity*; D.2.m [**Software Engineering**]: Miscellaneous—*rapid prototyping*
General Terms: Designs, Documentation
Additional Key Words and Phrases: software development methods

Received 1/83; accepted 8/83

Author's Present Address: Pamela Zave, AT&T Bell Laboratories, Room 3D-426, Murray Hill, NJ 07974

Operational Specification as the Basis

for

Rapid Prototyping

Robert M. Balzer

Neil M. Goldman

David S. Wile

Information Sciences Institute / USC

27 September 1982

ABSTRACT

This paper describes a set of freedoms which both simplify the task of specifing systems and make the resulting specification more comprehensible. These freedoms eliminate the need, in specific areas, to consider: the mechanisims for accomplishing certain capabilities, the careful coordination and integration of separate operations, the costs of those operations, and other detailed concerns which characterize implementation.

These freedoms are partitioned into the areas of efficiency, method, and data, and providing them has resulted in a novel formal specification language, Gist. The main features of this language are described in terms of the freedoms it affords. An overview of the language is then presented together with an example of its use to specify the behavior of a real system.

1. INTRODUCTION

Gist is an operational specification language, using the term operational in its broadest sense. That is, Gist specifications can be evaluated to yield a behavior(a sequence of states) given an initial state. This evaluation is possible because Gist's semantics are defined in terms of how situations (states) are modified by the operations comprising a specification, and because a Gist specification defines a *closed* system of activity with no *unspecified* behavior influencing it. This closed system assumption can be contrasted with the usual interpretation of programming languages, in which certain aspects of activity are encapsulated, or closed off from possible outside interference, but some interface is left to an *unspecifiable* (within the language) external environment whose use of that interface can affect the behavior of the specified portion. By internalizing such interfaces as additional components which interact within the closed system, Gist not only allows the specification to be evaluated, but also enables the full power of the specification language itself to be used to describe any knowledge of how that "interface" is used.

Thus, theoretically, a Gist specification *is*, without implementation, a prototype of the specified system, and can be used as a prototype to assess the specified behavior. Unfortunately, such

The work reported herein was sponsored
by the Defense Advanced
Research Projects Agency under grant DAHC 15 72C 0308.

prototype useage is not possible directly because the evaluation of Gist specifications in intolerably slow. Two alternative techniques for allowing Gist specifications to be used as prototypes are presented in companion papers [Feather 82, Cohen et al 82]. One is based on making the evaluation more efficient by transforming the specification into a suitable execution form. The other is based on characterizing all possible behaviors of the prototype through symbolic evaluation techniques. This paper presents, the design of a language, Gist, capable of producing operational closed system specifications which can be used as prototypes. The presentation is organized around a set of specification freedoms incorporated in Gist which permit numerous implementation concerns to be isolated from the concerns of defining system behavior.

2. SPECIFICATION FREEDOMS

To the extent that a specification language is doing its job of describing intended behavior(WHAT) without prescribing a particular algorithm(HOW), it is providing a set of freedoms from various implementation concerns. These implementation concerns fall into three broad catagories: finding a METHOD for accomplishing something, providing the DATA required for that method, and making the combination EFFICIENT(some function of time, space, and other resources).

Gist was specifically designed to maximize freedom from these concerns. Its major constucts were predicated on the need to provide these freedoms. Thus, these freedoms provide a convenient framework in which to describe the major features of Gist.

Each of these freedoms represents a design success in which a single functionality(WHAT) replaces a large set of alternative mechanisms(HOW) which satisfy that functionality. This is a design success in two ways. First, it is an abstraction of the common functionality that all of the alternatives share. By suppressing the irrelevant details of any particular member of this set of alternatives, the specification becomes both more concise and understandable. Even more importantly, the functionality is achieved merely by stating it, no matter how complex the mechanisms are, or how many of them need to be integrated together, to accomplish this functionality. That is, responsibility for accomplishing the functionality has been tranferred from the specifier to the implementation. From the specifier's standpoint, this functionality has become self-organizing. Whatever is necessary to accomplish the stated functionality will be done. This provides tremendous leverage for the specifier by allowing him to concentrate on stating desired functionality without concern for implementation mechanisms.

By providing these freedoms in the specification, we have shifted the responsibility for dealing with them to the implementation phase [London & Feather 81]. We feel that this is entirely appropriate, and that both the specification and implementation phases benefit when this occurs.

3. EFFICIENCY Freedom

Since the EFFICIENCY concern subsumes both the METHOD and DATA concerns and is dependent upon the implementation mechanisms employed, it is clear that unless specification freedom is provided here, it can't be provided anywhere (i.e. the concern for efficiency destroys the very notion of specification freedom by preventing the use of specification constucts without concern for HOW they are implemented).

Thus, the design of Gist starts with eliminating the EFFICIENCY concern. At its most basic level, this addresses the meaning of a specification and its relationship to an implementation. In Gist, specifications define sets of acceptable behavior. Each behavior is a sequence of states and transitions between those states. The transitions are events that correspond to the observable activity in the application domain. These events modify the objects that exist in the application domain. These objects and their associations with one another constitute the state of the domain. Thus, a specification defines a set of alternative acceptable sequences of states of the objects(and their associations) that constitute the application domain. An *implementation* produces some non-empty subset of these behaviors.

Thus, a specification is merely a generator of such behaviors, in a convenient, and we hope readable, format. The structure of a specification itself is important only insofar as it results in observable behavior(i.e. changes to the modeled world). Thus, at the most basic level, the behaviors are all that is relevant, not how the specification is organized, or what mechanisms are employed within it to achieve those behaviors. This viewpoint completely removes EFFICIENCY concerns because they simply are not expressable in Gist. Two Gist specifications cannot be compared with respect to efficiency, only with respect to the set of behaviors they generate.

4. METHOD Freedom

Having thus disposed of the EFFICIENCY concern, we can now address the METHOD and DATA concerns. We begin with the METHOD concern. This concern addresses finding a detailed sequence of operations which generates the desired set of behaviors. There are three difficulties in determining such a sequence of operations: determining which operations to include in the sequence, determining their order, and determining which objects they manipulate.

In Gist, we have provided a specification freedom for the latter two, but only partially for the first. This specification freedom allows behavior to be specified nondeterministically (i.e. ambiguously). As in natural language, this nondeterminism is restricted to the subset of choices that allow the sequence of operations to proceed without trouble. That is, an implementation must determine appropriate choices for each nondeterministic construct so that the sequence is successfully completed. Such success depends not only on the requirements local to the choice point, but also others which apply to later stages of the behavior. The choices must anticipate these later requirements and also succeeding choices which must be consistent with those already made. In general, implementation of this would require arbitrary look-ahead, and can get extremely difficult, or even impossible without search, as the specification becomes more complex.

Avoiding such choice difficulties provides a major specification freedom, and, in fact, results in the primary Gist specification technique. A simple general method is specified which includes the desired behaviors, but also includes many others. These are pruned away by adding constraints to the specification. These constraints impose additional requirements which reject otherwise acceptable behaviors. They provide a powerful mechanism for fine-tuning a specification to generate only the desired set of behaviors. Thus, this primary Gist specification technique is to start with an overly general simple method and fine tune it. Nondeterminism is the generalization mechanism and constraints are the fine-tuning control.

This design success, achieved through nondeterminism and constraints, must be contrasted with a design failure for the other METHOD difficulty - building an ordered set of operations. We would like to be able to specify a plan, or sketch, of a method as we do in natural language, and have the system fill in intermediate operations necessary to successfully complete the plan. The difficulty is that we have been unable to identify a mechanism the specifier could use to define which subset of the resulting behaviors were acceptable. The key issue is which operations can be added to a plan, under what circumstances they can be added, and which objects they can manipulate. Because such a description has proved so elusive, we have been unable to provide a specification freedom which allows plans (or, by similar reasoning, goals).

5. DATA Freedom

The DATA concern addresses the issue of providing the data needed by the method in the required form. In designing Gist, we used the single guiding principle that all information gathering activies would be specification freedoms. This implied the need for specification freedoms for: data access, changes in the form of information, no distinction between explicit and derived information, fully accessable global information, and data accesses across time. Furthermore, none of these information gathering activities could result in observable behavior.

The simplest way to envision all of these freedoms is to imagine a data base interface through which all data is accessed. This interface hides the actual representation of the data and the method by which it is accessed. It also includes an inferencing capability which provides access to all information logically derivable from that contained in the data base, and a perfect memory so that information about the past remains accessible. Finally, the information in this data base defines the state of the world being modeled and it is changed only by actions described in the specification, not by any of the information gathering activity provided by this interface.

5.1. Data Access Freedom

To provide data access as a freedom, Gist has equated description with reference. That is, any description of an object can be used to reference that object. Since many different descriptions may denote the same object, and since these descriptions may involve both the "structure" of the object and its relationship with other objects, it is clear that the access to the denoted object must be derived from the elements of the description. This situation can be simplified if the distinction between the inner "structure" of an object and its relationship with other objects is removed. Gist accomplishes this by also describing the "structure" of an object in terms its relationship to other objects. Thus, objects have no "structure" anymore. They are defined via their relationship with other objects. The access problem is solved once any of the relationships that an object participates in, or any combination of them, can be used to access that object. This of course implies that the same relationship can be used to access any of the objects that participate in that relationship. In data base terminology, this means that the relationships are fully associative(or, equivalently, that the data base is fully inverted).

Thus, Gist uses fully associative relations as its representation for data because it solves the access problem in a symmetric way. Other possibilities include set membership in which members can be accessed from sets and vise versa or functional notations which have inverses for each function. The difficulty with the latter two choices is that they are not as convenient as the relational approach in representing associations involving more than two objects.

Since objects are defined totally via their relationships with other objects and have no internal structure, our earlier statement(in the EFFICIENCY Freedom section) that events modify *objects*, should really have been that events modify the *relationships* among objects.

This data access freedom implies that specifications can be written in terms of any information even though it may be known that such information will not be accessible in an implementation. Such non-accessablity in an implementation may arise from privacy concerns, imperfect memory(see Historical Reference Freedom below), distributed data bases, cost, etc. It may make implementation difficult, or even impossible(as can other implementation limitations). But since the specification merely defines acceptable behavior, and none of the information gathering activities, including data access, are part of such behavior, the specification may employ this perfect knowledge freedom.

5.2. Form Conversion Freedom

There are usually many different ways to express the same information, with well-defined rules for converting one into another. In an implementation, one often picks a canonical form for storing the information and all operations use this form as input and produce it as output. Other times, explicit coercions are performed for operations that manipulate or produce information in some other form. In the remaining cases, dual forms of information are stored and coercions back and forth are carefully maintained.

Gist eliminates the need for choice of a canonical form and/or for explicit coersions by allowing the individual consumers of information to use whatever form is most convenient for them. As long as the conversion rules have been defined(in the form of derivation rules), they will be used as needed.

5.3. Information Derivation Freedom

This freedom is really the same as the previous one, although it is frequently perceived as being different. From a given set of information, one can often deduce(or derive) other information not explicitly stated. This is accomplished by applying rules of inference(stated as Gist derivation rules) to the explicit information to derive "new" information. This "new" information, together with previous information, may allow the derivation of further "new" information. This process may continue indefinitely until all logical deductions of the known explicit information have been derived.

Gist avoids the need to explicitly form such derivation chains by automatically forming them as needed. Each information request may be satisfied by explicit information, derived information, or a combination of the two. Thus, the distinction between explicit and derived information has been eliminated. This freedom exists for all information requests, including those contained in constraints. These constraint requests are much more pervasive than other requests as they are constantly monitored.

This specification freedom, based on Gist derivation rules, and covering both form conversion and derived information, complements the METHOD freedom. The METHOD freedom allows simple general processes to be tuned for desired behavior, while this freedom allows needed information to be accessed as if it were already available. Since so much of computation is concerned with the manipulation of information(in anticipation of performing some action), this is a very powerful freedom.

5.4. Historical Reference Freedom

This freedom is a simple extension of the information gathering freedom across time. Without it, any needed information which was available previously, but no longer is(because the state of the modeled domain has changed), would have to be encoded(remembered) in the current state and accessed from that encoding. This need to anticipate consumer reqirements at potential producer sites and to choose a consistent set of conventions, is just the type of situation we avoided via the form conversion and derivation freedoms.

To extend these freedoms to historical information, we simply allow any information request to specify the state in which that request will be processed(the default is the current state). Such state specification is normally the most recent state in which some predicate was satisfied. Gist assumes the responsibility for remembering all previous states so that such historical information requests can be satisfied. Note that with this design historical information gathering is no different from information gathering in the current state, and that no "anticipation" burden is placed on information producers as requests are localized at the information consumers.

5.5. Unobservable Information Gathering

The unobservable nature of information gathering follows from providing it as a freedom. If information gathering activities were observable, then information gathering would not be a specification freedom because the mechanism chosen to implement that freedom could itself(rather than the information gathered) affect subsequent behavior. A further implication of this freedom is that information gathering activites happen instantly(i.e. no state changes result from, nor occur during information gathering). Such atomisity greatly simplifies specification of multi-participant systems because the world will not change while it is being examined, or between an examination and the initiation of activity based on the information gathered.

6. Components of a Gist Specification

A Gist specification defines a collection of *behaviors*. Each behavior is a (possibly infinite) sequence of situations and represents, by definition, *one* possible behavior of the specified system. A Gist specification is composed of:

1. Structural declarations, which define a space of potential states of the system

2. Stimulus-response rules, which define situations which initiate activity and the range of behaviors ensuing from those situations

3. Constraints, which prune the space of possible behaviors defined by the elements of the

previous two categories. It is this pruned space of behaviors which is considered to constitute the system defined by a Gist specification

6.1. Structural Declarations

The structural declarations provide a partial cognitive model of the application domain, permitting the rest of the specification to be written in domain-specific terms. These declarations name the types of objects in the domain, any relevant instances of those types, and the relationships which may exist between objects of the various types.

Gist also permits a specifier to place the named types in a hierarchy[1] defining some types as supertypes of others. By defining relations, procedures, stimulus-response rules, and constraints in terms of the most general applicable types, the fidelity of the specification as a cognitive model is enhanced, and information is better localized in the specification.

6.2. operations

All activity occurring in a system is modeled in Gist in terms of four primitive operations:

- creation of a new object

- destruction of an existing object

- insertion of a new relationship

- deletion of an existing relationship

These primitives are composed using forms familiar from programming languages -- sequencing, conditional execution, iteration, encapsulation as invokable procedures -- and a few forms whose presence is dictated by the design goals of Gist.

The goal that a Gist specification be a cognitive model of a system implies that the states of the specified behaviors correspond to states of that system. This in turn implies that the transitions in the behaviors be of a granularity appropriate to the system. The granularity of the four primitives, however, is dictated by the choice of object types and relations used to model the system domain, and is in general too fine to capture the cognitive granularity. That is, if each state of a behavior differed by only a single primitive from its predecessor, only a subset of the states would correspond to identifiable states of the modeled system. Gist deals with this by permitting an arbitrary collection of primitive operations to be composed as a single "atomic" operation.

The goal that a Gist specification be able to describe a range of possible behaviors ensuing from a given situation is achieved by a liberal use of non-determinism in the specification of what operations are to be performed in a given situation. The choice of operations to be performed, the selection of operands for a given operation, and the order in which operations are to be performed may be specified non-deterministically.

Given the ability to define composite activity which alters the state of a system, it remains to specify *which* operations occur *when*. This is achieved via stimulus-response rules. When a rule's stimulus, an arbitrary predicate, *becomes* true, the rule's response, an arbitrary statement, becomes an active *line of control*. The non-deterministic interleaving and merging of the activity specified by all active lines of control generates the space of possible behaviors ensuing from a given situation.

6.3. Constraints

The domain model provided by the structural declarations and the non-determinism in the operational component of the specification define an infinite space of possible situations and behaviors ensuing from them. The final component of the specification, the *constraints*, serves to prune from this space both situations and behaviors which are not considered to be part of the modeled system.

---

[1]Actually, an acyclic directed graph.

121

Constraints which prune out particular situations, and thus any behavior containing any of those situations, include such common cases as:

- restrictions on the *types* of objects participating in relationships

- restrictions on the *number* of objects related to other objects in relationships

- arbitrary *predicates* specifying conditions which are required or prohibited in every situation

Constraints which prune behaviors on the basis of system history and ongoing activity include:

- restrictions on *changes* that may occur to system state

- predicates attached to individual statements in the specification, restricting the range of situations in which those statements may initiate and terminate

- restrictions on the order in which events may occur

7. Implementation Issues Affecting Specification Development

The foregoing discussion might lead the reader to believe that system specifications are composed entirely independently of their implementations. That is too idealistic. In particular, the "closed system" assumption enunciated above will have been hedged somewhat when a human agent is described. Indeed, his behavior will have been abstracted to limit him to some particular set of interactions within the closed system; probably he will have been specified to have considerable nondeterministic choice over his actions. However, there is no sense in which he has been entirely operationalized--he will always be underspecified.

More generally, a closed system specification will be used for many purposes: simulation, symbolic evaluation and as a behavioral yardstick for implementation. Gist specifications are unusual in the several different purposes they may be used for. Although we normally think of a specification describing a software system which is to be implemented, a Gist specification may describe the hardware implementation in which the software system resides. Simultaneously it proscribes some behavior of even agents with free will (users).

Despite this ubiquitous use of the specification, it is the case that any particular implementer of the specification will bring to bear a perspective that dichotomizes the world into that which he will implement and that which he will assume has been implemented. This split leads to two major problems:

- First, because the system is no longer "closed," there is some behavior over which the implementer has no control. It may be difficult, or even impossible, for him to maintain within his portion of the system a system-wide constraint. If it is impossible, then the specification is unimplementable, because the environment is not forced to behave benignly.

- Secondly, the assumption of "perfect information" is never valid in an implementation-- usually a fairly narrow communication channel defines the exchange between an implementation and its environment. Somehow, mappings to this channel must be found for those accesses the implementation assumes available. In the case of historical references, this may involve introducing artificial communication which the environment would normally not even have represented. Also, the free information derivation assumption cannot be met in real implementations.

These issues are largely not specification issues, but they often feed back into a specification because they tend to cause the functionality--observable behavior--of specifications to change significantly as the implementation is developed. For example, the specification of the functionality of a network communication protocol tends to be trivial without regard to implementation: move a message from point a to b. Only the reality of the antagonistic communication medium (the environment) necessitates that the functionality be degraded to allow the possibility of missed messages, out of sequence messages and unfairness. These are still realistic problems which enter the functional specification very early in any conceivable specification methodology for protocols.

Presently, we have no formal way in Gist for introducing these implementation dependencies. However, we are working on a formal incremental development methodology for describing the design history of specifications. We do not believe that significant modification of the Gist language is appropriate to deal with this issue, but rather that a formal description of design and development histories is appropriate.

8. A Package Router Example

A somewhat realistic example will illustrate both the strengths and weaknesses of the Gist language as a specification vehicle.

The problem approached is basically a routing problem [Hommel 80]. In its most abstract form it may be specified: "At random times, a new package appears at a particular location called the source assigned to be routed to an arbitrary destination bin. Packages located at the source are moved to their destinations."

```
demon CREATE_PACKAGE()
  response
    create package.new || package.new:DESTINATION = a bin
             and package.new:LOCATED_AT
                 = the source;

demon MOVE_PACKAGE(package)
  trigger package :LOCATED_AT = the source
  response
    update :LOCATED_AT of package to package :DESTINATION ;
```

This trivial specification demonstrates several essential features of the Gist language.

First, the event based nature of the language is evident. Packages are created by the CREATE_PACKAGE demon and moved by the MOVE_PACKAGE demon. The activity of the demons occurs nondeterministically in parallel. Demons--stimulus/response pairs--react to events in the environment by being activated when their trigger patterns become true. Secondly, the demons share a global data base describing packages and their associated destinations. The association is indicated by the access notation ": attribute", here DESTINATION and LOCATED_AT. The entire activity--

observable behavior--of the system is the creation of packages with arbitrary destinations and the delivery of these packages to their appropriate destinations--indicated by the change to the global data base of their location from the source to the destination. Notice that updating the LOCATED_AT attribute of a package causes the old value of the attribute to be removed.

An interesting feature of this trivial specification is the use of nondeterminism to select arbitrary destination bins. Another guise in which nondeterminism appears here is in the triggering of the CREATE_PACKAGE demon. The lack of a specified trigger implies that the demon's response may be taken after any state transition occurs--i.e., after any event.

Technically, we must introduce declarations for the types package, source, location and bin:

```
type package(located_at | location)
type location supertype of < source; bin >
```

In fact, the real world in which this specification will be implemented makes this specification inadequate: the specification is actually for a controller of a process which moves packages. In particular, gravity is used as the "mover" of packages through a binary tree of pipes and switches. The actual specification task is for a controller of the switches to shunt the packages from the source to the destination bins. Hence, the following specification is slightly more accurate:

123

```
demon MOVE_PACKAGE(package)
  response
    update :LOCATED_AT of package
      to package : LOCATED_AT : SWITCH_SETTING;

demon CREATE_PACKAGE
  response
    create package.new || package.new:DESTINATION = a bin
      and package.new:LOCATED_AT = the source;

demon SET_SWITCH(switch)
  response
    update :SWITCH_SETTING of switch to switch:SWITCH_OUTLET;

always required PACKAGES_REACH_DESTINATIONS
    package :LOCATED_AT isa bin
      => package : LOCATED_AT = package :DESTINATION;

type switch(SWITCH_SETTING | location,SWITCH_OUTLET|location)
  subtype of < location>
```

Notice, we have introduced a new demon which provides information to the moving demon to which it reacts. We have also generalized the body of the MOVE_PACKAGE demon to move the package from location to location associated by the controller, the SET_SWITCH demon. It nondeterministically sets switches to any of their allowed outlets.

A constraint has been added to insure that intended behavior from before is maintained: packages must arrive at their destinations. This is particularly important. The specification without this constraint specifies behaviors in which packages may go to arbitrary bins. This constraint "trims the tree" of possible nondeterministic behaviors to allow only those which ultimately result in packages reaching their destination bins. Hence, packages now ultimately have their destinations changed from the source to the destination bins--, but we have begun to model their flow through the system more accurately.

At this point two different aspects of the specification may be pursued in parallel:

- The system is allowed to err. It must be possible for packages to be created which do not reach their destinations, for gravity may cause packages to "bunch up" and not allow time for a switch to be thrown when the second package comes through.

- The details of the tree-like network of switches leading to destination bins could be described.

In a real sense, the former aspect is more central to the specification, for the introduction of error is a functional change to the specification. This is one of the feedback situations in which the "original" specification is actually a compromise between the ideal specification--a perfect package router--and specification of an economically feasible, occasionally erroneous system.

In choosing the latter specification, the only additional behavior which arises is that when packages are misrouted, the misrouting must be signalled by an event. Of course, it is also desirable to specify that non-erroneous behaviors are preferable to those in which packages are unsuccessful in reaching their destinations. To signal misrouting, we merely add:

```
relation MISROUTED_PACKAGE_REACHED_BIN
        (package,bin.reached,bin.intended)
  definition package:LOCATED_AT = bin.reached
        and package:DESTINATION = bin.intended
        and bin.intended ~ = bin.reached
```

Because every state transition is "observable," this relation is merely an derived extension of the existing specification. In fact, the specification could test whether a particular package, pkg, had been misrouted by using the predicate:

MISROUTED_PACKAGE_REACHED_BIN(*pkg*,$,$)
     asof ever

(The "$" indicates a wildcard slot--any bins satisfy the retrieval.) This historical reference ability is another ramification of the "perfect knowledge" assumption at the basis of the design of Gist.

Now notice that the constraint PACKAGES_REACH_DESTINATIONS cannot be forced to hold in the specification if misrouting is ever to occur. Thus, it is necessary to change the specification to indicate that we "prefer" that packages reach their destinations. We fully intend to provide a construct to permit such a statement, but have had trouble convincing ourselves that our formalisations of the preference concepts we have experimented with match our intuitions about preference. Hence, the final specification of the package router has this preference encoded in the constraint DID_NOT_SET_SWITCH_WHEN_HAD_CHANCE, which we find to be a less intuitive, but easier to formalize, description of the same behavior.

The introduction of the actual network referred to above is mostly an extension to this specification--an elaboration of deferred information--rather than an actual modification to it. The notion of derived information or free information gathering dominates Gist specifications. In the final specification, for example, the actual demons to MOVE_PACKAGEs and SET_SWITCHes interact with derived relationships, viz.

demon MOVE_PACKAGE(*package*)
  response
   update :LOCATED_AT of *package*
    to MOVEMENT_CONNECTION(*package*:LOCATED_AT,*)

demon SET_SWITCH
  response
   update :SWITCH_SETTING of *switch* to *switch*:SWITCH_OUTLET;

relation MOVEMENT_CONNECTION(*LOCATION.1*, *LOCATION.2*)
   definition
     LOCATION.1:SWITCH_SETTING = *LOCATION.2*;

(The "*" indicates that a value of the indicated slot is the value of the enclosing relationship; e.g., sqrt(4,*) + 1 = 3.) Here, the relation MOVEMENT_CONNECTION is defined in terms of the SWITCH_SETTING attributes of *switch*es. This specification "costs no more" than the original--that is, the implicit derivation of the MOVEMENT_CONNECTION relation is just another manifestation of the free information principle.

The final package router specification is given in the appendix. It appears somewhat complex, due in part to the considerable number of relationships between objects in the modelled world. In the package router specification these declarations state that objects involved in the process can be variously classified as source stations, packages, switches, pipes, sensors, and bins, and that the following relationships, among others, can exists among these objects:

Relationship Between Objects	Semantic Relationship Modeled
CONNECTION_TO_SWITCH_OR_BIN(pipe, switch)	a pipe leading into a switch
SWITCH_OUTLET(switch, pipe)	a pipe leading out of a switch
SWITCH_SETTING(switch, pipe)	a pipe dynamically connected to a switch by the switch's setting
CONNECTION_TO_SWITCH_OR_BIN(pipe, bin)	a pipe leading into a bin
SOURCE_OUTLET(source, pipe)	a pipe leading out of a source station
DESTINATION(package, bin)	an intended destination of a package

The domain of the problem is further specified by several *constraints*, serving to prune from this space both situations and behaviors which are not considered to be part of the modeled process. In the package router specification, constraints serve to limit the process to:

- situations in which the types bin, package, pipe, switch, and source station are mutually exclusive

- situations in which the types bin, pipe, switch, and source station "partition" the type location

- situations in which the relationships between the locations ensure a configuration consisting of a "binary tree" having switches as "non-terminals", bins as "terminals", and pipes as "arcs"

- situations in which there is a single source station, connected to the root of the switching tree by a single pipe

- situations in which packages have exactly one destination and exactly one position

- situations in which the pipe dynamically connected to a switch by its setting is one of the two pipes leaving it in the "binary tree"

- behaviors in which packages do not "pass" one another

- behaviors in which switches do not change setting while a package is in them

Additional complexity arises from the inclusion of an "implementation specification" describing the environment/system split. Because behavior in the original specification becomes unobservable in the implementation, some events have been recast in order to describe the split simply.

9. Relationship to other Work

Although we certainly believe that the combination of ideas which comprise Gist have produced a unique language, there are certainly other languages and technologies with some analogous features. The nondeterminism in Gist is different from most languages which permit it. Some [Dijkstra 75] insist that the nondeterminism be unable to produce different results. Others, allow nondeterminism to produce the "undefined" result [Bauer 81]. Ours is much closer to the automata theory definition of nondetemisitic machines--their behavior is defined when any nondeterministic path reaches an accepting state [Hopcroft 69].

Another significant thread in the development of Gist has been the global database notion, especially in concert with automatic demon invocation. PLANNER and QLisp both introduced these notions into Artificial Intelligence languages in the early 1970s [Bobrow 74]. The use of semantic network/relational data has recently been espoused as the basis for language design by Smith and Smith [Smith 77].

Both the operational semantics and the closed system assumptions have been made by the simulation languages [Birtwistle 73]. Certainly the denonational semanticists [DenotationalSemantics] are of a kindred spirit in espousing an "operational" rather than "axiomatic" semantic basis. Certainly other specification languages exist which are basicallly operational in nature, such as Special [Special].

Finally, the perfect information concept seems to assumed by program verification advocates [Gerhart 80], wherein it is assumed that all important relationships have been specified as properties to be verified.

Acknowledgements

The authors wish to thank several colleagues whose ideas have contributed considerably to the design of Gist: Don Cohen, Lee Erman, Martin Feather, Phil London, and Bill Swartout.

I. The Package Router Example

To illustrate our approach, we choose as an example a routing system for distributing packages into destination bins. Figure 9-1 illustrates the routing network. At the top is a source station which feeds packages one at a time into the network, which is a binary tree consisting of switches connected by pipes. The terminal nodes of the binary tree are the destination bins.

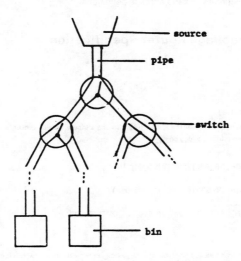

Figure 9-1: package router

When a package arrives at the source station, its intended destination (one of the bins) is determined. The package is then released into the pipe leading from the source station. For a package to reach its designated destination bin, the switches in the network must be set to direct the package through the network and into the correct bin.

Packages move through the network by gravity (working against friction), and so steady movement of packages cannot be guaranteed; so they may "bunch up" within the network and thus make it impossible to set a switch properly between the passage of two such bunched packages (a switch cannot be set when there is a package or packages in the switch for fear of damaging such packages). If a new package's destination differs from that of the immediately preceding package, its release from the source station is delayed a (pre-calculated) fixed length of time (to reduce the chance of bunching). In spite of such precautions, packages may still bunch up and become mis-routed, ending up in the wrong bin; the package router is to signal such an event.

Only a limited amount of information is available to the package router to effect its desired behavior. At the time of arrival at the source station but not thereafter, the destination of a package may be determined. The only means of determining the locations of packages within the network are sensors placed on switches and bins; these detect the entry and exit of packages but are unable to determine their identity. (The sensors will be able to recognize the passage of individual packages, regardless of bunching).

Key to font conventions and special symbols used in Gist

symbol	meaning	example
|	of type	*obj* | t - object *obj* of type t
||	such that	(<u>an</u> *integer* || *integer* > 3) - an integer greater than 3
_	may be used to build names, like this_name	
.	concatenates a type name with a suffix to form a variable name, e.g. *integer.1*	
	with the semantics that such variables with distinct suffices denote distinct objects.	

fonts	meaning	example
<u>underlined</u>	key word	<u>begin</u>, <u>definition</u>, <u>if</u>
lower case boldface	type name	**integer**
lower case italics	variable	*x*
UPPER CASE BOLDFACE	action, demon, relation and constraint names	
SMALL CAPITALS	role name	AGE (as in *person*:AGE)
SMALL CAPITAL ITALICS	role name being used as variable (in relation and attribute definitions)	

Package Router Specification

The network

<u>type</u> location() <u>supertype</u> <u>of</u>

< source(SOURCE_OUTLET | **pipe**);

> <u>Gist</u> <u>comment</u> - the above line defines source to be a type with one attribute, SOURCE_OUTLET, and only objects of type **pipe** may serve as such attributes. <u>end</u> <u>comment</u>

pipe(CONNECTION_TO_SWITCH_OR_BIN | (**switch** <u>union</u> **bin**));

switch(SWITCH_OUTLET | **pipe** :2, SWITCH_SETTING | **pipe**)
    <u>where</u> <u>always</u> <u>required</u>
        switch:SWITCH_SETTING = *switch*:SWITCH_OUTLET <u>end</u>;
bin()
>;

> <u>Spec</u> <u>comment</u> - of the above types and attribute, only the SWITCH_SETTING attribute of **switch** is dynamic in this specification, the others remain fixed throughout. <u>end</u> <u>comment</u>

> <u>Gist</u> <u>comment</u> - by default, attributes (e.g. SOURCE_OUTLET) of types (e.g. **source**) are functional - (e.g. there is one and only one pipe serving as the SWITCH_SETTING attribute of the **source**). The default may be overridden, as occurs in the SWITCH_OUTLET attribute of **switch** - there the ":2" indicates that each switch has exactly 2 pipes serving as its SWITCH_OUTLET attribute. <u>end</u> <u>comment</u>

<u>always</u> <u>prohibited</u> MORE_THAN_ONE_SOURCE
  <u>exists</u> source.1, source.2;

> <u>Gist</u> <u>comment</u> - constraints may be stated as predicates following either <u>always</u> <u>required</u> (in which case the predicate must always evaluate to true), or <u>always</u> <u>prohibited</u> (in which case the predicate must never evaluate to true). The usual logical connectives, quantification, etc. may be used in Gist predicates. Distinct suffixes on type names after <u>exists</u> have the special meaning of denoting distinct objects. <u>end</u> <u>comment</u>

<u>always</u> <u>required</u> PIPE_EMERGES_FROM_UNIQUE_SWITCH_OR_SOURCE
  <u>for</u> <u>all</u> *pipe* ||
  (<u>exists</u> <u>unique</u> *switch_or_source* | (**switch** <u>union</u> **source**) ||
   (*pipe* = *switch_or_source*:SWITCH_OUTLET <u>or</u>
    pipe = *switch_or_source*:SOURCE_OUTLET));

> <u>Gist</u> <u>comment</u> - the values of attributes can be retrieved in the following manner: if *obj* is an object of type t, where type t has an attribute ATT, then *obj*:ATT denotes any object serving as *obj*'s ATT attribute. <u>end</u> <u>comment</u>

<u>always</u> <u>required</u> UNIQUE_PIPE_LEADS_INTO_SWITCH_OR_BIN
  <u>for</u> <u>all</u> *switch_or_bin* | (**switch** <u>union</u> **bin**) ||
  (<u>exists</u> <u>unique</u> *pipe* ||
   (*pipe*:CONNECTION_TO_SWITCH_OR_BIN = *switch_or_bin*));

<u>relation</u> LOCATION_ON_ROUTE_TO_BIN(*LOCATION*,*BIN*)
  <u>definition</u>
   <u>case</u> *LOCATION* <u>of</u>
    bin => *LOCATION* = *BIN*;
    pipe => LOCATION_ON_ROUTE_TO_BIN(*LOCATION*:CONNECTION_TO_SWITCH_OR_BIN,*BIN*);
    switch => LOCATION_ON_ROUTE_TO_BIN(*LOCATION*:SWITCH_OUTLET,*BIN*);
    source => LOCATION_ON_ROUTE_TO_BIN(*LOCATION*:SOURCE_OUTLET,*BIN*);
   <u>end</u> <u>case</u>;

> <u>Spec</u> <u>comment</u> - this relation is defined to hold between a location and bin if and only if the location lies on route to the bin, i.e. the location is the bin, or the location is a pipe connected to a location leading to the bin (a recursive definition), or a switch either of the outlets of which leads to the bin, or a source whose outlet leads to the bin. <u>end</u> <u>comment</u>

always required SOURCE_ON_ROUTE_TO_ALL_BINS
for all *bin* || LOCATION_ON_ROUTE_TO_BIN(**the** *source,bin*) ;

Packages - the objects moving through the network

type package(LOCATED_AT | location, DESTINATION | bin) ;

relation MISROUTED(*PACKAGE*)
  definition
    not LOCATION_ON_ROUTE_TO_BIN(*PACKAGE*:LOCATED_AT, *PACKAGE*:DESTINATION) **or**
    SWITCH_SET_WRONG_FOR_PACKAGE(*PACKAGE*:LOCATED_AT,*PACKAGE*) ;

Software Portion

agent package_router() **where**

relation PACKAGES_EVER_AT_SOURCE(*PACKAGE_SEQ* | **sequence of** package)
  definition *PACKAGE_SEQ* =
    ({*package* || (*package*:LOCATED_AT = **the** source) **asof ever**}
    ordered temporally by start (*package*:LOCATED_AT = **the** source));

The source station

demon RELEASE_PACKAGE_INTO_NETWORK(*package.new*)
  trigger *package.new*:LOCATED_AT = **the** source
  response
    begin
      if (**the** *package.previous* || (*package.previous* **immediately** < *package.new*
                   wrt PACKAGES_EVER_AT_SOURCE(*))
        ):DESTINATION ≠ *package.new*:DESTINATION
      then WAIT[] ;

    update :LOCATED_AT **of** *package.new* **to** (**the** source):SOURCE_OUTLET
    end ;

The switches

relation SWITCH_IS_EMPTY(*SWITCH*)
  definition not exists *package* || *package*:LOCATED_AT = *SWITCH*;
  demon SET_SWITCH(*switch*)
    trigger RANDOM()
    response
      begin
        require SWITCH_IS_EMPTY(*switch*);
        update :SWITCH_SETTING **of** *switch* **to** *switch*:SWITCH_OUTLET
      end;

relation PACKAGES_DUE_AT_SWITCH(*PACKAGES_DUE* | <u>sequence</u> <u>of</u> **package**, *SWITCH*)
  <u>definition</u>
    PACKAGES_DUE =
      { <u>a</u> *package* ||
        LOCATION_ON_ROUTE_TO_BIN(*SWITCH*,*package*:DESTINATION) <u>and</u>
        <u>not</u> ((*package*:LOCATED_AT = *SWITCH*) <u>asof</u> <u>ever</u>) <u>and</u>
        <u>not</u> MISROUTED(*package*)
      } <u>ordered</u> <u>wrt</u> PACKAGES_EVER_AT_SOURCE(*) ;

> <u>Spec</u> <u>comment</u> · packages due at a switch are those packages for whom (i) the switch lies on their route to
> their destinations, (ii) they have not already reached the switch, and (iii) they are not misrouted. They are
> ordered by the order in which they were at the source. <u>end</u> <u>comment</u>

relation SWITCH_SET_WRONG_FOR_PACKAGE(*SWITCH*, *PACKAGE*)
  <u>definition</u>
    LOCATION_ON_ROUTE_TO_BIN(*SWITCH*,*PACKAGE*:DESTINATION) <u>and</u>
    <u>not</u> LOCATION_ON_ROUTE_TO_BIN(*SWITCH*:SWITCH_SETTING,*PACKAGE*:DESTINATION) ;

> <u>Spec</u> <u>comment</u> · A switch is set wrong for a package if the switch lies on the route to that package's
> destination, but the switch is set the wrong way. <u>end</u> <u>comment</u>

<u>always</u> <u>prohibited</u> DID_NOT_SET_SWITCH_WHEN_HAD_CHANCE
  <u>exists</u> *package*, *switch* ||
    (*package*:LOCATED_AT = *switch*
      <u>and</u>
      SWITCH_SET_WRONG_FOR_PACKAGE(*switch*,*package*)
      <u>and</u>
      ((*package* = <u>first</u>(PACKAGES_DUE_AT_SWITCH(*,*switch*)) <u>and</u>
        SWITCH_IS_EMPTY(*switch*)) <u>asof</u> <u>ever</u>)
) ;

> <u>Spec</u> <u>comment</u> · must never reach a state in which a package is in a wrongly set switch, if there has been an
> opportunity to set the switch correctly for that package, i.e. at some time that package was the first of those due
> at the switch and the switch was empty. <u>end</u> <u>comment</u>

Indicating arrival of misrouted package in bin

<u>demon</u> MISROUTED_PACKAGE_REACHED_BIN(*package*,*bin.reached*,*bin.intended*)
  <u>trigger</u> *package*:LOCATED_AT = *bin.reached* <u>and</u> *package*:DESTINATION = *bin.intended*
  <u>response</u> MISROUTED_ARRIVAL[*bin.reached*, *bin.intended*] ;

<u>action</u> MISROUTED_ARRIVAL[*bin.reached*, *bin.intended*]

<u>end</u>

The environment

<u>agent</u> environment() <u>where</u>

Arrival of packages at source

<u>demon</u> CREATE_PACKAGE()
  <u>trigger</u> RANDOM()
  <u>response</u>
    <u>create</u> *package.new* || (*package.new*:DESTINATION = <u>a</u> *bin* <u>and</u>
                    package.new:LOCATED_AT = <u>the</u> *source*) ;

> <u>Spec</u> <u>comment</u> · for the purposes of defining the environment in which the package router is to operate,
> packages with some random bin as their destination appear at random intervals (subject to the following
> constraint) at the source. <u>end</u> <u>comment</u>

<u>always</u> <u>prohibited</u> MULTIPLE_PACKAGES_AT_SOURCE
  <u>exists</u> *package.1*, *package.2* ||
    package.1:LOCATED_AT = <u>the</u> *source* <u>and</u> *package.2*:LOCATED_AT = <u>the</u> *source* ;

Movement of packages through network

<u>relation</u> MOVEMENT_CONNECTION(*LOCATION.1*, *LOCATION.2*)
  <u>definition</u>
   (<u>case</u> *LOCATION.1* <u>of</u>
     pipe => *LOCATION.1*:CONNECTION_TO_SWITCH_OR_BIN;
     switch => *LOCATION.1*:SWITCH_SETTING
    <u>end</u> <u>case</u>) = *LOCATION.2*;

<u>demon</u> MOVE_PACKAGE(*package*, *location.next*)
  <u>trigger</u> RANDOM()
  <u>response</u>
    <u>update</u> :LOCATED_AT <u>of</u> *package* <u>to</u> MOVEMENT_CONNECTION(*package*:LOCATED_AT,*);

       <u>Spec</u> <u>comment</u> - modelling of the unpredictable movement of packages through the network is achieved by having this demon at random move a random package from one location to the next MOVEMENT_CONNECTION location. <u>end</u> <u>comment</u>

<u>always</u> <u>prohibited</u> PACKAGES_OVERTAKING_ONE_ANOTHER
  <u>exists</u> *package.1*, *package.2*, *location*
  || <u>start</u> (*package.1*:LOCATED_AT = *location*) <u>earlier</u> <u>than</u>
     <u>start</u> (*package.2*:LOCATED_AT = *location*) <u>and</u>

     <u>finish</u> (*package.2*:LOCATED_AT = *location*) <u>earlier</u> <u>than</u>
      <u>finish</u> (*package.1*:LOCATED_AT = *location*) ;

       <u>Spec</u> <u>comment</u> - we are assured that packages do not overtake one another while they are moved through the network. <u>end</u> <u>comment</u>

<u>action</u> WAIT[] ;

Observable environment

       <u>Spec</u> <u>comment</u> - portions of environment to be used to describe observable information available to implementor. <u>end</u> <u>comment</u>

<u>type</u> sensor() <u>supertype</u> <u>of</u> < *switch*(); *bin*() > ;

<u>demon</u> PACKAGE_ENTERING_SENSOR(*package*,*sensor*)
  <u>trigger</u> *package*:LOCATED_AT = *sensor*
  <u>response</u> <u>null</u> ;

<u>demon</u> PACKAGE_LEAVING_SENSOR(*package*,*sensor*)
  <u>trigger</u> <u>not</u> *package*:LOCATED_AT = *sensor*
  <u>response</u> <u>null</u>

<u>end</u>

Implementation Specification

       <u>Spec</u> <u>comment</u> - this section is intended to capture the requirements placed on an implementor of the package router agent. <u>end</u> <u>comment</u>

<u>implement</u> **package_router**
  <u>observing</u>
    <u>attributes</u>
     SOURCE_OUTLET,
     CONNECTION_TO_SWITCH_OR_BIN,
     SWITCH_OUTLET,
     package:DESTINATION <u>when</u> *package*:LOCATED_AT = <u>the</u> *source*,
     package:LOCATED_AT <u>when</u> *package*:LOCATED_AT = <u>the</u> *source* ;

    <u>events</u>
     PACKAGE_ENTERING_SENSOR($,*sensor*),
     PACKAGE_LEAVING_SENSOR($,*sensor*) ;

  <u>effecting</u>
    <u>attributes</u>
     SWITCH_SETTING,
     package:LOCATED_AT <u>when</u> *package*:LOCATED_AT = <u>the</u> *source* ;

```
actions
    WAIT ;

exporting
events
    MISROUTED_ARRIVAL(bin.reached,bin.intended)

end implement;
```

References

[Bauer 81] Bauer, F. L., Broy, M., Dosch, W., Gnatz, R., Krieg-Brueckner, Laut, A., Matzner, T., Moeller, B., Partsch, H, Pepper, P., Samelson, K., Wirsing, M., and Woessner, H., *Report on a Wide Spectrum Language for Program Specification and Development*, Institute fuer Informatik, Technische Universitaet, Muenchen, Technical Report, May 1981.

[Birtwistle 73] Birtwistle, G. M., Dahl, O., Myhrhaug, B. and Nygaard, K., *SIMULA Begin,* Auerbach, 1973.

[Bobrow 74] Bobrow, D., and B. Raphael, "New programming languages for artificial intelligence research," *ACM Computing Surveys* 6, (3), September 1974, 153-174.

[Cohen et al 82] Cohen, D., Swartout, W. & Balzer, R., "Using symbolic execution to characterize behavior," in *Pre-Proceedings, ACM SIGSOFT Software Engineering Symposium on Rapid Prototyping*, pp. Paper-49, 1982.

[Dijkstra 75] Dijkstra, E. W., "Guarded commands, nondeterminancy, and formal derivation of programs," *Communications of the ACM*, (8), August 1975, 453-457.

[Feather 82] Feather, M., "Mappings for rapid prototyping," in *Pre-Proceedings, ACM SIGSOFT Software Engineering Symposium on Rapid Prototyping*, pp. Paper-47, 1982.

[Gerhart 80] Gerhart, S. L., et al., "An overview of *Affirm*: a specification and verification system," in *Proceedings IFIP 80*, pp. 343-348, Australia, October 1980.

[Hommel 80] Hommel, G., *Vergleich verschiedener Spezifikationsverfahren am Beispiel einer Paketverteilanlage*, Kernforschungszentrum Karlsruhe, Technical Report, August 1980.

[Hopcroft 69] Hopcroft, J. E. and Ullman, J. D., *Formal Languages and their Relation to Automata,* Addison-Wesley, 1969.

[London & Feather 81] London, P. & Feather, M.S., *Implementing specification freedoms*, ISI, 4676 Admiralty Way, Marina del Rey, CA 90291, Technical Report RR-81-100, 1981. Submitted to Science of Computer Programming

[Robinson 77] Robinson, L. and Roubine, O., *SPECIAL, a specification and assertion language*, Stanford Research Institute, Menlo Park, CA, Technical Report CSL-46, Jan 1977.

[Smith 77] Smith, J., and D. Smith, "Database abstractions: aggregation and generalization," *ACM Transactions on Database Systems* 2, (2), June 1977, 105-133.

[Tennet 76] Tennent, R. D., "The denotational semantics of programming languages," *CACM* 19, (8), August 1976, 437-453.

Operational Requirements Accommodation in Distributed System Design

STEPHEN W. SMOLIAR, MEMBER, IEEE

Abstract—Operational requirements are qualities which influence a software system's entire development cycle. The investigation reported here concentrated on three of the most important operational requirements: reliability via fault tolerance, growth, and availability. Accommodation of these requirements is based on an approach to functional decomposition involving representation in terms of potentially independent processors, called *virtual machines*. Functional requirements may be accommodated through hierarchical decomposition of virtual machines, while performance requirements may be associated with individual virtual machines. Virtual machines may then be mapped to a representation of a configuration of physical resources, so that performance requirements may be reconciled with available performance characteristics.

Index Terms—Distributed processing, fault tolerance, modularity, real-time systems, reliability, requirements engineering.

I. INTRODUCTION

REAL-TIME distributed systems constitute one of the most problematic design areas in contemporary computer science. Such systems must accommodate the basic problems of data communications which arise in computer networks, as well as the issues of resource sharing inherent in distributed database management. Since these systems generally are concerned with the monitoring and control of real-time devices, they also encompass that tightly coupled relationship between processing units and peripheral hardware which has come to be called an "embedded" system [1]. These systems are generally specified in terms of those tasks which they must perform (functional requirements), constraints concerned with the amount of time and other resources consumed in the performance of those tasks (performance requirements), and additional subjective qualities which will influence the system's developmental cycle. These latter ones are sometimes called *operational requirements* and may involve issues such as reliability, fault tolerance, growth, and availability.

The selection of a suitable representation for such a complex system's requirements has long been a major problem of software engineering. The tutorial volume of Mariani and Palmer [2] provides a thorough overview of the many approaches which have been taken to the formulation of specification languages and techniques. For the most part, these approaches

have all focused on representation of functional requirements, although the requirements specification language (RSL) also provides a framework for the expression of performance requirements. RSL is the base language of the software requirements engineering methodology (SREM) [3], which was explicitly designed with the concerns of embedded systems in mind. The SREM approach is based on analysis of the data exchanged (messages) at the interfaces between the processing system and its peripheral hardware. The assumptions are that the processing system generally must do "something" with each component of each type of input message, and the system likewise must provide transformations to develop each component of each output message. This technique thus tends to proceed inward from external interfaces.

The primary descriptive component of RSL is the *R-net* (requirements network). Each input message interface provides input to a distinct *R-net*, and the presence of data at that interface serves as an *enablement* condition for the *R-net*. An *R*-net may terminate in a number of ways, including generating an output message at an output interface. Processing within an *R*-net is highly sequential and synchronous, whereas the different *R*-nets which constitute a system may be regarded as asynchronously parallel components. The actual activity of an *R*-net is described in terms of *processing tasks* (called ALPHA's) and *events* (*E*-nodes), which describe the enablement of other *R*-nets.

Fig. 1 shows a typical set of *R*-nets for a simple radar control system. The triangular nodes simply represent initiation and termination points. The hexagonal nodes are external input and output interfaces. The rectangular nodes represent the ALPHA's, and the circular nodes are the *E*-nodes. The dashed arrows indicate the enablements, both by the *E*-nodes and through interaction with the radar. Notice that data elements are not shown in the *R*-nets, although data *are* described in the RSL text which serves to define the *R*-nets.

The general SREM approach to describing a system's behavior in terms of its interaction with external systems is a useful one, but it admits of more generality than is currently accommodated by the expressive capability of RSL. Section II presents an approach to operational requirements accommodation which generalizes the SREM approach to functional decomposition. Thus, every processing task may be viewed as the behavior of a potentially independent processor, called a *virtual machine*, following the terminology of Dijkstra [4]. Section III introduces a variation to the *R*-net notation as a notation for virtual machines. This new notation is called a *P-net*, and it is used to

Manuscript received January 19, 1981; revised June 13, 1981. This work was supported by the Ballistic Missile Defense Advanced Technology Center under Contract DASG60-78-C-0034.

The author was with the General Research Corporation, Santa Barbara, CA 93111. He is now with Schlumberger-Doll Research, Ridgefield, CT 06877.

Reprinted from *IEEE Transactions on Software Engineering*, Volume SE-7, Number 6, November 1981, pages 531-537. Copyright © 1981 by The Institute of Electrical and Electronics Engineers, Inc.

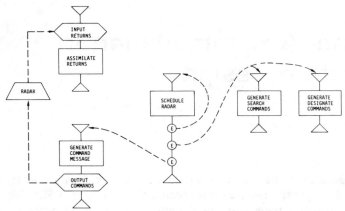

Fig. 1. *R*-net representation of radar control system.

discuss the accommodation of operational requirements in a case study. Section IV summarizes the features of *P*-nets which aid the overall requirements engineering task.

II. OPERATIONAL REQUIREMENTS

A. Reliability

In attempting to define "reliability" for distributed systems, there is a potential difficulty stemming from the fact that the definition of "errors" and "faults" is heavily dependent on being able to describe a system's behavior as a sequence of discrete, well-defined *states*. A survey by Randell, Lee, and Treleaven [5] defines an *erroneous state* to be one for which "there exist circumstances (within the specification of the use of the system) in which further processing, by the normal algorithms of the system, will lead to a failure which we do not attribute to a subsequent fault." (A *fault* is defined to be "the mechanical or algorithmic cause of an error," while the term "error" is reserved to isolate that particular part of an erroneous state which is "incorrect." However, the survey observes that such isolation is not always possible and recognizes that the terms "erroneous state" and "error" may be used as "casual equivalents.") Thus, within the framework of these definitions, a system's state space may be partitioned into those states which are erroneous and those which are not; *reliability* may then be regarded as a measure of the frequency of events which cause the system to enter one of its erroneous states.

Unfortunately, this framework tends to become unmanageable when one turns one's attention to distributed systems. While it generally makes sense to discuss the state of a single processor, the concept becomes much more awkward in a loosely coupled system of processors, all running under independent clocks. One can always take a direct sum approach, but the asynchrony of the components will introduce an unwieldy indeterminacy into the definition of transition rules. Any intuitive sense of concurrency will be totally lost within such a representation.

While any consideration of a global state of a distributed system may involve difficulties, it is still possible, in most respects, to talk about the state of a single processor. The behavior of the system as a whole may then be restricted to the "point of view" of each component processor. A processor may establish its view by conducting *transactions* with other

processors: retrieval of information and requests that certain information be updated.

This approach to reliability will obviously have an effect on how functional decomposition should be performed during requirements engineering. In particular, the approach tends to imply that functional decomposition should respect the following properties.

1) The units of decomposition should be *encapsulated*. That is, they should be free of side effects and should ultimately admit of implementation on totally disjoint and independent processing units.

2) All data-sharing among the units of decomposition should be achieved through *messages*. Not all of these messages need necessarily be implemented through communications primitives; but, at the level of specification, message-passing is the best trace of how all data are manipulated.

3) All units should exhibit simple behavior. (It is probably desirable that the behavior of any given unit be given as a mathematical function.) Consequently, each unit should admit of simple tests for erroneous behavior.

B. Growth

In many ways, growth is an even more subjective requirement than reliability, making any attempt at an objective characterization all the more difficult. Nevertheless, a specific example of accommodating growth may provide some useful ideas. Consider as such an example the radar control system illustrated in Fig. 1. The task of the ASSIMILATE RETURNS ALPHA is to scan all incoming radar returns and select those which should then be subjected to further processing. The reliability of this module will depend primarily on the reliability of those equations it uses to establish the validity of the data contained in a radar return. Both the structure and the coefficients of these equations may very likely be subject to change. Consequently, one should be prepared to "tune" these equations to agree with the properties of representative data, once these properties are known.

The implication of this observation is that the "tuning" of these equations should correspond, in a systematic manner, with the "tuning" of some set of critical parameters within the module under consideration. This requires, first of all, that all these parameters be represented by *explicit* data structures in the module (rather than depending implicitly on the manipulation of related data structures). Furthermore, these parameters should be localized in the resulting software structure in such a way that they may be easily changed. (This essentially complements the principle of "information hiding" advocated by Parnas [6]. These parameters constitute the information which should be "hidden" from other modules, but they must be readily accessible for the "tuning" of this particular module.)

Thus, accommodating growth is ultimately an issue of modularization. It begins with the explicit recognition of those components of the requirements specification which may be subject to change and some anticipation of the nature of the changes which may occur. It should eventually end with an implementation which is structured in such a way as to facilitate the realization of those changes, if and when they are introduced.

Once again, this approach will significantly influence the selection of criteria for functional decomposition. Fortunately, both encapsulation and data-sharing through messages, as cited in Section II-A, will greatly assist the development of systems with "tunable" parameters. Also, the above example should have demonstrated the high desirability of using a representation which corresponds as closely as possible to the underlying mathematics of a system's behavior. Many of the actual constructs of programming languages turn out to be little more than bookkeeping devices for the realization of a given mathematical expression [7], and these devices are more likely to disguise the actual "tunable" parameters than reveal them. In general, the closer one's mode of expression gets to basic mathematics, the more apparent will be the possibilities for change.

C. Availability

The operational requirement of availability is not so much concerned with the tasks performed by the resources which constitute a system as it is with the resources themselves. Thus, while reliability and growth may be accommodated by techniques concerned with functional decomposition, availability involves the performance requirements of the resulting units of decomposition. Once these performance requirements are determined, one must establish that in a given operational configuration, resources will actually be *available* to satisfy them. If such availability cannot be assured, then the performance characteristics of the configuration must be modified to account for resource access times.

Consequently, functional decomposition should be expressed in terms of a representation which will readily allow an expression of performance requirements in terms of the units of decomposition. In a similar manner a representation is needed which will accommodate the performance *characteristics* of the operational configuration which will actually realize these units of decomposition. Availability may then be accommodated in terms of a mapping of performance requirements onto performance characteristics—determining whether or not a given mapping is feasible and consistent.

D. Desiderata for Requirements Engineering Tools

On the basis of the preceding discussion, it is apparent that the accommodation of operational requirements will affect the elaboration of both functional and performance requirements. On the other hand, operational requirements can only be objectively expressed in terms of those functional and performance requirements which are being elaborated. Therefore, the most desirable quality of any tools to support requirements engineering is that they support a flexible approach to functional decomposition which may be successively embellished to accommodate functional, performance, *and* operational requirements. In other words, the specification of requirements may best be envisaged as the accumulation of a data base which will be progressively updated with information regarding functional, performance, and operational requirements [8].

To support this approach, every data processing task will be viewed as potentially the activity of an independent processor (sometimes called a *virtual machine*). Thus, following the principles of SREM, each task becomes an independent design problem which may be related to the entire system through its *interfaces*. Any need for a global data repository may be accommodated by a *file* element, where tasks interact with files by means of *transactions*, which embody the representation of retrievals and updates. However, as Dijkstra [4] has already demonstrated, individual files may themselves be regarded as virtual machines.

The analysis of performance and availability is concerned with *physical* resources, such as processors, communications channels, and storage devices, which may also be represented as virtual machines [9]. Performance analysis may then be defined in terms of a mapping from the virtual machines which represent data processing tasks to the virtual machines which represent physical resources. Such a mapping should ultimately provide enough information to generate a simulation of a system's performance characteristics on a given implementation environment [10].

It is also important that the representation of virtual machines allows for hierarchical decomposition. That is, one would like to view any individual virtual machine as being itself a system of virtual machines, with its own interfaces and files. This should greatly facilitate the accommodation of the growth requirement. This issue of the representation of virtual machines will now be considered in greater detail.

III. Accommodation Techniques

The representation and use of virtual machines may now be elaborated in terms of the radar control system illustrated in Fig. 1. In this example, the radar being controlled accepts two types of commands, called "search" and "designate." Search commands are scheduled according to some regular pattern through which the radar scans its entire field of view. Designate commands are scheduled to provide further processing of information returned from the radar in response to both search and designate commands; as described in Section II-B, any return which passes certain validity criteria will cause the generation of a new designate command. Search and designate commands are batched together in "command messages," which are dispatched to the radar at regular scheduling intervals.

Fig. 2 provides a representation of this system as a *configuration* of virtual machines. Each connected graph constitutes a single virtual machine. (The individual graphs will be called *process networks*, or *P-nets*, for short. *P*-nets are similar to *R*-nets in that they are independently enabled and may run asynchronously in parallel. The primary distinction between *R*-nets and *P*-nets is that all *P*-net enablement is determined through *interfaces*, still represented by hexagonal nodes. These interfaces serve to define the topology of the virtual machine configuration.)

Each *P*-net represents a single *processing task*, identified by its (unique) rectangular node. Every processing task is a strictly *data-driven function*. That is, a processing task may be viewed as a function which is applied to successive elements of an *input stream*, the successive results of application constituting its *output stream*; and the function may be *enabled* whenever there is an element in the input stream waiting to be processed.

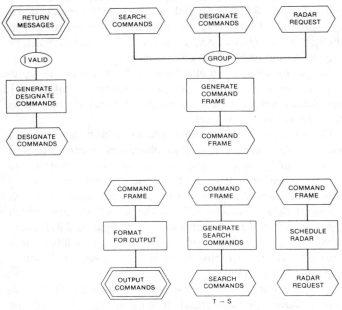

Fig. 2. A configuration of virtual machines.

The output stream is represented by the unique *output interface*, situated below the processing task node. The double hexagon around OUTPUT COMMANDS represents an *external* interface to another system (in this case, the radar), while single hexagons indicate *internal* interfaces among the *P*-nets within a single configuration. Internal output interfaces also appear as *input interfaces* to one or more *P*-nets. The elliptical nodes represent *synthesizers*, which collect data from the input interfaces to form the input streams for the processing tasks. (If a *P*-net has only a single input interface, then the absence of a synthesizer node implies that that interface may be assumed to be the input stream.)

This data-driven operation of *P*-nets arises from an interpretation of each interface as a queue [11]. The results of successive applications of a processing task are placed at the tail of the queue of its respective output interface. Synthesizers then collect data from the heads of their input interface queues to form the queue which represents the respective processing task's input stream. (In the absence of a synthesizer, the input interface queue is also the input stream queue.) Presence of data in the input stream queue thus constitutes the *activation condition* for the enablement of a processing task.

Note that a single output interface may provide input for several *P*-nets, as is the case for the COMMAND FRAME interface. All three *P*-nets which have COMMAND FRAME as an input interface will retrieve the *same* data from its associated queue. One may thus interpret this as the fact that every COMMAND FRAME message is actually replicated and sent to three distinct destinations.

The actual operation of the system illustrated in Fig. 2 may now be summarized as follows: the |VALID synthesizer creates an input stream for the GENERATE DESIGNATE COMMANDS processing task consisting only of those input returns from the radar which satisfy the VALID test. Thus, each VALID return from the radar will engender the creation of an element on the

DESIGNATE COMMANDS interface. The GROUP synthesizer collects these elements, together with elements on the SEARCH COMMANDS interface, until a RADAR REQUEST message is received. This will cause all accumulated SEARCH COMMANDS and DESIGNATE COMMANDS to be collected in a single tuple, which is then placed on the input stream for the GENERATE COMMAND FRAME processing task. The result of this processing task then serves to enable three *P*-nets. The first simply passes the command frame as output to the radar system. The second responds to this command frame with a new batch of search commands. This "batch" will be output as a single tuple by the GENERATE SEARCH COMMANDS processing task; but a *transfer function*, represented by the notation "$T \to S$," will convert this tuple of commands into a stream of commands, the appropriate input to GROUP. Finally, the third *P*-net which receives the command frame as input uses it simply to schedule the request for the next command frame.

The fact that each *P*-net contains only a single processing task allows for hierarchical decomposition. Every processing task may be regarded as an unspecified configuration of *P*-nets. The input and output streams for that processing task become, at the next level of decomposition, the external interfaces of a configuration to be elaborated. This decomposition arises from the fact that the processing tasks are strictly functional; hence, they may be implemented as encapsulated processes whose interactions will be expressed solely in terms of interfaces. Synthesizers may be decomposed in a similar manner, with an appropriate "binding" of external input interfaces.

Representation in terms of *P*-nets is particularly conducive to the accommodation of reliability and growth. Consider, for example, the problem of incorporating a new requirement (essentially a growth problem) which will enhance system reliability. Suppose it is decided that the VALID predicate should be specified in greater detail. This may be accommodated by a decomposition of the |VALID synthesizer. Suppose, further, that the activity of this synthesizer will involve the use of an *environmental map*. This could be interpreted as a file of information regarding the likelihood of noise or clutter in input returns, probably structured in such a way that it could be indexed by sky position. In fact, this file should not only be referenced during the determination of validity but also updated as a result of any additional criteria to be invoked by VALID.

This example illustrates a need for explicit representation of files, as proposed in Section II-D. However, this representation may be accommodated in terms of the interface construct. This is because any interface is nothing more than a manifestation of the *history* of outputs generated by a processing task [11], and a file may be regarded as a history of *states* arising from a sequence of updates. In these terms Fig. 3 illustrates the implementation of the environmental map as an internal interface in a configuration which serves as a decomposition of the |VALID synthesizer. Each input to |VALID is paired with the current state of the environmental map (by the & synthesizer) and passed to UPDATE, which creates a NEW MAP state. This updated state is then paired with the same input and passed to the validity test. The TEST function pairs

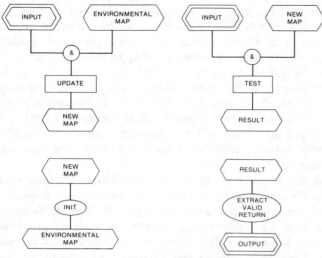

Fig. 3. Representing a file in a configuration.

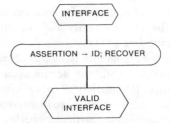

Fig. 4. An executable assertion.

the result of this test with the original input. The EXTRACT VALID RETURN synthesizer then extracts this input from those pairs for which the test result is true and discards those pairs for which the result is false. The sequence of map states is realized by the INIT synthesizer, which begins by placing an initial state on the ENVIRONMENTAL MAP channel and then continues by simply copying all elements placed on the NEW MAP channel.

(Note that the EXTRACT VALID RETURN and INIT synthesizers are connected directly to output interfaces. This is an abbreviation of a *P*-net whose synthesizer provides the input stream for an identity function. Thus, the output stream which appears on the output interface is identical to the input stream produced by the synthesizer.)

There are additional reliability issues, not directly related to growth, which are also accommodated by representation in terms of *P*-nets. One of these issues involves the validation of data across interfaces. The other concerns the implementation of fault tolerant processing.

Validation of data across interfaces may be implemented by associating *executable assertions* with all interfaces and transactions [12]. These provide a means for dynamic checking of all data structures before and after the activation of processing tasks. For example, one can determine valid value ranges for the individual components of an input return. If a given return has a value which is out of range, then one may associate one of several alternative *recovery actions* with the range assertion. The simplest action would be to reject the return and not commit the *P*-net to processing it. A more constructive action, given the constraints of real-time systems, however, might be to insert a default value in the data structure and pass the modified return to the processing task [13].

Fig. 4 illustrates how assertions and recovery actions may be expressed in terms of synthesizers. This is an example of a *conditional* synthesizer, which applies the predicate ASSERTION to successive elements in the INTERFACE queue and then applies the ID(entity) function to those elements which satisfy the predicate and the RECOVER function to those which do not. This form of expression then allows for further

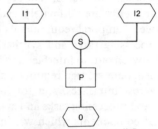

Fig. 5. A "paradigmatic" *P*-net.

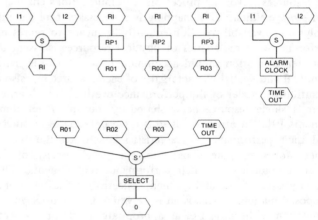

Fig. 6. Three-version redundancy.

elaboration of the functions ASSERTION and RECOVER. Once again, these elaborations may be represented as configurations of *P*-nets.

Fault tolerant processing is primarily achieved through the implementation of redundancy, coupled with a mechanism for voting on the results of redundant processing. Such redundancy is readily achieved when the processing tasks are encapsulated. For example, Fig. 5 is an illustration of a "paradigmatic" *P*-net consisting of two input interfaces $I1$ and $I2$, a synthesizer S, a processing task P, and an output interface O. Suppose one wants to enhance the reliability of P by providing three independent versions of it. Then such a three-version design may be represented by transforming the *P*-net in Fig. 5 into the configuration illustrated in Fig. 6. The synthesizer now passes input messages to a "redundant input" interface (RI). This interface provides input for three independent versions of P ($RP1$, $RP2$, and $RP3$, respectively); and each independent version has its own "redundant output" interface ($RO1$, $RO2$, and $RO3$, respectively). These output interfaces pass their data to a new synthesizer (S') which also receives TIME OUT messages provided by an ALARM CLOCK function, which assures activation of the SELECT function in time to meet any temporal performance requirements, even if not all versions have successfully completed their outputs within that time. S' may also be defined in terms of a function which maintains a "scoreboard" file of the "sanity" of the different sources of redundant output data [14].

Accommodation of availability is, as was observed in Section II-C, closely associated with the accommodation of performance requirements. Fortunately, P-nets provide a representation which may be readily extended to incorporate information related to performance. In particular, performance requirements may be factored in terms of the basic components of a P-net: processing tasks, interfaces, and synthesizers. All performance requirements are ultimately requirements concerning time or space. Temporal requirements include port-to-port timing, for processing tasks and synthesizers, and communication time (between output interface and input interface). "Spatial" requirements are storage requirements: for the messages which pass across interfaces, and for the control structures which implement processing tasks and synthesizers.

Each of the P-net components which was analyzed for performance requirements may now be mapped to specific physical resources, involving processors, communications channels, and storage units. This mapping is a necessary tool for the analysis of availability. Consequently, a means to represent performance characteristics of physical resources is essential. This representation should accommodate not only the basic temporal and spatial characteristics of each resource but also a quantitative model of the performance overhead which arises from a single resource being shared by multiple P-net components [9]. In other words, this representation of resources and their performance characteristics constitutes the "range space" for a mapping whose "domain space" consists of the P-net components and their performance requirements. The primary issue of availability, then, concerns the feasibility of a proposed mapping. This is an issue which is best resolved by simulation. The design of an appropriate simulator has been presented in another paper [10].

IV. CONCLUSIONS

The initial proposal for P-nets arose from an examination of the tools and languages provided by the TRW software requirements engineering methodology [3] concerned with their applicability to operational requirements accommodation [13]. There are three specific aspects of operational requirements accommodation which are handled by P-nets with greater facility than they would be handled by SREM. These aspects concern 1) the approach to reliability developed in Section II-A, 2) a desire to view systems development in terms of hierarchical decomposition, and 3) the need for a representation which will accommodate the synthesis of simulation. Section III discussed how P-nets address each of these aspects.

If P-nets had their origins in a "revisionist" view of R-nets, then these revisions were fueled by several significant approaches to the specifics of parallel processing and the generalities of software design and construction. While the appearance of the P-net is essentially a variation of that of the R-net, its associated interpretation establishes it as a notation for the "networks of parallel processes" which formed the basis for Kahn's formal semantics for parallel processing [11]. It is hoped that this noble ancestry will lead to the development of suitable analysis tools for systems represented as P-nets. Equally influential has been the work of Zave [1], who has long believed that applicative languages are the best notation for the design of distributed systems. The astute reader will quickly recognize the kinship between the application of a function and the activation of a P-net. In this respect, the most significant ancestor of this work is Backus, who, in his 1977 Turing lecture, vividly illustrated the limitations of thinking in terms of sequences of assignments of values to variables [15]. It is hoped that P-nets will provide ample opportunity for the task of software design to transcend the notorious von Neumann bottleneck.

In summary, P-nets provide for a representation of functional requirements in terms of a collection of data-driven processes. The data-driven operational semantics arise from the fact that the units of representation involve encapsulated processes (which do not share data through global variables) and explicit interfaces, both internal and external. Availability may be analyzed in terms of simulation of performance characteristics derived from representations of performance characteristics for the specific physical resources which constitute a data processing configuration: processors, communications channels, and storage units. P-nets also accommodate system growth by providing a basis for hierarchical system decomposition; they may be easily stored in a "development database" [8] whose internal structure may reflect this hierarchical decomposition.

ACKNOWLEDGMENT

The various "ancestors" of the P-net deserve thanks, not only for their theoretical achievements but also for their personal attention. J. Backus has followed the development of this work from its initial conception and has provided many constructive suggestions which have led to the current syntax and semantics for P-nets. Similarly, P. Zave has kept track of these accomplishments, albeit across a distance of 3000 miles. It may be fair to say that we are both at our most constructive when we are exchanging our most recent results. M. Alford has patiently heard me out on many an occasion and led me to considerations I would have otherwise overlooked. By imposing realistic deadlines, D. Palmer put me in a position where work *had to* and *could* get done; and waiting behind those deadlines, C. Davis was always ready with the feedback which would lead to consideration of new problems. Last, but not least, M. Thorpe has been assiduously responsible for the birth of every incarnation of this manuscript. All these individuals deserve more thanks than mere typescript can convey.

REFERENCES

[1] P. Zave, "The operational approach to requirements specification for embedded systems," Dep. Comput. Sci., Univ. Maryland, College Park, Tech. Rep. TR-976, Dec. 1980.

[2] M. P. Mariani and D. F. Palmer, *Distributed System Design.* New York: IEEE Press, 1979.

[3] M. W. Alford, "A requirements engineering methodology for real-time processing requirements," *IEEE Trans. Software Eng.*, vol. SE-3, pp. 60–69, Jan. 1977.

[4] E. W. Dijkstra, "Hierarchical ordering of sequential processes," in *Operating Systems Techniques*, C. A. R. Hoare and R. H. Perrott, Eds. New York: Academic, 1972, pp. 72–93.

[5] B. Randell, P. A. Lee, and P. C. Treleaven, "Reliability issues in computing system design," *Comput. Surveys*, vol. 10, pp. 123–165, June 1978.

[6] D. L. Parnas, "Information distribution aspects of design methodology," in *Information Processing 71*. Amsterdam, The Netherlands: North-Holland, 1971, pp. 339–344.

[7] R. E. Frankel and S. W. Smoliar, "Beyond register transfer: An algebraic approach for architecture description," in *Proc. 4th Int. Symp. Comput. Hardware Description Languages*, Oct. 1979, pp. 1–5.

[8] C. G. Davis and C. R. Vick, "The software development system," *IEEE Trans. Software Eng.*, vol. SE-3, pp. 69–84, Jan. 1977.

[9] E. R. Buley, R. E. Frankel, and S. W. Smoliar, "Data processing system modeling: A process-oriented approach," in *Proc. 11th Annu. Modeling Simulation Conf.*, May 1980, pp. 675–679.

[10] S. W. Smoliar, "Simulating distributed systems: A two-level approach," in *Proc. AIAA Comput. in Aerosp. III*, Oct. 1981, to be published.

[11] G. Kahn, "The semantics of a simple language for parallel programming," in *Information Processing 74*. Amsterdam, The Netherlands: North-Holland, 1974, pp. 471–475.

[12] D. M. Andrews, "Using executable assertions for testing and fault tolerance," in *Proc. 9th Annu. Int. Symp. Fault-Tolerant Comput.*, June 1979, pp. 102–105.

[13] D. F. Palmer *et al.*, *Distributed Data Processing (DDP) Technology Program Operational Requirements Accommodation: First Quarterly CY 80 Engineering Design Notebook*, General Res. Corp., Tech. Rep. CR-12-825, BMDATC Contract DASG60-78-C-0034, Apr. 1980.

[14] J. H. Wensley *et al.*, "SIFT: Design and analysis of a fault-tolerant computer for aircraft control," *Proc. IEEE*, vol. 68, pp. 1240–1255, Oct. 1978.

[15] J. Backus, "Can programming be liberated from the von Neumann style? A functional style and its algebra of programs," *Commun. Ass. Comput. Mach.*, vol. 21, pp. 613–641, Aug. 1978.

Stephen W. Smoliar (M'76) received the S.B. degree in mathematics and the Ph.D. degree in applied mathematics from the Massachusetts Institute of Technology, Cambridge, in 1967 and 1971, respectively.

From 1971 to 1973 he served as Instructor in the Department of Computer Science, Technion—Israel Institute of Technology, Haifa. From 1973 to 1978 he was Assistant Professor of Computer and Information Science at the University of Pennsylvania, Philadephia. At this time he was cosupervisor of a research project concerned with computer-assisted preparation and interpretation of dance notation scores. From 1978 to 1981 he was a member of the Technical Staff of the Santa Barbara Division of General Research Corporation. Currently, he is with Schlumberger-Doll Research, Ridgefield, CT. His research has been primarily concerned with distributed data processing requirements engineering and modeling and simulation of distributed systems for military applications. He has also published extensively in the areas of music theory and dance criticism.

Dr. Smoliar is a member of the Association for Computing Machinery and Sigma Xi.

Reprinted from *IEEE Transactions on Software Engineering*, Volume SE-12, Number 2, February 1986, pages 222-240. Copyright © 1986 by The Institute of Electrical and Electronics Engineers, Inc.

An Overview of JSD

JOHN R. CAMERON

Abstract—The Jackson System Development (JSD) method addresses most of the software lifecycle. JSD specifications consist mainly of a distributed network of processes that communicate by message-passing and by read-only inspection of each other's data. A JSD specification is therefore directly executable, at least in principle. Specifications are developed middle-out from an initial set of "model" processes. The model processes define a set of events, which limit the scope of the system, define its semantics, and form the basis for defining data and outputs. Implementation often involves reconfiguring or transforming the network to run on a smaller number of real or virtual processors. The main phases of JSD are introduced and illustrated by a small example system. The rationale for the approach is also discussed.

Index Terms—Design methodology, system design, systems analysis.

I. Introduction

THE Jackson System Development (JSD) approach aims to address most of the software lifecycle either directly or by providing a framework into which more specialized techniques can fit. JSD can be used from the stage in a project when there is only a general statement of requirements right through to the finished system and its subsequent maintenance. Many projects that have used JSD actually started slightly later in the lifecycle, doing the first steps largely from existing documents rather than directly with the users.

A JSD specification consists (mainly) of a distributed network of sequential processes. Each process can contain its own local data. The processes communicate by reading and writing messages and by read-only access to one another's data. The specification is developed middle-out starting with a particular set of "model" processes. Most of the data in the system belongs to these model processes. New processes are added to the specification by connecting them to the model. Usually the only direct connections in a network are between model and nonmodel processes and between nonmodel processes and the outside. Thus one model process is not directly connected to another or to the network boundary, and nonmodel processes only interact via the model processes. The exceptions to this general rule are discussed in Section V-B.

Direct implementations of this executable network are possible in principle and sometimes also in practice. Often, however, the network is reconfigured during the implementation phase by mapping the specification processes on to a smaller number (perhaps one) of implementation

Manuscript received April 8, 1985.

The author is with Michael Jackson Systems, Limited, London WIN 5AF, England.

IEEE Log Number 8405410.

processes. The reconfiguration involves fixing some of the scheduling that was left relatively unconstrained in the specification network. The other major concern in the implementation phase is the choice of storage structures (physical database design in an information system) to hold the data owned by the processes. The storage structures must also support the read-only access requirements of the other processes.

There are three main phases in the JSD method, the Model phase in which the model processes are selected and defined, the Network phase in which the rest of the specification is developed, and the Implementation phase in which the processes and their data are fitted on to the available processors and memory.

Sections II, III, and IV of this paper are concerned with, respectively, the model, network, and implementation phases. Section V contains the following five topics:

- A comparison of the JSD modeling approach to a more functional view of systems.
- A discussion of composition and of decomposition as general development strategies.
- A discussion of the variety of ways that the JSD steps can be mapped into the managerial framework of a project plan.
- A brief description of projects that are using or have used JSD.
- A brief description of available support tools.

II. The Modeling Phase

A. A Model with Only One Process Type

The modeling phase is concerned first with "actions" (or "events") about which the system has to produce displays, reports, signals, and other outputs. For most systems these events are mainly to be found in the world external to the system being built. They are selected and defined along with their associated attributes, and their mutual orderings described by a number of sequential processes.

Fig. 1, for example, is a list of eight actions taken from a simplified library system. By choosing these actions, and only these, we are defining a first scoping of the system. By "scoping" we mean a (indirect) definition of the range of functionality of the system. Later in the development a detailed choice will be made from this range.

We may imagine a pair of spectacles through which only the selected actions can be observed. The system to be built is like a person wearing these spectacles; its outputs can only be based on what has been observed of the world.

Action	Definition and Attributes
ACQUIRE	The library acquires the book. id, date, title, author, ISBN, price
CLASSIFY	The book is classified and catalogued. id, date
LEND	Someone borrows the book. id, date, borrower
RENEW	The borrower renews the loan. id, date
RETURN	The borrower returns the book to the library. id, date.
SELL	The book is sold. id, date, vendor, price
OUTCIRC	The book is taken out of circulation as part of the inter-library swop scheme. id, date, destination
DELIVER	The book is delivered to the other library. id, date

Fig. 1.

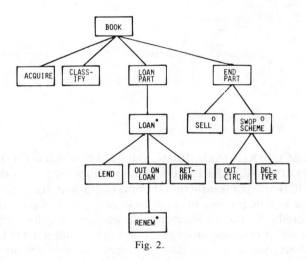

Fig. 2.

The diagram in Fig. 2 describes for one book the order in which the actions can happen. The diagram is a tree structure; the leaves are the actions; all the other components describe sequential relationships between actions or between groups of actions. Excepting the leaves there are three types of component—sequence, iteration, and selection. BOOK is a sequence of ACQUIRE, CLASSIFY, LOANPART, and ENDPART. That means that BOOK consists of one ACQUIRE, followed by one CLASSIFY, followed by one LOANSET, followed by one ENDPART. Similarly LOAN is a sequence of one LEND, then one OUTONLOAN, and then one RETURN.

LOANPART is an iteration of LOAN. That means LOANPART consists of zero or more LOAN's, one after the other. (An iteration is a generalization of a sequence.) Similarly, OUTONLOAN consists of zero or more RENEW's.

ENDPART is a selection component. That means ENDPART consists of either exactly one SELL or exactly one SWOPSCHEME. Sequences and selections can be of two or more parts; iterations can only be of one. Iterations and selections are denoted, respectively, by the "*" and "o"

in the top right corner of their constituent components. (Logically, but somehow not to the eye, the identifying symbol is in the wrong box.)

We are, of course, using a diagrammatic notation for regular expressions. We also use recursion within the diagrams, where appropriate.

Fig. 2 describes a set of sequences of actions. The following are two members of the set, two possible life histories for a book.

ACQUIRE, CLASSIFY, LEND, RETURN, LEND, RENEW, RETURN, SELL.
ACQUIRE, CLASSIFY, LEND, RENEW, RENEW, RETURN, OUTCIRC, DELIVER.

The complement of the set of sequences describes, by implication, what cannot happen. A LEND cannot immediately follow an ACQUIRE; a SELL cannot immediately follow a LEND. Later this information will be used to build some of the error-handling parts of the system.

If an input suggests that a book has been SOLD immediately after a LEND, we know that there has been some error on input because in accepting this diagram we are agreeing that a SELL cannot follow a LEND without an intervening RETURN.

The diagram describes orderings but it says nothing about how much time elapses between successive actions.

Each diagram describes the actions of one book. To describe the many books in the library we must have many instances of the diagram.

So far the diagram describes the library itself. Now we are also going to use the same diagram to describe a process type within our specification. The name of the process type is BOOK; there will be one instance for each book in the library; the purpose of a BOOK process is to model or mimic what is happening to the real book outside; to this end the process reads inputs, one for each action; the purpose of the input is to inform the BOOK model of what has happened so that the model can coordinate itself with the reality. A textual form of the process is shown in Fig. 3. This pseudocode is simply a transcription of the diagram with conditions added and reads inserted according to a read-ahead scheme. Note that one instance of this process will take as long to execute as the corresponding book is in the library. If we were able to observe the state of the partially excuted process we would know something, but not much, about the state of the corresponding book.

Having described what happens in the library, and built a process model that keeps track of what happens, we are in a position to define data. The diagrams and equivalent text in Figs. 4 and 5 define some example data items: IN-LIB, ONLOAN, LOANCT, TIMEONLOAN, and LOAN-DATE. Ignoring some of the technical details, the important points are as follows: the original model process is used as a framework for defining the data to be stored for one book; the meaning of the data is formally tied to the meaning of the actions and their attributes; a data item is local to a process instance; the mechanism for updating

```
BOOK seq
    read next input ;
    ACQUIRE seq
        read next input ;
    ACQUIRE end
    CLASSIFY seq
        read next input ;
    CLASSIFY end
    LOANPART iter  while (input = LEND)
        LOAN seq
            LEND seq
                read next input ;
            LEND end
            OUT-ON-LOAN iter while (input = RENEW)
                RENEW seq
                    read next input ;
                RENEW end
            OUT-ON-LOAN end
            RETURN seq
                read next input ;
            RETURN end
        LOAN end
    LOANPART end
    ENDPART select (input = SELL)
        SELL seq
        SELL end
    ENDPART alt (input = OUTCIRC)
        SWOPSCHEME seq
            read next input ;
        SWOPSCHEME end
        DELIVER seq
        DELIVER end
    ENDPART end
BOOK end
```

Fig. 3.

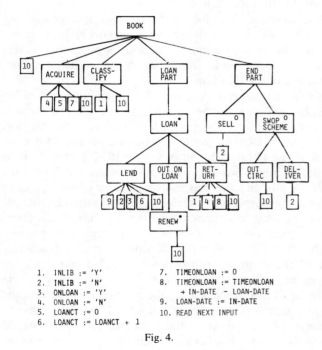

```
1.  INLIB := 'Y'          7.  TIMEONLOAN := 0
2.  INLIB := 'N'          8.  TIMEONLOAN := TIMEONLOAN
3.  ONLOAN := 'Y'             + IN-DATE - LOAN-DATE
4.  ONLOAN := 'N'         9.  LOAN-DATE := IN-DATE
5.  LOANCT := 0          10.  READ NEXT INPUT
6.  LOANCT := LOANCT + 1
```

Fig. 4.

the data is part of its definition, not something separate; the definition is in terms of event histories; as the model process executes to keep in step with the reality the data is also kept up to date; for this reason we have avoided problems of data integrity.

Defining these data begins a second, more restrictive scoping of the specification. The actions define what happens, the data define what is to be remembered about what has happened. The system can only use historical data in its outputs or in the conditions for producing outputs if that data has been stored. This also applies to simple items

```
BOOK seq
    read next input ;
    ACQUIRE seq
        ONLOAN := 'N';  LOANCT := 0;  TIMEONLOAN := 0;
        read next input;
    ACQUIRE end
    CLASSIFY seq
        INLIB := 'Y';
        read next input;
    CLASSIFY end
    LOANPART iter while (input = LEND)
        LOAN seq
            LEND seq
                LOAN-DATE := IN-DATE;  ONLOAN := 'Y';
                INLIB := 'N';
                read next input;
            LEND end
            OUT-ON-LOAN iter while (input = RENEW)
                RENEW seq
                    read next input;
                RENEW end
            OUT-ON-LOAN end
            RETURN seq
                INLIB := 'Y';  ONLOAN := 'N';
                TIMEONLOAN := TIMEONLOAN - IN-DATE + LOAN-DATE;
                read next input;
            RETURN end
        LOAN end
    LOANPART end
    ENDPART select (input = SELL)
        SELL seq
            INLIB := 'N';
        SELL end
    ENDPART alt (input = OUTCIRC)
        SWOPSCHEME seq
                .
                .
                .
                .
                .
```

Fig. 5.

like ACQUIRE-DATE, ISBN, and TITLE which are attributes of the ACQUIRE action and therefore are part of the ACQUIRE input transaction. Simple operations are needed in the BOOK process to store these data items, if they are required. (So far we have only shown how to define data in model processes; other processes may contain data; for example, we may introduce a process to hold the total numbers and values of books acquired in each of the last five weeks, or a process for each author to accumulate the number of LEND's in successive periods. These extra data are also part of the second scoping. Nevertheless, unless we remember every attribute of every action, the second scoping will be more restrictive than the first.)

For obvious reasons, we sometimes describe processes like the BOOK process as long-running processes. Only in some environments can such processes be executed directly. In others, an explicit suspend-and-resume mechanism has to be introduced. It could work as follows. When the process reaches a read it suspends itself; when a record becomes available, possibly several months later, the process resumes where it left off, executes as far as the next read, and suspends itself again. Between suspension and resumption, the values of any local variables and the resume point in the program (collectively called its "state vector") must be stored explicitly on some file or database. From the JSD point of view, the files or database of a system are simply the state vectors of the partially executed long-running processes that make up the specification.

A possible suspend-and-resume mechanism is illus-

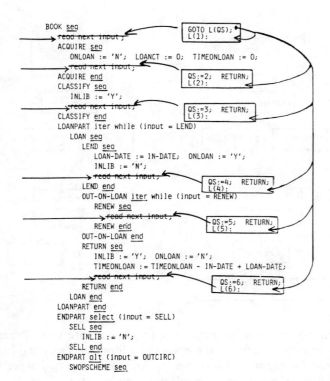

```
BOOK seq
    read next input;
    ACQUIRE seq
        ONLOAN := 'N';  LOANCT := 0;  TIMEONLOAN := 0;
        read next input;
    ACQUIRE end
    CLASSIFY seq
        INLIB := 'Y';
        read next input;
    CLASSIFY end
    LOANPART iter while (input = LEND)
        LOAN seq
            LEND seq
                LOAN-DATE := IN-DATE;  ONLOAN := 'Y';
                INLIB := 'N';
                read next input;
            LEND end
            OUT-ON-LOAN iter while (input = RENEW)
                RENEW seq
                    read next input;
                RENEW end
            OUT-ON-LOAN end
            RETURN seq
                INLIB := 'Y';  ONLOAN := 'N';
                TIMEONLOAN := TIMEONLOAN - IN-DATE + LOAN-DATE;
                read next input;
            RETURN end
        LOAN end
    LOANPART end
    ENDPART select (input = SELL)
        SELL seq
            INLIB := 'N';
        SELL end
    ENDPART alt (input = OUTCIRC)
        SWOPSCHEME seq
```

```
                        GOTO L(QS);
                        L(1):



                        QS:=2;  RETURN;
                        L(2):


                        QS:=3;  RETURN;
                        L(3):




                        QS:=4;  RETURN;
                        L(4):



                        QS:=5;  RETURN;
                        L(5):




                        QS:=6;  RETURN;
                        L(6):
```

Fig. 6.

trated in Fig. 6. Some details are omitted. For example, QS must be initialized before the first call, either by declaration or perhaps by the calling program. This mechanism converts the BOOK process into a BOOK subroutine. If several processes are similarly converted into subroutines of the same main program, then the several specification process will have been combined into a single implementation process.

The diagrams used in the first instance simply to describe and analyze the library later become part of the code of the final system. Model processes can be turned into update subroutines for the database, files, or other stored data.

We have digressed into a discussion of some issues to do with the implementation of model processes. We now return to the modeling phase and consider some more complicated models.

B. More Complicated Models

Fig. 7 introduces five new actions to the library system and discriminates between two cases of an existing action. There can be several copies of the same book, so a RESERVE refers to a title not to an individual book. Fig. 8 shows two more structures that describe the orderings of the actions, making three structures in all.

Several of the actions belong to more than one of the structures. The different structures describe intersecting subsets of actions; each structure describes a set of ordering constraints on its own actions. Thus we can view the same events in the same reality from different points of view. The constraints on any one action are the sum of the

A MORE COMPLICATED MODEL FOR THE LIBRARY

More Actions

Action	Definition and Attributes
JOIN	A new member joins the library member-id, name, address, lend-limit, date.
LEAVE	A member leaves the library, or through inactivity is deemed to have left. member-id, date.
CHANGE-DETAILS	A member's address, lend-limit or reserve-limit is changed. member-id, address, lend-limit, reserve-limit
RESERVE	A member reserves a title that isn't available member-id, title
CANCEL	A reservation is no longer wanted. member-id, title

In addition we have sometimes to distinguish two kinds of LEND action:

LEND-RESERVE	The LEND is the result of a reservation
LEND-NORMAL	The LEND is not the result of a reservation

Fig. 7.

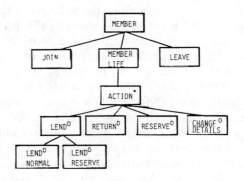

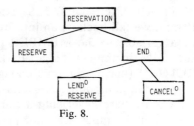

Fig. 8.

constraints imposed by the structures to which it belongs. The library only LEND's a BOOK to a MEMBER if the member has JOINED but not yet LEFT and if the BOOK has just been CLASSIFIED or RETURNED. Looking ahead to the error handling, a LEND input has to be checked against both relevant BOOK process and the relevant MEMBER process.

There is an implied CSP-like [1] parallel composition between processes (i.e., structures) that have actions in common, at least in as much as the processes describe the library itself.

The problem of data integrity is the problem of ensuring that several data items cannot take mutually inconsistent values. For data items within one process integrity is ensured by the process itself, which defines an appropriate update mechanism. When an action happens that is common to two processes, both must execute to keep in step with the external reality. Common actions therefore ensure integrity among data items that belong to different processes.

Interestingly, many systems deliberately allow their data to reach inconsistent states over controlled periods. For example, we may choose to run the BOOK and MEMBER processes as part of various on-line update transactions and the RESERVATION processes as part of a daily batch run; in this case the LEND-RESERVE in RESERVATION is not synchronized with the same action in BOOK and MEMBER.

Interfacing with existing systems also often leads to processes with common actions being left unsynchronized. For example, the BOOK processes may be part of an existing system to which a MEMBER and RESERVATION subsystem has to be added. The existing system already has a means of collecting an input for the LEND action. If the only convenient interface with the existing system is to extract periodically a file of LEND's then the BOOK and MEMBER processes cannot be synchronized.

Obviously, we want to avoid the kind of over-specification that excludes perfectly reasonable implementations. In the JSD specification, therefore, the processes that model BOOK's, MEMBER's, and RESERVATION's are not initially synchronized at their common actions. Synchronization can be added later if it is needed.

Allowing the same action in several processes improves the power of the notation, but still not enough to handle all circumstances conveniently. Suppose that no member is allowed to have more than some number, "lend-limit," of books on loan at one time. Lend-limit is defined from the JOIN and CHANGE DETAILS actions. To describe this constraint we fall back on an informal technique. We introduce a variable to the MEMBER process, set it to zero at the JOIN, increment it at a LEND, and decrement it at a RETURN (that is rigorous enough). Then we informally note the constraint ($N \leq$ lend-limit) beside the structure. We are here describing a library in which exceeding the limit is impossible, not just undesirable. So we are happy for subsequently defined error checking routines to reject a LEND if it would break the limit. If not, the constraint should not be added to the model. In practice this kind of constraint is only sensible if a member cannot take the book without the check being run.

Now consider the following description, in which the relevant actions/events are underlined.

"Film stars often <u>marry</u> but their marriages always end in <u>divorce</u>. They are frequently <u>hired</u> to work on a film but they are always <u>fired</u> for breaking one or other of the terms of their contract."

Fig. 9 describes one possible interpretation of this description and illustrates how there can be more than one struc-

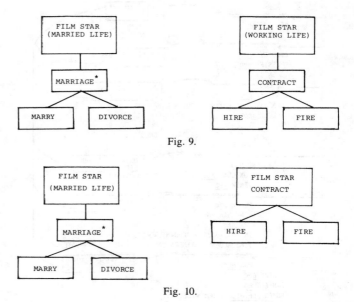

Fig. 9.

Fig. 10.

ture or process for the same entity. There are no ordering constraints between the events in a film star's married life and the events in his or her working life. The two aspects proceed in parallel. We call different structures that share the same identifier, different roles of the entity.

Any structure with more than one instance has to have an identifier, or some equivalent means of associating action inputs with their appropriate model instances. For example, a RETURN input has to be directed to the appropriate BOOK process. Thus, every action has to have among its attributes the identifiers of the structures to which it belongs. And if an action does not have a particular attribute, then it cannot belong to that structure; for example, RESERVE cannot be action of BOOK.

Fig. 9 reflects the assumptions that a film star can only have one spouse at a time and one contract at a time. A typical sequence of actions for a single film star is

$$M, H, D, M, D, M, F, H, F, D.$$

Fig. 10 relaxes the second of these restrictions. A typical sequence of actions for a single film star is

$$M, H_1, H_2, F_2, D, M, H_3, F_1, D, F_3$$

where the index on H and F is a contract-id.

More parallelism implies more and smaller structures. Drawing these structures is as much about parallelism as about ordering. A sequence of actions for many film stars is any interleaving of the sequences for individual film stars. (A qualification must be added if film stars can marry each other. MARRY and DIVORCE are then common actions of different instances of the same structure thus placing a constraint on their possible interleavings.)

An entity is defined in terms of its actions. It is simply the suitable name in the top box of a structure, the object on whose instances the ordering constraints apply. BOOK is not defined as a thing with lots of printed pages but as something which is ACQUIRED, CLASSIFIED, LENT, etc. Book would not be a good name if the library also had music cassettes which were ACQUIRED, CLASSI-FIED, LENT, and so on according to the same ordering rules as apply to things with printed pages. In practice a developer works with actions and entities together (best of all with phrases like "the member returns the book"). In theory, though, the actions come slightly first.

C. Event Models and Data Models

Database oriented approaches to the development of business systems start by building a data model of the enterprise (interpreting that term widely). Proponents argue, quite rightly, that the users' detailed requirements change very fast; that the stored data from which the requirements are calculated is much more stable; that therefore the key to robust systems is to get the database right; and the way to get the database right is to base it, via the stepping stone of a data model, on a description of the enterprise.

For data-processing systems, JSD can be viewed as a generalization of this approach, a generalization that includes the time dimension in the model of the enterprise. The state of a database (or equivalent files) does reflect the state of the enterprise. However, the way the database changes also reflects the way the enterprise evolves. We argue that it is just as important to capture the dynamics of the enterprise in the description which forms the basis of the system as it is to capture its static properties. In JSD we describe the dynamics first (what happens? in what order?) and then we define the states of the enterprise (the data) in terms of these dynamics (what is stored or remembered about what has happened?). Not only is this more powerful for almost all the problems to which the database approach does apply, but it also extends the applicability of the approach to real-time and other systems in which the data are not of central importance.

In making this generalization, we are also offering some clarification of some of the conceptual difficulties at the heart of data modeling. In his book *Data and Reality* [2], William Kent shows by a series of examples that the terms entity, attribute, and relationship, as commonly used, are very difficult to define and in particular very difficult to distinguish. He also argues that any record oriented description (let alone particular hierarchical, network, or relational descriptions) has important limitations and that these limitations are only difficult to see because our habits of thought are conditioned by available implementation techniques.

Events are the basic medium of JSD modeling, not *n*-tuples of data items. Events have the immediate advantage that they usually directly visible in the enterprise. Many data items are not (TIMEONLOAN, ACQUIREDATE, LOANCT, etc.), even though the data model is supposed to describe the enterprise. The concept of an event is fairly easy to define. The important point, apart from relevance to the system to be built, is that we must be prepared to regard the event as atomic, happening at a single instant of time. We are building a discrete simulation whether or

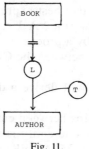

Fig. 11.

not the enterprise evolves continuously or discretely or both. The choice of actions determines the resolution of our simulation. Actions correspond to the smallest updates that can be made to the database or its equivalent.

An event can have any number of attributes, which simply further describe the event. (For example, in a system to support the use of JSD a single event "AMEND STRUCTURE DIAGRAM OF ENTITY," which was constructed by a whole session with a front-end editor, had the attributes developer-id, time, entity-id, version-id, and the whole of the new structure.)

We have defined the term "entity" as a process (or set of processes sharing the same identifier) that describes constraints on the orderings of the events. Data are defined for an entity by adding variables to its process. The variables can be declared in any way we choose. We can also introduce other processes to hold extra data that do not fit any entity process. For example, we may introduce AUTHOR processes to keep count of the number of LEND's of books by each author in successive periods of time.

(Fig. 11 shows an appropriate fragment of network. The BOOK processes output LEND messages to the appropriate AUTHOR process. The *T* messages define the end of the periods. Author is an attribute of ACQUIRE and not of LEND and so has to be stored within BOOK so the message can be sent to the right destination. These networks are described in Section III. Extra processes that hold data always feed off the basic entity processes in this way.)

Relationships: Relationships are, according to Kent [2], "the very stuff of which data models are made." Although relationships are not a fundamental concept in JSD, they can nevertheless be defined in terms of a JSD model in order to derive a data model of the desired flavor. Deriving a data model is useful if we are heading for a database implementation because most existing techniques of physical database design use some kind of "logical" data model as their starting point.

We would further argue a JSD model clarifies the definition of most relationships. For example, BOOK *X* "is-now-lent-to" MEMBER *Y* if LEND (*X*, *Y*, $\cdots$) but not yet the corresponding RETURN. The relationship is many–one because in the BOOK structure two LEND's must have an intervening RETURN whereas in the MEMBER structure there is no such constraint. BOOK *X* "has-been-lent-to" MEMBER *Y* if there has ever been a LEND (*X*, *Y*, · · ·).

Existence rules are also best expressed by considering the time dimension. The rule "A *Y* cannot exist unless an *X* exists" is described by a process in which the CREATE of a *Y* can only happen between the CREATE and the DELETE of the *X*.

The following rules will derive a data model from the JSD model.

1) Define relationships between entities where

   a) the identifier of one entity is part of the identifier of another (for example, MEMBER to RESERVATION if the identifier of RESERVATION is member.title);

   b) the identifier of one entity is part of the state vector of another (for example, MEMBER to BOOK if the borrower is stored in the BOOK process);

   c) part of the identifier of an entity is part of the state vector of another (for example, RESERVATION to BOOK where title is the relevant attribute).

2) Normalize any state vectors that are not already *n*-tuples, adding the obvious relationships between the separated parts. (For example, we could define within the BOOK process a list of all the MEMBERs who had ever borrowed the book. Normalization produces a new data modeling entity but not a new JSD entity.)

The JSD approach breaks down for data and relationships that cannot reasonably be defined in terms of histories of events, for example, for a database describing chemical compounds and their relationships. Except for correcting errors, such data are never changed. Data only need to be changed when something has happened (i.e., an event) that makes the current version inaccurate. The restriction to systems whose databases (or equivalent) evolve is not severe. Still, some static portions of an otherwise evolving database may not be amenable to the JSD approach.

Let us summarize some of the points in Section II. JSD models are defined in terms of events (or, synonymously, actions), their attributes, and a set of processes that describe their time orderings, and by implication possible parallelism. Processes are described by structure diagrams—tree structures whose leaves are the actions. The same action can appear in more than one structure. Usually the description requires multiple instances of a process type, in which case all the actions of a process must share an identifying attribute or attributes. Several processes can share the same identifier; each process is called a role of that entity. Data are defined directly in terms of the model either directly by adding variables to the existing processes or by adding new processes and adding variables to these; in either case data are defined in terms of event histories. The processes, called model processes, are the basis for the specification network.

Actions correspond to the transactions that cause database updates (or their equivalent in a real-time system). Model processes will be converted into database update subroutines. Stored data in the implemented system appears in the specification as the variables of long running processes, mainly of long running model processes.

III. THE NETWORK PHASE

A. Elaboration of the Model into a Specification

The JSD model consists of actions, attributes of actions, and a set of disconnected sequential processes that describe the time orderings of the actions. These sequential processes are the start of the network that will eventually comprise the specification. Development proceeds incrementally, by adding new processes to the network and by elaborating processes that are already there. Three issues must be addressed when a new process is added.

1) How is the new process connected to the rest of the network?

2) What elaboration is necessary to the existing processes to which it is connected? (For example, a new data item may have to be added to a model process, as described above.)

3) The internal workings of the new process must be defined. Unless there is a good reason to the contrary, the internal structure is expressed using the same sequence, selection, and iteration notation used for the model processes.

Processes are added for three main reasons. Data collection and error handling processes fit between the reality and the model. Their purpose is to collect information about the actions and make sure, so far as possible, that only error-free data are passed on to the model. Output processes extract information from the model, perform calculations and summaries, and produce the system outputs. Interactive functions are like output functions, except that instead of producing outputs they feed back into the model. They handle those cases, represented in the extreme by simulations, where the system can create or substitute for what would otherwise have been external events. Oversimplifying somewhat, the model processes hold the main data for the system along with its update rules. The other processes contain the algorithms that calculate and format outputs, and that drive the model either by collecting and checking inputs or by generating new actions.

Some examples of output and interactive functions are described below. We omit examples of input collection processes. For business and for real-time systems, typical examples are on-line data-collection programs and device drivers, respectively. The details of error handling are also omitted. (One technique is to add "guard" processes to filter inputs that look good but which do not fit the current state of the model. Before each read in a model process a write operation is inserted to send a message to its guard describing what the model is prepared to accept next.)

Fig. 12 shows how the four kinds of process in a JSD specification fit together. The network phase can be divided into three parallel subphases corresponding to the three kinds of process added to the network.

In a JSD network diagram the rectangles represent sequential process types and the circles and diamonds the two basic means of process communication, data stream and state vector communication, respectively. Data stream communication is by messages written by one process and

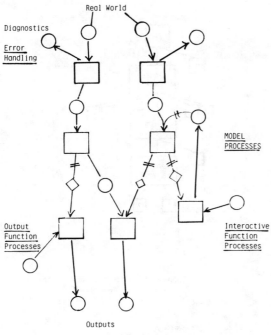

Fig. 12.

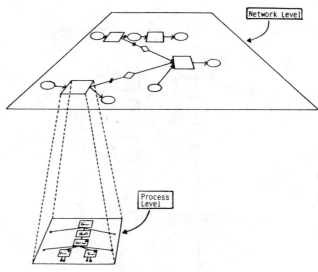

Fig. 13.

read by another. The writes and corresponding reads are not synchronized; the messages can build up in a FIFO queue. In the specification, we assume that the queue is big enough for processes never to be blocked on a write; however, a process is blocked on a read if no message is available. (The BOOK processes spend most of their time blocked waiting for an input.)

The state vector of a process consists of all its local variables including its text pointer. State vector inspection is a form of shared variable communication; one process is allowed read-only access to the other's state vector. We will see below how enquiries about the state of a particular book are answered by a process that examines the state vector of the corresponding BOOK model process.

The double bars in the network diagrams indicate relative multiplicity in the way process instances communicate—the double bars are on the side of the many. (Remember that communication is between process instances, but the rectangles represent process types.) Thus, Fig. 14 indicates that many instances of BOOK write messages to the same NEW BOOKS LISTER and that each process F_j, over its lifetime, examines many instances of the BOOK state vectors.

The merging of the input lines on two or more data streams indicates that the streams are merged before they are read. To the reading process they appear as one stream. The merging algorithm must not starve any stream, must preserve the ordering of messages from one stream, but is otherwise unspecified. This "rough-merging" introduces some indeterminacy into the specification, an indeterminacy that is limited by the kind of overall timing constraints discussed in Section III-C below. Section III-C also contains a discussion of the choice of data streams and state vector inspections as communication primitives.

Fig. 13 summarizes the nature of a JSD specification: there is a network of a large number of sequential pro-

cesses; each process is, in general, long-running; each process has its own internal structure consisting of sequences, selections, and iterations; the processes communicate by writing and reading messages and by a one-writer–many-readers form of shared variable communication; the state vectors of the processes, particularly the model processes, make up the files, databases, and other storage structures of typical implementations.

The network and the details of the processes are not quite the whole specification. We also need the definition of the actions to describe the way the network has to be embedded into the reality. These definitions fix the specification boundaries for most of the inputs. There must also be an equivalent agreed interpretation for the outputs from the specification. We need to know whether an output circle on the boundary describes a voltage difference, a screen display, or an invoice printed on gold-embossed paper.

We also need information about the desired speed of execution of the processes—this is not part of the definition of the network. Indeed, we are careful to ensure that correct operation of the network does not depend on some particular relative speed of the processes. Nevertheless, the system will be useless if it executes too slowly and we must complete the specification by describing, albeit informally, the required and desired limits on the speed of the processes.

B. Some Examples

First, we will add the following output functions, which can be based on the BOOK model process alone.

1) On input of a given book-id, output the whereabouts of the particular book.

2) On input of a given author, output the titles of the books of that author with counts of the number of books and the total number of loans for each title.

3) On input of a given title, output whether or not any books of that title are in the library and available for loan.

4) Periodically list the overdue books, grouped by borrower.

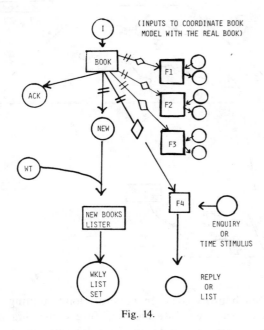

Fig. 14.

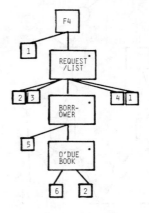

1. read next REQUEST
2. read next BOOK SV   (overdue books only, sorted by borrower)
3. write LIST-HDR
4. write LIST-TRLR
5. write BORROWER-HDR
6. write BOOK-LINE

Fig. 15.

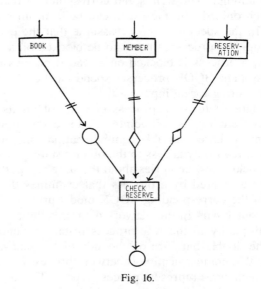

Fig. 16.

These functions are specified by the processes $F1$, $F2$, $F3$, and $F4$ in Fig. 14. Each Fj accesses the state vectors of the BOOK processes. Each Fj uses a particular ideal access path through the state vectors. These access paths are the raw material for the file design part of the implementation step. They are part of the definition of the state vector inspection.

For the above four functions the ideal access paths are as follows.
1) Direct access by book-id.
2) For a given author, grouped by title.
3) For a given title, books with INLIB = "Y".
4) Books grouped by borrower, with ONLOAN = "Y" and LENDDATE LT LIMIT.

In the implementation phase, some kind of file design will be chosen to hold the BOOK state vectors. A sophisticated design will support these access paths directly. A simple design will mean that extra components must be added in front of each Fj to extract from the state vectors actually accessed the ones Fj actually needs. In extreme cases sorting is also needed. The main point is that the network and the details of the Fj's are specified without any commitment to the file design or data storage structures that are to be used.

Fig. 15 describes the internal structure of $F4$.

The following two functions require data stream outputs from the model for their formal specification, as shown in Fig. 14.

1) Output an acknowledgment slip when a book is returned.

2) Output a periodic list of new books acquired since the last report. Include the cost of each book, the total value of books acquired in this period, and the brought forward and carried forward totals for the year.

Data streams are used when the model process has the initiative for the communication. The model sends a message to kick the other process into doing something, or at least because it is aware of the messages that need summarizing or further processing to produce the desired output.

State vector inspections are used when the initiative is with the function process. The communication takes place because the Fj's are triggered by enquiries or timing inputs to examine the state of the model.

Figs. 16 and 17 show the network part of the specification for two more complicated functions.

1) When a book is returned check if there are any reservations outstanding for that title and output the name and address of the member who has been waiting longest.

2) On request produce a list of overdue books (grouped by title) whose titles are reserved and also the name and address of the member who has borrowed them.

In the first function the BOOK process sends a message

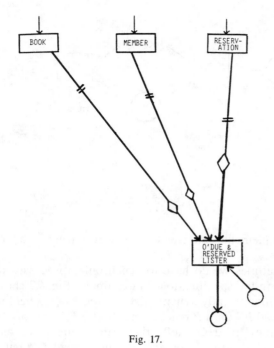

Fig. 17.

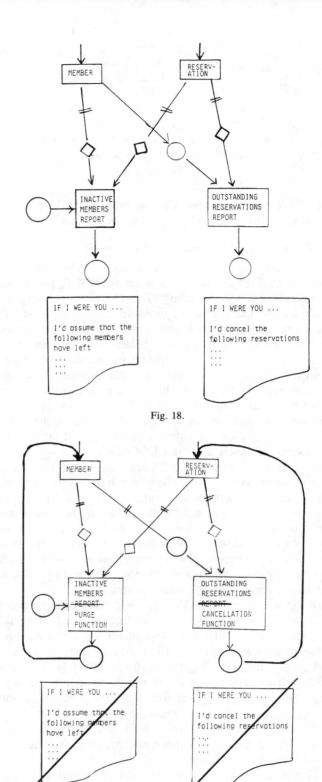

Fig. 18.

Fig. 19.

to CHECK RESERVE when the book is RETURNed; CHECK RESERVE then examines the state vectors of the RESERVATIONS, and if necessary the MEMBER, in order to output the result. The second function just needs state vector inspections.

The new processes do not communicate directly with each other. We only need to understand their connections with the model. That is why we only need to draw fragments of the network at a time and why each fragment contains some of the model processes.

In each case we have only considered the network part of the specification. We also have to consider the model processes we are connecting to. For each data stream we have to add appropriate write operations; for each state vector inspection we have to check that the data we expect to find has in fact been defined. These details have been omitted, as have the internal structures of the new processes. The JSP programming method [4]–[7] can be used to design these processes.

Fig. 18 shows the network part of the specification for two more functions.

1) When a member leaves, output a list of any outstanding reservations he or she may have.

2) On request output a list of members who have been inactive for at least a year.

Fig. 19 shows a modified specification. The output functions of Fig. 18 have been replaced by similar interactive functions. Now the system automatically cancels reservations when a member leaves, the system automatically makes inactive members leave (the library leaves the member), whether they like it or not.

The system is now generating actions that previously were happening only outside. In a simulation most or all of the actions are generated by interactive functions in this way. The exceptions, for example in a training simulation,

are the actions that are still happening externally and for which inputs have to be collected in the usual way. The model processes describe the reality that is to be simulated. The choice of actions and attributes determines the scope and resolution of the simulation. The interactive functions describe the rules by which the actions are deemed to have happened..

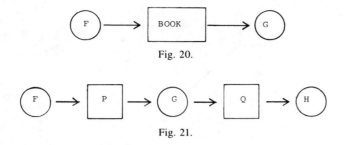

Fig. 20.

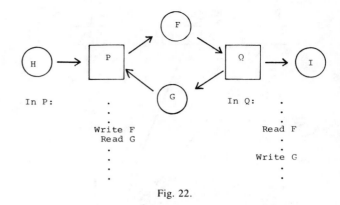

Fig. 21.

Fig. 22.

Our example also shows that we cannot just look to the external reality to find the initial set of actions.

C. The Choice of Communication Primitives

1) Asynchronous Writing and Reading: The tiny specification in Fig. 20 describes a set of BOOK processes each reading F's and writing G's. The processes are directly executable but the required speed of execution has not yet been specified. Of course the overall speed cannot be very fast—the whole point of these long-running processes is that they can be blocked for months at a read. However, there will be some execution speed of the operations between the reads which is so slow that the results appear on G too late to be useful. The specification has to include some description of required speeds. In the present state of JSD such constraints are specified informally by statements such as, "the BOOK's data must not be more than a day out-of-date" and, "any responses on G should occur within 5 seconds of the input of the triggering F record." Perhaps this informality is a weakness. However, we are reluctant to introduce a more formal notation because there is no means of embodying these timing constraints directly in an implementation in the way that BOOK processes can be converted into subroutines and embodied in the implementation. The extra precision would not really help the implementor.

In the specification in Fig. 21, there would be no point in using synchronous writing and reading on G. It would be unnecessarily restrictive. Any acceptable response time between an F and an H record could be met by making P and Q very fast and using up the time in the delay between writing and reading. Nor would synchronous communication save us if P or Q was too slow. The general reason for rejecting synchronous message-passing as our specification primitive is that it often leads to overspecification, that is, to specifications that unnecessarily exclude reasonable implementations.

That is not to say that we will not often choose to implement asynchronous writing and reading by a synchronous message passing mechanism. That is part of our implementation freedom. (In languages that do not support concurrency the easiest way is to implement the messages as parameters passed across a subroutine interface, for example, by introducing into Q a suspend-and-resume mechanism such as was described in Section II-A.) It is also part of our implementation freedom to buffer the G records for whatever period is consistent with the response constraints. For networks like Fig. 21 and many others,

this implementation freedom is worth plenty and costs nothing.

Sometimes we do have to synchronize processes more tightly in the specification. For example, Fig. 22 shows P and Q more tightly synchronized. Process Q is held up at the "read F" until P reaches the "write F." P is also held up at the "read G" (effectively the same place as the "write F") until Q not only reaches "read G" but also the "write G." This is the data stream equivalent of an Ada rendezvous.

2) State Vector Inspection: State vector inspection can be defined in terms of data streams, so it is not strictly necessary to have another communication primitive. However it is very attractive to be able to specify directly inspections of, for example, the data in the BOOK processes. In implemented systems generally there are very many components that have read-only access to stored data, so the extra complication of another primitive seems well worthwhile.

An informal description of state vector inspection uses such phrases as "only coherent states returned," "communication invisible to inspected process" and "a 'get SV of P' operation returns P's state vector without any operations being executed in P." These statements are correct but they skate around the mutual exclusion problem. A particular inspection may be invisible to P, but P still has to do enough to ensure that the results of inspections correspond only to particular coherent states, for example, to the states of P just before the execution of a read operation.

The mutual exclusion can be handled either on the state vector of P itself, or on a copy. The two cases correspond to slightly different definitions of state vector inspection. In the first P cannot be executing and being inspected at the same time; if P is not at one of the approved states the inspection must be delayed. In the second P writes a copy of each coherent state; the copy can be inspected while P is executing and the result of an inspection may now be out-of-date. Of course, the mutual exclusion problem does not disappear in the second case. An inspection must still be prevented while the copy is being updated.

At first sight surprisingly, we have chosen a definition that fits the second looser description. The reasons are similar to those for choosing asynchronous rather than

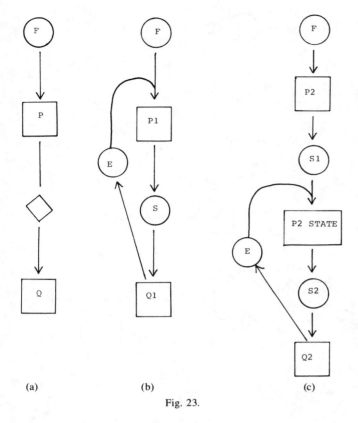

(a)   (b)   (c)

Fig. 23.

if G_i results in S_k and G_j results in S_1, then

$$i > j \Rightarrow k \geq l.$$

Let us now return to more practical matters. We have gained the freedom to implement state vector inspection using a second copy of the state vector. This freedom is particularly important in the following cases.

• In distributed implementations, local enquiries are answered by accessing a local copy of the data. The local copy is not necessarily exactly in step with the main copy.

• There is a trend in data processing towards having an operational database which is updated on-line and a decision support database which is periodically updated with an extract from the operational database. (IBM's new database system DB2 may mainly be used for this decision support role.)

• In real-time applications where virtual processors access the same global memory, second copies can reduce the problems of mutual exclusion and interrupt masking.

In our network the BOOK model already lags behind the real BOOK by some indeterminate amount, so there is no extra indeterminacy if the SV copy we access lags behind the real BOOK state vector. Descriptions of overall constraints on processor execution speeds like "for this enquiry the data accessed must be no more than 5 seconds (or 24 hours) behind the reality" limit the sum of the indeterminacies.

With the JSD style of distributed specification, we have to ensure that the problem really is solved in the specification. Because we often fix the relative scheduling of processes in the implementation phase, it is sometimes tempting to build a network that only "works" given particular relative processor speeds, in other words to anticipate the implementation. Certainly, it is unacceptable if some of the processes in the network execute too slowly; that would violate the extra, informally expressed timing constraints. But if a given set of processor speeds does meet all the constraints, then we should not be able to produce unacceptable results by making some of the processes run faster. The (small) price to pay for the implementation freedom we gain by using asynchronous message passing and the looser form of state vector inspection is occasionally some extra care in constructing the specification network.

IV. The Implementation Phase

There are two main issues in the implementation phase: how to run the processes that comprise the specification, and how to store the data that they contain. The first turns out to be particularly concerned with the data streams in the specification, the second with the state vector inspections.

Of course, there may be no work at all in the implementation phase. We only need to find a machine that will execute our executable network of processes. If we can, and if we meet the timing constraints that is fine. We are not looking for extra work.

The problem, though, is the number of (instances of)

synchronous message passing: we gain implementation freedom at little extra cost. Moreover, we are certainly not excluded from implementing the loose definition by using only one physical copy of the data.

The differences between the two possible definitions are clarified by considering their data stream equivalences. Fig. 23(b) is the equivalent of the first, tighter definition, and (c) is the equivalent of our chosen, looser definition. In both Q1 and Q2 the "get SV of P" operation has been replaced by a "write enquiry on E; read reply from $S(2)$" pair of operations. $P1$ is the process P elaborated to answer the enquiries; it answers by writing a copy of its state on S. The ordinary inputs F and the stream of enquiries E are merged; $P1$ reads the single stream F & E; since $P1$ is a sequential process, it cannot be processing an E and an F record at the same time.

$P2$ outputs its state on $S1$. P2STATE is very simple; it reads the merged stream E & $S1$; it stores the latest state from an $S1$ record; it answers enquiries from E by outputting this latest state. P2STATE executes concurrently with $P2$. The state stored in P2STATE may lag behind the real state of $P2$.

State vector inspection could be defined by Fig. 23(c) (plus the details of the internals of the processes), or more abstractly along the following lines.

Let $S_1, S_2, \cdots, S_m$ be the chosen coherent states reached during an execution of P. Let $G_1, G_2, \cdots, G_n$ be the "get SV of P" operations executed during an execution of Q. Then the result of each G_i is one of the S_k and:

processes in our specifications and the length of time it takes for their input to accumulate. In our library books last for up to 20 years and we have over 100 000 of them. Will our operating systems and concurrent languages allow us to run 100 000 processes concurrently for 20 years? We often have to combine and package the specification processes into a more familiar arrangement of "short-running" jobs and transaction-handling modules. Admittedly, our library example is fairly extreme. Many real-time environments do support some number of long-running processes, but probably still not as many as in our specifications.

A basic technique has already been introduced in Section II-A. A process can be converted into a subroutine by inserting a suspend-and-resume mechanism at its read statements and by passing the input records as parameters of the call. Every time the subroutine is called it executes part of the long-running program. It is passed an input record and returns control when it is ready to read another.

(The coding details of this suspend-and-resume mechanism can be found in [3]–[7]. The technique can be generalized to allow suspend points at the reads and writes on several or all of the data streams in a program.)

A. Data Design

After we have converted processes into subroutines, we can also easily separate the data (that is the state vector) from the subroutine text so that many instances of a process can be implemented by one copy of the subroutine and many copies of the data. For example, the state vector can be made a parameter of the subroutine. When the subroutine is called it is passed the input record and a state vector; this allows it temporarily to assume the identity of a particular instance; the subroutine executes and passes back the updated state vector when it returns; the calling program is responsible for storing and retrieving the state vectors. Alternatively, the extra parameter may only be the instance-id; the subroutine itself accesses the state vector by retrieval from a file or perhaps by using the id as a pointer into an array.

Once the data are separated, questions of storage and access can be considered. We deal with them here only briefly, not because they are unimportant, but because there is nothing new or special about the way physical data design is handled in JSD. From the specification we have a definition of the state vectors, that is of the data to be stored, and from the state vector inspections we have the definition of how the data are to be accessed. If we wanted we could also map the JSD model on to a data model of any desired flavor. We know the desired response times, the likely volumes, and we can add security and backup information as required. These are the essential inputs from the specification into database design or into the design of storage structures in main memory.

B. Combining Processes

First we show how an abstract network of programs can be combined into a main program and a hierarchy of sub-

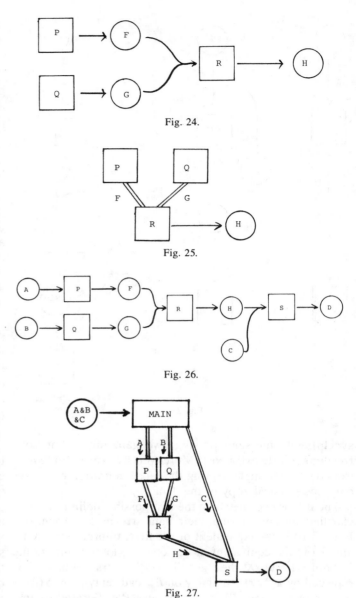

Fig. 24.

Fig. 25.

Fig. 26.

Fig. 27.

routines. Then we apply the technique to the library example.

Two or more rough merged data streams can be implemented by making the reading process a common subroutine of the several writing processes. In Fig. 24 P writes F, Q writes G, R reads the merged $F\&G$ as one stream. Fig. 25 is a subroutine hierarchy diagram in which P calls R passing F records as parameters, and in which Q calls R passing G records as parameters.

Now we will combine the four processes P, Q, R, and S in Fig. 26 so that they run as subroutines of a single main program. The technique works as follows. Imagine taking a knitting needle and threading it through all the external input streams, in this case A, B, and C. Pick up the needle and hold it horizontally. The programs will hang in the correct subroutine hierarchy, in this case as shown in Fig. 27. Each program is called by the supplier(s) of its input; all the programs return control upwards when they want to read a new input; the MAIN program is very sim-

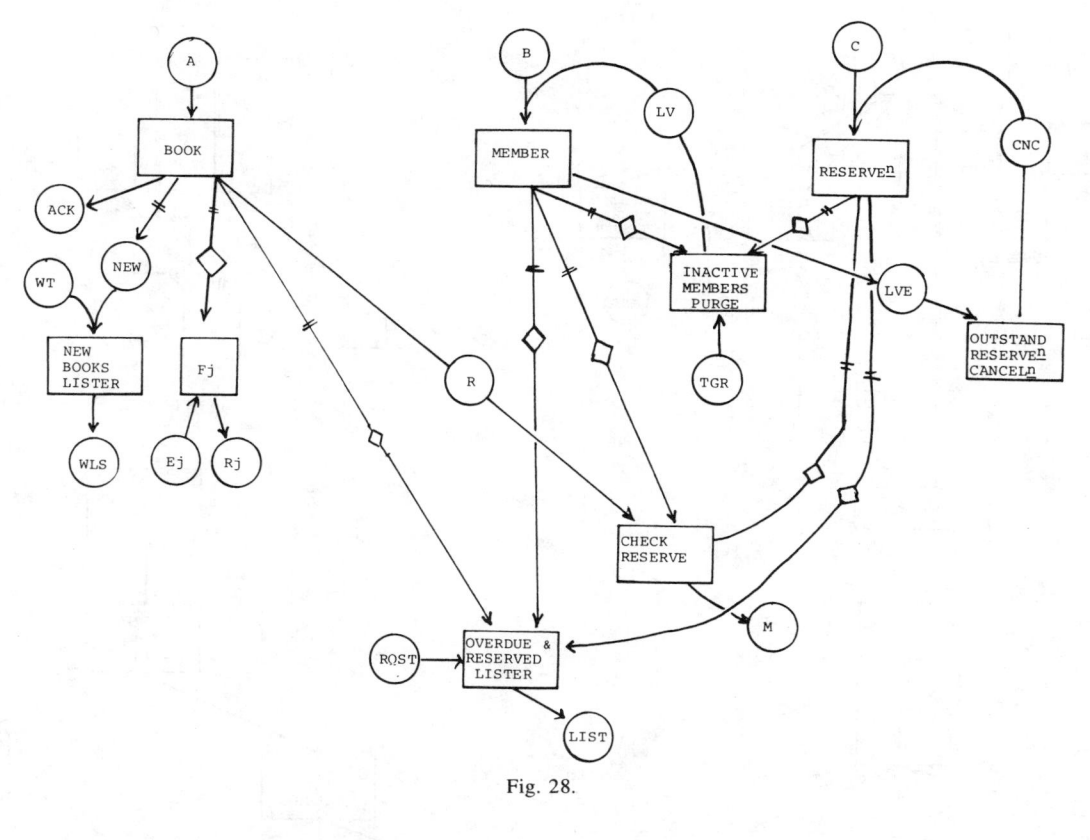

Fig. 28.

ple—it reads A&B&C and calls P, Q, and S with, respectively, the A, B, and C records as parameters.

This technique works provided every program only reads one input stream (the one stream may be the result of merging several) and provided there are no loops in the network. Loops are dealt with below. The treatment of programs with several input streams is omitted: the common special cases are easy; otherwise a more complex suspend-and-resume mechanism is needed.

State vector inspections in the network can simply be ignored. The subroutines will naturally access only a coherent version because the processes only give up control at read or write operations.

Fig. 28 shows the network for the library example. (We did not have to consider the whole of the network during the specification.) Fig. 29 shows the same network rearranged and with the state vector inspections removed. Fig. 30 shows the whole network implemented as a hierarchy of subroutines. A probable internal structure of MAIN is shown in Fig. 31. This style of implementation has no buffering on any of the internal data streams. It corresponds to a transaction oriented implementation in which one input and all its consequences are completely dealt wth before the next. MAIN has only been introduced as part of the implementation. It is a scheduling program; it controls the sequential interleaving of the processes in the network.

C. Internal Buffering

Fig. 32 is the same as Fig. 26, except for the extra data stream E from S to P, which introduces a loop into the network. There has to be some buffering on at least one of the data streams in the loop, on either F, H, or E. By

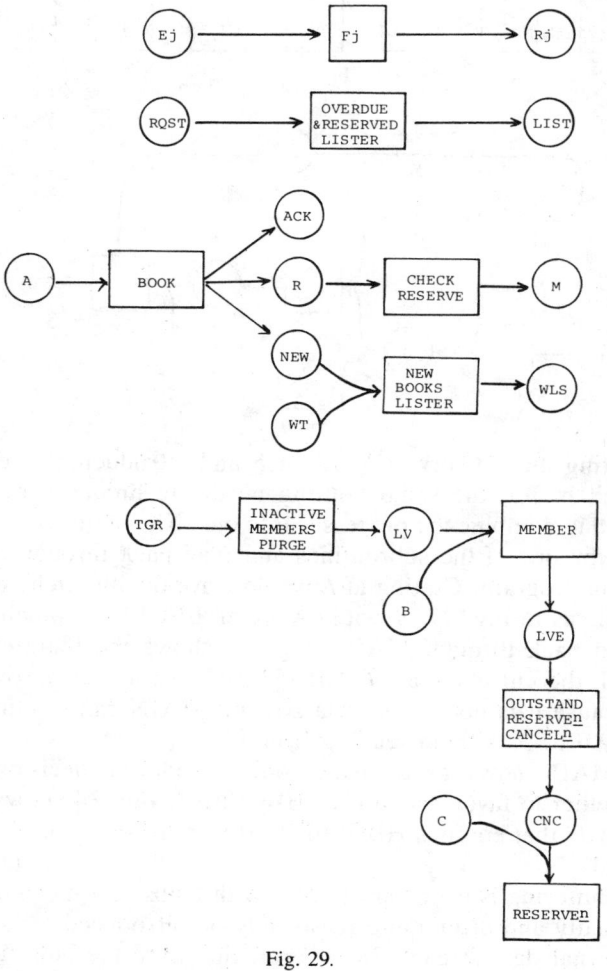

Fig. 29.

153

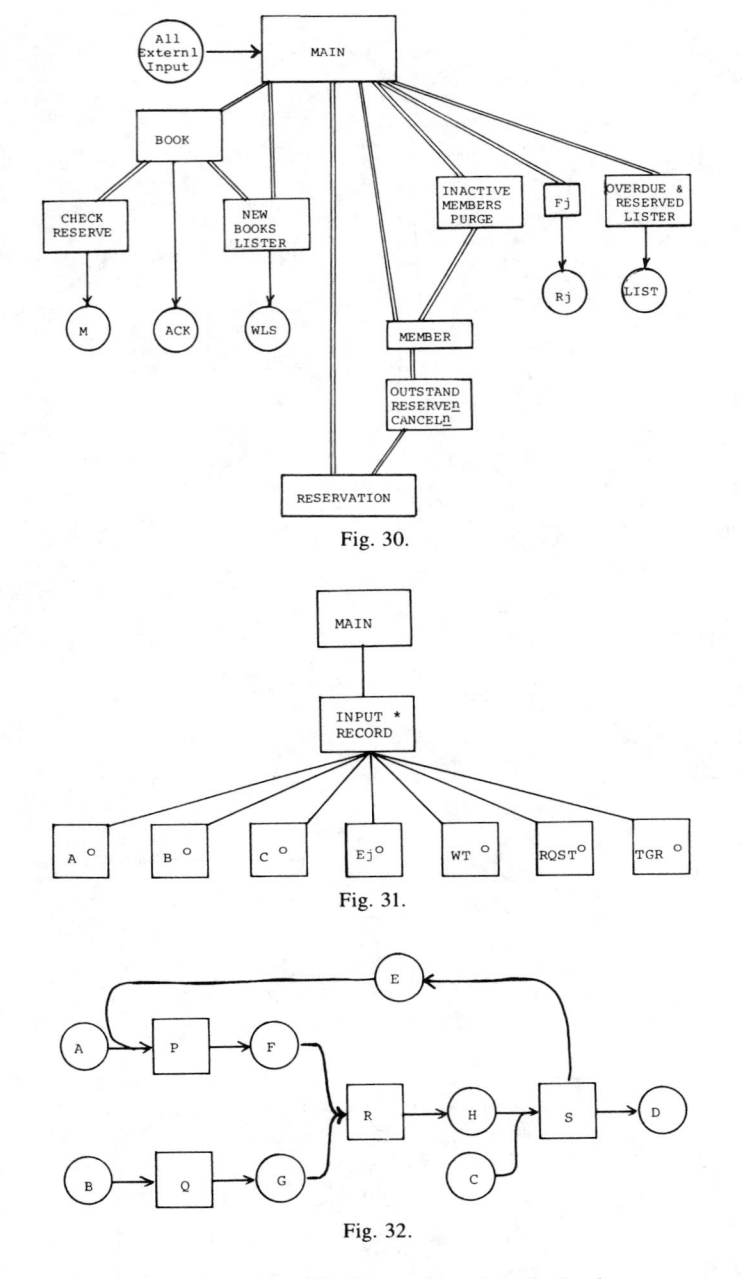

Fig. 30.

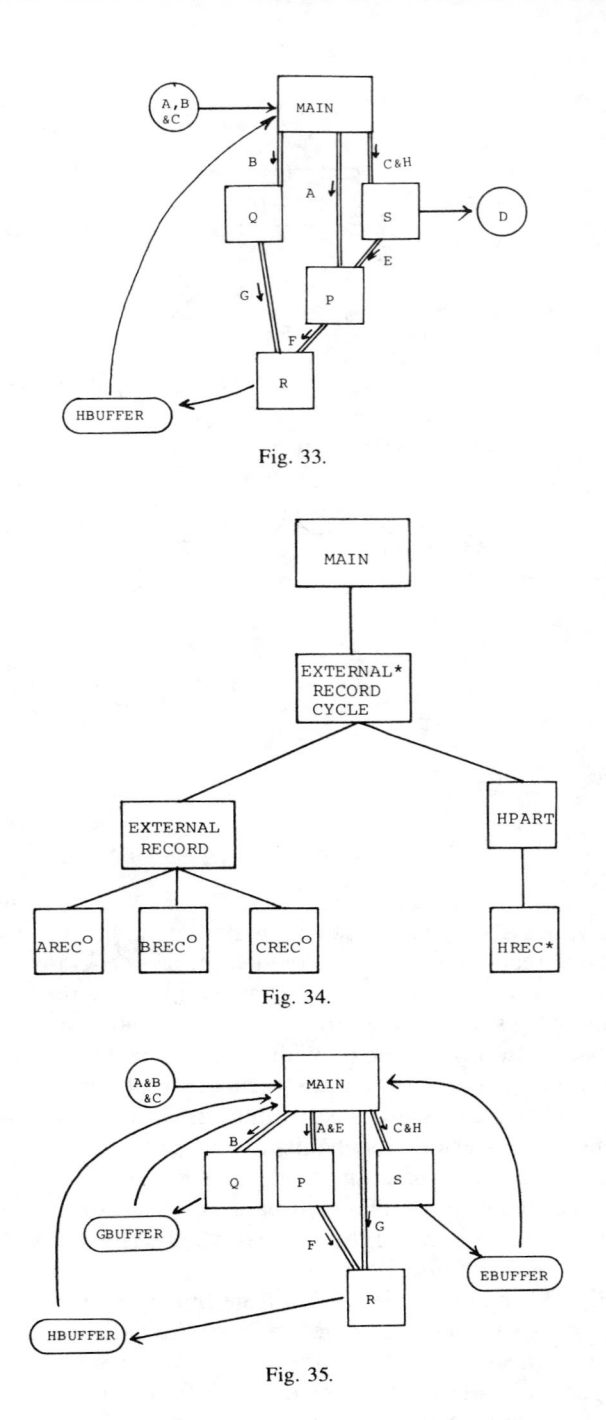

Fig. 33.

Fig. 31.

Fig. 34.

Fig. 32.

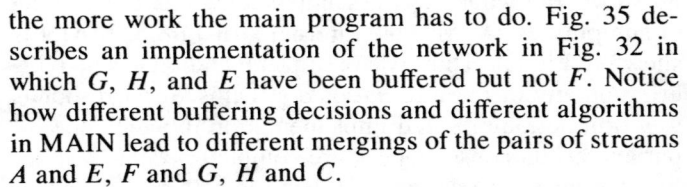

Fig. 35.

cutting the network at *F*, *H*, or *E* and introducing an explicit buffer, the same knitting needle technique can be used to combine the processes into one. The buffer is written by one of the subroutines and read back through the main program. Cutting at *E* would leave the hierarchy the same as in Fig. 27. *S* would write an EBUFFER which is read back through MAIN. Fig. 33 shows the hierarchy with the cut made at *H*. HBUFFER is shown as an oval because it is not a true data stream; MAIN can examine HBUFFER without reading from it.

MAIN now has to make some scheduling decisions; whether to favor *A&B&C* or HBUFFER. Fig. 34 shows a MAIN that empties HBUFFER after every *A*, *B*, or *C* record.

Buffering is necessary to deal with loops, but it can optionally and often quite reasonably be introduced for any internal data stream. In general, the more the buffering

the more work the main program has to do. Fig. 35 describes an implementation of the network in Fig. 32 in which *G*, *H*, and *E* have been buffered but not *F*. Notice how different buffering decisions and different algorithms in MAIN lead to different mergings of the pairs of streams *A* and *E*, *F* and *G*, *H* and *C*.

Fig. 36 shows the structure of a typical MAIN program for the kind of batch implementation that makes extensive use of buffering. Many long-running processes have been combined into one long-running program, which can be implemented by a combination of JCL and operator instructions. The bottom line is that if you do not have a long-running computer then you need a long-running operator.

154

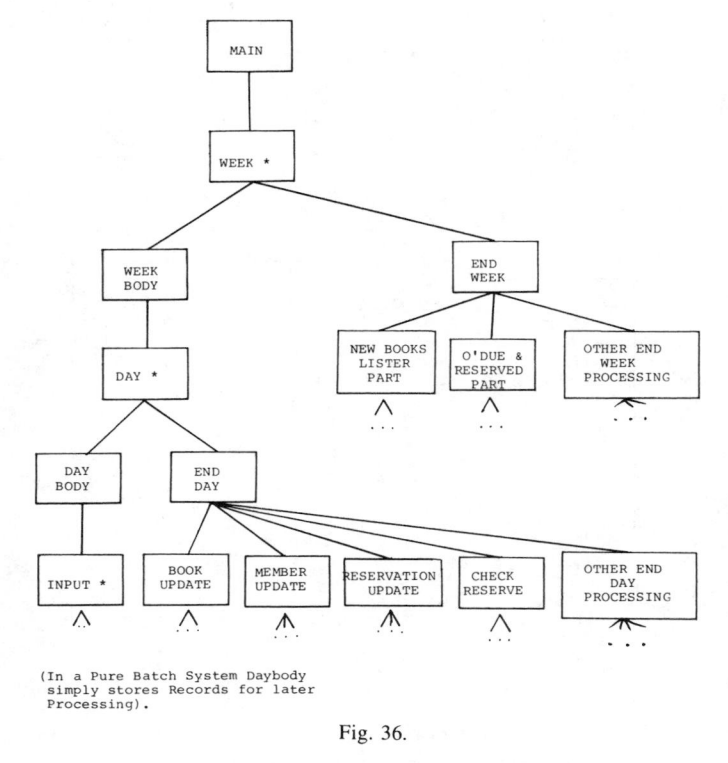

(In a Pure Batch System Daybody
simply stores Records for later
Processing).

Fig. 36.

D. Implementations with Several Processors

The above techniques combine a network into a single program with or without buffering. Often it is neither necessary nor appropriate to combine all the processes into one. Then the problem is to allocate all the processes to available processors, either real or virtual; to use the above techniques where there is more than one process on the same processor; and to implement the data streams and state vector inspections that pass between the processors.

Between virtual processors communicating via shared memory the state vectors can be put in the shared memory and the data streams implemented by, for example, a circular buffer. Care must be taken in both cases over mutual exclusion. Between real processors data streams will probably be simple messages. State vector inspection can be implemented either by an enquiry and reply pair of messages or by downloading and storing locally a copy of the state vector either periodically or on each update.

Alternatively and preferably we might be able to use directly the facilities of an operating system or of a language such as Ada that supports concurrency.

From among these many implementation possibilities, we have to choose the simplest that meets the informally laid down timing constraints. The plethora of possibilities is not a disadvantage, but a sign of success in separating specification from implementation.

V. Discussion

A. Why Modeling First?

The Meaning of System Outputs: Suppose that the librarian says at an early stage in the development of his system that he would like an output of the form

Number of books in the library = 5921

Average loan period = 12.3 days

What does this output mean? The librarian understands it by reference to the world he knows about. We, as developers, therefore have to understand the world of the library at least well enough to understand what the librarian is asking for. One major purpose of the modeling phase is to establish a basis for understanding and discussing the outputs of the system. That basis consists of the events in the JSD model, their attributes, and their orderings, and it is used not just to define the system outputs but also the data stored by the system and all the terms used in discussions with the users.

If you doubt the importance of establishing this basis, consider what the phrase "in the library" might mean. Is a book to be considered "in the library" if it has been ACQUIRED but not yet CLASSIFIED, or if it has been taken OUT of CIRCulation but not yet DELIVERED? Is the book in the library if it is really out of the library, that is, if it has been LENT but not yet RETURNed? There are many opportunities here for programming the wrong system. A specification document that is signed off, but which lacks a satisfactory model as a basis, is no guarantee of avoiding them.

Comparison to Physics: In any application of mathematics there is a bridge (a mapping) between the reality of the application domain and the formalism of the mathematics. The idea is that the mapping should capture in mathematical form some structure from the application domain. In physics, for example, we might define certain symbols as representing the charge on the electron, the speed of light, and so on; we manipulate the symbols according to some mathematical formalism; we then interpret the results back into the reality via the original definitions. In a similar way the definition of the events is the bridge between the reality of the library and the formal specification (and via the specification to the implementation) of the library system. The manipulations within the specification produce outputs which can be interpreted back into the world of the library via the definitions of events. In this sense building a library system is an application of mathematics to a library.

The bridge between the reality and the formalism can never be completely formal because the reality is not completely formal. Thus, the definitions of the actions are informal dictionary-type definitions whereas the data, for example, can be defined quite formally in terms of the actions.

One of the fundamental ideas in JSD is that the structure of the application domain should be directly reflected in the structure of the specification. The secondary assumption is that for a very wide class of information systems, real-time control and embedded systems and others, the important structure is sequential and should therefore be captured by sequential processes.

Contrast with the Functional View of Specifications: These arguments conflict directly with the widely supported functional view of specifications. According to this, view systems are functions mapping their inputs to their outputs; a specification should define the external behavior of the system, the behavior of the system as if it were a black box; internal structure is dealt with later in a design phase; no internal structure should be part of the specification.

With this view the output "number of books in the library = 5921" is explained in terms of the system inputs. This is, to say the least, uncomfortable for the librarian. Avoiding internal structure is supposed to avoid premature implementations commitments. We argue, however, that the sequential structure of BOOK, MEMBER, and RESERVATION is part of the problem statement and not an artifact of a particular implementation.

Maintenance: The second major purpose of JSD modeling is to clarify the problem of maintenance. The model is defined first and limits the scope of the system. A given model can support a whole family of outputs. The detailed functional requirements change much more quickly than the model on which they are based. Maintenance is easier because we can move relatively easily within the family of functions and, secondly, because we can explain up-front to a user what the family of functions is and therefore what the consequences are of choosing one or another model.

By including ideas of scoping (actually two scopings were discussed in Section II-A) and therefore of families of outputs, we can begin a serious discussion of maintenance. Maintenance is only comprehensible through some concept of families of functional requirements, through some idea of persistence of certain entities and structures through a number of changed specifications. The lack of such concepts is a serious weakness of the functional view. Extreme proponents sometimes argue that there is no such thing as maintenance, that a changed problem is a new problem. However, that is surely bending the facts to fit the theory.

Other Modeling Approaches: At least two other approaches similarly defer consideration of functionality and of outputs. Builders of simulation systems focus first on an abstraction of the reality to be simulated and defer consideration of reports and other outputs.

Database-oriented approaches use data models. We have argued in Section II-C that using events as the basic modeling tool is superior because it extends the modeling to include the time dimension as an integral part of the model and in so doing clarifies the semantics of data and of relationships, both of which are defined in terms of histories of events.

B. Composition and Decomposition

JSD cannot reasonably be called a top-down method (nor for that matter a bottom-up method).

• The network is not built by successive explosions of a process into a subnetwork of processes but middle-out from an initial set of model processes. The complexity of the network is not controlled by hierarchical description but by limitations on the interaction of nonmodel processes.

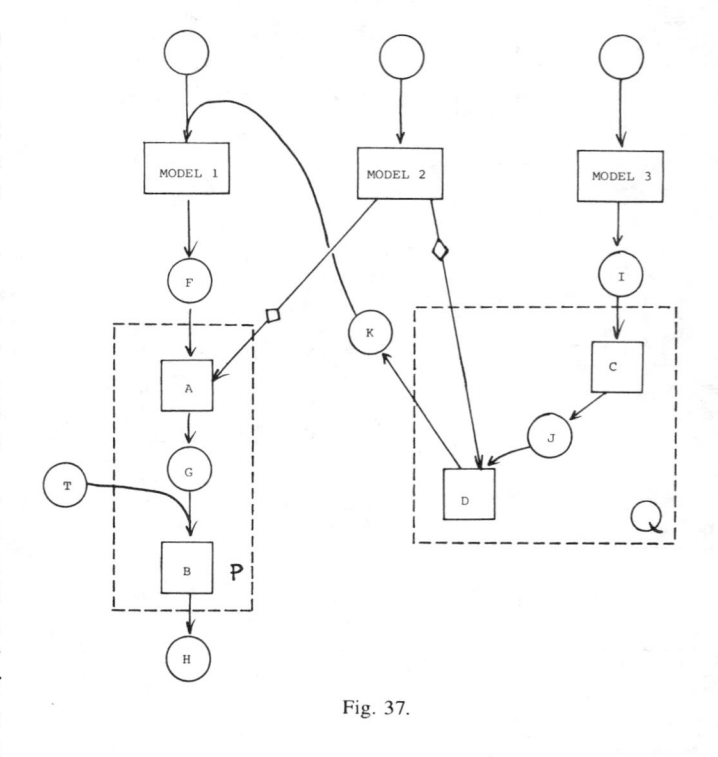

Fig. 37.

• The specification consists of an upper-level network and lower-level tree descriptions of the processes in the network. The whole of the first phase is concerned with the lower level, that is with the definition of the model processes. Then the network is developed middle-out. For each nonmodel process the lower level description is added. Development starts at the lower level of the specification and proceeds up, across, and down.

• Even the development of the tree structures in the modeling phase is not indisputably top-down. Consider the film star example from Section II-B. We started with the actions, the bottom level of the trees. We did not know at the outset whether there should be one top box or two, or even what the top boxes would be.

• Top-down development is characterized by the successive refinement of a single system structure. Using JSD the specification structure is (usually) repackaged into a completely different implementation structure. Fig. 33 and 35 (or 31 and 36) describe two different implementations; each has a different structure from that of the specification from which they were derived; the top levels of each did not even appear in the specification.

• The JSP programming method, used to develop the internals of nonmodel processes, starts with a number of data structure diagrams, composes them into a control structure of the program and then fleshes out the control structure. The data structure diagrams (and also the program structure) are abstractions of the whole program, not a description of its top levels.

Sometimes we do explode a process into a network of processes. Fig. 37 shows the output function process P decomposed into processes A and B and the interactive function process Q decomposed into processes C and D. In the Introduction we stated that nonmodel processes did not usually communicate with each other directly, that they interacted only via the model. That is true of P and Q, but obviously not of A and B or of C and D. The statement is true of the larger-scale structure of the network, that is, if the phrase "nonmodel process" is replaced by "non-model process or small subnetwork."

Even here we are just as likely to develop P incrementally by working outwards from the model. We might first add process A which does the basic calculations to produce the output G and only later add process B to do some device dependent formatting of the final output H.

The Weakness of Development by Decomposition: The idea of top-down decomposition (or stepwise refinement) is to develop software by successive decomposition. We start with a single box marked "system." If the system is not trivially simple it is decomposed into parts; the connections between the parts are defined; each part is then considered independently; any part which is not trivially simple is further decomposed.

The motivation is clear: small programs are easier than large programs; large programs are easier than small systems; small systems are easier than large systems. The idea is eminently saleable, especially to management. However, except in a very dilute form the idea is naive. If it were really possible for most developers to make good decompositions, the software problem would have been solved long ago.

The difficulty is this. That first box marked "system" is largely unknown, yet the first decomposition is a commitment to a system structure; the commitment has to be made from a position of ignorance. This dilemma is repeated at successive levels; the designer's ignorance decreases only as the decisions become less critical.

The same argument can be restated as follows. Each decision about the decomposition of a subsystem depends on the decisions that have led to that particular subsystem. This hierarchical decision structure makes the early decisions very critical. A bad early decision may not be discovered until very late. The designer must exercise tremendous foresight to make good decompositions.

We argue that decomposition or stepwise refinement only really works when a designer is effectively writing down a solution he already knows and understands. But then, he is using decomposition as a method of description, not of development. The distinction between the description of something known and thoroughly understood and the development of something largely unknown is often blurred, for example when a developer presents his design to a manager, or when the writer of a textbook presents a solution.

Proponents argue that most software development is on problems that are well understood. This view would be more convincing if most software projects met their deadlines.

If decomposition does not work, or does not work well for problems above a certain size, what is the alternative?

Development by Composition: The alternative is to develop software by composition. Instead of starting with a single box marked "system" we start with a blank piece of paper. Each increment added is precisely defined; an increment is any abstraction of the whole, not necessarily just a component of the whole; part of the system may have to be restructured, repackaged, or transformed in order to compose it with another part; at intermediate stages there is a well-defined incomplete system rather than an ill-defined complete system. JSD shows that such an approach is at least possible.

Finally, while it is a very appealing idea to make multiple descriptions of the same system, in effect to be allowed to view the same system from different perspectives, the idea does not really become useful unless there is some way to put the different descriptions together.

C. Technical Substance and Managerial Framework

Sensible managers of software projects always produce a plan dividing the project into phases. The manager is concerned with the deliverables at the end of each phase, the user signoff points, the usage of staff, the detection of slippage in time estimates, the political and organizational framework within which the project fits, and other similar issues. The managerial perspective is quite different from that of the technical staff doing the "real" work.

JSD is about the technical substance of a project. The technical substance of a project can be mapped on to a project plan in different ways. This flexibility is necessary because, even among technically similar projects, the managerial and organizational characteristics may vary widely.

For example, since a system may be needed quickly and for competitive or legal reasons, there is no possibility of not going ahead. The main uncertainty is over what and how much can be delivered in the first of several releases. A second system may have a much less certain cost justification, so that throughout the early stages the users only want to be committed to small increments of work, and they want the option of stopping the project as the end of each increment. The project plan, the phasing, and the phase-end deliverables ought not to be the same for these two projects even though they may be technically similar.

Some methodologies concentrate on the management framework rather than on its technical substance. The danger is that the development team gets locked into a framework that is totally inappropriate for their project. That is why many developers do not like methodologies and think them a waste of time. They are forced to produce documents which, in their circumstances, have little value. Their only option is to leave out some steps, which, they are told, means they are not using the methodology properly.

Obviously there are fairly standard mappings of the technical substance of JSD on to project plans. However, flexibility in choosing the mapping includes at least the following:

• considering the most critical implementation issues well before the specification is complete;

• doing a little of each of the model, network, and implementation phases as part of a feasibility or estimating study;

- iterating over the model, network, and implementation phases on a planned series of releases;
- building a low-volume prototype, amending the specification, and reimplementing to produce a high-volume production system.

We can summarize as follows. In JSD specification is strictly separated from implementation and, within the specification, model is strictly separated from the rest. But the ordering of model, network, and implementation is a local, not a global ordering. We need the BOOK model process before the output "Number of books in the library = 5921" can be formally added to the specification, but we do not need MEMBER or RESERVATION. We need part of the model but not all. Similarly, we need some knowledge of the specification to make implementation decisions, but we do not need a complete specification. A project plan fixes the ordering of the work more strictly than is implied by JSD alone; therefore JSD can be mapped in various ways on to a project plan.

D. Tools

Three JSD support tools are currently available, all from Michael Jackson Systems Ltd., 22 Little Portland St., London W1.

- PDF is a graphics editor for tree diagrams and lists of operations (as in Fig. 4) and a code generator from these diagrams into a variety of commonly used languages. The idea of the package is that the diagrams become the source of the program. PDF runs on the IBM PC, VAX VMS with VT100 type terminals and under Unix.
- SPEEDBUILDER is planned to be a series of JSD support products. So far only Unit One has been released. Unit One is a database for holding a JSD specification, a user-friendly editor for the database and a document maker that allows subsets of the database to be printed in a user-defined format. SPEEDBUILDER runs on the IBM PC.
- JSP-Cobol is a Cobol preprocessor that automates the insertion of suspend-and-resume mechanisms like the one described in Sections II-A and II-C, and provides a variety of testing aids. JSP-Cobol runs on a wide variety of mini and mainframe computers.

E. Projects

About 30 JSD or substantially JSD projects have been completed and perhaps as many again are underway. Most, but not all, are data-processing applications. The following are some brief notes about a sample.

- A Fleet Personnel system for a multinational oil company had a ship and employee as its main entities and kept track of people's careers, which ships they were on, where they could join a ship, etc. The system had 120 screen types, about 300 000 lines of procedural Cobol, had interfaces with an existing payroll system, and was implemented under IMS DB/DC.
- A Time Stamp project kept track of employees arriving for and leaving work. They work flexitime around core periods. Different shifts have different core periods, some employees work part-time, some employees are sick or on holiday. The implementation was distributed between IBM Series/1 and System 38 computers. Recovery problems were handled by running the on-line system under a batch scheduler.
- A Fingerprint Checking system restricts entry to a building by scanning in real-time the finger of the person trying to get in. Obviously, response times are critical. Implementation was in Fortran under the operating system RSX-11M.

Projects that are underway include the following:
- the redesign of a substantial part of the on-board software for a torpedo;
- the application software for a communications system to support air defense on the battlefield;
- a set of systems to support the merchandising function of a retail chain, the development of which will take several hundred man-years.

The experience from these projects deserves a more substantial treatment. Suffice here to report that the results have been generally favorable, although for no real project has JSD worked as cleanly or as clearly as it does on the Library example.

Acknowledgment

JSD has been developed (and is developing) within Michael Jackson Systems, Ltd. mainly by M. Jackson and the author, but also with contributions from A. McNeile, J. Kathirasoo, and T. Debling. M. Jackson and I. Smith both suggested a number of improvements to this paper.

References

[1] C. A. R. Hoare, "Communicating sequential processes," *Commun. ACM*, Dec. 1978.
[2] W. Kent, *Data and Reality.* Amsterdam, The Netherlands: North-Holland, 1978.
[3] M. A. Jackson, *System Development.* Englewood Cliffs, NJ: Prentice-Hall, 1982.
[4] ——, *Principles of Program Design.* New York: Academic, 1975.
[5] J. R. Cameron, *JSP and JSD: The Jackson Approach to Software Development.* IEEE Comput. Soc., 1983.
[6] L. Ingevaldsson, *JSP: A Practical Method of Program Design* (in Swedish). Studentlitteratur, 1977; (in English). Chartwell-Bratt, 1979.
[7] H. Jansen, *JSP-Jackson Struktureel Programmeren* (in Dutch). Academic Service, 1984.

John R. Cameron received the M.A. degree and Part III in mathematics from Cambridge University, Cambridge, England, 1973 and 1975, respectively.

From 1975 to 1977, he worked for Scicon, a British software company, mainly on simulations of communication networks. Since 1977 he has worked with Michael Jackson at Michael Jackson Systems Ltd. developing, teaching, consulting in, and building software tools to support the methods described in this tutorial. He is co-developer of the Jackson method of System Development and author of the IEEE Press tutorial book *JSP & JSD: The Jackson Approach to Software Development.*

An Operational Approach to Requirements Specification for Embedded Systems

PAMELA ZAVE

Abstract—The approach to requirements specification for embedded systems described in this paper is called "operational" because a requirements specification is an executable model of the proposed system interacting with its environment. The approach is embodied by the language PAISLey, which is motivated and defined herein. Embedded systems are characterized by asynchronous parallelism, even at the requirements level; PAISLey specifications are constructed by interacting processes so that this can be represented directly. Embedded systems are also characterized by urgent performance requirements, and PAISLey offers a formal, but intuitive, treatment of performance.

Index Terms—Applicative programming, distributed processing, embedded (real-time) systems, requirements analysis and specification, simulation models, system design and specification.

INTRODUCTION

RECENTLY the study of system requirements has emerged as a major area of research in software engineering. It has become clear that the stated requirements for a system have tremendous impact on the quality and usefulness of the ultimate product, and on the efficiency and manageability of its development. Yet, despite their leverage, relatively little is known about deriving and specifying good sets of requirements.

At the same time, the prominence of "embedded" (roughly equivalent to "real-time") systems has been increasing, due largely to hardware advances which have made them feasible for a broader category of applications than ever before. We will argue that embedded systems are characterized by the urgency of their performance requirements; to the extent that all computer systems would benefit from the ability to state and satisfy precise performance requirements, knowledge of embedded systems can be useful to developers of all types of system.

This paper presents a new approach to the problem of specifying the requirements for embedded systems. It offers a substantial increase in formality, expressive power, and potential for automation over the current widely known requirements technologies.

I. THE REQUIREMENTS PROBLEM

A. The Role of Requirements in the System Life Cycle

The development of a computer system begins with the perception of a need for it. During the requirements phase,

Manuscript received January 23, 1981; revised August 15, 1981. This work was supported in part by the U.S. Air Force Office of Scientific Research under Contract F49620-80-C-0001 at the University of Maryland.

The author is with Bell Laboratories, Murray Hill, NJ 07974.

analysts should arrive at a deep understanding of that need and propose a system to fill it. The product of the requirements phase is the requirements specification, which plays a unique and crucial role in the rest of development. It states what system is to be developed, at what costs, and under what constraints.

The project cannot be a complete success unless the requirements have the informed consent of everyone who will be involved, including members of the development organization (designers, programmers, and managers), the originating organization (managers or salespeople who determine the cost and value of the system), and the ultimate users of the system. This consensus can only be achieved through feedback and negotiation, with preliminary versions of the requirements specification being the major vehicle of communication.

During design and implementation, the requirements specification defines the "top" for top-down design, and the product toward which management effort is aimed. At the end of development, it is the standard against which the system is compared for success or failure, acceptance or rejection.

Requirements are often neglected, for reasons that are all too familiar: lack of awareness of their importance (which is disappearing), lack of useful requirements analysis and specification techniques, and natural reluctance to incur costs and delays at the beginning of a project. Yet the consequences of this shortsightedness, which include cancelled projects or unprofitable products, unhappy users, chaotically structured systems, budget and schedule overruns as endless changes are made, and even lawsuits, are so serious that no one involved in software engineering can afford to ignore them. Other introductions to the role of requirements in system development can be found in [8], [7], [39], [47], [24], [4], [12].

It should be noted that even with the most optimistic view of current progress on requirements analysis and specification, in which problems of communication and complexity can be solved, certain other problems will remain very difficult to deal with. One is that vital decisions must be based on forecasts of costs and even feasibility, while such forecasting is perhaps the weakest point of our software technology. Another is that the requirements are constantly changing, even as we try to write them down. And systems that are used evolve continually throughout their lifetimes [5], [32], creating "maintenance" costs which may eventually dwarf those of initial development.

As consciousness of the economic and technical importance of evolution in the system life cycle grows, we may develop a new concept of the life cycle based on iterated (re)develop-

Reprinted from *IEEE Transactions on Software Engineering*, Volume SE-8, Number 3, May 1982, pages 250-269. Copyright © 1982 by The Institute of Electrical and Electronics Engineers, Inc.

ments, large and small, as in [11]. In such a model, the requirements specification will evolve with the system, serving throughout its life as definition, documentation, and contract. Needless to say, this expanded role will place even greater demands on the quality and modifiability of our requirements specifications.

B. Goals for Requirements Specifications

Progress in software engineering has almost always been made from the bottom up: from machine language to axiomatic specifications, for example, we have proceeded first by learning to do something and then by understanding it well enough to find suitable abstractions of it. This paper takes the same approach to requirements. It seems unlikely that we will find really effective techniques for requirements analysis before we know how to write a good requirements specification recording the results of that analysis. Therefore we will concentrate on specification techniques (although useful results on specification cannot help but suggest analytic methods and principles).

Goals for requirements specifications have been examined by many of the cited authors, and are discussed at more length in [49]. In short, the things we do with requirements specifications are 1) use them as vehicles for communication, 2) change them, 3) use them to constrain target systems, and 4) use them to accept or reject final products.

For 1) and 2) they must be understandable and modifiable. For 3) they must be precise, unambiguous, internally consistent, and complete. They should also be minimal, i.e., define the smallest set of properties that will satisfy the users and originators. Otherwise the specification may overconstrain the target system, so that some of the best solutions to design problems are unnecessarily excluded. For 4) they should be formally manipulable (if verification is to be used) or testable (if acceptance testing is to be used).

The remainder of this paper is concerned with a requirements specification approach (and language) that promises to help us achieve many of these goals. It is also somewhat specialized for a particular class of systems, namely . . . .

II. Embedded Systems

Common examples of embedded systems are industrial process-control systems, flight-guidance systems, switching systems, patient-monitoring systems, radar tracking systems, ballistic-missile-defense systems, and data-acquisition systems for experimental equipment. The class of embedded systems is an important one, partly because it already includes some of our oldest and most complex computer applications, and partly because it is expanding rapidly in volume and variety as a result of the microprocessor revolution.

A. What Makes a System "Embedded"?

The term "embedded" was popularized by the U.S. Department of Defense in conjunction with its common languages (Ada) development project. "Embedded" refers to the fact that these systems are embedded in larger systems whose primary purposes are not computation, but this is actually true of any useful computer system. A payroll program, for instance, is an essential part of a business organization, which is a system whose primary purpose is selling products at a profit.

The common concept that unites the systems we choose to call "embedded" is *process control*: providing continual feedback to an unintelligent environment. This "theme" is easily recognized in flight-guidance systems and switching systems; even in a patient-monitoring system, sick patients are not exercising their intelligence in interacting with the system, and nurses can be viewed as providing a mechanical extension to the system's feedback loop.

The continual demands of an unintelligent environment cause these systems to have relatively rigid and urgent performance requirements, such as real-time response requirements and "fail-safe" reliability requirements. It seems that this emphasis on performance requirements is what really characterizes embedded systems, and causes us to be more aware of their roles in their environments than we are for other types of system.[1]

Fig. 1 shows an informal classification of systems, based on properties that show up at the requirements level. Requirements for "support systems" are generally much less definite than requirements for applications systems. And while the performance requirements for embedded systems may be couched in absolutes, the performance requirements for support systems will be relative to resources and resource utilization, and the performance requirements for data-processing systems will be relative to load, resources, and psychological factors. The most complex systems, such as nationwide airline-reservation systems, should probably be viewed as having subsystems of all three types.

B. The Special Problems of Embedded Systems

The special nature of embedded systems exacerbates many software engineering problems, and thus demands particular attention even during the requirements phase.

Few organizations have logged as much experience with embedded systems as the Department of Defense, which spends 56 percent of its approximately $3 billion annual software budget on them [15]. Here is a pointed summary of that experience:

> Embedded computer software often exhibits characteristics that are strikingly different from those of other computer applications. The programs are frequently large (50 000 to 100 000 lines of code) and long-lived (10 to 15 years). Personnel turnover is rapid, typically two years. Outputs are not just data, but also control signals. Change is continuous because of evolving system requirements—annual revisions are often of the same magnitude as the original development [15].

Clearly coping with complexity and change will not be easier in the domain of embedded systems.

In addition to the performance requirements, which have already been established as a major distinguishing factor, embedded systems are especially likely to have stringent resource requirements. These are requirements on the resources, mainly physical in this case, from which the system is constructed.

---

[1] Thus, "embedded" is almost synonymous with "real-time," but we prefer the newer term because it does not exclude performance requirements dealing with reliability.

TYPE	CHARACTERISTICS	EXAMPLES
embedded system	special-purpose (application) absolute performance requirements	industrial process-control system flight-guidance system
data-processing system	special-purpose (application) relative performance requirements	batch business program on-line database system
support system	general-purpose relative performance requirements	operating system software development tool

Fig. 1. A requirements-level system classification.

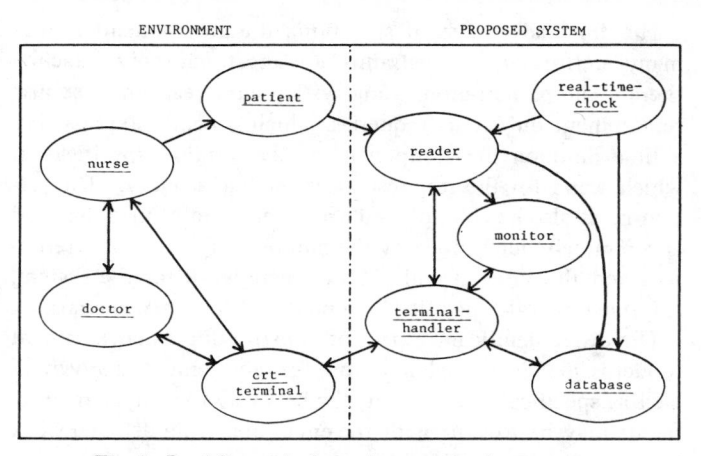

Fig. 2. Partial model of a patient-monitoring system.

This is because embedded systems are often installed in places (such as satellites) where their weight, volume, or power consumption must be limited, or where temperature, humidity, pressure, and other factors cannot be as carefully controlled as in the traditional machine room.

The interface between an embedded system and its environment tends to be complex, asynchronous, highly parallel, and distributed. This is another direct result of the "process control" concept, because the environment is likely to consist of a number of objects which interact with the system and each other in asynchronous parallel. Furthermore, it is probably the complexity of the environment that necessitates computer support in the first place (consider an air-traffic-control system)! This characteristic makes the requirements difficult to specify in a way that is both precise and comprehensible.

Finally, embedded systems can be extraordinarily hard to test. The complexity of the system/environment interface is one obstacle, and the fact that these programs often *cannot* be tested in their operational environments is another. It is not feasible to test flight-guidance software by flying with it, nor to test ballistic-missile-defense software under battle conditions.

III. AN "OPERATIONAL" APPROACH

The approach taken in this paper is to specify the requirements for an embedded system with an explicit model of the proposed system interacting with an explicit model of the system's environment. Both submodels consist of sets of asynchronously interacting digital processes, although some of the processes in the environment model may represent discrete simulations of nondigital objects such as people or machines. The entire model is executable, and the internal computations of the processes are specified in an applicative language.

We call this an "operational" approach because the emphasis on constructing an operating model of the system functioning in its environment provides its primary flavor. It has been embodied in a Specification Language which, since it is based on the ideas above and is therefore Process-oriented, Applicative, and Interpretable (executable), is named PAISLey.

In the remainder of this section, the basic ideas behind PAISLey will be explained, illustrated, and justified in detail. Section IV addresses apparent disadvantages of an operational approach, and Section V defines PAISLey.

A. Explicit Modeling of the Environment

Fig. 2 shows a partial requirements model for a simple patient-monitoring system. The "*patient*," "*nurse*," and "*doctor*" processes are all digital simulations of these natural objects. They represent, of course, only the roles played by these people with respect to patient-monitoring. The "*patient*" process also models a sensor attached to the patient (this model is only partial because the complete one would have multiple patients, sensors, terminals, etc.).

The "*reader*" process reads sensor data at specified intervals of real time, sending a warning to the terminal if the reading is so implausible as to suggest sensor malfunction. The "*monitor*" process checks the reading against medical safety criteria, sending a warning if it falls outside a safe range. Sensor data also go to the "*database*" process, which responds to queries from the terminal and also purges old data to maintain themselves at a reasonable size. Many parameters, such as sensor-reading frequencies and safe ranges, can be set by doctors and nurses.

The boundary between the environment and the proposed system is determined simply by which parts are "givens" for the contractor and which parts must be supplied by the contractor. The boundary is arbitrary (from a technical viewpoint), and is not even part of the formal PAISLey specification.

Including an explicit model of the environment has several advantages for requirements specification. The reason that the interface between an embedded system and its environment is complex, asynchronous, highly parallel, and distributed is that it consists of interactions among a number of objects which exist in parallel, at different places, and are not synchronized with one another. Organizing these interactions around the objects (processes) which take part in them is an effective way to decompose this sort of complexity. Furthermore, assumptions and expectations on both sides of the boundary can be documented. The result is a specification which is far more precise and yet comprehensible than could be obtained by treating either side of the interface as a "black box," which is what happens when the environment is not modeled.

Another reason for having an environment model is that the environment (when construed broadly enough) is the source of all changes to the system. Modeling it is therefore a promising way to anticipate changes and enhance the modifiability of both specification and target system.

The final advantage of specifying the environment is that many performance constraints are most naturally attached there. The patient-monitoring system has a real-time response requirement on database queries, which is neatly expressed as a time limit on the component of the terminal specification which waits for the response after sending a query. The system must also be able to handle a certain load. Since this load is completely determined by the numbers of sensors and terminals and the rates at which they create work for the system, it is most directly specified by a model of those peripherals.

The other significant aspect of constructing an environment model is that it is a valuable tool for requirements *analysis*, as well as specification. In fact, the best way to analyze requirements may be to start with the environment model, and work "outside-in" to a proposed system which supports a desirable model of operation in the environment. The extreme case is automation of an existing manual system--in the absence of changes to existing procedures, the requirements can be derived simply by modeling the current operation, and drawing a boundary to distinguish the automatable part! Yeh *et al.* [45], [46] discuss "conceptual models," which are models of system environments constructed for the purpose of requirements analysis.

In the patient-monitoring system, since only the "*patient*" and "*crt-terminal*" processes interact directly with the proposed computer system, only these are necessary for precise specification of the system interface. The "*nurse*" and "*doctor*" processes appear strictly as vehicles for requirements analysis. Wondering how doctors and nurses interact leads the analyst to ask which kinds of information a doctor expects to get from a nurse on duty, and which kinds he would like to find in the database. Wondering how nurses interact with patients and the display leads the analyst to ask how the display screen should be allocated to medical histories versus emergency messages, how often warnings concerning an ongoing crisis need be displayed, and whether information from the monitoring system is needed at the patient's bedside. These questions are never asked (or answered) in the numerous treatments of patient-monitoring systems appearing in the requirements literature.

Even if the analysts can achieve understanding of the requirements in some other way, early concentration on the environment may lead to better communication with users (who are much more interested in their environment than your system), and more open-minded problem-solving, unbiased by preconceived notions or similar systems the analysts have worked on.

B. Processes

Another key feature of the operational approach is that the primary units of specification are processes. A process is a simple, abstract respresentation of autonomous (distributed) digital computation. It is specified by supplying a "state space," or set of all possible states, and a "successor function"[2] on that state space which defines the successor state for each

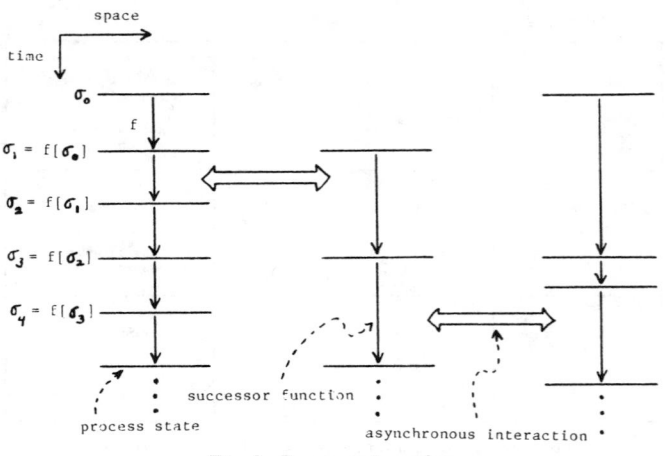

Fig. 3. Processes in action.

state. It goes through an infinite sequence of states (although a "halting" process can be specified by having it go into a distinguished "halted" state which it will never leave), asynchronously with respect to all other processes (Fig. 3).

A process is cyclic, with its successor function describing its natural cycle. The natural cycle of a process simulating a sick patient, for instance, would be a single step of the discrete simulation algorithm. The successor function of such a process might be declared as

$$\text{patient-cycle: } \textsc{patient-state} \rightarrow \textsc{patient-state},$$

where the set "PATIENT-STATE," which is its domain and range and also the state space of the process, contains values encoding possible states of the patient between simulation steps. The natural cycle of the "*doctor*" process might be to take one action, either asking one question of a nurse, giving one order to a nurse, or taking part in one transaction with the patient-monitoring system.

There can be no question about the *generality* of processes. They were originally used as abstractions of concurrent activities within multiprogramming systems [27], and many recent articles have shown that they can be used to represent I/O devices, data modules, tasks, monitors, buffers, or any other identifiable structure within a computer system (e.g., [26], [10], [33]). Process-based models of computation have been the focus of extensive theoretical work and the language Smalltalk [29]. Our varied examples are persuasive evidence that the notion of digital simulation of nondigital objects is similarly powerful in describing the environments of computer systems.

The *appropriateness* of using processes to specify requirements for embedded systems is based on our observation that in these systems asynchronous parallelism—among environment objects, between environment objects and the system, and within the system (if only for reasons of performance)—occurs naturally *at the requirements level*. One happy result of recognizing that parallelism is environment specifications which should be highly intuitive, even to naive users. This is because the specifications are populated by identifiable models of the same autonomous, interacting objects from which the real world is made.

Perhaps the best way to appreciate processes is to consider the alternatives: representations of processing used in other requirements languages. The one most commonly found in requirements documents is data access or "dataflow." Data-

---

[2]Throughout this paper mappings will be called "functions," despite the fact that mappings named in specifications are often relations. The reason is that "function" gives a more accurate impression: the intention is always to produce a unique value when the mapping is invoked in the eventual target system, even though that value cannot always be determined by a known functional expression.

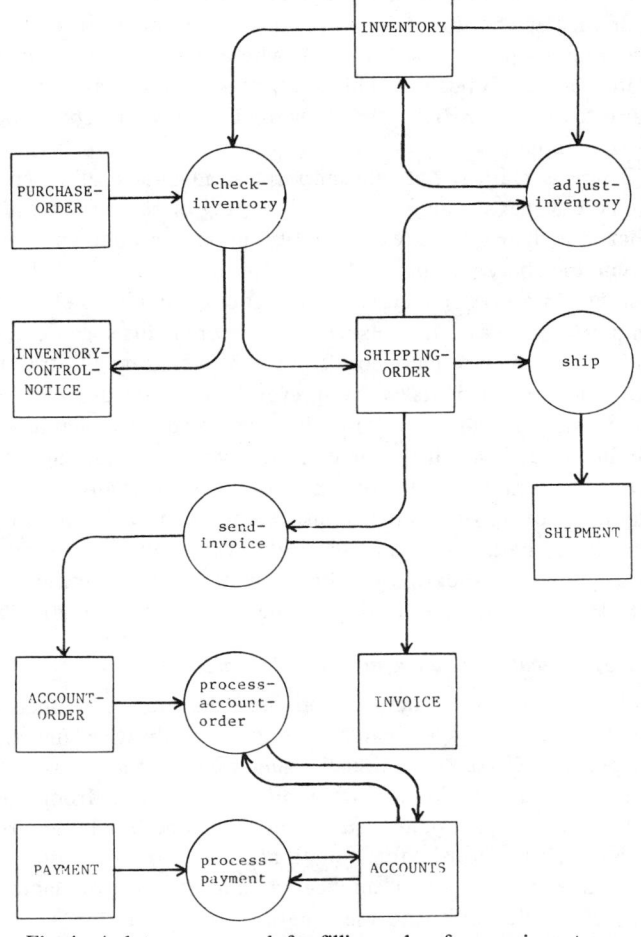

Fig. 4. A data-access graph for filling orders from an inventory.

access graphs show major system functions, and identify the data structures which are their inputs and outputs (e.g., Fig. 4). Data access is the basis of PSL/PSA [44] and SADT [38], [39], and has probably been rediscovered thousands of times by isolated requirements-writers.

Data access may be adequate for many data-processing systems, such as the one depicted in Fig. 4. This is because major subfunctions ("check-inventory," "send-invoice") are implemented as major subprograms, and subprograms are invoked in some implicitly understood sequence, whenever their input files are ready. Data access is seriously inadequate for embedded systems, however, because control is all-important in embedded systems and must be represented in any intelligible model. If a data-access graph is mistakenly interpreted as representing control as well, the concepts of control expressed will be simplistic and misleading.

In Fig. 4, for instance, the following problems would arise if control were implied. 1) A distinction must be made between inputs which are always present (such as the "INVENTORY" database) and inputs which invoke a function whenever a new instance appears (such as "PURCHASE-ORDER"). The situation is even more complex when there is an input value (such as the current output of a sensor attached to a hospital patient) which is always available, but only read at certain real-time intervals (and the interval itself is a variable stored in some

system database). 2) Functions (such as "process-account-order" and "process-payment") may have to be executed concurrently to meet performance requirements, in which case they must synchronize their uses of shared resources or databases (such as "ACCOUNTS"). 3) Functions may no longer execute in a predefined sequence (because of simultaneous access from multiple terminals, the need for internal housekeeping, etc.), and so a complex interplay of events and states must be anticipated.

The control arrow in SADT adds an explicit representation of control to data-access graphs (an illuminating discussion of its significance can be found in [38]), but its informality prevents it from being precise or expressive enough for embedded systems. Processes and their interactions, on the other hand, are well-suited to the task of specifying complex control, as would be expected from their historical origins in the specification of operating systems.

Other representations of processing appearing in requirements languages are stimulus-response paths in RSL [6], [2], [13] and finite-state machines [24], [12]. A finite-state machine is very much like a single process—permitting no explicit parallelism, decomposition of complexity, nor modeling of the environment.

Stimulus-response paths (e.g., Fig. 5) represent sequencing, control, and parallelism explicitly, and do make it possible to decompose the requirements. The "R-net" in Fig. 5 shows parallelism between "STORE_FACTOR_DATA" and "EXA-MINE_FACTORS," and is only one of several R-nets specifying the entire system. The fundamental differences between PAISLey and RSL appear to be as follows. 1) The PAISLey representation emphasizes the *cyclic* nature of system components, while the RSL representation emphasizes *sequences*. Both are obviously useful ways of characterizing embedded systems, and only time will tell if one is superior to the other in a majority of instances. 2) The PAISLey notation integrates data, processing, and control in a unified whole, while in RSL the various concepts are separated—R-nets for control, PSL/PSA-like notation for data-access properties, etc. We believe that the unified approach will ultimately prove stronger in terms of comprehensibility, modifiability, and ability to determine internal consistency.

C. Executability

In the operational approach, requirements specifications are executable. This means that, under interpretation, the specification becomes a simulation model generating behaviors of the specified system.

It is of vital importance to be able to interpret specifications regardless of their level of abstraction. Not only are requirements by their nature abstract in many respects, but they must also be developed by successive refinements of understanding, each version of which should benefit from this facility. We will defer until Section III-D a discussion of *how* this can be done, and only deal here with the advantages of doing so.

Executability is a powerful tool for understanding a specification in all its ramifications. An executable specification can be tested and debugged by the analysts who wrote it. Its be-

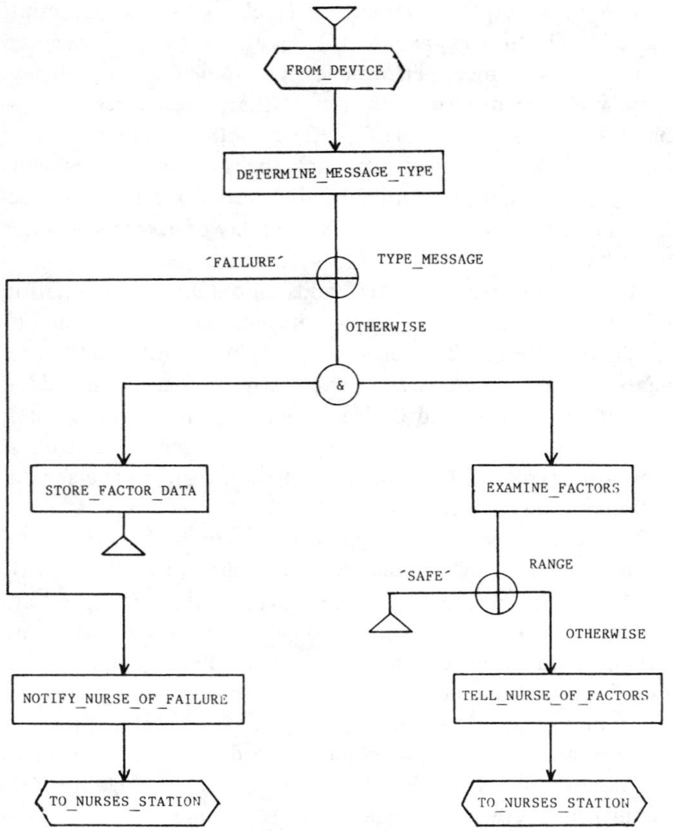

Fig. 5. A stimulus-response path (part of a patient-monitoring system) specified in RSL (from [2]).

havior can be validated by users in the course of demonstrations. If developed in enough detail, it can even be released on a small scale as a prototype of the proposed system.[3]

The ability to test is no panacea, as must be obvious from the literature on program testing—and with embedded system specifications there is the additional complication that any test must choose one of many relative-rate-dependent process execution sequences. Nevertheless, the problems inherent in testing programs have never caused us to give up on it, and requirements testing, once established in common practice, might seem likewise indispensable.

Furthermore, an executable requirements model can continue to be useful after the requirements phase. The environment part of the model can be used as a test bed during system development, which will be particularly valuable for embedded systems because of the aforementioned difficulties of testing them "in the field" (in fact, it is almost always necessary to write an environment simulator for exactly this purpose). The model of the proposed system can be used to generate sample behaviors for acceptance testing.

It is also possible to attach performance constraints in such a

[3]In most cases a practical requirements specification, even if executable, will be far more abstract (less detailed) than the system it specifies. Other differences between executable specifications and implementations lie in their performance, resource, and accessibility properties. A prototype falls somewhere between an executable specification and an implementation, because it must get some exposure in the field, and this requires performance, resource, and accessibility properties which are adequate at some minimal level.

way that they can be simulated along with the functional requirements, and this is done in PAISLey. Simulation can then be used to predict performance where it is too complex to determine analytically. This type of simulation is an important feature of SREM, the integrated set of tools by which RSL is supported.

There is a final, critically important, advantage of executability that has nothing to do with testing or simulation. It is that the demands of executability impose a coherence and discipline—because the parts of a specification must "fit together" in a very strong sense—that could scarcely be obtained in any other way. If an executable requirements specification is shown to be internally consistent, that means it will continue to generate behaviors without ever halting, deadlocking, or going into an undefined state. In other words, it is guaranteed to be a valid specification of *some* system interacting with *some* environment. Clearly this is the utmost that any formally defined notion of internal consistency could do for us, since deciding whether they are the *right* system and environment is a matter of validation by the originator/user, or verification of consistency with externally defined axioms of correctness.

D. Specification in an Applicative Language

Within a process, computation (i.e., the successor function of the process) is specified using a purely applicative language. "Applicative" (or "functional") languages are those based on side-effect-free evaluation of expressions formed from constants, formal parameters, functions, and functional operators ("combining forms" for functions, such as composition). Well-known examples of applicative languages are the lambda calculus, pure LISP, and the functional programming systems of [3].

1) Advantages of Applicative Languages: Applicative languages are currently receiving a great deal of favorable attention because of their numerous theoretical and practical advantages ([3], [30], [43], [18]–[22], among others), most of which can be exploited in requirements specifications. To begin with, because applicative languages are interpretable, they support the executability property: processes are executed by repeatedly replacing their current states by successor states, and successor states are discovered by interpreting the applicative expressions which define them.

For purposes of high-level specification, the most important property of applicative languages is their tremendous powers of abstraction, i.e., of decision deferment. Consider, for instance, the functional expression "f[(g[y], h[z])]," which says that the function "g" is to be applied to the argument "y" and "h" is to be applied to "z" (the "[ ]" symbols denote function application or composition). Then "f" is to be applied to the values produced (the "( )" symbols are used to construct tuples of data). The expression says exactly what is needed to compute the desired value, but does not otherwise constrain the data, control, processor, or other resource structures used to do so. Are "g[y]" and "h[z]" evaluated sequentially or in parallel? In what data structures are their values stored? Perhaps the arguments "y" and "z" are even shipped off to special "g"- and "h"-processors, respectively, at different nodes of a network!

Furthermore, a primitive function has several interesting interpretations, all of which enable additional decompositions of complexity. A primitive function can represent a set of deferred decisions, to be made later by defining the function in terms of simpler primitives. It can also represent a mapping which will always remain nondeterministic from the perspective of the requirements model, because it depends on factors outside the scope of the model. For instance, in specifying a terminal we might declare a primitive function

think: DISPLAY → INPUT,

where "DISPLAY" is the set of all CRT screen images and "INPUT" is the set of all input lines, to represent the human user's thought processes. Finally, in PAISLey a primitive function can be an abstraction for an interprocess interaction (see below). Because of these many options, applicative languages have been used successfully to describe phenomena ranging in level of abstraction from digital hardware to distributed system requirements [17], [42].

An interpreter for an abstract specification language makes expedient and non-functionally-significant decisions about such matters as control and space allocation. The only other thing needed for interpretation is some sort of implementation of functions and sets left primitive in the abstract specification. This can be done in many ways, perhaps the simplest of which is to choose values of primitive functions randomly or by default. Another way to interpret primitive functions is to display their arguments at a terminal and ask the analyst to supply a value, thereby creating an interactive testing system. In either case, the effect is to simulate the decisions which have been made, without interference from the decisions that have not been made.

Other advantages of applicative languages are that they are well-suited to formal manipulations such as verification, and may have great potential for efficient implementation (see [3]). In procedural languages, on the other hand, assignment statements thwart top-down thinking, complicate the formal semantics, and force memory to be referred to and accessed one word at a time.

2) PAISLey as an Applicative Language: PAISLey is not a purely applicative language because states in general, and process states in particular, are not applicative concepts. In [51] it is explained that, while many aspects of even embedded systems can be specified applicatively, the specification of most performance requirements, real-time interfaces with the environment, and certain resource requirements all necessitate the introduction of some nonapplicative structure such as processes.

In fact, the process structure makes PAISLey specifications easier to write than typical large applicative programs. The system is decomposed into processes, and process computations are decomposed into cycles or steps, before applicative programming comes into use. The current state of a process "remembers" all its relevant history. Thus the applicative expressions which must be written are quite simple relative to the complexity of the system as a whole.

Since PAISLey is a blend of the applicative world and the nonapplicative world of processes and states, the "seam" must be a smooth one. The two worlds meet at the mechanism for interprocess interaction, which is necessitated by the existence of processes but designed to fit smoothly into the applicative framework. Interactions take place through a set of three primitives called "exchange functions" which carry out the side effect of asynchronous interaction, but look and behave *locally* (intraprocess) exactly like primitive functions. Exchange functions are defined and explained in Section V-C. They are a unique mechanism which seems to fulfill our purposes very well, and also offers an interesting new perspective on asynchronous interaction mechanisms for distributed processes.

Applicative languages have, in some circles, a reputation for unreadability and general unsuitability for large-scale software engineering. We believe that this reputation is due to typelessness and recursion, neither of which is present in PAISLey.

Recursion is what purely applicative languages use to specify repetitive computation, and is analogous to looping (iteration) in procedural languages. Both are analogous to the repetitive application of a successor function to produce successive process states, which is how unbounded repetition is specified in PAISLey.

In most applicative languages, the only type of data object is the list or sequence, and all functions are applied to one list and produce one list. Since every function should be prepared to accept argument lists of any internal structure, there must be a distinguished "undefined" value produced whenever the internal structure of the argument is unsuited to the semantics of the function (as in [3])—and this mismatch must first be detected! Multiple arguments to or values from functions must be packaged in single lists, yet the existence of this substructure (or any other substructure, for that matter) cannot be explicitly acknowledged.

Of course, deliberate substructure in data items is ubiquitous, and it is common practice to document it with the use of data types. Furthermore, typing in a language provides a useful form of redundancy which is susceptible to automated checks of internal consistency.

In PAISLey nonprimitive sets can be defined using set union ("A ∪ B"), cross-product ("A × B"), enumeration ("{'true,' 'false' }"), and parenthesization. The domain and range sets of every function, primitive or not, must be declared (although a function need not have arguments). The domain and range declarations can use arbitrary set expressions. Here are three example declarations:

$$f: \; \rightarrow A \,;$$
$$g: \; B \times C \rightarrow D \cup E \,;$$
$$h: \; S \rightarrow T.$$

When a function is applied to arguments, their types must be consistent with the domain declaration of the function. Consistency can be defined with the assistance of coercion, however, so that the composition "h[g[f]]" is perfectly legal if the definitions

$$A = B \times C \,;$$
$$S = \text{INTEGERS} \,;$$
$$D = \{\, 0, 2, 4, 6, 8 \,\} \,;$$
$$E = \{\, 1, 3, 5, 7, 9 \,\}$$

have been made. This notion of typing provides all the documentation and redundancy desirable for engineering goals, without sacrificing any of the flexibility attributable to typelessness. All that it requires is the ability to compare any two set expressions for containment, which is easily done *given this particular language of set expressions*.

IV. QUALMS ABOUT OPERATIONAL REQUIREMENTS

Despite the obvious advantages of operational requirements, one cannot help but have certain reservations about the idea. In this section we examine its apparent disadvantages.

A. Encroaching on Design

Are not operational specifications actually *design* specifications rather than *requirements* specifications? This question is often prompted by the precision, potential for detail, and executability of PAISLey specifications.

From a certain technical viewpoint, requirements should specify only the functional and performance properties of the proposed system. Design begins when resources are introduced. The physical resources from which the system is to be built must be managed so that performance goals are met. The human resources who will implement and maintain the system must be managed so that they are used effectively; this depends on skillful modularization of the code to be written. Adopting this as a definition of the boundary between requirements and design, a requirements specification does not stray into design if it avoids unnecessary management of resources and unnecessary structuring of code.

PAISLey enables the requirements analyst to do this. This point is illustrated copiously in [49], using as an example the specification of a process-control system from [54]. We will confine ourselves here to explaining why one aspect of a PAISLey specification, its process structure, does not overconstrain resource management or code structure.

Processes are virtual structures, and a specification is partitioned into processes on the basis of factors such as functionality, synchronization, and performance—all of which belong to the requirements level. Thus a requirements analyst should use as many processes as "make sense" to him. Only in design should there be concern about how a large number of virtual processes are to be realized on a smaller number of physical processors, perhaps through time-multiplexing with priority scheduling. And the processes, representing dynamic structure of the target system, say nothing about its static code structure at all.

This technical view of requirements is elegant and satisfying, but it is not the whole story. Pragmatically, a requirement is any property of the proposed system that is necessary to satisfy the originating organization of the acceptability of the system, and these properties may very well include decisions about resources. Use of a particular computer or software subsystem may be required because the originating organization already owns it, and management insists that it be used. The new system may have to interface with an existing computer system, and thus be compatible with its resource management policies. The capabilities of the proposed system may even have to be trimmed to fit the resources available. This is

common with really large systems such as ballistic-missile-defense systems and massive database systems. Another example would be a system to monitor experimental equipment on a satellite. Since facilities must be shared with other experiments, the amount of memory in the on-board computer allocated to each experiment is an administrative decision which must be made (at least tentatively) before work on the individual projects can begin.

The reality is that a system develops through a hierarchy of decisions, each decision constraining those below it in the hierarchy. No system is developed in a political or economic vacuum, and almost no system performs its function without interfacing with any preexisting computer system. Thus, even though resource decisions may be premature at the requirements level, any requirements language which is unable to record them will be terribly fragile, performing adequately only in the most idealized of situations.

PAISLey can record resource decisions because resource structures are like any other structures occurring in digital systems. They can definitely be specified if there is a general model of digital computation, which PAISLey offers. Hardware and software modules, for instance, can be specified as processes, and then included as part of the environment of the proposed system. This is a great strength of the operational approach—the promise of no unpleasant surprises when new applications, constraints, or economic contexts are encountered.

The ultimate test of whether or not a decision belongs in the requirements is whether or not the system could be constructed in any other way. This is illustrated in [49], using the requirements from an early real-time simulation system [1]. It is shown that decisions about the communication network, time-stamps, and the simulation time frame, while seemingly design decisions, are actually derivable during requirements analysis from feasibility considerations. The specification in PAISLey of each such decision is also described.

B. Too Much Precision

There can be little question that specifications written in PAISLey are too precise, and based on too many technical principles, for customers, end users, managers, and other untrained personnel to understand. At the same time, their rigor can be invaluable to the trained analysts who will write them (this is based on numerous experiences of being confronted by surprise with the vagueness of my own ideas about a system). Informal analysis must always come first, but we have not yet fully exploited the potential of formal languages for expressing approximate or incomplete knowledge and real-world concepts.

There is not really a conflict here, simply because nontechnical people do not have to use the same representations that the analysts do. Analysts can communicate with them using simplified diagrams and narrow views derived from the current PAISLey specification. A process diagram such as Fig. 2, for instance, can have its interaction arrows labeled with the types of data being transferred. If this is done, the diagram does not differ substantially in form or content from the ever-popular data-access graph!

The single most successful feature of SREM (RSL) and PSL/PSA is that specifications are stored in a database from which a variety of up-to-date reports can be generated automatically. We envision PAISLey's being installed in such a database, and hope that user-oriented reports and diagrams could likewise be produced by tools running on the current specification.

C. Interface with Data-Oriented Specification Techniques

Other researchers have investigated the problem of requirements for data-processing systems, using as a starting point for their formalisms data definition languages, i.e., languages originally developed to describe the "conceptual schemas" (abstract, virtual, semantic structures) of databases. The notion that a requirements model should be an explicit representation of the proposed system interacting with its environment has also been derived in this context. A philosophy of data-oriented modeling is presented in [4], while [46], [40], [35], [41], and [23] exemplify it.

It is clear that a data-oriented technique is a more natural way than using PAISLey to develop requirements for data-processing systems. Yet data-processing systems cannot ignore performance and concurrency, and embedded systems cannot ignore data. Thus our goal is to view both process-oriented PAISLey specifications and data-oriented specifications as projections of the same underlying, all-encompassing model (Fig. 6). In this view the two types of specification are compatible and complementary, so that analysts are free to use either or both (in parallel) as the application domain and phase of development suggest. It is argued in [49], by describing the data definition facilities of PAISLey in traditional database terms, that the structure of PAISLey is not inconsistent with this goal.

V. THE PAISLey LANGUAGE

In this section full details of PAISLey are presented, including a new mechanism for process interactions and specification of performance requirements. An LALR grammar for PAISLey in BNF form can be found in the Appendix.

A. Language Philosophy

PAISLey is intended to be simple. In particular, only features which are directly associated with run-time semantics are included.

For production purposes the language must be supported by a system which, in addition to storing specification fragments and collecting them into executable configurations (not to mention providing tools for static analysis and report generation), offers such conveniences as scopes, versions, macros, parameters, libraries, meta-notations, etc. The current frenzy of research on "programming environments" makes it plain that the design of such an environment is not a trivial task, and should probably not be undertaken simultaneously with development of the specification semantics. Specifications prepared using any of the above features would be translated into PAISLey (as currently defined) before interpretation.

Stylistically, PAISLey follows APL in using distinct symbols for distinct operators (but has far fewer of them!). This leads to a concise notation in which essentially all words are user-chosen mnemonics. In this decision and the one above, we apply exactly the same philosophy as [26].

One other important principle is that every operational structure must be realizable with a bounded amount of resources (time and space). There is a bounded number of processes, no process state can require an unbounded amount of storage, and no process step can require an unbounded amount of evaluation time. The purpose of this is performance, i.e., making it possible to design systems which are guaranteed to meet their performance requirements. Clearly, if a computational path contains an unbounded loop, or may have to construct a data structure of unbounded size, no guarantee that it meets an absolute time constraint is possible. In PAISLey the only unbounded "structure" is the infinite succession of process steps of each process, and this one exception cannot be avoided.

Boundedness is enforced by requiring the sizes of system structures to be fixed. This gives the specification a static character which will greatly facilitate proofs of internal consistency, correctness, and other formal properties.

B. Sets, Functions, Processes, and Systems

Statements in PAISLey are delimited by semicolons, and comments are enclosed in double quotation marks.

Names are typed for greater readability. The names of functions are always in lowercase letters, and the names of sets are always in small capital letters (hyphens and integers may be used in either, but they must begin with alphabetic strings). Constants are either numbers, or strings enclosed in single quotation marks.

There are four kinds of statement: system declarations, function declarations, set definitions, and function definitions. Since a system is a fixed tuple of processes, we use the tuple-construction notation for a system declaration. A process is declared using a function application which applies its successor function to an expression evaluating to its initial process state. Thus a system consisting of four processes, three being terminals and the fourth being a shared database, would be declared as

    (terminal-1-cycle[blank-display],
     terminal-2-cycle[blank-display],
     terminal-3-cycle[blank-display],
     database-cycle[initial-database]
    ),

where the following domain-range declarations would be appropriate:

    terminal-1-cycle: DISPLAY → DISPLAY;

    blank-display: → DISPLAY;

    . . .

    database-cycle: DATABASE → DATABASE;

    initial-database: → DATABASE.

Terminal processes have the contents of the current displays as their process states. Note that there is no explicit naming of processes or systems, as it is not needed for the run-time semantics.

Function declarations give *properties* of functions, i.e., specify their domains and ranges or their performance (see Section V D). All function declaration statements begin with

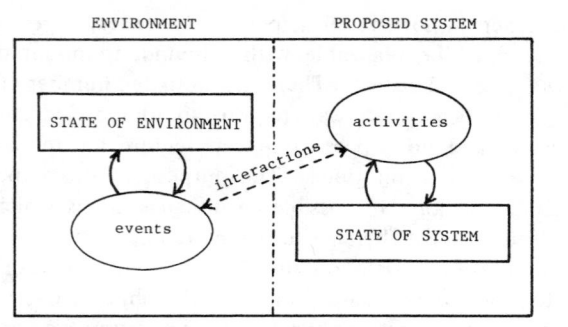

Fig. 6. The conceptual model underlying both process-oriented and data-oriented system specifications.

the function name and a colon. Domain-range declarations (of which we have seen many) are mandatory for all functions except intrinsic ones. (This is because intrinsic functions are either intrinsically typed or may have to handle several different types in the same specification.) Domain-range declarations are optional for intrinsic functions, and performance declarations are optional for all functions.

When a function is nonprimitive (defined), its declarations may be redundant, because its properties may be deducible from its definition. Declarations of nonprimitive functions can and should be checked for consistency with their definitions.

Set definitions define set names in terms of set expressions, which use set union, cross-product (which has precedence over union), enumeration, and parenthesization (all but parenthesization shown in Section III-D2). Note that the size of all data structures is bounded, because all tuples (members of sets defined by cross-product) are of fixed size.

Function definitions define function names in terms of function expressions, and may use formal parameters to do so. The structure of the argument may be imitated in a formal parameter list, thus giving names to argument substructures. Here, for instance, are some possible beginnings for function definition statements:

new-func-1 = . . . ;

new-func-2[p] = . . . ;

new-func-3[(p,q)] = . . . ;

new-func-4[(p,(q,(r,s)))] = ...

Now in a defining function expression (for all but "new-func-1") the argument's first component can be referred to as "p," as an alternative to selectors such as "car" and "cdr" in LISP. Formal parameters have the same syntax as function names; the argument structure must, of course, agree with the function's domain declaration.

Function expressions may use function names, formal parameters, constants, applications of functions to arguments, tuple construction, and conditional selection. Conditional selection (the "McCarthy conditional") has the syntax "/p1 : f1, p2 : f2, . . . 'true' : fn/" and evaluates to the value of the first functional expression "fi" such that the predicate (Boolean-valued functional expression) "pi" evaluates to '"true'." Note that there is no unbounded iteration, such as would be provided by "*while* . . . *do* . . . ," nor is recursion allowed. Fixed iteration can be specified using composition. The result is that the number of

primitive operations to evaluate any function, including a successor function, can be bounded *a priori*.

As a simple example, consider the following specification of the successor function of a process representing a CRT terminal:

terminal-cycle: DISPLAY → DISPLAY ;

terminal-cycle[d] = display
$$[\text{display-and-transact}$$
$$[(d, \text{think-of-request}[d])]] ;$$

think-of-request: DISPLAY → REQUEST ;

display-and-transact:
    DISPLAY X REQUEST
 → DISPLAY X (RESPONSE ∪ ERROR-MESSAGE);

display-and-transact[(d,r)] = (display [(d,r)] , transact [r]);

transact: REQUEST → RESPONSE ∪ ERROR-MESSAGE ;

display:
    DISPLAY X (REQUEST ∪ RESPONSE ∪ ERROR-MESSAGE)
 → DISPLAY .

The process handles one transaction per process step, reflecting both the request and the response in the display. The primitive function "display" can carry out scrolling or whatever other formatting is desired.

Even aiming for a minimum of conveniences, it is impossible to do without some feature for defining groups of nearly identical items. In PAISLey this is done at all levels using the same index notation, as seen in

VECTOR = #1 . .10< X INTEGER >,

which defines members of the set "VECTOR" to be 10-tuples of integers. Index notation always denotes a sequence of the expression in angle-brackets, with the first symbol in the brackets used as the sequence delimiter. The integers after the "#" give the lower and upper bounds of the sequencing count. The only index notation without a delimiter symbol is the one for bounded functional composition (application), which makes "#1 . . 3 <func> [arg]" equivalent to "func[func[func [arg]]]."

In most cases what we want is a group of statements or expressions which differ slightly. This is done by operating on names, which are defined so that "syllables" (alphabetic substrings delimited by hyphens) are semantically meaningful. If the header for an index notation begins with a "syllable" before the "#," any syllable matching it in a name in the repeated expression will be replaced by successive integers from the lower bound to the upper bound.[4] Thus,

BIG-SET = J#1 . .3< ∪ LITTLE-SET-J >

is equivalent to

BIG-SET = LITTLE-SET-1 ∪ LITTLE-SET-2 ∪ LITTLE-SET-3,

and the system declaration

[4]The matching of index syllables does not discriminate between upper- and lowercase letters, so that an index syllable has scope over set and function names alike.

(k#0..9999<,terminal-k-cycle[blank-display]>,
  database-cycle[initial-database]
)

creates a system with 10 000 terminal processes (an airline reservation system!), where the successor function of the thirteenth one is "terminal-12-cycle."

Index notation can even extend over groups of statements. Suppose we want our 10 000 terminals to be identical, except that some identification must be built into "transact," the primitive function whose elaboration will send to and receive from the central system. This can be done by making slight modifications to the terminal specification already given, as follows:

k#0..9999

< ; terminal-k-cycle: DISPLAY → DISPLAY ;

  terminal-k-cycle [d] =
    display
      [display-and-k-transact
        [(d, think-of-request [d])]] ;

  display-and-k-transact:
    DISPLAY X REQUEST
  → DISPLAY X (RESPONSE ∪ ERROR-MESSAGE);

  display-and-k-transact [(d,r)] =
    (display [(d,r)], k-transact [r]);

  k-transact: REQUEST → RESPONSE ∪ ERROR-MESSAGE;

>;

think-of-request: DISPLAY → REQUEST;

display:
    DISPLAY X (REQUEST ∪ RESPONSE ∪ ERROR-MESSAGE)
  → DISPLAY.

C. Asynchronous Interactions

1) Definition of Exchange Functions: Asynchronous interactions between processes are specified using three types of primitive functions known collectively as "exchange functions." An exchange function carries out two-way point-to-point mutually synchronized communication. It has one argument, which provides a value to be output, and always returns a value which was obtained as input. Thus within the process an exchange function looks like any other primitive function; it has, however, the side effect of carrying out a process interaction. By making interaction primitives masquerade as functions, we achieve compatibility with applicative notation.

An exchange function whose evaluation has been initiated interacts by "matching" (to be explained) with another pending exchange function. The two *exchange* arguments and terminate, so that each returns as its value the argument of the other.

Each exchange function has two attributes to be specified, namely a type ("x," "xm," or "xr") and a channel (a user-chosen identifier which has the syntax of a function name). The exchange function with type "x" and channel "chan" is named "x-chan," the exchange function with type "xr" and channel "real-time" is named "xr-real-time," etc. Only exchange functions with the same channel can match with each other.

The "x" is the basic type of exchange function. It can match with any other pending exchange function on its channel, including another of type "x." If no other exchange is pending, it will wait until one is. If there are several pending match possibilities, a match will be chosen nondeterministically, with the proviso that there must be no lockout (a situation where a pending exchange waits indefinitely while its match opportunities are given to other, more recently evaluated, exchange functions).

Competitive situations occur in most systems. To enable succinct specification of them we have exchanges of type "xm," which behave exactly like "x"'s except that two "xm"'s on the same channel cannot match with each other. They can then compete to match with an exchange of some other type, as the examples will show.

Embedded systems typically have real-time interfaces, especially with the processes in their environments. To specify these we need a third type of exchange function, the "xr," which behaves like the others except that it *will not wait* to find a match. If evaluation of an "xr" is initiated and there is no other pending exchange on its channel, the "xr" terminates immediately without matching, returning its own argument as its value. It is always possible to determine whether or not an "xr" matched by giving it an argument distinct from any that it could obtain by exchanging.

Fig. 7(a) shows the possible matches of exchange types within a channel. Fig. 7(b) (contributed to the understanding of exchange functions by Friedman [16]) shows the derivation of the three types. There must be both fully synchronized primitives ("synchronizing"), and also those which do not synchronize themselves ("free-running"). There must be exchanges which can match with their own kind and those that compete with their own kind. This makes four possibilities, except that a free-running type which exchanges with its own kind would be impossible, because it would require "matching" two simultaneous, instantaneous events.

2) Examples of Fully Synchronized Interactions: In this section we will use exchange functions to specify the interactions between multiple transaction-processing terminals and a central database. "transact" in the terminal specification of Section V-B can be elaborated as follows:

transact [r] =
    receive-response[send-request[r]] ;

send-request: REQUEST → FILLER ;

send-request [r] = xm-requ [r] ;

receive-response: FILLER → RESPONSE ∪ ERROR-MESSAGE ;

receive-response [null] = x-resp ['null'],

169

where "FILLER" is an intrinsic set whose only element is the constant "'null'." The database process successor function is specified as follows:

database-cycle[d] =
    finalize-transaction
      [perform-transaction
        [(d,receive-request)]];

receive-request: → REQUEST;

receive-request = x-requ['null'];

perform-transaction:
    DATABASE × REQUEST → DATABASE × RESPONSE;

finalize-transaction:
    DATABASE × RESPONSE → DATABASE;

finalize-transaction[(d,r)] =
    proj-2-1[(d,send-response[r])];

send-response: RESPONSE → FILLER;

send-response[r] = x-resp[r].

By renaming (redefining) the exchange functions, we are able to give them mnemonic names, and also to attach explicit types at the most meaningful place.

"send-request" in a terminal and "receive-request" in the database match with each other to transmit the request. Note that the type "xm"'s in the terminals compete for the type "x" in the database; if nothing but "x"'s were used, two evaluations of "send-request" in different terminals might match with each other! Since the "xm" and "x" are symmetric with respect to synchronization, either may have to wait for the other.

After the request is processed against the database, "finalize-transaction" disposes of the results. It is defined in terms of the intrinsic function "proj-2-1," which projects an ordered pair onto its first component, in this case the updated database. The second component is evaluated only for its side-effect of sending the response back; the "'null'" value it returns is thrown away.

"receive-response" could have been defined using type "xm," but an "x" is also correct, because precedence constraints enforced by the functional nesting of "send-request" inside "receive-response" ensure that at most one instance of "receive-response" will be in evaluation at any one time, namely that of the process whose request is now being processed. Thus matching on the channel "resp" is always unique.

"FILLER" and "'null'" are used as place-holders whenever syntactic rules dictate that there must be a set or value, but no semantics need be carried. "send-request," for instance, returns the value "'null'" because every function must have a value. And "receive-response" has "FILLER" as its domain simply because it is composed with "send-request," although the reason for the composition is sequencing rather than transfer of values. "receive-request" does not need a domain (because a function does not require one), but "x-requ" must have an argument—and so "'null'" is used.

3) Examples of Free-Running Interactions: A "free-running" process is one whose only interactions occur via "xr," so that it will never wait to synchronize with another process. The prototypical free-running process is a real-time clock, which "ticks" once per process step, and could not fulfill its intended function if it had any synchronizing interactions. Such a process is specified:

(clock-cycle[0], ...);

clock-cycle: TIME → TIME;

TIME = INTEGER;

clock-cycle[t] = proj-2-1[(increment[t],offer-time[t])];

increment: TIME → TIME;

offer-time: TIME → FILLER ∪ TIME;

offer-time[t] = xr-time[t].

Any process wishing to read the current time must evaluate

current-time: → TIME;

current-time = xm-time['null'].

Concurrent "xm-time"'s will compete to match with "xr-time," implying for this particular specification that no two readers will ever get the same clock value.

Another common type of free-running process is a digital simulation of a nondigital, unintelligent environment object. Here is the top-level specification of the processes representing the machines in the environment of a process-control system [54]:

j#1..3

< ; machine-j-cycle: MACHINE-STATE → MACHINE-STATE;

    machine-j-cycle[m] =
      proj-2-1
        [(simulate-machine[(m,feedback-j-if-any)],
        offer-machine-j-data[sense[m]]
)];

    feedback-j-if-any: → FEEDBACK ∪ FILLER;

    feedback-j-if-any = xr-j-back['null'];

    offer-machine-j-data:
      SENSOR-DATA → FILLER ∪ SENSOR-DATA;

    offer-machine-j-data[s] = xr-j-sens[s]

> ;

    simulate-machine:
      MACHINE-STATE × (FEEDBACK ∪ FILLER)
    → MACHINE-STATE;

    sense: MACHINE-STATE → SENSOR-DATA.

During each process step two things are done in parallel: 1) "simulate-machine" computes the next process state, which is an element of "MACHINE-STATE" encoding the machine's

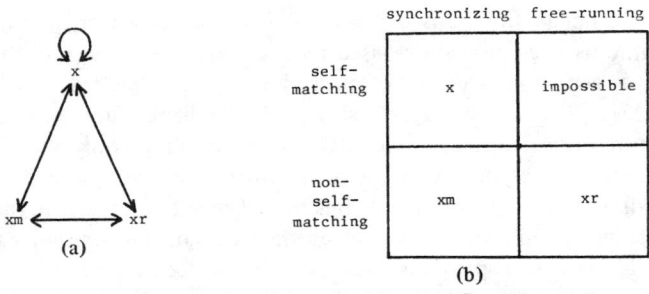

	synchronizing	free-running
self-matching	x	impossible
non-self-matching	xm	xr

(a)   (b)

Fig. 7. The three types of exchange function. (a) Possible matches on a channel. (b) Derivation of the types.

current status, and 2) the current output of sensors attached to the machine ("sense[m]") is offered to the control system via "xr-j-sens." If the control system is ready to accept the data from this machine cycle an exchange will take place; otherwise the data will be gone forever.

"simulate-machine" has two arguments: the current machine state and the value returned by "feedback-j-if-any." This function is defined as "xr-j-back," an exchange function which interacts with several sites in the control system which provide controlling feedback to the jth machine. If some actuator is being activated at the moment "xr-j-back" is evaluated, an exchange takes place and a value in "FEEDBACK" is returned. Otherwise the argument "'null'" is returned, indicating that no actuators are being used.

Our final example of a free-running process is a producer-consumer buffer. Its process state is the current buffer contents, and its successor function is:

next-buffer: BUFFER → BUFFER;

next-buffer[b] = give-to-consumer[get-from-producer[b]];

get-from-producer: BUFFER → BUFFER;

get-from-producer[b] =
  /full[b] : b,
   'true' : put-on-tail[(b,xr-prod['null'])]
  /;

give-to-consumer: BUFFER → BUFFER;
  /empty[b] : b,
   'true' : put-on-head[(xr-cons[first[b]],rest[b])]
  /.

On each process step "get-from-producer" provides the opportunity to put one new element in the buffer (assuming it is not already full). If some producer has a pending "xm-prod[new-element]," "new-element" will be returned as the value of "xr-prod" and inserted. Otherwise "xr-prod" returns "'null'," which "put-on-tail" will simply ignore.

Likewise, on each process step "give-to-consumer" offers the element at the head of the buffer ("first[b]") to any process evaluating "xm-cons['null']." If such an evaluation is pending an exchange will take place and "xr-cons[first[b]]" will return "'null'," which "put-on-head" will ignore. Otherwise the unconsumed "first[b]" will be returned, and "put-on-head" will reinstate it.

The expected behavior of this process (at least under light loading) will be to cycle very fast, checking for interactions but not having any on most process steps. This shows that exchange functions are in some sense more primitive than synchronization mechanisms which enable a process to wait for any one of several events to occur. The payoff is a much simpler implementation for exchange functions, and the choice is in keeping with the PAISLey philosophy of simplicity and minimal semantics. It is also arguable that the above specification is as perspicuous as any, largely because of the benefits of applicative style.

4) Implementation: Exchange functions can be implemented straightforwardly, even on distributed networks (assuming a simple message-passing facility). In almost all cases the pattern of matches on a channel is one-to-one or many-to-one, the latter for resource competition. In this section we present an efficient distributed algorithm for implementing exchange matching in these cases.

Consider first an exchange channel with many "xm"'s and one "x" (or just two "x"'s, in which case one of them takes the role of the "xm" in this description), all residing at different nodes of a network (see Fig. 8). When an "xm" is initiated, a message carrying its argument is sent to the node where the matching "x" resides. These messages are queued up in arrival order. When the "x" is initiated, if the queue is empty, it waits until it is not. When the queue is not empty, it removes the first entry as the "match," takes the value stored there as its own value, sends a termination message containing its argument to the matching "xm," and continues. Computation can continue at the "xm" as soon as the termination message (with its value) is received.

This implementation uses only two messages per match, and automatically prevents lockout with FIFO queueing. For channels with one "xr" and either one "x" or many "xm"'s, the queue is formed at the site of the "xr," and the only modification necessary is that if the "xr" is initiated when the queue of possible matches is empty, then it does not go into the wait state. For channels with many "xr"'s and one "x," matching is done at the site of the "x," but no queue forms. If an "xr" sends an initiating message but the "x" is not pending, a termination message with the original argument is sent back to the "xr" immediately.

In the rare cases where one party to all matches on a channel is *not* predetermined by the static specification structure, matching on a channel can be implemented by a "channel controller" situated anywhere in the network. The initiation of any exchange causes a message containing its type and argument to be sent to the controller. The controller queues and matches as appropriate, notifying an exchange function that it has been matched by sending it a termination message containing the value. This is less desirable than the previous strategy only because it requires four messages per match.

5) Further Properties and Justifications: Because exchange functions are only "pseudofunctions" and have side effects, expressions containing them cannot be optimized to avoid evaluation of expressions whose *values* are not needed. The most common example of this is a successor function with the form "proj-2-1[(a,b)]," where expression "a" computes the next state and "b" interacts with other processes.

There is also a potential problem with distributing values

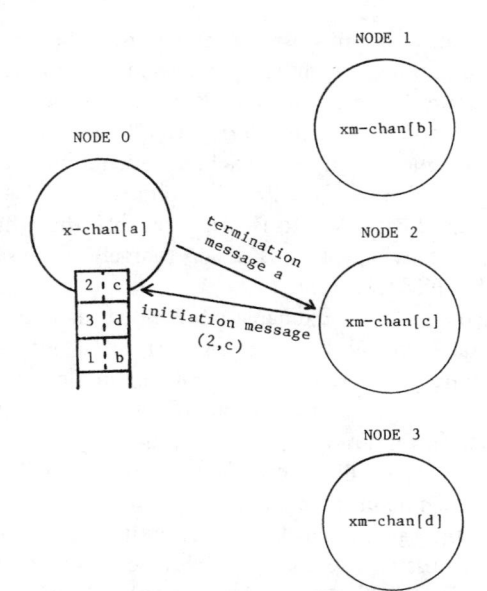

NODE 1

xm-chan[b]

NODE 0

x-chan[a]

NODE 2

xm-chan[c]

termination message a

initiation message (2,c)

2 | c

3 | d

1 | b

NODE 3

xm-chan[d]

Fig. 8. Distributed implementation of exchange matching.

obtained by interaction, but the formal parameter mechanism does this nicely. Suppose the effect of

/equal[(x-denom['null'],0)] : 'divide-check',
  'true':   divide[(numerator,x-denom['null'])]
/

is wanted, where both usages of the value returned by an exchange are supposed to result from a single evaluation. This can be specified unambiguously by defining "quotient" as

quotient[(n,d)] = /equal[(d,0)] : 'divide-check',
                     'true'   : divide[(n,d)]
                  /,

and then using it in the invocation "quotient[(numerator, x-denom['null'])]."

Establishing the internal consistency of a specification with exchange functions requires some attention. The range of a user-chosen function defined as an exchange must agree with the domains of all those with which it can exchange. Furthermore, precedence constraints caused by nested evaluation structures can cause exchange deadlocks. But the channel of an exchange function has been made a constant attribute rather than an argument to it just so that exchange patterns would yield to static analysis, and simple arguments do establish deadlock-freedom in many common cases. For instance, the process hierarchy constructed in [54] expresses the acyclic "dependency" structure of the interactions in the system; the argument that this prevents deadlock is a common one in the operating system literature (e.g., [9]).

There are so many proposals for distributed interaction mechanisms current today that comparison and justification are essential. Most properly, exchange functions are motivated and justified by our goal of fitting processes and asynchronous interactions into an applicative framework, and in this role they are almost unique (see also [34]). Their generality is established by Fig. 7(b) and by extensive experience with them, which indicates that the only kind of interaction they cannot specify is *unbounded* broadcast.

Exchange functions can also be justified, however, on the same basis as procedure-based mechanisms, which fall into the two general categories of procedure-call mechanisms [10], [25], [28] and message-passing [36]. Exchange functions are more primitive than procedure calls because they only specify interaction at one point in time rather than two (procedure call and return). They are thus more general and easier to implement, while the mutual synchronization of the communicating processes provides much of the structure and control usually associated with procedure-call mechanisms.

It is the mutual synchronization that most distinguishes exchange functions from message-passing mechanisms, where (usually) messages are automatically buffered, so that the sender transmits the message and continues, while the message is queued until the receiver is ready for it. The decision against this scheme is based on our concern with performance. Consider a set of terminals sending updates to a central database. With exchange functions a terminal cannot create new work for the system until the system has accepted its previous work. If a terminal could simply send an update message and continue, its speed could increase (unchecked by the ability of the system to handle the work), the queue at the database could grow to unbounded lengths, and no bounds on the performance of the system could ever be established.

At the same time, there is nothing wrong with *bounded* buffering, but this can always be specified in PAISLey. Introducing bounds within an abstract, general-purpose interaction mechanism (such as "message passing up to some bound") would seem a most unfortunate mixture of specification and implementation.

Given that synchronization is going to be two-way, it costs very little in the implementation to preserve the possibility of two-way data transfer, although it is seldom used. It also keeps the number of primitives down by a factor of two, since otherwise each of the three exchange function types would have to come in a "sending data" and a "receiving data" version.

Of all the well-known interaction mechanisms, the most similar to exchange functions is Hoare's input/output primitives [26]. In Hoare's language a pair of statements, "P?input" in process Q and "Q!output" in process P, will come together in the same mutually synchronized manner that two matching exchanges do. "output" is an expression whose value is assigned to the variable "input," assuming appropriate type correspondences. In addition to the relatively unimportant data asymmetry, Hoare's primitives seem to be different from exchange functions in three fundamental ways. 1) There is no way to specify real-time or free-running interactions. 2) There is no straightforward way to specify resource sharing, since all "matches" are one-to-one by process name. In Hoare's language a process representing a shared resource must have a separate command for each process with which it can communicate, and guard that command [14] with an input command naming the appropriate process of the many. The guard (and statement) to be executed are chosen nondeterministically from the processes that are ready to communicate. These multiple statements seem distinctly clumsy compared to an "xm"/"x" exchange match. Furthermore, the full knowledge each process must have about the names of the processes with

172

which it communicates makes modularity difficult to achieve. 3) Hoare's primitives belong in a procedural, rather than applicative, framework. The destination of a data transfer, for instance, is specified by an address.

D. Performance Requirements

1) Definition of Performance Requirements: So far the only structure that has been needed for complete and formal specification of performance requirements is attachment of timing and reliability attributes to functions in the "functional" requirements specification. A timing attribute refers to the evaluation time of the function. It is a random variable, and any information about its distribution, such as lower or upper bounds, mean, or the distribution itself, may be given.[5]

A reliability attribute can only be attached to a function whose range is divided into two subsets (e.g. "→ SUCCESS-RESULT ∪ FAILURE-RESULT"), the first for the values returned by successful evaluations and the second for values returned when the evaluation fails. The attribute itself is a discrete (binary) random variable whose two outcomes denote successful or failed evaluations, and any information about its distribution may be given.

When a primitive function fails it simply returns a value in its failure range. An exchange function fails in the same way, except that even when it fails it must still match another exchange, so that failures do not affect or complicate analysis of exchange patterns. Furthermore, if matching exchange functions *both* have reliability properties, they must succeed or fail together.

Failure of a nonprimitive function simply means that the function delivers a value in the second subset of its range. It is up to the function's definition to ensure that this happens with the specified frequency, since the function is evaluated according to its definition under all circumstances.

Reliability is a difficult and little-understood subject, but this definition of it has several appealing properties. It forces the specified system to have the primary characteristic of a reliable system, namely going into a well-defined and previously anticipated state when something fails. It makes reliability independent of timing and functionality, since a function evaluation must satisfy its timing requirements and deliver a value in its declared range regardless of whether it succeeds or fails. In fact, we have deemed this property so important that we have sacrificed some realism for it: only primitive functions can *really* fail (since nonprimitive ones are always evaluated according to their definitions). Much more knowledge of reliability is needed before we can be sure how successful this approach will be, but its formality and tractability are strong arguments in its favor.

These performance requirements can be simulated by the specification interpreter, and checked (in principle!) for internal consistency, just as the functional ones are. This means, for instance, that if "f[x]" is defined as "g[h[x]]," and there are upper bounds on the evaluation times of all three, then the

upper bound on "f" must be strictly greater than (allowing time for invocation/argument transfer) the sum of the upper bounds on "g" and "h."

2) Examples of "Synchronous Closed-Loop" Performance Requirements: An on-line database system can be called a "synchronous closed-loop" system—"closed-loop" because the entire feedback loop realized by the system is explicitly represented, and "synchronous" because the terminal process (on behalf of the cooperative person behind it) waits for responses, i.e., synchronizes itself with the system. For these systems the basic performance requirements are particularly easy to specify, and all are attached to the terminals. We will refer to the functional terminal specification in Section V-B, and give performance requirements typical of airline reservation systems [31].

Distributions have been left as comments in the PAISLey syntax because we have not yet settled on a formal language for them. Timing requirements normally call for the maximum, minimum, mean, or constant value of the random variable, while reliability requirements normally specify a lower bound on the probability of success.

A response-time limit of 3 s is specified by

transact: ! → "maximum = 3 sec."

An average load of 200 transactions/s, assuming 10 000 terminals in the system, is specified by

terminal-cycle: ! → "mean = 50 sec,"

which says that on the average a terminal demands a transaction (goes through a cycle) every 50 s. Finally, the requirement that at least 99 percent of all transactions must be processed successfully is expressed as

transact: % → "prob { 'success' } >= .99"

which, of course, can only be attached to "transact" because its range is divided into success ("RESPONSE") and failure ("ERROR-MESSAGE") subranges.

3) Examples of "Asynchronous Closed-Loop" Performance Requirements: Process-control systems can be called "asynchronous closed-loop" systems—"asynchronous" because the machines, which are the sources and destinations of the feedback loops realized by these systems, are free-running. The systems must keep up with them without their cooperation. Performance requirements for these systems are more of a challenge, but the operational approach enables us to specify them straightforwardly. "Open-loop" specifications, in which not all of the feedback loop (ultimately, the purpose of *any* embedded system is to realize feedback loops) is included explicitly in the model, have performance requirements similar to these. An example of an open-loop specification would be a patient-monitoring system in which treatment of patients was not represented, only display of warning messages.

In [54] a variety of timing requirements for a process-control system are given. These include: 1) the granularity of the discrete simulation of the machines in the environment, 2) a real-time limit on the fully automatic feedback loop realized by the system, 3) a real-time limit on the partially

---

[5]More generally, the sequence of evaluations of the function over the lifetime of the system could be associated with a stochastic process, so that the time of each evaluation would be a separate random variable, but let us hope such generality will never be needed.

manual feedback loop realized by the system, specified as separate response requirements on the human operator and on the computer system, and 4) a *derived* performance requirement on the system's internal database component which will guarantee that other system components can meet their own performance requirements. Despite the subtleties involved, each one of these requirements is specified simply by attaching a timing constraint to the successor function of a single process!

4) "Real-World" Properties: Time and reliability (the fact that sometimes digital components do not do what their definition says they will, for physical reasons forever beyond the reach of digital logic) are nondigital properties that incontrovertibly affect the digital domain. In [50] many other such physical ("real-world") properties are mentioned, weight and distance, for example. Why are these not formalized as performance requirements as well?

The answer is that, to the extent that we know them, the effects of these properties on the computational (digital) domain can be specified in terms of functions, timing, and reliability. Weight constraints, for instance, only affect how many functions can be realized. Even if we did attach weight attributes to components of PAISLey specification, there is nothing that an interpreter could do with them. Therefore an informal comment is just as satisfactory.

Distance is a more interesting example because its effects on the computational domain are more varied. Distance increases the relative time for interprocess interactions, decreases component reliability, and increases the logical complexity of interfaces which must cope with these factors. Yet these three effects are directly expressable in terms of timing, reliability, and functional requirements, respectively.

Factors such as these can nevertheless have a profound effect on requirements. In an airline reservation system, for instance, it may be necessary to divide the response-time or transaction-reliability allowances into portions for the data-communication subsystem and portions for the database subsystem. Although such allocation is technically a design decision, two reasons for doing it during the requirements phase are 1) to enable feasibility analyses of two very different technologies and 2) to contract the work to different organizations.

These allocated requirements can be specified in PAISLey. We have constructed a requirements model in which time limits are given for, and failures can occur in, each of three stages: input transmission, transaction processing, and output transmission. Failure at any stage aborts subsequent stages and propagates an appropriate error measage. This is the source of elements in the set "ERROR-MESSAGE" found in the range of "transact" in the terminal specification.

VI. EVALUATION AGAINST GOALS FOR REQUIREMENTS SPECIFICATIONS

A thorough evaluation of PAISLey cannot be made until an interpreter has been implemented and specifications of large systems have been written. In the meantime, we present the reasons why we believe our goals for requirements specifications will be met.

It was stated in Section I-B that in order to constrain the target system, a requirements specification should be precise, unambiguous, internally consistent, complete, and minimal. The formal nature of a PAISLey specification leaves no doubt as to its precision and lack of ambiguity. If it 1) is syntactically correct, 2) has all its domain declarations in agreement with all its function applications, 3) has all its range declarations in agreement with its function definitions, and 4) can be shown to be free of exchange deadlock, then it is internally consistent. The arguments in Section IV-A suggest that PAISLey does not obstruct the writing of minimal specifications.

The issue of completeness deserves special attention, because the worst failing a requirements specification language can have is to be unable to express what the requirements analyst wants to say. *This* is the problem that makes analysts revert to English! PAISLey has been used to specify requirements for a wide variety of embedded systems (small examples), and never yet found wanting. In addition to the examples used or referred to here, it was also used to specify (in some 33 pages, see [48]) a distributed design for an innovative interactive numerical system that was actually implemented directly from the specification [53], [52]. Furthermore, the prompt feedback provided by executable requirements should help to protect against omissions.

Of course, this refers only to properties relevant to the computational domain—it says nothing about constraints on the development process itself, such as deadlines, cost limits, methodological standards, and routine maintenance procedures. PAISLey does not address these, nor does it offer any particular help in posing alternate or prioritized requirements [47]. And the need to supplement formal requirements with diagrams, comments, and other informal avenues of human communication will never disappear.

A requirements specification must be formally manipulable or testable, so that it can be determined whether the final product meets its requirements. Any property of a PAISLey specification relating to the behavior of the system in a given situation is clearly testable, because the behavior of the executable specification can be compared directly to the behavior of the target system. PAISLey specifications should also be suitable for verification, because they are based on a few simple and formal concepts, but this aspect has not yet been explored.

Finally, requirements specifications should be understandable and modifiable. Although these qualities are vague and subjective, there is reason to believe that they can both be achieved by attaining two other qualities which are at least identifiable, if still subjective. These two qualities are 1) providing modeling capabilities which are abstract, intuitive, and close to human perceptions of the environment to be modeled and 2) providing means by which complexity can be decomposed. The latter is necessary because a complex specification must be understood (and changed) one small piece at a time. The former is important for understanding because it allows people to think in familiar, problem-oriented terms. It may also be important for modifiability, as explained in [23]. They argue that, since our current best definition of modifiability is that a small change in the environment causes a correspondingly small change in the specification, the property is most possessed by those specifications which are the most direct translations of the natural environment into formalism.

We contend that PAISLey models can be intuitive and close to the natural way people think about embedded systems. The objects in the system's environment can be modeled directly as autonomous parallel processes, using a language with the power to specify simulations of great verisimilitude. The internal process structure of the proposed system model is largely determined by the environment structure and user-oriented system "functions" or capabilities (see Section VII-B).

PAISLey also enables nontrivial decomposition of complexity. The division of a specification into processes is especially useful, for instance, because it decomposes both static and dynamic properties, and because it seems to correlate with divisions meaningful to users. The partitioning even extends to execution of specifications, because any subset of processes can be executed in isolation, simply by leaving all interactions with missing processes as unelaborated primitives in a form such as "receive-message: → MESSAGE." The interpreter will evaluate this "interaction site" by choosing some message at random. This capability was used in [54] to develop a specification in five versions, each independently executable, and each obtained from the last by adding new processes/functions in an "outside-in" sequence. Decomposition of complexity is discussed further in [49].

VII. PLANS FOR FUTURE RESEARCH

A. Execution of Specifications

We are currently planning the implementation of a system for executing specifications. Specifications will be checked for consistency and compiled into fully parallel runtime process-and-interaction structures. These structures will then be interpreted under interactive control. The most important questions to be answered are: What is it like to test a specification? What kind of control over the course of execution does the analyst need? What display, report, and trace facilities can be used to produce an intelligible outcome?

B. Methodology

This work on requirements *specification*, which has been pursued so far with small examples, must be extended in the directions of requirements *analysis*, and "scaling-up" to large systems. In other words, we need to pursue the implications of process-based specifications for a requirements methodology.

The most obvious problem is that process-based descriptions are not intrinsically hierarchical. It is not clear, however, that top-level system requirements are hierarchical either. Preliminary studies indicate that a complex system carries out several parallel functions for its environment, none of which is subservient to any other. ("Top-level" is important here because once the process structure of a PAISLey specification is determined, further decisions are recorded by elaboration of successor functions—which is completely hierarchical.)

This observation has suggested an alternate methodological approach, in which parallel functions are identified and translated into PAISLey processes or hierarchically arranged groups of them (similar to "subsystems" in DDN, see [37]). Preliminary work with three process-control examples has even revealed a set of rules which can be used to identify user-oriented functions of these systems; functions defined according to these rules have a one-to-one correspondence with processes in the subsequent PAISLey specification.

Complexity is then decomposed through incremental development: the specification is written and tested one function/process at a time. The language semantics already support this mode of use, as explained in Section VI, and our investigations of the interpreter's human interface are also being carried out with the incremental mode in mind.

These ideas are still highly speculative, but they do establish that hierarchical abstraction is not the only approach to a practical requirements methodology. At the highest levels of system description, "flat" structure may not be incompatible with good structure.

C. Design

It has been pointed out that PAISLey is capable of specifying the results of design decisions. A logical extension of this is to investigate its properties as a design specification language. The benefits are potentially great, because a uniform language for requirements and design should make possible substantial improvements in the traceability and automatability of design. It might also lead to a better theoretical understanding of design decisions as resource/performance tradeoffs.

APPENDIX
A GRAMMAR FOR PAISLey

This grammar is LALR, and is written in BNF with nonterminals underlined. Comments are transparent, and can therefore appear anywhere. Blanks are also transparent, except inside an ascii-string.

comment ::= "ascii-string"

---

spec ::= spec ; statement |

    statement |

    spec ; index-head < ; spec > |

    index-head < ; spec >

index-head ::= lower-string # integer .. integer |

    upper-string # integer .. integer |

    # integer .. integer

statement ::= system-decl |

    func-decl |

    set-defn |

    func-defn

---

system-decl ::= (process-list)

process-list ::= process-list , process |

        process |

        process-list , index-head < , process-list > |

        index-head < , process-list >

process ::= func-name [func-exp]

---

func-decl ::= func-name : func-property

func-property ::= domain-range |

        timing-attribute |

        reliability-attribute

domain-range ::= set-exp → set-exp |

        → set-exp

timing-attribute ::= ! → comment

reliability-attribute ::= % → comment

---

set-defn ::= set-name = set-exp

set-exp ::= set-exp ∪ set-term |

        set-term |

        set-exp ∪ index-head < ∪ set-exp > |

        index-head < ∪ set-exp >

set-term ::= set-term × set-item |

        set-item |

        set-term × index-head < × set-term > |

        index-head < × set-term >

set-item ::= set-name |

        (set-exp) |

        { const-list }

set-name ::= upper-string - set-name-string |

        upper-string

set-name-string ::= set-name-string - set-syll |

        set-syll

set-syll ::= upper-string |

        integer

const-list ::= const-list , const-name |

        const-name

const-name ::= 'ascii-string' |

        integer |

        real-number

---

func-defn ::= func-name = func-exp |

        func-name formal-params = func-exp

formal-params ::= [param-list]

param-list ::= param-list , func-name |

        func-name |

        param-list , (param-list) |

        (param-list)

func-exp ::= func-name |

        const-name |

        func-appl |

        (func-list) |

        / pred-pair-list , 'true' ; func-exp /

func-appl ::= func-name [func-exp] |

        index-head < func-name > [func-exp]

func-list ::= func-list , func-exp |

        func-exp |

        func-list , index-head < , func-list > |

        index-head < , func-list >

pred-pair-list ::= pred-pair-list , pred-pair |

        pred-pair |

        pred-pair-list , index-head < , pred-pair-list > |

        index-head < , pred-pair-list >

pred-pair ::= func-exp : func-exp

func-name ::= lower-string |

        lower-string - func-name-string

func-name-string ::= func-syll - func-name-string |

        func-syll

func-syll ::= lower-string |

        integer

Primitives of the grammar.

ascii-string ::= any string of ASCII characters

upper-string ::= any string of uppercase alphabetical characters

lower-string ::= any string of lowercase alphabetical characters

integer ::= any string of numerals

real-number ::= any string of numerals with a single embedded period

Intrinsic sets.

FILLER = { 'null' }

BOOLEAN = { 'true,' 'false' }

INTEGER = the set of all integers representable on the host machine

REAL = the set of all real numbers representable on the host machine

STRING = the set of all string constants with length less than or equal to some bound

---

Typeless intrinsic functions.

x-lower-string | xm-lower-string | xr-lower-string

proj-integer-integer

equal

Typed intrinsic functions.

sum: INTEGER X INTEGER → INTEGER

difference: INTEGER X INTEGER → INTEGER

product: INTEGER X INTEGER → INTEGER

quotient: INTEGER X INTEGER → INTEGER

remainder: INTEGER X INTEGER → INTEGER

greater-than: INTEGER X INTEGER → BOOLEAN

less-than: INTEGER X INTEGER → BOOLEAN

greater-than-or-equal: INTEGER X INTEGER → BOOLEAN

less-than-or-equal: INTEGER X INTEGER → BOOLEAN

ACKNOWLEDGMENT

Many people have contributed to the work presented here. My thanks especially to D. R. Fitzwater, with whom the foundations for PAISLey were laid, to S. Smoliar, A. Conn, and R. Mittermeir, for stimulating discussions on requirements, to P. Fowler, for the chance to try these ideas on a class at Bell Labs, to G. Cole, for diligent and able assistance, to R. Hamlet, who would read this stuff before anyone else would (or could), to the referees, and to R. Yeh, for support, encouragement, ideas, and good advice.

REFERENCES

[1] U.S. Air Force, "Air Force weapons effectiveness testing (AFWET) instrumentation system," Air Proving Ground Center, Eglin Air Force Base, FL, R&D Exhibit PGVE 64-40, 1965.

[2] M. W. Alford, "A requirements engineering methodology for real-time processing requirements," *IEEE Trans. Software Eng.*, vol. SE-3, pp. 60-69, Jan. 1977.

[3] J. Backus, "Can programming be liberated from the von Neumann style? A functional style and its algebra of programs," *Commun. Ass. Comput. Mach.*, vol. 21, pp. 613-641, Aug. 1978.

[4] R. Balzer and N. Goldman, "Principles of good software specification and their implications for specification language," in *Proc. Specifications of Reliable Software Conf.*, Cambridge, MA, Apr. 1979, pp. 58-67.

[5] L. A. Belady and M. M. Lehman, "The characteristics of large systems," in *Research Directions in Software Technology*, Peter Wegner, Ed. Cambridge, MA: M.I.T. Press, 1979, pp. 106-138.

[6] T. E. Bell, D. C. Bixler, and M. E. Dyer, "An extendable approach to computer-aided software requirements engineering," *IEEE Trans. Software Eng.*, vol. SE-3, pp. 49-60, Jan. 1977.

[7] T. E. Bell and T. A. Thayer, "Software requirements: Are they really a problem?," in *Proc. 2nd Int. Conf. Software Eng.*, San Francisco, CA, Oct. 1976, pp. 61-68.

[8] B. W. Boehm, "Software engineering," *IEEE Trans. Comput.*, vol. C-25, pp. 1226-1241, Dec. 1976.

[9] P. Brinch Hansen, *The Architecture of Concurrent Programs*. Englewood Cliffs, NJ: Prentice-Hall, 1977.

[10] —, "Distributed processes: A concurrent programming concept," *Commun. Ass. Comput. Mach.*, vol. 21, pp. 934-941, Nov. 1978.

[11] A. P. Conn, "Maintenance: A key element in computer requirements definition," in *Proc. COMPSAC '80*, Chicago, IL, Oct. 1980, pp. 401-406.

[12] A. M. Davis and T. G. Rauscher, "Formal techniques and automatic processing to ensure correctness in requirements specifications," in *Proc. Specifications of Reliable Software Conf.*, Cambridge, MA, Apr. 1979, pp. 15-35.

[13] C. G. Davis and C. R. Vick, "The software development system," *IEEE Trans. Software Eng.*, vol. SE-3, pp. 69-84, Jan. 1977.

[14] E. W. Dijkstra, "Guarded commands, nondeterminacy, and formal derivation of programs," *Commun. Ass. Comput. Mach.*, vol. 18, pp. 453-457, Aug. 1975.

[15] D. A. Fisher, "DoD's common programming language effort," *Computer*, vol. 11, pp. 24-33, Mar. 1978.

[16] R. E. Filman and D. P. Friedman, *Languages and Models for Distributed Computing*, to be published.

[17] D. R. Fitzwater and P. Zave, "The use of formal asynchronous process specifications in a system development process," in *Proc. 6th Texas Conf. Comput. Syst.*, Austin, TX, Nov. 1977, pp. 2B-21-2B-30.

[18] D. P. Friedman and D. S. Wise, "Aspects of applicative programming for file systems," in *Proc. ACM Conf. Language Design for Reliable Software*, Raleigh, NC, Mar. 1977, pp. 41-55.

[19] D. P. Friedman and D. S. Wise, "Aspects of applicative programming for parallel processing," *IEEE Trans. Comput.*, vol. C-27, pp. 289-296, Apr. 1978.

[20] —, "Unbounded computational structures," *Software–Practice and Experience*, vol. 8, pp. 407-416, July-Aug. 1978.

[21] —, "An approach to fair applicative multiprogramming," *Semantics of Concurrent Computation (Lecture Notes in Comput. Sci.)*, vol. 70, G. Kahn, Ed. Berlin: Springer-Verlag, 1979, pp. 203-226.

[22] —, "An indeterminate constructor for applicative programming," in *Proc. 7th Annu. ACM Symp. Principles of Programming Languages*, Las Vegas, NV, Jan. 1980, pp. 245-250.

[23] N. M. Goldman and D. S. Wile, "A relational data base foundation for process specifications," in *Entity-Relationship Approach to Systems Analysis and Design*, P. P. Chen, Ed. Amsterdam: North-Holland, 1980.

[24] K. L. Heninger, "Specifying software requirements for complex systems: New techniques and their application," in *Proc. Specifications of Reliable Software Conf.*, Cambridge, MA, Apr. 1979, pp. 1-14.

[25] C.A.R. Hoare, "Monitors: An operating system structuring concept," *Commun. Ass. Comput. Mach.*, vol. 17, pp. 549-557, Oct. 1974.

[26] —, "Communicating sequential processes," *Commun. Ass. Comput. Mach.*, vol. 21, pp. 666-677, Aug. 1978.

[27] J. J. Horning and B. Randell, "Process structuring," *Comput. Surveys*, vol. 5, pp. 5-30, Mar. 1973.

[28] J. D. Ichbiah *et al.*, "Rationale for the design of the Ada programming language," *SIGPLAN Notices*, vol. 14, June 1979, part B.

[29] D.H.H. Ingalls, "The Smalltalk-76 programming system design and implementation," in *Proc. 5th Annu. ACM Symp. Principles of Programming Languages*, Tucson, AZ, Jan. 1978, pp. 9-16.

[30] K. E. Iverson, "Notation as a tool of thought," *Commun. Ass. Comput. Mach.*, vol. 23, pp. 444-465, Aug. 1980.

[31] J. R. Knight, "A case study: Airlines reservations systems," *Proc. IEEE*, vol. 60, pp. 1423-1431, Nov. 1972.

[32] M. M. Lehman, "Programs, life cycles, and laws of software evolution," *Proc. IEEE*, vol. 68, pp. 1060-1076, Sept. 1980.

[33] W. T. Mao and R. T. Yeh, "Communication port: A language concept for concurrent programming," *IEEE Trans. Software Eng.*, vol. SE-6, pp. 194–204, Mar. 1980.

[34] G. Milne and R. Milner, "Concurrent processes and their syntax," *J. Ass. Comput. Mach.*, vol. 26, pp. 302–321, Apr. 1979.

[35] R. T. Mittermeir, "Semantic nets for modeling the requirements of evolvable systems—An example," Inst. Digitale Anlagen, Tech. Univ. Wien, Vienna, Austria, May 1980.

[36] R. Rao, "Design and evaluation of distributed communication primitives," Univ. Washington, Seattle, Comput. Sci. Rep. 80-04-01, Apr. 1980.

[37] W. E. Riddle *et al.*, "Behavior modeling during software design," *IEEE Trans. Software Eng.*, vol. SE-4, pp. 283–292, July 1978.

[38] D. T. Ross, "Structured analysis (SA): A language for communicating ideas," *IEEE Trans. Software Eng.*, vol. SE-3, pp. 16–34, Jan. 1977.

[39] D. T. Ross and K. R. Schoman, "Structured analysis for requirements definition," *IEEE Trans. Software Eng.*, vol. SE-3, pp. 6–15, Jan. 1977.

[40] N. Roussopoulos, "CSDL: A conceptual schema definition language for the design of data base applications," *IEEE Trans. Software Eng.*, vol. SE-5, pp. 481–496, Sept. 1979.

[41] J. M. Smith and D.C.P. Smith, "A data base approach to software specification," in *Proc. Software Develop. Tools Workshop*, Pingree Park, CO, May 1979, W. E. Riddle and R. E. Fairley, Eds. New York: Springer-Verlag, 1980, pp. 176–200.

[42] S. W. Smoliar, "Using applicative techniques to design distributed systems," in *Proc. Specifications of Reliable Software Conf.*, Cambridge, MA, Apr. 1979, pp. 150–161.

[43] ——, "Applicative and functional programming," *Software Engineering Handbook*, C. V. Ramamoorthy and C. R. Vick, Eds. Englewood Cliffs, NJ: Prentice-Hall, to be published.

[44] D. Teichroew and E. A. Hershey, III, "PSL/PSA: A computer-aided technique for structured documentation and analysis of information processing systems," *IEEE Trans. Software Eng.*, vol. SE-3, pp. 41–48, Jan. 1977.

[45] R. T. Yeh *et al.*, "Software requirement engineering—A perspective," Univ. Texas, Austin, Comput. Sci. Rep. SDBEG-7, Mar. 1979.

[46] R. T. Yeh, N. Roussopoulos, and P. Chang, "Systematic derivation of software requirements through structured analysis," Univ. Texas, Austin, Comput. Sci. Rep. SDBEG-15, 1979.

[47] R. T. Yeh *et al.*, "Software requirments: A report on the state of the art," Univ. Maryland, College Park, Comput. Sci. Rep. TR-949, Oct. 1980; to appear as "Software requirements: New directions and perspectives," in *Software Engineering Handbook*, C. V. Ramamoorthy and C. R. Vick, Eds. Englewood Cliffs, NJ: Prentice-Hall, to be published.

[48] P. Zave, "The formal specification of an adaptive, parallel finite-element system," Univ. Maryland, College Park, Rep. TR-715, Dec. 1978.

[49] ——, "The operational approach to requirements specification for embedded systems," Univ. Maryland, College Park, Rep. TR-976, Dec. 1980.

[50] ——, "Real-world properties in the requirements for embedded systems," in *Proc. 19th Annu. Washington D.C. ACM Tech. Symp.*, Gaithersburg, MD, June 1980, pp. 21–26.

[51] ——, "Extending applicative specification techniques to embedded systems," to be published.

[52] P. Zave and G. E. Cole, Jr., "A quantitative evaluation of the feasibility of, and suitable hardware architectures for, an adaptive, parallel finite-element system," to be published.

[53] P. Zave and W. C. Rheinboldt, "Design of an adaptive, parallel finite-element system," *ACM Trans. Math. Software*, vol. 5, pp. 1–17, Mar. 1979.

[54] P. Zave and R. T. Yeh, "Executable requirements for embedded systems," in *Proc. 5th Int. Conf. Software Eng.*, San Diego, CA, Mar. 1981, pp. 295–304.

Pamela Zave received the A.B. degree in English from Cornell University, Ithaca, NY, in 1970, and the M.S. and Ph.D. degrees in computer sciences from the University of Wisconsin, Madison, in 1972 and 1976.

From 1976 to 1981 she was an Assistant Professor of Computer Science at the University of Maryland, College Park. Since 1981 she has been with the Electronic and Computer Systems Research Laboratory of Bell Laboratories, Murray Hill, NJ. Her research interests include requirements analysis, system design, embedded and distributed systems, and models of parallel processing.

Dr. Zave is a member of the Association for Computing Machinery, SIGSOFT, SIGOPS, and the IEEE Computer Society.

A Case Study Extending Operational Specification to a Nonembedded System

William W. Agresti
Computer Sciences Corporation

Abstract

The method of operational specification is extended to the case of a nonembedded system. An operational model is introduced to capture essential relations among system elements and to provide the basis for interpreting the specification. Executability of the operational specification is demonstrated by considering a representative user scenario. The motivation for pursuing operational specification and the observed benefits of using it are discussed.

Introduction

How does an applications software group respond when it is charged with developing a completely different type of system? This was the situation that led our organization to consider alternatives to the traditional software development life-cycle. In this paper, we will discuss

- The circumstances that motivated a different approach to software development

- The resulting operational specification, which has innovative features

- The perceived benefits of the operational specification

The Motivation for a New Development Approach

The software development organization of interest builds flight dynamics software for the National Aeronautics and Space Administration (NASA)/Goddard Space Flight Center (GSFC). The software applications comprise spacecraft attitude determination and control, mission planning and analysis, and orbit determination. A typical system consists of 30,000 to 120,000 lines of FORTRAN with some assembly language, developed over 6 to 18 months. Further characteristics of the application software environment are described by Card et al. [82].

The software group works alongside analysts and researchers who conduct orbit and attitude studies that result in the computational methods used in the applications software. The researchers needed a more hospitable environment to develop and modify their analysis programs, written mostly in FORTRAN. They wanted to reconfigure program components easily, so that they could study the effect of different algorithms and models on spacecraft orbit and attitude. The Flight Dynamics Analysis System (FDAS) was proposed to meet this need.

It seemed natural to call upon the applications software group to design and develop FDAS because of their familiarity with the flight dynamics environment. Of course, FDAS presented a different set of challenges. One basic difference was the shift from applications to systems software. FDAS would provide source code control, simplified module interfaces instead of COMMON blocks, and libraries of reusable functions.

An immediate issue for the software group was to identify the steps necessary to develop FDAS. A well-defined development process was in place for building flight dynamics applications software [Agresti et al. 84]. Should those same life-cycle phases be used for FDAS? Facing the development of a different type of software caused the organization to focus on the assumptions that underlie their standard development process. The most critical assumption dealt with understanding and expressing requirements. For flight dynamics applications software, the requirements were both written and used by a staff that was very experienced with the applications. Generally, writers of requirements documents make assumptions, often implicitly, about the reader's familiarity with the application area. This high degree of shared understanding between writer and reader manifests itself in the requirements document. For example, references to the functioning of software from earlier projects are included. Also, some of the logical connections among requirements items are omitted on the belief that the reader is familiar with them. With FDAS, no such shared understanding of requirements existed.

Another key departure from the standard development process was the absence of any external source of hard requirements. With applications software, the hardware of the spacecraft and the characteristics of the mission serve as a touchstone on which the software requirements are founded. An attitude ground support system, for example, models and interacts with hardware and sensors onboard the spacecraft to determine and control its attitude. The mission support plan requires that the attitude be controlled to a specific accuracy. The physical features of the spacecraft and the physics of attitude dynamics provide an "envelope" of reality within which any support software must remain.

FDAS had no convenient "envelope" to constrain its requirements. The FDAS developers could not point to any mission support plan for ultimate reckoning. The users' "wish list" of FDAS capabilities no longer had the self-limitation that derived from physical laws or spacecraft hardware. These two conditions—lack of shared understanding of the subject and absence of an external requirements envelope—led the software group to question whether its typical life-cycle development process would be effective for FDAS.

The FDAS Operational Specification

The development team began looking for an alternative methodology for specifying the requirements. Previous experience applying automated requirements processors in the flight dynamics environment indicated that they would not be effective [Scheffer, Velez 78]. Also, the use of such requirements tools would not address the basic differences between FDAS development and typical projects. Operational specification appeared promising because it was executable. It would allow the development team to show users the results of FDAS processing without waiting until the implementation phase. In this way, users would be able to react to FDAS output and iteratively refine their understanding of the requirements. Published reports on operational specification had established its value with embedded systems [Zave 82], but its effectiveness outside that domain was not obvious. Another influence on the development team was a report on the Software Development System (SDS), which nominally addressed the definition of specification languages but in fact also provided a coherent rationale for specification in general [Levene, Mullery 82].

For FDAS, we sought to combine the strengths of SDS with those of "traditional," operational specification (i.e., for embedded systems). The FDAS operational specification has a world view that derives from SDS and, more generally, from the entity-relationship approach. The FDAS process descriptions, however, have the detail and precision found in the operational specification of embedded systems.

In the world view of the FDAS operational specification, objects in the requirements are components that are grouped into categories. Specific relationships may exist between components in different categories. For example, the relation CAUSE is shown in Figure 1 to hold between components of category EVENT and those of category PROCESS.

This view of requirements is hardly novel [Ramamoorthy, So 78]. However, the FDAS operational specification exploits this view to define executability and to provide a visual operational model.

Executability is provided by a relational semantics in the following way. An execution of FDAS may be described as a sequence of relations, each of the form r_{ij} (C_i, C_j), where r_{ij} is an allowed relation between C_i and C_j, which are components of categories i and j, respectively. Using Figure 1, a step in an FDAS execution may be CAUSE (time limit exceeded, supply default values), which relates the EVENT "time limit exceeded" to the PROCESS "supply default values."

The requirements for a real system produce many relations and categories of components. We define an *operational model* as the directed graph in which nodes are categories of components and arcs are allowed relations between components of different categories.

The FDAS operational model is shown in Figure 2. Four categories of components exist: users, actions, processes, and files. FDAS may be thought of as having one user at a time. The *user* can accomplish work on FDAS by selecting *actions*, which are one-line commands. *Processes* describe the internal behavior that is necessary for the actions to have their intended effect. Processes operate on *files* that capture the retained data that FDAS needs to support its functioning.

Completing the operational model in Figure 2 are six allowed relations:

SELECT—A user selects the action desired.

ACTIVATE—An action activates a process to accomplish the internal tasks required to satisfy the action.

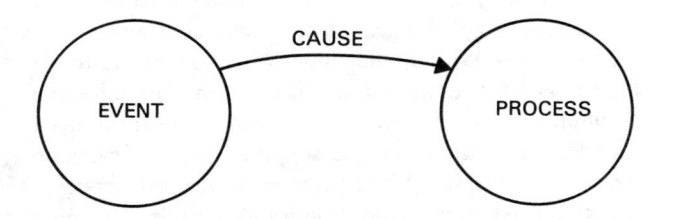

Figure 1. Sample Relation Between Components

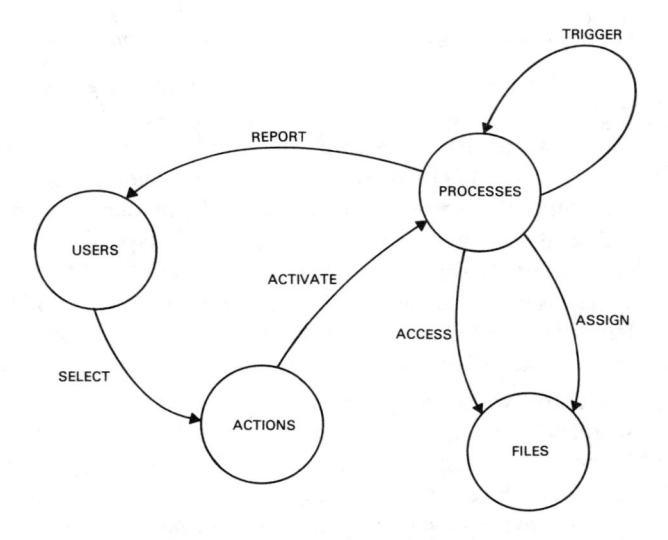

Figure 2. The FDAS Operational Model

TRIGGER—A process triggers other processes when necessary.

ACCESS—A process accesses files to obtain information.

ASSIGN—A process assigns new or changed information to files.

REPORT—A process reports information to the user.

The operational model expresses the executable aspect of FDAS. Of the four categories, only users are *active agents*; the only nondeterminism in FDAS resides with them. We cannot predict which actions they will select. Actions comprise the visible parts of FDAS. Once an action is selected, FDAS behaves deterministically. Actions, processes, and files are *passive agents* that cannot initiate behavior. FDAS is being modeled as a deterministic abstract machine in which state information is maintained in the files category. The user's interaction with the system is limited to selecting actions from an available set. All actions eventually lead to information being reported to the user. From the reports, the user can determine if the action had the desired effect and select another action accordingly.

Every step in an FDAS execution must correspond to a relation in the operational model. Whenever a category is both a source and a terminus of a relation, a question arises as to the progress of an execution through that node. Users, actions, and processes have this characteristic. For users, the effect that the REPORT relation has on SELECT is nondeterministic, as we have said, and not modeled in the FDAS operational specification. For actions, a one-to-one mapping exists—a SELECTed action results in an ACTI-VATEd process of the same name. Appendix A lists some of the FDAS actions.

Processes are the most complex category, figuring in five of the six relations. Process descriptions are written similar to those used in the operational specification of embedded systems. When a process is activated by an action, the process description expresses the required FDAS behavior. This behavior may include triggering other processes, accessing file data, assigning quantities to files, and reporting information to the user. Some of the processes, namely those with names identical to actions, may be viewed as high-level, action-handling processes. The remaining processes, unable to be directly activated by actions, perform support roles triggered by process descriptions. Appendix B lists some of the processes, and Appendix C shows a sample process description.

Files exist only at the termini of relations in Figure 2. Of course, data will flow from the files to the processes that accessed them. But the direction of the arrows in Figure 2 shows that the order of the ACCESS and ASSIGN relations is from processes to files.

Files capture state information on FDAS and serve as the repository for retained data critical to its functioning. The file structure was designed to simplify the writing of process descriptions for accessing and assigning file data. A *file* consists of one or more *records*, each organized into one or more *items*. Each item may require one or more *lines*. A line containing a distinguished symbol identifies the last line corresponding to an item. Each line contains either a single object or a pair of objects separated by a comma. Figure 3 shows the file structure, emphasizing the hierarchy of file, record, item, and line.

The simple file structure was never intended to carry over as the actual file layouts when FDAS was implemented. In this sense, operational specification afforded the group the freedom to ignore issues of practicality or efficiency in file implementation. The file structure simply served as a way of logically organizing data that processes could access and assign.

Every file has an owner who alone is entitled to alter the contents of the file. Read access to entire files or individual records is possible if the file owner enables an access flag. This ability to provide for sharing of information is impor-

```
FILE
    RECORD #1
        ITEM #1
            LINE 1
            LINE 2
                .
                .
                .
            LINE n₁
        ITEM #2
            LINE 1
            LINE 2
                .
                .
            LINE n₂
                .
                .
                .
        ITEM #m
            LINE 1
            LINE 2
                .
                .
            LINE nₘ
    RECORD #2
                .
                .
                .
    RECORD #N
```

Figure 3. Basic File Structure

tant to FDAS users. The file contents reflect the basic FDAS concept of reconfiguration, which is introduced briefly in the next section.

The FDAS Concept

The FDAS concept is embodied in five elements: experiment, function, software unit, data unit, and experiment control procedure (ECP).

The *experiment* is the unit of analytical work in FDAS. An example in flight dynamics would be a study of the Cowell orbit propagator. The analyst may want to investigate the effects of various integration methods or force models on an orbit. Before FDAS, such a study required the analyst to find and change source code in the Cowell software. The FDAS approach is to recognize the basic structure of the Cowell propagator as consisting of a set of *functions* in an invocation hierarchy, as shown in Figure 4. The objective of FDAS is to allow the analyst to manipulate these functional building blocks while being spared from making changes at the level of statements in the source code. (Of course, many other environments share this objective of component assembly [Bassett, Giblon 83]).

Under FDAS, trying a different aerodynamic drag model would entail only plugging in a new *software unit* for the existing one, where both software units are implementations of the DRAG function in Figure 4. (Accomplishing this reconfigurability draws attention to the required functional interfaces that every candidate software unit must satisfy. Such consideration is not the subject in this paper and is pursued elsewhere [Snyder et al. 84].)

Two elements, data unit and ECP, remain to be introduced. A *data unit* is associated with every software unit, identifying the values of data items needed as input to that software unit. An *ECP* describes the high-level control of the experiment. For example, an ECP for the Cowell propagator may contain procedural statements that

- Invoke the experiment
- Change the data unit, giving a different integration step size
- Reinvoke the experiment
- Compare the results of both experiments

From the viewpoint of operational specification, the important issue is to identify the information that any FDAS implementation must retain to provide the execution reconfiguration capabilities above. In the files of the operational specification, this essential information is identified.

The two files below are owned by the FDAS executive system:

- Status File—Contains the dynamic state of an FDAS session
- Valid Users File—Contains names of users allowed to use FDAS

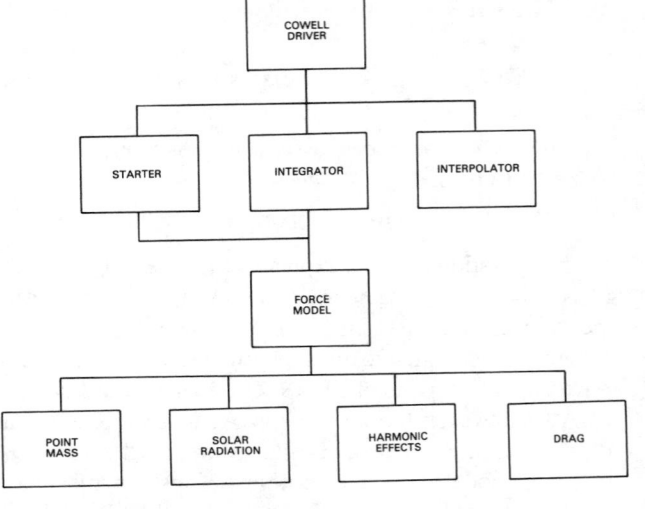

Figure 4. Major Functions of the Cowell Orbit Propagator

The remaining files constitute a set that is used for FDAS experiments. One set is owned by the system, thereby providing an inventory of frequently used functions and services. A set of the following files is also owned by each user to keep applications software that pertains to projects or individual analytical work:

- Header File—Contains information about the files: number of items and current record count
- Experiment File—Contains required information about every analytical experiment: name, description, and relationships between generic functions and corresponding software units
- Function File—Contains information on every function: name, description, input/output data items, and the names of corresponding software units
- Software Unit File—Contains name, description, associated functions, and source text for each software unit
- Data Unit File—Contains pairs giving data item names and corresponding values
- Experiment Control Program (ECP) File—Contains source text of (generally) brief, high-level procedures to control the execution of experiments

Appendix D contains the record descriptions for these files.

Operational Scenarios

The FDAS operational specification permits the consideration of various operational scenarios. In this way, the specification is exercised to determine if typical processing needs of the user can be met.

Appendix E presents one such scenario, emphasizing software reconfiguration. The sequence of user actions and FDAS responses is consistent with the operational model in Figure 2.

182

Benefits of Operational Specification

The FDAS operational specification had a wide range of beneficial effects. It served as an executable, testable representation of the system. The form of the specification made it accessible to users. By constructing operational scenarios, developers were able to demonstrate, in the domain of the user, that realistic processing needs could be met.

The operational specification is a new product that is produced early in the development process. It is more precise and revealing than a narrative, system specification and is a very useful product with which to start preliminary design because several important issues have been resolved. In particular, the files offer a clear statement of the necessary state information that FDAS requires. The actions present a concise set of capabilities that may be mapped into options available to the user. Process descriptions explain the required interaction between user actions and the FDAS state.

Developing the operational specification had unexpected benefits regarding personnel. Programmers generally prefer to work on design and implementation rather than specification. The operational specification gave developers the opportunity to work with specification using the more precise procedural notation, with which they were more comfortable. No longer was specification equated with the onerous task of documentation through the writing of a long narrative statement of system needs. Now the task was more like programming. Further, the style and precision of the specification made it easier to divide the work among staff members while understanding the connections among the parts of the specification.

The FDAS operational specification succeeded in capturing the essential element of the operational paradigm of software development. Developers were able to discuss and specify internal behavior of the system much earlier than if they used the traditional life-cycle model. The natural instincts of the staff to pursue descriptions of necessary internal system functioning were not rebuffed by unrealistic admonitions to state the "what" and not the "how" of the system. Yet, in specifying internal behavior, the developers were not claiming to have created a design; for example, they did not need to consider efficiency concerns. They created an executable specification that behaved as the system would need to do to meet its requirements.

CONCLUSIONS

The FDAS project demonstrated that the method of operational specification can be extended to embrace nonembedded systems. The resulting specification allowed the development team to make progress in understanding both the user's needs and the necessary system behavior to satisfy those needs.

Acknowledgments

The support of F. McGarry and K. Tasaki and the contributions of G. Snyder, S. Waligora, G. Klitsch, D. Solomon, and U. Saggare are gratefully acknowledged.

Appendix A—Actions in the Fdas Operational Specification

The following is a partial list of actions available in the FDAS operational specification:

- Initiating and terminating a session
  LOGON (<user-name>)
  LOGOFF
- Executing applications software
  EXECUTE (<file-owner>, <ECP-name>)
  ENTER (<text>)
- Displaying FDAS state information
  SHOW-RECORD (<file-owner>, <file-name>,
    <record-name>)
  SHOW-ITEMS (<file-owner>, <file-name>,
    <show-item-list>)
  COND-SHOW-ITEMS (<file-owner>, <file-name>,
    <cond-item-#>, <match-text>,
    <show-item-list>)
- Changing FDAS state information
  CREATE-RECORD (<file-name>, <record-name>)
  DELETE-RECORD (<file-name>, <record-name>)
  COPY-RECORD (<file-name>,
    <from-file-owner>, <from-record-name>,
    <to-record-name>)
  ADD-LINE (<file-name>, <record-name>,
    <item-#>, <line-#>, <new-contents>)
  DELETE-LINE (<file-name>, <record-name>,
    <item-#>, <line-#>)
  REPLACE-LINE (<file-name>, <record-name>,
    <item-#>, <line-#>, <new-contents>)

Appendix B—Processes in the FDAS Operational Specification

For every action in Appendix A, an FDAS process exists to accomplish the action. There are also internal processes that do not correspond to actions but instead are triggered (see Figure 2) by other process descriptions. Examples of some of these internal processes are as follows:

LOGON-CHECK—Checks that user has logged on to FDAS.

ENTER-CHECK—Checks enter-enable flag of status file. If FDAS is expecting the user to enter text (for example, in response to a query), FDAS reports to the user that the action cannot be performed until text is entered.

IS-MATCH (<file-owner>, <file-name>, <record-name>, <item-#>, <match-text>)—Returns true if any line in <item-#> matches <match-text>.

QUERY (<question>, <response>)—Reports <question> to the user and suspends itself until the user gives <response> by entering text.

REPORT (<text>)—Reports <text> to user; satisfies REPORT relation in Figure 2 to provide information to the user.

IS-ACCESS-ALLOWED (<file-owner>, <file-name>, <record-name>)—Checks item 3 of records to determine if read-access is allowed.

ASSIGN-LINE (<file-owner>, <file-name>, <record-name>, <item-#>, <line-#>, <new-contents>)—Satisfies ASSIGN relation in Figure 2; changes FDAS state by assigning <new-contents> to a line in a file record.

ACCESS-LINE (<file-owner>, <file-name>, <record-name>, <item-#>, <line-#>, <contents>)—Satisfies ACCESS relation in Figure 2; obtains <contents> from a line in a file record.

Appendix C—Sample Process Description

Process descriptions are presented in the following format:

Process process-name (list of parameters)
List of relations it initiates to components in other categories

Begin
Pseudocode of the process
End—Process name

The process description for the action-handling process COND-SHOW-ITEMS, which displays items in a file conditional on a particular item matching a text string, follows. For example, the user may select COND-SHOW-ITEMS with the following parameters:

COND-SHOW-ITEMS (SYSTEM, SOFTWARE UNIT, 4, 'INTEGRATOR', (1, 2))

This action activates the action-handling process of the same name. The user is requesting the following information: From among the software units owned by the system, display the name and description (items 1 and 2) for those associated with the function (item 4) "integrator."

Process COND-SHOW-ITEMS (<file-owner>, <file-name>, <cond-item-#>, <match-text>, <show-item-list>

—Relations (potentially) initiated by this process
ACCESSES Header File, <file-name> of <file-owner>
TRIGGERS—LOGON-CHECK, ENTER-CHECK, ACCESS-LINE,
    IS-ACCESS-ALLOWED
REPORTS—User

Begin
LOGON-CHECK—To ensure that the user has logged on
ENTER-CHECK—To ensure that the system does not have a suspended process waiting for the user to execute an ENTER action
Set MATCH to FALSE
Get the number of records in <file-name> from Header File of <file-owner>
FOR each record in <file-name>
  LOOP
      IF access to the record is allowed THEN
          IF <match-text> matches any line in <cond-item-#> of record THEN
          Set MATCH to TRUE
          Report every line of all items in <show-item-list>
          END IF
      END IF
      IF NOT MATCH THEN
          REPORT ('No items match the given text')
      END IF
  END LOOP
End COND-SHOW-ITEMS

Appendix D—Record Descriptions of Files in FDAS Operational Specification

Record descriptions for the eight files in the FDAS operational specification are presented below. The owner of each file is listed in parentheses following the file name. SYSTEM refers to a file owned by the FDAS executive system; SYSTEM or User-name refers to a file that exists for the SYSTEM and each user.

File Name (Owner)	Record Item Number	Description
Status File (SYSTEM)	1	Current user name or 0 if FDAS is idle
	2	Enter-enable flag—used when FDAS is ready to accept user text via ENTER action
Valid User File (SYSTEM)	1	User-name
Header File (SYSTEM or User-name)	1	Name of file
	2	Number of items defined for file
	3	Number of records currently in file
Experiment File (SYSTEM or User-name)	1	Experiment name
	2	Experiment description
	3	Read-access flag
	4	Experiment category (e.g., orbit propagator)
	5	Names of ECPs that involve this experiment
	6	Experiment relations: Pairs of the form <function name, software unit name>
Function File (SYSTEM or User-name)	1	Function name
	2	Function description
	3	Read-access flag
	4	Names of experiments associated with
	5	Names of software units that correspond
	6	Input data items
	7	Output data items
Software Unit File (SYSTEM or User-name)	1	Software unit name
	2	Software unit description
	3	Read-access flag
	4	Function associated with
	5	Names of functions called by this software unit
	6	Name of data unit used for input data items
	7	Source text of software unit
Data Unit File (SYSTEM or User-name)	1	Data unit name
	2	Data Unit description
	3	Read-access flag
	4	Names of software units associated with
	5	Pairs of <data item, value>
ECP File (SYSTEM or User-name)	1	ECP name
	2	ECP description
	3	Read-access flag
	4	Names of experiments caled by this ECP
	5	Source text of ECP

Appendix E—Sample Operational Scenario

A typical use of FDAS would be the reconfiguration of an analytical experiment. Consider the user who wants to study the effect of a more sophisticated aerodynamic drag model on an orbit propagator. Shown below is the sequence of user actions and the responses of the FDAS operational specification.

Actions Selected by User	Explanations and Assumptions	Responses by FDAS to USER
LOGON ('ID # XXX')	Assume ID # XXX is a valid user	Displays "welcome to FDAS"
COND-SHOW-items (XXX, Experiment File, 4, ORBIT PROPAGATOR, (1,2))	Requests the name and description (items 1 and 2) of all records in Experiment File that have ORBIT PROPOGATOR as experiment category (item 4)	Displays the requested information
SHOW-RECORD (XXX, Experiment File, COWELL)	Assume user wanted to get details of the COWELL orbit propagator	Displays complete record of experiment named COWELL, including item 6 giving the functions and corresponding software units for the experiment
SHOW-RECORD (XXX, Function File, AERO DRAG)	Assume user wanted to see details of aerodynamic drag function	Displays complete record of function named AERO DRAG including item 5 giving the names of all software units corresponding to that function
REPLACE-LINE (Experiment File, COWELL, 6, 19, 'AERO DRAG, NEWDRAG')	Assume user wanted to use software unit named NEW DRAG to implement the function AERO DRAG	Displays a message confirming that COWELL experiment has been changed
EXECUTE (XXX, ORBIT TESTER)	Assume user is satisfied with the reconfigured experiment and wants to run the experiment using ECP named ORBIT TESTER	Displays results of execution

REFERENCES

Agresti, W.W, F.E. McGarry, D.N. Card, et al., *Manager's Handbook for Software Development*, SEL-84-001, Software Engineering Laboratory, NASA/Goddard Space Flight Center, April 1984

Bassett, P., and J. Giblon, "Computer Aided Programming (Part I)," *Proceedings of the IEEE SOFTFAIR*. Washington, D.C.: Computer Society Press, 1983, pp. 9-20

Card, D.N., F.E. McGarry, G. Page, et al., *The Software Engineering Laboratory*, SEL-81-104, Software Engineering Laboratory, NASA/Goddard Space Flight Center, February 1982

Levene, A.A., and G.P. Mullery, "An Investigation of Requirements Specification Languages: Theory and Practice," *Computer*, vol. 15, no. 5, May 1982, pp. 50-59

Ramamoorthy, C.V., and H.H. So, "Software Requirements and Specifications: Status and Perspectives," *Tutorial: Software Methodology*. Washington, D.C.: IEEE Computer Society Press, 1978, pp. 43-164

Scheffer, P. and T. Velez, *GSFC Software Engineering Research Requirements Analysis Study*, SEL-78-006, Software Engineering Laboratory, NASA/Goddard Space Flight Center, November 1978

Snyder, G., W. Agresti, G. Klitsch, and U. Saggare, *Operational Specifications and Requirements for the Flight Dynamics Analysis System (FDAS)*, CSC/TM-84/6108, Computer Sciences Corporation, December 1984

Zave, P., "An Operational Approach to Requirements Specification for Embedded Systems," *IEEE Transactions on Software Engineering*, vol. SE-8, No. 3, May 1982, pp. 250-269 (included in this tutorial)

Part V. Transformational Implementation

The method of transformational implementation begins with a program specification and ends with a program, in which respect it is identical to the conventional paradigm. However, progress is made between these two points by using automation to apply a series of transformations that successively alter some characteristics of the current version of the program to produce the next version. Transformations may involve specializing or generalizing the current representation, choosing a data structure, changing a control structure to improve efficiency, or countless other alterations. Ideally, all transformation rules preserve correctness, such that the final product will satisfy the original specification.

Transformational implementation is the basis for a new paradigm of software construction. The benefits of this paradigm arise from several sources:

- Automation of the application of transformations, which reduces the labor intensity of software development
- Safety of applying transformations that can be expressed formally to ensure that they preserve correctness and are free of side effects
- Effective elimination of final product testing, which is replaced by verification of the program specification (a task that should be easier because the specification is more easily expressible in the domain of the user)
- Ability to capture specialized programming knowledge in small units that can be combined to produce desired transformations
- Flexibility to include the programmer "in the loop" to help guide the selection of transformations at each iteration

Program generators are being used effectively by some companies in specific application areas, although they do not provide all of the benefits listed above. The reality of a general transformational implementation paradigm is that it is not yet a candidate for organizations to adopt as their primary means of developing large software systems. When transformational implementation becomes an effective paradigm for general use, it will have benefited from the current work, which has necessarily been focused on relatively small programs.

The articles in this section present some leading examples of these current efforts. The selections aim for broad coverage of the various approaches to program transformation.

There is a bias toward work that is likely to provoke fundamental change in the process of developing software. In contrast, research efforts that seek automation in support of the programmer's conventional life-cycle phases are not represented.*

The first article, by Partsch and Steinbrüggen, is an excellent survey of the state of the art in program transformation systems. Especially useful is the discussion of the several dimensions along which to characterize transformation systems.

Under Partsch and Steinbrüggen's category of "General Transformation Systems" is the work of Balzer and his associates at the Information Sciences Institute (ISI) of the University of Southern California. The next two articles in this section are examples of this research. First, Balzer presents a detailed example of transformational implementation. Working from a formal specification for the eight queens problem, he shows how the transformation rules are applied to generate a program.

In the second of the ISI articles, Wile considers the recording of transformation progress in an object called a program development. The subject is much more significant and intriguing than is apparent to the casual observer. With transformational implementation, it is possible to capture the sequence of transformation steps as a computer-processible object. Such a record would be invaluable as a description of the design decisions that led to a particular program.

Bauer's article is an extremely readable essay on the role of formal reasoning in program construction. His example illustrates the reasoning involved in choosing transformations at each step. The article references other work by Bauer and his colleagues at the Technical University of Munich, another center for program transformation research.

Kant and Barstow report on an implemented expert system for synthesizing programs from specifications. Coding rules and searching rules interact at each step to accomplish the transformation. An example illustrates the operation of the system.

---

*Also not included in this section are program development methods that may use a well-defined refinement procedure but are not supported by automation. For example, [Schaul 85] reports on a rigorous program development process (derived from [Linger et at. 79]) that is based on abstraction and the successive refinement and verification of both functions and data.

The final article, by Cheatham, Holloway, and Townley, is an example of a program transformation system that is part of a more comprehensive environment. The intention is to promote reusability by maintaining abstract programs that can be made concrete through the use of program transformations.

This collection of articles provides both breadth (Partsch and Steinbrüggen) and representative examples on transformational implementation. The annotated bibliography provides additional guidance to the literature on this subject.

References

Linger, R.C., H.D. Mills, and B.I. Witt, *Structured Programming: Theory and Practice*. Reading, Mass.: Addison-Wesley, 1979

Schaul, M, "Design Using Software Engineering Principles: Overview of an Educational Program," *Proceedings, 8th International Conference on Software Engineering*, Washington, D.C.: IEEE Computer Society, 1985, pp. 201-208

Program Transformation Systems

H. PARTSCH AND R. STEINBRÜGGEN

Institut für Informatik, Technische Universität München, Munich, West Germany

Interest is increasing in the transformational approach to programming and in mechanical aids for supporting the program development process. Available aids range from simple editorlike devices to rather powerful interactive transformation systems and even to automatic synthesis tools. This paper reviews and classifies transformation systems and is intended to acquaint the reader with the current state of the art and provide a basis for comparing the different approaches. It is also designed to provide easy access to specific details of the various methodologies.

Categories and Subject Descriptors: D.1.2 **[Programming Techniques]**: Automatic Programming; D.2.6 **[Software Engineering]**: Programming Environments; D.3.4 **[Programming Languages]**: Processors—*optimization*; F.3.1 **[Logics and Meanings of Programs]**: Specifying and Verifying and Reasoning about Programs—*mechanical verification*; I.1.3 **[Algebraic Manipulation]**: Languages and Systems—*special-purpose algebraic systems*; I.2.2 **[Artificial Intelligence]**: Automatic Programming; I.2.3 **[Artificial Intelligence]**: Deduction and Theorem Proving

General Terms: Algorithms, Design, Documentation, Verification

Additional Key Words and Phrases: Transformational programming, transformation system

INTRODUCTION

"The time is clearly ripe for program-manipulation systems" [Knuth 1976].

Programming is a difficult task characterized by the problem of mastering complexity. There are many steps between the analysis of a problem and its efficient solution. Even between a formal (descriptive) specification of a problem and its accommodation to a given programming environment on a particular machine, a huge gap must be bridged. There is widespread agreement that the difficulties involved in constructing correct programs can only be overcome if the whole task is broken into sufficiently small and formally justified steps. This insight is not restricted to academic circles. Industrial environments also recognize the need for formally justified software and for tools for supporting the development process. The effort to develop a programming environment for the Department of Defense language, Ada,[1] is one example of this recognition.

In any programming methodology—whether it emphasizes a "synthetic" process of deducing the program from its formal specification or a more "analytic" process of deducing properties from the already finished program—pure creativity goes hand in hand with many automatable activities. Substantial support for program

---

[1] Ada is a trademark of the U.S. Department of Defense.

Computing Surveys, Vol. 15, No. 3, September 1983

CONTENTS

———————◆———————

development can already be expected if the automatable parts are performed by a machine and the programmer is free to concentrate on the creative aspects.

Software development systems are gradually becoming indispensable devices for programming. Within this class a small subclass, that of program transformation systems, is playing an increasingly important role [Pepper 1984].

This paper surveys the present capabilities of such transformation systems and how they actually support programming. This survey is not a tutorial on the methodological background of transformational programming;[2] rather, it provides an over-

view on the state of the art for readers who already have a basic understanding of the transformational programming paradigm.

1. A GENERAL VIEW OF TRANSFORMATION SYSTEMS

Since designers' intentions differ, existing transformation systems cannot be compared readily. In this section we establish a general framework of common criteria by which such systems can be classified and compared. We start by defining, in a deliberately informal way,[3] what we mean by a "transformation system."

1.1 Basic Notions

The word "program" is to be read in its ordinary sense: A *program* is a description of a method of computation that is expressible in a formal language. A *program scheme* is the representation of a class of related programs; it originates from a program by parameterization. Programs, conversely, can be obtained from program schemes by instantiating the schema parameters. In its most general form a *transformation* is a relation between two program schemes P and P'. It is said to be *correct* (or *valid*), if a certain semantic relation holds between P and P'.

The most important semantic relation in this context is *equivalence*. Secondary relations are the *weak equivalence* or the *descendant relation*. In contrast to equivalence, weak equivalence "ignores" undefined situations for P (e.g., program nontermination, given certain input) and assumes the designer does not care what happens to erroneous data. The descendant relation is important if P is a nondeterministic program (if P may generate different results, given the same input); it means that, for the same input, the possible results of P' are included in the set of possible results of P.

In general, arbitrary semantic relations [Broy et al. 1980] could be proposed pro-

---

[2] Introductions to the basic principles of transformational programming can be found in Balzer et al. [1976], Bauer [1976], Burstall and Feather [1978],

Darlington [1979], Loveman [1977], or Manna and Waldinger [1979]; for a comprehensive treatment of the subject see Bauer and Wössner [1982].
[3] A formal treatment of the mathematical foundations may be found in Steinbrüggen and Partsch [1984].

vided they have ordering and monotonicity properties. Ordering properties, such as *reflexivity* and *transitivity*, are required to compose transformations. *Monotonicity* guarantees that the global correctness is not affected by correct local changes.

Transformation rules[4] are partial mappings from one program scheme to another such that an element of the domain and its image under the mapping constitute a correct transformation. They are represented either by some procedure (*procedural rules*) or by a pair of related schemes (*schematic rules*). *Applying a transformation rule* simply means applying the respective mapping. Since this mapping may be partial, *enabling conditions*, that is, predicates over program schemes, are used to restrict the domain of a transformation rule.

Transformational programming is a methodology of program construction by successive applications of transformation rules. Usually this process starts with a (formal) *specification*, that is, a formal statement of a problem or its solution, and ends with an executable program. The individual transitions between the various versions of a program are made by applying correctness-preserving transformation rules. It is guaranteed that the final version of the program will still satisfy the initial specification.

Although the particular emphasis in transformational programming may vary (some may emphasize correctness, others efficiency), the *constructive approach* to program development remains constant. This contrasts, for example, with pure verification approaches, where the question of how to obtain the program to be verified is ignored.

A *transformation system*, finally, is an implemented system for supporting transformational programming. Not only must one learn about technical details (input, output, mode of operation, internal representations, and implementation techniques used) but one must also understand those capabilities (such as automatic rule selection, use of efficiency information in mak-

---

[4] Frequently, these are called just *rules* or *transformations*. Sometimes they are also called *source-to-source translations*.

ing design decisions, and mechanisms for rule composition) that depend on the specific underlying philosophy.

1.2 A Framework for Classifying Transformation Systems

To compare the various systems, we introduce a multidimensional classification scheme in which each dimension represents a major issue concerning transformation systems. Within the respective dimensions (each discussed in separate subsections below), the range of variation will be marked by identifying characteristic "values" on the respective scale.

1.2.1 Intentions of Transformational Programming

Before we look at different transformational programming goals, a more global distinction among transformation systems should be made. Consider the input to a system. Some systems take as input and manipulate *fixed specifications*. Others take a tentative, incomplete specification and gradually develop it into a complete one. By their very nature, transformations in the latter, *general software development systems*, are only one tool among many, whereas in the former, *proper transformation systems*, they play the dominant role.

In addition to occupying different positions in the software development process, transformations are used to achieve different specific goals. The most common goal is that of *general support for program modification*. This includes the *optimization* of control structures, the efficient *implementation* of data structures, and the adaptation of given programs to particular styles of programming (e.g., applicative, procedural, machine oriented). If modification is not restricted to proper programs but is extended to include program schemes, the system also may be used to formally derive new transformation rules (which are correct by construction). Hence, to some extent, modification also comprises *rule generation*.

A second goal of program transformation is *program synthesis*, the generation of a program from a (formal) description of the problem. Here the respective systems vary with regard to the formulation of the input. Program synthesis may start from specifications in (restricted) natural language, from examples in some formal language, or from mathematical assertions. (Synthesis by modifying similar programs is a somewhat different approach.)

A third goal is that of *program adaptation* to particular environments. For example, the designer might want to adapt a program written in one language to a related language with different primitives.

Other goals include *program description* (by exhibiting the derivation history or by building up "family trees" of related algorithms) and deduction-oriented *verification* of programs' correctness.

1.2.2 Range of System Support

Of course, each transformation system, whether general or special purpose, has a *component for dealing with transformations.* Usually this component consists of a facility for keeping the (predefined) collection of available transformations, called a catalog, and a mechanism for applying them. Frequently, systems allow this collection to be extended by the definition of new rules, but most systems expect these new rules to be proved by the user. Only a few systems allow the proof or derivation of new rules within the system by means of built-in composition operators. Some systems also provide some form of guidance for selecting rules from the collection.

Nearly all transformation systems are *interactive.* Even the "fully automatic" ones require an initial user input and rely (interactively) on the user to resolve unexpected events. *Input/output facilities* vary with respect to the user's comfort: The spectrum ranges from ad hoc implementation-dependent interfaces to high-level structured command languages. The system's reaction to input may include automatic checks on the "reasonableness" of given commands, as well as incremental interactive parsing using correction mechanisms. Usually the output of the system is filtered and presented to the user in a well-formatted *prettyprinted* form, sometimes even annotated with further information.

Most systems also have some *facility for documenting the development process*—one of the promising aspects of the transformational approach. These facilities include internal preservation of the source program, of final output, and of all intermediate versions. The documentation itself ranges from a simple sequential log of the terminal session (*bookkeeping*) to rather sophisticated database mechanisms. The most clever of these are even able to automatically redo a particular program development starting from a (slightly) changed input—a nontrivial task, particularly if the development is not a simple linear sequence but a graphlike structure (*decision tree*). In this "automatic redo" sense, the documentation facility plays an active part in the process of transformation selection.

Assessment of programs can be supported in qualitatively different ways: The system may incorporate some execution facility, such as an interpreter or a compiler to some target level, or it may utilize aids for "testing," such as symbolic evaluators. Occasionally the system will also have tools for program analysis, either for aiding in the selection of transformation rules or simply for "measuring" the effect of some transformation.

1.2.3 Organization and Types of Transformations

Most systems have a *predefined collection of transformation rules*, which is in some sense extensible. (The PDS approach, described in Section 4.1, in which the user alone supplies the development process with suitable transformations, is a notable exception.) In principle, there are two contrary methods for keeping transformations in the system: the *catalog approach* and the *generative set approach*. The borderline between them is somewhat hazy, and there is an evident tendency to move from the former toward the latter: Recent versions of systems that originally worked with catalogs now experiment with small sets of rules supplemented by suitable tactics or strategic means for generating new, more complex rules from simpler ones.

A *catalog of rules* is a linearly or hierarchically structured collection of transformation rules relevant for a particular aspect of the development process. Catalogs may contain, for example, rules about *programming knowledge* (i.e., available solution strategies, such as "a good way to search in an ordered list is by dichotomic search"), optimizations based on *language features*, such as recursion removal or loop fusion, or rules reflecting *data domain knowledge*, such as arithmetic and Boolean algebra, arrays, or sets. Additionally, some systems have catalogs of *efficiency information* or codified knowledge for *automatic data structure selection*. Systems based on the catalog approach are also frequently referred to as *knowledge-based systems*. The main problems of the catalog approach are completeness and structure, in particular, the availability of and the rapid access to individual rules.

By a *generative set* we mean a small set of powerful elementary transformations to be used as a basis for constructing new rules. Since these language-independent principles cannot be complete (in the sense that all imaginable transformations cannot be produced from them), they are used in connection with further knowledge about data structures and the specific programming task. This knowledge is presented to the system as another restricted set of rules about certain object domains. If elementary transformations are additionally coupled with a rather restricted language, a certain restricted kind of completeness may be achieved. In the generative set approach the main problem is to find the order in which to apply these elementary rules to achieve some bigger transformation.

1.2.4 Forms of Transformation Rules

We have already said that a transformation rule, as a (partial) mapping from program to program, can be represented in two ways: in the form of an algorithm, taking a program and producing a new one (*procedural rule*), or as an ordered pair of program schemes (*schematic rule* or *pattern replacement rule*), usually separated by some replacement symbol such as "⇔" for equivalence or "⇒" for descendance. Although the latter, syntax-oriented representation seems better suited to human perception,

it has the disadvantage that it is badly suited for expressing semantic knowledge or global information. Consequently, the schematic representation is used mainly in connection with *local rules*, and the algorithmic form is usually employed for *global rules*.

Typical *locally* applicable rules (*refinement rules*) serve to do the following:

(1) Relate *language constructs* (*syntactic rules*),[5] such as

> L: **if** B **then** S; **goto** L **fi**
> ⇔ **while** B **do** S **od**.[6]

(2) Describe *algebraic properties* relating different language constructs, such as

> 1 + **if** B **then** x **else** y **fi**
> ⇔ **if** B **then** $1 + x$ **else** $1 + y$ **fi**.

(3) Express *domain knowledge* (*domain rules*) in the form of data-type properties, such as

$$\text{pop}(\text{push}(s, x)) \Leftrightarrow s$$

$$\text{(for unbounded stacks } s\text{),}$$

or

$$b \wedge b \Leftrightarrow b \quad \text{(for Booleans } b\text{).}$$

Global rules, sometimes also called *semantic rules*, make up flow analysis, consistency checks, global cleanup operations, or representation of programming techniques and paradigms, such as the "divide-and-conquer" technique.

There are also hybrids between local and global rules used to codify certain *programming knowledge*. Two common hybrids are the UNFOLD and FOLD rules:

> UNFOLD is the replacement of a call by its body, with appropriate substitutions.
> FOLD is the inverse transformation, the replacement of some piece of code by an equivalent function or procedure call.

Hybrids are also used to represent *implementation details* (*implementation rules*),

---

[5] They even may be used for the formal definition of the semantics of a language [Pepper 1979].
[6] For denoting language constructs we use a self-explanatory ALGOL-like language.

Computing Surveys, Vol. 15, No. 3, September 1983

such as "a bounded stack may be represented by an array and an index variable."

1.2.5 Performance of the Transformation Process

All program transformation systems successively apply elementary transformation rules. The systems' differences lie in *user control*, that is, in the amount of work that is required from the user.

Obviously the simplest implementation is one that makes the *user responsible* for every single transformation step. Such an approach is only practical if the system provides some means for building up compact and powerful transformation rules, such as *remove recursion* or *implement data structure*.

Fully automatic systems, on the other hand, enable the selection and application of appropriate rules to be completely determined by the system using built-in heuristics, machine evaluation of different possibilities, or other strategic considerations. Such systems, however, work satisfactorily only for restricted domains of application.

Between the two extremes lie the *semiautomatic systems*, which, for predefined subtasks, work autonomously; however, for unsolvable problems the user becomes responsible. Usually these systems offer the user assistance in evaluating criteria for design decisions, depending either on the program version alone or on some predefined goal as well.

In addition to the different rule selection mechanisms, there are different techniques for *matching*, that is, for identifying the concrete instances of a certain rule. The simplest case is *first-order matching*, where only instances of object variables (*ordinary scheme parameters*) must be identified. If program schemes having both object and function variables are used, *second-order matching* is necessary.[7] Second-order matching is a more flexible and powerful technique, but unlike first-order matching, which is completely mechanizable, second-order matching sometimes needs assistance by the user.

---

[7] For a theoretical treatment of second-order matching, see the work by Huet and Lang [1978].

Matching can be also done in technically different ways. *Pattern-directed invocation*, a technique like that provided by QLISP, where applicable rules are identified if their left-hand sides match some piece of the currently considered program, or *anchored patterns*, which we describe later in Section 5.2.2., are typical examples.

In all systems the set of rules is supplemented by additional "advice" on how to apply them, at least in the form of *enabling conditions* for guaranteeing correct application. Other additions include *strategic conditions*, information for selecting rules that depends on some goal to be achieved; *assertions*, properties of the objects of manipulation; *continuation information*, which rule(s) to try next; and *information about the scope of application*, where in the program to try another rule.

1.2.6 Languages

Language sheds considerable light on a system's abilities. We are less interested in the languages used for implementation, although this is an important factor with respect to portability, but rather in the *kind* (or *style*) *of program* that is treated by the system. Although some systems are conceptually independent of a particular language, each implementation is in the end tied to a particular language.

Depending on the particular purposes of the systems, many conceptually different languages can be used as input. These languages may be separated into *specification languages*, which support the formal statement of problems, and *programming languages*, which are used for formulating solutions to problems. The borderline is hazy, since certain languages, such as the applicative languages of NPL or HOPE, may be associated with either of these categories.

Specification languages range from formalized natural language, over purely descriptive formal languages, such as mathematical notation or predicate logic, languages with both descriptive and operative constructs, such as CIP-L (Section 2.6.1), and fully operational specification languages, such as GIST (Section 2.1.3), to the aforementioned applicative languages, including also recursion equations or algebraic axioms.

For programming languages, a global distinction can be made between functionally oriented ones, such as LISP, and purely procedural ones, such as FORTRAN. Other frequently used programming languages include subsets of ALGOL, Pascal, or PL/I, which allow both applicative and procedural formulations, or particular languages such as EL1, CIP-L, or MENTOL (Section 4.2).

Data structures differ in how they are incorporated into the language: The languages either have fixed data types or provide mechanisms for generating new types.

Which kind of (input) language is used depends on the particular methodology and the specific purpose of the respective system. For the same reason the "output languages" differ. Whereas input and output language will be the same for systems aiming primarily at optimization, they will differ for synthesis systems.

1.2.7 *Range of Applicability*

From a practical viewpoint, the most interesting aspect of a transformation system is the range of problems it can handle. That this range may be too limited is a main source of criticism of the transformational approach (see Dijkstra [1976a]). In principle, there is no such limitation. However, all the described transformation systems originated in research institutions and, at present, must be considered mainly as experimental tools with restricted abilities.

A precise statement on the relative power of each system is impossible, owing to the lack of detailed technical information. We confine ourselves to giving an impression of each system's capabilities by indicating which examples it has successfully treated.

1.3 About This Survey

It is difficult to contrast transformation systems to related systems such as *general AI systems* [Biermann 1976], *production systems* [Davis and King 1975], *expert systems* [Michie 1979, 1981], *verification systems* [Igarashi et al. 1975], *data structure selection systems* [Low 1978; Schonberg et

al. 1979], or general software development environments [Hesse 1981; Hünke 1981]. As the main criterion for inclusion we have concentrated on systems having a proper *transformation component*. There still remain systems that fall exactly on the borderline, such as Hewitt's PLANNER [Hewitt 1971]. Occasionally, to provide background information, we also report on side developments (within bigger projects), even though they are not transformation systems in the strict sense. Furthermore, to be included in the survey, at least part of the system should actually be *implemented*.[8]

It is difficult to favor any one of the criteria given in the previous section. In contrast to an earlier work [Partsch and Steinbrüggen 1981] on the subject of this paper, we decided here to first distinguish proper transformation systems from general software development systems. Within the transformation systems, we further separated general systems from special-purpose ones. We are fully aware, though, that our classification is arbitrary (as is any other).

Within the respective section on each system, we give a brief summary of its overall performance and then concentrate on its specific properties in detail. Instead of ignoring the nomenclature of each system, we relate it to the notions introduced above, to ease the reader's access to the original literature.

2. GENERAL TRANSFORMATION SYSTEMS

In this section we review some transformation systems that we classify as general systems. They are restricted neither to a particular aspect of the software development process nor to specific kinds of transformation rules. Even though the published material does not explicitly stress their generality, it can be inferred from the basic system concept.

2.1 The SAFE/TI Project at ISI

The activities headed by R. Balzer at the Information Science Institute (ISI) in Los

---

[8] In this respect, we have relied mainly on published information.

Angeles emerged from earlier ideas on automatic programming [Balzer 1973]. ISI's activities aim at machine support for software development and are organized into two projects: The first, SAFE (Specification Acquisition From Experts [Wile et al. 1977; Balzer et al. 1978]), deals with the synthesis of formal specifications from informal ones, and the second, TI (Transformational Implementation) [Balzer et al. 1976], concentrates on the derivation of efficient programs from formal specifications by means of transformations.

2.1.1 The SAFE System

The basis for the SAFE synthesis system is the observation that precise formal and accurate specifications are not only difficult to write by hand, but are also hard to understand owing to the enormous amount of detail. Partial problem descriptions, on the other hand, focus both the writer's and reader's attention on the relevant issues and thus condense a specification. SAFE is an effort to provide a mechanism for resolving the ambiguity introduced into a specification by partial descriptions and for incorporating refinements of, and modifications to, structures produced from the text of a specification.

The input to SAFE is an informal description of the problem and its solution in a natural language, which is parenthesized to avoid parsing problems. This input first passes through a linguistic phase where it is translated into a series of *event descriptors*. These descriptors correspond approximately to procedure definitions that are built from basic actions and relations known to the system as either primitives or domain-specific actions. Typical types of basic event descriptors are *events* from verbs, *objects* and *sets* from nouns and plurals, and *conditionals*, *conjunctions*, and *loops* from verbs with set objects. The planning phase looks at the partial sequencing information contained in the input, then determines the overall operation sequencing for the program outline. In the next phase, *actions* are defined as sequences or refinements of events. And in the final phase, the fine details are resolved by symbolic evaluation (*metaevaluation*) to produce the formal specification.

SAFE tries to find out what the user means. Like an "intelligent reader," it performs a number of elementary tasks, such as finding missing operands, performing implicit coercions, or detecting terminology changes. If any ambiguity cannot be solved automatically, SAFE asks for the user's intention. SAFE tests the "adequacy" of the resulting formal specification by checking heuristics that assess its semantic reasonableness.

Examples handled by SAFE include a message processor and components of a satellite communication system [Balzer et al. 1978].

2.1.2 The TI Project

The TI project provides technologies for automating aspects in the second part of the software development process to bridge the gap between a formal specification and its implementation as an efficient program. Developing an implementation from a specification is seen as a continuous process of applying transformations, either to replace pure specification constructs with algorithmic ones [London and Feather 1981] or to simplify algorithmic constructs. The result of this process is a program in a subset of the specification language GIST (Section 2.1.3), which is automatically translatable into an existing programming language.

The main activity of the transformation process is the programmer's selection of appropriate transformations from a pre-existing catalog. If an appropriate transformation does not yet exist in the catalog, the programmer may either extend the catalog or modify the program directly through an interactive editor. In either case the responsibility for the correctness of a transformation rests with the user. The transformations in the catalog [Balzer et al. 1976] include UNFOLD, certain domain-dependent transformations such as $x \in \{y : p(y)\} \Leftrightarrow p(x)$ for sets, different forms of loop merging, rules for conditionals, and substitution of data structures with their representation. In this latter substitution transformation, both the objects and their characteristic operations must be replaced. An interesting aspect of TI with respect to transformation application is *jittering*: TI automatically modifies a program to match a transformation that previously failed to match because of some technical detail.

The system, implemented in INTER-LISP, tries to relieve some of the implementor's burden by providing

- an interactive transformation engine, a mechanism for applying selected transformations to the program being developed (provided by POPART; see Section 2.1.3);
- support for the development process, such as source-text maintenance or *bookkeeping* (see PADDLE, Section 2.1.3), that is, automatic documentation that allows one to redo a development using a modified specification;
- a catalog of transformations reflecting the knowledge of how to implement certain specification constructs or certain optimization techniques;
- a mechanism for translating the fully developed program into some target language.

Examples that have been treated within the TI approach include, among others, several versions of a line justifier [Balzer 1977], a text editor [Balzer et al. 1976], a text compressor [Wile 1981b], the "eight-queens" problem [Balzer 1981b], and a package router [London and Feather 1981].

2.1.3 Further Activities

Most of the tools for developing programs within the TI approach have been produced by Wile's POPART (Producer of Parsers and Related Tools) system [Wile 1981a]. These tools include, notably, a parser, editors, and the system for performing transformations. It should be noted that this system does not depend on a particular language but produces these tools for an arbitrary context-free language.

Currently, transformations are applied sequentially in the TI system. Ideas for imposing some structure on the development, in order to model the developer's

thoughts more appropriately, are condensed in PADDLE (POPART's Development Language) [Wile 1981b]. PADDLE contains primitive commands such as "apply transformation" and a facility for specifying goal structures. These facilities are intended to support a global strategy for program development along a goal/refinement structure. This attempt to impose structure on the collection of transformations contributes to the solution of the catalog-oriented approach's administrative problem. It also supports reimplementation as another benefit. Since POPART is language independent, it can be applied to PADDLE, which means that programs in the development language themselves can be manipulated via POPART.

Work in the TI project also concentrates on a specification language called GIST [Goldman and Wile 1980; Balzer, 1981a], which was developed to

- provide the flexibility and ease of expression necessary for describing the full range of acceptable system behaviors;
- be *wide spectrum*, that is, to be not only a reasonable specification language, but also an implementation language for describing efficient programs whose behavior coincides with the specification. (Here "implementation" is to be understood in an abstract sense, since at a certain level automatic translation is desired.)

A GIST specification is a formal description of valid behaviors of systems. It is composed of a set of states (determined by object types and relations between them), transition between states (defined by asynchronous responses to stimuli also known as actions and demons), and a set of constraints on states and state transitions. GIST's main effort has been to provide formal equivalents of the specificational expressiveness of natural languages. The expressive capabilities of GIST include historical reference to past process states, a relational and associative data model, and an *inference* global declaration for describing relationships among data. Because all constructs in GIST are operational, it can be used for *rapid prototyping* [Balzer et al. 1982; Cohen et al. 1982; Feather 1982a] by allowing operational simulation models of an intended system to be run with test data.

2.1.4 The GLITTER System

Within the TI environment, the GLITTER system (GoaL-directed jITTERer) [Fickas 1982] was designed to partially automate the design process of mapping an abstract program into an efficient, compilable one. In the GLITTER approach, recording a formal machine-usable history of the design process (including design goals and subgoals, competing methods, and selection criteria used to reach an implementation) plays an important role.

Program development with GLITTER begins with the user stating (in GIST) some design goal to a *problem solver*, which in turn either asks the user for details or checks its (extensible) *method catalog*. This catalog of methods for achieving goals contains both source-to-source transformations (*tactical knowledge*) and planning techniques (*strategic knowledge*). If there are several applicable methods, GLITTER uses the *selection rule catalog* to decide which to choose. Methods are ordered not only by the current planning state, but also by postplanning states. The *applier* applies the chosen method, thereby changing the problem state and recording it in the *history*.

The basic methods to be applied are essentially the same as those in the TI approach, methods for mapping specification freedoms, checking applicability conditions, or simplifying by jittering. These simplification methods, unlike the automatic invocation in PADDLE, are user invoked.

The GLITTER system is not fully automatic. The user is expected to guide the overall development by providing development goals for GLITTER to achieve. Besides providing development organization, the user also will probably be asked to supply information that is unavailable to the system and to fill in the missing portions of the respective catalogs.

GLITTER is implemented in Hearsay-III, a framework for constructing knowledge-based expert systems. In addition to implementing numerous toy examples,

GLITTER has been successfully used to develop a controller for a mechanical postal package router. In the router development, the system was able to generate automatically a significant number of steps of the development.

2.2 The PSI System

The PSI system (produced mainly at Stanford [Green 1976, 1977, 1978; Green et al. 1979]) is a large LISP system designed to synthesize efficient programs. PSI takes as its input a specification obtained from a dialogue with the user, which includes natural language or partial traces of computations (with sample input–output pairs being a special case). It is designed as a collection of knowledge-based *experts* for various tasks. One group of experts, the *acquisition group*, is responsible for acquiring specifications from the user. The group consists on an English parse–interpreter, a trace expert, a discourse expert, and an application domain expert, all of which extract information from the dialogue and convert it into program fragments that serve as input for another acquisition expert, the program model builder. This model builder, in turn, produces a complete *program model* and uses that model as its interface to the *synthesis group*, consisting of a coding expert and an efficiency expert.

2.2.1 The Program Model Builder

The main role of PMB (Program Model Builder) [McCune 1977, 1979] is to build a complete and consistent *program model*, an abstract, implementation-independent, annotated program in a high-level language, corresponding to the desires of the user. The inputs to PMB are program fragments, which may be incomplete, ambiguous, inconsistent, and arbitrarily ordered. Building such a complete model is an incremental process of extracting information and then updating a partial model. While updating, PMB also performs appropriate consistency checks to ensure a legal (with respect to the language semantics) and correct (with respect to the user's intention) model. If any problem cannot be resolved within PMB itself, it asks the other acquisition experts or, finally, the user for advice.

PMB's expertise is implemented in INTERLISP as a set of approximately 200 procedural rules, scheduled by a rule interpreter. These rules also include knowledge of program-model equivalence transformations to map equivalent expressions into a canonical form.

2.2.2 The Coding Expert

The coding expert, called PECOS [Barstow 1977c, 1979a] takes an abstract program description produced by PMB and successively refines this description by applying transformation rules that reflect coding knowledge. The description consists of essentially two parts:

- a collection of about 400 transformation rules about symbolic programming [Barstow 1979c] organized as an extensible knowledge base [Barstow, 1977a, 1977b];
- a task-oriented control structure based on the paradigm of developing programs by successive refinements.

The extensible catalog contains rules of essentially three types: *refinement rules* containing the coding knowledge, *property rules* to specify additional properties of a program description, and *query rules* to answer the experts' queries about a description, used to ensure the applicability of other rules. The refinement rules represent only the coding knowledge about the particular domain of symbolic programming. Early ideas on how to combine this knowledge-based approach with deduction-oriented ones can be found in Barstow's work [1979b]. The transformation rules in the catalog deal with general program constructs such as implementation for iterators or correspondences, with particular domains such as data representation or task-specific knowledge, or with properties of the target language such as table-oriented implementations for correspondences, linked-list or array representations for sets, and rules for enumeration [Barstow 1979c; Green and Barstow 1975, 1978].

The development essentially consists of a step-by-step successive refinement of the program description until a running LISP program[9] evolves. Both the algorithm and the data structure are refined interdependently. To drive a refinement, PECOS uses a simple task-oriented control structure. In each cycle a task (*refine, property, query*) is selected, and a rule is applied to the task. While PECOS is working on a given task, it may generate subtasks, which are handled in a last-in, first-out manner. When several rules are applicable, the refinement is split, with each rule applied in a different branch of the tree of program descriptions. The root of this tree is the original specification, the tree's leaves are programs in the target language, and each path from the root to a leaf constitutes a refinement sequence; thus the entire tree actually represents a family of algorithms [Green and Barstow 1978].

The critical issue in the whole approach is the size of this tree of partially developed programs. To keep the tree to a reasonable size, certain possible refinement steps are rejected and usually only one path is taken, following advice from the user, some heuristics, and the automated efficiency expert.

2.2.3 The Efficiency Expert

The purpose of the efficiency expert, LIBRA [Kant 1977, 1979], is to give advice to the coding expert and thus help make design decisions. LIBRA provides techniques for pruning the tree of partially refined programs and for directing the order of further expansion of the tree. Its expertise is codified in an extensible knowledge base of approximately 100 rules. New rules can be derived semiautomatically from new transformations or can be gained by asking appropriate questions of the user. A typical new rule would be a *planning* rule, derived from the previous analyses of how to make particular implementation decisions. Other examples include rules for grouping related decisions, and rules about scheduling and resource allocation that reflect the importance of a coding decision and of its expected consequence.

---

[9] The program is actually written in a subset of INTERLISP. There have also been experiments with other target languages, such as SAIL [Barstow 1977b].

For each decision not made by planning rules, LIBRA uses flow analysis and incrementally computes upper and lower bounds on the estimated costs. For this cost analysis LIBRA occasionally needs additional information from the user about things such as the number of elements in a set or the probabilities of the alternatives of a branching instruction. From this information LIBRA then computes measures such as the average storage requirement or the average number of times a loop is executed. LIBRA maintains its cost analysis of a program at every level of refinement for comparison between different refinements or branch-and-bound search. In particular, this cost analysis identifies parts that will lead to a bottleneck in the refinement process, so that refinement resources can be concentrated on those parts.

2.2.4 The Synthesis Phase

The synthesis phase of PSI also can be used as an independent subsystem, PSI/SYN, for transforming specifications given in the model builder's formal high-level language [Kant and Barstow 1981]. Here, in contrast to earlier ideas [Barstow and Kant 1976], the roles of PECOS and LIBRA are interchanged: Whereas in the earlier concept PECOS asked LIBRA for its advice, now part of LIBRA's knowledge, the *searching knowledge*, is used in each stage of refinement to call on either the coding rules to generate legal refinements or the cost-estimation rules to provide an evaluation function for the alternative implementations.

2.2.5 Experiences

The examples treated within the PSI efforts all were of moderate size. They comprised number-theoretic algorithms for computing prime numbers [Barstow 1979a; Kant and Barstow 1981], set algorithms [Barstow and Kant 1976], concept formation [Barstow 1979a; McCune 1977], a simple learning program [Kant 1977], a simple retrieval program [Kant 1979], and an algorithm dealing with the reachability of nodes in graphs [Barstow 1979a]. A hypothetical dialogue with the system for synthesizing a sorting program for linked lists

(70 steps, 150 transformations) can be found in work by Green and Barstow [1976]. Later, they approach the sorting problem again [Barstow 1979a; Green and Barstow 1978] and derive a whole family of sorting algorithms.

2.2.6 The CHI System and the Algorithm Design Project

The CHI system (for a collection of individual papers see Green et al. [1982]) is a more recent attempt to use some of the PSI technology, specifically that of PECOS and LIBRA, to build a knowledge-based programming environment. Instead of autonomous experts, though, CHI uses a homogeneous collection of tools sharing common databases. These tools enable the user to query all parts of the environment in a uniform way.

The major system components are

• an object-oriented database of programming knowledge that contains static refinement rules (for implementing sets, mappings, enumerations in terms of lists, arrays, hash tables, etc.) and a dynamic program-refinement workspace;
• the *knowledge-base manager*, a database that enables contexts and multiple versions and that manages the file utilities for storing and loading from disk storage;
• a structure-based editor used to modify programs and synthesis rules;
• an agenda mechanism to control user guidance and heuristic search.

CHI's essential difference from the former PSI system is its use of a more humanly readable wide-spectrum language, called *V.* that covers both high-level program specification and programming knowledge (synthesis rules, synthesis plans, constraints on programs). The primitives in V include sets, mappings, relations, enumerations, and state transformation sequences. Both declarative and procedural statements are allowed, as are facts about program efficiency or algorithm analysis. V is *uniformly extensible*, in that it allows continuous change and development of the objects used in programming.

Synthesis rules can be applied by name, by effect, or by analogy (by indicating a related rule having a similar effect). With respect to naming by effect, CHI shows some analogies to GLITTER (Section 2.1.4).

CHI is a *self-described programming environment*, meaning that the environment itself is described in terms that the modification rules understand. Consequently, the environment may be modified using the tools it, itself, provides.[10] Adding new rules to this system, therefore, does not necessarily imply a decrease in performance due to increased search time, but may even increase performance.

CHI has successfully been used to redevelop the system's rule compiler and has resulted in a program that is ten times shorter than the original one [Green et al. 1982]. Other, less comprehensive examples were several programs of differing complexity for computing even squares.

Strongly connected to the CHI activities is the Algorithm Design project [Green et al. 1982], which is aimed at providing tools to assist the user in the more creative aspects of new algorithms development. As an intermediate result, a set of *methods* has been formalized and partly implemented in CHI. In these methods, algorithm design principles are expressed in the form of *synthesis plans* (or *paradigm algorithms* [Darlington 1981b]). Typical of such principles are *generator incorporation* (usually known as *filter promotion* [Darlington 1981a]), *divide-and-conquer*, and *store versus recompute* (better known as *dynamic programming* [Aho et al. 1974] or *tabulation techniques* [Bird, 1980]).

Examples of problems that the Algorithm Design project has tackled include the *shortest path in a graph* problem and different versions of *prime finding*.

2.3 The Edinburgh School

Whereas the systems described in the previous sections are based on the catalog approach, the systems described below rely on the generative set approach.

2.3.1 The Early Work of Darlington and Burstall

The early work of Darlington and Burstall [Darlington 1972; Darlington and Burstall

1973, 1976] was based on a schema-driven method for transforming applicative recursive programs into imperative ones with improving efficiency as the ultimate goal. The system worked largely automatically, according to a set of built-in rules, with only a small amount of user control. The rules were complex transformations, including recursion removal, elimination of redundant computations, unfolding, and structure sharing. The main objection to this very early system was the incompleteness of the rule set, on one hand, and the difficulty of extension, on the other.

2.3.2 The Work of Burstall and Darlington

On the basis of experiences gained with their first system, in particular the observation that significant improvements can and should be done on an applicative level of formulation, Burstall and Darlington [1975, 1977] implemented a second system. This system, implemented in POP-2, was designed to manipulate applicative programs.

Their second system is a typical representative of the generative set approach and consists of only six rules: *definition*, *instantiation*, *unfolding*, *folding*, *abstraction*, and *laws* (actually a set of data-structure-specific rules). The basic idea of this system, the *unfold/fold method*, is simple but nevertheless rather powerful. Definition allows the introduction of new functions (in the form of recursion equations), which may be additionally structured using abstraction. After unfolding calls on the right-hand side of the equations, the right-hand sides may be further manipulated using substitution instances (introduced by instantiation) and the laws. These manipulations always try to allow a subsequent folding and thus an independent definition of a new and (it is to be hoped) more efficient function.

The theoretical background of the unfold/fold method—including sophisticated criteria to guarantee total correctness for folding—has been studied by Kott [1978, 1982].

In addition to synthesizing functions defined by implicit equations, the system is designed to improve user-provided func-

---

[10] The problem of correctness preservation is the user's responsibility.

tions. The user presents these functions as an appropriate set of explicit equations, written in a slightly restricted subset of NPL, an applicative language for first-order recursion equations [Burstall 1977]. The output of the system is again a program in NPL, but a less complex one (e.g., tree-like recursion will have been transformed into tail recursion).

The system works largely automatically, using *forced folding*. Within the currently considered equation, the system proposes foldings that the user either accepts or rejects, asking for another proposal. The user's duty is to supply the system with appropriate definitions and to provide clever ideas in the form of *Eurekas*.

The user must also supply laws for the data structures, give explicit reduction rules, preset switches to control the system's search for folds, and allow or disallow generalizations of expressions during the unfold/apply-law/fold process.

Examples of programs that have been treated with this system include algorithms for computing Fibonacci numbers or Cartesian products, an algorithm for diagonal search, a string-matching algorithm [Darlington 1981a], set algorithms [Darlington 1975], and the synthesis of sorting algorithms [Darlington 1978]. Ideas for using the unfold/fold method to develop implementations of abstract types can be found in work by Darlington and Moor [Darlington 1978; Moor and Darlington 1981].

2.3.3 The ZAP System

The ZAP system [Feather 1978a, 1979, 1982b] is based on the Burstall/Darlington system with a special emphasis on software development by supporting large-program transformation. The principle of the system is, again, the fold/unfold method. And the input/target language of the system is the same as in the previous Burstall/Darlington system, NPL.

In contrast to its predecessors, the ZAP system substantially supports the program development by providing the user with advanced means for concisely expressing guidance. It allows the user to write *meta-programs* to be applied to NPL programs,

and thus to direct the transformation of these programs in a high-level, hierarchical fashion. An overall *transformation strategy* is hand-expanded by the user into a set of *transformation tactics* such as *combining*, *tupling*, or *generalization*. These, in turn, are expanded, with some machine assistance, into *pattern-directed transformations* (i.e., transformation rules where the user gives only the approximate form of the expected answer, in the form of a pattern, and the system fills in the missing details). The pattern-directed transformations are commands to ZAP, which the system automatically expands into sequences of elementary manipulations (essentially those of the previous Burstall/Darlington system).

Also new—compared with the former Edinburgh systems—is the possibility of restricting ZAP's search for an applicable rule. The user can specify a context by indicating equations to be used for fold/unfold, lemmas to be used during unfold, and functions that may occur within the answer. For more details on these technical aspects, see the work by Feather [1978a].

Additional features for the convenient use of the system have been incorporated. These include an extended control language, defaults (in particular, certain standard patterns for pattern-directed transformations), a bookkeeping facility (for introducing, testing, and saving program versions, and a mechanism for rerunning developments), and a *discovery* capability, with which the system is able to suggest alternative transformations.

The examples dealt with by the system range from "toy" problems to comprehensive ones such as the telegram problem [Feather 1978b], a small compiler, and a text formatter [Feather 1979]. Preliminary investigation of the use of this approach for supporting maintenance and modifications of programs can be found in joint work by Darlington and Feather [1979].

2.3.4 Recent Developments

A richer metalanguage system, based on Feather's ZAP system and experiences from the Edinburgh LCF project [Gordon et al. 1977], is now used in Darlington's system at Imperial College [Darlington 1981b]. In this system, HOPE, an applicative language based on NPL [Burstall et al. 1980] is used for the formulation of programs to be transformed and also for writing the metaprograms. These metaprograms are composed of *first-level tactics*, the basic rules of the unfold/fold system, out of which can be built the *second-level tactics*, higher level operators, such as *merge loop* or *convert-to-iteration*. Still being researched are ways to express *paradigm algorithms*, such as the general divide-and-conquer paradigm and other general strategies. This concept of unifying the development, maintenance, and modification of ordinary and metalanguage programs is the next step of importance in research on transformational programming. A feeling for this advanced methodology may be obtained by studying the Hammings problem example [Darlington, 1981b].

2.4 Stanford Transformation Systems

The Stanford University work on program transformations, like the Edinburgh activities, can be best understood when broken into different phases, according to the techniques applied and the purposes of the program transformations.

2.4.1 The Work of Dershowitz and Manna

On the basis of their previous work [Dershowitz and Manna 1975], Dershowitz and Manna [1977] implemented a system in QLISP (an extension of INTERLISP with pattern-directed function invocation and backtracking) for modifying programs by using transformations. The basic idea of this approach is to find an *analogy* between the specification of an already constructed program and that of the program to be constructed. This analogy is then used as a basis for transforming the existing program to meet the new specification. This process is performed in three major steps:

(1) First, in a *premodification phase*, the old program is hand-annotated with assertions that constitute its specification. This specification and that of the intended new program are then rephrased (in a user–

system dialogue) to bring out their similarities.

(2) Then, in the *modification phase*, the system discovers the analogy between the old and the new specifications, and presents it to the user in the form of a set of transformations. Some of the transformations must be checked for validity; if valid, they are then applied to the old program. Applying valid transformations might result in unexecutable statements, as could be the case if a variable were replaced by an expression that then showed up on the left side of an assignment. Then the user must rewrite these statements into executable ones.

(3) Finally, in the *postmodification phase*, again performed interactively with the user, code for unachieved parts of the new specification is added and the new program is further optimized, if possible.

The examples treated with the system were simple numerical problems, such as the transformation from "bad" real division to "good" real division and array-manipulation problems, such as the search for the minimal element. More recent theoretical considerations on the same topic can be found in work by Dershowitz [1980, 1981].

2.4.2 The DEDALUS System

The DEDALUS system (DEDuctive ALgorithm Ur-Synthesizer) by Manna and Waldinger [1978a, 1979], earlier referred to as the SYNSYS system [Manna and Waldinger 1977a, 1977b], is also implemented in QLISP. Its goal is to derive LISP programs automatically and deductively from high-level input–output specifications in a LISP-like representation of mathematical–logical notation.

The task of synthesizing a program can be viewed as that of achieving some goal expressed in the specification. By use of meaning-preserving transformations, this goal is modified in steps until nonprimitive constructs of the specification language have been replaced by equivalent LISP constructs.

The truth or falsity of the respective enabling conditions is established using the system's *theorem-proving rules*. If a condition cannot be proved, a conditional expression is introduced by case analysis (*conditional introduction rule*). Superfluous synthesis of conditionals is avoided by using the *redundant-test stategy*.

If, among the consecutive subgoals, the system recognizes an instance of the top-level goal, and if termination is guaranteed, the system introduces a recursive call (*recursion formation rule*, the same as FOLD, described in Section 1.2.4). Similarly, instances of lower level goals trigger the system to introduce and call auxiliary functions (*procedure-formation rule*).

The transformations, QLISP programs, include knowledge about the programming language or programming techniques and rules expressing facts about certain subject domains. In addition to the logical enabling conditions, the transformation rules are supplemented by strategic conditions and ordered to prevent foolish applications.

DEDALUS is able to create a program, a correctness proof, and a proof of termination (via well-founded sets) simultaneously for programs not involving mutual recursion. To achieve a certain subgoal, DEDALUS selects candidate rules by *pattern-directed invocation* (see Section 1.2.5) and tries those rules sequentially, according to their ordering. DEDALUS selects the transformation that best substantiates the termination proof. If no rule applies to a given subgoal, DEDALUS automatically backtracks using the backtracking directly available from QLISP. The synthesis fails if the system runs out of backtracking possibilities and succeeds if the system can achieve all goals. The output of a successful synthesis is a running LISP program.

In addition to describing a not yet implemented *generalization rule*, incorporating the knowledge that a slightly general goal is sometimes easier to achieve than any given particular goal, Manna and Waldinger [1979] also outline how to integrate their earlier ideas about variables, loops, and side effects in program synthesis [Manna and Waldinger 1975, 1978b]. In essence, this integration would lead to an extension of the specification language to allow sequential subgoals and the formulation of side effects. It would also require

extending DEDALUS by corresponding elementary transformations such as the *variable-assignment rule*, rules for the *wp-operator* [Dijkstra 1976b], and further technical rules for coping with the interaction between these new rules and those already in the system. Parts of these additional rules have been implemented in a separate system [Waldinger 1977].

Although based on only a few general principles, the DEDALUS system actually contains more than a hundred individual transformations. By the introduction of new rules, the system can be simply expanded to handle a new subject domain.

DEDALUS is considered by its designers to be a laboratory tool rather than a practical tool. Hence the examples that have been treated by DEDALUS are in some sense toy examples: different versions of the greatest-common-divisor function, the modulo function, some list algorithms (maximum number of elements, intersection of two lists, or relation of one element to all others), and basic set operations, such as union or intersection.

2.4.3 Recent Work

Recently, Manna and Waldinger [1980] have come up with ideas for a new, not-yet implemented, deduction-oriented synthesis system. This new approach regards program synthesis as a theorem-proving task and relies on a method that combines unification, mathematical induction, and transformation rules.

The basic entity in the new system is a structural unit called a *sequent*, consisting of assertion and goal specifications written in first-order logic and output expressions formulated in a LISP-like language. The meaning of such a sequent is that, if all instances of each of the assertions are true, some instance of at least one of the goals is true and the corresponding instance of its output expression satisfies the respective specification.

The system operates by adding new assertions and goals and their corresponding new output expressions to the sequent without changing its meaning. New entries in a sequent can be constructed from existing ones by means of logical rules, such as those for splitting conjunctions or disjunctions, transformation rules, resolution rules for eliminating certain subexpressions, polarity strategies for restricting the resolution rules, and mathematical induction. In addition, rules already available in the DEDALUS system can be used, such as recursion formation rules, generalization, and formation of auxiliary procedures.

This new system has simpler structure and greater flexibility (e.g., in searching for applicable rules) than does the DEDALUS system. Although they exceed the capabilities of the DEDALUS system, the examples that have been treated (quotient of two integers, last element of a list) belong to the same class of toy problems. Recently, a more interesting example, an algorithm for unification [Manna and Waldinger 1981], has been treated along the proposed derivation technique.

2.5 The PUC System

Arsac's system [Arsac 1978] was designed to interactively manipulate imperative programs formulated in a language containing conditionals, iteration with nested exits, and basic assignment and input/output statements. It is currently used at the Institut de Programmation in Paris and was first implemented in SNOBOL at the Pontificia Universidade Catolica (PUC) de Rio de Janeiro.

Transformations are applied sequentially, and the user must indicate both the transformation and the program location at which it is to be applied. If a specified transformation step violates the applicability condition, an error message is displayed and the user is asked for another transformation. Because there is an inverse for each (syntactic) transformation, previous development steps can be restored in the case of a blind alley.

To avoid retrieval problems, the catalog of transformations is deliberately small and does not contain more involved transformations, such as changing data structure representations. The tools for performing transformations, though, are sufficiently flexible and powerful to cope with the more

involved transformations if necessary. There are approximately 50 transformation rules in the system, falling into five categories:

(1) *Syntactic transforms* are source-to-source transformations that preserve the flow of computation and are entirely checked by the system. They were first suggested by Arsac [1974] and were proved to be complete by Cousineau [1976]. A more detailed treatment can be found in the later work of Arsac [1979]. These rules comprise interchanging of the **if–fi** construct and other statements (*simple absorption*), moving statements into and out of loops (*simple expansion, false iteration*), rearrangement of loops (*inversion*), loop unrolling (*repetition*), and reduction of nested loops into single ones (*double iteration*).

(2) *Regular program equations* [Arsac 1977a] form a system of parameterless procedures (*actions*) without local variables, which are connected by terminal calls that may only appear as the last action of a statement body. The rules for solving such regular program equations are substitution, replacement of tail recursion by iteration, and elimination of dead code.

(3) There are two possibilities for dealing with nonterminal recursion, both of which simulate the stack mechanism by explicitly keeping track of the flow of control, either by using a system-generated activation counter or by using a user-defined discriminating predicate.

(4) *Local semantic transforms* are source-to-source transformations that change the flow of computation but rely on local program properties. Defining these transforms is the user's own responsibility, and they can include rules for assignment combination, loop simplification, the removal of unreachable alternatives, and the elimination of redundant tests.

(5) The *editing rules* include *prettyprinting* and unchecked textual modifications.

One strategy for using these basic transformations is to "translate the program into actions, build up a system of regular program equations, and solve that regular system"; this strategy has been applied to recursion removal [Arsac and Kodratoff

1979]. Owing to the possibility of unrestricted textual modification,[11] the system is powerful. Examples that have been treated with the proposed methodology[12] include a sorting program, the Chinese Rings (*Baguenaudier* [Arsac 1978]), permutations in lexicographical order, partitions [Arsac 1979], tree printing, Towers of Hanoi, Fibonacci numbers [Arsac and Kodratoff 1979, 1982], Ackermann's function [Arsac 1977b], and others [Arsac 1977a].

2.6 The Munich CIP Project

A research group directed by F. L. Bauer and the late K. Samelson at the Technical University of Munich also concentrates on the transformational approach to programming (for an overview see work by Bauer and others [Bauer 1976; Bauer and Wössner 1982; Möller et al. 1983]). The project, called CIP (Computer-aided, Intuition-guided Programming), consists of two main parts: the design of a programming language and the development of a program-transformation system.[13]

The project focuses on correctness-preserving, source-to-source program transformations at all levels of formulation, ranging from nonalgorithmic specifications, via purely applicative formulations, to imperative and even machine-oriented styles. This work also includes corresponding transformations on the data structure side.

The algorithmic language, CIP-L [Bauer et al. 1978, 1981a, 1981b], was especially designed for the methodology of transformational programming just described. CIP-L is a *wide-spectrum language* comprising all the aforementioned different styles of programming within one coherent syntactic and semantic frame. It is a *scheme language* (i.e., a language without a fixed set of basic data types) based on a suitably defined, treelike, abstract data type. Moreover, it is an abstract language with several

concrete representations (e.g., ALGOL- or Pascal-like dialects). A small kernel language of CIP-L is defined by a mathematical semantics. All other language constructs are viewed as extensions of that kernel, made by *definitional transformations* [Pepper 1979]. The language is described as a hierarchy of algebraic abstract data types [Broy et al. 1982]: The syntax of the language defines a term algebra, context conditions form predicates in this algebraic theory, and conditional equations (corresponding to transformation rules with enabling conditions) define the semantics. This algebraic language definition not only allows a modular description but also makes it easy to extend the language.

To provide a homogeneous formal basis for the whole transformational approach, the CIP transformation system, too, is founded on an algebraic view of the program-formulating language and is itself specified in a hierarchical algebraic way. This has the particular advantage that both the definition of the system and its implementation are independent of a particular language. The running prototype of the CIP-system operates on abstract trees [Luckmann 1979]. Within this prototype, programs in every language having both an appropriate string-to-tree precompiler and a facility for the tree-to-string retranslation can be manipulated.[14]

The purpose of the CIP system is to manipulate program schemes (of which concrete programs are a special case). Program schemes are terms of the underlying algebraic language definition, with scheme parameters as subterms. This ordinary concept of schemes (see Section 1.1) has been extended by introducing *context parameters* [Steinbrüggen 1980a], which allow the user to mark fragmentary terms (*contexts*), as well as subterms, as replaceable. In this way, whole classes of rules, differing only in varying contexts, can be compressed into a single rule. For example, consider the following rule:

F [**if** C **then** A **else** B **fi**]
   $\Leftrightarrow$ **if** C **then** $F[A]$ **else** $F[B]$ **fi**
(where A, B, and C are scheme parameters, and F is a context parameter)

---

[11] The possibility of arbitrary textual modification, in some sense, contradicts the idea of program transformations. By the way, the same remark holds for the TI system (Section 2.1.2) and the Programmer's Apprentice (Section 4.3).

[12] From the literature it is not clear which of the examples have been done with the system.

[13] A prototype transformation system has been specified and implemented by R. Steinbrüggen's group.

---

[14] Both are provided for the ALGOL dialect of CIP-L.

This rule states the distributivity of the **if–then–else** construct with anything else. Applied to the statement

$x := a * \textbf{if } x \geq 0 \textbf{ then } x \textbf{ else } -x \textbf{ fi}$

it yields

if $x \geq 0$ **then** $x := a * x$
  else $x := a * (-x)$ **fi**.

The reason for considering schemes as manipulation objects is that, since transformation rules themselves consist of three schemes—source template, target template, and enabling condition—they can also be manipulated by the system.

In addition to *rule application* [Erhard 1981], *expansion* and *composition* of transformation rules [Steinbrüggen 1981a] are realized. The basic operations allow the formal derivation of more complex rules from elementary ones within the system.[15] According to the language definition, the set of elementary rules is composed of the following:

- the fundamental rules (such as FOLD or UNFOLD) of the language kernel that are verified with respect to the mathematical semantics;
- the definitional rules for the additional language constructs that hold axiomatically;
- the axioms of the algebraic data types (characterizing certain subject domains) that can be defined within individual programs.

The system has no means for automatically performing transformations. Instead, transformation rules must be selected by the user. This might seem burdensome, but the system offers a metalanguage for formulating transformational algorithms. Despite its expressive poverty (this metalanguage has only a few simple constructs, viz., *union*, *product*, *closure*[16]), it provides the full computational power (of a Turing machine [Steinbrüggen 1982]). Nonetheless, to ease the formulation of transformational

algorithms, an extension to the full CIP-L vocabulary is planned.

To support communication with the user, the CIP system also provides an interactive shell responsible for the user dialogue. In addition to making the aforementioned functions available to the user, this subsystem provides functions for textual program modifications. More details on this subsystem and a sketch of its formal derivation can be found in Riethmayer [1981].

Currently, the means for (automatically) recording the history of a program development are lacking. Early work toward such a capability has been done [Bauer et al. 1977].

The development of the running prototype system has proceeded from prealgorithmic specifications [Steinbrüggen 1980b] to an applicative version and, finally, to a Pascal version, through a half-dozen intermediate stages. The main transitions are documented by program transformations. Because of this, the running system is proved to meet its specifications.

The system has been used to prove parts of its own development [Brass et al. 1982]. Currently, it is being used by students to develop algorithms and to prove, via derivation chains, theorems about abstract types. A new transformation system is currently being developed using the running prototype system [Partsch 1984].

2.7 The SETL Project and Related Activities

The transformational activities in connection with the SETL project [Schwartz 1975a; Dewar et al. 1979a] at the Courant Institute of New York University concentrate on three areas: an optimizer; an interactive, semiautomatic development system; and a verification/manipulation system.

Work on the SETL optimizer is strongly related to transformation systems. Although it is not a transformation system in a strict sense, it does use transformational techniques, particularly for selecting data structures and ensuring efficient data-type representation [Schwartz 1975b; Schonberg et al. 1979, 1981]. By adding type declarations to the program, the user can choose among a variety of ready made implementations for *tuple*, *set*, and *map* types,

---

[15] Occasionally, induction principles fit into this framework too.

[16] Essentially, these are the regular set theory operations. The difference in computational power is due to rule application.

which the system provides. If declarations are missing, concrete representations are automatically chosen by the SETL optimizer.

The second contribution to the transformational approach is an experimental interactive system for supporting the semiautomatic development of reliable and efficient software, using source-to-source transformations. This system, RAPTS (Rutgers Abstract Program Transformation System), implemented in SETL by R. Paige [1983] at Rutgers University emphasizes the strict stepwise refinement of programs by successive application of manually selected powerful correctness-preserving transformations. These transformations are based on *finite differencing*, also known as *formal differentiation*, a general form of strength reduction [Paige and Schwartz 1977; Paige 1981; Paige and Koenig, 1982; Sharir 1979a, 1979b, 1981]. If applicable, this technique always improves efficiency. In Paige's system it is strongly coupled with the data-type facilities provided by the input language SETL. Most other features supported by the system are fairly standard. Paige (private communication, 1981) plans to develop program analysis routines to automate the verification of applicability conditions associated with transformations. This task is known to be complex for nonsyntactic transformations. Currently, control-flow and data-flow analyses have been implemented, and type and perturbation analyses are being developed.

The third area of concentration is the SETL verification/manipulation system [Schwartz 1977; Deak 1980, 1981]. It can be briefly characterized as a semantically knowledgeable editor that allows programs to be changed when written in a SETL-like language and annotated with assumptions, if the resulting program remains correct. If the system cannot verify a change, it adds new assumptions to the program, which the user later verifies. This approach is catalog oriented. The catalog contains proof rules (for verifying assumptions) and transformation rules. Typical proof rules include assumption introduction, assertion elimi-

nation, propagation, induction, and proof-checker rules. Transformation rules include expression- or selection-substitution rules, refinement rules (selection refinement, insertion, and deletion), rules for labels and jumps, and some other optimization techniques well known from compiler construction.

Problems that have been dealt with by the SETL project range from the simple to the complex, such as a minimal path in a graph [Schonberg et al. 1979], garbage collection algorithms [Dewar et al. 1979b], and the Cocke–Younger parsing algorithm [Deak 1981]. For a fair comparison with other systems, though, it should be added that even though the latter developments are detailed case studies, they contain a great deal of informal reasoning and thus would require more technical work before they would be treatable by any system. Recently, Paige and Koenig have begun applying program transformations to database transaction optimization [Koenig and Paige 1981; Paige 1982].

3. SPECIAL-PURPOSE SYSTEMS

As mentioned in Section 1, it is difficult to differentiate between general and special-purpose transformation systems. Whereas general transformation systems support various aspects of the transformational approach to software development, special-purpose systems use the transformational concept to achieve a specific goal. All special-purpose systems may be characterized by the particular facet of the transformational activity (e.g., optimization, synthesis, verification, or adaptation) on which they focus and the particular class of programs that they manipulate. Examples of restricted programs include array-manipulating programs, programs specified by algebraic equations, and programs restricted to both a particular language (FORTRAN) and a special application area (numerical algorithms).

3.1 The Irvine SPECIALIST

The Irvine transformation system, called SPECIALIST [Kibler 1978], is implemented in LISP at the University of California at Irvine. On the basis of experiences gained with an earlier system [Kibler et al. 1977] SPECIALIST is restricted in two respects: It deals only with the optimization of executable programs and only in the domain of matrix problems. The input for the system is an ALGOL-like program, bearing *local predicate* constraints on data structures, such as "the matrix used is a diagonal matrix." The target is a simplified ALGOL-like program.

The transformation catalog is extendable and consists of about 50 rules. All the rules are syntactic or semiprocedural, and most are independent of the specific language, ALGOL. In particular, the rules dealing with control constructs are directly transferable to other languages. Most of the rules are simply rewrite rules called *productions*. A few others, such as those for useless-assignment elimination, empty-statement elimination, and constant propagation, need additional enabling conditions. The correctness of the rules in the catalog has been proved by an adaptation of Dijkstra's weakest precondition methodology [Dijkstra 1976b].

The area covered by the transformations concentrates on simplification of matrix computations,[17] although there are also rules specific to other domains (e.g., definitions, axioms, theorems, or optimizations for arithmetic or Boolean algebra). For handling local, temporary information, *dynamic transformations* are defined and used. These dynamic transformations are mainly applied by simple expansion as in, for example,

Diagonal-matrix (x)
$$\Rightarrow (\textbf{if } i \neq j \textbf{ then } x[i, j] = 0 \textbf{ fi}).$$

The transformations in SPECIALIST always assume correct, executable program versions. During the development process, SPECIALIST will not modify an algorithm's general strategy. Thus, for example, a transformation from linear search to binary search is impossible. There is no pos-

---

[17] Rules going beyond matrix problems can be found in earlier Irvine work on transformational programming [Standish et al. 1976a, 1976b].

sibility for treating global constraints, such as "the matrix used is invertible," and none of the optimizing transformations depend on global flow analysis or execution monitors. Global optimization is instead achieved by *chaining* simple local transformations.

Chaining [Kibler 1978] is based on the observation that, within the scope of any special problem field, a successful application of a transformation will provide information for significantly reducing the search space for the next step. By knowing where the last transformation was applied, the scope or *locality* (a node in the internal tree representation) of the next transformation in the program can be limited. The information about which transformation was applied provides hints for possible next-rule candidates. Each transformation is augmented by a list of *directions*. Each direction consists of a relative specification of a new locality, followed by an unordered list of successor rules. Because a reasonable ordering of that list would obviously speed the development process, suitable criteria, such as expense of applicability test, expense of performance, probability of applicability, and user intuition, are still being investigated. A successful transformation application causes the first direction to be tried and the others to be kept on a treelike *agenda* structure to enable directed backtracking, if necessary.

Given a program, local constraints, and a user-specified initial locality, the system automatically produces an optimized program. During this process, up to 90 transformations can be automatically chained without backup or user assistance. The system also provides the user assistance for entering new rules in the catalog. It does so by supporting the incremental derivation of new rule augmenting, using an appropriate list of directions (see above).

Examples that have been treated with Kibler's system concentrate—as do the transformation rules—on matrix computations [Kibler 1978]. A typical example, the development of matrix multiplication given diagonality or symmetry constraints, has been treated in complete detail [Kibler et al. 1977].

3.2 An Orsay System

Guiho's system [Bidoit et al. 1979; Guiho et al. 1980] in Orsay (Université Paris-Sud) is also restricted in two ways: (1) As with Kibler's system, it only deals with array-manipulating programs; (2) unlike Kibler's system, it aims only at one specific transformation task, that of synthesis from given specifications, with no effort toward optimization.

The system, which is implemented in LISP, takes as input high-level, nonalgorithmic specifications and produces ALGOL-like recursive programs. Although restricted to arrays, this system is based on the more general approach of algebraically specified abstract data types, and extensions are therefore possible. Typical examples of admissible specifications to the system include "Find index, such that P (index, input) holds," "Test P(input)," "Construct an array such that P(index, input) holds," and combinations of these.

The system employs two kinds of heuristics. The first is based on the interplay between constructors and selectors in abstract data types: Selectors decompose the problem; constructors synthesize a solution. In the special case of arrays, this interaction reduces to: "If the array is empty, then no operation; otherwise, operate on one element and then on the rest of the array." This rule corresponds to the conditional-formation rule in the DEDALUS system, given in Section 2.4.2. The second kind of heuristic deals with general programming knowledge such as *formation of recursive calls* (folding), generalization (used if a direct folding fails), and introduction of subsidiary programs. The system uses first-order matching to detect tail-recursive calls, second-order matching to select transformation rules (a simple keyword detection similar to the pattern-directed invocation described in Section 1.2.5), and a theorem prover, which, although "naive," proved sufficient for the examples it handled.

The examples are, of course, all array based and include those of element insertion, maximal element, test for sortedness, membership test, array reversal, test for identity of two arrays, and computation of two arrays' intersection.

3.3 The ISI AFFIRM System

The AFFIRM system at the Information Science Institute of the University of Southern California (ISI) [Erickson 1981; Gerhart et al. 1980] is based on algebraic data-type specifications having algebraic axioms[18] to characterize sets of objects according to the interrelation of their characteristic operations. AFFIRM is a verification system and not, in the strictest sense, a transformation system. But since algebraic axioms are specific kinds of transformations (see the algebraic view in the CIP project, Section 2.6), the classification of AFFIRM as a special-purpose transformation system seems plausible. In addition to this restricted kind of transformation, AFFIRM also has a limited scope of application: It is primarily an experimental system for the algebraic specification and verification of Pascal-like programs, using algebraically defined abstract types.

The purpose of the system is to help the user prove properties. The system's assistance essentially consists of the axiom applications (considered to be rewrite rules) and support for induction proofs, in which AFFIRM generates the cases of the induction.

Responsibility for the strategy of the proof rests solely with the user. The user must find the right set of axioms, the theorems to be proved, and the lemma structure of the proof. The system makes no effort to find proofs beyond repeatedly applying the axioms until no further rewriting is possible and doing some automatic simplification (mainly in the area of **if–then–else** constructs). However, because the system performs recording, undoing, and redoing of proof steps, it helps the user in the mechanical parts of a proof derivation.

The constituents (called *abstract machines*) of the AFFIRM system belong to several categories. The basic stock of transformations consists of the *rewrite rules*, the

---

[18] These axioms are usually equations, sometimes restricted by certain definedness conditions.

set of rewrite expressions based on the user-defined axioms. For performing transformations, the *specification* provides facilities for creating, modifying, destroying, and listing data-type specifications (including certain well-formedness checks). The *logic* comprises the usual propositional calculus, as well as the more advanced features of skolemization, normalization, unification, instantiation, and *case analysis*, the latter being a transformation to interchange function calls and the **if–fi** construct. The *theorem prover* maintains the treelike proof structure and provides means for interactively moving around the tree and modifying it. The service component includes the *executive*, which handles communication with the user and among the system's constituents, a *verification condition generator*, and *formula input/output*.

The AFFIRM system is strongly influenced by its implementation language, INTERLISP. The rewrite rules are simply translated into LISP functions, the INTERLISP history list acts as a bookkeeping device, and the automatically produced transcript is used as a proof session record. In addition, components such as the parser and structured editors of the implementation system are directly used.

As in the CIP system (Section 2.6), the AFFIRM system's specification and verification follow their own particular theoretical and programming paradigms:

(1) algebraic specification of abstract data types,
(2) verification by rewrites rules.

Of course, this does not mean that AFFIRM has been used to create itself, but rather that the respective proofs had been done by hand along the lines of the incorporated methodology.

Examples of problems treated by AFFIRM include many data-type specifications and proofs of associated properties [Musser 1979; Thompson et al. 1981], some simple problems using induction [Gerhard 1980], different versions of a message system [Gerhart and Wile 1979], and communication protocols [Thompson et al. 1981]. And Lee et al. [1981] report an incident in which the system helped in finding a design error in a distributed system.

3.4 The Argonne TAMPR System

The TAMPR (Transformation-Assisted Multiple Program Realization) system [Boyle and Dritz 1974; Boyle 1976; Boyle and Matz 1977] at the Argonne National Laboratory again is a special-purpose transformation system, since its primary goal is to use transformations to adapt numerical algorithms to particular hardware, software, and problem environments. (For a perspicuous outline of the underlying philosophy, see work by Boyle [1980].) TAMPR is designed to abstract from the details of several numerical subroutine packages for slightly different machines or languages and to express their commonality in the form of a *prototype program*, a program from which a set of variant, systematically related mathematical subroutines can be automatically derived. For the derivation of these variants, or *realizations*, sets of schematic transformation rules relating different FORTRAN[19] programs or program schemes are used. These sets of rules are known as *realization functions*. The transformation rules are also called *intragrammatical transformations*[20] because they guarantee syntactic correctness of the transformed program and serve to connect realizations either with the prototype program or with each other.

In the implementation, these transformations are carried out on a representation of the program written in an *applicative* language called *structured FORTRAN*. In detail, a given FORTRAN program is first translated into a parse tree and then into a *canonical abstract form* in structured FORTRAN. The system then applies the transformations to this canonical abstract form. From every intermediate version of the program, TAMPR is able to produce executable FORTRAN. Experiments with other

---

[19] Although the ideas are, in principle, language independent, all the actual work has been done in FORTRAN.

[20] Early ideas, in particular those about implementing intragrammatical transformations, can be found in work by Boyle [1970].

Computing Surveys, Vol. 15, No. 3, September 1983

languages, such as PL/I, also have been successfully carried out.

The transformations mainly focus on the transition from Basic Linear Algebra subroutines to in-line FORTRAN code. Typical examples [Boyle and Matz 1977; Boyle 1978, 1981] include some forms of unfolding, loop unrolling, conversion of a complex function to its real counterpart, converting single precision to double precision, and changing two-dimensional arrays into one-dimensional ones. TAMPR has been successfully applied to widely used numerical subroutine packages.

4. GENERAL PROGRAMMING ENVIRONMENTS

There are many general software development systems (for a typical example, see Alberga et al. [1981]; for a comprehensive survey and classification, see Hesse [1981]), but very few of them include a component for program transformations or provide tools for transformational programming. All the systems described in this section are general, rather than special-purpose, systems. When compared with the systems described in earlier sections, they are even more general, in the sense that the performance of program transformations is only a small aspect of the whole system.

4.1 The Harvard PDS

Built on the basis of experiences from the ECL project [Wegbreit 1972; Cheatham and Wegbreit 1972; ECL 1974], the Harvard PDS (Program Development System) [Cheatham et al. 1979b; Cheatham 1981; Townley 1981] is a programming environment consisting of an integrated collection of interactive tools to support definition, testing, and maintenance of large programs or program families whose members must be maintained in synchrony. The PDS puts special emphasis on program derivation from abstract specifications by nontrivial refinements.

The PDS system views a program as a hierarchical collection of modules used to solve a certain programming task. Each module consists of entities such as procedural expressions, data definitions, and documentation. Relationships among the modules are given by interface specifications whose consistency is checked by the PDS. A module may have several descendants, all of which are considered as refinements of the original parent module. Thus a program is defined at several levels, and a fundamental goal of the PDS is to support this multilevel view of a program by providing appropriate structures and means for maintaining the different program versions.

The PDS constructs and uses a database of facts about a program and its constituents, including a representation of the modules' interdependence and a history of their refinement, organized to enable automatic incremental rederivation, given a modified abstract specification. The interface to the user is provided by the executive of the PDS. Other available components include specification tools, analysis tools such as a symbolic evaluator [Cheatham et al. 1979a], and execution tools.

Refinement of an entity or module can be specified either by an incremental definition/redefinition of the respective entity via its attributes (name, derivation number, time of creation, etc.), by the history mechanism (the set of previously used refinements), or by the rewrite facility, that is, the transformation component of PDS [Cheatham et al. 1981]. In contrast to most of the other systems, which rely on pre-existing cataloged transformations, the PDS transformations must be defined by the user.[21] They represent design decisions in the stepwise refinement sequence and, as programs, are encapsulated in modules.

Transformation rules are represented schematically. They consist of a syntactic input pattern (with scheme parameters and iterable constructs explicitly marked), optionally augmented with a semantic predicate for applicability, and a syntactic output pattern, the *replacement part*.

Transformations are used to introduce nomenclature, implement an abstract notion (notational extension, similar to the

---

[21] From the literature it is not clear whether PDS supports individual user-defined transformation catalogs.

Computing Surveys, Vol. 15, No. 3, September 1983

definitional transformations in the CIP system given in Section 2.6) or certain aspects of the behavior of an abstract data type, and derive realizations of an abstract program.

In the PDS, the refinement of an abstract program consists of a series of steps leading from a program and a refinement module to a new program module. The entities in these modules may be divided into named groups to provide local scoping and to control the local application of a transformation. Instructions within the refinement module may specify which rules apply to which entities of the program module. Nesting transformations (in which transformations act as constituents of another transformation's replacement part) enable local transformations to be done by limiting the scope of applicability.

Rule application does not consist of a single replacement step but is performed in repeated passes over the evolving program module until no further rules apply. Transformations that are not intended to be used in the further development of their own "right side" can be marked for solitary application.

Examples of large programs that have already been developed with the PDS include the symbolic evaluator, a family of interpreters for EL-1 (the language of the ECL system), a family of interprocess communication handlers, a formula simplifier, and the PDS itself. Townley has done a detailed development of an efficient algorithm for reducing a deterministic automaton [Townley 1982].

4.2 The MENTOR System

The MENTOR system at INRIA [Donzeau-Gouge et al. 1975, 1980] was also designed for developing "realistic" programs. Its purpose is to realize an interactive programming environment in which the programmer can design, implement, document, debug, test, validate, and maintain programs or modify them for transportation purposes. Although MENTOR is, in principle, independent of language and development methodology, nearly all of the work actually done has focused on Pascal programs [Mélèse 1981]. By bootstrapping a small system core written in Pascal, MENTOR could be used to do most of its own development[22] and maintenance. In particular, MENTOR was used to develop its transportation from the IRIS 80 to the PDP-10 computer. The authors' philosophy is that a programming environment is a set of specialized interpreters for helping programmers do various computations and rearrangements on their programs. Hence MENTOR is not only extensible but also allows the structured editing of Pascal programs, including simple transformations such as parentheses insertion or *pretty-printing* in different type fonts. In addition, MENTOR allows normalization of Pascal programs (by rearranging declarations or cleaning up scope information) and, of course, different source-level transformations, such as constant propagation, consistent renaming of identifiers, and recursion removal for tail recursion.

MENTOR is a processor designed for manipulating structured data represented by abstract syntax trees. The translation between Pascal programs and abstract syntax trees is done by the system. For driving MENTOR, a special-purpose tree-manipulating language, called MENTOL, is used.

MENTOL is an interactive language designed for editing. It has side-effect-free expressions, commands with side effects, procedures with different calling mechanisms, a sophisticated facility for comments, and a built-in facility for pattern matching. Expressions are used for operations such as selecting and displaying marked subtrees of an abstract syntax tree. Typical commands modify or evaluate the selected subtree. The latter is most important, since, together with the possibility for defining schemes (constructable by commands or input through the parser) and pattern matching, it supports the implementation of transformations in terms of *tree-rewriting* operations. From basic commands, more complex ones can be built by using conventional language features such as sequencing, grouping, bound iteration, and conditional and case statements.

---

[22] From the literature it is not clear which parts have been implemented.

Furthermore, the language provides good debugging aids, including a trace package, an interrupt facility, and file manipulation primitives. Finally, it has its own abstract syntax, which allows a mixed development of both Pascal and MENTOL programs. In particular, it is possible (for experts only) to modify Pascal manipulation programs written in MENTOL.

4.3 The Programmer's Apprentice

The PA (Programmer's Apprentice) [Rich and Shrobe 1978; Rich et al. 1979] is a "knowledge-based editing approach" [Waters, 1982]. As such, it lies between an aid to an improved programming methodology and a knowledge-based automatic programming system.

Programmer and system work together (see "partnership" in GLITTER, Section 2.1.4) during all phases of development and maintenance. The programmer performs the "difficult" tasks such as design and implementation, and the PA acts as a junior partner and critic by keeping track of details and assisting in documentation, debugging, and maintenance.

PA's assistance mainly concentrates on two activities. First, given a LISP program, PA is able to analyze its underlying structure and recognize the structure's known building blocks or *plans*. Second, given an abstract or incomplete description of an algorithm, PA helps fill in details and debug incorrect portions. The result of this second activity is an executable LISP program, together with a layered description of its top-down construction process.

Program structures are represented as plans, conceptual units of behavior that are either primitive or hierarchically composed of other plans. A plan's basic entity is a *segment*, defined by *specs*, formal statements of input expectations and output assertions, based on a relational view of data. The relationship between individual plans are kept by *dependency links* comprising syntactic relations (data and control flow) and semantic relations (knowledge of how the behavior of a plan is inferred from the behavior of its components).

PA's knowledge is embodied in a *plan library*, a hierarchically organized knowledge base[23] of formalized general knowledge about nonnumerical programming. Typical plans include knowledge about the concept of a loop and its specializations into enumeration loops or search loops, or knowledge about general techniques for manipulating trees, lists, arrays, and the like.

On the basis of its understanding of the logical structure of a program, PA is able to reason deductively about plans. In particular, the system can verify that a plan matches some portion of a concrete program, point out bugs by finding discrepancies between its understanding and the actual program operations, and reason about consequences of modifying existing programs by determining what parts are affected by the change.

PA is based on an informal and flexible editing paradigm. The particular knowledge representation by plans allows both synthesis and analysis, and moving from the abstract to the concrete, or vice versa. By producing a low-level plan structure from a given program, the system helps to analyze already written programs. On the other hand, a user may construct a LISP program with assistance from the system, by naming general algorithms (plans from the plan library) and refining their abstract components into LISP code (by naming more concrete plans or filling in literal values).

There is neither a formal specification in the PA approach, nor are the changes required to be correctness preserving. This implies that, within the bounds of plan compatibility, arbitrary changes to a program can be made (see also the PUC system, Section 2.5). It is especially for this reason that PA can be considered a transformation system only in a rather broad sense.

4.4 The Draco System

The Draco System [Neighbors 1980] is a general mechanism for software construc-

---

[23] This knowledge base is similar to that of PECOS, Section 2.2.2, except for the explicit representation of the logical structure of programs.

tion based on the paradigm of "reusable software." "Reusable" here means that the analysis and design of some library program can be reused, but not its code. Draco is an interactive system that enables a user to refine a problem, stated in a high-level problem-domain-specific language, into an efficient LISP program.

Accordingly, Draco supplies mechanisms for defining problem domains as special-purpose domain languages and for manipulating statements in these languages into an executable form.

Initially, Draco contains domains that represent conventional, executable computer languages. On this basis, a hierarchy of new domains may be defined by providing the syntax of the (new) domain language in a Backus-Normal-Form (BNF) -like formalism defining the semantics by appropriate mappings (*refinements*) from the statements in the new language into statements of one or more previously defined languages, and by giving, finally, a set of optimizing (source-to-source) transformations for the new language.[24]

The user may then formulate a specific problem in terms of the new domain language. The transformations allow the user to "strip away generalities" and specialize the general components of the domain language according to his or her own particular use. While guiding a refinement, using the semantic mappings mentioned above, the user may make individual modeling and implementation choices among competing refinements presented by the system or rely on user-defined tactics to guide the semi-automatic refinement process. Design choices have enabling conditions and, if used, make assertions about the resulting program. If these conditions and assertions

ever conflict, backward movement to a safe, nonconflicting earlier development stage is necessary.

The complete refinement history then is a top-down description of the final program. Each schematic transformation rule is given an application code (identifying what it does and how desirable its application is) when it is defined. This code implies a partial order among transformations which is used to build up metarules, rules that relate the rules of a given fixed set to each other.

When a program formulated in terms of the domain language is parsed into the domain's internal tree form, Draco generates, upon request, for each node, an agenda of applicable transformations in the order of application code. The transformation mechanism then allows the application of rules within a user-selected *locale* in an instance of a domain. By providing the metarule mechanism and different application policies, Draco circumvents the need for transformation algorithms (*procedural transformations*).

The interesting aspect of the Draco approach is its way of achieving implementation-independent representation of algorithms: Draco enables the user to define his or her own level of abstraction. This has the additional advantage that powerful transformations are easily expressible. A typical example is given by the domain language for augmented transition networks; in this language, elimination of an unreadable transition state, which is difficult to capture in LISP code, can be simply formulated.

The Draco ideas have been implemented in a prototype system running under TOPS-10 on a DEC PDP-10 computer. However, owing to memory restriction, only small programs can be created using this prototype. An example that has been treated is a program for finding roots in a quadratic equation, originally formulated in a 10-line ALGOL program that was refined into approximately 80 lines of LISP. Another example was a natural language parser specified in the above-mentioned augmented transition networks.

---

[24] This is similar to the CIP approach (see Section 2.6), where a new problem domain can be defined by means of a suitable abstract type; the signature of the type defines the syntax, and the axioms serve as semantic definition as well as transformation rules. The essential difference lies in how the semantics of the new domain are defined. In Draco, an operational definition is given, whereas in the abstract data-type approach of the CIP project an axiomatic, algebraic one (which leaves freedom for various operational realizations) is used.

5. FURTHER ACTIVITIES

In addition to the projects described so far, there are other efforts that, from the present points of view, play only a minor role in the field. Nevertheless, they show some interesting properties and deserve mention.

5.1 Former Systems

The systems described in this section have in common the fact that there is no information about their implementor's current activities.

5.1.1 Haraldsson's System

Haraldsson's system REDFUN-2 [Haraldsson 1974, 1977, 1978], implemented in INTERLISP, is designed to simplify arbitrary LISP programs. This is achieved through the application of many algorithms. Among these, *partial evaluation* [Beckmann et al. 1976] of procedures (in different versions) based on partial information about the variables is most prominent. The concept of partial evaluation (also *mixed computation* [Ershov 1978, 1982]) is simple: If, for example, a function is defined with two arguments but actually depends on only one of them (i.e., the other is constant), it may be changed into an equivalent function with only one argument. Other techniques used are global analysis, β-*expansion* (unfolding), constant propagation, and certain collapsing rules to remove redundant code.

5.1.2 Rutter's System

Rutter's system [Rutter 1977] for improving the efficiency of LISP programs can be seen as a forerunner of Kibler's system, since its main contribution to the research on program transformations is an attempt to automatically chain rule applications. It consists of about 200 language-dependent rules. These rules are stored in a list and sequentially applied to the different program versions; applicable rules are found by binary search, depending on previous successes. The improvement process terminates when no rule is applicable. Some of the optimizations additionally require global flow analysis, the ordering of condi-

tionals, or the choice of data structures, as determined by an *execution monitor*.

5.1.3 Loveman's System

Loveman's ideas [Loveman 1977; Loveman and Faneuf 1975] for a transformation system are partly implemented in the IVTRAN compiler (FORTRAN compiler for ILLIAC-IV). In addition to "classical" transformations such as constant propagation, dead-variable elimination, and code motion, the system also contains about two dozen rules focusing on loop constructs (case splitting, loop unraveling, loop fusion, and interaction between loops and conditionals). Note that this approach, too, allows rules to be augmented with a set of possible-next-candidate rules.

Even more interesting is Loveman's attempt to incorporate transformations designed to execute loops on a parallel machine with a finite number of processors. The techniques used are the *coordinate method* for transforming well-behaved sets of nested loops into concurrent loops for several asynchronously operating processors, the *hyperplane method* for transforming well-behaved sets of nested loops into simultaneous loops for processors operating in a "lock-step" fashion, and *strip mining* for adjusting a given parallel loop to a machine with a fixed number of processors.

5.2 Recent Projects

Although there are now many groups working on program transformations, we shall briefly mention only some of those that recently became active in the field.

5.2.1 The CROPS/Pascal System

The CROPS (Conversational Restructuring, Optimizing, and Partitioning System)/Pascal system [Chusho 1980] is an interactive optimization system implemented in Pascal for Pascal programs that perform matrix computations. The system is characterized by having a generative set of basic rules (*commands*) out of which new rules can be built. Supporting this aspect of the system is a slightly different view of program transformations (*optimization com-*

mands): Transformations are not considered as preverified theorems on programs but rather as interactively specified replacement steps whose correctness must still be verified. However, by hierarchically basing arbitrary commands on more primitive ones, this correctness proof is strongly supported by the system and individual proof techniques are only occasionally needed. More primitive commands include predefined optimization commands; commands for testing, debugging, or verifying optimization commands; and edit commands for line/character manipulating and restructuring. Typical examples of predefined optimization commands include rules for changing the structure of loops (split, merge, move, rotate, expand), renaming variables, moving parts of code, doing expansion, performing strength reduction, and implementing a simple form of symbolic execution.

5.2.2 The IPMS

The IPMS (Interactive Program Manipulation System) [de Rivières 1980] can be characterized as a hybrid of a structured editor and a transformation catalog.

Starting with a functionally correct Pascal program[25] as input, the user gives standard structured editing commands (such as insertion, deletion, movement, or replacement) for modification or optimization. The IPMS attempts to carry out the command by finding a sequence of primitive, correctness-preserving, source-to-source transformations (similar to those in Kibler's system, Section 3.1) that achieves the desired result. Within this sequence, competing applicable rules are chosen in the order in which they appear in the catalog. Infinite sequencing of rules is prevented by a system-defined threshold. In case of failure the program is not altered and the programmer is informed about the difficulties encountered; otherwise, the command is performed and an optimized program version is produced as output.

The rules provided by IPMS are schematic quintuples: name, goal, left-hand-side pattern, right-hand-side pattern, enabling condition. In addition to the usual kind of patterns, one called *anchored pattern*,[26] which requires little or no searching, is used. These anchored patterns contain a bound variable, the *anchor*, which is identified first during matching. The remaining parts of the pattern are then searched for around the anchor. Instead of a right-hand-side replacement pattern, the rules may contain further goals to achieve. Thus IPMS (like GLITTER, Section 2.1.4) addresses both program space and problem space.

The collection of transformation rules is indexed by the editing functions they perform. Accordingly, rules that can perform more than one function have several index terms. For selecting applicable rules, a form of *pattern-directed invocation* (see DEDALUS, Section 2.4.2) is used. If there are enabling conditions, they are checked by inspecting control paths in the program tree leading to and from the site of application. For handling program-specific transformations, that is, transformations depending on values of variables, *dynamic transformations* (where equivalence is ensured by the specific context) are used.

From its conception, but also with respect to its abilities, IPMS is obviously another special-purpose system (see Section 3). Unfortunately, from the literature it is not clear whether the system really has been implemented. However, if it has not been, an implementation could be done straightforwardly, thanks to the technically detailed description given by de Rivières [1980].

5.2.3 The FOO System

The FOO system [Mostow 1981] is a system for AI problem solving by "operationalizing" a problem description stated at the problem-domain level into a procedure. This transformation is done relying only on actions that are executable by a *task agent* in the *task environment*. Roughly speaking, in Neighbors' terminology (see Section 4.4), this is the same as deriving an

---

[25] Actually a subset of Pascal, restricted to basic data types and a few simple control constructs, is used.

[26] There is a similar mechanism in SNOBOL.

operative solution for a problem in terms of already available components. One of the techniques used in the derivation of such a procedure is based on the "pigeonhole principle": A limited number of possible solutions is filtered by conclusions derivable from available facts.

The FOO system is catalog oriented and contains approximately 300 rules. From these, the user repeatedly selects appropriate ones and indicates where in the actual problem expression they should be applied. A selection among competing instantiations of the same rule must be made by the user.

Mostow's work [Mostow 1981] also contains a proposal for automating portions of the operationalization process (which again bears some resemblance to that of GLITTER, Section 2.1.4) by suggesting *means–end analysis* to guide the rule selection. The user provides the left-hand-side pattern of some rule that he or she finally wants to be applied. The *means–end module* then computes the *difference* between the pattern and the current problem expression and uses the computed difference as an index to selecting rules that might help reduce the difference.

5.2.4 Goad's System

Goad [1982] has introduced a system for "special-purpose automatic programming." This system is designed to increase the efficiency of computations by synthesizing, for particular classes of problems defined in ordinary mathematical terms, fast special-purpose programs from more general solutions.

As well as being denoted as relations rather than functions, the original solutions must have the property of *sweep coherence*, meaning that the result depends on two arguments, one of which changes slowly, and one rapidly. The basic idea of the approach may be characterized as a mixture of partial evaluation (Section 5.1.1) and formal differentiation (Paige's system, Section 2.7). By expanding (repeated unfolding, see Section 1.2.4) a partial call of the given solution into its complete decision tree, a special variant of the solution is synthesized and then analyzed

and appropriately modified. This process is repeated for all values of the slowly changing parameter and produces a family of special-purpose programs that covers the original solution.

Of course, to be profitable, a proceeding such as this requires that the effort in constructing the special-purpose programs not exceed the effort in running the original general-purpose program.

On the basis of the general principles, a program for the synthesis of special-purpose priority sorting programs has been implemented in MACLISP on a DEC PDP-10 computer. This program has been applied to the problem of "hidden surface elimination from displays of three-dimensional scenes" and resulted in special-purpose algorithms an order of magnitude faster than the best available general-purpose algorithms.

5.2.5 The Leeds Transformation System

The intention of the LTS (Leeds Transformation System) [Maher and Sleeman 1983] is to transform existing programs into "tidier," better readable, better structured programs. Owing to this restricted area of application, the LTS must also be considered a special-purpose system. On the basis of the observation that programmers vary in what they consider to be an acceptable form of a program, the system is *data driven*, and is independent of a particular language. The class of suitable languages is only restricted to languages without pointers, in which the flow of control is syntactically decidable. The translation between a particular language and the system's internal form is done by respective pre- and postprocessors (see also the CIP system, Section 2.6).

The transformation process is split into three independent phases: In the first phase, controlled by the user, the internal form of the program is restructured using a set of syntactic transformation rules (similar to those in Kibler's system, Section 3.1). By *variable usage transformations*, in the second phase, redundant variables, redundant statements, and loop-invariant statements are automatically eliminated until no further changes can be made (see also the Harvard PDS, Section 4.1). In the third phase, certain structuring features are introduced to replace more basic statements. This *modularization* phase again relies on the user to set appropriate bounds for the search processes involved.

The data-driven view requires that the user supply the system with information on the syntactic structures (language syntax in BNF, tables of language-specific constructs, transformation rules for the redefinition of statements), on statements effecting the flow of control, and on the effect of particular statements on variables.

Since the set of syntactic transformation rules is supplied as data, it is extensible and modifiable. The responsibility for the correctness of the rules rests exclusively with the user (as it did in the PA system, Section 4.3, or in the CHI system, Section 2.2.6). Furthermore, the transformation process assumes syntactically valid programs; programs containing semantic run-time errors are not excluded. Potential uses of the system are the following:

- transforming a program into its structured counterpart (e.g., FORTRAN into RATFOR);
- transforming an existing program to meet an installation standard;
- transforming unsupported features on "imported" programs into those supported by the system;
- optimizing programs in different ways (e.g., "peephole optimization," or transforming high-level constructs into more efficient lower level ones).

Because of the amount of pattern matching and replacement involved with syntactic transformations, the system was implemented in a dialect of SNOBOL called SPITBOL, on a DEC PDP-10 computer. Examples that have been treated include medium-size FORTRAN programs (500–1000 lines of code), numerous ALGOL-60 programs, and some small PL/I programs.

6. PERSPECTIVES FOR THE FUTURE

There is a widespread demand for safe, verified, and reliable software. This demand arises from economic considerations (production of correct chips), ethical reasons (protection of privacy), safety requirements (critical software, as for nuclear power stations), and strategic demands (reliability of weapon systems). Transformational programming can clearly make a valuable contribution toward this goal. But there are additional advantages: Programmers tend to underestimate the complexity of given problems and overrate their own mental capacity. Formal methods, integrated in transformational programming, safeguard against this human tendency. Since an initial problem specification is normally independent of any machine considerations, it can be used for deriving final programs not only for the sequential, storage-programmed, von Neumann computer but also for new architectures such as dataflow machines and array processors, provided that suitable transformation rules are available.

Because of these advantages, many people are enthusiastic about transformational programming as a programming methodology. There are also many people who object to the idea of mechanically supported transformational programming. Some people do not believe that automating the selection of transformations via an artificial intelligence problem solver is feasible and worry that, without such automation, the user would be forced into too much detail. Other people hope to avoid such burdensome detail by accomplishing the development in a few large conceptual steps. If, however, formal rigor really is their goal, transformational programming cannot exist without a computer-implemented transformation system.

As mentioned earlier, today's transformation systems are experimental and the problems they are capable of coping with are still more or less toy problems. However, work is under way worldwide, not only to investigate as yet unsolved theoretical problems, but also to check the methodology's feasibility on medium-size and large problems from many application areas.

In the systems themselves, the trend is away from generalized huge catalogs, and toward individual, problem-oriented subsystems based on small sets of powerful rules allied with advanced metalanguages. Of course, this does not mean that the systems will not support any storing of transformation rules. But, in order to be conveniently manageable, the catalogs must be more specific for certain groups of users and restricted to particular problem domains (e.g., sorting, graph problems, parsing). It is only by this restriction that individual rules can be made powerful enough to become widely accepted, valuable engineering tools.

Among the current approaches to the construction of formally verified software, transformational programming is certainly the most advanced and the most flexible. It already covers several phases of the classical software engineering life cycle and shows promise of covering the remaining ones. Transformational programming is likely to become a standard topic in computer science, analogous to deductive methods in mathematics. Consequently, transformation systems will become integrated parts of future software development support systems.

ACKNOWLEDGMENTS

The authors wish to thank their colleagues from the CIP group, notably, F. L. Bauer, M. Broy, A. Laut, and B. Möller, and the anonymous referees of COMPUTING SURVEYS for critical remarks and helpful suggestions on earlier versions of this paper. Comments by J. Darlington, M. Feather, and B. Paige on their part of the work reported on are also gratefully acknowledged. Special thanks go to R. Bird, R. Hyerle, and ACM's technical editor, R. Rutherford, who improved the English formulation, and to M. Krämer, I. Dippold, and S. Figura for their excellent and speedy typing.

REFERENCES

AHO, A. V., HOPCROFT, J. E., AND ULLMAN, J. D. 1974. *The Design and Analysis of Computer Algorithms.* Addison-Wesley, Reading, Mass.

ALBERGA, C. N., BROWN, A. L., LEEMAN, G. B., JR., MIKELSONS, M., AND WEGMAN, M. N. 1981. A program development tool. In *Proceedings of 8th ACM Symposium on Principles of Programming Languages* (Williamsburg, Va., Jan. 26–28). ACM, New York, pp. 92–104.

ARSAC, J. 1974. Languages sans etiquettes et transformations de programmes. In *Proceedings of 2d International Colloquium on Automata, Languages, and Programming.* Lecture Notes in Computer Science, vol. 14. Springer-Verlag, New York.

ARSAC, J. 1977a. *La Construction de Programmes Structures.* Dunod, Paris.

ARSAC, J. 1977b. Emploi de méthodes constructives en programmation. Un dossier: la fonction d'Ackermann. *RAIRO Theor. Comput. Sci. 11,* 2, 91–112.

ARSAC, J. 1978. An interactive program manipulation system for non naive users. LITP Res. Rep. 78-10, Institut de Programmation, Paris.

ARSAC, J. 1979. Syntactic source to source transforms and program manipulation. *Commun. ACM 22,* 1 (Jan.), 43–54.

ARSAC, J., AND KODRATOFF, Y. 1979. Some methods for transformation of recursive procedures into iterative ones. LITP Res. Rep. 79-2, Institut de Programmation, Paris.

ARSAC, J., AND KODRATOFF, Y. 1982. Some techniques for recursion removal from recursive functions. *ACM Trans. Program. Lang. Syst. 4,* 2 (Apr.), 295–322.

BALZER, R. 1973. A global view of automatic programming. In *Proceedings of the 3rd International Joint Conference on Artificial Intelligence* (Stanford, Calif.), pp. 494–499.

BALZER, R. 1977. Correct and efficient software implementation via semi-automatic transformations. USC/ISI Internal Rep., Information Science Institute, Univ. of Southern California, Marina del Rey.

BALZER, R. 1981a. Final report on GIST. Information Science Institute, Univ. of Southern California, Marina del Rey.

BALZER, R. 1981b. Transformational implementation: An example. *IEEE Trans. Softw. Eng. SE-7,* 1, 3–14.

BALZER, R., GOLDMAN, N., AND WILE, D. 1976. On the transformational implementation approach to programming. In *Proceedings of 2nd International Conference on Software Engineering* (San Francisco, Oct. 13–15). IEEE, New York, pp. 337–344.

BALZER, R., GOLDMAN, N., AND WILE, D. 1980. Informality in program specifications. *IEEE Trans. Softw. Eng. SE-4,* 2, 94–103.

BALZER, R. M., GOLDMAN, N. M., AND WILE, D. S. 1982. Operational specifications as the basis for rapid prototyping. *SIGSOFT Softw. Eng. Notes (ACM) 7,* 5 (Dec.), 3–16.

BARSTOW, D. R. 1977a. Automatic construction of algorithms and data structures using a knowledge base of programming rules. Ph.D. dissertation, Stanford Univ., Stanford, Calif.

BARSTOW, D. R. 1977b. A knowledge base of organization for rules about programming. *SIGART Newsl. (ACM) 63,* (June), 18–22.

BARSTOW, D. R. 1977c. A knowledge-based system for automated program construction. *Proceedings of the 5th International Joint Conference on Artificial Intelligence* (Cambridge, Mass.). M.I.T., Cambridge, Mass., pp. 382–388.

BARSTOW, D. R. 1979a. An experiment in knowledge-based automatic programming. *Artif. Intell.* *12*, 73–119.

BARSTOW, D. R. 1979b. The roles of knowledge and deduction in program synthesis. In *Proceedings of the 6th International Joint Conference on Artificial Intelligence* (Tokyo, Aug. 20–23). International Joint Council on Artificial Intelligence, Inc., Stanford, Calif., pp. 37–43.

BARSTOW, D. R. 1979c. On convergence toward a data base of programming rules. Paper distributed at *2nd Program Transformation Workshop* (Cambridge, Mass., Sept.).

BARSTOW, D. R., AND KANT, E. 1976. Observations on the interaction between coding and efficiency knowledge in the PSI program synthesis system. In *Proceedings of the 2nd International Conference on Software Engineering* (San Francisco, Oct. 13–15). IEEE, New York, pp. 19–31.

BAUER, F. L. 1976. Programming as an evolutionary process. In *Language Hierarchies and Interfaces*, F. L. Bauer and K. Samelson, Eds. Lecture Notes in Computer Science, vol. 46. Springer-Verlag, New York, pp. 153–182.

BAUER, F. L., AND WÖSSNER, H. 1982. *Algorithmic Language and Program Development.* Springer-Verlag, New York.

BAUER, F. L., PARTSCH, H., PEPPER, P., AND WÖSSNER, H. 1977. Notes on the project CIP: Outline of a transformation system. TUM-INFO-7729, Institut für Informatik, Technische Univ. München, Munich, West Germany.

BAUER, F. L., BROY, M., GNATZ, R., HESSE, W., KRIEG-BRÜCKNER, B., PARTSCH, H., PEPPER, P., AND WÖSSNER, H. 1978. Towards a wide spectrum language to support program specification and program development. *SIGPLAN Not.* (ACM) *13*, 12 (Dec.), 15–24.

BAUER, F. L., BROY, M., DOSCH, W., GEISELBRECHTINGER, F., HESSE, W., GNATZ, R., KRIEG-BRÜCKNER, B., LAUT, A., MATZNER, T., MÖLLER, B., PARTSCH, H., PEPPER, P., SAMELSON, K., WIRSING, M., AND WÖSSNER, H. 1981a. Report on a wide spectrum language for program specification and development. TUM-I8104, Institut für Informatik, Technische Univ. München, Munich, West Germany.

BAUER, F. L., BROY, M., DOSCH, W., GNATZ, R., KRIEG-BRÜCKNER, B., LAUT, A., LUCKMANN, M., MATZNER, T., MÖLLER, B., PARTSCH, H., PEPPER P., SAMELSON, K., STEINBRÜGGEN, R., WIRSING, M., AND WÖSSNER, H. 1981b. Programming in a wide spectrum language: A collection of examples. *Sci. Comput. Program. 1*, 73–114.

BECKMANN, L., HARALDSSON, A., OSKARSSON, Ö., AND SANDEWALL, E. 1976. A partial evaluator and its use as a programming tool. *Artif. Intell. 7*, 319–357.

BIDOIT, M., GRESSE, C., AND GUIHO, G. 1979. A system which synthesizes array-manipulating programs from specifications. In *Proceedings of 6th International Joint Conference on Artificial Intelligence* (Tokyo, Aug. 20–23). International Joint Council on Artificial Intelligence, Inc., Stanford, Calif., pp. 63–65.

BIERMANN, A. W. 1976. Approaches to automatic programming. In *Advances in Computers*, vol. 15. Academic Press, New York, pp. 1–63.

BIRD, R. S. 1980. Tabulation techniques for recursive programs. *ACM Comput. Surv. 12*, 4 (Dec.), 403–417.

BOYLE, J. M. 1970. A transformational component for programming language grammar. Rep. ANL-7690, Argonne National Laboratory, Argonne, Ill.

BOYLE, J. M. 1976. An introduction to transformation-assisted multiple program realization (TAMPR) system. In *Cooperative Development of Mathematical Software*, J. R. Bunch, Ed. Dept. of Mathematics, Univ. of California, San Diego.

BOYLE, J. M. 1978. Extending reliability: Transformational tailoring of abstract mathematical software. In *Proceedings of Programming Environment for Mathematical Software* (Pasadena, Calif., Oct. 18–20). ACM, New York, pp. 27–30.

BOYLE, J. M. 1980. Software adaptability and program transformation. In *Software Engineering*, H. Freeman and P. M. Lewis, Eds. Academic Press, New York, pp. 75–93.

BOYLE, J. M. 1981. Practical applications of program transformation. Unpublished manuscript.

BOYLE, J. M., AND DRITZ, K. W. 1974. An automated programming system to facilitate the development of quality mathematical software. In *Information Processing 74*. Elsevier North-Holland, New York, pp. 542–546.

BOYLE, J. M., AND MATZ, M. 1977. Automating multiple program realizations. In *Proceedings of the MRI Symposium*. Computer Software Engineering, vol. 24. Polytechnic Press, Brooklyn, N.Y., pp. 421–456.

BRASS, B., ERHARD, F., HORSCH, A., RIETHMAYER, H.-O., AND STEINBRÜGGEN, R. 1982. CIP-S: An instrument for program transformation and rule generation. TUM-I8211, Institut für Informatik, Technische Univ. München, Munich, West Germany.

BROY, M., PARTSCH, H., PEPPER, P., AND WIRSING, M. 1980. Semantic relations in programming languages. In *Information Processing 80*, S. H. Lavington, Ed. Elsevier North-Holland, New York, pp. 101–106.

BROY, M., PEPPER, P., AND WIRSING, M. 1982. On the algebraic definition of programming languages. TUM-I8204, Institut für Informatik, Technishe Univ. München, Munich, West Germany.

BURSTALL, R. M. 1977. Design considerations for a functional programming language. In *Proceedings of Infotech State of the Art Conference* (Copenhagen). Infotech Ltd., Maidenhead, UK.

BURSTALL, R. M., AND DARLINGTON, J. 1975. Some transformations for developing recursive programs. In *Proceedings of International Conference on Reliable Software* (Los Angeles). IEEE, New York, pp. 465–472.

BURSTALL, R. M., AND DARLINGTON, J. 1977. A transformation system for developing recursive programs. *J. ACM 24*, 1 (Jan.), 44–67.

BURSTALL, R. M., AND FEATHER, M. S. 1978. Program development by transformation: An overview. In *Les fondements de la programmation. Proceedings of Toulouse CREST Course on Programming*, M. Armirchahy and D. Neel, Eds. IRIA-SEFI, Le Chesnay, France.

BURSTALL, R. M., McQUEEN, D. B., AND SANNELLA, D. T. 1980. HOPE: An experimental applicative language. Internal Rep., Dept. of Computer Science, Edinburgh Univ., Scotland.

CHEATHAM, T. E., JR. 1981. Overview of the Harvard program development system. In *Software Engineering Environments*, H. Hünke, Ed.

CHEATHAM, T. E., JR., AND WEGBREIT, B. 1972. A laboratory for the study of automatic programming, In *Proceedings of AFIPS Spring Joint Computer Conference* (Atlantic City, N.J., May 16–18), vol. 40. AFIPS Press, Reston, Va., pp. 11–21.

CHEATHAM, T. E., JR., HOLLOWAY, G. H., AND TOWNLEY, J. A. 1979a. Symbolic evaluation and the analysis of programs. *IEEE Trans. Soft. Eng. SE-5*, 4, 402–417.

CHEATHAM, T. E., JR., TOWNLEY, J. A., AND HOLLOWAY, G. H. 1979b. A system for program refinement. In *Proceedings of 4th International Conference on Software Engineering* (Munich, West Germany, Sept. 17–19). IEEE, New York, pp. 53–62.

CHEATHAM, T. E., JR., HOLLOWAY, G. H., AND TOWNLEY, J. A. 1981. Program refinement by transformation. In *Proceedings of 5th International Conference on Software Engineering* (San Diego, Calif., Mar. 9–12). IEEE, New York, pp. 430–437.

CHUSHO, T. 1980. A good program = a structured program + optimization commands. In *Information Processing 80*, S. H. Lavington, Ed. Elsevier North-Holland, New York, pp. 269–274.

COHEN, D., SWARTOUT, W., AND BALZER, R. 1982. Using symbolic execution to characterize behavior. *SIGSOFT Soft. Eng. Notes* (ACM) 7, 5 (Dec.) 25–32.

COUSINEAU, G. 1976. Transformations de programmes iteratifs. In *Programmation*, B. Robinet, Ed. Dunod, Paris. pp. 53–74.

DARLINGTON, J. 1972. A semantic approach to automatic program improvement. Ph.D. dissertation, Dept. of Machine Intelligence, Univ. of Edinburgh, Scotland.

DARLINGTON, J. 1975. Applications of program transformation to program synthesis. In *Proceedings of International Symposium on Proving and Improving Programs* (Arc-et-Senans, France, July 1–3). IRIA, Le Chesnay, France, pp. 133–144.

DARLINGTON, J. 1978. A synthesis of several sort programs. *Acta Inf. 11*, 1, 1–30.

DARLINGTON, J. 1979. Program transformation: An introduction and survey. *Comput. Bull.* (Dec.), 22–24.

DARLINGTON, J. 1981a. An experimental program transformation and synthesis system. *Artif. Intell. 16*, 1–46.

DARLINGTON, J. 1981b. The structured description of algorithm derivations. In *Algorithmic Languages*, J. W. deBakker and H. van Vliet, Eds. Elsevier North-Holland, New York, pp. 221–250.

DARLINGTON, J., AND BURSTALL, R. M. 1973. A system which automatically improves programs. In *Proceedings of 3d International Joint Conference on Artificial Intelligence* (Stanford, Calif.). SRI, Menlo Park, Calif., pp. 479–485.

DARLINGTON, J., AND BURSTALL, R. M. 1976. A system which automatically improves programs. *Acta Inf. 6*, 41–60.

DARLINGTON, J., AND FEATHER, M. 1979. A transformational approach to modification. Paper presented at the 25th meeting of IFIP WG 2.1 (Summit, N.J., Apr.). Available from authors.

DAVIS, R., AND KING, J. 1975. An overview of production, systems. STAN-CS-75-524, Dept. of Computer Science, Stanford Univ., Stanford, Calif.

DEAK, E. 1980. A transformational approach to the development and unification of programs in a very high level language. Courant Computer Science Rep. 22, Courant Institute, New York Univ., New York.

DEAK, E. 1981. A transformational derivation of a parsing algorithm in a high-level language. *IEEE Trans. Softw. Eng. SE-7*, 1, 23–31.

DE RIVIÈRES, J. 1980. The design of an interactive program manipulation system. Master's thesis, Dept. of Computer Science, Univ. of Toronto, Canada.

DERSHOWITZ, N. 1980. The evolution of programs. Ph.D. dissertation, Dept. of Applied Mathematics, Weizmann Institute of Science, Rehovot, Israel; available as Rep. R-80-1017, Dept. of Computer Science, Univ. of Illinois, Urbana Ill.

DERSHOWITZ, N. 1981. The evolution of programs: Program abstraction and instantiation. In *Proceedings of 5th International Conference on Software Engineering* (San Diego, Calif., Mar. 9–12). IEEE, New York, pp. 79–88.

DERSHOWITZ, N., AND MANNA, Z. 1975. On automating structured programming. In *Proceedings of International Symposium on Proving and Improving Programs* (Arc-et-Senan, France, July 1–3). IRIA, Le Chesnay, France.

DERSHOWITZ, N., AND MANNA, Z. 1977. The evolution of programs: Automatic program modification. *IEEE Trans. Softw. Eng. SE-3*, 6, 377–385.

DEWAR, R. B. K., GRAND, A., LIU, S-C., AND SCHWARTZ, J. T. 1979a. Programming by refinement as exemplified by the SETL representation sublanguage. *ACM Trans. Program. Lang. Syst. 1*, 1 (July), 27–49.

DEWAR, R. B. K., SHARIR, M., AND WEIXELBAUM, E. 1979b. On transformational construction of garbage collection algorithms. Paper presented at the 26th meeting of IFIP WG 2.1 (Brussels, Dec.). Available from authors.

DIJKSTRA, E. W. 1976a. Why naive transformation systems are unlikely to work. EWD-636, privately circulated manuscript.

DIJKSTRA, E. W. 1976b. *A Discipline of Programming.* Prentice-Hall, Englewood Cliffs, N.J.

DONZEAU-GOUGE, V., HUET, G., KAHN, G., LANG, B., AND LEVY, J. J. 1975. A structure oriented program editor: A first step towards computer assisted programming. In *Proceedings of International Computing Symposium 1975* (Antibes, France). Also, Lab. Rep. 114, IRIA, Le Chesnay, France.

DONZEAU-GOUGE, V., HUET, G., KAHN, G., AND LANG, B. 1980. Programming environments based on structured editors: The MENTOR Experience. Res. Rep. 26, INRIA, Le Chesnay, France.

ECL 1974. ECL programmer's manual. TR-23-74, Center for Research in Computing Technology, Harvard Univ., Cambridge, Mass.

ERHARD, F. 1981. Programmtransformation im CIP System. Notizen zum interaktiven Programmieren 6, GI Fachausschuss 2, GI, Bonn, West Germany.

ERICKSON, R. W., Ed. 1981. AFFIRM collected papers. Information Science Institute, Univ. Southern California, Marina del Rey.

ERSHOV, A. P. 1978. On the essence of compilation. In *Proceedings of IFIP Working Conference on Formal Description of Programming Concepts* (St. Andrews, Canada, 1977), E. J. Neuhold, Ed. Elsevier North-Holland, New York, pp. 391–420.

ERSHOV, A. P. 1982. Mixed computation: Potential applications and problems for study. *Theor. Comput. Sci. 18,* 41–67.

FEATHER, M. S. 1978a. ZAP program transformation system: Primer and user manual. Res. Rep. 54, Dept. of Artificial Intelligence, Univ. of Edinburgh, Scotland.

FEATHER, M. S. 1978b. Program transformation applied to the telegram problem. In *Program Transformations,* B. Robinet, Ed. Dunod, Paris, pp. 173–186.

FEATHER, M. S. 1979. A program transformation system. Ph.D. dissertation, Univ. of Edinburgh, Scotland.

FEATHER, M. 1982a. Mappings for rapid prototyping. *SIGSOFT Softw. Eng. Notes 7,* 5 (Dec.) 17–24.

FEATHER, M. S. 1982b. A system for assisting program transformation. *ACM Trans. Program. Lang. Syst. 4,* 1 (Jan.) 1–20.

FICKAS, S. F. 1982. Automating the transformational development of software. Ph.D. dissertation, Univ. of California, Irvine.

GERHART, S. L. 1980. Complete and recursion induction in current AFFIRM. Affirm-Memo-33-SLG, Information Science Institute, Univ. Southern California, Marina del Rey.

GERHART, S. L., AND WILE, D. S. 1979. The DELTA experiment: Specification and verification of a multiple-user file updating module. In *Proceedings of Specifications of Reliable Software Conference* (Cambridge, Mass., Apr.). IEEE, New York, pp. 198–211.

GERHART, S. L., MUSSER, D. R., THOMPSON, D. H., BAKER, D. A., BATES, R. L., ERICKSON, R. W., LONDON, R. L., TAYLOR, D. G., AND WILE, D. S. 1980. On overview of AFFIRM: A specification and verification system. In *Information Processing 80,* S. H. Lavington, Ed. Elsevier North-Holland, New York, pp. 343–347.

GOAD, C. 1982. Automatic construction of special purpose programs. Rep. STAN-CS-82-897, Dept. of Computer Science, Stanford Univ., Stanford, Calif.

GOLDMAN, N., AND WILE, D. 1980. A relational data base foundation for process specification. In *Entity Relationship Approach to Systems Analysis and Design,* P. P. S. Chen, Ed. Elsevier North-Holland, New York.

GORDON, M. J., MILNER, R., AND WADSWORTH, C. 1977. Edinburgh LCF. Rep. CSR-11-77, Dept. of Computer Science, Edinburgh Univ., Scotland.

GREEN, C. 1976. The design of the PSI program synthesis system. In *Proceedings of 2d International Conference on Software Engineering* (San Francisco, Calif., Oct. 13–15). IEEE, New York, pp. 4–18.

GREEN, C. 1977. A summary of the PSI program synthesis system. In *Proceedings of 5th International Joint Conference on Artificial Intelligence* (Cambridge, Mass.). M. I. T., Cambridge, Mass., pp. 380–381.

GREEN, C. 1978. The PSI program synthesis system 1978: An abstract. In *Proceedings of 1978 National Computer Conference* (Anaheim, Calif., June 5–8), AFIPS Press, Reston, Va., pp. 673–674.

GREEN, C., AND BARSTOW, D. 1975. Some rules for the automatic synthesis of programs. In *Advance Papers of the 4th International Joint Conference on Artificial Intelligence* (Tbilisi, Georgia, USSR, Sept. 3–8). International Joint Council on Artificial Intelligence, Inc., Stanford, Calif.

GREEN, C., AND BARSTOW, D. 1976. A hypothetical dialogue exhibiting a knowledge base for a program understanding system. In *Machine Representations of Knowledge,* E. W. Elcock and D. Michie, Eds. Wiley, New York, pp. 335–359.

GREEN, C., AND BARSTOW, D. 1978. On program synthesis knowledge. *Artif. Intell. 10,* 241–279.

GREEN, C., GABRIEL, R. P., KANT, E., KEDZIERSKI, B. J., McCUNE, B. R., PHILLIPS, J. V., TAPPEL, S. T., AND WESTFOLD, S. J. 1979. Results in knowledge based program synthesis. In *Proceed-*

ings of 6th International Joint Conference on Artificial Intelligence (Tokyo, Aug. 20–23). International Joint Council on Artificial Intelligence, Inc., Stanford, Calif., pp. 342–344.

GREEN, C., PHILIPS, J., WESTFOLD, S., PRESSBURGER, T., KEDZIERSKI, B., ANGEBRANNDT, S., MONT-REYNAUD, B., AND TAPPEL, S. 1982. Research on knowledge-based programming and algorithm design—1981. Rep. Kes. U. 81.2, Kestrel Institute, Palo Alto, Calif.

GUIHO, G., GRESSE, C., AND BIDOIT, M. 1980. Conception et certification de programmes a partir d'une décomposition par les données. *RAIRO Inf. 14*, 4, 319–351.

HARALDSSON, A. 1974. PCDB—A procedure generator for a predicate calculus data base. In *Information Processing 74*. Elsevier North-Holland, New York, pp. 375–379.

HARALDSSON, A. 1977. A program manipulation system based on partial evaluation. Ph.D. dissertation, Dept. of Mathematics, Linkoping Univ., Sweden.

HARALDSSON, A. 1978. A partial evaluator and its use for compiling iterative statements in LISP. In *Proceedings of 5th Annual Symposium on Principles of Programming Languages* (Tucson, Ariz., Jan. 23–25). ACM, New York, pp. 195–202.

HESSE, W. 1981. Methoden und Werkzeuge zur Software-Entwicklung: Einordnung und Oberblick. In *Werkzeuge der Programmiertechnik*, G. Goos, Ed., Informatik-Fachberichte, vol. 43. Springer, New York, pp. 113–153.

HEWITT, C. 1971. Desciption and theoretical analysis (using schemata) of PLANNER: A language for proving theorems and manipulating models in a robot. Ph.D. dissertation, Massachusetts Institute of Technology, Cambridge, Mass.

HUET, G., AND LANG, B. 1978. Proving and applying program transformations expressed with second-order patterns. *Acta Inf. 11*, 31–55.

HÜNKE, H., Ed. 1981. *Software Engineering Environments*. Elsevier North-Holland, New York.

IGARASHI, S., LONDON, R. L., AND LUCKHAM, D. C. 1975. Automatic program verification I: Logical basis and its implementation. *Acta Inf. 4*, 145–182.

KANT, E. 1977. The selection of efficient implementations for a high-level language. In *Proceedings of 4th ACM Symposium on Artificial Intelligence and Programming Languages* (Rochester, N.Y., Aug. 15–17). *SIGPLAN Not. (ACM) 12*, 8 (Aug.)/ *SIGART Newsl. (ACM) 64* (Aug.), 140–156.

KANT, E. 1979. A knowledge-based approach to using efficiency estimation in program synthesis. In *Proceedings of 6th International Joint Conference on Artificial Intelligence* (Tokyo, Aug. 20–23). International Joint Council on Artificial Intelligence, Inc., Stanford, Calif., pp. 457–462.

KANT, E., AND BARSTOW, D. R. 1981. The refinement paradigm: The interaction of coding and efficiency knowledge in program synthesis. *IEEE Trans. Softw. Eng. 7*, 458–471.

KIBLER, D. F. 1978. Power, efficiency, and correctness of transformation systems. Ph.D. dissertation, Univ. of California, Irvine.

KIBLER, D. F., NEIGHBORS, J. M., AND STANDISH, T. A. 1977. Program manipulation via an efficient production system. In Proceedings of Symposium on Artificial Intelligence and Programming Languages, (Rochester, N.Y., Aug. 15–17). *SIGPLAN Not. (ACM) 12*, 8 (Aug.)/*SIGART Newsl. (ACM) 64* (Aug.), 163–173.

KNUTH, D. E. 1974. Structured programming with **goto** statements. *ACM Comput. Surv. 6*, 4 (Dec.), 261–301.

KOENIG, S., AND PAIGE, R. 1981. A transformational framework for the automatic control of derived data. In *Proceedings of 7th International Conference on Very Large Data Bases* (Cannes, France, Sept. 9–11). IEEE, New York, pp. 306–318.

KOTT, L. 1978. About a transformation system: A theoretical study. In *Program Transformations*, B. Robinet, Ed. Dunot, Paris.

KOTT, L. 1982. Unfold/fold program transformations. Res. Rep. 155, INRIA Centre de Rennes, France.

LEE, S., ERICKSON, R. W., AND GERHART, S. L. 1981. Finding a design error in a distributed system: A case study. In *Proceedings of IEEE Symposium on Reliability in Distributed Software and Database Systems* (Pittsburgh, Pa., July 21–22). IEEE Computer Society, Los Alamitos, Calif.

LONDON, P., AND FEATHER, M. 1982. Implementing specification freedoms. Res. Rep. 81-100, Information Science Institute, Univ. of Southern California, Marina del Rey.

LOVEMAN, D. B. 1977. Program improvement by source-to-source transformation. *J. ACM 24*, 1 (Jan.) 121–145.

LOVEMAN, D., AND FANEUF, R. 1975. Program optimization—Theory and practice. In Proceedings of Conference on Programming Languages and Compilers for Parallel and Vector Machines. *SIGPLAN Not. 10*, 3 (Mar.), 97–102.

LOW, J. R. 1978. Automatic data structure selection: An example and overview. *Commun. ACM 21*, 5 (May) 376–385.

LUCKMANN, M. 1979. CIP-Baummodul (Benutzeranleitung). Report, Institut für Informatik, Technische Univ. München, Munich, West Germany.

MAHER, B., AND SLEEMAN, D. H. 1983. Automatic program improvement: Variable usage transformations. ACM *Trans. Program. Lang. Syst. 5*, 2 (Apr.) 236–264.

MANNA, Z., AND WALDINGER, R. 1975. Knowledge and reasoning in program synthesis. *Artif. Intell. 6*, 2, 175–208.

MANNA, Z., AND WALDINGER, R. 1977a. The automatic synthesis of recursive programs. In Proceedings of Symposium on Artificial Intelligence and Programming Languages (Rochester, N.Y., Aug. 15–17). *SIGPLAN Not. (ACM) 12*, 8 (Aug.)/ *SIGART Newsl. (ACM) 64* (Aug.), 29–36.

MANNA, Z., AND WALDINGER, R. 1977b. The automatic synthesis of systems of recursive programs. In *Proceedings of 5th International Joint Conference on Artificial Intelligence* (Cambridge, Mass., Aug. 22–25). M. I. T., Cambridge, Mass., pp. 405–411.

MANNA, Z., AND WALDINGER, R. 1978a. The synthesis of structure-changing programs. In *Proceedings of 3rd International Conference on Software Engineering* (Atlanta Ga., May 10–12). IEEE, New York, pp. 175–187.

MANNA, Z., AND WALDINGER, R. 1978b. DEDALUS—The DEDuctive Algorithm Ur-synthesizer. In *Proceedings of National Computer Conference* (Anaheim, Calif., June 5–8), vol. 47. AFIPS Press, Reston, Va., pp. 683–690.

MANNA, Z., AND WALDINGER, R. 1979. Synthesis: Dreams ⇒ Programs. *IEEE Trans. Softw. Eng. SE-5*, 4, 294–328.

MANNA, Z., AND WALDINGER, R. 1980. A deductive approch to program synthesis. *ACM. Trans. Program. Lang. Syst. 2*, 1 (Jan.), 90–121.

MANNA, Z., AND WALDINGER, R. 1981. Deductive synthesis of the unification algorithm. *Sci. Comput. Program. 1*, 5–48.

McCUNE, B. P. 1970. The PSI program model builder: Synthesis of very high-level programs. In *Proceedings of Symposium on Artificial Intelligence and Programming Languages* (Rochester, N.Y., Aug. 15–17). *SIGPLAN Not.* (ACM) *12*, 8 (Aug.)–*SIGART Newsl.* (ACM) 64 (Aug.), 130–139.

McCUNE, B. P. 1979. Building program models incrementally from informal descriptions. Ph.D. dissertation, STAN-CS-79-772, Computing Science Dept., Stanford Univ., Stanford, Calif.

MÉLÈSE, B. 1981. MENTOR: L'environnement PASCAL. Tech. Rep. 5, INRIA Centre de Roquencourt, Le Chesnay, France.

MICHIE, D., ED. 1979. *Expert Systems in the Micro Electronic Age.* University Press, Edinburgh, Scotland.

MICHIE, D. ED. 1982. *Introductory Readings in Expert Systems.* Gordon and Breach, New York.

MÖLLER, B., PARTSCH, H., AND PEPPER, P. 1983. Programming with transformations: An overview of the Munich CIP project. Submitted for publication.

MOOR, I. W., AND DARLINGTON, J. 1981. Formal synthesis of an efficient implementation for an abstract data type. Unpublished manuscript.

MOSTOW, D. J. 1981. Mechanical transformation of tasks heuristics into operational procedures. Ph.D. dissertation, Rep. CMU-CS-81-113, Carnegie-Mellon Univ., Pittsburgh, Pa.

MUSSER, D. R. 1979. Abstract data type specification in the AFFIRM system. In *Proceedings of Specifications of Reliable Software* (Cambridge, Mass., Apr. 3–5). IEEE, New York, pp. 47–57.

NEIGHBORS, J. M. 1980. Software construction using components. Ph.D. dissertation, Tech. Rep. 160, Univ. of Calif., Irvine.

PAIGE, R. 1981. Expression continuity and formal differentiation of algorithms. Rep. LCSR-TR-9, Laboratory for Computing Science Research, Rutgers Univ., New Brunswick, N.J.

PAIGE, R. 1982. Applications of finite differencing to database integrity control and query/transaction optimization. In *Advances in Database Theory*, vol. 2, J. Minker, J. M. Nicolas, and H. Gallaire, Eds. Plenum Press, New York.

PAIGE, R. 1983. Transformational programming—Application to algorithms and systems. In *Proceedings of 10th ACM Symposium on Principles of Programming Languages* (Austin, Tex., Jan. 24–26). ACM, New York, pp. 73–87.

PAIGE, R., AND KOENIG, S. 1982. Finite differencing of computable expressions. *ACM. Trans. Program. Lang. Syst. 4*, 3 (July), 402–454.

PAIGE, R., AND SCHWARTZ, J. T. 1977. Expression continuity and the formal differentiation of algorithms. In *Proceedings of 4th ACM Symposium on Principles of Programming Languages* (Los Angeles, Calif., Jan. 17–19). ACM, New York, pp. 58–63.

PARTSCH, H. 1984. The CIP transformation system. In *Program Transformation and Programming Environments*, Pepper, P., Ed. Lecture Notes in Computer Science. Springer-Verlag. New York, to be published.

PARTSCH, H., AND STEINBRÜGGEN, R. 1981. A comprehensive survey on program transformation systems. Rep. TUM I8108, Institut für Informatik, Technische Univ. München, Munich, West Germany.

PEPPER, P. 1979. A study on transformational semantics. In *Program construction*, F. L. Bauer and M. Broy, Eds. Lecture Notes in Computer Science, vol. 69. Springer-Verlag, New York, pp. 322–405.

PEPPER, P., ED. 1984. *Program Transformation and Programming Environments.* Lecture Notes in Computer Science. Springer-Verlag, New York. To be published.

RICH, C., AND SHROBE, H. E. 1978. Initial report on a LISP programmer's apprentice. *IEEE Trans. Softw. Eng. SE-4*, 6.

RICH, C., SHROBE, H. E., WATERS, R. C. 1979. Overview of the programmer's apprentice. In *Proceedings of 6th International Joint Conference on Artificial Intelligence* (Tokyo, Aug. 20–23).

RIETHMAYER, H.-O. 1981. Die Entwicklung der Bedienungskomponente des CIP Systems. Notizen zur interaktiven Programmierung 6, GI-Fachausschuss 2, GI, Bonn, West Germany.

RUTTER, P. E. 1977. Improving programs by source-to-source transformations. Ph.D. dissertation, Univ. of Illinois, Urbana.

SCHONBERG, E., SCHWARTZ, J. T., AND SHARIR, M. 1979. Automatic data structure selection in SETL. In *Proceedings of 6th ACM Symposium on Principles of Programming Languages* (San Antonio, Tex., Jan. 29–31). ACM, New York, pp. 197–210.

SCHONBERG, E., SCHWARTZ, J. T., AND SHARIR, M. 1981. An automatic technique for selection of data representations in SETL programs. *ACM Trans. Program. Lang. Syst. 3*, 2 (Apr.), 126–143.

SCHWARTZ, J. T. 1975a. On programming: An interim report of the SETL project. Courant Institute, New York Univ., New York.

SCHWARTZ, J. T. 1975b. Automatic data structure choice in a language of very high level. *Commun. ACM 18*, 722–728.

SCHWARTZ, J. T. 1977. Correct program technology. Courant Computer Rep. 12, Courant Institute, New York Univ., New York.

SHARIR, M. 1979a. Some observations concerning formal differentiation of set-theoretic expressions. Tech. Rep. 16, Computer Science Dept., Courant Institute, New York Univ., New York.

SHARIR, M. 1979b. Algorithm derivation by transformations. Tech. Rep. 021, Computer Science Dept., Courant Institute, New York Univ., New York.

SHARIR, M. 1981. Formal integration: A program transformation technique. *Comput. Lang. 6*, 35–46.

STANDISH, T. A., HARRIMAN, D. C., KIBLER, D. F., AND NEIGHBORS, J. M. 1976a. The Irvine program transformation catalogue. Dept. of Information and Computer Science, Univ. of California, Irvine, Calif.

STANDISH, T. A., KIBLER, D. F., AND NEIGHBORS, J. M. 1976b. Improving and refining transformations by program manipulation. In *Proceedings of Annual Conference*, (Houston, Tex., Oct. 20–22). ACM, New York, pp. 509–516.

STEINBRÜGGEN, R. 1980a. The use of nested scheme parameters in the system CIP. In *GI-10. Jahrestagung Saarbrücken*, R. Wilhelm, Ed. Informatik Fachberichte, 33. Springer-Verlag, New York. (Extended abstract.)

STEINBRÜGGEN, R. 1980b. Pre-algorithmic specifications of the system CIP. Part 1. Rep. TUM-I8016, Institut für Informatik, Technische Univ. München, Munich, West Germany.

STEINBRÜGGEN, R. 1981. The composition of schemes for local program transformation. In *Proceedings of 3d Hungarian Computer Science Conference* (Budapest, Jan.), M. Arato and L. Varga, Eds. Akademiai Kiado, Budapest, pp. 111–124.

STEINBRÜGGEN, R. 1982. Program development using transformational expressions. Rep. TUM-I8206, Institut für Informatik, Technische Univ. München, Munich, West Germany.

STEINBRÜGGEN, R., AND PARTSCH, H. 1984. Mathematical foundation of transformation systems. Tech. Rep., Institut für Informatik, Technische Univ. München, Munich, West Germany. To appear.

THOMPSON, D. H., SUNSHINE, C. A., ERICKSON, R. W., GERHART, S. L., AND SCHWABE, D. 1981. Specification and verification of communication protocols in AFFIRM using state transition models. RR-81-88, Information Science Institute, Univ. of Southern California, Marina del Rey.

TOWNLEY, J. A. 1981. PDS user's manual. Center for Research in Computing Technology, Harvard Univ., Cambridge, Mass.

TOWNLEY, J. A. 1982. The use of transformations to implement an algorithm. In *Proceedings of International Symposium on Programming* (Turin, Italy, Apr. 6–8). Lecture Notes in Computer Science, vol. 137. Springer-Verlag, New York, pp. 381–406.

WALDINGER, R. J. 1977. Achieving several goals simultaneously. In *Machine Representations of Knowledge*, Machine Intelligence, vol. 8, E. W. Elcock and D. Michie, Eds. Ellis Horwood, Chichester, England, pp. 94–136.

WATERS, R. C. 1982. The programmer's apprentice: Knowledge based program editing. *IEEE Trans. Softw. Eng. SE-8*, 1, 1–12.

WEGBREIT, B. 1971. The ECL programming system. In *Proceedings of AFIPS Fall Joint Computer Conference* (Las Vegas, Nev., Nov. 16–18), vol. 39. AFIPS Press, Reston, Va., pp. 253–262.

WILE, D. 1981a. Program developments as formal objects. USC/ISI Tech. Rep. Information Science Institute, Univ. of Southern California, Marina del Rey.

WILE, D. 1981b. POPART: Producer of parsers and related tools, system builder's manual. USC/ISI Tech. Rep., Information Science Institute, Univ. of Southern California, Marina del Rey.

WILE, D., BALZER, R., AND GOLDMAN, N. 1977. Automated derivation of program control structure from natural language program descriptions. In Proceedings of Symposium on Artificial Intelligence and Programming Languages (Rochester, N.Y., Aug. 15–17). *SIGPLAN Not.* (ACM) *12*, 8 (Aug.)–*SIGART Newsl.* (ACM) 64 (Aug.), 77–84.

Received July 1981; final revision accepted January 1984.

Transformational Implementation: An Example

ROBERT BALZER

Abstract—A system for mechanically transforming formal program specifications into efficient implementations under interactive user control is described and illustrated through a detailed example. The potential benefits and problems of this approach to software implementation are discussed.

Index Terms—Optimization, program manipulation system, program reliability, programming techniques, program transformation.

MUCH recent work has focused on the investigation of program manipulation systems [1], [5]-[8], [12], [14], [17] as an alternative programming paradigm in which the *processes* of design and implementation are themselves the subject of study. They are captured and recorded to provide documentation of the program, the basis for its validation, and the framework within which future maintenance will occur.

This extension of the conventional programming paradigm to include the development of the program as a computer processable object in addition to the program itself is quite profound.

It is comparable to the early recognition that programs could themselves be treated as data, enabling computer languages to be developed. Correspondingly, by capturing and recording the development processes, a set of tools can be developed which use these processes as data.

Although such tools do not yet exist, it is easy to foresee some of their capabilities: automatically generated, up-to-date, and accurate documentation of the program relating the implementation back to its specification; explicating all the assumptions utilized within the development, and identifying the decisions made therein; validation of an implementation based not on an analysis of the resulting program, but rather upon the process by which it was produced; maintenance performed by modifying the development process rather than by attempting to modify the optimized program; and automatic instrumentation to test the performance assumptions implicit in critical design and implementation decisions.

Before such possibilities can be realized, however, the development process which currently only exists within peoples' heads must be made explicit and recorded. How can this be accomplished?

A key insight of the program manipulation approach is that transformations provide a sufficient basis for the development process. Each development decision can be represented as a transformation applied to the program. Thus, a development

is merely a linear sequence of transformations applied to the program. (Unfortunately, such linear sequences are unintelligible, and like programs, must be structured to be understandable.) But what programs are the transformations applied to? Since the object of the development is to produce a program, the resulting program is obviously not the one to which transformations are applied.

Instead, transformations are applied to the *program* resulting from the previous stage of development. Each stage of the development corresponds to the transformation of a program treated as a specification into another treated as implementation. Thus, development is an iterative (and as we will see later, sometimes a recursive) process of successive refinement in which a specification is gradually transformed into an implementation.

This implies that the original specification of the program is itself a program (so that it can be transformed). To be a program, the specification language must have a formal semantics (thus precluding pseudocode type languages) so that validity of transformations and of the development process is a meaningful concept.

Since the motivation of this program manipulation approach is to capture and record the development process, it is essential that the specification be rather directly stated, and that it is taken as the starting point for the development. Since the intent of a specification is to state *what* is required, while the intent of an implementation is to state *how* those requirements are to be satisfied with minimal expenditure of computing resources, quite different languages for specification and implementation are implied.

This wide disparity between the specification and implementation language and the avoidance of determining *how* requirements should be satisfied within the specification suggests to us that the development (embodied as a sequence of transformations) must be humanly guided (rather than automatically generated), because such global optimization issues are not well enough understood to automate (although this view is not universally held [4], [6], [16]). Thus, we have constructed an interactive system in which a user guides the system by specifying which transformations the system should apply. The rest of this paper is a description of the development process in such an interactive program manipulation system (as embodied in a prototype we have built) through consideration of a simple example. This particular example was chosen to be simple enough to cover within this paper, yet complex enough to demonstrate the type of issues which arise during development. In addition, only well-known examples were considered so that the example chosen did not have to be explained and motivated.

Manuscript received June 30, 1980. This work was supported by the National Science Foundation under Grant MCS 768390.

The author is with the Information Sciences Institute, University of Southern California, Marina del Rey, CA 90291.

Reprinted from *IEEE Transactions on Software Engineering*, Volume SE-7, Number 1, January 1981, pages 3-14. Copyright © 1981 by The Institute of Electrical and Electronics Engineers, Inc.

The Problem

Write a program which, given a set of eight queens, finds a way of positioning them on different squares of a chessboard so that no queen may capture any other.

The Formal Specification

Before the development processes of design and implementation can begin, the problem must be expressed in a formal specification. This specification should express as much as possible *what* the program is to do without expressing *how* it is to be accomplished. The *what* specification will then be systematically converted into a *how* implementation during the development process.

We have developed a formal specification language [2] in which this problem can be directly stated. This language allows the definition of a world (Chess) in terms of the objects (the chess board, the squares of which it is composed, the rows and columns, the various chess pieces, etc.) of that world; the relationships that may exist among those objects (the immediate adjacency of two squares, the squares which comprise a row, pieces occupying a square, etc.); the actions that exist in that world (placing a piece on a square, moving a piece, capturing a piece, etc.); the constraints that the objects of the world must satisfy (two pieces cannot occupy the same square); and the rules of inference within that world (a piece can capture another if it can move to the square occupied by that piece, etc.). These declarations define the environment within which the program will operate. An initial configuration of the objects in the world can be specified (in this case that the chess board is empty (no pieces are on the board) and that eight queens exist). The program portion of the specification then describes either the resulting configuration desired (preferred) or the behavior desired (acceptable). This latter option is provided because many real tasks cannot be simply stated in terms of a goal state, but rather are more naturally specified in terms of their desired behavior (such as a payroll system which periodically issues checks satisfying certain criteria). These behavioral specifications would naturally contain as much "resulting configuration" description as possible so as to least constrain the ultimate implementation. As the development proceeds, the "resulting configuration" portions are converted into behavior specifications which are then specialized and optimized.

For the "eight queens" problem, the formal specification is shown in Fig. 1. For the sake of conciseness and perspicuity, the definition of objects, relationships, and actions have been suppressed, as has the specification of the initial configuration (which defines the structure of the chess board, the fact that no pieces are on any of the squares, and the existence of eight queens) and the inference rule defining queen capture.

The formal specifications indicate that subject to two constraints (that two pieces cannot occupy the same square, and that queens cannot be placed so that they can capture each other), each queen in the set of (presumably eight) queens is to be placed somewhere on the chess board. Although this specification is not the most abstract possible (a completely "resulting state" specification is quite straightforward), and

```
PROGRAMS:
    QUEENS: (LAMBDA  (QUEEN-SET)
              (LOCAL  (BOARD-POSITION)
               (FOR  QUEEN IN-SET  QUEEN-SET DO
                (DETERMINE  BOARD-POSITION FROM
                      (CHESS-BOARD  BOARD-POSITION))
                (ASSERT  (PIECE-ON-BOARD  QUEEN
                                          BOARD-POSITION)
CONSTRAINT: TWO-PIECES-CAN'T-OCCUPY-SAME-SQUARE
    PATTERN: (AND  (PIECE-ON-BOARD  PIECE#1  BOARD-POSITION)
                   (PIECE-ON-BOARD  PIECE#2  BOARD-POSITION))
    PATTERN-VARIABLES: (PIECE#1  PIECE#2  BOARD-POSITION)

CONSTRAINT: QUEEN-CAN'T-CAPTURE-ANOTHER-QUEEN
    PATTERN: (AND  (PIECE-ON-BOARD  QUEEN#1  BOARD-POSITION#1)
                   (PIECE-ON-BOARD  QUEEN#2  BOARD-POSITION#2)
                   (QUEEN-CAPTURE  BOARD-POSITION#1
                                   BOARD-POSITION#2))
    PATTERN-VARIABLES: (QUEEN#1  QUEEN#2  BOARD-POSITION#1
                                 BOARD-POSITION#2)
```

Fig. 1.

although a minor implementation restriction has been imposed (the requirement of queens not capturing each other is only logically imposed on the resulting solution, and need not necessarily be true while the solution is being constructed, as is the case in the formal specification of Fig. 1), this specification has been chosen to reduce the amount of unconventional specification constructs considered in this example.

The Development Plan

The development of this specification into an implementation progressed in three main phases: explication, reorganization, and representation selection. In the explication phase, implicit structures within the specifications are made explicit and constraints are dealt with as early as possible in an attempt to gain an understanding of the algorithmic structure implied by the specification. In the reorganization phase, the sources of computational expense are identified and the program reorganized to mitigate these expenses. Representation suitable for the reorganized programs are selected in the third phase.

This phase-based conceptualization of the development process is not yet part of our prototype system and is introduced here to help the reader understand our development plans. We theorize that in more complex tasks, many cycles of this basic plan occur (it is also clear that the representation selection may precede the reorganization). If so, then some structure must exist among these cycles. Such structure, arising partially *a priori* (plan) and partially *a posteriori* (documentation), represents the explanation of the development.

Currently, a much more primitive development explanation is maintained by the system (see Appendix I). It consists of a linear sequence of state descriptions. Each description is composed of the state name, a comment entered by the developer, and the action taken in that state (such as applying a transformation, loading the initial specification, etc.). Structure is added to the linear sequence only when the action taken within the state fails. Development proceeds within the suspended state until the failing action succeeds.

For the development explanation shown in Appendix I, the explication phase corresponds to states 1 through 7, the reorganization phase corresponds to states 8 and 9, and the representation phase corresponds to state 10.

The Development Process

The development of the implementation from the formal specification is described informally here. The actual form of the program at each step is given in Appendix II which highlights (in bold face) the changes from state N into state $N + 1$. These program displays are produced by the system as part of the automatic documentation of a development [9].

In the text that follows, the informal description of the transition into a state will be preceded by its state description as given in Appendix I.

[State 2 (Unfold Both Constraints) (Apply Transformation: Unfold-Constraint)]

As the first step in making implicit structures explicit, both constraints contained in the original formal specifications are "unfolded." That is, rather than relying on the interpreter of the language to check the constraints after each (revelant) operation and to backtrack in case the constraint is violated, an analysis is performed to determine where explicit checks should be inserted in the program (after assertions which could affect the truthfulness of the constraint predicate), and the appropriate checking and backtracking code is added there. This analysis is performed by the unfold-constraint transformation. As part of its analysis, a simplification of the constraint predicate is performed (because the assertion which the check follows will be true and need not be rechecked). If this predicate is satisfied, then the constraint has been violated and the call to constraint-violation is executed which invokes the backtracking mechanism to reevaluate the most recent nondeterministic statement (the choice of a board position on which to place the queen).

Both constraints are unfolded by this transformation, and since each contains two instances of the fact being asserted, each generates two checks which are inserted in the program. The constraints, having been unfolded, are removed from the program.

[State 3 (Simplify: Remove Redundant Unfolded Constraint Checks) (Manual Effort)]

Because of the symmetry that existed in the constraint patterns, one of the two checks generated by the previous transformation for each constraint is redundant. The current system does not include an automatic simplifier, so either transformations for this particular type of simplification must be applied or else the redundant code must be manually removed. The latter option was chosen to illustrate this facility within the system.

It is assumed that situations will inevitably arise for which the appropriate transformation does not already exist within the catalog. Therefore, the developer may either define a new transformation (thus extending the catalog) or modify the program directly through the interactive editor (i.e., manually modify the program). It must be recognized that both options result in an unvalidated modification of the program (merely defining a transformation does not ensure its validity). In both cases the unvalidated step becomes part of the documentation of the development which can later be reviewed by the others and judged acceptable or not.

The redundancy of the first pair is based on simple renaming of free variables, while the second also depends upon determining that queen capture is a symmetric relation. The second element of each pair of checks was manually edited out of the program.

[State 4 (Make Backtracking Explicit so that It Can be Minimized) (Apply Transformation: Unfold-Consequential-Backtracking)]

The second step in making implicit structure explicit is now attempted by applying the transformation to unfold backtracking (other backtracking transformations can be found in reference [10], [13]). This transformation converts the implicit control structure necessary to support resumption of control at a nondeterminism point from the arbitrary failure into a format in which the nondeterminism is embedded in an iterative loop through all the possibilities searching for an acceptable one as determined by the loop body which contains all the possible failure points reexpressed as loop continuation statements.

The activation pattern for this transformation assumes a recursive format for the routine containing the nondeterminism. Unfortunately, when the transformation is applied to the program in State 3, this activation pattern fails to match. This causes the system to ask whether the developer would like to modify ("jitter") the program so that the activation pattern will match or whether to abort the application of the current transformation. The developer responded that jittering was desired. The system then enters a subgoaling mode in which further development proceeds under the direction of the developer until the suspended activation pattern successfully matches the modified program. At that point, the development pops out of the subgoal mode and continues application of the suspended transformation.

[State 4-1 (Convert Iteration to Recursion) (Jitter Transformation: Make-Set-Iteration-Recursive)]

In the subgoal development the developer applies a transformation (recorded as a jitter transformation because the developer is attempting to get the program to conform to the requirements of a suspended transformation) which converts the iteration to a recursion.

It is instructive to digress for a moment and consider in detail the application of this transformation which is shown in Fig. 2. The transformation contains a comment, an activation pattern, a list of modifications and declaration of variables used within the transformation. In addition, it could contain properties that the program and/or data had to satisfy in order for the transformation to be applicable or properties known to be true after the transformation was applied.

The pattern contains variables and literals (all names not declared to be variables). The variables will be matched against a single expression in the program to which the transformation is applied or against a sequence of expressions (if the variable begins with an exclamation mark). When this pattern is applied to the program in State 3, a unique match is found in which SET1 is bound to QUEEN-SET, P2 is bound to (BOARD-POSITION), the segment variables !S1 is bound to everything following the DO in the FOR statement (the DETERMINE and

```
COMMENT: CONVERT SIMPLE SET ITERATION THROUGH THE (ONLY)
         PARAMETER INTO A RECURSION

PATTERN: [LAMBDA (SET1)
               (LOCAL P2 (FOR O1 IN-SET SET1 DO IS1)
                IS2]

MODIFICATIONS: [(BIND R1 FROM FNAME)
               (BIND P3 FROM (CONS O1 P2))
               (REPLACE-PATTERN
                ((LAMBDA (SET1)
                       (LOCAL P3 (TERMINATION-TEST:
                                 (IF (EMPTY SET1)
                                     THEN
                                     IS2
                                     (RETURN)))
                        (REMOVE O1 FROM SET1)
                        IS1
                        (RECURSIVE-CALL: (R1 SET1)

PATTERN-VARIABLES: (SET1 IS1 O1 P2 IS2 P3 R1)
```

Fig. 2.

inner LOCAL statements), etc. If more than a single match were found, the developer would have been asked which match to use. If no match were found, the developer would have been asked whether the program should be jittered or the transformation aborted.

Following the pattern match, the applicability properties to be satisfied are checked (there are none in this transformation). These properties fall into two categories—properties which must be satisfied before the transformation can be applied and properties which eventually must be satisfied to validate the applicability of this transformation but which need not be considered immediately. Such properties are quite important because they build up "requirements" on the program and/or data which must eventually be satisfied, but which because they can be delayed, can be used as guidance for the subsequent development. If any immediate properties were not satisfied, then the system would attempt to prove them (currently only through special purpose property provers). Failing that, it would enter a subgoaling mode until further development established the immediate property.

After the applicability properties are satisfied (or delayed), the modifications are performed. These modifications are a linear sequence of actions. The prototypical action is to replace the portion of the program matched by the applicability pattern by some new pattern composed of literals and variables. The variances used in this replacement pattern can either be bound by the applicability pattern (such as SET1) or ones calculated from those variables (such as R1 and P3) through the BIND action. This sequence of BIND actions calculating new values which become part of the replacement pattern is quite typical of the transformations we have studied (and separates them from simpler so-called "syntactic" transformations which involve only pattern replacement).

In addition to these actions, other transformations can be applied (providing a means to package transformations), arbitrary functions can be invoked, or a simple plan established through goals to be achieved.

In the current transformation, the BIND action is used to calculate values for the recursive call of the program being transformed (in variable R1) and for the addition of the program iteration variable (QUEEN) to the declaration of variables in the LOCAL statement (in the transformation variable P3).

```
COMMENT: MAKE BACKTRACKING EXPLICIT

PATTERN: (LOCAL V1 (TERMINATION-TEST: (IF P2 THEN IS5 (RETURN)))
               IS1
               (DETERMINE O1 FROM P1)
               IS2
               (RECURSIVE-CALL: S3)
               IS4)

NECESSARY-PROPERTIES: ((CONSEQUENTIAL-NON-DETERMINISM-FREE IS1)
                      (CONSEQUENTIAL-NON-DETERMINISM-FREE IS2)
                      (CONSEQUENTIAL-NON-DETERMINISM-FREE IS4)
                      (CONSEQUENTIAL-NON-DETERMINISM-FREE IS5))

MODIFICATIONS: [(BIND IS2* FROM
                     (UNFOLD-CONSEQUENTIAL-BACKTRACKING-BUILDER IS2))
               [BIND IS2UNDO FROM (UNDO-OF (ACTIVE-PREDECESSORS-OF
                                          NIL IS2]
               [BIND IS1UNDO FROM (UNDO-OF (ACTIVE-PREDECESSORS-OF
                                          NIL IS1]
               (BIND IS5* FROM (UNFOLD-CONSEQUENTIAL-BACTRACKING-BUILDER
                IS5 T))
               (REPLACE-PATTERN
                ((LOCAL V1 (TERMINATION-TEST: (IF P2 THEN IS5*
                                             (EXIT SUCCESSFUL)))
                 IS1
                 (FOR ALL P1 THEREIS IS2*
                     (IF (SUCCESSFUL (RECURSIVE-CALL: S3))
                         THEN
                         (LOOP-RETURN CHOICE-ACCEPTED)
                         ELSE
                         (UNDO-ACTIONS: IS2UNDO)
                         (LOOP-RETURN FORCE-ANOTHER-CHOICE))
                     THEN
                     IS4
                     (EXIT SUCCESSFUL)
                     ELSE
                     (UNDO-ACTIONS: IS1UNDO)
                     (EXIT UNSUCCESSFUL]

PATTERN-VARIABLES: (IS1 IS2 IS4 IS2* IS2UNDO IS1UNDO V1 P2 P1
                   S3 O1 IS5* IS5)
```

Fig. 3.

These values are then used, along with several found directly by the applicability pattern, to form the replacement pattern.

The resulting program has annotations in the form of labels (names ending with a colon), which describe the teleological function of that portion of the program [15]. These annotations may well help later transformations access and analyze appropriate parts of the program. But as these annotations are currently part of the program text, they must be dealt with by succeeding transformations whether they are interested in these annotations or not. This has proved most bothersome. One solution used in the MENTOR system [11] is to place these annotations into orthogonal dimensions which are accessible only by special commands so that for those uninterested, they are invisible. We expect to employ this solution for all annotations including the maintenance of properties.

After applying the jittering transformation of State 4-1, the modified program successfully matches the applicability pattern of the suspended Unfold-consequential-backtracking transformation, and so processing of this transformation is resumed. The transformation (shown in Fig. 3) is similar in structure to the previous transformation as its modifications consists of a series of BIND actions followed by a REPLACE-PATTERN action. Unlike the previous transformation, this one contains some NECESSARY-PROPERTIES which must be satisfied before the transformation can be applied. The properties are arbitrary predicates applied to the various objects of the system being implemented (such as its programs, code segments, and data structures). In this transformation, there are four instances of the same property applied to single (but different) arguments consisting of a code segment identified by the match of the transformation applicability pattern. Aside from a small number of built-in properties directly relating to the semantics of the specification language (and produced and maintained by an analysis package soon to be incorporated within the system), all other properties must be defined either in terms of other properties (theorem proving techniques will be used to determine whether or not the property is satisfied) or self-defined through direct generation as the result (the KNOWN property) of some transformation(s) and/or deduction through special purpose property provers. Typically for self-defined properties, no explicit formal definition exists.

The property (CONSEQUENTIAL-NON-DETERMINISM-FREE) used in this transformation is defined only through its special purpose property prover. Informally, the property means that the code segment to which it is applied does not contain any "meaningful" nondeterminism. The reason this is important is that this transformation rearranges the program so that any "backtracking point" is part of the still active loop so that backtracking can be accomplished by merely continuing that loop (after undoing any actions taken within the loop). It assumes that only a single such backtracking point exists, and uses the property to validate this assumption. The concern is that only a single backtracking point exists and the existence of "incidental" nondeterminism is of no consequence. In the program of State 4-1, there are two nondeterministic statements, the selection of a queen and the determination of where to place it on the chessboard. The first of these is incidental in that it does not matter which queen is selected. But the second is consequential because the course of subsequent processing is highly dependent upon the choice made. Thus, in backtracking, only the nondeterminism of the selection of a board position should be considered as the other, incidental choice of a queen, does not affect the subsequent processing.

After the applicability pattern of the transformation has been matched, the system attempts to verify that the necessary properties are satisfied. The first property is CONSEQUENTIAL-NON-DETERMINISM-FREE applied to the segment !S1 which is bound to the statement (REMOVE QUEEN FROM QUEEN-SET). The method of verifying this property is to invoke its special purpose property prover which fails because it is unable to tell that this nondeterminism is incidental. Because a necessary property could not be verified the system enters a subgoal mode (through a self-generated ACHIEVE command which results in State 4-2) under which further development will continue until the necessary property is achieved. An appropriate message to this effect is given to the developer.

[State 4 2-1 (Mark "REMOVE" as Incidental Nondeterminism) (Apply Transformations: Mark-Incidental-Nondeterminism)]

The developer responds to this problem by applying a transformation which marks the REMOVE statement as incidental (by converting it to REMOVE*). This transformation has as a required property that the choice of the object being removed (queen) is incidental. Since this is a required rather than an immediate property, it need not be verified immediately, and so it is added as an UNPROVED-PROPERTY of the current state. Such properties must either be proved (by one of the methods described previously) or claimed (assumed by the user to be

true) before the development is completed. Any claims (developer assumptions) become part of the documentation of the development.

After each step of the development in the subgoal mode, the system attempts to determine whether the property to be achieved can be verified. Here, the appropriate method is to reinvoke the special purpose property prover on code segment !S1. However, the transformation just applied modified this code segment and the new value must be used. This is accomplished by rematching the suspended applicability pattern to obtain the appropriate code segment. In fact, since the subgoal development logically precedes the suspended transformation, the suspended transformation is reprocessed after each subgoal development step.

With !S1 rebound to (REMOVE* QUEEN FROM QUEEN-SET), the special purpose property prover is successful in verifying the CONSEQUENTIAL-NON-DETERMINISM-FREE property.

Verification of the first instance of the CONSEQUENTIAL-NON-DETERMINISM-FREE property completes the processing of the subgoal ACHIEVE state, and processing of State 4 resumes with attempts to verify the other instances of this property, all of which succeed.

Processing then continues with the modification steps. The second and third BIND actions find the active statements within some code segment and then build a sequence which undoes their effects (so that when control is returned to the "back-tracking point" (now in the form of an interactive loop) the program state has been restored to its state when control was last there). The first and last BIND action locate any CONSTRAINT-VIOLATION statements which occur in the program and replace them by the undo of the active statements which precede the CONSTRAINT-VIOLATION statement (and follow the nondeterministic choice) followed by a loop continuation statement (to the loop being introduced by this transformation). After all the BIND actions have been processed, the replacement pattern is constructed and substituted for the portion of the program matched by the transformation's applicability pattern.

[State 5 (Assimilate Constraint into Generator) (Apply Transformation: Assimilate-Test-in-Thesis-Loop)]

The final stage in explicating the underlying structure of the algorithm is to incorporate the constraints that a board position must satisfy into its selection. Here, these constraints are tested after a queen is placed on the board at the selected position (because the constraints were originally stated in terms of pieces on the board), and if the position is unacceptable, then the queen is removed from the board and another selection made. In general, more efficient processing results when a selection is based on all such restrictions that it must satisfy. Towards this end, the developer attempts to apply a transformation to assimilate one of these restrictions into the generator of board positions. (This same transformation will be applied again to assimilate the other restrictions.) Unfortunately, the applicability pattern of this transformation requires that the restrictions being assimilated be the first statement of the body of the for-loop in which the generator occurs and this fails to match the program. As before, the system asks the developer whether jittering is desired, and when affirmed, initiates a subgoal development (which will take several steps before the suspended applicability pattern can be matched).

[State 5-1 (Merge the Locals) (Jitter Transformation: Merge-Locals)]

As the first step in the jittering process, the developer attempts to merge the LOCAL inside the for-loop with the outer LOCAL. Again the applicability pattern fails because the two LOCAL's being merged must be separated by only a single level of nesting (here the inner LOCAL is inside the for-loop which is inside the LOCAL), and so (after confirmation by the developer), another level of jittering is initiated.

[State 5-1-1 (Extract LOCAL from For-Loop) (Jitter Transformation: Extract-Local-from-For-Loop)]

The developer applies a transformation which extracts the LOCAL from within the for-loop. This transformation enables the suspended applicability pattern of the Merge-locals transformation to succeed and so ends this level of jittering.

The suspended applicability pattern matched the jittered program and the transformation's modification steps are performed. First a BIND statement is used to calculate the combined set of variable declarations, and then the replacement pattern is formed which contains the combined declarations and in which the statements of the inner LOCAL are embedded within the outer one (as noted previously, the current system does not yet employ orthogonal annotation dimensions [11]. Here the LOCAL statements are used solely to scope variables. If this variable scoping were handled as an annotation it would not impede the development as it does here).

[State 5-3 (Move Constraint Test Ahead of Assertion) (Jitter Transformation: Move-Constraint-Uphill)]

The restriction has now been moved to the top level of the for-loop body, but it follows the assertion (rather than preceding it as required by the suspended assimilation applicability pattern). The developer applies the Move-constraint-uphill to interchange the order of the restriction and the assertion which precedes it.

To interchange these two statements, their mutual interactions must be revised to select the new ordering. This leaves the assertion unchanged since it has no dependence on the restriction. However, both the predicate and body of the restriction must (in general) be updated to reflect knowledge of the existence of the assertion which now follows them. Thus, if the predicate depended, in part, on the existence of the assertion, it must be modified to incorporate this dependence without actually accessing the date (because it will not yet exist). In the current case, the predicate is independent of the assertion, and so is not changed. On the other hand, the THEN clause denies the assertion before forcing another iteration of the selection loop, and thus, is highly dependent upon the assertion. The semantics of the program is maintained if

the denial is removed (whenever another iteration is forced the assertion will not exist). These modifications to the program are calculated by special purpose analysis routines (called as part of the transformation's BIND actions), incorporated into the replacement pattern, and substituted into the program.

[State 5-5 (Simplify: Suppress Null Else Clause) (Jitter Transformation: Else-Suppression)]

Although the restriction is now in the right location (as the first statement in the for-loop body), the suspended applicability pattern still does not match because it requires the restriction to be an IF-THEN statement (with no ELSE clause), and this restriction has an ELSE clause whose body is NIL. The fact that this match fails because of this trivial problem points up two difficulties with the current system. First, no automatic simplification exists. Such simplification would (if it existed) certainly have removed this null ELSE clause when it was created (by the unfold-constraint transformation in State 2). Secondly, given that a simple mismatch exists between the applicability pattern and program, rather than have jittering be a manual process (as it currently is), the system should automatically jitter the program so that the desired transformation can be applied (we are working to resolve both these deficiencies). Here, the developer had to apply a simplification transformation to remove the null ELSE clause. This modification enabled the suspended applicability pattern to succeed, and so, processing of the jittering subgoal development is completed.

The suspended applicability pattern succeeds, and the replacement pattern is formed by composing a new loop predicate consisting of the conjunctions of the old loop predicate and the negation of the restriction predicate. The rest of the restriction (the IF-THEN structure and the body of the THEN clause) is deleted and its semantics are now part of the loop itself.

[State 6 (Assimilate Remaining Constraint into Loop Generator) (Apply Transformation: Asismilate-Test-in-Thesis-Loop)]

The sequence of State 5 (without having to bother with the LOCAL's) is repeated (interchanging the order of the restriction and the assertion, and surpressing the null ELSE clause) to incorporate the remaining restriction into the loop generator.

[State 7 (Simplify: Remove Embedded AND in Loop Generation) (Apply Transformation: Simplify-AND)]

The embedded conjunction within the loop predicate is merged with the outer conjunction. Automatic simplification would, when added to the system, remove the need for this step.

[State 8 (Maintain Acceptable Board Positions Incrementally) (Apply Transformation: Calculate-Predicate-Incrementally)]

The simplification performed in the previous state completes the explication phase of the development whose purpose was to reveal the underlying structure of the algorithm implicit in the original specification. This structure is quite clear in State

7. A simple recursive program exists in which on each recursive level, a queen is removed from the set of queens and placed on a position on the chessboard which is not already occupied and which is not capturable by any queen already on the chessboard. The recursion is then carried out at the next level and if it (and all its recursive calls) were successful, the algorithm terminates. If not, the queen is removed from the board and another position selected.

The computationally expensive part of this algorithm is finding an acceptable board position. The developer recognizes that this same calculation (in a slightly altered environment with an extra queen placed on the board) is carried out at each level, and decides that rather than repeat these similar calculations, the set of acceptable board positions should be maintained incrementally. That is, as actions occur within the program which affect the membership of the set, appropriate maintenance actions are inserted to update the set membership accordingly. The actions which can affect set membership are the assertion and/or denial of facts which interact with the set definition predicate. Such statements are either preceded (assertions) or followed (denials) by the necessary maintenance actions. Furthermore, the iteration through the elements of the set is changed from a generative format (FOR ALL <predicate> . . .) to simple membership in a preexisting set (FOR <X> IN-SET <set> . . .).

These modifications are all made automatically by the Calculate-predicate-incrementally transformation. The calculation of the precise predicate to use to update the set membership is quite complex (see [3] for the details, and Paige paper (1977) for the foundations of these ideas), but the general idea is straightforward. Given the newfound truth (or falseness) of a fact, what else must necessarily be true to make the set definition pattern change its value (that it become true or become false, or equivalently, to have the support of the corresponding set element(s) change) and to ensure that no other support exists for these elements. That is, what must be true to detect the creation of the first support of an element or the deletion of its last support, because only then should it be added to, or deleted from, the set.

For the set of board positions, this maintenance predicate, following the placement of a queen on the board or its removal, is determined to be the set of board positions which are on the chessboard, are not occupied by any other piece, which *are* capturable by the queen being placed on the board or removed from it, and which are not capturable by any other queen already on the board.

Actually, since the PIECE-ON-BOARD pattern occurs twice in the set definition predicate, two maintenance action loops are generated. The first of these is concerned only with the position occupied by the queen (or about to be occupied by it), while the second maintenance loop is the one described above.

[State 9 (Simplify: Remove Redundant Loop from Maintenance Actions) (Manual Effort)]

The single position handled by the first maintenance loop is also handled by the second, more general, loop. It is therefore

redundant, and the developer used the editor to manually remove the first maintenance loop (both the occurrence preceding the assertion and the occurrence following the denial).

[State 10 (Pick a Representation for Board Positions) (Manual Effort)]

State 9 completes the reorganization phase of the development accomplished by deciding to employ incremental set maintenace. The final phase deals with determining representations appropriate for the processing. At this stage, the expensive part of the processing is determining within the maintenance actions whether particular positions are capturable by any queen. Is there a representation in which this operation can be more easily performed?

The time has come for the developer to introduce a little creative magic (it is at just these points that a purely automatic approach seems most suspect). By switching the viewpoint from positions to lines (i.e., rows, columns, and diagonals), the problem is greatly simplified. That is, rather than incrementally maintaining the set of remaining board positions explicitly, the set of remaining lines is incrementally maintained and the remaining board positions are generated from them (as the intersection of four of the remaining lines: a row, column, and two diagonals). In this representation, maintaining the set of remaining lines when a queen is placed on the board (or removed from it) merely involves deleting (or adding) the corresponding lines (the row, column, and two diagonals) without any search. Furthermore, the iteraction through the remaining board positions becomes a quadruply nested loop through the remaining rows, columns, and left and right diagonals finding four lines which intersect at a single position. Since a position is uniquely determined by a row and column, the inner two loops can be replaced by checks of whether the corresponding diagonals remain.

These modifications produce the program in State 10. It was produced by manual editing, but we are investigating how this step can be formulated as a representation alteration transformation (called type transformations [18]).

REMAINING OPTIMIZATIONS

A few steps remain to complete the optimization and convert the program into conventional form. They include removing the outer loop through the rows (since each row must have a queen and failure to place a queen in a row cannot be resolved by reconsidering that row again later), eliminating the use of the set of queens used only to determine termination (by using any one of the other sets which become empty at the same time), explicitly collecting the set of queen placements as the result of the computation rather than having it be implicit in the set of assertions in the data base, and using lists (or arrays) instead of sets.

We have not yet worked on these optimizations pending resolution of the representation selection issue.

CONCLUSIONS

Using a transformation system to develop the implementation of a small, but nontrivial example, such as the "eight queens" problem presented here, is both instructive and disconcerting.

Developing an implementation through the application of formalized transformations forces a more careful consideration of the strategy to be employed, and the tradeoffs involved. This highly beneficial result represents a shift in focus away from maintaining consistency, which almost completely consumes today's programmers, towards a concern with tradeoffs between alternative implementations. With the system assuming the responsibility for maintaining consistency, the developer should be free to concentrate on these higher level issues. Such consideration of the implementation tradeoffs heightens the need for adequate specifications which merely define the required behavior without determining how it is to be achieved.

However, it is quite evident from the development presented here, that the developer has not been freed to consider implementation tradeoffs. Instead of a concern for maintaining consistency, the equally consuming task of directing the low-level development has been imposed. While the correctness of the program is no longer an issue, keeping track of where one is in a development and how to accomplish each step in all its fine detail diverts attention from the tradeoff question.

It is quite clear that if transformation systems are to become useful, this difficulty must be removed. Automatic simplification and jittering, as discussed in this paper, will help considerably (see also [12]). But equally important is the ability to state, represent, refine, and display implementation plans. The current lack of an adequate framework in which the development proceeds is a major source of conceptual overload.

Also, major improvements are needed in the documentation of developments to make them understandable. The ability to highlight changes between successive states, as illustrated in Appendix II, is but a first step. The structure of the development plan must become an integral part of its documentation and understanding.

Finally, if implementation tradeoffs are to gain prominence, and if systems developed via transformations are to be maintained, the ability must be created to replay a slightly altered development (i.e., the altered development becomes the implementation plan to be carried out largely or completely automatically).

All of the above benefits and problems are present only on the assumption that people are involved in the development process. If this process were totally automated, then none of these issues would arise. However, given the growing concern with starting a development from a very high level (and largely noncomputational) specification, and the paucity of information known about strategic optimization which is central to implementating such specifications, it seems unlikely that fully automatic systems could deal effectively with such specification languages. Rather, one would expect to see a gradual raising of the level of the languages which can be automatically optimized. Thus, the role of interactive transformation systems will be to provide a validated mapping between the high-level specifications and the "programming language" from which automatic optimization can proceed.

APPENDIX I
DEVELOPMENT DOCUMENTATION

```
(STATE-1 (ENTER SPECIFICATION FOR EIGHT QUEENS PROBLEM)
         (LOAD FILE EIGHT-QUEENS.SPEC))

(STATE-2 (UNFOLD BOTH CONSTRAINTS)
         (APPLY TRANSFORMATION . UNFOLD-CONSTRAINT))

(STATE-3 (SIMPLIFY: REMOVE REDUNDANT UNFOLDED CONSTRAINT CHECKS)
         (MANUAL EFFORT))

(STATE-4 (MAKE BACKTRACKING EXPLICIT SO THAT IT CAN BE MINIMIZED)
         (APPLY TRANSFORMATION . UNFOLD-CONSEQUENTIAL-BACKTRACKING))

  (STATE-4-1 (CONVERT ITERATION TO RECURSION)
             (JITTER TRANSFORMATION . MAKE-SET-ITERATION-RECURSIVE))

  (STATE-4-2 (ACHIEVE A NECESSARY PROPERTY OF A TRANSFORMATION)
             (ACHIEVE THE FOLLOWING PROPERTY:
                 CONSEQUENTIAL-NON-DETERMINISM-FREE
                 (REMOVE QUEEN FROM QUEEN-SET)))

    (STATE-4-2-1 (MARK "REMOVE" AS INCIDENTAL NON-DETERMINISM)
                 (APPLY TRANSFORMATION .
                        MARK-INCIDENTAL-NON-DETERMINISM))

    (STATE-4-2-2
      NIL
      ((CONSEQUENTIAL-NON-DETERMINISM-FREE (REMOVE* QUEEN FROM
                                            QUEEN-SET))
       PROVED BY NO-CONSEQUENTIAL-NON-DETERMINISM))

  (STATE-4-3
    (ACHIEVE A NECESSARY PROPERTY OF A TRANSFORMATION)
    ((CONSEQUENTIAL-NON-DETERMINISM-FREE
      (LOCAL . . . )
      PROVED BY NO-CONSEQUENTIAL-NON-DETERMINISM))

  (STATE-4-4 (ACHIEVE A NECESSARY PROPERTY OF A TRANSFORMATION)
             ((CONSEQUENTIAL-NON-DETERMINISM-FREE)
              PROVED BY NO-CONSEQUENTIAL-NON-DETERMINISM))

(STATE-5 (ASSIMILATE CONSTRAINT INTO GENERATOR)
         (APPLY TRANSFORMATION . ASSIMILATE-TEST-IN-THEREIS-LOOP))

  (STATE-5-1 (MERGE THE LOCALS)
             (JITTER TRANSFORMATION . MERGE-LOCALS))

    (STATE-5-1-1 (EXTRACT LOCAL FROM FOR LOOP)
                 (JITTER TRANSFORMATION .
                         EXTRACT-LOCAL-FROM-FOR-LOOP))

  (STATE-5-3 (MOVE CONSTRAINT TEST AHEAD OF ASSERTION)
             (JITTER TRANSFORMATION . MOVE-CONSTRAINT-UPHILL))

  (STATE-5-5 (SIMPLIFY: SUPPRESS NULL ELSE CLAUSE)
             (JITTER TRANSFORMATION . ELSE-SUPPRESSION))

(STATE-6 (ASSIMILATE REMAINING CONSTRAINT INTO LOOP GENERATOR)
         (APPLY TRANSFORMATION . ASSIMILATE-TEST-IN-THEREIS-LOOP))

  (STATE-6-1 (MOVE REMAINING CONSTRAINT AHEAD OF ASSERTION)
             (JITTER TRANSFORMATION . MOVE-CONSTRAINT-UPHILL))

  (STATE-6-3 (SIMPLIFY: SUPPRESS NULL ELSE CLAUSE)
             (JITTER TRANSFORMATION . ELSE-SUPPRESSION))

(STATE-7 (SIMPLIFY: REMOVE EMBEDDED APAND IN LOOP GENERATOR)
         (APPLY TRANSFORMATION . SIMPLIFY-APAND))

(STATE-8 (MAINTAIN ACCEPTABLE BOARD POSITIONS INCREMENTALLY)
         (APPLY TRANSFORMATION . CALCULATE-PREDICATE-INCREMENTALLY))

(STATE-9 (SIMPLIFY: REMOVE REDUNDANT LOOP FROM MAINTENANCE ACTIONS)
         (MANUAL EFFORT))

(STATE-10 (PICK <ROW# COLUMN#> AS REPRESENTATION OF BOARD POSITION.
           RECOGNIZE THAT COMPONENTS ARE ORTHOGONAL AND CAN BE
           INDEPENDENTLY SELECTED. FURTHERMORE, RECOGNIZE THAT ROW
           AND COLUMN DETERMINE NE-DIAGONAL AND SE-DIAGONAL. FINALLY,
           RECOGNIZE THAT POSSIBLE-BOARD-POSITIONS CAN BE GENERATED
           FROM THE INTERSECTION OF THE REMAINING ROWS, COLUMNS,
           AND DIAGONALS, AND THAT INCREMENTAL UPDATE OF
           POSSIBLE-BOARD-POSITIONS MERELY INVOLVES REMOVING THE
           CHOSEN ROW, COLUMN, AND TWO DIAGONALS BECAUSE THE
           MAPPING IS ONE-TO-ONE IN BOTH DIRECTIONS.)
          (MANUAL EFFORT))
```

APPENDIX II
HIGHLIGHTED STATE TRANSITIONS

This Appendix contains program displays in which the changes from one state into another are highlighted in boldface type. The additions and modifications are highlighted to show the changes into the next state. They were produced automatically as part of the documentation of the development [9].

```
(LAMBDA (QUEEN-SET)
    (LOCAL (BOARD-POSITION)
        (FOR QUEEN IN-SET QUEEN-SET DO
            (DETERMINE BOARD-POSITION FROM
                (CHESS-BOARD BOARD-POSITION))
            (ASSERT (PIECE-ON-BOARD QUEEN BOARD-POSITION)
```

CHANGES INTO STATE-2

```
(LAMBDA (QUEEN-SET)
    (LOCAL (BOARD-POSITION)
        (FOR QUEEN IN-SET QUEEN-SET DO
            (DETERMINE BOARD-POSITION FROM
                (CHESS-BOARD BOARD-POSITION))
            (LOCAL (BOARD-POSITION#2 BOARD-POSITION#1 QUEEN#2 QUEEN#1
                    PIECE#2 PIECE#1)
                (ASSERT (PIECE-ON-BOARD QUEEN BOARD-POSITION))
                (IF (PIECE-ON-BOARD PIECE#2 BOARD-POSITION)
                    THEN
                        (CONSTRAINT-VIOLATION
                            TWO-PIECES-CAN'T-OCCUPY-SAME-SQUARE)
                    ELSE NIL)
                (IF (PIECE-ON-BOARD PIECE#1 BOARD-POSITION)
                    THEN
                        (CONSTRAINT-VIOLATION
                            TWO-PIECES-CAN'T-OCCUPY-SAME-SQUARE)
                    ELSE NIL)
                (IF (AND (PIECE-ON-BOARD QUEEN#2 BOARD-POSITION#2)
                        (QUEEN-CAPTURE BOARD-POSITION
                            BOARD-POSITION#2))
                    THEN
                        (CONSTRAINT-VIOLATION
                            QUEEN-CAN'T-CAPTURE-ANOTHER-QUEEN)
                    ELSE NIL)
                (IF (AND (PIECE-ON-BOARD QUEEN#1 BOARD-POSITION#1)
                        (QUEEN-CAPTURE BOARD-POSITION#1
                            BOARD-POSITION))
                    THEN
                        (CONSTRAINT-VIOLATION
                            QUEEN-CAN'T-CAPTURE-ANOTHER-QUEEN)
                    ELSE NIL)
```

CHANGES INTO STATE-3

```
(LAMBDA (QUEEN-SET)
    (LOCAL (BOARD-POSITION)
        (FOR QUEEN IN-SET QUEEN-SET DO
            (DETERMINE BOARD-POSITION FROM
                (CHESS-BOARD BOARD-POSITION))
            (LOCAL (BOARD-POSITION=2 BOARD-POSITION=1 QUEEN=2 QUEEN=1
                    PIECE=2 PIECE=1)
                (ASSERT (PIECE-ON-BOARD QUEEN BOARD-POSITION))
                (IF (PIECE-ON-BOARD PIECE=2 BOARD-POSITION)
                    THEN
                        (CONSTRAINT-VIOLATION
                            TWO-PIECES-CAN'T-OCCUPY-SAME-SQUARE)
                    ELSE NIL)
                (IF (AND (PIECE-ON-BOARD QUEEN=2 BOARD-POSITION=2)
                        (QUEEN-CAPTURE BOARD-POSITION
                            BOARD-POSITION=2))
                    THEN
                        (CONSTRAINT-VIOLATION
                            QUEEN-CAN'T-CAPTURE-ANOTHER-QUEEN)
                    ELSE NIL)
```

CHANGES INTO STATE-4-1

```
(LAMBDA (QUEEN-SET)
    (LOCAL (QUEEN BOARD-POSITION)
        (TERMINATION-TEST: (IF (EMPTY QUEEN-SET)
                THEN
                    (RETURN)))
        (REMOVE QUEEN FROM QUEEN-SET)
        (DETERMINE BOARD-POSITION FROM (CHESS-BOARD BOARD-POSITION))
        (LOCAL (BOARD-POSITION=2 BOARD-POSITION=1 QUEEN=2 QUEEN=1
                PIECE=2 PIECE=1)
            (ASSERT (PIECE-ON-BOARD QUEEN BOARD-POSITION))
            (IF (PIECE-ON-BOARD PIECE=2 BOARD-POSITION)
                THEN
                    (CONSTRAINT-VIOLATION
                        TWO-PIECES-CAN'T-OCCUPY-SAME-SQUARE)
                ELSE NIL)
            (IF (AND (PIECE-ON-BOARD QUEEN=2 BOARD-POSITION=2)
                    (QUEEN-CAPTURE BOARD-POSITION BOARD-POSITION=2)
                THEN
                    (CONSTRAINT-VIOLATION
                        QUEEN-CAN'T-CAPTURE-ANOTHER-QUEEN)
                ELSE NIL))
        (RECURSIVE-CALL: (QUEENS QUEEN-SET)
```

CHANGES INTO STATE-4-2-1

```
(LAMBDA (QUEEN-SET)
    (LOCAL (QUEEN BOARD-POSITION)
        (TERMINATION-TEST: (IF (EMPTY QUEEN-SET)
                THEN
                    (RETURN)))
        (REMOVE= QUEEN FROM QUEEN-SET)
        (DETERMINE BOARD-POSITION FROM (CHESS-BOARD BOARD-POSITION))
        (LOCAL (BOARD-POSITION=2 BOARD-POSITION=1 QUEEN=2 QUEEN=1
                PIECE=2 PIECE=1)
            (ASSERT (PIECE-ON-BOARD QUEEN BOARD-POSITION))
            (IF (PIECE-ON-BOARD PIECE=2 BOARD-POSITION)
                THEN
                    (CONSTRAINT-VIOLATION
                        TWO-PIECES-CAN'T-OCCUPY-SAME-SQUARE)
                ELSE NIL)
            (IF (AND (PIECE-ON-BOARD QUEEN=2 BOARD-POSITION=2)
                    (QUEEN-CAPTURE BOARD-POSITION BOARD-POSITION=2))
                THEN
                    (CONSTRAINT-VIOLATION
                        QUEEN-CAN'T-CAPTURE-ANOTHER-QUEEN)
                ELSE NIL))
        (RECURSIVE-CALL: (QUEENS QUEEN-SET))
```

CHANGES INTO STATE-4

```
(LAMBDA (QUEEN-SET)
    (LOCAL (QUEEN BOARD-POSITION)
        (TERMINATION-TEST: (IF (EMPTY QUEEN-SET)
                THEN
                    (EXIT SUCCESSFUL)
        (REMOVE= QUEEN FROM QUEEN-SET)
        (FOR ALL (CHESS-BOARD BOARD-POSITION)
            THEREIS
            (LOCAL (BOARD-POSITION=2 BOARD-POSITION=1 QUEEN=2 QUEEN=1
                    PIECE=2 PIECE=1)
                (ASSERT (PIECE-ON-BOARD QUEEN BOARD-POSITION))
                (IF (PIECE-ON-BOARD PIECE=2 BOARD-POSITION)
                    THEN
                        (UNDO-ACTIONS: (DENY (PIECE-ON-BOARD QUEEN
                                BOARD-POSITION))
                        (LOOP-RETURN FORCE-ANOTHER-CHOICE)
                    ELSE
                    NIL)
                (IF (AND (PIECE-ON-BOARD QUEEN=2 BOARD-POSITION=2)
                        (QUEEN-CAPTURE BOARD-POSITION
                            BOARD-POSITION=2))
                    THEN
                        (UNDO-ACTIONS: (DENY (PIECE-ON-BOARD QUEEN
                                BOARD-POSITION))
                        (LOOP-RETURN FORCE-ANOTHER-CHOICE)
                    ELSE
                    NIL)
                (IF (SUCCESSFUL (RECURSIVE-CALL: (QUEENS QUEEN-SET))
                    THEN
                        (LOOP-RETURN CHOICE-ACCEPTED)
                    ELSE
                        (UNDO-ACTIONS: (DENY (PIECE-ON-BOARD QUEEN
                                BOARD-POSITION))
                        (LOOP-RETURN FORCE-ANOTHER-CHOICE))
            THEN
            (EXIT SUCCESSFUL)
            ELSE
            (UNDO-ACTIONS: (ADD QUEEN TO QUEEN-SET))
            (EXIT UNSUCCESSFUL)
```

CHANGES INTO STATE-5-1

```
(LAMBDA (QUEEN-SET)
    (LOCAL (QUEEN BOARD-POSITION BOARD-POSITION#2 BOARD-POSITION#1 QUE
            QUEEN#1 PIECE#2 PIECE#1)
        (TERMINATION-TEST: (IF (EMPTY QUEEN-SET)
                THEN
                    (EXIT SUCCESSFUL)))
        (REMOVE= QUEEN FROM QUEEN-SET)
        (FOR ALL (CHESS-BOARD BOARD-POSITION)
            THEREIS
            (ASSERT (PIECE-ON-BOARD QUEEN BOARD-POSITION))
            (IF (PIECE-ON-BOARD PIECE=2 BOARD-POSITION)
                THEN
                    (UNDO-ACTIONS: (DENY (PIECE-ON-BOARD QUEEN
                            BOARD-POSITION))
                    (LOOP-RETURN FORCE-ANOTHER-CHOICE)
                ELSE NIL)
            (IF (AND (PIECE-ON-BOARD QUEEN=2 BOARD-POSITION=2)
                    (QUEEN-CAPTURE BOARD-POSITION BOARD-POSITION=2))
                THEN
                    (UNDO-ACTIONS: (DENY (PIECE-ON-BOARD QUEEN
                            BOARD-POSITION))
                    (LOOP-RETURN FORCE-ANOTHER-CHOICE)
                ELSE NIL)
            (IF (SUCCESSFUL (RECURSIVE-CALL: (QUEENS QUEEN-SET)))
                THEN
                    (LOOP-RETURN CHOICE-ACCEPTED)
                ELSE
                    (UNDO-ACTIONS: (DENY (PIECE-ON-BOARD QUEEN
                            BOARD-POSITION))
                    (LOOP-RETURN FORCE-ANOTHER-CHOICE))
            THEN
            (EXIT SUCCESSFUL)
            ELSE
            (UNDO-ACTIONS: (ADD QUEEN TO QUEEN-SET))
            (EXIT UNSUCCESSFUL)
```

CHANGES INTO STATE-5-1-1

```
(LAMBDA (QUEEN-SET)
    (LOCAL (QUEEN BOARD-POSITION)
        (TERMINATION-TEST: (IF (EMPTY QUEEN-SET)
                THEN
                    (EXIT SUCCESSFUL)))
        (REMOVE= QUEEN FROM QUEEN-SET)
        (LOCAL (BOARD-POSITION=2 BOARD-POSITION=1 QUEEN=2 QUEEN=1
                PIECE=2 PIECE=1)
            (FOR ALL (CHESS-BOARD BOARD-POSITION)
                THEREIS
                (ASSERT (PIECE-ON-BOARD QUEEN BOARD-POSITION))
                (IF (PIECE-ON-BOARD PIECE=2 BOARD-POSITION)
                    THEN
                        (UNDO-ACTIONS: (DENY (PIECE-ON-BOARD QUEEN
                                BOARD-POSITION))
                        (LOOP-RETURN FORCE-ANOTHER-CHOICE)
                    ELSE NIL)
                (IF (AND (PIECE-ON-BOARD QUEEN=2 BOARD-POSITION=2)
                        (QUEEN-CAPTURE BOARD-POSITION
                            BOARD-POSITION=2))
                    THEN
                        (UNDO-ACTIONS: (DENY (PIECE-ON-BOARD QUEEN
                                BOARD-POSITION))
                        (LOOP-RETURN FORCE-ANOTHER-CHOICE)
                    ELSE NIL)
                (IF (SUCCESSFUL (RECURSIVE-CALL: (QUEENS QUEEN-SET))

                    THEN
                    (LOOP-RETURN CHOICE-ACCEPTED)
                    ELSE
                    (UNDO-ACTIONS: (DENY (PIECE-ON-BOARD QUEEN
                            BOARD-POSITION))
```

```
                (LOOP-RETURN FORCE-ANOTHER-CHOICE))
          THEN
            (EXIT SUCCESSFUL)
          ELSE
            (UNDO-ACTIONS: (ADD QUEEN TO QUEEN-SET))
            (EXIT UNSUCCESSFUL))
```

CHANGES INTO STATE-5-3

```
(LAMBDA (QUEEN-SET)
    (LOCAL (QUEEN BOARD-POSITION BOARD-POSITION=2 BOARD-POSITION=1 QUEEN=2
            QUEEN=1 PIECE=2 PIECE=1)
        (TERMINATION-TEST: (IF (EMPTY QUEEN-SET)
                            THEN
                                (EXIT SUCCESSFUL)))
        (REMOVE= QUEEN FROM QUEEN-SET)
        (FOR ALL (CHESS-BOARD BOARD-POSITION)
            THEREIS
                (IF (PIECE-ON-BOARD PIECE=2 BOARD-POSITION)
                    THEN
                        (LOOP-RETURN FORCE-ANOTHER-CHOICE)
                    ELSE NIL)
                (ASSERT (PIECE-ON-BOARD QUEEN BOARD-POSITION))
                (IF (AND (PIECE-ON-BOARD QUEEN=2 BOARD-POSITION=2)
                         (QUEEN-CAPTURE BOARD-POSITION BOARD-POSITION=2))
                    THEN
                        (UNDO-ACTIONS: (DENY (PIECE-ON-BOARD QUEEN
                                                 BOARD-POSITION)))
                        (LOOP-RETURN FORCE-ANOTHER-CHOICE)
                    ELSE NIL)
                (IF (SUCCESSFUL (RECURSIVE-CALL: (QUEENS QUEEN-SET)))
                    THEN
                        (LOOP-RETURN CHOICE-ACCEPTED)
                    ELSE
                        (UNDO-ACTIONS: (DENY (PIECE-ON-BOARD QUEEN
                                                 BOARD-POSITION)))
                        (LOOP-RETURN FORCE-ANOTHER-CHOICE))
          THEN
            (EXIT SUCCESSFUL)
          ELSE
            (UNDO-ACTIONS: (ADD QUEEN TO QUEEN-SET))
            (EXIT UNSUCCESSFUL))
```

CHANGES INTO STATE-5-5

```
(LAMBDA (QUEEN-SET)
    (LOCAL (QUEEN BOARD-POSITION BOARD-POSITION=2 BOARD-POSITION=1 QUEEN=2
            QUEEN=1 PIECE=2 PIECE=1)
        (TERMINATION-TEST: (IF (EMPTY QUEEN-SET)
                            THEN
                                (EXIT SUCCESSFUL)))
        (REMOVE= QUEEN FROM QUEEN-SET)
        (FOR ALL (CHESS-BOARD BOARD-POSITION)
            THEREIS
                (IF (PIECE-ON-BOARD PIECE=2 BOARD-POSITION)
                    THEN
                        (LOOP-RETURN FORCE-ANOTHER-CHOICE))
                (ASSERT (PIECE-ON-BOARD QUEEN BOARD-POSITION))
                (IF (AND (PIECE-ON-BOARD QUEEN=2 BOARD-POSITION=2)
                         (QUEEN-CAPTURE BOARD-POSITION BOARD-POSITION=2))
                    THEN
                        (UNDO-ACTIONS: (DENY (PIECE-ON-BOARD QUEEN
                                                 BOARD-POSITION)))
                        (LOOP-RETURN FORCE-ANOTHER-CHOICE)
                    ELSE NIL)
                (IF (SUCCESSFUL (RECURSIVE-CALL: (QUEENS QUEEN-SET)))
                    THEN
                        (LOOP-RETURN CHOICE-ACCEPTED)
                    ELSE
                        (UNDO-ACTIONS: (DENY (PIECE-ON-BOARD QUEEN
                                                 BOARD-POSITION)))
                        (LOOP-RETURN FORCE-ANOTHER-CHOICE))
          THEN
            (EXIT SUCCESSFUL)
          ELSE
            (UNDO-ACTIONS: (ADD QUEEN TO QUEEN-SET))
            (EXIT UNSUCCESSFUL))
```

CHANGES INTO STATE-5

```
(LAMBDA (QUEEN-SET)
    (LOCAL (QUEEN BOARD-POSITION BOARD-POSITION=2 BOARD-POSITION=1 QUEEN=2
            QUEEN=1 PIECE=2 PIECE=1)
        (TERMINATION-TEST: (IF (EMPTY QUEEN-SET)
                            THEN
                                (EXIT SUCCESSFUL)))
        (REMOVE= QUEEN FROM QUEEN-SET)
        (FOR ALL (APAND (CHESS-BOARD BOARD-POSITION)
                        (NOT (PIECE-ON-BOARD PIECE=2 BOARD-POSITION))
            THEREIS
                (ASSERT (PIECE-ON-BOARD QUEEN BOARD-POSITION))
                (IF (AND (PIECE-ON-BOARD QUEEN=2 BOARD-POSITION=2)
                         (QUEEN-CAPTURE BOARD-POSITION BOARD-POSITION=2))
                    THEN
                        (UNDO-ACTIONS: (DENY (PIECE-ON-BOARD QUEEN
                                                 BOARD-POSITION)))
                        (LOOP-RETURN FORCE-ANOTHER-CHOICE)
                    ELSE NIL)
                (IF (SUCCESSFUL (RECURSIVE-CALL: (QUEENS QUEEN-SET)))
                    THEN
                        (LOOP-RETURN CHOICE-ACCEPTED)
                    ELSE
                        (UNDO-ACTIONS: (DENY (PIECE-ON-BOARD QUEEN
                                                 BOARD-POSITION)))
                        (LOOP-RETURN FORCE-ANOTHER-CHOICE))
          THEN
            (EXIT SUCCESSFUL)
          ELSE
            (UNDO-ACTIONS: (ADD QUEEN TO QUEEN-SET))
            (EXIT UNSUCCESSFUL))
```

CHANGES INTO STATE-6-1

```
(LAMBDA (QUEEN-SET)
    (LOCAL (QUEEN BOARD-POSITION BOARD-POSITION=2 BOARD-POSITION=1 QUEEN=2
            QUEEN=1 PIECE=2 PIECE=1)
        (TERMINATION-TEST: (IF (EMPTY QUEEN-SET)
                            THEN
                                (EXIT SUCCESSFUL)))
        (REMOVE= QUEEN FROM QUEEN-SET)
        (FOR ALL
            (APAND (CHESS-BOARD BOARD-POSITION)
                   (NOT (PIECE-ON-BOARD PIECE=2 BOARD-POSITION))
            THEREIS
                (IF (AND (PIECE-ON-BOARD QUEEN=2 BOARD-POSITION=2)
                         (QUEEN-CAPTURE BOARD-POSITION BOARD-POSITION=2))
                    THEN
                        (LOOP-RETURN FORCE-ANOTHER-CHOICE)
                    ELSE NIL)
                (ASSERT (PIECE-ON-BOARD QUEEN BOARD-POSITION))
                (IF (SUCCESSFUL (RECURSIVE-CALL: (QUEENS QUEEN-SET)))
                    THEN
                        (LOOP-RETURN CHOICE-ACCEPTED)
                    ELSE
                        (UNDO-ACTIONS: (DENY (PIECE-ON-BOARD QUEEN
                                                 BOARD-POSITION)))
                        (LOOP-RETURN FORCE-ANOTHER-CHOICE))
          THEN
            (EXIT SUCCESSFUL)
          ELSE
            (UNDO-ACTIONS: (ADD QUEEN TO QUEEN-SET))
            (EXIT UNSUCCESSFUL))
```

CHANGES INTO STATE-6-3

```
(LAMBDA (QUEEN-SET)
    (LOCAL (QUEEN BOARD-POSITION BOARD-POSITION=2 BOARD-POSITION=1 QUEEN=2
            QUEEN=1 PIECE=2 PIECE=1)
        (TERMINATION-TEST: (IF (EMPTY QUEEN-SET)
                            THEN
                                (EXIT SUCCESSFUL)))
        (REMOVE= QUEEN FROM QUEEN-SET)
        (FOR ALL
            (APAND (CHESS-BOARD BOARD-POSITION)
                   (NOT (PIECE-ON-BOARD PIECE=2 BOARD-POSITION))
            THEREIS
                (IF (AND (PIECE-ON-BOARD QUEEN=2 BOARD-POSITION=2)
                         (QUEEN-CAPTURE BOARD-POSITION BOARD-POSITION=2))
                    THEN
                        (LOOP-RETURN FORCE-ANOTHER-CHOICE))
                (ASSERT (PIECE-ON-BOARD QUEEN BOARD-POSITION))
                (IF (SUCCESSFUL (RECURSIVE-CALL: (QUEENS QUEEN-SET)))
                    THEN
                        (LOOP-RETURN CHOICE-ACCEPTED)
                    ELSE
                        (UNDO-ACTIONS: (DENY (PIECE-ON-BOARD QUEEN
                                                 BOARD-POSITION)))
                        (LOOP-RETURN FORCE-ANOTHER-CHOICE))
          THEN
            (EXIT SUCCESSFUL)
          ELSE
            (UNDO-ACTIONS: (ADD QUEEN TO QUEEN-SET))
            (EXIT UNSUCCESSFUL))
```

CHANGES INTO STATE-6

```
(LAMBDA (QUEEN-SET)
    (LOCAL (QUEEN BOARD-POSITION BOARD-POSITION=2 BOARD-POSITION=1 QUEEN=2
            QUEEN=1 PIECE=2 PIECE=1)
        (TERMINATION-TEST: (IF (EMPTY QUEEN-SET)
                            THEN
                                (EXIT SUCCESSFUL)))
        (REMOVE= QUEEN FROM QUEEN-SET)
        (FOR ALL
            (APAND (APAND (CHESS-BOARD BOARD-POSITION)
                          (NOT (PIECE-ON-BOARD PIECE=2 BOARD-POSITION))
                   )
                   (NOT (AND (PIECE-ON-BOARD QUEEN=2 BOARD-POSITION=2)
                             (QUEEN-CAPTURE BOARD-POSITION
                                     BOARD-POSITION=2)
            THEREIS
                (ASSERT (PIECE-ON-BOARD QUEEN BOARD-POSITION))
                (IF (SUCCESSFUL (RECURSIVE-CALL: (QUEENS QUEEN-SET)))
                    THEN
                        (LOOP-RETURN CHOICE-ACCEPTED)
                    ELSE
                        (UNDO-ACTIONS: (DENY (PIECE-ON-BOARD QUEEN
                                                 BOARD-POSITION)))
                        (LOOP-RETURN FORCE-ANOTHER-CHOICE))
          THEN
            (EXIT SUCCESSFUL)
          ELSE
            (UNDO-ACTIONS: (ADD QUEEN TO QUEEN-SET))
            (EXIT UNSUCCESSFUL))
```

CHANGES INTO STATE-7

```
(LAMBDA (QUEEN-SET)
    (LOCAL (QUEEN BOARD-POSITION BOARD-POSITION=2 BOARD-POSITION=1 QUEEN=2
            QUEEN=1 PIECE=2 PIECE=1)
        (TERMINATION-TEST: (IF (EMPTY QUEEN-SET)
                            THEN
                                (EXIT SUCCESSFUL)))
        (REMOVE= QUEEN FROM QUEEN-SET)
        (FOR ALL
            (APAND (CHESS-BOARD BOARD-POSITION)
                   (NOT (PIECE-ON-BOARD PIECE=2 BOARD-POSITION))
                   (NOT (AND (PIECE-ON-BOARD QUEEN=2 BOARD-POSITION=2)
                             (QUEEN-CAPTURE BOARD-POSITION
                                     BOARD-POSITION=2)
            THEREIS
```

```
(ASSERT (PIECE-ON-BOARD QUEEN BOARD-POSITION))
(IF (SUCCESSFUL (RECURSIVE-CALL: (QUEENS QUEEN-SET)))
    THEN
        (LOOP-RETURN CHOICE-ACCEPTED)
    ELSE
        (UNDO-ACTIONS: (DENY (PIECE-ON-BOARD QUEEN
                                    BOARD-POSITION)))
        (LOOP-RETURN FORCE-ANOTHER-CHOICE))
    THEN
        (EXIT SUCCESSFUL)
    ELSE
        (UNDO-ACTIONS: (ADD QUEEN TO QUEEN-SET))
        (EXIT UNSUCCESSFUL))
```

CHANGES INTO STATE-8

```
(LAMBDA
 (QUEEN-SET POSSIBLE-BOARD-POSITIONS)
 (LOCAL (QUEEN BOARD-POSITION BOARD-POSITION#2 BOARD-POSITION#1 QUEEN#2 QUEEN#1
         PIECE#2 PIECE#1)
  (TERMINATION-TEST: (IF (EMPTY QUEEN-SET) THEN (EXIT SUCCESSFUL)))
  (REMOVE* QUEEN FROM QUEEN-SET)
  (FOR (BOARD-POSITION) IN-SET POSSIBLE-BOARD-POSITIONS THEREIS
   (MAINTENANCE-ACTIONS: (FOR ALL
       (APAND (CHESS-BOARD BOARD-POSITION)
           (NOT (AND (PIECE-ON-BOARD QUEEN#3 BOARD-POSITION#3)
                 (QUEEN-CAPTURE BOARD-POSITION BOARD-POSITION#3)))
           (NOT (PIECE-ON-BOARD PIECE#2 BOARD-POSITION)))
       LBIND (BOARD-POSITION#3 QUEEN#3)
       DO (DELETE BOARD-POSITION FROM POSSIBLE-BOARD-POSITIONS))
      (FOR ALL
       (APAND (CHESS-BOARD BOARD-POSITION#3)
           (NOT (PIECE-ON-BOARD PIECE#3 BOARD-POSITION#3))
           (QUEEN-CAPTURE BOARD-POSITION#3 BOARD-POSITION)
           (NOT (AND (PIECE-ON-BOARD QUEEN#2 BOARD-POSITION#2)
                 (QUEEN-CAPTURE BOARD-POSITION BOARD-POSITION#2))
       LBIND (BOARD-POSITION#3 PIECE#3)
       DO (DELETE BOARD-POSITION#3 FROM POSSIBLE-BOARD-POSITIONS)))
   (ASSERT (PIECE-ON-BOARD QUEEN BOARD-POSITION))
   (IF (SUCCESSFUL (RECURSIVE-CALL: (QUEENS QUEEN-SET)))
   THEN (LOOP-RETURN CHOICE-ACCEPTED)
   ELSE
   (UNDO-ACTIONS:
    (DENY (PIECE-ON-BOARD QUEEN BOARD-POSITION))
    (MAINTENANCE-ACTIONS: (FOR ALL
        (APAND (CHESS-BOARD BOARD-POSITION)
            (NOT (AND (PIECE-ON-BOARD QUEEN#3 BOARD-POSITION#3))
                  (QUEEN-CAPTURE BOARD-POSITION BOARD-POSITION#3)))
            (NOT (PIECE-ON-BOARD PIECE#2 BOARD-POSITION)))
        LBIND (BOARD-POSITION#3 QUEEN#3)
        DO (ADD BOARD-POSITION TO POSSIBLE-BOARD-POSITIONS))
       (FOR ALL
        (APAND (CHESS-BOARD BOARD-POSITION#3)
            (NOT (PIECE-ON-BOARD PIECE#3 BOARD-POSITION#3))
            (QUEEN-CAPTURE BOARD-POSITION#3 BOARD-POSITION)
            (NOT (AND (PIECE-ON-BOARD QUEEN#2 BOARD-POSITION#2)
                  (QUEEN-CAPTURE BOARD-POSITION BOARD-POSITION#2))
        LBIND (BOARD-POSITION#3 PIECE#3)
        DO (ADD BOARD-POSITION#3 TO POSSIBLE-BOARD-POSITIONS)
    (LOOP-RETURN FORCE-ANOTHER-CHOICE))
   THEN (EXIT SUCCESSFUL)
   ELSE (UNDO-ACTIONS: (ADD QUEEN TO QUEEN-SET))
        (EXIT UNSUCCESSFUL))
```

CHANGES INTO STATE-9

```
(LAMBDA (QUEEN-SET POSSIBLE-BOARD-POSITIONS)
   (LOCAL (QUEEN BOARD-POSITION BOARD-POSITION#2 BOARD-POSITION#1 QUEEN#2
          QUEEN#1 PIECE#2 PIECE#1)
     (TERMINATION-TEST: (IF (EMPTY QUEEN-SET)
                   THEN (EXIT SUCCESSFUL)))
     (REMOVE* QUEEN FROM QUEEN-SET)
     (FOR (BOARD-POSITION) IN-SET POSSIBLE-BOARD-POSITIONS
            THEREIS
            (MAINTENANCE-ACTIONS:
            (FOR ALL
              (APAND (CHESS-BOARD BOARD-POSITION#3)
                  (NOT (PIECE-ON-BOARD PIECE#3 BOARD-POSITION#3))
                  (QUEEN-CAPTURE BOARD-POSITION#3
                         BOARD-POSITION)
                  (NOT (AND (PIECE-ON-BOARD QUEEN#2
                         BOARD-POSITION#2)
                     (QUEEN-CAPTURE BOARD-POSITION
                         BOARD-POSITION#2)
              LBIND (BOARD-POSITION#3 PIECE#3)
              DO (DELETE BOARD-POSITION#3 FROM
                     POSSIBLE-BOARD-POSITIONS)
     (ASSERT (PIECE-ON-BOARD QUEEN BOARD-POSITION))
     (IF (SUCCESSFUL (RECURSIVE-CALL: (QUEENS QUEEN-SET)))
     THEN (LOOP-RETURN CHOICE-ACCEPTED)
     ELSE
     (UNDO-ACTIONS:
      (DENY (PIECE-ON-BOARD QUEEN BOARD-POSITION))
      (MAINTENANCE-ACTIONS:
      (FOR ALL
        (APAND (CHESS-BOARD BOARD-POSITION#3)
            (NOT (PIECE-ON-BOARD PIECE#3
                     BOARD-POSITION#3))
            (QUEEN-CAPTURE BOARD-POSITION#3
                     BOARD-POSITION)
            (NOT (AND (PIECE-ON-BOARD QUEEN#2
                     BOARD-POSITION#2)
               (QUEEN-CAPTURE BOARD-POSITION
                     BOARD-POSITION#2)
        LBIND (BOARD-POSITION#3 PIECE#3)
        DO
        (ADD BOARD-POSITION#3 TO
               POSSIBLE-BOARD-POSITIONS)
     (LOOP-RETURN FORCE-ANOTHER-CHOICE))
     THEN (EXIT SUCCESSFUL)
     ELSE
     (UNDO-ACTIONS: (ADD QUEEN TO QUEEN-SET))
        (EXIT UNSUCCESSFUL))
```

CHANGES INTO STATE-10

```
(LAMBDA (QUEEN-SET REMAINING-ROWS REMAINING-COLUMNS
         REMAINING-NE-DIAGONALS REMAINING-SE-DIAGONALS)
   (LOCAL (QUEEN BOARD-POSITION BOARD-POSITION#2 BOARD-POSITION#1 QUEEN#2
          QUEEN#1 PIECE#2 PIECE#1)
     (TERMINATION-TEST: (IF (EMPTY QUEEN-SET)
                   THEN (EXIT SUCCESSFUL)))
     (REMOVE* QUEEN FROM QUEEN-SET)
     (FOR ROW IN-SET REMAINING-ROWS THEREIS
      (FOR COLUMN IN-SET REMAINING-COLUMNS
       WHEN
       (PROGN (DETERMINE* NE-DIAGONAL FROM
                  (CORRESPONDING-NE-DAGONAL ROW COLUMN))
          (DETERMINE* SE-DIAGONAL FROM
                  (CORRESPONDING-SE-DIAGONAL ROW COLUMN))
          (APAND (IN-SET? NE-DIAGONAL REMAINING-NE-DIAGONALS)
              (IN-SET? SE-DIAGONAL REMAINING-SE-DIAGONALS)
          ))
       THEREIS
       (MAINTENANCE-ACTIONS: (REMOVE* ROW FROM REMAINING-ROWS)
              (REMOVE* COLUMN FROM
                     REMAINING-COLUMNS)
              (REMOVE* NE-DIAGONAL FROM
                     REMAINING-NE-DIAGONALS)
              (REMOVE* SE-DIAGONAL FROM
                     REMAINING-SE-DIAGONALS))
          (DETERMINE* BOARD-POSITION FROM
                  (CORRESPONDING-BOARD-POSITION BOARD-POSITION
                     ROW COLUMN))
       (ASSERT (PIECE-ON-BOARD QUEEN BOARD-POSITION))
       (IF (SUCCESSFUL (PECURSIVE-CALL: (QUEENS QUEEN-SET
                     REMAINING-ROWS
                     REMAINING-COLUMNS
                     REMAINING-NE-DIAGONALS
                     REMAINING-SE-DIAGONALS)
       THEN (LOOP-RETURN CHOICE-ACCEPTED)
       ELSE (UNDO-ACTIONS: (DENY (PIECE-ON-BOARD QUEEN
                     BOARD-POSITION))
              (MAINTENANCE-ACTIONS: (ADD ROW TO
                     REMAINING-ROWS)
                  (ADD COLUMN TO
                     REMAINING-COLUMNS)
                  (ADD NE-DIAGONAL TO
                     REMAINING-NE-DIAGONALS)
                  (ADD SE-DIAGONAL TO
                     REMAINING-SE-DIAGONALS)
          (LOOP-RETURN FORCE-ANOTHER-CHOICE))
     THEN (EXIT SUCCESSFUL)
     ELSE (UNDO-ACTIONS: (ADD QUEEN TO QUEEN-SET))
        (EXIT UNSUCCESSFUL))
```

REFERENCES

[1] J. Arsac, "Syntactic source to source transforms and program manipulation," *Commun. Ass. Comput. Mach.*, vol. 22, Jan. 1979.

[2] R. Balzer and N. Goldman, "Principles of good software specification and their implications for specification languages," in *Proc. Conf. Specifications Reliable Software*, Boston, MA, 1979, p. 58.

[3] R. Balzer, "Set maintenance in a dynamic environment," unpublished.

[4] D. Barstow, "A knowledge-based system for automatic program construction," in *Proc. 5th Int. Joint Conf. Artificial Intelligence (IJCAI)*, Cambridge, MA, Aug. 1977, pp. 382–388.

[5] F. L. Bauer, "Programming as an evolutionary process," in *Proc. 2nd Int. Conf. Software Eng.*, San Francisco, CA, Oct. 1976, pp. 223–234.

[6] J. M. Boyle and M. Metz, "Automating multiple programs realizations," in *Proc. MRI Int. Symp. XXIV, Comput. Software Eng.* Brooklyn, NY: Polytechnic Press, 1977.

[7] R. M. Burstall and J. L. Darlington, "A transformation system for developing recursive programs," *J. Ass. Comput. Mach.*, vol. 24, pp. 44–67, Jan. 1977.

[8] T. Cheatham, G. Holloway, and J. Townley, "Symbolic evaluation and the analysis of program," Center for Res. in Comput. Technol., Harvard Univ., Tech. Rep. TR-19-78, 1978.

[9] W. Chiu, "Structure comparison," Inform. Sci. Inst., Univ. Southern California, Draft Rep., 1979.

[10] J. Cohen, "Interpretation of non-deterministic algorithm in higher level languages," *Inform. Processing Lett.*, vol. 3, Mar. 1975.

[11] Donzeau-Gouge, G. Huet, G. Kahn, R. Lang, and J. J. Levy, "A structure-oriented program editor: A first step towards computer assisted programming," in *1975 Proc. Int. Comput. Symp.* Amsterdam, The Netherlands: North-Holland, 1975.

[12] M. Feather, "ZAP," Program Transformation System Primer and User's Research Report 54, Dep. Artificial Intelligence, Univ. Edinburgh, Aug. 1978.

[13] S. L. Gerhart and L. Yelowitz, "Control structure abstractions of

the backtracking programming technique," *IEEE Trans. Software Eng.*, vol. SE-2, Dec. 1976.

[14] G. Huet and B. Lang, "Providing and applying program transformations expressed with second-order patterns," *Acta Informatica*, vol. 11, pp. 31–55, 1978.

[15] C. Rich and H. E. Shrobe, "Initial report on Lisp programmer's apprentice," *IEEE Trans. Software Eng.*, vol. SE-4, Nov. 1978.

[16] J. T. Schwartz, "Some syntactic suggestions for transformational programming," *SETL Newsletter*, vol. 205, Courant Inst., New York, NY, 1978.

[17] T. A. Standish, D. C. Harriman, D. F. Kibler, and J. M. Neighbors, "Improving and refining programs by program manipulation," in *Proc. 1976 ACM Annu. Conf.*, Oct. 1976, pp. 509–516.

[18] D. Wile, "Type transformations," this issue, pp. 32–39.

Robert Balzer, for a photograph and biography, see this issue, p. 1.

"Program Developments: Formal Explanations of Implementations" by D.S. Wile from *Communications of the ACM*, Volume 26, Number 11, November 1983, pages 902-911. Copyright 1983, Association for Computing Machinery, Inc., reprinted by permission.

RESEARCH
CONTRIBUTIONS

Programming
Techniques and
Data Structures

Ellis Horowitz
Editor

Program Developments: Formal Explanations of Implementations

DAVID S. WILE *USC/Information Sciences Institute*

Author's Present Address:
David S. Wile,
USC/Information Sciences
Institute, 4676 Admiralty
Way, Marina del Rey, CA
90291.

1. INTRODUCTION: TRANSFORMATIONAL IMPLEMENTATION

The programming paradigm considered here involves implementing a very high-level specification through the use of *correctness-preserving transformations*. The implementor—a person—chooses different transformations on the basis of his knowledge of the domain in which the program will ultimately run and appropriateness. The computer actually applies the transformations and displays the results so that he can consider further transformations.

These transformations accomplish two separate tasks [34]: 1) implementation—selecting realizations of abstract constructs in terms of more concrete ones; and 2) optimization—rearranging a set of operations so as to minimize their execution cost. To get around the confusion between implementation of the specification and optimization of the implementation in the programming language, it has become common to simply speak of "optimization of programs" in a "wide-spectrum language" [8]. Such a language encompasses both specifications and programs. To do so, every construct must be operational, i.e., even the highest level constructs are executable (though very inefficiently). Hence, all transformations are potential optimizations. Throughout this report, we will call the person performing the optimization and implementation the "implementor"; his task is "implementation of specifications" or equivalently, "optimization of programs."

Although proponents of this paradigm have been active for several years [5, 7, 10, 32, 39], no production-level system for transformational optimization has been designed [35]. Several problem areas for the paradigm have become evident:

This research was supported by the National Science Foundation under Contract No. MCS-7918792. Views and conclusions contained in this report are the author's and should not be interpreted as representing the official opinion or policy of NSF, the U.S. Government, or any person or agency connected with them.

- Constructing a library of transformations that adequately captures most useful optimizations (for any specification/programming language). Standish [39], Barstow [6], and Rich [36] have done pioneering work in this area.

- Indexing such a library so that one can browse through it to find transformations suitable to the purpose at hand. This is an essential component recently considered by Neighbors [34] as a classification issue. A different approach to the problem is to develop *generic* transformations, encapsulating some large chunk of knowledge about several different, but related, transformations.

- Verifying and validating transformations to be correctness–

ABSTRACT: Automated program transformation systems are emerging as the basis for a new programming methodology in which high-level, understandable specifications are transformed into efficient programs. Subsequent modification of the original specification will be dealt with by reimplementation of the specification. For such a system to be practical, these reimplementations must occur relatively quickly and reliably in comparison with the original implementation. We believe that reimplementation requires that a formal document—the program development—be constructed during the development process explaining the resulting implementation to future maintainers of the specification. The overall goal of our work is to develop a language for capturing and explaining these developments and the resulting implementations. This language must be capable of expressing: 1) the implementor's goal structure; 2) all program manipulations necessary for implementation; and 3) optimization and plans of such optimizations. We discuss the documentation requirements of the development process and then describe a prototype system for constructing and maintaining this documentation information. Finally, we indicate many remaining, open issues and the directions to be taken in the pursuit of adequate solutions.

preserving. Work by Gerhart [23] and Broy and Pepper [9] has provided a technology for transformation verification, though its adequacy has yet to be tested on any significant set of transformations.

- Designing a mechanism for dynamically verifying that conditions in the program pertain, enabling the application of transformations. In its worst guise, this is the automatic theorem-proving problem; it may suffice to use flow-analysis techniques developed for traditional compilers [2, 25] along with specialized *predicate pushing mechanisms* developed in program verification efforts [18, 19] and transformation system designs [13].

- Automating large parts of the transformation process. Enormous chains of primitive transformation applications are necessary to optimize even the most trivial specifications. *Simplification* [30] and *conditioning* [22] (getting the program into shape for a desired transformation) are two approaches to this problem. These are tied together by the work of Feather [20], in which the implementor describes how he would like the resulting program to look, along with some key (insightful) transformations the system should use in obtaining it. Naturally, all work on optimizing compilers is relevant here [1, 37, 45].

- Describing what the implementor did in optimizing the program, i.e., describing the design decisions as well as the particular steps he went through in producing the final program. Such information must be available for modifiers to an optimization design to be able to maintain the original specification. Feather [20], Feather and Darlington [16], and Sintzoff [38] have laid the groundwork for this largely unexplored problem.

- Scaling up—problems of *size*. For realistic applications, enormous numbers of transformations, transformation applications, intermediate program states, intermediate predicate states, etc., must be dealt with quickly. This makes size the most crucial problem to be solved.

However, not all problems need to be solved to obtain a useful, albeit incomplete, system. Currently, it is possible to maintain predicates correctly (or approximately correctly) with considerable success. Thus, it does not appear that proofs of programs or transformations are crucial; we can (temporarily) continue to rely on people to perform these tasks informally. Also, it is quite reasonable to expect that the automation problems—simplification and conditioning—will become more tractable and that an acceptable level of automation can be achieved through techniques such as preprocessing sets of transformations, using the ideas of Kibler [30] and Knuth and Bendix [31]; automatic data structure optimization, as begun by Low [33]; and automation of conditioning transformations, as begun by Feather [20] and developed by Fickas [22]. While these capabilities are being developed, a useful transformation system must rely on more intervention by the user. Hence, arriving at a useful, large catalog of transformations, supporting its perusal, and documenting the development process itself seem to be the unsolved problems most critical to realizing a practical transformation system.

We focus on the last of these problems—documenting the development of optimization for the purpose of maintaining specifications and subsequently reimplementing them. What we call a *program development* is a formal document explaining the implementation of a specification for subsequent use by maintainers. The efforts of Feather and Darlington [16, 17, 20] expose the fundamental principle: If the application of transformations is expressed in a way that captures the *structure* or *optimization strategy* being pursued, it may be read later to understand how subsequent specification changes might impinge on the original optimization, and whether or

not the original implementation strategy is still valid. (N.B.: Feather and Darlington made the crucial observation that a *formal* structure representing the optimization has the potential to be *replayed* automatically—reapplied to a changed specification.) Sintzoff [38] precisely defines the notion of design decision and develops several commonly used structuring facilities. Cheatham [14] provides a mechanism for replaying the *historical* development of the program on subsequent versions. Swartout [40] has designed a system to generate explanations automatically, given appropriate formal documentation of the primitives from which a program is constructed and the goals which they accomplish. The relationship of these bodies of work to ours will be detailed in the relevant sections which follow.

Our work concerns the nature of the formal object we call *development structure*, which is *applied* to specifications to produce implementations. The characterization of development structures as objects applied to produce other programs allows our development structures to encompass the related notions of developments, strategies, transformations, and editors. Transformations obviously satisfy this characterization. Editors are simply programs (usually interactive) for applying sequences of transformations (not necessarily equivalence- or correctness-preserving). Strategies represent the intent, or plan, behind such sequences, and developments are the combination of all these capabilities into a coherent structure.

Below we list the properties required of a development description language and relate this language to the development process itself and its use in replay. We then describe POPART [44], a prototype system we have built for experimenting with developments, transformations, and other program manipulations.

2. DEVELOPMENT LANGUAGE PROPERTIES

Recall that the principal reason for the development language is to enable future (re)implementors to understand how the original implementation was made. This does not actually necessitate a *formal* development language in and of itself. As we mentioned above, the desire arises from the observation that developments expressed in a formal language could be reapplied to changed specifications (automatically) and, in some cases, would produce an appropriate reimplementation. Hence, it is not the formal properties of the language that determine the desired characteristics for the development, but rather those properties of the language that will allow suitable explanation for reimplementation purposes.

In particular, the primary property of the development language is that it should allow the optimizer (human) to clearly explain (to the human reimplementer) the motivations and design decisions made in the original development of a program. At the very least, this implies a *structuring* of goals and explanations into goals with subordinate goals or ways of achieving them. Hence, some mechanism for *subordination* will be required: traditional mechanisms achieving these include *named subfunctions* and *explicit refinements* ("do X by doing Y and Z").

In addition, goals at the same conceptual level must be related to one another; hence, the need for mechanisms conveying *goal dependencies* as perceived by the implementor. For example, it will certainly be essential to understand that two subgoals are independent. The maintainer should be able to ignore independent subgoals that deal with sections of the specifications unaffected by a change.

The particular goal structures we have foreseen include the following:

- Sequential dependency (composition): Goal A must be achieved before Goal B.
- Goal independence: Goal A may be achieved in parallel with Goal B.
- Choice: Goal A was chosen from a set of possible goals {A, B, ...} all of which supported the same overall goal.
- Conditional goals: Goal A need only be achieved if Goal B could not be achieved.
- Repetitive goals: Achieve a set of goals {A_1, A_2, A_3 ...}.

Other primitive goals structures may become important as we gain more experience with developments and development languages.

More complex goal structures should also be expressible and, most importantly, *definable*, for these correspond to *plans*, or *strategies*, in design activities. Certainly they need to be parameterizable as well. We see a spectrum of plan-like objects spread along the axis of "completeness" or "degree of parameterization." In particular, a low-level, single-purpose transformation is a complete plan that is quite certain to succeed with little intervention from the implementor. Transformations with "free parameters" are a little less transformation-like and a little more strategic—for example, a transformation that introduces an arbitrary predicate to break out a special case. At the "less complete" end of the spectrum, a plan for "divide and conquer" that reads "split off parts, apply function to parts, and then combine results" is a highly parameterized, incomplete plan. It is clear that the implementor must be able to define and invoke the whole spectrum of plan types.

Interestingly enough, Sintzoff has independently arrived at essentially the same goal structuring facilities for recording design decisions. He includes an *inductive* decision type; we substitute several forms of conditionality, including loops and recursive plan invocation, to achieve the same ends. It would be surprising if any great differences were exhibited in such a minimal-semantics, decision-structuring language! The main source of differences lies in the primitives filling the structure and the interpretation of the structure.

Until now the discussion has not required any properties of the development language dependent on the choice of specification/programming language. Appropriately so, for the whole notion of implementation strategy and documentation is primarily language independent, relying only on "programming knowledge" (currently) locked inside the experts' heads. The only real constraint on the development language that relates to the programming language is that all commands necessary to describe program manipulation be expressible in the language. This requires that the development language be grounded in some language for manipulating programs and program properties. If an extremely powerful underlying mechanism were present, this could be as simple as the single command "*achieve goal.*" For our experiments, we have chosen a quite basic editing language, but other quite different (primitive) languages could have been chosen and used successfully within our development language.

To summarize, the overall goal is to explain the implementation using a formal development language which is capable of expressing: a) a rich goal structure; b) *all* program manipulations necessary to optimization; and c) plans for optimization, as well as detailed optimizations.

3. THE DEVELOPMENT LANGUAGE
The development language we have designed and imple-

mented (called **Paddle**[1]) primarily emphasizes *structure*. The structural aspects of the language seem almost independent of the programming/specification language whose objects are being transformed. That independence is emphasized below, where the structural facilities are introduced first, followed by the actual primitives that manipulate the specifications.

3.1 Definition and Refinement
The need for definition facilities for transformations, strategies, plans, etc., was mentioned above. Although there may be strict distinctions between these various definable entities, we are not yet sure where to draw the boundaries. Hence, our development language currently supports only a single definition facility: the *command*, consisting of a name, a set of parameters, and a body. Let's define the well known problem-solving paradigm "divide and conquer." We would like to capture the essence of this paradigm in an abstract plan. We begin by defining the following Paddle command:

command DivideAndConquer(function, set) =
  begin
    split set into subsets, s_1, s_2, . . .;
    compute a related function, f_1, on the subsets;
    combine values of f_1 on subsets via a new function, f_2;
    note You must insure that function applied to set = f_2
      applied to {$f_1(s_1)$, $f_1(s_2)$, . . .}
  end

The **begin/end** pair indicates the *sequential composition* of goals to be satisfied by the implementor, i.e., the goals must be satisifed in the order stated. "Split," "compute," and "combine" are not understood by the development system as predefined commands. Rather, the user must *refine* these "stubs" to deal with the situation at hand when the command is actually invoked. In particular, we could refine the "split" stub into a binary decomposition of the set using the following syntax for *refinement* (a refinement is simply an in-place definition):

split set into subsets s_1, s_2, . . .
  by
    binary partitioning into $s_1 = \{e_1 \ldots e_{k/2}\}$ and
             $s_2 = \{e_{k/2+1} \ldots e_k\}$;

The use of the reserved word **by** indicates that what follows the description is what was actually meant by the commentary before it. This will be indented and, thus, appropriately subordinate to the concept it implements. Thus, as with Caine and Gordon's Program Design Language [11], our development language provides a skeletal structure for English description leading ultimately to primitive Paddle commands.

3.2. Goal Structures
The examples above already illustrate two different goal structures: *sequential composition* and *refinement subordination*. Another goal type that arises frequently is an *and* goal: the optimizer wishes to convey independence of subgoals. Paddle allows this using the *each* construct. There are at least two varieties of *and* goal: each must be *achieved* independently or each must be *achievable* independently (but the order chosen may be relevant). The latter interpretation has been adopted in Paddle; the former may have to be introduced later.

---

[1] From POPART's Development Language: a homonym.

Another Paddle goal type is a *choice* goal. For example, the transformation/plan designer may wish to convey more information about the alternative possible methods for doing the split above. This is accomplished using the **choose from** construct:

split set = {$e_1, e_2, \ldots$} into subsets $s_1, s_2, \ldots$;
  by
    choose from
      partitioning into $s_1 = \{e_1\}$ and $s_2 = \{e_2, e_3, \ldots\}$;
      binary partitioning into $s_1 = \{e_1 \ldots e_{k/2}\}$ and
                           $s_2 = \{e_{k/2+1} \ldots e_k\}$;
      basis partition $s_0, s_1, s_2, s_4, \ldots s_2^i$,
      where each e_n is a linear combination of the s_2^j
    end

Presently, such choices are not made automatically; the implementor decides in each situation what the appropriate selection should be.

Conditional structures, are used to make automatic choices. Currently the only conditional structure, **first of**, is like LISP's COND, in which the first goal to succeed is the one chosen.[2] For example, the following indicates successively worse implementations (slower or requiring more space) for sequences:

first of
  ArrayImplementation;
  LinkedListImplementation;
  DoublyLinkedListImplementation;
  HashedImplementation
end

If each of the "implementations" is a transformation, then the first one to be usable in the current situation will be the goal achieved. The failure of each goal is the conditionality for the attempt of the next alternative.

Finally, there is a *loop* goal structure that enables the body to be executed (achieved) repeatedly *while* (or *until*) another goal is satisfied. An example of such a loop structure is one that implements all sets by repetitively applying the above conditional set implementation transformation to each unimplemented set.

These goal structures provide Paddle with a general programming capability so that arbitrary developments can be constructed. Our goal is to make such developments both convenient and understandable.

3.3. Relationship with the Program Manipulation System
Paddle is a language for structuring goals. How these goals are achieved is an orthogonal issue dependent entirely on how the terminal nodes of the goal structures are defined. As we mentioned earlier, a single primitive command, **achieve**, could be used as the terminal node for all goal statements, which would leave to the transformation system the choices of how to achieve the primitive goals. We could be slightly less ambitious and allow "hints" to the transformation system by introducing Feather's **using** statement:[3] the goal is to be accomplished automatically, but it must **use** a set of named transformations in its achievement [20].

Alternatively, a large set of primitive commands could be used to describe very particular ways of achieving goals; some may appear to be actions rather than goals. Although all of

these options are acceptable, we have chosen the last, in the form of an editing language, as the primitive Paddle node language expressing how to accomplish the goals stated in the development. This choice was thought to be both universal and easily implementable; further, as higher levels of automation are achieved (as is planned), more abstract "primitives" can be added. In the meantime, we will continue to have a functioning, usable system.

Notice that the process is potentially recursive in two ways: conditioning the program may require that further subgoals in the process be met, and applying the strategy itself may require modification of several pieces of the program (as in the divide-and-conquer example above). This recursive structure must eventually be reflected in the development. It can be incorporated wholly beforehand (*a priori*) or afterward (*a posteriori*) as the explanation of that development.

An implementor normally switches back and forth between these two modes during any single session.

3.4 Operational Interpretation
In fact, the set of primitive commands is actually a parameter to Paddle; however, the fact that the goal structure is given an *operational interpretation* is fixed and crucial to the actual kinds of problem solving/design activity that can be expressed. In particular, the overall model of program manipulation used by Paddle is as follows: there is at all times a specification/program affected by Paddle expressions. This specification/program, together with the active goal structure(s), forms the data and control portion of the state of the "abstract Paddle machine." The development structure is applied to an initial state to produce a new state. That application is a relatively straightforward interpretation of the development language as though it itself were a programming language. In particular, it is a depth first, left-to-right tree traversal of the goal structure represented by the development.

The state into which the initial state is transformed depends on whether the development process contains any errors or is incomplete. In such situations, the new state represents "progress so far"; facilities are provided for fixing the Paddle "program" and continuing. When there are no errors, the development is entirely automatic, and the Paddle program indeed represents the entire implementation history of the specification: the final state is the implementation. N.B.: It is the *automatic* application of a development structure to a specification to yield the final implementation which guarantees the fidelity of the implementation explanation.

We emphasize that Paddle is executed as a programming language; we have no facilities to interpret Paddle breadth-first or in some other nonoperational manner. To illustrate the significance of this decision, consider the problem of choosing two different data structures in different parts of the program. An implementor may interactively decide which choices to make "in any order," using whatever strategy he feels is appropriate (breadth-first examination of alternatives, for example). The system, when it is *applying* the development to the program (for example, during a replay), will completely elaborate one of the choices and its dependencies even before introducing the other choice.

This distinction involves the differences between the development *process* and the development *structure*, to be described presently.

4. THE DEVELOPMENT PROCESS
Although the development structure is applied like a program to a specification to yield an implementation, the process of

---

[2] A syntactic variant, in the form of an if-then-else statement, is also planned.
[3] Also used in Hewitt's (full) Planner.

designing the implementation and its explanation is by no means so stylized. In general, the following scenario captures the normal activity of the implementor:

- Focus on a program fragment;
- Find an appropriate implementation strategy;
- Get the program into "condition" to allow application of the strategy;
- Apply the strategy;
- Simplify the resulting program.

4.1 *A Priori* Explanations

An *a priori* explanation corresponds to planning, or using an existing implementation strategy. This is certainly a frequent initial implementation approach, for high-level specifications are usually so intrinsically inefficient that previous experience with similar problems suggests an overall implementation design. For example, while text-processing systems are best specified as multiple pass algorithms, most programmers will implement such systems as single-pass algorithms. Hence, most implementors will choose multiple-pass merging as their topmost strategy.

To produce an *a priori* explanation using our system, the implementor must indicate the focus of attention on the program in the development, as well as the actual implementation plan. He generally creates a piece of development structure to express both the implementation plan and the focus of attention. He then applies the development structure to the specification.

When using an *a priori* explanation, and therefore, applying a development to a specification, the implementor needs feedback as to exactly what is happening to the specification, in case his expectations are not met. Hence, in our system, the application of the development structure is *traced*. This gives the implementor exactly the same feedback as he would have had if he had done the transformations *a posteriori*.

Normally, something goes wrong during *a priori* development. Either the development plan contains undefined steps or a transformation's pattern or enabling conditions fail to match. When this happens the implementor becomes problem-driven rather than strategy-driven: he will produce an *a posteriori* explanation.

4.2 *A Posteriori* Explanations

When the implementor is not sure what transformation to apply next, or what portion of the program to focus on, or when problems arise with a planned development, he will switch his attention to the program itself. He may change the program, using editing commands and transformations. Often, such commands are used to condition the program for the transformation that was being attempted. When this happens, he may want the editing steps to be "bundled up" and inserted into the development structure, or he may want to make a new transformation which generalizes his editing steps and insert a call to it in the development. Support for both of these processes is provided in our system.

We emphasize that ultimately, it is the entirely automatic application of a development to a program to produce the resulting implementation that gives credence—and self-confidence— to the optimizer. Despite excursions into *a posteriori* explanations, the final implementation must appear to subsequent maintainers to have been produced entirely *a priori*.

5. REPLAY OF DEVELOPMENTS

Of course, the reason for having the development structure as a formal object in the first place is so that replaying the

development (in part) on changed specifications is the normal mode of operation. Unfortunately, simply having the explanation for the implementation does not guarantee the ability to replay developments accurately. There are two basic problems: (a) replaying the development and getting errors when it was expected to work; and (b) replaying the development and getting no error when the replay should not work. Naturally, the latter problem is the most insidious, for the implementor will not know that the new development is flawed. These can arise from insufficient identification of assumptions in the original development or implicit assumptions in the system.

5.1 Unexpected Errors

We have no real-world experience with replay, since we have not "maintained" (i.e., changed) any of the example specifications yet. Nevertheless, a fair amount of it occurs even in a normal design: midstream in the design, one often decides to try the whole thing "from scratch," as though the entire development were designed *a priori*, in order to test the accuracy of our development structure. From this experience, it is clear that the problems related to the development failing when we thought it would work are often problems of *focus*. The language we use is inadequate for expressing exactly which portion of the specification or development is being transformed. Generally, the language is simply too low level— it does not identify the pieces being transformed by using labeled program segments or high-level descriptions, e.g., "the loop over characters." High-level editing notions as suggested by [43] must be incorporated to avoid this problem.

5.2 Unreported Errors

We have begun to use conventions to forestall problems of the second type above. First, we often express a "map" or "template" of what we believe the implementation looks like at different, key stages in the development.

Second, we have started identifying key stages in the development structure where a dynanic snapshot of the implementation should be presented to the implementor. In particular, although the tracing facility is extremely useful during the design of the development, it is just like any other tracing facility when the traced object becomes large: it is overwhelming. Hence, looking back to it for information during reimplementation would be time consuming.

We have found it quite useful to identify *major steps* in the development and print out the entire implementation state before and after those steps. Subsequent maintenance versions can be compared with the original major steps to decide on new strategies. Basically, this is one mechanism which allows the maintainer to check that his newly created development is "on track" with the old one when he intends for it to be.

Of course, the major issue of checking that (implicit) assumptions match is most difficult. Recent work on semantic matching by [15] has solved part of the problem; systems can automatically compare two implementations and present semantic explanations of their differences to the user. However, this area remains completely open for solutions.

6. THE UNDERLYING PROGRAM MANIPULATION SYSTEM: POPART

POPART[4] [44] is a system developed in Interlisp [42] to provide the basis for a programming environment for *arbitrary*

---

[4] Producer of Parsers and Related Tools.

programming languages—in fact, for arbitrary languages describable in BNF. The tools provided for objects described in BNF grammars[5] include a parser, an editor, a pretty printer, a lexical analyzer, and a language-independent, pattern-matching and replacement mechanism. In fact, the transformation system itself is one of these language-independent tools! A "pure" parser was produced intially as a reaction of systems that embed semantic processing in the syntactic parsing mechanism [27]—LISP itself seemed to be a preferable medium for expressing the semantics of parsed sentences. In fact, to support the set of tools mentioned, an abstract representation of all the information in the source language must be maintained, i.e., a "pure" parser must be used for such systems. The idea to provide tools for manipulating expressions in these languages arose from proposals by Balzer [3, 4] and Yonke's Ph.D. dissertation establishing its feasibility [46]. POPART is certainly related to recent efforts on programming language environments, such as Gandalf [28, 21] and the environments for PL/CS [41] and Pascal [29]. It also defines a language for program manipulation, and is thus related to the recent work of Cameron and Ito on grammar-based metaprogramming systems [12].

A BNF grammar is used to generate an *abstract syntax* for the language; expressions are subsequently parsed by POPART into this abstract syntax. Thereafter, no other representation of the program exists, i.e., no stream of lexemes or characters. All tools work with the abstract syntax, variously converting strings into it and it into strings when communication with the user is necessary: the user always views and enters *source language*—he never sees the abstract syntax representation itself. This is quite different from the Gandalf system, but is consonant with Kahn's Pascal system, Mentor. POPART is embedded in the Interlisp interactive environment: it is a set of "commands" invoked just like any other Interlisp commands (EVALQUOTE). Hence, we should think of POPART not as a system, but as a set of augmentations to the already extensive Interlisp environment, provided to deal uniformly with objects described in BNF grammars.

POPART itself is intended to be a set of tools from which a *system designer* constructs and customizes a system. The default mechanism provided to the designer support an environment in which a single object is always being edited (for each grammar known to POPART). The *user* of the editor has commands for moving about in the abstract representation of the object; he may go in, out, forward, and backward in the structure. He also can change the object, but only in ways that maintain the grammatical integrity of the object.

It is not the intent of this report to describe the POPART system in detail. Those portions relevant to understanding the transformation system (component) will be dealt with as they are encountered.

7. STRUCTURES EXPRESSED IN THE PADDLE LANGUAGE

The single most powerful feature of the POPART/Paddle system is that since Paddle itself is described as a language with a formal syntax, Paddle developments themselves may be manipulated by the user using the POPART primitives! This is the nature of the synergism derived from using generic, tool-based systems rather than pat encapsulations isolating users from the environment system.

The fact that the Paddle language is independent of the programming language means that the development structure

---

[5] Of course, a variant allowing regular expressions.

mechanism can be a POPART tool. As was mentioned above, POPART editing *commands* can be written using Paddle's program manipulation facilities. Introducing Paddle comes full circle: we use POPART on Paddle, and then use Paddle in POPART.[6]

The Paddle development language is used to describe four different structures to POPART: Global Commands, Simplifications, Conditioners, and the Development.

7.1. Global Commands

The global commands are simply parameterized macros that can be used in any of these POPART structures and that may be explicitly invoked as editing instructions when editing the program itself. For example, if one wanted an abbreviated way to find a conditional statement, he might define the command:

command FindIf( ) =
    Find !ConditionalStatement

This innocuous definition represents much of the complexity of the Paddle/POPART marriage, so we will belabor it a bit. First, there are conceptually three different languages involved here:

- the language of the development system, Paddle;
- the primitive commands of the development system (chosen to be POPART's editing commands);
- the programming language that represents the program being transformed.

Font Conventions   Different font conventions have been adopted for each of the different languages to help the reader differentiate them, as follows:

Paddle
    Development Language—optimize body, comments, and so forth
    Development Keywords—**each, by, first**. . .
    Global Command Names—MergeLoops, FindCall. . .

Popart
    Primitive Command Names—*Find, Top, ReplaceAll*. . .

Programming Language
    Programming Language—text, character, vary3. . .
    Programming Language Keywords—***begin, end, procedure***. . .

Notice that the Paddle global command FindIf above is defined to be the POPART editor *Find* command of a pattern in the programming language: !ConditionalStatement. It is necessary for POPART to support switching between grammars for such expressions to be parsed. The expression !ConditionalStatement indicates that anything syntactically derivable from the grammar nonterminal "ConditionalStatement" should match. ConditionalStatement represents a pattern variable in the pattern language used for the *Find* and *Replace* commands.

What are normally considered to be transformations are also definable as commands. For example, to replace a conditional whose predicate is the constant ***true*** with its ***then*** clause one could write the following:

---

[6] Note: We have not yet used POPART and Paddle to implement POPART and Paddle.

```
command REPLACEWITHTHEN( ) =
  begin
    first of
      Match if true
                then !Statement;
      Match if true
                then !Statement
                else !Statement#
    end;
    Replace !Statement
  end
```

The POPART editing commands *Match* and *Replace* are the primitives of the Paddle development language. Notice that here in a simple transformation we have used the conditional goal satisfaction mechanism of the Paddle language—the **first of** command.[7] Either pattern may match (an **if** statement with or without an **else** clause). The *Match* command differs from the *Find* command in that it is an "anchored search" for the pattern. The statement matched will subsequently be replaced by the **then** part. This replacement will only occur if (some option within) the **first of** command succeeded. Otherwise, the **first of** command will fail.

Finally, plans or strategies as described above may be included among the global commands;

```
command DIVIDEANDCONQUER(function, set) =
  begin
    split set={e₁, e₂, . . . } into subsets s₁, s₂, . . . ;
      by
        choose from
          partitioning into s₁ = {e₁} and s₂ = {e₂, e₃, . . . };
          binary partitioning into s₁ = {e₁ . . . e_{k/2}} and
                                   s₂ = {e_{k/2+1} . . . e_k};
          basis partition s₀, s₁, s₂, s₄, . . . s₂ʲ,
              where each eₙ is a linear combination of the s₂ʲ
        end
    compute a related function, f₁, on the subsets;
    combine values of f₁ on subsets via a new function, f₂;
    note You must insure that function applied to set =
        f₂ applied to {f₁(s₁), f₁(s₂), . . . }
  end
```

Notice, in this command, the only predefined command is the *note* command!

7.2 Simplifications
Paddle is also used to describe **simplifications** to the editor. Each time a *Replace* command is called in the editor, the resulting expression is checked for various simplifications. Some of these are described by the grammar designer to POPART, such as automatic removal of extra parentheses when nested constructs replace expressions in which the nesting is unnecessary. In addition, a single Paddle **Simplication** command is always applied to the modified program when a replacement is made. For example, the REPLACE-WITHTHEN command defined above would be a reasonable simplification command to try. If we had an analogous command, REPLACEWITHELSE,

```
command REPLACEWITHELSE( ) =
  begin
    Match if false
         then !Statement
         else !Statement#;
    Replace !Statement#
  end
```

we might include these in the simplification structure:

```
first of
  REPLACEWITHTHEN;
  REPLACEWITHELSE
          * * *
end. . .
```

7.3 Conditioning
During the transformation process, it is frequently the case that a transformation's pattern will fail to match when the implementor thought it would (or should). He will then have to divert his attention from transforming to "getting the program into condition" to be transformed. Normally, this process of conditioning[8] the program will merely involve the application of a simple, equivalence-preserving transformation to the program.

POPART provides conditioning at the syntactic level within the *Find* and *Match* commands. The system builder builds tables which direct this activity by classifying productions as having associative, commutative, or nested fields. POPART will then automatically rewrite expressions using this information to condition it to match.

Conditioning is also provided for in the Paddle language in a manner analogous to simplification: A conditioning command is applied to the current expression to attempt to change it so that it will match a pattern that has failed to match.[9] For efficiency reasons, this will require preprocessing of the conditioning commands, to see if the pattern being matched could be produced by a *Replace* command in the conditioning command. For example, if the following conditioning commands were given to the system

```
begin
  command INTRODUCETHEN( ) =
    begin
      Match !Statement
      Replace if true
                  then !Statement
    end;
  command INTRODUCEELSE( ) =
    begin
      Match !Statement;
      Replace if false
                  then null
                  else !Statement
    end
end
```

and the user attempted

Match **if** !Predicate **then** !ActionInvocation

when the current expression was

TextRemove[text, character]

---

[7] Lack of an "option" in the pattern language forces the use of the first of command. We contemplate the future use of POPART's BNF to specify patterns, thus eliminating this difficulty.

[8] We previously called this "jittering," but find the connotation distasteful.
[9] This is not yet implemented.

the conditioner would have to notice that the INTRODUCETHEN command produces a conditional statement with the same format as the pattern being matched (the argument to the *Match*). It would then attempt to execute the command. If it succeeded, and the resulting expression matches, it is done.

if true then TextRemove[text, character]

Otherwise, it has a choice: it can either attempt to make the command succeed or try other conditioning commands. We will probably implement this mechanism as a breadth-first search with a very early cutoff (depth 2). This mechanism is significant because Paddle is used to express all program manipulations and because much of the conditionality currently embedded in plans and developments to handle local variability can be factored out and put into the conditioning mechanism. This will greatly simplify and clarify the plans and developments while insuring that this conditioning capability is uniformly applied.

7.4 The Development Process: A Simple Example
Of course, the development structure itself is the major focus of attention here. However, it is instructive to examine actual transcripts of the development process to understand the relationship between it and the resulting development structure. Hence, a set of four (lengthy) appendices to this article is available from the author, illustrating this relationship in considerable detail.

Appendix II is an actual transcript of a development of an implementation for the toy specification designed in Appendix I. The two transcripts together—Appendix I and Appendix II—have been constructed to be "self-explanatory"; many details of the POPART/Paddle system can be gleaned from careful reading of them.

The development process described in the Appendix typifies the nature of interactive program and development manipulation. Two characteristics stand out: (a) The development process is much more verbose and tedious than the final development explanation. (b) The development process is quite error-prone. Both argue strongly that a transcript of the development process is inappropriate documentation of the optimization itself.

7.5 Text Compression: An Extended Example Development
The actual development structure arrived at in the above example was too trivial to actually demonstrate most of the interesting issues involved in structuring explanations for later consumption. Hence, a related but considerably longer example development has been presented in its final form in Appendix III. This describes the partial implementation of the program

begin
    action
        savet[text | list of character, pred | predicate]
        definition loop(*any* character) **suchthat** character *in* text
            unless pred(character)
            do removet[text, character];
    relation
        redundant space(character, seq | list *of* character)
        definition successort(seq, *, character) *isa* space
            and character *isa* space;
    loop(*any* linefeed) **suchthat** linefeed *in* text
        do atomic insert linefeed *isa* space;
            delete linefeed *isa* linefeed
        end atomic;

savet[text, *'a* character ‖ character *isa* alphanumeric *or*
           character *isa* space];
  loop(*any* space) **suchthat** space *in* text *and* redundant ←
           space (space, text)
      do removet[text, space]
end . . .

This example was first worked out (manually, without system aids) in [5]. In that paper, approximately the same development strategy as we are now able to describe formally was suggested as the desirable way of accomplishing the optimization. Our formal representation of that strategy is now[10]

begin
  Pretty;
  MajorStep substitute savet definition for call
    by Unfold savet;
  MajorStep obtain a single loop
    by !POTAndCommands;
  MajorStep optimize loop body
    by !POTSeqCommands;
  MajorStep pick data representations
end . . .

The primitive command *MajorStep* causes the program to be printed out after its refinement has been executed. As was mentioned above, the verbatim trace of the executed primitive commands is not very valuable after-the-fact documentation. It is much more informative for the development structure to dynamically identify key steps which subsequent optimizers should use as "checkpoints" that the maintenance they perform is "on track" with the previous optimization. Thus, Appendix IV is included as an important (though easily regenerated) adjunct to the formal development. It represents the actual application of the development in Appendix III to the initial program. The tracing of the primitive commands has been turned off, yielding a much clearer picture of the development process itself.

8. PROBLEMS AND FUTURE RESEARCH
We believe we are in an excellent position to begin to do experimental research on development styles and the fundamental support necessary to make transformation systems realistic. The POPART and Paddle facilities are all implemented and function as described. Extensions to the system will arise from extensive experiments with large, realistic examples. I expect future experience to duplicate the past: Paddle commands are defined to approximate some facility that seems desirable. Experimentation with it leads to its inclusion as a primitive command or its rejection.

We are aware that these specific areas still need considerable attention.

8.1 A. Separate Goal Structure
Some goals cannot actually be expressed as independent, even though there appear to be two separate tasks being accomplished. For example, in the divide-and-conquer plan above, f_1 and f_2 are neither independent nor sequentially dependent. This defect may require that a separate goal structure be maintained (a noninterpretable structure). This is actually necessary for any reasonable interpretation of codependent goals or even entirely independent goals: the operational-

---

[10] The summarization of this development has been produced automatically using the POPART pretty-printer's level control mechanism. The references to !POTAnd Commands and !POTSeqCommands have been inserted automatically; they are merely "stubs" whose values are printed subsequently in the transcript.

ity of the development structure is too constraining to express these concepts adequately.

8.2 Styles to Support Maintenance
Exactly what mechanisms—like checkpoint snapshots of the optimization in progress—are necessary to facilitate maintenance activities on the specifications? How should the optimizer describe the editor's focus of attention on the program so as to remain general enough so that simple changes do not cause the attention to "drift," and yet be specific enough that replays do not work with just any new specification?

Although we described the development structure as "an explanation" of the development, there are other explanatory styles of more utility. For example, [40] uses a similar structure to produce answers to individual questions (about programs); the same might be used to justify development steps on a more localized basis.

8.3 Generic Transformations
The sequential composition, refinement subordination, and choice constructs provide the basis for creating packages that encapsulate a structured knowledge base of interrelated decisions. Their use results in selection of an implementation for some higher level goal (for example, "divide and conquer"). Packaging development strategies in ways that exhibit intelligent reaction to information provided by the user is an important issue for future research: how to describe or suggest the appropriateness of certain choices and to order dynamically the consideration of decisions.

8.4 Increased Automation
It is clear that automatic facilities are necessary for a useful system. Two major areas need work: predicate maintenance—flow analysis as well as domain dependent "predicate pushing," and automatic conditioning—including choosing appropriate transformations based on hints from the user.

8.5 Developments in Other Domains
We mentioned above that the set of primitive commands underlying Paddle need not be an editing language. We have two applications to quite different domains in which we wish to study the use of Paddle. First, we have already experimented with the use of Paddle in Affirm. Affirm [24] is a program verification/theorem proving system. Its command set has been used as a Paddle primitive node language. In that context, Paddle provides a mechanism for defining and invoking proof strategies. Paddle developments are applied to a state consisting of a set of theorems to be proved and a set of program specifications to be verified. The developments (may) represent entire program validations. A language-dependent version of some of these same Paddle development notions is captured in the proof metalanguage for LCF [26].

Another application in which Paddle may be useful is for specification design. In particular, the design decisions used in arriving at an initial specification should be documented as thoroughly as those used to arrive at an implementation. With a primitive node language devoted to describing the goals achieved when features are introduced into specifications we expect Paddle to provide a suitable framework for such design documentation. This will not be like Caine and Gordon's PDL [11], but will instead document the design process; i.e., the final development structure will not contain the program pieces in the leaves, but rather will tell how the specification changes between design stages.

We must emphasize that the directions taken for the future work will be based principally on the necessities demanded by a large example. If predicate maintenance does not seem to be a significant bottleneck, we will ignore it to the benefit of other areas. We believe we have laid the groundwork for extensive experimentation into the appropriate facilities for realistic transformation systems of the future.

Acknowledgments. Many thanks to Bob Balzer, Steve Fickas, Susan Gerhart, Neil Goldman, and Bill Swartout for their helpful comments on early drafts of this report. I would also like to thank Martin Feather and Phil London for helping to debug the Paddle system (as guinea pigs, of course). Most of the ideas in this report arose from discussions with these individuals, and Don Cohen and Lee Erman. Thanks to Nancy Bryan for her critical corrections to the final draft of this report. And finally, particular thanks to the *CACM* referee who suggested major structural improvements to this report.

REFERENCES

1. Allen, F.E. Bibliography on program optimization. Tech. Rep. RC 5767, IBM Research, Yorktown Heights, New York, 1975.
2. Babich, W.A., and Jazayeri, M. The method of attributes for data flow analysis: Parts I and II. *Acta Inf. 10,* 3 (1978), 245–264, 265–272.
3. Balzer, R.M. EXDAMS—extendable debugging and monitoring system. Spring Joint Computer Conference, IFIP, 1969, pp. 567–580.
4. Balzer, R.M. Language-independent programmer's interface. Tech. Rep. RR-73-15, USC/Information Sciences Institute, Marina del Ray, California, 1973.
5. Balzer, R., Goldman, N., and Wile, D. On the transformational implementation approach to programming. *Proc. 2nd International Conf. Softw. Eng.,* 1976, pp. 337–343.
6. Barstow, D.R., *Knowledge-based Program Construction.* Elsevier, North Holland, 1979.
7. Bauer, F.L. Programming as an evolutionary process. *Proc. 2nd International Conf. Softw. Eng.,* 1976, pp. 223–234.
8. Bauer, F.L., Broy, M., Partsch, H., Pepper, P. et al. Report on a Wide Spectrum Language for Program Specification and Development. Tech. Rep. TUM-18104, Technische Universitaet Muenchen, May 1981.
9. Broy, M., and Pepper, P. Program development as a formal activity. *IEEE Trans. Softw. Eng. 1* (January 1981), 14–22.
10. Burstall, R.M., and Darlington, J. A transformation system for developing recursive programs. *J. ACM 24,* 1 (1977), 44–67.
11. Caine, S.H., and Gordon, E.K. PDL—a tool for software development. In *Proc. National Computer Conference,* AFIPS, 1975.
12. Cameron, R.D., and Ito, M.R. Grammar-based definition of meta-programming systems. University of British Columbia, Vancouver, January 1982.
13. Cheatham, T.E., Holloway, G.H., and Townley, J.A. Symbolic evaluation and the analysis of programs. *IEEE Trans. Soft. Eng. 5,* 4 (July 1979), 402–417.
14. Cheatham, T.E., Holloway, G.H., and Townley, J.A. Program refinement by transformation. *Proc. 5th Int. Conf. Softw. Eng.,* IEEE, March 1981, pp. 430–437.
15. Chiu, W. *Structure Comparison and Semantic Interpretation of Differences.* Ph.D. Th., University of Southern California, 1981.
16. Darlington, J., and Feather, M. A Transformational Approach to Modification. Tech. Rep. 80/3, Imperial College, London, 1979.
17. Darlington, J. The structured description of algorithm derivations. Algorithmic Languages: Proc IFIP TC-2 International Symposium, 1982.
18. Deutsch, L. P. *An Interactive Program Verifier.* Ph.D. Th., University of California, Berkeley, June 1973.
19. Dijkstra, E.W., *A Discipline of Programming.* Englewood Cliffs, New Jersey: Prentice-Hall, 1976.
20. Feather, M.S. *A System for Developing Programs by Transformation.* Ph.D. Th., University of Edinburgh, Department of Artificial Intelligence, 1979.
21. Feiler, P.H., and Medina-More, R. An Incremental Programming Environment. Carnegie-Mellon University, April 1980.

22. Fickas, S. Automatic goal-directed program transformation. *Proc. 1st Annual Nat. Conf. Artif. Intell.*, The American Association for Artificial Intelligence, 1980, pp. 68–70.

23. Gerhart, S.L. Knowledge about programs: A model and a case study. *Proc. Int. Conf. Reliable Softw.*, IEEE, 1975, pp. 88–95.

24. Gerhart, S.L., et al. An overview of *Affirm*: A specification and verification system. Proceedings IFIP 80, Australia, October, 1980, pp. 343–348.

25. Geschke, C.M. *Global Program Optimizations*. Ph.D. Th., Carnegie-Mellon University, 1972.

26. Gordon, M., Milner, R. et al. A metalanguage for interactive proof in LCF. In *Proc. Conference Symp. Principles of Programming Languages*, 1978, pp. 119–130.

27. Griss, C., Griss, M., and Marti, J. META/LISP. Tech. Rept. Operating Note No. 24, University of Utah, Utah Computational Physics Group, 1976.

28. Habermann, A.N. An overview of the Gandalf project. In *CMU Computer Science Research Review 1978–79*, Carnegie-Mellon University, 1980.

29. Donzeau-Gouge, V., Huet, G., Kahn, G., Lang, B., and Levy, J.J. A structure-oriented program editor: A first step towards computer assisted programming. International Computing Symposium, 1975, 1975, pp. 113–120.

30. Kibler, D.F. *Power, Efficiency, and Correctness of Transformation Systems*. Ph.D. Th., University of California, Irvine, 1978.

31. Knuth, D.E., and Bendix, P.B., Simple word problems in universal algebras. In Leech, J., Ed., *Computational Problems in Abstract Algebra*, New York: Pergamon Press, 1970, pp. 263–297.

32. Loveman, D.B. Program improvement by source to source transformation. *J. ACM 24*, 1 (Jan. 1977), 121–145.

33. Low, J.R. Automatic Coding: Choice of Data Structures. Tech. Rep. 1, University of Rochester, Computer Science Department, 1974.

34. Neighbors, J.M. *Software Construction Using Components*. Ph.D. Th., University of California at Irvine, 1980.

35. Partsch, H., and R. Steinbrueggen. A comprehensive survey on program transformation systems. Tech. Rep. TUM 18108, Technische Universitaet Muenchen, July, 1981.

36. Rich, C. A formal representation for plans in the Programmer's Apprentice. In *Proc. 7th Int. Joint Conf. Artif. Intell.*, August 1981.

37. Schwartz, J.T. On Programming, An Interim Report on the SETL Project. New York University, Courant Institute of Mathematical Sciences, June 1975.

38. Sintzoff, M. Suggestions for composing and specifying program design decisions. In *4th Int. Symp. Progr.*, Paris, April 1980.

39. Standish, T.A., Harriman, D.C., Kibler, D.F., and Neighbors, J.M. Improving and refining programs by program manipulation. ACM National Conference Proceedings, ACM, 1976, pp. 509–516.

40. Swartout, W.R. Explaining and justifying expert consulting programs. *Proc. 7th Int. Joint Conf. Artif. Intell.*, August 1981.

41. Teitelbaum, T., and Reps, R. The Cornell program synthesizer: A syntax-directed programming environment. *Comm. ACM 24*, 9 (September 1981), 563–573.

42. Teitelman, W. *Interlisp Reference Manual*. Xerox Palo Alto Research Center, 1978.

43. Waters, R.C. "The Programmer's apprentice: Knowledge based program editing." *IEEE Trans. Soft Eng 8*, 1 (January 1982), 1–12.

44. Wile, D.S. *POPART: Producer of Parsers and Related Tools, System Builder's Manual*. USC/Information Sciences Institute, TM-82-21, 1982.

45. Wulf, W.A., Johnsson, R.K., Weinstock, C.B., Hobbs, S.O., and Geschke, C.M. *The Design of an Optimizing Compiler*. American Elsevier, New York, 1975.

46. Yonke, M.D. A knowledgeable, language-independent system for program construction and modification. Tech. Rep. RR-75-42, USC/Information Sciences Institute, October 1975.

CR Categories and Subject Descriptors: 4.12 [**Compilers and generators**], 4.20 [**Programming languages**]: general, 4.43 [**Program maintenance**], 5.23 [**Formal languages**]: grammars

Additional Key Words and Phrases: program design, program development, program optimization, program transformation, programming environments, replay, structure editors

Received 6/81; revised 11/81; accepted 11/82

From Specifications to Machine Code:
Program Construction through Formal Reasoning

by Friedrich L. Bauer

Institut für Informatik
Technische Universität München
Munich, Germany

Abstract

Due to modern technology, software will to an increasing extent be frozen into hardware. This is just one example for situations where bugs in the software are absolutely intolerable. Therefore programming must soon become a safe process of program construction; that is, it has to be organized as a sequence of steps of rational reasoning. Starting from an elaborate formal problem specification using elements of predicate logic, set theory and primitives from some algebras, the application of formal rules leads to algorithmic versions and finally to programs oriented towards the instruction repertoire of particular concrete machines.

A genuine program construction process needs strict formalization throughout. All versions including the specifications can conveniently be represented by one programming language comprising the complete spectrum of descriptive, applicative and procedural styles. Such a language includes the concept of nondeterminism, which makes the development process transparent and extremely flexible, and it is to be interpreted by some model of the underlying abstract data types. The use of formally proved transformation rules guarantees this correctness.

In addition, the transformational approach is universal in the sense that the collection of rules can be adapted to the application in question: Although initially envisaged and mainly used now for the construction of software for classical sequential stored-program machines, the approach can be extended to other computational models corresponding to the often cited innovative hardware architectures.

I. INTRODUCTORY REMARKS

What is program construction?

The word "construction" has its particular meaning in engineering disciplines: it denotes the actual building of an engineering product. In Software Engineering, it should be taken as a provocation, as compared with tinkering.

In geometry the word has its special connotation, too, which refers to Euklid. Descartes and Spinoza, in the 17th century, used the phrase 'more geometrico' to indicate the role rational reasoning should play in philosophy. Today, we should expect rational reasoning to play a top role in the program production process. But the real situation is somewhat like a backwoods scenery: Programs are concocted in moonshine distilleries; the humdrum day of a programmer is full of alchemy.

Why is program construction interesting?

In some areas, there are critical demands on correctness, for instance in Spaceships, Power plants, Weapon systems.

Correctness can also be mandatory by

. Political demands (control of government money spending by the parliament)
. Social demands (protection of privacy)
. Economic demands (frozen software on chips).

Moreover, the essence of software engineering is to see a program as a quality product, including guarantee of correctness.

Correct software construction is in the long run more economic: it

. allows timing of the design process
. makes 'maintenance' obsolete
. is a prerequisite of reliable software

Finally, correctness should be the result of self-esteem of the software designer and user. Correctness is but one of several advantages of rigourous program construction.

A chain of construction steps

An old principle of data processing is the following: Data flow should not be interrupted by human transmission, there should be no reading and retyping. Analogously, there is the rule:

> The program development process should be a chain of uninterrupted formal reasoning. No step is to be done unchecked: the weakest link determines the strength of a chain.

Finding a suitable chain of construction steps is of course the real difficulty. As a rule, it needs intuition and is based on ingenuity.

Reprinted from *The Proceedings of the 6th International Conference on Software Engineering*, 1982, pages 84-91. Copyright © 1982 by The Institute of Electrical and Electronics Engineers, Inc.

Performing the single construction step can be done mechanically. It needs concentration, attentiveness, accuracy - it is thus left to a machine, to a closed system which works according to fixed patterns best.

The need for formalization

Why do we need formalization? The need for formalization is inherent in computer science. The computer itself is absolutely formal in its contact with people. It will obey the 'sorcer's apprentice' verbally, but it will not accept 'do what I mean', nor will it understand 'see what I mean'.

Powerful tools for expressing formalities in a very compact way have been created first by people working in formal logic and then by theoretical computer scientists. These tools are much too compact, however, for a typical von Neumann computer. (Recent attempts to bring computers conceptually closer to these powerful tools, e.g. reduction machines, have not yet had an impact on the use of existing computers.)

Where do we start from, and where do we end?

A program can be *constructed* only with respect to some (formally) given specification. A (correct) program's value lies in its aptness for some given machine. Different machines may demand different programs, even totally different algorithms. Specification is machine-independent, of course. Early steps of program development are preferably kept uncorrupted by machine considerations.

What about verification?

Programs do not fall from heaven.
Programs which have been constructed from specifications by chains of uninterrupted formal reasoning are eo ipso correct and do not *need* verification. Programs which are not constructed this way - may they be the result of a brainstorm, an inspiration, a day-dream - are, as a rule, incorrect (- not terribly, just a little bit) and thus do not *allow* verification.[1]

II. AN ANALYSIS OF THE PROGRAM CONSTRUCTION PROCESS

Stages of the program construction process

I see the program construction process as consisting of three stages:[2]

Stage One: On the interface Purchaser/Programmer the specification is worked out and

---

[1] Verification methods with joint construction of program and proof are special cases of transformational methods.

[2] In the following, we deal mainly with Stage One, where more questions are open.

brought into formal form
Stage Two: The construction process proper starts from the (formal) specification and goes (in a number of steps) to the likewise formal machine-oriented algorithmic description, to machine code. Specification and machine code form the software product.
Stage Three: On the interface Programmer/Purchaser the software product is certified.

Comparing this with the claimed "life-cycle" of an industrial product (see e.g. Zelkowitz 1978), we see that *requirement analysis* and *definition* falls into Stage One, *design*, *implementation* and *coding* belong to Stage Two and show a floating transition between each other; *installation* and *service* falls into Stage Three, as well as *testing* and *maintenance*, if there is any.

> In the stage of construction proper, program tests and program maintenance have logically no place, provided all the construction steps are properly done, i.e. are formally sound and form an uninterrupted chain.

In reality, testing and maintenance may be worthwhile between successive acts of Stage Two: Intermediate forms of the programs can be viewed as new specifications and can be used to strengthen the agreement between programmer and purchaser (see below). Feedback of this kind (fig. 1) is natural and may even lead to a number of modifications in the specification.

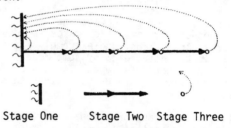

Stage One   Stage Two   Stage Three

Fig. 1   Short feedbacks between acts of program construction

Anyhow, the final software product, if it deserves this name, needs no debugging and to speak of maintenance of an incorrect software product is close to fraud. The existing unreliable environments have a demoralizing effect on the profession.

The conflict between problem-oriented and machine-oriented description

There is a fundamental conflict between a problem-oriented formalization - which can be very compact due to the powerful tools used in it - and a machine-oriented formalization, which is usually long and messy. However formalized it is, it is humanly incomprehensible, but this is not true for the problem-oriented formalization, and the need for it is two-fold: a machine program has to be derived from it and this can hardly be done in a predictable way if the problem-oriented specification is not sufficiently formalized. Moreover, as the basis of a contract between purchaser and programmer, a strict code can only be helpful.

III. STAGE ONE : PURCHASER AND PROGRAMMER DRAFTING
     THE (FORMAL) SPECIFICATION
     ("REQUIREMENT ENGINEERING")

It should go without saying that specifications are an indispensable requisite for any rational construction process. There is the rule:

> Decide first what to compute before you think about how to compute.

Apart from the situation where a student or a researcher writes a program for himself, there is usually a difference between the person or institution which orders a program, and the person or institution which delivers the program. The specification is a contract between them, and both sides have to understand that contract. It is this understanding which is at a low point in the profession.

Finding the specification can be a difficult job: most purchasers do not have a precise imagination of what they want. The crucial task is not to formalize the problem, but to find out which (formalizable) problem actually should be solved.

The conflict between Purchaser and Programmer

This conflict cannot be blamed solely on the partners. Communication between persons or groups always shows inherent difficulties, especially when one of the groups may have a better understanding of the subject matter of the problem while the other may have better training in formal methods of problem formulation and solution.

What can be done in such a situation? The programmer or computer scientist can try to acquire more knowledge in the problem area. To some extent, this will happen automatically if he is working in the same application area for a long time. Normally, however, the programmer will be no substitute for the specialist; and if he is wise he will not try to surpass him, although he may sometimes feel tempted to do so. Generally speaking, the computer scientist and even the programmer have had (or should have had) an education that makes them flexible and adaptive. This is not always true of the other partner.

Aversion to Formalization

High-ranking people in industry, commerce, science, administration, the armed forces and politics seldom have the time to acquire the fundamental knowledge of a computer scientist; formalization, which is a powerful tool, can only be learned by practical use. Apart from lack of time, however, there is a widespread superstition in these circles that 'these mathematical symbols' are witchcraft; that formalization is unintelligible and logical rigour is simultaneously both wonderful and appalling. The mere mention of even the simplest mathematical fact can make some people go cold all over.

Nevertheless today's computer scientist should not hesitate to start conversation with vice-presidents, MP's and colonels about how to express their intentions for the use of a computer. We have to approach them, however, in a language which they are able to understand. In practice these customers are intelligent enough to understand what computer scientists can tell them, provided we can translate it into their language. This argument is backed by an observation in the law field. Certain laws are quite involved and comprise a network of clauses, conditions, dependencies and so on that is comparable in complexity with a program system of medium size. Trained lawyers are able to understand such a law (some of course do better than others) - in the parallel case the same is true of programmers The leading people in the law field are also paid high fees for their services, which correspondingly are worthwhile. Furthermore, the law field uses a particular language - sublanguage of the natural language - which is enriched by technical terms and is, to some extent, a jargon, but basically distinguished from usual language by a high degree of formalization behind the façade of plain English, French or German.

Formalized and yet 'human' form of a language

Instead of trying in vain to teach vice-presidents, MPs and colonels our formalized symbol-ridden, mathematically corrupted language, we have to map specifications and translate programs into a language the customer thinks is his own, thus removing the language barrier. We can trust that the customer will then be able to understand even very complicated things, at least if he has the intellectual level that would allow him to pass law school.

I shall mention below some of the techniques to be used for such a translation and I shall give some small examples which **should** be typical.

Responsibility

I must first explain, however, why I propose to translate programs into a language the customer can absorb. Why cannot the customer be content to be told that the program has been made, delivered and paid for? Why should he bother to understand it?

The answer is responsibility. Professional and moral ethics or even financial worries make it advisable that the customer be able to check what is done in his name - even if these checks are only carried out by sampling. Many people are feeling more and more uneasy about their inability to understand what they are liable to be made responsible for.

We can make the customer take responsibility for the products produced in his name if we use a formalized specification which we read out in verbal form to him. The task of deriving a formalized program from such a formalized specification rests completely with the computer scientists. In practice, however, it will rarely be so simple that a computer scientist gets an order for a program, writes it and hands back a 'human' version for the purchaser, together with a portable machine form. Even medium-size programs need development. Such a development frequently includes (see above) a refinement of the original intentions. Therefore, a process of interaction will take place between the purchaser and the computer scientist. This process needs even more mutual understanding; thus translation to the 'human' form of specifications will be required many times. As our examples will show, the translation often amounts to nothing more than reading out a formalized text abbreviated by using 'these mathematical symbols'.

Nevertheless, large-scale programs will, in the human form, amount to hundreds of pages, and even if they are well-structured and thus broken down to some hundred pieces with a maximal hierarchical depth of, say, five to ten, the whole work is enormous. Even if each of the pieces is small enough and independent enough to be understood safely within not more than one hour of intensive study - the mere number of hundreds of such pieces will prevent many high-ranking people from going through all of them. The customer's staff might deal with appropriate subsets. However, what about responsibility? Would a court accept the apology: 'I was unable to afford these hundreds of one-hour sessions of intensive study, and so I trusted my staff to make the right decisions'?

Compact specifications

The answer to this question is that indeed the person in charge should not have to read the whole program, as the general of the army will not personally read all the instructions and commands that go down to regiments and battalions. The proper form of the material to be submitted to him is not the general program. In fact, it would be too late anyhow to make this the basis of a contract. What we will see are compact specifications which may not even be fully algorithmic.

The contract mentioned before is to be made on the basis of such a very compact specification paper that the purchaser can read and sign in the 'human' form, while the computer scientist can consider the 'formal' form as the basis for his work of deriving a machine program. The 'formal' specification is the pivot. Translation from the 'formal' to the 'human' form can be thought of as being done by mechanical transliteration, and responsibility for the operative fulfilment of the contract rests fully with the computer scientist who also has the technical skill to verify that his program fulfils the specification. This means, however, that the specification is to be performed in a much more formal way than has previously been the case. Neverthe-

less, we are convinced that this is feasible.

Specification tools

The formal essence of rational specifications can - according to our knowledge today - be expressed under the headings

> algebraic abstract types,
> predicate logic,
> non-determinism,
> higher order functionals.

The following examples will show the use of the first three of these tools. They work with strings, the abstract definition of which may run as follows:

Based on char as a parameter, there are, operating on string,

Primitives:
$body:$ $\underline{string} \to \underline{string}$
$tail:$ $\underline{string} \to \underline{char}$ (partial: undefined for $empty$)
$head:$ $\underline{string} \to \underline{char}$ (partial: undefined for $empty$)
$empty:$ $\underline{string}$
&: $\underline{string} \times \underline{string} \to \underline{string}$
≤: $\underline{char} \times \underline{char} \to \underline{bool}$

Laws:
$head(a) \& body(a) = a$

$head(x \& a) = \begin{cases} head(x) & \text{if } x \neq empty \\ head(a) & \text{if } x = empty \end{cases}$

$body(x \& a) = \begin{cases} body(x) \& a & \text{if } x \neq empty \\ body(a) & \text{if } x = empty \end{cases}$

etc.

An example of a specification

Our example will necessarily be of moderate size, and it will not be farfetched. It could be just one piece out of a many-piece specification. It could read in a 'human' form like this:

> 'For a given sequence of characters, the result of sorting should be a sequence of characters which
>
> (i) is a permutation of the given sequence and
> (ii) is sorted.'

The computer scientist would probably draft this in his shorthand:

> $\underline{funct}$ $sorting \equiv (\underline{string}\ a)\ \underline{string}:$
> $\underline{some}\ \underline{string}\ x : ispermutation(x,a)$
> $\wedge\ issorted(x)$

and would read it out to the customer as follows:

> The function $sorting$ with a string of characters a as a parameter has a string of characters as the result, which is defined as some string x such that x is a permutation of a and x is sorted

which says essentially the same as the verbal form above, and forms the contract.

Of course this formulation is so simple because it merely reduces the problem to the two still unspecified predicates *issorted* and *ispermutation*. But this is the trick: divide and conquer. Formalized specifications of these predicates have to follow. We concentrate on the (simpler) predicate *issorted* and assume that the partners have reached agreement about its meaning as follows:

> The predicate *issorted* with a string of characters *s* as a parameter is true if and only if for all pairs *p*, *q* of characters that occur in the string *s*, *p* is less than or equal to *q* whenever *p* is situated before *q* in the string.

The computer scientist would then draft this in his shorthand, and similarly go on with the predicate *ispermutation*.

Intentional vagueness

It has been remarked in software engineering circles that such a formal specification would not be liberal enough in the practical design and development process. The example shows that some *intentional vagueness* is compatible with formal specification and in fact is even an important design principle: the definition of sorting leaves the question of which way sorting is to be done algorithmically completely open. The formulation of *issorted*, on the other hand, immediately suggests an algorithm, but nobody would really want to work in this totally exhaustive way. Thanks to transitivity, a more efficient algorithm exists which works with neighbouring pairs only, but it needs a slightly more complicated description, according to the rule: 'what you gain in efficiency, you lose in clarity'. It is the simplicity of the description above which makes it just good for definition.

But even some quite efficient other versions of the predicate *issorted* can still be understood easily and thus could alternatively be made the basis of the contract. I shall give here two rather similar examples, the first one being in the computer scientist's shorthand:

$$\textbf{funct } \textit{issorted} \equiv (\underline{\text{string}}\ \ s)\ \underline{\text{bool}}:$$
$$s = empty$$
$$\lor\ body(s) = empty$$
(a)
$$\lor\ \ \exists\ \underline{\text{string}}\ u,\ \underline{\text{string}}\ v:$$
$$u \neq empty \land v \neq empty \land u\ \&\ v = s$$
$$\land\ issorted(u) \land issorted(v)$$
$$\land\ tail(u) \leq head(v)$$

which is read as follows:

> The predicate *issorted* with a string of characters *s* as a parameter is true if and only if
>
> the string *s* is the empty string
>
> or else the body of the string *s* is the empty string

or else there exists a string *u* and a string *v* such that

	u is not the empty string
and	*v* is not the empty string
and	*u* concatenated with *v* is the string *s*
and	both *u* and *v* are sorted
and	the tail of *u* is less than or equal to the head of *v*

This version does not speak of all pairs of all neighbouring pairs, and since it only requires the existence of some suitable pair, it is finished as soon as it is successful in finding one. It is, furthermore, recursive: in its body, the predicate *issorted* itself occurs. This has the advantage that it gives hints for a recursive solution of the function *sorting* which we are aiming at.

This is even more so in the following version:

$$\textbf{funct } \textit{issorted} \equiv (\underline{\text{string}}\ \ s)\ \underline{\text{bool}}:$$
$$s = empty$$
$$\lor\ body(s) = empty$$
(b)
$$\lor\ (\ \eta\ \underline{\text{string}}\ u,\ \underline{\text{string}}\ v:$$
$$u \neq empty \land v \neq empty \land u\ \&\ v = s;$$
$$issorted(u) \land issorted(v)$$
$$\land\ tail(u) \leq head(v))$$

which is read as follows:

> The predicate *issorted* with a string of characters *s* as a parameter is true if and only if
>
> the string *s* is the empty string
>
> or else the body of the string *s* is the empty string
>
> or else
>
> (let some string *u* and some string *v* be such that

	u is not the empty string
and	*v* is not the empty string
and	*u* concatenated with *v* is the string *s*)

> both *u* and *v* are sorted
> and the tail of *u* is less than or equal to the head of *v*

Textually, the difference seems small: here an existential quantifier ∃, there the choice operator η of BERNAYS. In essence, once a suitable choice has been made, only a test of whether *u* and *v* fulfill the second group of conditions is necessary. The choice is quite arbitrary; this gives another instance of intentional vagueness and shows what a useful tool the non-deterministic choice operator is. Intentional vagueness is also inherent in the use of abstract types which may allow even non-isomorphic models (polymorphism, Broy et al. /79/, Bauer, Wössner /81/, /82/), among which frequently different interesting implementations can be found.

The equivalence of all subsequent versions with the original version can be shown formally by a program transformation (see below) but the customer will probably agree intuitively that all the versions given express his intentions.

IV. STAGE TWO: STEPWISE REFINEMENT

Almost as a rule, the construction process proper is influenced by some particular machine architecture which determines the appearance of the machine program wanted. But even so, quite often the first steps of the development can be carried out without taking this into account. Mostly, the very first step will involve elimination of quantifiers which are a nuisance to almost every machine architecture.

Under conditions of strict formalization, programs can truly be derived by the computer scientist in an evolutionary process. For large tasks, this process will go through several levels of increasing machine orientation, which will lead to greater efficiency at the expense of simplicity.

In addition, more and more structuring of programs and of data will be introduced. The aforementioned final program with its hundreds of pieces may well be the result of such a process, starting with a few pieces, each of which can be understood in a few minutes. This will be particularly true as soon as people have learned to start with very compact pre-algorithmic specifications. These specifications may even involve non-deterministic elements without losing rigour, as we have seen.

Assuming for a moment that the target machine is somewhat close to a sequential machine with adressable storage, transitions may go through levels as indicated in fig. 2. Not too surprising, there is a connection between the steps on the control structure and on the data structure side.

General predicate calculus	abstract types
general recursion	recursively defined types (CH-2)
linear recursion	linear recursively defined types
tail recursion	tuples, variants, star (CH-3, regular expr.)
iteration	arrays
go to's	store organized with pointers
jump addresses	store organized with addresses

Fig. 2 Corresponding levels on program and data side on the way to a von Neumann machine

Unconventional machine architecture

The target machine may, however, have an unconventional architecture. Then various criteria influence the development process. For example, the target machine may be friendly to linear recursion or even to general recursion (reduction machines),

or it may show particular profits in parallelizing actions, it may in particular favour data streams (data flow machines). It is conceivable that at specification time it is completely left open which machine architecture is to be used in the end, and the task may just be to derive for a given problem a particularly well-suited one. This may be of advantage if the derived software is finally to be frozen on a chip together with the hardware on which it is running.

Our example : The construction process

With one of the above versions of *issorted* in the contract, the computer scientist will in Stage Two go ahead to obtain an algorithmic solution of *sorting*. It may be the following, still rather general recursive scheme suggested by the specification (b):

$$\underline{\text{funct}} \ \textit{sorting} \equiv (\underline{\text{string}} \ a) \ \underline{\text{string}} :$$
$$\underline{\text{if}} \ a = \textit{empty} \ \underline{\text{then}} \ a$$
$$\underline{\text{elsf}} \ body(a) = \textit{empty} \ \underline{\text{then}} \ a$$
$$\underline{\text{else}} \ \mathbf{\eta} \ \underline{\text{string}} \ u, \ \underline{\text{string}} \ v;$$
$$u \neq \textit{empty} \wedge v \neq \textit{empty} \wedge u \ \& \ v = a;$$
$$merging(sorting(u), \ sorting(v)) \quad \underline{\text{fi}}$$

which is based on the following recursive algorithm for merging two sorted strings:

$$\underline{\text{funct}} \ \textit{merging} \equiv (\underline{\text{string}} \ b, \ \underline{\text{string}} \ c: \textit{issorted}(b)$$
$$\wedge \ \textit{issorted}(c)) \ \underline{\text{string}} :$$
$$\underline{\text{if}} \ b = \textit{empty} \ \underline{\text{then}} \ c$$
$$\mathbb{\square} \ c = \textit{empty} \ \underline{\text{then}} \ b$$
$$\underline{\text{elsf}} \ head(b) \leq head(c) \quad \underline{\text{then}} \ head(b) \ \&$$
$$merging \ (body(b), \ c)$$
$$\mathbb{\square} \ head(c) \leq head(b) \quad \underline{\text{then}} \ head(c) \ \&$$
$$merging \ (body(c), \ b) \ \underline{\text{fi}}$$

sorting still contains an arbitrary choice for u and v, it still is a non-deterministic algorithm. Deterministic implementations can be obtained by fixing the choice. Taking $head(a)$ for u and $body(a)$ for v, the scheme simplifies to linear merge-sorting. By breaking a into two parts of fairly equal length, a more efficient binary merge-sort algorithm is obtained which may lead to heapsort. From any of these algorithms, iterative solutions can be derived, and one of them will be handed back to the customer.

Rather than going into the technicalities of, say, the process of eliminating quantifiers (and thus arriving completely formally at (a) or (b)) or of simplifying recursion (*sorting* still shows non-linear, cascade-type recursion, *merging* does not yet show tail-recursion), I would like to refer to the rich literature on this subject; a bibliography can be found in Bauer, Wössner /81/. In particular, I would want to mention work done at my university in Munich, Germany, within the project CIP, where a suitable computer-aided program transformation system, based on a wide spectrum of language concepts (Bauer et al. /81/), together with a program development methodology, has been worked out.

Programs as formal objects

In these program transformation systems programs themselves are treated as formal objects.

Even if someone prefers to understand his programs intuitively, of course every hardware and software system precisely defines an interpretation for every program given for that system. And even if a programming language is not formally defined, a program written in that language represents a formal object, at least with respect to every particular implementation. Hence one must clearly admit that programs are formal objects, but does this imply that it is also worthwhile to treat programs in a formal way?

Extensive research efforts have clearly exposed the inherent mathematical complexity of many of such transformations. This may be the reason for some people to question the practicability of formal methods. Nevertheless one cannot have much confidence in a software product dealing with a problem for which the known theory seems to be quite complex, the software product being therefore produced without relying on any theory, just based on the programmer's intuition.

However, in some cases the situation is even worse. For some of our problems in software engineering the theories are not yet fully developed at the moment, and thus a mathematically satisfying treatment is currently not yet possible. A drastic example can be found in the programming language ADA recently developed for the U.S. Department of Defense, the preliminary formal description of which leaves out a formal description of the issues of tasking by the words (cf. /ADA 79/):

> "However, the State of the Art in formal semantics does not allow (as in Spring 1979), in the opinion of the authors, to give a mathematically meaningful semantics for parallelism ..."

Perhaps it would be better in such a situation not to have a finger in every pie, and to wait until a more satisfactory situation (Broy /81/) is achieved.

Unconventional (machine) solutions

On the background of a sufficiently general theory which is now at hand (e.g. Bauer, Broy /81/), the program transformation methodology can lead (rigorously) to very efficient, but rather unorthodox machine solutions. From sorting, for example, or rather its binary descendant mentioned above, one may derive a very efficient data flow solution as was shown in Bauer /81/.

V. STAGE THREE : CERTIFICATION OF THE SOFTWARE PRODUCT

There is, of course, no need to prove correctness of a (correctly) derived software product: such a product is automatically correct with respect to the original specification. And testing in the low moral sense of 'debugging' is pointless. But is the original specification really the wanted one? Does it properly reflect the customer's wishes and intentions, vague as they may happen to be?

Before paying the fee, the customer should ascertain whether the product obeys the specification. Concerning correctness, he may do better than testing it - he may verify it and should even consider asking a different software house to do the verification. Or, he may require a stringent documentation of the computer scientist's development, including proofs of the correctness of the derivation steps. In this way, he does not only gain insight - some cornerstone versions can be easily translated into 'human' form - he may even get back more than he ordered: the scheme *sorting/merging* allows the later derivation of variants. Why should the customer not also profit from the design rule: keep generality as long as possible, e.g. delay decisions.

And is the software product efficient? This *performance evaluation* is the essential remaining task of Stage Three. Often, a trade-off is to be made, e.g. of time vs. storage, and an inefficient solution being unacceptable, return to Stage Two may be necessary until sufficient efficiency is reached.

Our Example : Fulfilment of the contract

We wish to come back to the start of our story and to see how the contract is fulfilled. Assume that the task did originate in a trade branch where addresses of interested people are collected. Certainly, each address is to be kept only once, and in sorting the addresses, which are the 'characters' in our problem, multiple occurrences should be thrown out. The customer will be disappointed that the solution the software house delivers does not suit this demand. Fortunately, we have the contract which speaks clearly of a permutation of the given string. In this case, the customer will have to pay the fee and the judge will have no difficulties in seeing this even without having studied formal logic. In other cases, the computer scientist may be caught: if he fails to meet the specifications, a simple counter-example will suffice to prove this to the satisfaction of the judge.

Professional morals require looking at programming as the fulfilment of a contract. The difficulties are less than most people would expect, provided the language barrier between customer and programmer can be lowered. The necessary theoretical background is available, but should not be used to frighten the customer. The responsible decisions should be made with common sense.

VI. CONCLUDING REMARKS

Shortcomings of today's practice

Up to the present time, there is an abundance of examples of unreliable software. Shortcomings of the widely used programming techniques are

. Lack of sufficient understanding of the theoretical basis, e.g. pointers, goto's, concurrency
. Lack of precise interface description
. Lack of established, naturally grown standards
. Lack of awareness on the users' side of difficulties.

All this falls under the rule:

> Programmers tend to underestimate the complexity of any given problem and to overrate their mental capacity.

Formal methods are a safeguard against this 'human' tendency, they force the programmer into intellectual discipline.

A treasury of formal methods needs a methodology.

Aims of a scientifically based programming methodology

. Analysis and classification of observable phenomena of software systems in the light of a suitable theory
. Derivation of a software production methodology based on engineering-type techniques and tools ("software engineering").

Scientific methodology does not render the program development process "easier, cheaper or simpler", but

. elucidates the process
. uncovers inherent difficulties
. eliminates uncertainties and decisions at random
. gives reliable software.

Software *construction* is to replace software *production*

Since 1968, the information processing field has made important steps towards a genuine software engineering discipline. Formal methods will for the rest of the century determine the trend in a scientifically based programming methodology which is centered on program construction through formal reasoning.

Acknowledgement: My sincere thanks are due to the members of the CIP group in Munich for their contributions to this paper, in particular to M. Broy and H. Partsch. B. Möller, P. Pepper, H. Wössner and A. Laut have carefully read the draft.

References:

/ADA 79/
Preliminary Ada Reference Manual. SIGPLAN Notices 14:6, Part A (1979); Ichbiah, J.D., Heliard, J.C., Roubine, J.G.P., Krieg-Brückner, B., Wichmann, B.A.: Rationale for the Design of the Ada Programming Language. SIGPLAN Notices 14:6, Part B (1979)

/Bauer 81/
Bauer, F.L.: New Aspects of, and New Prospects for a Software Engineer's Programming Methodology. Proc. COMPSAC 81, Chicago, Ill., November 18-20, 1981, p. 315-323.

/Bauer, Wössner 81/
Bauer, F.L., Wössner, H.: Algorithmische Sprache und Programmentwicklung. Berlin-Heidelberg-New York: Springer 1981

/Bauer, Wössner 82/
Bauer, F.L., Wössner, H.: Algorithmic Language and Program Development. Berlin-Heidelberg-New York: Springer 1982 (to appear)

/Bauer et al. 81/
Bauer, F.L., Broy, M., Dosch, W., Gnatz, R., Krieg-Brückner, B., Laut, A., Luckmann, M., Matzner, T.A., Möller, B., Partsch, H., Pepper, P., Samelson, K., Steinbrüggen, R., Wirsing, M., Wössner, H.: Programming in a Wide Spectrum Language: a Collection of Examples. Science of Computer Programming 1, 73-114 (1981)

/Broy 81/
Broy, M.: Prospects of New Tools for Software Development. In: Duijvestijn, A.J.W., Lockemann, C.P. (eds.): Trends in Information Processing Systems. Lecture Notes in Computer Science 123. Berlin-Heidelberg-New York: Springer 1981, p 106-121

/Broy, Bauer 81/
Broy, M., Bauer, F.L.: A Rational Approach to Language Constructs for Concurrent Programs. In: Cavalli, E. (ed.): Design of Numerical Algorithms for Parallel Processing, New York: Academic Press, 1982 (to appear)

/Broy et al. 79/
Broy, M., Dosch, W., Partsch, H., Pepper, P., Wirsing, M.: Existential Quantifiers in Abstract Data Types. In: Maurer, H.A. (ed.): Automata, Languages and Programming - Sixth Colloquium, Graz, July 1979. Lecture Notes in Computer Science 71. Berlin-Heidelberg-New York: Springer 1979, p. 73-87

/Zelkowitz 78/
Zelkowitz, M.V.: Perspectives on Software Engineering. Computing Surveys 10:2, 197-216 (1978)

Reprinted from *IEEE Transactions on Software Engineering*, Volume SE-7, Number 5, September 1981, pages 458-471. Copyright © 1981 by The Institute of Electrical and Electronics Engineers, Inc.

The Refinement Paradigm: The Interaction of Coding and Efficiency Knowledge in Program Synthesis

ELAINE KANT AND DAVID R. BARSTOW

Abstract—A refinement paradigm for implementing a high-level specification in a low-level target language is discussed. In this paradigm, coding and analysis knowledge work together to produce an efficient program in the target language. Since there are many possible implementations for a given specification of a program, searching knowledge is applied to increase the efficiency of the process of finding a good implementation. For example, analysis knowledge is applied to determine upper and lower cost bounds on alternate implementations, and these bounds are used to measure the potential impact of different design decisions and to decide which alternatives should be pursued. In this paper we also describe a particular implementation of this program synthesis paradigm, called PSI/SYN, that has automatically implemented a number of programs in the domain of symbolic processing.

Index Terms—Automatic programming, program development, program efficiency, program synthesis, refinement paradigm, stepwise refinement.

I. Introduction

ONE approach to reducing software costs is to specify systems in a very high-level language and use an automatic system to produce efficient code in a lower level language. We assume that it is possible to develop specification languages that are easy for people to understand and make changes in. The problem is then to develop a translation system. This problem differs from that of traditional compiler optimization in several ways. Since the source language is more abstract, many more combinations of implementations are possible, and the best should be chosen. For the sake of target program efficiency, we would like to allow different instances of the same high-level constructs to be implemented differently within the same program. For the sake of efficiency in the translation process, we would like to reimplement selective parts of the system when changes are made to the specification—only those parts of the program affected by the change (including parts whose efficiency is affected) should have to be reimplemented. For this and other reasons, we will save a history of how the implementation is related to

Manuscript received August 15, 1980. This work was supported by the National Science Foundation under a Fellowship, the Fannie and John Hertz Foundation under a Fellowship, the Stanford Artificial Intelligence Laboratory under ARPA Order 2494, Contract MDA903-76-C-0206, and by Systems Control, Inc. under ARPA Order 3687, Contract N00014-79-C-0127. This work was conducted at Stanford University, Stanford, CA 94305.

E. Kant is with the Department of Computer Science, Carnegie-Mellon University, Pittsburgh, PA 15213.

D. R. Barstow is with Schlumberger-Doll Research, Ridgefield, CT 06877.

the specification and of what implementation decisions were made and why.

This paper describes a general refinement paradigm for implementing high-level specifications in a low-level target language. Coding and analysis knowledge work together to produce an efficient program in the target language. Since there are many possible implementations, searching knowledge is applied to make the program synthesis process (the "compilation") itself efficient. We believe that the paradigm is similar to those used by good programmers.

We also describe a particular implementation of the paradigm PSI/SYN. This system was developed as part of a larger program synthesis system, called PSI [12], in which programs are specified by a dialogue with PSI's acquisition phase using a subset of English and example input/output pairs. PSI/SYN functions both as the synthesis phase of PSI and as an independent system whose specifications are in a formal high-level language. Within PSI/SYN, coding knowledge is represented as coding rules in a subsystem called PECOS [3], [4] and the efficiency knowledge (analysis and searching rules) is in a subsystem called LIBRA [13], [14].

II. The Refinement Paradigm

A. Refinement Trees

PSI/SYN is based on a refinement paradigm similar to paradigms discussed with respect to programming methodology (for example, see [29] or [9]). The original specification, described in terms of abstract concepts, is transformed through a sequence of descriptions using successively more refined constructs. The end result is the fully implemented program using the constructs of the target language. The process may be diagrammed as shown in Fig. 1.

The first description is the abstract specification, and the last is the fully implemented program; each intermediate description is slightly more concrete than the previous one. Each step in such a *refinement sequence* is produced by applying a single *coding rule*. Note that the constructs used within any particular description need not all be at the same level of abstraction.

Since more than one rule may be applicable at some step in a refinement sequence, the concept may be generalized to a *refinement tree*, as shown in Fig. 2. The root of the tree is the original specification, the leaves (terminal nodes) are alternative implementations, and each path is a refinement sequence. Intermediate nodes are partially implemented program descriptions.

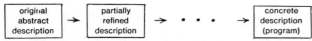

Fig. 1. A refinement sequence.

Although the paradigm does not require it, we believe that the steps in the refinement sequences should be relatively small. Most steps involve the application of a single refinement rule to a single instance of an abstract construct. The effect is essentially a replacement of the instance by a description in terms of slightly more refined constructs. For example, in PSI/SYN the process of refining a collection[1] into a linked list representation actually involves four different rules, tracing through the intermediate constructs of "explicit collection," "stored collection," and "sequence." Our preference for the smaller rules and changes is motivated largely by a concern for modularity in the programming knowledge and a desire to have every design decision reflected explicitly in the tree. The price paid, of course, is that our refinement trees can be quite large. It may take five or so steps to completely refine one abstract concept, and for an entire program of about twenty lines of specification, some refinement sequences may be as long as a thousand steps.

An important feature of such trees is that the nodes (program descriptions) all represent "correct" programs (assuming correctness of the coding rules). Each node represents a step in a path from the abstract specification to some concrete implementation of it. When paths cannot be completed (as happens occasionally), the cause is generally the absence of rules for refining a particular construct within a program description, rather than any inherent problem of the description itself. The use of refinement rules enables the system to proceed directly toward correct implementations, without any need for testing different combinations of primitive constructs to see if they are correct.

B. A Search Space of Correct Programs

Different implementations of abstract concepts are often appropriate under different situations. Given some measure of "appropriateness" (for example, an efficiency measure), the refinement tree provides a space that can be searched for the most appropriate implementation. Our experience with such trees suggests that they provide a relatively convenient way to deal with the variability and complexity that seem a necessary part of real-world programming.

Theoretically, the system could build the entire search tree, compute the efficiency measure of each terminal node, and select the best. Since the number of reasonable implementations of a given abstract algorithm can be combinatorially high (tens or even hundreds for small specifications), techniques for pruning the tree and limiting the search are clearly needed. Our approach combines many variants of the standard techniques; for example, it employs heuristic rules to prune the coding rules and estimates program costs to prune the tree (with branch and bound) and to guide its construction accord-

[1] The term "collection" is used since the rules do not distinguish between multisets, which may have repeated elements, and sets, which may not.

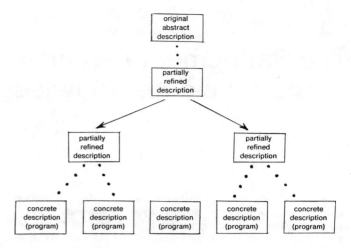

Fig. 2. A refinement tree.

ing to a mixture of best-first search with look-ahead and dynamic programming.

Within the framework of this search space, the roles of coding and efficiency knowledge can be simply stated. Coding knowledge plays the role of a "legal move generator" for a space of correct programs. Efficiency knowledge plays two separate roles. First, analysis knowledge is used to determine the cost of executing the programs represented by nodes in the space; that is, analysis knowledge plays the role of an "evaluation function." Second, searching knowledge is used to reduce the cost of finding the desired (or at least, an adequate) terminal node in the tree.

C. The Role of the Target Language

While any implementation of the refinement paradigm must necessarily involve some target language, the paradigm itself seems to be independent of any particular programming language. At some point in the refinement process, the descriptions begin to be expressed in terms of the target language. As refinement progresses, target-specific constructs play an increasingly dominant role in the descriptions. In fact, a terminal node in the tree is characterized by the fact that the description is expressed solely in target-specific terms: it is a program in the target language.

Since different target languages have constructs corresponding to different levels of abstraction, the languages can take over at varying points in the refinement process. For example, a language in which sets were implemented directly could take over much earlier than a language like Lisp. The same language may even support different levels of abstractions. For example, Pascal has a set data type but not a linked-list data type; Lisp has linked lists but not sets.

D. Implementation

We have implemented this refinement paradigm twice. In the first implementation we viewed the coding knowledge as being "in charge" of the process. When choice points were encountered (that is, when more than one coding rule was applicable), efficiency knowledge was used to select the best alternative. The details of the first implementation are available elsewhere [2]. Our principal conclusion was that the bandwidth for communication between coding and efficiency knowledge was too low.

In the second implementation, PSI/SYN, we reversed our model of who was in charge. The part of efficiency knowledge referred to earlier as "searching knowledge" controls the application of coding and analysis knowledge to build the part of the space that is actually explored in the process of finding the desired program. In this implementation, processing goes through a series of cycles, each consisting of the following steps.

1) Pick some node of the refinement tree to expand, based on cost estimates for the active nodes (which are nonterminal leaves).

2) Pick some part of the program described by that node to refine, based on the relative importance of different parts.

3) Find the coding rules that can be used to refine that part.

4) Prune those rules that fail to satisfy plausibility requirements.

5) Expand the tree by applying each of the remaining coding rules to create new program description nodes.

6) Compute cost estimates for the new nodes by applying the analysis rules.

In this process, branch-and-bound techniques are used to limit the search based on the cost estimates for the nodes in the refinement tree. Two cost estimates are associated with each node: "optimistic" (lower bound) estimates are computed assuming that each abstract construct can be implemented in the most efficient way without regard to possible interactions among the decisions; "achievable" (upper bound) estimates are computed assuming that each abstract construct will be implemented with a default technique that is known *a priori* to be feasible and free from interactions. It is not necessary to expand any node whose optimistic cost estimate is greater than the achievable cost estimate for some other node. These techniques are used primarily in step 1).

In addition, resource-management techniques are used to ensure that limited resources will be spent on the decisions that are most critical. Analysis techniques are used to determine the relative importance of different decisions [reflected in step 2)], and, for the less important decisions, more weight is attached to plausibility criteria [reflected in step 4)].

In a sense, PSI/SYN's coding rules define programming constructs implicitly in terms of more and less abstract constructs. In implementing the refinement paradigm we have found it helpful to include more explicit characterizations of the constructs. We call these characterizations *prototypes*. For example, the analysis knowledge makes use of default implementation costs that are associated with individual constructs. The intermediate constructs also provide convenient "hooks" for incorporating PSI/SYN's knowledge about its own behavior. For example, the plausibility criteria are associated with individual constructs. Also, the analysis rules need to know the structure of each construct to compute its time and space costs. In general, we have found it important to include in PSI/SYN's knowledge base descriptions of a variety of different kinds of relationships among the programming constructs that PSI/SYN employs.

NEWS

DATA STRUCTURES
  database: mapping from *story* to *keywords*;
  story: string;
  keywords: collection of *key*;
  key: string;
  command: alternative "quit" or *key*;

ALGORITHM
  database ← input();
  loop:
    command ← input();
    if *command* = "quit" then exit;
    forall S in domain-of(*database*) when *command*
      in *database*[S] do output(S);
    repeat;

Fig. 3. Initial program description for NEWS.

III. An Example

To illustrate the refinement paradigm, we will show how PSI/SYN constructs a simple retrieval program. The problem is to write a program, called NEWS, whose behavior is described by the following abstract algorithm.

> Read in a database of news stories. Each story has an associated collection of keywords. Repeatedly accept a keyword and print out a list of the names of the stories in the database that contain that keyword. If the keyword "quit" is entered, stop the process.

A human-readable form of PSI/SYN's specification-language version of NEWS is given in Fig. 3. (This version is a translation of the internal specification given to PSI/SYN. The internal representation is a kind of semantic net; its exact description is not relevant to this discussion.) As part of the specification, the user can provide information about data structure sizes and about the probabilities of taking different branches of a conditional. If the relevant information is not provided in the specification, PSI/SYN will ask the user for it at the beginning of the synthesis session.

A. Alternate Implementation Paths for NEWS

PSI/SYN can generate several versions of NEWS. Under different assumptions about the size of the database or the cost function to be used, different implementations are selected. A refinement tree showing several implementations and the critical decision points is presented in Fig. 4. Only nodes involving a choice of coding rules are shown. Achievable and optimistic cost estimates for each node are given in parentheses. (Cost estimates are in millisecond-pages, a result of a cost function that contains a product of running time measured in milliseconds and space measured in pages, and have been rounded for convenience of explanation.) The major choices to be made are the representation for the *database* mapping from stories to keywords and the representation for the *keywords* collection.

One refinement sequence, leading to node G in the search tree of Fig. 4, is explained in more detail in the following sections. It involves representing *database* internally as a hash table of stories, with each story in turn having a hash table to represent *keywords*. The cost function used in this case is the product of running time and number of pages in use. In this

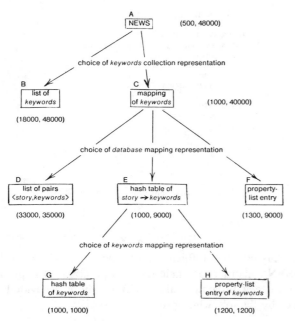

Fig. 4. Overview of alternate refinements of NEWS.

run, PSI/SYN questions the user to determine critical parameters. It finds that the expected number of stories in the database is 80, the average number of keywords per story is 100, the expected number of iterations of the loop is 300, and the probability that the command is a keyword of the average story is 0.01. PSI/SYN eventually chooses a hash-table representation for *keywords* because there are many keywords for each story. The time to convert the collection of keywords into a hash table (from the linked-list representation used for input) is balanced by the time savings from the membership test, which is faster as a hash-table lookup than as a search through a list of keywords (for large keyword collections). The *database* representation decision is similar. Both choices are reinforced by the fact that the main loop is executed many times before exiting with "quit." (This is about the best possible implementation given PSI/SYN's current set of coding rules.)

Under other assumptions, a path through node *B* would be taken and a linked-list representation would be selected for *database*. For example, if the loop is executed only a few times or if the number of keywords associated with a story is small, then the time required to convert the database from the list of pairs (<story, keywords>) representation to a hash-table representation is not outweighed by the fast hash-table lookup operations. If space is a critical factor in the cost function, another path through *B* might be taken in which the original representation of a list of pairs is preserved. This avoids using any more space than absolutely necessary, but at a cost in time.

A different tree than the one pictured in Fig. 4 may also be searched under different assumptions. Suppose there are only a few keywords per story, many stories, and a cost function dominated by running time. Then the representation of the *database* mapping would be a more critical decision than the representation of the *keywords* collection because the time for

the membership test would not differ greatly for the different representations. Section V describes how critical decisions are identified by the potential impact method.

If fewer resources are available for synthesis than in the examples described above, then some of the choices may be made by heuristic rules rather than by efficiency computations. For example, nodes *F* and *H* will not be considered if a plausibility rule that prefers hash-table representations to property-list entries is applied.

B. Initial Refinements in NEWS

The following sections show more details of the refinement sequence leading to node *G*. Recall that a dialogue with the user revealed that about 80 stories, 100 keywords per story, and 100 loop iterations are expected and that the probability that the command is a keyword is 0.01.

PSI/SYN first calls on the coding rules to make refinements that do not involve any decisions. For example, the format of the *database* on input is refined to a Lisp list of pairs (<story> . <keywords>), where *keywords* is a Lisp list of *keys*. These are the default input formats.

Also, the "forall" statement enumerating the domain of *database* is refined into an explicit enumeration of the items of the domain by the following coding rule (which is the only one applicable).

> The process of performing an action *A* for all elements of a collection may be implemented as a total enumeration of the elements; if a predicate is specified, the action for each element consists of testing the predicate and performing *A* if the test succeeds; if no predicate is specified, the action for each element is *A*.

To decide how to refine the enumeration, more information about the representation of the domain is needed. In this case, the following rules about plausible implementations are sufficient to constrain the choice to a single possibility.

> If the only uses of a collection *A* are for enumerations over *A*, and if *B* is another representation for *A* that is easily enumerable, then use the same representation for *A* and *B*.

> If all the uses of a collection are for enumerations, or as pointers to positions in it, or as tests of the state of the enumerations, and if the target language is Lisp, then refine the collection into a linked list.

These rules determine that the domain collection, which is used only for enumeration and is not an alternate representation of some other collection, should be refined into a linked list. Therefore, the following sequence of coding rules is applied.

- A collection may be represented explicitly.
- An explicit collection may be stored in a single structure.
- A stored collection may be represented using a sequence.
- A sequence may be represented as a linked list.

Some of the details of constructing the domain list and the enumeration of the domain are postponed by resource management rules because it is predicted that no decisions will be in-

NEWS

```
DATA STRUCTURES
    database: LISP list of pairs (story,keywords);
    db1: mapping from story to keywords1;
    story: string;
    keywords: LISP list of key;
    keywords1: collection of key;
    key: string;
    command: alternative "quit" or key;

ALGORITHM
    database ← input();
    ddb ← domain-of(database);
    loop:
        command ← input();
        if command = "quit" then exit;
        enumerate-items S in ddb
            if member(command,database[S])
                then output(S);
    repeat;
```

Fig. 5. Intermediate program description for NEWS.

volved and the cost estimate for that part of the program will not change significantly. Other choices that arise and cannot be resolved by rules about plausible implementations are also postponed until other useful refinements or design choices are made.

C. Identifying the Most Important Decision

All of the changes above take place before node A of Fig. 4 is reached. The partial program description at this stage of the refinement is shown in Fig. 5.

During this refinement several choices were postponed. These choices are: 1) how to refine the *database* mapping used inside the "forall" (which is now an "enumerate-items"), and 2) how to refine the *keywords* collection within that mapping. What are the effects of the two choices to be made in this example?

The internal representation of *database*, called *db1*, is used to retrieve the map value *keywords* of stories once per story per command. Possible implementations for mappings range from a linked list format that makes retrieval linear in the number of stories to associative structures that have constant expected retrieval time. The keyword collections in *db1* (called *keywords1*) are used in the "member(*command,database*[S])" test. This test is executed once per story for each iteration of the loop. Possible implementations give membership tests with times ranging from linear in the number of keywords to constant.

Since the user said that the number of keywords is greater than the number of stories, the keyword representation choice has the largest difference in cost between the default implementation and the optimistic estimate of the cost when the right decision is made. Thus, this part of the code is more likely to be a bottleneck in the final program if care is not taken in the representation choice. According to a resource management rule about making important decisions first, the next step is to look at the possible refinements of *keywords1*.

To make this decision, search resources must be assigned. Currently, the resources measured are the CPU time used in carrying out the refinements and the number of construct instances in the program descriptions. The resources needed to complete a program implementation without making choices are estimated and subtracted from the total available

resources. Decision-making resources from the remainder are assigned in proportion to the estimated importance of the decision. Then separate program descriptions are set up in which each of the alternate coding rules are applied. In this decision the applicable rules allow either refining *keywords1* into an explicit collection, leading to node B, or into an explicit mapping, leading to node C.

D. Exploring Two Implementations for Keywords1

PSI/SYN's goal is to refine the alternatives (B and C) enough that the comparison among implementations will be informative. The resources previously divided among the alternatives give upper limits on the time and space to be spent on getting more accurate estimates of the program costs of the implementations being explored. As part of the resource-management strategies, each program description has a "purpose" to be fulfilled and a set of program parts that is to be the focus of attention of processing. In this case the *keywords1* data structure, the representation conversion from the input representation, and the membership test are included in the focus set. Processing of the program description continues until the resources run out or until there are no more tasks relevant to refining the parts of the program under focus.

In the first program description, node B, the explicit-collection rule is applied and refinement proceeds until all relevant tasks are satisfied (resources are sufficient). At the conclusion, the keyword collection for each story has been refined, after the application of several coding rules, into a Lisp list, and the membership operation has been refined into a list search.

Refinement of node C, the program description in which the explicit-mapping rule was applied, also halts because all relevant tasks have been accomplished. Here the keyword collection is refined to a mapping and membership is tested by seeing if there is a mapping for the given key. There is also a representation conversion since the keyword collection is represented as a list in the input.

The efficiency rules then compute optimistic and achievable bounds on the cost of the whole program for each program description. In the linked-list implementation, node B, the optimistic estimate is 18 000 millisecond-pages, and the achievable bound is 48 000 (Section V gives more details about how these bounds are computed). The optimistic and achievable cost estimates for the mapping representation, node C, are 1000 and 40 000, respectively. Branch and bound is applied to eliminate any implementations with optimistic estimates worse than the achievable estimate of some other implementation. Neither implementation is eliminated in this case, although later in the refinement of NEWS this technique will be fruitful. In general, the comparison of alternatives includes all active program descriptions, not just those involved in the most recent decision. In this case node C has the best optimistic estimate and is chosen for further refinement.

E. Refining the Rest of NEWS

The remaining decisions include choosing a refinement for the explicit-mapping of *keywords1* and choosing a refinement for *db1*. The database decision (*db1*) is chosen by resource management rules as the most important decision to be made.

(If resources were running out at this stage, the rules about plausible implementations would make standard refinement choices to avoid the expense of comparing alternate implementations.)

Three program descriptions are set up to consider the three applicable refinement rules—one to consider refining the *db1* mapping to a list of pairs (node *D*), one to consider a stored mapping (node *E*), and one to consider a distributed mapping (node *F*). The relevant parts of the program, those related to the *db1* decision, are then refined in each program description. For example, the stored mapping is refined to a hash table. Next, the resulting program descriptions are compared with each other and with other program descriptions that have been temporarily abandoned, such as node *B*. As Fig. 4 shows, nodes *B* and *D* can be eliminated from further consideration because even their optimistic bounds are worse than the achievable bound on node *E*. The most promising implementation, node *E*, is then chosen and refinement continues.

The final decision to be made is how to represent the *keywords1* collection, which has been refined into a mapping. As in the refinement of node *C*, there are three applicable coding rules, but in this case the "collection of pairs" rule is eliminated by a rule about plausible implementations. This plausible-implementation rule (which was not applicable in the developments at node *C*) states that when refining a mapping that is itself a refinement of a collection, it is not worth pursuing the collection-of-pairs implementation. Thus, only two coding rules are considered. These rules are both tested, in nodes *G* and *H*. The stored mapping, leading to the hash-table representation in node *G*, proves to be the best choice. At this point, the cost estimate is precise enough to eliminate all the other possibilities.

Thus, the best possibility is the implementation of both the keyword collection and the mapping *db1* as hash tables. As refinement continues, several other choices of coding rules are resolved by rules about plausible implementations. These decisions include the choice to recompute rather than store values that are easy to compute. The program description is finally refined into the one page Lisp program given in Fig. 6.

IV. CODING KNOWLEDGE

PSI/SYN's coding knowledge is represented in the form of refinement rules, each of which describes a technique for implementing an abstract construct in terms of (slightly) more concrete constructs. Several of PSI/SYN's coding rules are given below as English paraphrases of the internal representation; the details of the representation language are available elsewhere [3], [4].

• A collection may be represented as a mapping of objects to Boolean values; the default range object is FALSE.

• If the enumeration order is linear with respect to the stored order, the state of an enumeration may be represented as a location in the sequential collection.

• If a collection (or mapping) is input, its representation may be converted into any other representation before further processing. If it is used inside an enumeration construct, its representation may be converted into any other representation during the loop's initialization.

```
(NEWS  [LAMBDA NIL
(PROG (DDB DATABASE)
    [SETQ DATABASE (CONS (QUOTE "HEAD")
                         (PROGN (PRIN1 "DATABASE?") (TERPRI) (READ]
    (SETQ DDB (PROG (G1 C1)
                    (SETQ C1 (CONS (QUOTE "HEAD") (QUOTE NIL)))
                    (SETQ G1 DATABASE)
              RPT1  (COND ((NULL (CDR G1)) (GO L1)))
                    (RPLACD C1 (CONS (CAR (CAR (CDR G1))) (CDR C1)))
                    (SETQ G1 (CDR G1))
                    (GO RPT1)
              L1    (RETURN C1)))
    (PROG (DB1)
          (SETQ DB1 (PROG (G2 C2)
                          (SETQ C2 (HARRAY 100))
                          (SETQ G2 DATABASE)
                    RPT3  (COND ((NULL (CDR G2)) (GO L2)))
                          (PUTHASH (CAR (CAR (CDR G2)))
                                   (PROG (G3 X C3)
                                         (SETQ C3 (HARRAY 100))
                                         [SETQ G3 (CDR (CAR (CDR G2]
                                   RPT4  (COND ((NULL G3) (GO L3)))
                                         (SETQ X (CAR G3))
                                         (PUTHASH X T C3)
                                         (SETQ G3 (CDR G3))
                                         (GO RPT4)
                                   L3    (RETURN C3))
                                   C2)
                          (SETQ G2 (CDR G2))
                          (GO RPT3)
                    L2    (RETURN C2)))
          RPT2 (PROG (KEY COMMAND)
                     (SETQ COMMAND (PROGN (PRIN1 "COMMAND?")
                                          (TERPRI) (READ)))
                     (COND ((EQ COMMAND (QUOTE XYZZY)) (GO L4)))
                     (SETQ KEY COMMAND)
                     (PROG (G4 Y)
                           (SETQ G4 DDB)
                     RPT4  (COND ((NULL (CDR G4)) (GO L5)))
                           (SETQ Y (CAR (CDR G4)))
                           (COND ((GETHASH KEY (GETHASH Y DB1))
                                  (PRINT Y)))
                           (SETQ G4 (CDR G4))
                           (GO RPT4)
                     L5    (RETURN)))
          (GO RPT2)
    L4    (RETURN])
```

Fig. 6. The final Lisp program for NEWS.

• If a linked list is represented as a Lisp list without a special header cell, then a retrieval of the first element in the list may be implemented as a call to the function CAR.

• An association table whose keys are integers from a fixed range may be represented as an array subregion.

The concepts covered by PSI/SYN's coding rules are all taken from the domain of symbolic programming. They deal generally with three categories of implementation techniques: representation techniques for collections, enumeration techniques for collections, and representation techniques for mappings. Overviews of these three categories of rules are given below. (In addition, PSI/SYN includes rules about low-level aspects of symbolic programming and about programming in Lisp, but these will be omitted from this discussion.)

A. Representation of Collections

Conceptually, a collection is a structure consisting of any number of substructures, each an instance of the same generic description. (As noted earlier, PSI/SYN's rules do not distinguish between sets and multisets.) The diagram in Fig. 7 summarizes the representation techniques that PSI/SYN currently employs for collections, as well as several (indicated by dashed lines) that it does not. Each branch in the diagram represents a refinement relationship. For example, a sequence may be refined into either a linked list or an array subregion. These refinement relationships are stored in the knowledge base as refinement rules. Of course, the diagram does not indicate all of the details that are included in the rules (for example, that

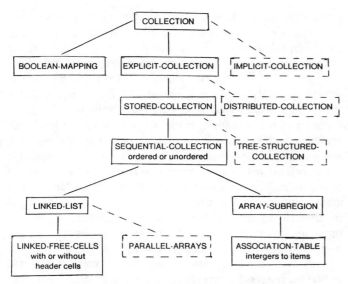

Fig. 7. Overview of collection representations.

an array subregion includes lower and upper bounds as well as allocated space).

As can be seen in the diagram of Fig. 7, PSI/SYN knows primarily about the use of Boolean mappings and sequences. Although "distributed-collection" occurs in a dashed box, PSI/SYN can implement a collection using property list markings by following a path through a Boolean mapping to a distributed mapping. The most significant missing representations are the use of trees (such as AVL trees or 2-3 trees) and implicit collections (such as lower and upper bounds to represent a collection of integers).

Note the extensive use of intermediate-level abstractions. For example, there are four constructs between "collection" and "linked free cells." As noted earlier, such intermediate levels help to economize on the amount of knowledge that must be represented and also facilitate making choices.

B. Enumerations Over Stored Collections

In its most general form, enumerating the elements of a collection may be viewed as an independent process or coroutine. The elements are produced one after another, one element per call. The process must guarantee that every element will be produced on some call and that each will be produced only once. In addition, there must be some way to indicate that all of the elements have been produced, as well as some way to start up the process initially. The process of constructing an enumerator for a stored collection involves two principal decisions: selecting an appropriate order for enumerating the elements and selecting a way to save the state of the enumeration.

There are several possible orders in which the elements can be produced. If the enumeration order is constrained to be according to some ordering relation, then clearly that order should be selected. If it is unconstrained, a reasonable choice is to use the stored (first-to-last) order, either from the first cell to the last (for linked lists) or in order of increasing index (for arrays). In some cases, it may be useful to use the opposite (last-to-first) order.

The enumeration state provides a way for the enumerator to remember which elements have been produced and which have

not. There are many ways to save such a state. Whenever the enumeration order is first-to-last (or last-to-first), an indicator of the current position is adequate: all elements before (or after, for last-to-first) the current position have been produced and all elements after (before) the position have not. PSI/SYN's rules handle these cases, as well as the case in which the enumeration order is constrained and the collection is kept ordered according to the same constraint, in which case a position indicator is also adequate for saving the state.

The situation is somewhat more complex for nonlinear enumerations (in which the enumeration order is not the same as the stored order or its opposite); finding the next element typically involves some kind of search or scan of the entire collection. During such a search, the state must be interrogated somehow to determine whether the element under consideration has already been produced. There are basically two kinds of nonlinear enumeration states, destructive and nondestructive. PSI/SYN's rules deal with one destructive technique, the removal of the element from the collection. A technique not covered by the rules is to overwrite the element. The rules also do not cover any nondestructive techniques.

C. Representation of Mappings

A mapping is a way of associating objects in one set (range elements) with objects in another set (domain elements).[2] A mapping may (optionally) have a default image. If there is no stored image for a particular domain element, a request to determine its image can return the default image. For example, when a Boolean mapping is used to represent a collection, the default image is FALSE.

The diagram of Fig. 8 summarizes representation techniques for mappings. As with collection representations, there are several intermediate levels of abstraction for mappings. Note that an association-list representation is determined by following the path from a "mapping" to a "collection" whose elements are domain/range pairs; the refinement path in the collection diagram given earlier then leads to a linked list of pairs. Property lists give a distributed mapping whose domain is the set of atoms. A plex (or record structure) with several fields would constitute a mapping whose domain is the set of field names. The most significant mapping representations missing from PSI/SYN's rules are implicit mappings (such as function definitions) and discrimination nets. The rules currently deal with only one small aspect of hash tables: the use of Interlisp's hash arrays.

V. Analysis Knowledge

PSI/SYN uses analysis knowledge to make cost estimates for a program description (or any part of one) at any stage of the refinement process and uses the resulting efficiency information for branch-and-bound comparisons, to identify potential bottlenecks in the target program, and for quantitative descriptions in the plausible-implementation rules. Given a program description and a cost function, PSI/SYN's *analysis-maintenance rules* incrementally update the analysis information associated

---

[2] PSI/SYN's rules only deal with many-to-one mappings and not with more general correspondences or relations.

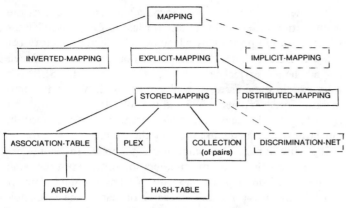

Fig. 8. Overview of mapping representations.

with the developing program; the *cost-estimation rules* compute summary cost information as needed. The lowest-cost implementation may vary under different assumptions about the input data characteristics and the cost function. The execution cost function can be any (user-supplied) polynomial in runtime and storage use that reflects the performance measure desired by the user (for example, the product of space and the square of time).

The top-down, incremental analysis process allows cost estimation for programs that would be difficult to analyze if only the target program were given. Another advantage of combining the stepwise refinement with this sort of analysis is that classes of implementations can be compared by considering the cost estimates for intermediate program descriptions rather than by explicitly expanding the refinement tree to compare many target-language programs. For example, in NEWS, the collection of keywords corresponding to a news story can be refined into a mapping (leading to a hash table, bit mapping, or property list) or to a sequence (leading to a linked list or array, ordered or unordered). Since the collection is used primarily for membership tests, PSI/SYN estimates that the mapping representation will give a faster execution time (a small constant) than the sequence (time is linear in the number of keywords) and therefore decides that the mapping refinement can be made without explicitly considering the list and array representations.

A. Updating Analysis Information

Information about the runtime characteristics of a program is needed to analyze efficiency; this includes statement running times and execution frequencies, data structure sizes, and data structure usage (where created, referenced, and modified). The user provides the needed information for the abstract specification, and then PSI/SYN updates the analysis information during refinement and keeps it associated with the relevant construct instances in the program descriptions of the refinement tree. In the NEWS program, the information provided with the specification is the expected number of stories (80), the average number of keywords per story (100), the probability that the command item is in a story (0.01), and the number of times the main loop in the program will be executed for a given database (300). In later stages information such as the size of the hash table is added.

PSI/SYN makes analysis transformations in parallel with refinements so that more accurate cost estimates can be associated with succeeding nodes in the search tree. Some of the analysis-maintenance rules are associated with particular coding rules. For example, when a "subset (A, B)" test is refined to "true-for-all x in A, member(x, B)," the probability that x is a member of B is computed automatically (as a function of the probability p that the subset test is true) by an analysis-maintenance rule associated with that coding rule. Many rules, such as those for analyzing Boolean combinations, are associated with coding constructs rather than with specific coding rules. For example, the probability of an "and" statement being executed is the product of the probabilities of all its arguments (assuming independence). Similarly, when new operation instances are added to a program description, the prototype for the operation is checked to see whether the arguments to the operation are modified or merely inspected so that the reference information for the data structure instances in the program can be updated.

B. Estimating Execution Costs

Cost-estimation rules use analysis information to estimate program execution costs. Rules for finding the space for data structures and the running time for operations are attached to the prototypes for the corresponding constructs. For example, a rule attached to the hash-table prototype says to estimate storage as 1.5 words times the size of the set being stored. Two rules are stored for runtimes of operations to give upper and lower bound estimates. The upper bound is an achievable estimate that is calculated by introducing standard (or default) implementation choices for each programming construct and by assuming that the standard implementation choices are made for the rest of the refinement process. For example, the achievable estimate for a membership test assumes that the default implementation of a collection is a list (when Lisp is the target language) and that the average running time is therefore a constant times $n(1 - 0.5p)$, where p is the probability that the test succeeds and n is the size of the set. For the membership test in NEWS (with a constant of 0.015), this is 0.015 $(100(1 - 0.005))$, which is approximately 1.5 ms. The lower bound is an optimistic cost estimate that is based on lower bounds for implementations known to the program, not a theoretical lower bound or a best case value. For the membership test, for example, the optimistic bound is a small constant (0.01) because representing the set with a mapping such as a hash table is a possibility.

The cost estimate functions for the target-language constructs obviously have to be hand-coded. However, the cost-estimation rules for constructs that can be constructed from lower level constructs (typically in more than one way) should *not* be arbitrary functions since consistency must be maintained. PSI/SYN uses a bottom-up process for constructing the time-estimation rules from time-estimation rules for other constructs. This process is described in more detail in [14].

In addition to the rules about the time and storage for the individual programming constructs, there are a small number of rules about how to combine the cost estimates for individual constructs into cost estimates for a control structure, including for the entire program. Cost estimates are generally prepared only when requested by other components, such as resource management rules, and can be made at varying levels of detail and precision, depending on the resources available for the computation. For example, the space in use for the program can be reestimated for each statement, for each control block, or just taken as the maximum over the whole program; similarly, the number of executions of a loop can be calculated exactly or estimated. A standard cost-computation process uses different cost-prototypes to make either optimistic or achievable cost estimates and to perform either a quick estimate or a more detailed (and usually more expensive) analysis. To calculate a global achievable cost for a partial program description, the cost-estimation rules simply combine the achievable costs estimates (of the desired level of precision) for the individual constructs. Global optimistic costs are estimated by assuming optimistic costs for each of the constructs in the program and by assuming that no representation conflicts occur.

Rather than having many specific rules for each construct, PSI/SYN uses only a few general cost-estimation rules that inspect the information in the prototypes. General prototypes of construct classes (such as enumerations) and specific prototypes for each construct (such as the "forall" statement) make the structure of the constructs explicit. For example, the prototypes tell how to find the substructures of a data structure, how to find the arguments to an operation, and how to tell which parts of a control construct are local memory, loop initialization, loop exits, and loop body. Cost-estimation rules can then use this information. For example, one rule computes the time used by a control-structure construct and its subparts by summing the time for loop initialization steps, the product of loop-exit probabilities and the time for the corresponding exit actions, and the product of the number of loop executions and the time for one iteration.

Using these cost-computation rules, PSI/SYN estimates that the achievable cost of the program of Fig. 5 is $(a + 300(b + 80 (c + d)))$, where a is the achievable cost to input the database and find its domain, b is the cost to input and test the command, c is the cost for the membership test inside the enumerate-items, and d is the cost to find the keywords corresponding to the command. (The cost function in NEWS is a space–time product, but since space is measured in pages and in this example everything fits on one page, cost is the same as time.) Since other rules estimate that a is approximately 10 and b, 0.05, and since c is approximately 1.5 (the achievable time for a membership test as described above), and d is approximately 0.5 (for reasons similar to the membership test analysis), then the global time (and cost) is therefore $10 + 300 (0.05 + 80(2))$, or about 48 000, as noted in Section III. Similarly, substituting $(0.01 + 0.01)$ for $(c + d)$ gives an optimistic time (cost) of about 500.

C. Computing Potential Impacts

Maintaining both optimistic and achievable estimates permits the assessment of a decision's *potential impact*. This is the difference between the achievable cost estimate and the execution cost estimate when optimistic costs are used for all parts of the program involved in the decision (and achievable esti-

mates are used for parts not involved in the decision). This measure of potential impact is used to identify critical choices and to assign resources. For example, consider the potential impact of the decision about the *keywords* representation in the NEWS. The set of *keywords* (computed by database$[S]$) are referenced in the "member(command, database $[S]$)" operation. From the cost expression given above, the potential impact is about $24\,000(2 - 0.51)$, or 35 760 millisecond-pages (ignoring differences in the optimistic and achievable estimates of a and b, which are small; PSI/SYN does compute the exact value). A similar calculation for the effect of how *database* is represented yields $24\,000(2 - 1.51)$ or 11 760, so the *keywords* decision is more important.

VI. Searching Knowledge

PSI/SYN controls the search for an efficient implementation with two types of searching rules that sometimes call on the coding rules to generate legal implementations and sometimes on the cost-estimation rules to provide an evaluation function for the alternate implementations. Agendas of synthesis tasks, one associated with each node in the refinement tree, serve as the workspace for recording the state of the search.

Resource-management rules choose a node (program description) in the refinement tree, and then a part of that program, to work on. These rules assign priorities to tasks to ensure that the tasks are carried out within the limits of the resources. When refining a part of a program, all relevant coding rules are retrieved and tested for applicability. If more than one rule is applicable, *plausible-implementation rules* help decide which coding rule to apply. These rules contain precomputed analyses that may restrict the possible coding rules to those that seem reasonable in the given program situation, thus pruning the search tree. If several coding rules are judged to be plausible, separate children of the current node are produced by each of the rules. The alternatives are refined and compared under the control of resource-management rules.

PSI/SYN's search space has several interesting regularities that influence the search strategies used. First of all, most of the implementations in terms of known coding constructs are reachable, so refinement failure only occurs when no coding rules are applicable, which happens only rarely. Second, the current set of coding rules generates a fixed set of programming constructs, which can be partially ordered by level of abstraction. The ordering on the constructs allows the plausible-implementation rules to predict good paths. Because most implementations are reachable and because the potential refinements of abstract constructs can be found from the partial ordering, the analysis rules can compute reasonably tight bounds on the costs of implementations even when the programs are specified in terms of abstract constructs. Of course, the rules may fail to predict the costs correctly if all lower bounds are not simultaneously achievable. In such cases an implementation can often be constructed by using representation changes, but at a higher cost than originally expected.

The size of the search space is rather large because more than one representation of the same type of data structure (or operation) is allowed. PSI/SYN allows different representations of the same data type, and even different representations of one instance of a data structure at different points in the program. If several representations of the same data were maintained at the same time, which is a reasonable implementation technique, the search space would be even larger. Thus, it is important for the searching knowledge to limit the possibilities considered. The plausible-implementation rules are one technique by which PSI/SYN ensures that multiple representations are only considered when there is a chance that they improve efficiency.

A. Assigning Priorities to Decisions

Unfortunately, coding decisions cannot always be made independently. For example, if the cost function involves a product of space and time, then the terms of the cost expression representing the product of the space occupied by one data structure and the time for operations not involving that data can be significant. Since all combinations of implementations cannot be considered in equal detail, the quality of the decisions depends on the order in which they are considered and on the depth to which the consequences of alternatives are explored before making a commitment. PSI/SYN's resource-management rules schedule tasks and allocate synthesis resources to balance the final program performance with the cost of choosing and constructing the implementations. These rules seem largely domain-independent. They make sense only in the context of a search space with properties similar to those described above, but do not depend on the domain being program synthesis.

PSI/SYN has three types of resource-management rules as follows.

1) Priority-setting rules limit the resources available to explore a particular branch in the refinement tree and decide which branches should be pursued in which order. These rules enforce global strategies such as branch and bound and best-first search with look-ahead. These rules, combined with a plausible-implementation rule that eliminates implementations that are worse in space and time than their alternatives, produce behavior similar to a dynamic programming algorithm. (See [27] for a good discussion of dynamic programming in implementation selection.)

2) Task-ordering rules determine the order for attempting different refinement tasks within a particular branch of the refinement tree. Ordering principles include postponing choices of coding rules while working on more clear-cut refinements to gather additional information, exposing choices by early expansion of complex programming constructs such as "subset," and postponing low-level coding details until the major decisions have been made.

3) Choice-ordering rules find an order for considering the decisions that must be made if several have been postponed along a particular branch of the refinement tree. One of these rules suggests allocating the most resources to the decisions that are likely to lead to bottlenecks and making those decisions first. The decisions with the highest potential impact (as defined in the section on analysis) are assumed to be those most likely to lead to bottlenecks. However, these values are adjusted to reflect the accuracy of the cost estimates for the current level of program development and the expected cost of completing the refinement process (based on the minimum number of refinements needed to complete the program). Without this, a highly refined implementation might be abandoned in favor of a very abstract description with a slightly better optimistic estimate that is probably not achievable.

B. Grouping Related Implementation Decisions

The number of implementations constructed for comparison can be reduced by grouping related refinement decisions. This reduces both the number of decisions and number of interactions between decisions. Better decisions can be made at a lower cost since, for example, all uses of a data structure will be considered at once.

Whenever possible, a program is factored into "costwise independent" groups—program parts that are independent (or nearly so) in terms of the global cost function. These parts are then refined separately without considering interactions with other program parts. A more frequently realizable technique is for the resource-management rules to apply the "information-structure" grouping. In this method related decisions such as the representation of a data structure and the implementation of all operations that reference it are considered as a group, which makes cost tradeoffs more explicit. Before choosing an implementation of one program part, the efficiency rules identify the related program parts and base the decision on the group's global cost impact. Also, when alternate choices of implementations are compared along different branches of the refinement tree, refinements are initially limited to those parts of the program related to the decision group.

C. Suggesting Plausible Implementations with Stored Analyses

The plausible-implementation rules are used to filter the coding rules. They help compare implementations without the expense of explicit construction and evaluation of the global execution costs of all alternatives. For example, if implementation X is better than implementation Y in both space and time, then Y can be eliminated without comparing the global costs of the programs that would result. The plausible-implementation rules typically describe the situations under which data structure representations are or are not appropriate, under which different sorting operations are plausible, or under which more than one representation for a data structure should be considered. For example, these rules determine that it is worth considering an additional representation for the database inside the loop of the NEWS program to facilitate faster access and membership testing. When the domain of the database is extracted and used only for enumeration, the plausible-implementation rules suggest a sequential representation. When the keyword collection decision is considered, the plausible-implementation rules for refining collections are checked. One of them says that for collections used only for membership tests and for inserting and deleting elements, some reasonable implementations are a linked list and a mapping function such as a hash table.

The plausible-implementation rules are structured condition-action rules. The condition of a rule about data structures, for example, states the critical uses of a data structure that make the rule relevant. Analysis information such as the size of a data structure and the number of executions of a statement may be used in rule condition. The rule action can set a Boolean combination of constraints for a set of program parts requiring that they be refined, or not refined, to a particular programming construct. A three-valued propositional logic (satisfied, possible, impossible) is used to check constraints.

The reliability of plausible-implementation rules may vary. In theory, a "reliability index" could be associated with each rule; in practice, two classifications are defined. A more reliable set of decision rules is always applied. They are assumed to be correct, and must explicitly set backup points if failure is anticipated. The less reliable rules are used only when a quick decision is needed and more accurate comparisons are not affordable or not potentially profitable. These rules contain the standard implementation choices. For example, one rule says to use lists rather than arrays to represent sequences in Lisp.

VII. ANOTHER EXAMPLE

The following problem is taken from Knuth's textbook series [15].

7.1-32.[22] (R. Gale and V. R. Pratt.) The following algorithm can be used to determine all odd prime numbers less than N, making use of sets S and C.

P1. [Initialize] Set $j \leftarrow 3, C \leftarrow S \leftarrow \{1\}$. (Variable j will run through the odd numbers $3, 5, 7, \cdots$. At step **P2** we will have

$$C = \{n|n \text{ odd}, 1 \leqslant n < N, n \text{ not prime, and } \text{gpf}(n) \leqslant p(j)\},$$

$$S = \{n|n \text{ odd}, 1 \leqslant n < N/p(j), \text{ and } \text{gpf}(n) \leqslant p(j)\},$$

where $p(j)$ is the largest prime less than j and $\text{gpf}(n)$ is the greatest prime factor of n; $\text{gpf}(1) = 1$.)

P2. [Done?] If $j \geqslant N/3$, the algorithm terminates (and C contains all the nonprime odd numbers less than N).

P3. [Nonprime?] If $j \in C$ then go to step **P5**.

P4. [Update the sets.] For all elements n in S do the following: If $nj < N$ then insert nj into S and into C, otherwise delete n from S. (Repeat this process until all elements n of S have been handled, including those which were just newly inserted.) Then delete j from C.

P5. [Advance j.] Increase j by 2 and return to **P2**.

Show how to represent the sets in this algorithm so that the total running time to determine all primes $< N$ is $O(N)$. Rewrite the above algorithm at a lower level (i.e., not referring to sets) using your representation.

[Notes: The number of set operations performed in the algorithm is easily seen to be $O(N)$, since each odd number $n < N$ is inserted into S at most once, namely when $j = \text{gpf}(n)$, and deleted from S at most once. Furthermore, we are implicitly assuming that the multiplication of n times j in step **P4** takes $O(1)$ units of time. Therefore you must simply show how to represent the sets so that each operation needed by the algorithm takes $O(1)$ steps on a random-access computer.]

Since PSI/SYN's rules do not cover enumeration over collections that are being modified during the enumeration, a slightly modified version of the original algorithm was given to PSI/SYN. In this version, the set S has been replaced by two collections $S1$ and $S2$, and the collection P is created to output the set of primes (the complement of C).

DATA STRUCTURES

N, J, K, X: integer
$C, S1, S2, P$: set of integer

ALGORITHM

```
N ← input();
J ← 3;
C ← {1};
S1 ← {1};
loop:
    if 3*J ⩾ N then exit;
    if J is not a member of C then
        S2 ← S1;
        S1 ← {};
        loop until S2 is empty:
            for any X in S2:
                remove X from S2;
                if J*X < N then
                    add X to S1;
                    add J*X to S2;
                    add J*X to C;
        remove J from C;
    J ← J+2;
    repeat;
K ← 3;
P ← {};
loop:
    if N < K then exit;
    if K is not a member of C
        then add K to P;
    K ← K + 2;
    repeat;
output P as a linked list.
```

The key here is to implement the collections $S1$, $S2$, and C differently. The only operations being performed on $S2$ are addition, removal, and taking "any" element. The "any" operation suggests that a Boolean mapping may be inappropriate and the frequent destructive operations suggest that an array may be relatively expensive. Thus, an unordered linked list is a reasonable selection. Since the value of $S1$ is assigned to $S2$, a representation conversion can be avoided by using the same representation for both collections. This is especially useful here, since the only operation applied to $S1$, the addition of elements, is relatively simple with unordered linked lists. The only operations applied to C are addition, removal, and two membership tests. Such operations are fairly fast with Boolean mappings. Since the domain elements of the mapping are integers with a relatively high density in their range of possible values, an array of Boolean values is a reasonable representation of C. PSI/SYN derived this implementation, and the resulting program exhibited linear behavior when it was tested.

VIII. Related Research

A logical extension of historical attempts to automate programming is to "compile" a very high level language. This is perhaps best exemplified by work on SETL [24]. SETL's specification language contains primarily mathematical concepts similar to PSI/SYN's sets and mappings. The implementation involves choosing from a small number of parameterized implementations by an algorithmic procedure based on sophisticated analysis of data flow and subset relations between sets. A wider variety of implementations is allowed in systems designed by Low and Rover [17], [22], with choices based on partitioning data structures into equivalence classes and using hill-climbing to select combinations of implementations. Programs are analyzed by monitoring default implementations. These approaches use only one level of refinement—they go from the high-level construct to the alternatives represented in the target language. Rovner's system can be noted for allowing multiple representations and for using heuristics for decision making that are built in but clearly identified. Other approaches to implementation selection use dynamic programming algorithms [19], [27].

Support for more gradual implementation (as well as for verification) is provided by languages such as CLU and Alphard [16], [30], in which a human user is allowed to define intermediate types or encapsulations. Automatic choice among alternatives is not available. Recently, work on specifying and verifying performance properties of programs has begun [25]. There has also been some work on automatic implementation selection systems with a few intermediate levels of refinement [19], [21], [23]. In addition, knowledge-based approaches similar to PSI/SYN have been successful in implementing lower level language compilers [7], [10].

There has been much recent work on transformations as a method for developing programs [1], [6], [8]. The last of these systems, PDS, with its explicit maintenance of a "family tree" of programs, is most clearly related to PSI/SYN's refinement paradigm. PDS allows a user to apply transformations that can refine abstract concepts or extend existing constructs and also provides some analysis tools. Work by Wegbreit [28] includes goal-directed transformations that explicitly use efficiency information based on theoretical lower bounds to drive search.

Another approach to automatic programming involves the use of theorem proving (for example, by Manna and Waldinger in [18]). Axiomatic definitions of program properties, rather than rules, are used to describe implementation techniques. This approach has been reasonably successful with the addition of some programming and domain-specific knowledge to the mathematical axioms.

Green and Barstow's sorting work [11] is another example of an application of the refinement paradigm. Also closely related in some ways is the plan-analysis approach in the Programmer's Apprentice project [20], [26].

IX. Observations

A. The Knowledge-Based Approach

The knowledge-based approach (the use of rules and prototypes) of our implementation of the refinement paradigm has proved to be quite successful. It provides a framework that facilitates the codification of programming knowledge, which is an experimental development process. New implementation techniques can be added simply by adding new coding rules. As new coding knowledge is added, the corresponding analysis knowledge is also added so that the system can always analyze what it can create. The knowledge-based approach also allows the system to include knowledge about its own capabilities, such as searching rules that know about the current deadends in the coding rules. Once a reasonably stable system is developed, it might be possible to "compile" a more efficient implementation, but during development the knowledge-based approach seems most appropriate.

We have also found that relatively small steps in the refinement sequences make the coding rules more modular and make it easier to reflect the design decisions explicitly in the search tree. The small or medium sized steps correspond roughly to human-sized steps of decision making, which makes it easier for people to build and understand the system. For example, new target languages can be produced by adding new low-level coding rules. Also, the operation of the system is more efficient because the intermediate level abstractions provide islands in the search space from which classes of implementations can be considered as a group. The job of analysis is also easier if the step size is small and the analysis can go hand in hand with refinement.

B. The Interaction of Coding and Efficiency Knowledge

Our first experience with writing a program synthesis system convinced us that the interaction between coding, analysis, and search knowledge is inherently complex and that a high bandwidth for communication between the different types of knowledge is a necessity. The refinement paradigm provides an organization in which that kind of communication can be achieved. The search tree serves as a workspace in which the coding decisions or analysis conclusions can be recorded for use by any type of rule. The prototypes provide a static representation of programming constructs that can be used, for example, to allow analysis rules to interpret coding knowledge and to attach analysis processes to either general coding constructs or particular coding rules. Searching knowledge can include domain-independent concepts such as tree search or branch and bound, and can make use of domain-specific information about coding rules in something like the plausible-implementation rules. The refinement paradigm also allows resource-limited searching to focus effort on the parts of a program that the analysis knowledge identifies as important.

Optimizing compilers also include both coding and efficiency knowledge, but the communication between the different types of knowledge is usually less explicit. Most optimizing compilers make relatively local, syntactic transformations to increase efficiency. The transformations are always applied without checking whether they improve performance for a particular program or for specific input data characteristics (such as list length). This prohibits the use of transformations that may optimize significantly in some situations but produce less efficient code in others. Traditional optimizing compilers cannot make major global improvements such as changing an algorithm. They tend to optimize by redistributing existing code, spreading around the coding decisions without leaving a record or what they have done, or why.

C. Limitations

The refinement paradigm seems general enough to be extended along several dimensions, but we have not tested this hypothesis in the PSI/SYN system. For example, what would happen if we attempted to write larger programs or systems of programs is an open question. We believe that the current search techniques would be sufficient to combat combinatorial explosion, but we did not test this hypothesis because the current implementation would not be able to hold all the intermediate representations of large programs in core. And although the coding rules cover the most common implementation techniques, many other coding rules could be added. Also to be determined is the feasibility of the analysis of more complex programs resulting from the addition of new coding rules.

Considering the refinement paradigm as a software design technique raises some other interesting issues. We have considered design decisions related to implementation, but what about design considerations for program specification and maintenance? We have not addressed the issues of specifying program decompositions or explaining implementation decisions to the user. The paradigm does not seem inconsistent with these activities, but again, we have not rigorously tested these hypotheses. Also, the current approach assumes that when modifications are to be made, the original specification is changed and the whole program is reimplemented; there is no obvious way to move back into the middle or compute which of the design decisions are affected by the change(s).

There are several dimensions along which it does seem fruitful to extend the paradigm. For example, it could be of value in the algorithm design process and as part of a system development repository (see the following sections).

D. Algorithm Design

In our use of the refinement paradigm we have focused on the process of algorithm implementation as opposed to algorithm design. (Of course, it is difficult to draw a clear boundary between the two activities: is it "design" or "implementation" to refine an enumeration by deciding to enumerate the items of a set in increasing order and to save the state by deleting enumerated items?) Nonetheless, we believe that the paradigm will also be of value in the algorithm design process. We expect that algorithm design through refinement will be characterized by the following features.

1) The refinement rules will often be of the form: "if the problem is of type X, then try using strategy Y."

2) As a consequence, the initial period of refinement will be subject to many more dead-end paths than later periods of the implementation process.

3) In testing the applicability conditions of the rules, there will be a need for a much stronger deductive component.

4) The analysis will be more difficult for design than for implementation.

In fact, we believe that there will be a gradual transition from the design to the implementation phases and that the re-

finement process will change gradually from one to the other. An extended discussion of the roles of knowledge and deduction in the algorithm design process is available elsewhere [5].

E. A System Development Repository

One of the important directions for future development in automatic programming systems will be the development of models of the design process, including ways to encode the decisions that were made in the development process and the relationships between specifications and low level implementations. As such models are developed, the result of programming will no longer simply be a program in some target language, but rather a detailed description of the entire design and development process, what we may call a "system development repository" (SDR). Such an SDR should be of great assistance in maintaining and enhancing a program, since it would allow the maintainer to "understand" the program more easily by providing direct access to every decision and the reasons for making it.

An SDR will be much more than simply a textual database; it will contain a highly structured and interrelated body of knowledge about a particular program and its design. In building such an SDR, it will be important to exploit whatever structures are naturally available as part of the programming process. We feel that the refinement paradigm provides such a structure—the refinement tree for a program constitutes an elementary form for an SDR, since all of the design and development decisions are encoded explicitly. Since the coding and analysis rules are understandable by a person as well as by a machine, pointers from the tree into the base of programming knowledge should be of great value in understanding the resulting program.

ACKNOWLEDGMENT

The authors would like to thank C. Green for providing a supportive environment and technical suggestions for the development of the PSI system. The research has also benefited from interaction with other members of the PSI group. B. McCune helped develop the specification language; J. Ludlow helped clarify the coding rules; they and R. Gabriel, J. Phillips, T. Pressburger, L. Steinberg, and S. Tappel provided much help and encouragement. They would also like to thank J. Bentley and the referees for their helpful comments on previous versions of the paper.

REFERENCES

[1] R. Balzer, "Transformational implementation: An example," *IEEE Trans. Software Eng.*, vol. SE-7, pp. 3–14, Jan. 1981.
[2] D. R. Barstow and E. Kant, "Observations on the interaction between coding and efficiency knowledge in the PSI program synthesis system," in *Proc. 2nd Int. Conf. Software Eng.*, Long Beach, CA, Oct. 1976, pp. 19–31.
[3] D. R. Barstow, *Knowledge-Based Program Construction*. New York: Elsevier, 1979.
[4] —, "An experiment in knowledge-based automatic programming," *Artificial Intell.*, vol. 12, Aug. 1979.
[5] —, "The roles of knowledge and deduction in algorithm design," in *Machine Intelligence*, D. Michie and Y. H. Pao, Eds. New York: Wiley, 1981.
[6] R. Burstall and J. Darlington, "A transformation system for developing recursive programs," *J. Ass. Comput. Mach.*, vol. 24, Jan. 1977.

[7] R. G. G. Cattell, "Formalization and automatic derivation of code generators," Dep. Comput. Sci., Carnegie-Mellon Univ., Pittsburgh, PA, Tech. Rep. CMU-CS-78-115, Apr. 1978; also, Ph.D. dissertation.

[8] T. E. Cheatham, J. A. Townley, and G. H. Holloway, "A system for program refinement," in *Proc. 4th Int. Conf. Software Eng.*, Sept. 1979, pp. 53–63.

[9] O. J. Dahl, E. W. Dijkstra, and C.A.R. Hoare, *Structured Programming*. New York: Academic, 1972.

[10] C. W. Fraser, "Automatic generation of code generators," Ph.D. dissertation, Dep. Comput. Sci., Yale Univ., New Haven, CT, 1977.

[11] C. C. Green and D. R. Barstow, "On program synthesis knowledge," *Artificial Intell.*, vol. 10, 1978.

[12] C. C. Green, R. Gabriel, E. Kant, B. Kedzierski, B. McCune, J. Phillips, S. Tappel, and S. Westfold, "Results in knowledge-based program synthesis," in *Proc. 6th Int. Joint Conf. Artificial Intell.*, Tokyo, Japan, Aug. 1979, pp. 342–344.

[13] E. Kant, "A knowledge-based approach to using efficiency estimation in program synthesis," in *Proc. 6th Int. Joint Conf. Artificial Intell.*, Tokyo, Japan, Aug. 1979, pp. 457–462.

[14] ——, "Efficiency considerations in program synthesis: A knowledge-based approach," Dep. Comput. Sci., Stanford Univ., Stanford, CA, Tech. Rep. STAN-CS-79-755, Sept. 1979; also, Ph.D. dissertation.

[15] D. E. Knuth, "Bit manipulation," *The Art of Computer Programming*, Draft of Section 7.1.

[16] B. Liskov, A. Snyder, R. Atkinson, and C. Schaffert, "Abstraction mechanisms in CLU," *Commun. Ass. Comput. Mach.*, vol. 20, Aug. 1978.

[17] J. R. Low, "Automatic data structure selection: An example and overview," *Commun. Ass. Comput. Mach.*, vol. 21, May 1978.

[18] Z. Manna and R. Waldinger, "Synthesis: Dreams = > programs," *IEEE Trans. Software Eng.*, vol. SE-5, July 1979.

[19] M. Morgenstern, "Automated design and optimization of management information system software," Ph.D. dissertation, Lab. Comput. Sci., Massachusetts Inst. of Technol., Sept. 1976.

[20] Charles Rich, "Inspection methods in programming," Ph.D. dissertation, Massachusetts Inst. of Technol., June 1980.

[21] S. J. Rosenschein and S. M. Katz, "Selection of representations for data structures," in *Proc. Symp. Artificial Intell. Programming Lang.*, Aug. 1977, pp. 147–154; also in *Joint SIGPLAN Notices*, vol. 12, no. 8, and *SIGART Newsletter*, vol. 64.

[22] P. D. Rovner, "Automatic representation selection for associative data structures," Dep. Comput. Sci., Univ. of Rochester, Tech. Rep. TR10, Sept. 1976.

[23] L. A. Rowe, "A formalization of modelling structures and the generation of efficient implementation structures," Ph.D. dissertation, Dep. Comput. Sci., Univ. of California, Irvine, June 1976.

[24] J. T. Schwartz, "On programming: An interim report on the SETL project, revised," Dep. Comput. Sci., Courant Inst. of Math. Sci., New York Univ., June, 1975.

[25] M. Shaw, "A formal system for specifying and verifying program performance," Dep. Comput. Sci., Carnegie-Mellon Univ., Tech. Rep. CMU-CS-79-129, June, 1979.

[26] H. E. Shrobe, "Dependency directed reasoning for complex program understanding," Massachusetts Inst. of Technol., Tech. Rep. 503, Apr. 1973.

[27] F. Tompa, and R. Ramirez, "An aid for the selection of efficient storage structures," Dep. Comput. Sci., Univ. of Waterloo, Tech. Rep. CS-80-46, Oct. 1980.

[28] B. Wegbreit, "Goal-directed program transformation," presented at 3rd Annu. Symp. Principles of Programming Lang. ACM SIGPLAN/SIGACT, Jan. 1976.

[29] N. Wirth, "Program development by stepwise refinement," *Commun. Ass. Comput. Mach.*, vol. 14, Apr. 1971.

[30] W. A. Wulf, R. L. London, and M. Shaw, "Abstraction and verification in Alphard: An introduction to language and methodology," Dep. Comput. Sci., Carnegie-Mellon Univ., 1976.

Elaine Kant received the B.S. degree in mathematics from the Massachusetts Institute of Technology, Cambridge, in 1973 and the M.S. and Ph.D. degrees in computer science from Stanford University, Stanford, CA, in 1975 and 1979, respectively.

Since 1980 she has been an Assistant Professor of Computer Science at Carnegie-Mellon University, Pittsburgh, PA. In 1979 she was a Research Computer Scientist at Systems Control, Inc., Palo Alto, CA. Her research interests are in the areas of artificial intelligence and programming environments with the focus on the automatic design, construction, and analysis of algorithms and programs.

Dr. Kant is a member of the Association for Computing Machinery, the American Association of Artificial Intelligence, and Sigma Xi.

David R. Barstow, for a photograph and biography, see this issue, p. 450.

PROGRAM REFINEMENT BY TRANSFORMATION*

Thomas E. Cheatham, Jr., Glenn H. Holloway, and Judy A. Townley

Center for Research in Computing Technology
Harvard University, Cambridge, MA 02138

Abstract

Program maintenance is simplified when the program to be modified can be viewed as an abstract algorithm to which clearly documented implementation decisions have been applied to produce an efficient realization. The Harvard Program Development System (PDS) [8] is a programming support environment that encourages users to take this view of programs. A user of the PDS creates transformations that incorporate implementation choices, and the system uses these transformations to refine concrete programs from their abstract counterparts. In addition to simplifying maintenance, this method supports the use of notational extensions and the development of program families. We describe the transformation facilities available to the user of the PDS, and we discuss aspects of the implementation of these facilities.

I. Introduction

Most modern programming methodologies encourage the use of abstraction. While the details of various disciplines for program design, specification, and implementation may differ, there is consensus on the value of developing and adhering to clear abstractions for data and control. Less widely accepted, but just as plausible, is the idea that abstract specifications and programs should be expressible in notations that are natural to the problem domain and that support the data and control abstractions.

This consensus about abstraction stems from the realization that for a large, long-lived software project, the existence of an accurate, readable model or specification that captures the essence of its behavior can be as important as the existence of an efficient implementation of it. Without such a model and a strict discipline for keeping it up to date, maintenance is a costly, error-prone process that often degrades the quality of the software it is intended to enhance.

Given such a model, deriving an efficient implementation from it is not always a simple process that can be left to a compiler. The derivation process, which we call refinement, may require as much insight as the creation of the abstract algorithms. Like the abstract descriptions of a system, the description of its refinement must be well structured and must be kept up-to-date as the system evolves.

Furthermore, many software projects, such as operating systems, compilers, or communications controllers, produce families of programs, each obeying the same abstract specification and each tailored to a particular running environment. Separating the abstract model from its individual implementations and giving the system designer full control of refinement facilitates the development of such families.

Before describing our approach to refinement, let us briefly review the ways current programming languages support this process.

A. Programming Language Facilities for Abstraction

The classical way to specify abstract computations is by procedure calls. A top-down or outside-in structured programming approach to coding encourages the use of such abstractions. One interpretation of this approach (e.g., [22]), views the development of a program as the development of a succession of virtual machines. At the topmost level, an algorithm is expressed using idealized machine operations. The primitive procedures of each virtual machine are then implemented in terms of procedures at the next lower level of abstraction, bringing the whole closer to the actual computational facilities available.

As user-defined data types became standard in programming languages, the need arose for a means of encapsulating the concrete details of abstract data types, just as procedures hide the details of control and simple data abstractions. Several programming languages [11, 13, 21, 23, 26, 28] now include type encapsulation facilities for this purpose. A type encapsulation typically contains the state variables and procedures for defining new operations appropriate to the type abstraction. Some languages also allow the user to overload basic operators, like assignment and component selection, for use with the encapsulated type. The encapsulation isolates the implementation details of the abstraction from the programs making use of it. But again, the procedure is the fundamental tool for implementing the abstract behavior.

There are three reasons why these devices -- procedures and type encapsulation -- are not always adequate. They do not address the desire for notational abstraction. They do not allow the implementer enough control over the derivation of efficient concrete realizations from abstract programs. And there are certain abstractions that are particularly difficult and clumsy to implement even with type encapsulation.

*This research was supported in part by the Advanced Research Projects Agency, under contract N00039-78-G-0020 with the Department of the Navy, Naval Electronic System Command.

Reprinted from *The Proceedings of the 5th International Conference on Software Engineering*, 1981, pages 430-437. Copyright © 1981 by The Institute of Electrical and Electronics Engineers, Inc.

To illustrate this last point, suppose we have a program that uses integer sequences. For example, if A were the name of a particular integer sequence, the program would refer to the I-th element of the sequence by the selection A[I], and it would change the I-th element by the assignment A[I] <- E. Suppose further that, because the sequences are known to be sparse, we choose to represent them at the concrete level by linked lists. Each element of such a list contains the index and value of a non-zero component. A selection A[I] is implemented by a loop that searches the list representing A for an element containing the index I and returns the value stored there; if no such element is found, zero is returned. The assignment A[I] <- E is also implemented by a search of the list representing A. Depending on the value of E, it may be necessary to insert, delete, or merely modify an element of the list.

Typical data type encapsulation mechanisms identify a set of standard operators that the programmer may overload in order to attribute special behavior to particular types. For example, the standard operators Select and Assign might handle selections and assignments, so that A[I] <- E would be interpreted as if written Assign(Select(A, I), E). While this is adequate for many type abstractions, it is not well suited to the linked list implementation of sparse sequences. Here the element assignment operation is best implemented by a single primitive, say AssignElement(A, I, E), in which the new element value E is known at the time the search for the old element is performed.

Advocates of function over form might argue that the expression A[I] <- E, if it is to have a special realization, should be given a name of its own, e.g., that it should be written AssignElement(A, I, E) at the abstract level. But such a requirement would interfere with the purpose of abstract programming. Frequently, what is primitive in one realization of an abstraction is compound in another. Moreover, form is very important. A designer should be able to choose the notation that is most natural to the problem domain, in this case the domain of integer sequences. The derivation of an acceptable concrete program must not depend on bending the abstract algorithm to suit particular realizations. This has been called the principle of uniform reference [16].*

It is also often desirable for the implementations of conceptually orthogonal abstract notions to interact. For instance, the high-level description of an operating system might include the concepts of general queues and process control records, the latter being a data type whose definition

---

*In [16], Geschke and Mitchell attempt to incorporate a rule in Mesa [25] for associating abstract expressions with data type operators that will handle the sparse sequence example without obfuscating the more usual cases. Under their rule, for instance, the evaluator of A[I] <- E would first look for an interpretation of ASSIGN(I, A, E). Failing to find one, it would consider the possibility that A names an element assignment procedure: A(I, E). Another failure would lead to more conventional interpretations. This rule seems hard to learn and easy to misuse. It has not been included in the published description of Mesa.

makes no reference to any queues. At the concrete level, it might be convenient for queues of process control records to be threaded through extra components of the records themselves instead of being handled by the general-purpose queue implementation. This would be difficult to achieve with procedures or type encapsulation facilities alone.

B. The Transformational Approach to Implementing Abstractions

To address such problems, we use program transformation, in addition to procedures and data encapsulation facilities, to implement abstractions. For example, the sparse sequence assignment statement A[I] <- E may be implemented by a transform consisting of a pattern that identifies the relevant assignment statements and a replacement that either adds, deletes, or changes a link in A's underlying list representation. The other example mentioned above, the process queue implementation, can be handled by transforms for augmenting the type definition of process control records with components to serve as queue threads and selectively refining the operations over the appropriate queues to take advantage of those thread components.

The transformational approach is more than an alternative programming language facility. It is an alternative way of deriving concrete programs from abstract ones. Moreover, we treat the reduction of high-level algorithms to concrete ones as a multi-step process over which the implementer has control.

By not compressing a high-level program and its lower-level realization into a single conceptual parcel, the transformational approach promotes the creation and maintenance of program families, whose different members are obtained by applying different groups of transformations to the same abstract model program. Parnas [27] has observed that there are two complementary methods of organizing the creation and maintenance of program families; he calls these "stepwise refinement" and "specification of information hiding modules." Our approach combines these methods. Transformations supplied by the user represent design decisions in the stepwise refinement sequence that leads from the abstract model of the family as a whole to a particular class of concrete family members. However, both programs and transformations are encapsulated in information hiding modules whose interdependencies must be explicitly declared. Such module interface declarations, together with the derivation history of each family member, make it possible to trace the effects of changing a design decision in order to correct a problem or to develop a new family member.

The refinement-by-transformation approach also fits nicely with the use of notational extensions. Extensions that introduce nomenclature, such as iteration expressions and abstract declarations, would be clumsy or impossible to handle procedurally. With transforms it is easy to give definitions for new dictions.

Program transformation has been proposed, and in some cases implemented, by a number of other researchers as a method for producing efficient realizations of algorithms while maintaining correctness. The TAMPR transformation system [5] has been used since 1975 to maintain families of mathematical packages written in FORTRAN; more recently, the use of TAMPR to produce concrete implementations of abstract programs has been investigated. The PSI system [17] has a catalog of transformation rules encoding programming knowledge that is used to synthesize programs from abstract specifications. The TI project of Balzer and coworkers [3] is similar, although it is designed to depend more on user guidance than PSI. Both systems employ powerful builtin transformations; both have been used experimentally for the refinement of small, intricate algorithms. Feather's thesis [14] demonstrates the feasibility of using the elegant transformation method of Burstall and Darlington [6] for the development of application programs, and it deals with issues of system maintenance; however, it does not attempt refinement below the level of a purely applicative, side-effect free programming language. Arsac [2], Gerhart [15], and a group led by Bauer [4] have studied transformation as a formal technique for program development, and Bauer's group plans to implement a system to support such manipulations. Kibler [19] and Loveman [24] have experimented with source level program optimizers based on catalogues of correct program transformations.

Our contribution lies in having implemented a system that uses transformation for the development and maintenance of sizable programs, by non-trivial refinement of abstract specifications. Our approach is unusual in its emphasis on user-defined (as opposed to pre-existing, catalogued) transforms, created and maintained along with the conventional procedural realizations of abstractions. We have embedded our tools for transformation -- and the means for recording their role in the refinement process -- in a programming support environment called the Program Development System (PDS) [8].

In section II we briefly discuss the issue of notational extensions. Section III gives some examples of the kinds of transformations we use for refinement; sections IV and V describe our transformation facility and discuss some of the issues addressed in its implementation. In the concluding section we discuss our experiences using the facility and indicate what we expect to do with it next.

II. Notational Extensions

Most programming language designers take pains to ensure that values with built-in data types can be manipulated using familiar and natural notation. For matrices of numbers, for example, it is generally accepted that

$$A[i,j] <- B[i,k] * C[k,j] + d$$

is preferable to

    Assign(Select(Select(A,i),j),
           Plus(Times(Select(...),Select(...)),d))

It is no less important to be able to use familiar, suggestive notations for data and control abstractions that are user-defined.

Suppose we are developing a data abstraction for mathematical sets. We would want to overload existing operators to accept sets and to define new ones that resemble the familiar notation of set algebra. For example one would rather read

$$S \text{ Union } (T - \{e\})$$

than

$$Union(S, Difference(T, CreateSet(e)))$$

We would similarly want to employ control abstractions in developing an abstract model of an algorithm to allow the reader to concentrate on the essence of the algorithm. For example, the following description of the bubble sort algorithm [20] uses a control abstraction to defer the details of the order in which the sequence being sorted is scanned:

    WhileExists I In 1 .. |A|-1
      SuchThat A[I] > A[I+1]
        Do Exchange(A[I], A[I+1]) End

The procedure Exchange is assumed to be a programmer-defined routine to interchange its arguments in place. The expression m..n represents the integer range [m,n] and |A| denotes the length of a sequence A. The abstract iteration

    WhileExists variable In domain
      SuchThat predicate Do body End

binds a new local variable to an element of the domain that satisfies the predicate, executes the body, and then repeats the operation until no such element can be found.

Given that one understands the meaning of the notation, the definition of the bubble sort algorithm and its correctness are clear. From this abstract model, one can derive a number of alternative realizations, incorporating desired optimizations and whatever specializations are appropriate for particular data representations.

Opponents of notational extension argue that it leads to a proliferation of dialects and results in code that is unreadable by anyone other than the author. There is no question that programmers can produce unreadable code in any programming language; any facility intended to promote clarity can be misused, leading to obscurity. These problems are best addressed by good training and, in some cases, organizational or management control.

Most technical organizations develop phrases and abbreviations to enhance communication among co-workers. Similarly, in most organizations there is a natural pressure that controls the unwarranted expansion of dialects to avoid misunderstanding. An individual joining the organization necessarily must be introduced to the language, and it may take time and/or training to become conversant with the parlance.

The use of notational extensions in programming is a comparable phenomenon. Dialects are created to facilitate the design and implementation of a software product; their semantics can be precisely specified, and their definitions as procedures or transformations can be carefully controlled. Such disciplined use of appropriate notation can be the means for producing more readable, and therefore more easily maintained, software.

We use a simple method for specifying notational extensions; it does not require the programmer to be familiar with the BNF grammar of the base language. Instead he is given several ways of defining new operators, and he can add new phrases to the language that are analogous to existing sentential forms. Any valid identifier may be turned into an operator. A programmer may compose a valid identifier either from the usual alphanumeric characters or from a pool of "operator-like" characters, such as +, ., {, and so on. Thus == might be a user-defined identifier.

The programmer can declare the symbols of his choice to act as prefix or infix operators, or both, and he may specify precedence and associativity attributes for them. We also have a category of operator pairs called matchfix operators. The declaration MatchFix("{","}"), for instance, adds a new bracketing construct to the language. Subsequent to the declaration, the expression {X, Y+2, A[J]} would be a legal utterance, and when evaluated, it is equivalent to a call on the left brace operator ({) with the three operands shown.

Longer phrases, such as the WhileExists notation given above, are added by analogy with existing ones. For example,

EquatePhrase
("WhileExists -- In -- SuchThat -- Do -- End",
 " For -- From -- To -- Repeat -- End")

means that each terminal symbol of the new phrase will be treated by the parser like the corresponding token from the old phrase. The internal form produced by the parser contains the tokens actually used so that the conversion from internal to external representation can be made correctly.

An implementer can refine such notation either by binding procedure definitions to the new operators or by using transformation rules.

III. Examples of Refinement by Transformation

A transformation rule consists of a syntactic pattern part, optionally augmented by a semantic predicate, and a replacement part. The symbol <-> separates the pattern (including any predicate) from the replacement. A $ preceding an identifier indicates that the identifier is a parameter of the pattern, with the understanding that a parameter may match an arbitrary expression. A ? preceding an identifier indicates a parameter that matches a sequence of arbitrarily many expressions or statements. Thus a general transformation rule has the form

        pattern Where predicate <-> replacement

The predicate is any Boolean expression and may involve the parameters of the pattern.

The most common kind of transform that we use is one that carries no semantic predicate and simply serves to implement some abstract notation. For example, the following rule provides an implementation for notation designating the addition of an element to the end of a queue:

    Insert $E Into $Q <->
      Begin
        $Q.Count <- $Q.Count + 1;
        $Q.Rear <-
          CreateQueueMember($E, $Q.Rear)
      End

Transforms are sometimes the most convenient way to implement certain aspects of the behavior of an abstract data type. For instance, the type SymbolicExpression might have abstract components called Op, Arg1, Arg2, and so on. If we represented SymbolicExpressions by LISP-like lists, we might use transforms to implement the component selections:

        $X.Op   <-> $X.Car
        $X.Arg1 <-> $X.Cdr.Car
        $X.Arg2 <-> $X.Cdr.Cdr.Car

We also use transforms to introduce nomenclature. Suppose we are writing a program that references numerous components of a record. It would be convenient to create an abstract declaration that introduces the relevant components of the chosen record into the current scope as simple variables. For example,

            Use <X,Y,Z> From S

could identify X with S.X, Y with S.Y and so on, for the remainder of the current block. (The Pascal WITH-statement serves a similar purpose.) To implement this declaration we use two rules:

    Use < > From $S <-> {| |}

    Use <$X, ?L> From $S <->
      {| Declare $X:Any Sharing $S.$X;
         Use <?L> From $S |}

Note that the parameter ?L matches a sequence of expressions, including the empty sequence. The brackets {| |} are a meta-notation used by the transformation mechanism. On the right side of a transform, they indicate that the statements inside the brackets constitute the replacement, with the brackets themselves being dropped. Thus the first of these transforms deletes a statement; the second replaces a single statement by two. Note also that the right side of the last transform contains abstract notation. Transformations are automatically applied in replacements as well as in the original program, so that the right sides of rules need not be entirely in concrete terms. For those situations in which one does not want a particular transformation to be used in the further refinement of its own right-hand side, there is a special transform operator <---> that defines "once-only" rules, as in

    Diag[$I,$J] <--->
      If $I ≠ $J Then 0 Else Diag[$I, $I]

User-defined iteration abstractions are usually refined by transformation since they also introduce nomenclature. For example, the WhileExists loop mentioned in section II could be defined as follows:

```
WhileExists $variable In $domain
   SuchThat $predicate Do ?body End <->


Repeat
   Declare Found:Bool Initially False;
   ForEach $variable in $domain
     Do If $predicate Then
        Begin ?body; Found <- True End;
     End;
     If Not Found Then ExitLoop;
   End;
```

If the base language contained a general-purpose ForEach iterator, this transform would complete the definition of WhileExists. If not, then the meaning of the ForEach loop would need to be given for relevant domains, as in

```
ForEach $E In $R Do ?body End
   Where $R HasType Range(Integer)  <->


For $E From $R.Lower To $R.Upper
   Repeat ?body End
```

Here the semantic precondition in the Where clause limits the application of the transform to ForEach iterators over integer ranges (such as 1 .. |A|-1). Another realization of the same syntactic form for a different domain is shown in section IV.B.

Our final example illustrates the use of transformations, not to implement some notation, but to derive a particularly efficient realization of an abstraction. Suppose we are representing an abstract array by a linked list. Certain combinations of array operators, such as X[I] <- Y[I], may occur so frequently that we want to make sure they are implemented efficiently. Transformation rules allow us to identify these combinations and define their implementations, as in the following example:

```
$A1[$I] <- $A2[$I]
   Where $A1 HasType Array And
         $A2 HasType Array    <->


   Begin
     Declare L1:List Initially Lower($A1,List);
     Declare L2:List Initially Lower($A2,List);
     To $I-1 Repeat
        If L1 = Nil Then
           Raise("Selection Fault", $A1, $I);
        If L2 = Nil Then
           Raise("Selection Fault", $A2, $I);
        L1 <- L1.NextElement;
        L2 <- L2.NextElement;
     End;
     L1.Item <- L2.Item;
   End
```

(Lower(A,T) coerces the abstract object A to its underlying data type T, and Raise(...) indicates an exception.) This rule encodes the programmer's knowledge that a single search loop suffices for both selections, on the assumption that a compiler is unlikely to perform this optimization. Whatever the state of the compiling art, there will always be insights of this kind that a mechanical optimizer cannot be expected to perceive and that can be conveniently expressed as transformations by the implementer.

IV. Controlling the Application of Transformations

When using our tools, the implementer has a number of ways of limiting and guiding the application of transformation rules. The syntactic pattern and the optional Where clause are the primary means of controlling applicability. There are other means, however, both passive and active. Scope rules may be used for implicit control, and the user may give explicit instructions specifying the order of application of (groups of) transforms to (groups of) program entities.

A. Uses of the Where Clause

As has been mentioned, the phrase

Where predicate

appearing to the left of the <-> operator in a transform causes the predicate to be evaluated once the syntactic pattern has matched successfully. The predicate may refer to the match parameters that have been bound during syntactic matching. If it evaluates to True, the transformation takes place; if its result is False, no replacement occurs.

The Where clause can be used for additional syntactic matching. For example, we may want to require that a particular match parameter be bound to an identifier or to an expression in some other syntactic category. If necessary, the pattern matcher of the transformation tool may be invoked as part of a predicate.

More typically, however, the Where clause is used to test semantic preconditions, usually concerning data types. We saw an instance of this in the refinement of the ForEach iterator in section III. The Where clause permits us to use a single notation for a single abstract notion even though it may have radically disparate realizations for different data types. Unlike type encapsulation schemes [23, 28] that require type-dependent operators to be keyed to a single data type, the transformational approach allows us to define refinements based on several constituent data types. Consider

```
$C = $R Where
   ($C HasType Cartesian And
    $R HasType Polar)    <->


$C.Abscissa = $R.Radius * Cos($R.Theta) And
$C.Ordinate = $R.Radius * Sin($R.Theta)
```

(Type-dependent transformations can be viewed as a generalization of the idea of procedure overloading, found in Mesa [25] and Ada [1].)

Another use of the Where clause is to ensure that two subexpressions identify the same program location. A syntactic match alone would not be sufficient since an intervening declaration can cause two occurrences of the same identifier to have different meanings. An example of a transform that incorporates such a predicate is presented in the next subsection.

The use of Where predicates for semantic preconditions depends on the existence of a program analyzer providing the semantic information about program expressions for use during transformation. In our system, abstract programs need not be "strongly typed"; that is, it may be non-trivial to determine the data type of an arbitrary expression. The analyzer currently available in our system [18] propagates data types and detects and evaluates certain statically reducible expressions. Because it was designed for other purposes, however, it is not entirely adequate. We discuss its weaknesses and our plans for its improvement in section VI.

B. Scoping and Sequencing of Transformations

In the PDS, the refinement of an abstract program takes place in a series of steps of the form

Transform(A1,R) -> A2

where A1 stands for a module containing abstract program entities, e.g., procedure and data declarations, and R is a refinement module. The refinement module may contain new entities, lower-level replacements for some of the entities in A1, transformation rules, and instructions to control the application of the rules. A2, the result of applying R to A1, is a module that presumably is a less abstract realization of A1. A2 itself may be the target of further transformation.

The entities in these modules may be divided into named groups, both to provide local scoping of entity names within modules, and to control the application of transforms. Refinement instructions within R may specify that a rule or group of rules from R is to be applied to one or more named groups from A1.

A user may also define a transform whose scope is limited to a small group of expressions or statements. By placing a transform inside a procedure body or in the replacement part of another transform, the user limits its scope to the remainder of the block in which it appears. No special notation is required to distinguish the local transforms. For example, suppose we have a linear list data abstraction that includes an operator for inserting elements:

Insert $E1 After $E2 In $L

This expression is implemented by scanning down the list $L until the element $E2 is found and then inserting $E1 after it. Within the body of a list iterator, however, certain insertions can be performed without making an extra scan through the list. We can express this with a transform having another, local transform as part of its replacement:

```
ForEach $E In $L Do ?body End
   Where $L HasType LinearList      <->

      Begin
         Declare Tail,Next:LinearList Initially $L;
         Repeat
            If Tail = Nil Then ExitLoop;
            Next <- Tail.NextElement;
            Declare $E:Element Sharing Tail.Item;

            Insert $E1 After $E2 in $L2
               (Where $E2 IsIdenticalTo $E And
                      $L2 IsIdenticalTo $L)   <->
               (Tail.NextElement <-
                  CreateListElement($E1,Tail.NextElement))

            ?body;
            Tail <- Next;
         End;
      End
```

Here the embedded transform applies only to the statements of the loop body, locally overriding the implementation of the general list insertion operator for this common special case. Note the use of the semantic predicate $E1 IsIdenticalTo $E2 which assures not only the syntactic but also the semantic identity of its operands.

In theory, these mechanisms allow the user to control the application of transformation rules to the same extent that would be possible with a production system [12]. It is typical for a PDS user to think of a transformation as the self-contained definition of a high-level concept in lower-level terms. There has not been enough need for elaborate sequencing of transformations to warrant the introduction of a more complex sequencing algorithm, such as that in a production system interpreter.

V. Implementation of the Transformation Tools

Our transformation tools operate on a tree-structured internal representation of programs. All components of the PDS share this internal form. The external, character representation of programs is converted to tree form by a common parser; the inverse conversion to formatted strings is performed by a tool called the unparser.

Transforms are also converted to a tree form by the parser, so that the transformation process is simply subtree matching and replacement. Because nearly all of the transformations we use are structure-preserving, we rarely have need of rules capable of manipulating lexeme or character strings. More importantly, preparsing programs and transforms offers numerous advantages. We avoid such parsing issues as balanced delimiter checks that would arise during matching in a string-based system. Since our interpreter, compiler, and analyzers all use the same internal form, no conversion between representations is required. The transformed result may be unparsed and is thus easy to read. And the user is protected against producing syntactically ill-formed programs.

The computation tree representation is also conducive to the accumulation of the semantic information propagated by analyzers. Without modifying the program, an analyzer can associate facts with its subexpressions, e.g., by using a hash table in which expression subtrees serve as keys. In this way, an elastic and readily accessible store of facts can be attached to any part of the program.

The actual transformation algorithm consists of repeated passes over the evolving program tree until no further rules are applicable. Most rules are applied during the top-down portion of the tree walk. If a match succeeds and a replacement occurs, then matching proceeds in the newly installed subtree. Only the once-only rules (P <---> R) are applied during the bottom-up portion of the first pass of the tree walk. This ensures that such a rule will never be applied to an instance of its own right hand side.

VI. Conclusion

The principal weakness of our transformational facility is its analysis component. The current analyzer propagates information about data types, performs constant folding, and allows us to test for semantic identity of variables. It does not attempt other data flow analysis, and its results do not take into account information from the path predicates in the program.

We have developed another analyzer, called the symbolic evaluator [9], that takes path predicates and aliasing patterns into account in describing the values of program expressions and attempts to analyze the effects of loops. The current symbolic evaluator, however, is not efficient enough for general use by the transformation facility. What we need is a spectrum of analyzers, and one aspect of our future work will be to investigate such a spectrum.

There is another dimension in which our analyzers are inadequate -- that is, they can only analyze the concrete behavior of programs. To make full use of the transformation paradigm, we need analysis of abstract behavior. Such analysis would gracefully handle programs with incompletely defined constructs -- programs that not only contain references to procedures, variables, and data types whose definitions are not yet available, but also contain user-created notations whose full definitions at the concrete level are determinable only after some analysis. The design and development of such an analyzer is under way.

The use of transformations based upon semantic information introduces the issue of maintaining this information during refinement. The replacement expression inserted by a transformation may need analysis for its further refinement. The current analyzer has to reanalyze the entire procedure in which the replacement occurs if a Where predicate must be tested and the matched expression lacks analysis. We hope to develop techniques for deriving this analysis incrementally.

Even with these limitations in our analysis tools, we have used the transformational approach extensively for program development. It has played a

major role in five large programming projects developed over the last four years: a symbolic evaluator for programs [9], a family of interprocess communication handlers [7], a formula simplifier, a family of interpreters for EL1 (the base language of the PDS), and the PDS itself [8].

The PDS is designed to facilitate the use of transformations. It creates and maintains a history of the development of programs, keeping track of the multiple levels of refinement and the tools used for refinement. The history enables automatic incremental rederivation of concrete code after a change at the abstract level. It is particularly important to be able to make a small change in an abstract algorithm and to have it quickly and automatically reflected in the concrete counterpart. To this end, the PDS takes into account the nature of each change to a module and uses simple but usually effective rules for bringing dependent modules up-to-date with a minimum of retransformation.

Our experiences suggest that the use of transformation, in addition to conventional refinement techniques, significantly improves the quality and maintainability of the resulting product. With this method, we tend to create more and better abstractions, thus producing more readable programs. Debugging and maintenance are easier because of the added separation of concepts from implementation. And, in spite of greater use of abstractions, the end products can be highly efficient.

REFERENCES

1. "Reference manual for the Ada programming language," U. S. Dept. of Defense, July 1980.

2. Arsac, J.J., "Syntactic source to source transforms and program manipulation," CACM, Vol. 22, No. 1, January 1979.

3. Balzer, R., N. Goldman, and D. Wile, "On the transformational implementation approach to programming," Proc. 2nd Int. Conf. on Software Engineering, San Francisco, CA, 1976.

4. Bauer, F.L., "Programming as an evolutionary process," Proc. 2nd Int. Conf. on Software Engineering, San Francisco, CA, 1976.

5. Boyle, J.M., "Program adaptation and program transformation," Proc. Workshop on Software Adaptation and Maintenance, (R. Ebert, J. Leugger, and R. Goecke, Eds.), Elsevier-North Holland, Amsterdam, 1980.

6. Burstall, R.M., and J. Darlington, "A transformation system for developing recursive programs," J. ACM, Vol. 24, No. 1, January 1977.

7. Bush, W.R., "Refinement of an abstract model of MSG," Center for Research in Computing Technology, Harvard University, TR-06-80, April 1980.

8. Cheatham, T.E., Jr., J.A. Townley, and G.H. Holloway, "A system for program refinement," Proc. 4th Int. Conf. on Software Engineering, September 1979, pp. 53-63.

9. Cheatham, T.E., Jr., G.H. Holloway, and J.A. Townley, "Symbolic evaluation and the analysis of programs," IEEE Trans. on Software Engineering, Vol. SE-5, No. 4, July 1979.

10. Conrad, W.R., "Rewrite user's guide," Center for Research in Computing Technology, Harvard University, Memo, August 1976.

11. Dahl, O.-J., B. Myhrhaug, and K. Nygaard, "The Simula 67 common base language," Norwegian Computing Centre, Forskingeien 1B, Oslo 3, Norway, 1968.

12. Davis, R., and J. King, "An overview of production systems," Department of Computer Science, Stanford University, STAN-CS-75-524, October 1975.

13. "ECL programmer's manual," Center for Research in Computing Technology, Harvard University, TR-23-74, December 1974.

14. Feather, M.S., "A system for developing programs by transformation," University of Edinburgh, Ph.D. thesis, 1979.

15. Gerhart, S.L., "Correctness-preserving program transformations," Proc ACM Symp. on Principles of Programming Languages, January 1975.

16. Geschke, C.G., and J.G. Mitchell, "On the problem of uniform references to data structures," IEEE Trans. on Software Engineering, Vol. SE-1, No. 2, June 1975.

17. Green, C.C., and Barstow, D.R., "On programming synthesis knowledge," Artificial Intelligence, Vol. 10, No. 3, North-Holland, November 1978.

18. Holloway, G.H., "User's guide to the expression analyzer and query facility," Center for Research in Computing Technology, Harvard University, Memo, May 1976.

19. Kibler, D.F., "Power, efficiency, and correctness of transformation systems," Ph.D. thesis, Computer Science Dept., University of California at Irvine, 1978.

20. Knuth, D.E. Sorting and Searching, Addison-Wesley, 1973.

21. Lampson, B.W., J.J. Horning, R.L. London, J.G. Mitchell, and G.J. Popek, "Report on the programming language EUCLID," SIGPLAN Notices, Vol. 12, No. 2, February 1977.

22. Linger, R.C., H.D. Mills, and B.I. Witt, Structured Programming: Theory and Practice, Addison-Wesley, 1979.

23. Liskov, B., A. Snyder, R. Atkinson, and C. Schaffert, "Abstraction mechanisms in CLU," CACM, Vol. 20, No. 8, August 1977.

24. Loveman, D.B., "Program improvement by source to source transformation," J. ACM, Vol. 24, No. 1, January 1977.

25. Mitchell, J.G., W. Maybury, and R. Sweet, "Mesa language manual," Xerox Palo Alto Research Center, CSL-78-1, February 1978.

26. Mitchell, J.G., and B. Wegbreit, "Schemes: a high-level data structuring concept," Xerox Palo Alto Research Center, CSL-77-1, January 1977.

27. Parnas, D.L., "On the design and development of program families," IEEE Trans. on Software Engineering, Vol. SE-2, No. 1, March 1976.

28. Wulf, W.A., R.L. London, and M. Shaw, "An introduction to the construction and verification of Alphard programs," IEEE Trans. on Software Engineering, Vol. SE-2, No. 4, December 1977.

GUIDE TO THE LITERATURE AND ANNOTATED BIBLIOGRAPHY

William W. Agresti
Computer Sciences Corporation

The literature concerning new paradigms for software development is organized according to the four major sections in this tutorial:

- Critiques of the Conventional Life-Cycle Model
- Prototyping
- Operational Specification
- Transformational Implementation

The selection of reference items was influenced by the following guidelines:

- Only references in the open literature were included.
- Items describing the conventional life-cycle model were not included. (Agresti's article, "The Conventional Software Life-Cycle Model: Its Evolution and Assumptions," in this tutorial may be consulted for such references.)

This bibliography focuses on work that affects the sequence and nature of the activities constituting the software development process. This orientation has especially influenced the selection of references in Part V, Transformational Implementation. This section is slanted toward real, implemented systems that have been motivated by the long-range goal of economically developing large software systems by using a transformation-based paradigm. Certain references in this section serve as points of departure for readers who want to pursue other aspects of program transformation:

- [Frenkel 85]: Knowledge-based approaches to software development and programmer assistance
- [Biermann et al. 84]: Program synthesis research that is not now associated with implemented systems
- [Burstall, Darlington 77]: Source-to-source program translation

[Partsch, Steinbrüggen 83] should be consulted for a wider range of references to the literature on program transformation.

I. Critiques of the Conventional Life-cycle Model

General Critiques

[Blum 82]	[Freeman 81]	[Giddings 84]
[Hall 82]	[Jackson 78]	[Jackson 81]
[Martin 84]	[McCracken 81]	[Riddle 84]
[Weinberg 82]	[Zave 84a]	[Zvegintzov 82]

Lack of User Involvement

[Lucas 78]	[McCracken, Jackson 81]

Ineffectiveness in Requirements Phase

[Gladden 82]	[McCracken 81]	[McCracken, Jackson 81]

Inflexibility To Accommodate Prototypes

[Alavi 84]	[Gremillion, Pyburn 83]

Unrealistic Separation of Specification From Design

[Giddings 84]	[Jackson 81]	[Jackson 82]
[McHenry 77]	[Swartout, Balzer 82]	

Inability To Accommodate Reused Software

[Silverman 85]

Maintenance-Related Problems

[Balzer et al. 83]   [Lehman 80]   [Zvegintzov 82]

Alternatives to the Conventional Life-Cycle Model

[Balzer et al. 83]	[Blum 84]	[Conner 81]
[Gladden 82]	[Jackson 82]	[Kerola, Freeman 81]
[Lucas 78]	[Tajima, Matsubara 84]	[Wegner 84]
[Zave 84a]		

II. Prototyping

Comprehensive, Book-Length Coverage

[ACM SIGSOFT 82]   [Boar 84]

General Discussion-Role and Benefits of Prototyping

[Blum, Houghton 82]	[Carey, Mason 83]	[EDP Analyzer 81]
[Gomaa 83]	[Gregory 84]	[Gremillion, Pyburn 83]
[Kowalski 84]	[McCracken 81]	[McCracken, Jackson 81]
[Patton 83]	[Scharer 83]	[Taylor, Standish 82]
[Weiser 82]	[Zelkowitz 82]	[Zolnowski, Ting 82]

How To Prototype

[Boar 84]	[Gomaa 83]	[Scharer 83]
[Taylor, Standish 82]		

Data on Prototype Development

[Alavi 84]	[Boehm et al. 84]	[EDP Analyzer 81]
[Gehani 82]	[Gomaa 83]	[Gomaa, Scott 81]
[Mason et al. 82]	[Sukri, Zelkowitz 83]	

Integrating Prototype Into the Life-Cycle

[Alavi 84]   [Carey, Mason 83]   [MacEwen 82]

A Separate Life-Cycle for Building Prototypes

[Boar 84]   [MacEwen 82]   [Scharer 83]

Transforming a Prototype Into a Complete System

[Blum 83]	[Duncan 82]	[EDP Analyzer 81]
[Keus 82]	[Taylor, Standish 82]	

A Specification as a Prototype

[Balzer et al. 82]	[Cheatham 84]	[Cohen et al. 82]
[Davis 82]	[Dixon et al. 82]	[Feather 82b]
[Goguen, Meseguer 82]		

A Design as a Prototype

[Bonet, Kung 84]   [Riddle et al. 78]   [Stavely 82]

To Learn About Requirements

[Alavi 84]	[Dodd 80]	[Gomaa 83]
[Gomaa, Scott 81]	[Hooper, Hsia 82]	[McCoyd, Mitchell 82]
[Scharer 81]		

Systems for Prototyping

   PDS: [Cheatham 84] [Cheatham et al. 79]
            [Klausner, Konchan 82]

TEDIUM: [Blum 83]

USE: [Wasserman 81] [Wasserman, Shewmake 82]

Languages and Tools for Prototyping

ACT/1:   [Mason et al. 82] [Mason, Carey 83]
Ada*:   [Duncan 82]
ATOL: [Dodd et al. 82]
FORTRAN: [Sukri, Zelkowitz 83]
HIBOL: [Mittermeir 82]
LISP: [Heitmeyer et al. 82] [McCoyd, Mitchell 82]
OBJ: [Goguen, Meseguer 82]
Pascal: [Bonet, Kung 84]
RAMIS: [EDP Analyzer 81]
SNOBOL: [Zelkowitz 80]
UNIX: [Gehani 82]

Applications of Prototyping

Applicative Language System Development: [Zelkowitz 80]
Commercial Data Processing: [Mittermeir 82]
                                [Naumann, Jenkins 82]
Expert Systems: [Barstow 82]
File Processing: [Ramanathan, Shubra 82]
Form Definition: [Gehani 82] [Gehani 83]
Information Systems: [Blum 83] [Wasserman 81]
                        [Wasserman, Shewmake 82]
Language Development: [Ford, Marlin 82]
Medical Systems: [Blum 83] [Gill et al. 82]
Military Systems: [Heitmeyer et al. 82]
Operating System: [MacEwen 82]
Personnel System: [EDP Analyzer 81]
Real-Time Systems: [Duncan 82]
Relational Data Base: [Klausner, Konchan 82]
Text Processing: [Dodd et al. 82]
User Interface: [Hemenway, McCusker 82] [Mason, Carey 83]
                    [Mason et al. 82] [Mittermeir 82]
                    [Strand, Jones 82] [Wasserman 81]
                    [Wasserman, Shewmake 82]

III. Operational Specification

General Approaches

[Balzer et al. 83]   [Cameron 82]   [Cohen et al. 82]
[Martin 84]   [Zave 84a]

Models for Operational Specification

[Cameron 82]   [Jackson 82]   [Kowalski 84]
[Riddle et al. 78]   [Smoliar 81]   [Smoliar 82]
[Zave 84a]

---

*Ada is a registered trademark of the U.S. Government [Ada Joint Program Office].

Algebraic Operational Specification

[Goguen, Meseguer 82]   [Smoliar 82]

Languages and Tools

Descartes: [Urban 82]
     GIST: [Balzer et al. 82]
      JSD: [Cameron 82] [Jackson 82]
      OBJ: [Goguen, Meseguer 82]
    P-net: [Smoliar 81]
 PAISLey: [Zave 82] [Zave 84b] [Zave, Yeh 81]

Applications

Commercial Data Processing: [Jackson 82]
Embedded Systems: [Zave 82] [Zave, Yeh 81]
Distributed, Real-Time Systems: [Smoliar 81]

IV. Transformational Implementation

Comprehensive, Book-Length Coverage

[Barstow 79]   [Biermann et al. 84]
[Partsch, Steinbrüggen 83]   [Pepper 84]

General: Program Transformation

[Balzer 81]   [Bauer 82]   [Broy, Pepper 81]
[Burstall, Darlington 77]   [Deak 81]   [Feather 82a]
[Wile 83]

Knowledge-Based Transformation

[Barstow 79]   [Barstow 82]   [Barstow et al. 82]
[Frenkel 85]   [Green 76]   [Kant, Barstow 81]
[Kowalski 84]   [Waters 82]

Languages, Systems, and Projects

    ALICE: [Darlington 84]
      CIP: [Bauer 82] [Partsch 84]
     HOPE: [Darlington 84]
      PDS: [Cheatham 84] [Cheatham et al. 79] [Cheatham et al. 81]
      PSI: [Green 76]
  PSI/SYN: [Kant, Barstow 81]
    TAMPR: [Boyle, Muralidharan 84]
       TI: [Balzer 81] [Balzer et al. 76]
      ZAP: [Feather 82a]
      $\emptyset_o$:   [Barstow et al. 82]

Bibliography

[ACM SIGSOFT 82]   ACM SIGSOFT, "Working Papers: ACM SIGSOFT Rapid Prototyping Workshop," ACM SIGSOFT *Software Engineering Notes*, vol. 7, no. 5, Dec. 1982, 184 pp.

Thirty working papers from the ACM SIGSOFT Rapid Prototyping Workshop held in Columbia, Maryland, April 19-21, 1982, are presented. Topics covered include effect of prototyping on the life-cycle, relation of software development and VLSI issues, impact of prototyping on environments, and tools and techniques of prototyping.

[Alavi 84]   M. Alavi, "An Assessment of the Prototyping Approach to Information Systems Development," *Communications of the ACM*, vol. 27, no. 6, June 1984, pp. 556-563

The effectiveness of prototyping is investigated through field interviews and a laboratory experiment. The interviews (of managers and analysts from 12 projects using prototypes) found that prototyping helps user-designer communication but makes the projects more difficult to manage. The experiment compared prototyping with the conventional life-cycle and led to recommendations about when to use prototyping (e.g., when requirements are unclear).

[Balzer 81]   R. Balzer, "Transformational Implementation: An Example," *IEEE Trans. Software Engineering*, vol. SE-7, no. 1, Jan. 1981, pp. 3-14

A prototype program transformation system is described, along with an example using the system to transform the eight queens specification into code. The paper also presents a good discussion of the transformational approach to software development. A key idea is to consider the recorded development of a program as a computer-processable object.

[Balzer et al. 76]   R. Balzer, N.M. Goldman, and D.S. Wile, "On the Transformational Implementation Approach to Programming," *Proceedings, Second International Conference on Software Engineering*, New York: Computer Society Press, 1976, pp. 337-344

Causes of the "software problem" and alternative approaches to programming are discussed. Transformational implementation is introduced, and its advantages and disadvantages are discussed. An editing example using the approach is also presented.

[Balzer et al. 82]   R. Balzer, N.M. Goldman, and D.S. Wile, "Operational Specification as the Basis for Rapid Prototyping," ACM SIGSOFT *Software Engineering Notes*, vol. 7, no. 5, Dec. 1982, pp. 3-16

The major features of the operational specification language GIST are described. The paper discusses the facilities of the language as they provide freedom from implementation concerns—a potentially useful organizing concept for specification tools generally. That the specification itself in GIST if the prototype fits squarely with the operational paradigm. The specification of a package router in GIST is shown as an example.

[Balzer et al. 83]   R. Balzer, T.E. Cheatham, Jr., and C. Green, "Software Technology in the 1990's: Using a New Paradigm," IEEE *Computer*, vol. 16, no. 11, Nov. 1983, pp. 39-45

An automation-based software development paradigm is introduced as an alternative to be investigated as part of the Department of Defense STARS program. Some of the weaknesses of the conventional paradigm are identified. The projected role of an automated assistant to support implementation is well summarized.

[Barstow 79]   D. Barstow, *Knowledge-Based Program Construction*, New York: Elsevier North-Holland, 1979

This book describes the knowledge-based paradigm of program construction. The interaction of transformation rules with a knowledge base provides a program synthesis system that is discussed in detail.

[Barstow 82]   D. Barstow, "Rapid Prototyping, Automatic Programming, and Experimental Sciences," ACM SIGSOFT *Software Engineering Notes*, vol. 7, no. 5, Dec. 1982, pp. 33-34

The rapid prototyping of objects other than software systems is discussed. An automatic programming system is used to support the petroleum science activity of quantitative log interpretation. The system may be viewed as one that provides rapid prototypes of models. The paper provides a good discussion of the role of domain knowledge in any specification language or rapid prototyping system.

[Barstow et al. 82]   D. Barstow, R. Duffey, S. Smoliar, and S. Vestal, "An Automatic Programming System To Support an Experimental Science," *Proceedings, Sixth International Conference on Software Engineering*, Washington, D.C.: IEEE Computer Society Press, 1982, p. 360

A program synthesis system, ϕ_o, operates in the domain of drilling oil wells, specifically quantitative log interpretation. The input to the system is a specification by the user in the form of a computational model (input, output, and a system of equations). The output is the program that incorporates the computational model.

[Bauer 82]   F.L. Bauer, "From Specifications to Machine Code: Program Construction Through Formal Reasoning," *Proceedings, Sixth International Conference on Software Engineering*, Washington, D.C.: IEEE Computer Society Press, 1982, pp. 84-91

The program construction process is discussed. An example illustrates the reasoning that should accompany programming. Program transformation is introduced as a beneficial paradigm.

[Biermann et al. 84]   A.W. Biermann, G. Guiho, and Y. Kodratoff (eds.), *Automatic Program Construction Tech-*

niques, New York: Macmillan, 1984

This collection of papers is edited from a meeting on automatic program construction. The focus is not on large, automated programming systems but rather on program synthesis techniques.

[Blum 82]   B. I. Blum, "The Life Cycle—A Debate Over Alternate Models," ACM SIGSOFT *Software Engineering Notes,* vol. 7, no. 4, Oct. 1982, pp. 18-20

The suitability of life-cycle models from the viewpoints of problem comprehension and ease of implementation is considered. This consideration leads to two general models for software development: (1) system architecture, in which all necessary information is known before implementation, and (2) system sculpture, in which knowledge of the requirements grows and changes during implementation.

[Blum 83]   B. I. Blum, "Still More About Rapid Prototyping," ACM SIGSOFT *Software Engineering Notes,* vol. 8, no. 3, July 1983, pp. 9-11

This paper offers the view that "throwing prototypes away" should not be part of the definition of prototyping. Prototypes are generally discarded because the tools to retain them effectively are lacking. Some emerging software environments (e.g., ACT/1 and TEDIUM) provide for very rapid implementation and should be considered to provide rapid prototyping capabilities even though the prototypes are not discarded. In fact, these environments provide a welcome opportunity for the prototype to make a greater contribution to the final product.

[Blum 84]   B.I. Blum, "Three Paradigms for Developing Information Systems", *Proceedings, Seventh International Conference on Software Engineering,* Washington, D.C.: IEEE Computer Society, 1984, pp. 534-543

The three paradigms discussed are (1) conventional, (2) tool-enhanced, and (3) fully automated. A design data base (DDB) captures the total knowledge about a development project. The three paradigms differ on the extent to which they automate and use the DDB. An overview is given of the DDB model in TEDIUM, an environment that supports the third paradigm.

[Blum, Houghton 82]   B.I. Blum and R.C. Houghton, Jr., "Rapid Prototyping of Information Management Systems," *ACM SIGSOFT Software Engineering Notes,* vol. 7, no. 5, Dec. 1982, pp. 35-38

A very general overview of various aspects of prototyping information systems is presented. Some of the available tools and some implications for the development cycle are discussed.

[Boar 84]   B. H. Boar, *Application Prototyping,* New York: John Wiley & Sons, 1984, 210 pp.

Whereas other literature on prototyping encourages organizations to start using it, this book describes how to introduce prototyping into an organization. Prototyping is primarily viewed as a tool for understanding require-ments. The book is practical in its style and even describes the staffing of a Productivity Center, an example of which is in operation at the author's company, AT&T.

[Boehm et al. 84]   B.W. Boehm, T.E. Gray, and T. See-waldt, "Prototyping Versus Specifying: A Multiproject Experiment," *IEEE Transactions on Software Engineering,* vol. SE-10, no. 3, May 1984, pp. 290-303

The experiment involved seven teams developing software products in response to the same set of needs (an interactive version of the COCOMO software cost estimation package). Four teams wrote requirements specifications; three used prototyping. The results were as follows: (1) There was no difference in the performance of the final products. (2) Prototyping led to products having 40 percent less code. (3) Prototyping teams expended 45 percent less effort. (4) Specifying teams' products scored better on functionality, robustness, ease of integration, and coherence of design. (5) Prototyping team products scored better on ease of use and ease of learning.

[Bonet, Kung 84]   R. Bonet and A. Kung, "Structuring Into Subsystems: The Experience of a Prototyping Approach," *ACM SIGSOFT Software Engineering Notes,* vol. 9, no. 5, Oct. 1984, pp. 23-27

The authors' experiences in designing a file system in Pascal are reported. Prototyping was used in the design phase to represent internal system specifications to pseudocode level. The resulting prototype was reviewed and the process repeated three times. The prototyping process, as it is used here, is really "iterative detailed design."

[Boyle, Muralidharan 84]   J.M. Boyle and M.N. Muralidharan, "Program Reusability Through Program Transformation," *IEEE Transactions on Software Engineering,* vol. SE-10, no. 5, Sept. 1984, pp. 574-588

The automatic transformation of a pure applicative LISP program into FORTRAN is described. Reusability is achieved by considering the LISP program to be an abstract specification. The TAMPR program transformation system is introduced. The paper provides a good discussion of the role of a transformation strategy to guide the use of the automated tool. The practicality of using program transformation is demonstrated: the 1300-line, 42-function LISP program was transformed in 4 hours into a 3000-line FORTRAN program that runs 25 percent faster than the LISP version.

[Broy, Pepper 81]   M. Broy and P. Pepper, "Program Development as a Formal Activity," *IEEE Transactions on Software Engineering,* vol. SE-7, no. 1, Jan. 1981, pp. 14-22

A formal approach to program development using transformation rules is presented. Various aspects of transformation rules are discussed--their representation, semantics, and correctness. The relationship to abstract data types and assertions is explored. As an extended example, the Warshall algorithm is developed via transformation from its formal specification.

[Burstall, Darlington 77]   R. M. Burstall and J. Darlington, "A Transformation System for Developing Recursive Programs," *Journal of the ACM*, vol. 24, no. 1, Jan. 1977, pp. 44-67

Various program transformation rules are described and applied to examples. Simple programs (expressed as first-order recursion equations) are transformed into more efficient programs. A system to automate the transformations is sketched. This article was an early and influential contribution.

[Cameron 82]   J.R. Cameron, "Two Pairs of Examples in the Jackson Approach to System Development," *Proceedings, 15th Hawaii International Conference on System Sciences*, 1982

The specification produced by applying the Jackson System Development (JSD) methodology is an abstraction of the external world and a realization of the abstraction as a set of sequential processes. This JSD modeling philosophy is discussed and applied to four examples.

[Carey, Mason 83]   T.T. Carey and R.E.A. Mason, "Information System Prototyping: Techniques, Tools, and Methodologies," *INFOR - The Canadian Journal of Operational Research and Information Processing*, vol. 21, no. 3, Aug. 1983, pp. 177-191

Prototyping, especially for use with commercial data processing systems, is reviewed. The paper discusses prototypes as aids to understanding requirements, classifications of prototypes, tools, and the relationship to conventional life-cycle phases. A good table reviewing case studies drawn from 45 references is provided.

[Cheatham 84]   T.E. Cheatham, "Reusability Through Program Transformations," *IEEE Transactions on Software Engineering*, vol. SE-10, no. 5, Sept. 1984, pp. 589-594

A software development methodology is introduced that begins with the creation of an abstract program. Excerpts from abstract programs are given using the EL1 language. Custom tailoring of the abstract program transforms it into a family of concrete programs. The abstract program can also serve to generate rapid prototypes by suitable choice of transformations. Reusability is achieved via these abstract programs, not concrete ones. The transformation support environment, the Harvard Program Development System (PDS), is briefly described.

Cheatham et al. 79]   T.E. Cheatham, J.A, Townley, and G.H. Holloway, "A System for Program Refinement," *Proceedings, Fourth International Conference on Software Engineering*, Washington, D.C.: IEEE Computer Society, 1979, pp. 53-62

The Harvard Program Development System (PDS), the development environment that includes program transformation tools, is introduced. The process of program refinement and its use on an example, changing an abstract version into a concrete one, are discussed.

[Cheatham et al. 81]   T.E. Cheatham, Jr., G.H. Holloway, and J.A. Townley, "Program Refinement by Transformation," *Proceedings, Fifth International Conference on Software Engineering*, Washington, D.C.: IEEE Computer Society, 1981, pp. 430-437

A software construction paradigm using program transformation in the Harvard Program Development System (PDS) environment is described. An abstract program is used as a starting point, and transformations are then applied to produce an efficient target version.

[Cohen et al. 82]   D. Cohen, W. Swartout, and R. Balzer, "Using Symbolic Execution To Characterize Behavior," *ACM SIGSOFT Software Engineering Notes,* , vol. 7, no. 5, Dec. 1982, pp. 25-32

The paper explores various aspects of the operational paradigm of development in which the specification is the prototype. It serves as a basis of communication between specifier and developer. Symbolic execution allows the characterization of large classes of behavior. A small example of the symbolic execution of a GIST specification is provided.

[Conner 81]   M.F. Conner, "An Integrated View of the Computer Software Application Development Life Cycle," *Systems Analysis and Design--A Foundation for the 1980's*, W. W. Cotterman et al., eds., New York: Elsevier North-Holland, 1981, pp. 540-550

Life-cycles are described and their role considered. A three-level life-cycle having organization, information system, and software application elements is introduced. This new generalized life-cycle accommodates different approaches to software development.

[Darlington 84]   J. Darlington, "Program Transformation in the ALICE Project," *Program Transformation and Programming Environments*, [P. Pepper, ed], Berlin, Heidelberg, New York, Tokyo: Springer-Verlag, 1984, pp. 347-353

The ALICE (Applicative Language Idealized Computing Engine) Project at Imperial College seeks to create a software development environment based on using declarative languages (i.e., with simple substitution properties). This article sketches the program transformation system of ALICE. HOPE is used as a metalanguage to express a transformation plan that embodies the design of the target program.

[Davis 82]   A.M. Davis, "Rapid Prototyping Using Executable Requirements Specifications," ACM SIGSOFT *Software Engineering Notes*, vol. 7, no. 5, Dec. 1982, pp. 39-44

A tool called the Feature Simulator, which is being developed as part of a set of tools that automate the requirements specification task, is introduced. After the requirements are captured in a processible language, the Feature Simulator can produce early prototypes of system behavior.

[Deak 81]   E. Deak, "A Transformational Derivation of a Parsing Algorithm in a High-Level Language," *IEEE Transactions on Software Engineering*, vol. SE-7, no. 1, Jan. 1981, pp. 23-31

A program transformation system based on a variant of the SETL language is described. The system behaves like an editor to make basic transformations such as substitute, insert, delete, and move. At each step, the system either verifies the correctness of the transformation or introduces new assumptions into the text. The Cocke-Younger parsing algorithm is developed as an example.

[Dixon et al. 82]   J.K. Dixon, J. McLean, and D.L. Parnas, "Rapid Prototyping by Means of Abstract Module Specifications Written as Trace Axioms," *ACM SIGSOFT Software Engineering Notes*, vol. 7, no. 5, Dec. 1982, pp. 45-49

Trace axioms, which are abstract specifications of modules, are introduced. Trace axioms can specify modules with delayed or hidden effects without reference to internal data structures. The desirability of computer aids to interpret the specifications to form rapid prototypes is discussed.

[Dodd 80]   W.P. Dodd, "Prototyping Programs," *Computer*, vol. 13, no. 2, Feb. 1980, p. 81

Prototyping is recommended as an improved medium for discussion between the customer and the engineer. Although arguments against prototyping have been based on its costliness, the author observes that maintenance costs may be expected to decrease if prototypes were used.

[Dodd et al. 82]   W.P. Dodd, P. Ramsay, T.H. Axford, and D.G. Parkyn, "A Prototyping Language for Text-Processing Applications," *ACM SIGSOFT Software Engineering Notes*, vol. 7, no. 5, Dec. 1982, pp. 50-53

The ATOL language is offered as an effective language for prototyping text processing applications. No examples of ATOL are provided.

[Duncan 82]   A. G. Duncan, "Prototyping in Ada: A Case Study," *ACM SIGSOFT Software Engineering Notes*, vol. 7, no. 5, Dec. 1982, pp. 54-60

Ada is used to prototype an example of an automatic bakery oven controller. The author views a prototype as a first version that is enhanced to reach a production system. Some Ada code is shown for the example.

[EDP Analyzer 81]   EDP Analyzer, "Developing Systems By Prototyping," *EDP Analyzer*, vol. 19, no. 9, Sept. 1981, 14 pp.

Examples of prototyping are described. Prototyping is estimated to require 10 to 20 percent of the development time for a large system. It is recommended for consideration especially for the development of decision support systems. The steps to refine the prototype into a final system are also discussed.

[Feather 82a]   M.S. Feather, "A System for Assisting Program Transformation," *ACM Transactions on Programming Languages and Systems*, vol. 4, no. 1, Jan. 1982, pp. 1-20

This effort was directed at practical aspects of following the transformation approach in [Burstall, Darlington 77]. The ZAP system takes as input the simple program (serving as the specification) and the metaprogram (the sequence of commands telling ZAP how to transform the simple program). An example using ZAP to produce part of a compiler is provided.

[Feather 82b]   M.S. Feather, "Mappings for Rapid Prototyping," *ACM SIGSOFT Software Engineering Notes*, vol. 7, no. 5, Dec. 1982, pp. 17-24

Approaches for converting GIST specifications into implementations are presented. Potentially effective techniques are considered for transformations of each of the basic GIST constructs: historical reference, constraints and nondeterminism, derived information, demons, and perfect knowledge.

[Ford, Marlin 82]   R. Ford and C. Marlin, "Implementation Prototypes in the Development of Programming Language Features," *ACM SIGSOFT Software Engineering Notes*, vol. 7, no. 5, Dec. 1982, pp. 61-66

To develop the ACL language, a base language (Pascal) was successively extended by adding one new language feature at a time. The prototypes are really successive versions in an iterative enhancement paradigm.

[Freeman 81]   P. Freeman, "Why Johnny Can't Analyze," *Systems Analysis and Design—A Foundation for the 1980's*, W.W. Cotterman et al., eds., New York: Elsevier North-Holland, 1981, pp. 321-329

The difficulty encountered by systems analysts in understanding and communicating user's needs is found to be due in part to the conventional life-cycle.

[Frenkel 85]   K.A. Frenkel, "Toward Automating the Software-Development Cycle," *Communications of the ACM*, vol. 28, no. 6, June 1985, pp. 578-589

A summary of current efforts to provide automated support for software development is presented. The author identifies 33 expert systems applications that are either implemented or well advanced.

[Gehani 82]   N.H. Gehani, "A Study in Prototyping," ACM SIGSOFT *Software Engineering Notes*, vol. 7, no. 5, Dec. 1982, pp. 71-74

UNIX tools were used to prototype a form definition facility. The prototype consisted of 2000 lines of C, developed over 5 to 6 weeks.

[Gehani 83]   N.H. Gehani, "An Electronic Form System An Experience in Prototyping," *Software—Practice and Experience*, vol. 13, no. 6, June 1983, pp. 479-486

A successful use of prototyping is reported. The application was a form definition system, using abstract data types. The benefits of the prototype in serving as a test bed for the form definition language are discussed.

[Giddings 84]   R.V. Giddings, "Accommodating Uncertainty in Software Design," *Communications of the ACM*, vol. 27, no. 5, May 1984, pp. 428-434

Many of the problems with effectively managing software projects are found to be due to using a conventional life-cycle model that is inappropriate for several classes of projects. A class of domain-dependent software needing a different life-cycle is distinguished and described. The paper offers good insight into the relationships between the software and characteristics of the problem domain.

[Gill et al. 82]   H. Gill et al., "Experience From Computer-Supported Prototyping for Information Flow in Hospitals," *ACM SIGSOFT Software Engineering Notes*, vol. 7, no. 5, Dec. 1982, pp. 67-70

The successful use of prototyping in a special-purpose language in a medical records application is reported.

[Gladden 82]   G.R. Gladden, "Stop the Life-Cycle, I Want to Get Off," *ACM SIGSOFT Software Engineering Notes*, vol. 7, no. 2, April 1982, pp. 35-39

The life-cycle concept is criticized because it cannot accommodate the requirements changes that are so often required because of vague and incomplete requirements. A new software development model is proposed that is based on hardware mockups, software prototypes, and live demonstrations of system behavior.

[Goguen, Meseguer 82]   J. Goguen and J. Meseguer, "Rapid Prototyping in the OBJ Specification Language," *ACM SIGSOFT Software Engineering Notes*, vol. 7, no. 5, Dec. 1982, pp. 75-84

OBJ provides user-definable abstract objects and syntax and provides for algebraic specification of programs. Because the resulting specifications are executable, they may be considered prototypes. Several examples of OBJ usage are provided.

[Gomaa 83]   H. Gomaa, "The Impact of Rapid Prototyping on Specifying User Requirements," *ACM SIGSOFT Software Engineering Notes*, vol. 8, no. 2, April 1983, pp. 17-28

A successful use of prototyping to help with the specification of user requirements is reported. Specific areas are identified in which the prototyping process made contributions. The prototyping effort cost less than 10 percent of the total development cost of software to control an integrated circuit fabrication facility. Sound, practical suggestions are presented for guiding the prototyping process, especially with its relationship to the user community.

[Gomaa, Scott 81]   H. Gomaa and D.B.H. Scott, "Prototyping as a Tool in the Specification of User Requirements," *Proceedings, Fifth International Conference on Software Engineering*, Washington, D.C.: IEEE Computer Society, 1981, pp. 333-342

Prototyping was used to help specify the requirements of a computer system to manage and control a semiconductor processing facility at General Electric. The prototype cost less than 10 percent of the total software development cost. A good discussion of experiences in building and using the prototype is presented.

[Green 76]   C. Green, "The Design of the PSI Program Synthesis System," *Proceedings, Second International Conference on Software Engineering*, Washington, D.C.: IEEE Computer Society, 1976, p. 4

A desired program is specified in a natural-language dialog between the user and PSI. The system design includes modules that are expert at acquiring from the dialog a model of the desired program. The synthesis modules (coding expert and efficiency expert) transform the model into a LISP target program. Excerpts from examples are provided.

[Gregory 84]   S.T. Gregory, On Prototypes vs. Mockups," *ACM SIGSOFT Software Engineering Notes*, vol. 9, no. 5, Oct. 1984, p. 13

The paper observes that "prototype" is inappropriately used in computer science. "Mockup" is a better term to show resemblance with the final product only at a surface level.

[Gremillion, Pyburn 83]   L.L. Gremillion and P. Pyburn, "Breaking the Systems Development Bottleneck," *Harvard Business Review*, vol. 61, no. 2, March-April 1983, pp. 130-137

Prototyping is presented as an alternative for systems development. Three properties—commonality, impact, and structure--determine when to use prototyping or the conventional life-cycle. Prototyping is recommended for projects having low commonality (no existing packages), high impact (broad effect on the company), and low structure (poorly understood problem and proposed solution).

(Hall 82]   P.A.V. Hall, "In Defence of Life Cycles," *ACM SIGSOFT Software Engineering Notes*, vol. 7, no. 3, July 1982, p. 23

This note encourages readers not to interpret the software life-cycle and its phases too rigidly. There can exist many life-cycles tailored to the needs of individual projects but still following some general guidelines, such as being structured as phases over which iterations may occur.

[Heitmeyer et al. 82] C. Heitmeyer, C. Landwehr, and M. Cornwell, "The Use of Quick Prototypes in the Secure Military Message Systems Project," *ACM SIGSOFT Software Engineering Notes*, vol. 7, no. 5, Dec. 1982, pp. 85-87

Experiences are shared on the prototyping of a military message system in LISP.

[Hemenway, McCusker 82] K. Hemenway and L. McCusker, "Prototyping and Evaluating a User Interface," *Proceedings, IEEE Computer Software and Applications Conference (COMPSAC)*, New York: Computer Society Press, 1982, pp. 175-180

As part of developing a new system for telephone customer service representatives, a prototype of the user interface for the new system was constructed. An experiment with 12 service representatives compared their performance using the prototype versus the current manual procedure. The article discusses the experimental procedure but not the development of the prototype.

[Hooper, Hsia 82] J.W. Hooper and P. Hsia, "Scenario-Based Prototyping for Requirements Identification," *ACM SIGSOFT Software Engineering Notes*, vol. 7, no. 5, Dec. 1982, pp. 88-93

User scenarios are recommended as "prototypes" to help understand system requirements.

[Jackson 78] M.A. Jackson, "Information Systems: Modeling, Sequencing, and Transformations," *Proceedings, Third International Conference on Software Engineering*, Washington, D.C.: IEEE Computer Society, 1978, pp. 72-81

The paper observes that the conventional development process has disadvantages arising from its functional orientation. It is recommended that a development process should first include a model of the real system.

[Jackson 81] M.A. Jackson, "Some Principles Underlying a System Development Method," *Systems Analysis and Design—A Foundation for the 1980's*, W.W. Cotterman et al., eds., New York: Elsevier North-Holland, 1981, pp. 185-198

A set of principles for software development methods is advanced: decomposing the process into distinct and ordered tasks, modeling the real world outside the computer system, using an active (not inert) model, and separating design activities from implementation activities. Jackson System Development (JSD) is introduced via an example.

[Jackson 82] M.A. Jackson, *System Development*, Englewood Cliffs, New Jersey: Prentice-Hall, 1982

JSD, Jackson System Development, is explained. The JSD modeling philosophy leads to the development of an operational specification.

[Kant, Barstow 81] E. Kant and D.R. Barstow, "The Refinement Paradigm: The Interaction of Coding and Efficiency Knowledge in Program Synthesis," *IEEE Transactions on Software Engineering*, vol. SE-7, no. 5, Sept. 1981, pp. 458-471

A program development paradigm is described that is based on successive refinements starting with a high-level specification. Refinements are applications of coding rules. The selection of a coding rule at each step is guided by efficiency knowledge. A program synthesis system is described in which the coding rules and efficiency knowledge are stored. The system is applied to generate a sample program from its specification.

[Kerola, Freeman 81] P. Kerola and P. Freeman, "A Comparison of Lifecycle Models," *Proceedings, Fifth International Conference on Software Engineering*, New York: IEEE Computer Society, 1981, pp. 90-99

The Finnish PSC systemeering model, which derives from general systems theory and semiotics, is introduced. PSC includes four perspectives: pragmatic, input-output, constructive, and operative. In a comparative study, PSC is shown to have a more encompassing world view than the conventional life-cycle.

[Keus 82] H.E. Keus, "Prototyping: A More Reasonable Approach to System Development," *ACM SIGSOFT Software Engineering Notes*, vol. 7, no. 5, Dec. 1982, pp. 94-95

Rapid specification prototyping (throwaway) and rapid cyclic prototyping (iterative enhancement) are identified and compared.

[Klausner, Konchan 82] A. Klausner and T.E. Konchan, "Rapid Prototyping and Requirements Specification Using PDS," *ACM SIGSOFT Software Engineering Notes*, vol. 7, no. 5, Dec. 1982, pp. 96-105

The Harvard Program Development System (PDS) is briefly introduced to show how it supports rapid prototyping. Excerpts are provided from an example of a relational data base system prototype.

[Kowalski 84] R. Kowalski, "AI and Software Engineering," *Datamation*, vol. 30, no. 18, Nov. 1, 1984, pp. 92-102

This is an excellent essay on the role of logic programming and rule-based knowledge representation on the software development process. The prospects for logic-based software technology are explained to enable prototyping and executable specification in a new development paradigm.

[Lehman 80] M.M. Lehman, "Programs, Life Cycles, and Laws of Software Evolution," *Proceedings of the IEEE*, vol. 68, no. 9, Sept. 1980, pp. 1060-1076

A broad-based discussion of software development is presented, including the classification of programs into specification-based, problem-solving, and embedded. Life-cycle phases and the role of maintenance are discussed, and the "Laws of Program Evolution" are introduced. Data on evolution dynamics are used to demonstrate the self-regulating aspect of the program evolution process.

[Lucas 78]   H.C. Lucas, Jr., "The Evolution of an Information System: From Key-Man to Every Person," *Sloan Management Review*, vol. 19, no. 2, Winter 1978, pp. 39-52

In the context of developing business information systems, the author faults the conventional life-cycle for giving too much responsibility to the professional systems designer with too little user involvement. An alternative "evolutionary design" model is proposed, featuring user-controlled logical design and special attention to the user interface. An example (a model to predict the effect of an employee stock ownership plan on a company) is discussed to illustrate the role that users can serve in design.

[MacEwen 82]   G.H. MacEwen,"Specification Prototyping," *ACM SIGSOFT Software Engineering Notes*, vol. 7, no. 5, Dec. 1982, pp. 112-119

Prototyping would be more effective if it followed a special life-cycle of its own. Such a life-cycle is described in this article; its phases correspond to successive levels of detail about a specification. At each level, an opportunity exists for a particular style of prototype (e.g., requirements prototype, design prototype). A case study of a secure operating system is traced throughout this new life-cycle, showing where prototypes were built.

[Martin 84]   J. Martin, *An Information Systems Manifesto*, Englewood Cliffs, New Jersey: Prentice-Hall, 1984

Chapter 11 deals with the inflexibility of the conventional life-cycle to accommodate tools and techniques that are recommended throughout this book: nonprocedural languages, computable specification languages, automation, prototyping, etc.

[Mason et al. 82]   R.E.A. Mason, T.T. Carey, and A. Benjamin, "ACT/1: A Tool for Information Systems Prototyping," *ACM SIGSOFT Software Engineering Notes*, vol. 7, no. 5; Dec. 1982, pp. 120-126

An approach to building prototypes of screen interactions using ACT/1 is explained. In a comparative example, ACT/1 required 25 percent fewer lines of code than a corresponding COBOL implementation.

[Mason, Carey 83]   R.E.A. Mason and T.T. Carey "Prototyping Interactive Information Systems," *Communications of the ACM*, vol. 26, no. 5, May 1983, pp. 347-354

A development methodology is introduced that stresses the importance of the users being able to understand the developers' interpretation of the system's requirements. ACT/1 is used as a tool to prepare screens and scenarios

quickly, and excerpts from a sample use of ACT/1 are presented. ACT/1 is found to be valuable as a prototyping tool to help with the specification of a system.

[McCoyd, Mitchell 82]   G.C. McCoyd and J.R. Mitchell, "System Sketching: The Generation of Rapid Prototypes for Transaction Based Systems," *ACM SIGSOFT Software Engineering Notes*, vol. 7, no. 5, Dec. 1982, pp. 127-132

A functional system sketch is identified by the author as a kind of prototype showing what the user has required in the encoded PSL-derivative requirements language called PSLAIR. A processor written in LISP interprets PSLAIR requirements statements to produce the system sketch. Examples of PSLAIR and its syntax are provided.

[McCracken 81]   D.D. McCraken, "A Maverick Approach to Systems Analysis and Design," *Systems Analysis and Design—A Foundation for the 1980's*, W.W. Cotterman et al., eds., New York: Elsevier North-Holland, 1981, pp. 446-451

The paper discusses two reasons why formal detailed specifications should not be used for large systems: they do not work and they are static. Prototyping and the use of fourth-generation languages and tools (RAMIS, NOMAD, and FOCUS) are recommended.

[McCracken, Jackson 81]   D.D. McCracken and M.A. Jackson, "A Minority Dissenting Position," *Systems Analysis and Design—A Foundation for the 1980's*, W.W. Cotterman et al., eds., New York: Elsevier North-Holland, 1981, pp. 551-553

Also appeared as "Life Cycle Concept Considered Harmful" *ACM SIGSOFT Software Engineering Notes*, vol. 7, no. 2, Apr. 1982, pp. 29-32

The life-cycle concept is criticized for its failure to accommodate a variety of development approaches and its unrealistic assumptions about the user. The life-cycle concept does not embrace prototyping or high end-user involvement in development. Another deficiency is that the life-cycle does not acknowledge that users' needs are not completely known and stable during the development process.

[McHenry 77]   R.C. McHenry, "A Proposed Software Development Process," *Proceedings, Tenth Hawaii International Conference on System Sciences*, 1977, pp. 228-229

This is an early, brief recommendation for what would later be called a "wide-spectrum language," extending the notion of specification across the conventional life-cycle.

[Mittermeir 82]   R.T. Mittermeir, "HIBOL—A Language for Fast Prototyping in Data Processing Environments," *ACM SIGSOFT Software Engineering Notes*, vol. 7, no. 5, Dec. 1982, pp. 133-140

HIBOL is a business data processing language for users who are not professional programmers. It permits easy definition of screens and so is useful as a prototyping language. Examples of HIBOL use are provided.

[Naumann, Jenkins 82]   J.D. Naumann and A.M. Jenkins, "Prototyping: The New Paradigm for Systems Development," *Management Information Systems Quarterly*, Sept. 1982, p. 29

The authors offer a model for systems development based on prototyping. The following phases are included: identification of the user's basic requirements, development of a working prototype, use of the prototype to refine the user's requirements, and revision and enhancement of the prototype.

[Partsch 84]   H. Partsch, "The CIP Transformation System," *Program Transformation and Programming Environments*, P. Pepper, (ed.), Berlin, Heidelberg, New York, Tokyo: Springer-Verlag, 1984, pp. 305-322

The Computer-aided, Intuition-guided Programming (CIP) Project at the Technical University of Munich includes a prototype transformation system that is written in Pascal. This article describes the system: its overall design, its use of rules, and its specification.

[Partsch, Steinbrüggen 83]   H. Partsch and R. Steinbrüggen, "Program Transformation Systems," *ACM Computing Surveys*, vol. 15, no. 3, Sept. 1983, pp. 199-236

An excellent overview of the state of the art in program transformation systems is presented. A framework for classification distinguishes systems as to their input, their relation (if any) to other tools in an environment, their goals, their approaches for maintaining rules, and their ranges of applicability.

[Patton 83]   B. Patton, "Prototyping—A Nomenclature Problem," *ACM SIGSOFT Software Engineering Notes*, vol. 8, no. 2, April 1983, pp. 14-16

The issue of the correct definition of prototyping is raised. "Expendable prototype" and "evolutionary prototype" are suggested to refer to cases in which the prototype is discarded or kept, respectively. A list of 24 articles on prototyping is included.

[Pepper 84]   P. Pepper (ed.) *Program Transformation and Programming Environments*, Berlin, Heidelberg, New York, Tokyo: Springer-Verlag, 1984, 374 pp.

This is a report on the NATO Advanced Research Workshop held in Munich in September 1983. Papers and position statements from many of the leading researchers in program transformation are presented. Also included are well-edited discussions organized around several themes: software management, formal methods in program development, software specification, and program transformation.

[Ramanathan, Shubra 82]   J. Ramanathan and C. J. Shubra, "Use of Annotated Schemes for Developing Prototype Programs," *ACM SIGSOFT Software Engineering Notes*, vol. 7, no. 5, Dec. 1982, pp. 141-149

Over 200 programs in the file-processing domain were analyzed to identify reusable programming patterns. Each pattern was defined by an input/output specification, a control structure, and a generic functional description. Prototypes are quickly constructed by composing these patterns in various ways.

[Riddle 84]   W.E. Riddle, "Report on the Software Process Workshop," ACM SIGSOFT *Software Engineering Notes*, vol. 9, no. 2, Apr. 1984, pp. 13-20

The activities of a workshop held February 6-8, 1984, in Egham, England, are reviewed. Brief summaries are given of the presentations, which cover the spectrum of approaches to software development: design tools, support environments, transformational, and knowledge-based. A valuable commentary by the author articulates the need for a base model of the software process from which specific models can be derived. Key elements of the base model are information accumulation and information transformation.

[Riddle et al. 78]   W. E. Riddle, J.C. Wileden, J.H. Sayler, A.R. Segal, and A.M. Stavely, "Behavior Modeling During Software Design," *IEEE Transactions on Software Engineering*, vol. SE-4, no. 4, July 1978, pp. 283-292

The DREAM (Design Realization, Evaluation and Modeling) System includes a design language that allows for the specification of the behavior of system components. The authors have used DREAM to obtain formal descriptions of complex software systems. The design descriptions can be analyzed for consistency. The system is modeled as subsystems, monitors, and events. Excerpts are provided from the description in DREAM of the HEARSAY speech recognition system.

[Scharer 81]   L. Scharer, "Pinpointing Requirements," *Datamation*, vol. 27, no. 4, Apr. 1981, pp. 139-151

This paper recognizes prototyping as valuable for understanding requirements. It presents a good practical discussion of general requirements problems and the different perspectives of user and analyst.

[Scharer 83]   L. Scharer, "The Prototyping Alternative," ITT *Programming*, vol. 1, no. 1, 1983, pp. 34-43

A step-by-step methodology for prototyping is proposed: preliminary fact-finding, pregeneration design, prototype generation, and prototype refinement iterations. Some often-neglected topics—organizational impact of prototyping, new documentation, and deliverable products—are discussed.

[Silverman 85]   B. G. Silverman, "Software Cost and Productivity Improvements: An Analogical View," *Computer*, vol. 18, no. 5, May 1985, pp. 86-96

Analogies are used by software developers when they recall previous designs or code that can contribute to a new system. The conventional life-cycle model does not, however, cover the systematic reuse of old designs and code. Results from NASA and DOD surveys show the value of analogy to software developers. The creation of a corporate memory of reusable "building blocks" is recommended. Four development paradigms, using various degrees of analogy, are identified.

[Smoliar 81]   S. W. Smoliar, "Operational Requirements Accommodation in Distributed System Design," *IEEE Transactions on Software Engineering*, vol. SE-7, no. 6, Nov. 1981, pp. 531-537

The specification of operational requirements (reliability, growth, and availability) is illustrated for real-time distributed systems. The requirements are captured by extending the R-nets of SREM to become P-nets (process networks), which are configurations of virtual machines. An example of a radar control system is represented by P-nets.

[Smoliar 82]   S.W. Smoliar
"Approaches to Executable Specifications," *ACM SIGSOFT Software Engineering Notes*, vol. 7, no. 5, Dec. 1982, pp. 155-159

The lambda calculus, functional expressions, data flow constructs, and algebraic representations are discussed to determine their ability to provide executable specifications.

[Stavely 82]   A.M. Stavely, "Models as Executable Designs," *ACM SIGSOFT Software Engineering Notes*, vol. 7, no. 5, Dec. 1982, pp. 167-168

If the model of a system design is executable, it can be viewed as a prototype because it illustrates behavior earlier than with the conventional life-cycle. However, the executable design, although useful to developers, does not represent behavior as the users would experience it.

[Strand, Jones 82]   E.M. Strand and W.T. Jones, "Prototyping and Small Scale Software Projects," *ACM SIGSOFT Software Engineering Notes*, vol. 7, no. 5, Dec. 1982, pp. 169-170

A tool was developed to ease the building and sequencing of displays for small interactive applications. Examples of the display frame (instructions) and a generated display are provided.

[Sukri, Zelkowitz 83]   J. Sukri and M.V. Zelkowitz, "Characteristics of a Prototyping Experiment," *Proceedings, Eighth Annual Software Engineering Workshop*, NASA/Goddard Space Flight Center, Nov. 1983, 22 pp.

The results of an experiment in prototyping the Flight Dynamics Analysis System in FORTRAN are reported. The data showed that the ratio of design effort to coding effort was greater with the prototype than with other projects in the environment. The prototype also succeeded in revealing some trouble spots in the software.

[Swartout, Balzer 82]   W. Swartout and R. Balzer, "On the Inevitable Intertwining of Specification and Implementation," *Communications of the ACM*, vol. 25, no. 7, July 1982, pp. 438-440

This paper discusses why the conventional life-cycle model is unrealistic in its separation of specification from implementation. An example is presented to show the problems of specifying a package-router control program.

[Tajima, Matsubara 84]   D. Tajima and T. Matsubara, "Inside the Japanese Software Industry," *Computer*, vol. 17, no. 3, March 1984, pp. 34-43

An extremely interesting overview of software development activities at Hitachi Software Engineering (HSK) is presented. Recruitment and education of employees, lifetime employment, home programming, and the company lifestyle are discussed. Noteworthy is the precision of the process description for SKIPS II, the HSK software development process.

[Taylor, Standish 82]   T. Taylor and T.A. Standish, "Initial Thoughts on Rapid Prototyping Techniques," *ACM SIGSOFT Software Engineering Notes*, vol. 7, no. 5, Dec. 1982, pp. 160-166

Some technical approaches to prototyping—heavily parameterized models, reusable software, prefabrication, prototyping languages, and reconfigurable test harnesses—are discussed. A working prototype can be incrementally redeveloped to become the complete system. Prototyping does not help developers and users learn about some aspects of a system: ease of altering, behavior under stress, and interaction with other elements of an environment.

[Urban 82]   J.E. Urban, "Software Development With Executable Functional Specifications," *Proceedings, Sixth International Conference on Software Engineering*, New York: IEEE Computer Society, 1982, pp. 418-419

An overview of the executable specification language, Descartes, is presented. A Multics PL/1 interpreter has been written to accept Descartes specifications. A few example statements in Descartes are given.

[Wasserman 81]   A.I. Wasserman, "User Software Engineering and the Design of Interactive Systems," *Proceedings, Fifth International Conference on Software Engineering*, New York: IEEE Computer Society, 1981, pp. 387-393

The User Software Engineering (USE) environment facilitates rapid prototyping of interactive information systems. Desired user interfaces are encoded as transition diagrams that are processed by the Transition Diagram Interpreter of USE to produce an executable program simulating the interface.

[Wasserman, Shewmake 82]   A.I. Wasserman and D.T. Shewmake, "Rapid Prototyping of Interactive Information Systems," *ACM SIGSOFT Software Engineering Notes* vol. 7, no. 5, Dec. 1982, pp. 171-180

The USE tool called RAPID (RApid Prototypes of Interactive Dialogues) supports prototype development. Desired user-computer interactions are described by transition diagrams. RAPID links these diagrams to procedures or data manipulation facilities so that the resulting prototype can possess any degree of functionality. An example of a transition diagram and its encoding are provided.

[Waters 82]   R.C. Waters, "The Programmer's Apprentice: Knowledge Based Program Editing," *IEEE Transactions on Software Engineering*, vol. SE-8, no. 1, Jan. 1982, pp. 1-12

The intermediate ground between human and automatic programming is described. The Programmer's Apprentice is LISP software, which works as a second active agent along with the human programmer to develop programs. A new model of program development activity at the level of the individual programmer is presented. The paper also provides an important representation of program fragments as plans.

[Wegner 84]   P. Wegner, "Capital Intensive Software Technology—Part 2: Programming in the Large," *IEEE Software*, vol. 1, no. 3, July 1984, pp. 24-32

Software development process models are viewed as a progression: static waterfall model, dynamic operational model, and futuristic knowledge-based model. Aspects of capital-intensive software technology, such as reusability and application generators, are discussed.

[Weinberg 82]   G.M. Weinberg, "Overstructured Management of Software Engineering," *Proceedings, Sixth International Conference on Software Engineering*, Washinghton, D.C.: IEEE Computer Society, 1982, pp. 2-8

As part of a wider discussion of software project management, it is observed that the conventional life-cycle paradigm is too idealized. Unsuccessful projects should be killed early, even though some managers claim it is unrealistic to expect them to admit the mistake. It is suggested that the killing of projects should be recognized as a reasonable expectation. Managers should strike a balance between the two errors: attempting to build a system that should not be attempted and failing to attempt a system that should be attempted.

[Weiser 82]   M. Weiser, "Scale Models and Rapid Prototyping," *ACM SIGSOFT Software Engineering Notes*, vol. 7, no. 5, Dec. 1982, pp. 181-185

A prototype may be viewed as a scale model if, for some features, the accuracy is representative of the completed system while, for other features, the prototype is inaccurate. A natural classification of scale models arises by identifying the aspect that is accurately modeled: the user interface, functionality, or performance.

[Wile 83]   D.S. Wile, "Program Developments: Formal Explanations of Implementations," *Communications of the ACM*, vol. 26, no. 11, Nov. 1983, pp. 902-911

With program transformation systems, the recorded sequence of transformation steps (i.e., the program development) is a potentially valuable trace of design decisions. This paper discusses the capturing of this transformation record using the POPART/Paddle tools developed at the Information Sciences Institute of the University of Southern California.

[Zave 82]   P. Zave, "An Operational Approach to Requirements Specification for Embedded Systems," *IEEE Transactions on Software Engineering*, vol. SE-8, no. 3, May 1982, pp. 250-269

A thorough introduction to operational specification is presented, and the need for such an approach to address the special circumstances of embedded systems is noted. The PAISLey language for specification is introduced. Excerpts from an example of a patient-monitoring system are also included.

[Zave 84a]   P. Zave, "The Operational Versus the Conventional Approach to Software Development," *Communications of the ACM*, vol. 27, no. 2, Feb. 1984, pp. 104-118

The operational and conventional approaches to software development are compared and contrasted, and the strengths and weaknesses of each are determined. The paper sketches the design of a solution to a problem, using each approach to demonstrate the differences. This is a very accessible introduction to the operational approach.

[Zave 84b]   P. Zave, "An Overview of the PAISLey Project," *ACM SIGSOFT Software Engineering Notes*, vol. 9, no. 4, July 1984, pp. 12-19 (correction in vol. 9, no. 5, Oct. 1984]

PAISLey is a process-oriented specification language oriented to real-time systems. It handles parallelism and timing considerations well but is "rather awkward" when dealing with static objects such as abstract data types. Excerpts from examples are provided, and the execution system that processes PAISLey specifications is described.

[Zave, Yeh 81]   P. Zave and R.T. Yeh, "Executable Requirements for Embedded Systems," *Proceedings, Fifth International Conference on Software Engineering*, Washington, D.C.: IEEE Computer Society, 1981, pp. 295-304

The PAISLey applicative specification language is used to develop an executable specification. Excerpts from the example, a process-control system, are presented. The paper compares this operational approach to data-oriented specification techniques.

[Zelkowitz 80]   M. V. Zelkowitz, "A Case Study in Rapid Prototyping," *Software—Practice & Experience*, vol. 10, no. 12, Dec. 1980, pp. 1037-1042

The use of prototyping on an implementation of an applicative programming system is discussed. The prototype was written in SNOBOL; the final version, in Pascal. The benefits of obtaining an early operational version and the effectiveness of SNOBOL for prototyping are reported.

[Zelkowitz 82]   M.V. Zelkowitz, "Software Prototyping in the Software Engineering Laboratory," *Proceedings, Seventh Annual Software Engineering Workshop*, NASA/Goddard Space Flight Center, Dec. 1982, 22 pp.

Issues relating to the use of prototyping—goals, tools, evaluation, etc.—for a NASA flight dynamics analysis software system are discussed.

[Zolnowski, Ting 82]   J. C. Zolnowski and P. D. Ting, "An Insider's Survey on Software Development," *Proceedings, Sixth International Conference on Software Engineering*, Washington, D.C.: IEEE Computer Society, 1982, pp. 178-187

A survey of the effectiveness of tools, methodologies, etc., on software development at Bell Laboratories showed prototyping to be the secondmost effective methodology (after distinct testing phases).

[Zvegintzov 82]   N. Zvegintzov, "What life? What cycle?," *Proceedings of the National Computer Conference*, Reston, Virginia: AFIPS Press, 1982, pp. 563-568

It is proposed that the conventional life-cycle is not a cycle and does not cover a system's productive life during its operation and maintenance (evolutionary) phase. A starting-gate model is offered as a more realistic representation. A good description of the practical aspects of modification —handling change requests and making changes—is provided.

Biography

William W. Agresti is a senior computer scientist with Computer Sciences Corporation (CSC) in Silver Spring, Maryland. His applied research and development projects support the Software Engineering Laboratory (SEL) at NASA's Goddard Space Flight Center and include co-authoring the SEL's *Manager's Handbook for Software Development*. He is task leader on software engineering for flight dynamics and project leader of a joint NASA-CSC team that is designing and developing a spacecraft dynamics simulator in Ada as an experiment on the effectiveness of Ada in the NASA environment.

From 1973-83, he held various faculty and administrative positions at The University of Michigan-Dearborn, including founding Director of Computer and Information Sciences, Associate Professor of Industrial and Systems Engineering, and Associate Dean of the School of Engineering. During this period, he was a consultant to Ford Motor Company and other businesses and agencies, senior partner in the engineering consulting firm of Alpha Associates, and a founder of the software products firm of AIS International, Inc., which produced application development systems.

He has published in the areas of software engineering, computer science, simulation, and operations research. He has received a journal best paper award and an inventor award for his design of a microcomputer-based data acquisition system. His current research interests are in software process engineering and software measurement.

He received the B.S. degree from Case Western Reserve University, and the M.S. and Ph.D. from New York University. He is a member of the IEEE Computer Society and the Association for Computing Machinery, having served as president of the Metropolitan Detroit Chapter in 1979-80.